HISTORY OF ROME.

BY

THOMAS ARNOLD, D. D.,

LATE REGIUS PROFESSOR OF MODERN HISTORY IN THE UNIVERSITY OF OXFORD,
HEAD MASTER OF RUGBY SCHOOL,
AND MEMBER OF THE ARCHÆOLOGICAL SOCIETY OF ROME.

THREE VOLUMES IN ONE.

REPRINTED ENTIRE, FROM THE LAST LONDON EDITION.

NEW-YORK:
D. APPLETON & COMPANY,
443 & 445 BROADWAY.
1868.

PREFACE.

In attempting to write the History of Rome, I am not afraid of incurring the censure pronounced by Johnson upon Blackwell,* that he had chosen a subject long since exhausted; of which all men knew already as much as any one could tell them. Much more do I dread the reproach of having ventured, with most insufficient means, upon a work of the greatest difficulty; and thus by possibility deterring others from accomplishing a task which has never yet been fulfilled, and which they might fulfil more worthily. The great advances made within the last thirty years in historical knowledge have this most hopeful symptom, that they have taught us to appreciate the amount of our actual ignorance. As we have better understood what history ought to be, we are become ashamed of that scanty information which might once have passed for learning; and our discovery of the questions which need to be solved has so outrun our powers of solving them, that we stand humiliated rather than encouraged, and almost inclined to envy the condition of our fathers, whose maps, so to speak, appeared to them complete and satisfactory, because they never suspected the existence of a world beyond their range.

Still, although the time will, I trust, arrive, when points now altogether obscure will receive their full illustration, and when this work must be superseded by a more perfect history, yet it may be possible in the mean while to render some service, if I shall be able to do any justice to my subject up to the extent of our present knowledge. And we, who are now in the vigor of life, possess at least one advantage which our children may not share equally. We have lived in a period rich in historical lessons beyond all former example; we have witnessed one of the great seasons of movement in the life of mankind, in which the arts of peace and war, political parties and principles, philosophy and religion, in all their manifold forms and influences, have been developed with extraordinary force and freedom. Our own experience has thus thrown a bright light upon the remoter past: much which our fathers could not fully understand, from being accustomed only to

* In his review of Blackwell's Memoirs of the Court of Augustus.—Works, Vol. II. 8vo. 1806.

quieter times, and which again, from the same cause, may become obscure to our children, is to us perfectly familiar. This is an advantage common to all the present generation in every part of Europe; but it is not claiming too much to say, that the growth of the Roman commonwealth, the true character of its parties, the causes and tendency of its revolutions, and the spirit of its people and its laws, ought to be understood by none so well as by those who have grown up under the laws, who have been engaged in the parties, who are themselves citizens of our kingly commonwealth of England.

Long before Niebuhr's death I had formed the design of writing the History of Rome; not, it may well be believed, with the foolish notion of rivalling so great a man, but because it appeared to me that his work was not likely to become generally popular in England, and that its discoveries and remarkable wisdom might best be made known to English readers by putting them into a form more adapted to our common taste. It should be remembered, that only the two first volumes of Niebuhr's History were published in his lifetime; and although careful readers might have anticipated his powers of narration even from these, yet they were actually, by the necessity of the case, more full of dissertations than of narrative; and for that reason it seemed desirable to remould them for the English public, by assuming as proved many of those results which Niebuhr himself had been obliged to demonstrate step by step. But when Niebuhr died, and there was now no hope of seeing his great work completed in a manner worthy of its beginning, I was more desirous than ever of executing my original plan, of presenting in a more popular form what he had lived to finish, and of continuing it afterwards with such advantages as I had derived from a long study and an intense admiration of his example and model.

It is my hope, then, if God spares my life* and health, to carry on this history to the revival of the western empire, in the year 800 of the Christian era, by the coronation of Charlemagne at Rome. This point appears to me its natural termination. We shall then have passed through the chaos which followed the destruction of the old western empire, and shall have seen its several elements, combined with others which in that great convulsion had been mixed with them, organized again into their new form. That new form exhibited a marked and recognized division between the so-called secular and spiritual powers, and thereby has maintained in Christian Europe the unhappy distinction which necessarily prevailed in the heathen empire between the church and the state; a distinction now so deeply seated in our laws, our language, and our very notions, that nothing less than a miraculous interposition of God's providence seems capable, within any definite

* Dr. Arnold died June 12th, 1842. He had completed the present volume, with the exception of adding a running commentary to the last part of it.

time, of eradicating it. The Greek empire, in its latter years, retained so little of the Roman character, and had so little influence upon what was truly the Roman world, that it seems needless, for the sake of a mere name, to protract the story for six hundred and fifty years fur ther, merely to bring it down to the conquest of Constantinople by the Turks.

For the whole of the period, from the origin down to the capture of Rome by the Gauls, in the middle of the fourth century before the Christian era, I have enjoyed Niebuhr's guidance; I have everywhere availed myself of his materials as well as of his conclusions. No acknowledgment can be too ample for the benefits which I have derived from him: yet I have not followed him blindly, nor compiled my work from his. It seemed to be a worthier tribute to his greatness, to endeavor to follow his example; to imitate, so far as I could, his manner of inquiry; to observe and pursue his hints; to try to practise his master-art of doubting rightly and believing rightly; and, as no man is infallible, to venture sometimes even to differ from his conclusions, if a compliance with his own principles of judgment seemed to require it. But I can truly say, that I never differ from him without a full consciousness of the probability that further inquiry might prove him to be right.

The form and style in which I have given the legends and stories of the first three centuries of Rome may require some explanation. I wished to give these legends at once with the best effect, and at the same time with a perpetual mark, not to be mistaken by the most careless reader, that they were legends and not history. There seemed a reason, therefore, for adopting a more antiquated style, which, otherwise, of course would be justly liable to the charge of affectation.

It might seem ludicrous to speak of impartiality in writing the history of remote times, did not those times really bear a nearer resemblance to our own than many imagine; or did not Mitford's example sufficiently prove that the spirit of modern party may affect our view of ancient history. But many persons do not clearly see what should be the true impartiality of an historian. If there be no truths in moral and political science, little good can be derived from the study of either: if there be truths, it must be desirable that they should be discovered and embraced. Skepticism must ever be a misfortune or a defect: a misfortune, if there be no means of arriving at truth; a defect, if while there exist such means we are unable or unwilling to use them. Believing that political science has its truths no less than moral, I cannot regard them with indifference, I cannot but wish them to be seen and embraced by others.

On the other hand, it must not be forgotten that these truths have been much disputed; that they have not, like moral truths, received that universal assent of good men which makes us shrink from submitting them to question. And, again, in human affairs, the contest has never been between pure truth and pure error. Neither, then, may we assume political conclusions as absolutely certain; nor are political truths ever wholly identical with the professions or practice of any party or individual. If, for the sake of recommending any principle, we disguise the errors or the crimes with which it has been in practice accompanied, and which, in the weakness of human nature, may perhaps be naturally connected with our reception of it, then we are guilty of most blamable partiality. And so it is no less, if, for the sake of decrying an erroneous principle, we depreciate the wisdom, and the good and noble feelings with which error also is frequently, and in some instances naturally, joined. This were to make our sense of political truth to overpower our sense of moral truth; a double error, inasmuch as it is at once the less certain, and, to those who enjoy a Christian's hope, by far the less worthy.

While, then, I cannot think that political science contains no truths, or that it is a matter of indifference whether they are believed or no, I have endeavored also to remember, that be they ever so certain, there are other truths no less sure; and that one truth must never be sacrificed to another. I have tried to be strictly impartial in my judgments of men and parties, without being indifferent to those principles which were involved more or less purely in their defeat or triumph. I have desired neither to be so possessed with the mixed character of all things human, as to doubt the existence of abstract truth; nor so to dote on any abstract truth, as to think that its presence in the human mind is incompatible with any evil, its absence incompatible with any good.

In the first part of my History, I have followed the common chronology without scruple; not as true, but as the most convenient. Where the facts themselves are so uncertain, it must be a vain labor to try to fix their dates minutely. But when we arrive at a period of greater certainty as to the facts, then it will be proper to examine, as far as possible, into the chronology.

Those readers who are acquainted with Niebuhr, or with the history written by Mr. Maldon, for the Society for the Diffusion of Useful Knowledge, may be surprised to find so little said upon the antiquities of the different nations of Italy. The omission, however, was made deliberately: partly, because the subject does not appear to me to belong essentially to the early history of Rome, and still more, because the researches now carried on with so much spirit in Italy, hold out the hope that we may obtain, ere long, some more satisfactory knowledge than is at present attainable. Pelasgian inscriptions, written in a character clearly distinguishable from the Etruscan, have been discovered very recently, as I am informed, at Agylla or Cære. And the study and comparison of the several Indo-Germanic languages is making such progress, that if any fortunate discovery comes in to aid it, we may hope to see the mystery of the Etruscan inscriptions at length unravelled. I was not sorry, therefore, to defer any detailed inquiry into the antiquities of the Italian nations, in the expectation that I might be able hereafter to enter upon the subject to greater advantage.

Amongst the manifold accomplishments of Niebuhr's mind, not the least extraordinary was his philological knowledge. His acquaintance with the manuscripts of the Greek and Roman writers was extensive and profound; his acuteness in detecting a corrupt reading, and his sagacity in correcting it, were worthy of the critical ability of Bentley. On no point have I been more humbled with a sense of my own inferiority, as feeling that my own professional pursuits ought, in this respect, to have placed me more nearly on a level with him. But it is far otherwise. I have had but little acquaintance with manuscripts, nor have I the means of consulting them extensively; and the common editions of the Latin writers in particular, do not intimate how much of their present text is grounded upon conjecture. I have seen references made to Festus, which, on examination, have been found to rest on no other authority than Scaliger's conjectural piecing of the fragments of the original text. But, besides this, we often need a knowledge of the general character of a manuscript or manuscripts, in order to judge whether any remarkable variations in names or dates are really to be ascribed to the author's having followed a different version of the story, or whether they are mere blunders of the copyist. For instance, the names of the consuls, as given at the beginning of each year in the present text of Diodorus, are in many instances so corrupt, that one is tempted to doubt how far some apparent differences in his Fasti from those followed by Livy, are really his own or his copyist's.

There are some works which I have not been able to consult; and there are points connected with the topography of Rome and its neighborhood, on which no existing work gives a satisfactory explanation. On these points I have been accustomed to consult my valued friend Bunsen, Niebuhr's successor in his official situation as Prussian minister at Rome, and his worthy successor no less in the profoundness of his antiquarian, and philological, and historical knowledge.

There has lately appeared in the second volume of Niebuhr's life and letters, a letter written by him to a young student, containing various directions and suggestions with respect to his philological studies. Amongst other things, he says, "I utterly disapprove of the common practice of adopting references, after verifying them, without naming the source whence they are taken; and, tedious as the double reference is, I never allow myself to dispense with it. When I cite a passage simply, I have found it out myself. He who does otherwise, assumes the appearance of more extensive reading than belongs tc him."

The perfect uprightness of Niebuhr's practice in this point is well worthy of him, and is deserving of all imitation. But I should find it difficult in all cases to say whether I had first noticed a passage myself, or had been led to it by a quotation in another writer. I have availed myself continually of Niebuhr's references, and of those made by Freinsheim in his supplement of Livy; but it has happened, also, that passages referred to by them had been taken by myself directly from the original source, without recollecting, or, indeed, without knowing, that they had been quoted previously by others. Niebuhr's reading was so vast, and his memory so retentive, that he may be presumed never to have overlooked any thing which could illustrate his subject: it is probable, therefore, that every quotation made in this volume may be found previously made by Niebuhr, unless it happen to relate to a matter which he has not written on. But yet, some quotations were made by me with so little consciousness of their existing in Niebuhr, that in one instance I searched his volume to see whether he had noticed a passage, because I did not remember to have observed any quotation of it by him, and yet I felt sure, as proved to be the case, that he had not overlooked it.

I have only, therefore, to state that many passages have been quoted by me from Pliny, Valerius Maximus, Frontinus, and other writers, for the knowledge, or at least for the recollection of which, I was indebted either to Niebuhr or to Freinsheim, or to some other modern writer. And yet I can truly say, that not a single paragraph has been written on a mere verifying of the references made by preceding writers, but that my own reading and comparison of the ancient authorities has been always the foundation of it. This is not said as laying claim to any remarkable degree of diligence or of learning, but simply to establish my right to call this history an original work, and not a mere compilation from Niebuhr or from others who have gone over the ground previously.

But I shall be believed by all who are acquainted with Niebuhr's third volume, when I say that the composition of this period in mine has been throughout a most irksome labor; inasmuch as I was but doing, with manifest inferiority in every point, what Niebuhr had done in all points admirably. In the first part, although all the substance of it and much more, was to be found in Niebuhr, yet in its form I might hope to have some advantage, as putting his matter into a more popular shape. But his third volume is no less eloquent than wise; and is as superior in the power of its narrative as in the profoundness of its researches. And yet, this portion of the history was to be written as a necessary part of my own work. I was obliged, therefore, to go through with it as well as I could, feeling most keenly all the while the infinite difference between Niebuhr's history and mine.

It may be thought by some that this volume is written at too great length. But I am convinced, by a tolerably large experience, that most readers find it almost impossible to impress on their memory a mere abridgment of history: the number of names and events crowded into a small space is overwhelming to them, and the absence of details in the narrative makes it impossible to communicate to it much of interest; neither characters nor events can be developed with that particularity which is the best help to the memory, because it attracts and engages us, and impresses images on the mind as well as facts. At the same time I am well aware of the great difficulty of giving liveliness to a narrative which necessarily gets all its facts at second-hand. And a writer who has never been engaged in any public transactions, either of peace or war, must feel this especially. One who is himself a statesman and orator, may relate the political contests even of remote ages with something of the spirit of a contemporary; for his own experience realizes to him, in great measure, the scenes and the characters which he is describing. And, in like manner, a soldier or a seaman can enter fully into the great deeds of ancient warfare; for, although in outward form ancient battles and sieges may differ from those of modern times, yet the genius of the general and the courage of the soldier, the call for so many of the highest qualities of our nature which constitutes the enduring moral interest of war, are common alike to all times, and he who has fought under Wellington has been in spirit an eye-witness of the campaigns of Hannibal. But a writer whose whole experience has been confined to private life and to peace, has no link to connect him with the actors and great deeds of ancient history, except the feelings of our common humanity. He cannot realize civil contests or battles with the vividness of a statesman and a soldier; he can but enter into them as a man; and his general knowledge of human nature, his love of great and good actions, his sympathy with virtue, his abhorrence of vice, can alone assist him in making himself, as it were, a witness of what he attempts to describe. But these even by themselves will do much; and if an historian feels as a man and as a citizen, there is hope that, however humble his experience, he may inspire his readers with something of his own interest in the events of his history: he may hope, at least, that a full detail of these events, however feebly represented, will be worth far more than a mere brief summary of them, made the text for a long comment of his own.

RUGBY, *May 28th*, 1840.

CONTENTS.

CHAPTER XIV.

CHAPTER XV.

CHAPTER XVI.

CHAPTER XVII.

CHAPTER XVIII.

CHAPTER XIX.

CHAPTER XX.

CHAPTER XXI.

CHAPTER XXII.

CHAPTER XXIII.

CHAPTER XXIV.

CHAPTER XXV.

CHAPTER XXVI.

CHAPTER XXVII.

CHAPTER XXVIII.

pened that the river at that time had flooded the country; when, therefore, the two children in their basket were thrown into the river, the waters carried them as far as the foot of the Palatine Hill, and there the basket was upset, near the roots of a wild fig-tree, and the children thrown out upon the land. At this moment there came a she-wolf down to the water to drink, and when she saw the children, she carried them to her cave hard by, and gave them to suck; and whilst they were there, a woodpecker came backwards and forwards to the cave, and brought them food.[17] At last one Faustulus, the king's herdsman, saw the wolf suckling the children; and when he went up, the wolf left them and fled;[18] so he took them home to his wife Larentia, and they were bred up along with her own sons on the Palatine Hill; and they were called Romulus and Remus.[19]

How it was found out who they were.

When Romulus and Remus grew up, the herdsmen of the Palatine Hill chanced to have a quarrel with the herdsmen of Numitor, who stalled their cattle on the hill Aventinus. Numitor's herdsmen laid an ambush, and Remus fell into it, and was taken and carried off to Alba. But when the young man was brought before Numitor, he was struck with his noble air and bearing, and asked him who he was. And when Remus told him of his birth, and how he had been saved from death, together with his brother, Numitor marvelled, and thought whether this might not be his own daughter's child. In the mean while, Faustulus and Romulus hastened to Alba to deliver Remus; and by the help of the young men of the Palatine Hill, who had been used to follow him and his brother, Romulus took the city, and Amulius was killed; and Numitor was made king, and owned Romulus and Remus to be born of his own blood.

How they disputed which should give his name to the city, and of the sign of the vultures.

The two brothers did not wish to live at Alba, but loved rather the hill on the banks of the Tiber, where they had been brought up. So they said, that they would build a city there; and they inquired of the gods by augury, to know which of them should give his name to the city. They watched the heavens from morning till evening, and from evening till morning;[20] and as the sun was rising, Remus saw six vultures.[21] This was told to Romulus; but as they were telling him, behold there appeared to him twelve vultures. Then it was disputed again, which had seen the truest sign of the god's favor: but the most part gave their voices for Romulus. So he began to build his city on the Palatine Hill. This made Remus very angry; and when he saw the ditch and the rampart which were drawn round the space where the city was to be, he scornfully leapt over them,[22] saying, "Shall such defences as these keep your city?" As he did this, Celer, who had the charge of the building, struck Remus with the spade which he held in his hand, and slew him; and they buried him on the hill Remuria, by the banks of the Tiber, on the spot where he had wished to build his city.

How Romulus opened a place of refuge, and how his people carried off the women of the neighboring people.

But Romulus found that his people were too few in numbers; so he set apart a place of refuge,[23] to which any man might flee, and be safe from his pursuers. So many fled thither from the countries round about; those who had shed blood, and fled from the vengeance of the avenger of blood; those who were driven out from their own homes by their enemies, and even men of low degree who had run away from their lords. Thus the city became full of people; but yet they wanted wives, and the nations round about would not give them their daughters in marriage. So Romulus gave out that he was going to keep a great festival, and there were to be sports and games to draw a multitude together.[24] The neighbors came to see the show, with their wives and their daughters: there came the people of

17 Ovid, Fasti, III. 54. Servius, Æn. I. v. 273.

18 Ennius, Annal. I. 78.

19 Gellius, Noct. Attic. VI. c. 7, quoted from Messurius Sabinus.

20 Ennius, Annal. I. v. 106, 107.

21 Livy, I. 7.

22 Ovid, Fasti, IV. 842.

23 The famous Asylum. See Livy, I. 8.

24 Livy, I. 9.

Cænina, and of Crustumerium, and of Antemna, and a great multitude of the Sabines. But while they were looking at the games, the people of Romulus rushed out upon them, and carried off the women to be their wives.

How for this cause the Sabines made war on them, and of the treason of the fair Tarpeia.

Upon this the people of Cænina first made war upon the people of Romulus:[25] but they were beaten, and Romulus with his own hand slew their king Acron. Next the people of Crustumerium, and of Antemna, tried their fortune, but Romulus conquered both of them. Last of all came the Sabines with a great army, under Titus Tatius, their king. There is a hill near to the Tiber, which was divided from the Palatine Hill by a low and swampy valley; and on this hill Romulus made a fortress, to keep off the enemy from his city. But when the fair Tarpeia, the daughter of the chief who had charge of the fortress, saw the Sabines draw near, and marked their bracelets and their collars of gold, she longed after these ornaments, and promised to betray the hill into their hands if they would give her those bright things which they wore upon their arms.[26] So she opened a gate, and let in the Sabines; and they, as they came in, threw upon her their bright shields which they bore on their arms, and crushed her to death. Thus the Sabines got the fortress which was on the hill Saturnius; and they and the Romans joined battle in the valley between the hill and the city of Romulus.[27] The Sabines began to get the better, and came up close to one of the gates of the city. The people of Romulus shut the gate, but it opened of its own accord; once and again they shut it, and once and again it opened. But as the Sabines were rushing in, behold, there burst forth from the Temple of Janus, which was near the gate, a mighty stream of water, and it swept away the Sabines, and saved the city. For this it was ordered that the Temple of Janus should stand ever open in time of war, that the god might be ever ready, as on this day, to go out and give his aid to the people of Romulus.

How the god Janus saved the city from the Sabines.

How the women who had been carried off made peace between their fathers and their husbands; and how the Romans and the Sabines lived together.

After this they fought again in the valley; and the people of Romulus were beginning to flee, when Romulus prayed to Jove, the stayer of flight, that he might stay the people;[28] and so their flight was stayed, and they turned again to the battle. And now the fight was fiercer than ever: when, on a sudden, the Sabine women who had been carried off ran down from the hill Palatinus, and ran in between their husbands and their fathers, and prayed them to lay aside their quarrel.[29] So they made peace with one another, and the two people became as one: the Sabines with their king dwelt on the hill Saturnius, which is also called Capitolium, and on the hill Quirinalis; and the people of Romulus with their king dwelt on the hill Palatinus. But the kings with their counsellors met in the valley between Saturnius and Palatinus, to consult about their common matters; and the place where they met was called Comitium, which means "the place of meeting."

Soon after this, Tatius was slain by the people of Laurentum, because some of his kinsmen had wronged them, and he would not do them justice.[30] So Romulus reigned by himself over both nations; and his own people were called the Romans, for Roma was the name of the city on the hill Palatinus; and the Sabines were called Quirites, for the name of their city on the hills Saturnius and Quirinalis was Quirium.[31]

[25] Livy, I. 10.

[26] Livy, I. 11.

[27] Macrobius, Saturnalia, 1. 9. Macrobius places the scene of this wonder at a gate "which stood at the foot of the hill Viminalis." It would be difficult to reconcile this story with the other accounts of the limits of the two cities of Romulus and Tatius; and certainly a gate at the foot of the Viminal could not have existed in the walls of the city of Romulus, according to the historical account of their direction and extent, as given by Tacitus, Annal. XII. 24. Yet Macrobius relates the wonder as having happened at one of the gates of the Roman city, when the Romans were at war with Tatius; and it seemed needless to destroy the consistency of the whole story by the unseasonable introduction of a topographical difficulty.

[28] Livy, I. 12.

[29] Livy, I. 13.

[30] Livy, I. 14.

[31] Perhaps I hardly ought to have embodied Niebuhr's conjecture in the legend, for certain-

How Romulus ordered his people.

The people were divided into three tribes;[32] the Ramnenses, and the Titienses, and the Luceres: the Ramnenses were called from Romulus, and the Titienses from Tatius; and the Luceres were called from Lucumo, an Etruscan chief, who had come to help Romulus in his war with the Sabines, and dwelt on the hill called Cælius. In each tribe there were ten curiæ, each of one hundred men;[33] so all the men of the three tribes were three thousand, and these fought on foot, and were called a legion. There were also three hundred horsemen, and these were called Celerians, because their chief was that Celer who had slain Remus. There was besides a council of two hundred men, which was called a senate, that is, a council of elders.

How he vanished suddenly in the field of Mars, and was worshipped as a god.

Romulus was a just king, and gentle to his people: if any were guilty of crimes, he did not put them to death, but made them pay a fine of sheep or of oxen.[34] In his wars he was very successful, and enriched his people with the spoils of their enemies. At last, after he had reigned nearly forty years, it chanced that one day he called his people together in the field of Mars, near the Goats' Pool:[35] when, all on a sudden, there arose a dreadful storm, and all was as dark as night; and the rain, and thunder and lightning, were so terrible, that all the people fled from the field, and ran to their several homes. At last the storm was over, and they came back to the field of Mars, but Romulus was nowhere to be found; for Mars, his father, had carried him up to heaven in his chariot.[36] The people knew not at first what was become of him; but when it was night, as one Proculus Julius was coming from Alba to the city, Romulus appeared to him in more than mortal beauty, and grown to more than mortal stature, and said to him, "Go, and tell my people that they weep not for me any more; but bid them to be brave and warlike, and so shall they make my city the greatest in the earth." Then the people knew that Romulus was become a god; so they built a temple to him, and offered sacrifice to him, and worshipped him evermore by the name of the god Quirinus.

THE LEGEND OF NUMA POMPILIUS.

How for one whole year the Romans had no king.

When Romulus was taken from the earth, there was no one found to reign in his place.[37] The Senators would choose no king, but they divided themselves into tens; and every ten was to have the power of king for five days, one after the other. So a year passed away, and the people murmured, and said, that there must be a king chosen.

How Numa Pompilius was chosen king.

Now the Romans and the Sabines each wished that the king should be one of them; but at last it was agreed that the king should be a Sabine, but that the Romans should choose him.[38] So they chose Numa Pompilius; for all men said that he was a just man, and wise, and holy.

Of his wise and pious ordinances; and of the favor shown him by the nymph Egeria.

Some said that he had learnt his wisdom from Pythagoras, the famous philosopher of the Greeks;[39] but others would not believe that he owed it to any foreign teacher. Before he would consent to be king, he consulted the gods by augury, to know whether it was their pleasure that he should reign.[40] And as he feared the gods at first, so did he even to the last. He appointed many to minister in sacred things,[41] such as the Pontifices, who were to see that all things relating to the gods were duly observed by all; and the Augurs, who taught men the pleasure of the gods concerning things to come; and the Flamens, who ministered in the temples;

ly no ancient writer now extant speaks of the town "Quirium." Yet it seems so probable a conjecture, and gives so much consistency to the story, that I have ventured to adopt it.

32 Livy, I. 13. Varro de Lin. Lat. § 55. Ed. Müller. Servius, Æn. V. 560.

33 Paternus, quoted by Lydus, de Magistratibus, c. 9.

34 Cicero de Republica, II. 9.

35 Livy, I. 16.

36 —————————"Quirinus
Martis equis Acheronta fugit."
Horat. III. Carm. 3.

37 Livy, I. 17.

38 Dionysius, II. 58.

39 Livy, I. 18. Dionysius, I. 59.

40 Livy, I. 18.

41 Livy, I. 19.

and the virgins of Vesta, who tended the ever-burning fire; and the Salii, who honored the god of arms with solemn songs and dances through the city on certain days, and who kept the sacred shield which fell down from heaven. And in all that he did, he knew that he should please the gods; for he did every thing by the direction of the nymph Egeria, who honored him so much that she took him to be her husband, and taught him in her sacred grove, by the spring that welled out from the rock, all that he was to do towards the gods and towards men.[42] By her counsel he snared the gods Picus and Faunus in the grove on the hill Aventinus, and made them tell him how he might learn from Jupiter the knowledge of his will, and might get him to declare it either by lightning or by the flight of birds.[43] And when men doubted whether Egeria had really given him her counsel, she gave him a sign by which he might prove it to them. He called many of the Romans to supper, and set before them a homely meal in earthen dishes;[44] and then on a sudden he said, that now Egeria was come to visit him; and straightway the dishes and the cups became of gold or precious stones, and the couches were covered with rare and costly coverings, and the meats and drinks were abundant and most delicious. But though Numa took so much care for the service of the gods, yet he forbade all costly sacrifices;[45] neither did he suffer blood to be shed on the altars, nor any images of the gods to be made.[46] But he taught the people to offer in sacrifice nothing but the fruits of the earth, meal and cakes of flour, and roasted corn.

Of his goodness towards his people, and how there were no wars in his reign.

For he loved husbandry, and he wished his people to live every man on his own inheritance in peace and in happiness. So the lands which Romulus had won in war, he divided out amongst the people, and gave a certain portion to every man.[47] He then ordered landmarks to be set on every portion;[48] and Terminus, the god of landmarks, had them in his keeping, and he who moved a landmark was accursed. The craftsmen of the city,[49] who had no land, were divided according to their callings; and there were made of them nine companies. So all was peaceful and prosperous throughout the reign of king Numa; the gates of the temple of Janus were never opened, for the Romans had no wars and no enemies; and Numa built a temple to Faith, and appointed a solemn worship for her;[50] that men might learn not to lie or to deceive, but to speak and act in honesty. And when he had lived to the age of fourscore years, he died at last by a gentle decay, and he was buried under the hill Janiculum, on the other side of the Tiber; and the books of his sacred laws and ordinances were buried near him in a separate tomb.[51]

THE LEGEND OF TULLUS HOSTILIUS.

How Tullus Hostilius was chosen king.

When Numa was dead, the Senators again for a while shared the kingly power amongst themselves. But they soon chose for their king Tullus Hostilius, whose father's father had come from Medullia, a city of the Latins, to Rome, and had fought with Romulus against the Sabines.[52] Tullus loved the poor, and he divided the lands which came to him, as king, amongst those who had no land. He also bade those who had no houses to settle themselves on the hill Cælius, and there he dwelt himself in the midst of them.

Of his war with the Albans, and of the combat between the Horatii and the Curiatii.

Tullus was a warlike king, and he soon was called to prove his valor; for the countrymen of the Alban border and of the Roman border plundered one another.[53] Now Alba was governed by Caius Cluilius, who was the dictator; and Cluilius sent to Rome to complain of

[42] Livy, I. 19, 20. Ovid, Fasti, III. 276.
[43] Ovid, Fasti, III. 289, et seqq. Plutarch, Numa, 15.
[44] Plutarch, Numa, 15. Dionysius, II. 60.
[45] Cicero de Repub. II. 14.
[46] Plutarch, Numa, 8. Varro, apud Augustin. Civit. Dei, IV. 31.
[47] Cicero de Rep. II. 14.
[48] Dionysius, II. 74. Plutarch, Numa, 16.
[49] Plutarch, Numa, 17.
[50] Livy, I. 21.
[51] Plutarch, Numa, 22.
[52] Dionysius, III. 1.
[53] Livy, I. 22, et seqq.

the wrongs done to his people, and Tullus sent to Alba for the same purpose. So there was a war between the two nations, and Cluilius led his people against Rome, and lay encamped within five miles of the city, and there he died. Mettius Fufetius was then chosen dictator in his room; and as the Albans still lay in their camp, Tullus passed them by, and marched into the land of Alba. But when Mettius came after him, then, instead of giving battle, the two leaders agreed that a few in either army should fight in behalf of the rest, and that the event of this combat should decide the quarrel. So three twin brothers were chosen out of the Roman army, called the Horatii, and three twin brothers out of the Alban army, called the Curiatii. The combat took place in the sight of both armies; and after a time all the Curiatii were wounded, and two of the Horatii were slain. Then the last Horatius pretended to fly, and the Curiatii each, as they were able, followed after him. But when Horatius saw that they were a great way off from one another, he turned suddenly and slew the first of them; and the second in like manner, and then he easily overcame and slew the third. So the victory remained to the Romans.

How Horatius slew his sister, and of the judgment passed upon him for the deed.

Then the Romans went home to Rome in triumph,[54] and Horatius went at the head of the army, bearing his triple spoils. But as they were drawing near to the Capenian gate, his sister came out to meet him. Now she had been betrothed in marriage to one of the Curiatii, and his cloak, which she had wrought with her own hands, was borne on the shoulders of her brother; and she knew it, and cried out, and wept for him whom she had loved. At the sight of her tears Horatius was so wroth that he drew his sword, and stabbed his sister to the heart; and he said, "So perish the Roman maiden who shall weep for her country's enemy." But men said that it was a dreadful deed, and they dragged him before the two judges who judged when blood had been shed. For thus said the law,

"The two men shall give judgment on the shedder of blood.
If he shall appeal from their judgment, let the appeal be tried.
If their judgment be confirmed, cover his head.
Hang him with a halter on the accursed tree;
Scourge him either within the sacred limit of the city or without."

So they gave judgment on Horatius, and were going to give him over to be put to death. But he appealed, and the appeal was tried before all the Romans, and they would not condemn him because he had conquered for them their enemies, and because his father spoke for him, and said, that he judged the maiden to have been lawfully slain. Yet as blood had been shed, which required to be atoned for, the Romans gave a certain sum of money to offer sacrifices to atone for the pollution of blood. These sacrifices were duly performed ever afterwards by the members of the house of the Horatii.

Of the fearful punishment of Mettius Fufetius, and of the destruction of Alba.

The Albans were now become bound to obey the Romans;[55] and Tullus called upon them to aid in a war against the people of Veii and Fidenæ. But in the battle the Alban leader, Mettius Fufetius, stood aloof, and gave no true aid to the Romans. So, when the Romans had won the battle, Tullus called the Albans together as if he were going to make a speech to them; and they came to hear him, as was the custom, without their arms; and the Roman soldiers gathered round them, and they could neither fight nor escape. Then Tullus took Mettius and bound him between two chariots, and drove the chariots different ways, and tore him asunder. After this he sent his people to Alba, and they destroyed the city, and made all the Albans come and live at Rome; there they had the hill Cælius for their dwelling-place, and became one people with the Romans.

After this, Tullus made war upon the Sabines, and gained a victory over

[54] Livy, I. 26. [55] Livy, I. 27, et seqq.

How king Tullus, having offended the gods, was killed by lightning.

them.[56] But now, whether it were that Tullus had neglected the worship of the gods whilst he had been so busy in his wars, the signs of the wrath of heaven became manifest. A plague broke out among the people, and Tullus himself was at last stricken with a lingering disease. Then he bethought him of good and holy Numa, and how, in his time, the gods had been so gracious to Rome, and had made known their will by signs whenever Numa inquired of them. So Tullus also tried to inquire of Jupiter, but the god was angry, and would not be inquired of, for Tullus did not consult him rightly; so he sent his lightnings, and Tullus and all his house were burnt to ashes. This made the Romans know that they wanted a king who would follow the example of Numa; so they chose his daughter's son, Ancus Marcius, to reign over them in the room of Tullus.

THE STORY OF ANCUS MARCIUS.

Of the good reign of Ancus Marcius.

Ancient story does not tell much of Ancus Marcius. He published the religious ceremonies which Numa had commanded, and had them written out upon whited boards, and hung up round the forum, that all might know and observe them.[57] He had a war with the Latins and conquered them, and brought the people to Rome, and gave them the hill Aventinus to dwell on.[58] He divided the lands of the conquered Latins amongst all the Romans;[59] and he gave up the forests near the sea which he had taken from the Latins, to be the public property of the Romans. He founded the colony at Ostia, by the mouth of the Tiber.[60] He built a fortress on the hill Janiculum, and joined the hill to the city by a wooden bridge over the river.[61] He secured the city in the low grounds between the hills by a great dyke, which was called the dyke of the Quirites.[62] And he built a prison under the hill Saturnius, towards the forum, because, as the people grew in numbers, offenders against the laws became more numerous also.[63] At last king Ancus died, after a reign of three-and-twenty years.[64]

CHAPTER II.

THE EARLY HISTORY OF ROME.

Ἐκ τῶν εἰρημένων τεκμηρίων τοιαῦτα ἄν τις νομίζων μάλιστα ἃ διῆλθον, οὐχ ἁμαρτάνοι· καὶ οὔτε ὡς ποιηταὶ ὑμνήκασι περὶ αὐτῶν, ἐπὶ τὸ μεῖζον κοσμοῦντες, μᾶλλον πιστεύων, οὔτε ὡς λογογράφοι ξυνέθεσαν ἐπὶ τὸ προσαγωγότερον τῇ ἀκροάσει ἢ ἀληθέστερον, ὄντα ἀνεξέλεγκτα καὶ τὰ πολλὰ ὑπὸ χρόνου αὐτῶν ἀπίστως ἐπὶ τὸ μυθῶδες ἐκνενικηκότα, εὑρῆσθαι δὲ ἡγησάμενος ἐκ τῶν ἐπιφανεστάτων σημείων, ὡς παλαιὰ εἶναι, ἀποχρώντως.—THUCYDIDES, I. 21.

I HAVE given the stories of the early kings and founders of Rome, in their own proper form; not wishing any one to mistake them for real history, but thinking them far too famous and too striking to be omitted. But what is the real history, in the place of which we have so long admired the tales of Romulus and Numa? This is a question which cannot be satisfactorily answered: I shall

56 Livy, I. 31.
57 Livy, I. 32. Dionysius, III. 36.
58 Cicero de Repub. II. 18. Livy, I. 33.
59 Cicero de Repub. II. 18.
60 Cicero, ib. Livy, I. 33. Dionys. III. 44.
61 Livy, I. 33.
62 Livy, I. 33.
63 Livy, I. 33.
64 Cicero de Repub. II. 18. Livy says, "twenty-four years." I. 35.

content myself here with giving the few points that seem sufficiently established; referring those who desire to go deeply into the whole question, to that immortal work of Niebuhr, which has left other writers nothing else to do, except either to copy or to abridge it.

The first question in the history of every people is, What was their race and language? the next, What was the earliest form of their society, their social and political organization? Let us see how far we can answer these questions with respect to Rome.

Language of the Romans.

The language of the Romans was not called Roman, but Latin. Politically, Rome and Latium were clearly distinguished, but their language appears to have been the same. This language is different from the Etruscan, and from the Oscan; the Romans, therefore, are so far marked out as distinct from the great nations of central Italy, whether Etruscans, Umbrians, Sabines, or Samnites.

Partly connected with that of Greece.

On the other hand, the connection of the Latin language with the Greek is manifest. Many common words, which no nation ever derives from the literature of another, are the same in Greek and Latin; the declensions of the nouns and verbs are, to a great degree, similar. It is probable that the Latins belonged to that great race which, in very early times, overspread both Greece and Italy, under the various names of Pelasgians, Tyrsenians, and Siculians. It may be believed, that the Hellenians were anciently a people of this same race, but that some peculiar circumstances gave to them a distinct and superior character, and raised them so far above their brethren, that in after ages they disclaimed all connection with them.[1]

Partly with that of the Oscans.

But in the Latin language there is another element besides that which it has in common with the Greek. This element belongs to the languages of central Italy, and may be called Oscan. Further, Niebuhr has remarked, that whilst the terms relating to agriculture and domestic life are mostly derived from the Greek part of the language, those relating to arms and war are mostly Oscan.[2] It seems, then, not only that the Latins were a mixed people, partly Pelasgian and partly Oscan; but also that they arose out of a conquest of the Pelasgians by the Oscans: so that the latter were the ruling class of the united nation; the former were its subjects.

Differences between the Romans and the other Latins.

The Latin language, then, may afford us a clue to the origin of the Latin people, and so far to that of the Romans. But it does not explain the difference between the Romans and Latins, to which the peculiar fates of the Roman people owe their origin. We must inquire, then, what the Romans were, which the other Latins were not; and as language cannot aid us here, we must have recourse to other assistance, to geography and national

[1] The Pelasgians, in the opinion of Herodotus, were a barbarian race, and spoke a barbarian language.—I. 57, 58. This merely means that they did not speak Greek. No one doubts the connection between Greek and Latin; yet Plautus, speaking of one of his own comedies, the story of which was borrowed from Philemon, says,

"Philemo scripsit, Plautus vertit barbarè."—
Trinummus, Prolog. v. 19.

That is, "translated into Latin." The discovery of affinities in languages, when they are not so close as to constitute merely a difference of dialect, belongs only to philologers. Who, till very lately, suspected that Sanskrit and English had any connection with each other?

[2] He instances, on the one hand, Domus, Ager, Aratrum, Vinum, Oleum, Lac, Bos, Sus, Ovis; while on the other hand, Duellum, Ensis, Hasta, Sagitta, &c., are quite different from the corresponding Greek terms. See Niebuhr, Rom. Gesch. Vol. I. p. 82. Ed. 1827.

The word "scutum" was, in the first edition of this work, introduced inadvertently into the list of Latin military terms, unconnected with Greek; as it is evidently of the same family with σκῦτος: but yet there are so many words of the same family in the other languages of the Indo-Germanic stock, that the connection belongs rather to the general resemblance subsisting between all those languages, than to the closer likeness which may subsist between any two of them towards one another. And this more distant relationship exists, I doubt not, between the Oscan and even the Etruscan languages, and the other branches of the Indo-Germanic family; and so far Greek, as well as Sanskrit, Persian, or German, may be rightly used as an instrument to enable us to decipher the Etruscan inscriptions. Lanzi's fault consisted in assuming too close a resemblance between Greek and Etruscan; in supposing that they were sisters, rather than distant cousins.

traditions. And thus, at the same time, we shall arrive at an answer to the second question in Roman history, What was the earliest form of civil society at Rome?

Distinct geographical position of Rome.

If we look at the map, we shall see that Rome lies at the farthest extremity of Latium, divided from Etruria only by the Tiber, and having the Sabines close on the north, between the Tiber and the Anio. No other Latin town, so far as we know, was built on the Tiber;[3] some were clustered on and round the Alban hills, others lined the coast of the Mediterranean, but from all these Rome, by its position, stood aloof.

Intermixture of Sabine and Etruscan institutions and people.

Tradition reports that as Rome was thus apart from the rest of the Latin cities, and so near a neighbor to the Etruscans and Sabines, so its population was in part formed out of one of these nations, and many of its rites and institutions borrowed from the other. Tradition describes the very first founders of the city as the shepherds and herdsmen of the banks of the Tiber, and tells how their numbers were presently swelled by strangers and outcasts from all the countries round about. It speaks of a threefold division of the Roman people, in the very earliest age of its history; the tribes of the Ramnenses, Titienses, and Luceres. It distinctly acknowledges the Titienses to have been Sabines; and in some of its guesses at the origin of the Luceres, it connects their name with that of the Etruscan Lucumones,[4] and thus supposes them to have been composed of Etruscans.

We know that for all points of detail, and for keeping a correct account of time, tradition is worthless. It is very possible that all Etruscan rites and usages came in with the Tarquinii, and were falsely carried back to an earlier period. But the mixture of the Sabines with the original people of the Palatine Hill cannot be doubted; and the stories of the asylum, and of the violence done to the Sabine women, seem to show that the first settlers of the Palatine were a mixed race, in which other blood was largely mingled with that of the Latins. We may conceive of this earlier people of Mamers, as of the Mamertini of a more historical period: that they were a band of resolute adventurers from various parts, practised in arms, and little scrupulous how they used them. Thus the origin of the highest Roman nobility may have greatly resembled that larger band of adventurers who followed the standard of William the Norman, and were the founders of the nobility of England.

Division of the Roman people into three tribes.

The people or citizens of Rome were divided into the three tribes of the Ramnenses, Titienses, and Luceres,[5] to whatever races we may suppose them to belong, or at whatever time and under whatever circumstances they may have become united. Each of these tribes was divided into ten smaller bodies called curiæ; so that the whole people consisted of thirty curiæ: these same divisions were in war represented by the thirty centuries which made up the legion, just as the three tribes were represented by the three centuries of horsemen; but that the soldiers of each century were exactly a hundred, is apparently as unfounded a conclusion, as it would be if we were to argue in the same way as to the military force of one of our English hundreds.

I have said that each tribe was divided into ten curiæ; it would be more cor-

[3] I had forgotten what may be the single exception of Ficana, which, according to Festus, stood on the road to Ostia, at the eleventh milestone from Rome: that is, according to Sir W. Gell and others, at the spot now called Tenuta di Dragoncella. But Westphal places Ficana at Traphusa, which is at some distance from the Tiber; so that, according to him, the statement in the text would be absolutely correct.

[4] So Junius Gracchanus, as quoted by Varro, de L. L., V. sec. 55; and so also Cicero, de Republicâ, II. 8.

[5] These in Livy's first book are called merely "Centuriæ equitum," ch. 13. But in the tenth book, ch. 6, they appear as "Antiquæ tribus." Both expressions come to the same thing, for the three centuries of horsemen, as appears by the story of Tarquinius Priscus and the augur, Attus Navius, were supposed to represent the three tribes, and their number was fixed upon that principle: just as the thirty centuries of foot soldiers represented the thirty curiæ.

Tribes made up of Curiæ; curiæ of houses.

rect to say, that the union of ten curiæ formed the tribe. For the state grew out of the junction of certain original elements; and these were neither the tribes, nor even the curiæ, but the gentes or houses which made up the curiæ. The first element of the whole system was the gens or house, a union of several families who were bound together by the joint performance of certain religious rites. Actually, where a system of houses has existed within historical memory, the several families who composed a house were not necessarily related to one another; they were not really cousins more or less distant, all descended from a common ancestor. But there is no reason to doubt that in the original idea of a house, the bond of union between its several families was truly sameness of blood: such was likely to be the earliest acknowledged tie; although afterwards, as names are apt to outlive their meanings, an artificial bond may have succeeded to the natural one; and a house, instead of consisting of families of real relations, was made up sometimes of families of strangers, whom it was proposed to bind together by a fictitious tie, in the hope that law, and custom, and religion, might together rival the force of nature.

The houses and their clients.

Thus the state being made up of families, and every family consisting from the earliest times of members and dependents, the original inhabitants of Rome belonged all to one of two classes: they were either members of a family; and if so, members of a house, of a curia, of a tribe, and so, lastly, of the state: or they were dependents on a family; and, if so, their relation went no further than the immediate aggregate of families, that is, the house: with the curia, with the tribe, and with the state, they had no connection.

These members of families were the original citizens of Rome; these dependents on families were the original clients.

The commons, or plebs.

The idea of clientship is that of a wholly private relation; the clients were something to their respective patrons, but to the state they were nothing. But wherever states composed in this manner, of a body of houses with their clients, had been long established, there grew up amidst or close beside them, created in most instances by conquest, a population of a very distinct kind. Strangers might come to live in the land, or more commonly the inhabitants of a neighboring district might be conquered, and united with their conquerors as a subject people. Now this population had no connection with the houses separately, but only with a state composed of those houses: this was wholly a political, not a domestic relation; it united personal and private liberty with political subjection. This inferior population possessed property, regulated their own municipal as well as domestic affairs, and as free men fought in the armies of what was now their common country. But, strictly, they were not its citizens; they could not intermarry with the houses, they could not belong to the state, for they belonged to no house, and therefore to no curia, and no tribe; consequently they had no share in the state's government, nor in the state's property. What the state conquered in war became the property of the state, and therefore they had no claim to it; with the state demesne, with whatever, in short, belonged to the state in its aggregate capacity, these, as being its neighbors merely, and not its members, had no concern.

Such an inferior population, free personally, but subject politically, not slaves, yet not citizens, were the original Plebs, the commons of Rome.

Their settlement on the Aventine Hill.

The mass of the Roman commons were conquered Latins.[6] These, besides receiving grants of a portion of their former lands, to be held by them as Roman citizens, had also the hill Aventinus assigned as a residence to those of them who removed to Rome. The Aventine was without the walls, although so near to them: thus the commons were, even in the nature of their abode, like the Pfalburger of the middle ages,—men not admitted to live within the city, but enjoying its protection against foreign enemies.

[6] See Niebuhr's chapter "Die Gemeinde und die plebeischen Tribus."

It will be understood at once, that whatever is said of the people in these early times, refers only to the full citizens, that is, to the members of the houses. The assembly of the people was the assembly of the curiæ; that is, the great council of the members of the houses; while the senate, consisting of two hundred senators, chosen in equal numbers from the two higher tribes of the Ramnenses and Titienses, was their smaller or ordinary council.

Members of the houses were the only citizens.

The power of the king was as varied and ill-defined as in the feudal monarchies of the middle ages. Over the commons he was absolute; but over the real people, that is, over the houses, his power was absolute only in war, and without the city. Within the walls every citizen was allowed to appeal from the king, or his judges, to the sentence of his peers; that is, to the great council of the curiæ. The king had his demesne lands,[7] and in war would receive his portion of the conquered land, as well as of the spoil of movables.

The king's power over the citizens, and over the commons.

CHAPTER III.

OF THE CITY OF ROME, ITS TERRITORY, AND ITS SCENERY.

"——— Muros, arcemque procul, ac rara domorum
Tecta vident.———
Hoc nemus, hunc, inquit, frondoso vertice collem,
Quis Deus incertum est, habitat Deus."
Virgil, Æn. VIII.

If it is hard to carry back our ideas of Rome from its actual state to the period of its highest splendor, it is yet harder to go back in fancy to a time still more distant, a time earlier than the beginning of its authentic history, before man's art had completely rescued the very soil of the future city from the dominion of nature. Here also it is vain to attempt accuracy in the details, or to be certain that the several features in our description all existed at the same period. It is enough if we can image to ourselves some likeness of the original state of Rome, before the undertaking of those great works which are ascribed to the later kings.

Early state of the city of Rome.

The Pomœrium of the original city on the Palatine, as described by Tacitus,[1] included not only the hill itself, but some portion of the ground immediately below it; it did not, however, reach as far as any of the other hills. The valley between the Palatine and the Aventine, afterwards the site of the Circus Maximus, was in the earliest times covered with water;

The original Pomœrium.

[7] Cicero de Republicâ, V. 3.

[1] Tacitus, Annal. XII. 24.—It is evident, by the minuteness of his description, that the consecrated limits of the original city had been carefully preserved by tradition; and this is exactly one of the points on which, as we know by our own experience with regard to parish boundaries, a tradition kept up by yearly ceremonies may safely be trusted. The exact line of this original Pomœrium is thus marked by Bunsen in his description of Rome, Vol. I. p. 137: "It set out from the Forum Boarium, the site of which is fixed by the Arch of Septimius Severus, at the Janus Quadrifons" (this must not be confounded with the Arch of Severus on the Via Sacra, just under the capitol), "and passed through the valley of the circus, so as to include the Ara Maxima, as far as the Ara Consi, at the foot of the hill. It then proceeded from the Septizonium (just opposite the church of S. Gregorio, at the foot of the Palatine), till it came under the baths of Trajan (or Titus), which were the Curiæ Veteres. From thence it passed on to the top of the Velia, on which the Arch of Titus now stands, and where Tacitus places the Sacellum Larium."

so also was the greater part of the valley between the Palatine and the Capitoline, the ground afterwards occupied by the Roman forum.

The original seven hills.

But the city of the Palatine Hill grew in process of time, so as to become a city of seven hills. Not the seven famous hills of imperial or republican Rome, but seven spots more or less elevated, and all belonging to three only of the later seven hills, that is, to the Palatine, the Cælian, and the Esquiline. These first seven hills of Rome were known by the names of Palatium, Velia, Cermalus, Cælius, Fagutal, Oppius, and Cispius.[2] Of this town the Aventine formed a suburb; and the dyke of the Quirites, ascribed in the story to Ancus Marcius, ran across the valley from the edge of the Aventine to that of the Cælian Hill near the Porta Capena.[3]

They did not include all the seven hills of the later city.

At this time Rome, though already a city on seven hills, was distinct from the Sabine city on the Capitoline, Quirinal, and Viminal Hills. The two cities, although united under one government, had still a separate existence; they were not completely blended into one till that second period in Roman history which we shall soon have to consider, the reigns of the later kings.

The Ager Romanus.

The territory of the original Rome during its first period, the true Ager Romanus, could be gone round in a single day.[4] It did not extend beyond the Tiber at all, nor probably beyond the Anio; and, on the east and south, where it had most room to spread, its limit was between five and six miles from the city. This Ager Romanus was the exclusive property of the Roman people, that is, of the houses; it did not include the lands conquered from the Latins, and given back to them again when the Latins became the plebs or commons of Rome. According to the augurs,[5] the Ager Romanus was a peculiar district in a religious sense; auspices could be taken within its bounds, which could be taken nowhere without them.

Scenery of the neighborhood of Rome.

And now what was Rome, and what was the country around it, which have both acquired an interest such as can cease only when earth itself shall perish? The hills of Rome are such as we rarely see in England, low in height, but with steep and rocky sides.[6] In early times the natural wood still remained in patches amidst the buildings, as at this day

It followed nearly the line of the Via Sacra, as far as the eastern end of the Forum Romanum. But Tacitus does not mention it as going on to join the Forum Boarium, because in the earliest times this valley was either a lake or a swamp, and the Pomœrium could not descend below the edge of the Palatine Hill. Nibby, in his work on the walls of Rome, places the Curiæ Veteres on the Palatine, and the Sacellum Larium between the Arch of Titus and the Forum on the Via Nova. The position of the Curiæ Veteres is certainly doubtful. Niebuhr himself (Vol. I. p. 288. Note 785. Eng. Tr.) thinks that the Pomœrium can scarcely be carried so far as the foot of the Esquiline; and the authority for identifying the Curiæ Veteres with the site of the Baths of Titus or Trajan is not decisive; for it only appears that Biondo, writing in 1440, calls the ruins of the Baths "Curia Vecchia," and says that in old legal instruments they were commonly so called. (Beschreibung Roms, Vol. III. part 2, p. 222.) Now considering the general use of the word Curia, and that the name is in the singular number, it by no means follows that Biondo's Curia Vetus must be the Curiæ Veteres of Tacitus.

[2] For the account of this old Septimontium, see Festus, under the word "Septimontio." Festus adds an eighth name, Suburra. Niebuhr conjectures that the inhabitants of the Pagus Sucusanus (which was the same district as the Suburra, and lay under the Esquiline and Viminal Hills, near the church of S. Francesco di Paola, where a miserable sort of square is still called Piazza Suburra) may have joined in the festival of the inhabitants of these seven hills or heights, although they were not themselves "Montani" (see Varro de L. L., VI. 24. Ed. Müller), to show that they belonged to the city of the Palatine, and not to the Sabine city of the Capitoline Hill. For the exact situations of the other seven spots, see Bunsen, description of Rome, Vol. I. p. 141. Velia was the ascent on the northeast side of the Palatine, where the Arch of Titus now stands. Cermalus, or Germalus, was on the northwest side of the Palatine, just above the Velabrum: Fagutal is thought to have been the ground near the Porta Esquilina, between the Arch of Gallienus and the Sette Sale. Oppius and Cispius were also parts of the Esquiline; the former is marked by the present church of S. Maria Maggiore, and the latter lay between that church and the baths of Diocletian.

[3] See Niebuhr, Vol. I. p. 403. Ed. 2d. and Bunsen. Beschreibung Roms, Vol. I. p. 620.

[4] See Strabo, Lib. V. p. 253. Ed. Xyland, and compare Livy, I. 23. "Fossa Cluilia, ab Urbe haud plus quinque millia." And II. 39. "Ad Fossas Cluilias V. ab Urbe M. P. castris positis, populatur *inde Agrum Romanum.*

[5] See Varro de L. L., V. 33. Ed. Müller.

[6] The substance of this description, taken from my journals and recollections of my visit

it grows here and there on the green sides of the Monte Testacco. Across the Tiber the ground rises to a greater height than that of the Roman hills, but its summit is a level unbroken line, while the heights, which opposite to Rome itself rise immediately from the river, under the names of Janiculus and Vaticanus, then sweep away to some distance from it, and returned in their highest and boldest form at the Monte Mario, just above the Milvian bridge and the Flaminian road. Thus to the west the view is immediately bounded; but to the north and northeast the eye ranges over the low ground of the Campagna to the nearest line of the Apennines, which closes up, as with a gigantic wall, all the Sabine, Latin, and Volscian lowlands, while over it are still distinctly to be seen the high summits of the central Apennines, covered with snow, even at this day, for more than six months in the year. South and southwest lies the wide plain of the Campagna; its level line succeeded by the equally level line of the sea, which can only be distinguished from it by the brighter light reflected from its waters. Eastward, after ten miles of plain, the view is bounded by the Alban hills, a cluster of high, bold points rising out of the Campagna, like Arran from the sea, on the highest of which, at nearly the same height with the summit of Helvellyn,[7] stood the Temple of Jupiter Latiaris, the scene of the common worship of all the people of the Latin name. Immediately under this highest point lies the crater-like basin of the Alban lake; and on its nearer rim might be seen the trees of the grove of Ferentia, where the Latins held the great civil assemblies of their nation. Further to the north, on the edge of the Alban hills looking towards Rome, was the town and citadel of Tusculum; and beyond this, a lower summit, crowned with the walls and towers of Labicum, seems to connect the Alban hills with the line of the Apennines just at the spot where the citadel of Præneste, high upon the mountain side, marks the opening into the country of the Hernicans, and into the valleys of the streams that feed the Liris.

Character of the Campagna.

Returning nearer to Rome, the lowland country of the Campagna is broken by long green swelling ridges, the ground rising and falling, as in the heath country of Surrey and Berkshire. The streams are dull and sluggish, but the hill sides above them constantly break away into little rocky cliffs, where on every ledge the wild fig now strikes out its branches, and tufts of broom are clustering, but which in old times formed the natural strength of the citadels of the numerous cities of Latium. Except in these narrow dells, the present aspect of the country is all bare and desolate, with no trees nor any human habitation. But anciently, in the time of the early kings of Rome, it was full of independent cities, and in its population and the careful cultivation of its little garden-like farms, must have resembled the most flourishing parts of Lombardy or the Netherlands.

Such was Rome, and such its neighborhood; such also, as far as we can discover, was the earliest form of its society, and such the legends which fill up the place of its lost history. Even for the second period, on which we are now going to enter, we have no certain history; but a series of stories as beautiful as they are unreal, and a few isolated political institutions, which we cannot confidently connect with their causes or their authors. As before, then, I must first give the stories in their oldest and most genuine form; and then offer, in meagre contrast, all that can be collected or conjectured of the real history.

to Rome in 1827, was inserted some time since in the History of Rome published by the Society for the Diffusion of Useful Knowledge. I am obliged to mention this, lest I might be suspected of having borrowed from another work without acknowledgment what was in fact furnished to that work by myself.

[7] The height of Monte Cavo is variously given at 2938 or 2965 French feet. See Bunsen, Vol. I. p. 40. Helvellyn is reckoned at 3055 English feet, by Col. Mudge; by Mr. Otley, in his Guide to the Lakes, it is estimated at 3070.

CHAPTER IV.

STORIES OF THE LATER KINGS.

"Quis novus hic nostris successit sedibus hospes?
Quem sese ore ferens, quam forti pectore et armis?"
VIRGIL, Æn. IV.

STORY OF L. TARQUINIUS PRISCUS.

In the days of Ancus Marcius there came to Rome from Tarquinii, a city of Etruria, a wealthy Etruscan and his wife.[1] The father of this stranger was a Greek,[2] a citizen of Corinth, who left his native land because it was oppressed by a tyrant, and found a home at Tarquinii. There he married a noble Etruscan lady, and by her he had two sons. But his son found, that for his father's sake he was still looked upon as a stranger; so he left Tarquinii, and went with his wife Tanaquil to Rome, for there, it was said, strangers were held in more honor. Now as he came near to the gates of Rome, as he was sitting in his chariot with Tanaquil his wife, an eagle came and plucked the cap from his head, and bore it aloft into the air; and then flew down again and placed it upon his head, as it had been before. So Tanaquil was glad at this sight, and she told her husband, for she was skilled in augury, that this was a sign of the favor of the gods, and she bade him be of good cheer, for that he would surely rise to greatness.

Of the birth of Tarquinius, and how he came to Rome.

Now when the stranger came to Rome, they called him Lucius Tarquinius;[3] and he was a brave man and wise in council; and his riches won the good word of the multitude; and he became known to the king. He served the king well in peace and war, so that Ancus held him in great honor, and when he died he named him by his will to be the guardian of his children.

Of his favor with king Ancus.

But Tarquinius was in great favor with the people, and when he desired to be king, they resolved to choose him rather than the son of Ancus. So he began to reign, and he did great works, both in war and peace. He made war on the Latins, and took from them a great spoil.[4] Then he made war on the Sabines, and he conquered them in two battles, and took from them the town of Collatia, and gave it to Egerius, his brother's son, who had come with him from Tarquinii. Lastly, there was another war with the Latins, and Tarquinius went round to their cities, and took them one after another; for none dared to go out to meet him in open battle. These were his acts in war.

Of his deeds in war.

He also did great works in peace;[5] for he made vast drains to carry off the water from between the Palatine and the Aventine, and from between the Palatine and the Capitoline Hills. And in the space between the Palatine and the Aventine, after he had drained it, he formed the Circus, or great race-course, for chariot and for horse races. Then in the space between the Palatine and the Capitoline he made a forum or market-place, and divided out the ground around it for shops or stalls, and made a covered walk round it. Next he set about building a wall of stone to go round the city; and

Of his works in peace

[1] Livy, I. 34.
[2] Livy, ibid. Dionys. III. 46–48. Cicero de Republicâ, II. 19.
[3] Cicero, Livy, and Dionysius, in locis citatis.
[4] Livy, I. 35–38.
[5] Livy, I. 38. 35. Dionysius, III. 67, 68.

he laid the foundations of a great temple on the Capitoline Hill, which was to be the temple of the gods of Rome. He also added a hundred new senators to the senate, and doubled the number of the horsemen in the centuries of the Ramnenses, Titienses, and Luceres, for he wanted to strengthen his force of horsemen; and when he had done so, his horse gained him great victories over his enemies.

Of the famous augur, Attus Navius.

Now he first had it in his mind to make three new centuries of horsemen, and to call them after his own name. But Attus Navius, who was greatly skilled in[6] augury, forbade him. Then the king mocked at his art, and said, "Come now, thou augur, tell me by thy auguries, whether the thing which I now have in my mind may be done or not." And Attus Navius asked counsel of the gods by augury, and he answered, "It may." Then the king said, "It was in my mind that thou shouldst cut in two this whetstone with this razor. Take them, and do it, and fulfil thy augury if thou canst." But Attus took the razor and the whetstone, and he cut, and cut the whetstone asunder. So the king obeyed his counsels, and made no new centuries; and in all things afterwards he consulted the gods by augury, and obeyed their bidding.

How Tarquinius chose Servius Tullius to be his heir, and how he was murdered by the sons of Ancus.

Tarquinius reigned long and prospered greatly; and there was a young man brought up in his household, of whose birth some told wonderful tales, and said that he was[7] the son of a god; but others said[8] that his mother was a slave, and his father was one of the king's clients. But he served the king well, and was in favor with the people, and the king promised him his daughter in marriage. The young man was called Servius Tullius. But when the sons of king Ancus saw that Servius was so loved by king Tarquinius, they resolved to slay the king, lest he should make this stranger his heir, and so they should lose the crown forever. So they[9] set on two shepherds to do the deed, and these went to the king's palace, and pretended to be quarrelling with each other, and both called on the king to do them right. The king sent for them to hear their story; and while he was hearing one of them speak, the other struck him on the head with his hatchet, and then both of them fled. But Tanaquil, the king's wife, pretended that he was not dead, but only stunned by the blow; and she said that he had appointed Servius Tullius to rule in his name, till he should be well again. So Servius went forth in royal state, and judged causes amidst the people, and acted in all things as if he were king, till after a while it was known that the king was dead, and Servius was suffered to reign in his place. Then the sons of Ancus saw that there was no hope left for them; and they fled from Rome, and lived the rest of their days in a foreign land.

THE STORY OF SERVIUS TULLIUS.

"Long live the Commons' King, King James."
LADY OF THE LAKE.

How king Servius enlarged the city.

Servius Tullius was a just and good king;[10] he loved the commons, and he divided among them the lands which had been conquered in war, and he made many wise and good laws, to maintain the cause of the poor, and to stop the oppression of the rich. He made war with the Etruscans,[11] and conquered them. He added the Quirinal and the Viminal Hills[12] to the city, and he brought many new citizens to live on the Esquiline; and there he lived himself amongst them. He also raised a great mound of earth to join the Esquiline and the Quirinal and the Viminal Hills together, and to cover them from the attacks of an enemy.

[6] Livy, I. 36. Dionysius, III. 70, 71. Cicero de Divinat. I. 17, § 32.
[7] Dionysius, IV. 2. Ovid, Fasti, VI. 627.
[8] Cicero de Repub. II. 21.
[9] Livy, I. 40.
[10] Dionysius, IV. 13-15. 40.
[11] Livy, I. 42.
[12] Livy, I. 43.

He built a temple[13] of Diana on the Aventine, where the Latins, and the Sabines, and the Romans, should offer their common sacrifices; and the Romans were the chief in rank amongst all who worshipped at the temple.

Of his good laws; and how he divided the people into classes and centuries.

He made a new order of things for the whole[14] people; for he divided the people of the city into four tribes, and the people of the country into six-and-twenty. Then he divided all the people into classes, according to the value of their possessions; and the classes he divided into centuries; and the centuries of the several classes furnished themselves with arms, each according to their rank and order: the centuries of the rich classes had good and full armor, the poorer centuries had but darts and slings. And when he had done all these works, he called all the people together in their centuries, and asked if they would have him for their king; and the people answered that he should be their king. But the nobles hated him, because he was so loved by the commons: for he had made a law that there should be no king after him, but two men chosen by the people to govern them year by year. Some even said that it was in his mind to give up his own kingly power, that so he might see with his own eyes the fruit of all the good laws that he had made, and might behold the people wealthy, and free, and happy.

How he married his two daughters to the two sons of king Tarquinius.

Now king Servius had no son,[15] but he had two daughters; and he gave them in marriage to the two sons of king Tarquinius. These daughters were of very unlike natures, and so were their husbands: for Aruns Tarquinius was of a meek and gentle spirit, but his brother Lucius was proud and full of evil; and the younger Tullia, who was the wife of Aruns, was more full of evil than his brother Lucius; and the elder Tullia, who was the wife of Lucius, was as good and gentle as his brother Aruns. So the evil could not bear the good, but longed to be joined to the evil that was like itself; and Lucius slew his wife secretly, and the younger Tullia slew her husband, and then they were married to one another, that they might work all the wickedness of their hearts, according to the will of fate.

How Lucius Tarquinius plotted against him and caused him to be murdered.

Then Lucius plotted with the nobles,[16] who hated the good king; and he joined himself to the sworn brotherhoods of the young nobles, in which they bound themselves to stand by each other in their deeds of violence and oppression. When all was ready, he waited for the season of the harvest, when the commons,[17] who loved the king, were in the fields getting in their corn. Then he went suddenly to the forum with a band of armed men, and seated himself on the king's throne before the doors of the senate-house, where he was wont to judge the people. And they ran to the king, and told him that Lucius was sitting on his throne. Upon this the old man[18] went in haste to the forum, and when he saw Lucius he asked him wherefore he had dared to sit on the king's seat. And Lucius answered that it was his father's throne, and that he had more right in it than Servius. Then he seized the old man, and threw him down the steps of the senate-house to the ground; and he went into the senate-house, and called together the senators, as if he were already king. Servius meanwhile arose, and began to make his way home to his house; but when he was come near to the Esquiline Hill, some whom Lucius had sent after him overtook him and slew him, and left him in his blood in the middle of the way.

How the wicked Tullia drove her chariot over her father's dead body.

Then the wicked Tullia[19] mounted her chariot, and drove into the forum, nothing ashamed to go amidst the multitude of men, and she called Lucius out from the senate-house, and said to him, "Hail to thee, king Tarquinius!" But Lucius bade her go home; and as she was going home, the body of her father was lying in the way. The driver of the chariot stopped short, and showed to Tullia where her father lay in his blood. But

[13] Livy, I. 45.
[14] Dionysius, IV. 16-20. Livy, I. 43. Cicero de Republicâ, II. 22.
[15] Livy, I. 46.
[16] Livy, I. 46. Dionysius, IV. 30.
[17] Dionysius, IV. 38.
[18] Livy, I. 48.
[19] Livy, I. 48.

she bade him drive on, for the furies of her wickedness were upon her, and the chariot rolled over the body; and she went to her home with her father's blood upon the wheels of her chariot. Thus Lucius Tarquinius and the wicked Tullia reigned in the place of the good king Servius.

THE STORY OF LUCIUS TARQUINIUS THE TYRANT.

Τύραννος——νόμαιά τε κινεῖ πάτρια, καὶ βιᾶται γυναῖκας, κτείνει τε ἀκρίτους.—HERODOTUS, III. 80.

——Superbos
Tarquinî fasces.—HORACE, Carm. I. 12.

Of king Tarquinius and his great power.

Lucius Tarquinius gained his power wickedly, and no less wickedly did he exercise it. He kept a guard[20] of armed men about him, and he ruled all things at his own will: many were they whom he spoiled of their goods, many were they whom he banished, and many also whom he slew. He despised the senate, and made no new senators in the place of those whom he slew, or who died in the course of nature, wishing that the senators might become fewer and fewer, till there should be none of them left. And he made friends of the chief men among the Latins, and gave his daughter in marriage to Octavius Mamilius of Tusculum; and he became very powerful amongst the Latins, insomuch that when Turnus Herdonius of Aricia had dared to speak against him in the great assembly of the Latins, Tarquinius accused him of plotting his death, and procured false witnesses to confirm his charge; so that the Latins judged him to be guilty, and ordered him to be drowned. After this they were so afraid of Tarquinius, that they made a league with him, and followed him in his wars wherever he chose to lead them. The Hernicans[21] also joined this league, and so did Ecetra and Antium, cities of the Volscians.

Of his buildings, and how he prepared the ground for his new temple.

Then Tarquinius made war upon the rest of the Volscians, and he took[22] Suessa Pometia, in the lowlands of the Volscians, and the tithe of the spoil was forty talents of silver. So he set himself to raise mighty works in Rome; and he finished what his father had begun; the great drains to drain the low grounds of the city, and the temple on the Capitoline Hill. Now the ground on which he was going to build his temple, was taken up with many holy places of the gods of the Sabines, which had been founded in the days of king Tatius. But Tarquinius consulted the gods by augury whether he might not take away these holy places, to make room for his own new temple. The gods allowed him to take away all the rest, except only the holy places of the god of Youth,[23] and of Terminus the god of boundaries, which they would not suffer him to move. But the augurs said that this was a happy omen, for that it showed how the youth of the city should never pass away, nor its boundaries be moved by the conquests of an enemy. A human head was also found, as they were digging the foundations of the temple, and this too was a sign that the Capitoline Hill should be the head of all the earth. So Tarquinius built a mighty temple, and consecrated it to Jupiter,[24] and to Juno, and to Minerva, the greatest of the gods of the Etruscans.

Of the strange woman who brought the books of the Sibyl to the king.

At this time there came a strange woman[25] to the king, and offered him nine books of the prophecies of the Sibyl for a certain price. When the king refused them, the woman went and burnt three of the books, and came back and offered the six at the same price which she had asked for the nine; but they mocked at her, and would not take the books. Then she went away, and burnt three more, and came back and asked still the same price for the remaining three. At this the king was astonished, and asked of the augurs what he should

[20] Livy, I. 49–52.
[21] Dionysius, IV. 49.
[22] Livy, I. 53, 55, 56.
[23] Dionysius, III. 69 He tells the story of the elder Tarquinius.
[24] Dionysius, IV. 6[illegible]
[25] Dionysius, [illegible] 62. A. Gellius, I. 19.

do. They said that he had done wrong in refusing the gift of the gods, and bade him by all means to buy the books that were left. So he bought them; and the woman who sold them was seen no more from that day forwards. Then the books were put into a chest of stone, and were kept under ground in the Capitol, and two men[26] were appointed to keep them, and were called the two men of the sacred books.

How Tarquinius won Gabii through the treachery of his son Sextus.

Now Gabii[27] would not submit to Tarquinius, like the other cities of the Latins; so he made war against it; and the war was long, and Tarquinius knew not how to end it. So his son Sextus Tarquinius pretended that his father hated him, and fled to Gabii: and the people of Gabii believed him and trusted him, till at last he betrayed them into his father's power. A treaty was then made with them, and he gave them the right of becoming citizens of Rome,[28] and the Romans had the right of becoming citizens of Gabii, and there was a firm league between the two people.

How he oppressed his people, and made them work like slaves.

Thus Tarquinius was a great and mighty king; but he grievously oppressed the poor, and he took away all the good laws of king Servius, and let the rich oppress the poor, as they had done before the days of Servius. He made the people labor at his great works: he made them build his temple, and dig and construct his drains; he laid such burdens[29] on them, that many slew themselves for very misery; for in the days of Tarquinius the tyrant it was happier to die than to live.

CHAPTER V.

THE HISTORY OF THE LATER KINGS OF ROME, AND OF THE GREATNESS OF THE MONARCHY.

'Επὶ μέγα ἦλθεν ἡ βασιλεία ἰσχύος.—THUCYD. II. 97.

'Αποφανῶ οὔτε τοὺς ἄλλους οὔτε αὐτοὺς 'Αθηναίους περὶ τῶν σφετέρων τυράννων ἀκριβὲς οὐδὲν λέγοντας. —THUCYD. VI. 54.

The accounts even of the later kings are not historical.

THE stories of the two Tarquinii and of Servius Tullius are so much more disappointing than those of the earlier kings, inasmuch as they seem at first to wear a more historical character, and as they really contain much that is undoubtedly true; but yet, when examined, they are found not to be history, nor can any one attach what is real in them to any of the real persons by whom it was effected. The great drains or cloacæ of Rome exist to this hour, to vouch for their own reality; yet of the Tarquinii, by whom they are said to have been made, nothing is certainly known. So also the constitution of the classes and centuries is as real as Magna Charta or the Bill of Rights; yet its pretended author is scarcely a more historical personage than King Arthur; we do not even know his name or race, whether he were Servius Tullius, or Mastarna,[1] a Latin or an Etruscan; the son of a slave reared in the palace of the Roman king, or a military adventurer who settled at Rome together with his companions in arms, and was received with honor for his valor. Still less can we trust

[26] See Livy, III. 10, and VI. 37. Dionysius gives "Ten," which was the later number. Gellius gives "Fifteen."

[27] Livy, I. 53, 54.

[28] Dionysius, IV. 58.

[29] Cassius Hemina, quoted by Servius, Æn. XII. 603.

[1] This is the name by which he was called in the Etruscan histories, quoted by the Emperor Claudius in his speech upon admitting the Gauls to the Roman franchise. This speech was engraved on a brass plate, and was dug up at Lyons about two centuries since, and is now preserved in that city. It was printed by Brotier at the end of his edition of Tacitus, and has been also published in the collections of inscriptions.

the pretended chronology of the common story. The three last reigns, according to Livy, occupied a space of 107 years; yet the king, who at the end of this period is expelled in mature but not in declining age, is the son of the king who ascends the throne a grown man in the vigor of life at the beginning of it: Servius marries the daughter of Tarquinius, a short time before he is made king, yet immediately after his accession he is the father of two grown-up daughters, whom he marries to the brothers of his own wife: the sons of Ancus Marcius wait patiently eight-and-thirty years, and then murder Tarquinius to obtain a throne which they had seen him so long quietly occupy. Still then we are, in a manner, upon enchanted ground; the unreal and the real are strangely mixed up together; but although some real elements exist, yet the general picture before us is a mere fantasy: single trees and buildings may be copied from nature, but their grouping is ideal, and they are placed in the midst of fairy palaces and fairy beings, whose originals this earth has never witnessed.

Three points connected with the three last reigns must be treated historically.

The reigns of the later Roman kings contain three points which require to be treated historically. 1st, The foreign dominion and greatness of the monarchy. 2d, The change introduced in the religion of Rome. And 3d, The changes effected in the constitution, especially the famous system of the classes and centuries, usually ascribed to Servius Tullius.

I. The greatness of the monarchy. Its great works. The walls of Servius Tullius.

1st. The dominion and greatness of the monarchy are attested by two sufficient witnesses; the great works completed at this period, and still existing; and the famous treaty with Carthage, concluded under the first consuls of the Commonwealth, and preserved to us by Polybius. Under the last kings the city of Rome reached the limits which it retained through the whole period of the Commonwealth, and the most flourishing times of the empire. What are called the walls of Servius Tullius continued to be the walls of Rome for nearly eight hundred years, down to the Emperor Aurelian. They enclosed all those well-known seven hills, whose fame has so utterly eclipsed the seven hills already described of the smaller and more ancient city. They followed[2] the outside edge of the Quirinal, Capitoline, Aventine, and Cælian Hills, passing directly across the low grounds between the hills, and thus running parallel to the Tiber between the Capitoline and the Aventine, without going[3] down to the very banks. From the outer or southern side of the Cælian they passed round by the eastern side of the hill to the southern side of the Esquiline; and here, upon some of the highest ground in Rome, was raised a great rampart or mound of earth with towers on the top of it, stretching across from the southern side of the Esquiline to the northern side of the Quirinal. For the Esquiline and Quirinal Hills, as well as the Viminal, which lies between them, are not isolated like the four others, but are like so many promontories running out parallel to one another from one common base,[4] and the rampart passing along

[2] See the account of the walls of Servius in Bunsen's Rome, vol. i., p. 623 et seqq., with the accompanying map, plate I. in the volume of plates.

[3] It is on this point that the German topographers of Rome differ from Nibby, and from all the common plans of ancient Rome, which make the walls go quite down to the river. Their reasons are, 1st, the description of the departure of the 300 Fabii, who are made to leave the city by the Porta Carmentalis; but if the walls came close down to the river, they must have re-entered the city again to cross by the Pons Sublicius: and 2d, Varro's statement, that one end of the Circus Maximus abutted upon the city wall; and that the fish-market was just on the outside of the wall. The first argument seems to me valid; the second cannot be insisted on, because the text of Varro in both places is extremely doubtful. See Varro de L. L., V. § 146. 153. Ed. Müller.

[4] The back of a man's hand when slightly bent, and held with the fingers open, presents an exact image of this part of Rome. The fingers represent the Esquiline, Viminal, and Quirinal, and a line drawn across the hand just upon the knuckles would show the rampart of Servius Tullius. The ground on the outside of the rampart falls for some way like the surface of the hand down to the wrist, and the later wall of Aurelian passed over the wrist instead of over the knuckles, at the bottom of the slope instead of the top of it.

This comparison was suggested to me merely by a view of the ground. It is a strong presumption in favor of its exactness, that the same resemblance struck Brocchi also. Speaking of the Pincian, Quirinal, Viminal, and Esquiline

the highest part of this base formed an artificial boundary, where none was marked out by nature. The circuit of these walls is estimated at about seven Roman miles.

The line of the mound or rampart may still be distinctly traced, and the course and extent of the walls can be sufficiently ascertained; but very few remains are left of the actual building. But the masonry with which the bank of the Tiber was built up, a work ascribed to the elder Tarquinius, and resembling the works of the Babylonian kings along the banks of the Euphrates, is still visible. So also are the massy substructions of the Capitoline temple, which were made in order to form a level surface for the building to stand on, upon one of the two summits of the Capitoline Hill. Above all, enough is still to be seen of the great Cloaca or drain, to assure us that the accounts left us of it are not exaggerated. The foundations of this work were laid about forty feet under ground, its branches were carried under a great part of the city, and brought at last into one grand trunk which ran down into the Tiber exactly to the west of the Palatine Hill. It thus drained the waters of the low grounds on both sides of the Palatine; of the Velabrum, between the Palatine and the Aventine; and of the site of the forum between the Palatine and the Capitoline. The stone employed in the Cloaca is in itself a mark of the great antiquity of the work; it is[5] not the peperino of Gabii and the Alban hills, which was the common building stone in the time of the Commonwealth; much less the travertino, or limestone of the neighborhood of Tibur, the material used in the great works of the early emperors; but it is the stone found in Rome itself, a mass of volcanic materials coarsely cemented together, which afterwards was supplanted by the finer quality of the peperino. Such a work as the Cloaca proves the greatness of the power which effected it, as well as the character of its government. It was wrought by taskwork, like the great works of Egypt; and stories were long current of the misery and degradation which it brought upon the people during its progress. But this taskwork for these vast objects shows a strong and despotic government, which had at its command the whole resources of the people; and such a government could hardly have existed, unless it had been based upon some considerable extent of dominion.

The Cloaca Maxima.

What the Cloaca seems to imply, we find conveyed in express terms in the treaty with Carthage.[6] As this treaty was concluded in the very first year of the Commonwealth, the state of things to which it refers must clearly be that of the latest period of the monarchy. It appears then that the whole coast[7] of Latium was at this time subject to the Roman dominion: Ardea, Antium, Circeii, and Terracina,[8] are expressly mentioned as the

Treaty with Carthage.

Hills, he adds; "Pr darne una sensibile imagine non saprei meglio paragonarle che alle dita di una mano raffigurando la palma il mentovato piano a cui tutte si attaccano."

Suolo di Roma, p. 84.

[5] It is the "Tufa litoide" of Brocchi; one of the volcanic formations which is found in many places in Rome. Brocchi is positive that this is the stone employed in the Cloaca; and the masses of it, he adds, taken from the older walls of Servius, are still to be seen in the present walls not far from the Porta S. Lorenzo.

Suolo di Roma, p. 112.

[6] Polybius, III. 22. See Niebuhr, vol. I. p. 556, ed. 2d.

[7] Niebuhr supposes that the coast eastward of Terracina was also included at this time under the name of Latium, because the treaty speaks of a part of Latium which was not subject to Rome, and because the name of Campania was not yet in existence. But if Polybius has translated his original correctly, the expression ἐάν τινες μὴ ὦσιν ὑπήκοοι would rather seem to provide for the case of a Latin city's revolting from Rome and becoming independent, and for an uncertain state of relations between Rome and Latium, such as may well be supposed to have followed the expulsion of Tarquinius; a state in which the Romans could not know what Latin cities would remain faithful to the new government, and what would take part with the exiled king. On the other hand there is no authority for extending the limits of Latium beyond Terracina. The name Campania, it is true, did not exist so early, but Thucydides calls Cuma a city of Opicia, not of Latium; and the Volscians or Auruncans must have already occupied the country on the Liris, and between that river and Terracina, although their conquests of Terracina itself as well as of Antium took place some years later. For the annals speak of Cora and Pometia revolting to the Aurunci as early as the year 251, which shows that they must at that time have been powerful in the neighborhood of Latium; not to mention the alleged Volscian conquests of the last king Tarquinius in the lowlands even of Latium proper.

[8] A fourth name is added in the MSS. of Polybius, 'Αρεντίνων. The editors have gener-

subject allies (ὑπήκοοι) of Rome. Of these, Circeii is said in the common story to have been a Roman colony founded by the last Tarquinius; but we read of it no less than of the others as independent, and making peace or war with Rome, during the Commonwealth down to a much later period. Now it is scarcely conceivable that the Romans could thus have been masters of the whole coast of Latium, without some corresponding dominion in the interior; and we may well believe that Rome was at this time the acknowledged head of the Latin cities, and exercised a power over them more resembling the sovereignty of Athens over her allies than the modern supremacy of Lacedæmon. On the right bank of the Tiber the Romans seem to have possessed nothing on the coast; but the stories of Etruscan conquests which we find in the common accounts of Servius Tullius, are so far justified by better testimony as to make it probable that in the direction of Veii the Roman dominion[9] had reached beyond the Tiber, and that the territory thus gained from the Etruscans formed a very considerable part of the whole territory of Rome. It is well known that the number of local tribes established by the later kings was thirty; whereas a few years after the beginning of the Commonwealth we find them reduced to twenty. Now, as even the common account of the war with Porsenna describes the Romans as giving up to the Veientians a portion of territory formerly conquered from them, it becomes a very probable conjecture that the Etruscans, soon after the expulsion of the kings, recovered all the country which the kings had taken from them; and that this was so considerable in extent, that by its loss the actual territory of the Roman people was reduced by one third from what it had been before.

Probable connection of Rome with Etruria.

It may thus be considered certain that Rome under its last kings was the seat of a great monarchy, extending over the whole of Latium on the one side, and possessing some considerable territory in Etruria on the other. But how this dominion was gained it is vain to inquire. There are accounts which represent all the three last kings of Rome, Servius Tullius no less than the two Tarquins, as of Etruscan origin. Without attempting to make out their history as individuals, it is probable that the later kings were either by birth or long intercourse closely connected with Etruria, inasmuch as at some early period of the Roman history the religion and usages of the Etruscans gave a deep and lasting coloring to those of Rome; and yet it could not have been at the very origin of the Roman people, as the Etruscan language has left no traces of itself in the Latin; whereas if the Romans had been in part of Etruscan origin, their language, no less than their institutions, would have contained some Etruscan

ally adopted Ursini's correction, Λαυρεντίνων: Niebuhr proposes Ἀρικηνῶν, observing that Aricia was a much more important place than Laurentum, and that Arician merchant vessels are mentioned by Dionysius, VII. 6. Yet Laurentum appears as one of the thirty Latin states which concluded the treaty with Sp. Cassius; and Larentum and Laurentum are but different forms of the same word, as appears in the name of the wife of Faustulus, who is called both Larentia and Laurentia.

[9] Müller in his very able work on the Etruscans believes rather that the later reigns of the Roman kings represent a period in which an Etruscan dynasty from Tarquinii ruled in Rome, and extended its power far over Latium; so that it was a dominion of Etruscans over Latins rather than the contrary. He considers this dominion to have been interrupted by the reign of Ser. Tullius, or Mastarna, an Etruscan chief from Volsinii, of a party wholly opposed to that of the princes or Lucumones of Tarquinii; and then to have been restored and exercised more tyranically than ever, in the time described by the Roman writers as the reign of Tarquinius the tyrant. Finally, the expulsion of the Tarquinii he regards as the decline of the power of the city Tarquinii, and the restoration of the independence of the Latin states, Rome being one of this number, which had been hitherto in subjection to it.—Etrusker, Vol. I. p. 115, et seqq.

I need not say that this is contrary to the opinion of Niebuhr, who believes the Tarquinii to have been Latins, and not Etruscans. But I should agree with Müller, in regarding the reigns of the two Tarquinii as a period during which an Etruscan dynasty ruled in Rome, introducing Etruscan rites, arts, and institutions. It is wholly another question whether these princes regarded Rome as their capital or Tarquinii; but the probability is, that they were kings of Rome, and they may very possibly have used the help of their Latin subjects even to make conquests for them in Etruria; just as the Norman kings of England soon found that England was more than Normandy, and Henry I. conquered Normandy from his brother, chiefly by the help of English men and money. And yet we retain the marks of the Norman conquest impressed on every part of our institutions down to this very hour.

elements. The Etruscan influence, however introduced, produced some effects that were lasting, and others that were only temporary; it affected the religion of Rome down to the very final extinction of Paganism; and the state of the Roman magistrates,[10] their lictors, their ivory chairs, and their triumphal robes, are all said to have been derived from Etruria. A temporary effect of Etruscan influence may perhaps be traced in the overthrow of the free constitution ascribed to Servius Tullius, in the degradation of the Roman commons under the last king, and in the endeavors of the patricians to keep them so degraded during all the first periods of the commonwealth. It is well known that the government in the cities of Etruria was an exclusive aristocracy, and that the commons, if in so wretched a condition they may be called by that honorable name, were like the mass of the people amongst the Sclavonic nations, the mere serfs or slaves of the nobility. This is a marked distinction between the Etruscans, and the Sabine and Latin nations of Italy; and, as in the constitution of Servius Tullius a Latin spirit is discernible, so the tyranny which, whether in the shape of a monarchy or an aristocracy, suspended that constitution for nearly two centuries, tended certainly to make Rome resemble the cities of Etruria, and may possibly be traced originally to that same revolution which expelled the Sabine gods from the capitol, and changed forever the simple religion of the infancy of Rome.

II. Changes in religion introduced in the time of the later kings.

II. It is a remarkable story[11] that towards the end of the sixth century of Rome, the religious books of Numa were accidentally brought to light by the discovery of his tomb under the Janiculum. They were read by A. Petillius, the Prætor Urbanus, and by him ordered to be burned in the comitium, because their contents tended to overthrow the religious rites then observed in Rome. We cannot but connect with this story what is told of Tarquinius the elder, how he cleared away the holy places of the Sabine gods from the Capitoline Hill, to make room for his new temple; and the statement which Augustine quotes from Varro,[12] and which is found also in Plutarch, that during the first hundred and seventy years after the foundation of the city, the Romans had no images of their gods. All these accounts represent a change effected in the Roman religion; and the term of 170 years, given by Varro and Plutarch, fixes this change to the reigns of the later kings. It is said[13] also, that Jupiter, Juno, and Minerva, the three deities to whom the Capitoline temple was dedicated, were the very powers whose worship, according to the Etruscan religion, was essential to every city; there could be no city without three gates duly consecrated, and three temples to these divinities. But here again we gain a glimpse of something real, but cannot make it out distinctly. Images of the gods belong rather to the religion of the Greeks than of the Etruscans; and the Greek mythology, as well as Grecian art, had been familiar in the southern Etruscan cities from a very early period, whether derived from the Tyrrhenians, or borrowed directly from Hellas or the Hellenic colonies. Grecian deities and Greek ceremonies may have been introduced, in part, along with such as were purely Etruscan. But the science of the Haruspices, and especially the attention to signs in the sky, to thunder and lightning, seems to have been conducted according to the Etruscan ritual; perhaps also from the same source came that belief in the punishment of the wicked after death, to which Polybius ascribes so strong a moral influence over the minds of the Romans, even in his own days. And Etruscan rites and ordinances must have been widely prevalent in the Roman commonwealth, when, as some writers asserted, the Roman nobility[14] were taught habitually the Etruscan language, and when

[10] Livy, I. 8. Dionysius, III. 62.

[11] Livy, XL. 29.

[12] Varro, Fragments, p. 46. Edit. Dordrecht. Plutarch, Numa, c. 8.

[13] Servius, on Virgil, Æn. I. v. 422. Miratur molem Æneas, &c. "Miratur" non simplicitur dictum volunt, quoniam prudentes Etruscæ disciplinæ aiunt, apud conditores Etruscarum urbium non putatas justas urbes, in quibus non tres portæ essent dedicatæ et votivæ, et tot templa, Jovis, Junonis, Minervæ,

[14] Livy, IX. 36. Habeo auctores, vulgo tum (in the middle of the fifth century of Rome), Romanos pueros sicut nunc Græcis ita Etruscis

the senate[15] provided by a special decree for the perpetual cultivation of the Etruscan discipline by young men of the highest nobility in Etruria; lest a science so important to the commonwealth should be corrupted by falling into the hands of low and mercenary persons.

III. Changes in the constitution introduced by the later kings.

III. Nothing is more familiar to our ears than the name of the classes and centuries of Servius Tullius; nothing is more difficult, even after the immortal labor of Niebuhr, than to answer all the questions which naturally arise connected with this part of the Roman history. But first of all, in considering the changes effected in the Roman con stitution during the later period of the monarchy, we find another threefold divi sion of them presenting itself. We have, 1st, the enlargement of the older constitution, on the same principles, in the addition to the number of senators and of the centuries of the knights, commonly ascribed to Tarquinius Priscus. 2nd, we have the establishment of a new constitution on different principles, in the famous classes and centuries of Servius Tullius. And, 3rd, we have the overthrow, to speak generally, of this new constitution, and the return to the older state of things, modified by the great increase of the king's power, in the revolution effected by Tarquinius Superbus, and in his subsequent despotism.

The alterations effected by the elder Tarquinius.

I. The old constitution was enlarged upon the same principles, in the increase of the number of senators, and of the centuries of the knights. It has been already shown that the older constitution was an oligarchy, as far as the clients and commons were concerned; it is no less true, that it was democratical, as far as regarded the relations of the citizens, or members of the houses, to each other. Both these characters, with a slight modification, were preserved in the changes made by Tarquinius Priscus. He doubled,[16] it is said, the actual number of senators, or rather of patrician houses; which involved a corresponding increase in the numbers of the senate; but the houses thus ennobled, to use a modern term, were distinguished from the old ones by the titles of the lesser houses; and their senators did not vote till after the senators of the greater houses. According to the same system the king proposed to double the number of the tribes, that is to divide his newly created houses into three tribes, to stand beside the three tribes of the old houses, the Ramnenses, Titienses, and Luceres. Now as the military divisions of the old commonwealths went along with the civil divisions, the tribes of the commonwealth were the centuries of the army; and if three new tribes were added, it involved also the addition of three new centuries of knights or horsemen; and it is in this form that the proposed change is represented in the common stories. But here it is said that the interest of the old citizens, taking the shape of a religious objection, was strong enough to force the king to modify his project. No new tribes were created, and consequently no new centuries;[17] but the new houses were enrolled in the three old centuries, so as to form a second division in each, and thus to

literis erudiri solitos. Livy rather believes that a knowledge of the Etruscan language was a peculiar accomplishment of the Fabius who went on the enterprise, namely, that of penetrating through the Ciminian Forest, and exploring Etruria. But the story of this enterprise comes evidently from the Fabian Family Memoirs, and its authenticity is most suspicious. Whereas the statement of the writers whom Livy refers to, is extremely unsuspicious and probable.

[15] See the famous passage of Cicero, de Divinatione, I. 41. § 92. I agree with Müller that the "Principum filii" here spoken of are Etruscans, and not Romans. The term "Principes" to express the Lucumones of Etruria is common enough: I doubt whether it is ever used to express the Roman patricians, or any class of men in Rome. "Principes civitatis" is used to express the most distinguished individuals of the commonwealth, not an order; besides, the passage in the treatise de Legibus seems to decide the question, II. 9, § 21, "Etruriæque principes disciplinam docento;" that is, "Let them instruct the government in their discipline, when any occasion arises for consulting them." Valerius Maximus, I. 1, § 2, has I believe borrowed his story from Cicero, and misunderstood his meaning.

[16] Duplicavit illum pristinum Patrum numerum: et antiquos Patres "majorum gentium" appellavit, quos priores sententiam rogabat, a se adscitos "minorum." Cicero, de Republicâ, II. 20.

[17] Neque tum Tarquinius de equitum centuriis quidquam mutavit: numero alterum tantum adjecit. . . . "Posteriores" modo sub iisdem nominibus qui additi erant appellati sunt. Livy, I. 36.

continue inferior in dignity to the old houses in every relation of the commonwealth. It may be fairly supposed, that these second centuries in the army were also second tribes and second curiæ in the civil divisions of the state; and that the members of the new houses voted after those of the old ones no less in the great council, the comitia of the curiæ, than in the smaller councils of the senate.

Their object.

The causes which led to this enlargement of the old constitution may be readily conceived. Whether Tarquinius was a Latin or an Etruscan, all the stories agree in representing him as a foreigner, who gained the throne by his wealth and personal reputation. The mere growth of the Roman state would, in the natural course of things, have multiplied new families, which had risen to wealth, and were in their former country of noble blood; but which were excluded from the curiæ, that is, from the rights of citizenship at Rome; the time was come to open to them the doors of the commonwealth; and a foreign king, ambitious of adding to the strength of his kingdom, if it were but for the sake of his own greatness, was not likely to refuse or put off the opportunity. Beyond this we are involved in endless disputes and difficulties; who the Luceres were, and whether Tarquinius had any particular reasons for raising them to a level with the old tribes, we never can determine. That there were only four vestal virgins before,[18] and that Tarquinius made them six, would certainly seem to show, that a third part of the state had hitherto been below the other two-thirds, at least in matters of religion; for it was always acknowledged that the six vestal virgins represented the three tribes of the Ramnenses, Titienses, and Luceres, two for each tribe. But in the additions made to the senate and to the centuries, the new citizens must have been more than a third of the old ones; and indeed here the story supposes that in military matters, at any rate, the Luceres were already on an equality with the Ramnenses and Titienses. It is enough, therefore, to say, that there had arisen at Rome so great a number of distinguished families, of whatever origin, or from whatever causes, that an extension of the rights of citizenship became natural and almost necessary: but as these were still only a small part of the whole population, the change went no further than to admit them into the aristocracy; leaving the character and privileges of the aristocracy itself, with regard to the mass of the population, precisely the same as they had been before.

Constitution of Servius Tullius.

II. But a far greater change was effected soon afterwards; no less than the establishment of a new constitution, on totally different principles. This constitution is no doubt historical, however uncertain may be the accounts which relate to its reputed author. "The good king Servius and his just laws," were the objects of the same fond regret amongst the Roman commons, when suffering under the tyranny of the aristocracy, as the laws of the good king Edward the Confessor amongst the English after the Norman conquest; and imagination magnified, perhaps, the merit of the one no less than of the other: yet the constitution of Servius was a great work, and well deserves to be examined and explained.

His object in forming it.

Servius, like Tarquinius, is represented as a foreigner, and is said also, like him, to have ascended the throne to the exclusion of the sons of the late king. According to the account which Livy followed, he was acknowledged[19] by the senate, but not by the people; and this, which

[18] See Dionysius, III. 67; and compare Livy, X. 6.

[19] Primus injussu Populi, voluntate Patrum regnavit. Livy, I. 41. Dionysius, confusing as usual the curiæ and the commons, and supposing that the most aristocratical body in the state must needs be the senate, represents him as chosen by the people in their curiæ, but not confirmed by the senate. Cicero says, "Non commisit se Patribus, sed, Tarquinio sepulto, Populum de se ipse consuluit, jussusque regnare, legem de imperio suo curiatam tulit." De Republicâ, II. 21. If indeed there existed a genuine "Lex Regia curiata de imperio" of the reign of Servius Tullius, then it must belong to a later period of his reign, when having established his power by means of his new constitution, the curiæ would have had no choice, but to acknowledge him; and this according to Livy's narrative was the case; for he says that

seemed contradictory so long as the people, populus, and the commons, plebs, were confounded together, is in itself consistent and probable, when it is understood that the people, who would not acknowledge Servius, were the houses assembled in their great council of the curiæ, and that these were likely to be far less manageable by the king whom they disliked, than the smaller council of their representatives assembled in the senate. Now supposing that the king, whoever he may have been, was unwelcome to what was then the people, that is, to the only body of men who enjoyed civil rights; it was absolutely necessary for him, unless he would maintain his power as a mere tyrant, through the help of a foreign paid guard, to create a new and different people out of the large mass of inhabitants of Rome who had no political existence, but who were free, and in many instances wealthy and of noble origin; who therefore, although now without rights, were in every respect well fitted to receive them.

He establishes thirty tribes for the commons.

The principle of an aristocracy is equality within its own body, ascendency over all the rest of the community. Opposed to this is the system, which, rejecting these extremes of equality and inequality, subjects no part of the community to another, but gives a portion of power to all; not an equal portion, however, but one graduated according to a certain standard, which standard has generally been property. Accordingly, this system has both to do away with distinctions, and to create them; to do away, as it has generally happened, with distinctions of birth, and to create distinctions of property. Thus at Rome, in the first instance, the tribes or divisions of the people took a different form. The old three tribes of Ramnenses, Titienses, and Luceres, had been divisions of birth, real or supposed: each was made up of the houses of the curiæ, and no man could belong to the tribe without first belonging to a curia, and to a house; nor could any stranger become a member of a house except by the rite of adoption, by which he was made as one of the same race, and therefore a lawful worshipper of the same gods. Each of these tribes had its portion of the Ager Romanus, the old territory of Rome. But now as many others had become Romans in the course of time, without belonging to either of these three tribes, that is, had come to live under the Roman kings, many in Rome itself, and had received grants of land from the kings beyond the limits of the old Ager Romanus, a new division was made including all these; and the whole city and territory[20] of Rome, except the Capitol, were divided into thirty

after the institution of the Comitia Centuriata, Servius "ausus est ferre ad populum, 'vellent juberentne se regnare?' tantoque consensu quanto haud quisquam alius ante, rex est declaratus," I. 46. On the other hand Livy, or the annalist whom he followed, may have added the circumstance "voluntate Patrum regnavit," because he could not conceive how Servius could have reigned without the consent of either senate or curiæ. But if we adopt the Etruscan story, and suppose that the king whom the Romans called Servius Tullius had gained his power in the first instance as the leader of an army, which after various adventures in Etruria had been driven out from thence, and had taken possession of the Cælian Hill in Rome, it is very conceivable that he may have reigned at first independently of the consent of any part of the old Roman people, whether senate or burghers; and that he may only have asked for that consent after his creation of a new Roman people, formed perhaps in part out of his own soldiers, when he would wish to reign according to all the old legal forms, and to be no longer king by the choice of a part of his subjects only, but with the approbation of all.

[20] Every reader who is acquainted with the subject knows the difficulties which beset the whole question respecting the original number of the tribes. On the whole I agree with Niebuhr in preferring the statement of Fabius, preserved by Dionysius, IV. 15, that the country tribes in the Servian constitution were six and twenty. But the great difficulty relates to three points; the Capitol, the Aventine, and the Ager Romanus. The four city tribes or regions, for tribe as a local division is synonymous with region, included neither the Capitol, nor the Aventine. This we know from that curious account preserved by Varro of the situation of the twenty-four Argean chapels in these regions; a passage which has been considered and corrected both by Müller and Bunsen, and may be now read in an intelligible form either in Müller's edition of Varro, I. § 45–54; or in Bunsen's and Platner's Beschreibung Roms, Vol. I. pp. 688–702. But there is this farther perplexity, that the chapels of the Argei are said by Varro to have been distributed through twenty-seven parts of the city; and yet the wooden figures called Argei, which were every year thrown by the Pontifices into the Tiber, are by Varro himself, according to the MSS. said to have been twenty-four, and by Dionysius thirty. [Antiqq. Rom. I. 38.] Bunsen adopts this latter number, and supposes that the three cellæ of the Capitoline Temple, and the three of the old Capitol on the Quirinal, were included in the reckoning,

tribes, four for the city, and twenty-six for the country, containing all the Romans who were not members of the houses, and classing them according to the local situation of their property. These thirty tribes corresponded to the thirty curiæ of the houses; for the houses were used to assemble, not in a threefold division, according to their tribes, but divided into thirty, according to their curiæ: and the commons were to meet and settle all their own affairs in the assembly of their tribes, as the houses met and settled theirs in the assembly of their curiæ.

The centuries, a military division, to include both the burghers and the commons.

Thus then were two bodies existing alongside of each other, analogous to the house of lords and the house of commons of our own ancient constitution, two estates distinct from and independent of each other, but with no means as yet provided for converting them into states-general or a parliament. Nor could they have acted together as jointly legislating for the whole nation; for the curiæ still regarded themselves as forming exclusively the Roman people, and would not allow the commons, as such, to claim any part in the highest acts of national sovereignty. There was one relation, however, in which the people and the commons felt that they belonged to one common country, in which they were accustomed to act together, and in which therefore it was practicable to unite them into one great body. This was when they marched out to war against a foreign enemy; then, arrayed in the same army, and fighting under the same standard, in the same cause, the houses and the commons, if not equally citizens of Rome, felt that they were alike Romans. It has ever been the case, that the distinctions of peace[21] vanish amidst the dangers of war; arms and courage, and brotherhood in perils, confer of necessity power and dignity. Thus we hear of armies[22] on their return home from war stopping before they entered the city walls to try, in their military character, all offences or cases of misconduct which had occurred since they had taken the field: whereas when once they had entered the walls, civil relations were resumed, and all trials were conducted according to other forms, and before other judges. This will explain the peculiar constitution of the comitia of centuries, which was a device for uniting the people and the commons into a national and sovereign assembly in their capacity of soldiers, without shocking those prejudices which as yet placed a barrier between them as soon as they returned to the relations of peace.

But in order to do this with effect, and to secure in this great assembly a

This appears to me unsatisfactory, but I can offer nothing better. However, the exclusion of the Capitol from the four city tribes is consistent enough; for the Capitol as the citadel of Rome, and the seat of the three protecting gods of the city, was reserved exclusively for the patricians, or old citizens, and no plebeian might dwell on it: whereas in the other parts of the city both orders dwelt promiscuously, till the famous Icilian law appropriated the Aventine to the plebeians alone, as the Capitol was appropriated to the patricians. It will be remembered that the Eupatridæ at Athens were distinguished in the old state of things by the title *οἱ κατ' ἄστυ οἰκοῦντες*, and the *ἄστυ* in the earliest times would be the Acropolis of a later age. With regard to the Aventine, it must I conceive have been included in one of the country tribes; nor is this to be wondered at, as the Aventine was still considered properly as a suburb, although it was included within the walls. It is not to be supposed that the whole of the land in the country tribes was the property of the plebeians; much of it undoubtedly remained as domain land, and as such became "possessed," in the Roman sense of the term, by the patricians; as appears in the account of the state of the Aventine Hill, before the passing of the Lex-Icilia. But as such possession or occupation was not property, the patricians might possess land in a tribe without becoming members of it. But if the Ager Romanus had formed a tribe, then we might be led to suppose that the patricians must have been members of this tribe, and so the tribes would cease to be an exclusively plebeian body, which Niebuhr, rightly, as I think, supposes them to have been in the outset. It is possible, however, that the whole territory, not excepting even the Ager Romanus, might locally have been included within the tribes, inasmuch as no district would be wholly without plebeian lands; and yet the patricians themselves, as belonging to a different political body, might have had nothing to do with the tribe politically: just as the estates of our peers are geographically included within some county, and yet no peer may be elected as knight of the shire, nor even vote at any election.

[21] "For he to-day who sheds his blood with me
Shall be my brother; be he ne'er so vile,
This day shall gentle his condition."
HENRY V.

[22] This was the case at Argos. *τὸν Θράσυλλον ἀναχωρήσαντες ἐν τῷ Χαράδρῳ οὗπερ τὰς ἀπὸ στρατιᾶς δίκας πρὶν ἐσιέναι κρίνουσιν, ἤρξαντο λεύειν.* Thucyd. V. 60.

Change in the organization of the army.

preponderance to the commons, a change in the military organization and tactic of the army became indispensable. In all aristocracies in an early stage of society, the ruling order or class has fought on horseback[23] or in chariots; their subjects or dependents have fought on foot. The cavalry service under these circumstances has been cultivated, that of the infantry neglected; the mounted noble has been well armed and carefully trained in warlike exercises, whilst his followers on foot have been ill armed and ill disciplined, and quite incapable of acting with equal effect. The first great step then towards raising the importance of the infantry, or, in other words, of the commons of the state, was to train them to resist cavalry, to form them into thick masses instead of a thin extended line, to arm them with the pike instead of the sword or the javelin. Thus the phalanx order of battle was one of the earliest improvements in the art of war; and at the time we are now speaking of, this order was in general use in Greece, and must have been well known, if only through the Greek colonies, in Italy also.[24] Its introduction into the Roman army would be sure to make the infantry from henceforward more important than the cavalry; that is, it would enable the commons to assert a greater right in Rome than would be claimed by the houses, inasmuch as they could render better service. Again, the phalanx order of battle furnished a ready means for giving importance to a great number of the less wealthy commons, who could not supply themselves with complete armor; while, on the other hand, it suggested a natural distinction between them and their richer fellows, and thus established property as the standard of political power, the only one which can in the outset compete effectually with the more aristocratical standard of birth; although in a later stage of society it becomes itself aristocratical, unless it be duly tempered by the mixture of a third standard, education and intelligence. In a deep phalanx, the foremost ranks needed to be completely armed, but those in the rear could neither reach or be reached by the enemy, and only served to add weight to the charge of the whole body. These points being remembered, we may now proceed to the details of the great comitia of Servius.

Details of the institution of the centuries. The six suffragia and plebeian centuries of knights.

He found the houses, that is to say, the nobility or citizens of Rome, for I cannot too often remind the reader that in this early period of Roman history these three terms were synonymous, divided into three centuries of knights or horsemen, each of which, in consequence of the accession to its numbers made by the last king, contained within itself two centuries, a first and a second. The old citizens, anxious in all things to keep up the old form of the state, had then prevented what were really six centuries from being acknowledged as such in name; but the present change extended to the name as well as the reality; and the three double centuries of the Ramnenses, Titienses, and Luceres, became now[25] the six votes (sex suffragia) of the new united assembly. To these, which contained all the members of the houses, there were now added twelve new centuries[26] of knights, formed, as usual in the Greek states, from the richest members of the community, continuing, like the centuries below them, to belong to the thirty tribes of the commons.

The centuries of infantry. The five classes.

It remained to organize the foot soldiers of the state. Accordingly, all those of the commons whose property was sufficient to qualify them for serving even in the hindmost ranks of the phalanx, were

[23] Homer's battles are a sufficient example of this: it explains also the name of ἱππῆς applied to the three hundred Spartans of the king's guard, and retained long after the reality had ceased, and the guard no longer consisted of cavalry or chariots, but of infantry. See Thucydides, V. 72. See also Aristotle, Politics, IV. 13. ἡ μὲν ἐξ ἀρχῆς (πολιτεία ἐγένετο) ἐκ τῶν ἱππέων. τὴν γὰρ ἰσχὺν καὶ τὴν ὑπεροχὴν ἐν τοῖς ἱππεῦσιν ὁ πόλεμος εἶχεν· ἄνευ μὲν γὰρ συντάξεως ἄχρηστον τὸ ὁπλιτικόν, αἱ δὲ περὶ τῶν τοιούτον ἐμπειρίαι καὶ τάξεις ἐν τοῖς ἀρχαίοις οὐχ ὑπῆρχον, ὥστ' ἐν τοῖς ἱππεῦσιν εἶναι τὴν ἰσχύν.

[24] Again, if Ser. Tullius was an Etruscan, he would have introduced the tactic of his own country, in arming the Roman infantry with the long spear and shield: for these were the weapons used by the Etruscans as well as by the Greeks. See Diodorus Siculus, XXIII. 1. Fragm. Mai.

[25] Festus in Sex Suffragia.

[26] Livy, I. 43. Cicero de Republ. II. 22.

divided[27] into four classes. Of these, the first class contained all whose property amounted to or exceeded one hundred thousand pounds weight of copper. The soldiers of this class were required to provide themselves with the complete arms used in the front ranks of the phalanx; the greaves, the coat of mail, the helmet and the round shield, all of brass; the sword, and the peculiar weapon of the heavy-armed infantry, the long pike. And as these were to bear the brunt of every battle, and were the flower of the state's soldiers, so their weight in the great military assembly was to be in proportion; they formed eighty centuries; forty of younger men, between the ages of fifteen and forty-five years[28] complete; and forty of elders, between forty-five and sixty: the first to serve in the field, the second to defend the city. The second class contained those whose property fell short of one hundred thousand pounds of copper, and exceeded or amounted to seventy-five thousand. They formed twenty centuries, ten of younger men, and ten of elders; and they were allowed to dispense with the coat of mail, and to bear the large oblong wooden shield called scutum, instead of the round brazen shield, clipeus, of the first ranks of the phalanx. The third class contained a like number of centuries, equally divided into those of the younger men and elders; its qualification was property between fifty thousand pounds of copper, and seventy-five thousand; and the soldiers of this class were allowed to lay aside the greaves as well as the coat of mail. The fourth class, again, contained twenty centuries; the lowest point of its qualification was twenty-five thousand pounds of copper, and its soldiers were required to provide no defensive armor, but to go to battle merely with the pike and a javelin. These four classes composed the phalanx; but a fifth class, divided into thirty centuries, and consisting of those whose property was between twenty-five thousand pounds of copper, and twelve thousand five hundred, formed the regular light-armed infantry of the army, and were required to provide themselves with darts and slings.

The Accensi and Velati, and the Proletarii.

The poorest citizens,[29] whose property fell short of twelve thousand five hundred pounds, were considered, in a manner, as supernumeraries in this division. Those who had more than one thousand five hundred pounds of copper, were still reckoned amongst the tax-payers, Assidui, and were formed into two centuries, called the Accensi and Velati. They followed the army, but without bearing arms, being only required to step into the places of those who fell; and, in the mean time, acting as orderlies to the centurions and decurions. Below these came one century of the Proletarii, whose property was between one thousand five hundred pounds and three hundred and seventy-five. These paid no taxes, and in ordinary times had no military duty; but on great emergencies arms were furnished them by the government, and they were called out as an extraordinary levy. One century more included all whose property was less than three hundred and seventy-five pounds, and who were called Capite Censi; and from these last no military service was at any time required, as we are told, till a late period of the republic.

The Fabri, Cornicines, and Tubicines.

Three centuries of a different character from all the rest remain to be described, centuries defined, not by the amount of their property, but by the nature of their occupation; those of carpenters and smiths, Fabrorum; of horn-blowers, Cornicines; and of trumpeters, Tubicines, or, as Cicero calls them, Liticines. The first of these was attached to the centuries of the first class, the other two to the fourth. The nature of their callings so connected them with the service of the army, that this peculiar distinction was granted to them.

The position held in the comitia by the patricians' clients is involved in great

[27] See, for all this account of the census, Livy, I. 43, and Dionysius, IV. 16–19.

[28] See Niebuhr, vol. I. p. 459. Ed. 2.

[29] See Niebuhr, p. 465, and the authorities there quoted. I have gone over the ground myself, and have verified the accuracy of Niebuhr's quotations, if, indeed, any could suspect it; and having been fully satisfied with his results, I have thought it best to refer to his work, rather than to the original writers, as the combined view of the several facts belongs to him, and not to them.

obscurity. We know that they had votes, and probably they must have been enrolled in the classes according to the amount of their property, without reference to its nature: at the same time, Niebuhr thinks that they did not serve in the regular infantry along with the plebeians. It would seem from the story of the three hundred Fabii, and from the adventures related of Caius Marcius,[30] that the clients followed their lords to the field at their bidding, and formed a sort of feudal force quite distinct from the national army of the commons, like the retainers of the nobles in the middle ages, as distinguished from the free burghers of the cities.

Such is the account transmitted to us of the constitution of the comitia of centuries. As their whole organization was military, so they were accustomed to meet[31] without the city, in the Field of Mars; they were called together, not by lictors, like the comitia of the curiæ, but by the blast of the horn; and their very name was, "the Army of the City," "Exercitus Urbanus."[32]

The constitution was soon destroyed, and never entirely restored.

It is quite plain that this constitution tended to give the chief power in the state to the body of the commons, and especially to the richer class among them, who fought in the first ranks of the phalanx. For wherever there is a well-armed and well-disciplined infantry, it constitutes the main force of an army; and it is a true observation of Aristotle,[33] that in the ancient commonwealth the chief power was apt to be possessed by that class of the people whose military services were most important; thus, when the navy of Athens became its great support and strength, the government became democratical; because the ships were chiefly manned by citizens of the poorer classes. But we know that for a very long period after the time of Servius, the commons at Rome, far from being the dominant part of the nation, were excluded from the highest offices in the state, and were grievously oppressed, both individually and as a body. Nay, further, whenever we find any details given of the proceedings of the comitia, or of the construction of the army, we perceive a state of things very different from that prescribed by the constitution of Servius. Hence have arisen the difficulties connected with it; for, as it was never fully carried into effect, but overthrown within a very few years after its formation, and only gradually and in part restored; as thus the constitution with which the oldest annalists, and even the law-books which they copied, were familiar, was not the original constitution of Servius, but one bearing its name, while in reality it greatly differed from it; there is a constant confusion between the two, and what is ascribed to the one may often be true only when understood of the other.

Servius appoints judges for the commons out of their own order.

Other good and popular institutions were ascribed to the reign of Servius. As he had made the commons an order in the state, so he gave them judges out of their own body to try all civil[34] causes; whereas before they had no jurisdiction, but referred all their suits either to the king or to the houses. These judges were, as Niebuhr thinks, the centumviri, the hundred men, of a later period, elected three from each tribe, so that in the time of Servius their number would probably have been ninety.

The festivals of the Paganalia and Compitalia.

To give a further organization to the commons, he is said also to have instituted the festivals called Paganalia and Compitalia. In the tribes in the country, many strongholds on high ground, pagi,[35] had been fixed

[30] Dionysius, VII. 19, 20.

[31] A. Gellius, XV. 27, quoted from Lælius Felix.

[32] Varro, de L. L., VI. 93.

[33] Politics, V. 4. VI. 7 Ed. Bekker.

[34] Dionysius calls these causes ἰδιωτικά, as opposed to τὰ ἐς τὸ κοινὸν φέροντα, IV. 25; but afterwards he expresses himself more freely, when he calls these laws, laws which hindered the commons from being wronged by the patricians as formerly, περὶ τὰ συμβόλαια, IV. 43. The Ephori, in like manner, at Sparta were judges in τὰς τῶν συμβολαίων δίκας. Aristot. Polit. III. 1. Ed. Bekker.

[35] It does not appear from Dionysius' account whether there were one or more pagi in every tribe. It would be most natural to suppose that there was but one, as otherwise the numbers of the people would have been taken according to a different division than that into

upon as a general refuge for the inhabitants and their cattle in case of invasion. Here they all met once a year, to keep festival, and every man, woman, and child paid on these occasions a certain sum, which, being collected by the priests, gave the amount of the whole population. And for the same purpose,[36] every one living in the city paid a certain sum at the temple of Juno Lucina for every birth in his family, another sum at the temple of Venus Libitina for every death, and a third at the temple of Youth for every son who came to the age of military service. The Compitalia[37] in the city answered to the Paganalia in the country, and were a yearly festival in honor of the Lares or guardian spirits, celebrated at all the compita, or places where several streets met.

Other laws ascribed to Servius.

Other laws and measures are ascribed to Servius, which seem to be the fond invention of a later period, when the commons, suffering under a cruel and unjust system, and wishing its overthrow, gladly believed that the deliverance which they longed for had been once given them by their good king, and that they were only reclaiming old rights, not demanding new ones. Servius, it is said,[38] drove out the patricians from their unjust occupation of the public land, and ordered that the property only, and not the person, of a debtor should be liable for the payment of his debt.

Further, to complete the notion of a patriot king, it was said that he had drawn out a scheme of popular government, by which two magistrates, chosen every year, were to exercise the supreme power, and that he himself proposed to lay down his kingly rule to make way for them. It can hardly be doubted that these two magistrates were intended to be chosen the one from the houses and the other from the commons, to be the representatives of their respective orders.

The constitution of Servius succeeded by a tyranny.

III. But the following tyranny swept away the institutions of Servius, and much more prevented the growth of that society, for which alone his institutions were fitted. No man can tell how much of the story of the murder of the old king and of the impiety of the wicked Tullia is historical; but it is certain that the houses, or rather a strong faction among them, supported Tarquinius in his usurpation: nor can we doubt the statement that the aristocratical brotherhoods or societies served him more zealously than the legal assembly of the curiæ; because these societies are ever to be met with in the history of the ancient commonwealths, as pledged to one another for the interests of their order, and ready to support those interests by any crime. Like Sylla, in after times, he crushed the liberties of the commons, doing away with the laws[39] of

tribes; which does not seem probable. The pagus was in a manner the town of the tribe, or rather would have become so, had this state of things continued. Dionysius connects pagus with the Greek πάγος, which is likely enough; although afterwards the word merely signified a district or canton, whether in a plain country, or in a hilly. Nor do Varro's words (L. L. V. p. 49. Edit. Dordr. 1619), "Feriæ non populi sed montanorum modo, ut Paganalibus, qui sunt alicujus pagi," imply that the Pagani were montani: for the whole passage, when rightly stopped, and as Müller has now printed it, runs thus:—"Dies Septimontium, nominatus ab his septem montibus in queis sita urbs est, feriæ non populi sed montanorum modo: ut Paganalibus, qui sunt alicujus pagi." "Montani" refers to the inhabitants of the seven hills (the seven hills of old Rome, existing before the time of Servius); and Varro says that the Septimontium was a festival kept not by the whole people, but by the inhabitants of those hills only; just as, at the Paganalia, the inhabitants of the pagus alone shared in the festival. See Festus, in Septimontio, "Septimontio ut ait Antistius Labeo, hisce montibus Feriæ," &c.

[36] Dionysius, IV. 15.

[37] Dionysius, IV. 14. What Dionysius here calls the Compitalia, and which he says were kept a few days after the Saturnalia, are not marked in the calendars, because, though the seasons at which they fell was fixed, the day was not so: they were amongst the "conceptivæ Feriæ," or festivals announced every year by the magistrates, of which the precise day in some instances varied. (Macrobius, Saturnal. I. 16.) They must not be confounded with the festival of the Lares Præstites on the first of May. The Lares were the spirits of the dead, δαίμονες, who watched over their living posterity; thence Dionysius calls them ἥρωες, because the heroes were deified men, like Hesiod's δαίμονες, whom he calls φύλακες θνητῶν ἀνθρώπων. The name of Lares is Etruscan, Lar is prince or mighty one. Yet as spirits, and belonging to the invisible world, they were called also the children of Mania (Macrobius, Saturnal. I. 7), a horrible goddess, whose name was given to frightful masks, the terror of children. Mania is clearly connected with the Dii Manes, who were also the spirits of a man's departed ancestors.

[38] Dionysius, IV. 9.

[39] Dionysius, IV. 43.

Servius, and, as we are told, destroying the tables on which they were written; abolishing the whole system of the census, and consequently the arrangement of the classes, and with them the organization of the phalanx; and forbidding even the religious meetings of the Paganalia and Compitalia, in order to undo all that had been done to give the commons strength and union. Further, it is expressly said,[40] that he formed his military force out of a small portion of the people, and employed the great bulk of them in servile works, in the building of the Circus and the Capitoline Temple, and the completion of the great drain or cloaca; so that in his wars his army consisted of his allies, the Latins and Hernicans, in a much greater proportion than of Romans. His enmity to the commons was all in the spirit of Sylla; and the members of the aristocratical societies, who were his ready tools in every act of confiscation, or legal murder, or mere assassination, were faithfully represented by the agents of Sylla's proscription, by L. Catilina and his patrician associates. But in what followed, Tarquinius showed himself, like Critias or Appius Claudius, a mere vulgar tyrant, who preferred himself to his order, when the two came into competition, and far inferior to Sylla, the most sincere of aristocrats, who, having secured the ascendancy of his order, was content to resign his own personal power, who was followed therefore by the noblest as well as by the vilest of his countrymen, by Pompeius and Catulus no less than by Catilina. Thus Tarquinius became hated by all that was good and noble amongst the houses, as well as by the commons; and both orders cordially joined to effect his overthrow. But the evil of his tyranny survived him; it was not so easy to restore what he had destroyed as to expel him and his family: the commons no longer stood beside the patricians as an equal order, free, wealthy, well armed, and well organized; they were now poor, ill armed, and with no bonds of union; they therefore naturally sunk beneath the power of the nobility, and the revolution which drove out the Tarquins established at Rome not a free commonwealth, but an exclusive and tyrannical aristocracy.

CHAPTER VI.

MISCELLANEOUS NOTICES OF THE STATE OF THE ROMANS UNDER THEIR KINGS.

"Ad nos vix tenuis famæ perlabitur aura."
VIRGIL, Æn. VII.

THE last chapter was long, yet the view which can be derived from it is imperfect. Questions must suggest themselves, as I said before, to which it contains no answers. Yet it seemed better to draw the attention first to one main point, and to state that point as fully as possible, reserving to another place much that was needed to complete the picture. For instance, the account of the classes of Servius leads naturally to questions as to the wealth of the Romans, its sources, its distribution, and its amount: the division of the people into centuries excites a curiosity as to their numbers: the mention of the change of the Roman worship, and the introduction of Etruscan rites, dispose us to ask, how these rites affected the moral character of the people; what that character was, and from whence derived. Again, when we read of the great works of the later kings, we think what advance or what style of the arts was displayed in them; and the laws of king Servius written on tables, with the poetical and uncertain nature of the story of his reign, make us consider what was the state of the human mind, and what

[40] Dionysius, IV. 44.

use had as yet been made of the great invention of letters. It is to these points, so far as I am able, that the following chapter will be devoted.

Of the wealth of the Romans under the later kings. Their copper money.

I. Niebuhr has almost exhausted the subject of the Roman copper money. He has[1] shown its originally low value, owing to the great abundance of the metal; that as it afterwards became scarce, a reduction in the weight of the coin followed naturally, not as a fraudulent depreciation of it, but because a small portion of it was now as valuable as a large mass had been before. The plenty of copper in early times is owing to this, that where it is found, it exists often in immense quantities, and even in large masses of pure metal on the surface of the soil. Thus the Copper Indians of North America found it in such abundance on their hills that they used it for all domestic purposes; but the supply thus easily obtained soon became exhausted: and as the Indians have no knowledge of mining, the metal is now comparatively scarce. The small value of copper at Rome is shown not only by the size of the coins, the *as* having been at first a full pound in weight, but also by the price of the war-horse, according to the regulation of Servius Tullius, namely, ten thousand[2] pounds of copper. This statement, connected as it is with the other details of the census, seems original and authentic; nor considering the great abundance of cattle, and other circumstances, is it inconsistent with the account in Plutarch's life of Publicola, that an ox, in the beginning of the commonwealth, was worth one hundred oboli, and a sheep worth ten; nor with the provisions of the Aternian law, which fixed the price of the one at one hundred ases and the other at ten.

Their principal sources of wealth.

The sources of wealth amongst the Romans, under their later kings, were agriculture, and also, in a large proportion, foreign commerce. Agriculture, indeed, strictly speaking, could scarcely be called a source of wealth; for the portions of land assigned to each man, even if from the beginning they were as much as seven jugera, were not large enough to allow of the growth of much superfluous produce. The ager publicus, or undivided public land, was indeed of considerable extent, and this, as being enjoyed exclusively by the patricians, might have been a source of great profit. But in the earliest times it seems probable that the greatest part of this land was kept as pasture;[3] and only the small portions of two jugera, allotted by the houses to their clients, to be held during pleasure, were appropriated to tillage. The low prices of sheep and oxen show that cattle must have been abundant; the earliest revenue, according to Pliny, was derived from pasture; that is, the patricians paid so much to the state

[1] Vol. I. p. 474, et seqq. Ed. 2. See also Müller, Etrusker, I. 4. § 13.

[2] "Ad equos emendos dena millia æris ex publico data." Livy, I. 43. It has been doubted whether this sum be meant as the price of one horse or two: Niebuhr supposes that it includes the purchase of a slave to act as groom, and also of a horse for him. And this seems confirmed in some degree by Festus, who says that the Romans used two horses in battle, to have a fresh one to mount when the first one was tired; and that the money given to furnish these two horses was called Pararium. Festus in "Pararium," and "Paribus equis." Yet I find in Von Raumer's account of the prices of Things in the middle ages (Geschichte der Hohenstaufen, V. p. 436, et seqq.), that in the year 1097, at the siege of Antioch, an ox was sold cheap at five shillings; and in 1225, at Verona, the average price of a horse was twenty-five pounds. This is reckoning by the Italian lira or pound, divided into twenty solidi or shillings; but the value of both the pound and the shilling differed so much in different times and places, that the comparison cannot be depended on without further examination. We should like to know from what Greek writer Plutarch borrowed his statement of the price of an ox in the time of Publicola. Was it from Timæus, from whom Pliny learnt that Servius Tullius was the first person who stamped money at Rome? And if so, at what did he reckon the as? Polybius reckoned the light as of his time at half an obolus, which would make the denarius, as it was already equivalent to sixteen ases, equal to eight oboli, or a drachm, and one-third. (II. 15.) By a comparison with the Aternian law, one would suppose that the obolus was meant to be equivalent to the as; if so, copper had so risen in value, that although the as of half an ounce weight was equal to half an obolus, the as, when it weighed twenty-four times as much, that is, a full pound, had only been worth twice as much; a diminution in value of twelve hundred per cent.

[3] "Diu," says Pliny, XVIII. 3. "pascua solum vectigal fuerant." Varro says, "Quos agros non colebant propter silvas, aut id genus ubi pecus posset pasci, et *possidebant*, ab usu suo Saltus nominarunt." De L. L. V. § 36. "Possidere," as Niebuhr's readers well know, is the proper term for the occupation of the public land. And the Scholiast on Thucydides, I. 139, rightly considers γῆς ἀορίστου to be equivalent to οὐ σπειρομένης, because undivided land was commonly left in pasture.

for their enjoyment of the ager publicus, which was left unenclosed as pasture ground; and all accounts speak of the great quantities of cattle reared in Italy from time immemorial. Cattle then may have been a source of wealth; but commerce must have been so in a still greater degree. The early foundation of Ostia at the mouth of the Tiber, ascribed to Ancus Marcius, could have had no object, unless the Romans had been engaged in foreign trade; and the treaty with Carthage, already alluded to, proves the same thing directly and undeniably. In this treaty the Romans are allowed to trade with Sardinia, with Sicily, and with Africa westward of the Fair Headland, that is, with Carthage itself, and all the coast westward to the Pillars of Hercules; and it is much more according to the common course of things that this treaty should have been made to regulate a trade already in activity, than to call it for the first time into existence. By this commerce great fortunes were sure to be made, because there were as yet so many new markets[4] open to the enterprising trader, and none, perhaps, where the demand for his goods had been so steadily and abundantly supplied as to destroy the profit of his traffic. But although much wealth must thus have been brought into Rome, it is another question how widely it was distributed. Was foreign trade open to every Roman, or was it confined to the patricians and their clients, and in a still larger proportion to the king? The king had large domains of his own,[5] partly arable, partly pasture, and partly planted with vines and olives; hence he was in a condition to traffic with foreign countries, and much of the Roman commerce was, probably, carried on by the government for its own direct benefit, as was the case in Judæa, in the reign of Solomon. The patricians also, we may be sure, exported, like the Russian nobility, the skins and wool of the numerous herds and flocks which they fed upon their public land, and were the owners of trading ships, as it was not till three centuries afterwards that a law[6] was passed with the avowed object of restraining senators, a term then become equivalent with patricians, from possessing ships of a large burden. Nor can we suppose that the new plebeian centuries of knights, who had been chosen from the richest of the commons, were excluded from those commercial dealings which their order in later times almost monopolized. All these classes, then, might, and probably did, become wealthy; but it may be doubted whether the plebeian landholders had the same opportunities open to them. Agriculture was to them the business of their lives; if their estates were ill cultivated, they were liable to be degraded from their order; nor had they the capital which could enable them to enter with advantage upon foreign trade. It is possible, indeed, that foreign trade may have been one of the privileges of the higher classes, as it is at this day in Russia;[7] but surely Niebuhr is not warranted by the passage which he quotes from Dionysius, in asserting that the plebeians were excluded from commerce as well as from handicraft occupations; retail trade,[8] which is all that Dionysius speaks of, was

[4] Thus Herodotus speaks of the enormous profits made by a Samian ship which accidentally found its way to Tartessus; observing, τὸ δὲ ἐμπόριον τοῦτο ἦν ἀκήρατον τοῦτον τὸν χρόνον. IV. 152.

[5] Cicero de Republicâ, V. 2. These were the Greek τεμένη, which the kings always had assigned to them. See Herodot. IV. 161.

[6] By Caius Flaminius, a short time before the second Punic war. See Livy, XXI. 63.

[7] Of the "Merchants of the three Guilds," only those of the first guild, possessing a capital of at least fifty thousand francs (something more than two thousand pounds), are allowed to own merchant ships, and to carry on foreign trade. Those of the second guild may only trade within the Russian empire; those of the third guild may only carry on retail trades. See Schnitzler, Statistique de l'Empire de Russie, p. 117.

[8] Οὔτε κάπηλον οὔτε χειροτέχνην βίον ἔχειν, IX. 25. It is true that Dionysius had just before used the term ἐμπόρων, but I think that it is ἐμπόρων which he uses in an improper sense, and not κάπηλον. Cicero distinguishes between them in a well-known passage. "Sordidi etiam putandi qui mercantur a mercatoribus quod statim vendant; (κάπηλοι) opificesque omnes (χειρότεχναι) in sordidâ arte versantur. * * * Mercatura autem, si tenuis est, sordida putanda est: sin magna et copiosa multa undique apportans, multisque sine vanitate impertiens, non est admodum vituperanda." De Officiis, II. prope finem. Cicero wrote at a time when all trade was considered degrading to a senator, and his language breathes the spirit of modern aristocracy. Yet even he distinguishes between the merchant and the petty trader or shopkeeper. The plebeians were excluded from following the latter callings by positive institution; from the former they might have been virtually excluded by their poverty.

Since writing the above note, I see that Nie-

considered by the ancients in a very different light from the wholesale dealings of the merchant with foreign countries.

Beyond this we have scarcely the means of proceeding. Setting aside the tyranny ascribed to Tarquinius, and remembering that it was his policy to deprive the commons of their lately acquired citizenship, and to treat them like subjects rather than members of the state, the picture given of the wealth and greatness of Judæa under Solomon, may convey some idea of the state of Rome under its later kings. Powerful amongst surrounding nations, exposed to no hostile invasions, with a flourishing agriculture, and an active commerce, the country was great and prosperous; and the king was enabled to execute public works of the highest magnificence, and to invest himself with a splendor unknown in the earlier times of the monarchy. The last Tarquinius was guilty of individual acts of oppression, we may be sure, towards the patricians no less than the plebeians; but it was these last whom he labored on system to depress and degrade, and whom he employed, as Solomon did the Canaanites,[9] in all the servile and laborious part of his undertakings. Still the citizens or patricians themselves found that the splendor of his government had its burdens for them also; as the great majority of the Israelites, amid all the peace and prosperity of Solomon's reign, and although exempted from all servile labor, and serving only in honorable offices,[10] yet complained that they had endured a grievous yoke, and took the first opportunity to relieve themselves from it by banishing the house of Solomon from among them forever.

Population.

Of the population of Rome under its later kings nothing can be known with certainty, unless we consider as historical the pretended return of the census taken by Servius Tullius, eighty-four thousand seven hundred. Nor is it possible to estimate the numbers of the army from the account of the centuries. We are expressly told that the centuries were very unequal in the number of men contained in them; and even with regard to the centuries of the first class, we know not whether they consisted of any fixed number. It is possible that the century in the Roman army, like the τάξις in the Athenian, bore two different senses; the Athenian heavy-armed infantry were divided into ten τάξεις, but the number contained in each of these must necessarily have been indefinite. We read, however, of τάξεις and ταξίαρχοι in particular expeditions, by which, apparently, we are to understand certain drafts from the larger τάξεις with their commanders, and the numbers here would be fixed according to the force required for the expedition. So the centuriæ[11] of the different classes must have each furnished their contingents for actual service on a certain fixed proportion, and these contingents from the centuries would be called centuries themselves; but we do not know either their actual force, or their force comparatively with one another; a century of the fifth class, consisting of light-armed soldiers, must have contained many more men than a century of heavy-armed soldiers of the first class.

Moral and political character of the Romans.

II. It is difficult to form a clear idea of the moral character of the Roman people under its kings, because we cannot be sure that the pictures handed down to us of that period were not copied from the manners of a later time, and thus represent, in fact, the state of the commonwealth rather than that of the monarchy. Thus the simple habits of Lucretia seem copied from the matrons of the republic in the time of its early poverty, and cannot safely be ascribed to the princesses of the magnificent house of the Tarquinii. Again, we can scarcely tell how far we may carry back the origin of those char-

buhr has himself tacitly corrected his mistake in the second volume, p. 450, 2d Ed. by translating κάπηλον in this same passage of Dionysius, "wer *Kramhandel* erwählte," instead of "*Handel.*" "Kramhandel" is "retail trade."

[9] 1 Kings, ix. 20, 21.

[10] 1 Kings, v. 22. Compare xii. 4–16.

[11] I propose to reserve all consideration of the numbers and constitution of the early Roman legion for the next volume, when we shall for the first time have any historical accounts in detail of the military operations of the Roman armies.

acteristic points in the later Roman manners, the absolute authority possessed by the head of a family over his wife and children. But it is probable that they are of great antiquity; for the absolute power of a father over his sons extended only to those who were born in that peculiar form of marriage called Connubium, a connection which anciently could only subsist between persons of the same order, and which was solemnized by a peculiar ceremony called Confarreatio; a ceremony so sacred, that a marriage thus contracted could only be dissolved by certain unwonted and horrible rites, purposely ordered, as it seems, to discourage the practice of divorce. All these usages point to a very great antiquity, and indicate the early severity of the Roman domestic manners, and the habits of obedience which every citizen learned under his father's roof. This severity, however, did not imply an equal purity; connubium could only be contracted with one wife, but the practice of concubinage was tolerated, although the condition of a concubine is marked as disreputable by a law so old as to be ascribed to Numa.[12] And the indecency of some parts of the ancient religious worship, and the license allowed at particular festivals, at marriages, and in the festal meetings of men amongst themselves, belong so much to an agricultural people, as well as to human nature in general, that these, too, may be safely presumed to be coeval with the very origin of the Roman nation.

Their love of institutions and law.

But the most striking point in the character of the Romans, and that which has so permanently influenced the condition of mankind, was their love of institutions and of order, their reverence for law, their habit of considering the individual as living only for that society of which he was a member. This character, the very opposite to that of the barbarian and the savage, belongs, apparently, to that race to which the Greeks and Romans both belong, by whatever name, Pelasgian, Tyrrhenian, or Sikelian, we choose to distinguish it. It has, indeed, marked the Teutonic race, but in a less degree: the Kelts have been strangers to it, nor do we find it developed amongst the nations of Asia: but it strongly characterizes the Dorians in Greece, and the Romans; nor is it wanting among the Ionians, although in these last it was modified by that individual freedom which arose naturally from the surpassing vigor of their intellect, the destined well-spring of wisdom to the whole world. But in Rome, as at Lacedæmon, as there was much less activity of reason, so the tendency to regulate and to organize was much more predominant. Accordingly, we find traces of this character in the very earliest traditions of Roman story. Even in Romulus, his institutions go hand in hand with his deeds in arms; and the wrath of the gods darkened the last years of the warlike Tullus, because he had neglected the rites and ordinances established by Numa. Numa and Servius, whose memory was cherished most fondly, were known only as lawgivers; Ancus, like Romulus, is the founder of institutions as well as the conqueror, and one particular branch of law is ascribed to him as its author, the ceremonial to be observed before going to war. The two Tarquinii are represented as of foreign origin, and the character of their reigns is foreign also. They are great warriors and great kings; they extend the dominion of Rome; they enlarge the city, and embellish it with great and magnificent works; but they add nothing to its institutions; and it was the crime of the last Tarquinius to undo those good regulations which his predecessor had appointed.

Of the state of the arts.

It is allowed, on all hands, that the works of art executed in Rome under the later kings, whether architecture[13] or sculpture,[14] were of Etruscan origin; but what is meant by "Etruscan," and how far Etruscan

[12] Pellex aram Junonis ne tangito . . . si tanget, Junoni crinibus demissis agnum fœminam cædito. Festus in "Pellex."

[13] Intentus perficiendo templo, fabris undique ex Etruriâ accitis, &c. Livy, I. 56.

[14] Before the ornamenting of the temple of Ceres at Rome, near the Circus Maximus, by two Greeks, Damophilus and Gorgasus, all works of painting or sculpture, according to Varro, had been Etruscan. (Pliny, XXXV. 12.) Micali supposes the temple here meant to have been the one vowed by A. Postumius, dictator at the battle of the lake Regillus (Tacitus, Annal. II. 49), described as a temple, "Libero, Liberæque et Cereri, juxta Circum Maximum." At any rate, the two Greek artists must belong to a period later than the foundation of the capitol.

art was itself derived from Greece, is a question which has been warmly disputed. The statue of Jupiter[15] in the capitol, and the four-horsed chariot on the summit of the temple, together with most of the statues of the gods, were at this period wrought in clay; bronze was not generally employed till a later age. There is no mention of any paintings in Rome itself earlier than the time of the commonwealth; but Pliny speaks of some frescoes at Ardea and at Cære, which he considered to be older than the very foundation of the city, and which in his own age preserved the freshness of their coloring, and in his judgment were works of remarkable merit. The Capitoline Temple[16] itself was built nearly in the form of a square, each side being about two hundred feet in length; its front faced southwards, towards the Forum and the Palatine, and had a triple row of pillars before it, while a double row inclosed the sides of the temple. These, it is probable, were not of marble, but made either of the stone of Rome itself, like the cloaca, or possibly from the quarries of Gabii or Alba.

Language and intellectual character of the Romans.

The end of the reign of the last king of Rome falls less than twenty years before the battle of Marathon. The age of the Greek heroic poetry was long since past; the evils of the iron age, of that imperfect civilization, when legal oppression has succeeded to the mere violence of the plunderer and the conqueror, had been bewailed by Hesiod three centuries earlier; Theognis had mourned over the sinking importance of noble birth, and the growing influence of riches; the old aristocracies had been overthrown by single tyrants, and these, again, had everywhere yielded to the power of aristocracies under a mitigated form, which in some instances admitted a mixture of popular freedom. Alcæus and Sappho had been dead for more than half a century; Simonides was in the vigor of life; and prose history had already been attempted by Hecatæus of Miletus. Of the works of these last, indeed, only fragments have descended to us; but their entire writings, together with those of many other earlier poets, scattered up and down through a period of more than two hundred years, existed till the general wreck of ancient literature, and furnished abundant monuments of the vigor of the Greek mind, long before the period when history began faithfully to record particular events. But of the Roman mind under the kings, Cicero knew no more than we do. He had seen no works of that period, whether of historians or of poets; he had never heard the name of a single individual whose genius had made it famous, and had preserved its memory, together with his own. A certain number of laws ascribed to the kings, and preserved, whether on tables of wood or brass, in the capitol, or in the collection of the jurist Papirius, were almost the sole monuments which could illustrate the spirit of the early ages of the Ro-

[15] Pliny, XXXV. 12, quotes Varro, as saying "Turrianum a Fregellis accitum, cui locaret Tarquinius Priscus effigiem Jovis in capitolio dicandam." He had just before said that all the images of this period were Etruscan; how, then, do we find the statue of Jupiter himself ascribed to an artist of Fregellæ, a Volscian town on the Livis, with which the Romans in Tarquinius' reign are not known to have had any connection? Besides, "Turrianus" is apparently only another form of "Tyrrhenus," and seems to mark the artist as an Etruscan. Are we, then, to read Fregenæ instead of Fregellæ, or are we to suppose the artist's fame to have been so eminent that the people of Fregellæ had first invited him thither from his own country, and the Roman king afterwards brought him from Fregellæ to Rome? In this manner, Polycrates of Samos sent for Democedes, the physician, from Athens; and the Athenians had invited him from Ægina, where he had first settled after leaving his own country, Croton. Herodotus, III. 131.

But the question still returns, What is meant by Etruscan art? Are we to understand this term of the Etruscans, properly so called, the conquerors of the Tyrrhenian Pelasgians, or of these Tyrrheno-Pelasgians themselves, who must have held Agylla at least, if not other places on the coast, down to the time of the last kings of Rome; or, again, how much of Etruscan art was introduced directly into Italy from Greece itself, as is indicated in the story of Demaratus coming from Corinth to Tarquinii, with the artists Euchir and Eugrammus, "Cunning hand" and "Cunning carver?" The paintings at Ardea and Cære, mentioned by Pliny, both occur in towns of Pelasgian origin; and the arts may have thus been cultivated to a certain degree in Italy, even before the beginning of any communication with Greece. But the vases and other monuments now found in Etruscan towns, in the ruins of Tarquinii, for instance, and of Vulci, belong to a later period, and are either actually of Greek workmanship, or were executed by Etruscans to whom Greek art was familiar. See M. Bunsen's "Discours," in the 6th volume of the Annals of the Antiquarian Institute of Rome, p. 40, &c.

[16] Dionysius IV. 61.

man people. But even these, to judge from the few extracts with which we are acquainted, must have been modernized in their language; for the Latin of a law ascribed to Servius Tullius, is perfectly intelligible, and not more ancient in its forms than that of the fifth century of Rome; whereas the few genuine monuments of the earliest times, the Hymns of the Salii, and of the Brotherhood of Husbandry, Fratres Arvales, required to be interpreted to the Romans of Cicero's time, like a foreign language; and of the hymn of the Fratres Arvales we can ourselves judge, for it has been accidentally preserved to our days, and the meaning of nearly half of it is only to be guessed at. This agrees with what Polybius says of the language of the treaty between Rome and Carthage, concluded in the first year of the commonwealth; it was so unlike the Latin of his own time, the end of the sixth and beginning of the seventh century of Rome, that even those who understood it best found some things in it which, with their best attention, they could scarcely explain. Thus, although verses were undoubtedly made and sung in the times of the kings, at funerals and at feasts, in commemoration of the worthy deeds of the noblest of the Romans; and although some of the actual stories of the kings may, perhaps, have come down from this source, yet it does not appear that they were ever written, and thus they were altered from one generation to another, nor can any one tell at what time they attained to their present shape. Traces of a period much later than that of the kings may be discerned in them; and I see no reason to differ from the opinion of Niebuhr, who thinks that as we now have them they are not earlier than the restoration of the city after the invasion of the Gauls.

If this be so, there rests a veil not to be removed, not only on the particular history of the early Romans, but on that which we should much more desire to know, and which in the case of Greece stands forth in such full light, the nature and power of their genius; what they thought, what they hated, and what they loved. Yet although the legends of the early Roman story are neither historical, nor yet coeval with the subjects which they celebrate, still their fame is so great, and their beauty and interest so surpassing, that it would be unpardonable to sacrifice them altogether to the spirit of inquiry and of fact, and to exclude them from the place which they have so long held in Roman history. Nor shall I complain of my readers, if they pass over with indifference these attempts of mine to put together the meagre fragments of our knowledge, and to present them with an outline of the times of the kings, at once incomplete and without spirit; while they read with eager interest the immortal story of the fall of Tarquinius, and the wars with Porsenna and the Latins, as it has been handed down to us in the rich coloring of the old heroic lays of Rome.

CHAPTER VII.

THE STORY OF THE BANISHING OF KING TARQUINIUS AND HIS HOUSE, AND OF THEIR ATTEMPTS TO GET THEMSELVES BROUGHT BACK AGAIN.

"Vis et Tarquinios reges, animamque superbam
Ultoris Bruti, fascesque videre receptos?"
VIRGIL, Æn. VI.

WHILE king Tarquinius was at the height of his greatness, it chanced upon a time, that from the altar[1] in the court of his palace there crawled out a snake, which devoured the offerings laid on the altar. So the king thought it not enough to consult the soothsayers of the Etruscans whom he had with him, but he sent two of his own sons to Delphi, to ask counsel of the oracle of the Greeks; for the oracle of Delphi[2] was famous in all lands. So his sons Titus and Aruns went to Delphi, and they took with them their cousin Lucius Junius, whom men call Brutus, that is, the Dullard; for he seemed to be wholly without wit, and he would eat wild figs with honey.[3] This Lucius was not really dull, but very subtle; and it was for fear of his uncle's cruelty, that he made himself as one without sense; for he was very rich, and he feared lest king Tarquinius should kill him for the sake of his inheritance. So when he went to Delphi he carried with him a staff of horn, and the staff was hollow, and it was filled within with gold, and he gave the staff to the oracle[4] as a likeness of himself; for though he seemed dull, and of no account to look upon, yet he had a golden wit within. When the three young men had performed the king's bidding, they asked the oracle for themselves, and they said, "O Lord Apollo, tell us which of us shall be king in Rome?" Then there came a voice from the sanctuary and said, "Whichever of you shall first kiss his mother." So the sons of Tarquinius agreed to draw lots between themselves, which of them should first kiss their mother, when they should have returned to Rome; and they said they would keep the oracle secret from their brother Sextus, lest he should be king rather than they. But Lucius understood the mind of the oracle better; so as they all went down from the temple, he stumbled as if by chance, and fell with his face to the earth, and kissed the earth; for he said, "The earth is the true mother of us all."

How king Tarquinius, affrighted by a prodigy in his palace, sent two of his sons with Lucius Brutus to consult the oracle of Delphi.

Now when they came back to Rome, king Tarquinius was at war with the people of Ardea;[5] and as the city was strong, his army lay a long while before it, till it should be forced to yield through famine. So the Romans had leisure for feasting and for diverting themselves: and once Titus and Aruns[6] were supping with their brother

How, at the siege of Ardea, the Roman princes disputed about the worth of their wives, and how Lucretia was judged the worthiest.

[1] Ovid, Fasti, II. 711.
Ecce, nefas visu, mediis altaribus anguis
Exit, et extinctis ignibus exta rapit.

[2] Livy, I. 56, maxime inclitum in terris oraculum. The story of the last of the Roman kings sending to consult the oracle at Delphi, is in itself nothing improbable. We read of the Agyllæans of Agylla or Cære doing the same thing at an earlier period. Herodotus, I. 167. These were Tyrrhenians, or Pelasgians; and there was a sufficient mixture of the same race in the Roman people, to give them a natural connection with the religion of Greece.

[3] A. Postumius Albinus, cotemporary with Cato the censor, quoted by Macrobius, Saturnalia, II. 16. Grossulos ex melle edebat. "Ex melle," dipping them into the honey, and eating them when just taken out of it, *i. e.* with the honey clinging all about them. Compare Plautus, Merc. I. 2, 28, "Resinam ex melle devorato," where the sense of the preposition can hardly be distinguished from that of "cum." Grossi and grossuli are imperfect and unripe figs; either those of the wild fig which never come to perfection, or the young fruit of the cultivated fig gathered before its time.

[4] Per ambages effigiem ingenii sui. Livy, I. 56.

[5] Livy, I. 57. This is one of the incongruities of the story. Ardea, in the first year of the commonwealth, is mentioned as one of the dependent allies of Rome. See the famous treaty with Carthage, as given by Polybius, III. 22.

[6] Livy, I. 57.

Sextus, and their cousin Tarquinius of Collatia was supping with them. And they disputed about their wives, whose wife of them all was the worthiest lady. Then said Tarquinius of Collatia, "Let us go and see with our own eyes what our wives are doing, so shall we know which is the worthiest." Upon this they all mounted their horses, and rode first to Rome; and there they found the wives of Titus, and of Aruns, and of Sextus, feasting and making merry. They then rode on to Collatia, and it was late in the night, but they found Lucretia, the wife of Tarquinius of Collatia, neither feasting nor yet sleeping, but she was sitting with all her handmaids around her, and all were working at the loom. So when they saw this, they all said, "Lucretia is the worthiest lady." And she entertained her husband and his kinsmen, and after that they rode back to the camp before Ardea.

Of the wicked deed of Sextus Tarquinius against Lucretia.

But a spirit of wicked passion[7] seized upon Sextus, and a few days afterwards he went alone to Collatia, and Lucretia received him hospitably, for he was her husband's kinsman. At midnight he arose and went to her chamber, and he said that if she yielded not to him, he would slay her and one of her slaves with her, and would say to her husband that he had slain her in her adultery. So when Sextus had accomplished his wicked purpose, he went back again to the camp.

How Lucretia, having told the wickedness to her husband and her father, slew herself.

Then Lucretia[8] sent in haste to Rome, to pray that her father Spurius Lucretius would come to her; and she sent to Ardea to summon her husband. Her father brought along with him Publius Valerius, and her husband brought with him Lucius Junius, whom men call Brutus. When they arrived, they asked earnestly, "Is all well?" Then she told them of the wicked deed of Sextus, and she said, "If ye be men, avenge it." And they all swore to her that they would avenge it. Then she said again, "I am not guilty; yet must I too share in the punishment of this deed, lest any should think that they may be false to their husbands and live." And she drew a knife from her bosom, and stabbed herself to the heart.

How her father and her husband and Lucius Brutus excited the people to drive out king Tarquinius and his house.

At that sight[9] her husband and her father cried aloud; but Lucius drew the knife from the wound, and held it up, and said, "By this blood I swear, that I will visit this deed upon king Tarquinius, and all his accursed race; neither shall any man hereafter be king in Rome, lest he do the like wickedness." And he gave the knife to her husband, and to her father, and to Publius Valerius. They marvelled to hear such words from him whom men called dull; but they swore also, and they took up the body of Lucretia, and carried it down into the forum; and they said, "Behold the deeds of the wicked family of Tarquinius." All the people of Collatia were moved, and the men took up arms, and they set a guard at the gates, that none might go out to carry the tidings to Tarquinius, and they followed Lucius to Rome. There, too, all the people came together, and the crier summoned them to assemble before the tribune of the Celeres, for Lucius held that office.[10] And Lucius spoke to them of all the tyranny of Tarquinius and his sons, and of the wicked deed of Sextus. And the people in their curiæ took back from Tarquinius the sovereign power, which they had given him, and they banished him and all his family. Then the younger men followed Lucius to Ardea, to win over the army there to join them; and the city was left in the charge of Spurius Lucretius. But the wicked Tullia fled in haste from her house, and all,

[7] Livy, I. 58.

[8] Livy, I. 58.

[9] Livy, I. 59.

[10] The tribune of the Celeres was to the king what the master of the horse was afterwards to the dictator. It is hardly necessary to point out the extravagance of the story, in representing Brutus, though a reputed idiot, yet invested with such an important office. Festus says that Brutus, in old Latin, was synonymous with Gravis; this would show a connexion between the word and the Greek βαρύς. It is very possible that its early signification, as a cognomen, may have differed very little from that of Severus. When the signification of "dulness" came to be more confirmed, the story of Brutus' pretended idiotcy would be invented to explain the fact of so wise a man being called by such a name.

both men and women, cursed her as she passed, and prayed that the furies of her father's blood might visit her with vengeance.

Meanwhile[11] king Tarquinius set out with speed to Rome to put down the tumult. But Lucius turned aside from the road, that he might not meet him, and came to the camp; and the soldiers joyfully received him, and they drove out the sons of Tarquinius. King Tarquinius came to Rome, but the gates were shut, and they declared to him, from the walls, the sentence of banishment which had been passed against him and his family. So he yielded to his fortune, and went to live at Cære with his sons Titus and Aruns. His other son, Sextus,[12] went to Gabii, and the people there, remembering how he had betrayed them to his father, slew him. Then the army left the camp before Ardea, and went back to Rome. And all men said, "Let us follow the good laws of the good king Servius; and let us meet in our centuries, according as he directed,[13] and let us choose two men year by year to govern us, instead of a king." Then the people met in their centuries in the Field of Mars, and they chose two men to rule over them, Lucius Junius, whom men called Brutus, and Lucius Tarquinius of Collatia.

Of the driving out of king Tarquinius, and how two yearly magistrates were appointed in his room.

But the people[14] were afraid of Lucius Tarquinius for his name's sake, for it seemed as though a Tarquinius was still king over them. So they prayed him to depart from Rome, and he went and took all his goods with him, and settled himself at Lavinium. Then the senate and the people decreed that all the house of the Tarquinii should be banished, even though they were not of the king's family. And the people met again in their centuries, and chose Publius Valerius to rule over them together with Brutus, in the room of Lucius Tarquinius of Collatia.

How Lucius Tarquinius, the husband of Lucretia, was driven out also for his name's sake.

Now at this time[15] many of the laws of the good king Servius were restored, which Tarquinius the tyrant had overthrown. For the commons again chose their own judges, to try all causes between a man and his neighbor; and they had again their meetings and their sacrifices in the city and in the country, every man in his own tribe and in his own district. And lest there should seem to be two kings instead of one, it was ordered that one only of the two should bear rule at one time, and that the lictors, with their rods and axes, should walk before him alone. And the two were to bear rule month by month.

The laws of the good king Servius restored.

Then king Tarquinius[16] sent to Rome, to ask for all the goods that had belonged to him; and the senate, after a while, decreed that the goods should be given back. But those whom he had sent to Rome to ask for his goods, had meetings with many young men of noble birth, and a plot was laid to bring back king Tarquinius. So the young men wrote letters to Tarquinius, pledging to him their faith, and among them were Titus and Tiberius, the sons of Brutus. But a slave happened to overhear them talking together, and when he knew that the letters were to be given to the messengers of Tarquinius, he went and told all that he had heard to Brutus and to Publius Valerius. Then they came and seized the young men and their letters, and so the plot was broken up.

How certain of the young Romans plotted to bring back king Tarquinius.

After this there was a strange and piteous sight to behold. Brutus and Publius[17] sat on their judgment-seats in the Forum, and the young men were brought before them. Then Brutus bade the lictors to bind his own two sons, Titus and Tiberius, together with the others, and to scourge them with rods, according to the law. And after they had been

How Lucius Brutus sat in judgment upon his own sons.

[11] Livy, I. 60.

[12] Livy, I. 60. Dionysius makes Sextus live till the battle by the lake Regillus, and describes him as killed there. When the stories differ, I have generally followed Livy, as the writer of the best taste, and likely to give the oldest and most poetical version of them.

[13] Consules inde comitiis centuriatis—ex commentariis Ser. Tullii creati sunt. Livy, I. 60.

[14] Livy, II. 2.

[15] Dionysius, V. 2.

[16] Livy, II. 3, 4.

[17] Livy, II. 5.

scourged, the lictors struck off their heads with their axes, before the eyes of their father; and Brutus neither stirred from his seat, nor turned away his eyes from the sight, yet men saw as they looked on him that his heart was grieving inwardly[18] over his children. Then they marvelled at him, because he had loved justice more than his own blood, and had not spared his own children when they had been false to their country, and had offended against the law.

How the people of Veii and Tarquinii made war upon the Romans, and how Lucius Brutus was slain.

When[19] king Tarquinius found that the plot was broken up, he persuaded the people of Veii and the people of Tarquinii, cities of the Etruscans, to try to bring him back to Rome by force of arms. So they assembled their armies, and Tarquinius led them within the Roman border. Brutus and Publius led the Romans out to meet them, and it chanced that Brutus with the Roman horsemen, and Aruns, the son of king Tarquinius, with the Etruscan horse, met each other in advance of the main battles. Aruns seeing Brutus in his kingly robe, and with the lictors of a king around him, levelled his spear, and spurred his horse against him. Brutus met him, and each ran his spear through the body of the other, and they both fell dead. Then the horsemen on both parts fought, and afterwards the main battles, and the Veientians were beaten, but the Tarquinians beat the Romans, and the battle was neither won nor lost; but in the night there came a voice out of the wood that was hard by, and it said, "One man more[20] has fallen on the part of the Etruscans than on the part of the Romans; the Romans are to conquer in the war." At this the Etruscans were afraid, and believing the voice, they immediately marched home to their own country, while the Romans took up Brutus, and carried him home and buried him; and Publius made an oration in his praise, and all the matrons of Rome mourned for him for a whole year, because he had avenged Lucretia well.

How Publius Valerius was suspected by the people, and how he cleared himself.

When Brutus was dead,[21] Publius ruled over the people himself; and he began to build a great and strong house on the top of the hill Velia, which looks down upon the Forum.[22] This made the people say, "Publius wants to become a king, and is building a house in a strong place, as if for a citadel where he may live with his guards, and oppress us." But he called the people together, and when he went down to them, the lictors who walked before him lowered the rods and the axes which they bore, to show that he owned the people to be greater than himself. He complained that they had mistrusted him, and he said that he would not build his house on the top of the hill Velia, but at the bottom of it, and his house should be no stronghold. And he called on them to make a law,[23] that whoever should try to make himself king should be accursed, and whosoever would might slay him. Also, that if a magistrate were going to scourge or kill any citizen, he might carry his cause before the people, and they should judge him. When these laws were passed, all men said, "Publius is a lover of the people, and seeks their good:" and he was called Poplicola, which means, "the people's friend," from that day forward.

Then Publius called the people together[24] in their centuries, and they chose Spurius Lucretius, the father of Lucretia, to be their magistrate for the year in the room of Brutus. But he was an old man, and his strength was so much gone, that after a few days he died. They then chose in his room Marcus Horatius.[25]

Now Publius and Marcus cast lots which should dedicate the temple to Jupiter

[18] Eminente animo patrio inter publicæ pœnæ ministerium. Livy, II. 5.

[19] Livy, II. 6.

[20] Uno plus Etruscorum cecidisse in acie; vincere bello Romanum. Livy, II. 7.

[21] Livy, II. 7.

[22] It is the rising ground just under the Palatine, up which the Via Sacra passes. The arch of Titus is on the Velian Hill.

[23] Livy, II. 8.

[24] Livy, II. 8.

[25] The treaty with Carthage makes M. Horatius the colleague of Brutus: another proof of the irreconcilableness of the common story with the real but lost history.

on the hill of the Capitol, which king Tarquinius had built; and the lot fell to Marcus, to the great discontent of the friends of Publius.[26] So when Marcus was going to begin the dedication, and had his hand on the door-post of the temple, and was speaking the set words of prayer, there came a man running to tell him that his son was dead. But he said, "Then let them carry him out and bury him;" and he neither wept, nor lamented, for the words of lamentation ought not to be spoken when men are praying to the blessed gods, and dedicating a temple to their honor. So Marcus honored the gods above his son, and dedicated the temple on the hill of the Capitol; and his name was recorded on the front of the temple.

Of the dedicating of the temple on the Capitol by Marcus Horatius.

But when king Tarquinius found that the Veientians and Tarquinians were not able to restore him to his kingdom, he went to Clusium,[27] a city in the farthest part of Etruria, beyond the Ciminian forest, and besought Lars Porsenna,[28] the king of Clusium, to aid him. So Porsenna raised a great army, and marched against Rome, and attacked the Romans on the hill Janiculum, the hill on the outside of the city beyond the Tiber; and he drove them down from the hill into the city. There was a wooden bridge over the Tiber at the bottom of the hill, and the Etruscans followed close upon the Romans to win the bridge, but a single man, named Horatius Cocles, stood fast upon the bridge, and faced the Etruscans;[29] two others then resolved to stay with him, Spurius Lartius and Titus Herminius; and these three men stopped the Etruscans, while the Romans, who had fled over the river, were busy in cutting away the bridge. When it was nearly all cut away, Horatius made his two companions leave him, and pass over the bridge into the city. Then he stood alone on the bridge, and defied all the army of the Etruscans; and they showered their javelins upon him, and he caught them on his shield, and stood yet unhurt. But just as they were rushing on him to drive him from his post by main force, the last beams of the bridge were cut away, and it all fell with a mighty crash into the river; and while the Etruscans wondered, and stopped in their course, Horatius turned and prayed to the god of the river, "O father[30] Tiber, I pray thee to receive these arms, and me who bear them, and to let thy waters befriend and save me." Then he leapt into the river; and though the darts fell thick around him, yet they did not hit him, and he swam across to the city safe and sound.[31] For this the Romans set up his statue in the comitium, and gave him as much land as he could drive the plough round in the space of a whole day.

How king Porsenna made war upon the Romans, to make them take back king Tarquinius.

Of the worthy deed of Horatius Cocles.

But the Etruscans still lay before the city, and the Romans suffered much from hunger. Then a young man of noble blood, Caius Mucius[32] by name, went to the senate, and offered to go to the camp of the Etruscans, and to slay king Porsenna. So he crossed the river and made his way into the camp, and there he saw a man sitting on a high place, and wearing a scarlet robe, and many coming and going about him; and saying to himself, "This must be king Porsenna," he went up to his seat amidst the crowd, and when he came near to the man he drew a dagger from under his garment, and stabbed him. But it was the king's scribe whom he had slain, who was the king's chief officer; so he was seized and brought before the king,

How Caius Mucius sought the life of king Porsenna; and how he burned his own hand in the fire

[26] Livy, II. 8.

[27] Livy, II. 9.

[28] "Lars," like "Iucumo," is not an individual name, but expresses the rank of the person, like ἄναξ. Micali connects it with the Teutonic word "Lord."

[29] Livy, II. 10.

[30] "Tiberine pater, te sancte precor, hæc arma et hunc militem propitio flumine accipias." Livy, II. 10.

[31] Polybius says that he was killed, VI. 55. It is vain to attempt to write a history of these events; and none can doubt that the poetical story, which alone I am wishing to preserve, was that given by Livy.

[32] "Adolescens nobilis," Livy, II. 12. Niebuhr doubts whether the old story called him by any other name than Caius. Mucius, he thinks, was a later addition; because the Mucii had the same cognomen of Scævola; and he considers it inconsistent, because the Mucii were plebeians.

and the guards threatened[33] him with sharp torments, unless he would answer all their questions. But he said, "See now, how little I care for your torments;" and he thrust his right hand into the fire that was burning there on the altar, and he did not move it till it was quite consumed. Then king Porsenna marvelled at his courage, and said, "Go thy way, for thou hast harmed thyself more than me; and thou art a brave man, and I send thee back to Rome unhurt and free." But Caius answered, "For this thou shalt get more of my secret than thy tortures could have forced from me. Three hundred noble youths of Rome have bound themselves by oath to take thy life. Mine was the first adventure; but the others will each in his turn lie in wait for thee. I warn you, therefore, to look to thyself well." Then Caius was let go, and went back again into the city.

Of the peace made between king Porsenna and the Romans; and of the great spirit of the maiden Clœlia.

But king Porsenna was greatly moved,[34] and made the Romans offers of peace, to which they listened gladly, and gave up the land beyond the Tiber, which had been won in former times from the Veientians; and he gave back to them the hill Janiculum. Besides this, the Romans gave hostages to the king, ten youths and ten maidens, children of noble fathers, as a pledge that they would truly keep the peace which they had made. But it chanced, as the camp of the Etruscans was near the Tiber, that Clœlia, one of the maidens, escaped with her fellows, and fled to the brink of the river, and as the Etruscans pursued them, Clœlia spoke to the other maidens, and persuaded them, and they rushed all into the water, and swam across the river, and got safely over. At this king Porsenna marvelled more than ever, and when the Romans sent back Clœlia and her fellows to him, for they kept their faith truly, he bade her go home free, and he gave her some of the youths also who were hostages, to choose whom she would; and she chose those who were of tenderest age, and king Porsenna set them free. Then the Romans gave lands to Caius, and set up a statue of Clœlia in the highest part of the Sacred Way; and king Porsenna led away his army home in peace.

How Tarquinius sought for aid from the Latins.

After this king Porsenna[35] made war against the Latins, and his army was beaten, and fled to Rome; and the Romans received them kindly, and took care of those who were wounded, and sent them back safe to king Porsenna. For this the king gave back to the Romans all the rest of their hostages whom he had still with him, and also the land which they had won from the Veientians. So Tarquinius, seeing that there was no more hope of aid from king Porsenna, left Clusium and went to Tusculum of the Latins; for Mamilius Octavius, the chief of the Tusculans, had married his daughter, and he hoped that the Latins would restore him to Rome, for their cities were many, and when he had been king he had favored them rather than the Romans.

Of the war between the Romans and Latins on account of Tarquinius.

So after a time thirty cities of the Latins joined together and made Octavius Mamilius their general, and declared war against the Romans. Now Publius Valerius was dead, and the Romans so loved and honored him that they buried him within the city,[36] near the hill Velia, and all the matrons of Rome had mourned for him for a whole year: also because the Romans[37] had the Sabines for their enemies as well as the Latins, they had made one man to be their ruler for a time instead of two; and he was called the Master of the people, or the commander, and he had all the power which the kings of Rome had in times past. So Aulus Postumius was appointed Master of the people at this time, and Titus Æbutius was the chief or Master of the horsemen; and they led out the whole force of the Romans, and met the Latins by the lake Regillus, in the country of Tusculum; and Tarquinius himself

[33] Here I have followed Dionysius rather than Livy, because in Livy's story Mucius tells Porsenna in reward of his generosity no more than he had told him at first as a mere vaunt to frighten him.

[34] Livy, II. 13.

[35] Livy, II. 14, 15.

[36] Plutarch in Publicola, 23. Livy, II. 16.

[37] Livy, II. 18.

was with the army of the Latins, and his son and all the houses of the Tarquinii: for this was their last hope, and fate was now to determine whether the Romans should be ruled over by king Tarquinius, or whether they should be free forever.

There were many Romans who had married Latin wives,[38] and many Latins who had married wives from among the Romans. So before the war began, it was resolved that the women on both sides might leave their husbands if they chose, and take their virgin daughters with them, and return to their own country. And all the Latin women, except two, remained in Rome with their husbands: but the Roman women loved Rome more than their husbands, and took their young daughters with them, and came home to the houses of their fathers.

How the Roman women who were married to Latin husbands came home to Rome.

Then the Romans and the Latins joined battle by the lake Regillus.[39] There might you see king Tarquinius, though far advanced in years, yet mounted on his horse and bearing his lance in his hand, as bravely as though he were still young. There was his son Tarquinius, leading on to battle all the band of the house of the Tarquinii, whom the Romans had banished for their name's sake, and who thought it a proud thing to win back their country by their swords, and to become again the royal house, to give a king to the Romans. There was Octavius Mamilius, of Tusculum, the leader of all the Latins, who said, that he would make Tarquinius his father king once more in Rome, and the Romans should help the Latins in all their wars, and Tusculum should be the greatest of all the cities, whose people went up together to sacrifice to Jupiter of the Latins, at his temple on the high top of the mountain of Alba. And on the side of the Romans might be seen Aulus Postumius, the Master of the people, and Titus Æbutius, the Master of the horsemen. There also was Titus Herminius, who had fought on the bridge by the side of Horatius Cocles, on the day when they saved Rome from king Porsenna. There was Marcus Valerius, the brother of Publius, who said he would finish by the lake Regillus[40] the glorious work which Publius had begun in Rome; for Publius had driven out Tarquinius and his house, and had made them live as banished men, and now they should lose their lives as they had lost their country. So at the first onset king Tarquinius levelled his lance, and rode against Aulus; and on the left of the battle, Titus Æbutius spurred his horse against Octavius Mamilius. But king Tarquinius, before he reached Aulus, received a wound in his side, and his followers gathered around him, and bore him out of the battle. And Titus and Octavius met lance to lance, and Titus struck Octavius on the breast, and Octavius ran his lance through the arm of Titus. So Titus withdrew from the battle, for his arm could no longer wield its weapon; but Octavius heeded not his hurt, but when he saw his Latins giving ground, he called to the banished Romans of the house of the Tarquinii, and sent them into the thick of the fight. On they rushed so fiercely that neither man nor horse could stand before them; for they thought how they had been driven from their country, and spoiled of their goods, and they said that they would win back both that day through the blood of their enemies.

Of the great battle by the lake Regillus.

Then Marcus Valerius, the brother of Publius, levelled his lance and rode fiercely against Titus Tarquinius, who was the leader of the band of the Tarquinii. But Titus drew back, and sheltered himself amidst his band; and Marcus rode after him in his fury, and plunged into the midst of the enemy, and a Latin ran his lance into his side as he was rushing on; but his horse stayed not in his career till Marcus dropped from him dead upon the ground. Then the Romans feared yet more, and the Tarquinii charged yet more vehemently, till Aulus, the leader of the Romans, rode up with

How two horsemen on white horses appeared in the battle, and fought for the Romans.

[38] Dionysius, VI. 1.

[39] Livy, II. 19.

[40] Domesticâ etiam gloriâ accensus, ut cujus familiæ decus ejecti reges erant, ejusdem interfecti forent. Livy, II. 20.

his own chosen band; and he bade them level their lances, and slay all whose faces were towards them, whether they were friends or foes. So the Romans turned from their flight, and Aulus and his chosen band fell upon the Tarquinii; and Aulus prayed, and vowed that he would raise a temple to Castor and to Pollux,[41] the twin heroes, if they would aid him to win the battle; and he promised to his soldiers that the two who should be the first to break into the camp of the enemy should receive a rich reward. When behold, there rode two horsemen at the head of his chosen band,[42] and they were taller and fairer than after the stature and beauty of men, and they were in the first bloom of youth, and their horses were white as snow. Then there was a fierce battle when Octavius, the leader of the Latins, came up with aid to rescue the Tarquinii; for Titus Herminius rode against him, and ran his spear through his body, and slew him at one blow; but as he was spoiling him of his arms, he himself was struck by a javelin, and he was borne out of the fight and died. And the two horsemen on white horses rode before the Romans; and the enemy fled before them, and the Tarquinii were beaten down and slain, and Titus Tarquinius was slain among them; and the Latins fled, and the Romans followed them to their camp, and the two horsemen on white horses were the first who broke into the camp. But when the camp was taken, and the battle was fully won, Aulus sought for the two horsemen to give them the rewards which he had promised; and they were not found either amongst the living or amongst the dead, only there was seen imprinted[43] on the hard black rock[44] the mark of a horse's hoof, which no earthly horse had ever made; and the mark was there to be seen in after ages. And the battle was ended, and the sun went down.

How the two horsemen appeared at Rome in the evening, and told that the battle was won.

Now they knew at Rome[45] that the armies had joined battle, and as the day wore away all men longed for tidings. And the sun went down, and suddenly there were seen in the forum two horsemen, taller and fairer than the tallest and fairest of men, and they rode on white horses, and they were as men just come from the battle, and their horses were all bathed in foam. They alighted by the temple of Vesta, where a spring of water bubbles up from the ground and fills a small deep pool. There they washed away the stains of the battle, and when men crowded round them, and asked for tidings, they told them how the battle had been fought, and how it was won. And they mounted their horses and rode from the forum, and were seen no more; and men sought for them in every place, but they were not found.

The two horsemen were the twin heroes, Castor and Pollux.

Then Aulus and all the Romans knew how Castor and Pollux, the twin heroes, had heard his prayer, and had fought for the Romans, and had vanquished their enemies, and had been the first to break into the enemies' camp, and had themselves, with more than mortal speed, borne the tidings of their victory to Rome. So Aulus built a temple according to his vow to Castor and Pollux, and gave rich offerings; for he said, "These are the rewards which I promised to the two who should first break into the enemies' camp; and the twin heroes have won them, and they and no mortal men have won the battle for Rome this day."

How Tarquinius, after the ruin of his house, went to Cumæ, and died.

So perished the house of the Tarquinii, in the great battle by the lake Regillus, and all the sons of king Tarquinius, and his son-in-law, Octavius Mamilius, were slain on that battle-field. Thus king Tarquinius saw the ruin of all his family and of all his house, and he was left alone, utterly without hope. So he went to Cumæ,[46] a city of the Greeks, and there he

[41] Livy, II. 20.

[42] Dionysius, VI. 13.

[43] Cicero, de Naturâ Deorum, III. 5.

[44] The lake of Regillus is now a small and weedy pool surrounded by crater-like banks, and with much lava or basalt about it, situated at some height above the plain on the right hand of the road as you descend from the high ground under La Colonna, Labicum, to the ordinary level of the Campagna, in going to Rome. Cicero speaks of the mark being visible "in silice;" and silex is the name given by the Roman writers to the lava and basalt of the neighborhood of Rome.

[45] Dionysius, VI. 13.

[46] Livy, II. 21.

died. And thus the deeds of Tarquinius and of the wicked Tullia, and of Sextus their son, were visited upon their own heads; and the Romans lived in peace, and none threatened their freedom any more.

CHAPTER VIII.

ROME AFTER THE END OF THE MONARCHY—THE DICTATORSHIP—THE TRIBUNES OF THE COMMONS.

Ἡμεῖς δὲ ἀνδρῶν τῶν ἀρίστων ἐπιλέξαντες ὁμιλίην τούτοισι περιθέωμεν το κράτος· ἐν γὰρ δὴ τούτοισι καὶ αὐτοὶ ἐσόμεθα.—Herodot. III. 81.

The Roman history is still meager and uncertain.

Men love to complete what is imperfect, and to realize what is imaginary. The portraits of king Fergus and his successors in Holyrood palace were an attempt to give substance to the phantom names of the early Scotch story; those of the founders of the oldest colleges in the gallery of the Bodleian library betray the tendency to make much out of little, to labor after a full idea of those who are only known to us by one particular action of their lives. So it has fared with the early history of Rome; Romulus and Numa are like king Fergus; John of Balliol, and Walter of Merton, are the counterparts of Servius Tullius, and Brutus, and Poplicola. Their names were known, and their works were living; and men, longing to image them to their minds more completely, made up by invention for the want of knowledge, and composed in one case a pretended portrait, in the other a pretended history.

There have been hundreds, doubtless, who have looked on the portrait of John of Balliol, and, imposed upon by the name of portrait and by its being the first in a series of pictures of which the greater part were undoubtedly copied from the life, have never suspected that the painter knew no more of the real features of his subject than they did themselves. So it is that we are deceived by the early history of the Roman commonwealth. It wears the form of annals, it professes to mark accurately the events of successive years, and to distinguish them by the names of the successive consuls, and it begins a history which, going on with these same forms and pretensions to accuracy, becomes, after a time, in a very large proportion really accurate, and ends with being as authentic as any history in the world. Yet the earliest annals are as unreal as John of Balliol's portrait; there is in both cases the same deception. I cannot as yet give a regular history of the Roman people; all that can be done with the first years of the commonwealth, as with the last of the monarchy, is to notice the origin and character of the institutions, and for the rest, to be contented with that faint outline which alone can be relied upon as real.

The commons gained something by the expulsion of Tarquinius.

The particulars of the expulsion of the last king of Rome, and his family and house, can only be given, as they already have been, in their poetical form. It by no means follows that none of them are historical, but we cannot distinguish what are so. But we may be certain, whether Brutus belonged to the commons, as Niebuhr thinks, or not, that the commons immediately after the revolution recovered some of the rights of which the last king had deprived them; and these rights were such as did not interfere with the political ascendancy of the patricians, but yet restored to the commons their character of an order, that is, a distinct body with an internal organization of its own. The commons again chose their judges to decide ordinary civil causes when both parties belonged to their own order, and they again met in their Compitalia and Paganalia, the common festivals of the inhabitants of the same neighborhood in the city and in the country. They also gained the important privilege of being, even in criminal matters, judges of their own members, in case of an appeal from the sentence of the magistrate. As a burgher might appeal to the people or great council of the burghers, so a commoner might appeal to the commons assembled in their tribes, and thus in this respect the two orders of the nation were placed on a footing of equality. It is said also that a great many of the richest families of the commons who belonged to the centuries of knights, or horsemen, were admitted as new patrician houses into the order of the patricians, or burghers, or people of Rome; for I must again observe, that the Roman people or burghers, and the Roman commons, will still for a long period require to be carefully distinguished from each other.

Foreign relations of Rome. Rupture of the alliance with the Latins. The territory on the right bank of the Tiber is conquered by the Etruscans.

In the first year of the commonwealth, the Romans still possessed the dominion enjoyed by their king; all the cities of the coast of Latium, as we have already seen, were subjected to them as far as Terracina. Within twelve years, we cannot certainly say how much sooner, these were all become independent. This is easily intelligible, if we only take into account the loss to Rome of an able and absolute king, the natural weakness of an unsettled government, and the distractions produced by the king's attempts to recover his throne. The Latins may have held, as we are told of the Sabines[2] in this very time, that their dependent alliance with Rome had been concluded with king Tarquinius, and that as he was king no longer, and as his sons had been driven out with him, all covenants between Latium and Rome had become null and void. But it is possible also, if the chronology of the common story of these times can be at all depended on, that the Latin cities owed their independence to the Etruscan conquest of Rome. For that war, which has been given in its poetical version as the war with Porsenna, was really a great outbreak of the Etruscan power upon the nations southward of Etruria, in the very front of whom lay the Romans. In the very next year after the expulsion of the king, according to the common story, and certainly at some time within the period with which we are now concerned, the Etruscans fell upon Rome. The result of the war is, indeed, as strangely disguised in the poetical story as Charlemagne's invasion of Spain is in the romances. Rome was completely conquered; all the territory which the kings had won on the right bank of the Tiber was now lost.[3] Rome itself was surrendered to the Etruscan conqueror;[4] his sovereignty was fully acknowledged,[5] the Romans gave up their arms and recovered their city and territory on condition of renouncing the use of iron[6] except for implements of agriculture. But this bondage did not last long: the Etruscan power was broken by a great defeat sustained before Aricia; for after the fall of Rome the conquerors attacked Latium, and while besieging Aricia, the united force of the Latin cities, aided by the Greeks[7] of Cumæ, succeeded in de-

[1] Δίκας περὶ τῶν συμβολαίων. Dionysius, V. 2.

[2] Dionysius, V. 40.

[3] This is confessed in the poetical story: only it is added that Porsenna, out of admiration for the Romans, gave the conquered land back again to them after the war. But Niebuhr has well observed that the Roman local tribes, which were thirty in number in the days of Ser. Tullius, appear reduced to twenty in the earliest mention of them after the expulsion of Tarquinius; and it appears from the account of the Veientian war of 271, that the Roman territory could not then have extended much beyond the hill Janiculum.

[4] Tacitus, Histor. III. 72. Sedem Jovis optimi maximi,—quam non Porsenna deditâ urbe, neque Galli captâ, temerare potuissent. What "Deditio" meant may be seen by the form preserved by Livy, I. 38.

[5] The senate, says Dionysius, V. 34, voted him an ivory throne, a sceptre, a golden crown, and triumphal robe. These very same honors had been voted, according to the same writer, to the Roman king Tarquinius Priscus by the Etruscans, as an acknowledgment of his supremacy, III. 62.

[6] Pliny, XXXIV. 14. In fœdere quod expulsis regibus populo Romano dedit Porsenna, nominatim comprehensum invenimus, ne ferro nisi in agriculturâ uterentur. Compare 1 Samuel xiii. 19, 20. These passages from Tacitus and Pliny were first noticed by Beaufort in his Essay on the Uncertainty of the Early Roman History.

[7] Dionysius, V. 36, et VII. 2–11.

stroying their army, and in confining their power to their own side of the Tiber. Still, however, the Romans did not recover their territory on the right bank of that river, and the number of their tribes, as has been already noticed, was consequently lessened by one third, being reduced from thirty to twenty.

Thus, within a short time after the banishment of the last king, the Romans lost all their territory on the Etruscan side of the Tiber, and all their dominion over Latium. A third people were their immediate neighbors on the northeast, the Sabines. The cities of the Sabines reached, says Varro, from Reate, to the distance of half a day's journey from Rome, that is, according to the varying estimate of a day's journey,[8] either seventy-five or a hundred stadia, about ten or twelve miles. But with the more distant Sabines of Reate, and the high valley of the Velinus, our history has yet no concern. The line of mountains which stretches from Tiber to the neighborhood of Narnia was a natural division between those Sabines who lived within it, and those who had settled without it, in the lower country nearer Rome. These last were the Sabines of Cures,[9] twenty-four miles from Rome, of Eretum, five miles nearer to it, of Nomentum, about the same distance, of Collatia and Regillus, southward of the Anio, and in the midst of Latium; and at a more ancient period, these same Sabines possessed Crustumerium, Cænina, Antemnæ, and, as we have seen, two of the very hills which afterwards made up the city of Rome. But living so near to or even in the midst of the Latins, these more lowland Sabines had become in some degree Latinized, and some of their cities partook in the worship of Diana on the Aventine,[10] together with the Romans and the Latins, during the reign of the last king of Rome. Perhaps they also were his dependent allies, and, like the Latins, renounced their alliance with Rome immediately after his expulsion. At any rate, we read of a renewal of wars between them and the Romans four years after the beginning of the commonwealth, and it is said, that at this time Attus Clausus,[11] a citizen of Regillus, as he strongly opposed the war, was banished by his countrymen, and went over to the Romans with so large a train of followers, that he was himself received immediately as a burgher, gave his name to a new tribe, which was formed out of those who went over with him, and obtained an assignment of lands beyond the Anio, between Fidenæ and Ficulea. But when we read of the lake Regillus as belonging to the territory of Tusculum,[12] and when we also find Nomentum included amongst the thirty cities of the Latins, which concluded the great alliance with Rome, in the consulship of Spurius Cassius, we are inclined to suspect that the lowland Sabines about this time were forced to join themselves some with the Romans and some with the Latins, being pressed by both on different quarters, when the alliance between the three nations was broken up. Thus Collatia, Regillus, and Nomentum fell to the Latins; and then it may well have happened that the Claudii and Postumii, with their followers, may have preferred the Roman franchise to the Latin, and thus removed themselves to Rome; while if Niebuhr's conjecture be true, that the Crustuminian tribe as well as the Claudian was created at this time, we might suppose that Crustumeria, and other Sabine cities in its neighborhood, whose very names have perished, united themselves rather with the Romans: certain it is that from this time forward we hear of no Sabine city nearer to Rome than Eretum, which, as I have already said, was nineteen miles distant from it. It is certain also that the first enlargement of the Roman territory, after its great diminution in the Etruscan war, took place towards the northeast, between the Tiber and the Anio; and here were the lands of the only new tribes that were added to the Roman nation, for the space of more than one hundred and twenty years[13] after the establishment of the commonwealth.

Relations of Rome with the Sabines.

[8] Herodotus reckons the day's journey in one place at two hundred stadia, IV. 801, and in another place at one hundred and fifty stadia, V. 53.

[9] Bunsen, "Antichi Stabilimenti Italici," in the "Annali dell' Instituto di Corrispondenza Archeologica," Vol. VI. p. 133.

[10] As appears from the story in Livy, I. 45.

[11] Livy, II. 16. Dionysius, V. 40.

[12] Livy, II. 19, "ad lacum Regillum in agro Tusculano."

[13] The number of tribes continued to be twenty-one till three years after the invasion of

Of the pretended returns of the census during this period.

The chronology of this period is confessed by Livy[14] to be one mass of confusion; it was neither agreed when the pretended battle at the lake Regillus was fought, nor when the first dictator was created; and accordingly, Dionysius sets both events three years later than they are placed by Livy. But a far more surprising disorder is indicated by the returns of the census, if we may rely on them as authentic; for these make the number of Roman citizens between fifteen and sixteen years of age to have been one hundred and thirty thousand,[15] in the year following the expulsion of the Tarquinii; to have risen to one hundred and fifty thousand seven hundred[16] at the end of the next ten years, and again five years later to have sunk to one hundred and ten thousand.[17] It should be added, that these same returns gave eighty-four thousand seven hundred as the number of citizens, at the first census of Servius Tullius; and for this amount Dionysius quotes expressly the tables of the census. Now, Niebuhr rejects the census of Servius Tullius as unhistorical, but is disposed to admit the authenticity of the others. Yet surely if the censor's tables are to be believed in one case, they may be in the other; a genuine record of the census of Servius Tullius might just as well have been preserved as that of Sp. Lucretius and P. Valerius Poplicola. And it is to be noted, that although Dionysius gives the return of the census taken by the dictator T. Lartius, as one hundred and fifty thousand seven hundred, yet he makes Appius Claudius, five years afterwards, give the number at one hundred and thirty thousand;[18] and then, although Appius quotes this number as applying to the actual state of things, yet the return of the census, at the end of that same year, gives only one hundred and ten thousand. I am inclined to suspect that the actual tables of the census, before the invasion of the Gauls, perished in the destruction of the city; and that they were afterwards restored from the annalists, and from the records of different families, as was the case with the Fasti Capitolini. If this were so, different annalists might give different numbers, as they also give the names of consuls differently; and exaggeration might creep in here, as in the list of triumphs, and with much less difficulty. For although Niebuhr's opinion is no less probable than ingenious, that the returns of the census include the citizens of all those foreign states which enjoyed reciprocally with Rome each other's franchise, still the numbers in the period under review seem inconsistent, not only with the common arrangement of the events of these years, but with any probable arrangement that can be devised. For if the Latins and other foreigners are not included in the census of Poplicola, the number of one hundred and thirty thousand is incredibly large; if they are included, with what other states can we conceive the interchange of citizenship to have been contracted in the ten following years, so as to have added twenty thousand names to the return made at the end of that period? I am inclined, therefore, to think that the second pretended census of the commonwealth, taken by the dictator T. Lartius, which gives an amount of one hundred and fifty thousand seven hundred citizens within the military age, is a mere exaggeration of the annalist or poet, whoever he was, who recorded the acts of the first dictator.

Progress of distress amongst the commons.

But the really important part of the history of the first years of the commonwealth is the tracing, if possible, the gradual depression of the commons to that extreme point of misery which led to the institution of the tribuneship. We have seen that, immediately after the expulsion of the king, the commons shared in the advantages of the revolution; but within a few years we find them so oppressed and powerless, that their utmost hopes aspired,

the Gauls, when four new ones were added. Livy, VI. 5.

[14] II. 21. Tanti errores implicant temporum, aliter apud alios ordinatis magistratibus, ut nec qui consules secundum quosdam, nec quid quoque anno actum sit, in tantâ vetustate non rerum modo sed etiam auctorum digerere possis.

[15] Dionysius, V. 20.

[16] Dionysius, V. 75.

[17] Dionysius, V. 96.

[18] Dionysius, V. 6.

not to the assertion of political equality with the burghers, but merely to the obtaining protection from personal injuries.

The specific character of their degradation is stated to have been this: that there prevailed[19] among them severe distress, amounting in many cases to actual ruin; that to relieve themselves from their poverty, they were in the habit of borrowing money of the burghers; that the distress continuing, they became generally insolvent; and that as the law of debtor and creditor was exceedingly severe, they became liable in their persons to the cruelty of the burghers, were treated by them as slaves, confined as such in their workhouses, kept to task-work, and often beaten at the discretion of their taskmasters.

Its particular character, that they became involved in debt.

In reading this statement, a multitude of questions suggest themselves. Explanations and discussions must occupy a large space in this part of our history, for when the poetical stories have been once given, there are no materials left for narrative or painting; and general views of the state of a people, where our means of information are so scanty, are little susceptible of liveliness, and require at every step to be defended and developed. The perfect character of history in all its freshness and fulness is incompatible with imperfect knowledge; no man can step boldly or gracefully while he is groping his way in the dark.

A population of free landowners naturally engages the imagination; but such a state of society requires either an ample territory or an uninterrupted state of peace, if it be dependent on agriculture alone. The Roman territory might be marched through in a day; and after the overthrow of the powerful government of Tarquinius, which, by the extent of its dominion, kept war at a distance, the lands of the Roman commons were continually wasted by the incursions of their neighbors, and were actually to a large extent torn away by the Etruscan conquest. The burghers suffered less, because their resources were greater: the public undivided land, which they alone enjoyed, was of a very different extent from the little lots assigned to each commoner, and besides, as being chiefly left in pasture, it suffered much less from the incursions of an enemy; a burgher's cattle might often be driven off in time to one of the neighboring strongholds, while a commoner's corn and fruit-trees were totally destroyed. Again, if commerce were forbidden to a commoner, it certainly was not to a burgher; and those whose trade with Sicily, Sardinia, and Africa was sufficiently important to be made the subject of a special treaty, were not, like the commoners, wholly dependent on a favorable season, or on escaping the plundering incursions of the neighboring people. Thus it is easy to conceive how, on the one hand, the commoner would be driven to borrow, and on the other how the burgher would be able to lend.

The causes which led to this state of debt. The plundering invasions of the neighboring nations.

The next step is also plain. Interest was as yet wholly arbitrary; and where so many were anxious to borrow, it was sure to be high. Thus again the commons became constantly more and more involved and distressed, while the burghers engrossed more and more all the wealth of the community.

The high rate of interest.

Such a state of things the law of the Israelites had endeavored by every means to prevent or to mitigate. If a small proprietor found himself ruined by a succession of unfavorable seasons, or by an inroad of the Philistines or Midianites, and was obliged to borrow of his richer neighbor, the law absolutely forbade his creditor to take any interest at all. If he were obliged to pledge his person for payment, he was not to serve his creditor without hope, for at the end of seven years, at the farthest, he was restored to his freedom, and the whole of his debt cancelled. Or if he had pledged his land to his creditor, not only was the right secured to him and to his relations of redeeming it at any time, but even if not redeemed it was necessarily to return to him or to his

The severity of the law of debtor and creditor.

[19] See the story of the old centurion, in Livy, II. 23.

heirs in the year of jubilee, that no Israelite might by any distress be degraded forever from the rank of a freeman and a landowner. A far different fate awaited the plebeian landowner at Rome. When he found himself involved in a debt which he could not pay, his best resource was to sell himself to his creditor, on the condition that unless the debt were previously discharged, the creditor, at the expiration of a stated term, should enter into possession of his purchase. This was called, in the language of the Roman law, the entering into a nexum,[20] and the person who had thus conditionally sold himself was said to be "nexus." When the day came, the creditor claimed possession, and the magistrate awarded it; and the debtor, thus given over to his purchaser, addictus, passed, with all that belonged to him, into his power; and as the sons were considered their father's property, they also, unless previously emancipated, were included in the sale, and went into slavery together with their father. Or if a man, resolved not by his own act to sacrifice his own and his children's liberty, refused thus to sell himself, or, in the Roman language, to enter into a nexum, and determined to abide in his own person the consequences of his own debt, then he risked a fate still more fearful. If, within thirty days after the justice of the claim had been allowed, he was unable to discharge it, his creditor might arrest him, and bring him before the court; and if no one then offered to be his security, he was given over to his creditor, and kept by him in private custody, bound with a chain of fifteen pounds weight, and fed with a pound of corn daily. If he still could not, or would not, come to any terms with his creditor, he was thus confined during sixty days, and during this period was brought before the court in the comitium, on three successive market-days, and the amount of his debt declared, in order to see whether any one would yet come forward in his behalf. On the third market-day, if no friend appeared, he was either to be put to death, or sold as a slave into a foreign land beyond the Tiber; that is, into Etruria, where there was as yet no interchange of franchise with Rome, amidst a people of a different language. Or if there were several creditors, they might actually hew his body in pieces; and whether a creditor cut off a greater or smaller piece than in proportion to his debt,[21] he incurred no penalty.

Aulus Gellius, who wrote in the age of the Antonines, declares that he had never heard or read of a single instance in which this concluding provision had been acted upon. But who was there to record the particular cruelties of the Roman burghers in the third century of Rome? and when we are told generally that they enforced the law against their debtors with merciless severity, can we doubt that there were individual monsters, like the Shylock and Front de Bœuf of fiction, or the Earl of Cassilis of real history, who would gratify their malice against an obnoxius or obstinate debtor, even to the extremest letter of the law? It is more important to observe that this horrible law was continued in the twelve tables, for we cannot suppose it to have been introduced there for the first time; that is to say, that it made part of a code sanctioned by the commons, when they were triumphant over their adversaries. This shows, that the extremest cruelty against an insolvent debtor was not repugnant, in all cases, to the general feeling of the commons themselves, and confirms the remark of Gellius, that the Romans had the greatest abhorrence of breach of faith, or a failure in performing engagements, whether in private matters or in public. It explains also the long

[20] For this explanation of the term "Nexus," see Niebuhr, Vol. I. p. 601, et seqq. Ed. 2.

[21] See the Extracts from the law of the XII. tables in A. Gellius, XX. 1. § 45, et seqq. Some modern writers have imagined that the words "partes secanto" were to be understood of a division of the debtor's property, and not of his person. But Niebuhr well observes, that the following provision alone refutes such a notion; a provision giving to the creditor that very security in the infliction of his cruelty, which Shylock had in his bond omitted to insert. "Si plus minusve secuerunt, se fraude esto" ("se" is the old form for "sine"). Besides, the last penalty, reserved for him who continued obstinate, was likely to be atrocious in its severity. What do we think of the "peine forte et dure" denounced by the English law against a prisoner who refused to plead? a penalty not repealed till the middle of the last century, and quite as cruel as that of the law of the XII. tables, and not less unjust.

patience of the commons under their distress, and, when at last it became too grievous to endure, their extraordinary moderation in remedying it. Severity against a careless or fraudulent debtor seemed to them perfectly just; they only desired protection in cases of unavoidable misfortune or wanton cruelty, and this object appeared to be fulfilled by the institution of the tribuneship, for the tribune's power of protection enabled him to interpose in defence of the unfortunate, while he suffered the law to take its course against the obstinate and the dishonest.

Such a state of things, however, naturally accounts for the political degradation of the commons, and the neglect of the constitution of Servius Tullius. The Etruscan conquest had deprived the Romans of their arms: how, amidst such general distress, could the commons again provide themselves with the full arms of the phalanx; or how could they afford leisure for that frequent training and practice in warlike exercises, which were essential to the efficiency of the heavy-armed infantry? It may be going too far to say that the tactic of the phalanx was never in use after the establishment of the commonwealth; but it clearly never existed in any perfection. It is quite manifest, that if the heavy-armed infantry had constituted the chief force of the nation, and if that infantry, according to the constitution of Servius Tullius, had consisted exclusively of the commons, the commons and not the burghers would soon have been the masters of Rome; the comitia of the centuries would have drawn all power to itself, the comitia of curiæ would have been abolished, as incompatible with the sovereignty of the true Roman people. The comitia of the tribes would have been wholly superfluous, for where could the commons have had greater weight than in an assembly where they formed exclusively every century except six? Whereas the very contrary to all this actually happened: the commons remained for more than a century excluded from the government; the curiæ retained all their power; the comitia of tribes were earnestly desired by the commons, as the only assembly in which they were predominant; and when, after many years, we can trace any details of the comitia of centuries, we find them in great measure assimilated to those of the tribes, and the peculiarity of their original constitution almost vanished.

The distress of the commons led to their weakness politically.

But the comitia of centuries were not an assembly in which the commons were all-powerful. We are expressly told[22] that the burghers' clients voted in these centuries; and these were, probably, become a more wealthy and a more numerous body, in proportion as the commons became more and more distressed and miserable. If a third part of the commons had lost their lands by the event of the Etruscan war, if a large proportion of the rest were so involved in debts that their property was scarcely more than nominally their own, we may feel quite sure that there would be many who would voluntarily become clients, in order to escape from their actual misery. What they lost, indeed, by so doing, was but little in comparison of what they gained; they gave up their order, they ceased to belong to a tribe, and became personally dependent on their patron; but, on the other hand, they might follow any retail trade or manufacture; they retained their votes in the comitia of centuries, and were saved by the protection of their patron from all the sufferings which were the lot of the insolvent commoner. For as the patron owed his client protection, he was accounted infamous if he allowed him to be reduced to beggary: and thus we read of patrons granting lands to their clients, which, although held by them only at will, were yet, under present circumstances, a far more enviable possession than the freeholds of the commons. And whilst the clients had thus become more numerous, so they would also, from the same causes, become more wealthy, and a greater number of them would thus be enrolled in the higher classes, whilst the commons, on the other hand, were continually sinking to the lower.

Influence exercised by the burghers through their clients, on the comitia of centuries.

[22] Livy, II. 64. Irata plebs interesse consularibus comitiis noluit. Per patres, clientesque patrum consules creati.

Separation of the richer commons from the mass of their order.

Yet, amidst the general distress of the commons, we meet with an extraordinary statement in one of the speeches[23] in Dionysius, that more than four hundred persons had been raised in one year from the infantry to the cavalry service on account of their wealth. This, strange as it seems at first, is probable, and full of instruction. When money bore so high a rate of interest, capital was sure to increase itself rapidly, and in a time of distress, whilst many become poorer, there are always some also who, from that very circumstance, become richer. The rich commons were thus likely to increase their fortunes, whilst the poorer members of their order were losing every thing. It was, then, the interest of the burghers to separate these from the mass of the commons, and to place them in a class which already seems to have acquired its character of a moneyed and commercial interest; a class which resigned the troubles and the honors of political contests for the pursuit and safe enjoyment of riches. Further, the removal of the richest commoners from the infantry service rendered the organization of the phalanx more and more impracticable, and thus preserved to the burghers, whether serving as cavalry or heavy-armed infantry, their old superiority; for that the burghers in these times did sometimes serve on foot,[24] although generally they fought on horseback, is proved not only by the story of L. Tarquitius, whose poverty, it is said, had forced him to do so, but by the legend of the valiant deeds of Caius Marcius, and of the three hundred Fabii who established themselves on the Cremera. It is probable that, when occasion required it, they were the principes in rich armor who fought in the van of the infantry, although, in ordinary circumstances, they fought on horseback; and as the infantry of the neighboring nations was not better organized than their own, the horsemen in these early times are constantly described as deciding the issue of the battle.

The government becomes an exclusive aristocracy.

Thus the monarchy was exchanged for an exclusive aristocracy, in which the burghers or patricians possessed the whole dominion of the state. For, mixed as was the influence in the assembly of the centuries, and although the burghers through their clients exercised no small control over it, still they did not think it safe to intrust it with much power. In the election of consuls, the centuries could only choose out of a number of patrician or burgher candidates; and even after this election it remained for the burghers in their great council in the curiæ to ratify or to annul it, by conferring upon, or refusing to the persons so elected, "the Imperium;" in other words, that sovereign power which belonged to the consuls as the successors of the kings, and which, except so far as it was limited within the walls of the city, and a circle of one mile without them, by the right of appeal, was absolute over life and death. As for any legislative power, in this period of the commonwealth, the consuls were their own law. No doubt the burghers had their customs, which, in all great points, the consuls would duly observe, because otherwise, on the expiration of their office, they would be liable to arraignment before the curiæ, and to such punishment as that sovereign assembly might please to inflict; but the commons had no such security, and the uncertainty of the consuls' judgments was the particular grievance which afterwards led to the formation of the code of the twelve tables.

A. U. C. 253. A. C. 499. Institution of the dictatorship.

We are told, however, that within ten years of the first institution of the consuls, the burghers found it necessary to create a single magistrate with powers still more absolute, who was to exercise the full sovereignty of a king, and even without that single check to which the kings of Rome had been subjected. The Master of the people,[25] that is, of the

[23] That of M. Valerius on resigning his dictatorship in the year 260. See Dionysius, VI. 43–45.

[24] Instances of battles won by the cavalry, when they had left their horses and fought on foot, are given by Dionysius, VI. 33, and VIII. 67, and by Livy, II. 65. III. 62. IV. 38.

[25] "Magister populi." See Varro, de Ling. Lat. V. 82. Ed. Müller, et Festus in "optima lex."

burghers, or, as he was otherwise called, the Dictator, was appointed, it is true, for six months only; and therefore liable, like the consuls, to be arraigned, after the expiration of his office, for any acts of tyranny which he might have committed during its continuance. But whilst he retained his office he was as absolute within the walls of the city, as the consuls were without them; neither commoners nor burghers had any right to appeal from his sentence, although the latter had enjoyed this protection in the times of the monarchy. This last circumstance seems to prove that the original appointment of the dictator was a measure of precaution against a party amongst the burghers themselves, rather than against the commons; and gives a probability to that tradition[26] which Livy slighted, namely, that the consuls who were for the first time superseded by "the Master of the burghers," were inclined to favor the return of the exiled king. It is not likely that they were the only Romans so disposed: and if a strong minority amongst the burghers themselves, and probably a large portion of the commons, were known to favor the restoration of the old government, it is very intelligible that the majority of the burghers should have resolved to strengthen the actual government, and to appoint an officer who might summarily punish all conspirators, of whatever rank, whether belonging to the commons or to the burghers.

If the consuls were superseded by the dictator because they could not be relied upon, we may be quite sure that the appointment was not left to their free choice.[27] One of the consuls received the name of the person to be declared dictator from the senate; he then declared him dictator, and he was confirmed and received the imperium by a vote of the great council of the curiæ. The dictator must previously have held the highest magistracy in the state,[28] that is, he must have been prætor, the old title of the consuls. Thus, afterwards, when the powers of the original prætors were divided between the consuls and prætors of the later constitution, any man who had been prætor was eligible to the dictatorship, no less than one who had been consul.

The Master of the knights or horsemen.

Together with the Master of the burghers, or dictator, there was always appointed the Master of the knights or horsemen. In later times this officer was always named by the dictator himself, but at first it seems as if both alike were chosen by the senate. The Master of the knights was subject, like every other citizen, to the Master of the burghers; but his own authority was equally absolute within his own jurisdiction, that is, over the knights and the rest of the commons. Lydus expressly says that from his sentence there was no appeal; Varro says that his power was supreme[29] over the knights and over the accensi; but who are meant by this last term it is difficult to determine.

Secession of the commons to the Sacred Hill, and first appointment of the tribunes

Fifteen years after the expulsion of Tarquinius, the commons, driven to despair by their distress, and exposed without protection to the capricious cruelty of the burghers, resolved to endure their degraded state no longer. The particulars of this second revolution are as uncertain as those of the overthrow of the monarchy; but thus much is certain, and is remarkable, that the commons sought safety, not victory; they desired to escape from Rome, not to govern it. It may be true that the commons who were left in Rome gathered together[30] on the Aventine, the quarter appropriated to their order, and occupied the hill as a fortress; but it is universally agreed that the most efficient part of their body, who were at that time in the field as soldiers, deserted their generals, and marched off to a hill[31] beyond the Anio; that is, to a spot beyond the limits of the Ager Romanus, the proper territory of the

[26] Ex factione Tarquinia essent (consules), id quoque enim traditur, parum creditum sit. Livy, II. 81.

[27] See on this point Niebuhr, Vol. I. p. 591, et seqq.

[28] "Consulares legêre." Livy, II. 18. This, in the language of the time, would have been "prætorios legêre."

[29] "Magister equitum, quod summa potestas hujus in equites et accensos." Varro, de L. L., V. 82. Ed. Müller.

[30] "Piso auctor est in Aventinum secessionem factam." Livy, II. 32. So also Cicero, de Republicâ, II. 33, and Sallust, Fragm. Histor. I. 2.

[31] "Trans Anienem amnem est." Livy, II. 32.

burghers, but within the district which had been assigned to one of the newly created tribes of the commons, the Crustuminian.[32] Here they established themselves, and here they proposed to found a new city of their own, to which they would have gathered their families, and the rest of their order who were left behind in Rome, and have given up their old city to its original possessors, the burghers and their clients.

But the burghers were as unwilling to lose the services of the commons, as the Egyptians in the like case to let the Israelites go, and they endeavored, by every means, to persuade them to return. To show how little the commons thought of gaining political power, we have only to notice their demands. They required[33] a general cancelling of the obligations of insolvent debtors, and the release of all those whose persons, in default of payment, had been assigned over to the power of their creditors: and, further, they insisted on having two[34] of their own body acknowledged by the burghers as their protectors; and to make this protection effectual, the persons of those who afforded it were to be as inviolable as those of the heralds, the sacred messengers of the gods; whosoever harmed them was to be held accursed, and might be slain by any one with impunity. To these terms the burghers agreed; and a solemn treaty was concluded between them and the commons, as between two distinct nations; and the burghers swore for themselves, and for their posterity, that they would hold inviolable the persons of two officers, to be chosen by the centuries on the Field of Mars, whose business it should be to extend full protection to any commoner against a sentence of the consul; that is to say, who might rescue any debtor from the power of his creditor, if they conceived it to be capriciously or cruelly exerted. The two officers thus chosen retained the name which the chief officers of the commons had borne before: they were called Tribuni, or tribe-masters; but instead of being merely the officers of one particular tribe, and exercising an authority only over the members of their own order, they were named tribunes of the commons at large, and their power, as protectors in stopping any exercise of oppression towards their own body, extended over the burghers, and was by them solemnly acknowledged. The number of the tribunes was, probably, suggested by that of the consuls;[35] there were to be two chief officers of the commons, as there were of the burghers.

When these conditions had been formally agreed to, the commons returned to Rome. The spot on which this great deliverance had been achieved became to the Romans what Runnymede is to Englishmen: the top of the hill[36] was left forever unenclosed and consecrated, and an altar was built on it, and sacrifices offered to Jupiter, who strikes men with terror and again delivers them from their fear; because the commons had fled thither in fear, and were now returning in safety. So the hill was known forever by the name of the Sacred Hill.

[32] Hence Varro calls it "secessio Crustumerina," de L. L., V. 81. Ed. Müller.

[33] Dionysius, VI. 83-89.

[34] "Two" is the number given by Piso (Livy, II. 58), and by Cicero, Fragm. pro Cornelio, 23. Ed. Nobb., et de Republicâ, II. 34. "Two," according to Livy and Dionysius, were originally created, and then three more were added to the number immediately. According to Piso, there were only two for the first twenty-three years, and by the Publilian law they became five. Fourteen years after this, in 297, the number, according to Livy and Dionysius, was raised to ten. (Livy, III. 30. Dionys. X. 30.) But Cicero, in his speech for the tribune Cornelius, says that ten were chosen in the very next year after the first institution of the office, and chosen by the comitia curiata. So great are the varieties in the traditions of these times. Possibly, however, the number really was altered backwards and forwards; and it may have been raised to ten in the year 261, when Sp. Cassius was consul, and afterwards reduced to its original number, when his popular measures were repealed or set aside by the opposite party. With regard to the curiæ, I agree with Niebuhr, that their share in the appointment of the tribunes must have been rather a confirmation or rejection of the choice of the centuries, than an original election. This the curiæ would claim at every election made by the centuries; and it was the object of the Publilian law to get rid of this claim, amongst other advantages, by transferring the appointment to the comitia of the tribes.

[35] Or, as Niebuhr supposes, by the number of tribes, at this time reduced to twenty-one, so that each decury of tribes should have one tribune of its own. But the odd number, twenty-one, may seem to make against this supposition.

[36] Dionysius, VI. 90.

Thus the dissolution of the Roman nation was prevented; the commons had gained protection; their rights as an order were again and more fully recognized; their oppressions were abated; better times came to relieve their distress, and they became gradually more and more fitted for a higher condition, to become citizens and burghers of Rome in the fullest sense, sharing equally with the old burghers in all the benefits and honors of their common country.

CHAPTER IX.

SPURIUS CASSIUS—THE LEAGUE WITH THE LATINS AND HERNICANS—THE AGRARIAN LAW.—A. U. C. 261-269.

"The noble Brutus
Hath told you, Cæsar was ambitious.
If it were so, it was a grievous fault,
And grievously hath Cæsar answered it."

Οἱ προστάται τοῦ δήμου, ὅτε πολεμικοὶ γένοιντο, τυραννίδι ἐπετίθεντο· πάντες δὲ τοῦτο ἔδρων ὑπὸ τοῦ δήμου πιστευθέντες, ἡ δὲ πίστις ἦν ἡ ἀπέχθεια ἡ πρὸς τοὺς πλουσίους.—ARISTOT. Politic. V. 5.

BRUTUS and Poplicola were no doubt real characters, yet fiction has been so busy with their actions, that history cannot venture to admit them within her own proper domain. By a strange compensation of fortune, the first Roman whose greatness is really historical, is the man whose deeds no poet sang, and whose memory the early annalists, repeating the language of the party who destroyed him, have branded with the charge of treason, and attempted tyranny. This was Spurius Cassius. Amidst the silence and the calumnies of his enemies, he is known as the author of three works to which Rome owed all her future greatness; he concluded the league with the Latins in his second consulship, in his third he concluded the league with the Hernicans, and procured, although with the price of his own life, the enactment of the first agrarian law.

League with the Latins.

I. We know that the Latins were in the first year of the commonwealth subject to Rome. We know that almost immediately afterwards they must have become independent; and it is probable that they may have aided the Tarquinii in some of their attempts to effect their restoration. But the real details of this period cannot be discovered: this only is certain, that in the year of Rome 261, the Latin confederacy, consisting of the old national number of thirty cities, concluded a league with Rome on terms of perfect equality; and the record of this treaty, which existed at Rome on a brazen pillar[1] down to the time of Cicero, contained the name of Spurius Cassius, as the consul who concluded it, and took the oaths to the Latin deputies on behalf of the Romans. It may be that the Roman burghers desired to obtain the aid of the Latins against their own commons, and that the fear of this union led the commons at the Sacred Hill to be content with the smallest possible concessions from their adversaries; but there was another cause for the alliance, no less natural, in the common danger which threatened both Rome and Latium from the growing power of their neighbors on the south, the Oscan, or Ausonian, nations of the Æquians and the Volscians.

The thirty cities which at this time formed the Latin state, and concluded the

[1] Cicero pro Balbo, 23. Livy, II. 33.

A. U. C. 261. The thirty states of Latium. Conditions of the league.

league with Rome, were these:[2] Ardea, Aricia, Bovillæ, Bubentum, Corniculum, Carventum, Circeii, Corioli, Corbio, Cora, Fortuna or Foretii, Gabii, Laurentum, Lanuvium, Lavinium, Lavici, Nomentum, Norba, Præneste, Pedum, Querquetulum, Satricum, Scaptia, Setia, Tellena, Tibur, Tusculum, Toleria, Tricrinum, Velitræ. The situation of several of these places is unknown; still the list clearly shows to how short a distance from the Tiber the Roman territory at this time extended, and how little was retained of the great dominion enjoyed by the last kings of Rome. Between this Latin confederacy and the Romans there was concluded a perpetual league:[3] "There shall be peace between them so long as the heaven shall keep its place above the earth, and the earth its place below the heaven: they shall neither bring nor cause to be brought any war against each other, nor give to each other's enemies a passage through their land; they shall aid each other when attacked with all their might, and all spoils and plunder won by their joint arms shall be shared equally between them. Private causes shall be decided within ten days, in the courts of that city where the business which gave occasion to the dispute may have taken place." Further, it was agreed that the command of the Roman and Latin armies, on their joint expeditions, should one year[4] be given to the Roman general, and another to the Latin: and to this league nothing was to be added, and nothing taken away, without the mutual consent of the Romans and the confederate cities of the Latins.

A. U. C. 268. League with the Hernicans.

II. Seven years afterwards the same Spurius Cassius, in his third consulship,[5] concluded a similar league with the cities of the Hernicans. The Hernicans were a Sabine, not a Latin people, and their country lay chiefly in that high valley which breaks the line of the Apennines at Præneste, and running towards the southeast, falls at last into the valley of the Liris. The number of their cities was probably sixteen; but with the exception of Anagnia, Verulæ, Alatrium, and Ferentinum, the names of all are unknown to us. They, like the Latins, had been the dependent allies of Rome under the last Tarquinius; they, too, had broken off this connection after the establishment of the commonwealth, and now renewed it on more equal terms for mutual protection against the Æquians and Volscians. The situation of their country, indeed, rendered their condition one of peculiar danger; it lay interposed in the very midst of the country of these enemies, having the Æquians on the north, and the Volscians on the south, and communicating with the Latin cities and with Rome only by the opening in the Apennines already noticed under the citadel of Præneste.

[2] Dionysius, V. 61. I have followed the readings of the Vatican MS. given in the various readings in Reiske's Edition, with Niebuhr's corrections, Vol. II. p. 19, 2d Ed.

[3] Dionysius, VI. 95.

[4] Cincius de Consulum Potestate, quoted by Festus in "Prætor ad Portam." The whole passage is remarkable. "Cincius ait, Albanos rerum potitos usque ad Tullum regem: Albâ deinde dirutâ usque ad P. Decium Murem cos. populos Latinos ad caput Ferentinæ, quod est sub Monte Albano, consulere solitos, et imperium communi consilio administrare. Itaque quo anno Romanos imperatores ad exercitum mittere oporteret jussu nominis Latini, complures nostros in Capitolio a sole oriente auspiciis operam dare solitos. Ubi aves addixissent, militem illum qui a communi Latio missus esset, illum quem aves addixerant prætorem salutare solitum, qui eam provinciam obtineret prætoris nomine." Cincius lived in the time of the second Punic war, and his works on various points of Roman law and antiquities were of high value. His statement, which bears on the face of it a character of authenticity, is quite in agreement with what Dionysius reports of the treaty itself, and only gives an additional proof of the systematic falsehood of the Roman annals in their accounts of the relations of Rome with foreigners. It is true that the words of Cincius, "quo anno," do not expressly assert that the command was held by a Roman every other year; and it may be that after the Hernicans joined the alliance, the Romans had the command only once in three years. But as the Latin states were considered as forming one people, and the Romans another, it is most likely that so long as the alliance subsisted between these two parties only, the command shifted from the one to the other year by year.

[5] Dionysius, VIII. 69. Τὰς πρὸς Ἕρνικας ἐξήνεγκεν ὁμολογας· αὗται δ' ἦσαν ἀντιγραφοι τῶν πρὸς Λατίνους γενομένων. Amongst other clauses, therefore, of the treaty was one which secured to the Hernicans their equal share of all lands conquered by the confederates; namely, one-third part. This is disfigured by the annalist, whom Livy copied, in a most extraordinary manner; he represented the Hernicans as being deprived by the treaty of two-thirds of their own land. "Cum Hernicis fœdus ictum, agri partes duæ ademtæ." Livy, II. 41.

On the other hand, the Romans were glad to obtain the willing aid of a brave and numerous people, whose position enabled them to threaten the rear of the Volscians, so soon as they should break out from their mountains upon the plain of Latium or the hills of Alba.

Importance of these two treaties.

Thus by these two treaties with the Latins and Hernicans, Spurius Cassius had, so far as was possible, repaired the losses occasioned to the Roman power by the expulsion of Tarquinius, and had reorganized that confederacy to which, under her last kings, Rome had been indebted for her greatness. The wound was healed at the very critical moment, before the storm of the great Volscian invasions burst upon Latium. It happened of necessity that the Latins, from their position, bore the first brunt of these attacks; Rome could only be reached when they were conquered: whereas, had it not been for the treaty concluded by Spurius Cassius, the Volscians, on their first appearance in Latium, might have been joined by the Latins; or the surviving cities of the confederacy, after the conquest of some of their number, might have taken refuge under the protection of the conquerors.

Sp. Cassius proposes an agrarian law.

But in restoring the league with the Latins and Hernicans, Spurius Cassius had only adopted a part of the system of the Roman kings. Another, and a far more difficult part, yet remained: to strengthen the state within; to increase the number of those who, as citizens, claimed their share of the public land, and out of this public land to relieve the poverty of those who united the two inconsistent characters of citizenship and beggary. Spurius Cassius proposed, what tradition ascribed to almost every one of the kings as amongst his noblest acts, an agrarian law. But he was not a king; and it is but too often a thankless act in the eyes of the aristocracy, when one of their own members endeavors to benefit and to raise the condition of those who are not of his own order.

The true character of the agrarian laws was first explained by Niebuhr.

If, amongst Niebuhr's countless services to Roman history, any single one may claim our gratitude beyond the rest, it is his explanation of the true nature and character of the agrarian laws. Twenty-four years have not yet elapsed since he first published it, but it has already overthrown the deeply rooted false impressions which prevailed universally on the subject; and its truth, like Newton's discoveries in natural science, is not now to be proved, but to be taken as the very corner-stone of all our researches into the internal state of the Roman people. I am now to copy so much of it as may be necessary to the right understanding of the views and merits of Spurius Cassius.

Of the public or demesne land in the ancient commonwealths, and its occupation.

It seems to have been a notion generally entertained in the ancient world, that every citizen of a country should be a landholder, and that the territory of a state, so far as it was not left unenclosed or reserved for public purposes, should be divided in equal portions amongst the citizens. But it would almost always happen that a large part of it was left unenclosed; the complete cultivation of a whole country, without distinction of soil, being only the result of an excess of population, and therefore not taking place till a late period. The part thus left out of cultivation was mostly kept as pasture, and a revenue was raised from it, not only from every citizen who had turned out sheep or cattle upon it, but also from strangers, who, although incapable of buying land, might yet rent a right of pasture for their flocks and herds. But when a new territory was gained in war, the richer parts of it already in cultivation were too valuable to be given up to pasture; while, on the other hand, if they were divided, the division could only follow the general rule, and allot an equal portion to every citizen. In these circumstances, it was the practice at Rome, and doubtless in other states of Italy, to allow individuals to occupy such lands, and to enjoy all the benefits of them, on condition of paying to the state the tithe of the produce as an acknowledgment that the state was the proprietor of the land, and the individual merely the occupier. With regard to the state, the occupier was merely a tenant at will; but with respect to other citizens, he was like the owner of the soil, and could alienate the land which he occupied either for a term of years or forever, as much as if he had been its actual proprietor.

Portions of it were granted to new citizens.

This public land thus occupied was naturally looked to as a resource on every admission of new citizens. They were to receive their portion of freehold land, according to the general notion of a citizen's condition; but this land could only be found by a division of that which belonged to the public, and by the consequent ejectment of its tenants at will. Hence, in the Greek states, every large accession to the number of citizens[6] was followed by a call for a division of the public land; and as this division involved the sacrifice of many existing interests, it was regarded with horror by the old citizens,[7] as an act of revolutionary violence. For although the land was undoubtedly the property of the state, and although the occupiers of it were in relation to the state mere tenants at will, yet it is in human nature that a long undisturbed possession should give a feeling of ownership, the more so, as while the state's claim lay dormant, the possessor was in fact the proprietor; and the land would thus be repeatedly passing by regular sale from one occupier to another. And if there was no near prospect of the state's claiming its right, it is manifest that the price of land thus occupied would, after some years of undisturbed possession, be nearly equal to that of an actual freehold.

The occupiers of the public land could always be ejected at the pleasure of the state.

Under such circumstances the English law, with its characteristic partiality to individual and existing interests, would no doubt have decided, as it did in the somewhat similar case of the copyholds, that the occupier could not be ejected so long as he continued to pay his tithe to the state. The Roman law, on the other hand, in a spirit no less characteristic, constantly asserted the utterly precarious tenure of the occupier,[8] whenever the state might choose to take its property into its own hands. And accordingly, most of the kings of Rome are said to have carried an agrarian law, that is, to have divided a portion, more or less, of the public land amongst those whom they admitted to the rights of citizenship. Yet it was understood that these new citizens, the Roman commons, although they received their portion of land as freehold, whenever the public land was divided, had still no right to occupy it[9] while it lay in the mass unallotted; while the old burghers, who

[6] Λεοντῖνοι—πολίτας τε ἐπεγράψαντο πολλοὺς, καὶ ὁ δῆμος τὴν γῆν ἐπενόει ἀναδάσασθαι. Thucyd. V. 4. So, again, when the Cyrenæans in Africa wished to increase the number of their citizens, they invited over any Greek that chose to come, holding out the temptation of an allotment of land. Herodotus, IV. 159.

[7] Hence it was a clause of the oath taken by every member of the court of Heliæa at Athens, that he would allow no division of the land of the Athenians (Demosthen. Timocrat. p. 746); by which it was not meant that there was any dream of a division of the private property of Athenian citizens, but of the public land of the commonwealth, which being beneficially enjoyed by the existing citizens, could not, without loss to them, be allotted out to furnish freehold properties, κλῆροι, for any citizens newly admitted to the franchise.

[8] I have used the words "occupation" and "occupier," rather than "possession" and "possessor," to express the Latin terms "possessio" and "possessor," because the English word "possession" is often used to denote what is a man's own property, whereas it was an essential part of the definition of "possessio," that it could relate only to what was *not* a man's own property. Hence the clause in the Licinian law, "Ne quis plus quingenta jugera agri possideret," was understood by every Roman without the addition of the word "publici" to "agri," because the word "possidere" could not in a legal sense apply to private property, although there is no doubt that in common language it is often found in that signification.

[9] This was because the plebs was not yet considered to be a part of the populus: δῆμος and πόλις were still carefully distinguished, and the state, or people, or burghers, claimed the exclusive administration of what may be called the corporate property of the state. Those who are acquainted with the affairs of the colleges of the English universities will recollect the somewhat similar practice there with regard to fines. Whatever benefits arise out of the *administration* of the college property belong exclusively to the ruling part of the society: the fellows engross the fines to themselves, just as the burghers at Rome enjoyed the exclusive right of occupying the public land. But the rents of college lands are divided in certain fixed proportions amongst the fellows and scholars, the populus and plebs of the society. And a law which should prohibit the practice of taking a fine on the renewal of a lease of college property, and should order the land to be let at its full value, in order to secure to the scholars their due share in all the benefits aris-

enjoyed exclusively the right of occupation with regard to the undivided public land, had no share in it whatever when it was divided, because they already enjoyed from ancient allotment a freehold property of their own. Thus the public land was wholly unprofitable to the commons, so long as it was undivided, and became wholly lost to the burghers whenever it was divided.

Now twenty-four years after the expulsion of Tarquinius, there must have been at least as great need of an agrarian law as at any former period of the Roman history. The loss of territory on the right bank of the Tiber, and all those causes which had brought on the general distress of the commons, and overwhelmed them hopelessly in debts, called aloud for a remedy; and this remedy was to be found, according to precedent no less than abstract justice, in an allotment of the public land. For as the burghers who occupied this land had even grown rich amidst the distress of the commons, so they could well afford to make some sacrifice; while the reservation to them of the exclusive right of occupying the public land till it was divided, held out to them the hope of acquiring fresh possessions, so soon as the nation, united and invigorated by the proposed relief, should be in a condition to make new conquests.

An agrarian law was greatly needed at this period of Roman history.

Spurius Cassius accordingly proposed an agrarian law[10] for the division of a certain proportion of the public land, while from the occupiers of the remainder, he intended to require the regular payment of the tithe, which had been greatly neglected, and to apply the revenue thus gained to paying the commons, whenever they were called out to serve as soldiers. Had he been king he could have carried the measure without difficulty, and would have gone down to posterity invested with the same glory which rendered sacred the memory of the good king Servius. But his colleague, Proculus Virginius,[11] headed the aristocracy in resisting his law, and in maligning the motives of its author. His treaties with the Latins and Hernicans were represented as derogating from the old supremacy of Rome; and this cry roused the national pride even of the commons against him, as, four centuries afterwards, a similar charge of sacrificing the rights of Rome to the Italian allies ruined the popularity of M. Drusus. Still it is probable that the popular feeling in favor of his law was so strong, that the burghers yielded to the storm for the moment, and consented to pass it.[12] They followed the constant policy of an aristocracy,

Spurius Cassius proposes his law, which is violently opposed by the burghers.

ing out of the college property, would give no bad idea of the nature and objects of an agrarian law at Rome.

[10] I have here followed Niebuhr (Vol. II. 188, 2d ed.) in assuming as the original proposal of Cassius, what is represented in Dionysius as the proposal of A. Sempronius Atratinus, to which the senate assented. Dionysius, VIII. 75, 76.

[11] Livy, II. 41. This was the great quarrel between the nobles and the commons in Castile. The commons complained that the crown domains had been so granted away to the nobles, that now, as the nobles were exempt from taxation, the commons were obliged to defray all the expenses of the public service at their own private cost. And it was the commons' insisting that the nobles should give up the domains as being strictly public property, which determined the nobles to take part with the crown, in the famous war of the commons in the reign of Charles V. See Ranke, Fursten und Völker von Süd-Europa. Vol. I. p. 218.

[12] See Niebuhr, Vol. II. p. 196. He argues, that as the tribunes, before the Publilian laws, had no power of originating any legislative measure, and as we hear of their agitating the question of the agrarian law, year after year from the death of Cassius, the fact must have been that the law was passed, and its execution fraudulently evaded; and that the tribunes demanded no more than the due execution of an existing law. And he supposes that the words of Dionysius, τοῦτο τὸ δόγμα εἰς τὸν δῆμον εἰσενεχθεν, τόν τε Κάσσιον ἔπαυσε τῆς δημαγωγίας καὶ τὴν ἀναῤῥιπιζομένην ἐκ τῶν πενήτων στάσιν οὐκ εἴασε περαιτέρω προελθεῖν, VIII. 76, are taken from some Roman annalist, who by the words "ad populum latum" meant the old populus, the assembly of the burghers in their curiæ. At any rate, the words εἰς τὸν δῆμον εἰσενεχθεν seem to imply more than the mere communicating to the people the knowledge of a decree of the senate. They must apparently signify that the decree of the senate, as a προβούλευμα, was submitted to the people for its acceptance and ratification; and this "*people*" must have been the burghers in their curiæ, and by its being stated that the bringing the measure before the people put an end to the agitation, it must surely be conceived that the measure was not rejected, but passed. For the words, ἐσφέρειν εἰς τὸν δῆμον, as signifying "to submit a measure to the people for their confirmation of it," it can hardly be necessary to quote instances, τοὺς ξυγγραφέας—ξυγγράψαντας γνώμην ἐσενεγκεῖν ἐς τὸν δῆμον. Thucyd. VIII. 67.

to separate the people from their leaders, to pacify the former by a momentary resignation of the point in dispute, and then to watch their time for destroying the latter, that so when the popular party is deprived of its defenders, they may wrest from its hands that concession which it is then unable to retain.

Spurius Cassius is impeached before the burghers, condemned, and executed.

When, therefore, the year was over, and Spurius Cassius was no longer consul, the burghers knew that their hour of vengeance had arrived. Ser. Cornelius and Quintus Fabius[13] were the new consuls; Kæso Fabius, the consul's brother, and Lucius Valerius, were the inquisitors of blood, quæstores parricidii, who, as they tried all capital offences subject to an appeal to the burghers or commons, were also empowered to bring any offender at once before those supreme tribunals, instead of taking cognizance of his case themselves. Cassius was charged with a treasonable attempt to make himself king, and the burghers, assembled in their curiæ, found him guilty. He shared the fate of Agis and of Marino Falieri; he was sentenced to die as a traitor, and was, according to the usage of the Roman law, scourged and beheaded, and his house razed to the ground.

CHAPTER X.

ASCENDENCY OF THE ARISTOCRACY—THE FABII AND THEIR SEVEN CONSULSHIPS—THE PUBLILIAN LAW.—A. U. C. 269–283.

'Ησυχίαν εἶχεν ὁ δῆμος καὶ κατάπληξιν τοιαύτην ὥστε κέρδος ὁ μὶ πάσχων τι βίαιον, εἰ καὶ σιγῴη, ἐνόμιζε. —THUCYD. VIII. 66.

"Les abus récens avaient bravé la force et dépassé la prévoyance des anciennes lois: il fallait des garanties nouvelles, explicites, revêtues de la sanction du parlement tout entier. C'était ne rien faire que de renouveler vaguement des promesses tant de fois violées, des statuts si long-temps oubliés."—GUIZOT, Révolution d'Angleterre, Livre I. p. 45.

The burghers claim the exclusive appointment of the consuls.

THE release of all existing debts by the covenant concluded at the Sacred Hill, and the appointment of the tribunes to prevent any tyrannical enforcement of the law of debtor and creditor for the time to come, had relieved the Roman commons from the extreme of personal degradation and misery. But their political condition had made no perceptible advances; their election of their own tribunes was subject to the approval of the burghers; and their choice of consuls, subject also to the same approval, was further limited to such candidates as belonged to the burghers' order. Even this, however, did not satisfy the burghers; the death of Spurius Cassius enabled them to dare any usurpation; while on the other hand, they needed a more absolute power than ever, in order to evade their own concession in consenting to his agrarian law. Accordingly, they proposed to elect[1] the consuls themselves,

[13] Livy, II. 41.

[1] See Niebuhr, Vol. II. p. 202, et seqq. Dionysius and Livy both ascribe the election of Æmilius and Fabius to the influence of the patricians; but Dionysius (VIII. 83) further notices their coming into office as a marked period in the Roman history, and mentions the date, and the name of the archon at Athens for that year; as if there had been some important alteration then made in the constitution. And Zonaras, who copies Dion Cassius, says expressly that the commons, in the year 273, insisted on electing one of the consuls, for at that time both were chosen by the patricians. It seems, therefore, probable that the period from 270 to 273 was marked by a decided usurpation on the part of the burghers, and that during that time they alone elected both consuls.

and only to require the confirmation of them by the centuries; a form which would be as unessential as the crowd's acceptance of the king at an English coronation, inasmuch as it was always by the vote of the burghers in their curiæ that the imperium or sovereignty was conferred; and when a consul was already in possession of this, it mattered little whether the centuries acknowledged his title or not. In this manner were Lucius Æmilius, and Kæso Fabius, the prosecutor of Spurius Cassius, chosen consuls by the burghers; and it was in vain that the commons demanded the execution of the agrarian law; the consuls satisfied the object of those who had elected them, and the law remained a dead letter. The same spirit was manifested in the elections of the following year, and was attended with the same result; the other prosecutor of Cassius, L. Valerius, was now chosen by the burghers, and with him another member of the Fabian house, Marcus, the brother of Kæso and of Quintus.

A. U. C. 270.

A. U. C. 271.

But the complete usurpation of the consulship by the burghers served to call into action the hitherto untried powers of the tribuneship. In the year 271, the tribune Caius Mænius[2] set the first example of extending the protection of his sacred office to those of the commons, who on public grounds resisted the sovereignty of the consuls, by refusing to serve as soldiers. This was the weapon so often used from this time forwards in defence of the popular cause: the Roman commons, like those of England, sought to obtain a redress of grievances by refusing to aid the government in its wars; they refused to furnish men, as our fathers refused to furnish money. But the first exercise of this privilege was overborne with a high hand; the consuls held their enlistment of soldiers without the city; there the tribunes' protection had no force; and if any man refused to appear, and kept his person safe within the range of the tribunes' aid, the consuls proceeded to lay waste his land, and to burn and destroy his stock and buildings, by virtue of that sovereign power which, except within the walls of the city, was altogether unlimited. Accordingly the tribunes' opposition totally failed, and the consuls obtained the army which they wanted.

The tribunes protect the commons in their refusal to serve as soldiers.

But there is an undying power in justice which no oppression can altogether put down. Caius Mænius had failed, but his attempt was not entirely fruitless; a spirit was excited amongst the commons which induced the burghers the next year, after long disputes and delays, to choose for one of the consuls a man well affected to the cause of the commons; and the year afterwards it was agreed by both orders that the election should be divided between them; that one consul should be chosen by the burghers in their curiæ, and the other by the whole people in their centuries. Still, however, it must not be forgotten, that the votes of the burghers' clients were at this time so numerous in the centuries, as to give to their patrons no small influence even in the election of that consul who was particularly to be the representative of the commons. Yet the commons regarded the change as a triumph, and it was marked as a memorable event[3] in the annals, that in the year 273, Kæso Fabius was again chosen consul by the burghers, and that Spurius Furius was elected as his colleague by the people in their centuries.

The centuries recover the power of appointing one out of the two consuls.

A. U. C. 272.

The refusal of the burghers to execute the agrarian law still rankled in the minds of the commons; and when men were again wanted to serve against the Æquians and Veientians, Spurius Licinius,[4] one of the tribunes, again offered his protection to those who refused to enlist. But his colleagues betrayed him, and either as being a majority of the college overruled the opposition of Licinius, or by an abuse of their peculiar power, offered their protection to the consuls in enforcing their

A.U.C. 273. The Roman soldiers suffer themselves to be beaten in battle, rather than fight for the burghers.

[2] Dionysius, VIII. 87.
[3] Zonaras, VII. 17. Dionysius, IX. 1.
[4] Livy, II. 43.

orders against the refractory. Thus an army was raised; but the soldiers who followed Kæso Fabius into the field, regarded him and the burghers as more their enemies than the Veientians, and according to the Roman annalists, they refused to conquer, and retreated before an enemy whom they could have vanquished if they would. This is merely the habitual style of Roman arrogance; but that brave men may be found capable of allowing themselves to be slaughtered by the enemy rather than risk the possibility of winning a victory for a commander whom they detest, we know, not merely from the suspicious accounts of the Roman writers, but from the experience of our own naval service in the last war, in one memorable instance as melancholy as it was notorious.

A. U. C. 274. The house of the Fabii supports the cause of the commons.

Marcus Fabius was again chosen as the burghers' consul for the next year, and Cn. Manlius[5] was elected by the centuries. Another attempt to stop the raising of an army was made by the tribune Tiberius Pontificius,[6] and was again baffled by the opposition of his colleagues. But this year witnessed an accession to the cause of the commons, of importance more than enough to compensate for the defection of the majority of the tribunes. The Fabian house had now been in possession of one place in the consulship for six years without interruption, a clear proof that no other house among the burghers could compare with them in credit and in power. Standing at the head of their order, they had been most zealous in its cause, and had incurred proportionably the hatred of the commons. But they had men amongst them of a noble spirit, who could not bear to be so hated by their countrymen, as that their own soldiers should rather allow themselves to be slaughtered by the enemy than conquer under the command of a Fabius. Thus the new consul, Marcus Fabius, was resolved to conciliate the commons;[7] he succeeded so far as to venture to give battle to the Veientians; in the battle[8] he and his brothers fought as men who cared for nothing else than to recover their countrymen's love; Quintus Fabius, the consul of the year 272, was killed; but the Romans gained the victory. Then the Fabii, to show that they were in earnest, persuaded the burghers to divide amongst their houses the care of the wounded soldiers; they themselves took charge of a greater number than any other house, and discharged the duty which they had undertaken with all kindness and liberality. Thus, when the burghers named Kæso Fabius to be again their consul, he was as acceptable to the centuries as his colleague whom they themselves appointed, Titus Virginius.

A. U. C. 275. Migration of the Fabii to the Cremera, where they are cut off by the Veientians.

Kæso did not delay an instant in showing that his sense of the wrongs of the commons was sincere; he immediately[9] required that the agrarian law of Spurius Cassius should be duly carried into effect. But the burghers treated him with scorn; the consul, they said, had forgotten himself, and the applause of the commons had intoxicated him. Then Kæso and all his house, finding themselves reproached for having deserted their former cause, resolved to quit Rome altogether. The war with the Veientians showed them how they might still be useful to their old country: they established themselves on the Cremera, a little stream that runs into the Tiber from the west, a few miles above Rome. Here they settled with their wives and families,[10] with a large train of clients,[11] and with some of the burghers also who were connected with them by personal ties, and who resolved to share their fortune. The Fabii left Rome as the Claudii had left Regillus a few years before; they wished to establish themselves as a Latin colony in Etruria, serving the cause of Rome even while they had renounced her. But two

[5] Patres—M. Fabium consulem creant: Fabio collega Cn. Manlius datur. Livy, II. 43.

[6] Livy, II. 44.

[7] Neque immemor ejus, quod initio consulatus imbiberat, reconciliandi animos plebis, &c. Livy, II. 47. ad fin.

[8] Livy, II. 45–47.

[9] Livy, II. 48.

[10] See Niebuhr, Vol. II. p. 219. Aulus Gellius says, Sex et trecenti Fabii cum familiis suis —curcumventi perierunt.

[11] Πελάτας τε τοὺς ἑαυτῶν ἐπαγόμενοι καὶ φίλους· and again, a little below, τὸ μὲν πλεῖον πελατῶν τε καὶ ἑταίρων ἦν. Dionysius, IX. 15.

years afterwards they fell victims to the Veientians, who surprised them, put them all to the sword, and destroyed their settlement.

A. U. C. 277.

The commons had gained strength and confidence from the coming over of the Fabii to their cause; they gratefully honored the spirit which had made them leave Rome, and when they heard of their overthrow, they at once accused the burghers of having treacherously betrayed them. Titus Menenius, one of the consuls, had been quietly lying encamped[12] near the Cremera when the Fabii were cut off. He was accused, therefore, in the following year of treason, and was condemned; but the tribunes themselves pressed for no heavier sentence than a fine, although he actually died from vexation and shame at having been subjected to such a sentence. In the next year[13] another consul was accused by the tribunes, because he had been defeated in battle by the Veientians, but he defended himself manfully, and was acquitted.

The commons impeach the consuls for allowing the Fabii to be cut off.

A. U. C. 278.

A. U. C. 279.

This habit of acting on the offensive for two successive years emboldened the commons, and they now began again to call for the execution of the agrarian law of Cassius. The consuls L. Furius and C. Manlius resisted this demand during their year of office, but as soon as that was expired, Cn. Genucius,[14] one of the tribunes, impeached them both before the commons for the wrong done to that order.

Genucius impeaches the consuls for resisting the execution of the agrarian law.

A. U. C. 280.

The burghers were now alarmed, for they saw that the commons were learning their own strength, and putting it in practice. They desired, at any risk, to produce a reaction, and they acted at Rome as the Spartans some years afterwards treated their Helots, or as the Venetian nobles in modern times silenced those bold spirits whom they dreaded. On the night before the day fixed for the trial of the consuls, Genucius the tribune was found dead in his bed.[15]

A. U. C. 281. He is found dead in his bed before the trial.

The secrecy and treachery of assassination are always terrifying to a popular party, who have neither the organization among themselves to be able to concert reprisals, nor wealth enough to bribe an assassin, even if no better feeling restrained them from seeking such aid. Besides, the burghers were not satisfied with a single murder; others whom they dreaded were put out of the way by the same means as Genucius; and like the Athenian aristocratical conspirators in the Peloponnesian war, they freely used the assassin's dagger to secure their ascendency.[16] Thus the tribunes for awhile were silenced, and the consuls proceeded to enlist soldiers to serve against the Æquians and Volscians. Amongst the rest was one Volero Publilius,[17] who had served before as a centurion, and who was now called on to serve as a common soldier; he refused to obey, and being a man of great vigor and activity, he excited the commons to support him, and the consuls and their lictors were driven from the Forum. Here the disturbance rested for the time, but Volero was chosen to be one of the tribunes for the year ensuing.

Other assassinations; the tribune Volero Publilius comes forward.

Volero was a man equal to the need. The tribunitian power might be crippled by the influence of the burghers at the elections; the burghers' clients were so numerous in the centuries, that they could elect whom they would; and thus, in ordinary times, the college of tribunes might, perhaps, contain a majority who were the mere tools of the burghers, and who could utterly baffle the efforts of their colleagues. This Volero was impatient to prevent, and taking advantage of the excitement of the moment, when the commons were enraged by the murder of Genucius, he proposed a law that the tribunes, for the time to come,[18] should be chosen by the votes of the commons in their tribes, and not by those of the whole people in their centuries.

A. U. C. 282. The Publilian law.

[12] Livy, II. 52.
[13] Livy, II. 52.
[14] Livy, II. 54.
[15] Livy, II. 54.
[16] Zonaras, VII. 17. Dion Cass. Fragm. Vatic. XXII.
[17] Livy, II. 55.
[18] Livy, II. 56.

No tribune could be persuaded to betray the cause of his order and of public freedom by opposing Volero on this occasion; but the year passed away, and the burghers were thus long successful in obstructing the further progress of the law. It should be remembered that Volero could but propose his measure to the commons assembled in their tribes, and that even if accepted by them, it did not, therefore, become a law, but rather resembled the old petitions of the house of commons, which required the sanction of the king and the house of lords before they could become the law of the land. So any resolution of the tribes was no more than a petition addressed to the senate and burghers; but there is a moral power in such petitions which is generally irresistible, and the burghers well understood the policy of an aristocracy, to fight its battle in the assembly of the commons themselves, rather than to commit their order in an open contest with the whole order of the commons. Accordingly, the burghers labored to prevent Volero from carrying his petition in the assembly of the tribes. With this view, their method was delay: the tribes met to transact business only once in eight days, once, that is, in a Roman week;[19] and no measure could be proposed unless notice had been given of it two full weeks beforehand, while any measure that was not carried on the day that it was brought forward, was held to be lost, and could not be again put to the vote till after the lapse of two full weeks more. The object, therefore, of the burghers was so to obstruct the course of business, whenever the tribes met, as to spin it out to sunset without a division; then the measure was lost, and could not be brought on again till after a fortnight's interval. And they interrupted and delayed the business of the tribes, by appearing with their clients in the Forum, and purposely exciting a disturbance with the commons. Besides, we are told that Rome was this year visited with a severe epidemic disorder, which, though it lasted only a little while, was exceedingly fatal. This was an interruption to ordinary business, and this, together with the arts of the burghers, prevented the commons from coming to a resolution in favor of their measure throughout the whole course of the year.

It is violently opposed by the burghers.

Volero was re-elected tribune;[20] Appius Claudius was chosen consul by the burghers, and T. Quintius was elected as his colleague by the centuries. With Volero there was chosen also another tribune more active than himself, Caius Lætorius;[21] the oldest of all the tribunes, but a man endowed with a resolute spirit, and well aware of the duty of maintaining the contest vigorously. Fresh demands were added to those contained in Volero's first law: the ædiles were to be chosen by the tribes as well as the tribunes, and the tribes were to be competent[22] to consider all questions affecting the whole nation, and not such only as might concern the commons. Thus the proposed law was rendered more unwelcome to the burghers than ever, and Appius determined to resist it by force. Lætorius was provoked by the insulting language of the consul, and he swore that on the next day on which the law could be brought forward, he would either get it passed by the commons before evening, or would lay down his life upon the place.[23] Accordingly, when the tribes assembled, Appius stationed himself in the Forum, surrounded by a multitude of the younger burghers and of his own clients, ready to interrupt the proceedings of the commons. Lætorius called the tribes to vote, and gave the usual order that all strangers, that is, all who did not belong to any tribe, should withdraw from the Forum. Appius refused to stir;[24] the tribune sent his officer to enforce obedience, but the consul's lictors beat off the officer, and a general fray ensued, in

A. U. C. 283. But at last carried.

[19] In the Roman Kalendars which have been preserved to us, eight letters are used to mark the several days of the month, just as seven are used by us. Thus, the nones of the month fell always one Roman week before the ides; the term nonæ, like that of nundinæ to express the weekly market-day, having reference to the inclusive manner of reckoning, common to all the nations of antiquity.

[20] Livy, II. 56.

[21] Dionysius, IX. 46.

[22] Dionysius, IX. 43. Zonaras, VII. 17.

[23] Livy, II. 56.

[24] Livy, II. 56.

which Lætorius received some blows; and matters would have come to extremity, it is said, had not T. Quintius interposed, and with great difficulty parted the combatants. This, however, appears to be one of the usual softenings of the annals, which delighted to invest these early times with a character of romantic forbearance and innocence. Both parties were thoroughly in earnest; Lætorius had received such injuries as to rouse the fury of the commons to the utmost; again had the sacred persons of the tribunes been profaned by violence, and Lætorius might soon share the fate of Genucius. Accordingly, the commons acted this time on the offensive: they neither withdrew to the Sacred Hill, nor shut themselves up in their own quarter on the Aventine, but they attacked and occupied[25] the Capitol, and held it for some time as a fortress, keeping regular guard, under the command of their tribunes, both night and day. The occupation of the citadel in the ancient commonwealths implied an attempt to effect a revolution; and a popular tribune, thus holding the Capitol with his partisans, might, at any instant, make himself absolute, and establish his tyranny, like so many of the popular leaders in Greece, upon the ruins of the old aristocracy. The senate, therefore, and the wiser consul, T. Quintius, resisted the violent counsels of Appius and the mass of the burghers; it was resolved that the law, which we must suppose had been passed by the commons immediately before they took possession of the Capitol, should be immediately laid before the senate, to receive the assent of that body. It received the senate's sanction,[26] and with this double authority it was brought before the burghers in their curiæ, to receive their consent also; the only form wanting to give it the force of a law. But the decision of the wisest and most illustrious members of their own body overcame the obstinacy of the burghers: they yielded to necessity; and the second great charter of Roman liberties, the Publilian law, was finally carried, and became the law of the land. Some said that even the number of tribunes was now, for the first time, raised to five, having consisted hitherto of two only. At any rate, the names of the first five tribunes, freely chosen by their own order, were handed down to posterity; they were C. Siccius,[27] L. Numitorius, M. Duilius, Sp. Icilius, and L. Mæcilius.

In this list we meet with neither Volero nor Lætorius. Volero, as having been already tribune for two years together, and having been less prominent in the final struggle, may naturally have been passed over; but Lætorius, like Sextius at a later period, would surely have been the first choice of the commons, when they came to exercise a power which they owed mainly to his exertions. Was it, then, that his own words had been prophetic; that he had, in fact, given up his life in the Forum on the day when he brought forward the law; that the blows of Appius' burghers were as deadly as those of Kæso Quinctius, or of the murderers of Genucius, and that Lætorius was not only the founder of the greatness of his order, but its martyr also?

Thus, after a period of extreme depression and danger, the commons had again begun to advance, and the Publilian law, going beyond any former charter, was a sure warrant for a more complete enfranchisement yet to come. The commons could now elect their tribunes freely, and they had formally obtained the right of discussing all national questions in their own assembly. Thus their power spread itself out on every side, and tried its strength, against that time when, from being independent, it aspired to become sovereign, and swallowed up in itself all the powers of the rest of the community.

[25] Dionysius, IX. 48.
[26] Dionysius, IX. 49.
[27] Livy, II. 58. He borrows the names from the annals of Piso.

CHAPTER XI.

WARS WITH THE ÆQUIANS AND VOLSCIANS—LEGENDS CONNECTED WITH THESE WARS—STORIES OF CORIOLANUS, AND OF CINCINNATUS.

"Pandite nunc Helicona Deæ, cantusque movete:
Qui bello exciti reges; quæ quemque secutæ
Complerint campos acies; quibus Itala jam tum
Floruerit terra alma viris, quibus arserit armis."
VIRGIL, Æn. VII. 641.

Introduction to the foreign history of Rome.

NOTHING conveys a juster notion of the greatness of Roman history than those chapters in Gibbon's work, in which he brings before us the state of the east and of the north, of Persia and of Germany, and is led unavoidably to write a universal history, because all nations were mixed up with the greatness and the decline of Rome. This, indeed, is the peculiar magnificence of our subject, that the history of Rome must be in some sort the history of the world; no nation, no language, no country of the ancient world, can altogether escape our researches, if we follow on steadily the progress of the Roman dominion till it reached its greatest extent. On this vast field we are now beginning to enter; our view must be carried a little beyond the valley of the Tiber, and the plain of the Campagna; we must go as far as the mountains which divide Latium from Campagna, which look down upon the level of the Pontine marshes, and even command the island summits of the Alban hills: we must cross the Tiber, and enter upon a people of foreign extraction and language, a mighty people, whose southern cities were almost within sight of Rome, while their most northern settlements were planted beyond the Apennines, and, from the great plain of the Eridanus, looked up to that enormous Alpine barrier which divided them from the unknown wildernesses watered by the Ister and his thousand tributary rivers.

The Opicans or Ausonians, and the two Opican nations, the Æquians and Volscians.

In the days of Thucydides, the Greek city of Cuma[1] is described as situated in the land of the Opicans. The Opicans, Oscans, or Ausonians, for the three names all express the same people, occupied all the country between Œnotria and Tyrrhenia, that is to say, between the Silarus and the Tiber; but the sea-coast of this district was full of towns belonging to people of other nations, such as the Greek cities of Cuma and Neapolis, and those belonging to the Tyrrhenian Pelasgians, such as Tarracina, Circeii, Antium, and Ardea. The Opicans were an inland people, and it was only by conquest that they at last came down to the sea-coast, and established themselves in some of the Tyrrhenian towns. They had various subdivisions; but the two nations of them with whom the Romans had most to do, and whose encroachments on Latium we are now to notice, are known to us under the name of the Æquians and Volscians.

It is absolutely impossible to offer any thing like a connected history of the Volscian and Æquian wars with Rome during the first half century from the beginning of the commonwealth. But in order to give some clearness to the following sketch, I must first describe the position of the two nations, and class their contests with Rome, whether carried on singly or jointly, under the names respectively of the Æquian and Volscian wars, according to the quarter which was the principal field of action.

[1] Thucyd. VI. 4.

The Volscians, when they first appear in Roman history, are found partly settled on the line of highlands overlooking the plain of Latium, from near Præneste to Tarracina, and partly at the foot of the hills, in the plain itself. It has been already noticed, that just to the south of Præneste a remarkable break occurs in this mountain wall, so that only its mere base has been left standing, a tract of ground[2] barely of sufficient elevation to turn the waters in different directions, and to separate the source of the Trerus, which feeds the Liris, from the streams of the Campagna of Rome. This breach or gap in the mountains forms the head of the country of the Hernicans, who occupied the higher part of the valley of the Trerus, and the hills on its left bank downward as far as its confluence with the Liris. But at Præneste the mountain wall rises again to its full height, and continues stretching to the northward in an unbroken line, till it is again interrupted at Tibur or Tivoli by the deep valley of the Anio. Thus from the Anio to the sea at Tarracina, the line of hills is interrupted only at a single point, immediately to the south of Præneste, and is by this breach divided into two parts of unequal length, the shorter one extending from Tibur to Præneste, the longer one reaching from the point where the hills again rise opposite to Præneste as far as Tarracina and the sea. Of this mountain wall the longer portion was held by the Volscians, the shorter by the Æquians.

Their geographical position.

But it is not to be understood that the whole of this highland country was possessed by these two Opican nations. Latin towns were scattered along the edge of it overlooking the plain of Latium, such as Tibur and Præneste in the Æquian portion of it, and in the Volscian, Ortona, Cora, Norba, and Setia. The Æquians dwelt rather in the interior of the mountain country; their oldest seats were in the heart of the Apennines, on the lake of Fucinus, from whence they had advanced towards the west, till they had reached the edge overhanging the plain. Nor is it possible to state at what time the several Latin cities of the Apennines were first conquered, or how often they recovered their independence. Tibur and Præneste never fell into the hands of the Æquians, their natural strength helping, probably, to secure them from the invaders. The Æquians seem rather to have directed their efforts in another direction, against the Latin towns of the Alban hills, pouring out readily through the breach in the mountain line already noticed, and gaining thus an advanced position from which to command the plain of Rome itself.

Seat of the wars with the Æquians;

The Volscian conquests, on the other hand, were effected either in their own portion of the mountain line, or in the plain nearer the sea, or finally, on the southern and western parts of the cluster of the Alban hills, as the Æquians attacked their eastern and northern parts. Tarracina[3] appears to have fallen into their hands very soon after the overthrow of the Roman monarchy; and Antium[4] was also an early conquest. In the year 261, Bovillæ, Circeii, Corioli, Lavinium, Satricum, and Velitræ, were still Latin cities; but all[5] these were conquered at one time or other by the Vol-

with the Volscians. Volscian conquests in Latium.

[2] Taking a parallel case from English geography, the gap in the oolitic limestone chain of hills which occurs in Warwickshire, between Farnborough and Edge Hill, may be compared to the gap at Præneste; the line of hills northward and southward from this point, overlooking the lias plain of Warwickshire, may represent respectively the countries of the Æquians and Volscians; whilst Banbury and the valley of the Cherwell answer to the country of the Hernicans.

[3] It is mentioned as a Volscian town under the name of Anxur in the year 349. (Livy, IV. 59.) Its capture by the Volscians is nowhere recorded; but in the earliest Volscian wars, after the expulsion of the Tarquins, the seat of war lies always on the Roman side of it. It seems, therefore, to have fallen soon after the date of the treaty with Carthage, in which it is spoken of as a Latin city.

[4] It belonged to the Volscians in the year 261, the year in which the Roman league with the Latins was concluded. Livy, II. 33.

[5] The present text of Dionysius has Βολὰς or Βωλάς (VIII. 20). Plutarch has Βόλλας (Coriolanus, 29); but it appears that Bovillæ, and not Bola, is meant, because the conquest of Bola is mentioned separately by both writers, and because Plutarch gives the distance of Βόλλαι from Rome at one hundred stadia, which suits Bovillæ, but is too little for Bola. The conquest of Circeii, Corioli, Lavinium, and Satricum, is noticed by Livy, II. 39. Velitræ was taken by the Romans from the Volscians in the year 260,

scians, so that at the period of their greatest success they must have advanced within twelve miles of the gates of Rome. The legend of Coriolanus represents these towns, with the exception of Velitræ, as having been taken between the years 263 and 266, in the great invasion conducted jointly by Coriolanus and by Attius Tullius. But Niebuhr has given reasons for believing that these conquests were not made till some years later, and that they were effected not all at once, but in the course of several years. Be this as it may, it is certain that some of the towns thus taken, Satricum, for instance, Cerceii, and Velitræ, remained for many years in possession of the Volscians. Corioli was destroyed, and is no more heard of in history, while Bovillæ and Lavinium were in all probability soon recovered either by the Romans or by the Latins.

Æquian conquests.

Whilst the Volscians were thus tearing Latium to pieces on one side, the Æquians were assailing it with equal success on the other. Their conquests also are assigned by the legend of Coriolanus to his famous invasion, when he is said to have taken Corbio,[6] Vitellia, Trebia, Lavici, and Pedum. All these places, with the exception of Trebia, stood either on the Alban hills, or close to them, and three of them, Corbio, Lavici, and Pedum, are amongst the thirty Latin cities which concluded the treaty with Spurius Cassius in the year 261. They were retained for many years[7] by their conquerors; and thus Tibur and Præneste were isolated from the rest of Latium, and the Æquians had established themselves on the Alban hills above and around Tusculum, which remained the only unconquered Latin city in that quarter, and was so thrown more than ever into the arms of Rome.

These conquests were effected gradually, during a period of several years, at the close of the third century of Rome.

Now, had all these conquests been indeed achieved as early as the year 266, and within the space of one or two years, what could have prevented the Æquians and Volscians from effecting the total conquest of Rome, or what could their armies have been doing in the years from 273 to 278, when the Romans were struggling so hardly against the Veientians? Or how comes it, as Niebuhr well observes, if the Æquians had taken Pedum, and Corbio, and Lavici, in 266, that their armies are mentioned as encamping on Algidus for the first time in the year 289; a spot which from that time forwards they continued to occupy, year after year, till Rome regained the ascendency? It is much more probable that the first years of the war after 263 were marked by no decisive events; that the league with the Hernicans in 268 opposed an additional obstacle to the progress of the Opican nations; but that subsequently, the wars with the Veientians, and the domestic disputes which raged with more or less violence from the death of Spurius Cassius to the passing of the Publilian law, distracted the attention of the Romans, and enabled the Æquians and Volscians to press with more effect upon the Latins and Hernicans. But Antium was wrested from the Volscians by the three confederate nations in 286; and the great period of the Roman disasters is to be placed in the ten years following that event, unless we choose to separate the date of the Volscian conquests from those of the Æquians. We must, then, suppose that Corioli, Satricum, Lavinium, and the towns in that quarter, had been taken by the Volscians between 266 and 286, that some of these were afterwards recovered, and that the Romans during the latter part of the period

but it must afterwards have been lost again; for we find it in arms with the Volscians against Rome, and afterwards with the Latins; and although this is spoken of as the revolt of a Roman colony, as if the descendants of the colonists, sent there after its first conquest in 260, had always continued in possession of it, yet the well-known inscription found there, known by the name of "La Lamina Volsca," or "Borgiana," is written in the Oscan language, and contains the Oscan title "Medix." See Lanzi, Saggio di Lingua Etrusca, Vol. III. p. 616. I believe Niebuhr is right in considering such pretended revolts of Roman colonies to have been properly a revolt of the old inhabitants, in which the Roman colonists, as a matter of course, were expelled or massacred. See Vol. II. p. 44, 45. Engl. Transl.

[6] Livy, II. 39.

[7] Lavici was conquered by the Romans in 336. (Livy, IV. 47.) Corbio in 297. (Livy, III. 30.) No recapture of Pedum is mentioned; but the town probably joined the Latin confederacy again, when it shook off the Volscian yoke: it is mentioned in the time of the great Latin war as taking an active part on the Latin side.

had been regaining their lost ground, till in 286 they became, in their turn, the assailants, and conquered Antium. Then the Æquians united their arms more zealously with the Volscians; the seat of the war was removed to the frontier of Latium, bordering on the Æquians, and then followed the invasion of that frontier, the establishment of the Æquians on Algidus, and the repeated ravages of the Roman territory between Tusculum and Rome.

That period was also marked by the visitations of pestilence.

The period between the year 286 and the end of the century was marked by the visitations of pestilence as well as by those of war. A short but most severe epidemic had raged in the year 282;[8] it broke out again in 288,[9] and then in 291,[10] when its ravages were most fearful. It carried off both the consuls, two out of the four augurs, the Curio Maximus, with a great number of other persons of all ages and conditions; and this sickness, like the plague of Athens, was aggravated by the inroads of the Æquians and Volscians, which had driven the country people to fly with their cattle into Rome, and thus crowded a large population into a narrow space with deficient accommodations, while the state of the atmosphere was in itself pestilential, even had it been met under circumstances the most favorable. It is manifest that at this time the Romans were in possession of no fortified towns between Rome and the Æquian frontier; when the Roman armies could not keep the field, the enemy might march without obstacle up to the very walls of Rome itself; and there was nothing for them to win, except the plunder of the Roman territory, and the possession of the capital.

And by internal dissensions, which drove many Romans in exile, who joined the armies of the Æquians and Volscians.

Perhaps, too, these disastrous times were further aggravated by another evil, which the Roman annals were unwilling openly to avow. When matters came to such a crisis that the commons occupied the Capitol in arms, as was the case immediately before the passing of the Publilian law, when we read of dissensions so violent, that the consuls of three successive years were impeached by the tribunes, and a tribune was on the other hand murdered by the aristocracy; when again, at a somewhat later period, we read of the disputes about the Terentilian law, and hear of the banishment of Kæso Quinctius for his violences towards the commons on that occasion, we may suspect that the whole truth has not been revealed to us, and that the factions of Rome, like those of Greece, were attended by the banishment of a considerable number of the vanquished party, so that Roman exiles were often to be found in the neighboring cities, as eager to return as the Tarquinii had been formerly, and as little scrupulous as they of effecting that return through foreign aid. That this was actually the case, is shown by the surprise of the Capitol, in the year 294, when a body of men, consisting, as it is expressly said, of exiles and slaves,[11] and headed by Appius Herdonius, a Sabine, made

[8] Dionysius, IX. 42.

[9] Livy, III. 2. Dionysius, IX. 60.

[10] Livy, III. 6, 7. Dionysius, IX. 67.

[11] It is not, indeed, expressly said that the exiles were Roman exiles; and Livy, who, in his whole narrative of the transaction, says nothing of Kæso, or of his connection with the conspiracy, uses language which might be applicable to the case of exiles of other countries. He makes Herdonius say (III. 15), "Se miserrimi cujusque suscepisse causam, ut exules injuria pulsos in patriam reduceret; id malle populo Romano auctore fieri: si ibi spes non sit, Volscos et Æquos, et omnia extrema tentaturum et concitaturum." Still even these words, especially the expression "in patriam," instead of "in patrias," are most naturally to be understood of Roman exiles; if they had been all Sabines, or Æquians, or Volscians, the attempt would have been made on the citadel of Cures, or Lavici, or Anxur; not on the Capitol at Rome. But Dionysius' words (X. 14) admit of no doubt. Ἦν δὲ αὐτοῦ γνώμη μετὰ τὸ κρατῆσαι τῶν ἐπικαιροτάτων τόπων (of Rome, namely) τούς τε φυγάδας εἰσδέχεσθαι, καὶ τοὺς δούλους εἰς ἐλευθερίαν καλεῖν. These can certainly be no other than the exiles and the slaves of Rome.

The supposition in the text receives further confirmation from a remarkable statement in Dionysius, that in the year 262, just before the banishment of Coriolanus, many Roman citizens were invited by the neighboring cities to leave their country and to come and live with them, and enjoy their franchise of citizenship. And a great many πολλοὶ πάνυ left Rome with their families, he says, on these terms; some of whom returned afterwards, when better times arrived, but others continued to live in their new countries. See Dionys. VII. 18. This undoubtedly must mean that many Romans were obliged to go into banishment, and these availed themselves of the treaty with the Latins, which established an interchange of citizenship between Rome and Latium, and became citizens

themselves masters of the citadel of Rome. There is, therefore, in all probability, a foundation in truth for the famous story of Coriolanus, but it must be referred to a period much later than the year 263, the date assigned to it in the common annals; and the circumstances are so disguised, that it is impossible to guess from what reality they have been corrupted. It would be a beautiful story, could we believe that Coriolanus joined the conquering Æquians and Volscians with a body of Roman exiles; that the victories of foreigners put it in his power to procure his own recall and that of his companions, but that, overcome by the prayers of his mother, he refrained from doing such violence to the laws of his country; and, contented with the conquests of his protectors, he refused to turn them to his own personal benefit, and chose rather to live and die an exile than to owe his restoration to the swords of strangers. Be this as it may, the common story is so famous and so striking that it must not be suppressed; and the life and death of Coriolanus are no unworthy sequel to the story of the life and death of the last king Tarquinius.

Story of Coriolanus. Of his early prowess at the battle by the lake Regillus.

Caius Marcius[12] was a noble Roman, of the race of that worthy king, Ancus Marcius;[13] his father died when he was a child, but his mother, whose name was Volumnia, performed to him the part both of father and of mother; and Caius loved her exceedingly, and when he gained glory by his feats of arms, it was his greatest joy that his mother should hear his praises; and when he was rewarded for his noble deeds, it was his greatest joy that his mother should see him receive his crown. And he fought at the battle by the lake Regillus,[14] against king Tarquinius and the Latins, and he was then a youth of seventeen years of age; and in the heat of the battle he saw a Roman beaten to the ground, and his foe was rushing on him to slay him, but Caius stepped before him, and covered him, and slew the enemy, and saved the life of his fellow-soldier. So Aulus, the general, rewarded him with an oaken wreath, for such was the reward given to those who saved the life of a comrade in battle. And this was his first crown, but after this he won many in many battles, for he was strong and valiant, and none of the Romans could compare with him.

How he took the city of Corioli, and won the name of Coriolanus.

After this there was a war between the Romans and the Volscians; and the Romans attacked the city of Corioli.[15] The citizens of Corioli opened their gates and made a sally, and drove the Romans back to their camp. Then Caius ran forwards with a few brave men, and called back the runaways, and he stayed the enemy, and turned the tide of the battle, so that the Volscians fled back into the city. But Caius followed them, and when he saw the gates still open, for the Volscians were flying into the city, then he called to the Romans, and said, "For us are yon gates set wide rather than for the Volscians; why are we afraid to rush in?" He himself followed the fugitives into the town, and the enemy fled before him; but when they saw that he was but one man they turned against him, but Caius held his ground, for he was strong of hand, and light of foot, and stout of heart, and he drove the Volscians to the farthest side of the town, and all was clear behind him; so that the Romans came in after him without any trouble, and took the city. Then all

of some Latin city. And this is the simplest way of accounting for the name Coriolanus, to suppose that he settled at Corioli, and became a citizen there; and afterwards, when Corioli was conquered by the Volscians, joined their army in order to prosecute his revenge against Rome.

[12] Zonaras, copying Dion Cassius, and most of the MSS. of Livy, give the prænomen of Coriolanus as Cnæus, and not Caius. Historically the point is of no consequence; but the richest poetry in which the story of Coriolanus was ever recorded, Shakspeare's tragedy on that subject, has consecrated the name of Caius; and in this respect, as well as in calling the mother of the hero Volumnia, and his wife Virgilia, I have regarded Shakspeare's authority as decisive.

[13] Plutarch, Coriolanus, I. 4.

[14] Plutarch, Coriolanus, 3.

[15] Plutarch, Coriolanus, VIII. The story represents Corioli as a Volscian town, and as taken by the Romans in the consulship of Postumus Cominius, A. U. C. 261. The authentic monument of these times, the treaty between the Romans and Latins concluded in this very same year, shows that Corioli was then not a Volscian but a Latin town, and one of the thirty states which made the alliance with Rome.

men said, "Caius and none else has won Corioli;" and Cominius the general said, "Let him be called after the name of the city." So they called him Caius Marcius Coriolanus.[16]

After this there was a great scarcity of corn, and the commons were much distressed for want, and the king[17] of the Greeks in Sicily sent ships laden with corn to Rome: so the senate resolved to sell the corn to the poor commons, lest they should die of hunger. But Caius hated the commons, and he was angry that they had got tribunes to be their leaders, and he said, "If they want corn, let them show themselves obedient to the burghers as their fathers did, and let them give up their tribunes; and then will we let them have corn to eat, and will take care of them." The commons, when they heard this, were quite furious, and they would have set upon Caius as he came out of the senate-house and torn him to pieces, but the tribunes said, "Nay, ye shall judge him yourselves in your comitia, and we will be his accusers." So they accused Caius before the commons; and Caius knew that they would show him no mercy, therefore he stayed not for the day of his trial,[18] but fled from Rome, and took refuge among the Volscians. They and Attius Tullius, their chief, received him kindly, and he lived among them a banished man.

Caius offends the commons, and is banished.

He goes to the Volscians:

Attius said to himself, "Caius, who used to fight against us, is now on our side; we will make war again upon the Romans." But the Volscians were afraid; so that Attius was forced to practice craftily, to make them do what he wished, whether they would or no. Now the manner of his practice was as follows:[19] The great games at Rome were finished, but they were going to be celebrated over again with great pomp and cost, to appease the wrath of Jupiter. For Jupiter had spoken in a dream to Titus Latinius, a man of the commons, and said, "Go and bid the consuls to celebrate the games over again with great pomp, for one danced at the opening of the games[20] but now, whom I liked not; and vengeance is coming therefore upon this city." But Titus feared to go to the consuls, for he thought that every one would laugh at him, and so he did not obey the god. A few days after his son fell sick and died; and again the vision appeared to him in his sleep, and said, "Wilt thou still despise what I tell thee? Thy son is dead, but if thou go not quickly, and do my bidding, it shall be yet worse for thee." But Titus still lingered, so he was himself stricken with a palsy; and he could not walk, but they carried him in a litter. Then he delayed no longer, but said to his kinsmen, "Carry me into the forum, to the consuls." And they carried him in his litter, and he told the consuls the bidding of the god, and all that had befallen himself. When he had finished his story, the consuls remembered how that on the morning of the first day of the games, a burgher had taken his slave and scourged him in the midst of the circus where the games were to

Attius Tullius stirs up war between the Romans and Volscians. How he contrived to bring this about.

[16] The story of the taking of Corioli was an attempt to explain the name of Coriolanus, which in reality merely showed that Marcius had been settled at Corioli, and had become a citizen of that place after his banishment from Rome. The same explanation will serve, perhaps, for some other Latin surnames, such as Medullinus, Regillensis, Malventanus, and others, recording the connection of Roman families at some period or other with the towns from which they took their names. See note 11.

[17] Plutarch names Gelon, tyrant of Syracuse. Livy merely says that the corn came from Sicily; Dionysius calls Gelon "the most distinguished of the tyrants of Sicily at that time," without specifying whether, at the time of the famine at Rome, he was tyrant of Gela or of Syracuse. The old Roman annalists, Licinius Macer and Cn. Gellius, cared about Greek chronology as little as Shakspeare did about that of Rome; and as he makes Titus Lartius talk of Cato the censor, so they made Dionysius the tyrant contemporary with the battle of Marathon, and said that it was he who relieved the scarcity at Rome in the year 262.

[18] Livy, II. 35. Ipse quum die dictâ non adesset, perseveratum in irâ est. Dionysius, whom Plutarch follows, says that the tribunes fixed perpetual banishment as the penalty which the accused should suffer if found guilty; that he was found guilty by the votes of twelve tribes out of twenty-one, and banished accordingly. Dionysius and Plutarch seem to have forgotten that exile as a punishment was unknown to the Roman law till a much later period.

[19] Livy, II. 36.

[20] Visus Jupiter dicere, "Sibi ludis præsultatorem displicuisse." Livy, II. 36.

be held; and the burgher regarded it not, but Jupiter saw it and was wroth: for it was a holy day, and a day for mirth and gladness, and not for crying and for torment. So the consuls believed what Titus said, and brought him into the senate, and he told the story again to the senators. When lo! so soon as he had ended his story, the palsy left him, and his limbs became strong as before, and he needed no more to be carried in his litter, but walked home on his feet.

The Volscians are driven out of Rome at the celebration of the great games.

Thus the great games[21] were celebrated over again at Rome, and many of the Volscians went to Rome to see the sight. Then Attius went to the consuls privately, and said to them: "A great multitude of Volscians are now in Rome. I remember now on a like occasion, not many years since, the Sabines made a riot in this city, and great mischief was like to come of it; loth were I that my people should do aught of the same kind: but it becomes your wisdom rather to hinder evil than to mend it." When the consuls told this to the senate, the senate was afraid; and it was thought best to send the criers round the city, to give notice that every Volscian should be gone from Rome before the setting of the sun. The Volscians were very angry at this, for they said to one another, "Do these men then hold us to be so profane and unholy, that our presence is an offence to the blessed gods?" So they left Rome in haste, and went home towards their own country, full of indignation at the shame which was put upon them.

Attius meets them, and excites them to go to war with the Romans.

Their way home was over the hills of Alba,[22] by the well-head of the water of Ferentina, where the councils of the Latins had been used to meet of old. Attius knew that the Volscians would be driven from Rome, and would pass that way, so he waited there to meet them. At last they came up in a long train, each as he could go, and Attius spoke to them, and asked them what was the matter, that they had so suddenly left Rome. When they told him, he called them to follow him from the road, down to the grass which was by the side of the stream, and there they gathered round him, and he made a speech to them, and said, "What is it that these men have done to you? They have made a show of you at their games before all the neighboring nations. Ye, and your wives, and your children, were cast out at the voice of the crier, as though ye were profane and unholy, and as if your presence before the sight of the gods were a sacrilege. Do ye not count them for your enemies already, seeing if ye had not made such good haste in coming away ye would have been all dead men ere now? They have made war upon us: see to it, if ye be men, that ye make them rue their deed." So the Volscians eagerly listened to his words, and all their tribes made it a common quarrel, and they raised a great army, and chose Attius and Caius Marcius, the Roman, to command it.

How Caius and Attius marched against Rome.

When this great host took the field, the Romans feared to go out to battle against it. So Caius and Attius attacked the cities of the Latins, and they first took Circeii,[23] and afterwards Satricum, and Longula, and Polusca, and Corioli; and then they took Lavinium, which was to the Romans a sacred city, because Æneas was its founder, and because the holy things of the gods of their fathers were kept there. After this Caius and Attius took Corbio, and Vitellia, and Trebia, and Lavici, and Pedum; and from Pedum they went towards Rome, and they encamped by the Cluilian dyke, which was no more than five miles from the city; and they laid waste the lands of the commons of Rome, but they spared those of the burghers; Caius, for his part, thinking that his quarrel was with the commons only, and that the burghers were his friends; and Attius, thinking that it would cause the Romans to be jealous of each other, and so make Rome the easier to be conquered. So the host of the Volscians lay encamped near Rome.

[21] Livy, II. 37. [22] Livy, II. 38. [23] Livy, II. 39.

Within the city, meanwhile, there was a great tumult; the women ran to the temples of the gods to pray for mercy, the poorer peop.e cried out in the streets that they would have peace, and that the senate should send deputies to Caius and to Attius. So deputies were sent,[24] five men of the chief of the burghers; but Caius answered them, "We will give you no peace, till ye restore to the Volscians all the land and all the cities which ye or your fathers have ever taken from them; and till[25] ye make them your citizens, and give them all the rights which ye have yourselves, as ye have done to the Latins." The deputies could not accept such hard conditions, so they went back to Rome. And when the senate sent them again to ask for gentler terms, Caius would not suffer them to enter the camp.

The Romans sue for peace, but it is not granted.

After this[26] the senate sent all the priests of the gods, and the augurs, all clothed in their sacred garments, and bearing in their hands the tokens of the gods whom they served. But neither would Caius listen to these; so they too went back again to Rome.

The priests of the gods go to sue for mercy to Caius, but he will not hear them.

Yet, when the help of man had failed the Romans, the help of the gods delivered them; for among the women who were sitting as suppliants in the temple of Jupiter in the Capitol, was Valeria,[27] the sister of that Publius Valerius who had been called Poplicola, a virtuous and noble lady, whom all held in honor. As she was sitting in the temple as a suppliant before the image of Jupiter, Jupiter seemed to inspire her with a sudden thought, and she immediately rose, and called upon all the other noble ladies who were with her to arise also, and she led them to the house of Volumnia, the mother of Caius. There she found Virgilia, the wife of Caius, with his mother, and also his little children. Valeria then addressed Volumnia and Virgilia, and said, "Our coming here to you is our own doing; neither the senate nor any other mortal man have sent us; but the god in whose temple we were sitting as suppliants put it into our hearts, that we should come and ask you to join with us, women with women, without any aid of men, to win for our country a great deliverance, and for ourselves a name glorious above all women, even above those Sabine wives in the old time, who stopped the battle between their husbands and their fathers. Come then with us to the camp of Caius, and let us pray to him to show us mercy." Volumnia said, "We will go with you:" and Virgilia took her young children with her, and they all went to the camp of the enemy.

A noble lady, called Valeria, persuades the mother and wife of Caius to go and sue to him for mercy.

It was a sad and solemn sight[28] to see this train of noble ladies, and the very Volscian soldiers stood in silence as they passed by, and pitied them and honored them. They found Caius sitting on the general's seat in the midst of the camp, and the Volscian chiefs were standing round him. When he first saw them he wondered what it could be; but presently he knew his mother, who was walking at the head of the train; and then he could not contain himself, but leaped down from his seat, and ran to meet her, and was going to kiss her. But she stopped him and said,[29] "Ere thou kiss me, let me know whether I am speaking to an enemy or to my son; whether I stand in thy camp as thy prisoner or as thy mother." Caius could not answer her, and then she went on and said, "Must it be, then, that had I never borne a son, Rome never should have seen the camp of an enemy; that had I remained childless, I should have died a free woman in a free city? But I am too old to bear much longer either thy shame or my misery. Rather look to thy wife and children, whom if thou persistest thou art dooming to an untimely death, or a long life of bondage." Then Virgilia and his children came up to him and kissed him, and all the noble ladies wept, and bemoaned their own fate and the fate of their country. At last Caius cried out, "O mother, what hast

How his wife and mother prevailed with him, and how he led away his army.

24 Dionysius, VIII. 22.
25 Dionysius, VIII. 35. Plutarch, Coriolan. 30.
26 Livy, II. 39. Plutarch, Coriolan. 32.
27 Plutarch, Coriolan. 32, 33.
28 Plutarch, Coriolan. 34.
29 Livy, II. 40.

thou done to me?" and he wrung her hand vehemently, and said, "Mother, thine is the victory; a happy victory for thee and for Rome, but shame and ruin to thy son." Then he fell on her neck and embraced her, and he embraced his wife and his children, and sent them back to Rome; and led away the army of the Volscians, and never afterwards attacked Rome any more; and he lived on a banished man amongst the Volscians, and when he was very old, and had neither wife nor children around him, he was wont to say, "That now in old age[30] he knew the full bitterness of banishment." So Caius lived and died amongst the Volscians.

How the Romans honored the noble ladies for their deed.

The Romans, as was right, honored Volumnia and Valeria for their deed, and a temple was built and dedicated to "Woman's Fortune,"[31] just on the spot where Caius had yielded to his mother's words; and the first priestess of the temple was Valeria, into whose heart Jupiter had first put the thought to go to Volumnia, and to call upon her to go out to the enemy's camp and entreat her son.

Such is the famous story which has rendered the Volscian wars with Rome so memorable; the wars with the Æquians are marked by a name and a story not less celebrated, those of L. Quinctius Cincinnatus.

Story of Cincinnatus. The Æquians break the peace with Rome, and scorn the complaints of the Romans.

There had been peace between the Romans and the Æquians: but the Æquians and Gracchus Clœlius,[32] their chief, broke the peace, and plundered the lands of the people of Lavici and of the people of Tusculum. They then pitched their camp on the top of Algidus; and the Romans sent deputies to them to complain of the wrong which they had done. It happened that the tent of Gracchus was pitched under the shade of a great evergreen oak, and he was sitting in his tent when the deputies came to him. His answer was full of mockery: "I, for my part," said he, "am busy with other matters; I cannot hear you; you had better tell your message to the oak yonder." Immediately one of the deputies answered, "Yea, let this sacred oak hear, and let all the gods hear likewise, how treacherously you have broken the peace! They shall hear it now, and shall soon avenge it; for you have scorned alike the laws of the gods and of men." Then they went back to Rome, and the senate resolved upon war: and Lucius Minucius, the consul, led his legions towards Algidus, to fight with the proud enemy.

How the army of the consul Minucius fell into an ambush.

But Gracchus was a skilful soldier,[33] and he pretended to be afraid of the Romans, and retreated before them, and they followed him, without heeding where they were going. So they came into a narrow valley, with hills on either side, high, and steep, and bare; and then Gracchus sent men secretly, who closed up the way by which they had entered into the valley, so that they could not get back; and the hills[34] closed round the valley in front of them, and on the right and left, and on the top of these hills Gracchus lay with his army, while the Romans were shut up in the valley below. In this valley there was neither grass for the horses, nor food for the men; but

[30] "Multo miserius seni exilium esse." Fabius, quoted by Livy, II. 40.

[31] Livy, II. 40. Dionysius, VIII. 55. It is one of Niebuhr's most ingenious conjectures that the foundation of this temple, and the fact that Valeria was the first priestess of it, gave occasion to the date assigned to the story of Coriolanus, and to the introduction of Valeria into it, as the first suggester of the step which saved Rome. Niebuhr observes that Fortuna Muliebris had nothing to do with the successful embassy of Volumnia and Valeria, but corresponded to Fortuna Virilis; and that both were anciently worshipped; the one as influencing the fortunes of men, the other those of women. Vol. II. p. 115. 2d edit.

[32] Livy, III. 25.

[33] Dionysius, X. 23.

[34] This is just the description of the famous Furcæ Caudinæ, in which the Romans were blockaded by C. Pontius. It suits the character of the Apennine valleys, but I never saw any such spots on the Alban hills, where the scene of Cincinnatus' victory is laid. It is likely enough, however, that Dionysius, or the annalist whom he followed, did actually take their description from that of the Caudine Forks, and that it made no part of the old legend. Livy's account says nothing of any natural disadvantages of position: he merely says that the Romans kept within their camp through fear, and that this encouraged the Æquians to blockade them.

five horsemen had broken out, before the road in the rear of the Romans was quite closed up, and these rode to Rome, and told the senate of the great danger of the consul and of the army.

Upon this Quintus Fabius,[35] the warden of the city, sent in haste for Caius Nautius, the other consul, who was with his army in the country of the Sabines. When he came, they consulted together, and the senate said, "There is only one man who can deliver us; we must make Lucius Quinctius Master of the people." So Caius, as the manner was, named Lucius to be Master of the people; and then he hastened back to his army before the sun was risen.

The Romans at Rome were in great alarm.

This Lucius Quinctius let his hair grow,[36] and tended it carefully: and was so famous for his curled and crisped locks that men called him Cincinnatus, or the "crisp-haired." He was a frugal man,[37] and did not care to be rich; and his land was on the other side of the Tiber, a plot of four jugera, where he dwelt with his wife Racilia, and busied himself in the tilling of his ground. So in the morning early the senate sent deputies to Lucius to tell him that he was chosen to be Master of the people. The deputies went over the river, and came to his house, and found him in his field at work without his toga or cloak, and digging with his spade in his ground. They saluted him and said, "We bring thee a message from the senate, so thou must put on thy cloak that thou mayest receive it as is fitting." Then he said, "Hath aught of evil befallen the state?" and he bade his wife to bring his cloak, and when he had put it on he went out to meet the deputies. Then they said, "Hail to thee, Lucius Quinctius, the senate declares thee Master of the people, and calls thee to the city; for the consul and the army in the country of the Æquians are in great danger." There was then a boat made ready to carry him over the Tiber, and when he stepped out of the boat his three sons came to meet him, and his kinsmen and his friends, and the greater part of the senators. He was thus led home in great state to his house, and the four-and-twenty lictors, with their rods and axes, walked before him. As for the multitude, they crowded round to see him, but they feared his four-and-twenty lictors; for they were a sign that the power of the Master of the people was as sovereign as that of the kings of old.

They appoint Lucius Quinctius to be Master of the people.

Lucius chose Lucius Tarquitius[38] to be Master of the horse, a brave man, and of a burgher's house; but so poor withal that he had been used to serve among the foot soldiers instead of among the horse. Then the Master of the people and the Master of the horse went together into the Forum, and bade every man to shut up his booth, and stopped all causes at law, and gave an order that none should look to his own affairs till the consul and his army were delivered from the enemy. They ordered also that every man, who was of an age to go out to battle, should be ready in the Field of Mars before sunset, and should have with him victuals for five days, and twelve stakes; and the older men dressed the victuals for the soldiers, whilst the soldiers went about everywhere to get their stakes; and they cut them where they would, without any hinderance. So the army was ready in the Field of Mars at the time appointed, and they set forth from the city, and made such haste, that ere the night was half spent they came to Algidus; and when they perceived that they were near the enemy, they made a halt.

Lucius marches out to deliver the consul's army.

Then Lucius rode on, and saw[39] how the camp of the enemy lay; and he or-

[35] Dionysius, X. 23.

[36] Zonaras, VII. p. 346. Ed. Paris. p. 260. Ed. Venet.

[37] Livy, III. 26.

[38] Livy, III. 27.

[39] "Quantum nocte prospici poterat" is Livy's qualification of the story; but the original legend, in all probability, regarded darkness no more than distance; and as it had brought the Roman army from Rome to Algidus between sunset and midnight, though each soldier had to carry his baggage and twelve stakes besides, so it made Cincinnatus reconnoitre the enemy as soon as he arrived in their neighborhood, without considering that on its own showing his arrival took place at midnight.

He conquers the Æquians.

dered his soldiers to throw down all their baggage into one place, but to keep each man his arms and his twelve stakes. Then they set out again in their order of march as they had come from Rome, and they spread themselves round the camp of the enemy on every side. When this was done, upon a signal given they raised a great shout, and directly every man began to dig a ditch just where he stood, and to set in his stakes. The shout rang through the camp of the enemy, and filled them with fear; and it sounded even to the camp of the Romans who were shut up in the valley, and the consul's men said one to another, "Rescue is surely at hand, for that is the shout of Romans." They themselves shouted in answer, and sallied to attack the camp of the enemy; and they fought so fiercely, that they hindered the enemy from interrupting the work of the Romans without their camp; and this went on all the night, till when it was morning, the Romans who were without had drawn a ditch all round the enemy, and had fenced it with their stakes; and now they left their work, and began to take part in the battle. Then the Æquians saw that there was no hope, and they began to ask for mercy. Lucius answered, "Give me Gracchus and your other chiefs bound, and then I will set two spears upright in the ground, and I will put a third spear across, and you shall give up your arms, and your cloaks, and shall pass, every man of you, under the spear bound across as under a yoke, and then you may go away free." This was done accordingly; Gracchus and the other chiefs were bound, and the Æquians left their camp to the Romans, with all its spoil, and put off their cloaks, and passed each man under the yoke, and then went home full of shame.

But Lucius would not suffer[40] the consul's army to have any share of the spoil, nor did he let the consul keep his power, but made him his own under-officer, and then marched back to Rome. Nor did the consul's soldiers complain; but they were rather full of thankfulness to Lucius for having rescued them from the enemy, and they agreed to give him a golden crown; as he returned to Rome, they shouted after him, and called him their protector and their father.

Lucius marches back to Rome in triumph.

Great was now the joy in Rome, and the senate decreed that Lucius should enter the city in triumph, in the order in which the army was returning from Algidus, and he rode in his chariot, while Gracchus and the chiefs of the Æquians were led bound before him; and the standards were borne before him, and all the soldiers, laden with their spoil, followed behind. And tables were set out at the door of every house, with meat and drink for the soldiers, and they and the people feasted together, and followed the chariot of Lucius, with singing and great rejoicings. Thus the gods took vengeance upon Gracchus and the Æquians; and thus Lucius delivered the consul and his army; and all was done so quickly, that he went out on one evening, and came home the next day at evening victorious and triumphant.

General state of the wars between the Romans and the Opican nations at the end of the third century of Rome.

This famous story is placed by the annalists in the year of Rome 296, thirteen years after the passing of the Publilian law. In such a warfare as that of the Romans with the Æquians and Volscians, there are always sufficient alternations of success to furnish the annalists on either side with matter of triumph; and by exaggerating every victory, and omitting or slightly noticing every defeat, they form a picture such as national vanity most delights in. But we neither can, nor need we desire to correct and supply the omissions of the details of the Roman historians: it is enough to say, that at the close of the third century of Rome, the warfare which the Romans had to maintain against the Opican nations was generally defensive; that the Æquians and Volscians had advanced from the line of the Apennines and established themselves on the Alban hills, in the heart of Latium; that of the thirty Latin states which had formed the league with Rome in the year 261, thirteen[41] were now either destroyed, or were in the possession of the Opicans;

[40] Livy, III. 29.

[41] Carventum, Circeii, Corioli, Corbio, Cora, Fortona (if it be the same with Ortona), Lavici, Norba, Pedum, Satricum, Setia, Tolina, and

that on the Alban hills themselves, Tusculum alone remained independent; and that there was no other friendly city to obstruct the irruptions of the enemy into the territory of Rome. Accordingly, that territory was plundered year after year, and whatever defeats the plunderers may at times have sustained, yet they were never deterred from renewing a contest which they found in the main profitable and glorious. So greatly had the power and dominion of Rome fallen since the overthrow of the monarchy. We have now to notice her wars with another enemy, the Etruscans; and to trace on this side also an equal decline in glory and greatness since the reigns of the later kings.

CHAPTER XII.

WARS WITH THE ETRUSCANS—VEII—LEGEND OF THE SLAUGHTER OF THE FABII AT THE RIVER CREMERA.

"Our hands alone
Suffice for this;—take ye no thought for it.
While the mole breaks the waves, and bides the tempest,
The ship within rides safe: while on the mountain
The wind is battling with the adventurous pines,
He stirs no leaf in the valley. So your state,
We standing thus in guard upon the border,
Shall feel no ruffling of the rudest blast
That sweeps from Veii."

AFTER the great war of king Porsenna, the Etruscans, for several years, appear to have lived in peace with the Romans; and in the famine of the year 262, when the enmity of the Volscians would allow no supplies of corn to be sent to Rome from the country on the left bank of the Tiber, the Etruscan cities, we are told,[1] allowed the Romans to purchase what they wanted, and the corn thus obtained was the principal support of the people. But nine years afterwards, in 271, a war broke out, not with the Etruscans generally, but with the people of the neighboring city of Veii. The quarrel is said[2] to have arisen out of some plundering inroads made by the Veientian borderers upon the Roman territory; but it suited the Roman aristocracy at this period to involve the nation in foreign contests,[3] in order to prevent the commons from insisting on the due execution of Cassius' agrarian law; and quarrels, which at another time might easily have been settled, were now gladly allowed to end in open war.

Beginning of hostilities with Veii.

Veii[4] lay about ten miles from Rome, between two small streams which meet a little below the city, and run down into the Tiber, falling into it nearly opposite to Castel Giubileo, the ancient Fidenæ. Insig-

Situation and size of Veii.

Velitræ. Carventum seems to have been one of the towns of the Alban hills, and Niebuhr suggests that we should read Κορυεντανοὶ instead of Κοριολανοὶ in Dionysius, VIII. 19, as the people conquered by Coriolanus, for they are placed in the neighborhood of Corbia and Pedum; whereas the conquest of the real Coriolani is mentioned in another place (VIII. 36), and in their proper neighborhood. Sir W. Gell supposes Carventum to have been at Roca Massimi, a high point on the Volscian highlands near Cora. Another supposition, as Mr. Bunsen informs me, places it on Monte Ariano, the highest eastern point of that volcanic range of mountains of which Monte Cavo is the most western point. But nothing is really known on the question.

[1] Livy, II. 34.

[2] Dionysius, VIII. 81, 91.

[3] Dionysius, VIII. 81. Dion Cassius, Fragm. Vatican, XX.

[4] See Sir W. Gell's Map of the Campagna.

nificant in point of size, these little streams, however, like those of the Campagna generally, are edged by precipitous rocky cliffs, and thus are capable of affording a natural defence to a town built on the table-land above and between them. The space inclosed by the walls of Veii was equal to the extent[5] of Rome itself, so long as the walls of Servius Tullius were the boundary of the city: the citadel stood on a distinct eminence, divided by one of the little streams from the rest of the town, and defended by another similar valley on the other side. In the magnificence of its public and private buildings, Veii is said to have been preferred by the Roman commons to Rome;[6] and we know enough of the great works of the Etruscans to render this not impossible; but the language is too vague to be insisted on; and the Etruscan Veii was as unknown to the Roman annalists as to us. On the other hand, Rome had itself been embellished by Etruscan art, and had been under its kings the seat of a far mightier power than Veii.

Its government.

The government of Veii, like that of the other Etruscan cities, was in the hands of an aristocracy of birth, one or more of whom were elected annually by the whole body to command in war and administer justice. There were no free commons; but a large population of serfs or vassals, who cultivated the lands of the ruling class. In wars of peculiar importance,[7] we read from time to time of the appointment of a king, but his office was for life only, and was not perpetuated in his family. The hereditary principle prevailed, however, in the priesthoods; none but members of one particular family could be priests of Juno,[8] the goddess especially honored at Veii.

Character of its military force.

The Veientians, like the other Etruscans, fought in the close order[9] of the phalanx; their arms being the small round shield, and the long pike. We know not whether they ventured, like the Parthians, to trust their serfs with arms equal to their own, and to enrol them in the phalanx; but we may more probably suppose that they employed them only as light-armed troops; and if this were so, their armies must have encountered the Romans at a disadvantage, their regular infantry being probably inferior in numbers to the legions, and their light troops, except for desultory warfare, still more inferior in quality. To make up for this, they employed the services of mercenaries, who were generally to be hired from one or other of the states of Etruria, even when their respective countries refused to take part publicly in the quarrel.

The war between the Romans and Veientians, which began in the year 271,

[5] Dionysius compares the size both of Rome and Veii with that of Athens, II. 54. IV. 13. Sir W. Gell told me that the traces of the walls of Veii, which he had clearly made out, quite justified the comparison of Veii in point of extent with Rome. And his map shows the same thing.

[6] Livy, V. 24. Urbem quoque urbi Romæ vel situ vel magnificentiâ publicorum privatorumque tectorum ac locorum præponebant. This being no more than an expression of opinion ascribed to the commons, we cannot be sure that Livy had any authority for it at all, any more than for the language of his speeches. But suppose that he found it in some one of the older annalists, still it can hardly be more than the expression of that annalist's opinion, grounded possibly upon some tradition of the splendor of Veii, but possibly also upon nothing more than the fact that the Roman commons were at one time anxious to remove to Veii. And if the Roman commons had actually said that Veii was a finer city than Rome, when they were extolling its advantages, is such an assertion to be taken as an historical fact, to justify us in passing a judgment as to the comparative magnificence of the two cities?

[7] Livy, V. 1. His words, "Tædio annuæ ambitionis regem creavêre," imply that the government was commonly exercised by one or more magistrates annually chosen, like the consuls at Rome. Niebuhr refers to the case of Lars Tolumnius, who had been king of Veii thirty-four years before the time of which Livy is speaking; and he thinks that Livy is mistaken, in supposing the appointment of a king in the last war with Rome to have been any thing unusual. (Vol. I. p. 128. 2d ed. note 344.) But we read of no king after Lars Tolumnius till the period of the last war, nor of any before him in the earlier wars with Rome. And as the lucumo, or chief magistrate of a single Etruscan city, was appointed sometimes chief over the whole confederacy, when any general war broke out; so the annual lucumo may have been made lucumo for life in times of danger, if he were a man of commanding character and ability.

[8] Livy, V. 22.

[9] Diodorus. Fragm. Vatican. Lib. XXIII. Τυῤῥηνοὶ χαλκαῖς ἀσπίσι φαλαγγομαχοῦντες, for so we must correct the reading φάλαγγα μαχοῦντες, just as a little below in the same passage we read σπειραῖς, i. e. cohortibus, or manipulis, instead of πειραῖς, which Mai absurdly renders "cuspidibus."

lasted nine years. It is difficult to say what portion of the events recorded of it is deserving of credit; nor would the details,[10] at any rate, be worth repeating now. But it seems to have been carried on with equal fortune on both sides, and to have been ended by a perfectly equal treaty. The Romans established themselves on the Cremera, within the Veientian territory, built a sort of town there, and, after having maintained their post for some time, to the great annoyance of the enemy, they were at last surprised, and their whole force slaughtered, and the post abandoned. Then the Veientians, in their turn, established themselves on the hill Janiculum, within the Roman territory; retaliated, by their plundering excursions across the Tiber, the damage which their own lands had sustained from the post on the Cremera; held their ground for more than a year, and then were, in their turn, defeated and obliged to evacuate their conquest. Two years afterwards, in 280, a peace was concluded between the two nations, to last for forty years; and, as the Roman historians name no other stipulations, we may safely believe that the treaty[11] merely placed matters on the footing on which they had been before the war; the Romans gave up all pretensions to the town which they had founded on the Cremera; the Veientians equally resigned their claim to the settlement which they had made on the hill Janiculum.

Outline of the war from 271 to 280.

But whatever may be thought of the history of this war, it has been the subject of one memorable legend, the story of the self-devotion of the Fabii, and of their slaughter by the river Cremera. The truth of domestic events, no less than of foreign, has been, probably, disregarded by this legend; and what seems a more real account of the origin of the settlement on the Cremera, has been given in a former chapter. The story itself, however, I shall now, according to my usual plan, proceed to offer in its own form.

Story of the Fabii.

The Veientians dared not meet the Romans[12] in the open field, but they troubled them exceedingly with their incursions to plunder the country. And on the other side, the Æquians and the Volscians were making war upon the Romans year after year; and while one consul went to fight with the Æquians and the other with the Volscians, there was no one to stop the plunderings of the Veientians. So the men of the Fabian house consulted together, and when they were resolved what to do, they all went to the senate-house. And Kæso Fabius, who was consul for that year, went into the senate and said, "We of the house of the Fabii take upon us to fight with the Veientians. We ask neither men nor money from the commonwealth, but we will wage the war with our own bodies, at our own cost." The senate heard him joyfully; and then he went home, and the other men of his house followed him; and he told them to come to him the next day, each man in his full arms; and so they departed.

The Fabian house offers to take the war with the Veientians wholly upon itself.

The house of Kæso was on the Quirinal Hill; and thither all the Fabii came to him the next day, as he had desired them; and there they stood in array in the outer court of his house. Kæso then put on his vest, such as the Roman generals were used to wear in battle, and came out to the men of his house, and led them forth on their way. As they went, a

The Fabii establish themselves on the river Cremera

[10] The Roman accounts of the war may be found in Livy, II. 42–54, and in Dionysius, VIII. 81. 91. IX. 1–36. I imagine both the post on the Cremera and that on the Janiculum to have been designed for permanent cities; the one, probably, being as near to Veii as the other was to Rome. These were exactly the ἐπιτείχισματα of the Greeks, when executed on a larger scale as rival cities, and not mere forts. I may, perhaps, be allowed to refer to my note on Thucydides, I. 142, where the two kinds of ἐπιτείχισμα are distinguished.

[11] Niebuhr supposes that the septem pagi, which the Romans had lost in the war with Porsenna, were at this time recovered. But if so, the annalist would surely have boasted of the cessions of territory made by the Veientians, even if they had been consistent enough not to describe the country recovered as the very same which they had made Porsenna restore out of generosity more than thirty years before. Is there any reason to believe that the Romans advanced their frontier on the right bank of the Tiber opposite Rome, beyond the hills which bound the valley of the river, previously to their conquest of Veii?

[12] Livy, II. 48. et seqq.

great crowd followed after them and blessed them, and prayed the gods for their prosperity. They were, in all, three hundred and six men, and they went down from the Quirinal Hill and passed along by the Capitol, and went out of the city by the gate Carmentalis, by the right-hand passage of the gate. Then they came to the Tiber, and went over the bridge, and entered into the country of the Veientians, and pitched their camp by the river Cremera; for there it was their purpose to dwell, and to make it a stronghold, from which they might lay waste the lands of the Veientians, and carry off their cattle. So they built their fortress by the river Cremera, and held it for more than a year; and the Veientians were greatly distressed, for their cattle and all their goods became the spoil of the Fabians.

The Veientians lay an ambush for them, and kill them all.

But there was a certain day[13] on which the men of the house of the Fabians were accustomed to offer sacrifice and to keep festival together to the gods of their race, in the seat of their fathers, on the hill Quirinal. So when the day drew near, the Fabians set out from the river Cremera, three hundred and six men in all, and went towards Rome; for they thought that as they were going to sacrifice to their gods, and as it was a holy time, and a time of peace, no enemy would set upon them. But the Veientians knew of their going, and laid an ambush for them on their way, and followed them with a great army. So when the Fabians came to the place where the ambush was, behold the enemy attacked them on the right and on the left, and the army of the Veientians that followed them fell upon them from behind; and they threw their darts and shot their arrows against the Fabians, without daring to come within reach of spear or sword, till they slew them every man. Three hundred and six men of the house of the Fabians were there killed, and there was not a grown man of the house left alive: one boy only, on account of his youth, had been left behind in Rome, and he lived and became a man, and preserved the race of the Fabians; for it was the pleasure of the gods that great deeds should be done for the Romans by the house of the Fabians in after-times.

[13] This latter part of the story is one of the versions of it given by Dionysius, which he rejects as improbable. Of course I am not maintaining its probability, but I agree with Niebuhr in thinking it a far more striking story than that which Dionysius prefers to it, and which has been adopted by Livy and by Ovid. The devotion of the Fabians to the sacrifices of their house on the Quirinal was a part of their traditional character; a similar story was told of C. Fabius Dorso, who broke out from the Capitol while the Gauls were besieging it, and made his way to the Quirinal Hill to perform the appointed sacrifice of his house.

CHAPTER XIII.

INTERNAL HISTORY—THE TERENTILIAN LAW—APPOINTMENT OF THE TEN HIGH COMMISSIONERS TO FRAME A CODE OF WRITTEN LAWS.

A. U. C. 284–303.

'Ολιλαρχία δὲ τῶν μὲν κινδύνων τοῖς πολλοῖς μεταδίδωσι, τῶν δ' ὠφελίμων οὐ πλεονεκτεῖ μόνον, ἀλλὰ καὶ ξύμπαν ἀφελομένη ἔχει· ἃ ὑμῶν οἵ τε δυνάμενοι καὶ οἱ νέοι προθυμοῦνται, ἀδύνατα ἐν μεγάλῃ πόλει κατασχεῖν.—Thucydides, VI. 39.

Τέταρτον εἶδος ὀλιγαρχίας, ὅταν παῖς ἀντὶ πατρὸς εἰσίῃ, καὶ ἄρχῃ μὴ ὁ νόμος ἀλλ' οἱ ἄρχοντες. Καὶ ἔστιν ἀντίστροφος αὕτη ἐν ταῖς ὀλιγαρχίαις, ὥσπερ ἡ τυραννὶς ἐν ταῖς μοναρχίας, καὶ περὶ ἧς τελευταίας εἴπομεν δημοκρατίας ἐν ταῖς δημοκρατίαις.—Aristotle, Politic. IV. 5.

Nothing is more unjust than the vague charge sometimes brought against Niebuhr, that he has denied the reality of all the early history of Rome. On the contrary, he has rescued from the dominion of skepticism much which less profound inquirers had before too hastily given up to it; he has restored and established far more than he has overthrown. Ferguson finds no sure ground to rest on till he comes to the second Punic war. In his view, not only the period of the kings and the first years of the commonwealth, but the whole of two additional centuries,—not only the wars with the Æquians and Volscians, but those with the Gauls, the Samnites, and even with Pyrrhus,—are involved in considerable uncertainty. The progress of the constitution he is content to trace in the merest outline: particular events, and still more particular characters, appear to him to belong to poetry or romance, rather than to history. Whereas Niebuhr maintains that a true history of Rome, with many details of dates, places, events, and characters, may be recovered from the beginning of the commonwealth. It has been greatly corrupted and disguised by ignorant and uncritical writers, but there exist, he thinks, sufficient materials to enable us, not only to get rid of these corruptions, but to restore that genuine and original edifice, which they have so long overgrown and hidden from our view. And accordingly, far from passing over hastily, like Ferguson, the period from the expulsion of Tarquinius to the first Punic war, he has devoted to it somewhat more than two large volumes; and from much, that to former writers seemed a hopeless chaos, he has drawn a living picture of events and institutions, as rich in its coloring, as perfect in its composition, as it is faithful to the truth of nature.

Were I, indeed, to venture to criticise the work of this great man, I should be inclined to charge him with having overvalued, rather than undervalued, the possible certainty of the early history of the Roman commonwealth. He may seem, in some instances, rather to lean too confidently on the authority of the ancient writers, than to reject it too indiscriminately. But let no man judge him hastily, till, by long experience in similar researches, he has learnt to estimate sufficiently the instinctive power of discerning truth, which even ordinary minds acquire by constant practice. In Niebuhr, practice, combined with the natural acuteness of his mind, brought this power to a perfection which has never been surpassed. It is not caprice, but a most sure instinct, which has led him to seize on some particular passage of a careless and ill-informed writer, and to perceive in it the marks of most important truth; while, on other occasions, he has set aside the statements of this same writer, with no deference to his authority whatever. To say that his instinct is not absolutely infallible, is only to say that he was a man; but he who follows him most carefully, and thinks over the subject of his researches most deeply, will find the feeling of respect for his judgment continually increasing, and will be more unwilling to believe what Niebuhr doubted, or to doubt what he believed.

I have said thus much as a preface to the ensuing chapter, in which I am to trace the internal history of Rome, from the passing of the Publilian law to the appointment of the decemvirs. The detail itself will show how little Niebuhr has deserved to be charged with overthrowing the Roman history; while, on the other hand, if I have followed him even on ground on which, had he not pronounced it to be firm, I might myself have feared to venture, I have done it, not in blind or servile imitation, but in the reasonable confidence inspired by experience. For many years I had doubted and disputed Niebuhr's views on several points of importance, but having had reason at last to be convinced that they were right, I feel for him now a deference the more unhesitating, as it was not hastily given, nor without inquiry.

A. U. C. 288. A. C. 469. Campaign of Appius Claudius against the Æquians and Volscians.

Immediately after the passing of the Publilian law,[1] the consuls took the field against the Æquians and Volscians. It was now the period when those two nations were pressing most dangerously upon Latium, not only overrunning the territory both of the Latins and Romans with their plundering incursions, but taking or destroying the cities of the Latin confederacy. There was no choice, therefore, but to oppose them; and thus the hated Appius Claudius, as well as his colleague, T. Quinctius, led out an army from the city. But the mutual suspicion and hatred between him and the commons was so great that they could not act together. He was tyrannical, and his soldiers became discontented and disobedient. In this temper they met the Volscians and were beaten; and Appius, finding it hopeless to continue the campaign, began to retreat towards Rome. On his retreat he was again attacked and again beaten; the soldiers, it is said, throwing away their arms and flying at the first onset. Thus doubly embittered by the shame of his defeats, and having obtained some color for his vengeance, Appius, as soon as he had rallied his army on ground out of the reach of the enemy, proceeded to indulge his old feelings of hatred to the commons. By the aid of the Latin and Hernican troops who were present in the army, and, above all, of the Roman burghers, who formed the best armed and best trained part of his own forces, he was enabled to seize and execute every centurion whose century had fled, and every standard-bearer who had lost his standard, and then to put to death one out of every ten men of the whole multitude of legionary soldiers.

Appius is brought to trial. Different accounts of his subsequent fate.

A. U. C. 243. A. C. 468.

The maintenance of military discipline, by whatever degree of severity it was effected, was regarded by the Romans, not as a crime, but as a sacred duty; nor would even the commons have complained of Appius for simply punishing with rigor his cowardly or mutinous soldiers. But when new consuls were come into office, L. Valerius and T. Æmilius,[2] and both showed themselves inclined to carry into effect the agrarian law of Sp. Cassius, while Appius still opposed it, and was most forward in defeating the measure, then two of the tribunes, M. Duilius and C. Sicinius,[3] brought him to trial before the commons as the perpetual enemy of their order; accusing him of giving evil counsels to the senate, of having laid violent hands on the sacred person of a tribune in the disputes about the Publilian law, and lastly, of having brought loss and shame on the commonwealth, by his ill conduct in his late expedition against the Volscians. His bloody executions were not charged as a crime against him; but every friend or relation of his victims would feel, that he who had dealt such severe justice to

[1] Livy, II. 58, 59. Dionysius, IX. 50.

[2] Livy, II. 61. Dionysius, IX. 51–54.

[3] These were two of the tribunes elected when the Publilian law was passed. The tribunes and consuls came into office, it should be remembered, at different times of the year; the consuls at this period began their year on the first of August (Livy, III. 6); when the tribunes began theirs, before the decemvirate, is uncertain. See Niebuhr, Vol. II. p. 227, and note 492, 2d edit.

others, could claim no mitigation of justice towards himself; and Appius felt this also, and neither expected mercy from the commons, nor would yield to ask it. A most extraordinary difference prevails, however, in the accounts of his subsequent fate. The common story says that he died in prison before his trial, implying that he killed himself to escape his sentence; but, according to the Fasti Capitolini,[4] it was this same Appius who, twenty years afterwards, became decemvir; and we must suppose, therefore, that he now fled from Rome, and lived for some years in exile at Regillus, till circumstances enabled him to return, and to take part in public affairs once more.

A. U. C. 285. A. C. 467. Antium and its port taken by the Romans.

The two following years were marked[5] by continued contests about the agrarian law of Cassius, which still led to no result. The fortune of war, however, gave some relief to the necessities of the poorer commons: for, in the year 285, the port[6] of Antium was taken, and a quantity of merchandise was found there, which was all given up to the soldiers; and the year following Antium itself fell into the hands of the Romans; and on this occasion, also, the soldiers derived some profit from their conquest.

A. U. C. 286. A. C. 466.

In the year 287, Ti. Æmilius, one of the consuls, supported the demand of the tribunes for the execution of the agrarian law; and we are told that the senate,[7] in order to pacify the commons by a partial compliance, proposed to send a colony to Antium, and to allow the commons, as well as the burghers, to enrol themselves amongst the colonists. But as the colony was to consist equally of Romans,[8] Latins, and Hernicans, and would be placed in a position of great insecurity, being, in fact, no other than a garrison, which would have at once to keep down the old population of the city within, and to defend itself against enemies without, the relief thus offered to the commons was neither very considerable in its amount, nor in its nature very desirable.

Severe visitations of pestilence.

The next year began a period of distress and suffering so severe, and arising from such various causes, that political disputes were of necessity suspended, and for four years no mention is made of any demands for the agrarian law, or of any other proceeding of the tribunes. The middle of the fifth century before the Christian era was one of those periods in the history of mankind which, from causes to us unknown, have been marked by the ravages of pestilence; when a disease of unusual virulence has, in a manner, travelled up and down over the habitable world during the space of twenty, thirty, or even fifty years; returning often to the same place after a certain interval; pausing sometimes in its fury, and appearing to sleep, but again breaking out on some point or other within its range, till, at the end of its appointed period, it disappears altogether. Rome was first visited by one of these pestilences, as has been already mentioned, in the year 282, when it caused a very great mortality; it now returned again in 288,[9] and crippled the operations of the Roman army against the Æquians. Whether it continued in the following year is uncertain, but the Æquians plundered the Roman territory with great success; and although the Roman annalists pretend that, towards the end of the year, the consul, Q. Fabius, cut off the main body of the plunderers, and then in turn ravaged the lands of the enemy, yet it is manifest that the campaign was on the whole unfavorable to the Romans. So it was the next year

A. U. C. 289. A. C. 466.

[4] It had been long known that the Fasti called Appius the decemvir, "Ap. F. M. N." "Appii Filius, Marci Nepos;" whereas the common story makes him the grandson, as well as the son of an Appius. But one of the recently discovered fragments of the Fasti calls the decemvir, under the year 302, "Appius Claudius, Ap. F. M. N. Crassin. Regill. Sabinus, II.," clearly showing that by calling the consulship of 302 his second consulship, the author of the Fasti considered him to be the same man who had been consul in 283.

[5] Livy, II. 63–65. Dionysius, IX. 56–58.

[6] Livy calls this place Ceno; the Antiates, it seems, already had begun the piracies, of which Demetrius Poliorcetes complained long afterwards to the Romans; and the merchandise taken by the Romans was partly, it is said, obtained in this manner, probably from the Carthaginians. The situation of Ceno is unknown: Strabo speaks of Antium itself as being without a harbor, as standing high upon cliffs.

[7] Livy, III. 1.

[8] Dionysius, IX. 59.

[9] Livy, III. 2.

also: the united forces of the Romans, Latins, and Hernicans, could not prevent the total ravaging of the Roman territory; and the crowding[10] of the fugitives from the country into the city was a cause or an aggravation of the return of the pestilence, which broke out again in the autumn, soon after the appointment of the consuls for the year 291, with unparalleled fury. During the whole of this fatal year, the Romans were dying by thousands within the city, while the Æquians and Volscians were ravaging the whole country without opposition, and defeated with great loss the Latins and Hernicans, who vainly attempted to defend the territory of their allies and their own. At last the pestilence abated, and the new consuls, in the autumn of 292,[11] took the field, and made head against the enemy with some effect. Immediately on this first gleam of better times, the political grievances of the commons began again to excite attention and to claim redress.

A. C. 460.

We are told that one of the tribunes[12] again brought forward the question of the agrarian law; but that the commons themselves refused to entertain it, and resolved to put it off till a more favorable opportunity. This is ascribed by Dionysius to the zeal which all orders felt to take vengeance on their foreign enemies; but he forgets that another measure, no less obnoxious to the burghers, was brought forward in this year, and readily received by the commons: and the better explanation is, that the leaders of the commons began to see that they must vary their course of proceeding; that to contend for the agrarian law under the actual constitution, was expecting fresh and pure water from a defiled spring; the real evil lay deeper, and the commons must obtain equal rights and equal power with the burghers, before they could hope to carry such measures as most concerned their welfare. Accordingly, Caius Terentilius[13] Harsa, one of the tribunes, proposed a law for a complete reform of the existing state of things. Its purport was, that[14] ten commissioners should be chosen, five by the commons and five by the burghers, and that those so chosen should draw up a constitution, which should define all points of constitutional, civil, and criminal law; and should thus determine, on just and fixed principles, all the political, social, and civil relations of all orders of the Roman people.

First proposal of the Terentilian law.

Now, as a popular cry of reform has never originated in the love of abstract justice, or in the mere desire of establishing a perfect form of government, but has been always provoked by actual grievances, and has looked especially for some definite and particular relief, so the Roman commons, in supporting the Terentilian law, were moved by certain practical evils, which lay so deep in the existing state of things, that nothing else than a total reform of the constitution could remove them. These were, the extreme separation and unequal rights of the burghers and the commons, the arbitrary powers of the consuls, and the uncertainty and variety of the law; evils which affected every part of men's daily life; and the first of them, in particular, was a direct obstacle to that execution of Cassius' agrarian law, on which the actual subsist-

Actual grievances of the commons.

[10] Livy, III. 6.

[11] Livy, III. 8.

[12] Dionysius, IX. 69. The name of the tribune is corrupt, *Σέξτου Τίτου*. Gelenius proposes to read *Τιτίου*.

[13] Livy, III. 9. Niebuhr writes the tribune's name "Terentilius," according to some of the best MSS. of Livy. Dionysius calls him "Terentius."

[14] Livy speaks only of five; Dionysius of ten: Niebuhr reconciles the two statements in the manner given in the text.

These "high commissioners," "Decemviri legibus scribendis," were like the Greek *νομοθέται*, or, in the language of Thucydides (VIII. 67), which exactly expresses the object of the Terentilian law, *δέκα ἄνδρας ἑλέσθαι ξυγγραφέας αὐτοκράτορας—καθ' ὅ τι ἄριστα ἡ πόλις οἰκήσεται.* We are so accustomed to distinguish between a constitution and a code of laws, that we have no one word which will express both, or convey a full idea of the wide range of the commissioner's powers; which embraced at once the work of the French constituent assembly, and that of Napoleon when he drew up his code. But this comprehensiveness belonged to the character of the ancient *lawgivers;* a far higher term than *legislators*, although etymologically the same; they provided for the whole life of their citizens in all its relations, social, civil, political, moral, and religious.

ence of the poorer commons after the late times of misery and ruin might be said to depend.

Their original political condition was not suitable to their altered circumstances.

Society has almost always begun in inequality, and its tendency is towards equality. This is a sure progress; but the inequality of its first stage is neither unnatural nor unjust; it is only the error of preserving instead of improving which has led to injustice; the folly of thinking that men's institutions can be perpetual when every thing else in the world is continually changing. When the conquered Latins were first brought to Rome by those who were then the only Roman citizens, when they were allowed to retain their personal liberty, to enjoy landed property, and to become so far a part of the Roman people, it was not required that they should at once pass from the condition of foreigners to that of perfect citizens; the condition of commons was a fit state of transition from the one rank to the other. But after years had passed away, and both they and their original conquerors were, in fact, become one people; above all, when this truth had been already practically acknowledged by the constitution of Servius Tullius, to continue the old distinctions was but provoking a renewal of the old hostility: if the burghers and the commons were still to be like two nations, the one sovereign and the other subject, the commons must retain the natural right of asserting their independence on the first opportunity, of wholly dissolving their connection with those who refused to carry it out to its full completion. That their desire was for complete union, rather than for independence, arose, over and above all other particular causes, from that innate fondness for remaining as we are, which nothing but the most intolerable misery can wholly eradicate.

Means adopted by the burghers to oppose the Terentilian law. Impeachment of Kæso Quinctius.

The burghers resolved to resist the Terentilian law, but they wished, apparently, as in the case of the Publilian laws, to prevent its being passed by the commons in their tribes, rather than to throw it out in their own assembly of the curiæ or in the senate. Accordingly, they again proceeded by an organized system of violence; the younger burghers were accustomed to have their brotherhoods or clubs, like the young men of the aristocratical party in Athens; the members of these clubs were ready to dare any thing for the support of their order, and being far more practised in martial exercises than the commons, were superior in activity, if not in actual strength, and, by acting in a body, repeatedly interrupted all business, and drove their antagonists from the Forum. At the head of these systematic rioters was Kæso Quinctius,[15] the son of the famous L. Quinctius Cincinnatus; and he made himself so conspicuous, that A. Virginius, one of the tribunes, impeached him before the assemby of the tribes, and named a day on which he was to appear to answer to the charge.

Of the Icilian law, on which his impeachment was grounded.

This is the fifth instance of impeachment by the tribunes, which we have met with in the course of fifteen years, besides the famous case of Coriolanus. The right in the present case was grounded on the Icilian law, brought forward by a tribune, Sp. Icilius, which I have not noticed before, because the time at which it passed is doubted. Dionysius, who alone mentions it, places[16] it as early as the year 262, in the year after the first appointment of the tribunes; while Niebuhr thinks that it could not have been earlier than the year 284, and that it was one of the consequences of the success of the Publilian laws. It established the important point, that if any burgher interrupted a tribune when speaking to the commons in their own assembly, the tribune might impeach him before the commons, and might require him to give sureties to such an amount as the accuser should think proper; if he refused to give security, he was to be put to death and his property confiscated; if he demurred to the amount of the sum required, this question also was to be tried by the commons. The great object in this law was to assert the jurisdic-

[15] Livy, III. 11. Dionysius, X. 4, 5. [16] Dionysius, VII. 17.

tion of the commons over a burgher; hence the severity of the punishment if the accused refused to give the required security; he was then to be put to death as an open enemy; but if he complied, and appeared to answer to the charge, the ordinary sentence for a mere interruption of the business of the assembly of the tribes, would probably be no more than a fine; and this seems to have caused the confusion of Dionysius' statement, for he represents the sureties as required, not for the accused person's appearance at his trial, but for his payment of such a fine as the tribunes might impose, as if the sentence could, in no case, exceed a fine. Whereas the case of Appius Claudius, as well as that of Kæso, proved the contrary; and of Kæso, Livy says[17] expressly that the tribune impeached him for a capital offence, before the alleged charge of murder was brought against him. In fact, where there is no fixed criminal law, awarding certain punishments for certain offences, the relation of judge implies a power of deciding not only as to the guilt or innocence of the prisoner, but also as to the degree of his guilt, and the nature of the punishment to be inflicted. And much more would this be the case when the judgment was exercised, not by an individual magistrate, but by the sovereign society itself.

Kæso goes into exile before his trial.

According to the Icilian law, the tribune called upon Kæso Quinctius to give sureties for his appearance, and the amount of the security required was heavy; he was to find ten sureties,[18] at three thousand ases each. But in the mean time a witness, M. Volscius Fictor, who had been tribune some years before, came forward to charge Kæso with another and a totally distinct crime. "During the time of the plague," he said, "he and his brother, a man advanced in years, and not completely recovered from an attack of the pestilence, had fallen in with Kæso and a party of his club in all the license of riot in the Suburra. An affray had followed, and his brother had been knocked down by Kæso: the old man had been carried home, and died, as he thought, from the injury; but the consuls had every year refused to listen to his complaint, and try the offender." Outrages of this sort on the part of the young aristocracy were common even at Athens;[19] in aristocratical states they must have been far more frequent; and in all ordinary cases there is a sympathy with youth and birth, even amongst the people themselves, which is against any severe dealing with such excesses. But Kæso's offence was gross, and seemed to belong to his general character; the commons were indignant to the highest degree at this new crime, and could scarcely be prevented from tearing the offender to pieces. Even the tribune thought that no money security was sufficient when the charge was so serious; the body of the accused must be kept safe in prison, that he might abide the sentence of the law. But some of the other tribunes were prevailed on by the powerful friends of the criminal to extend to him their protection; they forbade the attachment of his person. Being thus left at large, he withdrew from justice, and fled across the Tiber into Etruria before his trial came on.[20] His relations, by whose influence justice had been thus defrauded, paid the poor compensation of their forfeited bail; and even here the punishment would not fall on the guilty, for when a burgher was fined, his clients were bound to contribute to discharge it for him.

Conspiracy to effect his return.

Kæso's flight provoked his associates to dare the last extremities. From mere rioters they became conspirators; and they played their game deeply. Still continuing their riots whenever the assembly of the tribes met, but taking care that no one of their body should be especially conspicuous, they, on all other occasions,[21] endeavored to make themselves popular: they would speak civilly to the commons, would talk with them, and ask them to their

[17] "A. Virginius Kæsoni capitis diem dicit." III. 11.

[18] Livy, III. 13.

[19] See the well-known speech of Demosthenes against Midias, and also the speech against Conon. See, too, the stories told in Plutarch of the manifold excesses of Alcibiades.

[20] Livy, III. 13.

[21] Livy, III. 14.

houses, well knowing how readily the poor and the humble are won by a little attention and liberality on the part of the rich and noble. Meanwhile, a darker plot was in agitation: Kæso held frequent communication with them; he had joined himself to a band of exiles and runaway slaves from various quarters, such as abounded in Italy then no less than in the middle ages: with this aid he would surprise the Capitol by night, his associates would rise and massacre the tribunes and the most obnoxious of the commons, and thus the old ascendency of the burghers would be restored, such as it had been before the fatal concessions made at the Sacred Hill.

A party of exiles and slaves surprise the Capitol by night; but it is recovered the next day, and the party who had seized it are cut to pieces.

Such was the information which the tribunes, according to Dionysius,[22] laid before the senate, soon after Kæso's flight from Rome. From what annalist he copied this statement does not appear; but Livy, who has followed some author far more partial to the Quinctian family, makes no mention of it, although it is really essential to the right understanding of his own subsequent narrative. For in the next year, according to the account of both Livy and Dionysius,[23] the Capitol was surprised by night by a body of slaves and exiles, and the leader of the party made it his first demand that all Roman exiles should be restored to their country. The burghers had great difficulty in persuading the cómmons to take up arms; till at last the consul, P. Valerius, prevailed with them, and relying on his word that he would not only allow the tribunes to hold their assembly for the consideration of the Terentilian law, but would do his best to induce the senate and the curiæ to give their consent to it, the commons followed him to the assault of the Capitol. He himself was killed in the onset; but the Capitol was carried, and all its defenders either slain on the spot, or afterwards executed.

Kæso's share in the enterprise not openly acknowledged.

The leader of this desperate band is said to have been a Sabine, Appius Herdonius; and in the story of the actual attempt, the name of Kæso is not mentioned. But we hear, in general terms,[24] of Roman exiles, whom it was the especial object of the enterprise to restore to their country; and we may be sure that Kæso was one of them. Appius Herdonius was, probably, a Sabine adventurer in circumstances like his own, whom he persuaded to aid him in his attempt. Had we the real history of these times, we should find, in all likelihood, that the truth in the stories of Kæso and Coriolanus has been exactly inverted; that the share of the Roman exile in the surprise of the Capitol has been as unduly suppressed as that of the Roman exile in the great Volscian war has been unduly magnified; that Kæso's treason has been transferred to Appius Herdonius, while the glory of the Volscian leader, Attius Tullius, has been bestowed on Coriolanus.

L. Quinctius, the father of Kæso, opposes the Terentilian law vehemently.

The burghers, as a body, would certainly be opposed, both from patriotic and selfish motives, to the attempt of Kæso; an exile forcing his return by the swords of other exiles, and seizing the citadel, was likely to set himself up as a tyrant alike over the burghers and the commons; and even his own father, L. Quinctius, would have been the first to resist him. But when he had fallen, and this danger was at an end, other feelings returned; and L. Quinctius would then hate the commons with a deeper hatred, as he would ascribe to them the miserable fate of his son; Kæso's guilt, no less than his misfortune, would appear the consequence of their persecution. So when he was elected consul in the room of P. Valerius, he seemed to set no bounds to his thirst for vengeance. The promise by which Valerius had prevailed on the commons to follow him to the recovery of the Capitol was utterly disregarded; L. Quinctius[25] openly set the tribunes at defiance, told them that they should never pass their law while he was consul, and declared that he would instantly lead forth the legions into the field against the Æquians and Volscians.

[22] Dionysius, X. 10, 11.
[23] Livy, III. 15. Dionysius, X. 14–16.
[24] See chap. XI. note 11.
[25] Livy, III. 19.

The tribunes[26] represented that they would not allow him to enlist any as soldiers: but Quinctius replied, that he needed no enlistment; "the men who took up arms under P. Valerius swore to assemble at the consul's bidding, and not to disband without his orders. The consul never disbanded them; and I, the consul," he said, "command you to meet me in arms to-morrow at the lake Regillus." But more was said to be designed than a simple postponement of the Terentilian law: the augurs were to attend,[27] in order to inaugurate the ground where the soldiers were to meet, and thus convert it into a lawful place of assembly; then the army, in its centuries, would be called upon to repeal all the laws which had been passed at Rome under the influence of the tribunes; and none would dare to oppose the consul's will, for, beyond the distance of one mile from the city, the tribunes' protection would be of no avail, nor did there exist any right of appeal. More than all, Quinctius repeatedly declared that, when his year of office was expired, he would name a dictator, that the tribunes might be awed by the power of a magistrate from whom there lay no appeal, even within the walls of Rome.

His violent measures.

A. U. C. 294. A. C. 458.

The Roman annalists who recorded these events[28] loved to believe that, in spite of all their provocations, the commons so respected the sacredness of an oath, that they would have kept the letter of it to their own hurt, even when its spirit in no way bound them to obedience. They say that the tribunes and the commons felt that they could not resist as a matter of right; that they appealed[29] to the mercy of the senate, and that the senate only prevailed with the consuls to abandon their purpose of taking the field, on condition that the tribunes would promise not to bring forward the question of the law again during that year. It may be, however, that the senate knew how far they could safely tempt the patience of the tribunes; threats might be held out, in order to claim a merit in abandoning them; but an actual attempt to march the legions out of the city, with the avowed purpose of making them the helpless instruments in the destruction of their own liberties, would be too bold a venture; at the last excess of insolent tyranny, Nemesis would surely awake to vengeance.

He is prevailed upon to abandon them.

At any rate,[30] it appeared that neither the tribunes nor the commons were disposed to let the Terentilian law be forgotten; for when the elections came on, the same tribunes who had already been in office for two years were re-elected for a third year, and again began to bring forward the disputed question. But again they gave way to the pressure of foreign war; for the danger from the Æquians and Volscians was imminent: the former had surprised the citadel of Tusculum; the latter had expelled the Roman colony from Antium, and recovered that important city. After a series of operations, which lasted for several months, the Æquians were dislodged from Tusculum, but Antium still remained in the possession of the Volscians.

A. U. C. 295. A. C. 457. The law is delayed by foreign war.

Thus the Terentilian law was again delayed:[31] but, in the mean time, the burghers, who retained a lively resentment for the fate of Kæso, were trying to establish a charge of false witness against M. Volscius, by whose testimony, as to his brother's murder, the event of Kæso's trial had been chiefly decided. The two quæstores parricidii, or chief criminal judges, proposed to impeach Volscius before the curiæ; but the tribunes refused to allow the trial to come on till the question of the law had been first decided. Thus the year passed away: but the tribunes were again, for the fourth time, re-elected.

Charge against M. Volscius for false witness in the trial of Kæso.

In the following year is placed the story already related of the dictatorship of L. Quinctius Cincinnatus, and his deliverance of the consul and his army, when they were blockaded by the Æquians. The continued

A. U. C. 296. A. C. 456.

[26] Livy, III. 20.

[27] Livy, III. 20.

[28] Livy, III. 20. Nondum hæc, quæ nunc tenet sæculum, negligentia Deum venerat: nec interpretando sibi quisque jusjurandum et leges aptas faciebat, sed suos potius mores ad ea accommodabat.

[29] Livy, III. 21.

[30] Livy, III. 21–23.

[31] Livy, III. 24.

absence[32] of the legions, which kept the field nearly the whole year, afforded the burghers a pretence for opposing the introduction of the law; but L. Quinctius availed himself of his dictatorial power to hold the comitia for the trial of Volscius, in defiance of the tribunes; and the accused, feeling his condemnation to be certain, left Rome, and availed himself of the interchange of citizenship between the Romans and Latins, to become a citizen of Lanuvium. The tribunes were again re-elected for a fifth time.

Dictatorship of L. Quinctius. Volscius goes into exile.

The year 297[33] was marked by the same dangers from the Æquians; and the Sabines are said, in this and in the former year, to have joined them, and to have carried alarm and devastation into a new part of the Roman territory, that which lay between the Tiber and the Anio. Thus the law made no progress: but the tribunes obtained an important point, that their number should henceforth be doubled. Ten tribunes were from this time forward annually elected; two from each of the five classes.

A. U. C. 297. A. C. 455. Increase in the number of the tribunes.

There can be no doubt that the annals of this period, as we now have them in Livy and Dionysius, present a very incomplete picture of these dissensions. The original source of the details must have been the memorials of the several great families; each successive version of these, as men's notions of their early history became more and more romantic, would omit whatever seemed inconsistent with the supposed purity and nobleness of the times of their forefathers; and acts of bloody vengeance, which the actors themselves, and their immediate descendants, regarded with pride rather than compunction, as Sulla gloried in his proscriptions and recorded them on his monument, were carefully suppressed by historians of a later age. The burghers of the third and fourth centuries thought it no dishonor that their own daggers,[34] or those of their faithful clients, should have punished with death the insolence and turbulence of the most obstinate of the commons; they would glory in breaking up the assemblies of their adversaries by main force, and in treating them, on other occasions, with all possible scorn and contumely; ejecting them from their houses[35] with a strong hand, insulting them and their families in their nightly revels, or in open day; abusing them in the streets, or besetting their doors[36] with armed slaves, and carrying off their wives and daughters.[37] Their own houses, built mostly on the hills of Rome, which were so many separate fortresses, and always, by their style of building, secure at once from public notice and from attack, favored the perpetration of all acts of violence. Others, besides insolvent debtors, might be shut up in their dungeons; and if hatred or fear prompted them to consign their victims to a yet surer keeping, the dungeon might readily become a grave,[38] and who would dare to search for those whom it contained, whether alive or dead?

The annals have not given a full picture of the disorders of these times.

One act in particular, in which its authors doubtless gloried as in a signal example of public justice, has been so concealed by the later annalists, that from the faint and confused notices of it which alone remain to us, we can neither discover its date, nor its cause, nor any

Obscure story about the burning of nine men as traitors.

[32] Livy, III. 29. [33] Livy, III. 30.

[34] Zonaras, VII. 17, who, as we now find, borrowed his statement from Dion Cassius. Dion's words are, *οἱ εὐπατρίδαι φανερῶς μὲν οὐ πάνυ, πλὴν βραχέων, ἐπιθειάζοντές τινα, ἀντέπραττον, λάθρα δὲ συχνοὺς τῶν θρασυτάτων ἐφόνευον.* Fragm. Vatic. XXII.

[35] This is implied in the "forcible occupation" noticed in the law, "de Aventino publicando."

[36] Such outrages must be alluded to in the speech ascribed to L. Quinctius, Livy, III. 19. "Si quis ex plebe domum suam obsessam a familiâ armatâ nunciaret, ferendum auxilium putaretis." The conduct of Verres at Lampsacus illustrates this; from the treatment of the provincials in the later times of the commonwealth, we may judge of that shown to the commons at an earlier period.

[37] The famous story of Virginia cannot have been a solitary instance. Virginia was the daughter of a centurion, and betrothed to no less a man than L. Icilius, the famous proposer of the law, "de Aventino publicando." If such an outrage could be ventured against a woman of such birth, and so connected, we may conceive what those of humbler condition were exposed to.

[38] The body of a murdered man was discovered to have been buried in the house of P. Sestius, a burgher, in the first year of the decemvirate. Livy, III. 33. The discovery of one such case implies that there were many others which were not discovered.

of its particulars. We only know, that at some time or other during the latter half of the third century of Rome, nine eminent men,[39] who advocated the cause of the commons, were burned alive in the Circus, such being the old punishment of the worst traitors. It appears, however, from the fragment of Festus, which undoubtedly relates to this event, that some of the victims in this execution were of patrician houses; and there is an obscure and corrupt passage of Dion Cassius in the Vatican fragments, which seems to indicate that some of the burghers did take part with the commons, whether from a sense of justice or from personal ambition.

A. U. C. 298. A. C. 454. Law of L. Icilius, for allotting out the Aventine to the commons.

The year 298, to return to our annals, was marked, on the part of the tribunes, by an important measure. First of all,[40] to prevent their increased number from being a source of weakness, by making differences amongst themselves more likely, they bound themselves to each other by solemn oaths, that no tribune should oppose the decisions of the majority of his colleagues, nor act without their consent. Then Lucius Icilius, one of their number, brought forward his famous law for allotting

[39] Ἐννέα ποτὲ δήμαρχοι πυρὶ ὑπὸ τοῦ δήμου ἐδόθησαν. Dion Cassius, Frag. Vatic. XXII., and copied by Zonaras, VII. 17. A confused vestige of the same story may be found in Valerius Maximus (VI. 3, 2); and the mutilated passage in Festus, beginning, in the common editions, with "Nauti consulatu," must clearly refer to it. Niebuhr's restoration and explanation of this last fragment may be found in his note 265 to the 2d volume of his History, p. 144, 2d edition. Both are highly ingenious, and that the fragment began with the word "novem," and not with "nauti," seems certain; inasmuch as the article before it begins with the word "novalis," and that which follows it begins with "novendiales." All the words now to be found in the MS. of Festus, half of the page having been accidentally destroyed by fire, are the following, and ranged in the following order as to lines:

T. Sicini Volsci
inissent adversus
co combusti feruntur
ne quae est proxime cir-
pide albo constratus.
Opiter Verginius
Lævinus, Postumus, Col-
lius Tolerinus, P. Ve-
onius Atratinus, Ver-
tius Scaevola, Sex. Fu-

Who can profess to fill up such a fragment with certainty? But I observe that Mutius Scævola belonged to a house which, so far as we know, was never patrician; and the preceding name, of which only the first syllable remains, Ver-, may also have denoted a plebeian, as we meet with a Virginius amongst the tribunes as early as the year 293. (Livy, III. 11.) But as all the others are patrician names, how can they have been tribunes; or how can there have been nine tribunes earlier than the year 297; or how can we find a place for such an event between 297 and the appointment of the decemviri; after which time it becomes wholly inconceivable? The words "adversarii" and "adversus eum," seem to me the most unlikely parts of Niebuhr's conjectural addition. The criminals would hardly have been described simply as the adversaries of T. Sicinius, nor their crime called a conspiracy against him. The story in Valerius Maximus represents one tribune as being a principal agent in the execution of his nine colleagues. We can thus explain the position of the name of Sicinius, if we read, "novem collegæ T. Sicinii Volsci," and "cum conjurationem" (or "consilia") "inissent adversus Remp." But what are we to call the office in which these ten men were colleagues together? Can it really have been the tribuneship? and are we to take Cicero's statement, in the fragments of his speech for Cornelius, that the number of tribunes was increased from two to ten in the very year after the first institution of the office? and is it possible that the patricians named in Festus' Fragments were the very persons whom Dion Cassius had in his mind, when he said that "many of the highest patricians renounced their nobility from being ambitious of the great power of the office, and became tribunes?" If this were so, T. Sicinius Volscus would be a member of the house of the plebeian Sicinii, and not the patrician who was consul in the year 267. The time of the execution I should place about the same time as the death of Cassius; and it is not incredible that even the people in their centuries may have believed that accusation of a conspiracy against the common liberty which was brought against Cassius, and may have sentenced nine of the tribunes to death as his accomplices, especially if one of their own colleagues, and a genuine plebeian, had denounced them as being really enemies to liberty, under the mask of opposing the aristocracy. And such a circumstance as the alleged treason of nine out of ten of the tribunes would have afforded a good pretence for again reducing their number to two or five, from which it was again finally raised to ten in the year 297. It must be remembered, that the whole period between the first institution of the tribuneship and the death of Cassius is one of the greatest obscurity, and that the remaining accounts are full of variations. Sempronius Atratinus is mentioned by Dyonisius as speaking in favor of the appointment of a commission of ten men to carry into effect the proposed agrarian law of Cassius, at least in a modified form; this was in the year 268. (Dionysius, VIII, 74.) I have sometimes thought whether the nine men may not have been members of this commission, and accused by their tenth colleague, T. Sicinius, the patrician, of abusing their powers to favor the tyranny of Cassius.

[40] Dionysius, X. 31.

the whole of the Aventine Hill to the commons forever, to be their exclusive quarter and stronghold. This hill was not, as we have seen, a part of the original city, nor was it even yet included within the pomærium, or religious boundary, although it was now within the walls; much of it was public or demesne land, having neither been divided out among the original citizens, the burghers, nor having in later times been assigned in portions to any of the commons. The ground, which was thus still public, was occupied, according to custom, by individual burghers; some had built on it, but parts of it were still in their natural state, and overgrown with wood. Yet this hill was the principal quarter in which the commons lived, and large parts of it had doubtless been assigned to them in the time of the kings, as the freeholds of those to whom they were granted. It appears that encroachments were made on these freeholds by the burghers; that the landmarks, which, according to Roman usage, always distinguished private property from common, were from time to time forcibly or fraudulently removed; the ground was then claimed as public, and, as such, occupied only by burghers; and in this way the ejectment of the commons, from what they considered as their own hill, seemed likely to be accomplished. Again, the Aventine is one of the steepest and strongest of the hills of Rome; if wholly in the hands of the commons, it would give them a stronghold of their own, such as the burghers enjoyed in the other hills; and this, in such stormy times, when the dissensions between the orders might at any instant break out into open war, was a consideration of the highest importance. Such were the reasons which induced the tribunes to suspend for a time the question of the Terentilian law, and to endeavor to obtain at once for their order the secure and exclusive property of the Aventine.

New mode of proceeding to procure the passing of the law.

A new course[41] was also adopted in the conduct of this measure. Instead of bringing it forward first before the commons, where its consideration might be indefinitely delayed by the violent interruptions of the burghers, L. Icilius called upon the consuls to bring it in the first instance before the senate, and he claimed himself to speak as counsel in its behalf. This was asserting not merely the right of petitioning, but the still higher right, that the petition should not be laid on the table, but that counsel should be heard in defence of it, and its prayer immediately taken into consideration. A story is told that the consuls' lictor[42] insolently beat away the tribunes' officer who was going to carry to them his message; that immediately Icilius and his colleagues seized the lictor, and dragged him off with their own hands, intending to throw him from the rock for his treason against the sacred laws. They spared his life only at the intercession of some of the oldest of the senators, but they insisted that the consuls should comply with the demands of Icilius; and accordingly the senate was summoned, Icilius laid before them what may be called his petition of right, and they proceeded to vote whether they should accept or reject it.[43]

The law is passed.

The majority voted in its favor, moved, it is said, by the hope that this concession would be accepted by the commons instead of the execution of the agrarian law. Then the measure thus passed by the senate was submitted by the consuls to the comitia of centuries, which, as representing the whole nation, might supersede the necessity of bringing it separately before the curiæ and the tribes. Introduced in a manner by the government, and supported by the influence of many of the burghers, as well as by the strong feeling of the commons, the bill became a law: its importance, moreover, led to its being confirmed with unusual solemnities; the pontifices and augurs attended; sacrifices were performed, and solemn oaths were taken to observe it; and, as a further security, it was engraved on a pillar of brass, and then set up in the temple of Diana on the Aventine, where it remained till the time of Dionysius.

[41] Dionysius, X. 31. [42] Dionysius, X. 31. [43] Dionysius, X. 32.

The provisions of the law were, "that so much[44] of the Aventine Hill as was public or demesne property, should be allotted out to the commons, to be their freehold forever. That all occupiers of this land should relinquish their occupation of it; that those who had occupied it, forcibly or fraudulently,[45] should have no compensation, but that other occupiers should be repaid for the money which they might have laid out in building upon it, at a fair estimate, to be fixed by arbitration." Probably also, as Niebuhr thinks, there was a clause forbidding any burgher to purchase or inherit property on the hill, that it might be kept exclusively for the commons. It is mentioned that the commons began instantly to take possession of their grant, and the space not sufficing to give each man a separate plot of ground, an allotment was given to two, three, or more persons together, who then built upon it a house, with as many flats or stories[46] as their number required, each man having one floor for himself and family as his freehold. The work of building sufficiently employed the commons for the rest of the year; the Terentilian law was allowed to rest; and an unusual rainy season, which was very fatal to the crops,[47] may have helped to suspend the usual hostilities with the Æquians and Volscians.

Its provisions.

The same tribunes were re-elected for the year following, and the Terentilian law was now again brought forward, but still, as formerly, before the assembly of the tribes; its rejection by the senate being supposed to be certain, if it were proposed there in the first instance. The consuls[48] headed the burghers in their opposition, and in their attempts to interrupt the assembly of the commons by violence; the tribunes, in return, brought some of the offenders to trial for a breach of the sacred laws, and, not wishing to press for the severest punishment, enforced, according to Dionysius, only the confiscation of the criminal's property to Ceres, whose temple was under the special control of the ædiles of the commons, and was the treasury of their order. But the burghers, it is said, advanced money out of their own treasury to buy the confiscated estates from those who had purchased them, and then gave them back to their original owners.

Fresh disputes about the Terentilian law.

The consuls of the year 300, Sp. Tarpeius and A. Aternius, appear to have been moderate men; and not only were the two consuls of the preceding year

[44] Dionysius, X. 32.

[45] In Dionysius' Greek version, *βεβιασμένοι* (or with the codex Vaticanus *βιασάμενοι*), *ἢ κλοπῇ λαβόντες*: in the original language "vi aut clam," as in the well-known form of the prætor's interdict, "eum fundum quem nec vi, nec clam, nec precario alter ab altero possidetis, ita possideatis." See Festus in "Possessio."

[46] Dionysius, X. 32. Houses thus divided amongst several proprietors, each being the owner of a single floor, were the *ξυνοικίαι* of the Greeks; and these were the "insulæ" of which we hear at Rome, and which are distinguished by Tacitus from "domus," the houses of a single proprietor, just as Thucydides speaks of the rich Corcyræans setting on fire *τὰς οἰκίας καὶ τὰς ξυνοικίας*, III. 74. Compare Tacitus, Annal. XV. 41, 43. The original sense of the word "insula," as given by Festus, "quæ non junguntur communibus parietibus cum vicinis, circuituque publico aut privato cinguntur," seems to show that the insula was ordinarily built like our colleges, or like the inns of court in London, a complete building in itself, and so large as to occupy the whole space from one street to the next which ran parallel to it.

[47] Livy, III. 31. Annonâ propter aquarum intemperiem laboratum est. Such notices of the weather and seasons come from the oldest and simplest annals, whether of the pontifices or of private families, and may safely be looked upon as authentic.

[48] Dionysius, X. 33–42. The events of this year are given by Dionysius at great length, in fifteen chapters; in Livy they do not occupy as many lines. The story of L. Siccius, under a somewhat different form, is given by the former under this year; although in its common version it occurs again in his history in its usual place under the decemviri. Whoever was the writer from whom Dionysius copied, he must have been one who had no wish to disguise the injustice of the burghers, but rather, perhaps, to exaggerate it; for they never appear in a more odious light than in the transactions of this year. One statement, however, is curious; that the houses most violent against the commons, and most formidable from the strength of their brotherhoods or societies, *ἑταιρίαι*, were the Postumii, Sempronii, and Clœlii. The former of these was an unpopular house, as may be seen from the story of the severity of L. Postumius Tubertus to his son (Livy, IV. 29), and of the murder of M. Postumius by his soldiers (Livy, IV. 49). The Sempronii also appear as a family of importance during the next fifty years; but the Clœlii are very little distinguished either in the early or in the later Roman history, only four members of this house occurring in the Fasti, and none of them being personally remarkable. Their coins, however, are numerous.

accused before the commons by the tribunes, and fined, without any opposition on the part of the burghers; but the new consuls themselves brought forward a law, which was intended probably to meet some of the objects of the Terentilian law, by limiting the arbitrary jurisdiction of the patrician magistrates. The Aternian law,[49] de multæ sacramento, fixed the maximum of the fines, which the consuls could impose for a contempt of their authority, at two sheep and thirty oxen; nor could this whole fine be imposed at once,[50] but the magistrate was to begin with one sheep, and if the offender continued obstinate, he might the next day fine him a second sheep, and the third day he might raise the penalty to the value of an ox, and thus go on, day by day, till he had reached the utmost extent allowed by the law. It would appear also by the use of the term sacramentum,[51] which was applied to money deposited in the judge's hands by two contending parties, to be forfeited or recovered, according to the issue of the suit, that this fine was not absolute, but might be recovered by the party who paid it, either on his subsequent submission, or on his appeal to the judgment of his peers, whether burghers or commons, and on their deciding in his favor.

The Aternian law, "de multæ sacramento."

But with regard to the Terentilian law itself, the tribunes could make no progress. The burghers absolutely refused to allow the commons any share in the proposed revision of the constitution; but they consented to send three persons beyond the sea[52] into Greece, to collect such notices of the laws and constitutions of the Greek states as might be serviceable to the Romans. These commissioners were absent for a whole year; and in this year the pestilence[53] again broke out at Rome, and carried off so many of the citizens, amongst the rest four out of the ten tribunes, that there was a necessary cessation of political disputes. And as the pestilence spread also amongst the neighboring nations,[54] they were in no condition to take advantage of the distressed state of the Romans.

Three commissioners are sent to Greece.

A. U. C. 301. A. C. 451.

In the next year the pestilence[55] left Rome free; and on the return of the commissioners from Greece, the disputes again began. After a long contention, the commons conceded the great point at issue; and it was agreed that the revision of the laws and constitution should be committed to a body of ten men, all of the order of the burghers, who should supersede all other patrician magistrates, and each administer the government day by day in succession, as during an interregnum. Two of these were the consuls of the new year, who had been just elected, Appius Claudius and T. Genucius; the warden of the city and the two quæstores parricidii, as Niebuhr thinks, were three more; and the remaining five were chosen by the centuries.[56]

A. U. C. 302. A. C. 452. It is resolved to appoint ten men to revise the laws and constitution.

A. U. C. 303. A. C. 449.

Such was the end of a contest which had lasted for ten years; and all its circumstances, as well as its final issue, show the inherent strength of an aristocracy in possession of the government, and under what manifold disadvantages a popular party ordinarily contends against it. Nothing less than some extraordinary excitement can ever set on a level two parties so unequal; wealth, power, knowledge, leisure, organization, the influence of birth, of rank, and of benefits, the love of quiet, the dread of exertion and of personal sacrifices, the instinctive clinging to what is old and familiar, and the indifference to abstract principles so characteristic of common minds in every

Conclusion of the struggle about the Terentilian law.

[49] Cicero de Republicâ, II. 35. The reading of the consul's name, as given in this passage of Cicero, Aternius, enables us to account for and to correct the corrupt reading in Dionysius, Τερμήνιος. We find it also correctly given in one of the recently discovered fragments of the Fasti Capitolini.

[50] See Varro, de Ling. Latinâ, V. 177, and Niebuhr, Vol. II. p. 341, 2d ed.

[51] See Varro, Ling. Lat. V. 180, and **Festus** in voce.

[52] Livy, III. 31.

[53] Livy, III. 32.

[54] Dionysius, X. 53.

[55] Dionysius, X. 54. Livy, III. 32.

[56] Vol. II. p. 350, 2d ed.

rank of life; all these causes render the triumph of a dominant aristocracy sure, unless some intolerable outrage, or some rare combination of favorable circumstances, exasperate or encourage the people to extraordinary efforts, and so give them a temporary superiority. Otherwise the aristocracy may yield what they will, and retain what they will; if they are really good and wise, and give freely all that justice and reason require, then the lasting greatness and happiness of a country are best secured; if they do much less than this, yielding something to the growing light of truth, but not frankly and fully following it, great good is still done, and great improvements effected; but in the evil which is retained, there are nursed the seeds of destruction, which falls at last upon them and on their country. The irritation of having reasonable demands refused, provokes men to require what is unreasonable; suspicion and jealousy are fostered beyond remedy; and these passions, outliving the causes which excited them, render at last even the most complete concessions thankless; and when experience has done its work with the aristocracy, and they are disposed to deal justly with their old adversaries, they are met, in their turn, with a spirit of insolence and injustice, and a fresh train of evils is the consequence. So true is it, that nations, like individuals, have their time of trial; and if this be wasted or misused, their future course is inevitably evil; and the efforts of some few good and wise citizens, like the occasional struggles of conscience in the mind of a single man when he has sinned beyond repentance, are powerless to avert their judgment.

CHAPTER XIV.

THE FIRST DECEMVIRS, AND THE LAWS OF THE TWELVE TABLES.

"The laws of a nation form the most instructive portion of its history."—GIBBON, Chap. XLIV.

Appointment of the decemvirs. Suspension of all other magistracies.

THE appointment of a commission invested with such extraordinary powers as those committed to the decemvirs, implies of itself a suspension of all such authorities as could in any degree impede or obstruct its operations. It was natural, therefore, that the tribunate[1] should be suspended as well as the patrician magistracies; besides, the appointment of the decemvirs was, even in its present form, a triumph for the commons, and they would be glad to show their full confidence in the magistrates whom they had so much desired. Again, the tribunes had been needed to protect the commons against the tyranny of the consuls; but now that there were no consuls, why should there be tribunes? And who could dread oppression from men specially appointed to promote the interests of freedom and justice? Yet, to show that

[1] This is Dionysius' statement in the most express terms (X. 56), ad finem. Livy's language appears to me to admit of a doubt; for he says, when speaking of the wish of the commons to have decemvirs elected for another year, "Jam plebs ne tribunicium quidem auxilium, cedentibus in vicem appellationi [codd. 'appellatione'] decemviris quærebat." (III. 34. ad finem.) And although, when mentioning the appointment of the first decemvirs, he had said, "Placet creari decemviros—et ne quis eo anno alius magistratus esset" (III. 32), yet it was sometimes made a question whether the tribuneship was properly called magistratus or no: and, at any rate, it would not in these times be called "magistratus populi," but only "plebis:" further, Livy expressly adds, that the "sacratæ leges" were not to be abolished. Niebuhr believes that the tribuneship was not given up till the second decemvirate. I think, on the whole, that Livy meant to agree with Dionysius; and the statement does not appear to me to possess any internal improbability.

the tribuneship was not to be permanently surrendered, the sacred laws were specially exempted from the decemvirs' power of revision, as was also that other law, scarcely less dear to the commons, or less important, which had secured to them the property of the Aventine.

The decemvirs begin their legislation.

With the ground thus clear before them, and possessing that full confidence and cheerful expectation of the people, which is a government's great encouragement, the ten proceeded to their work. They had before them the unwritten laws and customs of their own country, and the information, partly, we may suppose, in writing, which the commissioners had brought back from Greece. In this there would be much which, to a Roman, would require explanation: but the ten had with them an Ionian sophist,[2] Hermodorus of Ephesus, who rendered such important services in explaining the institutions of his countrymen, above all of the Athenians, the great glory of the Ionian race, that a statue was erected to his honor in the comitium.

They complete ten tables of laws.

The result of these labors, after a few months, was submitted to the examination of the people.[3] Ten tables were published, and set up in a conspicuous place for all to read them. Every man was then invited to make known to the ten such corrections as he might think needed; these were considered, and adopted as far as the ten approved of them: and the ten tables, thus amended, were then laid before the senate, the centuries, and the curiæ, and received the sanction of both orders of the nation. The laws were then engraved on tablets of brass,[4] and the tablets were set up in the comitium, that all men might know and observe them.

Only fragments of them have been preserved to us.

It cannot be doubted that the ten tables were a complete work, and intended to be so by their authors. All the circumstances of their enactment show this; it seems shown also by their number, which had reference to that of the ten commissioners, as if each commissioner had contributed an equal portion of their joint work. It is clear, also, that they satisfied the expectations of the people, and were drawn up in a spirit of fairness and wisdom; for whatever the Romans found fault with in the laws of the twelve tables, was contained in the two last of them; and the laws, as a whole, are spoken of with high admiration, and remained for centuries as the foundation of all the Roman law. Unhappily, we ourselves know little of them beyond this general character. Some fragments[5] of them have been preserved by ancient writers; but these are far too scanty to allow us to judge either of the substance or the order of the whole code.

Still[6] we may fitly avail ourselves of the occasion offered by this great period

[2] Pomponius, de origine juris, § 4, in the Digest or Pandects, 1 Tit. ii. Strabo, XIV. 1, § 25, p. 642. Hermodorus was the friend of Heraclitus, the philosopher, who reproached the Ephesians for having banished him from mere jealousy of his superior merit. See the story in Strabo, as already quoted, and in Cicero, Tusculan. Disputat. V. 36. Diogenes Laertius says that Heraclitus flourished in the sixty-ninth Olympiad, but Syncellus makes him contemporary with Anaxagoras, the elder Zenon, and Parmenides, which would render it very possible for his friend Hermodorus to have visited Rome in the time of the decemvirs. Strabo expressly identifies the Hermodorus of whom Heraclitus spoke, with the man of that name who helped the decemvirs in drawing up their laws. And the fact of his having been honored with a statue in the comitium (Pliny, Hist. Nat. XXXIV. 11) would seem to prove that the story of his having helped the decemvirs was not without foundation.

[3] Livy, III. 34.

[4] So Dionysius, στήλαις χαλκαῖς ἐλχαράξαντες αὐτούς. X. 57. Livy's simple expression "tabulæ" would lead one to suppose that they were written on wood.

[5] The authentic remains of the twelve tables are given by Haubold in his "Institutionum Juris Romani privati Lineamenta," as republished after his death by Dr. Otto, Leipzig, 1826. They are given also by Dirksen, with an elaborate criticism as to the text and the sources of each fragment. "Ubersicht der bisherigen Versuche zur Kritik und Herstellung des Textes der Zwölf-Tafel-Fragmente." Leipzig, 1824. The earlier collections of them contain clauses ascribed to the twelve tables on insufficient authority.

[6] I am well aware of the difficulty of writing on legal details without a professional knowledge of the subject. But history must embrace the subject-matter of every profession; and as no man can be properly qualified to write on all, the necessity of the case must excuse the presumption. It will be proper here to mention the works from which the present chapter has been chiefly compiled. 1st. The Institutes of Gaius. An epitome of the three first books of this great work had been long known, but the

State of the Roman law in its earliest known form.

in Roman legislation, to give something of a view of the Roman law as it was settled by the twelve tables, or as it existed in the oldest form in which it is now possible to trace it. And I shall adopt that division of constitutional law on the one hand, and civil law on the other, which Livy had in his mind when he called the twelve tables "fons omnis publici, privatique juris."

Jus Privatum divided into the I. Law of Persons, II. Law of Things, and III. Law of Actions.

To begin, then, with "Jus privatum," or the civil law of Rome. This, according to the Roman lawyers, related either to persons, or to things, or to actions, in the legal sense of the term. Let us first examine some of the principal points in the law as it regarded persons.

I. Law of Persons. Persons born free, persons made free, and slaves.

I. In later times the lawyers had occasion to notice three descriptions of persons: those born free, those who had been made free, and slaves. The distinctions of burghers and commons, patricians and plebeians, had long since vanished; and all free-born Roman citizens were legally regarded as equal. On the other hand, the condition of slaves admits of little variation so long as they remain slaves; and thus, with regard to these, the lapse of centuries produced little change. But the freedmen of a later age appear to represent the clients of the period of the twelve tables.

The freedmen of a later age resembled the clients of the period of the twelve tables.

That the relation of the freedman to his former master very nearly resembled that of the client to his lord, might be conjectured from this, that when a slave obtained his freedom, his former master, "dominus," became his "patronus," the very same name which expressed his relation to his clients. Previously to the decemvirate, this class of persons voted indeed in the comitia of centuries, which comprehended the whole Roman people, but they did not belong to any tribe, and therefore had no votes in the separate comitia of the commons. The decemvirs[7] procured their enrolment in the tribes, and thus added greatly to the influence of the aistocracy over the popular assemblies; for the tie between a patron and his clients or freedmen seems to have been a very kindly one, and much stronger, as yet, than any sense of the duty of advancing the cause of the great mass of the nation. Indeed, the freedman was held to belong so much to his patron, that if he died intestate, and without direct

whole work, in its genuine state, was first discovered by Niebuhr in 1816, in a palimpsest, or rewritten manuscript, of some of the works of S. Jerome, in the Chapter Library at Verona. I have used the second edition, published by Göschen, at Berlin, in 1824; and I have derived great assistance from Göschen's continued references to parallel passages in the other extant works of the Roman lawyers. 2d. The fragment of Ulpian from a MS. in the Vatican, published by Hugo in his "Jus Civile Antejustinianeum." Berlin, 1815. The fragments of Ulpian more recently discovered and published by Mai, I have not seen. 3d. I have read the Institutes of Justinian, and referred continually to the Digest or Pandects; but I cannot pretend to have read through the Digest, or to be deeply acquainted with its contents. 4th. Hugo's Geschichte des Römischen Rechts. 9th edit. Berlin, 1824. 5th. Haubold's Institutionum juris Romani lineamenta, and Dirksen's work on the Twelve Tables, noticed in a preceding note; as also Haubold's edition of the well-known work of Heineccius, "Antiquitt. Romanar. jurisprudentiam illustrantium syntagma." 6th. Savigny, "Recht des Besitzes," 5th edition; and some articles by the same great writer in the "Zeitschrift fur geschichtliche Rechtswissenschaft." In point of excellence, I could not, I suppose, have consulted higher authorities than these; but I am perfectly conscious of the insufficiency of a few months' study, even of the best writers, on a subject so vast as the Roman law. The other works which I have consulted will be noticed in their several places.

"The Fragments of Ulpian discovered and published by Mai" are not correctly described, as I had not seen the book when this note was written. I have only been able to procure it since the completion of the present volume, and I find that it contains the remains of several treatises by an unknown lawyer, on various legal subjects; these treatises consisting, for the most part, of quotations from the works of the most eminent lawyers, arranged in order, as in the Pandects. Amongst the rest there are, naturally, citations from Ulpian, and some of these were not known to us before Mai's discovery; others had been already preserved in the Pandects. The manuscript in which these treatises were found was a palimpsest, now in the Vatican library, and marked in the catalogue VMDCCCLXVI. It was brought to Rome from the library of the monastery at Bobbio, near Placentia, and these treatises were first published from it by Mai in 1823: they have been since reprinted at Bonn, in 1833, under the superintendence of Bethmann Hollweg; and I know them only in this German edition. They do not give us any additional information as to the laws of the Twelve Tables.

[7] On this point see Niebuhr, Vol. II. p. 318. Eng. Transl. It is admitted also by Haubold, in his Tabulæ Chronologicæ, as one of the institutions of the decemvirs.

heirs,[8] his patron inherited all his property; a law which applied also, as we cannot doubt, though perhaps with some qualification, to the client.

Looking at the domestic relations of free citizens, we find that the absolute power of a father over his children was in some slight degree qualified by the twelve tables; inasmuch as they enacted,[9] that if a father had sold his son three times, he should have no further control over him. Formerly, it appears, the independence of a son during his father's lifetime had been regarded as monstrous and impossible; he never could become sui juris. The father might transfer his right to another by selling his son; but if his new master set him free, the father's right revived, and the son became again in potestate. But by the new law, the father's right became terminable; and if, after he had thrice sold his son, the last purchaser gave him his freedom, then the son no longer reverted to his father's power, but remained his own master. Still, as if to show the peculiar sacredness of the father's power, he could not, by any one act of his own, make his son independent; he could not give him his liberty like a slave, but was obliged, if he wished to emancipate him, to go through the form of thrice selling him; and it was only when, according to the common practice, the son, after the third sale, was resold to his father, that then, the fatherly power being extinct, he could give him his freedom by a direct act of manumission. It should be remembered, also, that an emancipated son lost his relationship to his father, and could no longer inherit from him; and further, that by having been sold, and so passed into the state of slavery, he incurred[10] that legal degradation which the Romans called diminutio capitis, and consequently, remained liable, during the remainder of his life, to certain peculiar disqualifications.

Power of a father over his children.

As the father of a family enjoyed absolute power over his children in his lifetime, so was he equally absolute in his choice of a guardian for them, and in his disposal of his property after his death.[11] He might bequeath his whole fortune to any one child, to the exclusion of the rest, or to an absolute stranger, to the exclusion of them all. In this respect the twelve tables gave, probably, a legal sanction to a power which was become common in practice, but, strictly speaking, was as yet only a matter of indulgence, not of right. Hitherto, the will of every citizen had been read before the comitia,[12] whether of the curiæ or of the centuries; that the former in the case of a

His power of disposing of his property by will.

[8] Gaius, Institut. III. § 40. A man's direct heirs, "sui heredes," were, according to the Roman law, his children "in potestate," whether male or female, by birth, or by adoption; his son's children; his son's son's children; his wife in manu; and his daughter-in-law. See Gaius, Institut. III. § 2. For the application of this law to clients, see Nieuport, Ritt. Romanor. Sect. I. ch. IV. § 3, and the defence of his statement in Reiz's preface to the 5th edit. of Nieuport's work. Niebuhr also is of the same opinion. Hist. Rom. Vol. I. p. 320, Eng. Transl. The qualification alluded to is supposed by Reiz to have consisted in this, that a client's agnati would have inherited before his patron, whereas a freedman could have no agnati, his natural relationships in his state of slavery being reckoned as nothing.

[9] Si pater filium ter venum duit, filius a patre liber esto. Fragm. duodec. Tabb. 12, apud Haubold, Institut. jur. Rom. lineamenta.

[10] Minima capitis diminutio accidit in his qui mancipio dantur, quique ex mancipatione manumittuntur; adeo quidem ut quotiens quisque mancipetur aut manumittatur, totiens capite diminuatur. Gaius, Institut. I. § 162. The disqualifications incurred by a diminutio capitis included a forfeiture of the jus agnationis. A man's agnati are his relations derived "per virilis sexus personas;" such as his father's brother, or brother's son, or the son of an uncle by the father's side. These inherited in preference to the cognati, or relations derived "per fœminei sexus personas;" and thus an emancipated son could not be heir or guardian to his nephew on his brother's side, by virtue of the jus agnationis, as he had lost that right by having gone through the state of mancipatio during the process of his release from his father's authority.

[11] Uti legassit super pecuniâ tutelâve suæ rei, ita jus esto. Fragm. duodec. Tabb. 13, apud Haubold. See Gaius, Institut. II. § 224.

[12] Testamentorum autem genera initio duo fuerunt; nam aut calatis comitiis faciebant, quæ comitia bis in anno testamentis faciendis destinata erant, aut in procinctu, id est cum belli causâ ad pugnam ibant: procinctus est enim expeditus et armatus exercitus. Gaius, Institut. II. § 101. Ulpian, Fragm. XX. 2. "Calata comitia" are defined by Labeo to be those, "quæ pro collegio pontificum habentur aut regis aut flaminum inaugurandorum causâ." "Iisdem comitiis," says Gellius, by whom the passage from Labeo has been preserved, "et sacrorum detestatio et testamenta fieri solebant." Noct. Att. XV. 27, § 1, 3. And Labeo tells us that these calata comitia were either

burgher, the latter in the case of a plebeian, might confirm or reject it. The confirmation was generally, as we may suppose, become almost a matter of course; still it is evident that it might have been refused. But from this time forward it became a mere formality; the right of the father to dispose of his property as he chose was fully acknowledged; and it was conferred on him with such full sovereignty, that it was only when he died intestate that the next of kin could take the management of his inheritance out of the hands of his sons, if they were squandering it extravagantly; no degree of waste on the part of a son could justify the interference of his relations,[13] if he had succeeded by virtue of his father's will. The principle of this distinction is plain: when the father of a family had waived his right of bequeathing his property, it seemed, in some measure, to revert to the community, as a member of which, he or his ancestor had originally received it. This community was the gens in the last resort, and more immediately the family of which he was the representative. As then his property would go to the male representatives of his family in default of his own direct heirs, so they had an interest in preserving it unimpaired, and were allowed to enforce it when the son's title to his inheritance rested, like theirs, only on the general award of the law. But where the father had disposed of his property by will, then the individual right of ownership passed in full sovereignty to his children, and no one might interfere with their management of what was wholly their own. The later law did away with this distinction; and the prætor was accustomed to deprive an extravagant son of the administration of his inheritance, even when he had succeeded to it by his father's will. And this is natural, for as society advances in true civilization, its supremacy over all individual rights of property becomes more fully recognized; and it is understood that we are but stewards of our possessions with regard to the commonwealth of which we are members, as well as with respect to God.

Law with respect to women: 1, as to marriage;

We shall not be surprised to find that the usages of a rude people paid but little respect to women. A man could acquire a right over a woman by her having lived with him for a year; exactly as a year's possession gave him a legal title to a slave, or any other article of movable property. Here again the twelve tables so far interfered,[14] as to give the power to the woman of barring this prescription, by absenting herself from her husband during three nights in each year. By so doing, she avoided passing under her husband's power, "in manum viri;" and could not, therefore, like a wife in the fullest sense, inherit from him as a daughter. Still the connection was recognized as a lawful marriage,[15] "connubium;" and the children accordingly followed their father's condition, and were subject to his power, which was the case only with such children as were born in "connubium."

2, as to their being always under guardianship.

Again, the old Roman law, confirmed in this instance also by the twelve tables, obliged all women, at all times of their lives, and under all circumstances,[16] to be under guardianship. If a father died intestate, his daughters immediately became the wards of their

"curiata" or "centuriata;" so that we may safely conclude that the will of a patrician was read at the former, that of a plebeian at the latter. See Niebuhr, Vol. II. p. 336, Eng. Trans.

[13] A prætore constituitur curator—ingenuis qui ex testamento parentis hæredes facti male dissipant bona: his enim ex lege (scil. XII. Tabularum) curator dari non poterat. Ulpian, Fragm. XII. 3.

[14] Gaius, Institut. I. § 111.

[15] The formalities of a marriage, according to the Roman law, seem only to have affected the wife's property, and her power of inheriting from her husband, not the legitimacy of the children. A woman's guardians might prevent her from passing in manum viri either by prescription, "usus," or by coemptio, because then they lost their control over her property, and their right of inheriting from her (see Cicero pro Flacco, 34); but only her father's refusal of consent hindered her from forming a connubium, if her connection was with a Roman citizen, and one not related to her in any prohibited degree. See Ulpian, Fragm. V. 2–7.

[16] Gaius, I. § 144. The vestal virgins were alone excepted by the twelve tables, "in honorem sacerdotii." Afterwards, by the later law, a woman obtained the same privilege by acquiring the "jus trium liberorum," which did not, however, always imply that she had really borne three children, but that by the emperor's favor she had acquired the right granted by law to one who had actually been a mother.

brothers, or of their nearest male relations on their father's side;[17] nor could they, without their guardian's sanction, contract any obligation,[18] or alienate their land, or make a will. If a woman married, she became, in law, her husband's daughter; he could appoint her guardians by his will, or, if he died intestate, her nearest male relations succeeded by law to the office; so that it was possible, in despite of the laws of nature, that a mother might be under the guardianship of her own son. By these institutions, the apparent liberality of the law, which enabled a man's daughters to inherit on an equal footing with his sons, was in great measure rendered ineffectual.[19] A daughter might, indeed, claim an equal share with her brother of her father's land; but as she could neither alienate it during her lifetime, nor bequeath it by will without his consent, and as he was her legal heir, there was little probability of its passing out of the family. All this was greatly modified by the later law; but there were always found persons who regretted the change, and upheld the old system, with all its selfishness and injustice, as favorable to a wholesome severity of manners, and a proper check upon the weakness or caprice of a woman's judgment.

II. Law of Things. Importance of a knowledge of the law of real property, as throwing light on the history of every people.

II. If from persons we now turn to property, or, according to the language of the law, to things, our curiosity as to the provisions of the twelve tables, and the state of things which they recognized, can be but imperfectly gratified. Yet there are few points of more importance in the history of a nation: the law of property, of real property especially, and a knowledge of all the circumstances of its tenure and divisions, would throw light upon more than the physical condition of a people; it would furnish the key to some of the main principles prevalent in their society. For instance, the feudal notion that property in land confers jurisdiction, and the derivation of property, either from the owner's own sword, or from the gift of the stronger chief whose sword he had aided, not from the regular assignment of society, has most deeply affected the political and social state of the nations of modern Europe. At Rome, as elsewhere among the free commonwealths of the ancient world, property was derived from political rights, rather than political rights from property; and the division and assignation of lands to the individual members of the state by the deliberate act of the whole community, was familiarly recognized[20] as the manner in which such property was most

[17] Quibus testamento quidem tutor datus non sit, iis ex lege XII. agnati sunt tutores. Gaius, I. § 155.

[18] A woman's agnati, by the old law, were her tutores legitimi. And it was a well-known rule of law that she could make no valid will without their consent. Gaius, II. § 118. The whole right of her agnati to become her guardians was done away by the emperor Claudius. (Gaius, I. § 171.) But her father, and, if she were a freed woman, her patronus, still retained the same power; and even in the time of the Antonines, her will was good for nothing if it had not their sanction.

[19] See Hugo, Geschichte des Römischen Rechts, p. 209.

[20] This is one of those general statements which I think the reader of ancient history will readily admit, although it is not possible to bring any particular passage of an ancient writer as the authority for it. Nor is it to be denied, that conquest, and the lapse of years, introduced the greatest inequalities of property, quite as great as those subsisting in modern Europe. But the notion of an equal division of the land of a country amongst its citizens, which in modern Europe is so without example that it is looked upon as one of the wildest of impossible fancies, seems, in the ancient world, to have been rather the rule in theory, and, in the earliest recorded settlement of a people, to have been often actually carried into practice. The division of Canaan amongst the Israelites is a well-known example. Let any one compare this with the utterly capricious manner in which the Norman chiefs, from duke William downwards, appropriated to themselves, or granted away to their followers, the lands of England. Again, a similar equal division is said to have existed at one time in Egypt (Herodotus, II. 109); and even after the period of the distress, noticed in Genesis, had brought most of the property into the hands of the kings, yet still we find the principle of regular division recognized; for even in the last years of the Egyptian monarchy, the class of landed proprietors who received their land as an hereditary fief, on the tenure of military service, enjoyed each man an equal portion. (Herodotus, II. 164, et seqq.) In all the Greek colonies there was the same system; each citizen had his κλῆρος or portion, and in many states these were not allowed to be alienated. (Aristotle, Politic. VI. 4.) Thus the well-known division of Laconia, ascribed to Lycurgus, was nothing unprecedented: the remarkable feature in it was, that it was a return to the principle of regular assignation, after a long departure from

regularly acquired. This act conveyed the property of the land so granted in complete sovereignty; no seignorial rights were reserved on it; all on the soil and under it, was alike made over to the proprietor; and, as he was the absolute owner of it in his lifetime, so he could dispose of it to whom he would after his death. But he must leave it as unfettered as he had himself enjoyed it: he could not control the rights of his successor by depriving him of his power of disposing of it in his turn according to his pleasure; for this seemed an unjust encroachment on the power of posterity, and an unnatural usurpation on the part of any single generation. And a man's civil rights and duties were derived, not from his possession of property, but from his being a citizen of that society from whose law his property itself had come to him. He was bound to defend his country, not as the holder of lands, but as a member of the commonwealth; as a master, he had power over his slaves; as a father, over his children; as a magistrate, over his fellow-citizens; as a free-born citizen he had a voice in public affairs; but as a proprietor of land he enjoyed only the direct benefits of property, and no power or privilege, whether social or political.

All property in land at Rome was derived originally from the grant of the state.

Yet the sword had won no small portion of the actual territory of Rome, no less than of the feudal kingdoms of a later period. The sword won it for the state, but not for individuals. Slaves, cattle, money, clothing, and all articles of movable property, might be won by individuals for themselves; and the law[21] acknowledged this as a natural method of acquiring wealth; but whatever land[22] was conquered belonged immediately to the commonwealth. It could be converted into private property only by purchase or by assignation; and assignation always proceeded on regular principles, and awarded equal portions of land to every man. But the mass of the conquered territory was left as the demesne of the state; and it was out of land similarly reserved to the kings in the conquests of the German barbarians that fiefs were first created. This system was prevented among the Romans, by the general law, strengthened apparently by the sanctions of religion: the law which prescribed to all grants of land made out of the state demesne the one form of common and equal assignation. The land then was not granted away, its property remained in the state; it was sometimes left as a common pasture, sometimes

it; it was the bringing back of an old state to a new beginning, as it were, of its social existence. I think, then, it may be stated, as one of the characteristic points of the ancient world, that landed property was not merely sanctioned and maintained by law, but had originally been derived from it; and that even where the people as a body had gained their country by the sword, yet their individual citizens received their separate portion neither from their own sword, nor from the capricious bounty of their chiefs, but from the deliberate act of society, which proceeded, on regular principles, to allot a portion of its common property to each of its members. With respect to the statement at the end of this paragraph, that land conferred no political power, it may be objected that power was connected with landed property, inasmuch as the commons, it is said, were liable to be removed from their tribe by the censors, if they followed any other calling but agriculture. But this and other such regulations went on the principle, that it was desirable that a citizen should live by agriculture rather than by trade; a principle very generally admitted in the ancient world, but founded on considerations of what was supposed to be for the moral good of the community; and very different from the notion that he who had land ought to have jurisdiction and power. Besides, it was only a ground of censorian interference, if a citizen having had land, neglected it and followed any other calling; it certainly did not follow that every citizen received a grant of land, much less that his possession of land beforehand qualified him to become a citizen.

[21] Gaius, II. § 69. Quæ ex hostibus capiuntur, naturali ratione nostra fiunt; and in Justinian's Institutes this is expressly extended to slaves; "adeo quidem, ut et liberi homines in servitutem nostram deducantur." II. 1, § 17. De rerum divisiones, &c.

[22] Gaius, II. § 7. In provinciali solo dominium populi Romani est, vel Cæsaris; nos autem possessionem tantum et usum fructum habere videmur. Accordingly no land, in provinciali solo, could be sold by mancipatio, because it was not res mancipii. "Provinciale solum" was opposed to "Italicum solum," and expressed the condition of land which remained still in the state of a conquest, and had not been incorporated with the territory, "ager," of the conquerors. But, as is well known, all the land in the provinces in the imperial times was not "provinciale solum;" particular spots enjoyed the privileges of "Italicum solum," and this was the famous jus Italiæ which was so completely misunderstood by all writers on the Roman law and constitution before Savigny. He first showed that it was a privilege attached to land, not, as had been supposed, to persons.

farmed, sometimes occupied by individuals, in the same manner and under the same circumstances as in later times it was granted in fiefs, but with this essential difference, that this occupation was an irregular, and as far as regarded the state, a wholly precarious tenure. The occupiers possessed large tracts of land, and derived as much profit from them as if they had been their property; but they were only tenants at will, and there was nothing to give to these permitted rather than authorized possessions, the dignity and political importance which were attached to the great fiefs of modern Europe.

Property acquired by prescription.

This occupation of the public land could by no length of prescription be converted into private property; lapse of time could never bar the rights of the commonwealth; and therefore the "possessions" of the Roman patricians in early times, within a few miles of Rome, were on the same footing with all land in the provinces afterwards: in neither case could prescription or usucapio[23] confer a legal title on the possessor, because in both instances the property of the soil lay in the state. But with respect to the lands of private persons, the early Roman law[24] allowed possession to become property after a lapse of only two years, provided that the possession had not been obtained in the first instance[25] either by force or fraud. The object of this enactment was supposed to have been the speedy settlement of all questions of ownership;[26] one year's possession gave a right of property in a slave, or any other movable, and twice that time was thought sufficient for the owner of the land to establish his right against the occupier in a territory so small as that of Rome, unless through his own neglect. Probably, also, it was judged expedient to prevent the risk of any lands lying long uncultivated, by regarding land thus neglected as returned, in a manner, to a state of nature, and open to the first occupant. Another reason would sometimes operate strongly; the duty of keeping up the religious rites attached to particular places, which would fall into disuse during the absence of an owner. This feeling was so powerful in the case of the religious rites of particular families,[27] that if the heir neglected to enter upon his inheritance, another person might step in and take possession, and after the lapse of a single year, he acquired a legal title to the estate. But it cannot be doubted that the effect of this encouragement given to possession was favorable to the burghers, or patricians as we must now begin to call them, at the expense of the commons. The twelve tables[28] utterly denied the right of possession to a foreigner; against such a one the owner's title remained good forever. And although the commons were no longer regarded as altogether foreigners, yet they were still excluded from the right of occupying the public land; and we may be certain that they could neither take possession of the inheritance of a patrician, nor of any portion of his land on which there was any temple or altar; for it would have been a direct profanation, had a stranger ventured to perform the religious rites peculiar to his family and race. Besides, in point of fact, the patricians' lands were far less likely to be left open to occupation. A plebeian, whose land

[23] Provincialia prædia usucapionem non recipiunt. Gaius, II. § 46. It need not be repeated that the provinciale solum of Gaius' time, of which the property was vested only in the Roman people or the emperor, while individuals could only have the occupation and usufruct of it, was exactly in the condition of the ager publicus of the time of the XII. tables. Afterwards the distinction between provinciale and Italicum solum was done away by Justinian, and usucapio was admitted alike in each; but it could be completed not in two years, but, according to various circumstances, in ten, twenty, or thirty. See Justinian's Code, VII. Tit. 31. De usucapione transformandâ.

[24] Gaius, II. § 42. Ulpian, Fragm. XIX. § 8.

[25] Si modo eas bonâ fide acceperimus. Gaius, II. § 43. But even if the actual possessor acquired the possession of any thing bonâ fide, yet he could not acquire the property of it by prescription or usucapio, if it had been originally obtained by force or fraud; "si quis rem furtivam aut vi possessam possideat." Gaius, II. § 45.

[26] Ne rerum dominia diutius in incerto essent. Gaius, II. § 44.

[27] Gaius, II. § 53, 55. Voluerunt veteres maturius hereditates adiri ut essent qui sacra facerent, quorum illis temporibus summa observatio fuit.

[28] "Adversus hostem æterna auctoritas." Fragm. XII. Tabular. 19, apud Haubold. "Auctoritas" is the right of claiming our own property, to prevent another from acquiring it by prescription.

had been laid waste by the enemy, whose house had been burnt, and his sons killed or swept off by the plague, might often be actually unable to cultivate his property again, and might leave it in despair, to be possessed by the first person who chose to occupy it. Or if he were detained prisoner for debt in some patrician's prison, the same result might happen; his wife and children might seek protection with some relation or friend, and their home might thus be abandoned. And supposing justice to have been fairly administered, yet the delays of legal business, or the want of friends to undertake the cause, or the fear of provoking a powerful enemy, might often hinder the owner from making good his claim within two years, and so the property might be lost forever.

Distinctions as to various kinds of property. Res mancipii and nec mancipii.

As the Roman law attached no political power to landed property, so neither did it make a distinction between it and all other kinds of property, as to the formalities required in conveying it to another. Yet there was a distinction recognized; some things might be conveyed by bare delivery, a title to others could only be given by selling them with certain solemn formalities, known by the names of mancipatio and in jure cessio. This latter class[29] included not only land and houses, but also slaves, and all tame animals of draught or burden, and all these were classed under one common name, as res mancipii or mancipi; every other article of property was nec mancipii. The formality of mancipatio was one of the peculiar rights of Roman citizens;[30] no magistrate's presence was required, nor was there need of any written instrument: but five Roman citizens of an adult age were to be present as witnesses, and a sixth, called the weigher, or scalesman, was to produce a pair of scales to weigh the copper, which was, at this time, the only money in circulation. Then the purchaser laid his hand upon the thing which he was buying, and said, "This thing I declare to be mine according to the law of the Quirites; and I have bought it with this money duly weighed in these scales." In later times, when this form was still preserved, only slaves and animals were required to be literally seized by the purchaser; land might be disposed of at a distance.[31] But in the days of the decemviri, we cannot doubt that every sale of land by mancipatio was transacted on the spot, and that the purchaser laid his hand upon the house or ground which he was buying, no less than on the slave or the ox. The form called "in jure cessio" took place before a magistrate:[32] the purchaser claimed, "vindicavit," the purchase as his property; the seller, when asked by the magistrate if he disputed the claim, answered "that he did not;" and then the magistrate awarded the article in question to the purchaser or claimant. These transactions, by word of mouth only, without writing, were especially sanc-

Mancipi res sunt prædia in Italico solo—item jura prædiorum rusticorum, velut via, iter, actus, aquæductus; item servi et quadrupedes quæ dorso collove domantur, velut boves, muli, equi, asini. Cæteræ res nec mancipi sunt. Ulpian, Fragm. XIX. 1. It has been doubted whether this distinction was as old as the Twelve Tables (see Hugo, Geschichte des Röm. Rechts, p. 425); but it is, at any rate, recognized by the Cincian law, passed in the year 550 (see Hugo, p. 321), and was, in all probability, coeval with the earliest state of the Roman law, except as far as regards the jura prædiorum; for these, being res incorporales, could not pass by actual bodily seizure, and mancipatio no doubt always in its original meaning implied this. It may be conjectured that mancipatio was at first a matter of usage amongst the plebeian landowners, a method of effecting a purchase in the country before a man's immediate neighbors, without the necessity of his going up to Rome and transacting the business before a magistrate. If the law of the Twelve Tables gave a legal sanction to this mode of conveyance, and thus gratified the commons by recognizing their custom as law, we can understand why there should have been afterwards a sort of pride felt in the exercise of this right of mancipatio, and why it should have been kept as one of the peculiar rights of Roman citizens. And if it were originally the mode of conveyance practised by the plebeian landowners, we can account for its being restricted to land, and to what constituted the most valuable part of the live stock of land, slaves, horses, mules, asses, and oxen. In particular, we can thus understand why ships were res nec mancipii, because foreign commerce was wholly unknown to the agricultural commons, and ships were neither bought nor sold amongst them. I may observe that in the MS. published by Mai, entitled "De donationibus, ad legem Cinciam," we have the true form "res mancipii," instead of "mancipi." See Hugo, p. 321, and Niebuhr, Vol. I. p. 447. Note 1044.

[30] Gaius, I. § 119.

[31] Gaius, I. § 121.

[32] Gaius, II. § 24. Ulpian, Fragm. XIX. 9.

tioned by the twelve tables, which declared, that in buying and selling, "even as the tongue had spoken, so should be the law."[33]

The principle of the law of descent was that of qualified male succession without primogeniture.[34] All children who had not been emancipated[35] inherited their father's estate in equal portions, without distinction of sex or eldership. A man's wife, if she had fully come under his power (in manum convenerat), inherited as a daughter; and his son's children, if the son were dead, or had been emancipated,[36] succeeded to that son's share, and divided it equally amongst them; even the children of his son's son inherited on the same condition, if their father had ceased to be in his grandfather's power, either by death or by emancipation; but daughters' children, as belonging to another family, had no right of succession. All these were called a man's own heirs, "sui heredes;" and in default of these, his agnati,[37] or relations by the father's side, succeeded; the nearer excluding the more remote, and those in the same degree of relationship receiving equal shares. In default of agnati,[38] a man's inheritance went to the members of his gens.

Law of succession

III. The last division of the Roman private law relates to actions. "Legis actio" signifies, "the course of proceeding which the law prescribes to a man, in order to settle a dispute with his neighbor, or to obtain the redress of an injury." It stands opposed to all those acts of superstition or violence, by which the ignorance or passion of man has sought to obtain the same end; to the lot or the ordeal on the one hand, to the dagger of the assassin or the sword of the duellist on the other. But a proceeding at law, according to the notion of the decemvirs, was bound to follow the law to the very letter; nothing was understood of construction or of deductions, insomuch that he who brought an action against another for cutting down his *vines*[39] was held to have lost his cause, because the twelve tables forbade only the cutting down of *fruit trees* generally, without any particular mention of vines. The modes of action were five:[40] 1. Sacramento; 2. Per judicis postu-

III. Law of actions. Five sorts of actions.

[33] Quum nexum faciet mancipiumque, uti lingua nuncupassit ita jus esto. Fragm. XII. Tabular. 17, apud Haubold. See Dirksen, p. 397–406.

[34] I call it "qualified male succession," because although a man's daughters inherited along with his sons, yet his daughters' sons were altogether excluded, and his daughters, being under their brothers' guardianship, could not dispose of or devise their inheritance without their consent. By the Athenian law the sons alone inherited, but they were obliged to portion out their sisters, and public opinion would not allow this to be done niggardly.

[35] Gaius, III. § 2.

[36] The reason of this restriction was, that if the son were in his father's power, he was himself his father's heir, and his children were, of course, excluded; if he had lost his succession, either by death or by emancipation, then his children succeeded to his share as his representatives.

[37] Gaius, III. § 9, 10. By the law of the XII. tables, all relations by the father's side, whether male or female, were alike included under the title of agnati; but afterwards the meaning of the term was more limited, and female relations were excluded beyond the degree of a sister. A man's mother, if she had passed "in manum mariti," acquired the rights of a daughter, as regarded her husband, and thus was considered in the light of a sister to her son. See Justinian, Institutes, III. Tit. 2, § 3.

[38] Gaius, III. § 17. It is provoking that the part of Gaius' work, in which he had defined who were a man's "*gentiles*," is wholly illegible in the MS. It was to be found in his first book, between the 164th and 165th sections of the present division. There is no more difficult question in Roman law than to ascertain when and to what extent the plebeians acquired "jura gentilitatis." The whole institution of the gentes seems to have been essentially patrician; and it was the boast of the patricians, "se solos gentem habere," Livy, X. 8. Who, then, in the succession to the property of an intestate plebeian, stood in a position analogous to that of the members of his gens in the succession to the property of a patrician? For the noblest of the plebeian families, the Cæcilii, for instance, or the Decii, could have had no connection with any patrician gens such as subsisted between the plebeian and patrician Claudii, so that it does not appear who would have succeeded to the property of an intestate Cæcilius, in default of sui hæredes and agnati. Was it, as in the Athenian law, that cognati, a term which included relations by the mother's side as well as by the father's, were capable of inheriting? And if no relations at all were to be found, had the tribe any claim to the succession, or was the property considered to be wholly without an heir, and thus capable of being acquired by a stranger by occupation, possessio, and two years' prescription, usucapio? In this case there would be a possibility of the property of a plebeian being acquired by a patrician, whereas, so long as there existed a single member of his gens, the property of a patrician could never be without a patrician heir.

[39] Gaius, IV. § 11.

[40] Gaius, IV. § 12.

lationem; 3. Per condictionem; 4. Per manus injectionem; 5. Per pignoris captionem.

1st Action: sacramento.

1. The first[41] of these was the most generally adopted where no other specific action was prescribed by law. The contending parties each staked a certain sum of money, "sacramentum," on the issue of their suit, five hundred ases, if the value of the disputed property amounted to one thousand ases or more; and fifty, if it fell below that sum. Only if the suit related to the establishing of the freedom of any one claimed as a slave,[42] the sacramentum was fixed at the lower sum of fifty ases, lest his friends might be deterred from asserting his liberty, by the greatness of the sum they would have to forfeit if they failed in proving it. For the party who lost his cause forfeited his stake besides, and it went not to the other party, but to the state. Accordingly, the magistrate having named a judge to try the cause, the parties appeared before him, and first briefly stated to him the nature of their respective claims. Then the object in dispute, if it were any thing capable of moving or being moved, was brought into court also, and the plaintiff, holding a rod or wand in one hand,[43] and laying hold of the object which he claimed with the other, asserted that it belonged to him according to the law of the Quirites, and then laid his rod upon it. The defendant did the same, and asserted his own right to it in the same form of words. Then the judge bade them both to loose their hold, and this being done, the plaintiff turned to the defendant, and said, "Wilt thou tell me wherefore thou hast claimed this thing as thine?" The other answered, "I have fulfilled what right requires, even as I have made my claim." Then the plaintiff rejoined, "Since thou hast made thy claim wrongfully, I defy thee at law; and I stake five hundred ases on the issue." To which the defendant replied, "In like manner, and with a like stake, do I also defy thee." Then the judge awarded possession of the object in dispute to one or other of the parties till the cause should be decided, and called upon him to give security to his adversary, "litis et vindiciarum," that is, that he would make good to him both the thing itself, "litem," and the benefit arising from his temporary possession of it, "vindicias," if the cause were finally decided against him. Both parties also gave security to the judge that their stake, or sacramentum, should be duly paid. But if the dispute related to the personal freedom of any man, whether he were to be adjudged to be a slave or a freeman, the twelve tables expressly ordered that the vindiciæ, or temporary possession,[44] should be awarded in favor of freedom, that the man should remain at liberty, till it were proved that he was lawfully a slave. I have given all these details, partly from their affording so curious an illustration of the legal proceedings of the fourth century of Rome, partly from the light which they throw on the famous story of Virginia, presently to be related, and partly also from their novelty; our whole knowledge of the old actions at law being derived from the Institutes of Gaius, which in their entire and original form were first discovered by Niebuhr at Verona, in the year 1816.

2d and 3d Actions: Per judicis postulationem and Per condictionem.

2. 3. The account of the second and third modes of action has been lost out of the MS. of Gaius, so that we can neither fully understand their nature, nor how they differed from one another. So far as we can judge, the latter, actio per condictionem, appears to have been a sort of serving a notice on the adversary, calling on him to appear at the end of thirty days, to submit his cause to the judge. The former, per postula-

[41] Gaius, IV. § 13-17.

[42] In the case of a slave's liberty, it was not necessary that the person who brought the question to issue should have any connection with the slave, or any personal interest for him: it was the duty, or rather the privilege, of every man to save a freeman from the perpetual loss of his liberty. "In his quæ asserantur in libertatem, quivis lege agere potest." Livy, III. 45.

[43] "Festucam tenebat." This was apparently a rod or wand, as Gaius says afterwards, "Festucâ autem utebantur quasi hastæ loco, signo quodam justi dominii," § 16. It cannot, therefore, signify the wisp of straw or chaff, which Plutarch says was thrown on a slave when he received his liberty. See Facciolati in Festucâ.

[44] Vindiciæ secundum libertatem. See Livy, III. 44, 45.

tionem judicis, was an application to the magistrate that he would name a judge to try the matter in dispute.

4. The summary process, per manus injectionem, was allowed by the twelve tables[45] as a method of enforcing the fulfilment of the judge's sentence. If the defendant, after having lost his cause, and having been sentenced to pay a certain sum to the plaintiff, had neglected to do so, the plaintiff might lay actual hands on him, and unless he could find a vindex, or defender, to plead his cause for him, he being himself not allowed to do it, he was dragged to the plaintiff's house, and there kept in chains till he had paid all that was due from him.

4th Action: Per manus injectionem.

5. Lastly, the action per pignoris captionem[46] was a rude method of distress, in which a man was allowed, in certain cases, to compel his adversary to pay him what he owed him by carrying off articles of his property as a pledge. In some instances it rested solely on old unwritten custom, such as that which allowed the soldier,[47] if his pay were withheld, to distrain in this manner upon the goods of the officer whose business it was to give it him. The twelve tables allowed it in cases connected with religious worship; as, for instance, it was permitted against him who had bought a sheep or an ox for sacrifice, and had not paid for it; or against him who had not paid for the hire of a beast, which the owner had let for the very purpose of getting money to enable him to offer a sacrifice himself. In the first case, there was an impiety in a man's offering to the gods that which was not his own; in the second, the gods themselves were defrauded of their sacrifice, inasmuch as their worshipper was deprived of the means to offer it.

5th Action: Per pignoris captionem.

I have purposely postponed my notice of one part of the law, that which relates to obligations, because it affords an easy transition to another branch of the subject, the criminal law of the twelve tables; inasmuch as several offences, which we regard as crimes, or public wrongs, were by the Romans classed under the head of private wrongs, and the compensation which the offender was bound to make to the injured party, followed from one species of civil obligation, technically called obligationes ex delicto.

Law of obligations.

Over and above our general duties to our fellow-citizens, we put ourselves often, by our own voluntary act, under certain new and specific obligations towards them, either from some particular engagement contracted with them, or from our having done them some wrong. In the first case, there arises an obligation to fulfil our agreement; in the second, an obligation to repair our injustice. Hence the Roman law[48] divided all legal obligations into those arising from engagement, ex contractu, and those arising from a wrong committed, ex delicto.

Obligations ex contractu and ex delicto.

I. It will not be necessary to go minutely into the subdivisions of the former of these two classes of obligations. To the head of obligationes re contractæ belonged the law of debtor and creditor: the mere fact of having borrowed money[49] constituted the obligation to pay it, without any promise to that effect, verbal or written,[50] on the part of the borrower. But as the remarkable provisions of the law of the twelve tables, with regard to debtors, have been already noticed, it will not be needful to state them

I. Obligations ex contractu. Debts, interest of money.

[45] Gaius, IV. § 21–25.

[46] Gaius, IV. § 26–29. With regard to the orthography of the word, the text of Gaius varies, exhibiting in one passage the form "captionem," § 12, and in another that of "capionem," § 26. If the expression be made one single word, the form would be pignoriscapio. See Cato, as quoted by Gellius, Noct. Att. VII. 10.

[47] Gaius, IV. § 27.

[48] Gaius, III. § 88.

[49] Or any thing else which can be weighed, counted, or measured. This was called "mutuum," when the thing, whatever it be, is given to another for his use, with the understanding that he shall return to us hereafter not that very same thing, but one of the same nature and quality. "Commodatum" expressed that which is lent to another, with the understanding that the very same thing shall be restored to us again.

[50] The English law considers an obligatio re contracta as an implied contract; such a contract "as reason and justice dictate, and which, therefore, the law presumes that every man undertakes to perform." Blackstone, Comment. Book II. c. 30, § IX.

again. One part, however, of the engagements of debtors, their being bound to pay the interest as well as the principal of their debt, belonged to obligations of another class, those contracted by direct words of covenant; for whereas the payment of the principal was an obligation re contracta, the payment of interest was a matter of distinct stipulation between the contracting parties.[51] Yet although this may seem to be as much a matter of voluntary bargain as any dealing between man and man, still the contracting parties meet often on so unequal a footing, and the weaker is so little in a condition either to gain more favorable terms, or to do without the aid of which they are the price, that legislators have generally interfered either to prohibit such engagements altogether, or at any rate to prevent the stronger party from making an exorbitant use of his advantages; they have either made all interest of money illegal, or have fixed a maximum to its amount. Accordingly, the decemvirs, while they enforced the payment of debts with such fearful severity, thought themselves bound to save the debtor, if possible, from the burden of an extravagant interest; they forbade any thing higher than unciarium fœnus,[52] an expression which has been variously interpreted as meaning, in our language, either one per cent., or cent. per cent.; but which, according to Niebuhr,[53] signifies a yearly interest of one-twelfth, or eight and one-third per cent.; and this, being calculated for the old cyclic year of ten months, would give ten per cent. for the common year of twelve months, which was in ordinary use in the time of the decemvirs. This, according to our notions, is sufficiently high; yet the common rate of interest at Athens, at this time, was twelve per cent.;[54] and Niebuhr observes, that from this period forward for sixty years, till the distress which followed the Gaulish invasion, we hear no more of the misery of insolvent debtors.

Obligations arising from the force of certain peculiar words or forms.

A third class of obligations,[55] ex contractu, contained all promises or covenants expressed in a certain form of words; and here the Roman law acknowledged such only to be legally binding as were concluded in the form of question and answer. The party with whom the covenant was made asked him who made it, "Dost thou engage to do so and so?" And he answered, "I do engage." It is a curious circumstance, that as the Romans had a peculiar form of sale, mancipatio, which none but Roman citizens might use, so also they had one peculiar word to express an engagement, which was binding only on Roman citizens, and lost its force even on them if translated into another language. This favorite word was *spondeo.*[56] A Roman might make a binding covenant with a foreigner in any language which both parties understood; if it were drawn up in Latin, the words promitto, dabo, faciam, or any others to the like effect, retained their natural and reasonable force, and constituted an agreement recognized by law; but if he used the word spondeo, or its supposed equivalent, in any other language, the engagement was null and void. This, undoubtedly, is to be referred to the religious origin of

[51] Gibbon, Vol. VIII. chap. xliv. p. 85, 8vo. ed. 1807, considers the payment of interest to follow from an obligation ex consensu, and to come under the general head of letting and hiring, locatio and conductio, inasmuch as interest may be considered as the hire paid for the temporary use of money. The view given in the text is that of Heineccius, III. 15, § 6, and of Hugo, Geschichte des Röm. Rechts, p. 230, Ed. 9.

[52] Tacitus, Annal. VI. 16. "Duodecim tabulis sanctum, ne quis unciario fœnore amplius exerceret." Now, the uncia being the well-known twelfth part of the Roman as, or pound, and the heavy copper coinage of the old times being still the standard at Rome, unciarium fœnus would be a very natural expression for "interest of an ounce in the pound," that is, of a twelfth part of the sum borrowed. Thus, at Athens we have τόκος ἐπίτριτος, τόκος ἔφεκτος, &c., to express respectively "Interest of a third and of a sixth part of the sum borrowed." And as the Greek expressions denote the interest for a year, although interest was, in fact, paid every month, so the unciarium fœnus, in like manner, may mean interest of a twelfth part, or eight and one third per cent. per annum, although a part of it was at Rome also paid monthly.

[53] See his chapter "über den Unzialzinsfuss," in the third volume of his history, p. 61.

[54] See Böckh, "Staatshaushaltung der Athener," Vol. I. p. 143. In Demosthenes' time, twelve per cent. at Athens was considered low.

[55] "Obligationes verbis contractæ." Gaius, III. 92.

[56] Gaius, III. § 93.

the term; it is clearly connected with σπένδω, and denoted, probably, an oath taken with the sanction of certain peculiar rites, such as a stranger could not witness without profanation. We may be sure that *sponcleo* was a word as peculiar to the patricians originally as it was afterwards to the united Roman people of patricians and commoners: there was a time when it could have been no more used in a covenant with a plebeian, than it was afterwards allowed to be addressed to a Greek or an Egyptian.

II. Obligationes ex delicto. Law of theft and law of libel.

II. The second division of obligations included those which arise from our having wronged our neighbor, the obligation of making good, or making reparation for, the injury which we have done. We may injure either the person, or the property, or, thirdly, the feelings and character of another. 1. Injuries[57] to the person were divided by the twelve tables into three classes. α. If a limb or any member were irreparably injured, the law ordered retaliation, "eye for eye, tooth for tooth," unless the injured party chose to accept of any other satisfaction. β. If a bone were broken or crushed, the offender was to pay three hundred ases. γ. And all other bodily injuries were compensated by the payment of twenty-five ases. The poverty of the times, says Gaius, made these money penalties seem sufficiently heavy; but twenty-five ases could never have been a very heavy penalty to the majority of the patricians; and such a law was well calculated to encourage the outrages which Kæso and his associates and imitators were in the habit of committing against the poorer citizens. 2. Injuries[58] against property, on the other hand, were visited severely. A thief in the night[59] might be lawfully slain; or by day,[60] if he defended himself with a weapon. If a thief was caught in the fact, he was to be scourged and given over,[61] addicebatur, to the man whom he had robbed; and the lawyers doubted whether he was only to be kept in chains by the injured party till he had made restitution, probably fourfold, or whether he was to be his slave forever. Theft not caught in the fact was punished with twofold restitution.[62] If a man wanted to search a neighbor's house for stolen goods, he was to search naked,[63] with only a girdle round his loins, and holding a large dish or platter upon his head with both his hands; and if he found his goods, then the thief was to be punished as one caught in the fact. 3. But in no provision of the twelve tables does the aristocratical spirit of their authors appear more manifest than in the extreme severity with which they visited attacks upon character, and in the large extent of their definition of a punishable libel. They declared it an offence for which[64] a man should be visited with one of their heaviest

[57] Gaius, III. § 223.

[58] Gaius, III. § 189.

[59] "Sei nox furtum factum esit, sei im occisit joure caisus esto." Fragm. XII. Tabular. § 10, apud Haubold.

[60] Gaius, ad edictum provinciale, quoted in the Digest, XLVII. De furtis, l. 54, § 2.

[61] Gaius, III, § 189.

[62] Gaius, III, § 190.

[63] Gaius, III. 192, 193. The notion of this strange law was, that the man who searched, by being naked, and having his hands occupied, could not conceal any thing about him, which he might leave secretly in his neighbor's house, and then charge him with theft. It is curious that this extraordinary custom seems to have existed also at Athens. See the following passage from the Clouds of Aristophanes, v. 497, ed. Dindorf.

ΣΩΚΡΑΤΕΣ.—Ἴθι νυν, κατάθου θοἰμάτιον.
ΣΤΡΕΨΙΑΔΗΣ. ἠδίκηκά τί;
ΣΩΚΡ. οὔκ, ἀλλὰ γυμνοὺς εἰσιέναι νομίζεται.
ΣΤΡΕΨ. ἀλλ' οὐχὶ φωράσων ἔγωγ' εἰσέρχομαι.

[64] There have been various opinions as to the precise penalty awarded to libels in the twelve tables. The foundation of our knowledge on this subject, is the passage quoted by Augustine (de Civit. Dei, II. 9), from the fourth book of Cicero's treatise, De Republicâ. "Duodecim tabulæ cum perpaucas res capite sanxissent, in his hanc quoque sanciendam putaverunt, si quis occentavisset, sive carmen condidisset, quod infamiam faceret flagitiumve alteri." And Augustine in another place, II. 12, referring to this passage, expresses what he supposed to be its meaning in his own words thus: "Capite plectendum sancientes tale carmen condere si quis auderet." Augustine, living in an age when capital punishments, in our sense of the term, were common, understands Cicero's words as signifying the "punishment of death." But in Cicero's time, when the punishment of death was, so far as Roman citizens were concerned, unknown to the law, the expressions, capite sancire, and res capitalis, generally, as is well known, have a milder meaning, and caput refers to the civil rather than to the natural life of a citizen. Thus Gaius says expressly, "Pœna manifesti furti ex lege XII. tabularum capitalis erat," III. § 189. And then he goes on, "*Nam*

punishments, involving a diminutio capitis, if he publicly uttered in word or writing any thing that tended to bring disgrace upon his neighbor. Cicero refers to this law, as proving the existence of something of a literature in the times of the decemvirs; and he contrasts it with the license enjoyed by the comic poets at Athens. No doubt satirical songs are sufficiently ancient, and these were the literature which the decemvirs dreaded; the coarse jests which were uttered in the Fescennine verses, and which were allowed, as at a kind of Saturnalia, to the soldiers who followed their general in his triumph. But the effect of this law was to make the ancient poetry of Rome merely laudatory; and afterwards, when prose compositions began, they caught the same infection. If the poet Nævius could be persecuted by the powerful family of the Metelli, and obliged to leave Rome for no severer satire than his famous line, "Fato Romæ fiunt Metelli consules," we may readily understand how little an humble writer, in recording the actions of a great patrician house, would dare to speak of them truly. And hence it has happened that the falsehood of the Roman annals is so deeply rooted, and that there is scarcely an eminent person in the Roman history who is spoken of otherwise than in terms of respect. It may be said that the license of Athenian comedy spared neither the innocence of Nicias, nor the pure and heroic virtue of Pericles. But has history, therefore, done justice to their merit? And how different is the value of praise when given, on the one hand, by the free pens of the great historians of Greece, and on the other, by that uniform adulation which saw, even in Marius and Sulla, more matter for admiration than for abhorrence!

Penal law.

All the offences hitherto enumerated were considered as private rather than public wrongs; and if they were in any case punished capitally, it was rather that the law allowed the injured party to take into his own hands the extremest measure of vengeance, than that the criminal suffered death in consequence of the deliberate sentence of the judge. But some offences were regarded as crimes, or public wrongs in the strictest sense; they were tried, either by the people in the comitia of centuries, or by judges, like the quæstores parricidii, specially appointed by the people. Of this sort were parricide,[65]

liber verberatus addicebatur ei cui furtum fecerat." On the other hand, not to insist on Horace's line, "Vertere modum formidine fustis," Cornutus, the scholiast on Persius, says expressly, "Lege XII. tabularum cautum est, ut *fustibus feriretur*, qui publice invehebatur," &c. Yet still there is another question, for the military punishment of the fustuarium was notoriously often fatal; and it may be, that the expression "fusti ferire," included even a beating to death. Thus we read of Egnatius Metellus, "qui uxorem fuste percussam interemit," Valer. Max. VI. 3, § 9, where the words fuste percussam are, I think, meant to describe the manner of the death, rather than a punishment inflicted previously to the capital one. And yet fustigatio, in the estimate of the later law, was a milder punishment than flagellatio; and the Digest calls it "fustigationis admonitio."—See Heineccius, IV. 18, § 7.

If we look to the later law, in order to learn what was then the punishment of libel, we shall find that, according to Ulpian (Digest. De injur. et famosis libellis, l. 5, § 9), the libeller was to be intestabilis, that is, he could neither give evidence in a court of justice, nor make a will. And in the somewhat vague language of the Theodosian Code, IX. 34, § 10, libellers are to dread "ultorem suis cervicibus gladium." But "famosi libelli," in the Theodosian Code, means, perhaps, something different from the libellous carmina of the XII. tables.

On the whole, it is certain that the punishment of a libeller involved in it a diminutio capitis, and was thus, in the Roman sense of the term, capital. It may be, also, that the sentence "ut fuste ferietur," not being limited with the careful humanity of the Jewish law, was, when executed with severity, fatal; and that a man who had thus died under his punishment was considered as jure cæsus. It might thus be truly said, that libels were punished capitally, in the later sense of the term, if the punishment might, in fact, be made to amount to a sentence of death, at the discretion of those who inflicted it. But the law meant only, that the libeller should be beaten, and incur also a diminutio capitis; and this was sufficiently severe, when we find that the most grievous bodily injuries, although visited by punishment in kind, yet did not involve any forfeiture of civil rights.

65 Every one knows the famous punishment of the parricide, that he should be scourged, then sewn up in a sack, in company with a dog, a viper, and a monkey, and thrown into the sea. But it is not certain that this was a law of the twelve tables. Cicero mentions only the sewing up of the parricide in a sack, and throwing him into the river. And he merely says, "Majores nostri supplicium in parricidas singulare excogitaverunt," pro Roscio Amerino, 25. It may have been a traditional punishment, older than even the twelve tables. So, again, nothing is known of the law of the twelve tables respecting murder. Pliny only

and probably all murder, arson,[66] false witness,[67] injuring a neighbor's corn by night,[68] witchcraft,[69] and treason.[70] The punishment for these crimes was death, either by beheading, hanging, throwing the criminal from the Tarpeian rock, or in some cases by burning alive. This last mode of execution was adjudged by the twelve tables to the crime of arson: but a memorial has been preserved by the lawyers, confirmatory of the story already mentioned of the execution of the nine adversaries of the consul T. Sicinius, that there was a time when burning alive was the punishment of enemies and deserters.[71] The "enemies" here meant could not have been merely foreigners taken in war, for their punishment could have found no place in the civil or domestic law of Rome; they must rather have been those Roman traitors who, according to a form preserved till the latest period of the commonwealth, were solemnly declared to be enemies of their country.

Law of bail.

When we read of capital punishments denounced by the Roman law, and yet hear of the worst criminals remaining at liberty till the very end of their trial, and being allowed to escape their sentence by going into voluntary banishment, we are inclined to ask whether the law meant to threaten merely, and never to strike an offender. Niebuhr has explained this seeming contradiction with his usual sagacity; it will be enough to say here, that although the Roman law, like the old law of England, did not refuse bail for a man accused of treason or felony,[72] yet it was by no means a matter of course that it should be granted; and ordinary criminals, at least in these early times, were, in the regular course of things, committed to prison to abide their trial, nearly with as much certainty as in England.

Constitutional law.

And now we come to the constitutional law of the twelve tables, a subject almost of greater interest than the common law, but one involved in much greater obscurity. Four or five enactments alone have been preserved to us: 1. That there should be an appeal to the people[73] from the sentence of every magistrate. 2. That all capital trials[74] should be conducted before the comitia of the centuries. 3. That privilegia,[75] or acts of pain and penalties against an individual, should be unlawful. 4. That the last decision[76] of the people should supersede all former decisions on the same subject. 5. That the debtor whose person and property were pledged to his creditor, nexus,[77] and

says that the turning cattle into a neighbor's corn by night was punished by the twelve tables more severely than murder; insomuch as the offender was hanged up as devoted to Ceres, and so put to death. Histor. Natur. XVIII. 3. Of course murder was punished, and probably with death; but the criminal was beheaded, we may suppose, and this would be considered as a less punishment than hanging.

[66] Gaius, IV. ad Leg. XII. tabularum apud Digest. XLVII. Tit. IX. § 9. De incendio, ruinâ, naufragio.

[67] Aulus Gellius, XX. 1.

[68] Pliny, Hist. Natur. XVIII. 3.

[69] Pliny, Hist. Natur. XXVIII. 2.

[70] Digest. XLVIII. Tit. VI. § 2. Ad Legem Juliam Majestatis.

[71] Digest. XLVIII. Tit. XIX. De pœnis, l. 8, § 2. Hostes autem item transfugæ eâ pœnâ afficiuntur, ut vivi exurantur. Godefroy remarks that we never read of enemies so punished, and some have proposed to read "hostes, *i. e.* transfugæ," as if deserters alone were intended. I believe that the common reading is right, but that it relates, as I have observed, to the Romans, who were declared enemies of their country. That a foreign enemy, however, might be sometimes so treated, is not impossible, as is shown by the story of Cyrus' treatment of Crœsus.

[72] "By the ancient common law all felonies were bailable." Blackstone, Vol. IV. p. 298. The statute law has greatly restricted this power, so far, at least, as justices of the peace are concerned; for "the court of King's bench may bail for any crime whatsoever, be it treason, murder, or any other offence." Blackstone, IV. p. 299. This last doctrine, however, was contested by Junius, in his famous letter to Lord Mansfield, in which he contends, agreeably to the notion of the Greek and Roman law, that no power could bail a thief taken with the manner, that is, with the thing stolen upon him. In cases of crimes committed by persons of high birth, like Kæso Quinctius, the being allowed to offer bail was a means of evading justice; and so it was found to be in England, before parliament interfered to amend the common law. But humble and ordinary criminals would not equally be allowed to profit by it.

[73] Cicero, de Republicâ, II. 31.

[74] Cicero, de Legibus, III. 19.

[75] Cicero, de Legibus, III. 19.

[76] Livy, VII. 17; IX. 34.

[77] See Festus in "Sanates."—But it is right to say that the sentence has been conjecturally restored by Scaliger, all the words actually remaining in the MS. being these, which I have printed in the Roman character:

in xii nexo *solutoque*
forti sanati*que idem jus esto*.

he who remained the free master of both, solutus, should be equal in the sight of the law; that is, that the nexus should not be considered to be infamis. And the same legal equality is given, also, to the fortis and the sanas;[78] terms which were merely guessed at in the Augustan age, and which it is hopeless to attempt to understand now. A sixth enactment is expressly ascribed to the last two tables, which Cicero described as full of unequal laws,[79] namely, that between the burghers and the commons there should be no legal marriages; if a burgher married the daughter of a plebeian, his children followed their mother's condition, and were not subject to their father, nor could inherit from him if he died intestate.

The constitutional changes effected by the decemvirs were probably not contained in the twelve tables.

With no further knowledge than of these mere fragments, we can judge but little of the tenor of the whole law; but yet, if we had the entire text of the twelve tables before us, we should probably find in them[80] no direct mention of the great constitutional changes which the decemvirs are, with reason, supposed to have effected. Their code of laws was the expression of their legislative, rather than of their constituent power; it contained the rules hereafter to be observed by the Roman people, but would not notice those previous organic changes by which the very composition, so to speak, of the people itself, was so greatly altered.

These changes were wrought by virtue of that particular branch of their sovereign power, which was afterwards perpetuated in the censorship. When we

The words in Italics, which complete the lines, were supplied by Scaliger. It has already been mentioned, Chap. XIII. note 89, that the only existing MS. of Festus has suffered from a fire, by which half of many of the pages has been burnt away vertically from top to bottom, so that every line is left mutilated.

[78] Our whole knowledge of this enactment is derived from the mutilated article in Festus, on the word "Sanates." The epitome of Paulus gives a foolish etymology, and says that the Sanates were people dwelling above and below Rome, who first revolted, but soon afterwards returned to their duty, and were called "Sanates:" "quasi sanatâ mente." And the "Fortes," according to Paulus, were "boni qui nunquam defecerant a populo Romano." This is all improbable enough; but Niebuhr says that the terms sanas and fortis must probably be understood either of bondmen and freemen, or of those who had hitherto been vassals in the ancient colonial towns, and the colonists. It is impossible, in the present state of our knowledge, to give any thing more certain on the subject.

[79] Cicero, de Republicâ, II. 37.

[80] The twelve tables were extant down to the latest age of Roman literature, and their contents were familiarly known. Had they contained, therefore, many regulations of a constituent cast, such, for instance, as related to the powers of the several orders in the state, to the enrolment of the burghers and their clients in the tribes, the Roman writers could not possibly have showed such great ignorance of the early state of their constitution, as they have done actually. On one point, however, on which the twelve tables appear to have spoken expressly, the practice and the law in after times may seem to have been at variance. I allude to the famous provision, "De capite civis nisi per maximum comitiatum ne ferunto," a provision which appears to make the centuries the sole criminal court, and to require that every ordinary felon should be tried before them; which we know was not the case, and would have been, in fact, absurd and impossible. But, in the first place, the institution of the judices selecti, in later times, was intended to be a sort of representation of the whole people for judicial purposes; so that a condemnation by these judges was final, and could not be appealed against, like the sentence of a magistrate (Cicero, Philipp. I. c. 9). And, again, there was taken out of the jurisdiction of the centuries all those cases of flagrant and evident guilt, which, according to the Roman notions, needed no trial at all. The difference in the penalty affixed to the crimes of furtum manifestum and nec manifestum, is very remarkable: in the former case, the thief was scourged and given over, addictus, to the party whom he had injured; in the latter case he had only to restore twofold. So the man who attacked his neighbor in satirical songs, the murderer caught "red hand," the incendiary detected in setting fire to his neighbor's house or corn, would, like the fur manifestus, be hurried off at once to condign punishment, and all trial would be held unnecessary. And the same summary justice would be dealt to the false witness and to the rioter. It is probable, also, that the magistrates, using that large discretion which the practice of Rome gave them, would punish summarily crimes as to which the guilt of the accused was perfectly clear, even though he might not have been caught in the fact. When it is further remembered, that slaves and strangers were wholly subject to the magistrates' jurisdiction, and that there are states of society in which crimes of a serious description are extremely rare, it may be conceived that the criminal business of the centuries would not be very engrossing.

However, if M. Manlius was, as Niebuhr thinks, tried and condemned by the comitia of curiæ, and not by the centuries, it would have been a direct violation of the law of the twelve tables. But the story of Manlius, as we shall see hereafter, is too uncertain to be argued upon; and it will not, perhaps, be found necessary to suppose that he was really sentenced by the curiæ.

find the censor Q. Maximus[81] annihilating at once the political influence of a great portion of the people, by confining all freedmen to four tribes only; when we read of another censor, M. Livius,[82] disfranchising the whole Roman people, with the exception of one single tribe, an exercise of power so extravagant indeed as to destroy itself, yet still, so far as appears, perfectly legal, we can scarcely understand how any liberty could be consistent with such an extraordinary prerogative vested in the magistrate. But if common censors in ordinary times possessed such authority, much more would it be enjoyed by the decemviri. They therefore altered the organization of the Roman people at their discretion; the clients of the burghers, and even the burghers themselves, were enrolled in the tribes; and the list of citizens was probably increased by the addition of a great number of freedmen, and of the inhabitants of the oldest Roman colonies, mostly the remains of the times of the monarchy. But whether it was at this time that the comitia of centuries assumed that form in which alone they existed in the historical period of Rome, whether the tribes were now introduced to vote on the Field of Mars as well as in the Forum, is a question not to be answered. We may be more sure that whilst the patricians were admitted into the tribes of the commons, they still retained their own comitia of curiæ, and their power of confirming the election of every magistrate by conferring on him the imperium, and of voting upon every law which had been passed by the tribes or centuries.

They were effected by virtue of their censorian power.

But Niebuhr has further conjectured that the decemvirs were intended to be a perpetual magistracy, like the archons at Athens in their original constitution; that the powers afterwards divided amongst the military tribunes, the censors, and the quæstores parricidii, were to be united in a college of ten officers, chosen half from the patricians, and half from the plebeians, and to remain in office for five years. And as the plebeians were thus admitted to an equal share in the government, the tribunitian power, intended specially to protect them from the oppression of the government, was no longer needed, and therefore, as Niebuhr supposes, the tribuneship was not to exist in the future constitution.

Conjectures of Niebuhr as to the permanency of the decemvirate.

Niebuhr's conjectures in Roman history are almost like a divination, and must never be passed over without notice. But as the decemvirate, whether intended to be temporary or perpetual, was soon overthrown, it does not seem necessary to enter further into the question; and the common story appears to me to contain in it nothing improbable. Its details, doubtless, are traditional, and are full of the variations of traditional accounts; still they are not like the mere poetical stories of Cincinnatus or Coriolanus, and therefore I shall proceed to give the account of the second decemvirate, of the tyranny of Appius and the death of Virginia, not as giving full credit to every circumstance, but as considering it, to use the language of Thucydides, as being in the main sufficiently deserving of belief.

[81] Livy, IX. 46.

[82] Livy, XXIX. 37.

CHAPTER XV.

THE SECOND DECEMVIRATE—STORY OF VIRGINIA—REVOLUTION OF 305.

Μάλιστα εὐλαβεῖσθαι δεῖ τοὺς ὑβρίζεσθαι νομίζοντας, ἢ αὐτούς, ἢ ὧν κηδόμενοι τυγχάνουσιν· ἀφειδῶς γὰρ ἑαυτῶν ἔχουσιν οἱ διὰ θυμὸν ἐπιχειροῦντες.—ARISTOTLE, Politica, V. 11.

Decemvirs are elected for a second year. Appius Claudius.

THE first decemvirs, according to the general tradition[1] of the Roman annalists, governed uprightly and well, and their laws of the ten tables were just and good. All parties were so well pleased, that it was resolved to continue the same government at least for another year; the more so as some of the decemvirs declared that their work was not yet complete, and that two tables still required to be added. And now the most eminent of the patricians,[2] L. Quinctius Cincinnatus, T. Quinctius Capitolinus, and C. Claudius, became candidates for the decemvirate; but the commons had little reason to place confidence in any of them, and might well be afraid to trust unlimited power in their hands. Appius Claudius, on the contrary, had been tried, and had been found seemingly trustworthy: he and his colleagues had used their power moderately, and had done their duty as lawgivers impartially; and such men were more to be trusted than the well-known supporters of the old ascendency of the burghers. Appius availed himself of this feeling, and exerted himself strenuously to procure his re-election. But his colleagues, now becoming jealous of him, contrived[3] that he should himself preside at the comitia for the election of the new decemvirs; it being considered one of the duties of the officer who presided at, or, in Roman language, who held the comitia, to prevent the re-election of the same man to the same office two successive years, by refusing to receive votes in his favor if offered: and most of all would he be expected to prevent it, when the man to be re-elected was himself. But the people might remember, that within the last few years they had owed to the repeated re-election of the same tribunes some of their greatest privileges; and that then, as now, the patricians had earnestly endeavored to prevent it. They therefore elected Appius Claudius to the decemvirate for the second time, and, passing over all his former colleagues, and all the high aristocratical candidates, they elected with him four patricians, and, as Niebuhr thinks, five plebeians. The patricians[4] were M. Cornelius Maluginensis, whose brother had been consul nine years before; M. Sergius, of whom nothing is known; L. Minucius, who had been consul in the year 296, and Q. Fabius Vibulanus, who had been already thrice consul, in 287, 289, and 295. Kæso Duilius, Sp. Oppius Cornicen, and Q. Pœtelius, are expressly said by Dionysius to have been plebeians; and we know of none but plebeian families of the first and last of these names, nor, with one single exception,[5] of the second. The remaining two decemvirs were T. Antonius Merenda, and M. Rabuleius, and these we should judge from their names to have

[1] Livy, III. 33, 34.

[2] Livy, III. 35.

[3] Livy, III. 35.

[4] Livy, III. 35. Dionysius, X. 58.

[5] A vestal virgin of the name of Oppia is mentioned in the annals of the year 271 (Livy, II. 42), and she must have been a patrician. Nor is it improbable that there was, in the times of the decemviri, a patrician as well as a plebeian family of Duilii, just as there were patrician and plebeian Sicinii. And the same may be said of the Pœtelii, Antonii, and Rabuleii; and the patrician branches of these families may have become extinct long before the time when their names became famous in history. Livy seems to have regarded the decemviri as all patricians; and if their names had presented a manifest proof of the contrary, he surely must have been aware of it, the more so as the plebeian Duilius acts an important part in his narrative of this very period.

been plebeians also; but Dionysius distinguishes them from the three preceding them, and classes them with three of the patrician decemvirs, merely as men of no great personal distinction.

Their tyranny.

Experience has shown that even popular leaders, when intrusted with absolute power, have often abused it to the purposes of their own tyranny, yet these have commonly remained so far true to their old principles as zealously to abate the mischiefs of aristocracy; and thus they have done scarcely less good in destroying what was evil, than evil in withholding what was good. But to give absolute power to an aristocratical leader is an evil altogether unmixed. An aristocracy is so essentially the strongest part of society, that a despot is always tempted to court its favor; and if he is bound to it by old connections, and has always fought in its cause, this tendency becomes irresistible. So it was with Appius: the instant that he had secured his election, he reconciled himself with his old party,[6] and labored to convince the patricians that not their own favorite candidates, the Quinctii, or his own kinsman, C. Claudius, could have served their cause more effectually than himself. Accordingly the decemvirate rested entirely on the support of the patricians. The associations or clubs,[7] Kæso's old accomplices, were the tools and sharers of the tyranny; even the better patricians forgave the excesses[8] of their party for joy at its restored ascendency; the consulship, instead of being controlled, as the commons had fondly hoped, by fresh restraints, was released even from those which had formerly held it; instead of two consuls, there were now ten, and these no longer shackled by the Valerian law, nor kept in check by the tribuneship, but absolute, with more than the old kingly sovereignty. Now, indeed, said the patricians, the expulsion of the Tarquins was a real gain; hitherto it had been purchased by some painful condescensions to the plebeians, and the growing importance of those half aliens had impaired the majesty of what was truly Rome. But this was at an end; and by a just judgment upon their insolence, the very revolution which they had desired was become their chastisement; and the decemvirate, which had been designed to level all the rights of the patricians, was become the instrument of restoring to them their lawful ascendency.

They add two tables to complete the code of the twelve tables.

The decemvirate seems, indeed, to have exhibited the perfect model of an aristocratical royalty,[9] vested not in one person, but in several, held not for life, but for a single year, and therefore not confined to one single family of the aristocracy, but fairly shared by the whole order. Towards the commons, however, the decemvirs were, in all respects, ten kings. Each was attended by his twelve lictors, who carried not the rods only, but the axe,[10] the well-known symbol of sovereignty. The colleges of ordinary magistrates were restrained by the general maxim of Roman law, "melior est conditio prohibentis," which gave to each member of the college a negative upon the act of his colleagues. But the decemvirs bound themselves by oath[11] each to respect his colleagues' majesty; what one decemvir did, none of the rest might do. Then followed all the ordinary outrages of the ancient aristocracies and tyrannies; insult, oppression, plunder, and blood; and, worst of all, the license of the patrician youth was let loose without restraint upon the wives and daughters of the plebeians.[12] Meanwhile the legislation of the decemvirs was to complete

[6] Livy III. 36. Aliquandiu æquatus inter omnes terror fuit; paullatim totus vertere in plebem cœpit. Abstinebatur a patribus, in humiliores libidinose crudeliterque consulebatur.

[7] Patriciis juvenibus sepserant latera, eorum catervæ tribunalia obsederant. Livy, III. 37. Ἑταιρείαν ἕκαστοι συνῆγον, ἐπιλεγόμενοι τοὺς θρασυτάτους τῶν νέων καὶ σφίσιν αὐτοῖς ἐπιτηδειοτάτους. Dionysius, X. 60.

[8] Primores Patrum—nec probare quæ fierent, et credere haud indignis accidere; avide ruendo ad libertatem in servitutem elapsos juvare nolle. Livy, III. 37.

[9] Decem regum species erat. Livy, III. 36.

[10] Cum fascibus secures illigatas præferebant. Livy, III. 36.

[11] Intercessionem consensu sustulerant, is Livy's expression, III. 36. Dionysius adds, ὅρκια τεμόντες ἀπόῤῥητα τῷ πλήθει, X. 59. These oaths resembled those which were sometimes taken by the ruling members of the Greek oligarchies: καὶ τῷ δήμῳ κακόνους ἔσομαι, καὶ βουλεύσω ὅ τι ἂν ἔχω κακόν. Aristotle, Politica, V. 9.

[12] Dionysius, XI. 2.

the triumph of their party. The two tables which they added to the former ten are described by Cicero as containing "unequal laws;" the prohibition of marriages between the patricians and plebeians is expressly said to have been amongst the number. Not that we can suppose that such marriages had been hitherto legal, that is to say, they were not connubia: and therefore if a patrician, as I have said, married the daughter of a plebeian, his children became plebeians. Still they were common in fact; and as the object of the first appointment of the decemvirs was, in part, to unite the two orders into one people, so it was expected that they would henceforth be made legal. It was therefore like the loss of an actual right, when the decemvirs, instead of legalizing these marriages, enacted a positive law to denounce them, as if they intended for the future actually to prohibit them altogether.

They resolve to retain their power after the end of the year.

So passed the second year of the decemvirate. But as it drew near to its close, the decemvirs showed no purpose of resigning their offices, or of appointing successors. Whether it was really a usurpation, or whether they had been elected for more than a single year,[13] may be doubtful; but it is conceivable that even in the former case the great body of the patricians, however personally disappointed, should have supported the decemvirs as upholding the ascendency of their order, rather than incur the danger of reviving the power of the plebeians. At any rate, the government of the decemvirs seemed firmly established; and the outrages of themselves and their party became continually more and more intolerable, so that numbers of the people are said to have fled from Rome,[14] and sought a refuge amongst their allies, the Latins and Hernicans.

The Sabines and Æquians invade the Roman territory.

In this state of things, the foreign enemies of Rome proved again her best friends. Since the year 297 external wars seem to have been suspended, partly, perhaps, from the wasting effects of the great plague on the neighboring nations, partly because the Romans themselves were engrossed with their own affairs at home. But now we hear of an invasion both from the Sabines and the Æquians; the former assembled their forces at Eretum,[15] and from thence ravaged the lands along the left bank of the Tiber: the latter encamped as usual on Algidus, and plundered the territory of Tusculum which lay immediately below them. Then the decemvirs called together the senate, which, hitherto, it is said, they had on no occasion thought proper to consult. The high aristocratical party, headed by the Quinctii[16] and C. Claudius, showed symptoms of discontent with the decemvirs for still retaining their power; L. Valerius Potitus and M. Horatius Barbatus[17] were celebrated by posterity for following a more decided course, and upholding the general liberty of the Roman people. But the majority of the senate supported the decemvirs, and the citizens were called upon to enlist against the common enemy.[18] One army, commanded by three of the decemvirs, was led out to oppose the Sabines at Eretum; another marched towards Algidus to protect the Tusculans; Appius Claudius, with one of his colleagues, Sp. Oppius, remained in Rome to provide for the safety of the city.

[13] Niebuhr considers it as certain that the decemvirs were appointed for a longer period than a year. Vol. II. p. 328. Eng. Transl. Otherwise, he says, they would not have been required to resign their power, but interreges would, immediately on the expiration of their office, have stepped into their place. This, however, does not seem to follow. In peaceable times, Appius Claudius the Blind held his censorship beyond the legal term of eighteen months, in defiance of the Æmilian law, and it does not appear that the tribunes, or any other power, could actually turn him out of his office; he was only threatened with imprisonment if he did not resign. Livy, IX. 34. To deprive a magistrate of his office, "abrogare magistratum," was accounted a most violent measure; it was to be resigned, and not wrested from him by any other power. The senate ejected Cinna from the consulship; but Paterculus remarks on the act that "hæc injuria homine quam exemplo dignior fuit." They were not disposed to proceed to such an extremity against the decemvirs.

[14] Dionysius, XI. 2.

[15] Dionysius, XI. 3. Livy, III. 38.

[16] Dionysius, XI. 15.

[17] Livy, III. 39.

[18] Livy, III. 41.

Both armies, however, were unsuccessful; and both, after having been beaten by the enemy, fled, the one to Tusculum, the other to the neighborhood of Fidenæ,[19] within the Roman territory. Here they remained, or here, at least, the story leaves them, till the tidings of the last outrage of the decemvirs' tyranny aroused them, and showed them plainly that the worst enemies of their country were within the walls of Rome.

The Roman armies are beaten.

Appius Claudius[20] had stayed behind from the war to take care of the city. He saw a beautiful maiden named Virginia, the daughter of L. Virginius,[21] who was now serving as a centurion in the army sent against the Æquians; and her father had betrothed her to L. Icilius, who had been tribune some time since, and had carried the famous law for assigning out the Aventine to the commons. One day as the maiden, attended by her nurse, was going to the Forum to school (for the schools were then kept in booths or stalls round the market-place), Marcus Claudius, a client of Appius, laid hands on her, and claimed her as his slave. Her nurse cried out for help, and a crowd gathered round her, and when they heard who was her father, and to whom she was betrothed, they were the more earnest to defend her from wrong. But M. Claudius said that he meant no violence, he would try his right at law, and he summoned the maiden before the judgment-seat of Appius. So they went before the decemvir, and then Claudius said that the maiden's real mother had been his slave; and that the wife of Virginius, having no children, had gotten this child from its mother, and had presented it to Virginius as her own. This he would prove to Virginius himself as soon as he should return to Rome; meanwhile it was just and reasonable that the master should, in the interval, keep possession of his slave. The friends of the maiden answered, that her father was now absent in the commonwealth's service; they would send him word, and within two days he would be in Rome. "Let the cause," they said, "wait only so long. The law declares expressly, that in all cases like this, every one shall be considered free till he be proved a slave. Therefore the maiden ought to be left with her friends till the day of trial. Put not her fair fame in peril by giving up a free-born maiden into the hands of a man whom she knows not." But Appius said, "Truly, I know the law of which you speak, and I hold it just and good, for it was I myself who enacted it. But this maiden[22] cannot in any case be free; she belongs either to her father or to her master. Now as her father is not here, who but her master can have any title to her? Wherefore let M. Claudius keep her till L. Virginius come, and let him give sureties that he will bring her forth before my judgment-seat when the cause shall be tried between them." But then there came forward the maiden's uncle, P. Numitorius, and Icilius, to whom she was betrothed; and they spoke so loudly against the sentence, that the multitude began to be roused, and Appius feared a tumult. So he said, that for the sake of L. Virginius, and of the rights of fathers over their children, he would let the cause wait till the next day; "but then," he said, "if Virginius does not appear, I tell Icilius and his fellows, that I will support the laws which I have made, and their violence shall not prevail over justice." Thus the maiden was saved for the time, and her friends sent off in haste to her father, to bid him come with all speed to Rome: and they gave security to Claudius that she should appear before Appius the next day, and then they took her home in safety.

Story of Virginia. Claudius, a client of Appius Claudius, claims Virginia as his slave.

The messenger[23] reached the camp that same evening, and Virginius obtained leave of absence on the instant, and set out for Rome at the first watch of the night. Appius had sent off also to his colleagues, praying them not to let Virginius go: but his message came too late.

Virginius comes to Rome from the army.

[19] Livy, III. 42.

[20] Livy, III. 44, et seqq.

[21] Cicero calls him Decimus Virginius. De Republicâ, II. 37.

[22] In ea quæ in patris manu sit, neminem esse alium cui dominus possessione cedat. Livy, III. 45.

[23] Livy, III. 46.

Judgment of Appius, awarding possession of Virginia to her pretended master. Virginius kills his daughter.

Early in the morning Virginius,[24] in mean attire, like a suppliant, led his daughter down to the Forum; and some Roman matrons, and a great company of friends, went with him. He appealed to all the people for their aid; "for this," said he, "is not my cause only, but the cause of all." So also spoke Icilius; and the mothers who followed Virginius stood and wept, and their tears moved the people even more than his words. But Appius heeded nothing but his own wicked passion; and before Claudius had done speaking, without suffering Virginius to reply, he hastened to give the sentence. That sentence adjudged the maiden to be considered as a slave till she should be proved to be free-born; and awarded the possession of her in the mean while to her master Claudius. Men could scarcely believe that they heard aright, when this monstrous defiance of all law, natural and civil, was uttered by the very man who had himself enacted the contrary. But when Claudius went to lay hold on the maiden, then the women who stood around her wept aloud, and her friends gathered round her, and kept him off; and Virginius threatened the decemvir, that he would not tamely endure so great a wrong. Appius, however, had brought down a band of armed patricians with him; and, strong in their support, he ordered his lictors to make the crowd give way. Then the maiden was left alone before his judgment-seat, till her father, seeing there was no other remedy, prayed to Appius that he might speak but one word with her nurse in the maiden's hearing, and might learn whether she were really his child or no. "If I am indeed not her father, I shall bear her loss the lighter." Leave was given him, and he drew them both aside with him to a spot called afterwards the "new booths," for tradition kept the place in memory, and there he snatched a knife from a butcher, and said, "This is the only way, my child, to keep thee free," and plunged it in his daughter's heart. Then turning to Appius, "On thee, and on thy head," he cried, "be the curse of this blood!" In vain did Appius call out to seize him: he forced his way through the multitude, and still holding the bloody knife in his hand, he made for the gates, and hastened out of the city, and rode to the camp by Tusculum.

Tumult in the city; the decemvirs are driven from the Forum.

The rest may be told more briefly. Icilius[25] and Numitorius held up the maiden's body to the people, and bade them see the bloody work of the decemvir's passion. A tumult arose, and the people gathered in such strength, that the patrician friends of their cause, L. Valerius and M. Horatius, thought that the time for action was come, and put themselves at the head of the multitude. Appius and his lictors, and his patrician satellites, were overborne by force, and Appius, fearing for his life, covered his face with his robe, and fled into a house that was hard by. In vain did his colleague, Oppius, hasten to the Forum to support him; he found the people already triumphant, and had nothing else to do but to call together the senate. The senators met, with little feeling for the decemvirs, but with an extreme dread of a new secession of the commons, and a restoration of the sacred laws, and of the hated tribuneship.

The army of Algidus marches to Rome and occupies the Aventine.

The secession, however, could not be prevented. Virginius[26] had arrived at the camp, followed by a multitude of citizens in their ordinary dress. His bloody knife, the blood on his own face and body, and the strange sight of so many unarmed citizens in the midst of the camp, instantly drew a crowd about him: he told his story, and called on his fellow-soldiers to avenge him. One common feeling possessed them all: they called to arms, pulled up their standards, and began to march to Rome. The authority of the decemvirs was wholly at an end; the army entered the city; as they passed along the streets, they called upon the commons to assert their liberties and create their tribunes; they then ascended the Aventine, and there, in their own proper home and city, they established themselves in arms.

[24] Livy, III. 47, et seqq. [25] Livy, III. 48, 49. [26] Livy, III. 50.

When deputies from the senate were sent to ask them what they wanted, the soldiers shouted that they would give no answer to any one but to L. Valerius and M. Horatius. Meanwhile, Virginius persuaded them to elect ten tribunes to act as their leaders; and accordingly ten were created, who took the name of tribunes of the soldiers, but designed to change it, ere long, for that of tribunes of the commons.

The army near Fidenæ was also in motion.[27] Icilius and Numitorius had excited it by going to the camp, and spreading the story of the miserable fate of Virginia. The soldiers rose, put aside the decemvirs who commanded them, and were ready to follow Icilius. He advised them to create ten tribunes, as had been done by the other army; and this having been effected, they marched to Rome, and joined their brethren on the Aventine. The twenty tribunes then deputed two of their number to act for the rest, and waited a while for the message of the senate.

The army from Fidenæ joins it.

Delays, however, were interposed by the jealousy of the patricians. Had the senate chosen, it might, no doubt, in the fulness of its power, have deposed the decemvirs, whether their term of office was expired or no; as, long afterwards, it declared all the laws of M. Drusus to be null and void, and by its mere decree took away from L. Cinna his consulship, and caused another to be appointed in his room. But the patricians were unwilling to violate the majesty of the imperium merely to give a triumph to the plebeians; and the decemvirs, encouraged by this feeling, refused themselves to resign. The commons, however, were thoroughly in earnest; and finding that nothing was done to satisfy them, they quitted the Aventine,[28] on the suggestion of M. Duilius, not, however, we may presume, without leaving it guarded by a sufficient garrison, marched in military array through the city, passed out of it by the Colline gate, and established themselves once more on the Sacred Hill. Men, women, and children, all of the plebeians who could find any means to follow them, left Rome also and joined their countrymen. Again the dissolution of the Roman nation was threatened; again the patricians, their clients, and their slaves, were on the point of becoming the whole Roman people.

Both armies, followed by the mass of the people, retired to the Sacred Hill.

Then the patricians yielded, and the decemvirs agreed to resign.[29] Valerius and Horatius went to the Sacred Hill, and listened to the demands of the commons. These were, the restoration of the tribuneship and of the right of appeal, together with a full indemnity for the authors and instigators of the secession. All this the deputies acknowledged should have been granted even without the asking; but there was one demand of a fiercer sort. "These decemvirs," said Icilius in the name of the commons, "are public enemies, and we will have them die the death of such. Give them up to us, that they may be burnt with fire." The friends of the commons had met this fate within the memory of men still living, and certainly not for greater crimes; but a people, if violent, is seldom unrelenting; twenty-four hours brought the Athenians to repent of their cruel decree against the Mytilenæans; and a few words from Valerius and Horatius, men whom they could fully trust, made the Roman commons forego their thirst for sudden and extraordinary vengeance. The demand for the blood of the decemvirs was withdrawn: so the senate acceded to all that was required: the decemvirs solemnly resigned their power, and the commons returned to Rome. They occupied the Aventine as before,[30] and thither the pontifex maximus was sent by the senate to hold the comitia for the election of the tribunes; but they occupied more than the Aventine; they required some security that the terms of the peace should be duly kept with them; and accordingly now, as in the disputes about the Publilian law, they were allowed also to take possession of the Capitol.[31]

The decemvirs resign, and the commons return to Rome.

[27] Livy, III. 51.
[28] Livy, III. 52.
[29] Livy, III. 52, 53.
[30] Livy, III. 54.
[31] Cicero pro Cornelio, I. Fragment.

Election of tribunes and of consuls.

In the comitia on the Aventine ten tribunes of the commons were elected, amongst whom were Virginius, Icilius, Numitorius, C. Sicinius, a descendant of one of the original tribunes created on the Sacred Hill, and M. Duilius. Then the commons were assembled on the spot afterwards called the Flaminian Meadows,[32] outside of the Porta Carmentalis, and just below the Capitol; and there L. Icilius proposed to them the solemn ratification of the indemnity for the secession already agreed to by the senate. The consent of the commons was necessary to give it the force of a law; and so, in like manner, Duilius proposed to the commons that they should accept another measure, already sanctioned by the patricians, the election of two supreme magistrates in the place of the decemvirs, with the right of appeal from their sentence. It is remarkable that now, for the first time, these magistrates were called consuls,[33] their old title, up to this period, having been prætors or captains-general. Consul signifies merely "colleague," one who acts with others; it does not necessarily imply that he should be one of two only, and, therefore, the name is not equivalent to duumvir. And its indefiniteness seems to confirm Niebuhr's opinion, that the exact number of these supreme magistrates was not yet fully agreed upon, and that the appointment of two only, in the present instance, was merely a provisional imitation of the old prætorship, till the future form of the constitution should be finally settled. Thus, as the commons had recovered their tribunes, so the patricians had again their two magistrates with the imperium of the former prætors, limited, as that of the prætors had been, by the right of appeal; but the final adjustment of the relations of the two orders to each other was reserved for after discussion. Be that as it may, the form of the old government was once again restored, and two patrician magistrates were elected with supreme power; but an important change was established, that these two were both freely chosen by the centuries, whereas one had hitherto been appointed by the burghers in their curiæ, and had only been appointed by the centuries afterwards

The result of the election sufficiently showed that it was a free one. The new magistrates, the first two consuls, properly speaking, of Roman history, were L. Valerius and M. Horatius; and the executive government, for the first time since the days of Brutus and Poplicola, was wholly in the hands of men devoted to the rights of their country rather than to the ascendency of their order.

[32] Livy, III. 64.

[33] Zonaras, VII. 19. It may be observed that the two supreme magistrates in the municipia and colonies of a later period, whose office was analogous to that of the consuls at Rome, were called duumviri.

CHAPTER XVI.

INTERNAL HISTORY—CONSTITUTION OF THE YEAR 306—VALERIAN LAWS, AND TRIALS OF THE DECEMVIRS—REACTION IN FAVOR OF THE PATRICIANS—CANULEIAN LAW—CONSTITUTION OF 312—COUNTER-REVOLUTION.

"The seven years that followed are a revolutionary period, the events of which we do not find satisfactorily explained by the historians of the time."—HALLAM, Middle Ages, Vol. II. p. 458.

Obscurity of the history of this period.

WE read in Livy and Dionysius an account of the affairs of Rome from the beginning of the commonwealth, drawn up in the form of annals; political questions, military operations, what was said in the senate and the Forum, what was done in battle against the Æquians and Volscians, all is related with the full details of contemporary history. It is not wonderful that appearances so imposing should have deceived many; that the Roman history should have been regarded as a subject which might be easily and completely mastered. But if we press on any part this show of knowledge, it yields before us, and comes to nothing. Nowhere is this more manifest than in the story of the period immediately subsequent to the decemvirate. What is related of these times is indistinct, meagre, and scarcely intelligible; but scattered fragments of information have been preserved along with it, which, when carefully studied, enable us to restore the outline of very important events; and these, when thus brought forward to the light, afford us the means of correcting or completing what may be called the mere surface-view contained in the common narrative. The lines, hitherto invisible, being so made conspicuous, a totally different figure is presented to us; its proportions and character are all altered, and we find that, without this discovery, while we fancied ourselves in possession of the true resemblance, we should, in fact, have been mistaking the unequal pillars of the ruin for the original form of the perfect building.

Constitution of the year 306.

The common narrative of the overthrow of the decemvirs omitted, as we have seen, the important fact that the commons in that revolution occupied the Capitol. It mentions,[1] however, that the two popular leaders, Valerius and Horatius, were appointed the two chief magistrates of the commonwealth, and that they passed several laws for the better confirmation of the public liberty, without experiencing any open opposition on the part of the patricians. In fact, the popular cause was so triumphant that all, and more than all, of the objects of the Terentilian law were now effected; and a new constitution was formed, by which it was attempted at once to unite the two orders of the state more closely together, and to set them on a footing of entire equality.

The Valerian laws.

In the first place, the old laws for the security of personal liberty were confirmed afresh, and received a stronger sanction. Whoever, while presiding at the comitia,[2] should allow the election of any magistrate, with no right of appeal from his sentences, should be outlawed, and might be killed by any one with impunity. This was the law proposed and passed by Valerius; but even this, as we shall see presently, did not content the commons: they required and carried a still stronger measure. A second Valerian law[3] for-

[1] Livy, III. 55. Dionysius, XI. 45.
[2] Livy, III. 55.
[3] Quod tributim plebes jussisset populum teneret. Livy III. 55. Dionysius describes this law correctly. He calls it νόμον κελεύοντα τοὺς ὑπὸ τοῦ δήμου τεθέντας ἐν ταῖς φυλετικαῖς ἐκκλησίαις

inally acknowledged the commons of Rome to be the Roman people; a Plebiscitum, or decree of the commons, was to be binding on the whole people: so it is expressed in the annalists; but Niebuhr supposes that there was a restriction on this power of which the annalists were ignorant; namely, that the plebiscitum should have first received the sanction of the senate, and of the assembly of the curiæ. It is, indeed, certain that the assembly of the tribes was not made the sole legislative authority in the commonwealth; what was intended seems to have been nothing more than to recognize its national character; its resolutions or decrees,[4] where not directly interfered with by another power equally sovereign, were to embrace not the commons only, but the whole nation. In the same way, in the later constitution, the senate was not all-powerful; it could not legislate alone, and its decrees were liable to be stopped by the negative of the tribunes; but no one doubted that its authority extended over the whole people, and not over the members of its own order only. And this appears to have been the position in which the Valerian law placed the assembly of the tribes.

Division of all the magistracies of the commonwealth between the patricians and commons.

Thus far we follow the express testimony of the annals from which Livy and Dionysius compiled their narratives. But we are warranted in saying that the revolution did not stop here. Other and deeper changes were effected; but they lasted so short a time, that their memory has almost vanished out of the records of history. The assembly of the tribes had been put on a level with that of the centuries, and the same principle was followed out in the equal division of all the magistracies of the state between the patricians and the commons. Two supreme magistrates,[5] invested with the highest judicial power, and discharging also those important duties which were afterwards performed by the censors, were to be chosen every year, one from the patricians, and the other from the commons. Ten tribunes of the soldiers,[6] or decemviri, chosen five from the patricians and five from the commons, were to command the armies in war, and to watch over the rights of the patricians; while ten tribunes of the commons, also chosen in equal proportions from both orders, were to watch over the liberties of the commons. And as patricians were thus admitted to the old tribuneship, so the assemblies of the tribes[7] were henceforth, like those of the centuries, to be held under the sanctions of augury, and nothing could be determined in them if the auspices were unfavorable. Thus the two orders were to be made fully equal to one another; but at the same time they were to be kept perpetually distinct; for at this very moment[8] the whole twelve tables of the laws of the decemvirs received the solemn sanction of the people, although, as we have seen, there was a law in one of the last tables which declared the marriage of a patrician with a plebeian to be unlawful.

Horatian and Duilian laws.

There being thus an end of all exclusive magistracies, whether patrician or plebeian; and all magistrates being now recognized as acting in the name of the whole people, the persons of all were to be re-

νόμους, απασι κεῖσθαι Ρωμαίοις ἐξ ἴσου, τὴν αὐτὴν ἔχοντας δύναμιν τοῖς ἐν ταῖς λοχίτισιν ἐκκλησίαις τεθησομένοις, XI. 45. Now we know that at this time laws passed by the comitia of centuries were not valid without the sanction of the senate, and, therefore, laws passed by the tribes must equally have required it.

[4] Compare the difference between a resolution or an order of the house of commons (although that body cannot legislate without the consent of the house of lords and the king) and the canons of a synod of the clergy. A law which should enact that "quod clerus jussisset populum teneret" need not give to a synod the exclusive right of making laws; it would deserve its name if it merely placed it on a level with the house of commons; if it empowered it to represent the whole nation, and not only one single order of men.

[5] Diodorus, XII. 25.

[6] Diodorus, XII. 25. Δέκα αἱρεῖσθαι δημάρχους μεγίστας ἔχοντας ἐξουσίας τῶν κατὰ πόλιν ἀρχόντων, καὶ τούτους ὑπάρχειν οἱονεὶ φύλακας τῆς τῶν πολιτῶν ἐλευθερίας. This description does not suit the tribunes of the commons, and the expression, τῆς τῶν πολιτῶν ἐλευθερίας, instead of τῆς τοῦ δήμου ἐλευθερίας, seems to show that the patricians or burghers were intended rather than the commons.

[7] Zonaras, VII. 19. He mentions the fact without its connection; but it seems to me extremely valuable, towards confirming the view of all these arrangements which is given in this history.

[8] Diodorus, XII. 26. Livy, III. 57.

garded as equally sacred. Thus the consul Horatius proposed and carried a law which declared, that whoever harmed any tribune of the commons, any ædile, any judge, or any decemvir, should be outlawed and accursed;[9] that any man might slay him, and that all his property should be confiscated to the temple of Ceres. Another law was passed by M. Duilius, one of the tribunes, carrying the penalties of the Valerian law to a greater height against any magistrate who should either neglect to have new magistrates appointed at the end of the year,[10] or who should create them without giving the right of appeal from their sentence. Whosoever violated either of these provisions was to be burned alive, as a public enemy.

Decrees of the senate kept in the temple of Ceres.

Finally, in order to prevent the decrees of the senate from being tampered with by the patricians, Horatius and Valerius began the practice[11] of having them carried to the temple of Ceres on the Aventine, and there laid up under the care of the ædiles of the commons.

The state of affairs was not ripe for this constitution.

This complete revolution was conducted chiefly, as far as appears, by the two consuls, and by M. Duilius. Of the latter we should wish to have some further knowledge; it is an unsatisfactory history, in which we can only judge of the man from his public measures, instead of being enabled to form some estimate of the merit of his measures from our acquaintance with the character of the man. But there is no doubt that the new constitution attempted to obtain objects for which the time was not yet come, which were regarded rather as a triumph of a party, than as called for by the wants and feelings of the nation; and, therefore, the Roman constitution of 306 was as short-lived as Simon de Montfort's provisions of Oxford, or as some of the strongest measures of the long parliament. An advantage pursued too far in politics, as well as in war, is apt to end in a repulse.

Impeachment of Appius Claudius. He is cast into prison.

As yet, however, at Rome, the tide of the popular cause was at full flood, for the decemvirs were still unpunished, and the fresh memory of their crimes excited a universal desire for vengeance. Virginius singled out Appius and impeached him;[12] but Appius, with the inherent pride of his family, scorned the thought of submission, and appeared in the Forum with such a band of the young patricians around him, that he seemed more likely to repeat the crimes of his decemvirate than to solicit mercy for them. But the tide was not yet to be turned, and Appius only hastened his own ruin.

[9] See this memorable law in Livy, III. 55. "Qui tribunis plebis, ædilibus, judicibus, decemviris nocuisset, ejus caput Jovi sacrum esset, familia ad ædem Cereris liberi liberæque venum iret." The different interpretations given to the words "judicibus, decemviris," in this passage, are well known. Niebuhr understands the latter nearly as I do, but the "judices" he considers to have been the centumviri. But the order of the words is, I think, decisive against this last notion; the centumviri never could have been mentioned between the ædiles and decemviri. Whereas, according to my interpretation, the two old plebeian offices are mentioned first, and then the two new offices which they were thenceforward to share, those of judge or consul, and of decemvir, or tribune of the soldiers. Livy himself informs us that there were some who had extended this law to the patrician magistrates, and who explained the "judices" as I have done; but he objects that judex, as applied to the consul, was the later title, and that the consul at this time was called prætor. To which the reply is easy: that according to Zonaras, who derived his materials from Dion Cassius, the consuls *ceased* to be called prætors at this very time, and were now first called consuls or colleagues; and it is very likely that their military power, being transferred to the tribunes of the soldiers, their name of judices, which they are allowed by Livy himself to have borne afterwards (see also Cicero, de Legibus, III. 4), took its origin from this period.

I may add, also, that the supposition that there were to be ten tribunes of the soldiers and as many tribunes of the commons, would agree with the otherwise puzzling statement of Pomponius, de Origine Juris, § 25, "that there were sometimes twenty tribunes of the soldiers," for the two tribuneships must, under the constitution of 306, have so resembled each other in many important points, that they may easily have been represented as one magistracy.

[10] Livy, III. 55. Diodorus, XII. 25. Livy says, "Tergo et capite puniretur;" Diodorus, more correctly, ζῶντας κατακαυθῆναι. The connection of this law with that mysterious story of the burning alive of nine tribunes, for not providing successors for themselves in their office (see Valerius Maximus, VI. 3, § 2, and note 39 to chap. XIII. of this history), cannot but strike every one; the clue, however, only goes far enough to excite curiosity, but will not enable us to satisfy it.

[11] Livy, III. 55.

[12] Livy, III. 56.

Virginius refused to admit the accused to bail, unless he could prove[13] before a judge duly appointed to try this previous issue, "that he had not, in a question of personal freedom, assumed that the presumption was in favor of slavery; in having adjudged Virginia to be regarded as a slave till she was proved free, instead of regarding her as entitled to her freedom, till she was proved a slave." Appius dared not have this issue tried; he only appealed to the tribunes, the colleagues of Virginius, to save him from being cast into prison; and when they refused to interpose,[14] he appealed to the people. The meaning of this appeal was, that he refused to go before the judge as Virginius had proposed, and submitted his whole case to the judgment of the people in the assembly of centuries. This he might legally do; but on the other hand, his refusal to have the question of fact, as to his conduct in the affair of Virginia, tried before a judge, enabled Virginius to assume his guilt as certain. But bail was not to be given to notorious criminals: it was thus that Kæso had defrauded justice, and Appius would certainly fly from Rome before his trial; unless he were secured within the walls of a prison. Accordingly, Virginius ordered him to be thrown into prison, there to await the judgment of the people.

His death before his trial.

But that judgment he never lived to undergo. Livy chose to believe that he killed himself,[15] despairing of the event of the trial. Another account implies, that it was the accusers, and not the accused, who feared to trust to the decision of the centuries; the tribunes, it was said, ordered him to be put to death in prison.[16] It would be painful to believe that so great a criminal, like the dictator Cæsar, was not executed, but murdered; yet the utter uncertainty of a trial before the centuries, where so many other points were sure to be considered besides the fact of the criminal's guilt, and the strange latitude allowed by the Romans to their magistrates on the plea of the public safety, render it not improbable that the tribunes dealt with Appius as Cicero treated the accomplices of Catilina in the very same prison. Cicero's conduct on that

[13] "Ni judicem dices te ab libertate in servitutem contra leges vindicias non dedisse, in vincula te duci jubeo." Livy, III. 56. Niebuhr rejects the reading "judicem *dices*" as nonsense, and corrects "judicem *doces*." I should lay little stress on the authority of our MSS. of Livy, which are all extremely corrupt; but in this instance the common reading is supported by the similar expression "diem dicere" and the term "condictio," quâ "actor adversario denuntiabat ut ad judicem capiendum die XXX adesset." Gaius, IV. § 18. "Ni judicem dices" signifies, "Unless thou wilt give me notice to come before a judge with thee, to have this issue tried."

For the matter of the transaction itself it may be observed, that the judge would have had to try simply the question of fact, whether Appius had given vindiciæ, or possession, in favor of slavery or not. And it was manifest that if the judge found against Appius on this issue, such a verdict would have weighed strongly against him at his trial before the centuries. On the other hand, Appius wished to reserve his whole case for the judgment of the centuries; for there, as he well knew, the issue tried was far less narrow, and the sentence would depend, not on the evidence as to a particular fact, but on the general impression produced on the minds of the audience by the speakers on either side; and to produce this impression the feelings and interests of the judges were freely appealed to, so that the greatest criminal might hope to be acquitted, if his eloquence and the influence of his friends were sufficiently powerful.

[14] An obscure and corrupt passage of Diodorus would appear to intimate, that, by the new constitution, the act of one tribune could not be stopped by another: in other words, that the ordinary rule of Roman law, "melior est conditio prohibentis," was, in the case of the tribunes, at this time reversed. The words are *ἐὰν δὲ οἱ δήμαρχοι μὴ συμφωνῶσι πρὸς ἀλλήλους, κύριοι εἶναι τὸν ἀνὰ μέσον κείμενον μὴ κωλύεσθαι*, XII. 25. Wesseling and the other interpreters understand *τὸν ἀνά μέσον χρόνον*, "in the interval," which seems to me to be neither good Greek nor sense. I am inclined to read *τὸ ἀνὰ μέσον κείμενον*, "the matter that was between them:" "If the tribunes should disagree, they had authority in the matter that was disputed between them, so as not to be restrained by the veto of their colleagues." But I am not yet satisfied that this is the complete restoration of the passage.

[15] Livy, III. 58.

[16] Dionysius, XI. 46. "This," he says, "was the general opinion." *ὡς μὲν ἡ τῶν πολλῶν ὑπόληψις ἦν.* He must have copied this from some annalist, although the oldest annalist could know as little as Dionysius of the public opinion of the times of the decemvirs. Perhaps the statement came from the memorials of the Claudian family, which would naturally be glad to impute such a crime to the hated tribunes. But that Appius was put to death in prison, is also the account given by the author of the little work, "De Viris Illustribus;" and it is stated positively as a point which was not doubted. And if this work was compiled, as Borghesi and Niebuhr believe, from the inscriptions at the base of the statues in the forum of Augustus, it may be supposed to express the prevailing opinion in the Augustan age.

occasion was sanctioned by Cato, and by the majority of the senate; and certainly the crimes of Appius were neither less flagrant, nor less notorious, than those of Cethegus and Lentulus.

Another of the decemvirs, Spurius Oppius,[17] underwent a similar fate. He was particularly odious, because he had been left with Appius in the government of the city, while the other decemvirs were abroad with the legions; and because he had been a faithful imitator of his colleague's tyranny. His most obnoxious crime was his having cruelly and wantonly scourged an old and distinguished soldier, for no offence, as it was said, whatsoever. Bail, therefore, was refused to him also; he was committed to prison, and there died before his trial came on, either by the hands of the executioner or his own. The other decemvirs,[18] and M. Claudius, who had claimed Virginia as his slave, were all allowed to give bail, or to escape before sentence was executed; and accordingly they all fled from Rome, and went into exile. Their property, as well as that of Appius and Oppius, was confiscated and sold at the temple of Ceres.

Fate of the other decemvirs.

From this point the reaction may be said to have begun. Vengeance having been satisfied, compassion arose in its place; the patricians seemed the weaker party, and any further proceedings against them were received with aversion, as a generous spirit cannot bear to strike an enemy on the ground. Accordingly, there seems from this moment to have been a division amongst the popular leaders; some thinking that they had done enough, and that in order to carry into effect the new constitution, nothing was so much needed as conciliation; while others believed that the patricians would never endure an equal government, and that it was the truest wisdom, as they had once fallen, to keep them down forever. As far as we can discern any thing of individual character amid the darkness of these times, the two consuls and M. Duilius were of the former of these two opinions; L. Icilius and L. Trebonius were of the latter.

Reaction and division among the popular leaders.

The state required, as Duilius thought, a general amnesty; and accordingly he declared[19] that he would stop any further political prosecutions; that he would allow no man to be impeached, nor to be thrown into prison as unworthy of bail, during the remainder of the year. With the next year, as he hoped, the new constitution would come into force, and then the liberty of the commons, and the peace of the nation, would be secured forever.

Duilius stops all further prosecutions.

But, as far as appears, the patricians observed that there were symptoms of a turn of the tide; and they hoped for better things than to be obliged to submit to the constitution of Duilius. The two consuls[20] went out to battle against the Æquians and the Sabines, and returned, asserting that they had won great victories, and claiming the honor of a triumph. No doubt the boast of victories in that plundering warfare was often very unsubstantial; but in this case the defeat of the Sabines, at any rate, seems to have been real and signal, for we hear no more of wars with them for a hundred and fifty years afterwards. The patricians, however, would grant no honor to consuls whom they regarded as traitors to their order, and the triumphs were refused. But on this occasion the consuls threw themselves into the hands of the more decided popular party; they summoned the people to meet in their centuries,[21] and there L. Icilius, the tribune, with the consuls' sanc-

The consuls take the field, and are victorious over the enemy. The senate refuses them a triumph, but the people grant it to them.

[17] Livy, III. 58.

[18] Livy, III. 58. Dionysius, XI. 46.

[19] Livy, III. 59.

[20] Livy, III. 60-63.

[21] It is not clear whether the vote in favor of the consuls' triumph was passed by the centuries or by the tribes. Livy's expressions are, "tulit ad populum," not "ad *plebem*," and "populi jussu triumphatum est," not "*plebis* jussu." Yet the vote is passed on the motion of a tribune, and it is said that "omnes tribus eam rogationem acceperunt." On the other hand, Dionysius says that the consuls summoned the people to the assembly, and the tribunes are represented as seconding their representation, rather than originating the question themselves. *πολλὰ τῆς βουλῆς κατηγορήσαντες, συναγορευσάντων αὐτοῖς τῶν δημάρχων.* XI. 50. These circumstances suit best the comitia of centuries, for the consuls could not enter the city without

tion, moved that the Roman people, by its supreme authority, should order the consuls to triumph. In vain did the patricians oppose the motion to the utmost: they had taken up an ill-chosen position, and the reaction here availed them nothing: the people ordered as Icilius proposed, and the consuls triumphed.

Growing strength of the aristocratical party.

This, if the consular Fasti may be trusted, took place in August. Again the mist closes over the events of the remainder of the year, and we can only judge of their nature by the result. The reaction grew stronger, and was increased by all the inherent strength of an aristocracy, the most powerful of all governments so long as it retains any portion of its original vigor. The patricians were determined that the new constitution should never take effect; that there should be no plebeian consul, and no plebeian tribunes of the soldiers: whether, if these points were carried, they might be forced also to have no patrician tribunes of the commons, they cared but little.

Proceedings of Duilius at the election of new tribunes.

To meet this determination, the bolder part of the leaders of the commons resolved that the magistrates for the present year should be re-elected. "If the patricians will not have the constitution," they said, "we will at least keep matters exactly as they now are; we have two consuls whom we can trust to the death, we have ten true and zealous tribunes, the leaders of our late glorious deliverance. If we retain these, the patricians will gain little by their resistance." But here again the division in the popular party made itself manifest: the consuls shrunk from the odium of re-electing themselves; Duilius was equally opposed to the re-election of himself and his nine colleagues. The lot for holding the comitia for the election of the new tribunes happened to fall to him. He resolutely refused[22] to receive votes for any of the last year's tribunes; and as many of the voters would vote for no other candidate, it turned out that only five candidates could obtain that proportion of suffrages out of the whole number,[23] which was required to constitute the legal vote of a tribe. Accordingly, when the sun set, he pronounced the comitia to be dissolved, and as all elections were to end in a single day, he declared[24] that the voting for tribunes

laying aside their imperium, and so giving up their claim to a triumph, and would necessarily assemble the people without the walls. Besides, the question of a triumph might be more justly decided by the people in the military array of their centuries on the Campus Martius, than by the commons in their tribes in the Forum. If Livy's expression, "omnes *tribus* rogationem acceperunt," could be relied upon, it would go far to prove that the blending of the system of centuries with that of tribes, in the comitia centuriata, that most perplexing question of Roman constitutional history, began at least as early as the time of the decemvirs, and probably accompanied the admission of the patricians and their clients into the tribes. Fifty years later, in the year 359, Livy speaks of the "prærogativa tribus," and the "jure vocatæ tribus," at the comitia of centuries, without the least intimation that the system implied in those expressions was then of recent introduction. See Livy, V. 18.

[22] Livy, III. 64. "Cum ex veteribus tribunis, negaret ullius se rationem habiturum."

[23] "Cum alii candidati tribus non explerent." "Explere tribun," and "explere centuriam," signify the obtaining such an absolute number of votes out of the whole number contained in the tribe or century, as was required to constitute its suffrage: for if the votes of the tribes were divided amongst so many candidates, that no one had an absolute majority of the whole tribe in his favor, the tribe was held to have voted for no one. And so if no candidate had an absolute majority of the whole number of tribes in his favor, the comitia were held to have voted for no one, and there was no legal return.

[24] There is much difficulty here in Livy's narrative. After saying that Duilius dismissed the assembly when only five tribunes had been elected, and that he would not go on with the election on any future day, "concilium dimisit, nec deinde comitiorum causâ habuit," Livy goes on as follows, "satisfactum legi aiebat, quæ numero nusquam præfinito tribunis, modo ut relinquerentur sanciret, et ab iis qui creati essent cooptari collegas juberet. Recitabatque rogationis carmen," &c. Now this evidently implies that Duilius referred to his own law, passed in this very year, by which it was made a capital offence in any tribune to go out of office, or to let the year expire without providing for the election of new tribunes to succeed him: and it appears that this very law had contained a clause, authorizing the elected tribunes, if fewer than ten, to fill up their number by choosing their own colleagues. Niebuhr, on the other hand, supposes that this was a new law, now proposed by Duilius; and he therefore reads, "et ab iis qui creati essent cooptari collegas jubebat," referring the verb to Duilius, instead of the common reading "juberet," referring to the former law. I think, however, that the grammar is against this construction, for if Livy had meant that Duilius brought forward a new measure, which must have been done at a particular time and place, he would not have used the imperfect tenses "aiebat" and "recitabat," but rather "dixit" and "recitavit." And besides, what likelihood is there that such a measure would have been passed by

was duly finished; that the commons had elected no more than five, and that it must remain with these five to complete their own number. Accordingly, the five elected tribunes chose to themselves five colleagues, and two[25] of these are expressly said to have been moderate patricians. We may safely conclude that all five were patricians, and that Duilius, hoping to prevail by moderation and conciliation, took this opportunity to carry into effect one part of the new constitution, in the confidence that, after this proof of honorable dealing, the patricians, for very shame, would be forced to fulfil the rest of it.

In this, however, he was mistaken: they had no thought of fulfilling it, although by what means they were enabled to defeat it we can only conjecture. Many years afterwards the patricians habitually set the Licinian law at defiance, and prevented the election of a plebeian consul, whenever the comitia were held by a magistrate devoted to their interests. But how could they persuade Horatius and Valerius, whom they had so recently insulted, to enter into their feelings, and when the day of election came on, to refuse all votes given in favor of a plebeian candidate? Perhaps the opposition of the patricians was so determined, that the consuls could not but yield to it; they might know, that although the centuries should elect a plebeian, yet the curiæ would not confirm the election by conferring on him the imperium, or sovereign power; and, above all, they might feel that there was not in the mass of the commons so deep an interest in the point as could overpower even the most resolute resistance. Thus they abandoned the new constitution to its fate: there was no election of tribunes of the soldiers, nor of a plebeian consul; only two patricians of known moderation were chosen, Lars Herminius[26] and T. Virginius Cælimontanus, men who were not likely to abuse their power, and so to make the victory of the patricians insupportable.

The new constitution is set aside.

Thus the hopes of Duilius were altogether disappointed, and the tribuneship had been laid open to the patricians for nothing. The most moderate men now saw that they had been deluded, and L. Trebonius, one of the five plebeians, was loud in his complaints of the treachery of the patricians. He then proposed a law,[27] which enacted that the election of the tribunes of the commons should from henceforth be continued till the whole number of ten were elected. We read of no opposition to this law from any quarter; the patricians knew that they must abandon their hold on the tribuneship if they insisted on keeping all the curule offices to themselves, and probably they were anxious to leave no vestige of the new constitution in existence, lest the commons, while any part of it remained, should be tempted to demand the whole. Accordingly, all things returned to their old state: except that the two orders were rendered more distinct than ever by the positive law enacted by the decemvirs, and introduced into the twelve tables, by which intermarriage between them was strictly forbidden.

The Trebonian law.

It was impossible, however, that matters should so rest. The moderate consuls of the year 307 were succeeded by two men of a different character, M. Geganius Macerinus[28] and C. Julius. Immediately

A. U. C. 308. A. C. 444. Violences of the young patricians.

the commons at the very moment when they were complaining of Duilius's conduct? Whereas it is very conceivable that the clause appealed to by Duilius had been inserted by him in his former law, perhaps with a view to the very object which he now proposed to gain by it; namely, the securing the admission of some patricians into the number of tribunes. And the clause would then have been passed without suspicion, as it involved no new principle, as might seem intended merely to relieve the tribune presiding at the comitia from the fearful penalty of the law, in a case in which he might be perfectly innocent; for it might not be in his power to secure the election of ten tribunes in a single day, if there was a very great number of candidates. And thus the tenses aiebat and recitabat are quite right; for they express the defence which Duilius *was in the habit of making*, whenever his conduct was called in question.

[25] These were Sp. Tarpeius and A. Aternius, the consuls of the year 300, who had passed the law "De multæ sacramento." Livy, III. 65, and Cicero, de Repub. II. 35.

[26] Livy, III. 65. The consuls at this time came into office on the Ides of December. Dionysius, XI. 63. Livy, IV. 37.

[27] Livy, III. 65.

[28] Livy, III. 65.

we hear again of the young patricians, as in the time of the decemvir Appius and of Kæso Quinctius. The tribunes in vain endeavored to break up their organization, by impeaching the most forward individuals: the consuls took their part, and repressed, says Livy, the combination among the tribunes without attacking the tribunitian power in itself, and yet without compromising the dignity of the patricians. This can only mean that private influence, corruption, or intimidation, were used to deter the accusers from proceeding. Thus relieved from all restraint, the patricians went on more boldly; violence was constantly offered to individual plebeians; the young patricians, organized in their clubs, supported each other in their outrages: and even the tribunes, far from being able to protect their constituents, were themselves, in spite of the sacred laws, insulted and assaulted. The commons complained that they wanted tribunes like Icilius; that those whom they now had were no better than mere shadows. It requires, indeed, no ordinary man to act the part of popular leader against a powerful aristocracy. Even in the Forum the patrician clubs were now the strongest party; so great is the superiority of youth, high birth, training in martial exercises, and organization, over mere numbers. But when they left the Forum, the tribunes were but individuals, often advanced in life,[29] with few slaves and no dependents; exposed in their own persons, and still more in their families, to all the insults and oppressions which wealth, rank, and their numerous clients, enabled the patricians to offer. Whose spirit would not be broken by such a trial? Who but the very boldest and firmest of men would have scrupled to purchase security in private life from such constant persecution, by withdrawing, in his public capacity, that opposition which, after all, he might feel to be hopeless?

A. U. C. 309. A. C. 443. Consulship of T. Quinctius. The Canuleian law.

In the next year, a member of the Quinctian house was chosen consul, T. Quinctius Capitolinus. Accordingly, the story of the year is made up from some of the memorials of the Quinctian family, and is a mere panegyric of the consul's great qualities in peace and in war. The real history of the year is lost almost entirely; it is only said[30] that the irritation of the commons was continually becoming more violent, and that impeachments against individual patricians were constantly the occasion of fresh contests between the orders. Then the panegyric succeeds, and describes[31] how the Æquians and Volscians broke in upon the Roman territory, and carried their ravages up to the very walls of Rome; how there was no one who went out to oppose them; and how the consul then called the people together, and addressed them so earnestly, and with such effect, that all internal quarrels were suspended, every man followed the consul to the field, and a great victory was gained over the enemy. So ran the story; but on this occasion it has not found its way into the Fasti, and the annals of the year contain no record of a triumph obtained by either consul. When Quinctius and his panegyric disappear from the state, the story of internal disputes returns, and we find[32] the Equians and Volscians, together with the Veientians and Ardeatians, again threatening Rome from without. But the new college of tribunes contained a man of resolution, C. Canuleius, and one, to all appearance, as wise as he was bold. He chose that particular reform out of many in which the commons felt a deep interest, and in

A. U. C. 310. A. C. 442.

[29] Shakspeare has truly seized this point in the character of the tribuneship, that it was generally held by men of mature, or even of advanced age; the tribunes who oppose Coriolanus are elderly men, like the city magistrates of modern times; and the aristocratical party taunt them with their want of strength: "Aged sir, hands off." "Hence, rotten thing! or I will shake thy bones out of thy garments." So the popular leader of Syracuse, Athenagoras, complains of the youth and presumption of Hermocrates and his party. And this is natural; for he who has to make his own way to fame, cannot expect to be distinguished as early in life as those who are recommended at once to public notice by the celebrity of their family.

Afterwards, when the tribunes, as in the case of the Gracchi, were chosen from families, which, though not patrician, were yet in the highest degree noble, young men might be elected to the office, for then they enjoyed all the aristocratical advantages of hereditary distinction, although their office was still a popular one.

[30] Livy, III. 66.

[31] Livy, III. 66.

[32] Livy, IV. 1.

which many of the patricians sympathized with them; the repeal, namely, of that law of the twelve tables which forbade connubia between the two orders. Many families must have felt the hardship of this law; for marriages between patricians and plebeians were common, and as they were not in the highest sense legal, the children followed the mother's condition, not the father's, and were not subject to their father's power, nor could inherit from him if he died intestate. On this point there was a strong and general feeling; but the other nine tribunes,[33] encouraged by their colleague's boldness, attempted to revive the question of the admission of plebeians to the consulship, and they proposed a law, "that the consulship should be thrown open, without distinction, to the members of both orders."

Tumult on the Janiculum. The Canuleian law is carried.

Here, again, the family memorials, and the annalists who compiled their narratives from them, have left a blank in the story. No patrician made himself remarkable, either by his magnanimous opposition to the commons, or by his patriotic support of their claims; no memorable tale of outrage or of heroism was connected with these events, and thus they have been passed by almost unnoticed. But the short statement of Zonaras,[34] "that many violent things were said and done on both sides," acquires something more of distinctness from the mention made by Florus[35] of a tumult which broke out on the hill Janiculum, headed by the tribune Canuleius. It seems, then, that the commons again took up arms, and established themselves, not, as before, on the Aventine or the Sacred Hill, but beyond the Tiber, on a spot easily capable of being converted into a distinct city. Thus pressed, the patricians once more yielded, and the law of Canuleius, to repeal the decemvirs'[36] prohibition of intermarriages between the two orders, was carried without further opposition.

Disputes about the law proposed by his colleagues for opening the consulship to the commons.

The success of Canuleius encouraged his colleagues; and they now more vehemently urged their law for opening the consulship to the commons. But this measure, it seems, excited a less general interest in its behalf, while it awakened a yet fiercer opposition. We may suppose, however, that the commons again occupied, in military order, either the Aventine or the Janiculum: for the patricians held meetings amongst themselves,[37] which neither Valerius nor Horatius would attend; and C. Claudius, true to the spirit of his family, wanted to invest the consuls with full military power, and to commission them to attack the tribunes and the commons by force of arms. The Quinctii, however, so said their family accounts, would have no violence done on the sacred persons of the tribunes; and their milder counsels led to a temporary settlement of the contest. The consulship was to be suspended, but tribunes of the soldiers, with consular power, were to be appointed, and these might be either plebeians or patricians. What was to be the number of these tribunes is uncertain; three only were actually chosen; but Zonaras says,[38] that according to the constitution of the office there were to be six, three to be chosen from each order. Perhaps the number three had reference to the three old tribes of the Roman people, the Ramnenses, the Titienses, and Luceres, and as these, in the division of the centuries, were now six, the sex suffragia, it may have been intended, in like manner, that after three patrician tribunes had been elected, three plebeians should be added to their number, like the first and second centuries of the three tribes, according to the system ascribed to the elder Tarquinius. At any rate, three tribunes were elected; and, as Livy declares, three patricians: A. Sempronius Atratinus, L. Atilius, and Cloelius.[39]

[33] Livy, IV. 1.

[34] Πολλὰ κατ' ἀλλήλων καὶ βίαια ἔλεγόν τε καὶ ἔμπραττον. VII. 19.

[35] Tertiam seditionem incitavit matrimoniorum dignitas, ut plebeii cum patriciis jungerentur. Qui tumultus in monte Janiculo, duce Canuleio, tribuno plebis, exarsit. Florus, I. 25.

[36] Livy, IV. 6.

[37] Livy, IV. 6. Dionysius, XI. 55.

[38] VII. 19. Dionysius also agrees with him, XI. 60.

[39] In the MSS. of Livy, this last tribune is called "T. Celius," or "Cælius," or "Cæcilius;" Cæcilius is the reading followed in Drakenborch's edition, but Bekker has adopted the correction of Sigonius, "T. Cloelius." In Dio-

It is remarkable that two out of these three, Sempronius and Cloelius, were chosen from families especially noted, twelve years[40] earlier, for their violent hostility to the commons, and for the great strength of their bands of associated followers. This can hardly have been a mere accident: it looks as if the patricians had made every effort to bring them forward as efficient leaders in the struggle for which they were preparing. But again the details are lost; and Livy's story[41] merely relates that within three months the tribunes were called upon by the augurs to resign, from an alleged religious informality in their election; that there was then a dispute, whether other tribunes should be elected, or whether consuls should be appointed, as before; that T. Quinctius Barbatus, whom the patricians had appointed interrex, was on this occasion their leader; that the commons, feeling that only patricians would be elected, whether under the name of consuls or tribunes, thought it vain to dispute for nothing; and that thus, in the end, two consuls were appointed, L. Papirius Mugillanus, and another, Sempronius Atratinus, and all mention of the laws proposed by the tribunes of the commons was thus for several years laid to sleep.

The dispute ends in the appointment of consuls as before.

Another account[42] represents T. Quinctius, not as interrex, but as dictator, and says that in no more than thirteen days he put an end to the contest, and then laid down his office. And as we find the record of a treaty concluded in this year between Rome and Ardea, it has been conjectured[43] that the patricians may have availed themselves of foreign aid in putting down the opposition of the commons. It is certain that in the following year we meet, for the first time, with the name of a new patrician magistracy, the censorship; and Niebuhr saw clearly that the creation of this office was connected with the appointment of tribunes of the soldiers; and that both belong to what may be called the constitution of the year 312.

Varying accounts of these transactions.

This constitution recognized two points: a sort of continuation of the principle of the decemvirate, inasmuch as the supreme government was again, to speak in modern language, put in commission, and the kingly powers, formerly united in the consuls or prætors, were now to be divided between the censors and tribunes of the soldiers; and, secondly, the eligibility of the commons to share in some of the powers thus divided. But the partition, even in theory, was far from equal: the two censors, who were to hold their office for five years, were not only chosen from the patricians, but, as Niebuhr thinks,[44] by them; that is, by the assembly of the curiæ; the two quæstors who judged in cases of blood were also chosen from the patricians, although by the centuries. Thus the civil power of the old prætors was, in its most important points, still exercised exclusively by the patricians; and even their military power, which was professedly to be open to both orders, was not transmitted

New constitution. Censors, quæstors, and tribunes of the soldiers.

dorus the MSS. read Κόϊντος, for which the editors have corrected Κοΐντιος (Quintius, or Quinctius). In Dionysius, the common reading is Κλόσιον Σικελόν, but the cognomen enables us to correct this, and in the Vatican MS. it is rightly given Κλύλιον Σικελόν. Neibuhr says that L. Atilius must have been a plebeian, because the Atilii were a plebeian family, and the L. Atilius, who was tribune of the soldiers in 356, is expressly called a plebeian by Livy himself. But this is merely the same question which occurs with respect to some of the decemvirs; and it never can be shown that there were not some patrician houses of all those names, which, to us in the later history, occur only as plebeian, except where the plebeian family had been noble in some other city of Italy, and was not of Roman extraction. Thus we do not hear of any patrician Ælii or Cæcilii. It is more probable, I think, that the three tribunes first chosen were patricians, and that three plebeians were to have been added to their number; but that the patricians resisted this, and finally, to simplify the question, got rid of their own tribunes also, and returned to the government by consuls.

[40] Dionysius, X. 41.

[41] Livy, IV. 7.

[42] Lydus, de Magistratibus, I. 38. But the infinite confusions of the passage in which this statement occurs, render its authority extremely questionable.

[43] Niebuhr, Vol. II. p. 410, Engl. Transl.

[44] Vol. II. p. 394, Engl. Transl. It appears that in after times the election of the censors was confirmed by a lex centuriata, as that of the other curule magistrates was by a lex curiata. Both were, then, a mere formality; but Niebuhr infers from this difference between the censorship and the other magistracies, that the former was originally conferred by the curiæ, and confirmed by the centuries, as the others were conferred by the centuries, and confirmed by the curiæ.

to the tribunes of the soldiers, without some diminution of its majesty. The new tribuneship was not an exact image of the kingly sovereignty; it was not a curule office, and therefore no tribune ever enjoyed the honor of a triumph,[45] in which the conquering general, ascending to the Capitol to sacrifice to the guardian gods of Rome, was wont to be arrayed in all the insignia of royalty.

Its inequality as regarded the commons.

But even the small share of power thus granted in theory to the commons, was in practice withheld from them. Whether from the influence of the patricians in the centuries, or by religious pretences urged by the augurs, or by the enormous and arbitrary power of refusing votes which the officer presiding at the comitia was wont to exercise, the college of the tribunes was for many years filled by the patricians alone. And while the censorship was to be a fixed institution, the tribunes of the soldiers were to be replaced, whenever it might appear needful, by two consuls; and to the consulship no plebeian was so much as legally eligible. Thus the victory of the aristocracy may seem to have been complete, and we may wonder how the commons, after having carried so triumphantly the law of Canuleius, should have allowed the political rights asserted for them by his colleagues to have been so partially conceded in theory, and in practice to be so totally withheld.

Causes why this was quietly endured.

The explanation is simple, and it is one of the most valuable lessons of history. The commons obtained those reforms which they desired, and they desired such only as their state was ripe for. They had withdrawn in times past to the Sacred Hill, but it was to escape from intolerable personal oppression; they had recently occupied the Aventine in arms, but it was to get rid of a tryanny which endangered the honor of their wives and daughters, and to recover the protection of their tribunes; they had more lately still retired to the Janiculum, but it was to remove an insulting distinction which embittered the relations of private life, and imposed on their grandchildren, in many instances, the inconveniences, if not the reproach, of illegitimacy. These were all objects of universal and personal interest; and these the commons were resolved not to relinquish. But the possible admission of a few distinguished members of their body to the highest offices of state concerned the mass of the commons but little. They had their own tribunes for their personal protection; but curule magistracies, and the government of the commonwealth, seemed to belong to the patricians, or, at least, might be left in their hands without any great sacrifice. So it is that all things come best in their season; that political power is then most happily exercised by a people, when it has not been given to them prematurely, that is, before, in the natural progress of things, they feel the want of it. Security for person and property enables a nation to grow without interruption; in contending for this, a people's sense of law and right is wholesomely exercised; meantime, national prosperity increases, and brings with it an increase of intelligence, till, other and more necessary wants being satisfied, men awaken to the highest earthly desire of the ripened mind, the desire of taking an active share in the great work of government. The Roman commons abandoned the highest magistracies to the patricians for a period of many years: but they continued to increase in prosperity and in influence; and what the fathers had wisely yielded, their sons, in the fulness of time, acquired. So the English house of commons, in the reign of Edward III.,[46] declined to interfere in questions of peace and war, as being too high for them to compass; but they would not allow the crown to take their money without their own consent; and so the nation grew, and the influence of the house of commons grew along with it, till that house has become the great and predominant power in the British constitution.

[45] Zonaras, VII. 19. It might be a curious question whether the ovation, or inferior triumph, in which the conquering general walked on foot instead of riding in his chariot, was not first introduced in the case of a tribune of the soldiers; and whether it did not mark in its origin the inferior rank of the general who had gained it, rather than the less importance of his military successes.

[46] Hallam, Middle Ages, Vol. III. p. 71. ed. 1822.

If this view be correct, Trebonius judged far more wisely than M. Duilius; and the abandonment of half the plebeian tribuneship to the patricians, in order to obtain for the plebeians an equal share in the higher magistracies, would have been as really injurious to the commons, as it was unwelcome to the pride of the aristocracy. It was resigning a weapon with which they were familiar, for one which they knew not how to wield. The tribuneship was the foster nurse of Roman liberty, and without its care that liberty never would have grown to maturity. What evils it afterwards wrought, when the public freedom was fully ripened, arose from that great defect of the Roman constitution, its conferring such extravagant powers on all its officers. It proposed to check one tyranny by another; instead of so limiting the prerogatives of every magistrate and order in the state, whether aristocratical or popular, as to exclude tyranny from all.

CHAPTER XVII.

INTERNAL HISTORY FROM 312 TO 350—THE CENSORSHIP, AND THE LIMITATION OF IT BY MAMERCUS ÆMILIUS—SP. MÆLIUS AND C. AHALA—THE QUÆSTORSHIP LAID OPEN TO THE COMMONS—SIX TRIBUNES OF THE SOLDIERS APPOINTED, AND PAY ISSUED TO THE SOLDIERS.

"What can be more instructive than to observe the first principles of right springing up, involved in superstition and polluted with violence; until, by length of time and favorable circumstances, it has worked itself into clearness?"—BURKE, Abridgment of English History, Book III. Chap. IX.

THE period of nearly forty years on which we are now going to enter, so short a space in the history of a nation, so long to all of us individually, includes within it the whole of the Peloponnesian war. Whilst at Rome the very form and tendency of great political revolutions cannot be discovered without difficulty; whilst military events are wholly disguised by ignorance or flattery, and whilst we can as yet obtain no distinct ideas of any one individual, nor fully conceive the character of the national mind, Athens is, on the other hand, known to us almost in its minutest points of detail. During this time Thucydides was collecting materials for his history; and Herodotus, after having travelled nearly all over the world, was making the last additions to his great work in the country of his later years, on the southern coast of Italy. Pericles had passed all of his glorious life except its most glorious close; and Socrates, the faithful servant of truth and virtue, was deserving that common hatred of the aristocratical[1] and democratical vulgar, which made him at last its martyr. The arts and manufactures of Athens were well known at Rome; and those names and stories of the wars of Thebes and Troy, which their dramatists were continually presenting afresh to the memory of the Athenians, were familiar also in the heart of Italy, were adopted into the language and traditions of Etruria and of Rome, and employed the genius of

[1] The aristocratical hatred against Socrates is exhibited in the Clouds of Aristophanes; and the famous speech of Cleon on the question of the punishment of the revolted Mytilenæans, shows the same spirit in connection with the strong democratical party. Political parties are not the ultimate distinction between man and man; there are higher points, whether for good or evil, on which a moral sympathy unites those who politically are most at variance with each other; and so the common dread and hatred of improvement, of truth, of principle—in other words, of all that is the light and life of man, has, on more than one occasion, united in one cause all who are low in intellect and morals, from the highest rank in society down to the humblest.

Italian artists[2] as of those of their original country. But, during the period at which we are now arrived, central Italy became acquainted, not with Athenian art only, but with the fame of the Athenian arms. The Etruscans heard with delight that a mighty avenger of their defeat at Cuma[3] was threatening their old enemies of Syracuse; their cities gladly lent their aid to the invader; and the Romans must have heard with interest from their neighbors and friends of Cære or Agylla, how some of their countrymen had done good service in the lines[4] of the Athenian army, and how they had been involved in that sweeping ruin in which the greatest armament ever yet sent out by a free and civilized commonwealth had so miserably perished. But the Romans knew not, and could not know, how deeply the greatness of their own posterity, and the fate of the whole western world, was involved in the destruction of the fleet of Athens in the harbor of Syracuse. Had that great expedition proved victorious, the energies of Greece during the next eventful century would have found their field in the west no less than in the east: Greece, and not Rome, might have conquered Carthage; Greek, instead of Latin, might have been at this day the principal element of the languages of Spain, of France, and of Italy; and the laws of Athens, rather than of Rome, might be the foundation of the law of the civilized world.

The period now before us is marked, as far as Rome itself is concerned, with few events of great importance. The commons retained and asserted those rights which were the best suited to their actual condition; and thus became gradually fitted to desire and to claim others of a higher character. But for the first important advantage to their cause they were indebted to one of the wisest and best Romans of his time, who was at once trusted by them, and respected by his own order, the patrician Mamercus Æmilius. Nine years after the institution of the censorship, Mamercus, having been named dictator, to oppose a threatened attack from the Etruscans, proposed and carried a law[5] to limit the duration of the censorship. That office, in its powers and outward splendor a lively image of royalty, was held for a term of five years. By the law of Mamercus Æmilius it was to be held in future only for eighteen months; and as the election of censors still took place only at intervals of five years, this magistracy was always in abeyance for a longer time than it was in existence.

General character of the ensuing period.

A. U. C 321. A. C. 431.

The censorship was an office so remarkable, that, however familiar the subject may be to many readers, it is necessary here to bestow some notice on it. Its original business[6] was, to take a register of the citizens and of their property; but this, which seems at first sight to be no more than the drawing up of a mere statistical report, became, in fact, from the large discretion allowed to every Roman officer, a political power of the highest importance. The censors made out the returns of the free population; but they did more; they divided it according to its civil distinctions, and drew up a list of the senators,[7] a list of the equites, a list of the members of the several tribes, or

The censorship.

[2] In specimens of Etruscan vases and frescoes given by Micali in the atlas accompanying his History of the Ancient People of Italy, and in those published more recently by the Antiquarian Society of Rome, it is curious to observe how many of the subjects are taken from the story of the siege of Thebes, and still more from that of Troy. Many of the vases on which these subjects occur are thought to be actually of Athenian manufacture; others appear to be Italian imitations; but both equally prove that the stories of the heroic age of Greece were well known in Italy, and the works of Grecian art admired and sought after.

[3] The naval victory of Cuma was won by Hiero, the brother and successor of Gelon, over the Etruscans, in the year 474 B.C. Olymp. 76-3. It is commemorated by Diodorus, XI. 51, and by Pindar, Pyth. I. 140, and one of the helmets taken from the enemy on this day, and sent as an offering to the Olympian Jupiter, was discovered by an English traveller, in 1817, amongst the ruins of Olympia, and bears an inscription which tells its story, "that Hiero, the son of Dinomenes, and the Syracusans, offered it to Jove as a part of the Tyrrhenian spoil from Cuma." See Böckh, Corpus Inscript. Græc. tom. I. p. 34.

[4] Thucydides, VII. 53.

[5] Livy, IV. 24.

[6] Magistratus, cui scribarum ministerium custodiæque et tabularum cura, cui arbitrium formulæ censendi subjiceretur. Livy, IV. 8.

[7] See the accounts of the census in Livy, XXIV. 18, and XXXIX. 42, 44. See also Zonaras, VII. 19.

of those citizens who enjoyed the right of voting, and a list of the ærarians, consisting of those freedmen, naturalized strangers, and others, who, being enrolled in no tribe, possessed no vote in the comitia, but still enjoyed all the private rights of Roman citizens. Now the lists thus drawn up by the censors were regarded as legal evidence of a man's condition: the state could refer to no more authentic standard than to the returns deliberately made by one of its highest magistrates, who was responsible to it for their being drawn up properly. He would, in the first place, be the sole judge of many questions of fact, such as whether a citizen had the qualifications[8] required by law or custom for the rank which he claimed, or whether he had ever incurred any judicial sentence which rendered him infamous:[9] but from thence the transition was easy, according to Roman notions, to the decision of questions of right; such as whether a citizen was really worthy of retaining his rank, whether he had not committed some act as justly degrading as those which incurred the sentence of the law; and in this manner the censor gave a definite power to public opinion, and whatever acts or habits were at variance with the general feeling, he held himself authorized to visit with disgrace or disfranchisement. Thus was established a direct check upon many vices or faults which law, in almost all countries, has not ventured to notice. Whatever was contrary to good morals, or to the customs of their fathers, Roman citizens ought to be ashamed to practise: if a man[10] behaved tyrannically to his wife or children, if he was guilty of excessive cruelty even to his slaves, if he neglected his land,[11] if he indulged in habits of extravagant expense,[12] or followed any calling which was regarded as degrading,[13] the offence was justly noted by the censors, and the offender was struck off from the list of senators, if his rank were so high; or if he were an ordinary citizen, he was expelled from his tribe, and reduced to the class of the ærarians. Beyond this the censor had no power of degradation;[14] for the private rights of Roman citizens could not be taken away by any magistrate; the sentence could only affect his honors, or such privileges as were strictly political.

Power of the censors over the property of the people.

Yet the censors had a further hold even on the ærarians, nor was their power limited to the degrading a citizen from his rank; they could also affect his fortune. It was their business, as I have said, to make a return of the property of every Roman, and of its value; for the taxes were levied according to this return, and here, too, its evidence was decisive. Every citizen presented at the census a detailed account of his prop-

[8] For instance, whether a man claiming to belong to one of the tribes, followed any trade incompatible with the character of a plebeian; all retail trades being forbidden at this time to the commons. See Dionysius, IX. 25.

[9] This was called a "judicium turpe," and this was incurred in various actions, which are specified by the lawyers: as, for instance, if a man were cast in an actio furti, or vi bonorum raptorum, or tutelæ, or mandati, or pro socio, &c. See Gaius, Institutes, IV. § 182. And the disqualification thus incurred was perpetual, and could not be reversed by the censors. See Cicero, pro Cluentio, 42.

[10] Dionysius, XX. 3. Fragm. Mai.

[11] A. Gellius, IV. 12.

[12] Dionysius, XX. 3. See the well-known story of the censor Fabricius expelling Rufinus from the senate, because he had ten pounds' weight of silver plate in his possession.

[13] As, for instance, that of an actor. See Livy, VII. 2.

[14] There is a remarkable passage in Livy, XLV. 15, in which C. Claudius, one of the censors in the year 584, is represented as denying the right of the censor to deprive any man of his vote: he could remove him from a more honorable tribe to a less honorable, but he could not remove him from all the thirty-five tribes, and so, in effect, disfranchise him. And yet the expression "in ærarios referri," is equivalent to "in Ceritum tabulas referri," and this is a well-known designation of the "civitas sine suffragio;" for Gellius says expressly, that "in has tabulas censores referri jubebant, quos notæ causâ suffragiis privabant." XVI. 13. It would seem, however, that "tribu movere," and "in ærarios referre," were two distinct sentences, and that the former did indeed only imply a removal from a higher tribe to a lower (in which sense it probably is that Dionysius speaks of the censors as removing a man *εἰς τὰς τῶν ἀτίμων φυλάς*, XVIII. 22. Fragm. Mai); but that the latter was, for the time, equivalent to a judicium turpe, and deprived a citizen of all his political rights; but it could be reversed either by the censor's colleague, or by the next censors. But the question concerning the ærarians, like every other connected with the censors and the centuries, is beset with difficulties, from our ignorance of the changes introduced at different periods, and thus being apt to ascribe to one time what is applicable only to another.

erty; he stated the name[15] and situation of his landed estate, what proportion of t was arable, what was meadow, what vineyard, and what olive ground. He was even to number his vines and olive-trees, and to the whole thus minutely described he was to affix his own valuation. He was to observe the same rules with regard to his slaves, and undoubtedly with regard to his horses and cattle; for all these came under the same class of res mancipii. But the censor had an unlimited power of setting on all these things a higher valuation, and, consequently, of subjecting them to a higher rate of taxation. Further, we have instances[16] of a censor's calling for a return of other articles of property, such as clothing, jewels, and carriages, which were not returned in the regular order of the census; and on these he would set an extravagant valuation, to ten times their actual worth. Nor does it appear that in these cases there was any remedy for the person aggrieved: the censor's decision was final. On the return of taxable property thus made, the senate, in case of need, levied a certain rate, ordinarily,[17] as it seems, of no more than one per thousand; but raised, as circumstances might require, to two, three, or four per thousand. For it must be understood that this property tax, or tributum, was mostly a war tax, and not a part of the regular revenues of the state: it might happen, therefore, that no property tax was levied, and in that case the censor's surcharge, or over-valuation, would have been inoperative; but wars were so frequent, and the necessities of the state so great, in the early periods of the Roman history, that there was probably no one term of five years in which the tributum was not needed, and, consequently, no return of any censors which was not carried into effect. We are told also that the censors,[18] on some occasions, not only put their own valuation on the property returned at the census, but also fixed the rate to be levied upon it: being sure in this, as in so many other instances, to have their acts sanctioned by the senate, if it did not appear that they had been influenced by any unworthy motives.

Over the vectigalia, or property of the commonwealth.

In addition to this great power with regard to the taxes, or tributa, the censors had the entire management of the regular revenues of the state, or of its vectigalia.[19] They were the commonwealth's stewards, and to their hands all its property was intrusted. But these state demesnes were ample and various, including arable land, vineyards, pastures, forests, mines, harbors, fisheries, and buildings. The letting or farming of all these belonged wholly to the censors; the harbors including the portoria or customs, which appear to have been levied as a harbor, wharfage, and perhaps warehouse duty. They were thus a charge paid by the merchant for his use of the state's property; and this is the proper notion of vectigal as opposed to tributum; that the first was received by the state in its capacity of landlord or proprietor, the latter was paid to it as a political society; the vectigal was given by the farmer, trader, or consumer, as the price of some commercial or economical benefit; the tributum was the citizen's duty to his country. Besides all these sources of revenue, the state claimed a monopoly of salt;[20] and the right of

[15] See all these particulars in the "forma censualis," given by Ulpian, de Censibus, lib. III. quoted in the Digest, Tit. de Censibus, L. 4. (Lib. L. Tit. XV.)

[16] Livy, XXXIX. 44. Ornamenta et vestem muliebrem et vehicula . . . . in censum referre jussit: . . . . . . uti decies tanto pluris quam quanti essent æstimarentur.

[17] This was the proportion observed in the tribute imposed on the twelve defaulting colonies in the second Punic war; Livy, XXIX. 15; and Niebuhr concludes that it was the ordinary rate. "Three per thousand" is mentioned as the rate fixed by Cato and Valerius Flaccus in their severe censorship in 568. Livy, XXXIX. 44.

[18] Livy, XXXIX. 44.

[19] Ut vectigalia populi Romani sub nutu atque arbitrio (censorum essent). Livy, IV. 8.

[20] The salt works at the mouth of the Tiber were said to have been first established in the reign of Ancus Marcius. Livy, I. 33. According to Gronovius' excellent note on the well-known passage in Livy, II. 9, the government, in the early times of the commonwealth, kept the sale of salt in its own hands, and did not farm it, as was usual with the other vectigalia. But it was farmed, and the price at which it was to be sold was fixed by the censors in the year 548, when M. Livius, one of the censors, acquired from this very circumstance his nickname Salinator. Livy, XXIX. 37.

selling this most necessary article was also let by the censors on their own terms; for they fixed the price at which it was to be sold to the public. Why salt was thus considered as state property may probably be explained on the principle that the sea and the sea-shore belonged to no man; and in a country where the whole supply of salt comes from the sea, it would not appear unnatural that the state should take into its own hands the sale of a commodity so universally needed, and which was derived immediately from that element which no individual could claim as his property. At any rate, salt was at Rome, as afterwards in France, an article that could be sold only by the government.

With these almost kingly powers, and arrayed in kingly state, for the censor's robe[21] was all scarlet, and not merely bordered with a scarlet band, elected by the curiæ, and holding their office for five years, the censors might well seem too great for a free commonwealth, and the patricians, in retaining an office so important in their own exclusive possession, seemed to have more than compensated for their loss of a part of the military tribuneship, had the constitution of 312 been really acted on. It was a most welcome law, then, to the commons, when the dictator Mamercus Æmilius, in the year 321, proposed the shortening of the term of the censor's office to eighteen months. Nor did the patricians refuse their consent to the measure; for there were many of their body who felt that a magistracy held for five years could be accessible only to a few individuals of the highest distinction; and that the mass of the patricians, no less than of the commons, would be subject to the power of the censors, without being ever able to exercise it themselves.

The greatness of the censor's office has led me to depart a little from the chronological order of events, and to anticipate, by a few years, the regular mention of the Æmilian law. I now go back to the year 312, and the appointment of consuls in the room of tribunes of the soldiers, immediately after the institution of this latter office.

Consuls continued to be appointed for the next four years; but a memorable event which occurred in the year 316, again led to the election of tribunes. The year 315 had been a season of great scarcity:[22] a special officer had been named with the title of præfectus annonæ, or master of the markets, in order to relieve the general distress; but he had been able to do very little, and the suffering was so extreme that many of the poorer citizens threw themselves into the Tiber in despair. In this state of things,[23] Sp. Mælius, one of the richest of the commons, and a member of one of the plebeian centuries of knights or equites, a man of large mercantile dealings, and having thus many connections in the neighboring countries, succeeded in making large purchases of corn, and issued it to the poorer citizens either at a very low price, or even gratis. He thus became exceedingly popular, and was followed by a great multitude[24] whenever he appeared in the Forum; so that it was supposed that he would attempt to win a share of the consulship for the commons, and was likely himself to become the first plebeian consul. The patricians, resolved to prevent this, procured the appointment of one of the most eminent of their order, T. Quinctius Capitolinus; but the danger might be only delayed: the scarcity still continued, and Mælius was gaining fresh popularity every day: the harvest was still distant, and if the distress became greater, the mingled despair and gratitude of the commons might overbear all opposition, and the consulship might be wrested from the patricians in spite of all their efforts. On a sudden[25] it was announced that the old L.

A. U. C. 315. A. C. 437. Scarcity, and extensive liberalities of Sp. Mælius.

A. U. C. 316. A. C. 436.

[21] Polybius, VI. 53. And a censor's funeral, funus censorium, used to be voted even to the emperors, as the most honorable and magnificent of any. See Tacitus, Ann. IV. 15, and XII. 2, with Lipsius' note on the first quoted passage.

[22] Livy, IV. 12.

[23] Livy, IV. 13. Zonaras, VII. 20.

[24] Zonaras adds, that he had actually provided himself with men to seize the Capitol, and other strong positions in the city; for this must be the meaning of the expression, ἐπορίσατο φρουρούς.

[25] The senate, according to Zonaras, appoint-

Quinctius Cincinnatus had been named dictator by the consul T. Quinctius, in consequence of a meeting of the senate: the dictator had made C. Servilius Ahala his master of the horse; the patricians and the plebeian knights[26] had occupied the Capitol and the other strong places of the city during the night, and in the morning the dictator appeared in the Forum, with the array of his four-and-twenty lictors, all bearing along with their rods those well-known axes which denoted his sovereign power, while he was supported besides by his master of the horse, at the head of a numerous body of the younger patricians in arms.

He is put to death by C. Ahala.

The dictator took his seat at his tribunal, and sent C. Ahala to summon Mælius to appear before him. As master of the horse, all the members of the centuries of equites were under his immediate authority; and on this account, perhaps, he was chosen to deliver the summons. Mælius saw that his fate was determined; he endeavored to fly: his enemies charged him with snatching up a butcher's knife,[27] and endeavoring to repel the knights who were pursuing him; under somewhat similar circumstances the treacherous murder of Wat Tyler was excused by his pretended insolent behavior to the king; and Ahala, as eager as Sir William Walworth to do his work, slew Mælius on the spot, as guilty of disobedience. The old dictator[28] justified the deed to the multitude: "Mælius had aimed, not at the consulship, but at making himself king; the master of the markets had reported to the senate that secret meetings were held at his house, and arms collected. To meet this danger the senate had appointed a dictator; he had purposed to try Mælius, and judge him according to his guilt or innocence; but, as he had refused to obey his summons, and had resisted his own immediate commander, he had been lawfully slain."[29] Immediately afterwards, treating Mælius as a convicted traitor, he ordered his house to be levelled with the ground; thus the story of the concealed arms could never be disproved, for no time was allowed to the tribunes of the commons to search the house: Mælius' enemies might report whatever they pleased. The house stood under the Capitol, not far from the Mamertine prison,[30] and the site of it was, for ages after, called the Æquimælium, or the Mælian level.

The commons are indignant at his death.

Such is the story which the traditions or memoirs of the Quinctian and Servilian families handed down, and which the annalists adopted on their authority. Whatever ambitious designs Mælius may have had, nothing, even according to the statement of his enemies, was proved against him; and his aiming at the consulship would have been a sufficient crime in the eyes of the patricians to tempt them to violent measures. On the other hand, charity was so little familiar to the Greeks and Romans, that the splendid munificence of Mælius is in itself suspicious; a time of great distress would make it easy for a man of his wealth to engage a band of armed adventurers, sufficient to put him in possession of the Capitol by a sudden attack; and then his popularity with the commons, and their hatred of the patricians, would have rendered him ample service. However, the commons were indignant at his summary death; and there is a dim and confused account of disturbances consequent upon it. Ahala

ed L. Quinctius dictator before they left the senate-house; and they did not separate till evening, that the result of their measures might not be prematurely known. The occupation of the Capitol during the night, and the appearance of the dictator in the Forum early in the morning, ready to anticipate whatever might have been the designs of Mælius, remind us of the Doge of Venice, Gradenigo, and the energetic measures by which he met and baffled the conspiracy of the Querini and Thiepoli. See Daru, B. VII.

[26] Zonaras says that the Capitol was secured διὰ τῶν ἱππέων. This may include the plebeian centuries of knights, but it certainly applies mainly to the patricians, who were all enrolled in the sex suffragia, or patrician centuries of knights or cavalry. And so, after the death of Mælius, Ahala is described as returning to the dictator, "stipatus catervâ patriciorum juvenum." Livy, IV. 14.

[27] Dionysius, XII. 1. Fragm. Mai.

[28] Livy, IV. 15.

[29] "Jure cæsum pronuntiavit," an expression which seems as technical and official as our verdict of "justifiable homicide." Suetonius pronounces this same judgment on the murder of Cæsar, "Prægravant cætera facta dictaque ejus ut . . . jure cæsus existimetur." C. 76.

[30] Niebuhr, Vol. II. note 928. Bunsen, Beschreibung der Stadt Rom. Vol. III. p. 46. Varro, Ling. Lat. V. § 157. Ed. Müller.

was obliged to leave Rome;[31] and tribunes of the soldiers, instead of consuls, were chosen for the following year: thus much is intelligible; and the strength of the patricians in the comitia of the centuries, the immense power of the officer who presided at them, and perhaps, also, the natural leaning of the richer plebeians to the side of the patricians in a time of distress, when the contest was so likely to take the form of one between numbers and property, will sufficiently account for the election of three patricians, and, amongst them, of L. Quinctius, the son of the old dictator. But still the greatest number of votes was given to Mamercus Æmilius, who had been chosen one of the quæstores parricidii along with L. Valerius a few years before, and whose popular dictatorship four years later we have already noticed.

Story of L. Minucius having gone over to the commons, and of his popular acts.

There was, however, a much more mysterious story[32] to be found in some of the annalists from whom Livy compiled his history; that L. Minucius, that very master of the markets who is said to have given the first information of the dangerous designs of Sp. Mælius, now, in the disturbances that followed, went over from the patricians to the commons, was chosen by the ten tribunes to be their colleague, thus raising the number to eleven, and in this office put a stop to the dissensions. Further, he is said to have brought down the price of corn at the end of three market days to one as for the modius,[33] and to have become so popular, that the commons presented him, as their deliverer out of misery, with an ox with gilded horns to offer as a sacrifice;[34] and a statue was erected in his honor without the Porta Trigemina, made out of the bronze or brass coins which the commons subscribed for the purpose, each man contributing an ounce, or the twelfth part of the as, which was still of the weight of a full pound.

Remarks on this story.

Dion Cassius has preserved a statement, that in these times many patricians did, in fact, go over to the commons; and it is remarkable, that from this time forward we meet with none but plebeians of the name of Minucius, although patrician Minucii have hitherto occurred several times in the Fasti. And it is conceivable enough, that if any man had wished so to degrade himself, as the patricians would consider it, he might have done it with no opposition on their part: nay, they would have at once cast him out from their body as an unworthy member; for the feeling of later times, when P. Clodius was adopted into a plebeian family to enable him to stand for the tribuneship, and when the aristocracy opposed it as only furthering the purposes of his ambition, could not exist amongst the haughty patricians of the fourth

[31] Valerius Maximus, V. 3, § 2. And so Cicero, de Republicâ, I. 3. Offensio commemoratur Ahalæ. He had just before spoken of "Camilli exilium," and immediately afterwards mentions "invidia Nasicæ." Now offensio is in itself an ambiguous term, and may signify either exilium or invidia; either "the misfortune or calamity of Ahala," or "the odium which he incurred." But then this odium may have induced him to leave Rome, as Nasica did, without undergoing any formal trial; and then, when his party was strong enough, he may have returned, according to the statement of the pseudo-Cicero pro Domo, c. 32, and this may have been called a return from banishment without much exaggeration.

[32] Livy, IV. 16.

[33] Pliny, Hist. Nat. XVIII. 4. Livy describes this, as if Minucius had sold at this rate the corn which Mælius had collected, and which had been confiscated after his death. But Pliny's expression, "in trinis nundinis ad assem redegit," implies a more gradual, and, at the same time, a more extensive reduction of the price. If he proposed a law to fix a maximum, it would, of course, require three nundinæ to elapse before it could be passed; and this may be Pliny's meaning. Then the sale of Mælius' corn at a cheap rate may have taken place in the mean while; and if much corn had really been hoarded, it would naturally cause a great reduction of prices when brought suddenly into the market in the spring, especially if there was a promise of an abundant harvest in the coming summer.

[34] Livy mentions the ox, Pliny the statue, XVIII. 4, and XXXIV. 11, and both specify the place, extra portam Trigeminam, that is, on the bank of the Tiber, between the northeastern foot of the Aventine and the river. But as Livy's expression, "bove aurato extra portam Trigeminam est donatus," is rather strange, his editors have proposed various corrections, amongst which, the most plausible was that of Gronovius, who proposed to read "bove et prato." But a bos auratus, that is, auratis cornibus, was given by the consul to P. Decius, one of the tribunes of the soldiers, for saving his army in the first Samnite war, Livy, VII. 37; and Niebuhr's conjecture is simpler and more probable, that the words "et statuâ" have dropped out in Livy's text, between "bove aurato" and "extra portam Trigeminam."

century. On the other hand, Cicero treats these supposed passings over from one order to the other as mostly fictitious, and invented by plebeians, merely to claim for themselves kindred with an old patrician house of the same name. Nor is it probable that there could have been eleven tribunes at once; but it may be that L. Minucius so acted in concert with the tribunes as master of the markets,[35] that he was said to be like an eleventh member of their college. The rest is sufficiently probable, that he proposed and carried, after the regular period of three market days, a law to fix the maximum at which corn should be sold; and this, in a season of scarcity, when the evil is always attributed by the vulgar to the covetousness of corn-dealers, rather than to natural causes, would quite account for his popularity.

Dictatorship of Mamercus Æmilius.

In the following year, however, consuls were again chosen, and continued to be so for four years, that is, till 321, when Mamercus Æmilius was appointed dictator. His law for abridging the duration of the censor's office so offended the existing censors, one of whom was M. Geganius Macerinus, already known as a zealous partisan of his order in his consulship in 308, that they degraded him from his tribe,[36] and rated his property in the census at eight times as much as its real value. The commons were so indignant that they called aloud for military tribunes instead of consuls; and for the next two years tribunes were accordingly elected; but still no plebeian was chosen, nor even any patrician distinguished for his attachment to the popular cause.

The tribunes of the commons are applied to by the senate to compel the consuls to submit to its authority.

Again, for five years, we find the names of consuls in the Fasti, from 324 to 328 inclusive. But the power of the commons was silently and healthily advancing; and within this short period we find two remarkable instances of it. In 325,[37] T. Quinctius, a son of the old L. Cincinnatus, and C. Julius Mento, were consuls. The Æquians and Volscians had united their forces, and assembled a great army at their usual position on Algidus. A pestilence, nearly cotemporary with that which visited Athens so fearfully in the early years of the Peloponnesian war, had prevailed in Rome at intervals during the last four years, and had carried off great numbers of the people. This gave a sense of weakness; and, to increase it, the consuls, attacking the enemy on Algidus, were defeated. Then the senate resolved to appoint a dictator; but the consuls, jealous at this implied censure on themselves, refused to obey the senate's decree. Some party or family feuds, of which we know nothing, were most probably at work in this dispute; and it was proposed and carried, that the senate should call upon the tribunes for their aid. Niebuhr thinks that the tribunes were called upon to propose the senate's decree to the commons, that their acceptance of it might give it the force of a law. Livy's story is, that the tribunes threatened to throw the consuls into prison, if they persisted in disobeying the senate. However this be, there was, at any rate, an important acknowledgment of the power of the commons, when the patrician senate appealed to them to enforce its authority over the highest patrician magistrates.

The question of a war with Veii is submitted to the centuries.

Again, in 328, when a war with Veii was resolved on, the tribunes threatened[38] to stop the enlistments of soldiers, unless the question of going to war were first submitted to the people in their centuries. The senate had considered its own decree sufficient; but it had taught the tribunes, by its own conduct, not to regard it so; and accordingly the war

[35] Three of the tribunes, we are told by Livy, had taken no part in proposing the vote of the commons, which rewarded Minucius with his ox and his statue, but, on the contrary, continued to revile him, as he had been the first person to give information to the senate of the supposed treasonable designs of Mælius. But the other seven, constituting the majority of the college, must have gone along with him in his measures as master of the markets, and his acting in concert with them, perhaps, in some instances, against the wishes of the patricians, may have given rise to the story.

[36] Livy, IV. 24.

[37] Livy, IV. 26.

[38] Livy, IV. 30.

was proposed in the comitia, and sanctioned by the votes of all the centuries.

These were great constitutional points; another matter, deeply affecting individuals, had been provided for by a law passed three years before, which fixed a definite money computation for the fines of[39] sheep and oxen commonly imposed by the consuls for contempt of their jurisdiction. That the payment of these fines in kind would be often highly vexatious, is obvious: and if the consul were allowed to fix his own rate of commutation, it might bear hardly on the delinquent, especially if, as is probable, the brass money was now beginning to rise in value, so that the old money price of an ox or a sheep would be now more than it was worth. Cicero's statement[40] is, that the censors, L. Papirius and P. Pinarius, had imposed their fines in kind, and had thus seized so many cattle; that the consuls, to relieve the commons, fixed an easy rate of money commutation, at which the cattle might be redeemed.

A. U. C. 325. A. C. 427. Law for a fixed money commutation for the fines of sheep and oxen.

From the year 329 to 341 we have tribunes constantly, with the exception of only two years, instead of consuls. In 331, after a long interval,[41] we again hear of a call for an agrarian law; recent victories over the Volscians and Veientians had added, probably, to the amount of the demesne land; and the patricians who occupied it, either paid no acknowledgment for it at all, or if they did, it went not into the national treasury, but into that of their own order; the commons reaped no benefit from it. At the same time the commons had to serve at their own expense in war; and thus, as the poorer classes could ill support this burden, and could provide themselves only with inferior arms, the numbers and the efficiency of the regular infantry were much below what they might have been. Accordingly, the tribunes demanded that there should be a division of a portion of the demesne land amongst the commons; and that the occupiers of the remainder should pay their vectigal regularly, and that it should be devoted to the purpose of paying the soldiers. Here was a question in which the mass of the commons were interested; and it was likely that, during the continuance of this contest, the leaders of the commons would gain some of those points which they so longed for, but which were of far less importance, in the estimate of their followers, an admission to the higher magistracies.

A. U. C. 331. A. C. 421. New demand for an agrarian law.

A favorable opportunity presented itself three years afterwards, in 334: when the patricians[42] themselves proposed an increase in the number of the quæstores classici, those officers chosen by the centuries, and quite distinct from the quæstores parricidii, whose business it was to receive all money paid to the public treasury, and to make all payments from it. This was an office of great trust and dignity, and was usually regarded as entitled to a place in the senate; the censors, in drawing out their list of that body, generally included in it the quæstors of the last five years. Now, as wars were beginning to be carried on on a greater scale, and were attended with more success than formerly, it was desirable to have two new quæstors to accompany the armies to the field, and to take charge of the plunder that might be gained, or of the lands that might be conquered. But the tribunes naturally demanded, that if the college of quæstors were thus increased to four, two of them should be chosen from the commons. This the senate would not listen to, but proposed that the whole number should be taken indiscriminately from either order. When the tribunes refused to accept this compromise, having learned, from experience, that such a pretended free choice would always end in the exclusive election of patricians, the senate dropped the measure altogether. But the tribunes then brought it forward themselves, and, after long disputes, the compromise first proposed by the senate was accepted,

A. U. C. 334. A. C. 418. The office of the quæstores classici is thrown open to the commons.

[39] Livy, IV. 30.
[40] De Republicâ, II. 35.
[41] Livy, IV. 36.
[42] Livy, IV. 43.

and the quæstorship, with its four places, was declared by law to be open alike to the patricians and to the commons.

Here, again, the advantage gained by the commons as an order was great; but the individuals who had sown the seed did not reap the fruit; for again, owing to the great influence of the magistrate who presided at the comitia, none but patrician quæstors were chosen. Still the commons waxed stronger: three years afterwards, in 337, an agrarian law[43] was passed, by which fifteen hundred of the commons received allotments of two jugera a man out of the land lately conquered from the people of Lavici. But a larger division of the demesne land was demanded, and in a quarter where it could be enjoyed more securely; for the colonists sent to a frontier district would have continually to defend their new property with their swords, and men naturally longed for a division of the old demesne nearer home, which every new advance of the Roman boundary placed at a greater distance from danger. This, however, the patrician occupiers of this land were too powerful to permit; and the contest really turned upon the disposal of the new conquests. Thus, in 340, Bolæ was conquered, a town of the Æquians, not far from Lavici; and the commons required that a portion of this newly-won territory might, at least, be allotted to them. Even this was resisted, and by none more vehemently than by M. Postumius Regillensis,[44] one of the military tribunes of the year 341. He commanded one of the armies which were in the field against the Æquians, and, abusing his military power for political purposes, he threatened to visit upon his soldiers any display of feeling which they might have shown in favor of the proposed agrarian law. This excited universal indignation, which he heightened by refusing to his army any share of the spoil which they had won in recovering Bolæ from the Æquians. Open discontent then broke out, and Postumius, repressing it with extreme severity and the most merciless executions, provoked his soldiers to a mutiny, in which he was stoned to death.

Dispute about the agrarian law. Murder of M. Postumius by his soldiers.

A. U. C. 337. A. C. 415.

A. U. C. 340. A. C. 412.

A crime so rare in the Roman annals produced its natural and just consequence, a reaction against the cause which appeared to be connected with it. Consuls were chosen instead of tribunes of the soldiers; and the commons, to whom the senate had given the choice of the judge[45] in this cause, commissioned the consuls to inquire into the murder of Postumius, and to punish the guilty. This choice was sanctioned by the curiæ, and the judges thus appointed fulfilled their task with moderation, so that the influence which the patricians had gained by the whole transaction was marked by the undisturbed election of consuls for three years following. But by that time the feeling had changed: the continued opposition of the patricians to any agrarian law seemed a more present evil than the murder of Postumius; and, while that crime had been duly punished, the injustice of the patricians was triumphant. It is dangerous to overlook a change in public opinion, and still more to try to force in its old direction the tide which is beginning to turn. The patricians carried the election of consuls for a fourth year in spite of a strong feeling of discontent; but the commons were so roused, that in spite of all obstructions caused by the presiding officer, they elected, at the open comitia of quæstors,[46] no fewer than three plebeians.

Proceedings in consequence of this murder

A. U. C. 346. A. C. 406.

Then the agrarian law was demanded more vehemently than ever, and three

[43] Livy, IV. 47.

[44] Livy, IV. 49, 50.

[45] "A plebe consensu populi, consulibus negotium mandatur." Livy, IV. 51. A remarkable passage, which Niebuhr, as may be supposed, has not forgotten to appeal to, as a proof of the identity of the populus in old times with the patricians. It would seem as if the murder of Postumius was regarded as a crime committed by plebeians against the patrician order; it was then an act of moderation in the senate to allow the offending party to name the judge, and the patricians, to whom the injury had been done, would, at any rate, require that the nomination should be submitted to them for their approval.

[46] Livy, IV. 54.

Contest about the agrarian law continued.

tribunes, all of the Icilian family, were conspicuous as the leaders of the commons. The year passed away in these contests, but the commons insisted on having tribunes instead of consuls for the year following; and this was consented to,[47] but at the same time rendered nugatory by the condition annexed to it, that none of the tribunes of the commons of that year should be either re-elected to the same office, or be chosen tribunes of the soldiers. Thus those candidates being excluded whose claims were greatest, the patricians once more succeeded in defeating the plebeian candidates of less name, and in obtaining every place in the tribuneship for their own body.

A. U. C. 349. A. C. 403. Pay granted to the soldiers: number of tribunes of the soldiers increased to six.

Two years afterwards came the issue of the contest. A truce, which had been concluded for twenty years[48] with the Veientians, was now on the point of expiring; and as war, rather than peace, was supposed to be the natural state of things between two nations, unless some express treaty was interposed, so, at the end of the truce, hostilities would be resumed of course, unless either party wished to renew it, and was willing to purchase its continuance on the enemy's terms. Rome now felt itself much stronger than Veii, for that town had been lately torn with internal discords, so much more violent and injurious than those of Rome, in proportion as there was less of equal law and of acknowledged rights. The Romans, therefore, put a higher price on the renewal of the truce than the Veientians would consent to pay; and both nations prepared for war. This was the moment for the commons to press their claims, and they refused to vote for the law unless something was done to satisfy them. The patricians, looking forward to all the glory and dominion promised them by the expected conquest of Veii, or yielding to the power of justice, at last gave way. The vectigal,[49] or tithe, due from the occupiers of the public land, was to provide pay for the soldiers; if this were not sufficient, it was to be made good by a tax or tribute levied upon the whole people, according to the census of every citizen; and six tribunes of the soldiers were henceforth to be elected annually; one of whom, as Niebuhr thinks, was always to be a patrician, and to perform the important judicial duties afterwards discharged by the prætor urbanus; the other five were to be elected indiscriminately from either order. At any rate, six tribunes were elected from this time forwards, and this increased number gave the commons a greater likelihood of seeing some of the places filled by men of their own body. And so it happened, in fact; but for this the commons had yet to wait five years more.

A. U. C. 350. A. C. 402.

Accordingly pay[50] was issued to the soldiers, six tribunes of the soldiers were elected, and in the year 350, about the end of the Peloponnesian war, the Romans began their vast career of dominion by laying siege to the great Etruscan city of Veii.

[47] Livy, IV. 55.

[48] Livy, IV. 58. Livy says, that in the year 348 the truce had already expired; and, as it had been concluded, according to his own account, in the year 330, Niebuhr supposes that it must have been intended to last only twenty cyclic years, of ten months each. But we find that hostilities did not begin till 350, and no one will believe that the Romans allowed two years, in which they were, according to ancient notions, at war with Veii, to pass away without attacking their enemy, because the Veientians were involved in civil dissensions, and the Romans were too generous to take advantage of their weakness. We see from Thucydides, V. 14, that it was usual, when a truce was nearly expired, to negotiate as to the terms on which it might be renewed; and this, I doubt not, is the true explanation of the negotiations that went on during the years 348 and 349.

[49] This is not stated by Livy; but as it had been the great object insisted on by the tribunes, it is natural to suppose that it must either have been granted, or at any rate promised. It was probably, however, paid very irregularly, and hence the pay of the soldiers would, in point of fact, be provided chiefly out of the tax or tributum.

[50] Livy, IV. 59, 60, 61.

CHAPTER XVIII.

WARS OF THE ROMANS FROM 300 TO 364—THE ÆQUIANS AND VOLSCIANS—THE ETRUSCANS—SIEGE AND CAPTURE OF VEII.

Τὰ μὲν σπενδόμενοι, τὰ δὲ πολεμοῦντες—εὖ παρεσκευάσαντο τὰ πολέμια καὶ ἐμπειρότεροι ἐγένοντο, μετὰ κινδύνων τὰς μελέτας ποιούμενοι.—THUCYDIDES, I. 18.

The foreign history of Rome is even more uncertain than the domestic.

THE internal history of Rome in the first century of the commonwealth is obscure and often uncertain; nor can we venture to place full confidence in the details of events, or of individual characters. The family traditions and funeral orations out of which the oldest annalists compiled their narratives were often, as we find, at variance with each other, and dealt largely in exaggeration and misrepresentation. Yet still, up to a certain point, they were a check upon one another; there were necessarily limits to falsehood, when fellow-citizens, whether individuals or parties, were the subject on which it was exercised. But with regard to foreign enemies, even this check was wanting. Every family might claim victories over the Æquians or the Veientians: there was no sufficient knowledge of chronology to make it evident that the story of one victory and one triumph was fatal to the truth of others; the accommodating annalists found room for all. The account, then, of the early wars of the Romans cannot be trusted implicitly in its merest outline; we have the highest authority[1] for saying that victories, and even triumphs, were sometimes purely imaginary; a year which is filled with pretended successes of the Romans may have witnessed nothing but their defeats. We are reduced, therefore, not only to an outline, but to one made up from such scattered and almost accidental notices, that scarcely any one but Niebuhr would have attempted, far less have been able, to restore it. Here, as well as in the domestic history, the work is almost done to my hands: it were endless to make particular acknowledgments, when scarcely a page of this volume could have been written, had I not enjoyed the benefit of Niebuhr's guidance.

Advance of the Roman power between 300 and 364.

Our last notice of the foreign affairs of Rome stopped at that disastrous period, the end of the third century, when the Æquians and Volscians, having overrun Latium, having occupied many of the Latin towns, and established themselves on the Alban hills, were in the habit of carrying their plundering inroads up to the very walls of Rome. And whilst the Opican nations were thus formidable on the side of Latium, the Sabines made frequent descents into the Roman territory between the Tiber and the Anio, and sometimes spread their ravages on that side also as far as the immediate neighborhood of the city. Such nearly was the state of things about the year 300, which may be considered as the lowest point of the Roman fortunes. The next sixty years witnessed a wonderful change; at the end of that period the Roman power had spread itself out on every side, and the Opican nations, the Sabines, and the Etruscans, had all given way before it.

Successful war and peace with the Sabines.

Of these three enemies, the Sabines were the soonest and most effectually repelled. After the year 306, when M. Horatius Barbatus, the deliverer of the Roman commons from the decemvirs' tyranny, is said to have gained a great victory over them,[2] we read of them

[1] That, namely, of Cicero, in the often quoted passage of his Brutus, c. 16. "Multa scripta sunt in eis (scil. in mortuorum laudationibus) quæ facta non sunt, falsi triumphi," &c.

[2] Livy, III. 62, 63. Fasti Capitolini. "M. Horatius, M. F. Barbatus, de Sabineis (triumphavit) Ann. CCCIV. VII. K. Septembr."

no more during a period of more than a hundred and fifty years. A treaty of some sort or other must have followed this victory; perhaps it was only a truce for a certain number of years, which may have been continually renewed by mutual consent; the Romans having enough to do in Latium and in Etruria; and the Sabine youth finding a field for their enterprise, by joining their kinsmen the Samnites, who soon after this time began their conquests in Campania. Thus the Roman territory along the left bank of the Tiber was left in peace, and the frontier of the commonwealth on this side remained long unaltered, being bounded by the territory of the Sabine city of Eretum, which was situated about nineteen miles from Rome.

Wars with the Æquians and Volscians. Dictatorship and victory of A. Postumius Tubertus.

A far more obstinate and varied contest was maintained against the Æquians and Volscians. It is pretended that L. Valerius, the worthy colleague of M. Horatius, gained a great victory over them in the year 306;[3] but in 309[4] we find them again overrunning the Roman territory, and advancing unopposed, for the last time, as far as the walls of Rome by the Esquiline gate. In that same year T. Quinctius the consul is said to have gained a great victory over them, and there is this evidence of its reality, that the Romans established a garrison on the enemies' frontier at Verrugo;[5] a place undoubtedly on the Alban hills, but whether on Algidus above Tusculum, or on the side of Velitræ looking towards Antium and the Volscian lowlands, seems impossible to be ascertained. From this time we hear of no general efforts of the Æquians and Volscians for fifteen years; but in 324 the united armies of the two nations again appeared on Algidus,[6] and the Romans, in alarm, named A. Postumius Tubertus dictator to oppose them. That the danger was great, is shown by the dreadful story related of A. Tubertus,[7] that he executed his own son for having engaged with the enemy without orders, although successfully. This rigorous observance of discipline always occurs in Roman history, when the Roman arms were engaged in any contest more than ordinarily hazardous; and thus in the great Latin war about ninety years after this period, the act of A. Postumius Tubertus was again repeated in the more famous instance of T. Manlius. On the present occasion the Latins and Hernicans aided the Romans with their whole force, and the Opican nations were completely defeated. A truce of eight years was concluded with the Æquians;[8] the power of the Volscians, already shaken by their defeat, was further weakened by civil dissensions; the advocates for peace and war proceeding to the most violent extremities against each other.

A. U. C. 324. A. C. 428.

Eight years afterwards,[9] the Opican nations, first the Volscians, and soon after

[3] Livy, III. 61.

[4] Livy, III. 66.

[5] Livy, IV. 1.

[6] Livy, IV. 26.

[7] Livy, IV. 29, mentions the story, but wishes not to believe it. It is related, however, by Diodorus, XII. 64; by Valerius Maximus, II. 7, § 6; and by Aulus Gellius, XVII. 21. Gellius also speaks of "Posthumia" or "Posthumiana imperia et Manliana," I. 13, § 7; although it is one of Livy's reasons for not believing the story, that the common proverbial expression to denote power arbitrarily and cruelly exercised was "imperia Manliana non Postumiana."

[8] Livy, IV. 30.

[9] According to Livy, the Æquians had obtained a truce for eight years, in the beginning of the year 325. IV. 30. Five years afterwards, in 330, they are described as suing again for an extension of this term, and obtaining an additional truce for three years. IV. 35. The renewal of hostilities is placed in the year 334, Livy, IV. 43; but it may be concluded that it should in fact be placed a year earlier, and that the year 333, which with the Roman annalists is wholly devoid of military transactions, was indeed devoid of Roman victories, but not of defeats, or at least of disasters. For Livy begins the account of the next year with the words, "Non diutius fortuna Æquis indulsit, qui ambiguam victoriam Volscorum pro suâ amplexi fuerant." Now this "dubia victoria" had been won in 332, and the expression, "non diutius indulsit," would imply that for a certain time fortune had favored the Æquians; in other words, that they, encouraged by the Volscians' success in 332, took up arms themselves in the following year, and were during that year masters of the field. Thus it would seem that a truce of eight years, not cyclic, but common years, had been observed from 325 to 333; and the probability is, that the term originally agreed upon was five years, to which three were afterwards added; Livy's mistake consisting in this, that he supposes the whole eight years' truce to have been granted in 325, and that the three years added in 330 were an ad dition to this number.

the Æquians, again renewed the contest. The seat of war was again on the frontier of the Æquians: and there, in the year 332, the Romans received a check which we may not improbably conjecture to have been a serious defeat. But four years afterwards, in 336, the people of Lavici[10] are mentioned as joining the Æquians, and are spoken of as new enemies. Lavici, now La Colonna, placed on an isolated hill which rises as a sort of outwork at the northern extremity of the Alban cluster, had been one of the thirty Latin cities which signed the treaty of alliance with Rome in 261. Since that time the conquest of the Opican nations had separated it from its old confederacy, and it had possibly received an Æquian colony; but it had hitherto taken no active part against Rome. Now, however, it openly joined the Æquians; and its soldiers, after having ravaged the neighboring territory of Tusculum, encamped, together with their allies, in their old station on Algidus. They gained one victory, but it was speedily retrieved by the dictator Q. Servilius Priscus; Lavici was taken by the Romans,[11] its inhabitants massacred, expelled, or sold for slaves, and a large portion of its land was allotted to colonists of the Roman commons. This was a decided conquest, and gave the Romans possession of an advantageous post on their enemy's frontier. The victory seems also to have shaken the Æquian confederacy; for Bola, another town formerly belonging to the Latins, but wrested from them by the Opican conquerors, was allowed by the other Æquian states to fall unassisted, and another important post was thus occupied by the Romans. This happened in the year 341.[12]

War on the Æquian frontier. Lavici and Bola taken by the Romans.

The tide had now turned, and as ill success loosened the bond which held the Opican nations and cities together, so victory strengthened the alliance of the Romans, Latins, and Hernicans. In 342, this last people recovered Ferentinum,[13] one of their towns which the Volscians had formerly conquered; and as we hear, in two following years, of the ravage of the Latin and Hernican territory by the enemy, we cannot doubt that all the three confederate nations took an active part in the war. The Opicans, however, struggled vigorously; the frontier posts of Verrugo,[14] and of the castle of Carventum,[15] were taken and retaken; but the Æquians suffered so much from having the seat of war so continually on their frontier, that in the rally of the Opican league, which took place in the year 347, the lowland Volscians appear at the head of the confederacy, and the gathering-place of the army was at Antium. For two years nothing decisive happened; but in 349,[16] the Romans opened the campaign with their force divided into three small armies; and while one threatened Antium, and a second advanced upon Ecetræ, laying waste the country on every side to divert the enemy's attention, the third pushed direct for Anxur, or Tarracina, a most important place, standing at the very end of the plain of the Pontine Marshes, at the point where the Apennines of the Volscian highlands come down close upon the sea. Tarracina,[17] a Tyrrhenian city, had been subject to Rome in the last period of its monarchy; immediately afterwards it had been conquered by the Volscians, and from them received its name of Anxur; it is the natural gate of the country round Rome on the one hand, and of Campania on the other, and its capture would restore the Roman boundary to the extent which it had for-

Continued success of the Romans, Latins, and Hernicans.

They take Tarracina, or Anxur,

[10] Livy, IV. 45.
[11] Livy, IV. 47.
[12] Livy, IV. 49.
[13] Livy, IV. 51.
[14] Livy, IV. 55, 56, 58.
[15] Livy, IV. 53, 55. The position of Carventum and of its castle or citadel is wholly unknown. Sir W. Gell puts it doubtfully at Rocca Massimi, a high point on the Volscian highlands near Cora. Bunsen suggested to me the high ground of Monte Ariano, Mons Artemisius, the southeastern summit of the Alban hills, which rises above Velletri. I have not been able to find any notice of the place in Westphal's work on the neighborhood of Rome.
[16] Livy, IV. 59.
[17] It was probably a town belonging to the same race as Circeii and Ardea; that race which may be called either Tyrrhenian, Pelasgian, or Sikelian, and which, in language and religion, bore so close an affinity to the Greeks. Tarracina is mentioned as a dependent ally of Rome in the first treaty between Rome and Carthage, concluded in the first year of the commonwealth. See Polybius, III. 22.

merly reached under the Tarquinii. Its distance from the front of the war probably put its inhabitants off their guard, and it yielded to the sudden attack of the Romans with little resistance.[18] Twenty-five hundred of the inhabitants, who survived the storming of the town, were saved alive to be sold for slaves; and the two divisions which had covered the siege now came up to join their comrades, and the plunder of the town was given to the whole army without distinction. Two years afterwards the Romans invaded the Volscian highlands, and Artena,[19] on the edge of the mountains, looking across to the Alban hills at the back of Algidus, was taken, and razed to the ground. From henceforward the attention of Rome, for some years, was so much engaged by her wars on the Etruscan frontier, that she would have been well contented to have maintained and secured her conquests from the Æquians and Volscians, without endeavoring to extend them. And now was proved the advantage of the occupation of posts on the enemies' territory, and still more of the Roman system of colonies. When Anxur was taken, the neighboring Volscian cities seem to have concluded a truce with Rome to save their lands from ravage; at least, there was a free intercourse between them and the garrison, and the Roman soldiers were scattered[20] over the neighborhood to traffic with the inhabitants instead of plundering them. Advantage was taken of this, and Anxur was surprised by a sudden attack and recovered. But, as the Volscians are not charged with perfidy, we must either suppose that the assailants came from some of the more distant cities, which had not been included in the truce, or that the truce itself was concluded only for periods of a few days,[21] and continued by successive renewals; and that, at the end of one of these periods, the Volscians had refused to renew it, whilst the Romans had fully depended on its continuance. This was in 353, and two years afterwards Anxur was again recovered by a fresh surprise, the Volscians[22] neglecting to guard their walls whilst keeping a festival. It was recovered just in time; for as the war of the Romans with Veii and the neighboring cities still continued, the Opican nations seem to have renewed their league, and made another combined effort to retrieve their losses. In 358,[23] the Volscians were employed in besieging Anxur, while the Æquians were surrounding Lavici: had not the Romans possessed these two posts, the enemy might have again spread ravage over their whole territory, at a moment when a force could ill have been spared to check them. As it was, Anxur and Lavici were left to their own resources, and to the aid of the Latins and Hernicans, who, at this critical period, seem to have sustained the whole weight of the struggle with the Opican nations, for all the Roman armies were engaged elsewhere. Whether Lavici was taken or not, we know not; but in the next year Veii fell, and then the Æquians and Volscians solicited and obtained a truce.[24] The Romans availed themselves of it to establish a new colony in the country conquered from the Æquians, at Vitellia,[25] not far from Præneste, on the opposite side of the great gap or break by which the chain of the Apennines is there interrupted. They had found the benefit of their colony at Lavici; and this more distant settlement was made

and Artena.

Anxur is lost again by a surprise.

But again recovered.

The Romans establish a colony at Vitellia, on the Æquian frontier.

[18] Livy, IV. 59.

[19] Livy, IV. 61. The present Monte Fortino, according to Sir W. Gell; and according to Westphal also, if Artena, Ortona, and Virtona be, as is probable, only one and the same place. I learn, from a review of this history in the Dublin Review, No. XIII., that Nibby fixes the exact site of Artena at a place not more than a mile on the southeast of Monte Fortino, where the remains of a polygonal wall on a high level spot are still visible.

[20] Livy, V. 8.

[21] Like the ten days' truce, which was all that the Bœotians could be persuaded to agree to with Athens, when Lacedæmon concluded the peace of Nicias. See Thucydides, V. 26, 32.

[22] Livy, V. 13.

[23] Livy, V. 16.

[24] Livy, V. 23.

[25] Livy, V. 24, 29. Sir W. Gell places Vitellia at Valmonte, in the situation described in the text. Westphal puts it, but doubtfully, immediately under the northeast extremity of the Alban hills, on that shoulder of ground, raised above the ordinary level of the Campagna, which connects the roots of the Alban hills with the Apennines.

proportionably stronger; three thousand colonists were sent to occupy it instead of fifteen hundred. But the Æquians were more roused than daunted by this occupation of Vitellia, as they had already been taught the importance of such colonies. We hear nothing of the Volscians, so that they probably remained at peace; but the Æquians, though alone, dislodged the Romans from their old post of Verrugo,[26] and in the following year surprised the new colony of Vitellia. Four years after the fall of Veii, the whole force of Rome, under both consuls, was once more employed against the Æquians on the old battle-ground of Algidus;[27] which clearly shows that the Æquian frontier had again advanced, and that Vitellia and its territory were lost to Rome. An easy victory is, indeed, claimed for the Roman armies in this campaign, but the contest was not over, and its issue was still undecided, when in the next year the storm of the Gaulish invasion broke upon Latium, and crushed both of the contending parties; the Romans, however, for a short time only, the Æquians forever.

The Æquians destroy it.

The war undecided up to the time of the Gaulish invasion.

Thus in her long contest with the Opican nations, Rome had advanced, indeed, from her depressed state at the beginning of the century, yet had by no means reduced her enemies to submission. The occupation of Anxur on the side of the Volscians, and of Lavici and Bola on the Æquian frontier, was an important advantage; but the attempt to effect a settlement within the line of the Æquian highlands had been utterly defeated, and the Æquians, instead of defending their own country, were still able to fix the war on what may be called their advanced post of observation, the Alban hills; and from their advantage ground of Algidus, could still overhang Tusculum, and threaten devastation to the whole territory of Rome. It was in the opposite quarter, on the right bank of the Tiber, that the Romans made the first important addition to their dominion, and, for the first time, since the days of their kings, increased their power by an accession of new citizens from the population of the countries which they conquered.

Results of this long contest.

We have seen that in the year 280,[28] the Veientians had concluded a peace with the Romans for forty years. But in the year 317 the two nations were again involved in war; whether we are to suppose, with Niebuhr, that the truce was to last only for forty cyclical years of ten months each, and, therefore, that it had expired three years before, or whether it was brought to a premature termination, like the thirty years' peace between Athens and Sparta, which was cut short in the midst by the breaking out of the Peloponnesian war. The latter seems more probable, because the quarrel is especially said to have originated in the revolt of Fidenæ; whereas, had the truce been at an end, no particular cause of war would have been needed; hostilities would have been resumed as a matter of course.

Wars with Veii and Fidenæ.

The left bank of the Tiber, immediately above its confluence with the Anio, is skirted by a line of low hills at the distance of about half a mile. On one of these, which, like all the hills of the Campagna, break off into cliffs on their sides, stood the town of Fidenæ,[29] between five and six miles distant from Rome; the citadel, as some think, was on a higher point

Situation of Fidenæ. It is twice taken, and finally kept by the Romans.

[26] Livy, V. 28.

[27] Livy, V. 31. According to Diodorus, Velitræ and Satricum revolted from Rome at this period, and Circeii must have been lost previously and recently recovered again, as a colony was planted there in the year 362. It is clear, from this statement, that the Opican nations were rather roused than daunted by the fall of Veii, and were carrying on the war with Rome with unabated vigor, down to the very time of the Gaulish invasion. See Diodorus, XIV. 102, 106.

[28] See chapter XII.

[29] Westphal places Fidenæ at the site of the modern Villa Spada, just five miles from Rome; a spot which is now shown to strangers as the site of the villa of Phaon, Nero's freedman, and the place where Nero killed himself. According to Sir W. Gell, Fidenæ was about half a mile further on the road, and its citadel stood on the isolated hill of Castel Giubileo, which rises immediately above the Tiber. Westphal says that some inscriptions have been found which identify the spot. If so, and if I recognize his description, the excavations in the rock behind the Villa Spada, resembling those at Snenton, near Nottingham, would be, probably, the tombs of the citizens of Fidenæ.

of the ridge, separated from it by a valley, and rising immediately above the river. Fidenæ is described as an old Roman colony, established as early as the time of Romulus;[30] other accounts call it an Alban or Latin colony,[31] while it is represented as having been originally a city of the Etruscans.[32] It is said also to have twice revolted from Rome since the expulsion of the kings, and to have been twice reduced, the last time in the year 256,[33] and to have forfeited the half of its territory to the Roman garrison or colonists who occupied its citadel. All that can be gathered from these stories is, that the subject population in Fidenæ consisted chiefly of Etruscans; and that the ruling part of the inhabitants, the citizens of the colony, were Romans. In the year 317,[34] from some causes, of which we know nothing, the old Etruscan population rose against the Roman colonists, expelled them, and then put themselves under the protection of Veii. It is added that four Romans, sent to remonstrate with them upon their revolt, were murdered by them at the command of the Veientian king, who was become their new sovereign; and statues of the men thus slain were afterwards set up in the rostra; an honor that was paid two centuries later to the ambassadors murdered by the Illyrian queen Teuta. This revolt of Fidenæ, and the protection afforded to the revolters by the Veientians, led to a renewal of war between Rome and Veii; and the seat of the war was removed not only from the right to the left bank of the Tiber, but even, on more than one occasion, to the left bank of the Anio, that is to say, within three miles of Rome. In 320, however, Q. Servilius Priscus,[35] who was appointed dictator, is said to have taken Fidenæ, and new colonists were again sent to occupy the place; but in 329 we read of another revolt, accompanied by a massacre[36] of the colonists, and Mamercus Æmilius was named dictator to meet this new danger. He gained a great victory over the Veientians and Fidenatians, and again took Fidenæ; but this time the work was done effectually:[37] the Etruscan population were either massacred or sold for slaves, and the town and its territory remained from henceforth in the undisturbed possession of the Romans. At the same time a peace was concluded with the Veientians for twenty years.[38]

War with Veii.

This was in 330; but in the year 348, Livy says that the term of the truce had already expired;[39] so that Niebuhr conjectures that in this instance also we must reckon by cyclical years of ten months, and that the truce was only concluded for sixteen common years and eight months. On the other hand, if this were so, the truce must have expired early in 347, for there seems no foundation for Niebuhr's conjecture, that it had not begun before 331: it was surely likely that it would have been solicited immediately after the taking of Fidenæ, and concluded early, rather than late, in 330, much less can we suppose it to have been delayed till the year following. Besides, we read of no actual hostilities before the year 350, that is, till the end of twenty common years; and the story that the Romans forbore to press their demands on Veii during

[30] Compare Livy, I. 14 and 27.

[31] Dionysius, II. 53, says that Fidenæ, Nomentum, and Crustumeria were all of them Alban colonies, founded at the same time by three brothers. Virgil names Fidenæ along with Nomentum and Gabii, and also speaks of it as an Alban colony. Æn. VI. 73.

[32] Livy, I. 15. Strabo, V. 2, § 9, p. 226. Plutarch makes Fidenæ, Crustumeria, and Antemnæ to have been Sabine towns, Romulus, 17. Müller well remarks that in Fidenæ and Crustumeria, as in Rome, we find traces of these same three elements of the population, Latins, Sabines, and Etruscans. But at Fidenæ, the close connection of the place with Veii (to which place it seems to have been subject or dependent, as was also Capena), seems to show, that previously to its final conquest by the Romans, the Etruscan element was predominant. See Müller's Etrusker, Vol. I, p. 113, 361.

[33] Dionysius, V. 60.

[34] Livy, IV. 17. He speaks as if the Roman colonists had revolted; but Niebuhr seems right in supposing, that when we read of the revolt of a colony in these early times, we should understand it not properly speaking of the colonists, but of the subject population who arose and drove them out, and then asserted their own independence, or connected themselves with some people of their own race.

[36] Livy, IV. 21. The common editions of Livy, including Bekker's, call him A. Servilius, following in this most of our present MSS. But Glareanus says that most of the MSS. had "Quintus," and that "Aulus" was the reading of Aldus' MS., which he followed in his edition. Sigonius, Glareanus, Pighius, and Drakenborch, all prefer the reading "Quintus."

[36] Livy, IV. 31.

[37] Livy, IV. 34.

[38] Livy, IV. 35.

[39] Livy, IV. 58. Tempus induciarum exierat.

the year 348 out of magnanimity, because the Veientians were distracted by internal factions, is suspicious enough to throw discredit upon the whole narrative which involves it. It is far more probable that, as the expiration of the truce drew near, both parties tried what could be gained by negotiation.[40] The Romans were engaged in war with the Æquians and Volscians, and although successful in the campaign of 347, yet they had obtained no decided advantage. Thus the Veientians tried to spin out the negotiation till they should see the event of the next campaign, but as that was unfavorable to the Romans, the garrison at Verrugo being surprised and cut to pieces by the Volscians, the Veientians took courage, and refused to grant the Roman demands. The next year, however, greatly altered the face of affairs; the Romans were completely successful against the Volscians, and took the important city of Anxur: war with Veii was now looked forward to with delight, the commons were conciliated by the grant of pay to the soldiers, and thus, at the close of the twentieth year of the truce, apparently in the spring of 350, the Roman people voted for instant war with the Veientians; and the military tribunes of that year[41] commenced the invasion of the Veientian territory, and the occupation of fortified posts in the neighborhood of Veii.

Again, in the year following, 351, the Roman arms were called off from Veii by the Volscian war,[42] and nothing was attempted against the city. But in the next year the Volscians were quiet, and the siege of Veii was commenced in earnest. Livy's expressions[43] convey the notion that a double line of walls was carried all round the city, as at Platæa, the inner wall to blockade the besieged, the outer one to shelter the besiegers from any attempt to raise the siege on the part of the other states of Etruria. But the circuit of the walls of Veii, according to Sir W. Gell's measurements,[44] was above five miles; the besiegers' line, therefore, must have embraced a still larger space, and the deep valleys with rocky sides, between which the small streams of this district always flow, would have offered formidable interruptions to the work. Besides, it is manifest that if such a circumvallation had been completed, Veii must have been starved out within a year, instead of resisting for seven years, and not being even at last reduced by famine. It appears rather that the two Roman armies employed in the siege established themselves in two separate camps, and secured the communication between them as well as they could by detached forts, intending to carry on their circumvallation on each side from their camps, as the Athenians did at Syracuse, till it should meet and effectually inclose the city. And as it was necessary that the lines should be maintained through the winter, the Romans now, for the first time, became acquainted with war on a greater scale, and, instead of returning home after a few days' service, a considerable portion, at least, of the soldiers were to remain before Veii during the whole year. This was as strange and unwelcome to the Romans as it would have been to the Peloponnesians, but the national feeling was interested in the war, and the lines, after having been once taken by a sally of the besieged, were recovered and maintained by an army of volunteers.

The siege of Veii formed.

A. U. C. 352. A. C. 400.

Still there was no complete circumvallation: Veii was open and accessible to relief; and the people of the two neighboring cities of Capena and Falerii, being at length aroused to a sense of their own danger if Veii fell, exerted all their power to deliver it. They attacked the Roman lines,[45] stormed one of the two camps which formed the strongholds of the besieging army, and for the remainder of the year the communications of Veii with the surrounding country were carried on in freedom.

A. U. C. 353. A. C. 399. Attacks made on the besieging army.

[40] See note 48 of the last chapter.

[41] Livy, IV. 61. Ab his primum circumsessi Veii sunt.

[42] Livy, IV. 61.

[43] Livy, V. 1. Ita muniebant ut ancipitia munimenta essent, alia in urbem—versa, aliis frons in Etruriam spectans auxiliis, si qua forte inde venirent, obstruebatur. Compare Thucydides' description of the Peloponnesian lines round Platea: τὸ τεῖχος εἶχε δύο τοὺς περιβόλους, πρός τε Πλαταιῶν, καὶ εἴ τις ἔξωθεν ἀπ' 'Αθηνῶν ἐπίοι. III. 21.

[44] See the conclusion of the article "Veii," in his work on the topography of Rome and its vicinity.

[45] Livy, V. 8.

For five years after this, the siege, if so it may be called, made but little progress. The Romans retained their camps before Veii, as the Veientians had once held the Janiculum; they plundered the Veientian territory, and by their advanced position protected their own. The Capenatians and Faliscans could not again succeed in carrying the Roman camps, and the Tarquinensians, who took part in the contest in the year 358,[46] and ventured to invade the Roman territory, were repelled with loss. But this interference of the people of Tarquinii, one of the greatest and most influential of the Etruscan cities, and not the immediate neighbor of Veii, was probably a symptom of the dispositions of the whole Etruscan confederacy. A great council of the whole nation met at the temple of Voltumna,[47] the Panionium of Etruria; the question of aiding Veii with the united force of the twelve cities was debated: but at this critical moment the attention of the northern states of the league was drawn off to another and a more imminent danger. The Gauls had crossed the Alps, and were overrunning the country of the twelve cities of northern Etruria, between the Alps and the Apennines. With such an enemy so near them, the northern states of Etruria proper, Volteræ, Fæsulæ, Cortona, and Clusium, were not disposed to march their forces away to a contest on the banks of the Tiber, and to leave their own homes open to the inroads of the Gauls. Accordingly, the southern cities were left to their fate; and only Capena and Falerii took any part in the final struggle between Veii and Rome.

The other Etruscan states refuse their aid to the Veientians.

But the events of the last year of this struggle plainly showed what Rome would have had to fear from a coalition of all the twelve cities of Etruria. Two of the Roman military tribunes[48] were defeated by the Faliscans and Capernatians; one of them was killed in the battle; and the panic spread to the lines before Veii, and even to Rome itself, where the rumor prevailed, that the whole force of Etruria was on its march, that the lines before Veii were actually assailed by the enemy, and that his victorious bands might be expected every moment to advance upon Rome. So great was the alarm, that the matrons crowded to the temples to avert, by prayers and sacrifices, their country's peril; and the senate resolved to appoint a dictator.[49] The dictator thus chosen was the famous M. Furius Camillus.

A. U. C. 359. A. C. 393. The Romans defeated before Veii. Camillus appointed dictator.

During thirty years from this period Camillus was undoubtedly the most eminent man in Rome, and the favorite leader of the aristocracy, who twice made him their champion in the hour of their greatest need, once to put down M. Manlius, and again to prevent, if possible, the passing of the Licinian laws. Nor was the distinction of his family confined to him alone; one of his sons was the first prætor, and another was twice dictator, and twice consul, and gained a memorable victory over the Gauls. But in proportion to this high eminence of the Furian family, was the exaggeration of which they were the subject. The stories told of them were so popular, that they were not merely engrafted upon the brief notices contained in the genuine records of the time, but took the place of these altogether; so that it is through

The history of the fall of Veii has been supplanted by the poetical story.

[46] Livy, V. 16.

[47] Livy, V. 17. The situation of this temple is unknown, as well as the attributes of the goddess to whom it was dedicated. The assemblies held at the temple were composed only of the ruling caste, the Principes or Lucumones of Etruria: but they were connected with a religious festival, with games of various sorts, and especially with dramatic entertainments; so that people of all ranks came together on these solemnities, and the concourse attracted traders from foreign countries, as to a favorable opportunity of carrying on their traffic.

[48] Livy, V. 18.

[49] So strangely does the poetical story at this point supplant the real history, that Livy does not so much as mention the resolution of the senate to appoint a dictator, but after describing the alarm at Rome, and the prayers of the matrons, he passes abruptly to the legend, and merely says, "fatalis dux ad excidium illius urbis servandæque patriæ M. Furius Camillus dictator dictus magistrum equitum P. Cornelium Scipionem dixit." V. 19. It appears, however, that the master of the horse, according to the Fasti Capitolini, was not P. Cornelius Scipio, but P. Cornelius Maluginensis. See the "Frammenti nuovi," published by Borghesi.

the Greek writers only that we can learn the real issue of the Gaulic invasion, and the history of the taking of Veii has not been preserved at all. That the beautiful and romantic story of the fall of Veii belongs entirely to the traditions and funeral orations of the Furian family, is plain from this, that the events, even of the very last year of the war, are related historically down to the very time of the appointment of Camillus to the dictatorship; but then the history suddenly vanishes, and a mere romance succeeds in its place wherever the actions of Camillus are the subject, interspersed here and there with fragments of authentic history, where the story relates to the actions of other persons. Thus we do not really know how Veii fell, or by what means a contest which, in the beginning of the year 359, wore so unpromising an aspect, was, before the end of that same year, brought to a triumphant conclusion. It is mentioned[50] that the Latins and Hernicans, who seem hitherto to have taken no part in the war, joined the Romans with their whole force as soon as Camillus was made dictator. Probably the defeat sustained in the early part of the year, and the fear lest all Etruria should combine to relieve Veii, if any accident should turn the stream of the Gaulish invasion upon other countries, convinced the Romans that they must make the most of the present moment, whilst the Etruscans still stood aloof. An overpowering army of the Romans and their allies was brought against Veii; the siege of Platæa shows what great works for the reduction of a town could be completed within a short time by the united labor of a multitude of hands: a mound might be carried to the top of the loftiest walls; or their foundations might be undermined, and a breach opened in an instant; or, in the wide extent of Veii, some ill-guarded spot might be found, by which the enemy might effect an entrance without opposition. Be this as it may, the manner of the real capture of the place is irrecoverably lost; but it is certain that in the year 359, after a war of nine years, this old antagonist of Rome, the large, the wealthy, and powerful city of Veii, was taken by the Romans, and the political existence of its people destroyed forever.

Difference between the poetical legends and the wilful falsehoods of the family memoirs.

But before we finally quit the poetical legends of the early Roman history, the last of them, and not the least beautiful, that which relates to the fall of Veii, must find its place in this narrative. In the life of Camillus there meet two distinct kinds of fiction, equally remote from historical truth, but in all other respects most opposite to one another: the one imaginative, but honest, playing, it is true, with the facts of history, and converting them into a wholly different form, but addressing itself also to a different part of the mind; not professing to impart exact knowledge, but to delight, to quicken, and to raise the perception of what is beautiful and noble; the other, tame and fraudulent, deliberately corrupting truth in order to minister to national or individual vanity, pretending to describe actual events, but substituting in the place of reality the representations of interested or servile falsehood. To the former of these classes belongs the legend of the fall of Veii; to the latter the interpolation of the pretended victory of Camillus over the Gauls. The stories of the former kind, as innocent as they are delightful, I have thought it an irreverence to neglect; the fabrications of the latter sort, which are the peculiar disgrace of Roman history, it is best to pass over in total silence, that they may, if possible, be consigned to perpetual oblivion.

The poetical story of the fall of Veii is as follows:

Poetical story of the fall of Veii. The lake of Alba overflows its banks.

For seven years and more the Romans had been besieging Veii. Now the summer was far advanced,[51] and all the springs and rivers were very low; when on a sudden the waters of the lake of Alba began to rise; and they rose above its banks, and covered the fields and houses by the water-side; and still they rose higher and higher, till they reached the top of the hills which surrounded the lake as with a wall, and

[50] Livy, V. 19.

[51] Dionysius, XII. 11. Fragm. Mai.

they overflowed where the hills were lowest; and behold, the water of the lake poured down in a mighty torrent into the plain beyond. When the Romans found that the sacrifices[52] which they offered to the gods and powers of the place were of no avail, and their prophets knew not what counsel to give them, and the lake still continued to overflow the hills and to pour down into the plain below, then they sent over the sea, to Delphi, to ask counsel of the oracle of Apollo, which was famous in every land.

A prophet of Veii declares the meaning of the overflow.

So the messengers were sent to Delphi. And meanwhile the report of the overflowing of the lake was much talked of; so that the people of Veii heard of it. Now there was an old Veientian,[53] who was skilled in the secrets of the Fates, and it chanced that he was talking from the walls with a Roman centurion whom he had known before in the days of peace; and the Roman spoke of the ruin that was coming upon Veii, and was sorry for the old man his friend; but the old man laughed and said: "Ah! ye think to take Veii; but ye shall not take it till the waters of the lake of Alba are all spent, and flow out into the sea no more." When the Roman heard this he was much moved by it, for he knew that the old man was a prophet; and the next day he came again to talk with the old man, and he enticed him to come out of the city, and to go aside with him to a lonely place, saying that he had a certain matter of his own, concerning which he desired to know the secrets of fate. And while they were talking together, he seized the old man, and carried him off to the Roman camp, and brought him before the generals; and the generals sent him to Rome to the senate. Then the old man declared all that was in the Fates concerning the overflow of the lake of Alba; and he told the senate what they were to do with the water, that it might cease to flow into the sea: "If the lake overflow, and its waters run out into the sea, woe unto Rome; but if it be drawn off, and the waters reach the sea no longer, then it is woe unto Veii." But the senate would not listen to the old man's words, till the messengers should come back from Delphi.

The Romans dig through the mountains, and draw off the water of the lake.

After a time the messengers came back, and the answer of the god agreed in all things with the words of the old man of Veii. For it said,[54] "See that the waters be not confined within the basin of the lake: see that they take not their own course and run into the sea. Thou shalt let the water out of the lake, and thou shalt turn it to the watering of thy fields, and thou shalt make courses for it till it be spent and come to nothing." Then the Romans believed the oracle, and they sent workmen, and began to bore through the side of the hills to make a passage for the water. And the water flowed out through this passage under ground; and it ceased to flow over the hills; and when it came out from the passage into the plain below, it was received into many courses which had been dug for it, and it watered the fields, and became obedient to the Romans, and was all spent in doing them service, and flowed to the sea no more. And the Romans knew that it was the will of the gods that they should conquer Veii.

The Romans refuse peace to the Veientians.

So Marcus Furius Camillus was made dictator; and the Veientians sent to Rome to beg for peace,[55] but the Romans would not grant it. Now the Etruscans are skilled in the secrets of fate above all other nations; and one of the chief men of Veii, who had gone with the embassy, turned round as he was going out of the senate-house, and looked upon the senators, and said: "A goodly answer truly have ye given us, and a generous; for though we humble ourselves before you, ye will show us no mercy, but threaten to destroy us utterly. Ye heed neither the wrath of the gods nor the vengeance of men. Yet the gods shall requite you for your pride; and, as ye destroy our country, so ye shall shortly after lose your own."

[52] Dionysius, XII. 12.

[53] Dionysius, XII. 13. Livy, V. 15. Plutarch, Camillus, 4.

[54] Livy, V. 16.

[55] Dionysius, XII. 17.

Meanwhile Marcus Furius[56] pressed the city on every side; and he was at the head of a mighty army; for the Latins and the Hernicans had brought their aids; and he commanded his men to dig a way under ground, which should pass beneath the walls, and come out again to the light within the precinct of the temple of Juno, in the citadel of Veii. The men worked on by night and by day; for they were divided into six bands; and each band worked in turn and rested in turn; and the secret passage was carried up into the precinct of the temple of Juno; but it had not broken through the surface of the ground; so that the Veientians knew not of it.

A mine dug into the heart of the citadel of Veii.

Then every man[57] who desired to have a share of the spoil hastened from Rome to the camp at Veii. And Marcus, the dictator, made a vow, and promised to give the tenth part of all the spoil to Apollo, the god of Delphi; and he prayed also to Juno, the goddess of the Veientians, that she would be pleased to depart from Veii, and to follow the Romans home to their city, which from henceforth should be hers, and where a temple worthy of her majesty should be given her for her abode. After this, he ordered the Romans to assault the city on every side; and the Veientians ran to the wall to meet them; and the shout of the battle arose, and the fight was carried on fiercely.[58] But the king of the Veientians was in the temple of Juno in the citadel, offering a sacrifice for the deliverance of the city; and the prophet who stood by, when he saw the sacrifice, cried aloud, "This is an accepted offering; for there is victory for him who offers its entrails upon the altar!" Now the Romans were in the secret passage, and heard the words of the prophet. So they burst forth into the temple, and they snatched away the entrails from those who were sacrificing, and Marcus, the Roman dictator, and not the king of the Veientians, offered them upon the altar. Then the Romans rushed down from the citadel, and ran to the gates of the city, and let in their comrades; and all the army broke into the town, and they sacked and took Veii.

Veii is taken.

While they were sacking the city, Marcus looked down upon the havoc from the top of the citadel, and when he saw the greatness of the city and the richness of the spoil, his heart swelled within him,[59] and he said, "What man's fortune was ever so great as mine?" But then in a moment there came the thought, how little a thing and how short a time can bring the greatest fortune down to the lowest, and his pride was turned into fear, and he prayed, if it must be that in return for such great glory and victory, some evil should befall himself or his country, yet that it might be light and recoverable. Whilst he prayed he veiled his head,[60] as is the custom of the Romans in prayer, and turned round towards the right. But as he turned, his foot slipped, and he fell upon his back upon the ground. Yet he was comforted rather than dismayed by his fall, for he said, "The gods have heard my prayer, and for the great fortune of my victory over Veii they have sent me only this little evil."

Camillus vaunts himself of his victory.

Then he ordered some young men,[61] chosen out from all his army, to approach to the temple of Juno; and they had washed themselves in pure water, and were clothed in white, so that there was on them no sign or stain of blood and of slaughter; and they bowed low as they came to the temple, but were afraid to touch the image of the goddess, for no hand might touch it except the priest's who was born of the house that had the priesthood. So they asked the goddess whether it was her pleasure to go with them to Rome. And then there happened a wonder; for the image spake, and answered, "I will go;" and when they touched it, it moved from its place of its own accord, and it was carried to Rome. Thus Juno left her abode in the

The statue of Juno is carried from Veii to Rome.

56 Livy, V. 19.
57 Livy, V. 20, 21.
58 Livy, V. 21. Plutarch, Camillus, 5.
59 Dionysius, XII. 19.
60 Dionysius, XII. 22, 23. Plutarch, Camillus, 5.
61 Livy, V. 22.

citadel of Veii, and she dwelt in her temple at Rome, on the hill Aventinus, which the Romans built and dedicated to her honor.

Camillus triumphs proudly.

After this[62] there were rejoicings at Rome greater than had ever been known before; and there were thanksgivings for four days, and all the temples were filled with those who came to offer their thank-offerings. And Marcus entered the city in triumph, and he rode up to the Capitol in a chariot drawn by four white horses, like the horses of Jupiter and like the horses of the sun. But wise men thought that it was done too proudly; and they said, "Marcus makes himself equal to the blessed gods; see if vengeance come not on him, and he be not made lower than other men."

Increase of the Roman territory by the conquest of Veii.

To return from this famous legend to our imperfect history of the times, the Romans, by the fall of Veii, acquired a considerable addition to their territory. The inhabitants of several districts subject to the Veientians had revolted to the Romans during the war, or rather, to escape the ravage of the Roman armies, had surrendered themselves and their lands at discretion. The rest of the country, if any remained so long independent, must have fallen with the capital; and thus the Romans now extended their dominion along the right bank of the Tiber from its mouth to a distance of about thirteen miles above Rome,[63] whilst it stretched northwards from the Tiber as far as the Lago di Bracciano, Lacus Sabatinus,[64] and the edge of the actual Campagna at Monterosi; passing thence, in a line including the remarkable eminence of Monte Musino,[65] to the Tiber opposite the Ager Crustumerinus. But in the years immediately following the conquest of Veii, the Romans penetrated still deeper into Etruria. Capenia, which had stood by the Veientians to the last, fell in the very next year after its ally;[66] and its conquest put the Romans in possession of an additional portion of the right bank of the Tiber, above the territory just won from the Veientians. In the year after, we hear of the submission of Falerii, the sole remaining member of the alliance, situated either on or near the site of the modern town of Civita Castellana.[67] Camillus was the military tribune who reduced Falerii, and accordingly we have another tale in the place of history. A schoolmaster,[68] who had the care of the sons of the principal citizens, took an opportunity, when walking with his boys without the walls, to lead them to the Roman camp, and throw them into the power of the enemy. But Camillus, indignant at this treason, bade the boys to drive their master back into the town again, flogging him all the way thither, for the Romans, he said, made no war with children. Upon this the Faliscans, won by his magnanimity, surrendered to him at discretion, themselves, their city, and their country. Whether the city, however, was really surrendered at this time, may seem very doubtful; that it sued for and obtained peace is likely: it lost, also, a portion of its territory, for we read of a number of Faliscans as forming a part of the four new tribes[69] of Roman citizens, which were created immediately after the Gaulish invasion.

Submission of Nepete and Sutrium.

In the same year, or in the following year, may be placed also the submission of Nepete and Sutrium,[70] which appear immediately after the retreat of the Gauls as the dependent allies of Rome. They did not

[62] Livy, V. 23.

[63] Pliny, Hist. Nat. III. 9.

[64] This may be concluded, not only from the short distance between Veii and the Lacus Sabatinus, and from there being no independent city, so far as we know, between them; but it seems to follow, also, from the name of one of the new tribes which were formed immediately after the Gaulish invasion, the tribus Sabatina. The lands of this tribe must have been situated near the lake; and from whom could the Romans have conquered them at that period, except from the Veientians?

[65] See the description and sketch of Monte Musino, in Sir W. Gell's work on the neighborhood of Rome, under the title "Ara Mutiæ."

[66] Livy, V. 24.

[67] Westphal and Nibby place the Etruscan Falerii at Civita Castellana, and the later Roman colony at S. Maria di Falari, about half way between Civita Castellana and Ronciglione. Sir W. Gell places the Etruscan city at S. Maria di Falari.

[68] Livy, V. 27.

[69] Livy, VI. 4.

[70] Diodorus places in the same year the peace with the Faliscans, and something in connec-

surrender themselves, "dediderunt se," but obtained a treaty of alliance, such as we find so often between the weaker and the stronger states in Greece. Nepete still exists, with almost the same name, and is a well-known town on the Perugia road to Rome, standing in a beautiful country between the edge of the Campagna and the valley of the Tiber, a little to the north of Monterosi. Sutrium also exists in the modern town of Sutri, a little to the west of the present road from Monterosi to Ronciglione.

The Romans reach the ridge of the Ciminian mountains.

The Romans had now reached what may be called the extreme natural boundary of the basin of the Tiber on the side of Etruria. Sutrium and Nepete looked up immediately to the great and lofty ridge of the Ciminian mountains, that ridge which the traveller ascends as soon as he leaves Viterbo, while from its summit he catches his first view of the neighborhood of Rome, of the line of the Apennines skirting the Campagna to the northeast, and of the Alban hills in the farthest distance, and, although the particular objects cannot be distinguished, of that ever memorable plain in which stands Rome. This ridge, in short, separates the streams which feed the Tiber from the valley of Viterbo and the basin of the lake of Bolsena, or, to speak the language of the fourth century of Rome, it separated the territories of Veii and Falerii, the advanced posts, as it were, of the Etruscan confederacy, from those of Vulsinii and Tarquinii, two of the greatest and most distinguished states of the whole nation.

They cross them, and are engaged in war with the people of Vulsinii and the Salpinatians.

Eighty years after this period, the passage of the Ciminian mountains was regarded as a memorable event, as little less than the entrance into an unknown world.[71] But now, emboldened by their victories over the nearer Etruscan cities, and aware, no doubt, that the dread of the Gauls on the northern frontier would render a general gathering of the whole nation impossible, the Romans seemed anxious to cross their natural boundary, and to penetrate into the heart of Etruria. A war broke out, we know not on what grounds, between Rome and Vulsinii;[72] but in the first year the Romans were crippled, according to their own account, by a famine and pestilence; and the Vulsinians, aided by the Salpinatians, a neighboring people wholly unknown to us, invaded the Roman territory without opposition. In the next year, however, the Romans were able to act on the offensive; a great victory was gained over the Vulsinians; the Salpinatians did not risk a battle; and, after the lands of either people had been laid waste by the conquerors, the Vulsinians sued for and obtained a truce for twenty years,[73] on the condition of giving satisfaction to the Romans to the extent of their demands, and furnishing a year's pay for the army employed against them. Of the Salpinatians we hear no further mention, either now or at any future period.

A. U. C. 364. A. C 388.

Conclusion.

Thus Rome was gaining ground rapidly in Etruria, while in Latium she could not yet dislodge her old enemies the Æquians, even from the Alban hills. With so stubborn, so active, and so powerful an adversary on the south, any attempt to make extensive conquests on the north must ever have been full of danger; and an alliance between the Etruscan confederacy and the Opican nations, at this period of the Roman history, would probably have effected what the league between the Etruscan and Sabellian nations, ninety years afterwards, attempted in vain. But Providence, which designed that Rome should win the empire of the world, altered the course of events by turning the torrent of a Gaulish invasion upon Latium. This it was which crushed the Æquians forever; and which obliged the Romans, by its

tion with Sutrium. The present text is corrupt: Σoύτριον μὲν ὥρμησαν. Niebuhr proposes to supply ἐπὶ, but the corruption lies, I think, in the verb, and in the preceding conjunction, καί. See Diodorus, XIV. 98.

71 Livy, IX. 36.

72 Livy, V. 31.

73 Livy, V. 32.

consequences, to confine their attention again for a long period to the left bank of the Tiber. There, in many years of patient and arduous struggles, they laid deeper and firmer the foundations of their after greatness, by effectually subduing the remnant of their Opican enemies, and obtaining a more complete command than ever over the resources of the cities of the Latins. Thus the Gaulish invasion and conquest of Rome was but the instrument of her greater and surer advance to the dominion of Italy.

CHAPTER XIX.

INTERNAL HISTORY FROM 350 TO 364—PLEBEIAN MILITARY TRIBUNES—BANISHMENT OF CAMILLUS.

"SICINIUS.—He's a disease that must be cut away.
MENENIUS.—Oh, he's a limb that has but a disease:
Mortal to cut it off; to cure it easy."
SHAKSPEARE, Coriolanus.

Φοβηθέντες γὰρ αὐτοῦ οἱ πολλοὶ τὸ μέγεθος τῆς τε κατὰ τὸ ἑαυτοῦ σῶμα παρανομίας ἐς τὴν δίαιταν . . . . ὡς τυραννίδος ἐπιθυμοῦντι πολέμιοι καθέστασαν.—THUCYDIDES, VI. 15.

Advance of the plebeians.

IN the fourteen years which elapsed between the beginning of the last war with Veii and the invasion of the Gauls, the plebeian leaders reaped the fruit of the seed which their predecessors had sown so perseveringly. Now, for the first time, we find plebeians not only admitted into the college of military tribunes, but forming in it the majority. Yet even this was, as it were, only the first-fruits of the harvest; many years elapsed before the full crop was brought to the sickle.

The patricians interfere with the election of tribunes.

In the year 352, the third year of the war with Veii, the Romans intending, as has been mentioned, to blockade the city, were obliged to keep a part of their forces on duty during the winter. This was doubly unpopular, both as it obliged so many citizens to be absent from their homes for several months together, a term of service ill endured by an army of householders and agriculturists; and also as it increased the expense of the war, for the soldiers received pay only for those months in which they were actually under arms. Thus the tribunes began to complain of the burden of the siege, and the indecisive character of the war hitherto was likely to make it unpopular; but when news came that the Roman lines had been destroyed by a sally of the besieged,[1] national pride prevailed, and all ranks united in supporting the contest zealously. But the next year only brought fresh disasters:[2] Anxur was surprised by the Volscians, and the armies before Veii were completely defeated, and the blockade entirely raised. Then feelings of irritation revived; and these were so far shared by the senate, that they obliged all the military tribunes of the year to go out of office on the first of October,[3] two months and a half before the expiration of their year. The commons, however, were not satisfied; for the first act of the new military tribunes was to call out to military service, not only the citizens within the usual age,[4] but the older men also, who were to form a force for the defence of the city. Such a

A. U. C. 353. A. C. 399.

[1] Livy, V. 7. [2] Livy, V. 8. [3] Livy, V. 9. [4] Livy, V. 10.

call, just as winter was coming on, was most unwelcome; besides, every additional soldier rendered a heavier taxation necessary; and as the patricians were continually evading the payment of the vectigal for their occupation of the public land, so the tributum or property tax necessarily increased in amount. In this state of things, the patricians were so afraid of the possible effects of the tribunician power, that they ventured on the unusual step of tampering with the elections for new tribunes, which took place in December. The tribune who presided at the comitia must have been gained over to betray his trust; he refused votes, we must suppose, when given in favor of the most popular, and therefore the most obnoxious candidates, whilst others could not gain from the tribes themselves the requisite majority of suffrages. The consequence was that, in defiance of the Trebonian law, only eight tribunes were returned;[5] and these, by a second violation of the law, filled up the vacant places by choosing two colleagues for themselves.

Plebeians for the first time elected as tribunes of the soldiers.

But this overstraining broke the bow. One honest tribune of the college, Cn. Trebonius, was enough, where the cause was so manifestly just, to awaken the indignation of the commons. Three of the other tribunes,[6] men, as it seems, of those base natures which always follow the stream, now strove to avert their own unpopularity by impeaching the two unfortunate military tribunes who had been defeated before Veii. These were condemned and fined, but their punishment did not abate the storm. The tribunes then proposed an agrarian law; and when this was resisted, they positively refused to allow the tribute to be collected[7] for the benefit of the army at Veii. This stoppage of the supplies brought the soldiers almost to a state of mutiny. We have seen[8] that a custom, so old as to be held equivalent to law, authorized the soldier to practise a summary process of distress upon the paymaster, if his pay was not regularly issued. Thus the law itself seemed to sanction insubordination, if the soldier's right was denied him: so that if the tribunes persisted in forbidding the tribute to be levied, the siege of Veii was inevitably at an end. Then at last, after an interval of more than forty years, the constitution of the year 312 was fully carried into effect; the elections of military tribunes were left really free, and four out of six[9] of the members of the college were chosen from among the plebeians. A similar result attended the elections of the year following; four out of six of the tribunes of the soldiers were again chosen from the commons.

A. U. C. 355. A. C. 397.

A. U. C. 356. A. C. 396.

Endeavors of the patricians to recover the exclusive possession of the military tribuneship.

Such a choice, continued for two years successively, proves how deep was the indignation excited by the attempt of the patricians to tamper with the tribuneship of the commons. But the influence of an aristocracy acts through the relations of private life, which are in their very nature permanent, whilst it is opposed only by a strong feeling of anger, or

[5] Livy, V. 10.

[6] Livy, V. 11.

[7] Cum tributum conferri per tribunos non posset. Livy, V. 12.

[8] Pignoris capio. See Gaius, IV. § 27.

[9] The names, as given by Livy, are, P. Licinius Calvus, P. Manlius (Mænius being a mere correction by Sigonius), L. Titinius, P. Mælius, L. Furius Medullinus, and L. Publilius Volscus. He calls them all patricians, except Licinius; yet it is certain that all, except L. Furius and P. Manlius, were plebeians. The names are all plebeian; which, although not a decisive argument with respect to the very early times of the commonwealth, yet becomes a circumstance of great weight in the middle of the fourth century of Rome. Again, the reappointment of many of the tribunes of this year, four years afterwards, as colleagues of P. Licinius, is a confirmation of their being plebeians. And if we examine the several names, we find a M. Titinius elected tribune of the commons in the year 306, and a Sex. Titinius tribune in the year 316. And the fragments of the Fasti Capitolini describe P. Mælius as the son of Sp. Mælius, and give him the surname of Capitolinus; so that there is every reason to regard him as the son of that Mælius who was murdered by Servilius Ahala in 316, and whose house, as we know, stood sufficiently within the precincts of the Capitoline Hill to entitle him to the name Capitolinus. Lastly, Publilius Volscus is described in the Fasti as "Voleronis Nepos," and as bearing the surname of Philo; so that there can be no doubt that he was a descendant of the famous tribune who carried the Publilian law in the year 283, and of the family of the no less famous plebeian dictator who passed the Publilian laws of the year 416.

an urgent sense of public interest, both of which exist only in seasons of excitement, and wear out by the mere lapse of time. It happened also that in the last two years Rome had been visited by a winter of such unusual severity, as to appear preternatural, and afterwards, by a pestilence; and such calamities have a well-known tendency to engross men's minds with their own domestic affairs, and to make them regard political questions with indifference. Nor did the patricians fail to represent these visitations as proofs of the displeasure of the gods, who were offended that plebeians[10] had been elected even in the comitia of centuries, which professed to be regulated according to the divine will as observed and declared by the augurs. And still further to secure their object, when the election of military tribunes came on, the most eminent individuals of the noblest families of the patricians appeared as candidates. Accordingly, every place in the college for the year 357[11] was once more filled by a patrician; and the election of the following year presented the same result.

The commons resist them with success.

The tribunes of the year 358 appear, however, to have been moderate men; and there was a danger lest they should hold the comitia fairly, and lest some plebeians might thus again be elected as their successors. Accordingly the senate obliged them all, on religious pretences,[12] to resign before their year was expired; and an interrex was named to hold the comitia. But the discontent of the commons had been again growing; even in this very year the tribunes had opposed the enlistment of soldiers to meet a new enemy, the people of Tarquinii; and now, when the object of the patricians in appointing an interrex could not be mistaken, they interfered, and would not allow the comitia to be held. The dispute went on for some time, and lasted till a third interrex had been appointed, the famous M. Camillus. But even he, though one of the bitterest enemies of the commons, was, on this occasion, obliged to yield; either Veii must be relinquished, or the commons must have justice; and accordingly it was agreed that the elections should be held freely, so as to allow a majority in the college to the plebeians,[13] and four out of six of the military tribunes were again chosen from the plebeians.

But after the fall of Veii the patricians again prevail.

The defeat of two of these tribunes by the Faliscans and Capenatians led to the appointment of M. Camillus as dictator, and in this year Veii fell. Thus the patricians were no longer obliged to conciliate the commons; the opposition of the tribunes to the levying of the tribute was henceforward of no importance; and we hear no more of plebeian military tribunes. The entire college was composed of patricians in the years 360, 361, and 364; and in the years 362 and 363, the senate decreed that consuls should be created, instead of military tribunes; so that from the fall of Veii to the Gaulish invasion the patricians appear to have recovered their old exclusive possession of the highest magistracies.

Disputes about the tithe of the plunder of Veii.

Yet this period was by no means one of hopeless submission on the part of the commons; nor were there wanting subjects of dispute, which the tribunes followed up with vigor. Camillus had vowed to offer to Apollo the tithe of the spoil won at Veii; but the town had been plundered before Apollo's portion had been set apart for him; and the soldiers having disposed of all that they had gained, were unwilling to refund it afterwards.[14] The

[10] Livy, V. 14.

[11] Livy, V. 14, 16.

[12] Livy, V. 17.

[13] Livy, V. 18, Fasti Capitolini. Frammenti nuovi, Borghesi. According to Livy, the tribunes were P. Licinius, the son of the tribune of 355, L. Titinius, P. Mænius, P. Mælius, Cn. Genucius, and L. Atilius. But the fragments of the Fasti show that for P. Mænius we should here also read Q. Manlius; and the cognomen of Cn. Genucius, as appears from the Fasti for 356, was Augurinus; so that he belonged to the patrician Genucii, one of whom was elected consul, and afterwards decemvir, with Appius Claudius, in the year 303. Thus the plebeians were four to two in the college of 359, and not five to one; and this agrees with the stipulation made previously to the election, "ut major pars tribunorum militum ex plebe crearetur." Livy, V. 17.

[14] Livy, V. 23. The practice of devoting a tithe of the spoil to some god was adopted sometimes, in order to prevent an indiscriminate plunder: the spoil was first to be brought to the general, that the tithe might be duly separated from it, and the remainder was then to

pontifices, however, declared that the vow must be performed; and an appeal was made to the conscience of every individual, calling upon him to value his share of the plunder, and bring the price of the tithe of it into the treasury for the purchase of an offering of gold to Apollo. This call was slowly obeyed, and Camillus complained loudly of the profane neglect of the people: he urged further, that his vow had included the tithe, not only of the movable property of Veii, but also of the city and territory.[15] The pontifices decided that this too must be paid; and the money was accordingly advanced out of the treasury for this purpose. The money of the Romans at this period was all of copper; gold was dear, and could not readily be procured. Accordingly the Roman matrons are said to have brought to the treasury all their ornaments of gold;[16] and the senate showed its sense of their zeal by giving them permission to be drawn in a carriage about Rome on all occasions, and to use a peculiar and more luxurious sort of carriage at the games and solemn sacrifices. Yet, after all, the gold was not accepted as a gift; the senate ordered every matron's contribution to be valued, and the full price paid to her.

The commons desire to move to Veii.

This transaction irritated the minds of men against Camillus, as if his vow had been a mere pretence, in order to defraud the people of the spoil which they had so hardly won. But the conquest of Veii gave occasion to another dispute of a more serious character. T. Sicinius,[17] one of the tribunes, proposed a law for removing a portion of the patricians and commons to Veii, and for allotting to them the whole, or a considerable part, of the Veientian territory; so that the Roman commonwealth should consist of two cities, Rome and Veii. The peculiarity of this proposal, according to Roman notions, consisted in making Veii a co-ordinate state with Rome, instead of a colony. The unity of the commonwealth was in no way injured by the foundation of new colonies, because these became its subjects, and not its equals; whereas, if a portion of the Roman people lived in Veii, a city equal to Rome in extent and magnificence, the commonwealth must either be reduced to a mere confederacy, like that of the cities of the Latins, or else it would be a matter of dispute at which of the two cities the assemblies of the united people should be held, and which of them should be the home of the national gods. Accordingly the project was strenuously resisted by the patricians, who saw how fatal it would prove to the greatness of Rome, and they persuaded two of the tribunes to oppose it.[18] Thus the measure was resisted for that year, and it met with the same fate the year following, 361; both parties having obtained the re-election of the same tribunes, so that T. Sicinius and his friends again brought forward the law, and A. Virginius and Q. Pomponius, the two tribunes who sided with the patricians, were again ready to meet it with their negative.

The measure rejected through the influence of the patricians.

But in the year 362, Virginius and Pomponius were no longer re-elected tribunes, but were, on the contrary, impeached for their betrayal of their constituents' interests during the time of their magistracy. They were tried, and condemned to pay a heavy fine,[19] and the tribunes again brought forward their law, with a confidence that it would meet with no opposition. But the patricians now resolved to exert their influence in a fair and constitutional manner, and they exerted it with success. Leaving the decision of the question to the votes of the tribes,[20] and being prepared themselves to attend at the comitia and give their votes like the rest of their fellow-citizens, they endeavored, by their individual authority, to win the suffrages of their tribesmen, entreating and reasoning by turns, and imploring them not to pass a law which would put the conquered city of Veii on a level with its conqueror. Their arguments and solicitations were listened to with respect, and

be equitably divided. See the advice given by Crœsus to Cyrus after the taking of Sardis. Herodotus, I. 89.

[15] Livy, V. 25.

[16] Livy, V. 25.

[17] Livy, V. 24.

[18] Livy, V. 25, 29.

[19] Livy, V. 29.

[20] Livy, V. 30.

when the question was brought forward, it was negatived by the votes of eleven tribes out of twenty-one.

A grant of land in the territory of Veii made to the commons.

A victory thus fairly and honorably obtained, was likely to dispose the patricians to placable and kindly feelings. Immediately after the rejection of the law, the senate decreed a division of the Veientian territory[21] amongst the commons on a scale of unusual liberality. Each lot consisted of seven jugera; and not only fathers of families were considered in this grant, but they received an additional allotment of seven jugera for each free person in their household. Thus the dispute was, for the time, peaceably and advantageously settled.

Alteration of the time at which the tribunes of the soldiers entered on their office.

The year 363 is remarkable, as introducing another change in the time at which the curule magistrates entered on their office. The consuls, one of whom was M. Manlius, afterwards so famous, were obliged by the senate[22] to resign three months before the end of their year, so that their successors, the military tribunes of the year 364, came into office on the first of July. But why they were required to resign is doubtful. The ostensible reason was the state of their health; a dry and exceedingly hot season had ruined the crops, and given birth to a violent epidemic disorder, which attacked both of the consuls, and prevented them from taking the field against the Vulsiniensians. On the other hand, Niebuhr thinks that the real cause of their deposition was their having neglected to aid the people of Cære, the allies of Rome, when their harbor of Pyrgi was taken and sacked by Dionysius of Syracuse. Perhaps, too, personal feelings were concerned, for immediately on the resignation of the consuls, M. Camillus was appointed interrex, who was afterwards so strongly opposed to M. Manlius, and whose enmity may have already begun before this period. It should be observed that the six military tribunes elected for the following year were all patricians.

Charge of corruption against Camillus. He retires from Rome.

If Camillus had any undue share in effecting the resignation of the late consuls, he did not long enjoy his triumph. L. Appuleius,[23] one of the tribunes, impeached him for having appropriated secretly to his own use a portion of the plunder of Veii. It was said[24] that some doors of brass, the bullion of a country which at this time used only brass money, were found in his house; and that his numerous clients and friends told him plainly,[25] when he applied to them for their aid, that they were ready to pay his fine for him, but that they could not acquit him. We are startled at finding the great Camillus brought to trial on a charge of personal corruption; but that strict integrity which Polybius ascribes to the Romans seems not always to have reached as high as the leaders of the aristocracy, for the great Scipio Africanus was impeached on a similar charge, and his brother, the conqueror of Antiochus, was not only accused, but condemned. Nor were the eminent men of the Spartan aristocracy free from the same reproach; the suspicion attached itself to Leotychides, the immediate predecessor of Archidamus; to Pleistoanax, the son of Pausanias; and just before the banishment of Camillus, the famous Gylippus, the conqueror of the Athenians at Syracuse, had been driven from his country for a similar act of baseness. Other accounts,[26] as was natural, ascribed the condemnation of Camillus solely to the envy and hatred of the commons; while, according to others,[27] his punishment was a sort of ostracism, because the arrogance of his triumph, after the conquest of Veii, seemed inconsistent with the conduct of a citizen in a free commonwealth. It seems allowed by all, that no party in the state attempted to save him; and it is clear, also, that he incurred the forfeiture of all his civil rights in consequence of his not appearing to stand his trial, either as an outlawry, or because his withdrawal was held equivalent to

21 Livy, V. 30.
22 Livy, V. 31.
23 Livy, V. 32.
24 Plutarch, Camillus, 12.
25 Livy, V. 32.
26 Dionysius, XIII. 5. Fragm. Mai.
27 Diodorus, XIV. 117.

a confession of guilt, and a man convicted of furtum, incurred thereby perpetual ignominy, and lost all his political franchise. Perhaps his case was like that of the Spartan Pausanias; and the treasure which he secreted may have been intended to furnish means for making him tyrant of Rome. But at any rate, he withdrew from Rome before his trial came on, and retired to Ardea. The annalists reported[28] that as he went out of the gates, he turned round, and prayed to the gods of his country, that if he were unjustly driven into exile, some grievous calamity might speedily befall the Romans, and force them to call him back again. They who recorded such a prayer must have believed him innocent, and therefore forgave him for it; they even thought that the gods heard it with favor, and fulfilled its petition by sending the Gauls, in the very next year, to be ministers of vengeance on his ungrateful country.

CHAPTER XX.

STATE OF FOREIGN NATIONS AT THE PERIOD OF THE GAULISH INVASION—ITALY, SARDINIA, CORSICA.

Τὸ τῆς ἡμετέρας πραγματείας ἴδιον . . . . τοῦτό ἐστιν· ὅτι καθάπερ ἡ τύχη σχεδὸν ἅπαντα τὰ τῆς οἰκουμένης πράγματα πρὸς ἓν ἔκλινε μέρος, ... οὕτω καὶ διὰ τῆς ἱστορίας ὑπὸ μίαν σύνοψιν ἀγαγεῖν τοῖς ἐντυγχάνουσί τὸν χειρισμὸν τῆς τύχης, ᾧ κέχρηται πρὸς τὴν τῶν ὅλων πραγμάτων συντέλειαν.

POLYBIUS, I. 4.

Introduction to the view of the state of foreign nations.

THE farthest point hitherto reached by the soldiers of any Roman army was scarcely more than fifty miles distant from Rome. The southern limit of Roman warfare had been Anxur; its northern was Vulsinii. Nor do we read of any treaties or commercial intercourse by which Rome was connected with foreign powers, since the famous treaty with Carthage, concluded in the first year of the commonwealth. Still the nations of the ancient world knew more of one another than we are inclined to allow: for we do not enough consider how small a portion of their records has come down to us; how much must have been done of which mere accident has hindered us from hearing. About thirty[1] years later than the Gaulish invasion, the author of that most curious survey of the coasts of the Mediterranean, known by the name of the Periplus of Scylax, mentions Rome and Ancona alone of all the cities of Italy, with the exception of the Greek colonies; and this notice is the more remarkable, as Rome is not immediately on the coast, and the survey rarely extends to any place far inland. Aristotle also was not only acquainted with the fact that Rome was taken by the Gauls, but named an individual whom he called Lucius,[2] as its

[28] Livy, V. 32. Plutarch, Camillus, 12. Dionysius, XIII. 6.

[1] For the date of the Periplus of Scylax, see Niebuhr's essay in the first volume of his "Kleine Historische Schriften," Bonn, 1828, p. 105; or, as translated by Mr. Hare, in the second number of the Philological Museum. I have said that Scylax mentions no other Italian cities but Rome and Ancona, with the exception of the Greek colonies. It is true that, according to other writers, Ancona itself was a Greek colony, but Scylax does not describe it as such; whereas, in speaking of the cities on the Lucanian and Iapygian coast, he expressly notices their Greek origin.

[2] Plutarch, Camillus, 22. It need not be said, that in the old times men were designated by their prænomen rather than by their nomen or cognomen; and thus Aristotle would call L. Furius "Lucius," rather than "Furius," or "Camillus," just as Polybius calls Scipio "Publius," and Regulus "Marcus."

deliverer. Heraclides Ponticus[3] even spoke of Rome as a Greek city, which, while it shows the shallowness of his knowledge concerning it, proves also, that it was sufficiently famous in Greece, to make the Greeks think it worthy of belonging to their race and name; and we see, besides, that a wide distinction was drawn between the Latins and the Etruscans, the latter of whom they always regarded as foreigners, while in the former they did but exaggerate the degree of connection really subsisting between the two nations, whose kindred is proved by the resemblance of their languages. But the fame of the Gaulish invasion, the first great movement of barbarians breaking down upon the civilized countries of Europe from the north, which had occurred within historical memory, drew the attention of the Greeks more than ever towards Italy. And as this invasion led to a more general mixture of nation and nation, for less than twenty years afterwards we read of Gaulish cavalry in the service of Dionysius of Syracuse, and of their being sent by him to Peloponnesus to help the Lacedæmonians against Epaminondas; so I may at this period draw up the curtain which has hitherto veiled from our view all countries and people beyond the immediate neighborhood of the Tiber, and look as widely over the face of the world as the fullest knowledge of Greeks or Carthaginians enabled them at this time to see either eastward or westward.

The Etruscans.

The fall of Veii, and the submission of Capena and Falerii, have shown us that the greatness of the Etruscans was on the wane. In the days of their highest prosperity they had spread their dominion widely over Italy. The confederacy of their twelve cities, each of which was again the head of a smaller confederacy of the neighboring towns, occupied the whole country between the Tiber, the Macra, the Apennines, and the sea. But they were also to be found on the north of the Apennines,[4] and another Etruscan confederacy, consisting also of their favorite number of twelve cities, extended to the shores of the Adriatic, and possessed the plain of the Po, and of its tributary rivers to the north and south, from the sea as high as the Trebia. Bononia, under its older name of Felsina, Melpum, Mantua, and Atria, with Cupra on the coast of the Adriatic, were Etruscan towns. Nor had their dominion been confined to the north of the Tiber; a third confederacy of twelve cities had occupied Campania;[5] and amongst these were Capua, Nola, Surrentum, and Salernum.

[3] Plutarch, Camillus, 22. Heraclides noticed Rome in his treatise, Περὶ ψυχῆς; and said that a report had come from the west, telling how a host had come from the land of the Hyperboreans, without the Pillars of Hercules, and had taken a Greek city called Rome, which was situated somewhere in those parts about the great sea.

[4] This is the positive statement of the ancient writers; as Livy, V. 33, Strabo, V. p. 216, and Verrius Flaccus and Cæcina, quoted by the interpreters of Virgil, Æn. X. 198, in the Verona MS. Niebuhr, agreeably to his notion that the Etruscans came into Italy over the Alps, from the north, and not by sea from Asia, considers their settlements in the valley of the Po to have been older than those in Etruria. Müller believes them to have been of equal antiquity with each other; the Etruscans, or Rasena, he holds to have been an aboriginal people of Italy, settled from time immemorial both on the north and south sides of the Apennines.—(Etrusker, Einleitung, III. § 1.) Micali places the original seat of the Etruscans in the Apennines; he even ventures to fix on the precise spot, namely, the mountains which extend from the high point of La Falterona, above the valley of the Sieve, or of Mugello. (Storia degli antichi popoli Italiani, Vol. I. p. 106.) From thence they descended first into Etruria, and afterwards, having become a civilized people, they sent out their colonies into northern Italy. Without entering on the endless question of the origin of the Etruscans, or of the comparative antiquity of their several settlements, I have thought it sufficient merely to notice the limits which their nation reached at the time of its greatest power.

[5] It is well known that Niebuhr doubts the existence of this Campanian Dodecapolis; and he thinks that the whole statement of Etruscan settlements in Campania is a mere mistake, arising out of the common confusion between the Tyrrhenians and the Etruscans. He says that neither in the inscriptions found in Campania, nor in the works of art, is there to be observed any trace of an Etruscan population; and he thinks that in the days of the Etruscan greatness, that is, in the third century of Rome, we cannot conceive the possibility of Etruscan colonies being settled in Campania, while the intervening country between the Tiber and the Liris was occupied by the Romans and the Opican nations. See Vol. I. p. 74, 76, Eng. transl. Müller, on the contrary, receives the common account of the ancient writers as containing in it nothing improbable. Etrusker, Einleitung, IV. I. Polybius' testimony is positive that the Etruscans possessed the Phlegræan plains round Capua and Nola, at the time when they were also in possession of the plains round the Po, II. 17. And there were writers whom Velleius Paterculus quotes as saying that Capua and Nola were founded by the Etruscans, about forty-eight years before the common date of the foundation

Nay, there are traditions and names which have preserved a record of a still more extended Etruscan sovereignty: there was a time when their settlements in Campania must have been connected with those in Etruria by an uninterrupted line of conquered countries; the Volscians[6] were once subject to the Etruscans; the name of Tusculum seems to show that their power had penetrated into Latium; and it is stated generally that they had possessed nearly the whole of Italy.[7] But from this their height of greatness they had long since fallen. Within historical memory they were only to be found in Etruria, on the Po, and in Campania; but about half a century before the period at which we are now arrived, the Samnites had broken up their southern confederacy, and had wrested[8] from them Capua, and most of their other cities in that quarter; while more recently, in the last year of the siege of Veii,[9] the conquest of their northern confederacy was completed by the Gauls. Thus there only remained the central confederacy of Etruria Proper, and even this had been broken in upon, as we have seen, by the loss of Veii. Still there were left to them the powerful cities of Tarquinii, Vetulonium, Volaterræ, and Pisa, on or near the coast; and in the interior Vulsinii, Clusium, Perusia, Cortona, and Arretium.

Their relations with the Greeks.

We are told that in early times[10] the Etruscans had enjoyed the dominion of the neighboring seas, as well as the land of Italy. About one hundred and fifty years before the fall of Veii, the Etruscans and Carthaginians in the western part of the Mediterranean stood in nearly the same relation to the Greeks who ventured into those seas, as the Spaniards in the sixteenth and seventeenth centuries did to the English in the West Indies and in South America. The Greeks were treated as interlopers, and they in their turn seem to have held, that there was no peace beyond the Straits of Messina. Dionysius of Phocæa, when he fled from the ruin of the Ionian cause in Asia Minor, after the sea-fight off Miletus, considered the Etruscans[11] and Carthaginians as his natural prey, just as Raleigh regarded the Spaniards; and those treaties of commerce between Etruria and Carthage, of which Aristotle[12] has preserved the memory, provided, it is likely, not only for their relations with one another, but for their mutual defence against a nation whom both looked upon as their common enemy. But with the growth of the Greek cities in Sicily the maritime dominion of the Etruscans began to fall; and after the great naval victory gained over them at Cuma by Gelon's brother and successor, Hiero, they sank from sovereigns of the sea to pirates; and a few years afterwards, a very short time before the decemvirate at Rome, the Syracusans[13] sent a fleet to the coast of Etruria, with the

of Rome. When Paterculus further quotes Cato, as saying that Capua had been founded by the Etruscans, and yet that it had existed only two hundred and sixty years at the time of its conquest by the Romans in the second Punic war, there is indeed a calculation not very easy to be explained; for this would place the foundation of the Etruscan Capua, or Vulturnum, only about fifty years earlier than its conquest by the Samnites, and in the year of Rome 281, a period at which it is indeed difficult to conceive of the Etruscans as establishing themselves for the first time in Campania. The solution of the whole question is, probably, to be found in what Virgil says of Mantua: "Gens illi triplex: . . . . Tusco de sanguine vires." The ruling portion of these Campanian cities was Etruscan, but the bulk of the population was Oscan. Thus, when they were conquered by the Samnites, the marks of the Etruscan dominion speedily vanished, and the inscriptions which have reached our times are naturally Oscan, as that continued to be the language of the mass of the people. The foundation of Capua and Nola by the Etruscans may, in fact, have been no more than their occupation by some bands of Etruscan adventurers, who may have been engaged in the service of the Oscan inhabitants; just as Mastarna and his followers once occupied Rome, or as the Campanians afterwards occupied Messina. The Etruscan Dodecapolis, or confederacy of twelve cities, if indeed it ever existed in Campania, must have been founded undoubtedly at an earlier period; and yet we need not conceive it much earlier than the beginning of the commonwealth of Rome.

[6] Servius, Æn. XI. v. 567.

[7] Servius, Æn. XI. v. 567.

[8] Livy, IV. 37.

[9] Melpum, one of the richest cities in the country north of the Po, was said by Cornelius Nepos [Pliny, Hist. Natur. III. 17] to have been destroyed by the Gauls on the very day on which Camillus took Veii. What gave occasion to this story, representing the coincidence as so very exact, it is hard to guess; but that generally the fall of the northern Etruscan confederacy was contemporary with the siege of Veii, is rendered sufficiently probable by the appearance of the Gauls in Etruria Proper so soon afterwards.

[10] Livy, V. 33.

[11] Herodotus, VI. 17.

[12] Politic. III. 9.

[13] Diodorus, XI. 88.

avowed object of putting down their piracies. And yet we know there was an active commerce[14] carried on between Etruria and the cities of old Greece, so advantageous to both nations, that we can scarcely conceive how either of them could have allowed the robberies of its own people to hazard its interruption. It is possible, however, that what the Greeks call piracy was a system of vexations and violence carried on against Greek vessels in the Etruscan seas, with the view of keeping the trade exclusively in Etruscan hands; and the robberies of which the Greeks complained were committed by the people of the small towns along the coast, who, not possessing natural advantages or wealth enough to engage on a large scale in commerce, turned their seamanship and enterprise to account in another way, and fitted out small vessels for piracy instead of the large ships employed for trading voyages. Thus it is expressly mentioned that the people of Cære,[15] which was a large and wealthy city, possessing its harbor on the coast for the convenience of its trade, were wholly free from the reproach of piratical practices thrown by the Greeks upon the mass of their countrymen.

Sardinia.

Nothing can be more unequal than the fate of the three sister islands of Sicily, Sardinia, and Corsica. Whilst the first of them has rivalled in its fame the most distinguished countries of Europe, the two latter have remained in obscurity from the earliest times down to the present hour. They seemed to repel that kindling spark of Greek civilization, which found so congenial an element in Sicily; and, therefore, as they did not receive what was the great principle of life in the ancient world, they were condemned to perpetual inactivity and helplessness. Of what race were the earliest inhabitants of Sardinia, we have no records to inform us. Settlers from Africa, not Carthaginians, but native Lybians,[16] are said to have crossed over to the island at a very remote period. They were followed at intervals, such was the Greek tradition, by some adventurers or fugitives from Greece and Asia Minor; but these all belong to the mythic period, and the Greek settlements are said to have been afterwards utterly extirpated, whilst those from Asia, described as fugitives from Troy, were driven to the mountains and became barbarized. A more probable statement mentions a colony of Iberians from Spain, the founders of Nora,[17] the oldest city in the island; and during the height of the Etruscan dominion, the Etruscan colonists brought in a new element to the already mingled population. When the power of the Carthaginians began to grow, Sardinia soon attracted their notice; already, in the first year of the Roman commonwealth, eight-and-twenty years before the expedition of Xerxes, it is spoken of as belonging exclusively to their dominion, in their famous commercial treaty with Rome; and at the period of the great Persian invasion of Greece, Sardinia is mentioned, together with Corsica, as furnishing mercenary soldiers[18] to that great host with which Hamilcar invaded Sicily, and which was destroyed by Gelon at Himera. Yet a few years before, when the Persians were overpowering the Greek commonwealths in Asia Minor, Sardinia was more than once looked to by the Ionions,[19] as offering them a desirable refuge from the conquerors' dominion, and as affording every facility for a flourishing Greek colony. But it was to the Ionians of Asia like an unknown world; and no sufficient number of colonists could be induced to join in the enterprise, while a small body would have been utterly unable to maintain its ground against the Carthaginians. Thus Sardinia remained subject to Carthage; and as the Carthaginians wanted it chiefly to supply their armies with soldiers, and to provide harbors for their ships engaged in the trade with Etruria, they took no pains to improve its natural resources, but are said to have purposely kept waste[20] some

[14] We know this by the surest evidence, namely, by the vast quantities of Greek, and in particular of Athenian pottery, found in the recent excavations at Vulci and Tarquinii. See the "Discours de M. Bunsen," in the sixth volume of the "Annali dell' Instituto di corrispondenza archeologica," p. 40, et seqq.

[15] Strabo, V. 2, § 3, p. 220.

[16] Pausanias, X. 17.

[17] Pausanias, X. 17.

[18] Herodotus, VII. 165.

[19] Herodotus, I. 170, V. 124.

[20] Aristotle, De mirabil. 100.

of its most fertile districts, that no reports of its fertility might tempt thither what they above all things dreaded, a colony of Greeks.

Corsica.

Corsica had undergone nearly the same course of events as Sardinia. Its oldest inhabitants were Iberians and Ligurians; it was then occupied by the Etruscans, who after having, by the aid of the Carthaginians, effected the ruin of the Greek settlement of Aleria or Alalia,[21] and having shared the dominion of the island with their Carthaginian allies down to the time of the decemvirate at Rome, were now, in the general decline of their nation, leaving it entirely to the Carthaginians. Corsica was valuable for its timber and its mines, but its agriculture was of no account, and its native inhabitants were reckoned among the most untamable of barbarians.[22]

Campania.

These were the countries which bounded the horizon of Rome to the north and west. Southward and eastward, beyond that belt of mountain country held by the Opican nations, the Æquians and Volscians, which girt in Latium from the Anio to the sea, there lay a country, destined ere long to be the favorite battle-field of the Romans, but a stranger to them as yet both in the relations of peace and of war. Campania, inhabited in the most remote times by the Sikelians,[23] then wrested from them by the Opicans, receiving at a very early period the first germ of Greek civilization, in the Chalcidian colony of Cuma, and afterwards subjected, like so many other parts of Italy, to the wide-spreading dominion of the Etruscans, had lately, as we have seen, submitted to a new invader, the nation of the Samnites. The Samnites, a people of the Sabellian or Sabine race, had descended from their high valleys amidst the ranges of the divided line of the Apennines, and were now the ruling nation in Campania, although they had by no means extirpated the older races of its inhabitants On the contrary, they seem themselves to have almost melted away into the general mass of their mixed subjects; the conquered did not become Samnites, but the conquerors became Campanians, the Opican or Oscan being the prevailing language, but the influence of the Greek colonies, Cuma and Neapolis, spreading powerfully around them, as usual, the arts and the manners of Greece. But the Samnite invasion, and the revolution which followed it, produced great disorder; the old inhabitants, whom the conquerors despoiled of their property, were driven to maintain themselves by their swords; the conquerors themselves had many adventurers amongst them, who preferred war with the prospect of fresh plunder, to a peaceful life in the country which they had won; and thus for more than a century we read of numerous bands of Campanian or Opican mercenaries, partly Samnite and partly Oscan, employed in the wars of Sicily, as if foreign service had been one of the principal resources of the nation. It is mentioned that eight hundred of them were engaged by the Chalcidian Greeks of Cuma or Neapolis,[24] to serve in the Athenian armament against Syracuse; but that arriving in Sicily after the destruction of the Athenians, they were hired by the Carthaginians.

Invasion of the south of Italy by the Lucanians.

As a new people had thus arisen in Campania, so new names and a new power had lately come into notice in the south of Italy. From Thurii to Rhegium, on the shore of the Ionian sea, from Rhegium to Posidonia on the Tyrrhenian sea, the numerous Greek colonies which lined both coasts were settled in a country known to the early Greek writers by the names of Italia and Œnotria.[25] The natives of the interior, Œnotrians and Chonians, had for many years past wanted either the will or the power to offer serious annoyance to the Greeks; and when Sybaris was destroyed by its neighbor city Croton, the natives took no advantage of these internal quarrels, and a new Greek colony, Thurii, arose in the place of Sybaris, without any opposition on their part. But the latter part of the fifth century before the Christian æra, in other words, the early part of the fourth century of Rome, and the period of the

[21] Herodotus, I. 166.
[22] Strabo, V. 2, 6, 7, p. 224.
[23] Thucydides, VI. 2.
[24] Diodorus, XIII. 44.
[25] Aristotle, Politica, VII. 10. Herodotus, I. 167.

Peloponnesian war, was a time marked by natural as well as political calamities beyond all remembered example. The pestilences, which we have already noticed as causing such havoc at Rome and throughout Latium, travelled, we may be sure, into Samnium also; their visitations are often accompanied by unfavorable seasons, which cause scarcity or famine; and the distress occasioned by one or both of these scourges, may have led to those movements amongst the Samnites, which at this period so greatly changed the face of Italy. On one side, as we have seen, they broke in upon the Opicans of the valley of the Vulturnus and the country round Vesuvius; on another they overwhelmed the Œnotrians and Chonians,[26] and spread themselves as far as the Ionian sea. The tribe or mixed multitude which moved on this expedition southwards, was afterwards known by the name of Lucanians. It does not follow that they were numerous, far less are we to suppose that they extirpated the older inhabitants; but as conquerors they gave their name to the country, and till they gradually became a settled people, they were the terror of the Greek colonies. It is probable that many of the Œnotrians became barbarized by the oppressions and example of their conquerors, and that the whole population of the interior, known under one common name of Lucanians, carried on a restless plundering warfare against the Greek cities on both coasts of the peninsula. Posidonia fell into their hands, and the Greek inhabitants, like the Opicans of Capua, became a subject people in their own city; and so general was the terror excited by the Lucanian inroads, that the Greeks formed a league[27] amongst themselves for their mutual defence, and if any city was backward in coming to the rescue, when summoned to aid against the Lucanians, its generals were to be put to death. But whilst the barbarians were thus driving them to the sea, another enemy drove them back from the sea to the barbarians. Dionysius of Syracuse had formed an alliance with the Lucanians, hoping, with their aid, to obtain possession of the Greek cities; he repeatedly invaded Italy, destroyed Caulon and Hipponium, and made himself master of Rhegium.

Character of the Lucanians.

When the Lucanians first became formidable to the Italian Greeks, they were stigmatized as a horde of the lowest barbarians,[28] a mixed band of robbers, swelled by fugitive slaves, and desperate adventurers of every description. But when time had converted the invaders and plunderers of Œnotria into its regular inhabitants and masters, when the Lucanians had an opportunity of displaying the better points of their character, then the contrast between their simple and severe manners, and the extreme profligacy of the Greek colonies, could not fail to attract attention. "The Lucanians," says Heraclides Ponticus,[29] "are a hospitable and an upright people." And another testimony[30] declares that "amongst the Lucanians, extravagance and idleness are punishable crimes; and if any man lends money to a notorious spendthrift, the law will not enable him to recover it." We find similar praises bestowed by Scymnus of Chios on the Illyrians, who a century before his time had been infamous for their piracies. But when a rude people have lost somewhat of their ferocity, and have not yet acquired the vices of a later stage of civilization, their character really exhibits much that is noble and excellent, and both in its good and bad points it so captivates the imagination, that it has always been regarded by the writers of a more advanced state of society with an admiration even beyond its merits.

The extreme southeastern point, the heel of Italy, was the country of the

26 Strabo, VI. 1, § 2, 3, p. 253, 254.

27 Diodorus, XIV. 101.

28 We Athenians, says Isocrates, *ῥᾶον μεταδίδομεν τοῖς βουλομένοις ταύτης τῆς εὐγενείας ἢ Τριβαλλοὶ καὶ Λευκανοὶ τῆς αὑτῶν δυσκλεείας.* De Pace, § 62, p. 169.

29 De Politiis sive rebuspublicis. Artic. "Lucani." Heraclides Ponticus flourished in the latter part of the fourth century before the Christian æra: he was a disciple of Plato, Speusippus, and Aristotle. See Fynes Clinton, Fasti Hellen. Vol. III. Appendix XII.

30 Nicolas Damascenus, de moribus gentium. Artic. "Lucani." He lived in the Augustan age.

Iapygians or Apulians, the one being the Greek and the other the Latin form of the same name.[31] They stretched round the Iapygian cape, and were to be found along the coast of the Adriatic, as far as the headland of Garganus. But neither these nor the Sabellian nations immediately beyond them, nor the Umbrians, who lived again still further to the northwest, and joined the Etruscan settlements on the shores of the Adriatic, were, as yet, become famous in history.

Iapygia.

There was, however, a movement beginning about this period on the east of Italy, which threatened to lead to the most important consequences. Dionysius of Syracuse, unsatisfied with his Sicilian dominion, and looking to Greece itself as the most tempting field of ambition to every Greek, was desirous of getting a footing on the coast of Epirus, and of establishing a naval power in the Ionian sea and the Adriatic. Accordingly he entered into an alliance with the Illyrians,[32] and, unless there is a confusion between the two names, he occupied both the island of Issa,[33] the modern Lissa, and the town of Lissus[34] on the main land, a little to the north of Epidamnus, and kept a fleet regularly stationed at this latter settlement, to uphold the reputation of his power. But there is a statement in Pliny[35] and other writers, that Ancona, Mumana, and Adria, on the coast of Italy, were also Sicilian settlements. Adria is expressly said to have been founded by Dionysius, and his intercourse with these countries is further shown by the fact, that he was in the habit of importing the Venetian horses,[36] as the best breed for racing; the great games of Greece being to him, as they had been to Alcibiades, an object of peculiar interest and ambition. Strabo also calls Ancona a Syracusan colony,[37] but ascribes its foundation to some exiles who fled from the tyranny of Dionysius. That there was a Greek population there, and that the Greek language was prevalent, is proved by its coins; yet on the other hand, Scylax, though he names Ancona, does not call it a Greek city, a circumstance which he rarely or never admits, when he is speaking of Greek cities built on a foreign coast. The probability is, that the death of Dionysius, and the subsequent decline of his power, left these remote colonies to themselves; that their communication with Greece and Sicily was greatly checked by the growing piracies of the Illyrians, and that they admitted, either willingly or by necessity, an intermixture of barbarian citizens from the surrounding nations, which destroyed or greatly impaired their Greek character. But it marks the power of Dionysius, that at one and the same time he should have been founding colonies on the coast of the Adriatic, and that on the other side of Italy he should have been master of the sea without opposition, insomuch that, under pretence of restraining the piracies of

Interference of Dionysius of Syracuse in the affairs of south Italy.

[31] See Niebuhr, Vol. I. p. 151. Ed. 1827.

[32] Diodorus, XV. 13.

[33] Scymnus Chius, V. 413. Scylax also calls Issa a Greek city.

[34] Diodorus, XV. 13, 14. It is hard to account for the strange state of the actual text of Diodorus, in which, after mentioning the foundation of Lissus, it goes on, *ἐκ ταύτης οὐν ὁρμώμενος Διονύσιος κατεσκεύασε νεώρια. κ. τ. λ.* describing, in three lines, the great works of Dionysius at Syracuse, which Diodorus had already mentioned at length in the preceding book, and which have no intelligible connection with the foundation of Lissus. It is a curious specimen of the patchwork of so many of the ancient histories; for the whole passage, beginning at *Πάριοι κατά τίνα χρησμόν*, and going down to the end of the chapter, is taken apparently from some account either of Paros, or of the Greek settlements in the western seas, where the writer having been led accidentally to mention Dionysius, *συμπράξαντος αὐτοῖς Διονυσίου τοῦ τυράννου*, took the opportunity to give a brief sketch of the greatness of so famous a man. But Diodorus must have left out something in the middle of the passage, and joined the end with the beginning with most extraordinary carelessness; *ἐκ ταύτης* never could have referred to *τὴν πόλιν τὴν ὀνομαζομένην Λισσόν*, but, as I should suppose, to Syracuse, such as it was when Dionysius first became tyrant. Some mention of Syracuse must have preceded the description of the docks and walls, and the expression, *τῇ πόλει*, as at present the sentence is either wholly ungrammatical, or is mere nonsense. Mitford really supposes that *ἐκ ταύτης* refers to Lissus, and talks of the advantages derived from this colony giving Dionysius the means of building docks, &c., at Syracuse; an interpretation equally at variance with grammar and with history.

[35] Hist. Natural. III. 13. Numana a Siculis condita; ab iisdem colonia Ancona. Etymologic. Magn. in Ἄδρίας.

[36] Strabo, V. 1, § 4, p. 212.

[37] V. 4, § 2, p. 241.

the Etruscans, he appeared with a fleet of sixty triremes[28] on the coast of Etruria, passed the mouth of the Tiber almost within sight of Rome, landed on the territory of Cære, defeated the inhabitants who came out to resist him, sacked their sea-port of Pyrgi, and carried off from the plunder of the temple of Leucothea,[29] or Mater Matuta, a sum computed at no less than a thousand talents.

The mention of this eminent man leads me naturally to Sicily, to take some notice of the heart and root of that mighty dominion which spread out its arms so widely and so vigorously. Besides, the Roman history has hitherto presented us with nothing but general pictures, or sketches rather, of the state of the commonwealth as a whole: individuals have been as little prominent as the figures in a landscape: they have been too subordinate, and occupied too small a space in the picture, to enable us to form any distinct notion of their several features. But Dionysius outtopped by his personal renown the greatness of the events in which he was an actor; he stood far above all his contemporaries, as the most remarkable man in the western part of the civilized world. We may be allowed, then, to overstep the limits of Italy, and to consider the fortunes and character of a man who was the ruler of Syracuse and of Sicily, during a period of nearly forty years in the middle of the fourth century of Rome.

CHAPTER XXI.

DIONYSIUS THE ELDER, TYRANT OF SYRACUSE.

Πόπλιον Σκιπίωνά φασι ἐρωτηθέντα, τίνας ὑπολαμβάνει πραγματικωτάτους ἄνδρας γεγονέναι καὶ σὺν νῷ τολμηροτάτους, εἰπεῖν, τοὺς περὶ Ἀγαθοκλέα καὶ Διονύσιον τοὺς Σικελιώτας.—Καὶ περὶ μὲν τῶν τοιούτων ἀνδρῶν εἰς ἐπίστασιν ἄγειν τοὺς ἀναγινώσκοντας . . . . καὶ καθόλου προστιθέναι τὸν ἐπεκδιδάσκοντα λόγον—ἁρμόζει.—POLYBIUS, XV. 35.

State of Syracuse before the tyranny of Dionysius.

THE history of colonies seldom offers the noblest specimens of national character. The Syracusan people, made up, in the course of a long alternation of tyrannies and factions, out of the most various elements, had been bound together by no comprehensive code of laws, and, from their very circumstances, they could not find a substitute for such a code in the authority of ancient and inherited rites of religion, and of the manners and customs of their fathers.

Hermocrates and Diocles.

The richer citizens, who often possessed very large fortunes, were always suspected, and probably not without reason, of aiming at making themselves tyrants; whilst the people, possessing actual power, yet feeling that its tenure was precarious, were disposed to be suspicious, even beyond measure, and were prone to violence and cruelty. The Athenian invasion, by obliging the Syracusans to fit out a great naval force, had increased, as usual, the power of the poorer classes,[1] who always formed the great mass of the seamen in the Greek commonwealths: while, on the other hand, although Hermocrates, one of the most eminent of the aristocratical leaders, had personally displayed great courage and ability, and although the cavalry in which the

[28] Diodorus, XV. 14. Pseudo-Aristotle, Œconom. II. p. 1349. Ed. Bekker.

[29] Ἔλαβεν ἐκ τοῦ τῆς Λευκοθέας ἱεροῦ. Pseudo-Aristotle. "Leucothee Græcis, Matuta vocabere nostris." Ovid, Fasti, VI. 545.

[1] Aristotle, Politic. V. 4.

richest citizens served had always acquitted itself well, yet the heavy-armed infantry, which contained the greatest proportion of the upper classes, had gained little credit; and the victory over the invaders had been won by the seamen of Syracuse far more than by its soldiers. Thus the popular party became greatly strengthened by the issue of the invasion: Hermocrates and some of his friends were banished,[2] while Diocles, the head of the popular party, a man somewhat resembling the tribune Rienzi, a sincere and stern reformer, but whose zealous imagination conceived schemes beyond his power to compass, endeavored at once to give to his countrymen[3] a pure democracy, and to establish it on its only sure foundation, by building it upon a comprehensive system of national law.

Code of Diocles.

Of the details of this code we know nothing. Diodorus ascribes to it the high merits of conciseness and precision, and while he speaks of it as severe, he praises it for its discrimination in proportioning its punishments to the magnitude of the crime. But its best praise is, that it continued to enjoy the respect, not only of the Syracusans, but of other Sicilian states also, till the Roman law superseded it. This was the law of Syracuse, and Diocles was the lawgiver: while others, who in the time of Timoleon, and again in the reign of Hiero, either added to it, or modified it, were called by no other title than expounders of the law;[4] as if the only allowed object for succeeding legislators was to ascertain the real meaning of the code of Diocles, and not to alter it.

Efforts of the aristocratical party against it.

But democracy and law, when first introduced amongst a corrupt and turbulent people, require to be fostered under the shelter of profound peace. Unluckily for Diocles, his new constitution was born to stormy times; its promulgation was coincident with the renewal of the Carthaginian invasions of Sicily, after an interval of nearly a century. "War," says Thucydides,[5] "makes men's tempers as hard as their circumstances." The Syracusan government was engaged in an arduous struggle; the power of its enemy was overwhelming, while every failure in military operations bred an increase of suspicion and disaffection at home. Then the aristocratical party began, as they are wont to do, to use popular language, in order to excite the passions of the multitude, and thus make them the instruments of their own ruin. They encouraged the cry of treason and corruption against the generals of the commonwealth; and personal profligacy was united with party zeal. Hipparinus was a member of the aristocratical party; he was also a desperate man, because he had ruined himself by his extravagance;[6] both these causes united made him anxious to overthrow the popular government; and looking about for a fit instrument to accomplish his purpose, he found and brought forward Dionysius.

Early character of Dionysius.

There must have been no ordinary promise of character in Dionysius to lead to such a choice. He was a young man under five-and-twenty,[7] not distinguished for his birth or fortune, and his personal condition was humble; he was a clerk[8] in some one of the departments of the public business. But he had been a follower of Hermocrates, and had accompanied him in his attempt to effect his return from exile by force, and had been wounded[9] in the conflict which took place on that occasion, and in which Hermocrates was killed. He was brave, active, and eloquent; the wealth[10] and influence of a

[2] Xenoph. Hellenic. I. i. § 27. Thucydides, VIII. 85.

[3] Diodorus, XIII. 34, 35.

[4] Ἐξηγητὴν τοῦ νομοθέτου. Diod. XIII. 35.

[5] III. 82. Βίαιος διδάσκαλος, καὶ πρὸς τὰ παροντα τὰς ὀργὰς τῶν πολλῶν ὁμοιοῖ.

[6] Aristotle, Politica, V. 6.

[7] Cicero, Tusculan. Disputat. V. 20.

[8] Demosthenes, Leptines, prope finem.

[9] Diodorus, XIII. 75.

[10] It is said that at the beginning of his career, when he was fined, on one occasion, by the magistrates for addressing the people irregularly, Philistus, the historian, a man of large property, paid the fine for him, and told him to go on speaking as much as he pleased, and that as often as the magistrates fined him, so often would he continue to discharge the fine for him. Diodorus, XIII. 91.

powerful party supported him, and he came forward when men's minds were wrought up to the highest pitch of alarm and irritation; for Agrigentum, after a seven months' siege, had been taken and sacked by the Carthaginians, and the fugitives who fled to Syracuse for shelter, ascribed the loss of their city to the misconduct of the Syracusan generals, who had been sent to its relief, and had allowed it to fall unprotected.

Death of Diocles.

The popular party was no longer headed by Diocles. We do not know the exact time or occasion of his death, but the circumstances attending it are most remarkable. One of the laws of his code had denounced the penalty of death against any man who came into the market-place armed. This was especially directed, no doubt, against the aristocratical party, who were apt to resort to violence,[11] in order to break up or intimidate the assemblies of the people, or to revenge themselves on any of the more obnoxious popular leaders. It happened that Diocles had marched out of the city on an alarm of some hostile inroad, perhaps that very attempt[12] of Hermocrates to get back to Syracuse by force, which has been already noticed. But he was suddenly recalled by the news that the enemy were in the city, and, armed as he was, he hastened back to meet them, and found them already in possession of the market-place. A private citizen, most probably after the fray was over, when the death of so eminent a citizen as Hermocrates would be deeply felt, even by many of his political adversaries, called out to Diocles, in allusion to his having appeared in arms in the market-place, "Ah, Diocles, thou art making void thine own laws!" "Nay rather," was his reply, "I will ratify them thus;" and he instantly stabbed himself to the heart. Such a spirit, so sincere, and so self-devoted, might well have been the founder of freedom and of legal order for his country, and saved her, had his life been prolonged, from the selfish ambition of Dionysius.

Restoration of the aristocratical exiles.

His place at the head of the government was supplied, inadequately, as it appears, by Daphnæus and Demarchus.[13] Dionysius played the demagogue ably; inveighing against the incapacity of the generals, representing them as men of overweening influence,[14] and urging that the people would do well to choose in their place men of humbler means, whom they would be able more effectually to control. Accordingly the assembly deposed their actual generals, and elected others in their room, and amongst these was Dionysius. Thus far successful, he ventured on a more decisive measure, a general recall of exiled citizens.[15] It should be remembered, that in the continual struggles between the aristocratical and popular parties throughout Greece, the triumph of one side was accompanied by the banishment of the most forward supporters of the other. Every state had thus always its exiles, like the *fuorusciti* of the Italian republics, whose absence[16] was essential to the maintenance of the existing order of things, and whose recall was equivalent to a revolution.

[11] As the aristocrats at Corcyra broke into the council-house with daggers, and murdered the heads of the popular party to the number of about sixty, partly to escape from the payment of a fine which they had lawfully incurred, and partly to prevent the passing of a decree for an alliance with Athens. Thucyd. III. 70.

[12] It is true that, according to Diodorus, Diocles had been banished some time before [XIII. 75]; but his account of the affairs of Syracuse, between the Athenian expedition and the tyranny of Dionysius, is exceedingly fragmentary, and observes no chronological order. It may be, then, that Diocles had been recalled previously to the final attempt of Hermocrates; at least the circumstances of that attempt, and of the affray which led to the death of Diocles, bear a remarkable resemblance to each other. See Diodorus, XIII. 33 and 75.

[13] Diodorus, XIII. 96. Daphnæus had commanded the Syracusan troops which had been sent ineffectually to the relief of Agrigentum. Diodorus, XIII. 86. Demarchus was one of the generals sent to supersede Hermocrates in the command of the auxiliary force which was co-operating with the Peloponnesians, on the coast of Asia Minor, against the Athenians. Thucyd. VIII. 85.

[14] Diodorus, XIII. 91. Aristotle, Politica, V. 5. *Διονύσιος κατηγορῶν Δαφναίου καὶ τῶν πλουσίων ἠξιώθη τῆς τυραννίδος, διὰ τὴν ἔχθραν πιστευθεὶς ὡς δημοτικὸς ὤν.*

[15] Diodorus, XIII. 92.

[16] Thus it was one of the clauses in the oath taken by every member of the court of Heliæa, at Athens, "that he would not recall those citizens who were in exile." Demosthenes, Timocrates, p. 746.

The Syracusan exiles were the youth of the aristocratical party, the friends and comrades of Hermocrates, bold and enterprising, proud and licentious, the counterparts of Kæso Quinctius and of the supporters of the decemvir Appius; men whose natural hatred and scorn of the popular party was embittered by the recollection of their exile. An obdurate spirit is not the vice of a democracy; the kindly feelings of the people, their sympathies with youth and high birth, their hopes and their fears were alike appealed to; the tide was already setting towards aristocracy; the assembly decreed a general recall of the exiles, and the revolution from that moment became inevitable.

Dionysius appointed captain-general of the commonwealth.

The overthrow of the constitution of Diocles and of the popular party was sure; but it was owing to the terror of the Carthaginian arms, and the personal ascendency of Dionysius, that there was set up in its place the despotism of a single man, instead of an aristocracy. Dionysius continued to attack his colleagues,[17] no less than the generals who had preceded them; "they were selling Syracuse to the Carthaginians," he said; "they were withholding the soldiers' pay, and appropriating the public money to themselves; he could not endure to act with such associates, and was resolved therefore to lay down his office." A dictatorship is the most natural government for seasons of extraordinary peril, when there appears a man fit to wield it. The terror of the coalition drove the French, amidst the full freshness of their enthusiasm for liberty, to submit to the despotism of the committee of public safety; and Dionysius, bowing all minds to his ascendency by the mighty charm of superior genius, was elected sovereign commander of the commonwealth.[18] It is said that Hipparinus, who first brought him forward, was appointed as his nominal colleague; with as much of real equality of power as was enjoyed by Lebrun and Cambacérès when they were elected consuls along with Napoleon.

Length of his reign.

From this time forward Dionysius retained the supreme power in Syracuse till his death, a period of nearly forty years. When he first assumed the government, the Peloponnesian war was not yet ended: and one of his latest measures was to send aid to his allies the Lacedæmonians, when Sparta itself was threatened with conquest by an army of the Theban confederacy, headed by Epaminondas. In the course of this long reign he had to contend more than once with domestic enemies, and was always more or less engaged in hostility with Carthage. The first he crushed, and from the last, although reduced on one occasion to the extremest jeopardy, he came forth at last triumphant. Without entering into a regular account of his life and actions, it will be enough to take a general view of his government in some of its most important relations at home and abroad.

Internal affairs. State of parties.

Dionysius owed his elevation, as we have seen, to the ascendency of his own genius acting upon minds agitated by suspicion of their own government, and by intense fear of the progress of the Carthaginians. The recall of the exiles gave him a number of devoted partisans, and the war led to the employment of a large body of mercenary soldiers, who both from inclination and interest would be disposed to support an able and active general. These remained faithful to him[19] when his ill success against the Carthaginians, in the

[17] Diodorus, XIII. 94.

[18] Στρατηγὸς αὐτοκράτωρ. It is not to be supposed that this title conferred that unconstitutional and absolute power which the Greeks called "tyranny." It implied merely an unrestricted power of conducting the operations of the war, and released the general from the necessity of consulting the government at home as to his measures, and of communicating his plans to them. It was the title conferred on Nicias and his colleagues by the Athenians, when they sent their great expedition to Sicily; and after the Syracusans had sustained their first defeat, Hermocrates urged that their generals also should be invested with these full powers, and that the people should take the oath which, in fact, conveyed them, namely, "that they would let their generals exercise their command at their discretion." See Thucydides, VI. 26, 72. But as the perpetual dictatorship at Rome was equivalent to a tyranny, so Dionysius, by retaining his command for an unlimited time, and abusing the military power which it gave him for purposes wholly foreign to its proper objects, did, in fact, convert it into a political despotism.

[19] Diodorus, XIII. 112, 113.

very first year of his government, had shaken his popularity amongst the Syracusans, and encouraged them to attempt an insurrection. Nor was it the old popular party to whom he was most obnoxious, but the citizens of the richer classes, who as they would have rejoiced in the overthrow of the democracy, so were no way pleased to see it succeed by the despotism of a single man, under which they were sure to be the greatest sufferers. And partly, perhaps, from this very reason the poorer classes began to be better affected to his government, and he showed a desire to win their attachment. The knights, or richest class, fled from Syracuse in great numbers, or were banished, or put to death;[20] a great mass of landed property was thus placed at his disposal; and there was, besides, as in every state of the ancient world, a considerable amount also of public land, of which wealthy individuals had ordinarily a beneficial occupation. With all these means in his power, he put in practice the two grand expedients of revolutionary leaders, a large admission of new citizens, and a division of the public and confiscated land amongst them. The new citizens were many of them enfranchised slaves, to whom he assigned houses in Syracuse, as well as portions of land in the country. Thus the state of parties had assumed a new form; the better part of both the old aristocratical and popular interests were drawn together by their common danger, while Dionysius was supported by a few individuals of the richest class who shared in the advantages of the tyranny, by the mercenary soldiers, and by the lowest portion of the whole population, who owed to him their political existence.

Fruitless attempt to overthrow the power of Dionysius.

Accordingly, as the knights had shown their hostility to his government, so also did that large body of citizens of the middle classes, who in the ancient commonwealths composed the heavy-armed infantry. When Dionysius led them into the field to make war against the Sikelians (the old inhabitants of Sicily, whom the Greek colonies had driven from the coast into the interior of the island), they openly rose against his authority,[21] and invited the exiled knights to join them. This was one of the greatest dangers of his life; he fled to Syracuse, and was there besieged; but the strength of the walls protracted the siege, and time led to divisions and quarrels amongst the besiegers. Meantime Dionysius engaged the services of a body of those Campanian mercenaries,[22] whose reputation for valor was so high at this period in Sicily, and by their aid he defeated his antagonists. But, wishing to break effectually so formidable a combination, he offered an amnesty[23] to all who would return and live quietly in Syracuse; and finding that few only of the exiled knights accepted this offer, and feeling that the class of heavy-armed citizens was no less hostile to him, he took advantage of the ensuing harvest, when the citizens were engaged in getting in their corn in the country, and sent parties of soldiers[24] to their houses in Syracuse to carry off their arms. After this he began to increase his navy, the seamen being now the class of citizens on whom he could most rely, and further strengthened himself by raising an additional force of mercenaries.

Causes of the permanence of his government.

From this time till his death, a period of nearly thirty-seven years, the government of Dionysius met with no further disturbance from any domestic enemies. Eight years afterwards, indeed, when the great Carthaginian armament under Imilcon was besieging Syracuse, an attempt was made[25] by some of the knights to excite the people against him, and Theodorus is said to have attacked him in the public assembly as the author of all the calamities of his country. But the influence of the commander of a Lacedæmonian auxiliary force[26] then at Syracuse was exerted strongly in his favor; his

[20] Diodorus, XIII. 113, XIV. 7.

[21] Diodorus, XIV. 7.

[22] Diodorus, XIV. 8.

[23] Diodorus, XIV. 9.

[24] Diodorus, XIV. 10. This is the παραίρεσις τῶν ὅπλων, the disarming of these classes which usually possessed arms, one of the most well-known expedients of the Greek tyrants to obtain or to secure their power. Τὴν παραίρεσιν ποιοῦνται τῶν ὅπλων (scil. οἱ τύραννοι), says Aristotle, implying that it was their ordinary manner of proceeding. Politica, V. 10.

[25] Diodorus, XIV. 64, 65.

[26] Diodorus, XIV. 70.

own mercenaries were formidable; and in a season of such imminent danger from a foreign enemy, many even of those who disliked his government would think it inexpedient to molest it. On this occasion he tried all means to win popularity, mixing familiarly with the poorer citizens, gratifying some by presents, and admitting others to those common tables or messes of the soldiers, which were kept at the public expense.[27] But the permanent security of his dominion rested on his mercenary troops, who were ever ready to crush the beginnings of a tumult, on his own suspicious vigilance, on the ascendency of his firm and active character, and on the mutual jealousies and common weakness of the old aristocratical and popular parties, among whom there seems to have been no eminent man capable of opposing so able a tyrant as Dionysius. It should be remembered that the far weaker government of the second Dionysius was only overthrown, in the first instance, by the defection of a member of his own family; and when he was expelled a second time, the Syracusans could find no competent leader amongst themselves; they were obliged to invite Timoleon from Corinth.

His government was a tyranny.

All the ancient writers, without exception, call the government of Dionysius a tyranny.[28] This, as is well known, was with them no vague and disputable term, resting on party impressions of character, and thus liable to be bestowed or denied according to the political opinions of the speaker or writer. It describes a particular kind of government, the merits of which might be differently estimated, but the facts of its existence admitted of no dispute. Dionysius was not a king, because hereditary monarchy was not the constitution of Syracuse; he was not the head of the aristocratical party, enjoying supreme power, inasmuch as they were in possession of the government, and he was their most distinguished member: on the contrary, the richer classes were opposed to him, and he found his safety in banishing them in a mass, and confiscating their property. Nor was he the leader of a democracy, like Pericles and Demosthenes, all powerful, inasmuch as the free love and admiration of the people made his will theirs; for what democratical leader ever surrounded himself with foreign mercenaries, or fixed his residence in the citadel,[29] or kept up in his style of living and in the society which surrounded him the state and luxury of a king's court? He was not an hereditary constitutional king, nor the leader of one of the great divisions of the commonwealth: but he had gained sovereign power by fraud, and maintained it by force; he represented no party, he sought to uphold no ascendency but that of his own individual self; and standing thus apart from the sympathies of his countrymen, his objects were essentially selfish, his own safety, his own enjoyments, his own power, and his own glory. Feeling

[27] Diodorus, XIV. 70. *Τινὰς δὲ ἐπὶ τὰ συσσίτια παρελάμβανε.* That this institution of syssitia, or common tables, was not peculiar to the Lacedæmonians, is well known. It was practised at Carthage, and even its first origin was ascribed, not to any Greek people, but to the Œnotrians of the south of Italy. See Aristotle, Politic. II. 11, VII. 10. Aristotle blames the Lacedæmonians for altering the character of the institution by making each individual contribute his portion, instead of causing the whole expense to be defrayed by the public. The object of the common tables was to promote a social and brotherly feeling amongst those who met at them; and especially with a view to their becoming more confident in each other, so that in the day of battle they might stand more firmly together, and abide by one another to the death. With Dionysius, these common tables would be confined to his guards, or to such of the soldiers as he could most rely on; they would be maintained at his expense, and would be used as a means of keeping up a high and exclusive feeling amongst their members, as belonging to a sort of privileged order. And thus the offer of admission to such a society would be an effectual bribe to many, as being at once a benefit and a distinction.

[28] Even Xenophon calls him "Dionysius the tyrant." (Hellenic. II. 2, § 24.) It is remarkable, however, and confirms Niebuhr's opinion that the Hellenics contain two distinct works, and that the five last books were written many years later than the two first, when Xenophon's feelings were become more completely aristocratical or antipopular, that in the latter books Dionysius is not called tyrant, but is spoken of simply as "Dionysius," or as "the first Dionysius." The offensive appellation was not to be bestowed on the ally of Lacedæmon and Agesilaus.

[29] Mitford's mistake in supposing that the island at Syracuse was not the citadel; and arguing that Dionysius was not a tyrant, because he resided amongst the "nautic multitude," and not on the heights of Epipolæ, which Mitford imagines to have been the citadel, will be shown in a subsequent note.

that he had no right to be where he was, he was full of suspicion and jealousy, and oppressed his subjects with taxes at once heavy and capriciously levied, not only that he might enrich himself, but that he might impoverish and weaken them. A government carried on thus manifestly for the good of one single governor, with an end of such unmixed selfishness, and resting mainly upon the fear, not the love, of its people; with whatever brilliant qualities it might happen to be gilded, and however free it might be from acts of atrocious cruelty, was yet called by the Greeks a tyranny.

His taxes and spoliations.

It was no part of the policy of such tyrants to encourage trade or agriculture, that their own wealth might be the legitimate fruit of the general wealth of their people. On the contrary, their financial expedients were no other than blind and brute exactions, which satisfied their immediate wants; it mattered not at what cost of future embarrassment. Aristotle names Dionysius' government,[30] as exemplifying the tyrant's policy of impoverishing his people by an excessive taxation. The direct taxes were at one time so heavy,[31] that it was computed that in the course of five years, they equalled the entire yearly value of the property on which they were levied: then there was the old fraud of debasing the coin,[32] the oppression of forced loans, which he paid in a depreciated currency, direct robbery of his people under the pretence of ornamenting the temples of the gods, and an unscrupulous sacrilege, which appropriated the very offerings to the gods, so made, to his own individual uses. With such a system, it is not wonderful that plunder should have been one of his favorite resources. The sale of prisoners taken in war, one of the most important of the ways and means of the first Cæsar, was so much a matter of ordinary usage in the ancient world, that it brought no peculiar obloquy on Dionysius. But the sack of the wealthy temple of the Mater Matuta on the Etruscan coast, was considered as little better than piracy,[33] and it was reported that his settlement at Lissus, on the coast of Epirus, was mainly intended to further his design of plundering the very temple of Apollo at Delphi.[34] We read of his colonies up the Adriatic; but the only notice of any commerce carried on with those countries, mentions merely the importation of horses[35] from the country of the Veneti, in order that they might run in the chariots of Dionysius at the great games of Greece and of Sicily.

He fortifies and enlarges Syracuse.

Every strong and able government, however oppressive, is yet sure to accomplish some works at once magnificent and useful; and thus the extended walls of Syracuse, which included the whole slope of Epipolæ to its summit, in addition to the older city which the Athenians had be-

[30] Politica, V. 11.

[31] Aristotle's expression is, ἐν πέντε γὰρ ἔτεσιν ἐπὶ Διονυσίου τὴν οὐσίαν ἅπασαν εἰσενηνοχέναι συνέβαινε. This can only mean, I suppose, one of two things: either, as I have explained it in the text, that Dionysius imposed a property tax of twenty per cent., so that in five years a man might be said to have paid taxes to the amount of his whole income, or else that a man's property was valued much below its real worth; so that twenty per cent. on the rated amount of his property, not of his income merely, would be very much less than a fifth part of what he really possessed. It might be thus possible that a man might have paid in five years a sum equal to the rated amount of his whole property; but that he should literally have paid a sum equal to his whole real property seems to me an absurdity. To notice no other objections, was it ever known that the money in any country bore such a proportion to the value of the property in it as to render it possible in five years to convert all property into cash? For the rest, the period of five years here mentioned is remarkable, as it seems to indicate that the official valuation of property at Syracuse, as at Rome, took place every five years.

[32] This, and the following instance of Dionysius' exactions, are taken from the second chapter of the second book of the Œconomica, commonly ascribed to Aristotle. This chapter, however, is clearly not Aristotle's, but, as Niebuhr has shown (Kleine Historische Schriften, p. 412), must have been a later work, written in Asia Minor, and is a collection of all sorts of financial tricks and extortions, which are recommended to the imitation of the satraps and officers of the monarchies of Alexander's successors. And whoever reads the whole of the collection will find no reason to doubt the truth of the stories about Dionysius, as being unprecedented or unworthy of him.

[33] Diodorus, XV. 14. Strabo calls it the temple of Ilithyia, or Lucina; and adds, that Dionysius plundered it in the course of an expedition to Corsica. V. 2, § 8, p. 226.

[34] Diodorus, XV. 13.

[35] Strabo, V. 1, § 4, p. 212.

sieged, were the work of Dionysius. These were built[36] under the terror of a Carthaginian invasion; and his docks for two hundred ships, or, according to other accounts, for a far greater number, were constructed at once for defensive and offensive war against the same enemy. His works in the island of Ortygia had an object more directly selfish. This oldest and strongest part of the city of Syracuse, which had originally constituted the whole city, was now, since the town had spread over the adjacent parts of the mainland of Sicily, come to be regarded as the citadel. Here Dionysius fixed his residence,[37] and built a strong wall to cut off its communication with the rest of Syracuse; he also appropriated it exclusively to his own friends and his mercenary soldiers, allowing no other Syracusan to live in it. For the same reasons under the Roman government, the island was the residence of the Roman prætor and his officers,[38] and the Syracusans were still forbidden to inhabit it.

II. Foreign affairs. Wars with Carthage and the Italian Greeks.

Dionysius had owed his elevation to the terror inspired by the arms of Carthage; and the great service which he rendered to Greece and to the world, was his successful resistance to the Carthaginian power, and opposing a barrier to their conquest of Sicily. The very difficulty of his task, and the varied fortune of his wars, shows plainly that had Syracuse been under a less powerful government, it must have shared the fate of Selinus and of Agrigentum. We do not know the causes which seem to have roused the Carthaginians to such vigorous activity against the Sicilian Greeks, immediately after the destruction of the Athenian armament. Had that great expedition been successful at Syracuse, it was designed to attempt the conquest of the Carthaginian dominions,[39] and even of Carthage itself; and the Carthaginians are represented by Hermocrates[40] as living in constant dread of the power and ambition of Athens. Yet four or five years afterwards we find them sending out to Sicily so large a force, that they might well have defied the hostility of the Athenians; and the conquest of Selinus, Himera, and Agrigentum, proved to the Syracusans that they were again incurring the danger, from which they had been delivered about eighty years before by Gelon's great victory of Himera.

First treaty of Dionysius with Carthage.

In his first attempts to check the progress of the Carthaginians, Dionysius was unsuccessful. He was glad to conclude a peace with them, by which they were to retain possession of their own colonies, and of the Sicanian tribes in the west of Sicily. The survivors[41] of the people whom they had recently conquered, of Himera, Selinus, and Agrigentum; as also the inhabitants of Gela and Camarina who had abandoned their homes during the war, and had fled first to Syracuse, and afterwards to Leontini, might now, it was stipulated, return to their own countries and live in peace; but they were to pay a tribute to the Carthaginians, and were to live only in open villages; their cities were to remain dismantled and desolate. In the east of the island, Messana, Leontini, and all the Sikelian tribes were to be independent; these last were the old enemies of the Syracusans, and the Carthaginians naturally, therefore, made this stipulation in their favor. Thus Dionysius was left master of Syracuse alone; stripped of its dominion over the Sikelians, stripped of its old allies, the other Dorian cities of Sicily; while the dominion of Carthage, which a few years before had been confined to three settlements at the western corner of the island, was now advanced almost to the eastern coast, and by means of the Sikelian

[36] Diodorus, XIV. 18, 41, 42.

[37] Diodorus, XIV. 7. Those who understand the nature of the Greek citadels, that they always contained the temples of the peculiar gods of the people, and therefore were always the oldest part of the city, will understand that Epipolæ could not have been, according to Greek notions, the citadel of Syracuse. On the other hand, the strength of the island of Ortygia well fitted it for purposes of security, and although its walls were washed by both harbors, yet we may be sure that it was at no time the residence of the poorest classes, such as composed the seamen of the state, but was appropriated to the oldest and wealthiest families.

[38] Cicero, Verres, V. 32. He calls the island, "Locus quem vel pauci possint defendere."

[39] So Alcibiades told the Spartans; Thucyd. VI. 90, and added, *τοιαῦτα μὲν παρὰ τοῦ ἀκριβέστατα εἰδότος, ὡς διενοήθημεν, ἀκηκόατε.*

[40] Thucyd. VI. 34.

[41] Diodorus, XIII. 114.

tribes, whose independence had been just secured, it hemmed in, and in a manner overhung, the scanty territory which was still left to Syracuse.

This treaty was concluded in the last year of the Peloponnesian war, according to the chronology of Diodorus. It was virtually no more than a truce, delaying the decision of the quarrel between the two contracting parties, till one of them should be in a better condition to resume it. Dionysius had been crippled by his military disasters, and the Carthaginians were suffering from a pestilence which was at this time fatally raging in Africa. No sooner, then, was the peace concluded, than Dionysius began to undo its work. It had declared the Sikelian tribes independent; he found, or made a pretence for attacking them:[42] it had stipulated for the independence of Leontini; he compelled the inhabitants to leave their city,[43] and to come and dwell as citizens in Syracuse. He also destroyed the Chalcidian cities of Naxos and Catana,[44] and sold their inhabitants for slaves. He cultivated the friendship of Messana, Rhegium,[45] and the Greek towns of Italy; with Locri in particular he established a right of intermarriage, and he availed himself of it to take a Locrian lady as his own wife. He was busy in making arms and artillery[46] for the use of his armies, and in building ships, and arsenals to receive and fit them out becomingly. And after all his preparations were completed, finding that the pestilence was still raging in Africa,[47] he determined to declare war against Carthage. This was in the fourth year of the ninety-fifth Olympiad, about eight years after the conclusion of the last treaty.

He prepares to break it.

Dionysius had chosen his own time; the plague had weakened the Carthaginians, and the declaration of war against them, unexpected as it was, was preceded by a general plundering of their property,[48] and a massacre of their citizens in all the Greek cities of Sicily. Dionysius marched immediately towards the Carthaginian territories; the forces of the several Greek cities joined him as he advanced; and he laid siege to the city and island of Motya,[49] one of the three settlements which Carthage possessed in Sicily[50] before her conquest of Selinus. Motya was one of a group of small islands which lie off the western coast of Sicily, immediately to the north of Marsala or Lilybæum. It is about a mile and a half in circumference,[51] and about three-quarters of a mile from the main land, with which it was connected by a narrow artificial causeway. Like Tyre and Aradus in point of situation, it was like them flourishing and populous: and its inhabitants, being themselves of Phœnician blood, were zealous in their resistance to the Greek invader. Attacked by an overwhelming force,[52] and seeing their walls breached, and their ramparts swept, by engines and an artillery such as had never before been equalled, they did not yield even when the enemy had forced his way into their city, but availed themselves of their narrow streets and lofty houses to dispute every inch of his progress. The Greeks then brought up their movable towers, which had been built to match the height of the houses, and from these they threw out bridges to the roofs, and thus endeavored to board the enemy. Day after day this bloody struggle continued; the Greek trumpets regularly sounding a retreat when night fell, and calling off their combatants; till at length Dionysius turned this practice to his account, and as soon as the trumpets sounded as usual, and the Phœnicians supposed that the contest was at an end till the next day, he sent in a party of picked men, who, before the enemy suspected their design, had established themselves in a commanding situation from which they could not be dislodged again. Then the whole Greek army poured into the town by the moles or dykes

He suddenly declares war on the Carthaginians and lays siege to Motya.

42 Diodorus, XIV. 7, 14.
43 Diodorus, XIV. 15.
44 Diodorus, XIV. 15.
45 Diodorus, XIV. 44.
46 Diodorus, XIV. 41.
47 Diodorus, XIV. 45.
48 Diodorus, XIV. 46.
49 Diodorus, XIV. 47.
50 Thucydides, VI. 2.
51 See Captain Smyth's Memoir on Sicily.
52 Diodorus, XIV. 48–53.

which they had thrown across from the main land to the shore of Motya, and the place was taken by storm. Neither age nor sex were spared by the conquerors; a few only of the inhabitants saved their lives by running to the temples of those gods whom the Greeks honored in common with the Carthaginians, and these were afterwards sold for slaves. The whole plunder of the town was given to the victorious soldiers.

Dionysius attacks the Sicilian allies of Carthage.

While the siege of Motya was going on, Dionysius had employed a portion of his army in endeavoring to reduce the remaining colonies or allies of Carthage. The Sicanian tribes,[53] who were the principal inhabitants of the interior in the west of Sicily, submitted without opposition. But five places held out resolutely: Soloeis and Panormus, both of them, as well as Motya, Phœnician settlements; Egesta, whose quarrel with Selinus first brought the Athenians into Sicily, and afterwards the Carthaginians; Entella, and Halicyæ. It was in vain that Dionysius ravaged their lands, destroyed their fruit-trees, and attacked their towns; they remained unmoved in their fidelity; and even after the fall of Motya, when the Greek power seemed so irresistible that the people of Halicyæ then at last submitted to it, yet the other four still held out; and when Dionysius again ventured to besiege Egesta, the inhabitants sallied by night and set fire to his camp, and obliged him to abandon his enterprise with loss.

Great Carthaginian expedition to Sicily.

Here ended the circle of Dionysius' glory. The Carthaginians,[54] provoked by the suddenness of his attack, by his having taken advantage of their distressed condition, and by the inveteracy with which the Greeks were pursuing all of their name and race, were roused to extraordinary exertion. An immense army was raised of Africans and Spaniards; but the Gauls, so constantly employed in the Punic wars, had not yet crossed the Alps, or become known to the civilized nations of the south; so that there were none of them in the armament now collected for the invasion of Sicily. As it was, however, the Carthaginian force was estimated by Timæus at 100,000 men, and it was commanded by Imilcon, the supreme military chief of the commonwealth. The expedition landed at Panormus, and every thing gave way before it. Motya was instantly recovered; the Sicanians left Dionysius to join their old friends, the Carthaginians; Dionysius himself retreated upon Syracuse; and the seat of war was removed almost instantaneously from the western to the eastern extremity of the island, from Motya and Egesta to Syracuse.

The Carthaginians besiege Syracuse.

Imilcon advanced[55] along the northern coast towards Messina, being anxious to possess that important place, and so intercept any succors which might be sent to the aid of Dionysius, either from the Greek states of Italy, or from Greece itself. He took Messina, defeated the Syracusans in a sea fight off Catana, and then, being completely master of the field, he proceeded to lay siege to Syracuse by sea and land; his ships occupied the great harbor, while with his army he held all the most important points on shore: the headland of Plemyrium, which forms the southern side of the great harbor, the temple of Olympian Jupiter on the right bank of the Anapus, and the suburb of Neapolis, just without the walls of Acradina, and under the cliffs of Epipolæ. The position of Epipolæ itself, which the Athenians had at first occupied with so much effect, and which they afterwards neglected to their ruin, was now secured against the enemy by the walls lately carried round its whole extent by Dionysius.

Critical state of the Greek power in Sicily.

Thus the Greek power in Sicily was reduced, as it were, to one little spark, which the first breath seemed likely to extinguish; but on its preservation depended the existence of Rome and the fate of the world. Had Carthage become the sovereign of all Sicily, her power, in its full and unde-

[53] Diodorus, XIV. 48–54.
[54] Diodorus, XIV. 54, 55.
[55] Diodorus, XIV. 57–63.

cayed vigor, must have immediately come into contact with the nations of Italy; and the Samnite wars of Rome might have ended in the destruction of both the contending nations, when their exhausted strength had left them at the mercy of a powerful neighbor. But this was not to be, and Dionysius was inspired with resolution to abide the storm, that so he might fulfil that purpose of God's providence, which designed the Greek power in Sicily to stand as a breakwater against the advances of Carthage, and to afford a shelter to the yet unripened strength of Rome.

Dionysius proposes to escape from Sicily.

The condition of Dionysius seemed desperate. Blockaded by sea and land, with a people impatient of his despotism, with a force of mercenaries, who, the moment that he became unable to pay them, might betray him, either to the enemy without the walls or to his political adversaries within; he held a council with his friends in the citadel, and expressed his purpose of leaving Syracuse to its fate, and attempting to effect his own escape by sea. One of them boldly answered,[56] "A king's robe is a noble winding-sheet." At these words the spirit of Dionysius rose within him, and he resolved to live or die a king.

The Carthaginian armament crippled by an epidemic sickness.

But his deliverance was effected by another power than his own. The spots where the small Sicilian rivers make their way into the sea are, during the summer, notoriously unhealthy: a malaria fever is almost the certain consequence of passing a single night in any village so situated. The shore near the mouth of the Anapus, and the marshy plain immediately behind it, would be absolutely pestilential to an army quartered there during the heats of summer; and the Athenians, when besieging Syracuse seventeen years before, had severely suffered from its influence.[57] But now the season was unusually hot, and from the prevalence of epidemic disease in Africa about this period, it is likely that the constitutions of many of the Carthaginian soldiers would be more than usually susceptible of infection. Accordingly,[58] the disorder which broke out in the besieging army more resembled the most malignant pestilence than any ordinary form of marsh or malaria fever. The patients were commonly carried off in five or six days; and the disease was either really so contagious, or was imagined to be so, that no one dared to visit the sick, or to pay them the most necessary attentions: and thus all who were taken ill were left to die without relief.

Dionysius destroys their fleet.

This visitation broke both the power and the spirit of the Carthaginians. Dionysius[59] now made a sally, and attacked them both by sea and land. He carried their post at the temple of the Olympian Jupiter, and that at Dascon, at the very bottom of the harbor, on the right of the Anapus, where the Athenians first effected their landing. Here he found their ships drawn up on the beach, and he instantly set fire to them. Meanwhile the Syracusan fleet advanced right across the harbor, and surprised the enemy's ships before they could be manned and worked out from the shore to offer battle. Thus taking them at a disadvantage, the Greeks sunk or shattered them without resistance, or surrounded them and carried them by boarding. And now the flames began to spread from the ships on the beach to those which lay afloat moored close to the shore. These were mostly merchant ships, worked by sails like ours, and consequently, even while at anchor, they had their masts up and their standing rigging. As the flames caught these and blazed up into the air, the spectacle afforded to the Syracusans on their walls was most magnificent. The crews of the burning ships leaped overboard, and left them to their fate; their cables were burnt, and the blazing masses began to drift about the harbor, and to run foul of one another; while the crackling of the flames, and the crashing of the falling masts and of the sides of the ships in their mutual shocks, heard amidst volumes

[56] Καλόν ἐστιν ἐντάφιον ἡ τυραννίς. Isocrates. Archidamus, § 49, p. 125.

[57] Thucydides, VII. 47.

[58] Diodorus, XIV. 70, 71.

[59] Diodorus, XIV. 72–75.

of smoke and sheets of fire, reminded the Syracusans of the destruction of the giants by the thunder of Jove, when they had assayed in their pride to storm Olympus.[60]

Rejoicings of the Syracusans.

Thus called, as they thought, by the manifest interposition of heaven to finish the work, the very old men and boys of Syracuse could bear to look on idly from their walls no longer, but getting into the large punts or barges,[61] which were ordinarily used for ferrying men and cattle across the harbor, they put out to sea, to save and capture such of the enemy's ships as the fire had not yet destroyed. But the walls were crowded with fresh spectators, for as the report of the victory became more and more decided, the women, children, and slaves, all poured out from their houses, and hastened to enjoy with their own eyes the sight of this wonderful deliverance. When the day was over, the Carthaginian naval force was almost utterly destroyed, while Dionysius encamped on the ground which he had won near the temple of Olympian Jupiter, having the remnant of the besieging army shut in between his position on one side, and the walls of Syracuse on the other.

Retreat of the Carthaginians.

But Imilcon had no hope of continuing the contest with success any further. He offered all the treasure in his camp, amounting to three hundred talents, to purchase the unmolested retreat of the remainder of his armament. "This," said Dionysius, "cannot be granted; but I will consent that the native Carthaginians shall be allowed to escape by night to Africa," stipulating nothing for their subjects and allies. He foresaw that if the head were thus taken from the body, the body would instantly fall into his power; and he was not sorry to impress the Africans, Iberians, and Sikelians, with a strong sense of the selfish arrogance of the Carthaginians, who, thinking only of themselves, abandoned their allies to destruction without scruple. Accordingly, when the Carthaginians had escaped, the rest of the armament attempted to provide as they could for their own safety. The Sikelians and Africans were obliged to lay down their arms, after the former had endeavored in vain to make good their retreat to their own country; but the Iberians held together, and made so formidable a show of resistance, that Dionysius readily listened to their proposals of entering into his service. They became a part of his mercenary army; and while they helped to secure his power against his domestic enemies, they also added to the glory of his arms abroad: and in the strange vicissitudes of human fortune, these same Iberians, who had been enlisted in Spain, taken thence to Africa, and afterwards had crossed the sea to Sicily as invaders, were some years later sent over from Sicily to Greece,[62] as a part of the auxiliary force sent by Dionysius to aid the Lacedæmonians; and fought with distinction in Laconia under the eye of Agesilaus, against the invading army of Epaminondas.

State of the Carthaginian power in Sicily.

Thus was Dionysius saved from imminent ruin, and the Greek power in Sicily was preserved. His subsequent wars with Carthage were of no importance, for amidst much variety of fortune in particular engagements, the relations of the two states were never materially altered; the Carthaginians remained masters of all the western part of the island, while the eastern part continued to be under the dominion of Dionysius.

Dionysius prepares to attack the Italian Greeks.

After the destruction of this great armament, Dionysius felt himself able to carry on his plans of conquest against the Greeks of Italy. One of his first measures was to people the important city of Messana. The remains of the old citizens, who had been driven out by the

[60] Diodorus, XIV. 73. This whole description seems to have been taken from the history of Philistus, who was probably an eye-witness of the scene: so that the comparison is not to be regarded as the mere flourish of a writer, far removed in time and space from the action which suggested it, but as one which really arose in the minds of the Syracusans, amidst the excitement and enthusiasm of the actual spectacle.

[61] Τὰ πορθμεῖα. Diodorus, XIV. 74. This is one of the touches which seem to argue that the writer of the description was at any rate a Syracusan, familiar with the harbor of Syracuse. No explanation is given by him, because the use of these πορθμεῖα was to him so familiar, that he could not fancy that any was requisite.

[62] Xenophon, Hellenic. VII. 1, § 20.

Carthaginians, returned to their home after Imilcon's defeat; but their numbers were so thinned, that Dionysius added to them a large body of new citizens from Locri on the Italian coast, his old and firm ally, and from a Locrian colony,[63] Medama, on the Tyrrhenian sea, which had probably been lately conquered by the Lucanians. With these there were at first joined some exiles from old Greece, of the race of the old Messenians; but afterwards, to satisfy the jealousy of Lacedæmon, they were removed from Messana, and founded for themselves the new city of Tyndaris.[64]

Battle of the Helleporus, and conquest of Rhegium.

The principal object of Dionysius' hostility among the Greek cities of Italy was Rhegium. The Rhegians had favored his political adversaries, and had personally affronted him by refusing to allow him the right of intermarriage with their citizens. But his ambition led him to desire the dominion of all the coast of Italy on the Ionian sea; and he entered into a league with the Lucanians, as has been already mentioned, hoping that they might exhaust the Greek cities, by their constant plundering warfare, and that he might then step in to reap the harvest. His defeat of the combined army of the Italian Greeks on the banks of the Helleporus,[65] and his conquest of Rhegium,[66] Caulon,[67] and Hipponium,[68] are the principal events of this contest. He enlarged Syracuse, by removing thither the whole, or a great part, of the population of the conquered cities; and his increased power and influence on the Italian coast facilitated those further plans of aggrandizement which have been already noticed, his settlements at Issa and Lissus, and on the coast of Picenum, his alliance with the Illyrians, and his trade in the Adriatic.

Dionysius sends chariots to the Olympian games, and wins the prize of tragedy at Athens.

Thus powerful at home and abroad, and possessing a far greater dominion than any prince or state in old Greece, Dionysius yet felt that Greece was, as it were, the heart and life of the civilized world, and that no glory would be universal or enduring unless it had received its stamp and warrant from the genius of Athens. He sent chariots to Olympia, to contend for the prize at the Olympic games;[69] he sent over also rhapsodists most eminent for the powers of their voice and the charm of their recitation to rehearse his poems; and he was repeatedly a candidate for the prize of tragedy at Athens. Alexander, indeed, scorned to contend for victory at the Olympic games unless kings could be his competitors; but in such matters there was a wide difference between a king and a tyrant, between the descendant of a long line of princes,[70] sprung from Hercules, the son of Jove, and the humble citizen of Syracuse, whom his fortune had unexpectedly raised to greatness. There is a story that the public feeling at Olympia was so strong against Dionysius as a tyrant,[71] that the tents of his theori, or deputies to the Olympic assembly, were plundered, and the recitation of his verses drowned amidst the clamor and hisses of the multitude. But whether this be true or false, we know that at Athens his tragedies were by no means regarded as contemptible; he gained on different occasions the second and third prizes, and at last his tragedy, entitled "Hector Ransomed,"[72] was judged worthy of the highest prize.

This evident desire of intellectual fame, united with the powers of earning it, tempted the philosophers of Greece to believe that they should find in Dionys-

[63] Diodorus, XIV. 78. The present reading in the text of Diodorus is Μεδιμναίους, for which Cluverius has conjectured Μεδμαίους. Μεδαμαίους would be still nearer the present reading, and Μέδαμα is the name of the city in Strabo, VI. 1, § 5, p. 256, and, it is said, on one of its coins. Medama, or Mesma, is described as a Locrian colony by Strabo, in the passage above quoted, and by Scymnus Chius, V. 307.

[64] Diodorus, XIV. 78.

[65] Polybius calls the river "Elleporus," I. 6. Diodorus calls it "Helorus," XIV. 104. I suspect that the true reading in Polybius would be "Helleporus."

[66] Diodorus, XIV. 3.

[67] Diodorus, XIV. 106.

[68] Diodorus, XIV. 107.

[69] Diodorus, XIV. 109.

[70] In an earlier age, however, an ancestor of the great Alexander, the Macedonian king of the same name, who reigned during the Persian invasion, was anxious to be admitted as a competitor for the prize at the Olympic games, even in the foot race, and he ran accordingly in the stadium. See Herodotus, V. 22.

[71] Diodorus, XIV. 109.

[72] Diodorus, XV. 74.

His intercourse with Isocrates and Plato.

ius a man who could sympathize with them in spite of his political greatness, and would rejoice to associate with them on equal terms. Plato visited Syracuse,[73] and Isocrates,[74] at a safer distance, addressed to Dionysius a letter of compliment from Greece. As long as they remained on the opposite shores of the Ionian sea, the philosopher and the tyrant might correspond with each other without offence. But many are the stories which show the folly of supposing that an equality of mind can triumph over the differences of rank and power. No man can associate freely with another, when his life is at the mercy of his companion's caprice. Plato soon returned to Greece, with a lesson from some of the philosophers of Syracuse, "that men of their profession would do well either to shun the society of tyrants,[75] or else in their intercourse with them, to study how they could please them most." This advice is said to have been occasioned by a practical lesson given to Plato by Dionysius, which ought to have rendered it superfluous; the story ran, that the tyrant was so offended with something that Plato had said, that he sent him forthwith to the slave-market, and had him sold as a slave, but that the philosophers immediately redeemed him by a general subscription amongst themselves, and then urged him to quit Sicily. A similar story is told of the poet Philoxenus, whom Dionysius is said to have sent from his own table to his prisons in the quarries, because he had expressed an unfavorable opinion of the tyrant's poetry. These stories may deserve but little credit for the particular facts; yet the intercourse between Frederick of Prussia and Voltaire was interrupted in a similar manner, and the presumption of literary men on the one hand, and the pride of rank and power on the other, are likely to lead to such results.

His private life.

That the despot of Syracuse should not scruple to send a poet to the quarries and to sell a philosopher in the slave-market, is nothing wonderful. We may be more unwilling to believe the reports of the state of miserable fear to which suspicion could reduce one so able and so daring as Dionysius. "He could trust no man," it was said,[76] "but a set of miserable freedmen, and outcasts, and barbarians, whom he made his body-guard. He fenced his chamber with a wide trench, which he crossed by a draw-bridge; he never addressed the Syracusan people but from the top of a high tower, where no dagger could reach him; he never visited his wives without having their apartments previously searched, lest they should contain some lurking assassin; nay, he dared not allow himself to be shaved by any hands except his own daughters'; and even them he was afraid to intrust with a razor; but taught them how to singe off his beard with hot walnut-shells." Much of this is probably exaggeration, but the Greek tyrants knew that to kill them was held to be no murder; and it is no shame to Dionysius, if his nerves were overcome by the hourly danger of assassination, a danger which appalled even the iron courage of Cromwell.

Peculiar character of the ancient tyrannies.

The Greeks had no abhorrence for kings: the descendant of a hero race, ruling over a people whom his fathers had ruled from time immemorial, was no subject of obloquy, either with the people, or with the philosophers. But a tyrant, a man of low or ordinary birth, who by force or fraud had seated himself on the necks of his countrymen, to gorge each prevailing passion of his nature at their cost, with no principle but the interest of his own power, such a man was regarded as a wild beast that had broken into the fold of civilized society, and whom it was every one's right and duty by any means, or with any weapon, presently to destroy. Such monsters of selfishness Christian Europe has rarely seen. If the claim to reign by "the grace of God"

[73] Diodorus, XV. 7.

[74] Whether the letters professing to be written from Isocrates to Dionysius and Philip of Macedon, and published at the end of his orations, are genuine, may well be doubted; although the fact of his having corresponded with them may be true notwithstanding.

[75] Diodorus, XV. 7. Δεῖ τὸν σοφὸν τοῖς τυράννοις ἢ ὡς ἥκιστα ἢ ὡς ἥδιστα ὁμιλεῖν.

[76] Cicero, Tusculan. Disputat. V. 20.

has given an undue sanction to absolute power, yet it has diffused at the same time a sense of the responsibilities of power, such as the tyrants, and even the kings of the later age of Greece, never knew. The most unprincipled of modern sovereigns would yet have acknowledged that he owed a duty to his people, for the discharge of which he was answerable to God; but the Greek tyrant regarded his subjects as the mere instruments of his own gratification; fortune, or his own superiority, had given him extraordinary means of indulging his favorite passions, and it would be folly to forego the opportunity. It is this total want of regard for his fellow-creatures, the utter sacrifice of their present and future improvement, for the sake of objects purely personal, which constitutes the guilt of Dionysius and his fellow-tyrants. In such men all virtue was necessarily blighted; neither genius, nor courage, nor occasional signs of human feeling, could atone for the deliberate wickedness of their system of tyranny. Brave and able as Dionysius was, active, and temperate, and energetic, he left behind him no beneficial institutions; he degraded rather than improved the character of his countrymen; and he has therefore justly been branded with infamy, by the accordant voice of his own and of after ages; he will be known forever as Dionysius the tyrant.

CHAPTER XXII.

CARTHAGE—BARBARIANS OF WESTERN EUROPE—EAST OF EUROPE—GREECE—MACEDONIA—ILLYRIA.

"Cæterum—qui mortales initio coluerint, indigenæ an advecti, parum compertum."—TACITUS Agricola, XI.

Difficulties of ancient history.

THE enlarged researches of our own times, while they make us more sensible of the actual extent of our ignorance, yet encourage us with the hope that it will gradually be diminished. But he who attempts to write history in the interval between this awakened consciousness of the defects of our knowledge, and that fuller light which may hereafter remove them, labors under peculiar disadvantages. A reputation for learning was cheaply gained in the days of our fathers, by merely reading the works of the Greek and Roman writers, and being able to repeat the information which they have communicated.

But now we desire to learn, not what existing accounts may have recorded of a people or a race, but what that people or race really was, and did; we wish to conceive a full and lively image of them, of their language, their institutions, their arts, their morals; to understand what they were in themselves, and how they may have affected the fate of the world, either in their own times, or in after ages. These, however, are questions which the ancient writers were often as unable to answer as we are; happier, it may be thought, than we in this, that they had no painful consciousness of ignorance. To repeat what the Greek and Roman writers have left on record of Carthage, and its dominion in Spain and Africa, would be an easy task, but at the same time most unsatisfactory. We look around for other witnesses, we question existing languages, and races, and manners, in the hope of gleaning from them some fuller knowledge of extinct nations, than can be gained from the scanty accounts of foreigners or enemies.

Carthage.

The internal state of Carthage may fitly be reserved for a later period of this history. It will be enough now to fill up, so far as I can, that sketch of her dominion and foreign relations, which has been begun in some measure in the two preceding chapters.

In the middle of the fourth century before the Christian era, the Carthaginians possessed the northern coast of Africa, from the middle of the greater Syrtis to the pillars of Hercules, a country reaching from 19 degrees, east longitude, to 6 degrees, west; and a length of coast which Polybius[1] reckoned at above sixteen thousand stadia. But unlike the compactness and organization of the provinces of the Roman empire, this long line of coast was, for the most part, only so far under the dominion of the Carthaginians, that they possessed[2] a chain of commercial establishments along its whole extent, and with the usual ascendency of civilized men over barbarians, had obliged the native inhabitants of the country, whether cultivators of the soil or wandering tribes, to acknowledge their superiority. But in that part where the coast runs nearly north and south, from the Hermæan headland, or Cape Bon, to the lesser Syrtis, they had occupied the country more completely. This was one of the richest tracts to be found;[3] and here the Carthaginians had planted their towns thickly, and had covered the open country with their farms and villas. This was their περιοικὶς, the immediate domain of Carthage, where fresh settlements were continually made as a provision for the poorer citizens;[4] settlements prosperous, indeed, and wealthy, but politically dependent, as was always the case in the ancient world; insomuch that the term περίοικοι, which in its origin expressed no more than "men who dwelt not in, but round about a city," came to signify a particular political relation, theirs, namely, who enjoyed personal freedom, but had no share in the government of their country.

Extent of the Carthaginian dominion in Africa.

Distinct from these settlements of the Carthaginians themselves were the sister cities of Carthage, founded immediately, like herself, by the Phœnicians of Tyre and Sidon, although her fortune had afterwards so outgrown theirs. Amongst these Phœnician colonies were Utica,[5] more famous in Roman than in Carthaginian history, Adrumetum,[6] the two cities known by the name of Leptis, situated, the one near the western extremity of the great Syrtis, and the other on the coast between the lesser Syrtis and the Hermæan headland; and Hippo, a name so closely connected in our minds with the piety and energy of its great bishop, Augustine. These were the allies of Carthage, and some of them were again at the head of a small confederacy of states,[7] who looked up to them for protection, as they in their turn looked up to Carthage. They enjoyed their own laws, and were independent in their domestic government; but in their foreign relations they found, in common with all the weaker states of the ancient world, that alliance with a greater power ended sooner or later in subjection.

Phœnician colonies in Africa.

The Phœnician colonists, who founded Carthage, at first paid[8] a tribute to the native Africans on whose land they had settled, as an acknowledgment that the country was not their own. But in process of time they became what the Europeans have been in later times in India, no longer dependent settlers, but sovereigns; and the native Africans, driven back from the coast and confined to the interior, were reduced to the condition of strangers on

Condition of the African subjects of Carthage.

[1] Polybius, III. 39.

[2] Ὅσα γέγραπται πολίσματα ἢ ἐμπόρια ἐν τῇ Λιβύῃ ἀπὸ τῆς Σύρτιδος τῆς παρ' Ἑσπερίδας μέχρι Ἡρακλείων στηλῶν ἐν Λιβύῃ πάντα ἐστὶ Καρχηδονίων. Scylax, Periplus, p. 51, 52. Ed. Hudson.

[3] Polybius, III. 23. Diodorus, XX. 8. Scylax, p. 49.

[4] Aristotle, Politica, VI. 5. Within the last ten years an exact image of the relation of the ancient περίοικοι to their πόλις, and of the irritation occasioned by it, has been exhibited to the notice of Europe on more than one occasion in Switzerland. Liechstal was one of the περιοικίδες of Basel; and the disputes between the citizens of Basel and the inhabitants of Liechstal, and the other country towns, seemed, to those familiar with ancient history, like a revival of the political relations of Lacedæmon and Carthage.

[5] Justin, XVIII. 4.

[6] Sallust, Bell. Jugurth. 22, 80.

[7] In the second treaty between Rome and Carthage, the contracting parties on the one side are, "the people of Carthage, the people of Tyre, and the people of Utica, *with their allies*." Polybius, III. 24.

[8] Justin, XVIII. 5.

their own soil. They understood and practised agriculture, but we know not how far they were allowed to retain the property of the land, or to what extent the rich Carthaginians had ejected them, and employed them as tenants and cultivators of the soil of which they had been once proprietors. At any rate, the Africans were in the condition of a Roman province; they[9] were ruled despotically by the Carthaginian officers sent amongst them, and were subject to taxes, and to a conscription of their youth to serve as soldiers, at the discretion of their governors. In the first Punic war, they were taxed to the amount of fifty per cent. on the yearly produce of their land, and the oppression to which they were subjected made them enter readily and zealously into the quarrel of the mercenary soldiers, during their famous war with the Carthaginians.

Differences between the situation of Carthage and Rome with respect to their subjects and allies.

The contrast between Carthage exercising absolute dominion over her African subjects, and Rome surrounded by her Latin and Italian allies, and gradually communicating more widely the rights of citizenship, so as to change alliance into union, has been often noticed, and is indeed quite sufficient to account for the issue of the Punic wars. But this difference was owing rather to the good fortune of Rome and to the ill fortune of Carthage, than to the wisdom and liberality of the one and the narrow-mindedness of the other. Rome was placed in the midst of people akin to herself both in race and language; Carthage was a solitary settlement in a foreign land. The Carthaginian language nearly resembled the Hebrew; it belonged to the Semitic or Aramaic family. Who the native Africans were, and to what family they belonged, are among the most obscure questions of ancient history. But it is one of the consequences of that wider view of the connection of races and languages, which we have learnt of late to entertain, that the statements to be found in the traditional or mythic reports of the origin of nations, appear in some instances to contain in them a germ of truth, and we do not venture, as formerly, to cast them aside as mere fables. Thus in that strange account of the peopling of Africa, which Sallust[10] copied from Carthaginian books, the stream of migration is described as having poured into northern Africa at its western, not at its eastern extremity, by the straits of Gibraltar, not by the isthmus of Suez and by Egypt. And we read that the invaders were Medians and Persians, who had marched through Europe into Spain, as a part of the great army of Hercules. They found the north of Africa possessed by an older race of inhabitants, the Gætulians and Libyans, of whose origin no account is given. But the story of the expedition of Hercules, and of the Medians and Persians[11] following in his army, and entering Africa by crossing over thither from Spain, may at least lead us to inquire whether any affinity can be traced between the language of the Berbers, the descendants of the ancient Mauritanians, and that of the Basques, the descendants of the old Iberians; and whether the languages of the native tribes of north Africa, whether agricultural or wandering, may not be supposed to have belonged either wholly or in part to the Indo-Germanic family, rather than to the Semitic. These are the points in which we are standing half way between the equally extreme credulity and skepticism of the last two centuries, and that fuller knowledge which may be the portion of our posterity. But whatever may be discovered as to the African subjects of Carthage, they were become so distinct from their masters, even if they were originally sprung from a kindred race, that the two people were not likely to be melted together into one state; and thus they remained always in the unhappy and suspicious relation of masters and of slaves, rather than in that of fellow-citizens, or even of allies.

[9] Polybius, I. 72.

[10] Bell. Jugurthin. 20. Uti ex libris Punicis, qui regis Hiempsalis dicebantur, interpretatum nobis est.

[11] The Sigynnæ, a people whom Herodotus describes, V. 9, as living beyond the Danube, that is, in what is now Hungary, were said by some, he tells us, to have been a colony of the Medes, at which he naturally wonders. It is so difficult, in these stories, to distinguish what is mere confusion or invention from what contains a germ of truth, under more or less of disguise.

The dominion of Carthage in Africa, as it resembled in many other respects that of the British in India, had produced also, as in our Indian empire, a numerous half-caste population, sprung from intermarriages between the Carthaginians and the native Africans. This mixed race was known by the name of Liby or Afro-Phœnicians;[12] but whether they were regarded by Carthage as a source of strength, or suspected as dangerous enemies, we have no sufficient information to determine. Perhaps they were thought to be dangerous at home, but useful and trustworthy abroad; and thus they were sent as colonists to Spain,[13] and to the more remote parts of the coast of Africa, without the Pillars of Hercules, just as the poorer citizens of Carthage itself were sent, as we have seen, to settlements nearer home. If we can trust the text and the authenticity of the Greek version now existing of the voyage of Hanno, these Afro-Phœnician colonies were planted on a very large scale; for that voyage was undertaken for the purpose of settling no fewer than thirty thousand Afro-Phœnicians[14] along the shore of the Atlantic southward of the straits of Gibraltar.

Colonies of the Afro-Phœnicians, or people of half-caste.

In the seventh century before the Christian era, a Samian ship[15] bound for Egypt was caught in a violent storm, with the wind blowing strongly from the east. The ship was carried altogether out of her course, the wind continued to blow from the east, and at last she was actually driven through the Pillars of Hercules, and the first land which she succeeded in making was the coast of Tartessus or Tarshish, the southwestern coast of Spain. The Samians found that the storm had proved their best friend; they returned home enriched beyond all their hopes, for the port of Tarshish, says Herodotus, was at that time fresh[16] and undisturbed; the gold of its neighboring mines was a treasure not yet appreciated by its possessors; they bartered it to the Samian strangers in return for the most ordinary articles of civilized living, which barbarians cannot enough admire. This story makes us feel that we are indeed living in the old age of the world. The country then so fresh and untouched has now been long in the last stage of decrepitude: its mines, then so abundant, have been long since exhausted; and after having in its turn discovered and almost drained the mines of another world, it lies now like a forsaken wreck on the waves of time, with nothing but the memory of the past to ennoble it. In the middle of the fourth century of Rome, the coast of Spain,[17] both on the ocean and on the Mediterranean, was full of Carthaginian trading settlements, but these were mostly small, and of no great celebrity. Gadir, or Gades, on the other hand, a colony founded directly from Tyre,[18] had been long since famous. Here was one of the most celebrated temples of the Tyrian Hercules, and its trade and wealth were considerable; the neighboring country being rich in mines, while the sea yielded an inexhaustible supply of fish, which was commonly sold in the Athenian markets as early as the Peloponnesian war.[19] But except Gades, the Greek seamen knew of no other place of importance on the coast of Spain at this period, till they came north of the Iberus, to the country which was then inhabited by the Ligurians. Here there was the Greek settlement of Emporion,[20] an offshoot from the Phocæan colony of Massalia. If Saguntum was really a city of Greek or Tyrrhenian origin, founded by colonists from Zacynthus and Ardea, it seems to have retained no marks of the Greek character; it had no seaport, and though it was itself near the coast, yet it was not of sufficient importance to attract the notice of the Greek navigators.

Iberia, or Spain: Phœnician colony of Gadir, or Gades.

The great Spanish peninsula itself, and its original inhabitants, the various tribes of the Iberian race, were as yet but little known to the rest of the world. Sicil-

[12] Polybius, III. 33.
[13] Scymnus Chius, V. 195, 196.
[14] Hanno, Periplus, p. 1. Ed. Hudson.
[15] Herodotus, IV. 152.
[16] 'Ακήρατον.
[17] Scylax, Periplus, p. 1.
[18] Strabo, III. prope finem.
[19] Pollux, VI. 48. Eupoli, quoted by Stephanus Byzant. in Γάδειρα.
[20] Scylax, Periplus, p. 1.

Native Iberians; their race and character.

ian antiquarians[21] derived the oldest part of the population of their island, the Sicanians, from the northeastern coast of Spain. The Iberians had for some time been accustomed to serve in the Carthaginian armies; their name occurs amongst the various nations who composed the great host of Hamilcar[22] when he invaded Sicily in the time of Gelon, and was defeated in the famous battle of Himera. The Iberians were known to the Athenians[23] as amongst the most warlike of the barbarians of the west, whom they purposed to employ in conquering their Peloponnesian enemies, had success at Syracuse enabled them to fulfil their more remote designs; and we have seen Iberians distinguished above all the other soldiers in the same service, in the great Carthaginian expedition which Imilcon led against the tyrant Dionysius. Another circumstance removed them even more than their remarkable courage from the common mass of barbarians. Writing was common among them; and some of their tribes[24] possessed written records of their past history, not composed in verse, besides numerous poems, and large collections of laws and institutions in a metrical form, amounting, it was said, to about six thousand lines. We ourselves have, in some degree, a national interest in the Iberians, if it be true that colonies of their race crossed the Bay of Biscay, and established themselves on the coast of Cornwall. But their memory has almost utterly perished; we know not with what race of mankind they were connected; and although the Basque dialect, still spoken on both sides of the Pyrenees, is supposed to be a remnant of their language, yet its relation to other languages appears to have been not yet ascertained, so as to inform us to what family it belongs. It may be hoped that this, as well as the deciphering of the Etruscan monuments, may be amongst the discoveries reserved for our own generation, or for that of our children.

The Ligurians.

From the Pyrenees to the frontiers of Etruria,[25] the coast of the Mediterranean was occupied by the Ligurians, a people distinguished by the Greeks both from the Iberians and from the Kelts, although they are supposed to have been connected with the latter nation in their race and language. As the Ligurians dwelt on the coast, they became known to the Carthaginians; and thus Ligurians[26] are named together with Iberians amongst the soldiers of Hamilcar's expedition to Sicily, at the beginning of the fifth century before the Christian era. In the time of Scylax, a few years later than our present period, the Ligurians and Iberians were mixed together on the coast, between the Pyrenees and the Rhone, and the exclusive dominion of the Ligurians only extended from the Rhone to Etruria. But Thucydides mentioned it as an ascertained fact,[27] that at a very remote period they had dislodged the Sicanians from their land on the Sicanian river in Iberia, and that these, flying before their conquerors, went over and settled in Sicily. We cannot certainly tell what river is

21 Thucydides, VI. 2, following Antiochus.

22 Herodotus, VII. 165.

23 Thucydides, VI. 90.

24 Strabo, III. p. 139. Here again Niebuhr's sagacity has corrected the common reading, *νόμους ἐμμέτρους ἑξακισχιλίων ἐτῶν*, which, as he observes, would not be Greek, into *νόμους ἑξακισχιλίων ἐπῶν*.

When this page was written, I had not seen the excellent work of the lamented William Von Humboldt, "on the earliest inhabitants of Spain," although I was aware generally of its character, and of the conclusion which it endeavored to establish. He considers it to be certain that the present Basque language is substantially the same with the ancient Iberian: the names of places in the ancient geography of Spain being, for the most part, not only significant in Basque, but exhibiting in their sound, and in their omission of some letters, and their combinations of others, the peculiarities of the existing language. It appears that in the Basque country there are three distinct dialects, and that with regard to one of these nothing satisfactory had been published when Von Humboldt wrote, while the lexicon or vocabulary of another was far from perfect. I notice this, because words may exist in these dialects which may go far to establish the resemblance of the Basque language to others, or to prove its diversity; and may explain those names in the ancient geography of Spain which have not been hitherto interpreted. The Iberians, in Humboldt's judgment, were a people quite distinct from the Kelts; but they may have had the same degree of connection with them which subsisted between all the nations of the great Indo-Germanic family. He does not believe in the Iberian extraction of any part of the inhabitants of the British Islands.

25 Scylax, p. 2. Herodotus speaks of "the Ligurians who live above Massalia." V 9.

26 Herodot. VII. 165.

27 Thucydides, VI. 2.

meant, nor what limits Thucydides assigned to Iberia; but a migration to Sicily, rather than to Corsica or Sardinia, becomes probable, in proportion as we place the Sicanians further to the south, and nearer to the trading settlements of the Carthaginians or Phœnicians. Perhaps the Ligurians advanced along the coast from east to west, expelling or conquering the Iberian tribes; till at last, when the force of their irruption was spent, the Iberians recovered their former country, wholly between the Iberus and the Pyrenees, and partially between the Pyrenees and the Rhone. At any rate, it should be remembered that the Iberians, and not the Kelts, were the inhabitants of the country between the Pyrenees and the Garonne and the Cevennes, as is shown even to this day, by the existence of the Basque language in the south of France no less than in Spain.

The Kelts, or Gauls: why they were as yet so little known.

It may be true, indeed, that the Kelts or Gauls had long before the fourth century of Rome crossed the Alps, and established themselves in that country, which now forms the Lombard portion of the Austrian dominions in northern Italy. It may be true also that Keltic tribes were to be found in the heart of Spain; for, before civilization has asserted its power, nations, like rivers, are continually changing their boundaries, and take their own course almost at pleasure. But as the Kelts had most certainly neither crossed the Apennines, nor reached as yet the shores of the Adriatic, they had no connection with the civilized world; the Carthaginians had no opportunity of enlisting them into their armies, nor had the Greek traders acquired any direct knowledge of them. Their name was known only through the reports of those Phœnicians[28] who navigated the Atlantic and the Bay of Biscay, on their way to the tin mines of Britain. And this explains the strange description of their position given by Herodotus,[29] "that the Kelts dwell without the Pillars of Hercules, and that they border on the Kynesians, who live the farthest to the west of all the people of Europe." This is clearly the language of some Phœnician Periplus of the western coasts of France and Spain: the Kynesians[30] must have lived on the coasts of Portugal, Gallicia, and Asturias; perhaps on that of Gascony and Guienne: beyond these, as the voyager pursued his course along the land, he came to the country of the Kelts who occupied the whole coast north of the Garonne, and were, very probably, intermixed with the Iberian Kynesians on the coasts of Gascony and Navarre. The Greeks, when they read this account, little suspected that these same Kelts reached from the shores of the ocean inland as far as the Alps, and, possibly, nearly to the head of the Adriatic; and that while they heard of them only as dwelling without the Pillars of Hercules, they were advanced in the opposite direction, almost within the ordinary horizon of Greek observation, and in a very short time would unexpectedly appear like a wasting torrent in the heart of Italy. The narrow band of coast occupied by the Ligurian and Venetian tribes was as yet sufficient to conceal the movements of the Kelts from the notice of the civilized world. Thus immediately before that famous eruption which destroyed Herculaneum and Pompeii, the level ridge[31] which was then Vesuvius excited no suspicion; and none could imagine that there were lurking close below that peaceful surface the materials of a fiery deluge, which were so soon to burst forth, and to continue for centuries to work havoc and desolation.

We can trace with great distinctness the period at which the Kelts became familiarly known to the Greeks. Herodotus only knew of them from the Phœnician navigators: Thucydides does not name them at all: Xenophon only notices them as forming part of the auxiliary force sent by Dionysius to the aid of Lacedæmon. Isocrates makes no mention of them. But immediately afterwards, their incursions into central and southern Italy on the one hand, and into the countries between the Danube and Macedonia on the other, had made them objects of general interest and curiosity; and Aristotle notices several points in their habits and character in different parts of his philosophical works.

[29] II. 33, IV. 49.

[30] There is no mention of these Cynesians, so far as I remember, in any ancient writer, except in the two passages of Herodotus quoted above. Niebuhr places them to the north, rather than to the west, of the Kelts (Kleine Histor. Schriften, p. 142); but I do not see why this is necessary. The account in the text seems sufficiently to explain the description in Herodotus.

[31] Vicina Vesevo ora *jugo*. Since the eruption no one would ever have called the top of Vesuvius a "jugum."

Greece. Supremacy of Lacedæmon. Olynthian confederacy.

From the countries of western Europe, on which the first faint dawn of historical light had as yet scarcely broken, we turn to the heart of the civilized world, to those republics of Greece which had already reached their highest point of glory and advancement, and were now feeling the first approach of decay, like a plant when its seed is almost ripe, and ready to be shed or wafted by the winds to a distance, there to multiply the race of its parent. According to the synchronism of Polybius,[32] the invasion of Rome by the Gauls took place in the same year with the conclusion of the peace of Antalcidas, that is, in the second year of the ninety-eighth Olympiad. Probably it should be placed a few years later; but at any rate, it falls within the period of the Lacedæmonian supremacy in Greece, after the humiliation of Athens by the result of the Peloponnesian war, and before the rise of the power of Thebes. Never was dominion wielded by such unfit hands as those of the Spartans. Living at home under an iron system, which taught each successive generation that their highest virtue was to preserve and not to improve the institutions of their fathers, the Lacedæmonians were utterly unable to act the part of conquerors; for conquest, being the greatest of all possible changes, can only be conducted by those who know how to change wisely;[33] a conqueror who is the slave of existing institutions, is no better than a contradiction. Thus the Spartans had no idea of turning their triumph over Athens to any other account than that of their own pride and rapacity; neither the general intercourse between nation and nation, nor commerce, nor intellectual nor moral excellence, derived any benefit from their ascendency. It was therefore unnatural, and fulfilled no object of God's providence, except that of being an instrument for the chastisement of others; so that it could only sow the seed of future wars, till, having heaped up the measure of insult and oppression, it at last drew down its just judgment. But the growth of that spirit of organization and self-government, which the high intelligence of the Greek mind could not but foster, was seen in the formation of the Olynthian confederacy.[34] Among the Chalcidian and Bottiæan towns of the peninsula of Pallene and its neighborhood, places whose fate it had been hitherto to be the mere subjects of some greater power, we now witness the growth of an independent political system, of which the head was not to be Sparta nor Athens, but Olynthus. This was a proof that the vigor of the Greek character was developing itself in a wider circle than heretofore, and prepares us for the change so soon to be effected by the genius of Philip and Alexander, when the centre of the power and outward activity of Greece was to be found in Macedon, while Athens still remained the well-spring of its intellectual vigor.

Eastern coast of the Adriatic. Molossians and Thesprotians.

The eastern coast of the Adriatic is one of those ill-fated portions of the earth which, though placed in immediate contact with civilization, have remained perpetually barbarian. Unvisited, and indeed almost inaccessible to strangers from the robber habits of the population, the Dalmatian provinces of Austria, no less than those of Montenegro and Albania, which are not yet reunited to Christendom, are to this hour as devoid of illustrious names and noble associations, as they were in the fourth century before the Christian era. From the gulf of Ambracia, the northwestern boundary of Greece, up to the head of the Adriatic, the coast was occupied by the Molossians, Thesprotians, Chaonians, and beyond these, by the various tribes[35] of the great Illyrian nation, amongst whom Herodotus included even the Henetians or Venetians, at the northern extremity of this whole region. In remote times, before the Hellenic race began to assume a character so distinct from all its

[32] I. 6.

[33] Ἡσυχαζούσῃ μὲν πόλει τὰ ἀκίνητα νόμιμα ἄριστα· πρὸς πολλὰ δὲ ἀναγκαζομένοις ἰέναι πολλῆς καὶ τῆς ἐπιτεχνήσεως δεῖ. Thucyd. I. 71.

[34] Xenophon, Hellenica, V. 2, § 12, et seqq.

[35] Scylax distinguishes the Venetians, as well as the Istrians and Liburnians, from the Illyrians, pp. 6, 7. And so also does Livy, X. 2. But Herodotus, as I have said, reckons even the Venetians as Illyrians, I. 196, and Strabo calls the whole eastern coast of the Adriatic, Illyricum, as far as the very head of the gulf. VII. pp. 313, 314.

kindred nations, the Molossians, Thesprotians, and Chaonians, all of them, it is probable, Pelasgian tribes, were both, in their religion and in their traditions of their heroes, closely connected with the Greeks. The ancient temple of Dodona, once no less famous than Delphi became afterwards, belonged to the Thesprotians; the son of Achilles was said to have reigned over the Molossians; and even within historical memory, the names of Molossian kings and chiefs are of Greek origin, such as Alcon, one of the suitors of the fair Agaristé, the daughter of Clisthenes of Sicyon, and still later, Admetus, the protector of Themistocles in his disgrace, and Alcetas, the ally of Dionysius of Syracuse. But the mass of the people were considered to be barbarian, and their fortunes were distinct from those of Greece, till the brilliant reign of Pyrrhus, more than a century after our present period, for a time united them.

Illyrians.

The Illyrians were already notorious for their piracies, and it was remarked of them, that some of their tribes were governed by queens.[36] Their queen Teuta, and her wars with the Romans, will give me an opportunity of noticing them more fully hereafter; and so rapidly is our knowledge increasing, that ere long we may possibly gain some clue to assist us in discovering the race and language of the Illyrians, points which at present are involved in the greatest obscurity.

Macedon. Reign of Amyntas, the father of Philip.

We are within five-and-twenty years of the accession of Philip to the throne of Macedon, but so entirely was the Macedonian greatness his own personal work, that nothing as yet gave sign of what it was so soon to become. His father, Amyntas, was at this time king, and unable even to cope with the Olynthian confederacy, which had lately grown up in his neighborhood. Many of the cities of Macedonia were won by the Olynthians,[37] and Amyntas was most rejoiced to obtain the aid of Lacedæmon to establish him on his throne by putting down this formidable enemy. The Macedonians[38] were not allowed to be Greeks, although they were probably of a kindred stock, and although the Greek language was now in universal use among them. But their kings were of the noblest Greek blood, being Heraclidæ from Argos, claiming descent from Temenus, one of the three hero chiefs of the race of Hercules, who had established themselves in Peloponnesus by the aid of the Dorians. The people were stout, brave, and hardy, and more numerous than the citizens of the little Greek commonwealths; so that Philip afterwards found no difficulty in raising a considerable army, when he began to aspire to the honor of making himself the first power in Greece. But as yet, though Archelaus had made roads through the country,[39] and had collected large supplies of arms to arm his people, the friendship and the enmity of Macedon were of little value, and none could have imagined that the fatal blow to the independence of Greece was to come from a kingdom which as yet scarcely belonged to the Greek name, and in the struggles for dominion between Athens and Lacedæmon, had been only a subordinate auxiliary.

State of the Persian monarchy.

Further to the east, the great Persian monarchy still existed unimpaired in the extent of its visible dominion, although ready at the first touch to fall to pieces. All of Asia, of which the Greeks had any knowledge, from the shores of the Ægæan to the Indus and the Araxes, from the Erythræan sea southwards to the Caspian and the chain of Caucasus, obeyed, to speak generally, the great king. In Africa, however, it was otherwise: Egypt

[36] Λιβυρνοὶ γυναικοκρατοῦνται. Scylax, Periplus, p. 7. This is on the assumption that the Liburnians were either Illyrians, or, at any rate, of a kindred stock.

[37] Xenophon, Hellenica, V. 2, § 13, 3, § 9.

[38] Alexander, the son of Amyntas, when he went over with some secret information to the Greek camp, before the battle of Platæa, is represented by Herodotus (IX. 45) as accounting for his interest in the welfare of Greece by saying, that he himself was of Greek origin, alluding to his supposed descent from Temenus the Heraclid. This would have been needless, had his birth as a Macedonian made him a Greek. Again, Thucydides distinguishes the Macedonians from the Greeks who were settled on their coast, and even expressly includes them amongst the barbarians, IV. 124, 126.

[39] Thucydides, II. 100.

had been for some years in revolt, was again governed by a dynasty of its native princes, and had defied the efforts of the Persian kings to reconquer it. And this example, together with the long war carried on against the Persians by Evagoras, the tyrant of the little state of Salamis, in Cyprus, and the belt of Greek cities encircling the whole coast of Asia Minor, from Trapezus on the Euxine to Cnidus by the Triopian cape, was tending gradually to dissolve the Persian power. The great king's hold on Caria and Cilicia was loosened, and when Isocrates wrote his Panegyrical Oration, in the beginning of the hundredth Olympiad,[40] Tyre was in the possession of the king's enemies, and its naval force strengthened for a time the arms of Evagoras.

Conclusion.

Such was the state of the civilized world, when the Kelts or Gauls broke through the thin screen which had hitherto concealed them from sight, and began, for the first time, to take their part in the great drama of the nations. For nearly two hundred years they continued to fill Europe and Asia with the terror of their name; but it was a passing tempest, and if useful at all, it was useful only to destroy. The Gauls could communicate no essential points of human character in which other races might be deficient; they could neither improve the intellectual state of mankind, nor its social and political relations. When, therefore, they had done their appointed work of havoc, they were doomed to be themselves extirpated, or to be lost amidst nations of greater creative and constructive power; nor is there any race which has left fewer traces of itself in the character and institutions of modern civilization.

CHAPTER XXIII.

MISCELLANEOUS—PHYSICAL HISTORY.

"Postrema vero partitio historiæ civilis ea sit, ut dividatur in meram aut mixtam. Mixturæ celebres duæ: altera ex scientiâ civili; altera præcipue ex naturali."—BACON, De Augmentis Scientiar. II. 10.

Imperfection of the materials of physical history.

A GREAT work might be written on the connection between the revolutions of nature and those of mankind: how they act each upon the other; how man is affected by climate, and how climate is again altered by the labors of man; how diseases are generated; how different states of society are exposed to different disorders, and require different sorts of diet; how, as all earthly things are exhaustible, the increased command over external nature given by increased knowledge, seems to have a tendency to shorten the period of the existing creation, by calling at once into action those resources of the earth which else might have supplied the wants of centuries to come; how, in short, nature, no less than human society, contains tokens that it had a beginning, and will as surely have its end. But, unfortunately, the physical history of ancient times is even more imperfect than the political history; and in the place of those exact and uninterrupted records of natural phenomena, from which alone any safe conclusions can be drawn, we have only a few scattered notices; nor can we be sure that even these have recorded what was most worthy of our knowledge. Still, these scanty memorials, such as they

[40] Isocrates, Panegyric. § 188, p. 74.

are, must not be neglected; and as we gain a wider experience, even these may hereafter be found instructive.

The climate of Italy was anciently colder in winter than it is now.

The first question with regard to the physical state of ancient Rome is, whether the climate was such as it is at present. Now here it is impossible not to consider the somewhat analogous condition of America at this day. Boston is in the same latitude with Rome; but the severity of its winter far exceeds not that of Rome only, but of Paris and London. Allowing that the peninsular form of Italy must at all times have had its effect in softening the climate, still the woods and marshes of Cisalpine Gaul, and the perpetual snows of the Alps, far more extensive than at present, owing to the uncultivated and uncleared state of Switzerland and Germany, could not but have been felt even in the neighborhood of Rome. Besides, even on the Apennines, and in Etruria and in Latium, the forests occupied a far greater space than in modern times: this would increase the quantity of rain, and consequently the volume of water in the rivers; the floods would be greater and more numerous, and before man's dominion had completely subdued the whole country, there would be large accumulations of water in the low grounds, which would still further increase the coldness of the atmosphere. The language[1] of ancient writers, on the whole, favors the same conclusion, that the Roman winter, in their days, was more severe than it is at present. It agrees with this, that the olive, which cannot bear a continuance of severe cold, was not introduced into Italy till long after the vine: Fenestella[2] asserted that its cultivation was unknown as late as the reign of Tarquinius Priscus; and such was the notion entertained of the cold of all inland countries, even in the latitude of Greece, that Theophrastus[3] held it impossible to cultivate the olive at the distance of more than four hundred stadia from the sea. But the cold of the winter is perfectly consistent[4] with great heat in the summer. The vine is cultivated with success on the Rhine, in the latitude of Devonshire and Cornwall, although the winter at Coblentz and Bonn is far more severe than it is in Westmoreland; and evergreens will flourish through the winter in the Westmoreland valley far better than on the Rhine or in the heart of France. The summer heat of Italy was probably much the same in ancient times as it is at present, except that there

[1] It is by no means easy to know what weight is to be given to the language of the poets, nor how far particular descriptions or expressions may have been occasioned by peculiar local circumstances. Pliny's statement, Epistol. II. 17, that the bay-tree would rarely live through the winter without shelter, either at Rome, or at his own villa at Laurentum, if taken absolutely, would prove too much; for although the bay is less hardy than some other evergreens, yet how can it be conceived that a climate in which the olive would flourish, could be too severe for the bay? There must either have been some local peculiarity of winds or soil, which the tree did not like, or else the fact, as is sometimes the case, must have been too hastily assumed; and men were afraid, from long custom, to leave the bay unprotected in the winter, although, in fact, they might have done it with safety. Yet the elder Pliny, XVII. 2, speaks of long snows being useful to the corn, which shows that he is not speaking of the mountains; and a long snow lying in the valleys of central or southern Italy would surely be a very unheard-of phenomenon now. Again, the freezing of the rivers, as spoken of by Virgil and Horace, is an image of winter, which could not, I think, naturally suggest itself to Italian poets of the present day, at any point to the south of the Apennines. Other arguments, to the same effect, may be seen in a paper by Daines Barrington, in the 58th volume of the Philosophical Transactions. Gibbon, also, after stating the arguments on both sides of the question, comes to the same conclusion. Miscellaneous Works, Vol. III. p. 246. He quotes, however, the Abbé de Longuerue, as saying that the Tiber was frozen in the bitter winter of 1709.

[2] Pliny, Hist. Natur. XV. 1.

[3] Pliny, Hist. Natur. XV. 1.

[4] It is a common notion that climate follows latitude, and that a northern country will be cold, and a southern one warm, as compared with each other throughout the year. But this is by no means a universal rule; on the contrary, climate in England is more affected by the longitude of a place, than by its latitude; and the winters are often mildest in those parts where the summers are least genial. The whole eastern coast, from Kent to Caithness, is much colder in winter than the western; and this to such a degree, that Kent is not only colder than Cornwall, but colder than Cumberland, or Argyleshire. On the other hand, the eastern coast in summer enjoys a much greater share of steady fine weather and sunshine than the western. Wall-fruit will ripen in the neighborhood of Edinburgh far more surely than in Westmoreland, and wheat grows luxuriantly as far north as Elgin, while it is a rarity on the coast of Argyleshire.

were a great number of spots where shade and verdure might be found, and where its violence would, therefore, be more endurable. But the difference between the temperature of summer and winter may be safely assumed to have been much greater than it is now.

This perhaps had an effect on the healthiness of the neighborhood of Rome.

It then becomes a question whether the greater cold of the winter, and the greater extent of wood and of undrained waters which existed in the times of the Romans, may not have had a favorable influence in mitigating that malaria which is now the curse of so many parts of Italy, and particularly of the immediate neighborhood of Rome. On a subject so imperfectly understood, even by those who have had the fullest experience, it were most unbecoming in a foreigner to speak otherwise than with the greatest diffidence. We know, however, that the Campagna at Rome, which is now almost a desert, must, at a remote period, have been full of independent cities; and although the greater part of these had perished long before the fourth century of Rome, yet even then there existed Ostia, Laurentum, Ardea, and Antium on one side, and Veii and Cære on the other, in situations which are now regarded as uninhabitable during the summer months; and all the lands of the Romans, on which they, like the old Athenians, for the most part resided regularly, lie within the present range of the malaria.

The range of the malaria less extensive formerly than at present.

Some have supposed that, although the climate was the same as it is now, yet the Romans were enabled to escape from its influence, and their safety has been ascribed[5] to their practice of wearing woollen next to the skin, instead of linen or cotton. But not to notice other objections to this notion, it is enough to say that the Romans regarded unhealthy situations with the same apprehension as their modern descendants; it is one of the first cautions given by Cato[6] and Varro[7] to a man going to purchase land, that he should buy only where the air is healthy; "otherwise," says Varro, "farming is nothing else than a mere gambling with life and property." The truth seems to be, that the malaria, although well known and extremely fatal, was much more partial than at present, and that many spots which are now infected were formerly free from it. "The whole of Latium," says Strabo,[8] "is a flourishing and very productive country, with the exception of a few spots near the coast, which are marshy and unhealthy." And again, when speaking expressly of the Campagna between the Alban hills and Rome,[9] he says, "that the parts towards the sea are not so healthy; but that the rest is a good country to live in, and well cultivated accordingly." Now, although this is probably going too far, for the unhealthy spots could not have been confined altogether to the seacoast, yet with every allowance for exaggeration and careless writing, this is a description of the Campagna which no man in his senses would think of giving now.

Rome itself, then as now, was less unhealthy than its immediate neighborhood.

On the other hand, Cicero[10] and Livy[11] both speak of the immediate neighborhood of Rome as unhealthy, but at the same time they extol the positive healthiness of the city itself; ascribing it to the hills, which are at once airy themselves, and offer a screen to the low grounds from the heat of the sun. Bunsen, also, from an experience of many years, gives a favorable account of the healthiness of the city itself. "The site of Rome," he says, "taken generally, may be called healthy." It is true, that one of the most unhealthy parts of modern Rome, the Piazzi di Spagna and the slope of the Pincian hill above it, was not within the limits of the ancient city. Yet the praise of the healthiness of Rome must be understood rather com-

[5] By Brocchi, in his "Discorso sulla condizione dell' aria di Roma negli antichi tempi," printed at the end of his work on the Geology of Rome.

[6] Cato, de Re Rusticâ, II.

[7] Varro, de Re Rusticâ, II. 4.

[8] V. 3, § 5, p. 231.

[9] V. 3, § 12, p. 239.

[10] De Republicâ, II. 6. "Locum delegit (Romulus) in regione pestilenti salubrem."

[11] Compare VII. 38. "In pestilente atque arido circa urbem solo;" and V. 54. "Saluberrimos colles."

paratively with that of the immediate neighborhood than positively. Rome, in the summer months, cannot be called healthy, even as compared with the other great cities of Italy, much less if the standard be taken from Berlin or from London.

Again, the neighborhood of Rome is characterized by Livy as a "pestilential and parched soil." The latter epithet is worthy of notice, because the favorite opinion has been that the malaria is connected with marshes and with moisture. But it is precisely here that we may find, I think, the explanation of the spread of the malaria in modern times. Even in spring, nothing can less resemble a marsh than the present aspect of the Campagna. It is far more like the down country of Dorsetshire, and as the summer advances it may well be called a dry and parched district. But this is exactly the character of the plains[12] of Estremadura, where our soldiers suffered so grievously from malaria fever in the autumn of 1809. In short, abundant experience has proved, that when the surface of the ground is wet, the malaria poison is far less noxious than when all appearance of moisture on the surface is gone, and the damp makes its way into the atmosphere from a considerable depth under ground. After a wet and cold summer in 1799, when the whole face of the country was nearly flooded with water, the British army remained the whole autumn in one of the most unhealthy parts of Holland, without suffering in any remarkable degree from malaria fever. But in 1809, when the summer had been hot and fine, every one remembers the deadly effect in the autumn fevers on the soldiers who were holding Walcheren. If, then, more rain fell in the Campagna formerly than is the case now; if the streams were fuller of water, and their course more rapid; above all, if, owing to the uncleared state of central Europe, and the greater abundance of wood in Italy itself, the summer heats set in later, and were less intense, and more often relieved by violent storms of rain, there is every reason to believe that the Campagna must have been far healthier than at present; and that precisely in proportion to the clearing and cultivation of central Europe, to the felling of the woods in Italy itself, the consequent decrease in the quantity of rain, the shrinking of the streams, and the disappearance of the water from the surface, has been the increased unhealthiness of the country, and the more extended range of the malaria.

The Campagna has perhaps become less healthy from the winters having become milder, and from the diminution in the quantity of rain.

It must be observed also, that the present desolation of the Campagna, and even that comparative want of population which prevailed in it during the later times of the Roman republic and under the empire, are not wholly to be attributed to physical causes. The aguish districts of England continue to be inhabited, nor have the terrors of the yellow fever driven men away from the unhealthiest situations of the West Indies, or from Vera Cruz, Acapulco, or Carthagena. The old cities of the Campagna would have continued to defy the malaria; their population would have been kept down, indeed; many of their children would have died young, and the average length of human life would have been far short of threescore years and ten; but men do not readily leave their country, and they would have continued, as their fathers had done before them, to struggle with disease and death. When, however, political causes had destroyed the cities of the Campagna one after the other, and the land became the property of Roman citizens; when again, at a later period, the small properties disappeared, and whole districts fell into the hands of a few individuals; then it was natural that those who could afford to live where they chose, should

Causes of its gradual desolation.

[12] The view here given of some of the phenomena of marsh or malaria fevers was obtained from a paper by Dr. Ferguson of Windsor, "on the nature and history of the Marsh Poison," which was read before the Royal Society of Edinburgh in 1820. I directed Bunsen's attention to it, and he has made much use of it in his own paper on the "Aria Cattiva," in the first volume of his description of Rome. An unprofessional man's judgment of a medical work is worth little; but the subject of Dr. Ferguson's paper is one in which I have long felt a lively interest; and all that I have observed myself, or heard from medical men, in answer to my inquiries as to matters of fact, has been in agreement with his statements.

not fix themselves in a spot of even partial unhealthiness, and thus a great part of the Campagna was left only to the slaves by whom it was cultivated. In modern times, when slave labor was no longer to be had, and there were no attractions strong enough to induce a free population to migrate from their homes to an unhealthy district, the Campagna has remained a wilderness, and its harvests are reaped by a temporary immigration of laborers from other parts of the country. To repeople it under such circumstances is far more difficult than to keep up a population already existing; and if, as I believe, the physical state of the Campagna has become more and more unfavorable, it seems likely, without some extraordinary advances in our knowledge of the malaria, and in our ability to combat it, to remain a wilderness forever.[13]

Various epidemic disorders noticed in the annals.

The disorders produced by malaria, whether more or less fatal, so regularly accompanied the return of hot weather, that they were not likely to be recorded in the annals. The diseases which were noticed there were of a very different character, and belonged rather to another class of phenomena, those extraordinary sicknesses which, in obedience to a law hitherto undiscovered, visit the earth at different periods, prevail more or less extensively, and acting independently, as it seems, of any recognized causes of disease, are also beyond the reach of all known remedies. The first half of the fourth century of Rome was one of these calamitous periods, and the pestilences which occurred at the beginning of it have already been noticed. Seven others are recorded between the years 318 and 365; that is to say,[14] in 319, 320, 322, 327, 343, 356, and 363. They are described in general terms, with the exception of those of the years 327 and 363, which are ascribed to unusual droughts; and said also to have nearly resembled each other in their symptoms. The epidemic of 327 first, as we are told, attacked the cattle, the herdsmen, and others who tended the cattle, and lastly it became general. It appears to have been wholly inflammatory, and to have shown itself particularly on the skin; first, in the form of a violent rash,[15] accompanied with extreme irritation, and afterwards in the shape of erysipelas of a very malignant kind. This visitation took place just after the conclusion of the peace of Nicias, and we do not hear of any coincident prevalence of pestilence in Greece. The epidemic of 363[16] is described in similar terms; it was brought on by the same causes, an exceedingly hot and dry summer; and the symptoms were the same, an eruption terminating in large and painful ulcers, accompanied with such irritation, that their patients tore their flesh even to the bone. The date of this disorder falls about the beginning of the ninety-ninth Olympiad, that is to say, it coincides with the Olynthian war; and as it arose

[13] This opinion should be expressed with the greatest hesitation and diffidence, because Bunsen believes that the Campagna is reclaimable by encouraging human habitation in it; and he thinks that if the great landholders were to let out their property on leases to a number of small farmers, who would thus naturally create a resident population, the unhealthiness of the air would, in a great measure, be obviated. It is said that the breaking up of the surface of the ground is found to lessen the virulence of the malaria; and the fires which necessarily accompany human dwellings, are another known antidote to it. As a proof of this, Bunsen appeals to the great improvement thus effected by the duke of Zagarolo in the neighborhood of that little town, which stands on the edge of the Campagna, a few miles from Palestrina, about a mile on the left of the road coming from Rome. The air, which was decidedly unhealthy, has been purified; and the whole district, by having been peopled, has become actually capable of supporting a population in health and prosperity. However, without reckoning on the moral improbability of finding the great body of proprietors disposed to follow a new system, at variance with their old habits, it must be allowed that the duke of Zagarolo's experiment was made under circumstances unusually favorable. The country round Zagarolo is high ground; it forms a sort of shoulder, connecting the Alban hills with the Apennines, and forms the divortium aquarum, or water-shed, of the feeders of the Tiber on the one hand, and of the Garigliano on the other. Its character also is wholly different from the general aspect of the Campagna; it is not a country of long swelling slopes, notched as it were here and there with deep narrow stream beds; but a succession of nearly parallel ridges, rising to a considerable height, with valleys rather than gorges between them. To all appearance, therefore, it was more easily reclaimable than the great mass of the Campagna.

[14] Livy, IV. 21, 25, 30, 52. V. 13, 31.

[15] Dionysius, XII. 3. Fragm. Mai.

[16] Dionysius, XIII. 4. Fragm. Mai. Livy, V. 31. Dionysius appears to put this epidemic a year earlier than Livy, namely, 362.

from local causes, we cannot be surprised that we hear no mention of its having extended into Greece. But the epidemic of 322 and of the years almost immediately preceding it, was contemporary with the great plague of Athens: and that of 356 coincided, according to the chronology of Diodorus, with the violent sickness which destroyed Imilcon's army before Syracuse, and had been preceded by three or four years of epidemic disease in Africa.

Phenomena of the weather. Great frost of the year 355.

If from diseases we turn to the phenomena of the weather, with which they are, in all probability, closely connected, we find the years 327 and 363 marked, as has already been observed, by excessive droughts; and the summer of 356 is said by Diodorus[17] to have been of the same character. On the other hand, the winter of 355 had been one of unusual severity;[18] the Tiber was choked up with ice, the snow lay seven feet deep, where it was not drifted; many men and cattle were lost in it, and many of the cattle were killed by the extreme cold, or starved from want of pasture, the resources by which we now provide for their subsistence during the winter being then little practised. It is added that the fruit-trees, by which are meant the figs and olives in particular, either perished altogether, or suffered so severely that they did not bear for a long time afterwards; and that many houses were crushed by the weight of snow which lay on them, or carried away by its melting when the frost at last broke up. There is also a notice in Diodorus of the winter of 321,[19] which is described as having been excessively wet, so that the fruits of the following season never ripened properly, and the corn was considered unwholesome.

Volcanic phenomena. Earthquakes.

The period about the year 322 was remarkable in Greece for the frequency and severity of earthquakes; the numerous earthquakes which, from their occurring so nearly together, were remembered afterwards as an epoch, happened, says Thucydides,[20] at this time. In the same way the Romans were alarmed in the year 319 by reports[21] of frequent earthquakes in the country immediately adjoining Rome, and many houses were thrown down by the shocks. It is probable some phenomenon of this sort occasioned also the great overflow of the Alban lake during the war with Veii; an event remarkable in itself, and still more so as having led to the famous work existing to this day; the tunnel by which the water of the lake is carried through the range of hills which encircle it, and from thence is discharged into the Campagna.

The volcanic lakes of the neighborhood of Rome. Tunnel of the lake of Alba.

The lakes of Alba and Nemi, like others in the neighborhood of Rome, are of a peculiar character. In their elevation, lying nestled as it were high up in the bosom of the mountains, they resemble what in Cumberland and Westmoreland are called tarns; but our tarns, like ordinary lakes, have their visible feeders and outlets, their head which receives the streams from the mountain sides, and their foot by which they discharge themselves, generally in a larger stream, into the valley below. The lakes of Alba and Nemi lie each at the bottom of a perfect basin, and the unbroken rim of this basin allows them no visible outlet. Again, it sometimes happens that lakes so situated have their outlet under ground, and that the stream which drains them appears again to the day after a certain distance, having made its way through the basin of the lake by a tunnel provided for it by nature. This is the case particularly where the prevailing rock is the mountain or metalliferous limestone of Derbyshire, which is full of caverns and fissures: and an instance of it may be seen in the small lake or tarn of Malham in Yorkshire, and another on a much larger scale in the lake of Copais in Bœotia. But the volcanic rocks, in which the lake of Alba lies, do not afford such natural tunnels, or at

[17] XIV. 70.

[18] Livy, V. 13. Dionysius, XII. 8. Fragm. Mai. Bunsen observes that ice in the Tiber is now as unknown a phenomenon as it would be between the tropics. The winter of 355 is indeed described by Dionysius as one altogether unparalleled in the Roman annals, either before or since, down to his time. I cannot find any particulars of the freezing of the Tiber in 1709, already noticed in note 1.

[19] XII. 58.

[20] III. 89.

[21] Livy, IV. 21.

least they are exceeding small, and unequal to the discharge of any large quantity of water; so that if any unusual cause swells the lake, it can find no adequate outlet, and rises necessarily to a higher level. The Roman tradition reported that such a rise took place in the year 357; it was caused probably by some volcanic agency, and increased to such a height, that the water at last ran over the basin of hills at its lowest point,[22] and poured down into the Campagna. Traces[23] of such an outlet are said to be still visible; and it is asserted that there are marks of artificial cutting through the rock, as if to enlarge and deepen the passage. This would suppose the ordinary level of the lake in remote times to have been about two hundred feet higher than it is at present; and if this were so, the actual tunnel was intended not to remedy a new evil, but to alter the old state of the lake for the better, by reducing it for the time to come to a lower level. Possibly the discharge over the edge of the basin became suddenly greater, and so suggested the idea of diverting the water altogether by a different channel. But the whole story of the tunnel, as we have it, is so purely a part of the poetical account of the fall of Veii, that no part of it can be relied on as historical. The prophecy of the old Veientian, and the corresponding answer of the Delphian oracle, connecting the draining of the lake with the fate of Veii, must be left as we find them; only it is likely enough that any extraordinary natural phenomenon, occurring immediately after the visitation of pestilence, and in the midst of a long and doubtful war, should have excited unusual alarm, and have been thought important enough to require an appeal to the most famous oracle in the world. But other questions of no small difficulty remain: the length of the tunnel, according to the lowest statement given, exceeds two thousand one hundred yards;[24] according to others it exceeds two thousand six hundred;[25] and one estimate makes it as much as two thousand eight hundred:[26] its height varies from seven feet and a half to nine or ten feet; and its width is not less than four feet. Admitting that it was wholly worked through the tufo,[27] which is easily wrought, still the labor and expense of such a tunnel must have been considerable; and in the midst of an important war, how could either money or hands have been spared for such a purpose? Again, was the work exclusively a Roman one, or performed by the Romans jointly with the Latins, as an object of common concern to the whole confederacy? The Alban lake can scarcely have been within the domain of Rome; nor can we conceive that the Romans could have been entitled to divert its waters at their pleasure without the consent of the neighboring Latin cities. But if it were a common work; if the Latins entered heartily into the quarrel of Rome with Veii, regarding it as a struggle between their race and that of the Etruscans; if the overflow of the waters of their national lake, the lake which bathed the foot of the Alban mountain, where their national temple stood and their national solemnities were held, excited an interest in every people of the Latin name, then we may understand how their joint labor and joint contributions may have accomplished the work even in the midst of war; and the Romans, as they disguised on every occasion the true nature of their connection with the Latins, would not fail to represent it as exclusively their own.

[22] Dionysius, XII. 11. Fragm. Mai.

[23] Sir W. Gell, Topography of Rome, &c. Vol. I. p. 43.

[24] Westphal. Römische Kampagne, p. 25.

[25] Sir W. Gell, Topography of Rome, p. 39.

[26] Mr. Laing Meason, quoted by Sir W. Gell in a note to p. 53 of his Topogr. of Rome, Vol. I.

[27] Westphal says it is worked through lava. Sir W. Gell says it is excavated generally in the tufo. Mr. Meason, whose authority is considerable, as he had had much practical acquaintance with mining, and went into the tunnel for about 130 yards from the lake, speaks of the work as cut in the tufo.

CHAPTER XXIV.

THE GAULS INVADE CENTRAL ITALY—BATTLE OF THE ALIA—BURNING OF ROME—RANSOM OF THE CAPITOL AND OF THE CITY—RETREAT OF THE GAULS.

"Hark! the Gaul is at her gates!"
COWPER.

"Aurea cæsaries ollis, atque aurea vestis:
Virgatis lucent sagulis; tum lactea colla
Auro innectuntur: duo quisque Alpina coruscant
Gæsa manu, scutis protecti corpora longis."
VIRGIL, Æn. VIII. 658.

Common account of the settlements of the Gaulish tribes in Italy.

THE fourth century before the Christian æra brought the Gauls, as we have seen, for the first time within the observation of the civilized world. They then crossed the Apennines, and overran central and southern Italy; they then also broke in upon the Illyrian[1] tribes, established themselves between the Danube and Greece, and became known to the kings of Macedon.[2] But whether it was in this same century that they had first crossed the Alps as well as the Apennines, is a question much more difficult to answer. If we follow the well-known account of Livy,[3] we must fix their passage of the Alps two hundred years earlier: it was about six hundred years before the Christian æra, according to this statement, that there happened a vast emigration of the inhabitants of central Gaul; one great multitude, said the story, crossed the Rhine, and sought a home amidst the wilds of the Hercynian forest; another made its way over the Alps, descended into the plain of the Po, encountered and defeated the Etruscans, who were then the masters of the country, near the river Ticinus, and founded the city of Mediolanum. After this other tribes of central Gauls, entering Italy by the same course, and finding their countrymen already in possession of all to the westward of the Adda, penetrated still deeper, and extended the Gaulish settlements as far as the Adige. Again, at a later period, but how much later we are not told, the Boii[4] and Lingones set out from the east

[1] Justin, XXIV. 4. This is the great expedition which Scylax alludes to, when he describes the Gauls on the northwestern coast of the Adriatic, as "men who had stayed behind from their expedition;" ἀπολειφθέντες τῆς. The following words, ἐπὶ στενῶν, appear to me to be corrupt.

[2] In the very beginning of the reign of Alexander, when a Gaulish embassy came to congratulate him on his victory over the Getæ. Arrian, Exp. Alex. I. 4.

[3] Livy, V. 34, 35.

[4] The Lingones came from the neighborhood of Langres, that high table-land which looks down on the infant Marne to the north, and on the streams which feed the Saone to the south. The situation of the Boii in Gaul is not known; their nation is only to be traced in the countries to which it had emigrated, in Germany and Italy. It is remarkable that the story speaks of a simultaneous migration into Germany and Italy; and we find Boii in both of these countries. Again, the Senones, who are mentioned as having entered Italy last of all the Gauls, are also included amongst the tribes of the first swarm who founded Mediolanum. Both these circumstances seem to show, that in the view of the author of this account, all the migrations into Italy took place nearly continuously, and were the result of one and the same cause. This also seems to agree best with the fact, that the last comers, instead of attempting to dislodge those who had arrived before them, passed on quietly to a more distant settlement. This is very conceivable, if all had left their country from one and the same impelling cause, and in the course of one generation; but had the Boii and Lingones entered Italy a century or a century and a half later than the founders of Mediolanum, and from causes wholly unconnected with their migration, they would, in all probability, have tried to establish themselves between the Ticinus and the Adda, and would have paid little regard to the tie of a common extraction, when distance of time and place had done so much to weaken it.

and northeast of Gaul, made their way to the lake of Geneva, ascended the valley of the Rhone, crossed the Alps by the pass which now bears the name of the Great St. Bernard, and as the whole country on the north of the Po was already occupied, these new adventurers passed that river, and drove out the Etruscans and Umbrians from their possessions between the Po and the Apennines, from the neighborhood of the modern cities of Parma, Modena, and Bologna. Last of all, but again the time is not specified, came the Senones from the same quarter of Gaul, and following the track of the Boii and Lingones, crossed as they had done both the Alps and the Po, reached the coast of the Adriatic, and finally spread themselves along its shores from the neighborhood of Ravenna to that of Ancona.

Its chronology is suspicious.

The geographical part of this account appears to deserve our full belief; but it does not follow that its chronology is equally trustworthy. The narrative itself seems to imply that all these migrations were nearly continuous, and it is for many reasons most probable[5] that they were so; yet it is not credible that the Senones should have been settled on the coast of the Adriatic[6] for two hundred years before they crossed the Apennines; and there is a preponderance[7] of evidence to prove that their inroad into Etruria followed close upon their first establishment in north Italy. It is impossible to say at how early a period tribes of Gauls may have passed over the Cottian Alps, and settled in the valleys and plains of Piedmont. But the general overthrow of the Etruscan power between the Alps and the Apennines has every appearance of having been

[5] Partly for the reasons given in the preceding note, and also, because a general burst of migration at one particular period is more probable amongst a barbarian people than a succession of migrations to the same quarter, during a term of two hundred years.

[6] They crossed the Apennines, according to Diodorus and the author of the little work, "De Viris Illustribus," because their settlement on the Adriatic was parched and barren: they surely would have discovered this in less time than a hundred years. Niebuhr notices the general rapidity of barbarian incursions; they advance further and further till they meet with some invincible obstacle. And those who had exterminated the Etruscans from the north of the Apennines, would have had nothing to deter them from attacking the same enemies in their southern possessions in Etruria Proper.

[7] Diodorus, XIV. 113. Dionysius, XIII. 14, 15. Fragm. Mai. Pliny, Hist. Natur. III. 17, where he says that the Gauls destroyed the Etruscan city of Melpum in northern Italy in the same year and day on which the Romans took Veii. Justin, XXIV. 4, and XX. 5, and even Livy himself, in two passages referred to by Niebuhr, V. 17, and 37, where he makes the Etruscans speak of the Gauls as a people whom they had never seen, who were recently become their neighbors, and with whom they knew not whether they were to have peace or war; and where in the same way he speaks of the Gauls as a new enemy to the Romans, who were come upon them from the shores of the ocean and the extremities of the earth. The only plausible argument for the more ancient settlement of the Gauls in Italy (for little stress is to be laid on their pretended alliance with the Phocæan exiles who were founding Massilia), is to be found in the statement of Dionysius, VII. 3, which some understand as saying that the Greek city of Cuma in Campania was besieged in the reign of Tarquinius Superbus by some Etruscans who had dwelt on the shores of the Ionian gulf, and who had been in the course of time driven from their country by the Gauls. This is the interpretation of Dionysius' words, as Müller understands them. (Etrusker, Vol. I. p. 153, note 78.) Niebuhr, however, understands them differently; and the language is not sufficiently precise to enable us to be certain as to the writer's meaning. The words are, *Τυῤῥηνῶν οἱ περὶ τὸν Ἰόνιον κόλπον κατοικοῦντες, ἐκεῖθέν θ' ὑπὸ τῶν Κελτῶν ἐξελαθέντες σὺν χρόνῳ, καὶ σὺν αὐτοῖς Ὀμβρικοί τε καὶ Δαύνιοι καὶ συχνοὶ τῶν ἄλλων βαρβάρων ἐπεχείρησαν ἀνελεῖν (τὴν Κύμην).* Niebuhr thinks that this means, "those Etruscans who then were dwelling on the Ionian gulf, but who in the course of time were afterwards driven from thence by the Gauls." Müller objects that if this were the meaning, Dionysius must have written *οἱ τότε μὲν κατοικοῦντες, ὕστερον δὲ ἐξελαθέντες.* This would have been clearer, undoubtedly; but Dionysius does not write with the perfect clearness of Isocrates or Demosthenes, and the words *σὺν χρόνῳ* are meant to express the same thing as Müller's *ὕστερον*. But after all, what can be made of the passage under any interpretation? "The Etruscans on the Ionian gulf," that is, on the Adriatic, could not have been driven out by the Gauls as early as the sixty-fourth Olympiad, for all allow that the Senones, who expelled the Etruscans from the coast, entered Italy after all the other Gauls; and their invasion was so recent, that Scylax speaks of the Etruscans, as well as of the Umbrians and Daunians, as still dwelling on the shores of the Adriatic even in his time. Nor is there any reason for considering the expedition against Cuma as occasioned by the expulsion of the invaders from their own country by another enemy. The Umbrians and Daunians who took part in it were certainly never driven out from their country by the Gauls; and it is more probable that the Etruscans, who are named as the first people in the confederacy, were not a band of fugitives; but were rather attempting, in conjunction with their dependent allies, to extend their dominion still further over Italy; for this was the period of their greatest power,

effected suddenly, speedily, and not earlier than the middle of the fourth century of Rome, when some causes, to us unknown, set the whole Keltic or Gaulish nation in motion, and drove them southward and eastward to execute their appointed work of devastation and destruction.

To what Keltic race did the Gauls, who invaded Italy, belong?

Another question next presents itself. Can we recognize these Gaulish invaders of Italy as belonging to either of the existing divisions of the Keltic race? Were they Gael, or were they Kymry? or did they belong to some third division, distinct from each of these, which has since utterly perished? Much has been written upon the subject of the Kelts and their language; but we seem as yet unable to connect our knowledge of the existing Keltic races with the accounts which we have received of them from the writers of antiquity.

Diodorus' distinction between the Gauls and Kelts.

Diodorus[8] tells us that the Romans included under one common name of Gauls two great divisions of people: the one consisting of the Keltic tribes of Spain, of the south and centre of Gaul, and of the north of Italy; the other embracing those more remote tribes which lived on the shores of the ocean, and on the skirts of what he calls the Hercynian mountains, and eastward as far as Scythia. This last division, he says, were the proper Gauls, while the others were to be called Kelts. Niebuhr supposes that Diodorus learnt this distinction from Posidonius, and it is undoubtedly well worth noticing. Diodorus further says, that to these more remote tribes belonged the Kimbri, whom some writers identified with the old Kimmerians; and that these Kimbri were the people who took Rome, and sacked Delphi, and carried their conquests even into Asia.

Kelt and Gaul are but different forms of the same name.

It may be doubted, however, whether there be not in this statement a show of knowledge greater than the reality. Keltæ and Galatæ are undoubtedly only different forms of the same name; the first was the form with which the Greeks were earliest acquainted, at a time when their knowledge of the Kelts was confined to the tribes of Spain and Gaul. The great Gaulish migration of the fourth century before Christ, introduced the other and more correct form "Galatæ;" yet many writers[9] continued to use the old orthography, and in fact, with the exception of the Galatians of Asia Minor, the other Gauls, in all parts of the world, are generally called by the Greeks according to their old form of the name, not Galatæ, but Keltæ. These names, therefore, would in themselves rather show that the invaders of Italy and Greece were the same people with the old inhabitants of the west of Europe, than establish any diversity between them.

Yet the distinction of Diodorus is partly true,

But when we find from Cæsar,[10] that the Gauls on the shores of the ocean, that is, on the coasts of the British channel and the North sea, the Gauls whom he calls Belgians, were distinguished both in language and customs from the Gauls of the interior; when we consider that these more remote Gauls included, according to Diodorus, the people called Kimbri, and when we see that the people now calling themselves Kymry, namely, the Welsh, do actually differ in language and in customs from the Keltic tribes in Ireland and Scotland, the statement of Diodorus does appear to contain a real truth, and we begin to recognize in the Keltæ and Galatæ of his geography two great divisions of the same race, analogous to the Gael and Kymry existing at this day in Great Britain.

Yet the gleam of light thus gained is almost instantly overclouded. The Gauls of the north of Italy appear, according to every testimony,[11] to have been the

Diodorus, V. 32.

[9] Aristotle ascribes to the Keltæ a peculiarity in national manners, which Diodorus reports of the Galatæ. And in those notices of Keltic manners and character which occur in several places of his works, he must have been speaking of the Kelts of Pannonia and Thrace, that is, of the Galatæ of Diodorus, and not of the remote inhabitants of Gaul and Spain.

[10] De Bello Gallico, I. 1.

[11] Polybius, II. 15. Τρανσάλπινοί γε μὴν οὐ διὰ τὴν τοῦ γένους ἀλλὰ διὰ τὴν τοῦ τόπου διαφορὰν προσαγορεύονται.

but involved in much difficulty.

same people with the Gauls of the centre of France, or in the language of Diodorus, with the Keltæ. The names of their tribes, the Senones,[12] Lingones, Insubres, Cenomani, can be connected at once with particular districts of Keltic Gaul, which bore, it may almost be said which bear to this day, the same names, and from which their origin is distinctly traced. We find among them no traces of Belgian or Kimbrian names, or of their having come from the shores of the Northern ocean,[13] or the Hercynian mountains. How then can it be said that the invaders of central Italy were not Keltæ, but Galatæ; not Gael, but Kymry?

The Gauls who invaded Italy came from Keltic Gaul.

It has been maintained, indeed, that[14] the Boii, Lingones, and Senones, the tribes which were the last to enter Italy, and which crossed the Alps, not by the passes to the west of Turin, but by the Great St. Bernard, were of a different race from the earlier invaders, and that while those were Gael, these who came last were Kymry. But the Roman writers, and Polybius, who was well acquainted with the Cisalpine Gauls, acknowledged no such diversity. And though we cannot ascertain the country of the Boii, yet the Lingones and Senones both fall within the limits assigned by Cæsar to Keltic Gaul, as distinguished from the country of the Belgæ or Kymry.

But possibly the Kimbri, or Kymry, may have taken part in the invasion with them.

If, however, we are disposed to rely on the statement of Diodorus and Appian, that the Gauls who invaded Greece were Kimbri, it may be very possible that there was a more general movement among the Keltic tribes in the fourth century of Rome, than the Greek or Roman writers were aware of. The Kymry, breaking in upon the Gael from the east and north, may have persuaded or forced some of their tribes to join them in their march southwards; the two nations may have poured into Italy together, and while the Gaelic tribes settled themselves on the Po or on the coast of the Adriatic, the mass of the Kymrians may have pressed forward round the head of the gulf, and so penetrated into Pannonia and Thrace. Nor could we deny the possibility of some Kymrians having remained in Italy with the Gael; and if we believe that the name of Brennus[15] was really borne by the leader of the attack on Rome, and that this word is no other than the Kymrian "Brenhin,"[16] which signifies king or leader, then we must conclude that although the mass of the invaders were Gael, yet that not only were there Kymrians joined with them, but that a Kymrian chief commanded the whole expedition. This may have been so, but I can hardly think that there is sufficient evidence to require us to believe that it was so.

Difficulty of identifying the language of the Gauls who invaded Italy with any existing Keltic dialect.

Again, though I have called the Gauls of north Italy Gael, and have supposed that those who passed on to Illyricum and Thrace may have been Kymry, yet I am far from concluding that in the language of the former we should have recognized the exact Erse and Gaelic of Ireland and the Scotch Highlands, or in that of the latter the

[12] The Senones came from the neighborhood of Sens on the Yonne, the Lingones from that of Langres: the Insubres came from a district in the country of the Ædui, between the Loire and Saone; and the Cenomani from the neighborhood of Le Mans.

[13] The expression in Livy already referred to, "that the Gauls came from the shores of the ocean," must not be alleged here, inasmuch as the ocean is there used merely in opposition to the Mediterranean, and may quite as well be understood of the Bay of Biscay as of the German Ocean or the Baltic.

[14] By Thierry in his Histoire des Gaulois, Vol. I. p. 44, &c.

[15] It must be remembered always that Fabius, the oldest Roman historian, wrote about two hundred years after the Gaulish invasion, and borrowed largely from the Greek writers. They mentioned the attack on Rome, as we know, but not with its details; and it is not likely that they should have given the name of the Gaulish leader. In fact, Diodorus, whose narrative, as Niebuhr supposes, is copied from Fabius, does not give it at all. It is very likely that the name of Brennus was borrowed from the story of the Gaulish attack on Delphi, as so many of the embellishments of the Roman history have been taken from the famous stories of the history of Greece.

[16] Dr. Pritchard, whose authority in such questions is of the highest order, believes that Brennus is not the Welsh "Brenhin," but rather the proper name Bran, which occurs in Welsh history. I know not whether this name ever prevailed amongst the Irish or the Gael of Scotland.

exact form of the modern Welsh. The Keltic languages, which still exist in these islands, are in all likelihood the solitary survivors out of the multitude of languages or dialects, once spoken by the various branches of the great Keltic family, from the Atlantic to the sources of the Danube, from the Mediterranean to the northern extremity of the British isles. Length of time and remoteness of place introduce wonderful changes in a language; so that no one could expect to find an exact resemblance between the Keltic spoken in the fourth century before the Christian æra, by the Gauls of France and Italy, and the actual language of the inhabitants of Ireland and the north of Scotland. We may, therefore, find names of places and persons[17] among the ancient Gauls, which no Keltic language in its present state will enable us to interpret. Much more may it be impossible to trace such words in the written Welsh, or Erse, or Gaelic; although an exact acquaintance with the various spoken dialects in the several parts of Ireland or Wales might even now enable us to discover them. There are many German words[18] lost in our written English, which either exist in the names of places or in some of our provincial dialects; and doubtless the converse of this might be observed by any one who was familiar with the spoken dialects of Germany. For the language of the civilized nation was once no more than the dialect of some particular tribe, till some intellectual or political superiority of those who spoke it, caused it to be adopted in writing in preference to its sister dialects, and thus made its peculiarities from henceforth the common rule. Now, it may well happen in two nations speaking a common language, that the dialects[19] which shall

[17] Dr. Pritchard tells me that he cannot trace the terminations magus, briga, and briva, in any of the existing Keltic languages. Although I am myself ignorant of those languages, yet I can see that Thierry's pretended explanations of Keltic names of places are often quite extravagant. Bodencus, according to Polybius, was the name given by the people of the country to the river Po (Polyb. II. 16); and this word, according to Pliny, Hist. Natur. III. 16, signifies bottomless, "fundo carens." Metrodorus of Scepsis, from whom Pliny borrowed this account, said indeed that Bodencus, or Bodincus, as it is in our copies of Pliny, was a Ligurian word; but there was a town, Bodincomagus, which has evidently a Keltic termination. Can Bodincus, or Bodencus, be reasonably explained by the present Welsh or Irish languages? Again, the same Metrodorus derived Padus from the Gaulish Pades, which, he said, signified a pine-tree. Can this be traced in modern Keltic? It should be observed, that in explaining the names of places, and especially of terminations, it is not enough to produce Welsh or Irish words of similar sound, and capable of forming something of a significant word; but their combination must be agreeable to the usages of the language; and with regard to terminations, it should be shown either that they are common in names of places in Keltic countries now, or that some word of similar signification is so used. Attempts have been made within these few years by Welsh and German antiquaries to explain the names of ancient towns in Italy from the Keltic and Teutonic languages; and in either case it has not been difficult to find words of similar sound both in Welsh and German, which when combined give a possible signification. But in all these cases we see at once that of two different derivations one must be wrong; and it mostly happens, I think, that both are so.

Von Humboldt notices the terminations of magus, briga, and briva, as undoubtedly Keltic. The first and last of them do not occur in Spain; but Briga is frequently met within the limits occupied by the Keltiberians. Humboldt refers to the termination bria, which is met with in the geography of Thrace, as in the town of Selymbria and Mesembria. He thinks that the Basque "iri" and "uri" are connected with both; and that we can go no further than to say that there was an old root bri or bro, expressing land, habitation, settlement, with which also the Teutonic burg and the Greek πύργος may have been originally connected. In the Welsh and Breton languages "bro" is still, he says, not only a cultivated field, but generally a country or district; and the Scholiast on Juvenal, Sat. VIII. 234, explains the name of Allobrogæ as signifying strangers, men from another land, "quoniam brogæ Galli agrum dicunt, alla autem aliud." Briva is supposed to mean bridge; but Von Humboldt agrees with Dr. Pritchard in saying, that there is no similar word of a like signification known to exist in any of the surviving Keltic languages.

I find brog and brug in O'Brien's Irish Dictionary as signifying "a grand house or building, fortified place, a palace or royal residence." O'Brien connects it with briga and the Thracian Bria. I also find the substantive "brugaide" in O'Brien's Dictionary, as signifying "a husbandmen, ploughman, or farmer."

[18] Dorf, "a village," is a well-known instance; a word which now exists in English only in the form of "thorpe," a common termination of the names of places in several counties, and sometimes a name by itself. Again, the German "bach," a stream or brook, is in common use in the north of England, where the brooks or streams are invariably called becks.

[19] Many curious instances of this might be given. Horse and pferd are the classical English and German words for the same animal; but horse exists in German under the form ros, and is to be met with in poetry, and also sometimes on the signs of inns, as if it were now either an old or a merely provincial or familiar word. And, on the other hand, the English form of pferd, which is pad, has sunk still lower,

ultimately prevail in each, shall not be those which most nearly resemble one another; and thus, at an advanced period of their history, their languages shall present a far greater dissimilarity than existed between them in their infancy.

The differences between languages were anciently less marked than they have become in later times.

Thus, as we follow the stream of time backwards towards its source, it is natural that the differences, not of dialect only, but even of language, should become less and less; so that what are now distinct main branches of one great stock, may at a very remote period have formed the as yet undivided elements of one common trunk. There must have been a time when the Keltic[20] and Teutonic languages were parted far less widely than we find them now; even within historical memory, when the Keltic and Teutonic tribes were intermixed with each other, within the limits of what is now Germany, and when they were so confounded together in the eyes of the Greeks and Romans, as to be regarded only as one great people,[21] the real differences of manners and language may have been much less than they became afterwards, when their limits were more distinctly marked. What was working in the wide extent of central Europe during so many centuries of which no memorial remains, we should vainly seek to discover. Accident, to use our common language, may have favored the growth of improvements in some remote tribe, while the bulk of the people, although nearer to the great centre of human civilization, may have remained in utter barbarism; and thus Cæsar's statement may be perfectly true, that druidism, of which we find no traces amongst the Cisalpine Gauls, was brought to its greatest perfection in Britain, and that the Gauls in his own time were in the habit of crossing over thither as to the best and purest source of instruction in its mysteries.

Physical character of the Gauls.

There is one point, however, in which the difference between the Keltic race in ancient and modern times has been unduly exaggerated. The Greek and Roman writers invariably describe the Gauls[22] as a tall and light-haired race in comparison with their own countrymen; but it has been maintained that there must be some confusion in these descriptions between the Gauls and the Germans, inasmuch as the Keltic nations now existing are all dark-haired. This statement was sent to Niebuhr by some Englishman; and Niebuhr, taking the fact for granted on his correspondent's authority, was naturally much perplexed by it. But had he travelled ever so rapidly through Wales or Ireland, or had he cast a glance on any of those groups of Irish laborers, who are constantly to be met with in summer on all the roads in England, he would have at

and is merely a cant or ludicrous word in our present language.

[20] It is quite manifest from Dr. Pritchard's excellent work on the origin of the Keltic nations, that the Keltic and Teutonic languages belong to one common family, which is commonly called the Indo-Germanic. This appears not only from their containing a multitude of common words, but from a surer evidence, the analogy in their grammatical forms.

In order to judge of the connection between one language and another, something more is necessary than the being merely able to write and to speak those two languages. Sir W. Betham, in his work called "the Cymry and the Gael," gives a list of Welsh and Irish pronouns, to show that the Welsh language has no connection with the Irish. Whereas that very list furnishes a proof of their affinity to any one who has been accustomed to compare the various forms assumed by one and the same original word, in the several cognate languages of the same family.

[21] Dionysius divides the country of the Kelts, Κελτική, into two great divisions, which he calls Gaul and Germany, XIV. 2. Fragm. Mai. Strabo describes the Germans as the most perfect and genuine specimens of the peculiarities of the Gaulish race, and says that the Romans called them Germani, "true," "genuine," to intimate that they were genuine Gauls: *ὡς ἂν γνησίους Γαλάτας φράζειν βουλόμενοι.* VII. 1, § 2, p. 290.

[22] Diodorus calls them *εὐμήκεις, λευκοί* and *ταῖς κόμαις ξανθοί.* V. 28. Ammianus Marcellinus calls them "candidi et rutili," XV. 12. Virgil speaks of their "aurea cæsaries," and "lactea colla," Æn. VIII. 658, 9. Strabo says that the "Germans differ a little from the Gauls in being more tall and more light haired," *τῷ πλεονασμῷ τοῦ μεγέθους καὶ τῆς ξανθότητος.* VII. p. 290; and again he describes the Britons as "less light haired than the Gauls," IV. p. 200. Polybius also speaks of their "great stature," II. 15; and Livy mentions their "procera corpora, promissæ et rutilatæ comæ," XXXVIII. 17. Now after such multitudes of Gauls had been brought into the slave market by the conquests of the dictator Cæsar, the writers of the Augustan age, even though they might never have crossed the Alps, must have been as familiar with the appearance of a Gaul as the West Indians are with that of a negro. A mistake so general on a point so obvious is utterly impossible.

once perceived that his perplexity had been needless. Compared with the Italians, it would be certainly true that the Keltic nations were, generally speaking, both light-haired and tall.[23] If climate has any thing to do with the complexion, the inhabitants of the north of Europe, in remote times, may be supposed to have been fairer and more light-haired than at present; while the roving life, the plentiful food, and the absence of all hard labor, must have given a greater development to the stature of the Gaulish warrior who first broke into Italy than can be looked for amongst the actual peasantry of Wales or Ireland.

The Gauls cross the Apennines, and attack Clusium.

The Gauls then from beyond the Alps were in possession of the plain of the Po, and had driven out or exterminated the Etruscans, when in the year of Rome 364, they for the first time crossed the Apennines, and penetrated into central Italy. On the first alarm of this irruption[24] the Romans sent three of their citizens into Etruria to observe their movements; and these deputies arrived at Clusium just at the time when the Gauls appeared before its walls, and began, after their usual manner, to lay waste the country. The citizens made a sally, and the Roman deputies went out with them; they engaged with the Gauls, and one of the deputies encountered and slew a Gaulish chief. Roman patricians, said the Roman story,[25] could not be confounded with Etruscans; the Gauls instantly perceived that there were some strangers of surpassing valor aiding the citizens of Clusium; they learned that these strangers were Romans, and they forthwith sent deputies to Rome to demand that the man who had thus fought with them, and slain one of their chiefs, when there was no war between the Gauls and the Romans, should be given up into their hands, that they might have blood for blood. The senate thought that the demand of the strangers was reasonable, and voted that the deputy should be given over into their hands; but his father, who was one of the military tribunes for the year, appealed to the people from the sentence of the senate, and being a man of much influence, persuaded them to annul it. Then the Gauls, finding their demand rejected, broke up in haste from Clusium, and marched directly against Rome.[26]

Uncertainty of the accounts of the Gaulish war.

Thus the very outset of this Gaulish invasion, even as related by Diodorus, who gives the story in its simplest form, is disguised by the national vanity of the Romans. It is impossible to rely on any of the details of the narrative which has been handed down to us; the Romans were no doubt defeated at the Alia; Rome was taken and burnt; and the Capitol ransomed; but beyond this we know, properly speaking, nothing. We know that falsehood has been busy, to an almost unprecedented extent, with the common story; exaggeration, carelessness, and honest ignorance, have joined more excusably in corrupting it. The history of great events can only be preserved by contemporary historians; and such were in this case utterly wanting. But as we have an outline of undoubted truth in the story, and as the particulars which are given are exceedingly striking and in many instances not improbable, I shall endeavor at once to present such a view of the events of the Gaulish war as may be clear from manifest error, and to preserve also some of its most re-

[23] I should not have ventured to speak so confidently merely from my own observation; but Dr. Pritchard, who has for many years turned his attention to this question, assures me that he is perfectly satisfied as to the truth of the fact here stated. To me it is only surprising that any one should have thought of disputing it.

[24] Diodorus, XIV. 113.

[25] Livy, V. 36. Nec id clam esse potuit, quam ante signa Etruscorum tres nobilissimi fortissimique Romanæ juventutis pugnarent; tantum eminebat peregrina virtus.

[26] Diodorus, IV. 113, 114. This story, it will be observed, differs from Livy's in several points. According to Livy, the three deputies were all demanded by the Gauls; nothing is said of their father being military tribune, but it is said that they themselves were immediately elected military tribunes for the ensuing year. Diodorus does not name them; according to Livy they were three brothers, sons of M. Fabius Ambustus. Now no Fabius appears in the list of military tribunes for the year 364, either according to Diodorus or Livy; and though the list for 365, as given by Diodorus, is very corrupt, yet there are no traces of its ever having contained the names of more than two Fabii at the most.

markable details, which may be true, and are at any rate far too famous to be omitted.

The Gauls advance upon Rome.

We know that the Gauls needed no especial provocation to attack Clusium, or to penetrate beyond Rome into the south of Italy. Wherever there was a prospect of the richest plunder, there was to them a sufficient cause for hostility. But the cities of Etruria, surrounded by their massive walls, were impregnable except by famine; so that after the open country had been once wasted, the Gauls would naturally carry their arms elsewhere. From Clusium the valley of the Clanis would conduct them directly to the Tiber; that river, so far from its mouth, would be easily fordable; and then all the plain of Latium lay open to their attack. The season was now the middle of summer; the new military tribunes, who at this period came into office on the first of July, had just been elected; and expecting the Gauls to advance upon Rome, and supposing that they would approach by the right bank[27] of the Tiber, they summoned to the field the whole force of the commonwealth, they called on their Latin and Hernican[28] allies to aid them, and having thus collected all their strength, they marched out of Rome on the road to Etruria, intending to receive the enemy's attack in the neighborhood of Veii, which was now a sort of frontier fortress of the Roman territory, and which might serve as the base of their operations. The whole army thus assembled amounted, according to the statement of Plutarch,[29] to forty thousand men.

They cross the Tiber, and enter the country of the Sabines.

But the Gauls meantime had crossed the Tiber into Umbria, and were moving along the left bank of the river, through the country of the Sabines, towards the plain of Latium. The Roman writers, who pretend that their only object was Rome, and that as soon as they heard that their demand for satisfaction was rejected they hastened from Clusium to attack the Romans, forget that this is inconsistent with another part of their story, namely, that the deputies who had gone to Clusium were, as if in mockery of the Gauls, elected military tribunes immediately after the refusal to give them up. For as the tribunes did not enter on their office till the first of July, and the battle of the Alia was not fought till the sixteenth, the pretended hasty march of the Gauls from Clusium to Rome, a distance of about a hundred miles,[30] must have taken up more than a fortnight. But in all likelihood the Gauls went on plundering the country before them, without aiming exclusively at Rome: according to Diodorus, they had waited in Etruria before they began their march southwards, long enough to receive large reinforcements[31] from beyond the Apennines; and the provocation given them by the Romans was, we may suppose, gladly seized as a pretence for extending their attacks from the country of their old enemies, the Etruscans, to that of the other nations of central Italy.

When it was discovered that the Gauls were already on the left bank of the Tiber, and advancing by the Salarian road, which was the old communication be-

[27] Diodorus states positively that the Roman army marched out across the Tiber. It is true that he seems to have supposed the Alia to have been on the right bank of the Tiber; but this confusion arose probably from his finding no notice of the Romans recrossing the river before the battle. His first statement is probable, and seems to me to explain the extreme suddenness with which the battle on the Alia took place.

[28] "The Gauls," says Polybius, "defeated the Romans and those who were drawn up in the field along with them." *'Ρωμαίους καὶ τοὺς μετὰ τούτων παραταξαμένους.* II. 18. These could have been no other than the Latin and Hernican allies.

[29] Camillus, 18. According to Dionysius, XIII. 19, there were four legions of picked and experienced soldiers, and a still more numerous force of those who commonly stayed at home and did not serve in war; that is, of proletarians and ærarians. According to Diodorus, the left wing of the Roman army, consisting of the bravest soldiers, amounted to 24,000: that is, it contained the four regular legions spoken of by Dionysius, which amounted together to 12,000 men, and of an equal number of the allies. This would leave about 16,000 men for the raw and inferior troops, *τοὺς ἀσθενεστάτους*, who in the battle formed the right of the Roman army.

[30] Polybius underrates the distance at a three days' journey. II. 25. Strabo calls it eight hundred stadia. V. p. 226. The itineraries as corrected make it one hundred and two, and one hundred and three miles, and it cannot be much less.

[31] XIII. 114.

The Romans take post on the Alia.

tween the land of the Sabines and Rome, then the Romans were naturally thrown into the greatest alarm. The Tiber, for many miles above Rome, is not fordable; as there were no towns on the river there were probably no bridges, and boats could not be procured at such short notice for the passage of so large an army. The Romans therefore were obliged to go round by Rome, and without an instant's delay march out by the Salarian road, in order to encounter the enemy at as great a distance from the city as possible. They found the Gauls already within twelve miles of Rome; the little stream of the Alia, or rather the deep bed through which it runs, offered something like a line of defence;[32] and accordingly the Romans here awaited the attack of their enemy. Their right was posted on some high ground,[33] covered in front by the deep bed of the Alia, and with a hilly and wooded country protecting its flank; while the left, consisting of the regular legions, filled up the interval of level ground between the hills and the Tiber, and its extreme flank was covered by the river.

Battle of the Alia.

There seems in all these dispositions nothing of overweening rashness or of folly; it is doubtful what was really the disproportion of numbers between the two armies; if the Gauls had but recently been reinforced, the Roman generals may have supposed the enemy's numbers to have been no greater than they were at Clusium; and to fight was unavoidable, if they wished to save their country from devastation. But the Gaulish leader showed more than a barbarian's ability. With the bravest of his warriors he assailed the right of the Roman position: the soldiers of the poorer classes, unused to war, and untrained in the management of their arms, were appalled by the yells, and borne down by the strength of their enemies; and their wooden shields were but a poor defence against the fearful strokes of the Keltic broadsword. The right of the Romans was broken and chased from its ground; the course of the river had obliged the left of the army to be thrown back behind the right, so that the fugitives in their flight disordered the ranks of the regular legions; and the Gauls pursuing their advantage, the whole Roman army was totally routed. The vanquished fled in different directions; those on the left[34] plunged into the Tiber, in the hope of swimming across it and escaping to Veii; but the Gauls slaughtered them in heaps on the banks, and overwhelmed them with their javelins in the river, so that a large part of the flower of the Roman people was here destroyed. The fugitives on the right fled towards Rome; some took refuge in a thick wood[35] near the road, and there lay hid till nightfall; the rest ran without stopping to the city, and brought the tidings of the calamity.

The Gauls pass the night on the field of battle.

The Gauls did not pursue the fugitives far: we hear as yet nothing of that cavalry for which they were afterwards so famous; probably because they had not yet been long enough in Italy to have supplied themselves with the horses of that country; and the breed of Transalpine Gaul, like that of Britain, was too small to be used except for the

[32] It is well known that to identify the famous Alia with any existing stream is one of the hardest problems of Roman topography. Virgil and Livy agree in placing it on the left bank of the Tiber; and Livy's description seems as precise as possible, for he says that the armies met, "ad undecimum lapidem, qua flumen Alia Crustuminis montibus præalto defluens alveo haud multum infra viam Tiberino amni miscetur." V. 37. And Westphal accordingly says that "something less then eleven miles from Rome, there is a small brook with high banks," and that "on the right of the road at this spot you see the village of Marcigliana Vecchia." p. 127. But I cannot reconcile this with Sir W. Gell's map, or with his description in his article on the Alia in his topography of Rome; for there Marcigliana Vecchia is placed about two miles nearer to Rome. Both descriptions are given in such detail that this diversity is rather perplexing.

[33] Livy, V. 38. Diodorus, XIV. 114.

[34] Livy, V. 38. Diodorus, XIV. 114, 115.

[35] Festus in "Lucaria." The wood, according to this statement, was between the Salarian road and the Tiber. This shows that Sir W. Gell has rightly marked the old Salarian road on his map, where he makes it turn to the right over the hills away from the Tiber, about two miles beyond Castel Giubileo. Had the road followed the low grounds near the river, there could scarcely have been a wood between it and the Tiber, for the ground must have been then as now, nothing but a great expanse of meadows.

drawing of their war-chariots. Besides, they were themselves wearied with their march, and with their exertions in the battle; and it was of importance[36] to each man to collect and exhibit his trophies, the heads of the enemies whom he had slain; for these were the proof that the warrior had done his duty in the battle, and was entitled to his share of the spoil: these were to be carried home, and preserved to after ages in his family, as a memorial of his valor. Thus, according to the account of Diodorus, the Gauls passed the night after their victory on the field of battle.

The Romans resolve to defend the Capitol.

But the Romans found it impossible to defend their city; as the flower of the citizens of the military age, who had escaped from the battle, had retreated to Veii. It is probable that a large proportion of these were not sorry to have this opportunity of effecting what they had before attempted in vain, and wished to remain at Veii as their future country. Of the remaining inhabitants of Rome, the greater part dispersed, as the Athenians had done before the approach of Xerxes;[37] they took refuge with their families, and such of their effects as they could remove, in many of the neighboring cities. But it was resolved, as at Athens, to maintain the citadel,[38] for this, as in all the cities of the ancient world, was in a manner the sanctuary of the nation: it was the spot in which the temples of the nation's peculiar gods were built; and to this every feeling of patriotism, whether human merely or religious, was closely connected. This was the home of the true gods of Rome, and the citadel of the true Roman people, before the stranger commons, with their new gods, had pretended to claim the rights of Roman citizens; and many a patrician, indignant at the retreat of the legions to Veii, and regarding this desertion as another proof that the commons were no genuine sons of Rome, retired into the Capitol with a resolution never to abandon that country and those gods, which he felt and might justly claim to be indeed his own.

The Vestal Virgins with the eternal fire withdraw to Cære.

But the citadel might be taken; the genuine Romans who defended it might be massacred; the temple of the three guardian powers of Rome, Jupiter, Juno, and Minerva, of the Capitol, might be profaned and destroyed. Still there had been a time when other gods had possessed the Capitol, and yet even then there was Rome, and there were Romans. Other powers and other rites were the pledge of Rome's existence, and if they failed, she must be lost forever. The flamen of Quirinus,[39] the deified founder of the city, and the Vestal Virgins, who watched the eternal fire, the type and assurance of its duration, must remove their holy things beyond the reach of the enemy, or if all could not be removed, what was left must be so hidden that no chance should ever betray it. Accordingly the Flamen and the Virgins of Vesta buried some of their holy things in the ground, in a spot preserved afterwards with the strictest care from every pollution; and whatever they could remove, they carried with them to Agylla or Cære. They went on their way, said the story,[40] on foot; and as they were ascending the hill Janiculum, after having crossed the river and left the city, there overtook them on the ascent, a man of the commons, L. Albinius by name, who was conveying his wife and children in a carriage to a place of safety. But when Lucius saw them, he bade his wife and children to alight, and he put into the carriage in their room the holy virgins and their eternal fire; "For it were a shame," said he, "that I and mine should be drawn in a carriage, while the Virgins of Vesta with their holy things were going on foot." So he conveyed them safe in the carriage to Cære.

[36] Diodorus, XIV. 115. V. 29. Strabo, IV. p. 197. The practice of cutting off the heads of their enemies, and of preserving them in their houses, is ascribed directly to the Gauls. The presenting them to the general, as a title to a share of the spoil, is mentioned by Herodotus as a Scythian custom (IV. 64); but as in other respects the Scythian customs with regard to the heads of their enemies resemble what is related of the Gauls, I have ventured to transfer to the latter people this custom also.

[37] Diodorus, XIV. 115. Livy, V. 40.

[38] Diodorus, XIV. 115. Livy, V. 39. Florus says that the force which garrisoned the Capitol did not exceed a thousand men, I. 13.

[39] Livy, V. 40.

[40] Livy, V. 40.

Meantime the Gauls, it is said, hesitated for one whole day[41] to attack the city, suspecting that the apparent absence of all preparations for defence was but a snare to entice them to venture on an assault rashly. Thus the Romans gained a respite which was most needful to them; and when, on the third day after the battle, according to the ancient mode of reckoning, the enemy did force the gates and enter the city, the mass of the population had already escaped, and the Capitoline Hill was, as well as circumstances would allow, provisioned and garrisoned. When the Gauls entered, their chiefs it appears established themselves on some of the houses on the Palatine Hill,[42] exactly opposite to the Capitol; and in the rest of the city the work of plunder and destruction raged freely.

The Gauls enter Rome.

The mass of the commons had fled from Rome with their wives and children, or having escaped from the route of the Alia had taken refuge at Veii. The flower of the patricians, and of the citizens of the richer classes of an age to bear arms, had retired into the Capitol, to defend to the last that sanctuary of their country's gods. The flamen of Quirinus and the Vestal Virgins had departed with the sacred things committed to their charge out of the reach of danger. But there were other ministers of the gods,[43] whom their duty did not compel to leave Rome, whom their age rendered unable to join in the defence of the Capitol, and who could not endure to be a burden upon those whose strength allowed them to defend it. They would not live the few remaining years of their lives in a foreign city, but as they could not serve their country by their deeds, they wished at least to serve it by their deaths. So they, and others of the old patricians who had filled the highest offices[44] in the commonwealth, met together; and M. Fabius, the chief pontifex, recited a solemn form of words, which they each repeated after him, devoting to the spirits of the dead and to the earth, the common grave of all living, themselves and the army of the Gauls together with themselves, for the welfare and deliverance of the people of the Romans and of the Quirites.[45] Then, as men devoted to death, they arrayed themselves in their most solemn dress; they who had held curule offices, in their robes of white with the broad scarlet border;[46] they who had won

The old patricians devote themselves to death for their country.

[41] Diodorus makes them hesitate for two whole days, and thus to enter the city on the fourth day after the battle, according to the ancient manner of reckoning. The cause of the delay may indeed be a little misrepresented; after so great a victory, the conquerors indulged themselves for one whole day, as we can readily suppose, in excess, and in plundering all the surrounding country; and if their leader had pushed on to Rome, yet the force which he could induce to follow him might be so small, as to make him afraid to commence an attack upon so large a city. But it seems certain that the delay was of one day only, and not of two. Polybius says that the Gauls took Rome three days after the battle; that is, after the interval of one whole day. II. 18. And the statement of Verrius Flaccus, preserved by Gellius, V. 17, and which has all the precision of a quotation from some official record, says, "post diem tertium ejus diei urbem captam esse."

[42] Diodorus, XIV. 115.

[43] Οἱ τῶν ἄλλων θεῶν ἱερεῖς, is Plutarch's expression, after mentioning the departure of the Vestal Virgins. Camillus, 21.

[44] Qui curules gesserant magistratus. Livy, V. 41.

[45] Plutarch, Camillus, 21. Livy mentions this account, though he does not expressly adopt it. V. 41. I have borrowed the "carmen devotionis," the form in which the old men devoted themselves, from the story of Decius in the great Latin war. He who devoted himself to death for his country, intended to offer himself to the powers of death, as a willing victim on the part of his own countrymen, that the other victims required by fate might be taken from the army of the enemy. To have prayed for victory simply, without any sacrifice on the part of the conquerors, was a tempting of Nemesis; but if the sacrifice was first offered, then the wrath of Nemesis would be turned against the enemy, that they too might have their portion of evil. The devoted offered himself "diis manibus tellurique." Livy, VIII. 9. Strictly, the dii manes were the spirits of a man's own ancestors, but they are addressed here as representatives of the powers of death generally. Tellus is of course the notion of the grave.

[46] The toga prætexta, or bordered toga. The toga, it is well known, was rather a shawl than a robe, but the word shawl would suit so ill with our associations of ancient Rome, that it would not be worth while to introduce it. The triumphal toga, toga picta, was like a rich Indian shawl worked with figures of various colors; it was thrown over the tunica palmata, the coat or frock worked with figures of palm branches, probably in gold. The sella curulis was, as its name imports, the seat or body of the chariot, δίφρος, and when used by the curule magistrates at their tribunals, implied that they shared in the imperium or sovereign power held of old by the kings, one mark of which was the being borne in a chariot instead of walking on foot.

triumphs, in their robes of triumph overlaid with embroidery of many colors and with palm branches of gold, and took their seats each on his ivory chair of magistracy in the gateway of his house. When the Gauls saw these aged men in this array of majesty, sitting motionless amidst the confusion of the sack of the city, they at first looked upon them as more than human,[47] and one of the soldiers drew near to M. Papirius, and began to stroke reverently his long white beard. Papirius, who was a minister of the gods, could not endure the touch of profane barbarian hands, and struck the Gaul over the head with his ivory sceptre. Instantly the spell of reverence was broken, and rage and the thirst of blood succeeded to it. The Gaul cut down the old Papirius with his sword; his comrades were kindled at the sight, and all the old men, according to their vow, were offered up as victims to the powers of death.

Blockade of the Capitol.

The enemy now turned their attention to the Capitol. But the appearance of the Capitoline Hill in the fourth century of Rome can ill be judged of by that view which travellers obtain of its present condition. The rock, which is now so concealed by the houses built up against it, or by artificial slopings of the ground, as to be only visible in a few places, formed at that time a natural defence of precipitous cliff all round the hill; and there was one only access to the summit from below, the clivus or ascent to the Capitol. By this single approach the Gauls tried to storm the citadel, but they were repulsed with loss;[48] and after this attempt they contented themselves with blockading the hill, and extending their devastations over the neighboring country of Latium. It is even said that they penetrated into the south of Italy; and a Gaulish army is reported to have reached Apulia,[49] whilst a portion of their force was still engaged in blockading the Roman garrison in the Capitol.

Night assault on the Capitol repulsed by M. Manlius.

Meantime, the Romans who had taken refuge at Veii had recovered from their first panic, and were daily becoming more and more reorganized. It was desirable that a communication should be opened between them and the garrison of the Capitol; and a young man named Pontius Cominius[50] undertook the adventure. Accordingly, he set out from Veii, swam down the Tiber, climbed up the cliff into the Capitol, explained to the garrison the state of things at Veii, and returned by the same way unhurt. But when the morning came, the Gauls observed marks on the side of the cliff, which told them that some one had made his way there, either up or down; and the soil had in places been freshly trodden away, and the bushes which grew here and there on the face of the ascent had been crushed or torn from their hold, as if by some one treading on them or clinging to them for support. So, being thus made aware that the cliff was not impracticable, they proceeded by night to scale it. The spot being supposed to be inaccessible, was not guarded; the top of the rock was not even defended by a wall. In silence and in darkness the Gauls made their way up the cliff; no sentinel perceived them; even the watch-dogs, said the story,[51] heard them not, and gave no alarm. But on the part of the hill by which the enemy were ascending, stood the temple of the three guardian gods of the Capitol and of Rome, Jupiter, Juno, and Minerva; and in this precinct there were certain geese kept, which were sacred to Juno; and even amidst their distress for food, the Romans, said the old story, had spared the birds which were protected by the goddess. So now in the hour of danger, the geese heard the sound of the enemy, and began to cry in their fear, and to flap their wings; and M. Manlius, whose house was in the Capitol hard by the temple, was aroused by them; and he sprang up and seized sword and shield, and called to his comrades,

[47] Primo ut deos venerati deinde ut homines despicati interfecere. Auctor de viris illustr. in Camillo.

[48] Livy, V. 43.

[49] Diodorus, XIV. 117. It was apparently this portion of the Gauls which offered its services to Dionysius while he was engaged in his war with the Greeks of southern Italy. He enlisted some of them, and these were perhaps the very Gauls whom he afterwards sent into Greece to aid the Lacedæmonians against Epaminondas. Justin, XX. 5.

[50] Diodorus, XIV. 116.

[51] Livy, V. 47. Diodorus, XIV. 116.

and ran to the edge of the cliff. And behold a Gaul had just reached the summit, when Marcus rushed upon him and dashed the rim of his shield into his face, and tumbled him down the rock. The Gaul, as he fell, bore down those who were mounting behind him; and the rest were dismayed, and dropped their arms to cling more closely to the rock, and so the Romans, who had been roused by the call of Marcus, slaughtered them easily, and the Capitol was saved. Then all so honored the brave deed of Marcus Manlius, that each man gave him from his own scanty store one day's allowance of food, namely, half a pound of corn, and a measure containing five ounces in weight of wine.[52] Historically true in the substance, these stories are yet, in their details, so romantic, that I insensibly, in relating them, fall into the tone of the poetical legends.

The Gauls receive a sum of money from the Romans, and raise the blockade.

Six months,[53] according to some accounts, seven or even eight months,[54] according to others, did the Gauls continue to blockade the Capitol. The sickness of a Roman autumn did not, we are told, shake them from their purpose; the plunder which might be gained in other yet unwasted districts of Italy, did not tempt them to abandon it. But is it possible to believe that barbarians could have shown such perseverance, or that in one day of preparation, provisions could have been carried into the Capitol in sufficient quantities to hold out even for a small garrison, during a siege of six or eight months?[55] Thus much, however, may safely be believed, that the garrison of the Capitol was at last reduced to extremity;[56] they offered to ransom themselves by the payment of a large sum of money, and the Gauls were disposed, it is said,[57] to accept the offer, because they heard that the Venetians, that nation of Illyrian blood who dwelt around the northern extremity of the Adriatic, had made an inroad into their own country beyond the Apennines. They consented, therefore, to the terms offered by the Romans; and a thousand pounds' weight of gold were to be collected from the offerings in the Capitoline temple, and from the treasures which had been carried into the Capitol before the siege from every part of Rome, that for this ransom the blockade might be raised. Even in accepting these terms, the Gaulish leader felt that he was admitting to mercy enemies whom he had wholly in his power. His weights, said the Roman story,[58] were unfair; the Roman tribune of the soldiers, Q. Sulpicius, complained of the fraud, but the Gaul threw his heavy broadsword into the scale; and when the tribune again asked what he meant, he replied in words which may be best represented by an analogous English proverb, "It means that the weakest must go to the wall."[59]

Corruptions of the true story of the retreat of the Gauls.

Thus, according to the true version of this famous event, the Gauls returned from their inroad into Italy loaded with spoil and crowned with glory. That as soon as they were known to be retreating, the nations whom they had overrun should have recovered their courage, and have taken every opportunity to assail them on their march home, is perfectly probable; nor need we doubt that these attacks were sometimes successful, that many stragglers were cut off, and much plunder retaken. These stories were exaggerated, as was natural; and by degrees the Romans claimed the glory of them for themselves. We can almost trace the gradual fabrication of that monstrous falsehood which in its perfected shape so long retained its hold on Roman history. After the retreat of the Gauls from Rome, their country-

[52] "Quartarios vini." Livy, V. 57. The quartarius, or the fourth part of the sextarius, was the twenty-fourth part of the congius; and as the congius contained ten pounds' weight of water, the quartarius contained five ounces. It was a little more than the half of the Greek cotyle.

[53] Florus, I. 13.

[54] Polybius, II. 22, and Plutarch in Camill. 30, say, "seven." Servius, Æn. VIII. 652, says "eight."

[55] If the Gauls stayed in Rome for so long a time, they must have left it in the middle of winter. Now it is said that they hastened on their way homewards, because their own country was invaded by the Venetians; but barbarians would scarcely choose the depth of winter for an enterprise of this sort.

[56] Diodorus, XIV. 116.

[57] Polybius, II. 18.

[58] Livy, V. 48.

[59] "Væ victis esse."

men who had advanced into Apulia, returned from their expedition, and found the Romans in too weak a condition to do them any harm; but as they were on their march through the Roman territory, the people of Cære, or Agylla, laid an ambush for them, and cut off, it is said, the whole party.[60] To enhance the merit of this success, the Gauls who were cut off were next made to be the same party who had besieged the Capitol;[61] and it was added that the people of Cære recovered the very gold which had been paid for the ransom of Rome. But the glory of such a trophy could not be left to strangers; the victory was soon transferred to the Romans; and it was Camillus who found the Gauls, a long time after their retreat from Rome, employed in besieging a city[62] in alliance with the Romans, who defeated them utterly, and won from them all their spoil. Lastly, the story was to be more entirely satisfactory to the Roman pride; Rome[63] was never ransomed at all; Camillus appeared with the legions from Veii just as the gold was being weighed out; as dictator he annulled the shameful bargain, drove the Gauls out of Rome at the sword's point, and the next day defeated them so totally on their way home, eight miles from Rome, on the road to Gabii, that he left not a single man alive to carry to their countrymen the tidings of their defeat. Such a falsification, scarcely to be paralleled in the annals of any other people, justifies the strongest suspicion of all those accounts of victories and triumphs which appear to rest in any degree on the authority of the family memorials of the Roman aristocracy.

What was the real condition of Rome and the neighboring countries after this first Gaulish tempest had passed away; how the second period of Roman history begins in a darkness almost as thick as that which overhangs the beginnings of the first, but a darkness peopled by few of those forms, so beautiful though so visionary, which gave so great a charm to the times of the kings; how faintly we can trace the formation of that great fabric of dominion and policy which, when the light of day breaks, we find well-nigh in its complete proportions, it will be my endeavor to make appear in the succeeding portion of this history.

CHAPTER XXV.

HISTORY, FOREIGN AND DOMESTIC, FROM THE YEAR 365 TO 378—ROME AFTER THE RETREAT OF THE GAULS—ITS WEAKNESS, AND THE GREAT MISERY OF THE COMMONS—POPULARITY AND DEATH OF M. MANLIUS—WARS WITH THE NEIGHBORING NATIONS.

'Αθηναίων δὲ τὸ κοινὸν, ἐπειδὴ αυτοῖς οἱ βάρβαροι ἐκ τῆς χώρας ἀπῆλθον, διεκομίζοντο εὐθὺς ὅθεν ὑπεξέθεντο παῖδας καὶ γυναῖκας καὶ τὴν πέριοῦσαν κατασκευήν, καὶ τὴν πόλιν ἀνοικοδομεῖν παρεσκευάζοντο.

THUCYDIDES, I. 89.

The Roman history is still full of uncertainty.

LIVY begins his history of the period after the invasion of the Gauls by contrasting what he calls its greater clearness and certainty with the obscurity of the period which had preceded it. True it is, that

[60] Diodorus, XIV. 117.

[61] Strabo, V. p. 220.

[62] Diodorus, XIV. 117. The name of the city is wholly corrupt, Οὐεάσκιον.

[63] Livy, V. 49. If the Gauls who were besieging the Capitol received their ransom, and withdrew from Rome before the end of the autumn, while others of their countrymen remained in Italy through the winter, and did not return home till the first beginning of spring, Camillus may then have obtained some advantages over these last in their retreat, and may have obtained a triumph. In this case the exaggeration or confusion was easy, that the Gauls, after a stay of eight months in Rome, were at last driven out by Camillus; the period of their stay in Italy being mistaken for that of their occupation of Rome.

there was no subsequent destruction of public records such as had been caused by the burning of the city; and although many invaluable monuments perished in the great fire of the Capitol in the times of Sylla, yet these might have been, and in some instances we know that they had been, previously consulted by historians, so that all knowledge of their contents was not lost to the writers of the Augustan age. Yet still no period of Roman history since the first institution of the tribunes of the commons is really more obscure than the thirty years immediately following the retreat of the Gauls. And the reason of this is, that when there are no independent contemporary historians, the mere existence of public documents affords no security for the preservation of a real knowledge of men and actions. The documents may exist, indeed, but they give no evidence: they are neglected or corrupted at pleasure by poets and panegyrists; and a fictitious story gains firm possession of the public mind, because there is no one to take the pains of promulgating the truth. And thus it has happened that the panegyrists of Camillus and of the other great patrician families, finding ready belief in many instances from national vanity, have so disguised the real course of events, that at no other period of Roman history is it more difficult to restore it.

The Romans proceed to restore their city. Proposal for removing to Veii. Camillus persuades the people to remain at Rome.

The Gauls were gone, and the ruins of Rome were possessed again by the Romans. The Flamen of Quirinus and the Vestal Virgins returned from Cære; and the eternal fire, unextinguished by the late calamity, was restored to its accustomed place in the temple of Vesta. But the fugitives who had fled to Veii from the rout at the Alia, and who formed a large proportion of the Roman people, were most unwilling to leave the city which for several months had been their only country; at Veii they had houses already built, and perhaps they were not sorry to escape from the ascendency of the patricians, and to settle themselves in a new city of which they would be the original citizens.[1] Thus Rome was threatened anew with the dangers of a secession, with such a division of the strength of the commonwealth as must have insured its ruin; for some of the patricians would, no doubt, have removed to Veii, while others, with their clients, would as certainly have remained at Rome. At this period the name and ability of Camillus were most effectual in putting an end to the dissension, and in determining that the proposed secession to Veii should be utterly abandoned: but by what means or at what time his exile was reversed we cannot discover. It may be true,[2] that while the Gauls were in possession of Rome he had encouraged the people of Ardea, where he had become a citizen, to take up arms against the Gaulish plundering parties; he may also, in such a time of necessity, have been chosen commander by some of the Romans who had fled from the city, and with them he may have done good service, both in cutting off the enemy's stragglers, and, perhaps, in harassing their rear after they began to retreat. And if after these exploits he had led back his party to Rome rather than to Veii, and had thus proved that even in banishment his heart was true to his old country, there is no doubt that he would have been received as joyfully as the Athenians under similar circumstances received Alcibiades;[3] his exile would have been speedily reversed, and his entrance into Rome, like Cicero's in after-times, would have been celebrated with general rejoicings. Still more would this have been the case, had he really during his exile repaired to Veii, and brought back to Rome after the retreat of the Gauls any consider-

[1] That is, they would be the burghers or patricians of Veii, and around them a new plebs or commons would, in process of time, be formed, just as they themselves had grown up beside the patricians of Rome.

[2] See Livy, V. 43, 44.

[3] When Alcibiades returned to Athens in the 25th year of the Peloponnesian war, after his successes in the Hellespont and in Thrace, he had never been formally recalled from exile, and doubted, at first, it is said, how he should be received. But a sense of his great services, and of the necessities of the commonwealth, overpowered all other considerations, and the people did receive him with enthusiasm.—See Xenophon, Hellenic. I. 4. How refreshing is it, after the vagueness and uncertainties of the Roman traditions to turn for a moment to the narrative of a contemporary historian, even when, like Xenophon, he is far below the highest standard of excellence!

able portion of the soldiers who had made Veii their refuge. Then may have followed the discussion whether these soldiers should return to their countrymen at Veii, or whether all should unite once more at Rome. Then Camillus and the patricians opposed to the secession would naturally appeal both in the senate[4] and the forum to all the local attachments and religious feelings of which Rome alone could be the object; and when the excitement was great, and the smallest thing would incline men's wavering minds either the one way or the other, it may be true[5] that they received as an omen from heaven the casual words of a centurion, who, passing through the comitium with his century, and having occasion to halt in front of the senate-house, called aloud to the standard-bearer, "Pitch[6] thy standard here, for this is the best place to stop at."

The remaining monuments are collected, and the city begins to be rebuilt.

The secession, in whatever manner, having been prevented, and the mass of the commons having consented to remain at Rome, although many still refused to quit Veii, the senate proceeded to reconstruct, as well as they could, the shattered fabric of the commonwealth. The sites of the temples[7] were retraced as well as was possible amidst the ruins, their limits were again duly fixed by the augurs, and ceremonies were performed to expiate the pollution which they had undergone by having been profaned by the barbarians. Some relics which it was impossible to replace, were said to have been miraculously preserved; the lituus[8] or augural crook of Romulus, with which he was supposed to have marked out the quarters of the heavens, when in answer to his augury the gods sent him the famous sign of the twelve vultures, was discovered unhurt, so ran the tradition, under a heap of ashes. Then the day[9] in which the route of the Alia had taken place, the day after the ides of July, or the 16th, according to our reckoning, was pronounced by the pontifices to be a day of ill-omen; and no sacrifice could acceptably be offered, nor any business prosperously done, on that day forever. All[10] remaining records were sought for; the laws of the twelve tables, some laws ascribed to the kings, and some treaties with foreign nations, such as those with Carthage and with the Latins, were found to be still in existence; and parts of the laws were again fixed up in some place where they were accessible to the people at large; but the sacred or religious law, it is said, was not made public; the pontifices alone were to be acquainted with it. The city was to be rebuilt with all diligence; at present even the walls had been partially broken down, and the streets were a mere heap of ashes. There was no plan to show their old direction: men built wherever they found a spot clear of rubbish, and the first houses so erected, determined in great measure the position of the rest. Each citizen, no doubt, built upon his own hill, and, generally speaking, in his own quarter or parish, if I may use the expression, according to the division of the city marked by the sacraria or chapels of the Argei. But within these limits, the old distinctions of property were not duly observed, and there was a sort of scramble for the ground; so that the city was built irregularly, and the direction[11] of the cloacæ did not correspond with that of the streets. Meanwhile the government offered to furnish[12] roofing materials for the new houses at the public expense: and Niebuhr conjectures that these were chiefly obtained by unroofing the houses of Veii, and thus rendering the proposed seat of the secession uninhabitable, while it was made to

[4] See the speech ascribed to Camillus in Livy, V. 51–54.

[5] The story is given by Livy, V. 55, and by Plutarch, Camillus, 32.

[6] Signifer, statue signum hic manebimus optime.

[7] Livy, V. 50.

[8] Plutarch, Camillus, 32. Dionysius, XIV. 5. Fragm. Mai.

[9] Gellius, V. 17. Livy, VI. 1.

[10] Livy, VI. 1.

[11] Livy, V. 55.

[12] Livy, V. 55, tegula publice præbita est. We know from Cornelius Nepos, quoted by Pliny, Hist. Natur. XVI. 10, § 36, that the houses in Rome were roofed with wood (shingles), down to the time of the war with Pyrrhus. Either, then, tegula is a general word in this passage of Livy, signifying roofing materials, whether of shingles or of tiles; or if it mean tiles strictly, we must suppose that the people did not like the labor of fetching them from Veii, and preferred to use wood, according to their former practice.

contribute at tne same time to the rebuilding of Rome. Stone and timber might also be quarried and felled by any man from any public lands, provided he gave security that he would complete his house within the year. But with all these aids the building fell heavily upon the mass of the people; it was delayed also by the attacks of foreign enemies: the securities given for completing it within the year would in many instances be forfeited; and hence began again the old system of borrowing from the patricians, speedily to be followed, as before, by a train of intolerable distresses and oppressions.

Four new tribes added to the Roman people.

In the small states of Greece and ancient Italy, the loss of a great battle caused a sensible diminution of the population of free citizens. The defeat at the Alia had been bloody: many lives must have been lost in after skirmishes with the Gauls, and in their devastations of the surrounding country; and many fugitives who had taken refuge in the neighboring cities may have preferred remaining in their new homes. On the other hand, there was a large subject[13] population, chiefly, it is probable, of Tyrrhenian, that is, of Pelasgian origin, in the recently conquered territories of Veii, of Capena, and, as Livy adds, of Falerii. From these it was resolved to make up the losses occasioned by the Gauls, and to convert subjects, who would infallibly have soon revolted, into citizens, who would be a most seasonable accession of strength. Accordingly, they were admitted in a body to the full rights of Roman citizens: each head of a family had his portion of seven jugera of land duly granted to him in full property, and set with landmarks, according to the rules of the agrimensores, which constituted the legal freehold tenure of the Romans; and to show the great number of new citizens thus admitted, four new tribes[14] were formed out of them, and they thus constituted nearly a sixth part of the whole people in political weight, and, probably, a larger proportion in point of actual numbers. The tribes were thus increased from twenty-one to twenty-five.

The neighboring people attack the Romans. Camillus repels the Volscians and Etruscans.

I have noticed these measures without regard to the exact chronological order in which they are said to have occurred. They are all placed, however, with the exception of the creation of the four new tribes, in the first year after the retreat of the Gauls: in that year the new citizens were admitted, and received their grants of land: although the creation of the new tribes, in which they might exercise their franchise politically by voting at the comitia, is said to have happened two years[15] later. The magistrates still, as before the Gaulish invasion, came into office on the first of July;[16] thus the military tribunes who had commanded at the siege of the Capitol, were still in office for some months after the retreat of the Gauls; but they were not allowed to hold the comitia[17] for the election of their successors, because of the supposed ill-luck of their magistracy; they resigned therefore, and the comitia were held by an interrex, a fact which of itself confutes the story of Camillus' pretended dictatorship: for had he been dictator throughout the year, according to the tales of his exploits,[18] the comitia would naturally have been held by him, and there would have been no need of an interregnum. But immediately after the appointment of the new tribunes, that is, about the season of harvest, the favorite season for the plundering incursions of the Peloponnesians into Attica, the

[13] Livy, VI. 4, calls the new citizens, "qui Veientium Capenatiumque ac Faliscorum per ea bella transfugerant ad Romanos." Individual deserters could not be numerous enough to form four tribes; but when the cities of Veii and Capena were hard-pressed, their territory, inhabited chiefly by a subject population, περίοικοι in the political language of Greece, would be likely to revolt or submit to the Romans. The new citizens could scarcely have been Etruscans, as the difference of language would then have presented a serious barrier to their union with the Romans; but if they were Tyrrhenian Pelasgians, they were of the same stock as the Romans themselves, and their language and religion both bore a considerable affinity to those of Rome.

[14] Livy, VI. 5.

[15] That is, it took place at the next census, which was taken in the year 368; the preceding censors having been appointed in the year 363. Livy, V. 31.

[16] They continued to do so, it is said, for at least sixty years after this period. See Livy, VIII. 20.

[17] Livy, VI. 1.

[18] See Livy, VI. 1, and Plutarch, Camillus, 31.

Romans were alarmed by the reports of hostile attacks on every side; their forlorn condition, it is said, tempting even the smallest of the neighboring states to assail them. If we are to believe one tradition which has accidentally been preserved to us,[19] the people of Ficulea, Fidenæ, and other places round about, appeared in arms under command of Livius Postumius, the dictator, as he is called of the Fidenatians, and caused such a panic that the Romans fled before them; and the anniversary of this flight, the nones or 7th of July, was celebrated ever afterwards under the name of the day of the people's flight.[20] This, however, is an uncertain story,[21] in some respects improbable, and connected at any rate with circumstances which are clearly fabulous. It is more credible that the late destructive inroad of the Gauls should have shaken all old political relations, and that the Romans could no longer rely on the aid of the Latins and Hernicans. Emboldened by their knowledge of this, the Volscians took up arms, and advanced into Latium as far as the neighborhood of Lanuvium,[22] which stood on a sort of spur of high ground, running out from the very southern extremity of the Alban Hills. Here they encountered the Roman army commanded by the military tribunes, and were so superior in numbers that they presently confined the Romans within their camp. The tidings of their danger were carried to Rome; Camillus was named dictator, and he, taking the field with every man who could bear arms, hastened from Rome by a night-march,[23] and appeared at day-break on the rear of the Volscians. Then the Roman army under the military tribunes made a sally, and the Volscians, attacked both in front and rear, were totally routed. Scarcely was this danger repelled, when the dictator learned that an Etruscan army, probably from Tarquinii, had attacked the Roman frontier on the opposite side, on the right bank of the Tiber, and was besieging Sutrium. Camillus hastened to its aid, but on his way,[24] said the story of his exploits, he met the citizens of Sutrium in forlorn plight, they having been obliged to surrender their city, and having saved nothing but their lives. They fell on their knees before him, told him their sad case, and craved his assistance. He bade them be of good cheer, saying that it was now the turn of the Etruscans to wail and weep. Then he advanced upon Sutrium, and found, as he had expected, that the enemy kept no watch, and were thinking of nothing but plunder: he instantly forced his way into the place, and made a great slaughter, and a still greater number of prisoners; and Sutrium was thus, according to the story, "lost and recovered in a day again."[25] It is impossible to tell how much of exaggeration is mixed up with these details; but there is no reason to doubt that Camillus by his genius in this memorable year did truly save his country from destruction. The enemies of Rome were checked, and time was gained for the state to recover from its disorder and distress, and to meet its rivals on more equal terms. The very existence of the Roman people in after-ages proves how well they must have defended themselves

[19] By Varro, Ling. Lat. VI. 18, ed. Müller, and partly by Macrobius, Saturnal. I. 11.

[20] Poplifugia.

[21] It is uncertain, because a different account of the origin of the Poplifugia is given by Macrobius, Saturnal. III. 2, and by Dionysius, II. 56, and because we know how little reliance is to be placed on stories pretending to account for the origin of old traditional usages or festivals. It is improbable, because Fidenæ had been taken and colonized by the Romans forty years earlier, and from that time forward plays no part in history, and because Ficulea is never mentioned at all after the times of the Roman kings. Nor can we conceive how Fidenæ should have had a dictator, which was a title peculiar to the Latin towns; unless, indeed, we suppose that it had joined some Latin confederacy since the fall of the Roman power, and was now become Latin. Further, the story of the Fidenatian dictator is mixed up with the famous legend of Tutula and the female slaves, which is evidently fabulous.

[22] Diodorus, XIV. 117. Livy, VI. 2.

[23] The resemblance of this story to that of Cincinnatus is obvious, and is very suspicious. Livy merely describes the victory of Camillus, without saying any thing of the previous danger. Plutarch makes the Latins to have joined the Volscians, but he expressly says that Camillus marched to relieve the army of the military tribunes, which was besieged by the enemy.—Camillus, 34.

[24] Livy, VI. 3. Plutarch, Camillus, 35.

[25] The very passage from which this line is taken, in Shakspeare's Henry VI. Part I. shows how little reliance can be placed on a poetical version of events in themselves historical. The line refers to the capture of Rouen by the Maid of Orleans, and its recovery by Talbot on the same day; both the capture and recapture being, as every one knows, alike purely imaginary.

when attacked by two enemies at once in the hour of their most extreme helplessness and depression.

It were a mere wearying of the reader's patience to follow Livy through the details of the petty wars of this period—details which cannot be regarded as historical, and which, even though true, would be of little value. It will be enough to trace generally Rome's foreign relations down to the time of her great internal regeneration.

Extent of the Roman frontier. Its limit towards Etruria.

On the right bank of the Tiber, the Roman frontier neither advanced nor receded. Nepete and Sutrium, which had submitted to Rome three or four years before the Gaulish invasion,[26] and were the border towns of the Roman dominion, were twice, according to the story of Camillus, attacked by the Etruscans; once, as we have seen, in 366, and again in 369. They were both, according to the same authority, taken in 369, and immediately recovered.[27] It appears that the Etruscans, who were engaged in this affair, were the people of Tarquinii; and finding the strength of Rome greater than they had expected, they were probably glad to conclude a truce for a certain number of years; which was no less welcome to the Romans, as they saw that they should have enemies enough on their hands on their opposite frontier.

Its limits on the left bank of the Tiber.

On the left bank of the Tiber we hear of wars with the Volscians generally, almost every year, and particularly with the people of Antium. The scene of action was commonly the neighborhood of Satricum, a town which lay between Velitræ and Antium.[28] Satricum had originally been one of the thirty cities of the Latins; it had then been conquered by the Æquians and Volscians, had afterwards been taken by the Romans, and had lastly, a little while before the Gaulish invasion, revolted from them,[29] and was now again become Volscian. It is said to have been retaken by Camillus in 369,[30] and a Roman colony was sent to occupy it in the following year. Again, however, it was lost in 373,[31] and held for five years by the Volscians; after which time, when the people of Antium made peace with the Romans, and Satricum was to have been restored, it was burned, out of indignation by the Latins,[32] who had been allied with the Antiatians against Rome, and now found themselves deserted. Thus, on this side, the Roman frontier had considerably receded from the point which it had reached thirty years earlier. Then Anxur had been conquered, but now even Satricum could not be maintained, a place less than thirty miles distant from Rome. The loss of Anxur is nowhere expressly acknowledged; but it must have fallen either in the year 358, when we read of its being besieged by the Volscians;[33] or else it must have been lost, as well as Bola,[34] amidst the calamity of the Gaulish invasion; for it is not possible that it could have been retained by the Romans whilst the Volscians were fighting year after year at Satricum, nearly five-and-twenty miles nearer to Rome.

Altered relations of Rome with Latium.

But the peculiar feature of Rome's foreign relations, after the retreat of the Gauls, consisted in her altered position with respect to the Latins. Hitherto, during all the wars with the Æquians and Volscians, the alliance of the Latins and the Hernicans with the Romans had remained unbroken. It is true that some of the thirty Latin cities which had concluded the original treaty with Sp. Cassius in 261, had since been conquered by the Æquians and Volscians:[35] and thus as Niebuhr supposes, that treaty had long since been vir-

[26] See chap. xviii.

[27] Livy, VI. 9, 10.

[28] Its position is unknown: the Italian antiquaries fix it at a little place called Conca, on the edge of the Selva di Nettuno, in the supposed line of the old road from Velitræ to Astura and Antium. But nothing exists beyond a few shapeless ruins, which can determine nothing. Westphal, p. 40.

[29] Diodorus, XIV. 102.

[30] Livy, VI. 8, 16.

[31] Livy, VI. 22.

[32] Livy, VI. 33.

[33] Livy, V. 16.

[34] Camillus is made to recover Bola from the Æquians, in the year 366. Livy, VI. 2. It must therefore have been previously lost.

[35] Of the thirty Latin cities enumerated by Dionysius, eight are mentioned by Livy or Dionysius as having been conquered by the Volscians under the command of Coriolanus; Velitræ also became Volscian in the course of the

tually at an end: and while some of the Latin states were become Æquian or Volscian, or had drawn around themselves a distinct confederacy of the small towns in their immediate neighborhood; others, like Tusculum, were, from the equal, become no more than the dependent allies of Rome: for instance, Præneste, as Niebuhr thinks, must from its position have become Æquian, and Tibur stood aloof, and formed the centre of a small confederacy of its own. It does not, however, appear to me that we are compelled to adopt this supposition by the reason of the case; and external testimony,[36] such as it is, seems to be against it. The Æquians may have poured out upon the Campagna through that breach in the Apennine wall which lies open close below Præneste, and may have occupied Pedum in the plain, and Lavici on the roots of the Alban Hills; nay, they may have even taken Bola within the mountain-range itself, and yet the impregnable strength of Præneste, which, at a later period, so long defied the whole power of Sylla, may have remained in perfect security; and as the Hernicans were unconquered, and yet lay quite on the rear of the Æquians when they established themselves on Algidus, so Tibur and Præneste, safe in their mountain-holds, may have continued to belong to Latium, though almost isolated from the mass of the Latin people by the conquests of the Opican nations. On the other hand, it is very likely that amid the ruin of the Latin cities around them, many small Latin communities may have gathered under their protection; and that thus the disproportion in strength between them and the other remaining states of the Latin confederacy would have become greater than it had been before. This of itself, when Rome had been so crushed by the Gauls, would lead to an altered relation between them and the Romans. By the treaty concluded with Sp. Cassius, Rome stood as one contracting party, and the whole Latin confederacy as another: of the plunder or conquest made by the allied nations, the share of Rome alone was to be equal to that of all the Latin cities together; the allied armies were to be commanded alternately by a Roman and a Latin; but each particular Latin state would enjoy the command many times less often than Rome. Thus when Rome had sunk in power, and Præneste had risen, it would seem fair that they should stand towards each other on a different footing; that Præneste should be no longer a mere single member of the state of Latium, but should itself treat as state to state with Rome.

Wars with the Latin states.—Præneste.

Be this as it may, we find that after the Gaulish invasion, the treaty of Sp. Cassius, both with the Latins and Hernicans, was either imperfectly observed, or altogether violated for a period of nearly thirty years. Latin and Hernican volunteers in great numbers are said to have joined the armies of the Volscians;[37] then the Latins generally, without any mention of particular states, are described as at open war with Rome,[38] in alliance with the Volscians; and Lanuvium,[39] and above all, Præneste,[40] are especially noticed as taking a prominent part in these hostilities. On the other hand, Tusculum,[41] though on one occasion suspected, remained generally true to Rome: and so also did

wars with the Opican nations; and others of the thirty which are not noticed again in history, were, in all probability, destroyed.

[36] Livy says that "the Latins and Hernicans, since the battle at the lake Regillus, had remained faithful to Rome for nearly a century without interruption." VI. 2. This, as a general statement, and one clearly in some respects inaccurate, may not be entitled to much weight; but a variety of incidental notices in the accounts of the several years, seem to imply that the alliance between the three nations, Romans, Latins, and Hernicans, lasted without any material change down to the Gaulish war. Latins and Hernicans joined Camillus against Veii in 359. (Livy, V. 19.) Ferentinum, when taken from the Volscians, was given to the Hernicans as their share of the spoil in 342. (Livy IV. 51.) The Latin and Hernican lands are ravaged by the Æquians or Volscians in 346 (Livy, IV. 55), in 345 (id. IV. 53), and the Hernican lands in 342. (Id. IV. 51.) The Latins and Hernicans announce the intended invasion of the Opican nations in 332 and 324 (Livy, IV. 26, 37), and in 292 it is expressly mentioned that the lands ravaged by the Volscians were those of the Prænestines, Gabians, and Tusculans (Livy, III. 8): the three people belonging all alike at that period to the Latin confederacy.

[37] Livy, VI. 7, 13.

[38] Livy, VI. 30, 32, 33.

[39] Livy, VI. 21.

[40] Livy, V. 21, 22, 27, et seq. 30.

[41] Livy, VI. 21, 25, 26.

Gabii and Lavici.[42] It may be well conceived how greatly this altered disposition of the Latins added to the distress of the Roman commons. For some years past Latium had borne the brunt of the ravaging incursions of the Æquians and Volscians; its aid had enabled the Romans to carry the war at times into the enemies' country, while their own territory had rested in security. But now we read of the Roman territory being ravaged in all directions by the Volscians;[43] and on one occasion[44] the Prænestines, having laid waste the country between the Tiber and the Anio, a quarter most likely to have escaped the attacks of other enemies, at last even crossed the Anio, and advanced as far as the very walls of Rome. Under such circumstances any gleam of victory would be doubly welcomed; and an inscription in the Capitol[45] long recorded the successful campaign of T. Quinctius Cincinnatus, who having been appointed dictator to repel this invasion of the Prænestines, marched out against them, defeated them in a battle on the very banks of the ill-omened Alia, chased them into their own country, and stormed nine of their townships in as many days. But such successes, like those with which the Saxon kings of England sometimes relieved the disasters of the Danish invasions, were attended by no permanent fruits. The Prænestines were in the field again the very next year;[46] and the aspect of the Roman foreign affairs continued to be overclouded down to the very end of that period with which we are concerned in the present chapter.

Internal distress. Sufferings of the Roman commons.

But the prospect at home was not overclouded merely; it was the very deepest darkness of misery. It has been well said that long periods of general suffering make far less impression on our minds, than the short sharp struggle in which a few distinguished individuals perish; not that we over-estimate the horror and the guilt of times of open bloodshedding, but we are much too patient to the greater misery and greater sin of periods of quiet legalized oppression; of that most deadly of all evils, when law, and even religion herself, are false to their divine origin and purpose, and their voice is no longer the voice of God, but of his enemy. In such cases the evil derives advantage, in a manner, from the very amount of its own enormity. No pen can record, no volume can contain, the details of the daily and hourly sufferings of a whole people, endured without intermission, through the whole life of man, from the cradle to the grave. The mind itself can scarcely comprehend the wide range of the mischief: how constant poverty and insult, long endured as the natural portion of a degraded caste, bear with them to the sufferers something yet worse than pain, whether of the body or the feelings; how they dull the understanding and poison the morals; how ignorance and ill-treatment combined are the parents of universal suspicion; how from oppression is produced habitual cowardice, breaking out when occasion offers into merciless cruelty; how slaves become naturally liars; how they whose condition denies them all noble enjoyments, and to whom looking forward is only despair, plunge themselves, with a brute's recklessness, into the lowest sensual pleasures; how the domestic circle itself, the last sanctuary of human virtue, becomes at length corrupted, and in the place of natural affection and parental care, there is to be seen only selfishness and unkindness, and no other anxiety on the part of the parents for their children, than that they may, by fraud or by violence, prey in their turn upon that society which they have found their bitterest enemy. Evils like these, long working in the heart of a nation, render their own cure impossible: a revolution may execute judgment on one generation, and that, perhaps, the very one which

[42] Livy, VI. 21, 25, 26. [43] Livy, VI. 31.

[44] Livy, VI. 28.

[45] Livy, VI. 29, and Festus in "Triens." The inscription, as Niebuhr has restored it, ran thus:

Juppiter, atque Divi omnes hoc dederunt,
Ut Titus Quinctius dictator Romanus
Oppida novem diebus novem caperet.

From Jove and all the gods this favor did befall,
That Titus Quinctus, sometime Rome's captain-general,
Nine towns did in nine days assault and take withal.

[46] Livy, VI. 30.

was beginning to see and to repent of its inherited sins; but it cannot restore life to the morally dead; and its ill success, as if in this line of evils no curse should be wanting, is pleaded by other oppressors as a defence of their own iniquity, and a reason for perpetuating it forever.

Causes of the distress; severity of the treatment of insolvent debtors.

But it was the blessing of Rome, that this course of evils was, in her case, checked in time, when it had brought suffering only on one generation, before it had entailed moral corruption on the remotest posterity. Twenty years[47] of poverty and oppression, could we present to ourselves each individual case of misery, would seem a fearful amount of evil; but, happily, twenty years' suffering in the life of a nation are but like an attack of fever, severe indeed while it lasts, but too short to weaken the constitution permanently. Mere poverty, moreover, is an evil, the sense of which varies greatly according to differences of time and place; its actual privations depend much on climate; their intolerableness arises from contrast; where none are extravagant or luxurious, poverty must almost sink to beggary before its sting is felt acutely. The actual distress endured by the Roman commons in the loss of their houses, and the destruction of their cattle and fruit-trees, few of which could have escaped the hands of the Gauls during their long occupation of the city and territory of Rome, although severe for the time, would, nevertheless, have been diminished by the sense of its being the common portion, and would in time have been altogether relieved. But the attacks of foreign enemies rendered the tributum, as a war-tax, constant and heavy; and other taxes were imposed to defray the expense of building up the rock of the Capitol with large blocks of stone,[48] and probably of rebuilding the temples generally; whilst the obligation of completing the houses in the city within twelve months, was a pressure on the means of the less wealthy, coming at the very time when they were least able to meet it. Thus, as we have seen, debts were unavoidably contracted; and when there was a general demand for money, it was not possible that any positive law could keep the rate of interest low. Whether the enactment of the twelve tables, which fixed its yearly rate at one-twelfth of the principal, was actually repealed, or only disregarded by common consent, we cannot tell, but the re-enacting that rate[49] a few years later is a proof that at this period it was not observed; and it is expressly mentioned that the principal[50] of debts was sometimes paid many times over in interest before they were of five years' standing. It is not necessary to repeat the details of the extreme severity of the law towards insolvent debtors; they have been already noticed; but as the distress was far greater now than at any former time, this severity must have been more extensively felt than ever: every patrician house was become a private jail; but a jail in which the prisoners were kept to hard labor for the jailer's benefit, or were, at his caprice, loaded with irons and subjected to the lash.

Aggravations of their misery from particular causes.

Imprisonment for debt in its mildest form, and amidst the manifold money transactions of a great commercial country, in which the debtor must often be paying the penalty of his own imprudence, is yet beginning to shock the feelings of modern times, as being liable to the evil of confounding together misfortune and crime. How then should we regard the treatment of the Roman commons, whose debts were incurred by no

[47] The period, according to Niebuhr's chronology, was one of eighteen years, from 365 to 383: according to the common chronology, it lasted twenty-three years, from 365 to 388.

[48] Livy, VI. 4. "Capitolium saxo quadrato substructum est." This must mean that where the cliff had been proved to be accessible, and thus have been more or less of an inclined plane, it was so built up with large blocks of stone as to enlarge the upper surface of the hill, and make it perpendicular with the bottom of it. Similar substructions have enlarged the surface of the hill towards the Forum, where the remains of the Tabularium still exist.

The "saxum quadratum" of the Roman writers, is the "Steintuf" of the German geologists; the "Tufa litoide" of Brocchi: it is a volcanic conglomerate, found in Rome itself, and is the stone employed in the Cloaca.

[49] Livy, VII. 16.

[50] Livy, VI. 14. "Multiplici jam sorte exsolutâ, mergentibus semper sortem usuris." This is said of the year 370, only five years after the Gaulish invasion.

fault of their own, but were the consequence of an overwhelming national calamity, and of the want of consideration shown by the government for their state of distress? Yet it is remarkable that the severity of the law in itself seems even now to have excited no complaint; nor do we find that the tribunes extended their protection to the multitude of innocent debtors who were daily dragged off to labor amongst slaves in their creditor's workhouse; what excited general discontent was, in the first place, the high rate of interest exacted by the patricians, who thus seemed to make their profit out of the general misery; and next the harshness of obliging the commons to pay heavy taxes for the public service, while the state's domain land, the natural resource in extraordinary national emergencies, was appropriated to the benefit of individuals, and whilst the taxation itself was highly arbitrary, being regulated according to an old valuation of the property of the citizens,[51] and making no allowance for the enormous losses which had since so greatly reduced its amount. Above all, there was the intolerable suspicion that the taxes thus hardly wrung from the people were corruptly embezzled: a tax had been imposed to replace twofold the treasures borrowed from the temples to purchase the retreat of the Gauls; and it was whispered[52] that this money, instead of being restored to the gods, was secretly kept back by the patricians for their own use.

M. Manlius comes forward as the protector of the poor and the insolvent debtors.

Thus the evils of the times and the public irritation were great; but before they found their true and wholesome remedy, they gave occasion to one of those false shows of relief, which only aggravate the disease. M. Manlius, the preserver of the Capitol from the Gauls, was jealous of the high reputation of Camillus,[53] and alienated from the patricians generally, because his share of the high offices of the commonwealth was not such as his merits claimed. Thus he was ready to feel indignant at the severities practised against the debtors; and his better feelings also, the loftiness of his nature, and his sympathy with brave men, were all shocked by the scenes which he daily witnessed. One day[54] he saw a centurion, who had served with him, and whom he knew to be a distinguished soldier, now dragged through the Forum on his way to his creditor's workhouse. He hastened up, protested against the indignity, and himself paid the debt on the spot, and redeemed the debtor. The gratitude and the popularity which this act won for him, excited him to go on in the same course: he sold by public auction the most valuable[55] part of his landed property, and declared that he would never see a fellow-citizen made a bondsman for debt, so long as he had the means of relieving him. So well did he fulfil this promise that he was said to have advanced money to no fewer than four hundred debtors, without requiring any interest to be paid to him; and thus to have discharged their debts, and saved them from bondage. Such generosity obtained for him the unbounded affection of the people; he was called the "Father of the Commons;" and his house in the Capitol was always beset by a multitude of citizens, to whom he spoke of the cruelty of their creditors, and of their fraud and sacrilege in appropriating to themselves the money paid by the people to replace the treasures borrowed from the gods for the ransom of the Capitol.

A dictator had been[56] already appointed early in the year, with the double purpose of employing him against the Volscians abroad, and, if need should be, against the attempts of Manlius at home. The office had been conferred on A.

[51] See Niebuhr, Vol. II. p. 675.

[52] Livy, VI. 14.

[53] Livy, VI. 11. Plutarch, Camillus, 36.

[54] Livy, VI. 14. One is rather too much reminded here of the story of the brave old centurion, whose hard usage from his creditors excited such a tumult in the year of Rome 259.—See Livy, II. 23.

[55] "Fundum in Veienti," says Livy, "caput patrimonii." It could hardly, then, have been a part of the Veientian territory which had been conquered only eleven years before. But the Ager Veiens came down to the Tiber, and portions of it may have been conquered in earlier wars, or even in the earlier years, of the final war. The fundus in question was, probably, a "possessio," or a portion of the domain land held by occupation; but such estates were bought and sold amongst individuals as if they were property, subject always to the chance of their being reclaimed by the state.

[56] Livy, VI. 11.

His ambitious practices. His impeachment by the tribunes. His trial and death.

Cornelius Cossus, perhaps the same person who, in his consulship, eight-and-twenty years before, had taken cognizance of the murder of M. Postumius by his soldiers; and he was now recalled from the field to check the apprehended sedition. He summoned Manlius[57] before him, called upon him to prove his charge of the embezzlement of the sacred money, and on his failing to do so threw him into prison. This seems to have been merely the exercise of that power of arresting dangerous individuals, and so stopping their plans for a season, which is granted to, or assumed by, all governments in perilous times; it is remarkable, however, that the imprisonment of Manlius did not expire with the term of the dictator's office, but continued till the senate, fearing, it is said, that he would be released by force, passed a vote to restore him to his liberty. This might seem to have been an act of weakness, yet the event allows us to attribute it to a wise policy; for Manlius, when released, indulged in language more violent than ever, and at last, if we can rightly interpret[58] the doubtful language of the annalists, the assemblages at his house assumed a more threatening character; and the Capitol was occupied by him and his followers as a stronghold in defiance of the government, as it was many years afterwards by the tribune L. Saturninus. That his motives were not pure, and that his purposes were treasonable, seems evident from several circumstances. He did not unite with the tribunes, the natural leaders of the commons, nor concert with them any definite measure for the redress of the existing evils. This makes a wide distinction between him and the several honest popular leaders who, on other occasions, had opposed the aristocracy. Volero, Terentilius, Duillius, Icilius, Canuleius, and Trebonius, had each come forward with some distinct measure for the attainment of a particular end; but of Manlius we hear nothing but that he exercised great liberality towards distressed individuals, and so acquired an immense popularity; that he excited the passions of the people by vague charges and invectives against the aristocracy; and that he occupied the Capitol with a multitude of his partisans. It marks also the character of his proceedings, that the tribunes, forgetting the just grievances of their order, joined the patricians against him; and that Q. Publilius,[59] whose family was surpassed by none in its hereditary zeal for the true liberties of the commons, came forward to impeach him of high treason. What follows is told with some variations, and the real details cannot be recovered. According to the common account, Manlius submitted to take his trial before the centuries in the Campus Martius. I have already shown how much even the greatest criminals had to hope from the uncertainty of such a tribunal; how much weight was given to matters foreign to the question at issue; how a strong and eloquent appeal to the feelings of the judges might overpower the clearest evidence of the prisoner's guilt. If even the decemvir Appius had thought his acquittal by the centuries not impossible, how much more might Manlius expect from them a favorable sentence? Nor was his hope deceived. When he appeared in the Field of Mars, he brought forward four hundred debtors[60] whom he had relieved from bondage; he exhibited the spoils of thirty enemies whom he had slain in personal combat; he showed forty honorary rewards which he had at various times received from his generals in war; and amongst these, eight of those wreaths of oak, the famous civic crowns, which were given for saving the life of a fellow-citizen in battle. He produced, besides, some of the very men whom he had thus saved, living witnesses of his services, whose tears and entreaties in behalf of their preserver might strike to the hearts of all who saw them. Finally, he bared his own breast, covered with

[57] Livy, VI. 16.

[58] "Senatus de secessione in domum privatam plebis, . . . agitat."—Livy, VI. 19. The word "secessio" is either an exaggeration or denotes a positive act of insurrection, or, to speak more strictly, of a withdrawal of allegiance from the existing government.

[59] Livy, VI. 19. This Publilius was of the same family with Publilius Volero, and was the dictator Publilius Philo who passed the famous popular laws which bear his name some years afterwards.—Livy, VIII. 12.

[60] Livy, VI. 20.

honorable scars; and, looking up to the Capitol, which rose immediately above the Field of Mars, he implored the aid of those gods whose temples he had saved from barbarian pollution, and bade the people to look at the Capitol, and then give their judgment. The tribunes saw that the centuries, thus excited, would never find him guilty; and the trial was adjourned,[61] not to be brought forward again before the same tribunal. Yet how he was prevented from appealing to the centuries from the sentence of any other court that might have condemned him, does not appear. Nothing more is known with certainty than that Manlius was put to death as a traitor; the very manner[62] of his execution, as well as the authority by which he was condemned, are variously reported. All agree, however,[63] that his house was levelled with the ground; that a law was passed forbidding any one from henceforth to reside within the precincts of the Capitol; and that the members of the Manlian gens shared so deeply in the general sense of his guilt, as to make it a rule of their house, that no Manlius should ever hereafter receive the prænomen of Marcus.

Increased distress: the tribunes at last venture to interfere in behalf of the commons.

After this ill-omened opposition to the aristocracy, their power was, as usual, only the more confirmed. For four years the distress went on increasing, till the tribunes of the year 375 (we do not know their names) ventured to make a stand[64] in behalf of their constituents. Censors had been appointed in this year, to take a new valuation of the property of the citizens; but one of them having died, and it being accounted unlucky to fill up the place of a deceased censor, his colleague went out of office. Two censors were then elected, but the augurs pronounced their election invalid, and they also resigned without doing any business; after which a religious objection was made to any third election, as if the gods had manifested it to be their will that there should be no censors that year. This so provoked the tribunes, that when it was proposed to call the legions into the field against the people of Præneste, they had recourse to the old method of opposition practised by the tribunes in the preceding century, and protected every citizen in refusing to enlist; nay, they went still further, and declared that they would once for all redress the existing grievances, by forbidding any debtor to be given over to his creditor's power by the sentence of the magistrate. And though they did not persevere in their purpose, for the Prænestines,[65] by a sudden inroad up to the very gates of Rome, furnished an excuse for the appointment of a dictator, and made the war seem a matter of paramount necessity, yet the tribunes withdrew their opposition only on some compromise; and at the ensuing election of military tribunes, three out of six were, for the first time since the Gaulish invasion, chosen from among the plebeians.

Their interference seems unavailing.

This apparently brought some relief for the following year; but at the end of it only one[66] plebeian was elected amongst the military tribunes; and the year 377 was only marked by disappointment of all the hopes of the commons, and an actual increase of their burdens. Censors were

[61] Any objection of a religious kind on the part of the augurs, or a notice "that it thundered," was sufficient to break up the comitia. C. Rabirius was saved from condemnation by a sudden adjournment produced by the act of L. Metellus, who tore down the standard hoisted on the Janiculum, and thus, according to an old custom, obliged the comitia to separate.

[62] Livy, and most other writers, say that he was thrown from the Tarpeian rock. Cornelius Nepos related that he was scourged to death.—See Gellius, XVII. 21, § 24. Again, some said, that he was condemned by a "concilium populi," held in the Peteline grove without the Porta Flumentana; others said that he was condemned by the duumviri, or two judges created, according to the old law ascribed to the times of the kings, for the purpose of trying him as a public enemy. Further, what was the "concilium populi," and where was the "Lucus Petelinus?" for the present reading of "Porta Nomentana" in the editions of Livy, is a mere correction of Nardini, and not to be admitted; inasmuch as there was no Porta Nomentana before the enlargement of the walls by Aurelian. Then there is the curious story recorded by Dion Cassius, and which Niebuhr prefers as the most authentic of all the accounts. The question is too long to be discussed here: I have thrown it therefore into a note at the end of the volume.

[63] Livy, VI. 20. Plutarch, Camillus, 36. Auctor. de Viris illustr. in Manlio. Dion Cassius, Fragm. Peiresc. xxxi.

[64] Livy, VI. 27.

[65] Livy, VI. 28.

[66] Livy, VI. 31.

again elected, but a war with the Volscians was made a pretence for postponing the census; while, on the other hand, although the censors could not find opportunity for relieving the distress of the commons, they thought it necessary to contract for the building of a part of the city wall;[67] and to defray the expense of this work, additional taxes were imposed. Accordingly, in this and the following

A. U. C. 378.

year, the amount of debt in the state continued to increase, and the number of insolvent debtors condemned to bondage was greatly multiplied; while a sudden dissolution of the alliance between the Latins and Volscians, and the conclusion of a separate peace between the latter and Rome,[68] relieved the patricians from any immediate pressure of foreign warfare, and thus deprived the opposition of the tribunes of its most effectual weapon.

But deliverance is, notwithstanding, at hand.

From this apparently hopeless condition there sprung up suddenly a prospect of deliverance. Again we have conflicting traditions, idle stories, and party exaggerations in the place of history. But the result of the great struggle is certain, whatever obscurity hangs over the details. And L. Sextius and C. Licinius, though we cannot gain a distinct knowledge of them as individuals, yet deserve to be recorded amongst the greatest benefactors to the cause of good government and equal law, inasmuch as they brought forward and carried the Licinian laws.

CHAPTER XXVI.

THE LICINIAN LAWS.—378–384.

"Les mouvemens qui agitent les peuples peuvent être de deux sortes. Les uns sont produits par une cause directe, d'où résulte un effet immédiat. Une circonstance quelconque amène une nation, ou même une partie de la nation, à désirer un but déterminé; l'enterprise échoue ou réussit. . . . . Ce sont là les heureuses révolutions; on sait ce qu'on veut, on marche vers un point précis, on se repose quand il est atteint."—BARANTE, Tableau de la Littérature Française pendant le Dixhuitième Siècle.

SIX patrician military tribunes[1] had been elected at the comitia for the year 378, and had entered on their office on the first of July. The coalition between the Latins and Volscians, which had been so dangerous to Rome, was dissolved in this same summer, and the Volscians of Antium made a separate peace.[2] During the autumn the commons seemed to have utterly lost heart; the patricians were all powerful at home, and fortune seemed disposed to favor them equally abroad: the cause, in short, appeared so hopeless that the more eminent men[3] amongst the commons were discouraged from coming forward as candidates, even for the office of tribune of the commons; the tribune's power, they thought, would merely expose themselves to odium, while it would be unable to effect any good. Thus the elderly men, who generally held the tribuneship, now abandoned the helm in despair, and younger men, who would have given way to their higher claims under other circumstances, now found themselves called upon to come

[67] Livy, VI. 32.

[68] Livy, VI. 33.

[1] Livy, VI. 32.

[2] Livy, VI. 33. But they could scarcely have made an absolute surrender, "deditio," of their city and territory; for we hear of them again in little more than twenty years, as an independent and sovereign people; planting a colony on that very spot, Satricum, which they had conquered in the war now before us, and which they must have retained, therefore, at the peace of 378. See Livy, VII. 27. But a state which retains even its conquests at the end of a war is not likely to make at that same time an absolute surrender of its own city and territory.

[3] Livy, VI. 34.

forward, and brought with them strength and spirits better fitted for times so perilous. At the election in December, C. Licinius Stolo, a member of one of the richest[4] and most distinguished families amongst the commons, and a man in the full vigor of life, obtained a place amongst the ten tribunes, and L. Sextius, a young man of an active and aspiring spirit, and a personal friend of Licinius, was elected one of his colleagues.

Could we look into the private history of these times, we should find, no doubt, amongst the Roman patricians, as amongst the members of all aristocracies, a certain number of persons, who, from various motives, are opposed to the majority of their own order. By some of these, Licinius and Sextius were, we may be sure, encouraged and supported; the Licinian family had repeatedly intermarried with patricians:[5] the tribune himself was married to a Fabia, and others of his name had been similarly connected with the Manlii and the Cornelii. With all the advantages then of wealth and connection that could be enjoyed by a commoner, Licinius came forward to redress the grievances of his order, and to secure their rights for the time to come.

Some of the patricians are favorable to the cause of the commons.

He proposed in the assembly of the tribes, in conjunction with L. Sextius, three separate laws.[6] The first provided a strong remedy for the great actual evil, the overwhelming pressure of debt. It enacted, that whatever had been already paid in interest should be deducted from the amount of the principal;[7] and that the debt thus reduced should be discharged in three years, in three equal instalments. The second bill was intended to save the commons, when their debts were once relieved, from the necessity of running into debt again. It proposed therefore to provide for the poorer citizens by giving them grants of land out of the domain, or ager publicus; and in order to have land enough available for this purpose, it restrained the right of the occupation, by enacting that no man should occupy more than five hundred jugera of the public land in tillage,[8] nor feed more than a hundred oxen and five hundred sheep on those portions of it which were left in pasture. The third bill was dictated by the consciousness that the enjoyment of property is neither secure in itself, nor can satisfy the wants of a noble mind, without being united with a certain portion of political power. The commons, as an order, must be raised to a level with the patricians; the honors of their country must be laid open to them; they must have an opportunity of bequeathing nobility to their children. The institution of the military tribuneship was, in itself, an affront to the commons: it was only because it was so inferior in dignity to the consulship, that it had been made nominally accessible to them. The bill of Licinius, accordingly, did away with the military tribuneship, and restored the consulship.[9] That very image of the ancient royalty, with all its sacredness and display of sovereign state, was to be open to the commons no less than to the patricians. But expe-

The tribunes propose the three Licinian laws.

[4] This appears from what is related of him afterwards, that the amount of public land in his occupation exceeded the measure of 500 jugera, which had been fixed by his own law. Niebuhr observes also that this wealth of the Licinian family continued to the latest period of the republic, as is shown by the immense riches of M. Licinius Crassus.

[5] The Licinius who was a military tribune in the year 355 was a brother of Cn. Cornelius; and the Licinius who was master of the horsemen in 382–3 was related to the dictator of that year, P. Manlius. Livy, V. 12, VI. 39. If in the first of these two cases we suppose with Borghesi (Nuovi Frammenti, Parte 2, p. 89), that P. Licinius was a Cornelius by birth, and adopted into the family of the Licinii, it shows no less the high eminence of the Licinii and their intimacy with the noblest patrician houses, when even a Cornelius would not scruple to become their adopted son.

[6] Livy, VI. 35.

[7] "Ut deducto eo de capite quod usuris pernumeratum esset, id quod superesset triennio æquis portionibus persolveretur."—Livy, VI. 35.

[8] "Ne quis plus quingenta jugera agri possideret." If we remember the legal definition of possessio, quicquid apprehendimus cujus proprietas ad nos non pertinet, aut nec potest pertinere, hoc possessionem apellamus," De Verbor. Significat. 115 (Digest. Lib. L. tit. xvi.), we shall see that it was needless to add "publici" to "agri," because the only land which men ordinarily occupied without its being their own, was the "ager publicus."

For the clause limiting the number of cattle which might be fed on the public pasture land, see Appian, de Bell. Civil. I. 8.

[9] "Ne tribunorum militum comitia fierent, consulumque utique alter ex plebe crearetur."—Livy, VI. 35.

rience had shown that it was not enough to throw it open merely; one place must be secured to the commons by law, or the influence of the patricians at the comitia would forever exclude them from it. It was proposed, therefore, that one, at least, of the two consuls should of necessity be elected from the commons.

Operation of the system of debtor and creditor.

This last law requires no explanation; and the second, since Niebuhr has cleared up the whole subject of the agrarian laws, is equally intelligible. The first, however, involves in it some difficulty; for if the rate of interest had been high, and a debt had been of long standing, the sum paid in interest would not only have equalled, but must, in some instances, have actually exceeded the amount of the principal; so that the creditor, far from having any thing more to receive, would rather have had something to refund. To explain this, Niebuhr observes, that debts were ordinarily settled at the end of one year; and that if a debtor could not then pay, he was in the habit of borrowing money of a new creditor to discharge the principal and interest of his first account; a proceeding which, from its frequency, had a particular name, "Versura."[10] That a speedy settlement of debts was the ordinary practice, may indeed be collected from the clause in this very Licinian law itself, which required the whole debt remaining after the deduction of the already paid interest to be discharged within three years; and if the practice of versura was often repeated, it will be obvious that a debtor would have paid his original debt many times over in interest, although not under that name: a part of the principal of every new debt being, in fact, the interest of the preceding one. Still, as the distress had now lasted for thirteen years, there must have been many who could not have gone on so long upon this system; the amount of their debt must have so exceeded all their possible means of payment, that no new creditor could have been found to advance them the money to discharge it. Under these circumstances, what could the debtor do but enter into a nexum, and at the end of a certain term, on failing to redeem himself, submit to be given over as a bondman to his creditor; or else try to procure a further respite by offering an exorbitant rate of interest? In this latter case the interest so paid would, undoubtedly, be deducted from the amount of the principal, and thus it would happen that there would be a very small balance left for the creditor still to receive. But such cases would be very few: in most instances, when a man's credit was so exhausted that he could no longer practice the system of borrowing from a new creditor to pay his old one, he would be obliged to enter into a nexum, and being still insolvent, would, in the common course of things, become his creditor's bondman. Then whilst the debtor was giving his creditor all the benefit of his labor, we cannot suppose that the interest of the debt went on accumulating also; and thus, after he had remained some years in bondage, he might be redeemed by the mere payment of his original debt, from which there would be deducted only that interest which he had paid before he had been consigned to his creditor's power. But what we should most desire would be, to learn the fate of the great mass of debtors, who, in the course of the last thirteen years, had thus been reduced to slavery. Was there any limit of time beyond which they could not be redeemed? or, if the debt were never paid, did they or their posterity ever recover their freedom?[11] Are we, in short, to believe that many families of the

[10] Festus, or rather Paulus, in "Versura."

[11] There is a well-known passage in Quinctilian, VII. 3, § 27, which enters into the differences between the condition of a slave and that of one who was "addictus," or given over to his creditor into bondage. But it does not specially touch the questions which I have suggested. Some parts of it, however, are remarkable. "Ad servum nulla lex pertinet: addictus legem habet. Propria liberi quæ nemo habet nisi liber, prænomen, nomen, cognomen, tribum; habet hæc addictus." "Addictus legem habet;" that is, he could not be killed by his master, nor treated by him absolutely at his discretion, but might claim the protection of the law like a freeman; again, he could inherit property and acquire property, which a slave could not do. "Tribum habet" is remarkable, because it implies that the addictus did not undergo either the maxima or media capitis deminutio; he could not lose his rights of citizenship if he retained his tribe. But were these rights in abeyance, as the father's power over his children was suspended so long as he was

Roman commons, during this period, were finally lost to their country as free citizens; or was there any mitigation of the extreme rigor of their fate, and did the slave-debtor ever recover his personal liberty by consenting to become the client of his master? These are questions to which, I believe, it is impossible to give satisfactory answers.

The tribunes stop the election of curule magistrates.

To return, however, to our narrative; the promulgation of the three Licinian bills provoked, as was natural, the most determined opposition on the part of the aristocracy. Again the battle was to be fought in the assembly of the tribes; the great object of the patricians was to prevent the bills from being passed there. Some of the tribunes were attached to the aristocratical party, and these were persuaded to interpose their negative,[12] to forbid the reading of the bills to the people, and thus to stop them from ever being put to the vote. Licinius and Sextius, thus baffled, and being unable to proceed with their measures directly, determined to retaliate by obstructing, in like manner, the course of their opponents. When the month of July arrived, and the military tribunes for the last year went out of office, Licinius and Sextius forbade the election of any successors to them; they would allow no curule magistrates to be appointed; and they with the ædiles of the commons remained for a time the only magistrates of the republic.

But this time of anarchy did not last for five years.

But that this time continued for five years, according to the common report of the Roman Fasti and historians, is a thing altogether incredible.[13] An anarchy of five years; so long a period of the most extreme political excitement, nay, of the greatest extremities of revolutionary violence; the water boiling, as it were, with such intensity, and yet never boiling

a prisoner in the hands of the enemy, but returned to him as soon as he came home? or can we suppose that they continued to exist, and that a creditor might drive his addicti into the Forum to give their votes as he should require, and that such votes were legal? or would this be one of the many cases in which the officer who presided at the comitia exercised his discretion in objecting to them whenever he thought proper, or receiving them if it suited the interests of his party?

[12] Livy, VI. 35.

[13] It is utterly impossible to ascertain the real chronology of this period. The story of the five years' anarchy arose probably from an exaggerated interpretation of some expressions in the annalists, "that for five years the tribunes went on obstructing the elections," meaning, that whilst the contest lasted, this was their weapon, which they used from time to time, and never relinquished it without stipulating for some concession in turn. Afterwards, when the date of the Gaulish invasion had been fixed to the 2d year of the 98th Olympiad, and this was assumed as certain, the existence of the five years' anarchy was no longer questioned. The Fasti Capitolini acknowledge them as well as Livy; so also does Dionysius, for he speaks of the ten years' tribuneship of Licinius. (XIV. 22. Fragm. Mai.) And Polybius implies them, where he gives the dates of the several invasions of the Gauls, II. 18. The later writers, such as Eutropius, Cassidorus, and Rufus Festus, make the anarchy to have lasted for four years. So also does Zonaras; but then these four years are with him the whole period of the struggle, for he makes them to be followed immediately by the dictatorship of Camillus, and the pretended Gaulish invasion. They are then the years which, in the common Fasti, follow the five pretended years of anarchy; and which are marked by four colleges of military tribunes. It is to be observed, that about forty years afterwards we still find the consular year spoken of as beginning on the 1st of July (Livy, VIII. 20), which requires us to suppose either that one whole year passed without military tribunes, and that the elections were not again delayed; or that in the course of the five years' struggle, the elections were each year delayed for a time, so that at the end of the period the time lost in the several years, when added together, amounted to just a year in all, or, finally, we must believe that there was no period of anarchy at all; that the tribunes every year threatened to stop the elections, but allowed them, from consideration for the public service, to be held as usual, stipulating, perhaps, for the election of certain individuals known to be either favorable to their claims, or, at least, not violently adverse to them. Borghesi thinks that one college of military tribunes has been omitted by Livy in the year preceding the beginning of the anarchy, and he has restored it, partly from Diodorus, and partly from conjecture. Thus he places the election of L. Sextius as the first plebeian consul, exactly four-and-twenty years after the invasion of the Gauls. Striking out the five years of pretended anarchy, the consulship of L. Sextius falls nineteen years after the invasion of the Gauls, which agrees exactly with the chronology of Diodorus, when his confusions have been corrected, and the Gaulish invasion brought to its true date, according to his system, that is, to the third year of the 99th Olympiad. It agrees also with the statement of Orosius, III. 1, 4; and this is the nearest approximation to the truth at which I think it is possible to arrive; namely, to fix the consulship of L. Sextius in the 2d year of the 104th Olympiad, which is the date of the battle of Mantinea, and of the death of Epaminondas, 363–2, B. C.

over; a knot so perplexing, which none untied, and yet none were tempted to cut; a livelong strife, neither pacified by any compromise, nor exasperated into open violence, requires far better testimony than that of the Roman annalist removed two hundred years from the period of the struggle, to induce us to admit it as historical. What would have become of the ordinary course of business, if for five years the supreme courts of law had been closed, and the prætor's or prætorian tribune's judgment-seat so long left empty? Where was the restless enmity of the Latins, who, down to the beginning of this pretended anarchy, are described as so relentless in their hostilities, and who again appear in arms as soon as it is over? Unless the circumstances of the struggle were very different from all the representations of them which have reached our times, we can scarcely doubt that the Fasti, followed by Diodorus and Orosius, have preserved the truer account of these disputes; that one year at the most, perhaps even that not continuously, but at different intervals, was passed without curule magistrates; that the consulship of the first plebeian consul is to be placed not twenty-four but nineteen years only after the invasion of the Gauls.

Military tribunes again elected.

The length of the struggle, even when reduced in all from ten years to five, is sufficiently memorable. The tribunes had prevented the election of any curule magistrates; whether this state of things really lasted for a whole year, or only for a few weeks, it is not possible to determine; but it was ended by a fresh attack of the Latins on the old allies of Rome, the people of Tusculum;[14] the call for aid on the part of the Tusculans could not be resisted; the tribunes withdrew their veto, and the comitia for the election of military tribunes were duly held; but care was taken that only moderate men, or men friendly to the popular cause, should be chosen; there were two Valerii, the very name of whose house was an assurance to the commons, and a third tribune was Ser. Sulpicius, connected by marriage with C. Licinius, and with his patrician supporter, M. Fabius. After all, they were not allowed to enlist the soldiers for the legions without much opposition, nor probably without some stipulation on the part of the senate, that the military tribunes should not, like M. Postumius, abuse their power by visiting on their soldiers in the field the political offences of the commons at Rome. When the army did at last march, Tusculum was relieved, and Velitræ, which had been foremost in the attack upon it, was besieged in its turn; but the siege was not speedily ended, and the year came to a close before the place was reduced.

Plebeians chosen as commissioners of the sacred books.

Meanwhile the popular cause was gaining ground: amongst the new military tribunes was M. Fabius Ambustus,[15] the father-in-law of Licinius, and the zealous supporter of his bills, an advantage which more than counterbalanced the danger threatened by the appointment of two zealous members of the aristocratical party. These were A. Cornelius Cossus, who had been named dictator some years before to oppose the designs of M. Manlius, and Q. Quinctius Cincinnatus, of the house of that Cincinnatus, who, in his consulship, had proposed to repeal the laws passed in favor of the commons at Rome, by the votes of his soldiers, in an assembly to be held in the field beyond the protection of the tribunes, and who in his dictatorship had defended the murder of Sp. Mælius. Besides, the patrician interest in the college of the tribunes of the commons was becoming weaker and weaker; not only were Licinius and Sextius continually re-elected, but three others of their colleagues, it is said, now espoused their cause, and the remaining five, who had still pledged their veto to the patricians, so felt the difficulty of their position as to be obliged to lower their tone: their veto now professed only to suspend the discussion of the bills, and not to forbid it altogether: "A large proportion of the people,"[16] they said, "were engaged in foreign service at Velitræ: so great a question must be decided in a full assembly; till, therefore, the legions should return home, the bills must

[14] Livy, VI. 36.

[15] Livy, VI. 36.

[16] Livy, VI. 36.

not be brought forward." In such contests as these, delay is an advantage to the resisting party when the assailants are not keen in their attack, so that it may be possible to divert them from it by exhausting their patience; but when they are thoroughly in earnest, the flood gathers into a stronger head the longer it is opposed, and breaks in at last more overwhelmingly. So Licinius finding his three bills thus pertinaciously resisted, now proceeded to add to them a fourth,[17] enacting that the two keepers of the Sibylline books should be superseded for the future by a commission of ten, and that these ten should be chosen alike from the patricians and from the commons. The notion of a plebeian consul was most objected to on religious grounds; a plebeian, it was said, could not take the auspices, because his order could exercise no office connected with the service of the gods. Licinius resolved to destroy this objection most effectually, by attacking the religious exclusion itself. So far was he from allowing that a plebeian could not be consul because he could not be a priest, that he claimed for his order a share in the priestly offices as such; he required a distinct acknowledgment that the service of the gods might be directed, and their pleasure made known, by plebeian ministers as rightfully as by patricians. Perhaps, too, he had another and more immediate object; in seasons of extreme public danger, it was usual to consult the Sibylline books, and the keepers of them reported the answer which they found applicable to the emergency. Licinius might fear that this oracle, if left solely in the keeping of his adversaries, might be unfairly tampered with; and its answers shaped according to their interests. It was thus especially desirable that some of the commons should be made acquainted with their contents, to prevent the possibility of any forgery.

New military tribunes,[18] it is said, came into office before the army came home from Velitræ. This would be equally true whether we suppose that the soldiers came home to the harvest in July and August, or remained in the field till the close of the autumn. Amongst the new military tribunes we again find Ser. Sulpicius, and also Ser. Cornelius Maluginensis, a man so distinguished that he had already filled the same office six times before.[19] When the Licinian bills were again brought forward, the popular feeling in their favor was so strong as to make it apparent that the tribunes opposed to them would find it impossible to persist in interposing their negative; the patricians accordingly had recourse to their last expedient; it was pretended that the war with Velitræ required a dictator, and then Camillus, the bitterest enemy of the commons, was appointed to fill that office. It appears that he issued a proclamation[20] summoning the citizens within the military age to enlist and follow him to the field; whether his object was any thing more than delay must remain doubtful; but his edict was utterly disregarded, and the senate, to allay the storm, called upon him to resign his dictatorship. The Fasti recorded, that P. Manlius Capitolinus was named dictator shortly after, for the avowed purpose of putting an end to the domestic disturbances;[21] no record, however, remains to us of any thing that he did in his office; but it is evident that he was disposed to take no violent steps against the commons, for one branch of the Licinian family were his relations, and from them he chose C. Licinius Calvus, though a plebeian, to be his master of the horsemen. As if to show still further that the contest was drawing to a close, the bill[22] relating to the keepers of the Sibylline books was passed before the end of this year; but the other three were still delayed a little longer. Every nerve was, doubtless, strained by the patricians to preserve the exclusive possession of the consulship, and this was naturally the point to which

M. Camillus and P. Manlius dictators.

[17] Livy, VI. 37.

[18] Livy, VI. 38.

[19] This appears from the fragments of the Fasti Capitolini.

[20] Livy says, that he only threatened to issue such a proclamation, VI. 38. But Plutarch speaks of it as actually issued, προέγραψε στρατιᾶς κατάλογον.—Camillus, 39. And so the Fasti Capitolini; for the beginning of the line may be safely restored as Sigonius has supplied it. "*Ob Edict*um in milites ex S. C. abdicarunt."

[21] "Seditionisse dandæ et rei gerendæ causâ."

[22] Livy, VI. 42.

the mass of the commons attached the least importance, while they eagerly desired to pass the other two bills, relating to the public land, and to the debts. But the tribunes, being well aware of this feeling, and being anxious, on personal as well as public grounds, to secure the great point of an equal share of the highest magistracies, had resolved only to bring forward the three bills together, to be altogether either accepted or rejected. The more violent[23] of the aristocratical party remonstrated with hypocritical indignation against the arrogance of the tribunes, in thus dictating to the commons; and against their selfishness, in refusing to bring forward bills for the good of their whole order without stipulating at the same time for the gratification of their own ambition. But Licinius, trusting that the people would have the sense to reject the pretended sympathy of their worst enemies, persevered in his purpose; and told the commons in homely language,[24] "that they must be content to eat if they wished to drink."

On what grounds the better part of the aristocracy opposed the Licinian bills.

There is nothing viler than the spirit which actuates the vulgar of an aristocracy; we cannot sympathize with mere pride and selfishness, with the mere desire of keeping the good things of life to themselves, with the grasping monopoly of honors and power without nobleness of mind to appreciate the true value of either. All can conceive from what motive, with what temper, and in what language, the coarser spirits of the aristocratical party opposed the Licinian bills. But in all the uncorrupted aristocracies of the ancient world, there was another and a very different element also; there were men who opposed the advance of the popular party on the highest and purest principles; who regarded it as leading, in the end, to a general lawlessness, to a contempt for the institutions and moral feelings of men, and to a disbelief in the providence of the gods. Such men must have existed amongst the Roman patricians; and their views are well deserving of the notice of posterity. When Ser. Cornelius Maluginensis in his seventh military tribuneship opposed Licinius and Sextius in the assembly of the tribes, he might have expressed his feelings in something like the following language, and the soberest and wisest of the commons themselves would have been touched with a foreboding fear, while they could not help acknowledging that it was partly just:—[25]

Speech of Ser. Cornelius Maluginensis.

"I know, Quiretes, that ye account as an enemy to your order whoever will not agree to the passing of these three ordinances proposed by your tribunes, Caius Licinius and Lucius Sextius. And it may be that some who have spoken against them, are, in truth, not greatly your well-wishers; so that it is no marvel if your ill opinion of these should reach also to others who may appear to be treading in their steps. But I stand here before you as one who has been now, for the seventh time, chosen by you one of the tribunes of the soldiers;—six times have ye tried me before, in peace and in war, and if ye had ever found me to be your enemy, it had been ill done in you to have tried me yet again this seventh time. But if ye have believed me to have sought your good in times past, even believe this same thing of me now, though

[23] See the language which Livy has put into the mouth of Appius Claudius, VI. 40, 41.

[24] Εἰπὼν, ὡς οὐκ ἂν πίοιεν εἰ μὴ φάγοιεν. Dion Cassius, Fragm. Peiresc. 33, as corrected by Reimar.

[25] I am far from wishing to introduce into history the practice of writing fictitious speeches, as a mere variety upon the narrative, or an occasion for displaying the eloquence of the historian. But when the peculiar views of any party or time require to be represented, it seems to me better to do this dramatically, by making one of the characters of the story express them in the first person, than to state as a matter of fact, that such and such views were entertained. I believe it to be perfectly true, that the better part of the opposition to the advance of popular principles in the ancient world was grounded on the view of human affairs which I have ascribed to Ser. Maluginensis. And this view is exceedingly deserving of notice, because it so strongly illustrates one of the great uses of the Christian revelation; namely, that it provides a fixed moral standard independently of human law, and therefore allows human law to be altered as circumstances may require, without the danger of destroying thereby the greatest sanction of human conduct. I have not, then, put modern arguments into the mouth of a Roman of the fourth century of Rome; but I have made him deliver arguments not only which might have been, but which were undoubtedly used then, and which are so characteristic of ancient times, that they could not be repeated now without absurdity.

I may speak that which in the present disposition of your minds ye may perchance not willingly hear.

"Now, as regarding the ordinances for the relief of poor debtors, and for restraining the occupation of the public land, I could be well content that they should pass. I know that ye have borne much, and not through any fault of yours; and if any peaceable way can be found out whereby ye may have relief, it will be more welcome to no man than to me. I like not the taking of usury, and I think that ye may well be lightened of some part of the burden of your taxes by our turning the fruits of the public land to the service of the commonwealth. But if ye ask me, Why then dost thou oppose these ordinances? I must truly bid you go to your tribunes, Caius and Lucius, and demand of them your answer.[26] They can tell you that they will not suffer me to give my vote for these ordinances, nor will they suffer you to have your will. For they have said that these ordinances shall not have our votes, neither yours nor mine, unless we will vote also for a third ordinance, which they have bound to them so closely, as that none, they say, shall tear them asunder. Now, as touching this third ordinance, Quirites, I will deal honestly with you: there is not the thing in all the world so precious or so terrible as shall move me, either for love or for fear, to give my vote in its behalf.

"What is there, then, ye will say to me, in this third ordinance which thou so mislikest? I will answer you in few words. I mislike the changing of the laws of our fathers, especially when these laws have respect to the worship of the gods. Many things, I know, are ordered wisely for one generation, which, notwithstanding, are by another generation no less wisely ordered otherwise. There is room in human affairs for change; there is room also for unchangeableness. And where shall we seek for that which is unchangeable, but in those great laws which are the very foundation of the commonwealth; most of all in those which, having to do with the immortal gods, should be also themselves immortal. Now it belongs to these laws that the office of consul,[27] which is as it were the shadow of the majesty of Jove himself, should be held only by men of the houses of the patricians. Ye know how that none but the patricians may take any office of priesthood for the worship of the gods of Rome, nor interpret the will of the gods by augury. For the gods being themselves many, have set also upon earth many races of men and many orders; and one race may not take to itself the law of another race, nor one order the law of another order. Each has its own law, which was given to it from the beginning; and if we change these the whole world will be full of confusion. It is our boast[28] that we Romans have greater power over our children than the men of any other nation: with us the son is ever, so long as he lives, subject to his father's will, except his father be pleased to give him his freedom. Now, if a son were to ask why he should not, when he is come to full age, be free from his father's authority, what answer should we give than this, that the law of the Romans gave to fathers this power over their children, that to this law he had been born, as surely as to those other laws of his nature which appointed him to be neither a god nor a beast, but a man. These laws are not of to-day, nor of yesterday; we know of no time when

[26] This attack on the tribunes for their refusal to separate the three bills from each other is put by Livy into the mouth of Appius Claudius, VII. 40. It would, of course, be pressed by all the opponents of the measures; and it is too much to expect that even the best of the aristocratical party would have scrupled to avail themselves of it, although they would have dwelt on this point in a very different manner from their more violent associates.

[27] The religious argument, that a plebeian could not be created consul without profanation, is to be found twice in Livy, in the arguments used against the Canuleian bills, IV. 2–6, and again in the speech of Appius against the Licinian bills, VI. 41. The principle implied in this argument is not to be found in Livy, but is important to be stated, because it is as characteristic of polytheism, as the opposite principle, that all men are equal before God, except so far as their own conduct creates a difference between them, is characteristic of Christianity.

[28] "Fere enim nulli alii sunt homines, qui talem in filios suos habent potestatem qualem nos habemus."—Gaius, Institut. I. § 55.

they have not been: may neither we nor our children ever see that time when they shall have ceased to be!

"But if the mere will of the men of this generation can set aside these laws: if, breaking through that order which the gods have given to us, we elect for consuls those whom the gods allow not; see what will be the end. Within these fifteen years four tribes of strangers have been added to the commons of this city. Ye know, also, that many enfranchised slaves, men with no race, with no law, I had well-nigh said with no gods, are, from time to time, enrolled amongst our citizens. If all these are admitted into our commonwealth, to become Romans, and to live according to the laws of the Romans, it is well. But if we may alter these laws; if strangers come among us not to receive our custom, but to give us theirs, what thing is there so surely fixed in our state, that it shall not be torn up at our fancy? what law will be left for us to follow, save the law of our own fancies? Truly, if the gods had sent down one from heaven to declare to us their will; if, as our own laws were written by the decemvirs upon the twelve tables, so there were any tables to be found on which the gods had written their laws for all mankind, then we might change our own laws as we would, and the law of the gods would still be a guide for us. But as the gods speak to us, and will speak only through the laws[29] of our fathers, if we once dare to cast these aside, there is no stay or rest for us any more; we must wander in confusion forever.

"Nor is it a little thing that by breaking through the law of our fathers, and choosing men of the commons for consuls, we shall declare that riches[30] are to be honored above that rule of order which the gods have given to us. Riches, even now, can do much for their possessor, but they cannot raise him beyond the order in which he was born; they cannot buy for him—shame were it if they could!—the sovereign state of the consulship, nor the right to offer sacrifice to the gods of Rome. But once let a plebeian be consul, and riches will be the only god which we shall all worship. For then he who has money will need no other help to raise him from the lowest rank to the highest. And then we may suffer such an evil as that which is now pressing upon the cities of the Greeks in the great island of Sicily. There may arise a man from the lowest of the people with much craft and great riches, and make himself what the Greeks call a tyrant.[31] Ye scarcely know what the name means; a vile person seizing upon the state and power of a king, trampling upon all law, confounding all order, persecuting the noble and good, encouraging the evil, robbing the rich, insulting the poor, living for himself alone[32] and for his own desires, neither fearing the gods, nor regarding men. This is the curse with which the gods have fitly punished other people for desiring freedom more than the law of their fathers gave them. May we never commit the like folly to bring upon ourselves such a punishment!

"Therefore, Quirites, unless your tribunes can find for us another law of the gods to guide us in the place of that law which they are destroying, I cannot consent to that ordinance which they are so zealously calling upon us to pass. Not because I am proud, not because I love not the commons, but because, above all things else on earth, I love and honor law; and if we pull down law and exalt[33]

[29] *Τοῖς ἐρωτῶσι πῶς δεῖ ποιεῖν ἢ περὶ θυσίας ἢ περὶ προγόνων θεραπείας ἢ περὶ ἄλλου τινὸς τῶν τοιούτων, . . . ἡ Πυθία νόμῳ πόλεως ἀναιρεῖ ποιοῦντας εὐσεβῶς ἂν ποιεῖν.*—Xenophon, Memorab. I. 3, § 1. Compare the language of Archidamus, and of Cleon in Thucydides, I. 84, III. 37, and the argument against any alteration in the laws given by Aristotle in his review of the theoretical commonwealth of Hippodamus. *Ὁ γὰρ νόμος ἰσχὺν οὐδεμίαν ἔχει πρὸς τὸ πείθεσθαι, πλὴν παρὰ τὸ ἔθος. τοῦτο δ' οὐ γίγνεται εἰ μὴ διὰ χρόνου πλῆθος.*—Politic. II. 6.

[30] Compare the sentiments of Theognis and Pindar on this point, who constantly lament the increasing honor paid to riches in comparison with the declining estimation of noble birth.

[31] Thucyd. I. 13. *Δυνατωτέρας δὲ γιγνομένης τῆς Ἑλλάδος καὶ τῶν χρημάτων τὴν κτῆσιν ἔτι μᾶλλον ἢ πρότερον ποιουμένης τὰ πολλὰ τυραννίδες ἐν ταῖς πόλεσι καθίσταντο, τῶν προσόδων μειζόνων γιγνομένων.*

[32] Thucyd. I. 17. *Τὸ ἐφ' ἑαυτῶν μόνον προορώμενοι, ἔς τε τὸ σῶμα καὶ ἐς τὸ τὸν ἴδιον οἶκον αὔξειν δι' ἀσφαλείας ὅσον ἐδύναντο μάλιστα τὰς πόλεις ᾤκουν.*—Compare the description of a tyrant in Herodotus, III. 80, and V. 92.

[33] This is what Archidamus and Cleon, strik-

our own will in the place of it, truth, and modesty, and soberness, and all virtue will perish from amongst us; and falsehood, and insolence, and licentiousness, and all other wickedness will possess us wholly. And instead of that greater freedom which ye long for, the end will be faction and civil bloodshed,[34] and, last of all, that which is worse than all the rest, a lawless tyranny."

What was to be said in answer to the arguments of the speech of Ser. Cornelius.

To such language as this the tribunes might have replied by denying that its principle was applicable to the particular point at issue: they might have urged that the admission of the commons to the consulship was not against the original and unalterable laws of the Romans, inasmuch as strangers had been admitted even to be kings at Rome; and the good king Servius, whose memory was so fondly cherished by the people, was, according to one tradition, not only a stranger by birth, but a slave. And further they might have answered, that the law of intermarriage between the patricians and commons was a breaking down of the distinction of orders, and implied that there was no such difference between them as to make it profane in either to exercise the functions of the other. But as to the principle itself, there is no doubt that it did contain much truth. The ancient heathen world craved, what all men must crave, an authoritative rule of conduct; and not finding it elsewhere, they imagined it to exist in the fundamental and original laws of each particular race or people. To destroy this sanction without having any thing to substitute in its place was deeply perilous; and reason has been but too seldom possessed of power sufficient to recommend its truths to the mass of mankind by their own sole authority. On the other hand, good and wise men could not but see that national law was evidently, in many cases, directly opposed to divine law;[35] and that obedience and respect for it were absolutely injurious to men's moral nature; they felt sure, moreover, that the very truth was discoverable by man, and trusted that it must at last force its way if the ground were but cleared for its reception. They hoped, besides, as was the case with Aristotle, that by gaining the ear of statesmen they might see a system of national education established,[36] which would give truth all the power of habit; and knowing too that universal law, that if man does not grow better he must grow worse, and that to remain absolutely unchanged is impossible; they ventured to advance towards a higher excellence, even amidst the known dangers of the attempt, in the faith that God would, sooner or later, point out the means of overcoming them.

The events of the last year of this long struggle are even more obscure than those of the years preceding it. P. Manlius,[37] the late dictator P. Valerius, who had been five times tribune before, two Cornelii, Aulus and Marcus, the one of

ing specimens of the noblest and vilest advocates of an unchanged system, as opposed to one of continual progress, call "the wishing to be wiser than the laws." Archidamus boasts that the Spartans were trained *ἀμαθέστερον τῶν νόμων τῆς ὑπεροψίας*.—Thucyd. I. 84. Cleon describes good citizens as men who *ἀπιστοῦντες τῇ ἐξ ἑαυτῶν ξυνέσει, ἀμαθέστεροι τῶν νόμων ἀξιοῦσιν εἶναι*.—Thucyd. III. 37.

[34] So Theognis,

Κύρνε, κύει πόλις ἥδε· δέδοικα δὲ μὴ τέκῃ ἄνδρα
Εὐθυντῆρα κακῆς ὕβριος ὑμετέρης.
'Εκ τῶν γὰρ στάσις ἐστὶ, καὶ ἔμφυλοι φόνοι ἀνδρῶν·
Μούναρχος δὲ πόλει μήποτε τῇδε ἅδοι. 39–51.

[35] Hence the distinction insisted on by the philosophers between universal and municipal law, between natural and political justice.—See Aristotle, Ethics, V. 7, Rhetoric, I. 14. Hence the interest of the story of Antigone, who is represented as breaking the law of her country because it was at variance with the law of the gods: Sophocles invests her character with all the sacredness of a martyr; but Æschylus, who more entirely identified the laws of the land with the highest standard of human virtue, ends his tragedy of the "Seven Chiefs who warred on Thebes" with the expression of the opposite sentiment, which is evidently uttered from his heart. Half of the chorus go with Antigone to bury Polynices in defiance of the king's decree; urging in their justification:—

καὶ γὰρ γενεᾷ
κοῖνον τόδ' ἄχος, καὶ πόλις ἄλλως
ἄλλοτ' ἐπαινεῖ τὰ δίκαια.

But the other half follow the body of Eteocles, whose funeral was sanctioned by the law, exclaiming:—

ἡμεῖς δ' ἅμα τῷδ', ὥσπερ τε πόλις
καὶ τὸ δίκαιον ξυνεπαινεῖ.
μετὰ γὰρ μάκαρας καὶ Διὸς ἰσχὺν
ὅδε Καδμείων ἤρυξε πόλιν
μὴ 'νατραπῆναι, μηδ' ἀλλοδαπῶν
κύματι φωτῶν
κατακλυσθῆναι τὰ μάλιστα.

[36] Ethic. Nicomach. X. 9. *'Εκ νέου δὲ ἀγογῆς ὀρθῆς τυχεῖν πρὸς ἀρετὴν χαλεπὸν, μὴ ὑπὸ τοιούτοις τραφέντα νόμοις . . . διὸ νόμοις δεῖ τετάχθαι τὴν τροφὴν καὶ τὰ ἐπιτηδεύματα· οὐκ ἔσται γὰρ λυτηρὰ συνήθη γενόμενα.*

[37] Livy, VI. 42.

Last college of military tribunes. End of the contest. Institution of the prætorship.

the family of Cossus, the other of that of the Maluginenses; M. Geganius Macerinus, and L. Veturius, formed the last college of military tribunes which was to be known in Rome. Manlius and Valerius were likely to favor the bills; of Veturius we know little; but the two Cornelii[38] and Geganius, if they were true to the political sentiments of their families, would be strongly opposed to them. But the story of this year is again perplexed by an alleged dictatorship of M. Camillus, and a pretended inroad of the Gauls into Latium. It is said that an alarm of an approaching invasion from the Gauls led to the appointment of Camillus; and this may be true; for the senate would gladly avail themselves of the slightest rumor as an excuse for investing him with absolute power; but that the Gauls really did invade Latium at this time, and were defeated by Camillus in a bloody battle[39] near Alba, seems to be merely a fabrication of the memorials of the house of the Furii, the last which occurs in the story of Camillus, and not the least scrupulous. Setting aside this pretended Gaulish war, the annalists merely related, that after most violent contests, the Licinian bills were carried;[40] this must have taken place before the tribunes went out of office in December; and apparently they were not again re-elected, as if in the full confidence that the battle was won. But when the comitia for the election of consuls were held, according to the new law, and the centuries had chosen L. Sextius to be the first plebeian consul, the storm broke out again with more violence than ever, owing to the refusal of the curiæ to confirm the election and invest him with the imperium. No particulars are recorded of the following crisis; matters, it is said, came almost to a secession of the commons, and "to other terrible threats of civil contentions;"[41] words which seem to mean that the secession would not have been confined to mere passive resistance, but would have led to an actual civil war. But Camillus, who was still, it is said, dictator, acted on this occasion, if we may believe any story of which he is the subject, the part of mediator; both sides made some concessions: the patricians were to confirm the election of the plebeian consul; but the ordinary judicial power was to be separated from the consul's office, and conferred from hence-

[38] The two Cornelii Maluginenses were amongst the most zealous supporters of the second decemvirate, one of them being actually a colleague of Appius Claudius, at a time when even the patricians themselves were generally disgusted with it; and a Cornelius Cossus had been appointed dictator to oppose the supposed designs of Manlius. The consulship of M. Geganius Macerinus, two years after the end of the decemvirate, is marked as the period at which the reaction in favor of the patricians began; and the consuls of that year are contrasted with those of the year preceding, who are described as moderate men, not much inclined to either party. And M. Geganius was one of those censors who treated the dictator Mam. Æmilius with such unjust severity, because he had abridged the duration of the censor's office.

[39] The Fasti Capitolini state that Camillus was appointed dictator this year, "rei gerundæ causâ," that is, "to command an army in the field," as distinguished from the other objects for which a dictator was sometimes appointed, such as, "seditionis sedandæ causâ," "comitiorum habendorum causâ," or "clavi figendi causâ." But as the fragments of the Fasti are in this place very much mutilated, we cannot tell whether they contained any mention of his victory and triumph over the Gauls or no. Probably, however, they did, for the story seems to have established itself in the Roman history very generally; it is mentioned by Livy, by Plutarch, by Dionysius in the fragments of his 14th book, by Zonaras, by Appian, in a fragment which clearly refers to it, IV. 7, and it is implied, I think, in the short summary of Florus, I. 13. On the other hand, there is the notorious falsehood of the other stories of Gaulish victories gained by Camillus; there is the positive statement of Polybius, that the Gauls did not invade Latium again till thirty years after their first irruption; and that when they did come, and advanced to Alba, the scene of Camillus' pretended victory over them, the Romans did not dare to meet them in the field.—Polyb. II. 18. There is also the statement of Aristotle, quoted by Plutarch, Camillus, 22, and agreeing so completely with Polybius, "that Rome was delivered from the Gauls by Lucius; that is, by Lucius Camillus, the son of Marcus, who repelled the Gauls in the year 406 (or more properly 401), the first time, according to Polybius, that the Romans ever did meet them with advantage. Finally, the common stories of this pretended war are at variance with one another, some placing the famous combat of T. Manlius with the Gaulish giant in this year, and making the Gauls advance as far as the Anio; while others laid the scene of Camillus' victory on the Alban Hills, and placed the combat of Manlius ten years later. I believe, therefore, that the accounts of this last dictatorship of Camillus are as little to be relied on as those of his pretended defeat of Brennus, and freeing Rome from the shame of paying a ransom.

[40] Livy, VI. 42.

[41] "Terribilesque alias minas civilium certaminum."—Livy, VI. 42.

forth on a new magistrate, who was always to be a patrician, and who being appointed without a colleague was not to be called consul but prætor; a title of high dignity, which had been anciently borne by the consuls, and expressed particularly their supreme power, as the captains or leaders of the commonwealth. The first person who filled this new office[42] was Sp. Camillus, the son of the dictator; a compliment which his old father well deserved, if the last public act of his life of more than fourscore years was the reconciling of the quarrels of his countrymen, and the bringing a struggle of five years to a peaceful and happy termination.

Institution of the Curule Ædileship.

This union of the two orders was acknowledged also in the religious ceremonies of the republic. A temple[43] was built on the Capitoline Hill looking towards the Forum, and dedicated to "Concord;" and a fourth day was added to the three hitherto devoted to the celebration of the great or Roman games; as if to signify that the commons were from henceforth to take their place as a part of the Roman people, by the side of the three old patrician tribes, the Ramnenses, Titienses, and Luceres. To preside at these games, two new magistrates were appointed under the name of Curule Ædiles; and these were to be elected in alternate years from the patricians and from the commons. Their other duties and powers it is very difficult to define; but it appears that they exercised for a time[44] the jurisdiction which had formerly belonged to the Quæstores Parricidii, that they tried criminals for various offences, and if their sentence were appealed against, they appeared as prosecutors of the appellant before the comitia of the centuries.

The completion of the form of the constitution.

Thus, with no recorded instance of bloodshed committed by either party, the five years' conflict upon the Licinian bills was happily ended. From this time forward the consulship continued without interruption to the end of the republic; and, with the exception of a short period to be hereafter noticed, it was duly shared by the commons. The form of the constitution, such as we find it described in those times which began to have a contemporary literature, was now in its leading points completed; but many years must yet elapse before we can do more than trace the outline of institutions and of actions; the spirit and character of the times, and still more of particular individuals, must yet, for another century, be discerned but dimly.

[42] Livy, VII. 1.

[43] Plutarch, Camillus, 42. Livy, VI. 42.

[44] See Niebuhr, Vol. III. p. 42, and seqq. To what is there said, it may be added that the title Ædilis was common amongst the magistrates of the municipia and colonies at a later period; that we meet frequently, in inscriptions, with the title "Ædilis juri dicundo," that the ædiles in the municipia had a "tribunal," or judgment-seat, as a mark of their high dignity; and as Savigny thinks, they in the earlier period of the empire possessed even the "imperium." Savigny, Geschichte des Rom. Rechts im Mittelalt. Vol. I. p. 36. The two Scipios of the fifth century, whose tombs and epitaphs have been preserved to us, have their ædileships as well as their censorships and consulships recorded. This seems to imply that the office then was held in higher estimation than when Cicero could call the curule Ædile "paullo amplius quam privatus."—Verr. Act. I. 13.

CHAPTER XXVII.

GENERAL HISTORY, DOMESTIC AND FOREIGN, FROM THE ADMISSION OF THE COMMONS TO THE CONSULSHIP TO THE BEGINNING OF THE FIRST SAMNITE WAR—EVASION OF THE LICINIAN LAWS—WARS WITH THE GAULS, TARQUINIENSIANS, AND VOLSCIANS.—A. U. C. 389–412, LIVY; 384–407, NIEBUHR.

μυρίας δ μυρίος
χρόνος τεκνοῦται νύκτας ἡμέρας τ' ἰων,
ἐν αἷς τὰ νῦν ξύμφωνα δεξιώματα
δόρει διασκεδῶσιν ἐκ σμικροῦ λόγου.

Sophocles, Œdip. Colon. v. 617.

Chronology of the Licinian laws.

The first plebeian consulship coincides, as nearly as the chronology can be ascertained, with the great battle of Mantinea and the death of Epaminondas. At this point Xenophon ended his Grecian history; and as the writings of Theopompus and of the authors who followed him have not been preserved to us, we here lose the line of contemporary historians in Greece, after having enjoyed their guidance during a period of nearly one hundred and forty years. More than that length of time must still elapse before we can gain the assistance of a contemporary writer, even though a foreigner, for any part of the history of Rome.

Contrast between our knowledge of the Greeks and of the Romans at this period.

But as I have before observed that the Greek poets, long before the time of Herodotus, have done more than any mere annalists could have done to acquaint us with the most valuable part of history, that which relates to a people's mental powers and habits of thinking, so, when we close the Hellenics of Xenophon, we find in the great orators and philosophers of the next half century more than enough to compensate for the want of regular historians. What contemporary record of mere battles and sieges, of wars and factions, could afford such fulness of knowledge as to the real state of Greece, in all points that are most instructive, as we derive from the pamphlets, as they may be called, of Isocrates, from the dialogues of Plato, the moral and political treatises of Aristotle, and the various public and private orations of Isæus, Æschines, and Demosthenes? It is when we think of the overflowing wealth of Greece, that we feel most keenly the absolute poverty of Rome. The fifth century from the foundation of the city produced neither historian, poet, orator, nor philosopher; its whole surviving literature consists of three or four lines of a monumental inscription, and a short decree of the senate, the date of which is not, however, ascertained. I cannot too often remind the reader of the total want of all materials for a lively picture of the Roman character and manners under which we unavoidably labor. Still we are, as it were, working our way to light; the greatness of Rome is beginning to unfold itself; we are approaching the Samnite and the Latin wars, of which the first trained the Romans to perfection in all military virtues, by opposing to them the bravest and most unwearied of enemies; while the latter consolidated forever the mass of their power near home, by securing to them the aid of the most faithful of allies. And the great domestic struggles are almost ended; what required direct interference has been, for the most part, remedied; it must be left for time to complete the union of the two orders of the commonwealth, now that they have been freed from those positive causes of irritation which kept them so long not only distinct from each other, but at enmity.

We have seen the Licinian bills become laws of the land; we have next to endeavor to trace their results; to see how far they were fairly carried into effect, and what was their success in remedying the evils which had made them appear to be necessary.

Effects of the Licinian laws.

I. The Licinian law, which opened the consulship to the commons, was regularly observed during a period of eleven years.[1] After that time the patricians ventured to disregard it, so that in the fifteen following years, down to the great Latin war, it was violated six or seven several times.[2] But after the Latin war it was observed regularly, and we can only find one or two doubtful instances of a violation of it. In the twenty years of plebeian consulship which occur before the Latin war, there appear, however, the names of only eight plebeian families; the Sextii, the Genucii, the Licinii, the Pœtelii, the Popillii, the Plautii, the Marcii, and the Decii: two of these, the Marcii[3] and the Popillii, enjoyed the consulship four times each; the Genucii[4] and Plautii obtained it three times each; the Licinii and Pœtelii twice each; and the Sextii and Decii once each. Of the individual consuls none were eminent, except M. Popillius Lænas, C. Marcius Rutilus, and P. Decius Mus; the two former were each four times elected consul, and C. Marcius obtained besides the offices of dictator[5] and censor, being the first commoner who attained to either of them. The fame of P. Decius has been still greater, and more enduring; his self-devotion in the Latin war placed him in the fond remembrance of his countrymen on a level with the greatest names of Roman history, and from that time forward it could not be denied that commoners were to be found as worthy of the consulship as the proudest and noblest of the Fabii or the Cornelii.

1. Of the law respecting the consulship.

Thus it appears that the Licinian law was not passed till the state of the commonwealth was ripe for it. There were families amongst the commons fit to receive the highest nobility; whilst, on the other hand, so sound was the public feeling, that we read of no mere demagogue raised to the consulship as the reward of his turbulence and faction; even the two tribunes who had conducted the long contest with the patricians were each only once elected consul, and none of the other plebeian consuls are known to have been tribunes at all. No constitutional reform could be more happy than this; nothing could be more just or more salutary than to open the honors of the state to an order sufficiently advanced to be capable of wielding political power, but retaining so much simplicity and soberness of mind as to be in no danger of abusing it.

It was a seasonable and wholesome measure.

II. It has ever been found that social evils are far more difficult to cure than such as are merely political. It was easier to adjust the political relations of the patricians and commons, than the social relations of the great and the humble, the creditor and the debtor. We are told that the agrarian law of Licinius was carried; but what amount of public land was allotted under it to the poorer commons we have no means of discovering. Niebuhr concludes from a passage in Laurentius Lydus,[6] that now as in the time of Ti. Gracchus

2. Of the Agrarian law.

[1] Livy, VII. 18.

[2] That is to say, in the year 400, when a Sulpicius and Valerius were consuls, and in the two following years; again in 404, when a Sulpicius and a Quinctius were elected; then in 406, in 410, and lastly, in 412. This would amount to seven instances, but in the year 401 some annals made a plebeian, M. Popillius, the colleague of M. Fabius; although most authorities give this as a year of two patrician consuls. See Livy, VII. 18.

[3] C. Marcius Rutilus was consul in 398, in 403, in 411, and 413. And M. Popillius Lænas was consul in 396, in 399, in 405, and in 407.

[4] One of the Genucian family was consul in 390, 392, and 393, and a Plautius was consul in 397, in 408, and in 414.

[5] He was dictator in 399 (Livy, VII. 17), and censor in 404 (Livy, VII. 22).

[6] De Magistratibus, I. 35. *Εἶτα ἐπὶ πενταετίαν ἀναρχίαν ἐδυστύχει τὸ πολίτευμα· καὶ τὸ λοιπὸν τρεῖς νομοθέτας καὶ δικαστὰς προβληθῆναι πρὸς βραχὺ συμβέβηκε διὰ τὰς ἐμφυλίους στάσεις.* Niebuhr thinks that this is taken from Junius Gracchanus, and that it relates to the period immediately following the anarchy. But Lydus, whose confusions and blunders make his authority very suspicious, intended, I believe, only to notice all the extraordinary magistrates who had at any time been appointed at Rome; and thus after mentioning the famous decemvirs, he goes on to speak of the pontifices, and ædiles, as being in some sort magistrates; and then he names the military tribunes, and the five years' anarchy, as another anomalous period; and lastly, the

a commission of three persons was appointed, with those large powers ordinarily granted to a Roman commission, for the purpose of carrying into effect the new agrarian law, and that Licinius himself was one of these commissioners, which would account for his not having been chosen rather than Sextius to be the first plebeian consul. It would be the business of this commission to take away all public land occupied by any individual above the prescribed amount of five hundred jugera, and from the land thus become disposable, to assign portions to the poorer citizens. But their task would not be easy; for attempts of every sort would be made to defeat or to evade the law: land which had passed by purchase from one occupier to another, and which had been possessed without dispute for many years, would acquire, even in the eyes of unconcerned persons, something of the character of property; while in the feeling of those who held it, to take it from them without offering them any compensation was no better than robbery. Besides, the occupation of the public land had been for some time past, probably since the period of the last war with Veii, permitted to the commons as well as to the patricians; so that the occupiers were a larger and more influential body of men than they had ever been before, and the commissioners must have found it proportionably hard to compel them to observe the letter of the law.

Difficulties in carrying it into effect.

Thus, although we are told[7] that the patricians and commons, when the law was passed, had solemnly sworn to observe it, and though a penalty had been denounced against any violation of it, yet the commission, it seems, found it impossible to carry it into effect. The difficulties in the way of a speedy settlement were indeed manifold. In the first place, many of the occupiers emancipated their sons,[8] and then made over to them the land in their occupation beyond the legal amount of five hundred jugera; and in the same way probably their sheep and oxen, which were fed on the public pasture land, were also entered in the names of their emancipated sons, when they exceeded the number fixed by the law. In this manner large portions of land must have been retained in private hands, which the law had expected to make available for allotments to the commons. But further, the occupiers urged that they had laid out money of their own on the land which they occupied; they had erected buildings on it and planted trees; were they to lose these without receiving any equivalent? They were willing to resign what belonged to the state, but the improvements of the property had been made at their own expense, and on these the state could have no claim. Besides, it was not always easy to ascertain what was public land and what was private; for portions of both being held by the same persons, the boundary stones which, according to Roman practice, were to serve as so sure a mark of private property had been taken up, or suffered to be destroyed; and in the want of any regular surveys of the ground, the uncertainty and occasions of litigation were endless. In short, we may suppose that, generally speaking, the occupiers retained their land, either in their sons' names or in their own, and that the agrarian law of Licinius did but little towards relieving the distress of the commons.

C. Licinius himself is prosecuted for evading it.

We are told that nine years after the first plebeian consulship, in the year 398,[9] C. Licinius was himself impeached by M. Popillius Lænas, one of the curule ædiles, for having violated his own law by occupying a thousand jugera of the public land, half of which he held in his son's

government of the triumvirs, by whom he means, I believe, no other persons than the famous triumviri reipublicæ constituendæ, Augustus, Antonius, and Lepidus. But although I do not think that Lydus spoke of any extraordinary commissioners appointed after the passing of the Licinian laws, yet an agrarian law on an extensive scale necessarily implied a commission, whether of three, five, ten, or even fifteen members, to carry its provisions into effect. And the powers of such a commission, as may be seen from Cicero's speeches against the agrarian law of Rullus, were very great and very important; and it is extremely probable that Licinius would be appointed one of its members, almost as a matter of course.

[7] Appian, Bell. Civil. I. 8.

[8] Appian, Bell. Civil. I. 8. Livy, VII. 16.

[9] Livy, VII. 16.

name, having emancipated him in order to evade the law. Licinius was condemned to pay a fine of ten thousand ases; but in the meagerness of our knowledge of these times, we cannot tell in what spirit the prosecution was conducted; whether it originated in personal feelings of enmity to Licinius, or whether it was merely one out of a number of other prosecutions carried on with the intention of trying once more to carry the agrarian law into full effect. We know nothing of the character of M. Popillius; but from his having been chosen four times consul, and once curule ædile, it is scarcely possible to conceive that he could have been particularly obnoxious to the patricians; whereas we know that they never forgave any man who was an active supporter of an agrarian law. I am inclined to think therefore that the prosecution of Licinius[10] was rather instigated by a desire to lower his credit, and to punish him for his obnoxious laws, than by any wish to see those laws enforced more strictly.

3. Of the law for the relief of distressed debtors.

III. The failure of the agrarian law was of itself sufficient to prevent the success of the third of the Licinian bills, that for the relief of distressed debtors. It was something, no doubt, to free them from the double burden of both interest and principal, by deducting from the principal of every debt what had been already paid in interest, and to allow a lengthened term of payment, during which they might be free from the extremest severity of the law. But to men who had nothing, and had no means of earning any thing, this lengthened term was but a respite, and their debts, even when reduced by the deduction of the interest already paid, were more than they were able to discharge. Grants of public land made at such a moment might have delivered them from their difficulties; but as these were withheld, the evil after a short pause returned with all its former virulence. The Licinian law was not prospective, nor did it lay any restriction on the amount of interest which might be legally demanded. Accordingly, to pay their reduced debt within the term fixed by the law, the debtors were obliged to incur fresh obligations, and to give such interest as their creditors might choose to demand. Things grew worse and worse, till in the year 398, nine years after the passing of the Licinian laws, a bill was brought forward by two[11] of the tribunes, M. Duilius and L. Mænius, to restore the limitation of interest formerly fixed by the twelve tables, namely, the rate of the twelfth part of the sum borrowed, fœnus unciarium. But still this did not reach the root of the evil; the very principal itself could not be paid, and the number of nexi, or persons who were pledged to their creditors, and were to become their slaves if the debt was not discharged within a certain time, went on continually increasing.

Commission of five appointed. Its beneficial effects up to a certain point.

At length, in the year 403, fourteen years after the passing of the Licinian laws, the consuls, P. Valerius and C. Marcius Rutilus, the latter himself a plebeian, the former a member of that family which had always been eminent amongst the patricians for its constant zeal

[10] We should be glad, however, to be able to excuse the conduct of Licinius, which cannot be justified by any want of sincerity in the motives of his prosecutor. Ti. Gracchus made it a provision of his agrarian law that the commissioners for enforcing it should be a permanent magistracy, to be filled up by new elections from year to year. And it was this very clause which deprived the opponents of his law of all hope of evading it. (Appian, Bell. Civil. I. 10.) The commission in the present case was probably not renewed after the first year, and then the law became powerless. It is possible that the evasion of it practised by Licinius was very generally adopted; and he may have excused himself by that common sophism, that as the evil could not be prevented, he might as well share in the benefits to be derived from it. This is not conscientious reasoning certainly, but it is too common; and Licinius may well have deceived himself by it. His enemies would naturally triumph in his violation of his own law, and would care little though they themselves had set him the example of breaking it.

[11] Livy, VII. 16. It is pleasant to observe the traces of an hereditary political character in so many of the Roman families. The Mænii and Duilii appear to have been remarkable for their moderation and integrity; the conduct of the tribune M. Duilius, after the overthrow of the decemvirs' tyranny, has already been noticed; and another Duilius was appointed one of the five commissioners in 403, for the relief of the distressed commons, and distinguished himself in that office by his impartiality and diligence. We have seen also a Mænius taking part with the patricians against the dangerous designs of M. Manlius; and C. Mænius, the

for the welfare of the commons, determined that the government should itself interfere to relieve a distress so great and so inveterate. Five commissioners were appointed,[12] three plebeians and two patricians, with the title of mensarii, or bankers. These established their banks or tables in the Forum, like ordinary bankers, and offered in the name of the government to accommodate the debtors with ready money on the most liberal terms. It appears that one cause of the prevailing distress was the scarcity of the circulating medium.[13] A debtor, therefore, even though he possessed property in land, might yet be practically insolvent, inasmuch as he could not, except at an enormous loss, convert his land into money. Here, therefore, the five commissioners interposed: they furnished the debtor with ready money, when he had any property to offer as a security, or any friend who would be security for him; and they ordered that land and cattle should be received in payment at a certain valuation. In this manner much property, which had hitherto been unavailable, was brought into circulation; land and cattle became legal tender at a certain fixed rate of value; and thus a great amount of debt was liquidated, and, as Livy adds, to the satisfaction of the creditor as well as of the debtor. If he had any authority for saying this, the fact is remarkable, for when the dictator Cæsar remedied the evils arising from a scarcity of money, during the civil wars, by nearly a similar arrangement, he was accused of making the creditors sustain a loss of 25 per cent.;[14] and men are so apt to regard money as the only standard of value, that this feeling is still very general; and he who should pay his creditor a less sum in actual money than he had borrowed, would be thought to have defrauded him of his due, although, from an increase in the value of money, what he paid might really be fully equal in its command over other commodities, to the sum which he had originally received.

Other measures attempted, but with incomplete success.

After all, however, although these proceedings of the five commissioners were well calculated to relieve the embarrassments of those debtors, who, being really solvent, were yet unable, owing to peculiar causes, to convert their property into money, yet the case of the insolvent debtors was not affected by them. Five years afterwards, in 408, the interest of money was still further reduced to the twenty-fourth part of the sum borrowed, or $4\frac{1}{6}$ per cent.;[15] and in 411, several persons were brought to trial for a breach of the law,[16] and condemned to pay fourfold, as in an action for furtum manifestum.

Thus palliatives of the existing evil had been sufficiently tried; but all were found to be inadequate. The mischief came to a head in the year 413, and could be stopped only by the most decisive remedies; but the disturbances of that year so affected the whole state of the commonwealth, and were again so much mixed up with political grievances, that an account of them will be more fitly reserved for another place, when we shall have reached that period in the course of our general narrative.

upright dictator in the second Samnite war, was a worthy representative of the family character.

[12] Livy, VII. 21. Their names were C. Duilius, alluded to in the preceding note; P. Decius Mus, who devoted himself in the Latin war; Q. Publilius Philo, eminent both as a general, and as the author of the famous laws which bear his name; Ti. Æmilius, one of the most moderate of the patricians, the colleague of Q. Publilius in his consulship, and the man who named him dictator; and M. Papirius, of whom nothing, I believe, is known.

[13] Whether that great rise in the price of copper had yet begun, which led to the successive depreciations of the as, it is not possible to ascertain; but without taking this into the account, other and more temporary causes tended to raise the value of money at this time at Rome, as compared with that of land. A little before this period the Gauls had been plundering the country round Rome during four consecutive years; and the terror of such an enemy could not but depreciate the value of land exposed to their ravages, while money could be kept safely within the walls of cities which the Gauls did not attempt to besiege; and at such seasons of alarm the practice of hoarding money is always more or less prevalent, so that the circulating medium becomes perceptibly scarcer, and, accordingly, rises in value. If, added to these causes, the demands of commerce had already begun to draw away the copper of Italy into Greece and Asia, the difficulty of selling land to pay a debt contracted when money was more plentiful must have been proportionably greater.

[14] Suetonius, Julius Cæsar, c. 42.

[15] Livy, VII. 27.

[16] Livy, VII. 28. Cato de re rusticâ, ab initio.

I propose, then, first, to take a general view of the internal state of the commonwealth, during the period which intervened between the passing of the Licinian laws and the first Samnite war, and then to trace its foreign relations within the same space of time.

General internal history from 389 to 412.

The first part of our task has been nearly completed already, in the view which has been given of the effects of the three Licinian laws. One or two points, however, may still require to be noticed.

Between 389 and 412 we find the remarkable number of fourteen dictatorships. Four of these dictators are expressly said to have been named with a political object,[17] that they might preside at the election of consuls, and prevent the observance of the Licinian law. Two more,[18] those of 402 and 403, although nominally appointed to command against a foreign enemy, were yet really named for political purposes; and two,[19] those of 392 and 411, were appointed to perform a religious ceremony. Of the remaining six, three were named during the alarm of the Gaulish invasion in 394, 395, and 397;[20] and the other three were chosen in 393, 399, and 410, to act against the Hernicans, the Tarquiniensians, and the Auruncans.[21] But even in these last appointments there was something of a political feeling: they prevented a plebeian consul from obtaining the glory of defeating the enemy, and notwithstanding the Licinian law, kept the executive government in the hands of a patrician; and it is expressly mentioned, that App. Claudius was named dictator in 393, to conduct the Hernican war, because he had been so active in opposing the bills of Licinius.

Frequent dictatorships and their object.

It is thus evident that a soreness of feeling continued to exist between the patricians and commons; and that the former could not yet reconcile themselves to the inevitable change which was in progress. The attack of the Tiburtians in 396, is said to have stopped a rising quarrel between the two orders;[22] the inactivity of the dictator, C. Sulpicius, in the early part of the campaign of 397, was ascribed to the policy of the patricians,[23] who wished to keep the commons as long as possible in the field, to prevent them from passing any measures adverse to the patrician interest in the Forum. The Pœtelian law passed in that same year, and brought forward by C. Pœtelius,[24] one of the tribunes, with the sanction of the patricians, appears also to have been intended indirectly to undermine the Licinian law with respect to the consulship. Its professed object was to put down canvassing, "ambitus," and ambitus here seems to be taken in its literal sense, not as implying any bribery, but simply the practice of going round to the several markets and meetings, held, for whatever purpose, in the country, and thus acquiring an interest among the country tribes. It is expressly said, that this law was directed against plebeian candidates; and this is natural; for men whose names did not yet command respect from their old nobility, were obliged to rely on their personal recommendations, and a simple plebeian, if unknown to the country voters, could ill compete with the influence of an old patrician family, strong not only in its ancient fame, but in the actual votes of its own clients, and of those of the other patricians, a body of men who would be mostly resident in Rome. Be-

Pœtelian law against canvassing. Breach of the Licinian law respecting the consulship.

[17] M. Fabius in 404 (Livy, VII. 22), L. Furius Camillus in 405 (Livy, VII. 24), T. Manlius Torquatus in 406 (Livy, VII. 26), and another, whose name is unknown, in 407; the fragments of the Fasti Capitolini only containing under this year the words,
"Dict.
Comit. Habend. Caus . . ."

[18] T. Manlius in 402 (Livy, VII. 19), and C. Julius in 403 (Livy, VII. 21).

[19] L. Manlius in 392, "clavi figendi causa" (Livy, VII. 3, and Fasti Capitol.), and P. Valerius, "feriarum constituendarum causa," in 411 (Livy VII. 28).

[20] T. Quinctius in 394 (Livy, VII. 9, Fasti Capitol.), Q. Servilius Ahala in 395 (Livy, VII. 11, Fasti Capitol.), and C. Sulpicius Peticus in 397 (Livy, VII. 12, Fasti Capitol. Appian de rebus Gall. 1).

[21] App. Claudius in 393 (Livy, VII. 6, Fasti Capitol.), C. Marcius Rutilus in 399 (Livy, VII. 17, Fasti Captol.), and L. Furius Camillus in 410 (Livy, VII. 28).

[22] Livy, VII. 12.

[23] Livy, VII. 13.

[24] Livy, VII. 15.

sides, if he had not an opportunity of canvassing the country tribes generally, his interest might not extend beyond his own immediate neighborhood, and thus the total number of his votes in any given tribe might not be sufficient to give him the legal vote of that tribe, and two patrician candidates might obtain a majority of suffrages, merely because no one plebeian candidate had any general interest in his favor. This seems to have been the way in which the Licinian law was set aside three years afterwards, in 400. The majority of votes was in favor of two patrician candidates; one of these was a Valerius, and his name was sure to be popular amongst the commons; whilst the plebeian candidates, debarred from general canvassing by the Pœtelian law, had each of them probably so small number of votes in his favor, that they would not have been duly elected according to the Roman law, even had there been no candidate standing against them. Thus the interrex,[25] M. Fabius, was enabled to say that the people had themselves set aside the Licinian law; inasmuch as there was a legal majority in favor of two patrician candidates, and only a small minority for any plebeian.

Law "de vicesima eorum qui manumitterentur" passed by one of the armies in the field.

An event occurred in the year 398, which very properly alarmed the tribunes, although it does not seem to have originated in any evil intention. One of the consuls, Cn. Manlius,[26] was in the field with a consular army, to carry on the war against the Tarquiniensians and Faliscans; his colleague, C. Marcius Rutilus, was engaged with the Privernatians, and enriching his army, it is said, with the plunder of the enemy's country, which had been for many years untouched by the ravages of war. It is probable that the soldiers on this occasion made prisoners of many Privernatian families, and released them again on the payment of a large ransom. But prisoners taken in war, becoming, according to ancient law, the slaves of the captor, his release of a prisoner upon ransom was, in fact, the manumission of a slave. Accordingly, Cn. Manlius called his soldiers together in the camp near Sutrium, according to their tribes, and, as if they were assembled in regular comitia, he proposed to them a law, that five per cent. on the value of any emancipated slave should be paid by his master into the public treasury.[27] It might be argued that the state ought not to lose all benefit from the plunder acquired by its soldiers; and that, especially, if a soldier set an enemy at liberty for the sake of his ransom, some compensation should be made to his country, whom his act might be supposed to injure. There was some plausibility in this, and the army of Manlius might have felt also some jealousy at the better fortune of their comrades, and might have known that their own general would not, like C. Marcius, give up to them the full benefit of such plunder as they might acquire from the Etruscans. Accordingly the law was passed in the camp, and received the ready sanction of the curiæ and the senate at Rome. But the tribunes, dreading the precedent of a law passed at a distance from Rome, beyond the range of the tribunes' protection, and where every citizen was subject to the absolute power of his general, declared it to be a capital offence, if any one should for the future summon the tribes in their comitia in any other than their accustomed place of meeting.[28] Their bill to this effect was sure of the support of Marcius and his army; and its principle was so clearly just, that it was passed, so far as we hear, without meeting any opposition.

The years 390, 391, and 392, were marked by a pestilence,[29] which is said to

[25] Livy, VII. 17. "Fabius aiebat, in duodecim tabulis legem esse, ut quodcunque postremum populus jussisset, id jus ratumque esset; jussum populi et suffragia esse."

[26] Livy, VII. 16.

[27] "Legem de vicesimâ eorum qui manumitterentur." The time and place at which the law was passed justify the explanation which I have given of its meaning; for had the object been merely to check the increase of the class of freedmen it would scarcely have been brought forward in such an irregular manner. Similar laws were in force in some of our West Indian islands, at once to restrain emancipation, and to prevent the slave from becoming a burden upon the public, if the state received nothing as a compensation for the contingency of being obliged to maintain him as a freeman.

[28] "Ne quis postea populum *sevocaret*." Compare the well-known sense of *secessio*.

[29] Livy, VII. 1, 2.

have been very generally fatal; and in 391, the Tiber rose to an unusual height, overflowed the Circus Maximus,[30] and put a stop to the games which were going on there at that very time, as a propitiation of the wrath of heaven. It is difficult to say whether it was a similar flood two years afterwards, or the shock of an earthquake, which gave occasion to the famous legend of the filling up of the Curtian lake in the Forum. All know how the gulf, which had suddenly yawned wide and deep in the midst of the Forum,[31] could be filled up by no human power, till the gods at last declared, that the best and true strength of the Roman commonwealth must be devoted as an offering to the gulf; so should the state exist and flourish forever. While men were asking, what is the true strength of Rome? a noble youth, named M. Curtius, whose valiant deeds had made him famous, said that it were a shame to think that the true strength of Rome could lie in aught else but in the arms and in the valor of her children; and he put on his armor and mounted his horse, and plunged into the gulf. All the assembled multitude threw their offerings into it after him, and the gulf was closed, but the place bore his name forever. It were vain to inquire at what period and upon what foundation this remarkable story was first originated.[32]

Natural phenomena. Story of Curtius leaping into the gulf.

The first year of the pestilence was marked by the death of M. Camillus.[33] In him we seem to lose the last relic of early Rome, the last hero whose glory belongs rather to romance than to history. But the fame of the stories connected with him proves the high estimation in which he was held when living; and it was a beautiful conclusion to his long life, that his last public action was that of a peacemaker, his last interference in political contests was that of a patriot and not of a partisan. The glory of his name was supported for one generation by his son, L. Furius, and then sank forever.

Death of Camillus.

The same period of pestilence was also noted as the era at which the first and simplest form of dramatic entertainments[34] was introduced at Rome. Amongst the games ordered to be celebrated in the hope of propitiating the gods, one, it is said, consisting of a dance in dumb show, as an accompaniment to the music of the flute, was, for the first time, introduced from Etruria. The dumb show was afterwards succeeded by a song in which the dance was suited to the words; then came a dialogue, and, last of all, a regular acted story; but here the Romans did but translate or imitate the dramatists of Greece, and nothing in literature is less original, and therefore less valuable than the tragic and comic drama of Rome.

First introduction of stage acting and dancing.

What power of imagination can complete these few isolated facts into the full picture of the life of a people during three and twenty years? who can represent to himself the Senate or the Forum, such as they were at this period, either as to outward forms and scenes, or as to the men who frequented them? Much less can we conceive what was passing in the interior of every family, and realize to ourselves the names of our scanty history—the Fabii, the Valerii, the Sulpicii, or the Marcii, as they were talking and acting in the ordinary relations of life, abroad or at home. A period, of which there remains no contemporary literature, has virtually perished from the memory of after ages; some scattered bones of the skeleton may be left, but the face, figure, and mind of the living man are lost to us beyond recall.

In times so imperfectly known as those with which we are now engaged, the

[30] Livy, VII. 3.

[31] Livy, VII. 6. Valerius Maximus, V. 6. § 2.

[32] Another story derived the name of the Curtian lake in the Forum from one Curtius Mettius, a soldier of Tatius, the king of the Sabines; who, in the battle between Tatius and Romulus, had been nearly lost in a piece of boggy ground between the Capitoline and Palatine hills. Livy, I. 12, 13. A spot in the centre of the Forum, marked out by an altar, was known, even in the times of the emperors, by the name of the Curtian lake: Galba was thrown out of his litter and murdered close to it. (Tacitus, Hist. I. 41.) But the real origin of the name being unknown, various stories, as is usual, were invented to explain it.

[33] Livy, VII. 1.

[34] Livy, VII. 2.

Foreign history of Rome from 389 to 312.

geographical order of events is far more instructive than the chronological. I propose, therefore, to trace successively the relations of Rome with the several neighboring states, from 389 to 412, beginning with the wars with the Etruscans, who were divided by the Tiber from the Latins, Volscians, and Hernicans.

Wars with Tarquinii and the Faliscans.

I. The people of Tarquinii, sometimes aided by the Faliscans, were engaged in wars with Rome during a period of eight years, from 396 to 404. What may have been the cause of quarrel is unknown, if it were any thing more than the ordinary enmity between two neighboring nations, and the disputes which are forever occurring on their common border. But the war is rendered remarkable by the specimens displayed in it of the character and influence of the Etruscan religion. The Roman consul, C. Fabius,[35] having been defeated in a battle in the year 397, the Tarquinians sacrificed to their gods three hundred and seven Roman soldiers, who had been taken prisoners in the action; and two years afterwards, when the Faliscans had joined them, the priests of both cities, with long snake-like ribbons of various colors twisted in their hair, and brandishing burning torches in their hands,[36] fought in the front of their army, and struck such terror into the Roman soldiers, that they drove them back in confusion to their camp. The Etruscan priests, it should be remembered, were also the chiefs or lucumones of the nation, and they acted on this occasion, and with equal success, the same part which the two Decii performed for Rome in the Latin and Etruscan wars of a later period. Full of confidence in the support of the gods, the Etruscans followed up their victory; they entered the Roman territory and spread their devastations over the whole country on the right bank of the Tiber as far as the sea. It was to meet this danger that C. Marcius[37] was appointed dictator; he was named, we must suppose, by the plebeian consul of that year, M. Popillius Lænas, and was the first plebeian who ever obtained the dictatorship. His appointment gave great offence to the patricians, and was proportionably acceptable to his own order; all his commands were zealously obeyed; he repelled the invaders, and, like the popular consuls of the year 305, he obtained a triumph by a vote of the people when the senate refused to grant it.

Peace concluded for forty years.

In the year 401, the Roman annalists say that the butchery of the Roman prisoners by the Tarquinians four years before was signally avenged; the Tarquinians were defeated in a great battle, and three hundred and fifty-eight of the noblest of the prisoners were sent to Rome, and there scourged and beheaded in the Forum.[38] The war lingered on, however, for three years more; and was then ended by a peace concluded for forty years.[39] No conquests of towns or territory are recorded, and thus the Roman frontier still remained on the side of Etruria in the same position as it had been for the last forty years, since the conquest of Veii, Nepete, and Sutrium.

Wars in Latium.

II. Far more complicated was the scene on the left bank of the Tiber. There great changes took place; the relations of the several people to one another were materially altered; some nations almost vanish out of history, whilst Rome saw her territory enlarged, her population of citizens increased, her power and influence strengthened and extended beyond all former example. But the causes and circumstances of these changes are partly disguised by the dishonesty, and partly omitted through the mere meagerness of the Roman historians. Out of the confusion of Livy's narrative we must endeavor, if possible, to obtain a clear and consistent outline of the events of a period which contributed, in no small degree, to determine the future destinies of Rome and the world.

In the year 394, according to the common chronology, the Gauls again ap-

[35] Livy, VII. 15.
[36] Livy, VII. 17.
[37] Livy, VII. 17.
[38] Livy, VII. 19.
[39] Livy, VII. 22.

peared in Latium. This inroad lasted, according to the Roman annals, for four years, and was ended, as they pretend, by the total destruction of the invaders in the year 397. Eight years afterwards, in 405, we hear of another invasion; but this new attack was completely defeated in the following year, and from that time forward we never again find the Gauls in Latium.

Gaulish invasions.

The dates of these two invasions are, no doubt, correctly given. They are confirmed by Polybius,[40] although in all other points his account differs widely from that of the Roman writers. The Gauls penetrated into the heart of Latium thirty years after their first attack on Rome; they appeared at Alba, but the Romans, surprised by the suddenness of their inroad, and unable to collect their allies together, did not venture to meet them in the field. Twelve years afterwards, continues Polybius, they came again; but the Romans had now timely notice of their coming; their allies had joined them, and they marched out boldly to give the enemy battle. The Gauls were dismayed by this display of confidence; their chiefs quarrelled, and their whole multitude broke up under cover of night, and retreated like a beaten army to their own country. On this their last appearance in Latium, the Roman army opposed to them was commanded by Lucius Camillus; and this is the Lucius[41] whom Aristotle spoke of as the deliverer of his country from the Gauls. According to the Roman accounts, he defeated the Gauls in a general action; yet it is not pretended that he obtained a triumph.

Account of them given by Polybius.

These last invasions of the Gauls were marked, according to the Roman annalists, not only by many signal victories won by the Roman armies in general battles, but in particular by two brilliant single combats in which two of the noble youth of Rome gained for themselves an immortal memory. T. Manlius, the future conqueror of the Latins, fought with a gigantic Gaul[42] on the bridge over the Anio upon the Salarian road: he slew his enemy, and took from his neck his chain of gold (torques), which he wore on his neck in triumph, so that the soldiers called him Torquatus, and his descendants ever after bore that name. And again, before the last great victory won by Lucius Camillus, there was another single combat in the Pomptinian territory between a second giant Gaul and the young M. Valerius,[43] who afterwards

Stories of the Gaulish invasions. T. Manlius Torquatus, and M. Valerius Corvus.

[40] II. 18. It is well known, that the Roman writers claim three victories in the course of the invasion of 394–397 in which, according to Polybius, the Romans did not venture to meet the Gauls in the field. The victory of the dictator C. Sulpicius, in 397, is described very circumstantially by Appian, who, probably, copied Dionysius, as well as by Livy, and the Fasti Capitolini give the day of his triumph, the nones of May. On the other hand, the statement of Polybius is given simply and positively, and we know how completely the Romans corrupted the memory of many events in the Samnite war, and in other parts of their early history. We should be glad to know from what sources Polybius derived his knowledge of these events. The chronological exactness of his account seems to show, that it could not have been taken from any Greek writer who may have mentioned the Gaulish invasions of central Italy, but from some Roman annalist, and it is probable that Fabius, who, in spite of his national prejudices, had, in other instances, given a true report of transactions which later annalists utterly misrepresented, was the authority whom Polybius followed. It is not likely, on the other hand, that the pretended victories of the Roman generals are mere inventions, but that some trifling advantages gained over detached parties of the Gauls were magnified into general battles, and that the triumphs, if not altogether false, were granted by the policy of the senate, wishing to make the most of any advantage gained over an enemy so formidable as the Gauls.

[41] **Τὸν δὲ σώσαντα Λεύκιον εἶναι φησίν.** Plutarch, Camill. 22. It should be remembered, that the Romans, in old times, were known and called by their prænomina, or first names, as Polybius calls Scipio, "Publius," and Regulus, "Marcus." The prænomen was then much less likely to be mistaken than in after ages, when the nomen and cognomen were generally used instead of it, and when it was possible for a foreigner to be very familiar with the actions of Cæsar, without remembering whether his prænomen was Caius or Lucius. But Aristotle would have been no more likely to have mistaken one prænomen for another, than to have confounded two Greek brothers together, because together with their own peculiar names they had both the same patronymic.

[42] There is a striking description of this combat given by Q. Claudius Quadrigarius, an annalist of the seventh century of Rome, and preserved to us by A. Gellius, IX. 13.

[43] This combat is also given by Gellius from some of the old annalists, IX. 11. It is described too by Dionysius, XV. 1, 2, and by Livy, VII. 26.

defeated the Samnites at the great battle of Mount Gaurus. A wonderful thing happened in this combat, said the story; for as Marcus was going to begin the fight, all on a sudden a crow flew down and perched upon his helmet. When the two combatants closed with each other, the crow still sat on the Roman's helm, but ever and anon it soared up in the air, and then darted down upon the Gaul, and struck at his face and eyes with its beak and claws. So the Gaul, confounded and dismayed, soon fell by the sword of Marcus; and then the crow flew up again into the air, and vanished towards the east. For this wonderful aid thus afforded him M. Valerius was known ever afterwards by the name of Corvus, Crow, and the name remained to his posterity. These stories are the very counterpart of the combat between Sir Guy of Warwick and the Danish giant Colbrand before the walls of Winchester; or, as Manlius and Valerius Corvus are certainly more real personages than Sir Guy, we may compare them with the ballad of Chevy Chase, and consider how far we could recognize the historical battle of Otterburne, and the real Hotspur, in the battle on the Cheviot hills, and in the Earl Percy of the poem. As in this instance, the time,[44] place, circumstances, and issue of the poetical battle bear no resemblance to those of the real one, so also the poetical or romance accounts of these last Gaulish invasions retain scarcely a feature of that simple and real history of them which has been preserved to us by Polybius. That the triumphal Fasti have followed the fictitious rather than the true account, belongs to that peculiar blot on the Roman character which I have already noticed; that what with other people has been mere fanciful romance, has been by the Romans made to wear such an appearance of serious earnest as to be no longer romance but falsehood.

Effect of the Gaulish invasions on the relations of the several states of Italy.

What the Gauls did in Latium and against the Romans has been sufficiently disguised and perverted; but what they did in other parts of Italy is altogether unknown to us. We hear of them in Latium, and that they moved southwards from thence into Campania and Apulia;[45] but they do not seem to have touched Etruria, and their attacks on Rome were all made on the left bank of the Tiber. Perhaps the Etruscans had early concluded a peace with them, so that in their invasions of Latium and Campania they passed through Umbria and the country of the Sabines, descending upon Rome either by the Salarian road along the Tiber, or by the valley of the Anio. The Romans complained that two Latin cities, Tibur and Præneste,[46] had not scrupled, in their hatred of Rome, to ally themselves with these barbarians; and this was remembered afterwards against them when the issue of the great Latin war had placed them at the mercy of their old enemies. But it is not to be wondered at if they were glad to divert the torrent of the Gaulish invasion from themselves to the territory of strangers or rivals; perhaps they hired some of the Gaulish bands to enter into their service, and some advantages gained over these by the Roman generals may have been the origin of the pretended victories and triumphs recorded in the annals and in the Fasti. The main Gaulish army appears to have stationed itself principally on the Alban hills,[47] from whence, as from some island stronghold, they could attack and lay waste all the neighboring country. Twice they are said to have approached Rome, and once they advanced as far as the very Colline gate,[48] by which they had entered the city in their first

[44] The battle of Otterburne was fought in the reign of Richard the Second, of England, and Robert the Second, of Scotland; the poetical account of it places it in the reign of a King Henry in England, and a King James in Scotland. Otterburne is in Redesdale near Elsdon, the scene of battle in the poem is in the Cheviot hills; the historical battle did not arise out of any hunting excursion of Percy on the Scottish border, but from an inroad of the Scotch into Northumberland. In the real battle, Percy was taken prisoner, and the English were defeated; in the poetical battle, Percy is killed, but the English are victorious. And further, to show how slight actions may be magnified into great battles, the Scottish army at Otterburne which consisted really of 2300 men, is made in another ballad of the battle to amount to 44,000, of whom there "went but eighteen away."

[45] Livy, VII. 11. 26.

[46] Livy, VII. 11. VIII. 14.

[47] Polybius, II. 18. Livy, VII. 25. Dionysius, XIV. 12.

[48] Livy, VII. 11.

invasion. On one occasion we find them encamped at Pedum[49] in front of Præneste, an old Latin city which the Æquians had formerly conquered, but which afterwards, perhaps at this very time, got rid of its foreign masters and became again united to the Latin nation. None can tell what cities were destroyed, what people weakened, and what confederacies or dominions were broken up in the course of these Gaulish invasions. The Volscians seemed to have suffered more especially; for it was through their territory that the Gauls moved onwards from Latium to Campania, or returned from Campania to their quarters on the Alban hills; and it appears that their nation was from this time forward broken into fragments, each of which had from henceforth a destiny of its own. In order to understand this change fully, we must recollect that in the year of Rome 378 the Roman frontier had fallen back from Anxur to Satricum, that Satricum itself had been won by the Volscians, and afterwards burnt by the Latins[50] that it might not revert to Rome, and that the Roman territory in the maritime part of the Campagna scarcely reached to the distance of twenty-five miles from Rome. But in 397 we find that the Latins[51] renewed their alliance with the Romans; that two new tribes of Roman citizens were created,[52] the Pomptine and the Publilian; and that Velitræ and Privernum,[53] both of them Volscian towns, but the latter unmentioned hitherto in Roman history, were engaged alone in a war with Rome. This same year witnessed also the retreat of the Gauls from Latium, after they had been overrunning it at intervals during a period of three years; and finally, it was marked by what the Romans call a conquest of the Hernicans,[54] who for the last four years had been at open war with Rome. That there was a connection between all these events is manifest, although they appear in Livy as mere accidental coincidences. It should be remembered also that in this same year war was formally declared[55] between Rome and Tarquinii.

Renewal of the alliance between Rome and the Latins and Hernicans.

The complicated negotiations and the ever-changing alliances of the Greek states, between the peace of Nicias and the Athenian expedition to Sicily, cannot be comprehended readily, even though related by such an historian as Thucydides. In the last ten years of the fourth century of Rome, Latium and its neighborhood must have presented a tissue of events equally perplexed in themselves, without any contemporary historian like Thucydides to explain them to posterity. But by considering the mere fragments of information which have been preserved to us, we may attempt to combine them into something like the following form. A war with Tarquinii, in addition to one with the Hernicans, and that at a time when Tibur and Præneste were hostile, and when the Gauls might be expected to appear again in Latium as they had done regularly for the last three years, was clearly more than the strength of Rome could bear. The old alliance with the Hernicans, and with some at any rate of the Latin cities, must, at whatever price, be renewed. We can easily conceive that there must have been a party amongst the Latins and Hernicans equally well disposed to such a reunion. It was accordingly effected: the plebeian consul C. Plautius appears to have had the honor of restoring at this critical moment the great work of Sp. Cassius. The whole people of the Hernicans renewed their old alliance with Rome; but of the thirty Latin cities which had concluded the league with Sp. Cassius many had perished, and some had become separated from the Latin confederacy, and were now the heads of small confederacies of their own: we may safely conclude, however, that Aricia, Bovillæ, Gabii, Lanuvium, Laurentum, Lavinium, Nomentum, and Tusculum were among the cities which returned to their old connection, and became as heretofore the equal allies of the Romans. Thus a force was organized

49 "Gallos . . . circa Pedum consedisse auditum est." Livy, VII. 12.
50 Livy, VI. 33.
51 Livy, VII. 12.
52 Livy, VII. 15.
53 Livy, VII. 15.
54 "Hernici devicti subactique sunt."—Livy, VII. 15.
55 Livy, VII. 12. "Rebus nequicquam repetitis, novi consules jussu populi bellum indixere."

which might be able at last to meet the Gauls in the field, should they again venture to establish themselves on the Alban hills, or to overrun the plains of Latium.

But while Rome was thus strengthened by this reconciliation with her old allies, she also made an addition to the number of her own citizens. Two new tribes were created, making the whole number twenty-seven; and the new citizens thus received into the state appear to have been in part the inhabitants of the Ager Pomptinus, or Volscian lowlands, the country between Antium and Tarracina on the coast, and running inland as far as the roots of the Apennines which form the eastern wall of the Campagna. In the times of the later kings, the Romans, according to their own stories, had made several conquests over the Volscians in this region, which at any rate were all lost again during the subsequent advance of the Æquians and Volscians into Latium: but in the twenty years immediately preceding the Gaulish invasion, the Volscian frontier had again receded, and the Romans, as we have seen, extended their dominion for a time as far as Tarracina or Anxur. After the Gaulish invasion there followed another change of fortune; when the Latins no longer aided the Romans, but were for some time in alliance with the Volscians, the Romans again lost ground; Satricum became once more Volscian, and the intermediate country between it and Tarracina, the much contested Ager Pomptinus, must also have returned to its old masters. But whether it was that the Volscians had suffered even more than their neighbors from the Gaulish invasions, or whether the Samnites had already begun their attacks upon them in the valley of the Liris and on the side of Campania, or whether it is to be ascribed to internal divisions, and to the destruction of their old allies the Æquians, it seems at any rate that the Volscian nation was now declining, and utterly unable to withstand, as it had once done, the united forces of Rome and Latium. It is probable that much of its territory became at this period either Roman or Latin; exactly in the same manner as the Sabines of Regillus and Nomentum had lost their independence soon after the expulsion of the Tarquins. And as the Claudian and Crustuminian tribes were then formed out of those Sabines who became Romans, while Nomentum and Regillus fell to the share of the Latins, so a similar division in all probability took place now, and the Pomptine and the Publilian tribes must have been formed out of the Volscians who were assigned to Rome, whilst other portions of the Volscian territory and population fell to the share of the Latins. Thus the Volscian nation having been so dismembered, those states which still survived became henceforth more individually distinguished, and also, as was natural, more resolute to defend their independence. Amongst this number were the people of Privernum; and the ravages which they and the people of Velitræ are said to have carried into the Roman territory[56] in this same year, were doubtless more especially directed against those whom they would consider as traitors, their own Volscian countrymen, the new Roman citizens of the Pomptine and Publilian tribes.

Two new Roman tribes created.

This favorable aspect of the Roman affairs was still further improved four years afterwards, when in the year 401 both Tibur and Præneste[57] gave up their long-continued hostility, and obtained, perhaps at the price of some sacrifices of territory, a peace for a certain number of years with Rome. The peace with Tarquinii followed, as we have already seen, in the year 404.

Peace with Tibur and Præneste.

But in the year 402 we again hear of an attack made by the Volscians upon the Latins in the direction of Tusculum.[58] No particulars are mentioned, perhaps because the allied Romans and Latin forces were in this year commanded by a Latin general; but we may

The growth of the Samnite power draws the Romans and Latins more closely together.

[56] Livy, VII. 15. "Accessit . . . vastatio Romani agri, quam Privernates, Veliterni deinde, incursione repentina fecerunt."

[57] For the peace with Tibur, see Livy, VII. 19; and for the peace or rather truce with Præneste, see Diodorus, XVI. 45.

[58] Livy, VII. 19.

suppose that Privernum and Velitræ, with some of the cities of the Volscian highlands, were the part of the Volscian nation engaged in these hostilities. From this time for the next five years all was quiet: but in the year 407, Satricum, which had been burnt some years ago by the Latins, and the territory of which the Latins had appropriated to themselves in their late partition of the Ager Pomptinus with Rome, was again occupied and rebuilt by the Volscians of Antium.[59] Jealousies were arising about this time between Rome and Latium; and it appears probable that there was a party amongst the Latins disposed to form a separate alliance with the remaining independent states of the Volscians, in order to be strengthened by them against Rome. Thus when the Auruncans, or Ausonians, one of the most southern people of the Volscian stock, began to plunder the Ager Pomptinus in 410, the Romans, we are told, suspected that this inroad was actually made with the concurrence of the Latins, and expected[60] a war with the whole Latin confederacy. Their fears, however, were groundless for the present, and indeed the progress of the Samnite arms in Campania and on the Liris was a strong inducement both to the Romans and Latins to defer their jealousies of each other to a more convenient season. Two years afterwards, in 412, the first Samnite war broke out, in which both the Latins and Volscians to all appearance took part with Rome.

Increased power of Rome.

Thus in the course of three-and-twenty years Rome was finally delivered from the scourge of the Gaulish invasion; she had secured her northern frontier by a peace with the neighboring states of Etruria; her old alliance with the Latins and Hernicans, however doubtful might be its duration, had been restored in time to enable her to repel the Gauls and to crush the Volscians: and it was now ready to aid her in her coming struggle with the Samnites. She had not merely extended her dominion, but by granting the full rights of citizens to the Volscians of the Ager Pomptinus, she had enlarged and strengthened her own commonwealth. She was thus prepared for the events of the next ten years, which assured to her beyond dispute the first place among the nations of Italy.

Chronology.

We have seen that the date of the first plebeian consulship coincided with that of the death of Epaminondas at Mantinea. The first Samnite war broke out about two years before the establishment of the Macedonian supremacy in Greece by Philip's great victory at Chæronea.

CHAPTER XXVIII.

THE FIRST SAMNITE WAR—SEDITION OF THE YEAR 408—GENUCIAN LAWS.—A. U. C. 407-409 NIEBUHR: 410-412 FASTI CAPIT.: 412-414 LIVY.

"Majora jam hinc bella et viribus hostium et longinquitate vel regionum vel temporum spatio quibus bellatum est dicentur; namque eo anno adversus Samnites, gentem opibus armisque validam, mota arma."—LIVY, VII. 29.

Legend concerning the origin of the Samnites.

THE Sabines, who dwelt amidst the highest mountains of the Apennines, where the snow lies all the year long, and which send forth the streams to run into the two seas northward and southward, were[1]

[59] Livy, VII. 27.

[60] Livy, VII. 28.

[1] Strabo, V. p. 250. Dionysius, II. 49.

at war for many years together with their neighbors the Umbrians. At last they made a vow, that if they should conquer their enemies, all the living creatures[2] born in their land in that year should be devoted to the gods as sacred. They did conquer, and they offered in sacrifice accordingly all the lambs and calves and kids and pigs of that year, and such animals as might not be sacrificed, they[3] redeemed. But still their land would not yield its fruits, and when they thought what was the cause of it, they considered that their vow had not been duly performed; for all their own children[4] born within that year had been kept back from the gods, and had neither been sacrificed nor redeemed. So they devoted all their children to the god Mamers, and when they were grown up they sent them away to become a new people in a new land. When the young men set out on their way, it happened that a bull went before them; and they thought that Mamers had sent him to be their guide, and they followed him. He laid himself down[5] to rest for the first time when he had come to the land of the Opicans; and the Sabines thought that this was a sign to them, and they fell upon the Opicans, who dwelt in scattered villages[6] without walls to defend them, and they drove them out, and took possession of their land. Then they offered the bull in sacrifice to Mamers, who had sent him to be their guide; and a bull was the device[7] which they bore in after ages; and they themselves were no more called Sabines, but they took a new name and were called Samnites.

What truth is contained in it.

Such is the legendary account of the origin of that great people whose history is now beginning to connect itself with that of Rome. In two points it has preserved the truth; the Samnites were a people of Sabine extraction, and had established themselves as conquerors in the country of the Opicans. But the two races were, probably, not very remote from each other, and thus it is less surprising that the conquerors should have adopted the language of their subjects; for the Samnites spoke Opican, or Oscan, and the legends of their coins, and their remaining inscriptions are in the Oscan character. Still the two people were distinct; and the Samnites regarded neither their Opican subjects in Campania, nor their Opican neighbors, the Æquians and Volscians, as their own proper countrymen.

Notice of the Samnites in the Periplus of Scylax.

One single contemporary notice of the Samnites[8] in the days of their greatness has descended to our times; and this is contained in two short lines of the Periplus of Scylax, who describes the Samnites as living on the coast of the Lower Sea between the Campanians and Lucanians, and the length of their coast-line was no more, he tells us, than half a day's sail. The space which they occupied reached nearly from the Sarnus to

[2] The form of one of these vows is given by Livy, XXII. 10, "quod ver adtulerit ex suillo, ovillo, caprino, bovillo grege, quæque profana erunt, Jovi fieri."

[3] Τὰ μὲν κατέθυσαν, τὰ δὲ καθιέρωσαν. Strabo, V. p. 250. What was not sacrificed, but yet was consecrated to the gods, must have been redeemed before it could be employed for ordinary purposes.

[4] Strabo as before. Festus in "Mamertini."

[5] This reminds us of the story of the white sow which guided Æneas to the place where he was to build his city. A wolf was said to have done the same service to the Hirpinians, who were also of Samnite extraction.

[6] Ἐτύγχανον δὲ κωμηδὸν ζῶντες. Like the Ætolians in the time of the Peloponnesian war, Thucyd. III. 94; or like the Casali, which to this day contain the greatest part of the population in the valleys of the central Apennines.

[7] Micali gives an engraving of a coin, struck by the Italian allies during their great war with the Romans in the seventh century of Rome, which represents a bull, the emblem of the Samnites, goring a wolf, the well-known type of the Romans. Two or three specimens of this coin are to be seen in the British Museum.

[8] Καμπανῶν δὲ ἔχονται Σαυνῖται· καὶ παράπλους ἐστὶ Σαυνιτῶν ἡμέρας ἥμισυ, p. 3. Niebuhr reads Σαυνῖται instead of Δαυνῖται in the following page of Scylax, urging that the description is inapplicable to the Daunians, as they neither extended across all Italy from sea to sea, nor lived to the N. W. of Mount Drium or Garganus. I think that this conjecture is highly probable, because Scylax had not mentioned the Daunians in his description of the coasts of the Lower Sea, but had mentioned the Samnites; and the only other people who had stretched from sea to sea, the Etruscans or Tyrrhenians, are mentioned separately in the description of both coasts. If so, Scylax includes within the limits of the Samnites, not only the country of the Frentanians, who were notoriously of Samnite origin, but also that of their neighbors, the Marrucinians and Vestinians.

the Silarus; Neapolis, according to Scylax, is in Campania; Posidonia, or Pæstum, is in Lucania. But the Samnite possessions on or near the coast, even though they once included the famous cities of Herculaneum and Pompeii,[9] of Nola, Nuceria, and Abella, were a mere recent offshoot from the great body of the nation: the true Samnium lies wholly in the interior, and having been thus removed from the notice of the Greeks, from whom alone we derive our knowledge of the ancient world before the dominion of the Romans, it has been fated to remain in perpetual obscurity.

Geography of Samnium.—The Matese.

Nearly due north of Naples, there stands out from the central line of the Apennines, like one of the towers of an old castle from the lower and more retiring line of the ordinary wall, a huge mass of mountains, known at present by the name of the Matese. On more than three-fourths of its circumference it is bounded by the Volturno and its tributary streams, the Calore[10] and the Tamaro, which send their waters into the Lower or Tyrrhenian Sea; but on its northern side, its springs and torrents run down into the Biferno, and so make their way to the Adriatic. A very narrow isthmus or shoulder, high enough to form the watershed between the two seas, connects the Matese at its N. W. and N. E. extremities with the main Apennine line, and thus prevents it from being altogether insulated.

Its extent and character.

The circumference of the Matese, as above described, is between seventy[11] and eighty miles. Its character bears some resemblance to that of the district of Craven, in Yorkshire, or more closely to that of the Jura. It is a vast mass of limestone,[12] rising from its base abruptly in the huge wall-like cliffs or scars, so characteristic of limestone mountains, to the height of about 3000 feet; and within this gigantic inclosure presenting a great variety of surface, sloping inwards from the edge of the cliffs into deep valleys, and then rising again in the highest points of the centre of the range, and especially in the Monte Miletto, which is its loftiest summit, to an elevation computed at 6000 feet. Its upland valleys offer, like those of the Jura, a wide extent of pasture, and endless forests of magnificent beech-wood; it is rich in springs, gushing out of the ground with a full burst of water, and suddenly disappearing again into some of the numerous caverns in which such limestone rocks abound. In this manner the waters of a small lake in the heart of the mountain have no visible outlet;[13] but the people of the country say that they break out at the foot of a deep cliff or cove, about two or three miles distant, and form the full stream of the Torano.

On the highest points of the Matese the snow lies till late[14] in the summer; and such is their elevation, that the view from them extends across the whole breadth of Italy from sea to sea. No heat of the summer scorches the perpetual fresh-

[9] Herculaneum and Pompeii both stood, it is true, to the northward of the Sarnus; and Strabo expressly says that they were wrested by the Samnites from the Etruscans, V. p. 247. This, however, was the case also with Cuma and Capua; but as Scylax places these towns in Campania, and distinguishes it from the country of the Samnites, a little to the south of it, it is probable that at the time of the first Samnite war, which is nearly the date of Scylax's Periplus, most of this district had recovered its independence, and the Samnite possessions were reduced to the limits mentioned in the text.

[10] The Calore runs along the southern side of the Matese: the Tamaro, which bounds its eastern side, runs into the Calore from the north nearly at right angles.

[11] Mr. Keppel Craven says, that it is reckoned to measure seventy miles.—Excursions in the Abruzzi, &c. Vol. II. p. 166. Giustiniani gives it at sixty-two Neapolitan miles, which are more than seventy English ones.—See his Dizionario del Regno di Napoli, Parte 2, in "Matese."

[12] This limestone is, in some parts, bituminous, and contains some fossil remains of fish. There are some volcanic or tufaceous rocks in the Matese, resembling probably the beds of tuff which are found on the slopes of the Apennines in other places, as, for instance, on the road from Naples to Avellino in the pass of Monteforte.

[13] See Keppel Craven, Excurs. in the Abruzzi, Vol. I. p. 18. The English reader will remember Malham Tarn, and the full burst of water with which the Aire rushes out from under the rocks of Malham Cove. Similar phenomena are frequent in the limestone mountains of Peloponnesus.

[14] See Giustiniani, Dizionario. Mr. Keppel Craven found the upper half of the Matese covered with snow in May: it would remain much later on the highest summits.

ness of these mountain pastures; and during the hottest months[15] the cattle from the surrounding country are driven up thither to feed.

This singular mountain, with its subject valleys, was the heart of the country of the Samnites. Of the two principal divisions of the Samnites, one, the Caudinians, occupied the southern side of the Matese, and the other, the Pentrians, dwelt on its northern side. To the former belonged the towns of Allifæ[16] on the Vulturnus, of Telesia, the country of that Pontius Telesinus,[17] who struggled so valiantly against the fortune of Sylla in the great battle at the Colline gate, and of Beneventum.[18] To the Pentrians belonged Æsernia[19] on one of the first feeders of the Vulturnus, Bovianum[20] on the Biferno or Tifernus, and Sepinum[21] on the E. of the Matese, not far from the sources of the Tamaro.

Principal divisions and towns of Samnium.

Besides the Caudinians and Pentrians, there were, doubtless, other tribes more or less closely connected with the Samnite name, who took part in the great contest of their nation with Rome. The very names of some of these may have perished; for it is by mere accident that we hear of the Caracenians,[22] a tribe to the north of the Pentrians, who dwelt in the upper valley of the Sangro or Sagrus, and to whom belonged the town of Aufidena. The Frentanians, who reached down to the very shores of the Adriatic, are called a Samnite people;[23] yet in the accounts of the wars with Rome, they are spoken of as distinct; and they seem to have taken no part in the first war. And the Hirpinians, whose country is also included within the limits of Samnium, and who dwelt to the S. E. of the rest of their countrymen, occupying the upper valleys of the Calore and Sabbato on the south of the Apennines, and of the Ofanto or Aufidus on the northern side, are on some occasions[24] distinguished from the Sam-

Tribes connected with the Samnites.

[15] They are turned out about the end of June. See Keppel Craven, Vol. I. p. 20.

[16] Alife, which still retains its ancient name, ranks even now as a city, but the bishop resides at Piedimonte, a flourishing town about three miles distant, and Alife is at present almost depopulated from malaria. See Keppel Craven, Vol. I. p. 21.

[17] And according to the writer of the little work, "de viris illustribus," it was the country also of that still greater C. Pontius, who defeated the Romans at the Caudine Forks. The remains of Telesia are to be seen at the distance of about a mile to the N. W. of the modern town of Telese, which, like Alife, has almost gone to ruin from the influence of the malaria. See Keppel Craven, Vol. II. p. 173, 174.

[18] This is still a well-built and flourishing town, containing a population of 18,000 souls. See Keppel Craven's Tour in the southern provinces of Naples, p. 22, 28.

[19] The present town, still called Isernia, stands on a narrow ridge between two torrents, running down in very deep ravines, which meet a little below, and then fall into the Vandra, about two miles above its junction with the Volturno. It is a flourishing place, with various manufactures, and a population of about 7000 souls. Large remains of polygonal walls are still visible, which belong, probably, to the days of its independence as a Samnite city. The remarkable tunnel, hewn through the rock for about a mile, and still used, according to its original purpose, for supplying the town with water, is probably a work of the Roman times. See Keppel Craven, Abruzzi, Vol. II. p. 81–84.

[20] Bovianum, or Boiano, also contains remains of polygonal walls, built of very large stones, put as closely together as possible, and the smaller interstices filled up with remarkable nicety. It is a cold place, being shaded by the Matese, which rises directly to the south of it; and the Biferno so floods the valley, that it is a constant swamp, and the air is damp and foggy; but there is no malaria, because it has no severe heats in summer. Its population, according to Giustiniani, writing in 1797, was then 3500 souls. Mr. Keppel Craven rates it at present as low as 1500. Abruzzi, Vol. II. p. 164.

[21] The actual town of Sepino stands on a hill at some distance from the remains of the ancient city, which are to be seen in the valley below. These remains are very large and remarkably perfect, but they are of Roman, as I imagine, rather than of Samnite origin. One of the famous cattle-tracks (calles, tratturi, delle pecore), which have existed unaltered from time immemorial for the yearly migrations of the cattle from and to the coast, runs straight through the ruins of the ancient town from E. to W. See Keppel Craven, Abruzzi, Vol. II. p. 131, 135.

[22] The name is only noticed, I believe, by Zonaras and Ptolemy; unless it be the same with the Carentini of Pliny. The Italian writers, Romanelli, for instance, and Micali, propose to read Sariceni, as if the name were derived from the neighboring river Sarus or Sangro. But this is exceedingly uncertain. Alfidena, or Aufidena, contains at present about 1500 souls: it stands on the Rio Torto, a torrent which just below the town plunges down into a very deep and narrow glen, about a mile above its junction with the Sangro. There exists considerable remains of polygonal walls, and an Oscan inscription on the bridge which crosses the Rio Torto. Keppel Craven, Abruzzi, Vol. II. p. 58, 59.

[23] Strabo calls them Σαυνιτικὸν ἔθνος, V. p. 241; yet Livy represents them as suing for and obtaining peace as a distinct people, after a treaty had been concluded with the Samnites, IX. 45.

[24] As, for instance, "Hannibal ex Hirpinis in Samnium transit." Livy, XXII. 13.

nites; and it is by no means certain that they took part in the beginning of the contest with Rome; nor, on the other hand, that when they became involved in it, the other tribes which had been first engaged continued to maintain it without interruption.

The country of the Samnites still retains its ancient features, and our own eyes can inform us sufficiently of its nature. But of the Samnite people we can gain no distinct notions whatever. Unknown and unnoticed by the early Greek writers, they had been well-nigh exterminated before the time of those Roman writers whose works have come down to us; and in the Augustan age, nothing survived of them but a miserable remnant, retaining no traceable image of the former state of the nation. Our knowledge of the Samnites is literally limited to the single fact that they were a brave people, who clung resolutely to their national independence. We neither know what was the connection of the several tribes of the nation with each other, nor what was the constitution of each tribe[25] within itself. We know nothing distinct of their military system and tactic, except that they did not use the order of the phalanx; the sword and large shield[26] were their favorite arms, and not the small shield and pike. We do not know how they governed the countries which they conquered, nor how far they adopted the Roman system of colonies.[27] Their wealth, manner of living, and general civilization we can but guess at; and to add to all this, the very story of their wars with Rome having been recorded by no contemporary historian, has been corrupted, as usual, by the Roman vanity; and neither the origin of the contest, nor its circumstances, nor the terms of the several treaties which were made before its final issue, have been related truly.

Little is known of the state of the Samnite people.

Thus destitute of direct information, we may be pardoned for endeavoring to extract some further conclusions from the few facts known to us. The nature of their country makes it certain that the principal wealth of the Samnites consisted in their cattle. Wool and hides must have been the chief articles which they had to sell to their neighbors. But the high elevation of much of their country, as it preserved the pasture unscorched by the summer heats, was, on the other hand, especially exposed to the rigor of the winter; the snow lay so long on the ground that their cattle could not have found subsistence. And as, in like manner, the parched plains of Apulia yield no grass in the summer, the inhabitants of the centre of Italy, and of the coast of the Adriatic, must always have been dependent on each other; and the Samnites, either by treaty or by conquest, must have obtained the right of pasturing their cattle in winter in the low grounds near the sea, either on one side of the peninsula or on the other. On the shores of the Adriatic this was probably secured by their close connection with the Frentanians, a people of their own race; and by their constant friendly inter-

Their principal articles of produce.

Winter pasturage for their cattle on the sea-coast.

[25] Micali states that the Samnites were governed by a priestly aristocracy, like the Etruscans. He gives no authority for this, and certainly it is not proved by their mere practice of enlisting their soldiers on great emergencies with certain solemn religious ceremonies.

[26] Livy expressly speaks of them as scutati, and describes the form of their shield, IX. 40. The use of the scutum in itself implies that the sword, and not the spear, was the offensive weapon generally used; we are told also that the Campanians called their gladiators Samnites, because they equipped them with arms taken from the Samnites (Livy, IX. 40); and in such combats, as the very name shows, the sword was the common weapon. Add to this the story, whether well or ill founded, as to the particular fact, that the Romans borrowed their arms, offensive and defensive, "arma et tela," from the Samnites. Sallust, Bell. Catilin, 52. Athenæus, VI. 106, p. 273. Diodorus, XXIII. 1. Fragm. Vatic.

[27] Micali says that "their society was founded on a system of agrarian laws," and he quotes as his authority for this a fragment of Varro preserved to us by Philargyrius, one of the scholiasts on Virgil, in his note on Georgic. II. 167. The fragment runs thus: "Terra culturæ causâ attributa olim particulatim hominibus, ut Etruria Tuscis, Samnium Sabellis." But I do not understand this as saying any thing of agrarian laws, but merely that the earth became the property of particular portions and races of mankind, instead of being all common to all; and that thus Etruria was given (by the gods, I think, and not by an agrarian law) to the people of the Etruscans, and Samnium to the Sabellines.

course[28] with the Marrucinians and Vestinians; while their arms, by winning possession of Campania, procured for them an access to the coast on that side, and gave them the full enjoyment of that soft and sunny plain which extends along the shore of the Gulf of Salerno.

Their conquests in Campania.

It is not certain, as I have said, that the Samnites governed their Campanian conquests by means of colonies, but there is every probability that they did so. The Samnite colonists would thus constitute the ruling body in every city: and, like the early Roman patricians, might be called indifferently either the burghers or the aristocracy. Niebuhr supposes that the sixteen hundred Campanian knights, who in the great Latin war are said to have stood aloof from the mass of the people, and to have remained faithful to Rome, were the colony of the Samnite conquerors. And the frequent revolts which we read of, from one alliance to another, may mark a corresponding domestic revolution, in which the colony either lost or re-established its ascendency. Yet it may have happened that the colony, in some cases, had really identified itself with the old inhabitants, and felt with them more than with the people from whom they were themselves descended. In this manner the Samnite colonies may have become in feeling thoroughly Campanian, and have wished to make themselves independent of their own Samnite countrymen in Campanium; and thus, although the highest of the Campanian nobility were of Samnite extraction, yet Campania may have become, as it is represented, wholly independent of the Samnite nation within no long period after its first conquest.

How they were affected by the invasions of the Gauls.

Not the slightest notice remains of the effect produced on the Samnite dominion by the irruptions of the Gauls. Yet in the year 394–395 the Gauls had wintered[29] in Campania; and after their last appearance in Latium in 406, they are said to have retreated into Apulia[30] through the land of the Volscians and Falernians; so that they must have passed as it seems through a part of Samnium. The heart of the Samnite territory indeed they were not likely to assail; they were not expert in besieging walled cities, nor would they be tempted to invade the mountain fastnesses of the central Apennines. Thus if the Samnites did not choose to engage with them in the plains, their substantial power would be little impaired by their invasions; and they received from them perhaps no greater mischief than the ravaging of their territory in Campania, and the loss of their cattle, which might have been sent down to the coast for their winter pasture. It is possible, however, that a dread of the Gauls may have been one of the causes which led to a treaty of alliance between Rome and the Samnites[31] in the year 401.

The first Samnite war, which broke out eleven years afterwards, was no doubt

[28] The Vestinians join the Samnites in 424, and the Marsians, Pelignians, and Marrucinians, are represented as so closely connected with the Vestinians, that an attack on these would necessarily involve the Romans in a war with all the others. Livy, VIII. 29. I think it may be concluded that the Marsians and Palignians were on friendly terms with the Samnites, from the fact that the Latins, then in alliance with Rome, attacked the Pelignians in the first year of the Samnite war (Livy, VII. 38); and that as soon as peace is made between Rome and Samnium, the Roman armies march through the country of the Marsians and Pelignians, in order to reach Campania. Livy, VIII. 6.

According to Livy, IX. 13, the Apulians were hostile to the Samnites, because they were oppressed by them, and their country frequently laid waste. Had Livy any authority for this last expression, "campestria et maritima loca . . . ipsi montani atque agrestes depopulabantur," or did he put it in merely as a natural way of accounting for the ill-will of the Apulians towards their neighbor? But what if the injurious treatment of the Samnites consisted in compelling the Apulians to find pasture for their cattle in the winter; exactly as the Arragonese kings of Naples obliged all tenants holding of the crown in Apulia to let their lands during the winter to the cattle-owners of the Abruzzi; and although the French took off these restrictions, yet the present government has, in a great measure, reimposed them: and the Apulian proprietors are still obliged to reserve two-thirds of their land in pasture, and have only the cultivation of one-third left to their own disposal. See Keppel Craven, Abruzzi, Vol. I. p. 267–269.

[29] Livy, VII. 11.

[30] Livy, VII. 26.

[31] Livy, VII. 19. Diodorus, XVI. 45. It may be observed that Diodorus agrees with Livy in placing this treaty in the consulship of M. Fabius Ambustus, and T. Quintius; but the consulship is according to him the 2d year of the 107th Olympiad.

occasioned in part by the advance of the Samnite arms in the valley of the Liris, and by the war between Rome and the Auruncans in the year 410, which brought the Roman legions into the immediate neighborhood of Campania.[32] At this time Rome and Latium were in league together, and jointly pressing upon the Volscians; their power held out hopes to the Campanians that, by their aid, they might be defended against the Samnites. This aid was in the year 412 become highly needful; the Campanians, having ventured to defend the Sidicinians[33] against an attack of the Samnites, had drawn the hostilities of the Samnites upon themselves, and we find that a Samnite army occupied the ridge of Tifata immediately above Capua, and from thence descended like the Æquians and Volscians from Algidus, to the plain before the walls of the city. In this state of distress, Capua implored the protection of Rome and Latium, and obtained it.[34] A war between Samnium on the one hand, and the connected Romans, Latins, and Campanians on the other, was the immediate consequence.

Causes of the first war between the Romans and Samnites.

The Roman consuls in this year were M. Valerius Corvus, and A. Cornelius Cossus. Valerius is the hero of that famous legend already related, which told how he had vanquished in his early youth a gigantic Gaul by the aid of a heaven-sent crow. The acts of his consulship have been disguised by a far worse spirit; they were preserved, not by any regular historian, but in the mere funeral orations and traditional stories of his own family; and were at last still further corrupted by the flattery of a client of his house, the falsest of all the Roman writers, Valerius of Antium. Hence we have no real military history of the Samnite war in this first campaign, but accounts of the worthy deeds of two famous Romans, M. Valerius Corvus, and P. Decius Mus. They are the heroes of the two stories, and there is evidently no other object in either of them but to set off their glory. It seems to me to be a great mistake[35] to regard such mere panegyric as history.

Character of the accounts of the war.

All that history can relate is that the Romans, we know not with what allied

[32] Livy, VII. 28. Niebuhr supposes that by the name of Auruncans are meant the Volscians on the Liris, and that Sora was an Auruncan town. Vol. III. p. 101. Livy himself does not seem to have had this notion; for the Auruncan and Volscian wars are in his accounts carefully distinguished, and Sora is said to have been taken from the Volscians. The Auruncans, on the other hand, are mentioned again in the 8th Book, c. 15, and Suessa Aurunca is named as their chief town. Now Suessa is Sessa, a town standing on the crater of an old volcano, just above the modern road from Naples to Rome, a few miles to the east of the Garigliano or Liris. Is there any reason for thinking that these Auruncans were more closely connected with the Volscians of Sora and Arpinum than with those of Antium, or that the name Auruncan was at this period extended to any other Opican people than to those of the neighborhood of Sessa?

[33] Livy, VII. 29. The Sidicinians were close neighbors to the Auruncans, living on the same cluster of volcanic hills which form the boundary of the plain of Naples on the road towards Rome. Teanum, now Teano, was their principal town.

[34] Livy, VII. 31. But it is impossible to believe the statement in Livy that they applied to the Romans only, or that they purchased the Roman protection by a literal surrender, deditio, of themselves and their city to the sovereign disposal of Rome. Every step in the Samnite and Latin wars has been so disguised by the Roman annalists, that a probable narrative of these events can only be given by a free correction of their falsifications. The case of Capua applying for aid to Rome against the Samnites was exactly that of Corcyra asking help from Athens against Corinth. The motives which induced the Athenians to receive the Corcyræans into their alliance were the very same which influenced the Romans: the justice of the measure was in both cases equally questionable; but it may be doubted whether the Roman legions sent into Campania were ordered only to fight in the event of an actual attack made upon their allies, which was the charge given by Pericles' government to the ten ships sent to protect Corcyra. So truly is real history a lesson of universal application, that we should understand the war between Rome and Samnium far better from reading Thucydides' account of the war between Corinth and Corcyra, than from Livy's corrupted story of the very events themselves.

[35] Some of my readers may have seen a work which formed a sort of Appendix to the "Victoires, Conquêtes, &c. des Français," and was called "Tables du Temple de la Gloire." It consisted of an alphabetical catalogue raisonné of all Frenchmen, of whatever military rank, who had distinguished themselves, or thought that they had done so, in the course of the last war; and many of the articles were apparently contributed by the very individuals themselves who were the heroes of them. Now these notices had nothing of the license of a poetical account of events; they professed to be a real matter of fact narrative; they were published when the memory of the actions to which they relate was fresh, and in the face of the jealous

First campaign, and battl by Mount Gaurus.

force to aid them, took the field with two armies; that one of these was to protect Campania, while the other was destined to invade Samnium. The army in Campania was commanded by M. Valerius, and his panegyric, careless of historical details, brings him, without a word as to his previous march, to Mount Gaurus,[36] now Monte Barbaro, in a remote corner of Campania, close upon the sea above Pozzuoli. Here, says the story, he met the Samnites, and here, after a most bloody battle, he defeated them.

Unsuccessful invasion of Samnium.

The army which was to invade Samnium,[37] had scarcely entered the hills which bound the plain of Naples, apparently by the pass of Maddaloni, when it became involved in a deep defile, and was nearly cut off by the enemy. It was saved by the conduct and courage of the famous P. Decius, then one of the military or legionary tribunes; and thus his panegyrist gives the whole story in great detail, and ends with saying that the Roman army was not only saved from destruction, but gained a great victory over the enemy. As it is not pretended, however, that the Romans made any progress in Samnium beyond the scene of their victory, it is likely that their success was limited to their escaping from a very imminent danger, and being enabled to retreat with safety.

Result of the campaign.

The story of Valerius pretends that he won yet a second victory over the whole collected force of Samnium, which had been gathered to revenge their late defeat; and yet we are told that as soon as the Roman armies had returned to Rome, the Campanians[38] were obliged to send embassies to the senate, requesting that a force might winter in Campania for their protection, to keep off the attacks of the Samnites. This is the beginning of a totally different story, that of the sedition of the year 413, and the author of it having no concern with the Samnite war, did not think of reconciling his

criticism of all the nations of Europe, where there were thousands of witnesses both able and eager to expose any exaggeration. And yet, after all, what sort of history of any of the campaigns of the last war could be compiled from the "Tables du Temple de la Gloire?" I cannot therefore, persuade myself that the details of the battle by Mount Gaurus, or of the wise and valiant conduct of Decius in Samnium, deserve to be transcribed in a modern history of Rome. They have not obtained such celebrity as to be worth preserving as legends; they have not in their style and substance those marks of originality which would make them valuable as a picture of the times; and least of all, have they that trustworthiness which would entitle them to be regarded as historically true.

[36] Livy, VII. 32. "Consules . . . ab urbe profecti, Valerius in Campaniam, Cornelius in Samnium, ille ad montem Gaurum, hic ad Saticulam, castra ponunt." "What actions," says Niebuhr, "had forced the consul to fall back thither, and gave to the Samnites that assurance of victory with which they hastened to attack him,—this knowledge, as almost all else whereby the Samnite wars might have become more intelligible, is buried in everlasting night." Vol. III. p. 137.

[37] Livy, VII. 34–36. The account of the honors paid to Decius on this occasion by his fellow-soldiers, is characteristic of the time and people, and is worth transcribing. "After the battle, the consul called all the soldiers together, and made a speech, in which he commended all the worthy deeds which Decius had done." [Polybius especially mentions and praises this practice, VI. 39.] "He then, as was the custom, gave him divers gifts of honor, especially a crown of gold, and one hundred oxen, and one beautiful white ox over and above the number, with his horns bedecked with gold. To the soldiers who had been with him in his post of danger, the consul gave an ox to each man, and two coats; and told them that their daily allowance of corn should for the time to come be doubled. Then, when the consul had ended, all the soldiers of the legions gave to Decius a wreath of twisted grass, which was accustomed to be given by a beseiged or blockaded army to him who had delivered them; and it was put upon his head amidst the cheers of all the army. Another wreath also, of the like sort, was given to Decius by the soldiers of his own band. So Decius stood, wearing his crown of gold and his wreath of grass, and he forthwith offered in sacrifice to Mars the beautiful white ox with the gilded horns, and the other hundred oxen he gave to the soldiers who had followed him in his enterprise. And the other soldiers too gave each man to the soldiers of Decius a pound of corn from their own allowances, and a measure exceeding a pound in weight (sextarios) of wine. All the while that they were giving these honors to Decius and his soldiers, the whole army were shouting and cheering, for they knew not what to do for joy." Livy, VII. 37.

[38] Livy VII. 38. He adds that the people of Suessa sent an embassy to the same effect. This shows, that immediately after the retreat of the Roman armies, the Samnites were beginning, not only to overrun Campania again, but even to carry their ravages beyond the Vulturnus into the country of the Sidicinians and Auruncans.

account with the exaggerated representations given of the preceding campaign. That the Romans drove the Samnites from Campania is probable; but, on the other hand, they failed in their attack upon Samnium, and the Samnites were clearly no way dispirited as to the general result of the war.

It would seem from a short and obscure notice in Livy,[39] that the Samnites were assisted in this war by some of their neighbors; whether as equal or as dependent allies we know not. For it appears that the Latins, instead of being engaged in Campania or in Samnium, moved into the heart of Italy and attacked the Pelignians; so that we must suppose that the operations of this year were carried on on a most extensive scale, and we thus see how much greater was this contest with Samnium, than any other in which Rome had been engaged before.

The Latins engaged against the Pelignians.

The active campaign was short; for the consuls, so far as appears, still entered on their office on the 1st of July, and their triumphs took place on the 22d and 24th of September.[40] They themselves did not return to Campania, but parties of Roman soldiers, according to the request of the Campanians, were sent back to garrison the several cities, and a large force was thus kept on service during the winter. This state of things lasted through the following spring; the Romans would not commence offensive operations till the new consuls should come into office: of the movements of the Samnites we hear nothing; but it may be that their usual season of military service was the same as that of the Romans, and mere plundering parties would be deterred by the force left to keep them in check. But when the new consul, C. Marcius Rutilus, arrived after midsummer to take the command of the army, he found himself engaged in a very different duty from that of marching against the Samnites.

A Roman army winters in Campania.

Had we any history of these times, events so important and so notorious as the great disturbance of the year 413 must have been related in their main points clearly and faithfully. But because we have merely a collection of stories recording the great acts of particular families and individuals, and in each of these the glory of its own hero, and not truth, was the object: even matters the most public and easy to be ascertained are so disguised, that nothing beyond the bare fact that there was a disturbance, and that it was at length appeased, is common to the various narratives.[41] The panegyrists of the Valerian family claimed the glory of putting an end to the contest for M. Valerius Corvus, who was, they said, specially appointed dictator; while the stories of the Marcian and Servilian families said that every thing had been done by the two consuls, C. Marcius Rutilus, and Q. Servilius. One account represented the affair as a secession of the Roman commons, another described it as a mutiny of the army in Campania. The story which most of the annalists afterwards adopted, taking only the latter view of the case, and thinking that mutinous soldiers ought not to benefit by their mutiny, told only how they were pardoned for their crime, and how they obtained[42] no more than one or two insignificant concessions, which in no respect compromised the dignity of the government. But other accounts[43] preserved the memory of a secession headed by a tribune of the commons, and winning some of the most important constitu-

Domestic disturbances

[39] Livy, VII. 38. "Hujus certaminis fortuna... Latinos, jam exercitibus comparatis, ab Romano in Pelignum vertit bellum." This can only mean that the Latins directed their main force against the northern side of the Samnite confederacy, moving by the lake Fucinus upon Sulmo, and the country of the Pelignians, and thus threatening Samnium on the rear.

[40] See the Fasti Capitolini.

[41] "Adeo nihil," says Livy, "præterquam seditionem fuisse, eamque compositam, inter antiquos rerum auctores constat." VII. 42. We must not suppose that the "ancient authors" here spoken of were contemporary with these times; they were but the annalists of the sixth and seventh centuries of Rome, who followed each the traditions and memorials of a different family. Livy himself, in another place, VIII. 40, deplores the want of all contemporary writers for the times of the Samnite wars, as one great cause of the hopeless confusion in which the story of those wars was involved.

[42] Livy, VII. 41.

[43] Livy, VII. 42.

tional points which had ever yet been agitated; nay, they told how it forced from the patricians that which above all things they would be most loth to yield, both on public grounds and on private,—a general abolition of debts.[44]

The army in Campania mutinies and marches towards Rome.

The truth, however, in this instance, seems not difficult to disentangle. In spite of the successive lowerings of the rate of interest, there was a large amount of debt undischarged, because there had been no change for the better in the circumstances of the commons at large to enable them to pay off even the principal of what they owed. A multitude of men thus involved, many of them perhaps actually nexi, were kept on foreign service during the winter, a thing in itself extremely galling to them, and were quartered in the towns of Campania, where they witnessed a state of luxury such as they could never have conceived before. Nothing is more probable[45] than that they should have longed to appropriate those wealthy cities to themselves, to establish themselves at Capua, as their fathers, forty years before, would have fain done at Veii, and to make the Campanians their subjects, the commons of a state in which they themselves would be the burghers. Stories of their design were carried to Rome, and the commons there feeling that they too had their share of distress, proposed also to seek their remedy. Before the plans of the soldiers were yet ripe, attempts were made by their officers to break up their combinations, and detachments of those who were most suspected were ordered home, as if they were no longer wanted in Campania. But these, when they came to Lautulæ, a narrow pass between the sea and the mountains close to Tarracina, concerted their measures with the cohort which was there in garrison, and openly refused to obey their commanders. The example once set became contagious; the mass of the soldiers quartered in Campania joined the revolters, and all marched together[46] towards Rome, releasing on their way all the bondmen debtors whom they found working as slaves on their creditors' lands, till their number was swelled to 20,000 men.

The commons rise at Rome. M. Valerius Corvus dictator.

They halted on the slope of the Alban hills, near Bovillæ, fortified a regular camp, plundered the country as if it belonged to an enemy,[47] and seized upon a patrician, T. Quinctius, at his farm or country-house near Tusculum, and forced him to become their leader. The commons at Rome waited no longer; they too rose; they too laid hold on a patrician, C. Manlius, loving the name of their old champion and martyr M. Manlius: they marched out of the city, and established themselves in a spot four miles distant from the walls. Even now the patricians were not left helpless; besides themselves and their clients, a numerous body, they would on this occasion be

[44] Auctor de Viris Illustribus, in Valer. Corvo. Appian, Samnitic. Fragm. I. § 2.

[45] Perhaps I ought hardly to have expressed myself so strongly as to the probability of this part of the story, since Niebuhr considers it undeserving of credit. But Wachsmuth has well observed, that the eager desire of the commons to settle at Veii, proves sufficiently that they had no invincible attachment to Rome as their native country: he adds, with no less truth, "that a people whose innocence is the fruit of ignorance rather than of principle, is little able to resist the first strong temptation." How great were the excesses of the Spartans after the Peloponnesian war, when opportunities of indulgence were first offered to them! And why should we conceive that the Roman commons were men of greater simplicity of manners than the Samnites, who had formerly seized Capua in a similar manner, when they were inhabiting it jointly with the Etruscans? Compare also the stories of the forcible occupation of Smyrna by some Colophonian exiles who had been hospitably received there (Herodotus I. 150); and of the seizure of Zancle by the Samians (Herodotus, VI. 23), as showing that such acts were practised even by Greeks towards Greeks, at a period when manners had been as little corrupted by luxury and skepticism as they were at this time at Rome; whereas the Campanians were no countrymen of the Romans, and therefore, according to the too prevailing notions of the ancient world, were entitled to far less consideration.

[46] Appian, Samnitic. Fragm. I. § 1. The persons whom he speaks of as ἐπὶ τῶν ἔργων ἐν τοῖς ἀγροῖς δεδεμένους, must have been debtors working as slaves on the "possessiones" of their patrician creditors, on such portions of land lately conquered from the Volscians as had been occupied in the usual manner by individuals. Foreign-purchased slaves must have been too rare at Rome at this period, to have been employed in great numbers as agricultural laborers: and, in fact, the slaves who were confined to work in the workhouses of the patricians in these early times, are always described as insolvent debtors.

[47] "*Ex prædatoribus vagis* quidam compertum adtulerunt," &c.—Livy, VII. 39.

joined by all the noblest and richest of the commons, and by many, perhaps, of the best men even among the less wealthy, who would view with horror the disobedience of the soldiers, and the breach of their military oath. They prepared to put down the revolt; yet, not trusting to force alone, they named as dictator M. Valerius Corvus, the most popular man in Rome, born of a house whose members had ever befriended the commons, himself in the vigor of youth,[48] scarcely thirty, yet already old in glory, and now in the full renown of his recent victories over the Samnites. The dictator proceeded to meet the soldiers from Campania; the consuls were left to deal with the commons who had seceded from the city.

Reconciliation of the contending parties.

But when the opposing parties[49] approached each other, and citizens were seen arrayed in order of battle against citizens, all shrunk alike from bringing their contests to such an issue, and with a sudden revulsion of feeling the soldiers, instead of joining battle, first welcomed each other with friendly greetings, then, as they drew nearer, they grasped each other's hands, till at last, amidst mutual tears and expressions of remorse, they rushed into each other's arms. It may well be believed that not Valerius only, but the majority of the patricians, were noble enough to rejoice sincerely at this termination of the mutiny, although they foresaw that whatever were the demands of the soldiers and the commons, it would now be necessary to grant them.

Terms demanded by the soldiers, and granted.

But the insurgents were also brought to a softer temper, and asked little but what might have been given them unasked, as being in itself just and reasonable. First, an act of amnesty[50] was passed for the mutiny and the secession, and the dictator entreated the patricians and those of the commons who had sided with them, that they would never, even in private life, in jest or in earnest, reproach any man with having been concerned in these unhappy dissensions. Then there was passed and sworn to, with all religious solemnities,[51] a law which the soldiers regarded as their great charter, that no man's name who had been once enlisted should be struck off the list of the legions without his own consent, and that no one who had once been chosen military tribune should be afterwards[52] obliged to serve as a centurion. They deprecated the power of striking their names off the list of soldiers, partly because it degraded them to an inferior rank, that of the capite censi, who were

[48] He was three and twenty in his first consulship (Livy, VII. 40), and he was consul for the first time in the year 407. — See Livy, VII. 26.

[49] Livy, VII. 42. Appian, Samnitic. Fragm. I. § 2. This sudden burst of feeling is credible enough; for civil war seems shocking to men who are little scrupulous in shedding the blood of foreigners, however unjustly. In this respect, it needs the hardness and coldness of a later stage of society to overcome the natural shrinking from domestic warfare. The feudal times are, of course, an exception to this; for to the isolation and lawlessness of the feudal system the relations of countryman and fellow-citizen were almost unknown.

[50] Livy, VII. 41.

[51] "Lex sacrata militaris." A lex sacrata partook of the character of a treaty, and was sworn to by the two parties between whom it had been agreed to. Thus the term is applied only to such laws as settled points most deeply affecting the interests of the two orders in the state, and were therefore a sort of treaty of peace between them. Of this sort, besides the famous laws respecting the tribunes of the commons, was the law of Icilius, de Aventino publicando.

[52] It should be observed, that Livy gives to this petition a different object. The soldiers, he says, insisted that no one who had been once tribune should afterwards be made centurion, out of dislike to one P. Salonius, who had been made almost every other year one or the other, and who was obnoxious to them, because he had especially opposed their meeting. Both Niebuhr and Wachsmuth suppose, on the contrary, that P. Salonius was a popular man with the soldiers, and that the petition was made in his behalf, to save him from being obliged to go on serving in a lower rank, after having once served in a higher. Wachsmuth well compares the case of Volero Publilius, who complained of being required to serve as a common soldier, after having been once centurion. (Livy, II. 55.) Many motives may have joined, however, in suggesting this demand of the soldiers. It was a great thing for a deserving soldier, that if once appointed military tribune (six of whom were at this time chosen by the votes of the people themselves, Livy, VII. 5), he should be freed from the necessity of serving again, except in the same or a higher rank. And it was a great thing for the mass of the commons, that promotion should be kept as open as possible, and that it should be necessary every year to fill up the vacancies among the centurions with new men, instead of confining them to a certain number of individuals who might pass at pleasure from one command to another.

considered unfit to bear arms; partly because, whilst they were on military service, they were protected from being personally attached for debts; and partly, also, because service in Campania bore an agreeable aspect, and might furnish a poor man with the means of relieving himself from his embarrassments. The law about the military tribunes had, probably, various objects; amongst the rest it may have been intended to advance the dignity of that office, which offered to the commons the readiest means of acquiring distinction, and thus was a natural step to the highest political magistracies.

Terms demanded and refused.

Another demand was made in a different spirit; that the pay of the horsemen or knights should be lowered, they receiving at that period three times as much as the foot-soldiers. In requiring this the soldiers not only wished to reduce the public expenditure, and sc to lighten their own taxation, but there was also a feeling of enmity towards the knights, who had taken a decided part against them. But on this point the senate would not yield; and the soldiers, ashamed perhaps of the motives which had led them to ask for it, did not press their demand.[53]

Demands of the commons in Rome. The Genucian laws.

While the mutiny of the legions was thus ended, the commons, who had withdrawn from the city, returned to their homes again; and L. Genucius,[54] one of their tribunes, proposed to them in the Forum, certain political measures to which, it was understood, the patricians would offer no opposition. These were, "that no man should be re-elected to the same magistracy within ten years, nor hold two magistracies in the same year; and that both consuls *might* be plebeians, as the Licinian law had declared that one *must* be." The multiplication of various offices in the same hands is an evil of which we have no instance on record, because we have no lists of any of the magistrates of this period, except the consuls only. The frequent re-election of the same person to the consulship created an aristocracy within the aristocracy, and confined the highest offices to a number of great families; and now that the Licinian law was again observed, it would raise a few plebeian houses to an undue distinction, whilst the mass of the commons would be altogether excluded. It may be observed that C. Marcius, the plebeian consul of this very year, was now consul for the fourth time within a period of fifteen years.

General abolition of debts.

But there was another law passed, which Livy could not endure to record, and of which we know not who was the proposer:[55] a law whose very name all settled societies regarded with horror; a law which is, indeed, like war, an enormous evil, but which in this is most unlike war, that it has never been adopted, except when it was really necessary to prevent an evil still greater. In order to give the commons an opportunity of rising to a more healthful condition, they were to be freed once for all from the shackles thrown around them by a former period of unavoidable distress: the consequences of the burning of the city by the Gauls had never yet been shaken off, nor did it appear likely that in the ordinary state of things they ever would be. It was demanded, therefore, by the commons, and M. Valerius, it is said, advised compliance with their demand, that an act of grace should be extended to all debtors, and that their cred-

[53] As the commons were persuaded by Valerius and Horatius to abandon their demand for the summary execution of the decemvirs.—See chap. xvi.

[54] Niebuhr supposes, not unnaturally, that this Genucius belonged to the family of the tribune Genucius, who was murdered by the aristocracy in the year 281.—See p. 65. He was also, in all probability, of the same family with the plebeian consuls of the years 385, 387, and 388.

[55] It is attested by Appian, who, as Niebuhr thinks, copied this part of his work from Dionysius; and by the little work De Viris Illustribus. Appian's words are plain enough: ἡ βουλὴ—τὰς μὲν τῶν χρεῶν ἀποκοπὰς ἐψηφίσατο πᾶσι Ῥωμαίοις· τοῖς δὲ τότε ἐχθροῖς (namely, the revolted soldiers), καὶ ἄδειαν—Samnitic. Fragm. I. § 2. There is no mistaking the well-known expression χρεῶν ἀποκοπή.—"Num honestum igitur," asks Cicero with respect to Cæsar when he had just heard of his crossing the Rubicon, "χρεῶν ἀποκοπὰς, φυγάδων καθόδους, sexcenta alia scelera moliri,

τὴν θεῶν μεγίστην ὥστ᾽ ἔχειν τυραννίδα?"

Ad Atticum, VII. 11.

The expression in the Roman writer is no less decisive. M. Valerius, he says, "sublato ære alieno, seditionem compressit."

itors should not be permitted to enforce payment. In other words, all those who had pledged their personal freedom for the payment of their debts (nexi) were released from their bond; nor could the prætor give over to his creditor's power, addicere, any debtor who had refused, or might refuse, to enter into such an engagement. Thus the burden of actual debts was taken away; and to prevent the pressure of an equal burden hereafter, even the lowest rate of interest was declared illegal, and any man who received more than the actual sum which he had lent was liable to restore it fourfold.

This was a sort of national bankruptcy, yet surely it wore the mildest features of that evil, and in some respects did not deserve the name. The nation itself broke no faith; but it required one portion of its citizens to sacrifice their strict legal rights in favor of another portion for the common benefit of all. It was doing on a large scale and under the pressure of urgent necessity, what we see done every day on a smaller scale for an object, not of necessity, but of expediency; when individuals are forced to sell their property at a price fixed by others, in order to facilitate the execution of a canal or a railway. The patricians were, in like manner, obliged to part with the money which had been advanced as a loan either by themselves or by their fathers; and the compensation which they received was the continued existence of a state of society fraught to them above all their fellow-citizens with the highest means of happiness: they lost their money to preserve their country. Had such a sacrifice been made to the indolence, or carelessness, or dishonesty of their debtors, it would have been mischievous as a precedent, however urgent the necessity which led to it; but in the present case the debts of the commons had arisen out of a common calamity, not occasioned by their fault, nor to be remedied by their exertions: their distress, therefore, was fairly entitled to sympathy, and if there be any meaning in the term civil society, justice would require that its stronger members should bear the burdens of the weaker, and should submit to more than their share of the inconveniences of a common misfortune, rather than allow it to entail upon their fellow-citizens not inconvenience merely, but absolute ruin.

Its necessity and justice.

The domestic disturbances of this year produced important consequences abroad. The whole brunt of the Samnite war devolved on the Latins, and they sustained it so ably that their consideration amongst their allies was greatly increased, and Latium, rather than Rome, began to be regarded as the most powerful member of the league. The remains of the Volscians, such as the brave people of Privernum, and the Antiatians, together with those more distant tribes of the same stock who bordered on Campania, and were known to the Romans under the name of the Auruncans, began to gather themselves under the supremacy of Latium, and the Campanians, who had good reason to dislike the presence of Roman soldiers in their towns, may have hoped to find in a new confederacy, of which the Latins should be the head, protection at once against Rome and against the Samnites. Accordingly, the Romans felt that it was no time for them to continue their quarrel with Samnium; and in the very next year they concluded with the Samnites[56] a separate peace. Thus the relations of all these nations were entirely changed: Rome had connected herself with Samnium, and perhaps

Growing power of the Latins. Peace between Rome and Samnium.

A. U. C. 414. A. C. 340.

[56] The Roman story is (Livy, VIII. 1, 2), that when L. Æmilius, the consul, entered the Samnite territory he found no enemy to oppose him; that the Samnites humbly sued for peace, and purchased an armistice to allow them to send ambassadors to Rome, by giving the consul a year's pay for his army, and three months' allowance of corn. What would have been the account of a Latin writer? Would it not have been something of this sort? "That when the confederate armies of Rome and Latium were actually in the field, to invade the Samnite territory on different sides, the Romans suddenly and treacherously made a separate peace with the common enemy, and withdrew their army: and that, not content with this, they actually entered into an alliance with the Samnites, and were ready to join them against Latium."—Compare the extreme dissatisfaction of the former allies of Lacedæmon, when she suddenly formed her separate treaty with Athens soon after the conclusion of the peace of Nicias.—Thucydides, V. 27.

through the Samnites with their neighbors the Marsians and Pelignians; while, on the other side, stood a new confederacy, consisting of the Latins and all the people of Opican extraction who lay between them and the Samnite frontier, whether known by the name of Volscians, Auruncans, Sidicinians, or Campanians. In the same manner, after the Peloponnesian war, we find Thebes and Corinth, so long the close allies of Lacedæmon, organizing a new confederacy against her; and thus, at a later period, Athens was at one time supporting Thebes, and shortly after, having become jealous of her growing power and ambition, joined Lacedæmon against her former ally; so that in the last campaigns of Epaminondas, the free citizens of Athens and the barbarian mercenaries of Dionysius the tyrant were fighting in the same ranks in defence of the Spartan aristocracy.

CHAPTER XXIX.

THE GREAT LATIN WAR—BATTLE UNDER MOUNT VESUVIUS—THE PUBLILIAN LAWS—FINAL SETTLEMENT OF LATIUM.—A. U. C. 415-417 (410-412 NIEBUHR).

"Je me refuse à croire que des peuples confédérés puissent lutter long-temps, à égalité de force, contre une nation où la puissance gouvernmentale serait centralisée."—DE TOCQUEVILLE, De la Démocratie en Amérique; Tome I. p. 290.

Uncertain relations between Rome and Latium.

ALTHOUGH Rome had concluded a separate peace with Samnium, yet the old alliance with the Latins still subsisted in name unbroken. But it could not long remain so; for the Latins continued the war against the Samnites, and might undoubtedly have called upon the Romans to aid them, according to the terms of the alliance; while the Samnites[1] called upon the Romans to procure for them peace with Latium also. In fact, the existing state of things showed clearly that the relations between Rome and Latium must undergo some change; either the two nations must become wholly separate, or more closely united; if they were to act together at all, some scheme must be devised to insure that they should act unanimously.

The Latins make proposals for a union between Rome and Latium.

The general congress of the Latin cities took upon itself to propose such a scheme; and the two prætors for the year, L. Annius of Setia, and L. Numisius of Circeii, magistrates corresponding to the Roman consuls, and retaining the name which the consuls had borne down to the time of the decemvirate, were dispatched with ten of the principal deputies of the congress, to communicate their proposal to Rome.[2] The substance of it was that the two nations should be completely united; that they should both be governed by two consuls or prætors, one to be chosen from each nation; that there should be one senate, to consist of Romans and Latins in equal proportions;

[1] Livy's whole narrative proceeds on the assumption that the Latins were the dependent allies of Rome, and that the war was on their part a revolt. Now, this is certainly false, as we know from the terms of the original alliance preserved by Dionysius, V. 61 (see p. 58 of this history), and from the indisputable authority of Cincius (p. 58, note 4). Livy himself supplies a refutation of his own story; for he allows expressly, VIII. 2, that the Latins had the right of making war with whom they pleased: that is, in Greek language, they were αὐτόδικοι, or able to give and receive satisfaction in their own name, without being obliged to refer their quarrels to any superior; one of the characteristics of an equal as opposed to a dependent alliance.—See Thucyd. V. 18, 27. I have, therefore, tacitly corrected all Livy's false coloring in this matter, and given his facts in their true light.

[2] Livy, VIII. 5.

and a third similar provision must have been made for the popular branch of the government, so that a number of Latin tribes should be created, equal to that of the Roman, and the fifty-four tribes of the two nations should constitute one common sovereign assembly. In one point the Latins were willing to yield precedence to Rome; none of their cities was equal to Rome in size or greatness: Rome, therefore, was to be the capital of the nation and the seat of government; there the senate should sit, and the assembly of the tribes be held; the Roman Jupiter of the Capitol should be equal to the Latin Jupiter of the mountain of Alba; to both should the consuls of the united people offer their vows when they first came into office, and to the temples of both should they go up in triumph, when they returned home from war with victory.[3]

These proposals are rejected with indignation.

There were probably some in Rome who would have accepted this union gladly; but the general feeling, both of the patricians and of the commons, was strongly against it. It was viewed as a sacrifice of national independence and national pride. To the Latins, used already to a federal government, it was but taking another city into their union; but to the Romans, whose whole political life was centred in Rome, it was admitting strangers into the Forum and into the Senate, and allowing the majesty of the Roman Jupiter to be profaned by the entrance of a foreigner into his temple. Accordingly when the Latin prætors announced their proposal to the senate, which had assembled in the Capitol, it was rejected with indignation; and T. Manlius Torquatus,[4] who was one of the newly elected consuls, declared that if the senate should be so lost to itself as to receive the law from a man of Setia, he would come armed into the senate-house, and would plunge his sword into the body of the first Latin whom he saw within its walls. Then he turned to the image of the Capitoline Jupiter, and exclaimed: "Hear, O Jove, this wickedness! Wilt thou endure to behold a stranger consul and a stranger senate within the sacred precinct of thy temple, as though thou wert thyself vanquished and made captive?" To this the Latin prætor, L. Annius of Setia, made a reply which the Romans called insulting to their god. "But Jove," said the Roman story,[5] "taught the stranger to repent him of his scorn: for as soon as he had spoken his proud words, the lightning flashed and the thunder pealed, and as the Latin left the temple in haste, to go down by the hundred steps towards the Forum, his foot slipped, and he fell from the top of the steps to the bottom, and his head was dashed against a stone, and he died." Some of the annalists, struck perhaps by its being a notorious fact that L. Annius commanded the Latin army in the war, scrupled to say that he had been killed before its commencement; they said, therefore, that he had only been stunned by his fall: and they said nothing of the sudden burst of the lightning and thunder. No doubt, if the traditions of the family of L. Annius had been preserved, they would have given a different picture of his mission. But whatever were the particulars of it, its result is certain; the proposal for an equal union was rejected, and the sword was to decide whether Latium should from henceforth be subject to Rome, or Rome to Latium.

[3] If the Latins really consented, as is not improbable, to acknowledge Rome as the capital of the united nation, it accounts for their subsequent acquiescence in the settlement made by the Romans after the war, so far as this, that it shows their willingness to waive the mere feeling as to the name of their country, and their consciousness that Rome was so superior to every other Latin city, as to be fairly entitled to be the head of the united nation. What I have added in the text respecting the Jupiter of the mountain of Alba, seems warranted by the actual practice of later times, even after the Latins were in a state of acknowledged inferiority to Rome. It is well known, that one of the consul's first duties after entering upon his office, was to offer sacrifice at the great Latin festival on the mountain of Alba, as well as to sacrifice to the Roman Jupiter in the Capitol. Livy, XXI. 63, XXII. 1. And, although the instances are of more rare occurrence, yet we read of Roman generals triumphing at the Mons Albanus, and going up in solemn procession by the Via Triumphalis to the temple of the Latin Jupiter, as they went up usually by the Via Sacra to the Capitol. We cannot imagine, therefore, that the Latins, when proposing a perfectly equal union, should have consented to assign less honors to their national god, than he enjoyed even when they were become dependent.

[4] Livy, VIII. 5.

[5] Livy, VIII. 6.

The Romans, however, had made up their minds to this issue before they heard the proposals of the Latin ambassadors. They were anxious to engage in the war at a moment when they might be assisted by the whole force of the Samnites: the Latins, on the other hand, would gladly have reduced Samnium to submission before they came to an open breach with Rome. Resolved, therefore, on the struggle, and well aware of its importance, the Romans wished to anticipate the election of the new consuls,[6] that they might have more time for their preparations before the usual season for military operations arrived, which, as we have seen, was not till after the harvest. Accordingly, the consuls of the year 409 were required by a decree of the senate to resign their office before the end of their year, the middle of the summer, and two men of the highest military reputation were appointed to succeed them. One of these was T. Manlius Torquatus, renowned in his youth, like Valerius Corvus, for having slain a gigantic Gaul in single combat, and no less remarkable for a force of character, such as is best fitted for the control of great emergencies, when what in ordinary life is savageness becomes often raised and sobered into heroism. He had been consul only four years before; but a special act, we must suppose, dispensed in his case with the recent provisions of the Genucian law. His colleague was the deliverer of the Roman army from its imminent peril in Samnium in the first campaign of the late war, and a man no less distinguished nine years earlier for his moderation and equity as one of the five commissioners appointed to relieve the commons from the burden of their debts,[7] the famous P. Decius Mus.

The Romans prepare for war. T. Manlius and P. Decius are appointed consuls.

The Romans had good reason to prepare earnestly for the coming contest; for never had they been engaged in one so perilous. With two or three exceptions all the Latin cities were united against them; not all indeed with equal determination, but still all were their enemies. Tusculum,[8] whose true friendship they had so long experienced; Lavinium, the sacred city, which contained the holy things reported to have been brought by Æneas from Troy; Setia, Cerceii, and Signia, Roman colonies, were now joined with the mass of the Latin nation, with Tibur and Præneste, with Pedum, Nomentum, and Aricia. The Latin nobles were personally known to those of Rome, and in many instances connected with them by mutual marriages; the two nations speaking the same language, with the same manners, institutions, and religious rites, trained with the same discipline to the use of the same arms, were bound moreover to each other by the closeness of their long alliance; their soldiers had constantly served in the same camp, and almost in the same tents; the several parts of their armies[9] had constantly been blended together; legions, cohorts, and maniples had been made up of Romans and Latins in equal proportions; the soldiers, centurions, and tribunes of both nations were thus familiar with each other's faces: and each man would encounter and recognize in his enemy an old and tried comrade.

Importance of the contest.

"The Romans and Latins," says Livy,[10] "were alike in every thing, except in their courage." This is an unworthy slander. Even nations of different race, and climate, and institutions, when long trained together under a common system of military discipline, and accustomed to fight side by side in the same army, lose all traces of their original disparity. But what the Latins were, we know from the rank which they held

The Latin military character not inferior to the Roman.

[6] Livy, VIII. 2.

[7] "Quinqueviri mensarii." See Livy, VII. 21.

[8] Geminus Metius, who was slain by the young T. Manlius, commanded the horsemen of Tusculum.—Livy, VIII. 7. Lavinium, according to Livy, took no part in the first campaign, but the Fasti Capitolini says that the consul Mænius, in the year 417, triumphed over the Lavinians; and their disposition is evident from Livy's own story, VIII. 11. The prætors of the whole nation for the first year of the war came from Setia and Circeii, and they are especially said to have induced Signia to join the confederacy.

[9] Livy, VIII. 7, 8.

[10] "Adeo nihil apud Latinos dissonum ab Romanâ re præter animos erat."—VIII. 8.

amongst the nations of Italy, and from the families which they afterwards furnished to Rome, when it became their common country. The Latins were able to contend on equal terms with the Samnites and Volscians, with the countrymen of C. Pontius and C. Marius. From Latium Rome received the Fulvii,[11] a family marked at once with all the great and all the bad qualities of the Roman aristocracy; and what Roman house could ever boast of brighter specimens of every Roman virtue than the Latin house of the Catos of Tusculum? The issue of the contest was not owing to the superior courage of the Romans, but to the inherent advantages possessed by a single powerful state when contending against a confederacy whose united strength she can all but balance alone, while to each of its separate members she is far superior.

The Latin confederacy, and its weaknesses.

With the Latins were joined, as we have seen, the Campanians, the Sidicinians, the Auruncans, and the Volscians, including under this name the various remnants of that people, the Antiatians on the coast, and the several tribes or cities in the valley of the Liris. Laurentum, Ardea, and perhaps Lanuvium,[12] alone of all the Latin cities took part with Rome: Fundi and Formiæ stood aloof from the rest of their Volscian countrymen and remained neutral, allowing a free passage to the Roman armies through their territory.[13] It was a more remarkable circumstance, and one of ill omen for the unanimity and perseverance of the Latin confederacy, that the knights[14] or aristocracy of Capua, whether of Samnite extraction, or of mixed blood, Samnite, Etruscan, and Opican, protested as a body against the war with Rome, although for the present the influence of the Latin party overbore their opposition. But it was evident that on the first reverses they would regain their ascendency, and hasten to withdraw their countrymen from the league. We have also indications[15] of a Roman party in some of the cities of the Latins; and it is impossible to suppose that Tusculum in particular should not have contained many zealous supporters of the old alliance with Rome. Probably the Roman and anti-Roman parties were in most places more or less identical with the aristocracy and the party of the commons; and already, as in the second Punic war, Rome was regarded by the Italian aristocracies as the greatest bulwark of their ascendency.

Allies of Rome.

With Rome were united some few Latin towns,[16] some of her own colonies,[17] her old allies the Hernicans, and above all the Samnites and their

[11] L. Fulvius, who was consul in the year 427, had been chief magistrate of Tusculum only the very year before he was consul at Rome.—Pliny, Hist. Natur. VII. 43. Ed. Venet. 1559.

[12] I agree with Niebuhr and with Sigonius, that in Livy's narrative, VIII. 12, 13, Lavinio and Laviniis should be restored instead of Lanuvio and Lanuvinis. It is not only that the Fasti Capitolini name the people of Lavinium and not of Lanuvium as those over whom the consul Mænius triumphed, or that several MSS. of Livy support the correction; but in the settlement of Latium the Lanuvians are named apart, as if they had been treated with singular favor, which is scarcely to be conceived, if they had been among the last of the Latins to remain in arms. And that they were favorably treated appears also from the famous article "Municipium" in Festus, where they are classed along with the people of Fundi, Formiæ, and others, who we know were thought worthy of reward rather than punishment. Besides, Livy himself tells us that the Antiatians in the year 415 ravaged the district called Solonius (VIII. 12), and we know from Cicero, de Divinatione, I. 36, that this district was a part of the territory of Lanuvium. It is certain, therefore, that Lanuvium must have been friendly to Rome at that time, and if so, it is not conceivable that she could afterwards have joined the Latins, when their cause was almost desperate. But I am not sure that the mistake is not to be ascribed to Livy himself rather than to his copyists: for it seems a just remark of Drakenborch's that Livy calls the people of Lavinium not Lavinii, but Laurentes, as if he had confused the two towns together. Yet "Laurentes," in VIII. 11, must mean the people of Laurentum, not of Lavinium, from a comparison with Livy's own statement about Lavinium in the beginning of the same chapter; and that the two names really belong to two distinct places is proved by their being both found in the list of the thirty Latin towns given by Dionysius, V. 61.

[13] Livy, VIII. 14.

[14] Livy, VIII. 11.

[15] The Romans received information of the hostile designs of the Latins, says Livy, "per quosdam privatis hospitiis necessitudinibusque conjunctos." These, like the πρόξενοι in Greece, would undoubtedly form a party disposed to Rome, whose influence would be felt as soon as the fortune of the war turned against the Latins.

[16] The lands of the Ardeatians were ravaged by the Antiatians in 415 (Livy, VIII. 12). Ardea, therefore, must have been at that time in alliance with Rome.

[17] Such as Ostia, whose lands were also ravaged by the Antiatians in 415. (Livy, ibid.)

confederacy, including, it is probable, the warlike nations of the Marsians and the Pelignians.

The Romans commence the war unexpectedly, and both consuls march through Samnium into Campania.

When the Latins sent the two prætors as ambassadors to Rome, it is evident that no active warfare could be going on in Campania. Latin garrisons had probably wintered there to repel plundering parties of the Samnites; and the Latin army would march thither as soon as the season for military operations arrived, to renew their invasion of Samnium. No expectation seems to have been entertained that their proposal of an equal union would be answered by an immediate declaration of war. Certain it is that the breach of the old alliance was far more to be charged on the Romans than on them; for the Romans had deserted them in the midst of a war jointly undertaken by the two nations, and had made peace with the common enemy; and the Campanians, who had originally joined the alliance to obtain protection against the Samnites, had no choice but to follow the Latins, as from them alone was that protection now to be hoped for. But the opportunity was tempting, and the Romans, taking advantage[18] of the earliness of the season, when the Latins might scarcely be prepared for active operations, hastily declared war, and dispatched both consuls with two consular armies, not by the direct road into Campania by Tarracina or by the Liris, but by a circuitous route at the back of their enemies' country, through the territory of the Marsians and Pelignians[19] into Samnium. There the consuls were joined by the Samnite army; and their combined forces then descended from the mountains of Samnium, and encamped in presence of the enemy in the plain of Capua, with a retreat open into the country of the Samnites on their rear, but with the whole army and territory of the hostile confederacy interposed between them and Rome.

The son of T. Manlius engages the enemy contrary to his father's orders, and is executed.

While the Romans and Latins lay here over against each other, the consuls issued an order[20] strictly forbidding all irregular skirmishing, or single encounters with the enemy. They wished to prevent the confusion which might arise in chance combats between two parties alike in arms and in language; perhaps also they wished to stop all intercourse with the Latins, lest the enemy should discover their real strength, or lest old feelings of kindness should revive in the soldiers' minds, and they should begin to ask whether they had any sufficient grounds of quarrel. It was on this occasion that T. Manlius, the consul's son, was challenged by Geminus Metius, of Tusculum;[21] and, heedless of the order of the generals, he accepted the challenge and slew his antagonist. The young man returned in triumph to the camp, and laid his spoils at his father's feet; but the consul, turning away from him, immediately summoned the soldiers to the prætorium, and ordered his son to be beheaded before them. All were struck with horror at the sight, and the younger soldiers, from a natural sympathy with youth and courage, regarded the consul

When we consider that the usual season for hostilities at this period was the autumn, it may be doubted whether the Latin army which fought under Vesuvius was more than that force which had wintered in Campania to garrison the several towns, and as such very inferior in numbers to the two consular armies of the Romans. The rapid march of the consuls through the central countries of Italy may have been unknown to the Latins, and their sudden appearance in Campania in conjunction with the Samnites may have been as startling a surprise to the enemy, as that of Claudius Nero to Hasdrubal after his admirable march from Bruttium to join his colleague on the Motaurus; or as that of Napoleon to the Austrians when the army of reserve broke out from the Val d'Aosta on the plains of Lombardy in the campaign of 1800.

[19] Livy, VIII. 6.

[20] Livy, VIII. 6.

[21] Livy, VIII. 7. The same story may be told again with effect, even after it has been often told before, if we have received it from an original and independent source; because if twenty eye-witnesses give an account of the same event, the impression which it has made on each of them will have been different, and, therefore, each will tell the story in his own way, and it will contain something new and original. But when we derive all our knowledge from one single account, and that account has been once perfectly given, there is nothing to be done by later writers but to copy it, or simply to state its substance. Thus it is with Livy's famous description of the condemnation of T. Manlius by his father; the story cannot be better told than he has told it, and we have no means of adding to it or varying it from other original sources. I have therefore followed Niebuhr in simply stating its outline; for the finished picture the reader must consult Livy himself.

with abhorrence to the latest hour of his life; but fear and respect were mingled with their abhorrence, and strict obedience, enforced by so dreadful an example, was felt by all to be indispensable.

The two armies meet near Mount Vesuvius. Resolution of the Roman generals to devote themselves to death for the victory of their country.

The stories which we are obliged to follow, shifting their scene as rapidly and unconnectedly as our old drama, transport the two armies without a word of explanation from the neighborhood of Capua to the foot of Mount Vesuvius, where, on the road which led to Veseris, according to their own way of expressing it, the decisive battle was fought. What Veseris was,[22] or where it was situated, on which side of Vesuvius the action took place, or what had brought the two armies thither, are questions to which we can give no answers. But he who had been present at the last council held by the Roman generals before they parted to take their respective stations in the line, might have seen that, having planned for the coming battle all that skill and ability could devise, they were ready to dare all that the most heroic courage could do or suffer: the aruspices had been consulted[23] as to the import of the signs given by the entrails of the sacrifice: their answers had been made known to the principal officers of the army; and with it the determination of the consuls, that, on whichever side of the battle the Romans should first begin to give ground, the consul who commanded in that quarter should forthwith devote himself, and the hosts of the enemy with himself, to the gods of death and to the grave: "for fate," said they, "requires the sacrifice of a general from one party, and of an army from the other: one of us, therefore, will be the general that shall perish, that the army which is to perish also may be not ours, but the army of the Latins."

Similar dispositions of both armies.

We have seen that the arms and tactic of both armies were precisely similar. In each there were two grand divisions, the first forming the ordinary line of battle, and the second the reserve; the latter being, in point of numbers, considerably the strongest.[24] The first division, however, was subdivided into two equal parts, the first of which, known by the name of the Hastati, consisted of light and heavy armed soldiers, in the proportion of one-third of the former to two-thirds of the latter; the second part, called the Principes, contained the flower of the whole army, all heavy-armed men, in the vigor of their age, and most perfectly and splendidly accoutred. The reserve, forming in itself a complete army, contained a threefold subdivision; one-third of it was composed of veteran heavy-armed soldiers, the Triarii; another third of light-armed, Rorarii; and the remainder were mere supernumeraries, Accensi, who were destined to supply the places of those who should have fallen in the first line, or to act with the reserve in cases of the last extremity. These divisions being the same in both armies, the generals on either side knew precisely the force and nature of the enemy's reserve, and could calculate the movements of their own accordingly.

Tactic of the Roman legion at this period.

The tactic of the Romans was, at this period, in an intermediate state, between the use of the order of the phalanx, with the round shield and pike, and the loose array of the later legion, with the large oblong shield, sword, and pilum, such as it is described by Polybius. But the want of all co-

[22] "Apud Veserim fluvium," is the expression of the author "de Viris Illustribus" twice over, in his notices of P. Decius and of T. Manlius. Cicero twice mentions the name, but simply says "ad Veserim." There is no stream at present on either side of Vesuvius which will answer the description; but it is scarcely possible to calculate the changes effected in the geography of a country by volcanic action during a period of so many centuries.

[23] Livy, VIII. 6. Both consuls, said the story, had seen in the night the same vision; a figure of more than human stature and majesty appeared to them, and told them that the gods of the dead, and earth, the mother of all, claimed as their victims the general of one party, and the army of the other: the consuls then sacrificed, to see whether the sign observed in the entrails of the victim would speak the same language as their vision.

[24] See the famous description of the legion at this period in Livy, VIII. 8, and Niebuhr's comments upon it, Vol. I. p. 497, &c. Ed. 2, 1827, and Vol. III. p. 110, &c. The first line, comprising the hastati and principes, contained in each legion only 1890 men; the reserve, consisting of the triarii, rorarii, and accensi, amounted to 2790.

temporary accounts of this middle period makes it exceedingly difficult to comprehend it clearly. Reserving, therefore, for another place all minute inquiries into the subject, I shall here only take for granted some of the principal points, so far as they are essential to a description of the battle.

The Roman and Latin legions were, as we have seen, opposed to each other.

Order of battle of both armies.

The Samnites and Hernicans, who formed one wing of the Roman army, must, in like manner, have been opposed to the nations of their own or of a kindred stock, the Campanians, Sidicinians, and Volscians.

Of the Roman line itself, the legions on the right were commanded by Titus Manlius,[25] those on the left by Publius Decius.

Battle under Mount Vesuvius.

The battle began with the encounter of the hastati, who formed on each side, as we have seen, the first division of the first line. Consisting both of light and heavy armed soldiers, they closed with each other with levelled pikes, amidst showers of darts from their light-armed men, who either skirmished in the intervals between the maniples of the pikemen, or, sheltered behind them, threw their missiles over the heads of their comrades into the line of the enemy.

Roman first line in disorder.

In this conflict the right wing of the Latins prevailed, and the Roman hastati of the left wing fell back in disorder upon the principes, who formed what may be called the main battle.

P. Decius devotes himself.

Decius then called aloud for M. Valerius,[26] the pontifex maximus. "The gods," he said, "must help us now;" and he made the pontifex dictate to him the form of words in which he was to devote himself and the legions of the enemy to the gods of death. It should be remembered that to Decius, as one of the commons, all the ceremonies of the Roman religion were an unknown mystery. The pontifex bade him take his consular toga,[27] and wrap

[25] Livy, VII. 9.

[26] Who this M. Valerius was, we know not; whether it was the M. Valerius Poplicola, who was consul in 400 and 402, or M. Valerius Corvus, who had been already three times consul and once dictator, and of whom Pliny relates, that in the course of his long life, he was appointed to curule offices no fewer than one and twenty times. Hist. Natur. VII. 48.

[27] "Togam prætextam sumere jussit;" "sumere," because it was not commonly worn in battle. The form of words in which Decius devoted himself ran as follows: "Thou, Janus, thou, Jupiter, thou, Mars, our father, thou, Quirinus, thou, Bellona; ye, Lares, ye, the nine gods, ye, the gods of our fathers' land, ye, the gods whose power disposes both of us and of our enemies, and ye also gods of the dead, I pray you, I humbly beseech you, I crave, and doubt not to receive this grace from you, that ye would prosper the people of Rome and the Quirites with all might and victory; and that ye would visit the enemies of the people of Rome and of the Quirites with terror, with dismay, and with death. And, according to these words which I have spoken, so do I now, on the behalf of the commonwealth of the Roman people and the Quirites, on the behalf of the army, both the legions and the foreign aids, of the Roman people and the Quirites, devote the legions and the foreign aids of our enemies, along with myself, to the gods of the dead, and to the grave." No one can doubt the genuineness of this prayer, which, together with the rules to be observed in these solemn devotions, Livy has copied, he tells us, "verbis ipsis, ut tradita nuncupataque sunt:" VIII. 11; where "tradita," I may observe, does not refer to any oral tradition, but to the pontifical books: just as Cyprian, where he appeals to "traditio apostolica," means to refer to the apostolical writings in the New Testament. Livy himself may have copied the prayer immediately from one of the older annalists, either from Fabius Pictor, from whom Gellius quotes one or two similar notices of ancient religious observances, or from L. Cincius, whose treatise "de Re Militari" contained the form used by the Fetiales in declaring war, and that of the military oath. See Gellius, XVI. 4. Varro also was fond of recording ancient forms, carmina, in their own words; of which we have several instances in that almost solitary remnant of his voluminous works which has reached our times, his work on the Latin language. Forms of all sorts, and laws, may be relied on as perfectly genuine, even when ascribed to a period the history of which is good for nothing.

To notice more particularly the prayer of Decius, it may be seen that it addresses Janus before all other gods, even before Jupiter himself; in evident agreement with that ancient rite of opening the gates of Janus at the beginning of a war, which implied that he was in an especial manner the god whom the Romans wished to go out with them to battle. See p. 4. Mars *Pater*, like the Ζεὺς and Ἀπόλλων πατρῷος, has a manifest reference to the legend of the birth of Romulus. As a god of war, Mars, I should imagine, was of a later date in Italy than Janus; or, at any rate, that the two gods came to the Romans from different quarters. Virgil speaks of the opening of the gates of Janus as a Latin rite, older than the origin of Rome. The "lares" here spoken of, would be, I suppose, "lares militares" (see Orelli's Inscriptions, No. 1665), "lares," as is well known, being a general title, and denoting powers, or mighty ones; their particular character and office being expressed by a particular title, or implied by the nature of the case. Thus L. Æmilius, in the

it round his head, putting out his hand from under it, to hold it to his face, and to set his feet upon a javelin, and so to utter the set words which he should dictate. When they had been duly spoken, the consul sent his lictors to his colleague, to say that he had devoted himself to death for the deliverance of the Roman army. Then, with his toga wrapped around his body, after the fashion adopted in sacrifices to the gods, he sprung upon his horse, armed at all points,[28] plunged amidst the ranks of the enemy, and was slain. Such an example of self-devotion in a general is in all cases inspiriting; but the Romans beheld in this not only the heroic valor of Decius, but the certain devotion of their enemies to the vengeance of the gods; what was due from themselves to the powers of death Decius had paid for them; so, like men freed from a burden, they rushed on with light and cheerful hearts, as if appointed to certain victory.

The main battles on both sides engage.

The Latins, too, understood the meaning of Decius' death, when they saw his dress and heard his words of devotion; and no doubt it produced on their minds something of dismay. But, soon recovering, the main battles on both sides closed in fierce onset; and though the light troops of the Roman reserve were also brought into action, and skirmished amongst the maniples of the hastati and principes, yet victory seemed disposed to favor the Latins.

The Roman reserve decides the fate of the day.

In this extremity Manlius, well knowing that in a contest so equal the last reserve brought into the field on either side would inevitably decide the day, still kept back the veterans of his second line, and called forward only his accensi or supernumeraries, whom, for this very purpose, he had, contrary to the usual custom, furnished with complete arms. The Latins mistook these for the veterans, or triarii, and thinking that the last reserve of the Romans was now engaged, they instantly brought up their own. The Romans struggled valiantly, but at last were beginning to give way, when, at a signal given, the real reserve of the Roman veterans started forwards, advanced through the intervals of the wavering line in front of them, and with loud cheers charged upon the enemy. Such a shock at such a moment was irresistible; they broke through the whole army of the Latins almost without loss; the

war with Antiochus, when engaged in a sea-fight with the enemy, vowed to build a temple to the lares permarini, or "the powers or genii of the deep." Livy, XL. 52. Macrobius, Saturnalia, I. 10. Müller, Etrusker, Vol. II. p. 129, conf. p. 91. The war lares, to whom Decius prayed, are, apparently, the same powers that are represented on two Etruscan tombs, engravings of which are given by Micali in the plates accompanying his history, Pl. 105, 106. They are winged figures, male and female, who are present in a battle, taking part with the several combatants.

The "nine gods," "dii novensiles," are probably the nine gods of the Etruscan religion, who alone had the power of launching lightning and thunderbolts. See Müller, Etrusker, Vol. II. p. 84, note 10. According to another definition, Servius, Æn. VIII. 187, the dii novensiles were gods who had been deified for their good deeds; "quibus merita virtutis dederint numinis dignitatem."

By "the gods whose power disposes both of us and of our enemies," "divi quorum est potestas nostrorum hostiumque," may be meant either the especial tutelar powers of each nation, the "lares urbium et civitatum" (see Orelli, Inscription. Collect. 1668, 1670, and Müller, Etrusker, Vol. II. p. 91, 93), or the peculiar national gods of each, such as the Jupiter, Juno, and Minerva of the Capitol for Rome, and the Jupiter of the mountains of Alba for Latium. The gods of Latium might be addressed in the prayer, to show that the Romans did not treat them with that irreverence which the Latin ambassador had manifested towards the Jupiter of the Capitol.

Lastly, to end this long note, it has been doubted what is the meaning of the expression, "veniam peto *feroque*," which occurs in the prayer of Decius. I think the true interpretation of "fero" is "nanciscor;" and that as some have understood it (see the note on the words in Bekker's Livy), the words are added as of good omen, "the grace which I crave I feel sure that I shall also obtain;" in the well-known future sense of the present tense, in which "fero" signifies, "I am going to obtain." It may, perhaps, signify no more than an earnest wish, "I am ready to obtain," "I would fain obtain;" but, at any rate, "ferre veniam" must signify "to receive favor," as "petere" signifies to sue for it."

[28] "Armatus in equum insilivit," says Livy. Zonaras says, τὰ ὅπλα ἐκδύς (VII. 26). But this must refer only to the moments while he was uttering the prayer: when that was ended, he resumed the full arms of a Roman general; only his sacred character, as one devoted to the gods, was marked by the peculiar manner in which his toga was wrapped around him, the "cinctus Gabinus."

With respect to the nature and origin of the cinctus Gabinus, see Müller, Etrusker, Vol. II, p. 266.

battle became a butchery, and, according to the usual result of engagements fought hand to hand, where a broken army can neither fight nor fly, nearly three-fourths of the Latins were killed or taken.

Share of the Samnites in the battle.

How far the Samnites contributed to this victory, whether they, after having beaten the Volscians and Campanians, threatened the flank of the Latins at the moment of the last charge of the Roman veterans, there was no Samnite historian to tell, and no Roman annalist would tell truly. Nor need we wonder at this; for if we had only certain English accounts of the battle of Waterloo, who would know that the Prussians had any effectual share in that day's victory?

If the importance of a battle be a just reason for dwelling upon it in detail, then I may be excused for having described minutely this great action between the Romans and Latins under Mount Vesuvius; for to their victory on that day, securing to them forever the alliance of Latium, the Romans owed their conquest of the world.

The Latins are again defeated, and many cities submit.

The wreck of the Latin army retreated by different routes out of Campania; and the conquerors had suffered so severely that they were in no condition to pursue them. The fugitives first halted at Minturnæ;[29] then finding themselves not molested, they advanced again to Vescia, a town described as in the country of the Ausonians, one of the Greek forms of the name of the Opicans or Oscans, and situated apparently on the eastern or Campanian side of the Massican hills, where the streams run towards the Savone. Here they rallied, and L. Numisius, the Latin prætor, used every effort to revive their courage, and to procure reinforcements both from Latium, and from the Volscians; Campania having been wholly lost by the late battle. A large force was thus again assembled, and the Romans and Samnites, who had been themselves also reinforced, we may suppose, in the interval, from Samnium at any rate, if not from Rome, hastened a second time to encounter them. But the victory was easy and decisive; and as no third army could immediately be raised, the consul entered Latium without opposition, plundered the open country, and received the submission of several cities. The Latin confederacy was, in fact, broken up forever.

T. Manlius returns to Rome and triumphs.

According to the Fasti, the consuls of the preceding year must have resigned so long before the regular expiration of their office, that Manlius and Decius must have been appointed to succeed them almost before the end of the winter, and their great campaign was carried on in the early spring. Manlius made all haste, no doubt, to return home to his triumph; but as he triumphed on the 18th of May,[30] it is clear that he had greatly anticipated the usual season for military operations, and by so doing had perhaps taken the enemy by surprise. Great as had been his services, his triumph was regarded with no joy; such rejoicings seemed unbecoming[31] in one who had lost both his colleague and his own son in the course of the contest; and the younger Romans looked on him less as the conqueror of the Latins, than as the murderer of his son.

The Latin towns which had already submitted were deprived of all their public or domain land, and a like penalty was imposed on the Campanians.[32] But as

[29] Livy, VIII. 10, 11. It is plain from this that Samnium was altogether the base of the Roman army's operations, and that whatever was the exact scene of the great battle, the Romans fought with the enemy's army interposed between them and Rome. This sufficiently marks the grand scale of these operations, and also the enlarged military views of the Roman consuls. They ventured to abandon altogether the line of their own territory, and to carry the war directly into Campania, resting on the territory of their allies, and communicating with Rome by a route circuitous indeed, but secure from interruption, through the country of the Marsians and Pelignians.

[30] The notice in the fragments of the Fasti runs as follows:—

[T. M]anlius L. F. A. N. Imperiossus Torquatus [C]os III. De Latineis . Campaneis . Sidicineis . Aurunceis . A.CDXIII. xv. K. Junias.

[31] Dion Cassius, Fragm. XXIX. Mai.

[32] Livy, VIII. 11. Niebuhr thinks that the settlement of Latium was attended by many ex-

the Campanian aristocracy had been wholly opposed to the war with Rome, they were rather entitled to reward than punishment. They therefore received the franchise of Roman citizens, which enabled them to intermarry with Romans, and to inherit property, while their ascendency in their own country was abundantly secured; and as a compensation for the loss of their domain land, they were each to receive from the Campanian people 450[33] denarii a year.

The Campanian aristocracy rewarded for their attachment to Rome.

Whilst the consuls were absent in Campania, L. Papirius Crassus, the prætor, had been left at home with the command of the forces usually appointed to protect the city. He had watched the Antiatians, and checked their plundering inroads, but had been able to do nothing of importance. After the return of Manlius he was appointed dictator, as Manlius himself fell sick. It seems probable that he was appointed dictator for the purpose of holding the comitia, and that Manlius, having been left sole consul, and afterwards being himself disabled by illness, was required, like the consuls who had preceded him, to resign his office before the end of his year.[34] He was succeeded by Ti. Æmilius and Q. Publilius Philo.

L. Crassus, dictator.

The history of their consulship is obscure. The Latins are said to have renewed the war again,[35] to recover their forfeited domain; it is more likely that only some of their cities had submitted to Manlius, and that the treatment which these met with drove the rest to try the fortune of arms once again. They were defeated by the consul Publilius,[36] and more of their towns then submitted; some, however, still continued to resist, and amongst these Pedum, Tibur, and Præneste, are particularly named. The consul Ti. Æmilius laid siege to Pedum, but the defence was obstinate; and whatever was the true cause, Pedum remained to the end of his consulship unconquered.

The new consuls defeat the Latins again.

This was probably owing to the state of affairs in Rome. Out of the large tracts of domain land won in the last campaign, the assignations of land to the commons had in no case exceeded the amount of three jugera to each man: all the rest was occupied, as usual, by the great

Q. Publilius Philo dictator. He brings forward and passes the Publilian laws.

ecutions, which history, from a desire to soften the picture, has omitted, Vol. III. p. 159. The Romans, however, far from being ashamed of such executions, rather gloried in them, and even Livy himself relates with entire approbation the cruel vengeance taken upon Capua in the second Punic war. The moment that the war was at an end with any of the Latin states, it was the policy of Rome to avoid driving them again to despair by any bloody executions; and as the deportation of the senators of Velitræ is mentioned as an instance of remarkable severity, it seems reasonable to believe that no blood was shed except on the field of battle.

[33] Livy, VIII. 11. Mr. Twiss supposes that thirty talents were fixed upon as the annual payment to be made to each century of the Campanian equites, which would make one hundred and twenty talents for the whole four centuries; and as there were four hundred knights in each century, it allows just four hundred and fifty denarii or drachmæ to each individual. Niebuhr well observes that the yearly payment of so large a sum as one hundred and twenty talents gives us a high idea of the wealth of Capua. The coin paid is called by Livy "denarios nummos;" and although silver denarii were not coined at Rome till a later period, yet this proves nothing against their earlier use in Campania; and although Eckkel and Mionnet acknowledge only a copper coinage of ancient Capua, yet Micali gives an engraving of a silver coin, with an Oscan inscription, which must, undoubtedly, have belonged to Capua in the days of its independence. See plate 115 of Micali's Atlas.

[34] Something of this sort must be supposed, if Livy had any authority for his statement, that the consuls in the year 420, only ten years after this period, still came into office on the 1st of July. (Livy, VIII. 20.) For as Manlius entered on his consulship before the winter was well ended, and triumphed as early as May, the consular year must have begun from that time forwards, not in July, but in the early spring, unless it had again been altered by some subsequent change. But the whole chronology of this period is still so uncertain in its details, that it is impossible to arrive at any certain conclusion.

[35] Livy, VIII. 12.

[36] The dates for these years furnished by the Fasti are as follow:

T. Manlius triumphed on the 18th of May, 413. Q. Publilius Philo triumphed on the 13th of January, 414; and L. Camillus and C. Mænius triumphed on the 28th and 30th of September, 415. Now, as the Fasti reckon the years of Rome from the 21st of April (the Palilia), the traditionary date of the foundation of the city, it is obvious that between May, 413, and January, 414, there intervened twenty months, whilst between January, 414, and September, 415, there would be no more than eight. But whether these dates are correct is quite another question. I believe that it is impossible to fix the chronology of much of the fifth century of Rome with precision, because it is impossible to fix the history; and again, we cannot attempt to fix the history by the chronology, because that is in itself uncertain.

families of the aristocracy. Great discontent was excited at this, and other circumstances occurred, in all probability showing a design on the part of the patricians to take advantage of their successes abroad in order to recover their old ascendency. Niebuhr supposes that the majority of the senate was opposed to these projects, and cordially joined with the consuls in repressing them. Both the consuls were wise and moderate men; both had been amongst[37] the five commissioners for the relief of the general distress in the year 403, whose merits were so universally acknowledged by all parties. There is no likelihood that such men should have indulged a spirit of faction or personal pique at such a moment, or should have proposed and carried laws of the greatest importance without any especial call for them, and yet without encountering any formidable opposition. Nor is it consistent that the senate, after having had some months' experience, according to the common story, of the factious character of the two consuls, should have required them to name a dictator in order to get rid of them, when the very result which did take place might have been so easily foreseen, that Æmilius would name his own colleague. It is far more probable that the senate foresaw, and had in fact arranged that it should be so, in order that the reforms which were judged necessary might be supported and carried with the authority of the greatest magistracy in the commonwealth. The reforms now effected were purely constitutional, and consisted mainly, as far as appears, in destroying the power of the aristocratical assembly of the curiæ, a body necessarily of a very different character from the senate, and in which the most one-sided party spirit was likely to be predominant. General assemblies of the members of a privileged or separate order[38] are of all things the most mischievous; as they combine with the turbulence and violence of a popular assembly all the narrow-mindedness and exclusiveness of a particular caste. It seems that no greater benefit could have been conferred on Rome than the extinction of the power of the curiæ; and accordingly one of Publilius' laws deprived[39] them of their power as a branch of the legislature with regard to all laws passed by the comitia of tribes; and another reduced it to a mere formality with respect to all laws submitted to the comitia of the centuries:[40] whatever law was proposed by

[37] Livy, VII. 21. "Meriti æquitate curâque sunt ut per omnium annalium monumenta celebres nominibus essent."

[38] It scarcely needs to be observed that our house of lords resembles the Roman senate, and not the comitia of the curiæ. If our nobility were like that of the continent, so that all a peer's sons were noble, or like the patrician order at Rome, so that all his descendants in the male line were noble, a representative body chosen out of and by so large a privileged class, without any mixture of new creations, would be a very different thing from our house of peers, and would give a tolerable idea of the nature of the Roman comitia of curiæ. Compare also the spirit, at once factious and intolerant, which has marked the convocations of the clergy, and particularly the lower house of convocation as opposed to the upper; that is, again, the curiæ as opposed to the senate. Consider also that worst of all possible assemblies, the diet of the nobles of Poland.

[39] I have followed Niebuhr in his explanation of the Publilian laws. Vol. III. p. 169, et seqq. Livy says the purport of the first law was "ut plebiscita omnes Quirites tenerent:" evidently understanding it to have had the same purport with the Valerian and Horatian law of the year 306, which enacted, "ut quod tributim plebes jussisset populum teneret." III. 55. It is certainly possible that the same law having fallen into disuse, or rather being obstructed by the power of a party, should be again solemnly re-enacted; but Niebuhr's explanation is so consistent and so probable that I have been induced to adopt it.

[40] "Ut legum quæ comitiis centuriatis ferrentur ante initum suffragium patres auctores fierent." I need not say that "patres" here was generally supposed to mean the senate, and I have no doubt that Livy so understood it; but I think Niebuhr is right in understanding it of the patrician curiæ, who had before possessed a distinct voice as a branch of the legislature. The power of the curiæ was likely to be disputed earlier than that of the senate; the senate was now a mixed body, composed of the most eminent men of both orders; it was a true national council; and that such a body should exercise the power of deciding what questions should be submitted to the comitia of the people at large, was nothing more than what was common in Greece even at this very period; and it was held not to be incompatible with a democracy, provided that the body in which this power was vested was not of too narrow and exclusive a character. *Δεῖ μὲν γὰρ εἶναί τι τοιοῦτον ᾧ ἐπιμελὲς ἔσται τοῦ δήμου προβουλεύειν· . . τοῦτο δὲ, ἂν ὀλίγοι τὸν ἀριθμὸν ὦσιν, ὀλιγαρχικόν.* Aristotle, Politica IV. 15. See also the institution of the *νομοφύλακις* at Athens: *προγράφουσι δεὸ τῆς βουλῆς καὶ πρὸ τῆς ἐκκλησίας ὑπὲρ ὧν πρῖ χρηματίζειν.* Pollux, from Aristotle, VIII. § 95. It is not probable then that the senate at Rome should have thus early lost a power which still existed generally in Greece;

the senate to the centuries, and no measure could originate with the latter, was to be considered as having the sanction of the curiæ also: so that if the centuries passed it, it should have at once the force of a law. A third Publilian law enacted that one of the two censors should necessarily be elected from the commons; a fourth, as Niebuhr thinks, provided that the prætorship also should be thrown open, and that in each alternate year the prætor also should be a plebeian.

"The patres," says Livy, "thought that the two consuls had done the commonwealth more mischief by their domestic measures than service by their conduct of the war abroad." If the term patres be understood of the majority of the patrician order, Livy is probably right; but if he meant to speak of the senate, he must have judged them overharshly. That assembly contained the best and wisest of the aristocracy, but it did not represent the passions and exclusiveness of the patrician vulgar. The majority of the senate, whether patricians or commoners, saw the necessity of the Publilian laws, and had the rare wisdom to pass them in time. Accordingly, they were followed by no demands for further concessions; but by a period of such unbroken peace and order, that for many years the internal dissensions of the Romans are heard of no more; and the old contests between the patrician order and the rest of the people may be said to have ended forever. The Hortensian laws, about fifty years later, were occasioned by contests of another sort, such as marked the latter period of the commonwealth; contests of a nature far more dangerous—where the object sought for is not so much political power for its own sake, but as the means of obtaining bread.

The Publilian laws approved by a majority of the senate.

In the following year the war with the Latins was brought to a conclusion. The new consuls were L. Furius Camillus, perhaps a grandson[41] of the great Camillus, and C. Mænius. Camillus marched against Pedum, while his colleague attacked the Antiatians, who were supported by the people of Velitræ, Aricia, and Lavinium. Both were completely successful; Pedum was taken by Camillus,[42] and the people of Tibur and Præneste, who endeavored to relieve it, were defeated; while Mænius gained a victory over the Antiatians and their allies near the river, or rather stream, of Astura. Then all the cities of Latium severally submitted, as did also the people of Antium; garrisons were placed in them, and the future settlement of Latium was submitted by the consul, Camillus, to the decision of the senate. It appears that the case of each city was considered separately, and its fate was settled as justice or expediency might seem to dictate. Unluckily, Livy either could not find, or grew impatient of repeating, what was the particular sentence passed upon each state; he has only noticed the fate of a few, and we are left to conjecture what was determined with respect to the rest.

Final submission of Latium.

First of all, it was ordered as a general law, that there should be from henceforth no common meetings, assemblies, or councils for any two or more of the cities of Latium;[43] and that they should be made as foreigners to one another, with no liberty of intermarriage, or of

Settlement of Latium. Dissolution of the Latin confederacy.

but that the curiæ should be deprived of it was perfectly natural. And as Niebuhr observes, that the principal members of the senate, headed by the dictator and supported by the mass of the people, should have triumphed over the ultra aristocratical spirit of the curiæ, is easily conceivable: but the senate would not so readily have yielded an important prerogative of its own; and it is not possible to believe that had the senate joined the body of the patricians in resisting the dictator's measures, they could have been carried without some violent convulsions. Whereas the Publilian laws, very unlike the Hortensian, the Genucian, the Canuleian, or any other of the great measures carried by the commons against the inclination of the senate as well as of the patricians, were passed peaceably, and, so far as we hear, without a struggle.

41 He is called in the Fasti, "Spurii filius, Marci nepos." The great M. Camillus is known to have had a son named Spurius, who was the first prætor. Livy, VII. 1. The other consul, C. Mænius, must have belonged to one of the most distinguished families of the commons, for although we have no yearly lists of tribunes preserved, yet three tribunes of the name of Mænius are incidentally mentioned at different times by Livy, IV. 53, VI. 19, and VII. 16.

42 Livy, VIII. 13.

43 "Ceteris Latinis populis connubia commerciaque et concilia inter se ademerunt." Livy, VIII. 14.

purchasing or inheriting lands in each other's territories. All notion of a Latin state or union was to be utterly done away; and each city was to be isolated from its neighbors, that all community of interests and feelings between them might as much as possible be destroyed. This was the system on which the Romans settled the kingdom of Macedon after their final victory over Peresus: it was split up into four distinct portions,[44] and each of these was debarred from any interchange of the rights of citizenship with the other three.

Condition of the several Latin states. Tibur and Præneste.

Tibur and Præneste, the two most powerful cities of Latium, were deprived of their domain land,[45] and probably of any dominion which they may have exercised over the decayed towns or districts in their immediate neighborhood. They retained their own laws and municipal independence, and there was still to exist between them and the Romans the old mutual right of assuming at pleasure each other's citizenship, so far as regarded the concerns of private life. But in war they were bound to follow where Rome should lead, and to furnish soldiers as auxiliaries or allies to the the Roman legions.

Lanuvium, &c.

Lanuvium obtained the full rights of Roman citizenship, and its people formed the whole or a part of one of the new tribes which were created at the next census.[46] It is probable that several other districts of Latium obtained the same privilege: perhaps such as had been hitherto dependent on some of the larger towns, since the decay or destruction of their own cities. In this manner the inhabitants of Scaptia and Gabii, which once were among the thirty cities of Latium, but had since fallen to decay, may have become latterly subjects of the Tiburtians, and now, in all likelihood, received the full citizenship of Rome, and composed the Scaptian tribe, which was created five years afterwards.

Aricia, Pedum, &c.

Aricia,[47] Pedum, Nomentum, and perhaps Tusculum, obtained the Roman citizenship without political rights; in other words, they were placed in the condition of provincial towns, without any municipal or corporate privileges, and justice was administered amongst them by a præfect sent from Rome. Their law was altogether that of Rome; their citizens were enlisted in the legions, and their taxation was in all respects the same as that of the Romans.

In Velitræ, from some reason to us unknown, the aristocracy appear to have

[44] Livy, XLV. 29.

[45] Livy, VIII. 14. That Tibur remained a distinct state is proved by the language of Livy, IX. 30, where he speaks of the Romans sending ambassadors to the people of Tibur; and still more by the fact that Roman citizens might choose Tibur as a place of exile, as was also the case with Præneste. Late in the sixth century of Rome, we have instances on record of this, Livy, XLIII. 2; and Polybius, writing early in the seventh century, speaks of the same right as still existing, adding, as the reason of it, that the Romans were bound by solemn treaties to the people of these cities. These treaties, ὅρκια, are rightly understood by Niebuhr to have been the old terms of the Latin league, including the interchange of all the private rights of citizenship between the citizens of the two countries; ἰσοπολιτεία. On the other hand, the political dependence of Tibur and Præneste upon Rome is evident: Papirius Cursor, when consul, had a summary power of life and death over the general of the Prænestine auxiliary troops serving in his army, Livy, IX. 16, so that the alliance probably contained the famous clause which distinguished a dependent from an equal ally: "Majestatem populi Romani comiter conservato." See Cicero, pro Balbo, 16. Compare Livy, XXXVIII. 11.

[46] The Mæcian tribe was created in 422 by the censors, Q. Publilius and Sp. Postumius. It derived its name, according to Paulus, the epitomator of Festus, "a quodam castro." And Livy, VI. 2, speaks of a place near Lanuvium, which he calls "ad Mæcium." The probability is, therefore, that the Mæcian tribe contained in it the people of Lanuvium.

[47] This may seem at variance with Livy's statement, who says that they were admitted to the rights of Roman citizens on the same footing as the people of Lanuvium. But it is true that Lanuvium, immediately after the war, did receive no more than the civitas sine suffragio; it could not enjoy the full franchise till its people were admitted into some tribe; and this did not take place till the next census. But that from the time of the next census, Lanuvium was in a different condition from Aricia, and, probably, also from Pedum and Nomentum, appears from the famous article "Municipium" in Festus; Niebuhr's commentary on which (Vol. II. chap. 4, pp. 55–60, Eng. Transl.) is one of the best specimens of his unrivalled power in discerning the true political relations of the ancient world. I would refer the reader continually to this passage in Niebuhr, for a full explanation of the various rights included sometimes under the common term of "municipium."

been zealous supporters of the late war, while the people were well disposed to the Romans. Accordingly, the walls of the town were destroyed,[48] and all the senators deported beyond the Tiber, with a heavy penalty upon their return to Latium. All their lands, whether domain or private property, were taken from them and given to some Roman colonists who were sent to supply their place. Yet the people of Velitræ appear to have received the full Roman citizenship five years afterwards, and to have been included at that time in the new Scaptian tribe.[49]

Velitræ.

Larentum, which had taken no part in the war, remained, as before, municipally independent,[50] enjoying an interchange of all the private rights of citizenship with Rome, but bound to aid, or in other words, to serve, the Romans as an ally: and this, probably, was the condition also of Ardea.

Laurentum.

The relations of some Volscian and Campanian towns, which had taken part in the late contest, were also fixed at this time.

Relations of Volscian and Campanian towns.

The people of Antium[51] were obliged to surrender all their ships of war, and forbidden to send any more to sea for the time to come. A colony was to be sent thither, but the Antiatians might themselves, if they chose, be enrolled amongst the colonists; that is to say, their territory was to be divided into lots, according to the Roman method of assignation, and all former limits or titles of property were to be done away; but every Antiatian might receive a portion of land in the new allotment, as a member of the Roman colony of Antium. The municipal independence of Antium ceased, as a matter of course; the Roman laws superseded the old laws of the city; and the Antiatians became Roman citizens in all their private relations, but with no political rights.

Antium.

Fundi and Formiæ,[52] which had remained neutral, Capua, for whose fidelity its own aristocracy would be a sufficient guarantee, and several other Campanian towns, such as Cumæ, Suessula, Atella, and Acerræ, were either now, or shortly afterwards, made capable of enjoying the private rights of Roman citizens, but retained their own laws and government. Their soldiers in war formed distinct legions,[53] and were not numbered amongst the

Fundi, Formiæ, &c.

[48] Livy, VIII. 14.

[49] The Octavii belonged to the Scaptian tribe (Suetonius in Augusto, 40), and their original country was Velitræ. The tale which Suetonius adds, of their having come to Rome in the time of Tarquinius Priscus, and having been made patricians by Servius Tullius, but afterwards having chosen to become plebeians, is merely one of the ordinary embellishments of a great man's pedigree, invented after he has risen to eminence.

[50] "Cum Laurentibus renovari fœdus jussum, renovaturque ex eo quotannis post diem decimum Latinarum." Livy, VIII. 11.

[51] Livy, VIII. 14. Antium became a maritime colony, and as such was exempted from furnishing soldiers to the legions (Livy, XXVII. 38); it was obliged, however, to furnish seamen for the naval service. (Livy, XXXVI. 3.) With regard to the prohibition to send ships to sea, it must be understood only of triremes and quinqueremes; for that the Antiatians after this period not only had many smaller vessels, but were accustomed to sail even as far as the Greek seas, appears from the complaints of their piracies addressed to the Romans successively by Alexander and by Demetrius Poliorcetes. Strabo, V. p. 232.

[52] Livy, VIII. 14, compared with Festus in "Municipium." Acerræ is mentioned by Livy, VIII. 17, and by Festus in "Municipium," and in "Municeps." Atella is mentioned by Festus in "Municeps." Festus says expressly of Fundi, Formiæ, Cumæ, and Acerræ, that after a certain number of years they became Roman citizens, that is, in the full sense of the term, being enrolled in a tribe, and being made eligible to all public offices. But the "certain number of years" was about a century and a half; for the date of the admission of Fundi and Formiæ to the full citizenship happens to be known, and it did not take place till the year 564. (Livy, XXXVIII. 36.) What can be meant by the expression that the people of Cumæ and Acerræ after some years became Roman citizens, it is not easy to decide; but it may be that they received the full franchise later than the period included in the last remaining book of Livy; and for that subsequent period we have no detailed information.

[53] "In legione merebant," says Festus, in "Municeps." The Campanian soldiers who made themselves masters of Rhegium a little before the first Punic war, are called by Livy, Legio Campana; and the name of their leader, Decius Jubellius, is clearly Campanian. Yet these same soldiers are called by Polybius (I. 6. 7), and by Appian (Samnitic. Fragm. 9), "Romans," and Orosius calls them the "eighth legion" (IV. 3); nor should it be forgotten, that Polybius, in his list of the forces at the disposal of the Romans in the great Gaulish war of 529, reckons the Latins and the other Italian nations separately, but classes the Romans and Cam-

auxiliaries; a distinction which perhaps entitled them to a larger share of the plunder,—possibly also these states may have even received portions of conquered land to add to their domain.

Honors paid to the consuls. The rostra.

Equestrian statues of the two consuls by whom this great war had been brought to a conclusion, were set up in the Forum;[54] and the beaks of the Antiatian ships were affixed to the front of the circular stand or gallery, between the comitium and the Forum, from which the tribunes were accustomed to address the people. From this circumstance it derived its well-known name of rostra, or the beaks.

The war with Latium was ended naturally and beneficially for both parties.

Three years were sufficient to finish forever the most important war in which Rome was at any time engaged; whilst with the Samnites the contest was often renewed, and lasted altogether for more than seventy years. It was not that the Samnites were a braver people than the Latins, but that the Latin war found immediately its natural termination in a closer union, which it was hopeless and not desirable to disturb; whereas, in the Samnite contest, such a termination was impossible; and the struggle could end in nothing short of absolute dominion on one side, and subjection on the other. The Samnites were complete foreigners, remote in point of distance, with a different language and different institutions; they and the Romans were not likely to form one people, and neither were willing to be the others' mere subjects. But between Rome and Latium nature had given all the elements of union; and the peculiar circumstances of the Latins precluded that mischievous national pride which has sometimes kept two nations apart, when nature, or rather God speaking in nature, designed them to be one. Had Latium been a single state like Rome, neither party[55] would willingly have seen its distinct nationality merged in that of the other; but the people of Tusculum or Lanuvium felt no patriotic affection for the names of Tibur or Præneste: they were as ready to become Romans as Tiburtians; and one or the other they must be, for a mass of little states, all independent of each other, could not be kept together; the first reverses, appealing to the sense of separate interest in each, inevitably shattered it to pieces. Those states that received the full Roman franchise became Romans, yet did not cease to be Latins; the language and manners of their new country were their own. They were satisfied with their lot, and the hope of arriving in time at the same privileges was a prospect more tempting even to the other states than any thing which they were likely to gain by renewed hostilities. Tibur and Præneste, thus severed from their old confederates, could not expect to become sovereign states; they must, according to the universal practice of the ancient world, be the allies of some stronger power; and if so, their alliance with Rome was at once the most natural and the most desirable. Thus

panians together, and names the amount of their joint force. This seems to show that the connection between Rome and Campania from the great Latin war to the invasion of Hannibal was unusually intimate; and we know also that a mutual rite of intermarriage prevailed between the inhabitants of both countries. Livy, XXIII. 4.

[54] Livy, VIII. 13, 14. For the description of the rostra given in the text, see Niebuhr, Vol. III. note 268; and particularly Bunsen, "Les Forum de Rome," p. 41. Bunsen, judging from the views of the rostra given on two coins in his possession, supposes that it was a circular building, raised on arches, with a stand or platform on the top bordered by a parapet; the access to it being by two flights of steps, one on each side. It fronted towards the comitium, and the rostra were affixed to the front of it, just under the arches. Its form has been in all the main points preserved in the ambones, or circular pulpits, of the most ancient churches, which also had two flights of steps leading up to them, one on the east side, by which the preacher ascended, and another on the west side, for his descent. See Ducange, Glossar. Med. et Infim. Latinit. in "Ambo." Specimens of these old pulpits are still to be seen at Rome in the churches of St. Clement, and S. Lorenzo fuori le mure. Bunsen aptly compares the platform of the rostra, on which the speaker moved to and fro, as he wished to address different parts of his audience, to the hustings of an English election.

[55] The rights of succession in an hereditary monarchy may affect a union between two countries, by the crown of each devolving on the same person, which would have been utterly impracticable had either of them been a republic. As it was, the union of the crowns of England and Scotland preceded the union of the kingdoms by more than a century; and had not the crowns been united, what human power could ever have effected a union of the two parliaments?

the fidelity of the Latins was so secured that neither the victories of Hannibal, nor the universal revolt of all Italy in the social war, tempted it to waver: one strong proof amongst a thousand, that nations, like individuals, cheerfully acquiesce in their actual condition, when it appears to be in any degree natural, or even endurable; and that their desire of change, whenever they do feel it, is less the wish of advancing from good to better, or a fond craving after novelty, than an irresistible instinct to escape from what is clearly and intolerably bad, even though they have no definite prospect of arriving at good.

CHAPTER XXX.

GENERAL HISTORY TO THE BEGINNING OF THE SECOND SAMNITE WAR—PRIVERNUM—PALÆPOLIS—A. U. C. 418-428—413-423, NIEBUHR.

Τὴν διὰ μέσου ξύμβασιν εἴ τις μὴ ἀξιώσει πόλεμον νομίζειν οὐκ ὀρθῶς δικαιώσει.—Τοῖς γὰρ ἔργοις ὡς διῄρηται ἀθρείτω, καὶ εὑρήσει οὐκ εἰκος ὂν εἰρήνην αὐτὴν κριθῆναι.—THUCYDIDES, V. 26.

Alexander's conquests in Asia contemporary with the period immediately following the Latin war.

ACCORDING to the synchronism of Diodorus, the same year which witnessed the final settlement of Latium, was marked also by the first military enterprises of Alexander, by his expedition against the Illyrians, and his conquest of Thebes. During the twelve following years, the period nearly which I propose to comprise within the present chapter, Asia beheld with astonishment and awe the uninterrupted progress of a hero, the sweep of whose conquests was as wide and as rapid as that of her own barbaric kings, or of the Scythian or Chaldæan hordes; but far unlike the transient whirlwinds of Asiatic warfare, the advance of the Macedonian leader was no less deliberate than rapid: at every step the Greek power took root, and the language and the civilization of Greece were planted from the shores of the Ægæan to the banks of the Indus, from the Caspian and the great Hyrcanian plain to the cataracts of the Nile; to exist actually for nearly a thousand years, and in their effects to endure forever.[1] In the tenth year after he had crossed the Hellespont, Alexander, having won his vast dominion, entered Babylon; and, resting from his career in that oldest seat of earthly empire, he steadily surveyed the mass of various nations which owned his sovereignty, and revolved in his mind the great work of breathing into this huge but inert body the living spirit of Greek civilization. In the bloom of youthful manhood, at the age of thirty-two, he paused from the fiery speed of his earlier course; and for the first time gave the nations an opportunity of offering their homage before his throne. They came from all the extremities of the earth, to propitiate his anger, to celebrate his greatness, or to solicit his protection. African tribes[2] came to congratulate and bring presents to him as the sovereign of Asia. Not only would the people bordering on Egypt upon the west look with respect on the founder of Alexandria and the son of Jupiter Ammon, but those who dwelt on the east of the Nile, and on the shores of the Arabian gulf, would hasten to pay court to the great king

[1] I leave out of sight the question as to the greater or less influence exercised upon the civilization of India by the Greek or semi-Greek kingdoms of the extreme eastern part of Alexander's empire, and refer merely to the facilities afforded by the diffusion of the Greek language and civilization in Asia and Egypt to the early growth of Christianity.

[2] See Arrian, VII. 15.

whose fleets navigated the Erythræan sea, and whose power was likely to affect so largely their traffic with India. Motives of a different sort influenced the barbarians of Europe. Greek enterprise had penetrated to the remotest parts of the Mediterranean; Greek traders might carry complaints of wrongs done to them by the petty princes on shore, or by pirates at sea, to the prince who had so fully avenged the old injuries of his nation upon the great king himself. The conqueror was in the prime of life; in ten years he had utterly overthrown the greatest empire in the world: what, if having destroyed the enemies of Greece in the east, he should exact an account for wrongs committed against his nation in the west? for Carthaginian conquests, for Lucanian devastations, for Etruscan piracies? And he would come, not only having at his command all the forces of Asia, whose multitude and impetuous onset would be supported in time of need by his veteran and invincible Macedonians, but already the bravest of the barbarians of Europe were eager to offer him their aid; and the Kelts and Iberians, who had become acquainted with Grecian service when they fought under Dionysius and Agesilaus, sent embassies to the great conqueror at Babylon, allured alike by the fame of his boundless treasures and his unrivalled valor. It was no wonder, then, that the Carthaginians,[3] who had dreaded a century earlier the far inferior power of the Athenians, and on whose minds Timoleon's recent victories had left a deep impression of the military genius of Greece, dispatched their ambassadors to secure, if possible, the friendship of Alexander. But some of the Italian nations, the Lucanians and the Bruttians, had a more particular cause of alarm. They had been engaged in war for some years with Alexander, king of Epirus, the uncle by marriage of the conqueror of Asia. Alexander of Epirus had crossed over into Italy as the defender of the Italian Greeks against the injuries of their barbarian neighbors: in this cause he had fallen, after having long and valiantly maintained it, and his great kinsman could not have heard without indignation of the impious cruelty with which his enemies had outraged his lifeless body.[4] Thus the Lucanians and Bruttians are especially mentioned as having sent embassies to Alexander at Babylon: it is not unlikely that their kinsmen, the Samnites, who had been their allies in the war, joined with them also in their endeavors to escape the dreaded vengeance, although their name was either not particularly known, or not thought worthy of especial record by the great Macedonian officers who were their king's earliest and best historians.

Embassies from Italy to Alexander in Babylon.

"The Tyrrhenians also," said Aristobulus and Ptolemæus, "sent an embassy to the king to congratulate him upon his conquests." The ports of the western coast of Italy swarmed at this time with piratical vessels, which constantly annoyed the Greek traders in those seas, and sometimes ventured as far as the eastern side of the Ionian gulf. This reproach was not confined to the Etruscans; it was shared certainly by the people of Antium; it may be doubted whether Ostia, Circeii, and Tarracina were wholly free from it. These piracies had been reported to Alexander,[5] and he sent remonstrances to

[3] Arrian, VII. 15.

[4] Livy, VIII. 24. Livy sets the death of Alexander of Epirus in the consulship of Q. Publilius and L. Cornelius. This consulship, according to Diodorus, synchronizes with Olymp. 113-3, and he places the embassies to Babylon and the death of Alexander two years later, in Olymp. 114-1. But his reckoning in this place is confused, and his Fasti differ from those of Livy; for with him there is a year between the consulships of Publilius and Cornelius and Pœtelius and Papirius, which, according to Livy, were next to one another. Again, Livy places the death of Alexander of Epirus in the same year with the foundation of Alexandria. But Alexandria, according to Arrian, was founded in Olymp. 112-1, and, according to Diodorus, one year later, in Olymp. 112-2, which would bring the death of Alexander of Epirus to the consulships either of M. Valerius and M. Atilius in 420 (415), or of T. Veturius and Sp. Postumius, in the year following. Yet the treaty of Alexander of Epirus with Rome is placed in the consulship of A. Cornelius and Cn. Domitius, that is, in 422 (417); and this is likely to be a sure synchronism, because the treaty would naturally contain the names of the Roman magistrates who concluded it. It seems impossible to fix exactly the date of the death of Alexander of Epirus, but it seems from every calculation that we may safely place it so early as to make it certain that his nephew must have heard of it at the time when he received the Italian ambassadors at Babylon.

[5] Strabo, V. p. 232. *Διόπερ καὶ Ἀλέξανδρος πρότερον ἐγκαλῶν ἐπέστειλε, καὶ Δημήτριος ὕστερον.* Some

paid. The gods would not be mocked with the trickery of a childish superstition, which endeavored to abuse their holy names for the support of perfidy and injustice." So Sp. Postumius and his companions were given back to the Roman feciales, and returned unhurt to their own army.

Such is the account which the Roman annalists have given of the famous defeat and treaty of the pass of Caudium. It differs in many respects, probably, from the truth; yet it is accurate and trustworthy when compared with the stories of the transactions which followed. L. Papirius Cursor was one of the favorite heroes of Roman tradition; his remarkable swiftness of foot, his gigantic strength, his enormous capacities for food, and the iron strictness of his discipline, accompanied as it was by occasional touches of rough humor,[54] all contributed to make his memory popular, somewhat in the same way as Richard Cœur de Lion has been admired amongst us; and his countrymen boasted that he would have been a worthy champion to have fought against Alexander the Great, if Alexander had ever invaded Italy. This favorite leader was consul in the year immediately following the affair of the pass of Caudium; so great a warrior must have signally avenged that disgrace; and, accordingly, he was made to realize the most sanguine wishes of the national vanity; he retook Luceria,[55] the fatal town which had tempted the consuls of the last year to rush blindly into the defile of Caudium; and in it he recovered all the arms and all the standards which had been taken from the Romans, and, above all, he there found the six hundred Roman knights who had been given up as hostages, and delivered them all safe and sound. Thus every stain of the late disaster was wiped away; but the pride of the Samnites must also be humbled: seven thousand Samnite soldiers were taken into Luceria, and were sent away unhurt after having been made to pass half naked under the yoke, and C. Pontius himself, by the especial favor of the gods, was their commander, so that the ignominy which he had inflicted on the Romans was now worthily returned upon his own head. No wonder, after such a marvellous victory, L. Papirius should have entered Rome in triumph; and never, since M. Camillus had triumphed over the Gauls, had there been seen, it was said, so glorious a spectacle. The two triumphs, indeed, may well be compared with one another; both are equally glorious, and both also are either wholly or in part the inventions of national vanity.

Exaggerated stories of L. Papirius Cursor

The Fasti Capitolini for this year are, unluckily, only partially legible; but it is remarkable that they contain the names of three dictators, of only one of whom there is the slightest notice in Livy, and that they place the triumph of L. Papirius not in this year, but in the following, when, according to them, he was for the third time elected consul. One of the three dictators was L. Cornelius Lentulus; and as the Cornelian house was very numerous and powerful, there were not wanting writers who claimed for him the glory of all the supposed victories[56] of this year, which others had given to L. Papirius. Victories as unreal as the pretended conquest of Luceria might well be ascribed to different persons; that town had only been just taken by the Samnites, and it is impossible to believe that they would have kept their most precious trophies and the whole number of their hostages in a foreign and conquered city, rather than in the cities of Samnium itself. Besides, there is reason to doubt whether Luceria was recovered at all before the year 440, at which time Livy places what, according to him, was its second recapture, as it had just before revolted to the enemy. The real events of this year cannot be ascertained; but there is every probability that the Romans were, in truth, successful; that they did much to remove the feeling of discouragement from the minds of their own

But the Romans were really very successful.

[54] See the character given him by Livy, IX. 16, and the anecdotes related there, and by Dion Cassius, Fr. Mai, XXXIX.

[55] Papirius' campaign is given at length by Livy, IX. 13-15. Traces of the same story are to be found in Dion Cassius, Fragm. Mai, XXXVIII., in Dionysius, Fragm. Vaticana, XXXVI., and in Florus, I. 16.

[56] Livy, IX. 15.

that they were in the next year joined by the Opicans of Cales,[10] whom Livy calls Ausonians. Cales stood on the edge of the plain of Capua, not more than ten miles from the city:[11] its example might become contagious, and therefore the Romans now roused themselves in earnest, and sent both consuls to act against this new enemy; and, having driven both the Sidicinians and the Ausonians within their walls, they chose M. Valerius Corvus as consul for the succeeding year, and committed the war especially to his charge. He laid regular siege to Cales, and took the place: but although both he and his colleague, M. Atilius Regulus, proceeded afterwards to attack the Sidicinians, yet on them they could make no impression. And although Cales was immediately made a colony, and garrisoned with 2500 colonists,[12] yet the Sidicinians held out during the two following years; their lands were wasted, but their principal city, Teanum, was not taken, and as neither victories nor triumphs over them appear in the annals or in the Fasti, and the termination of the war is never noticed, we may suppose that they, after a time, obtained favorable terms, and preserved at least their municipal independence.

A. U. C. 419.

Before the close of this contest it was noticed in the annals[13] that Samnium was become suspected by the Romans. This was in 421, and the same thing is remarked of the year following; so that the Romans heard with pleasure in that year, that Alexander, king of Epirus, brother of Olympias, and thus uncle to Alexander the Great, had landed in Lucania,[14] near Pæstum, and had defeated the united armies of the Lucanians and Samnites. Immediately after this battle, the Romans concluded a treaty of peace with the conqueror; a treaty which could have no other object than to assure him of the neutrality of the Romans, and that the alliance, which had so lately subsisted between them and the Samnites in the Latin war, was now virtually at an end. Whether there were any stipulations for a division of the spoil, in the event of his making territorial conquests in Italy, must be merely matter of conjecture; but the Romans, at any rate, took advantage of Alexander's invasion; and when, in 424,[15] the Volscians of Fabrateria sent an embassy to solicit their protection against the Samnites, they received it favorably, and threatened the Samnites with war if they did not leave Fabrateria unmolested. And yet the Samnites, in attacking it, were but putting down the last remains of the Latin confederacy on the upper Liris, exactly as the Romans had done in Campania; the Volscians of Fabrateria and the Sidicinians had been alike allied with the Latins against Rome and Samnium, and as Rome was now engaged with the latter for her own separate advantage, so it was just that Samnium should gain her own share of the spoil by conquering the former. But the Romans treated the Samnites now as they treated the Ætolians after the battle of Cynocephalæ, or the Achæans after the defeat of Perseus: as soon as the common enemy was beaten down, the allies who had aided Rome in his conquest became her next victims. Two years afterwards, in 426,[16] the Romans went a step further, and actually planted a colony of their own at Fregellæ, a Volscian city, which, as we have seen, had been taken and destroyed by the Samnites, so that its territories were now lawfully, so far as the Romans were concerned, a part of Samnium. But fortune had now turned against Alexander of Epirus, and his power was no longer to be dreaded; the Samnites, therefore, were in a condition to turn their attention to

League between the Romans and Alexander of Epirus.

A. U. C. 422.

A. U. C. 424.

[10] Livy, VIII. 16.

[11] Cales is the modern Calvi, six Neapolitan miles from the modern Capua, and therefore about eight Neapolitan miles from the ancient Capua, which stood on the site of the modern village of S. Maria di Capua. But eight Neapolitan miles are about ten English ones, the Neapolitan mile being nearly 1¼ English mile.

[12] Livy, VIII. 16.

[13] In 422 it is said that "Samnium jam alterum annum turbari novis consiliis suspectum erat."—Livy, VIII. 17.

[14] Livy, VIII. 17.

[15] Livy, VIII. 19. Fabrateria is the modern Falvaterra, standing on a hill on the right bank of the Trerus or Tolero, a little above its junction with the Liris.

[16] Livy, VIII. 22.

other enemies; the war between Rome and the Greeks of Palæpolis and Neapolis immediately followed, as we shall see presently, and this led directly to an open renewal of the contest between Rome and Samnium.

In the mean time the Romans had gained a fresh accession of strength nearer home. The unconnected notices of these events recorded[17] that in 424 a war broke out with the people of Privernum, in which the people of Fundi took a part, notwithstanding the favorable terms of their late treaty with Rome. Not a word of explanation is given as to the causes of this war, but the name of its leader has been recorded: Vitruvius Vaccus, a citizen of Fundi, who, availing himself of the interchange of all private rights of citizenship between the inhabitants of the two countries, had acquired property at Rome, and actually possessed a house on the Palatine Hill. His influence at Privernum, as well as the fact of his having a house at Rome in such a situation, prove him to have been a man of great distinction; and probably he was ambitious of being admitted to the full rights of a Roman citizen,[18] and like Attus Clausus of Regillus in old times, of becoming a member of the senate, and obtaining the consulship. Disappointed in this hope, he would feel himself slighted, and seek the means of revenging himself. Privernum had been deprived of a portion of its domain after the late war, and had seen this land occupied by Roman settlers; motives, therefore, for hostility against Rome were not wanting; and hopes of aid from Samnium might encourage to an attempt which otherwise would seem desperate. But either these hopes were disappointed, or Vitruvius had rashly ventured on an enterprise which he could not guide. He was defeated in the field, and fled to Privernum after the battle: his own countrymen, the people of Fundi, disclaimed him, and made their submission; but the Privernatians held out resolutely against two consular armies till the end of the Roman civil year; and the new consuls, who continued to beset Privernum with the whole force of Rome, did not finish the war for some months afterwards. At length Privernum submitted;[19] Vitruvius Vaccus was taken alive, kept in the dungeon at Rome till the consuls' triumph, and then was scourged and beheaded; some others were put to death with him; the senators of Privernum, like those of Velitræ, were deported beyond the Tiber: the consuls, L. Æmilius and C. Plautius, triumphed,[20] and Æmilius obtained the surname of Privernas, in honor of his conquest over so obstinate an enemy.

War with Privernum. A. U. C. 424.

What follows is almost without example in Roman history, and though, like every other remarkable story of these times, its details are in some respects uncertain, yet its truth in the main may be allowed,[21] and it is well worthy of mention,

[17] Livy, VIII. 19.

[18] The case of L. Fulvius of Tusculum, a very few years later, seems to throw light upon the views of Vitruvius Vaccus. It is mentioned of Fulvius, that in one year he commanded a Tusculan army against Rome, and in the next was himself elected Roman consul, having in the interval obtained the full citizenship of Rome. Circumstances favored him, and were adverse to Vitruvius; but the object in view was, in both cases, probably the same.

[19] Livy, VIII. 20.

[20] See the Fasti Capitolini, which also give the consul Æmilius his title of Privernas.

The coins of the Plautian family, struck at the very end of the seventh century of Rome, still record the triumph over Privernum; in the legend, C. HVPSAE. COS. PREIVER. CAPT. Hypsæus was one of the cognomina of the Plautian family, and in later times the prevailing one; but the conqueror of Privernum, according to the Fasti, was C. Plautius *Decianus*. That is, apparently, he was a Decius adopted into the Plautian family, so that his name at full length would have run, C. Plautius Hypsæus Decianus.—See Eckhel, Doctr. Num. Vol. V. p. 275.

[21] The details are uncertain, because Dionysius places its date in the year 398, and ascribes the questions put to the Privernatians, not to a Plautius or Æmilius, but to a Marcius; that is to say, to C. Marcius Rutilus, the first plebeian dictator and censor. There are also some variations in the circumstances of the story. It appears to me that the story itself was of Privernatian origin, and that when the Privernatians became Roman citizens, they used to relate with pride this instance of the unflattering nobleness of their fathers. When it became famous at Rome, the Romans, as it reflected credit on them also, were glad to adopt it into their history, and then the several great families which had conducted wars at different periods against Privernum, were each anxious to appropriate it to themselves. Thus the Marcii wanted to fix it to the earlier war with Privernum, which had been carried on by an ancestor of theirs; while the Æmilii and Plautii claimed it for the last war,

Story of the bold language used by a Privernatian deputy before the Roman senate.

as a solitary instance of that virtue, so little known to the Romans, respect for the valor of a brave enemy. After their triumph, the consuls brought the case of the people of Privernum before the senate, and urging their neighborhood to Samnium, and the likelihood of a speedy war with the Samnites, recommended that they should be gently dealt with, to secure their fidelity for the future. Some of the senators were disposed to adopt a less merciful course; and one of these called to the Privernatian deputies, who had been sent to Rome to sue for mercy, and asked them, "Of what penalty, even in their own judgment, were their countrymen deserving?" A Privernatian boldly answered, "Of the penalty due to those who assert their liberty." The consul, dreading the effect of this reply, tried to obtain another of an humbler strain, and he asked the deputy, "But if we spare you now, what peace may we expect to have with you for the time to come?" "Peace true and lasting," was the answer, "if its terms be good; if otherwise, a peace that will soon be broken." Some senators cried out that this was the language of downright rebellion: but the majority were moved with a nobler feeling, and the consul, turning to the senators of highest rank who sat near him, said aloud, "These men, whose whole hearts are set upon liberty, deserve to become Romans." Accordingly, it was proposed to the people, and carried, that the Privernatians should be admitted to the rights of Roman citizenship: in the first instance, probably, they were admitted to the private rights only, but ten years afterwards two new tribes were formed, and one of these, the Ufentine, included among its members the inhabitants of Privernum.[22]

Alarm of a new Gaulish invasion.

The year 425 is further marked by an alarm of a new Gaulish invasion, which was thought so serious, that the workmen in the several trades, and even those whose business was altogether sedentary,[23] are said to have been enlisted as soldiers; and a large army, composed in part of such materials, marched out as far as Veii to look out for and oppose the expected enemy. A similar alarm[24] had led to the appointment of a dictator, and to an unusual strictness in the enlistment of soldiers, three years before; but in neither instance did any invasion actually take place. Polybius says,[25] that at this period, "the Gauls, seeing the growing power of the Romans, concluded a treaty with them:" he does not mention what were the terms of this treaty, and Livy seems to have known nothing of its existence. Probably the Gauls found that their arms might be turned against other nations with more advantage and less risk than against Rome; while the Romans, looking forward to a war with Samnium, would be glad to purchase peace on their northern frontier by some honorary presents to the Gaulish chiefs, and by engaging not to interfere with them, so long as they abstained from attacking the Roman territory.

The Romans found a colony at Anxur, or Tarracina.

On their southern frontier, the Romans, still with a view to the expected war with the Samnites, secured their direct communications with Campania, by sending a small colony or garrison of three hundred settlers to occupy the important post of Anxur,[26] or Tarracina. Each man received as his allotment of land no more than two jugera, so that the whole extent of ground divided on this occasion did not exceed 400 English acres. We are not to suppose that these three hundred colonists composed the whole population of the town; many of the old inhabitants, doubtless, still resided there,[27] and had continued to do so ever since the place had become subject

in which their ancestors had been the consuls. The Privernatian story, in all probability, mentioned no Roman general by name.

[22] Festus, in "Oufentina."

[23] "Sellularii." Livy, VIII. 20.

[24] Livy, VIII. 17.

[25] Livy, II. 18.

[26] Livy, VIII. 21.

[27] It is a part of the well-known definition of a Roman colony given by Servius, Æn. I. 12, that "deducti sunt in locum certum ædificiis munitum." The colonists were sent to inhabit a town already in existence, not to build a new one for themselves; and thus by the very nature of the case, they would generally form a part only of the whole population of such a town, as the old inhabitants would rarely be altogether extirpated.

to the Romans; but they had ceased to form a state or even a corporate society; all their domain was become the property of the Roman people, and they were governed by a magistrate or præfect sent from Rome. The Roman colonists, on the other hand, governed themselves and the old inhabitants also; they chose their own magistrates and made their own laws: and over and above the grant of two jugera to each man, a portion too small by itself to maintain a family, they had, probably, a considerable extent of common pasture on the mountains, the former domain of the city of Anxur, and of which the colonists would have not, indeed, the sovereignty, but the beneficial enjoyment. It should be remembered, too, that as they retained their Roman franchise, they could still purchase or inherit property in Rome, and intermarry with their old countrymen; and thus, if any of them returned to Rome at a future period, they would easily enrol their names again amongst the members of their old tribe, and so resume the exercise of all their political rights, which had been suspended during their residence in the colony, but not actually forfeited.

War with the Greeks of Parthenope.

Two years after the war with Privernum, there began that course of events which finally involved the Romans in open hostilities with the Samnites. When the Latin confederacy was broken up by the victory of Manlius and Decius, Capua, as we have seen, was punished for her accession to it by the loss of her domain land; and the territory thus ceded to Rome had been partly divided out by the government to the commons in small portions of three jugera to each settler, and partly had been occupied, after the usual manner, by families of the aristocracy. Thus a large body of strangers had been introduced into Campania; and disputes soon arose between them and the inhabitants of the Greek towns of the sea-coast.[28] Of these, Palæpolis and Neapolis, the old and new towns of Parthenope, were at this period almost the sole survivors. They were both Cumæan colonies; but Cumæ itself had, about eighty years before, been taken by the Samnite conquerors of Capua; and since that period it had ceased to be a purely Greek city: a foreign race, language, and manners were intermixed with those of Greece, and lately Cumæ, like the neighboring towns of Capua and Acerræ, had become intimately connected with Rome. The two Parthenopean towns, on the contrary, had retained their Greek character uncorrupted; when their mother city had been conquered, they opened their gates to the fugitives[29] who had escaped from the ruin, and received them as citizens of Parthenope; and although a short time afterwards they formed an alliance with the Samnites, perhaps from dread of the ambition of Dionysius of Syracuse, yet this connection had not interfered with their perfect independence. They kept up also friendly relations with the people of Nola, whose admiration and imitation of the Greeks was so great as to give them, in some respects, the appearance of a Greek people.[30] Now, for the first time, they were brought into contact with the Romans, who accused them of molesting the Roman settlers in Campania, and demanded satisfaction for the injury. Certainly the Greeks had no scruples to restrain them from making spoil of the persons and property of barbarians; but the hostility was generally mutual; the Greek cities in southern Italy had suffered greatly from the attacks of their Lucanian neighbors; and the Roman settlers and occupiers of land in Campania might sometimes relieve their own wants by encroaching on the pastures or plundering the crops of the Greeks of Parthenope.

What account the Neapolitans gave of the origin of their quarrel with Rome, we know not; but the Roman story was, that when their feciales were sent to

[28] Livy, VIII. 22. Dionysius' statement represents the wrong as offered to the Campanians themselves; and that the Romans took up the cause of their dependent allies, or, in the well-known Greek term, of those who were ὑπήκοοι τῆς Ῥωμαίων ἡγεμονίας. See Dionys. XV. 4. Fragm. Mai.

[29] Dionysius, XV. 6. Fragm. Mai.

[30] Νωλανῶν σφόδρα τοὺς Ἕλληνας ἀσπαζομένων. Dionys. XV. 5. The coins of Nola closely resemble those of Neapolis, and the legend is in the Greek, not in the Oscan character.

It involves the Romans in a war with the Samnites.

Palæpolis[31] to demand satisfaction, the Greeks, being a tongue-valiant people, returned an insulting refusal. Upon this the senate submitted to the centuries the resolution that war should be declared with the people of Palæpolis; and the centuries having approved of it, war was declared accordingly. Both consuls were sent into Campania; Q. Publilius Philo to attack the Greeks, L. Cornelius Lentulus to watch the Samnites, who were expected to aid them. It was said that a Samnite garrison of 4000 men,[32] together with 2000 men from Nola, were received into Palæpolis; and L. Cornelius reported to the senate that enlistments of men were ordered all over Samnium, and that attempts were making to excite the people of Privernum, Fundi, and Formiæ to rise in arms again against Rome. Upon this, the ambassadors were sent by the Roman government to the Samnites, to obtain redress for their alleged grievances. The Samnites wholly denied their having tampered with Privernum,[33] Fundi, and Formiæ; and the soldiers who had gone to Palæpolis were, they said, an independent body, who had volunteered into the Greek service, and had not been sent by any public authority. This was probable enough, at a period when Campanian, or Opican, or Samnite mercenaries,—for the same men were called indifferently by all these names,—bore such a high renown for valor, and were enlisted into the service of so many different nations. But the Samnites further charged the Romans with a breach of the treaty on their part, in having planted a Roman colony at Fregellæ; a place which, having been conquered by the Samnites from the Volscians in the late war with the Latin confederacy, belonged rightfully to them as their share of the spoil. The Roman annalists seem to have known of no adequate answer that was made to this charge: the Romans proposed, it is said, to refer the question to the decision of some third power, keeping possession, however, of Fregellæ in the mean time. But the Samnites thought their right so clear, that it was idle to refer the matter to any arbitration,[34] and to allow the Romans in the mean while to exclude them from entering upon their own land. They replied, that no negotiations, and no mediation of any third party, could decide their differences; the sword alone must determine them. "Let us meet at once in Campania," they said, "and there put our quarrel to issue." The answer was characteristic of the Romans: "Our legions march whither their own generals order them, and not at the bidding of an enemy." Then the Roman fecialis, or herald,[35] stepped forward: "The gods of war," he said, "will judge between us." And then he raised his hands to heaven and prayed, "If the Roman commonwealth has received wrong from the Samnites, and shall proceed to take up arms because she could obtain no justice by treaty, then may all the gods inspire her with wise counsels, and prosper her arms in battle! But if Rome has been false to her oaths, and declares war without just cause, then may the gods prosper neither her counsels nor her arms!" Having said thus much, the ambassadors departed; and L. Cornelius, it is said, crossed the frontier immediately, and invaded Samnium.

Q. Publilius Philo is made pro-consul.

But the year passed away unmarked by any decisive actions. Q. Publilius established himself between Palæpolis and Neapolis, so as to intercept all land communication between them, and to be enabled to lay waste their territory. He did not venture, however, to besiege either city,

[31] Dionysius, in all his account of these affairs, makes mention only of Neapolis; the name of Palæpolis does not once occur in his narrative. In the Roman story, Palæpolis holds the more prominent place; for no other reason, apparently, than because Palæpolis was conquered by force, and enabled Publilius to obtain the honor of a triumph, while Neapolis entered into a friendly treaty with Rome. But Palæpolis must really have been a very insignificant place; for it followed almost as an infallible rule, that whenever a new town, Neapolis, was founded in a more advantageous situation, the old town, or Palæpolis, went to decay.

[32] Livy, VIII. 23.

[33] Livy, VIII, 23.

[34] See the answer of the Corinthians when the Corcyræans, like the Romans, first besieged Epidamnus, and then offered to refer the dispute to the arbitration of some third party. Thucyd. I. 39.

[35] Dionysius, XV. 13. Fragm. Mai.

and as the sea was open to their ships, they were not likely to be soon reduced to famine. Thus when the consular year was about to close, Q. Publilius was empowered to retain his command as proconsul,[36] till he should have brought the war to a conclusion; and this is the first instance on record of the name and office of proconsul, and proves the great interest which Publilius must have had both in the senate and with the people at large; for certainly no urgent public necessity required that he should receive such an extraordinary distinction. It might have seemed of much greater consequence to leave the same general in the command of the army in Samnium; but Cornelius[37] was only excused from returning to Rome to hold the comitia, and was required to nominate a dictator for that purpose; as soon as the new consuls came into office, the conduct of the war was committed to them.

Patrician jealousies against a plebeian dictator.

The consul named as dictator M. Claudius Marcellus, a man who had been himself consul four years before, but was of a plebeian family. And here we may observe a confirmation of Niebuhr's opinion, that the spirit of the senate at this period was very different from that of the more violent patricians, or probably of a majority of the order. The senate had just conferred an unprecedented honor on the man whom the patricians most hated—on the author of the Publilian laws. This probably excited much bitterness; and although M. Claudius Marcellus seems to have given no personal cause of offence, yet as he was a plebeian, the more violent patrician party determined to vent their anger upon him. They could not stop the proconsulship of Publilius, for that was solely within the cognizance of the senate and people; but the dictatorship of Marcellus might be set aside by a power which was still exclusively patrician, and for that very reason was likely to be animated by a strong patrician spirit, the college of augurs. Reports were spread abroad that the dictator had not been duly appointed, that some religious impediment had occurred; and of this question the augurs were alone judges. It was referred to them, and they pronounced that in the appointment[38] the auspices had not been properly taken, and that it was therefore void. The dictator accordingly resigned his office; but the decision of the augurs, although not legally questionable, was openly taxed with unfairness. The consul, it was said, was in the midst of his camp in Samnium; he had arisen, as was his custom, at the dead of night, and had named the dictator when no human eye beheld him. He had mentioned nothing of evil omen to vitiate his act; there was no witness who could report any, and how could the augurs, whilst living quietly at Rome, pretend to know what signs of unlucky import had occurred at a given time and place in Samnium? It was plain to see that the real impediment to the dictator's appointment consisted in his being a plebeian.

Attempts to set aside the Licinian law.

The patricians appear to have been so encouraged by this victory, as to venture upon another attempt of a far more desperate nature: they seem to have tried to set aside the Licinian law, and to procure the election of two patrician consuls. This at least is the most likely explanation of the fact that after the dictator's resignation, when the comitia were to be held by an interrex, the election was so delayed[39] that thirteen interregna, a period of more than sixty-five days, were suffered to elapse before the new consuls were appointed. The fourteenth interrex was L. Æmilius Mamercinus, a man whose family, since the days of the good dictator Mamercus Æmilius, had always been opposed to the high patrician party, who was himself a friend[40] of Publilius Philo, and whose brother had been Publilius' colleague and associate in the year in which he had passed his famous laws. He brought on the election without delay, and took care that it should be conducted according

[36] Livy, VIII. 23.
[37] Livy, VIII. 23.
[38] Livy, VIII. 23. "Vitiosum videri dictatorem pronuntiaverunt."
[39] Livy, VIII. 23.
[40] He had named Publilius his master of the horse a few years earlier, when he was himself dictator. Livy, VIII. 16.

to law; and thus the efforts of the patricians were baffled, and a plebeian consul, C. Pœtelius,[41] was elected along with the patrician L. Papirius Mugillanus.

Feelings of both nations at the beginning of the second Samnite war.

It was an untimely moment for the renewal of party quarrels, when Rome was entering upon her second and decisive war with Samnium. In the first contests the two nations had met without animosity, and the war was ended between them soon and easily. But in the fourteen years which had since elapsed their feelings had become greatly changed. They were now well aware of each other's power and ambition; their dominions were brought into immediate contact; neither could advance but by driving back the other. The Latin states were now closely united with Rome, and it was become a question which of the two races, the Latin or the Sabellian, should be the sovereign of central and southern Italy. The second Samnite war, therefore, was carried on with feelings of bitter hostility; and instead of ending, like the first, within three years, it lasted, amidst striking vicissitudes of fortune, for more than twenty.

CHAPTER XXXI.

SECOND SAMNITE WAR—L. PAPIRIUS CURSOR—AFFAIR OF THE FORKS OR PASS OF CAUDIUM—BATTLE OF LAUTULÆ—Q. FABIUS, AND THE WAR WITH ETRURIA.—A. U. C. 428-450: 423-444, NIEBUHR.

"Samnites quinquaginta annis per Fabios et Papiriospatres, eorumque liberos, ita subegit ac domuit (populus Romanus), ita ruinas ipsas urbium diruit, ut hodie Samnium in ipso Samnio requiratur; nec facile appareat materia quatuor et viginti triumphorum."—FLORUS, I. 16.

Chronology of the second Samnite war.

THE second Samnite war brings us to the middle of the fifth century of Rome, and within little more than three hundred years of the Christian æra. Alexander died almost before it had begun; and neither Aristotle nor Demosthenes were living when the Romans, in the fifth year of the contest, were sent under the yoke at the memorable pass of Caudium. At its conclusion, sixteen years later, we are arrived at the second generation of Alexander's successors; Eumenes and Antipater were dead, Demetrius Poliorcetes was in the height of his renown; and Seleucus and Ptolemy had already assumed the kingly diadem, and founded the Greek kingdoms of Syria and of Egypt. So completely had Greece arrived at the season of autumn, while at Rome it was yet the early spring.

General nature and objects of the war.

The war on which we are going to enter lasted, on the lowest computation, about twenty years. It was full of action, but its events present so complicated a tissue, that it is not easy to comprehend its general principle. Here, however, as in the Peloponnesian war, it was a great object with either party to tempt the allies of the other to revolt; and thus the Roman armies were so often employed in Apulia, and in the valley of the upper Liris, while the Samnites were eager at every favorable opportunity to pour down into Campania. At first the fidelity even of the Latin states to Rome seemed doubtful; but that was secured by timely concessions, and Rome and Latium, firmly united, were enabled to send out armies so superior in number to those of the Samnites, that while revolt from the Romans was an attempt of the greatest

41 Livy, VIII. 25.

danger, revolt to them was prompted both by hope and fear. The Etruscan war, like all the other military attempts of that divided people, offered no effectual diversion; and at last Samnium saw her allies stripped, as it were, from around her, and was obliged herself to support the havoc of repeated invasions. She then yielded from mere exhaustion; but was so unsubdued in spirit that she only made peace till she could organize a new force of allies to assist her in renewing the struggle.

The Lucanians and Apulians become the allies of Rome.

Q. Publilius Philo,[1] in his new office of proconsul, was continuing his land blockade of the Greeks of Parthenope; while the new consuls of the year 428 with their united armies were ordered to invade Samnium. But the Romans, according to the policy which they invariably pursued in their later wars, did not choose to carry on a systematic war in their enemy's country till they had secured the alliance of some state in his immediate neighborhood. Thus, before they commenced their operations, they concluded treaties of alliance[2] with the Lucanians and Apulians, or, at any rate, with some particular states or tribes of these two nations. The Lucanians, although a kindred people to the Samnites, were politically distinct from them; and they had, moreover, their own internal factions,[3] each of which would gladly apply for foreign aid to enable it to triumph over its rival. Besides, they were the old enemies of the Greek cities on their coasts; and as Rome was now in open war with Neapolis, and on the brink of a quarrel with Tarentum, this very circumstance would dispose the Lucanians to seek her alliance. As for the Apulians, they were treated by the Samnites, it is said, almost as a subject people;[4] and they might, therefore, as naturally look to Rome for deliverance, as the allies of Athens in the Peloponnesian war were ready to revolt to Lacedæmon. But the Samnite government had not the active energy of the Athenian; and the Romans were still more widely distant from the pusillanimity and utter unskilfulness which marked the military plans of Sparta.

End of the war with the Greeks of Parthenope. Neapolis becomes the ally of the Romans.

We know nothing but the mere outside of all these transactions; the internal parties whose alternate triumph or defeat influenced each state's external relations, are mostly lost in the distant view presented by the annalists of Rome. But it is recorded[5] that the war with the Greeks of Parthenope was ended by the act of a citizen of Palæpolis, who, preferring the Roman to the Samnite connection, found means to admit the Romans into his city. Publilius obtained a triumph for his conquest, and Palæpolis is no more heard of in history; but Neapolis, warned in time by the fate of her sister city, did not allow one of her own citizens to place her at the enemy's mercy, but at once concluded peace for herself, and was admitted into the Roman alliance.[6] From that day forward the political history of Neapolis is a blank to us, till, in the revolutions of ages, the Chalcidian colony became the seat of an independent duchy, and afterwards of a Norman kingdom.

The people of Tarentum,[7] it is said, were greatly concerned at the issue of

[1] Livy, VIII. 25.

[2] Livy, VIII. 25.

[3] This, Niebuhr observes, appears from the statement that Alexander of Epirus, during his wars in Italy, was attended by about two hundred Lucanian exiles; and that tnese exiles treated with the opposite party, and purchased their return to their several estates by betraying him and murdering him.—Livy, VIII. 24. It is vexatious that Diodorus, or rather his work as it now remains to us, makes no mention of the affairs of Italy during this period. He notices the war between the Lucanians and Tarentum in the 110th Olympiad, in which Archidamus, the king of Sparta, fought on the side of the Tarentines and was killed; and which was exactly contemporary with the battle of Chæronea, and the beginning of the great Latin war. (Diodorus, XVI. 62-88.) But of the subsequent relations between Tarentum and the Lucinians we have not a word; the whole of the 17th and 18th books in their present state being devoted exclusively to the affairs of Greece and Asia; and the portion of the history which treated of the contemporary events in Sicily and the west, having been entirely lost.

[4] Livy, IX. 13. See chap. XXVIII. of this history, note 28.

[5] Livy, VIII. 25.

[6] Livy, VIII. 26, speaks of a "fœdus Neapolitanum," not "Palæpolitanum," which he accounts for by saying, "Eoenim (scil. Neapolin), deinde summa rei Græcorum venit." But see chap. XXX. note 31.

[7] Livy, VIII. 27.

The Lucanians revolt from Rome, and again join the Samnites.

this wăr, and were anxious by every means to stop the alarming growth of the Roman power. A strange story is told of their deceiving the Lucanians by false representations of outrages offerred by the Roman generals to some Lucanian citizens; and the effect of their trick, it is said, was so great, that the whole Lucanian nation, in the very same year in which they had concluded their alliance with Rome, revolted and joined the Samnites. But the Samnites, mistrusting this sudden change, obliged them to give hostages for their fidelity, and to receive Samnite garrisons into their principal towns.

Obscurity of these accounts. Operations of the first campaign.

It is quite evident that we have not here the whole explanation of the conduct of the Lucanians. Some internal revolution must have prepared the way for it, and then any stories, whether true or false, of the insolence of the Roman generals might be successfully employed to excite the popular indignation. But how the Roman party was so suddenly and completely overthrown, and why neither of the consular armies made any attempt to restore it, it is impossible to conjecture. The whole account of the operations of the two consuls is confined to the statement,[8] that they penetrated some way from Capua up the valley of the Vulturnus, and took the three towns of Allifæ, Callifæ, and Rufrium. But no success was obtained of sufficient importance to deserve a triumph, and the conquered towns were in all probability immediately abandoned, for the Romans could not as yet hope to maintain their ground permanently on the upper Vulturnus; and it appears that fifteen years afterwards Allifæ was still held by the Samnites. Thus, at the end of the first campaign, the aspect of the war was not favorable to Rome.

A. U. C. 429. Second campaign. War with the Vestinians.

The next year opened still more unpromisingly; for the Vestinians[9] joined the Samnite confederacy; and if the Romans attacked them, it was likely that the Marsians, Marrucinians, and Pelignians, would all take up arms in their defence. These four nations lay on the north and northwest of Samnium, and their territory reached from the coast of the Adriatic to the central chain of the Apennines, and to the shores of the lake Fucinus. If they were hostile, all communication between Rome and Apulia was rendered extremely precarious; and Samnium was secured from invasion except on the side of the valley of the Liris, or from Campania. The Romans, therefore, boldly resolved to declare war at once against the Vestinians, and by a sudden attack to detach them from the Samnite alliance. One of the new consuls, Dec. Junius Brutus, marched immediately into their country; the neighboring nations remained quiet, and the Vestinians, overpowered by a superior force, saw their whole country laid waste; and when they were provoked to risk a battle they were totally defeated, and were reduced for the rest of the season to disperse their army, and endeavor only to defend their several cities. Two of these,[10] however, were taken, and although it is not mentioned that the Vestinians sued for peace, yet the communication between Rome and Apulia seems for the future to have been carried on through their country without interruption.

L. Papirius Cursor dictator.

Meanwhile the other consul, L. Furius Camillus, who was to have invaded Samnium,[11] was taken ill, and became unable to retain his command. Being then ordered to name a dictator, he fixed upon L. Papirius Cursor, who accordingly appointed Q. Fabius Rullianus his master of the horse, and marched out to attack the Samnites. Livy's carelessness, and the extreme obscurity of the small towns and villages in Samnium, make it impossi-

[8] Livy, VIII. 25.

[9] Livy, VIII. 29.

[10] Cutina and Cingilia.—Livy, VIII. 29. Both names are entirely unknown, and both, therefore, as usual, are given with great variations in the MSS. The country of the Vestinians lay on the left bank of the river Aturnus, and it included that highest part of the whole range of the Apennines known by the name of "Il gran Sasso d' Italia." But the sites of the several small towns in it, which in all probability had perished long before the Augustan age, it is impossible to ascertain now.

[11] Livy, VIII. 29.

ble to ascertain the seat of this campaign exactly. We cannot even tell whether the Romans invaded Samnium,[12] or were obliged themselves to act on the defensive, and to meet the Samnite army in the valley of the upper Anio, under the Imbrivian or Simbrivian hills, about half way between Tibur and Sublaqueum.

Story of his severity towards Q. Fabius, his master of the horse.

The faint and obscure outline of the military transactions of this campaign affords a strong contrast to the lively and full picture of the dispute between the Roman dictator and his master of the horse, which the annals have given amongst the events of this year. As the story would be considered honorable to both the actors in it, the traditions and memoirs of both their families would vie with each other in recording it; and the historian, Fabius Pictor, in honor of his own name and race, was likely to give it a place in his history. It is told by Livy with his usual power and feeling; but here, as in the story of T. Manlius and his son, it will be best merely to repeat the outline of it, as we have no other knowledge of it than what we derive from Livy himself, and to give it again in detail would be either to translate him, or to describe with less effect what in him is related almost perfectly.

Q. Fabius appeals to the tribunes; and the people, by their entreaties, prevail on the dictator to spare his life.

When the auspices were taken,[13] as usual, by the dictator at Rome, previously to his marching out to war, the signs of the will of the gods were not sufficiently intelligible. It was necessary, therefore, to take them over again; and as they were auspices[14] which could only be taken lawfully within the precinct of the old Ager Romanus, the dictator was obliged for this purpose to return to Rome. He charged his master of the horse to remain strictly on the defensive during his absence; but Fabius disobeyed his orders, and gained some slight advantage over the enemy; an advantage which the annalists magnified into a decisive victory, with a loss to the Samnites[15] of 20,000 men. However, Papirius, as soon as he heard of this breach of his orders, hastened back to the camp, and would have executed Fabius immediately, had not the violent and almost mutinous opposition of the soldiers obliged him to pause. During the night Fabius fled from the camp to Rome, and immediately summoned the senate to implore their protection; but ere the senators were well assembled, the dictator arrived, and again gave orders to arrest him. M. Fabius, the father of the prisoner, then appealed to the tribunes for their protection, and declared his intention of carrying his son's cause before the assembly of the people. Papirius warned the tribunes not to sanction so fatal a breach of military discipline, nor to lessen the majesty of the dictator's office, by allowing his judgments to be reversed by any other power. The tribunes hesi-

[12] Livy fixes the scene of action in Samnium, and calls the place at which the action was fought "Imbrinium." VIII. 30. But Niebuhr observes, that the circumstances of the story which follows, imply that the Roman army could have been at no great distance from Rome; and the Imbrivian or Simbrivian hills of the upper valley of the Anio are well known. In this Samnite war, wherever we have any details of a battle, the geography of the campaign is generally more perplexed than ever; because such details always come from stories preserved by the several families of the aristocracy, whether in writing or traditionally; and these, caring nothing for the military history of the previous operations, only sought to describe the deeds of their hero in the battle.

[13] Livy, VIII. 30.

[14] This appears from the well-known passage in Varro, in which he gives the augurs' division of all countries, according to the rules of their art; that is, according to the several kinds of auspices which were peculiar to each of them. The ager Romanus and the ager Gabinus are classed apart, because in these two districts the auspices might be taken in the same way. All other countries were either ager peregrinus, or ager hosticus, or ager incertus; and these required different auspices.—See Varro, V. § 33. Ed. Müller.

[15] Livy, VIII. 30. Some writers, not content with this, asserted that two pitched battles had been fought during the dictator's absence, and that Fabius had been twice signally victorious. "In quibusdam annalibus tota res prætermissa est," says Livy; that is, the action was of no importance in itself, and therefore was omitted in those annals which did not enter into the details of the story of Papirius and Fabius. But, as it made a necessary part of that story, it was mentioned, of course, in every version of it; and both the Papirian and the Fabian traditions would be disposed to exaggerate its importance: the latter, from an obvious reason; but the former would be disposed to do it equally, for the glory of the character of Papirius was placed in his unyielding assertion of the sacredness of discipline; and this would be rendered the more striking, in proportion to the brilliancy of the action, which he, notwith standing, treated as a crime, because it had been fought contrary to his orders.

tated; they were unwilling to establish a precedent of setting any limits to the absolute power of the dictator, a power which was held essential to the office; and yet they could not bear to permit an exercise of this power so extravagantly severe as to shock the sense and feelings of the whole Roman people. They were relieved from this difficulty by the people themselves;[16] for the whole assembly, with one voice, implored the dictator to show mercy, and to forgive Fabius for their sakes. Then Papirius yielded; the absolute power of the dictator, he said, was now acknowledged: the people did not interfere to rescind his sentence,[17] but to entreat his mercy. Accordingly, he declared that he pardoned the master of the horse; "and the authority of the Roman generals was established," says Livy, "no less firmly by the peril of Q. Fabius than by the actual death of the young T. Manlius." This is true, if by peril we understand not only that he was in danger, but also that he was no more than in danger, and that he did not actually perish; for the execution of Fabius would, perhaps, have been more ruinous to discipline than any other possible result of the transaction, as the reaction of feeling produced by laws of extreme severity has a direct tendency to utter lawlessness. It may be observed also, that, according to this story, the tribunes possessed the power within the city of staying the execution, even of a dictator's sentence; and there is no doubt that in him, no less than in an inferior magistrate, it would have been a breach of the solemn covenant of the Sacred Hill to have touched the person of a tribune. And, in the same manner, the people in their centuries could, undoubtedly, have taken cognizance of the offence of Fabius themselves, and removed it out of the jurisdiction of the dictator. But neither the tribunes nor the people wished so to interfere, because it was held to be expedient that the dictator's power should be, in practice, unrestrained; and, therefore, it was judged better to save Fabius by an appeal to the clemency of Papirius, rather than by an authoritative reversal of his sentence.

Successes of Papirius. Truce for a year.

From this story we return again to the meagerness of the accounts of the war. It is said, that whilst Papirius[18] was absent in Rome, one of his foraging parties was cut off by the Samnites; and that after his return to the army, the soldiers were so unwilling to conquer under his auspices, that in a bloody battle, fought under his immediate command, with the enemy, the fortune of the day was left doubtful. Then, said the story,[19] Papirius saw how needful it was to win the love of his soldiers; he was assiduous in his attentions to the wounded; he commended them by name to the care of their respective officers; and he himself, with his lieutenants, went round the camp, looking personally into the tents, and asking the men how they were. The affections of the army were thus completely regained; another battle followed, and the victory of the Romans was so decisive, that the Samnites were forced to abandon the open country to the ravages of their enemies, and were even driven, so said the stories of the Papirian family, to solicit peace. The dictator granted an armistice, and ambassadors from the Samnites followed him to Rome, when he returned thither, about the end of February,[20] to celebrate his triumph. But as the terms of a lasting peace could not be agreed upon, nothing more was concluded than a truce for a single year; a breathing-time which both parties might find convenient.

Third campaign. Confusion of the history of this year. A. U. C. 431.

The new consuls, however, were engaged in hostilities with the Samnites in the course of their magistracy, so that the Roman annalists accused the Samnites of having broken the truce as soon as Papirius went out of office.[21] In the utter confusion of the chronology of this period, and the obscurity of its history, we cannot tell whether the charge was

[16] Livy, VIII. 35.

[17] "Non noxa eximitur Q. Fabius, sed noxæ damnatus donatur populo Romano, donatur tribuniciæ potestati, precarium non justum auxilium ferenti."—Livy, VIII. 35.

[18] Livy, VIII. 35.

[19] Livy, VIII. 36.

[20] See the Fasti Capitolini.

[21] Livy, VIII. 37. "Nec earum ipsarum (induciarum) sancta fides fuit: adeo, postquam Papirium abisse magistratu nuntiatum est, arrecti ad bellandum animi sunt."

well founded or no. But the events of this year, 431, according to the common chronology, have been more than ordinarily disguised and suppressed, for the annalists represent it as a year marked by no memorable action; whereas, in fact, it witnessed a coalition against Rome, which was indeed quickly dissolved, but in the mean time had exposed the republic to the most imminent jeopardy. We must attempt to restore the outline at least of the real but lost picture.

The consuls march into Apulia and Samnium.

The Samnites had employed the year of the truce in endeavoring to procure assistance for themselves amongst the allies and subjects of Rome. They succeeded, either wholly or in part, with the Apulians: some of whose cities[22] revolted from the Romans, and called in the Samnites to assist in reducing those who refused to join them. Thus when the truce was either ended, or broken, Q. Aulius Cerretanus,[23] one of the consuls, was obliged to march with one consular army into Apulia; whilst the other consul, C. Sulpicius Longus, was sent into Samnium. Whether he made his attack on the side of Campania, or from the country of the Pelignians and Marsians, we know not; but it appears, at any rate, that both consuls were engaged at a distance from Rome, and their communications with it would, therefore, be liable to great interruption.

Great rising of the cities near Rome to claim the full rights of citizenship. L. Fulvius consul of the Tusculans.

Five years had now elapsed since the rights of Roman citizenship had been bestowed on the people of Privernum; thirteen years had passed since the same privileges had been given to the Tusculans. But as this citizenship extended only to private rights, and conferred no political power (for neither the Privernatians nor the Tusculans were as yet included in any Roman tribe, and, consequently, they enjoyed no rights of voting), so it was felt to be a degradation rather than a benefit; or, at any rate, it was fitted only for a temporary measure, which ought to pave the way for a more perfect union. We may conjecture also, from what has taken place in other countries, that hopes had been held out, or even promises made, by the Romans, of which the fulfilment was afterwards indefinitely delayed; and the nobility of Privernum and Tusculum, connected with those of Rome in their private relations, and aspiring to share with them also their political distinctions, were especially impatient of their actual condition. The Samnite war, and, above all, the absence of both the consular armies in remote parts of Italy, seemed to afford them an opportunity of enforcing their claims, and obliging the Romans to grant them a full equality of rights. Suddenly, therefore, like the Irish volunteers of 1782, the people of Tusculum and Privernum flew to arms; and the spirit which actuated them must, indeed, have been general, if it be true that the people of Velitræ,[24] although already included in a Roman tribe, were yet persuaded to join them. One of their leaders was L. Fulvius Curvus, of Tusculum, and, like the leaders of the Italian allies in the great war of the seventh century, he was invested with the title of consul.[25] A Privernatian leader was, probably,

[22] Livy, VIII. 37.

[23] Livy calls him Q. Æmilius Cerretanus, but says "Aulium quidam annales habent." He himself calls him Aulius, however, when he mentions his second consulship in the year 429.—Livy, IX. 15.

[24] In the bill proposed afterwards by M. Flavius for the punishment of the Tusculans, it was proposed to punish all those "quorum ope ac consilia Veliterni Privernatesque populo Romano bellum fecissent." This can only allude to the short war of this year; but the account of these events in Livy is so meager that if we only followed his narrative the allusion would be unintelligible; for not a word had been said of Privernum since the war of 425, nor of Velitræ since the great Latin war. Drakenborch, therefore, is naturally at a loss to understand the meaning of the passage; but as the statement of the language of the bill is likely to be authentic, we might venture, even from that alone, to supply the defects of the other part of Livy's narrative, even if we had not Pliny's remarkable notice of L. Fulvius, which throws a light upon the whole transaction.

[25] "Est et L. Fulvius inter insignia exempla. Tusculanorum rebellantium consul; eodemque honore quum transisset exornatus confertim a populo Romano: qui solus eodem anno quo fuerat hostis Romæ triumphavit ex iis quorum consul fuerat." Pliny, Histor. Natur. VII. 44. Now, the title of consul was Roman exclusively, and not Latin; the Latins had prætors and dictators, but no consuls; which would naturally be the case, if the origin of the name at Rome were as accidental, and as connected with the peculiar circumstances of the time, as I have supposed it to have been. See p. 120. If, then,

associated with him in this dignity, in intimation that Tusculum and Privernum were resolved to form a distinct Roman commonwealth of their own, they too being Roman citizens, if the inhabitants of the capital persisted in excluding them from the government and honors of their common country.

Night march of L. Fulvius upon Rome. The demands of the insurgents are granted.

Their measures seem to have been taken with the most careful secrecy, and the execution of them fell upon the Romans like a thunderbolt. In the dead of the night, an alarm was given that an enemy was before the walls of Rome;[26] the citizens arose in haste, each man seized his arms, and ran to the Capitol, or to defend the walls and secure the gates of the city. The attempt of L. Fulvius to surprise Rome, not less bold than the march of C. Pontius Telesinus upon the Colline gate, was timely baffled; and, finding the city secured against a surprise, he retreated as rapidly as he had advanced. But although this single blow had failed, it still revealed the magnitude of the actual danger. If Velitræ had joined in the revolt, what hope was there that the other cities of Latium would remain faithful? and if the whole storm of the Latin war should again gather, when the Samnites were no longer allies of Rome, as in the last war, but her deadly enemies, what prospect was left of victory? The pride of the Roman aristocracy was obliged to yield; and the self-same conduct which in Vitruvius Vaccus five years before they had punished with death, they were now obliged, in the case of L. Fulvius Curvus, to reward with the consulship. What security they could give that they would keep their plighted faith, we know not; but L. Fulvius was so satisfied that he went over to the Romans, and his countrymen and their allies, assured that their demands would be granted, laid down their arms. A mad, if not a treacherous, attempt to disturb this understanding was made by M. Flavius,[27] one of the tribunes; he proposed a law for visiting with condign punishment those citizens of Tusculum who had been the instigators of the late insurrection. This must, undoubtedly, have included L. Fulvius himself; and had the law passed, the Latins, in indignation and despair, would have risen as one man; and the quarrel would have become utterly irreconcilable. One tribe, the Pollian, voted in favor of it, and even expressed its wish for a still bloodier vengeance on the whole people of Tusculum, such as the Athenians had taken upon the revolted Melians and Scionæans. But all the other tribes, to the number of eight and twenty, had the wisdom to reject the bill. In the very next census the Tusculans[28] and Privernatians received the full rights of citizenship; but L. Fulvius obtained the object of his ambition even without this short delay; he was elected at once Roman consul; and the man who in one year had led a hostile army to assail the very walls of Rome, was in the next year invested with the highest civil and military power in the Roman commonwealth.

Fulvius was really called consul, and not prætor, the title must have been chosen with the same feeling as in the Italian war; when the Italian allies, claiming to be the true representatives of the Roman nation, elected their two consuls and twelve prætors in opposition to the consuls and prætors of the city of Rome.

[26] Livy, VIII. 37. "Romæ nocturnus terror ita ex somno trepidam repente civitatem excivit, ut capitolium atque arx mœniaque et portæ plena armatorum fuerint, et cum concursatum conclamatumque ad arma omnibus locis esset, primâ luce nec auctor nec causa terroris comparuit." The story thus given is a mere absurdity; but it is probable enough, if explained as in the text. We read of a similar night attack made by the Æquians upon Tusculum towards the close of the third century of Rome, Livy, III. 23; and in the same manner Appius Herdonius had actually surprised the Capitol at Rome in the year 294. It may be that Fulvius expected to be joined by a party within Rome itself, and the failure of this co-operation may have ruined his design. That he should have retreated instantly, as soon as he found that he was discovered, was, of course, necessary; and thus there would have been no enemy to be seen from the walls of Rome when the day broke; and yet the alarm in the night was any thing but imaginary.

[27] Livy, VII. 37.

[28] This is known with regard to the Privernatians, because they were included in the tribe Ufentina, or Oufentina, which was created in 436. See Livy, IX. 20. Diodorus, XIX. 10. With regard to the Tusculans it is only a conjecture; but we never hear of them afterwards, except as full citizens; and their being enrolled in the Papirian tribe (which is known from Livy, VIII. 37) seems to suit with the supposition that they were admitted to the full franchise by L. Papirius Cursor, who, as appears from the Fasti Capitolini, was one of the censors of the year 436, when the Falerian and Ufentine tribes were created.

Fourth campaign of the war. Victories of the Romans.

What became of the consular armies in Samnium and Apulia, while these important events were passing in the neighborhood of Rome, we have no means of discovering. It is certain that they gained no victories; it is possible that they may have sustained some defeats, and that their ill fortune may have helped to break the spirit of Roman government, and to enforce a compliance with the demands of the Tusculans. But when the seeds of dissension near home were destroyed, and Tusculum and the other neighboring cities were cordially united with Rome, the war in Samnium assumed a different aspect. The Roman annals represent the year 432 as one marked by most brilliant victories; although some accounts[29] ascribed the merit of them to the consuls, Q. Fabius and L. Fulvius, while others gave it to a dictator, A. Cornelius Arvina. All agreed, however, in saying that the Samnites sustained a bloody defeat, insomuch that the party in Samnium which was favorable to peace obtained, for the moment, an ascendency. This party resolved to purchase the friendship of Rome by the humblest concessions: all prisoners[30] and all plunder taken from the Romans were to be restored; all the demands of the Romans before the war were to be fully satisfied; and Brutulus Papius, the leader of the war party, was to be given up to the Romans, as the man who had broken the peace between the two nations. Brutulus Papius, it is said, would not be given up alive; he killed himself, and only his lifeless body was offered to the vengeance of his enemies. But the Romans, thinking that a party which could yield so much would not dare to refuse any thing, rejected even these terms, and would be contented with nothing less than that the Samnites should acknowledge their supremacy, and become their dependent allies.[31] One unsuccessful campaign was not enough to reduce so brave a people to such a humiliation; the whole nation resolved to try the chance of war once more; and their choice of an imperator, or captain-general, for the approaching campaign fell on a man who has deserved to be called the Samnite Hannibal, or Caius Pontius of Telesia.[32]

Fifth campaign. The Romans invade Samnium from Campania.

The military history of the ensuing year is more than ordinarily obscure, because the annals were filled with nothing but the stories about the disaster of Caudium; and, as usual, these stories never think of connecting the event to which they relate with the circumstance which led to it, but plunge into the midst of it at once. The two new consuls, it is said, T. Veturius and Sp. Postumius, at the head of two consular armies, consisting each of two Roman legions, and a considerable force of auxiliaries, marched from Rome into Campania; as if it was intended to strike a blow at the great Samnite cities on the southern side of the Matese at Caudium, and Telesia, and Beneventum, or, as it was then called, Maleventum. The last campaign in Apulia had, probably, recovered the revolted cities in that country, and the Roman party amongst the Apulians was supposed to be strong enough to retain their countrymen in their alliance with Rome. Thus the seat of war was removed entirely to the southern frontier of Samnium; and C. Pontius, the Samnite general, was prepared to defend the passes which lead from the plain of Naples to Beneventum and the higher valleys within the line of the Apennines.

They enter the pass of Caudium.

But, in order to tempt the Romans to plunge blindly into these defiles, Pontius contrived to mislead them by a false report that the whole Samnite army was gone off into Apulia,[33] and was there busily engaged in besieging Luceria; as if trusting to the natural strength of their own

[29] Livy, VIII. 38, 39.
[30] Livy, VIII. 39. Dion Cassius, Fragm. Ursin. 143.
[31] Appian, III. Fragm. 4.
[32] He is called Pontius Telesinus by the author of the little work "de Viris Illustribus," in the notice of Sp. Postumius. The great Samnite leader who fought so obstinately against Sylla was also Pontius Telesinus, and, possibly, a descendant of the Pontius who defeated the Romans at the pass of Caudium.
[33] Livy, IX. 2. At what period in this campaign, or by what forces, Luceria was really won over to the Samnite alliance, it is not possible to say. A part of the Samnite forces may have been in Apulia when the Romans entered Samnium; and C. Pontius may have won his victory with an army much inferior in numbers to

country to withstand the invasion of the Roman consuls. The consuls believed this story, and, thinking on the one hand, that the danger of their allies made it necessary to choose the shortest route into Apulia, while the absence of the Samnite army would enable them to force their way through Samnium without difficulty, they entered the fatal pass of Caudium. This was a cut or valley in the outer line or wall of the Apennines, leading from the plain of Campania under the foot of Tiburnus to Maleventum. The modern road from Naples to Benevento still runs through it, and it is now called the valley of Arpaia.[34]

They are defeated, and their retreat is cut off.

In this valley the Roman army found itself on a sudden surrounded by the enemy, who showed themselves on both flanks and on the rear, as soon as the heads of the columns were stopped by the obstacles with which the Samnites had blocked up the road in front of them. Thus entangled in a situation nearly similar to that of Flaminius at Thrasymenus, the Romans were completely defeated.[35] Night, however, saved them from total destruction; but to retreat to the plains was impossible: the pass in their rear, by which they had entered the valley, was secured by the enemy; so that they had no other resource but to encamp in the valley, not far from the scene of their defeat, and there hopelessly to abide the issue. The Samnites, having thus got them in their power, waited quietly till famine should do their work for them. Occupying the road, both in front and on the rear of the Romans, and guarding every possible track by which the enemy might try to escape over the hills on either side of the valley, they easily repulsed some desperate attempts made by the Romans to break out; and a large army, surprised on its march, with all its communications cut off, and hemmed in within a single narrow valley, could not possibly have the means of subsistence beyond a very short period. Accordingly, the Romans soon threw themselves on the mercy of the conqueror: "Put us to the sword,"[36] they said, "sell us as slaves, or keep us as prisoners till we are ransomed: only save our bodies, whether living or dead, from all unworthy insults." They might have remembered how their own countrymen were accustomed to lead their captive enemies in triumph, and to execute them in cold blood in the common prison; nay, how they had lately demanded even the lifeless body of a noble Samnite, Brutulus Papius, to be given up to them, and had deprived it of the rites of burial. But now they could understand that it became a noble nature to show mercy, and that an unfortunate enemy deserved to be treated with compassion.

that of the Romans. But the history of this campaign cannot be completely restored.

[34] The situation of the pass of Caudium has been a matter of dispute. Mr. Gandy, in a memoir published by Mr. Keppel Craven, in his tour through the southern provinces of Naples, p. 12–20, places it in a narrow gorge on the little stream of the Isclero, above Sant' Agata de' Goti. But Niebuhr adheres to the common opinion that it was the valley between Arienzo and Arpaia, through which the present road from Naples to Benevento runs. A village in the midst of this defile is still called Forchia, and Niebuhr says that the defile itself was, even in the middle ages, distinguished by the name of la Furcula Caudina. The dispute has been only occasioned by the supposition that Livy's description of the scene was topographically correct, and by the difficulty of reconciling it with the actual character of the valley of Arpaia. But Livy's descriptions, unless we can be sure that they are taken from some writer who was careful about such matters, deserve no credit; and the picture which he gives of the pass of Caudium is but a representation of almost all mountain valleys, which contract at intervals into mere gorges, and expand between these gorges into something almost deserving the name of a plain. It is said that the valley of Arpaia is too open to suit such a description. Both Niebuhr and Mr. Keppel Craven call it, however, a narrow valley, and the Romans, as they have disguised every other part of the story, were likely also to exaggerate the natural difficulties of the ground, in order to lessen the shame of their defeat.

[35] Livy, as is well known, makes the Romans surrender without a blow, overcome by the insuperable difficulties of the ground where they had been entrapped. But Appian, when he enumerates the officers who signed the capitulation afterwards, names only twelve military tribunes, and says that those who signed were all who were surviving; *σύμπαντες ὅσοι μετὰ τοὺς διεφθαρμένους ἦρχον.*—III. Fragm. 4, § 6. Now two consular armies consisted of four legions, and had twenty-four military tribunes; so that half of the full number must have been either killed or disabled by their wounds. And Cicero, in two places, quoted by Niebuhr (De Officiis, III. 30, and De Senectute, 12), expressly says that there was a battle of Caudium, in which the Romans were defeated.

[36] Appian, III. Fragm. 4. § 2. Compare Dionysius, XVI. 4. Fragm. Mai.

They spoke to one who could feel this in the hour of triumph, and not merely when fortune had turned against him. The father of C. Pontius had been no stranger to the philosophy of Greece; his intercourse with the Tarentines had made him acquainted, it was said, with Archytas:[37] nay, he had even taken part in a philosophical conversation, respecting pleasure, so went the story, not with Archytas only, but with Plato. These particulars may not be historical: but the connection with Tarentum was likely to have an influence on the most eminent Samnites; and C. Pontius was probably far more advanced in cultivation of mind than any Roman general of that age. He resolved to use his victory generously, and to make it, if possible, the occasion of an equal, and therefore of a lasting peace.[38] "Restore to us," he said to the consuls, "the towns and the territory which you have taken from us; and call home your colonists whom you have unjustly settled upon our soil; and conclude with us a treaty which shall acknowledge each nation to be alike independent of the other. If ye will swear to do this, I will spare your lives, and let you go without ransom; each man of you giving up his arms merely, and keeping his clothes untouched; and you shall pass in sight of our army as prisoners whom we had in our power, and whom we set free of our own will, when we might have killed them, or sold them, or held them to ransom."

C. Pontius of Telesia. He offers terms to the Romans.

When Pontius had announced these terms, he called for the Roman fecialis, whose office it was to conclude all treaties and to take the oaths in behalf of the Roman people.[39] But there was no fecialis with the army; for the Romans had resolved to make no peace with the Samnites, and to receive no proposals from them but their absolute submission. So the consuls and all the surviving officers took the oaths; and six hundred Roman knights were to be delivered as hostages to the Samnites to insure the ratification of the peace by the Roman people.

The consuls accept them.

When the Spartans were hopelessly cut off from all aid in the island of Sphacteria, the Athenian commanders agreed to a truce,[40] in order to allow time to the Spartan government to send an embassy to Athens, and to purchase, if they could, the deliverance of their soldiers by consenting to reasonable terms of peace. Why Pontius did not act in a similar manner, and insist upon treating, not with the generals of the blockaded army, but with the senate and people of Rome, whose consent was obviously essential to the validity of any treaty of peace, the suspicious and imperfect accounts of the Roman writers will not enable us to explain. Did he know so little of the Romans as to expect that they would ratify the treaty because its terms were so moderate, and because he had spared the lives of so many thousands of their citizens? But, according to Roman notions, no peace was endurable unless they themselves dictated its conditions; and the mercy of an enemy was a deadly insult, because it reminded them that they had been vanquished. Or did he trust to the force of natural affection; that the six hundred knights whom he had demanded as hostages, and who were probably the sons

But the Roman government was not likely to observe them.

[37] Cicero, de Senectute, XII. § 41. Cicero makes Cato relate this story on the authority of Nearchus of Tarentum, whom he had himself personally known, and who had repeated it to him on the authority of some old men, as a Tarentine tradition. Cato is made to add, that according to his own calculation, Plato's visit to Tarentum had taken place in the consulship of L. Camillus and App. Claudius; that is, in the year of Rome 406, according to the common reckoning. Niebuhr thinks that Nearchus' story only means that Nearchus had himself written a dialogue περὶ ἡδονῆς, in which Archytas, Pontius, and Plato were made the speakers. (Vol. III. note 373.) But Aristoxenus, a scholar of Aristotle, and therefore removed from the time of Archytas only by one generation, in his life of Archytas, speaks of a discussion on bodily pleasures between him and Polyarchus, and he seems to give a reality to the conversation, by stating that Polyarchus came to Tarentum on an embassy, which had been sent thither by the younger Dionysius. (Athenæus, XII. 64.) At any rate, as Niebuhr himself allows, the very introduction of the name of C. Pontius into a philosophical dialogue with Archytas and Plato would show that the eminent Samnites had acquired, through their intercourse with Tarentum, an interest in and an acquaintance with the Greek philosophy.

[38] Appian, Samnitic. Fragm. IV. § 5. Livy, IX. 4.

[39] Appian, Samnit. Fragm. IV. § 5

[40] Thucydides, IV. 15, 16.

or near relations of the most influential members of the senate, would be so far regarded by their fathers, as to tempt them for their sakes to impair the majesty of Rome? But those fathers were the countrymen and contemporaries of T. Manlius, who had ordered his son to be put to death, even when victorious, rather than allow of any example which might be injurious to military discipline; how, then, could the lives of sons who had degraded themselves by becoming prisoners to the Samnites be purchased at the price of national humiliation? Or was Pontius really guilty of no such imprudence; and was it his only fault that he relied on the solemn faith of a people whose care was not to observe their treaties honestly, but to devise some pretext by which, whilst they broke the spirit, they might still save the letter? It is expressly mentioned[41] that not only the officers of the army, but two of the tribunes of the commons, gave their sanction to the treaty; and it seems certain that they gave it as tribunes, and that they were not merely elected tribunes after the surrender, having been at the time no more than tribunes of the soldiers. But if two tribunes of the commons, as such, signed the treaty, how came they to do so, or how was it that during the term of their sacred office they were abroad with the army, and not within the walls of Rome? Were they sent to the camp for the very purpose of deceiving the Samnite general, by accepting the treaty, and assuring him that it would be ratified; and did he, knowing their sacred character, and that they were the leaders and representatives of the Roman commons, rely too confidently on their word, without requiring that formal authority for it, which alone, according to the casuistry of the Romans, could make the nation responsible?

The Romans give up their arms and march out under the yoke.

When the consuls, quæstors, tribunes of the soldiers, and the two tribunes of the commons, had taken the oaths, the first fulfilment of the treaty immediately followed. The Romans gave up their arms, and marched out of their camp wearing or carrying with them nothing but one single article of clothing,[42] the campestre or kilt, reaching from the waist to the knees, and leaving the upper part of the body naked, now that the soldiers had been obliged to give up their coats of mail. Even the consuls were obliged to appear in this humble plight, for their war cloaks, paludamenta, were taken from them, and their lictors ordered to leave them the instant they came out of the camp. The six hundred knights were then delivered up to the Samnites, and the rest of the Roman army, stripped of their arms and baggage, passed in order through an opening purposely made for them in the Samnite lines of blockade.[43] Two spears were set upright in this opening, and a third was fastened across them at the top; and through this gateway the vanquished army marched out, as a token that they had been conquered in war, and owed their lives to the enemy's mercy. It was no peculiar insult devised for this occasion, but a common usage, so far as appears, in all similar cases;[44] like the modern cere-

[41] Cicero, de Officiis, III. 30, § 109. Cicero's words are, "Eodemque tempore, Ti. Numicius, Q. Mælius, qui tum tribuni plebis erant, quod eorum auctoritate pax erat facta, dediti sunt, ut pax Samnitium repudiaretur." The expression, "quod eorum auctoritate pax erat facta," shows, I think, that they were tribunes of the commons when they signed the treaty, and that the "auctoritas" here spoken of was the sanction of their sacred office. Livy also mentions the fact, that two men who were tribunes of the commons in that year were amongst those who signed the treaty, IX. 8.

[42] Ἕκαστον ὑμῶν σὺν ἱματίῳ.—Appian. Samnit. Fr. IV. § 5, "cum singulis vestimentis inermes." Livy, IX. 5. In this state Livy calls them "seminudi," IX. 6, because all the upper part of their bodies was naked: Dion Cassius less correctly calls them γυμνούς—Ἐκέλευον αὐτοὺς εἰς τὸ αὐτὸ ζυγὸν γυμνοὺς εἰσελθεῖν οὗπερ ἐλεηθέντες ἀφείθησαν. Frag. Mai. XXXVII. It may be observed that this condition of allowing each soldier to march out with a single article of clothing was granted by the Athenian commanders to the Potidæans, when Potidæa was taken in the second year of the Peloponnesian war; and that the Athenian government complained of the treaty as too favorable to the vanquished.—See Thucydides, II. 70.

[43] Ὁ μὲν Πόντιος παραλύσας τι τοῦ διατειχίσματος. Appian, Frag. IV. § 6. Διατείχισμα, "a cross or dividing wall," because the Samnite blockade would be effected merely by carrying two lines across the valley, one above the Roman camp and the other below it. The nature of the ground rendered a circumvallation, or περιτείχισμα, unnecessary.

[44] This is shown by the story of Cincinnatus, which represents the Æquians as made to pass under the yoke by Cincinnatus under similar circumstances. And Dionysius expressly calls it a Roman custom to make an enemy who had

mony of piling arms when a garrison or army surrender themselves as prisoners of war. So far, indeed, was Pontius from behaving with any unusual insolence, that he ordered carriages to be provided for the sick and wounded of the Roman army; and furnished[45] them with provisions sufficient to support them till they should reach Rome.

They retreat to Capua, and from thence return to Rome.

In far different plight, and with far other feelings than they had entered the pass of Caudium, did the Roman army issue out from it again upon the plain of Campania. Defeated and disarmed, they knew not what reception they might meet with from their Campanian allies; it was possible that Capua might shut her gates against them, and go over to the victorious enemy. But the Campanians behaved faithfully and generously;[46] they sent supplies of arms, of clothing, and of provisions to meet the Romans even before they arrived at Capua; they sent new cloaks, and the lictors and fasces of their own magistrates, to enable the consuls to resume their fitting state; and when the army approached their city the senate and people went out to meet them, and welcomed them both individually and publicly with the greatest kindness. No attentions, however, could soothe the wounded pride of the Romans: they could not bear to raise their eyes from the ground, nor to speak to any one; full of shame, they continued their march to Rome: when they came near to it, all those soldiers who had a home in the country[47] dispersed and escaped to their several houses, singly and silently; whilst those who lived in Rome lingered without the walls till the sun was set, and stole to their homes under cover of the darkness. The consuls were obliged to enter the city publicly and in the light of day, but they looked upon themselves as no longer worthy to be the chief magistrates of Rome, and they shut themselves up at home in privacy.

Grief and humiliation of the senate and people.

Nor was the blow less deeply felt by the senate and by the whole people. The actual loss in the battle, and the captivity of six hundred of the flower of the youth of Rome, were enough of themselves to throw the nation into mourning; how much more grievous were they when accompanied by such utter defeat and humiliation![48] All business was suspended; all orders put on mourning; the knights and senators laid aside their gold rings, and took off the well-known red border of their dress which marked their rank: in every house there was weeping and wailing for those who had returned home dishonored, no less than for those who were dead or captive: and all ceremonies of rejoicing, all festivals, and all private marriages, were suspended, till they could be celebrated in a year of better omen. A dictator[49] was named to hold the comitia for the election of new consuls; but the augurs declared that the appointment was null and void; another dictator was then chosen, but the same objection was repeated; till at last, as if the gods abhorred every magistrate of this fatal year, the elections were held by an interrex. This interrex was M. Valerius Corvinus, and the consuls chosen[50] were two of the most eminent citizens in the commonwealth, Q. Publilius Philo, the author of the Publilian laws, and L. Papirius Cursor, who had so sternly upheld military discipline in his late dictatorship.

It is resolved to break the treaty and to give up to the enemy the generals and officers who signed it.

We cannot suppose that the Samnites would have allowed their victory to remain long unimproved, without assuring themselves whether it was the intention of the Roman government to ratify the treaty or no. But the chronology and history of these events are alike so meager, or so wilfully falsified, that it is scarcely possible to ascer-

surrendered pass under the yoke, III. 22, p. 469, Reiske. The same thing is implied in the definition of the terms "jugum," and "sub jugum mitti," in Festus.

[45] Appian, Fragm. IV. § 6.

[46] Livy, IX. 6. Dion Cassius, Fragm. Mai, XXXVI.

[47] Appian, Fragm. IV. § 7. Livy, IX. 7.

[48] Appian and Livy, ubi supra.

[49] Zonaras says, that the consuls were obliged to resign their office immediately; παραυτίκα ἔπαυσαν, VII. 26.

[50] Livy, IX. 7.

tain either the dates or the real character of the transactions which followed. As soon as the new consuls came into office, the question of the ratification of the treaty[51] was brought before the senate. Sp. Postumius, one of the consuls of the last year, being called upon to deliver his opinion, declared at once that the treaty ought not to be accepted, but that himself and his late colleague, T. Veturius, with every officer who had taken the oaths to the Samnites, should be given up to them, as having promised what they were unable to perform. The senate embraced his proposal; and to many of the senators it involved a personal sacrifice scarcely less than that which he was making himself, inasmuch as they were exposing their sons, who were amongst the six hundred hostages, to the vengeance of the enemy. But the Romans were as regardless of their own individual feelings as of the laws of justice and good faith, when either was set in the balance against national pride and ambition. The consuls and all the other officers who had sworn with them to the Samnites, were committed to the charge of the feciales, and were by them conducted into Samnium. They were then half stripped, as when they passed under the yoke, their hands were bound behind their backs, and the feciales solemnly delivered them over to the Samnites as men whose persons were justly forfeited to them in atonement for their breach of faith. No sooner was this surrender completed, than Sp. Postumius struck the Roman fecialis[52] violently with his knee, his hands and feet being fettered; and cried out, "I now belong to the Samnites, and I have done violence to the sacred person of a Roman fecialis and ambassador. Ye will rightfully wage war with us, Romans, to avenge this outrage." It is hard to say whether this trickery, at once so base and so foolish, should be ascribed to mere hypocrisy or to fanaticism; for the fanatic is as prone to falsehood as to cruelty, and justifies to himself the one no less than the other, by holding that the end sanctifies the means.

Pontius refuses to accept them.

Yet it is a fanaticism, less wicked, indeed, but even more extraordinary, when a man like Livy can describe such a scene, and can represent, as he has done, the conduct of Pontius in such strong contrast with that of the Romans, without appearing to feel any admiration of the one or any shame for the other. Pontius refused the offered victims: "They were not the guilty persons,"[53] he said, "nor would he, by transferring the punishment to them, acquit their country. The Roman government had reaped all the advantages of the treaty of Caudium, but refused to fulfil its conditions. Either the legions should be replaced in their desperate position, from which nothing but that treaty could have delivered them, or the stipulated price of their deliverance should be

[51] Livy, IX. 8.

[52] Livy, IX. 10. Niebuhr supposes that there must have existed between Rome and Samnium at this period a relation of isopolity; that is, that the citizens of either country, on losing or relinquishing their own franchise, might take up at pleasure that of the other; and that in this sense Sp. Postumius, when given up by the Romans, and so having ceased to be a Roman citizen, immediately took up his franchise as a citizen of Samnium. But this supposition appears to me unnecessary and improbable. Sp. Postumius could have no choice of becoming a citizen of Samnium, for he was given up by the Samnites, deditus, and therefore had no rights whatever in relation to them, but became their absolute property. See the language held with respect to the Campanians when they surrendered themselves to Rome, according to the Roman story, to obtain protection against the Samnites. Livy, VII. 31. The meaning of Postumius' action and words was this: that he now belonged to the Samnites, and that they were responsible for his actions, as for those of their slaves. If the Samnite slaves had plundered the Roman territory, the Romans would have called upon the Samnites to give them satisfaction for the wrong; and in this sense a Samnite slave had now insulted a Roman fecialis, and Rome had thus received a wrong, for which she might either demand satisfaction, or seek it herself by arms. The latter course might lawfully be taken, unless there was a special treaty by which the contracting parties had bound themselves to appeal to negotiation in case of any dispute between them, before they had recourse to arms. And accordingly we find such a clause in the truce concluded between Athens and Lacedæmon, in the ninth year of the Peloponnesian war, Thucyd. IV. 118, where the parties mutually engage τὰ ἀμφίλογα δίκῃ διαλύειν ἄνευ πολέμου. But the Spartans at the beginning of the war had chosen to follow a different course, and to seek redress for their alleged grievances by a direct appeal to arms, without any negotiation.—See Thucyd. I. 86.

[53] Dion Cassius, Fragm. Mai, XXXVII. Livy, IX. 11.

paid. The gods would not be mocked with the trickery of a childish superstition, which endeavored to abuse their holy names for the support of perfidy and injustice." So Sp. Postumius and his companions were given back to the Roman feciales, and returned unhurt to their own army.

Such is the account which the Roman annalists have given of the famous defeat and treaty of the pass of Caudium. It differs in many respects, probably, from the truth; yet it is accurate and trustworthy when compared with the stories of the transactions which followed. L. Papirius Cursor was one of the favorite heroes of Roman tradition; his remarkable swiftness of foot, his gigantic strength, his enormous capacities for food, and the iron strictness of his discipline, accompanied as it was by occasional touches of rough humor,[54] all contributed to make his memory popular, somewhat in the same way as Richard Cœur de Lion has been admired amongst us; and his countrymen boasted that he would have been a worthy champion to have fought against Alexander the Great, if Alexander had ever invaded Italy. This favorite leader was consul in the year immediately following the affair of the pass of Caudium; so great a warrior must have signally avenged that disgrace; and, accordingly, he was made to realize the most sanguine wishes of the national vanity; he retook Luceria,[55] the fatal town which had tempted the consuls of the last year to rush blindly into the defile of Caudium; and in it he recovered all the arms and all the standards which had been taken from the Romans, and, above all, he there found the six hundred Roman knights who had been given up as hostages, and delivered them all safe and sound. Thus every stain of the late disaster was wiped away; but the pride of the Samnites must also be humbled: seven thousand Samnite soldiers were taken into Luceria, and were sent away unhurt after having been made to pass half naked under the yoke, and C. Pontius himself, by the especial favor of the gods, was their commander, so that the ignominy which he had inflicted on the Romans was now worthily returned upon his own head. No wonder, after such a marvellous victory, L. Papirius should have entered Rome in triumph; and never, since M. Camillus had triumphed over the Gauls, had there been seen, it was said, so glorious a spectacle. The two triumphs, indeed, may well be compared with one another; both are equally glorious, and both also are either wholly or in part the inventions of national vanity.

Exaggerated stories of L. Papirius Cursor

The Fasti Capitolini for this year are, unluckily, only partially legible; but it is remarkable that they contain the names of three dictators, of only one of whom there is the slightest notice in Livy, and that they place the triumph of L. Papirius not in this year, but in the following, when, according to them, he was for the third time elected consul. One of the three dictators was L. Cornelius Lentulus; and as the Cornelian house was very numerous and powerful, there were not wanting writers who claimed for him the glory of all the supposed victories[56] of this year, which others had given to L. Papirius. Victories as unreal as the pretended conquest of Luceria might well be ascribed to different persons; that town had only been just taken by the Samnites, and it is impossible to believe that they would have kept their most precious trophies and the whole number of their hostages in a foreign and conquered city, rather than in the cities of Samnium itself. Besides, there is reason to doubt whether Luceria was recovered at all before the year 440, at which time Livy places what, according to him, was its second recapture, as it had just before revolted to the enemy. The real events of this year cannot be ascertained; but there is every probability that the Romans were, in truth, successful; that they did much to remove the feeling of discouragement from the minds of their own

But the Romans were really very successful.

[54] See the character given him by Livy, IX. 16, and the anecdotes related there, and by Dion Cassius, Fr. Mai, XXXIX.

[55] Papirius' campaign is given at length by Livy, IX. 13–15. Traces of the same story are to be found in Dion Cassius, Fragm. Mai, XXXVIII., in Dionysius, Fragm. Vaticana, XXXVI., and in Florus, I. 16.

[56] Livy, IX. 15.

soldiers, and to lower the confidence of the Samnites. It appears that the victory of the pass of Caudium had not been a solitary advantage to the enemy; for they had also taken Luceria in Apulia, and driven the Roman colonists out of Fregellæ,[57] the occupation of which place had been one of the immediate causes of the war. The people of Satricum[58] also, in the heart of Latium, are said to have revolted to the Samnites; a fact which is thus barely noticed, with the remarkable addition, that the Satricans took an active part in the recovery of Fregellæ. Thus the consuls, Publilius and Papirius, had an arduous task to accomplish; and they well justified the confidence of their countrymen, who had selected them above all other citizens to retrieve the honor and the fortune of Rome.

The Roman consuls in Apulia.

Fregellæ, on the upper Liris, and Satricum, in the heart of Latium, the one on the upper road, the Via Latina, from Rome to Capua, the other nearly on the lower road, by Anxur and Fundi, were now fallen into the power of the enemy; and the war might, at any moment, by the revolt of the Hernicans, or of a greater number of the Latin or old Volscian cities, be brought under the very walls of Rome. Yet the Romans resolved at once to fix the seat of war in Apulia, in the same spirit of courage and wisdom which made them send troops to Spain, even when Hannibal was in the heart of Italy. Luceria had fallen, and unless the Romans could effectually support their party in Apulia, that whole country would soon be lost to them and strengthen the power of their enemy. Accordingly, L. Papirius Cursor marched[59] into Apulia by the longer but uninterrupted route through the country of the Vestinians and along the coast of the Adriatic; while Q. Publilius was to force his way through Samnium, and so effect a junction with his colleague. If the main force of the Samnites was employed in Apulia, it is possible that a Roman consular army, consisting of two Roman legions and an equal number of allied troops, might have found no army in Samnium strong enough to obstruct its march; and it would of itself avoid engaging in the siege of any of the Samnite cities. But the account of Publilius' exploit is so extravagant, and at the same time so vague,[60] that we cannot tell by what line he reached Apulia: it is only certain that both consuls were engaged on the other side of Italy during the whole campaign, and that, whether they retook Luceria or not, the progress of revolt in Apulia was effectually checked.

Successive dictatorships at Rome for the protection of the city.

Meanwhile the neighborhood of Rome could not be left defenceless; and the dictators of this year were, probably, appointed to provide for the safety of the capital, and to prevent the example of Satricum from spreading amongst the other cities of Latium. But traces of the old patrician party spirit may here be again observed, as in the dictatorship of M. Marcellus six years before. Q. Publilius had named C. Mænius[61] as dictator,

[57] Livy, IX. 12.

[58] Livy, IX. 12, 16.

[59] Livy, IX. 14. "Locis maritimis pervenerat Arpos."

[60] The account is vague, for it names no scene of action more definite than Samnium. "Publilius in Samnio substitit adversus Caudinas legiones." Livy, IX. 12. "Adversus Caudinas legiones" is also a vague expression, for it may signify either the troops that had lately been engaged at Caudium under C. Pontius, or the forces of the city of Caudium, or of the whole tribe or district of the Caudinians, one of the great divisions of the Samnite nation. And it is extravagant, because it represents the Samnites as flying from the field of battle in Samnium directly into Apulia, when they were in such a state of total rout that they did not venture to defend their own camp. Had this been the case, they would rather have fled for shelter to their own cities, than have gone to a foreign country, which was at that very time the seat of active warfare: to say nothing of the absurdity of an army accomplishing a march of such a distance in a disorderly and scattered flight. "Apuliam dissipati pettiêre."

[61] Only fragments of the Fasti Capitolini are here legible, so that the names of the three dictators of this year, and of their masters of the horse, are mutilated, and stand thus:

C. MA . . .
M. FOS . . .
L. CORN . . .
L. PAPIRIU . .
T. MANLI . . .
L. PAPIRIU . . .

That the first dictator and master of the horse were C. Mænius, spelt Mainius in the Fasti, and M. Foslius, admits of no doubt, as the Fasti, in noticing the dictatorship of C. Mænius six years later, call him then dictator for the second time. [II. DICT.] The second dictator is clearly

a man of a plebeian family like himself, and who, together with himself, was made the subject of a more violent attack from the patricians in his second dictatorship six years afterwards. The augurs, no doubt, declared his appointment to have been invalid, as they had done in the case of Marcellus; and, accordingly, he resigned, and a patrician was appointed to succeed him, P. Cornelius Lentulus. Thus far the accounts are intelligible; but why Lentulus also should have resigned, and the consuls have been required to make a third choice, it is not so easy to discover. This third dictator was T. Manlius, apparently the same Manlius who eighteen years before had gained the great victory over the Latins by Mount Vesuvius; and it is probable that by him were held the comitia for the following year, at which L. Papirius Cursor was again elected consul, together with Q. Aulius Cerpetanus. It may be that the patrician party were anxious to secure the re-election of Papirius; and that P. Lentulus had been opposed to it. Manlius, on the contrary, so much resembled Papirius in the sterner points of his character, that he was likely to agree with those who thought his re-election desirable.

Recovery of Satricum.

Papirius, in his military conduct, justified the confidence of his countrymen. He recovered Satricum,[62] while his colleague carried on the war with continued success in Apulia. The authors of the revolt of Satricum were executed; the people were disarmed, and the town secured by a strong garrison. Thus again the sparks of a Latin insurrection, the greatest of all dangers, were put out before they could burst into a flame.

Truce for two years.

In the next year the Samnites[63] are said to have concluded a truce with the Romans for two years; but it may be that this truce only restrained the two parties from directly invading each other's territories, while it left them at liberty to support their respective allies in Apulia. At any rate, the war continued in that country without intermission, but with uniform success on the side of the Romans. Teanum, Canusium, and Forentum,[64] submitted to Rome, and became her dependent allies; and Apulia was so far reduced that the consuls, towards the end of the second year of the truce, 437–8, proceeded to carry the war into Lucania, and took a place called Nerulum.[65] But no further progress was made in that quarter.

Two new Roman tribes created.

During these two years of truce the Romans were engaged in consolidating their power in their own immediate neighborhood. The censors, L. Papirius Crassus and C. Mænius, created two new tribes[66] in the years 436–7, the Ufentine and the Falerian, and enrolled in some of the old tribes an accession of citizens. The Roman settlers in Campania, who had received grants of land there after the Latin war, were put under the government of a præfect, who was yearly sent to Capua to administer justice amongst them and amongst the Roman citizens residing in Capua itself, according to the Roman law;[67] and a new constitution was given to the colony of Antium, probably im-

L. Cornelius Lentulus, who is mentioned by Livy, and the third is as certainly T. Manlius; but the two L. Papirii, who are named successively as masters of the horse, are very uncertain. Sigonius makes the latter of them to have been L. Papirius Crassus, who was censor two years afterwards, and the former, he thinks, was L. Papirius Cursor, the son of the consul, who was himself afterwards so distinguished in the third Samnite war. But the annals which Livy notices as having made L. Papirius Cursor master of the horse to L. Cornelius, meant, undoubtedly, L. Papirius the father, and not the son. This, however, could not have been the meaning of the Fasti Capitolini; for it is plain that they made L. Papirius consul in this year, although the names of the consuls do not exist on our present fragments, inasmuch as in the next year they call him "Cos: III."—I imagine, therefore, that the second L. Papirius, who was master of the horse in this year, must have been L. Papirius Mugillanus; the same man whom some annals, according to Livy, made consul instead of L. Papirius Cursor in the year following.

[62] Livy, IX. 16.

[63] Livy, IX. 20.

[64] Livy, IX. 20.

[65] Livy, IX. 20. If this place was the Nerulum of the Itineraries, the consuls must have penetrated deeply into Lucania; for the Nerulum of the Itineraries lay far to the south, nearly between the Greek cities of Laos on one sea, and Sybaris on the other.

[66] Livy, IX. 20. Diodorus, XIX. 10.

[67] Livy, IX. 20, and compare Niebuhr, Vol. III. 339.

proving the condition of the old Volscian population. The importance of Antium as a naval station made it desirable to leave there no seeds of disaffection; the more so, if the Tarentines, as is not improbable, furnished the Samnites with some naval assistance at this period, and made occasional descents on the coast of Latium.

Unsettled state of men's minds in Campania.

Whether there had been any interference of the Romans in the domestic affairs of the Campanian cities which excited jealousy; or whether the increasing success of Rome in the war of Samnium created a general alarm amongst her allies, lest they should be left without any power capable of checking her absolute ascendency, we find at any rate that about this time there was a general restlessness amongst the Campanians, and that the Samnites were encouraged to adopt the wiser policy of carrying the war into the territory of their enemies' allies, rather than abide the storm passively at home. The Falerian tribe, which had been recently created at Rome, included that part of Campania known by the name of the Falerian territory; the Roman settlers there would certainly be enrolled in it, while it did not comprise the inhabitants of Cales, Fundi, or Formiæ. Privileges granted to some are a source of discontent if denied to others; and the creation of a Roman tribe so near to them, into which they were not admitted, might make the Campanian towns more impatient of their relation of mere alliance. Thus Nuceria[68] had revolted in the preceding year, and other towns were ready, on the first opportunity, to follow its example.

The Samnites are successful on the upper Liris.

But here again the chronology and history are both involved in inextricable confusion. Livy's account is so imperfect and so unreasonable that it is clearly impossible to rely on it; that of Diodorus is far more sensible, yet it also has omissions which it is difficult to supply. As soon as the truce was over, the Samnites resolved to act on the offensive, and turned their attention to the valley of the Liris, where, as we have seen, they had recovered and still held Fregellæ. They attacked and stormed the town of Plistia,[69] an unknown place, but apparently situated somewhere in that neighborhood; they then prevailed on the Volscian population of Sora to massacre the Roman colonists who held their town, and to join the Samnite confederacy. It is impossible to believe that while these events were taking place, the Roman consuls were sitting idle at Rome; it is much more likely that one consular army was, as usual, in Apulia, and the other either watching the Samnites in the valley of the Liris, or invading Samnium from the side of Campania. But when the news arrived of the fall of Plistia and the revolt of Sora, it was judged necessary to appoint a dictator; and L. Æmilius,[70] who was the dictator fixed upon, immediately began to act on the offensive, and laid siege to Saticula. Whether this town belonged to the Samnites, or was only in alliance with them, and was still possessed by the old Opican population of Campania, is not easy to determine. The Samnites made a desperate effort to relieve the place, but they were defeated by the besieging army with considerable loss, and Saticula was obliged to surrender.[71]

[68] Diodorus, XIX. 65. Compare Livy, IX. 38, 41.

[69] Diodorus, XIX. 72.

[70] Fasti Capitolini, and Livy, IX. 21. But Livy makes the appointment of L. Æmilius precede the fall of Plistia and the revolt of Sora. I have followed the order of Diodorus, who, without naming Æmilius, places the siege of Saticula, which he conducted, after the other two events.

Saticula stood within the first line of hills which rise immediately from the plain of Naples, in a small valley which divides these first hills from the higher and bolder mountains of Taburnus.

[71] The Fasti Capitolini and Diodorus agree in stating, that in the following year, which, according to the Fasti, was the year of Rome 438, or 439, according to the common reckoning, and 434 according to Niebuhr, L. Papirius Cursor and Q. Publilius Philo were again elected consuls together; and Diodorus places the battle of Lautulæ expressly in their consulship. Niebuhr's latest criticism (Vol. II. p. 627, 2d edit.) seems to have rejected this consulship as an interpolation; and it is remarkable that Livy, although he certainly makes a year intervene between the consulship of Sp. Nautius and M. Popilius, and that of M. Pœtelius and C. Sulpicius, does not give the consuls' names. He says, moreover, that they, like the consuls of the preceding year, stayed at Rome and did

After the fall of Saticula the consuls of the new year, if these events really belong to two distinct years, proceeded on the one hand to invade Samnium on the side of Saticula, and on the other to march as usual into Apulia. The army which invaded Samnium overran the country in the neighborhod of Saticula, and then either forced its way into Apulia, or turned aside to the left up the valley of the Vulturnus, and from thence crossed over by the line of the Latin road to the valley of the Liris, and advanced upon Sora, in the hope of punishing it for its revolt. A movement was made, at any rate, which left Campania open; and the Samnites, seizing the opportunity, called out, it is said,[72] their whole population within the military age, and without withdrawing their armies from Apulia and Sora, they burst down into Campania with this third army, which, though hastily raised, was strong in its numbers and in its determined courage. All Campania was at once in a ferment, and the Romans were obliged to name Q. Fabius Maximus dictator, and to send him out with all speed with such a force as could be found or raised in and near Rome, in order to check the spirit of revolt. Fabius advanced beyond Anxur, and occupied the pass of Lautulæ between Anxur and Fundi, already noticed as a post of importance on the coast road from Rome to Campania. Here the Samnites attacked him, and notwithstanding his high military reputation, they defeated him with great slaughter. Q. Aulius Cerretanus, the master of the horse, sacrificed his life nobly in covering the retreat, but the Samnites remained masters of the country, and it is stated in general terms that every place in the neighborhood revolted to them,[73] and that all through Campania,[74] and even at Capua itself, the party opposed to the Roman alliance began to obtain the ascendency.

They defeat the Romans at Lautulæ.

How the consuls effected their retreat from Apulia and from Samnium we know not, nor how far the Samnites either improved or neglected their present opportunity. The Roman citizens of the new Falerian tribe must have been exposed to the greatest dangers; for the open country of Campania was now in the power of the enemy, and as the Roman settlers had no strong towns of their own, they must have either taken shelter in the several cities of their allies, or have made their escape within the pass of Tarracina into the old Volscian country, now the Ufentine tribe, or even to Rome itself. But within the limits of the Campagna we hear of no disposition to revolt; there the timely gift of the full Roman franchise had converted Volscians and Latins into Romans, and neither Privernum nor Tusculum gave any cause for suspicion in this emergency. The new consuls were C. Sulpicius Longus and M. Pœtelius Libo; the latter had not till now commanded an army; the former had indeed been already twice consul, and must now have been advanced in years; but we do not know that he had acquired any remarkable distinction.

Consequences of this defeat.

The principal seat of the war in the next campaign appears to have been the country between Tarracina and the Samnite frontier; and both of the consuls were employed in this quarter. Their business was to watch the Samnites, and to protect the allies of Rome, but they did not for some time venture to encounter the enemy in the field. In spite of all their endeavors, however, Suessa Aurunca and Calatia[75] either revolted or

Revolt of Capua and the other towns of Campania.

nothing, which in a time of such danger as this year must have been, even according to his own account, is an absolute impossibility. Diodorus places the revolt of Sora, the siege of Saticula, and the battle of Lautulæ, all in the same year, which according to him was the year of the consulship of Papirius and Publilius. Amidst all this confusion it is impossible to determine the order of events with certainty.

[72] Diodorus, XIX. 72.

[73] "Circa omnia defecerunt," are the words which Livy puts into the mouth of Fabius, when he is urging his soldiers to venture a second battle after the defeat at Lautulæ.—IX. 23.

[74] Livy, IX. 25, 26.

[75] This appears, because Calatia is mentioned as retaken by the Romans in the following year; and a Roman colony was sent to Suessa, which, it is said, "Auruncorum fuerat." That a colony was sent there implies that the place must have been conquered by the Romans, which could not have happened, unless it had previously revolted from them, or been otherwise in the enemy's power.

were taken; and Capua itself, as if judging that the battle of Lautulæ was now proved to have decided the fate of the war, broke off its alliance with Rome, and declared for the Samnites.[76] This last misfortune obliged the Romans to name a dictator; and C. Mænius, who had once before filled that office, was now again invested with it, and was sent out with a third army to act especially against Capua. An obscure report, barely noticed by Livy,[77] has acquainted us with the existence of another danger which beset Rome at this time, and which must have been more alarming than all the rest. Cabals, and even conspiracies, were formed amongst some of the Roman aristocracy, to turn the perilous crisis of their country to their own personal advantage. Who were the individuals concerned in these plots, or what was their special object, we know not; we can scarcely be mistaken, however, in supposing that Appius Claudius, who was censor two years afterwards, was one of them; and his subsequent conduct makes it probable that he wished to make a party amongst the lowest of the people, and by their help, combined with the strength of the more violent patricians, to overthrow the actual constitution, and restore the exclusive ascendency of the old burgher aristocracy. Disasters in war excite discontent, and discontent readily attacks the existing order of things, however unconnected it may be with the immediate evil; and in this manner the defeat of Lautulæ might be made instrumental to a patrician revolution.

The Ausonian cities are betrayed to the Romans.

But the domestic and foreign danger was alike dispelled by the military success of the consuls. While an aristocratical conspiracy at Rome was threatening the most extreme evils, a similar conspiracy in the Ausonian cities of Ausona, Minturnæ, and Vescia, occurred most critically to revive the cause of Rome in the neighborhood of Campania. Twelve of the young nobility[78] of those towns, dreading nothing so much as the ascendency of their political adversaries through Samnite assistance, offered to the Roman consuls to betray their respective countries into their hands. By their means Roman soldiers were put in possession of the gates of the three cities, and the mass of the people in each were put to the sword. Thus the Romans gained three places of considerable importance from their position; and the bloody execution done upon the inhabitants would spread the impression among the neighboring states, that to revolt from Rome might even yet be attended with danger.

Great victory of the Romans at Cinna. Submission of Capua.

Still the Samnite force was yet unbroken, and availing themselves of the effect produced by their victory at Lautulæ, the Samnite armies were still acting on the offensive. Where the great battle was fought which effectually turned the tide, it is not possible to ascertain. Livy places[79] the scene at the edge of the plain of Naples, where the road from Capua to Beneventum first ascends the hills of Samnium, apparently not far from the pass of Maddaloni. Diodorus fixes it at a place which he calls Cinna,[80] a name wholly unknown, nor will his account enable us so much as to guess its situation. But whatever was the scene of the action, the victory of the Romans was complete, and the threatening consequences of the defeat at Lautulæ were entirely prevented. The news of the battle instantly struck terror into the Campanians, and they at once[81] made their submission to the dictator, and agreed to give up to him the principal instigators of their revolt. Amongst these are particularly named two men of one of the noblest families in Capua, Ovius and Novius Calavius. They, like Vibius Virrius and his associates in the war of Hannibal, chose to perish by their own hands, rather than by the axe of the dictator's lictors, and the principal offenders having thus atoned for their revolt, the state of Capua was pardoned, and readmitted to its former alliance with Rome.

[76] Diodorus, XIX. 76.

[77] IX. 26. "Nec Capua ipsa crimine caruit: quin Romam quoque et ad principum quosdam inquirendos ventum est."

[78] Livy, IX. 25.

[79] Livy, IX. 27.

[80] Livy, XIX. 76.

[81] Diodorus, XIX. 76.

The strength of the two parties in the Samnite war was so essentially unequal that the loss of a battle pressed far more severely on the one than on the other. Accordingly, after the defeat which rendered their victory at Lautulæ fruitless, the Samnites were again reduced to the defensive, and saw the towns which they had won successively wrested from them. In the next two years[82] Fregellæ, one of the original causes of the war, Sora,[83] which had revolted just before the battle of Lautulæ, and Atina,[84] another Volscian city situated among the mountains which look down on the valley of the Melfa, one of the early feeders of the Liris, were all taken by the Romans; while in Campania and its neighborhood they made themselves masters of Suessa Aurunca, of Nola, and Calatia;[85] and in Apulia they finally obtained possession of Luceria.[86] They resolved, too, to secure these conquests by permanent occupation; and thus 2500[87] colonists were sent to Luceria; another colony was planted at Suessa Aurunca; a third in the island of Pontia;[88] and two more, to consist of 2000 colonists each, were ordered to be founded at Interamna on the Liris, and at Casinum on one of the feeders of the Liris.

Continued successes of the Romans. Colonies planted at Luceria, Suessa, Interamna, and Casinum.

These three last colonies were settled on ground which had formerly belonged to the Volscians: Interamna and Casinum were an advance of the Roman frontier on the upper road into Campania; but Pontia must have been colonized with a different object. Two years afterwards we find that two commissioners[89] for naval affairs were for the first time created by the Romans; and this appointment, coupled with the occupation of Pontia, make it probable that during the war with Samnium the Roman coasts were exposed to continual plundering descents, and the Roman merchant-vessels often intercepted on their voyages. Whether this annoyance proceeded from the Lucanians, or whether the Tarentines had really lent to the Samnites the aid of their maritime power in this long struggle, are amongst the many points in the history of these events of which we must be content to be ignorant.

The Samnite war lasted eight years longer; nor was even this latter period of the contest unchequered by some changes of fortune; still Rome was continually becoming more powerful, and the various attempts made by several of the Italian nations to check her growing supremacy served only to set in a clearer light the greatness of her resources. Etruria, which had remained at peace for nearly forty years, now, as if alarmed by the danger of the Samnites, exerted her whole strength against Rome, but in vain. The Umbrians, a people whose name we have scarcely hitherto had occasion to mention, attacked the Romans in entire ignorance of their own and their enemy's power, and were defeated and struck down in an instant. The Hernicans, so long united with Rome in a close alliance, revolted only to become more completely subjected; the hardy nations of the Marsians, Pelignians, and Marrucinians, after having from jealousy stood aloof hitherto from their Samnite kinsmen, now at last endeavored to aid them when it was too late, and did but involve themselves in their humiliation. Northwards, and southwards, in the central Apennines, and on the coast of the Adriatic, the Roman power was alike irresistible, and Rome towered above the nations who were jointly or severally assailing her, like one of the heroes of the Homeric poems when beset by a multitude of common men.

Superiority of the Roman power over that of all the nations opposed to it.

To those who estimate the power of a nation by its geographical extent, this

[82] Livy, IX. 28. Diodorus, XIX. 101.
[83] Livy, IX. 24.
[84] Livy, IX. 28.
[85] Livy, IX. 28. Diodorus, XIX. 101.
[86] Diodorus, XIX. 72. Livy, IX. 26.
[87] Livy, IX. 26.
[88] Livy, IX. 28. Diodorus, XIX. 101–105. Niebuhr observes, that the plural form, "Pontiæ," belongs only to the group of islands, or rather of rocks, in the largest of which, now Ponza, the Roman colony was founded. Ponza has a good harbor, and was taken possession of by the British in 1813. It is volcanic, and is about 14 Neapolitan miles in circumference (nearly 17¼ British), and exhibits several remains of ancient buildings. See Giustiniani, Dizionario del Regno di Napoli, in Ponza.
[89] Livy, IX. 30.

Its causes; the greater population of Rome and Latium: the central position of Rome, and the unity of its government.

constant superiority of Rome may appear extraordinary: for undoubtedly the portions of Italy possessed by the Etruscans, Umbrians, and Samnites, were many times larger than the territory of Rome and her allies. But their superiority in population was by no means equally great; nor is it likely that either Etruria or Samnium were peopled as densely as Latium and Campania. Livy does not give the returns of the several census taken at this period, but he states generally, that the number of Roman citizens averaged about 250,000;[90] to which the Latin and Campanian allies are to be added. Now we do not know what was the population of Samnium or Etruria at this time; but if we may at all be guided by the famous return of the military force of the several nations of Italy in the great Gaulish war of 529,[91] we may conclude that it fell far short of that of the Romans and their confederates. To this must be added the still greater advantages on the side of Rome, of a central position, a unity of counsels, and a national spirit, as systematic as it was resolute. A single great nation is incomparably superior to a coalition; and still more so when that coalition is made up not of single states, but of federal leagues; so that a real unity of counsels and of public spirit is only to be found in the individual cities of each league; which must each be feeble, because each taken separately is small in extent and weak in population. The German empire alone, setting aside the Spanish, Italian, and Hungarian dominions of the house of Austria, could never, even with the addition of the Netherlands, have contended on equal terms with France.

Etruscan war. A great Etruscan army besieges Sutrium. Campaign of Q. Æmilius on the Etruscan frontier, and of C. Junius in Samnium.

The sudden breaking out of the Etruscan war at this period was determined, no doubt, by the expiration of the forty years' peace which had been concluded with the Tarquinians in the year 404. As usual, when the term of peace was drawing to a close, there would be some negotiation between the two countries,[92] to ascertain whether the treaty would be renewed, or whether its close was to be followed by immediate war; and this explains Livy's statement,[93] that in the consulship of M. Valerius and P. Decius there arose rumors of hostilities with Etruria; and that great preparations were made by both nations, although no actual attack was begun by either till the year following. But if we may trust the Roman accounts,[94] not Tarquinii only, but all the Etruscan cities except Arretium took part in the renewed quarrel. This probably was owing to a jealousy of the Roman power on the one hand, and to the cessation of the Gaulish inroads into northern Etruria on the other, so that Clusium and Perusia and Cortona were no longer prevented by a nearer danger, as in the last war with Veii, from giving their aid to the cities on the southern frontier. Accordingly a

A. U. C. 433. B. C. 311.

great Etruscan army laid siege to Sutrium,[95] which was still, as it had been nearly eighty years before, the most advanced point of the Roman do-

[90] Livy, IX. 19. "Censebantur ejus ætatis lustris ducena quinquagena millia capitum."

[91] The return of free citizens within the military age, gave for the Samnites, Lucanians, Marsians, Marrucinians, Frentanians, and Vestinians, the number of 120,000 foot soldiers, and 14,000 horse. Polybius, II. 24. The Umbrians were 20,000; the Etruscans and Sabines together (the number of the Etruscans separately is not given) were 50,000 foot and 4000 horse. Here we have a total of 190,000 foot and 18,000 horse. But the same return reckons the Romans, Latins, and Campanians at 330,000 foot and 23,000 horse, besides the forces actually at that time in the field, which amounted to 50,000 Romans and Campanians more, and probably too at least 20,000 Latins, with not more than 40,000 of the Samnites, Lucanians, &c., on the very highest calculation, and probably much less. Thus the Romans, Latins, and Campanians, at the time of the great Gaulish war, were more numerous than the Etruscans, Umbrians, Samnites, and Lucanians, nearly in the proportion of two to one. And although, in the course of the eighty or ninety years which elapsed between the second Samnite war and the Gaulish invasion, the population of Etruria and Samnium may be supposed to have decreased, while that of Rome undoubtedly had increased by the accession of the Hernicans, Æquians, and a large part of the Sabines, to the rolls of Roman citizens, yet still, with every possible allowance that can be made, we must believe that the Romans and their allies in the second Samnite war considerably surpassed their enemies even in mere numbers.

[92] See of this history, chap. xvi. note 48, and chap. xviii. p. 147.

[93] IX. 29.

[94] Livy, IX. 32.

[95] Livy, IX. 32.

minion on the side of Etruria. Q. Æmilius Barbula, one of the consuls, marched with a single consular army to protect the Sutrians, and a battle was fought with no decisive result; but it was most obstinately contested, and the loss on both sides was immense. The Etruscans, however, continued to besiege Sutrium, and they apparently constructed lines around it, as the Romans had done at Veii, in which they proposed to keep a part of their army through the winter, that the blockade might not be interrupted. Meantime the campaign of this year in Samnium had been decidedly favorable to the Romans, although the details are utterly uncertain; for, if we compare Livy's account with that of Diodorus, no one would suspect that both writers were describing the events of the same war and the same period. According to Livy,[96] the scene of action lay in Samnium, and one consular army only, that of C. Junius Bubulcus, was engaged. By this army, Bovianum, the chief city of the Pentrian Samnites, on the north side of the Matese, is said to have been taken; and afterwards, when the Samnites had nearly surprised the consul by an ambuscade, the practised valor of the soldiers repelled the danger, and even obtained a complete victory. According to Diodorus,[97] both consuls were employed, and the seat of war was Apulia. Here the Romans, after a battle which lasted two days, gained a complete victory, and from that time forwards they remained masters of the field, overran the open country without opposition, and took by storm or by the terror of their arms several of the enemy's cities. In order to reconcile these apparent contradictions, we must suppose that Diodorus describes the winter campaign, and Livy that of the summer following: that both consuls, after entering upon their office in September or October, were employed in Apulia during the winter, which, as Niebuhr has observed, is the best season for military operations in that country; that in the summer of the following year the Etruscan war broke out, and that then Q. Æmilius was sent to relieve Sutrium, while C. Junius carried on the war in the centre of Samnium. The siege of Bovianum, where the climate is so cold, that the snow must render military operations impracticable till very late in the spring, and the ambuscade formed by the Samnites to surprise the Romans while pursuing the cattle into the high mountain pastures, clearly imply a summer campaign. And when C. Junius marched home with his army to celebrate his triumph on the 5th of August, he probably found his colleague still engaged with the Etruscans on the side of Sutrium.

A. U. C. 444. Campaign of Q. Fabius Maximus in Etruria.

Q. Fabius Maximus was elected one of the consuls for the new year; the same person who, when master of the horse fourteen years before, had so nearly forfeited his life for his disobedience to the orders of the dictator, L. Papirius Cursor. As the Fabian house was both powerful and popular, he was a favorite hero in the stories of these times; and his exploits in this campaign have been disguised by such exaggerations that it is difficult to appreciate his real merit justly. We can hardly believe that he defeated the whole united force of the Etruscan nation in a great battle under the walls of Perusia, with such slaughter that sixty thousand Etruscans were killed or taken; nor were the Ciminian mountains so impassable a barrier as to justify the statement, that, before the daring expedition of Fabius they had not even been crossed by any Roman traders, and that the country beyond was as unknown as the wilds of Germany before the conquests of Drusus. Yet the campaign of Fabius was, doubtless, in a very high degree, able, enterprising, and successful, and the triumph which he obtained in the following year for his victories over the Etruscans was assuredly well deserved.

He resolves to penetrate into the heart of the enemy's country.

According to Diodorus,[98] both the consuls, R. Fabius and his colleague, C. Marcius Rutulus, marched together to relieve Sutrium; and it was by their joint force that the Etruscan besieging army, which had ventured to attack them, was beaten and obliged to take refuge within

[96] IX. 31. [97] XIX. 26. [98] XX. 35.

its lines. But the employment of both the consular armies in Etruria was not unobserved by the indefatigable Samnites. They poured down into Apulia, and ravaged the territory of the allies of Rome in that country without meeting with any opposition. This obliged the Romans to recall C. Marcius from Sutrium, and to send him with his army against the Samnites. Fabius was thus left alone, and the Etruscan lines before Sutrium were too strong to be attacked with success. But it struck him that a sudden and rapid invasion of central Etruria might oblige the enemy to recall their army from Sutrium, and would, at the same time, enrich his soldiers with the plunder of a wealthy and untouched country. It was thus that Hannibal hoped to relieve Capua by his unexpected march upon Rome; and the same policy led Scipio into Africa, as the surest method of obliging Hannibal to evacuate Italy. Fabius sent to Rome to acquaint the senate with his purpose, that an army of reserve[99] might be raised to cover the Roman territory during his absence: he had also previously sent his brother[100] across the Ciminian mountains to collect information, and to persuade, if possible, some of the Umbrian states to ally themselves with Rome. His brother could speak the Etruscan language, and in the disguise of a shepherd, accompanied only by a single slave who had been brought up with him from a child, and also was acquainted with Etruscan, he penetrated through Etruria as far as Camerte or Camerinum in Umbria, a town on the northern side of the Apennines, near the modern road from Foligno to Ancona. The Camertians received him in the most friendly manner, and desired him to assure the consul, that if he came into their neighborhood their entire force should join his army, and that they would supply him with provisions during a whole month. With this encouraging message the Roman officer returned to his brother, and Q. Fabius resolved to lose no time in carrying his plan into execution, suspecting, perhaps, that if he delayed he might receive a peremptory order from the senate not to risk his army in so hazardous an enterprise.

The Ciminian hills. Fabius crosses them, and carries the war into Etruria. His victories there.

The Ciminian hills, for we should scarcely call them mountains, are the ridge which divides the valley of the Tiber from the basin of the lake of Bolsena, and from the valley which runs from the foot of the lake down to the sea. Where the road from Viterbo to Rome crosses them they are still covered with copse-wood, and the small crater of the lake of Vico, which lies high up in their bosom, is surrounded by the remains of the old forest. In the fifth century of Rome the woods were far more extensive; and the hills, having now become the boundary between the Roman and Etruscan nations, were, perhaps, studiously kept in their wild state in order to prevent collisions between the borderers of both frontiers. They are a remarkable point, because, as they run up to a crest, with no extent of table-land on their summits, they command a wide view on either side, reaching far away to the southeast over the valley of the Tiber, even to the Alban hills, whilst on the north and west they look down on the plain of Viterbo; and the lake of Bolsena is distinctly visible, shut in at the farthest distance by the wild mountains of Radicofani.

[99] That such an army was raised, appears from Livy, IX. 39; and Niebuhr well observes, that the mission of five senators, accompanied by two of the tribunes of the commons, who arrived in the camp before Sutrium too late to stop the expedition into Etruria (Livy, IX. 36), seems to imply that some earlier communications had passed upon the subject, and that Fabius having shown a disposition to disobey the prohibition of the senate, the two tribunes were sent to arrest him, which they alone, by virtue of their inviolable character, could do with safety.

[100] Livy, IX. 36. That the Camertians, who concluded the treaty with the Romans on this occasion, were the people of Camerinum, the modern Camerino, and not, as Dr. Cramer supposes, of the obscure place of Camerata, on the left bank of the Tiber, between Todi and Amelia, is proved decisively, if, indeed, it could ever have been reasonably doubted, by an inscription found at Camerino, in which the Camertians express their gratitude to the emperor Severus, for having confirmed to them "the equal rights of their treaty," "jure æquo fœderis sibi confirmato:" an allusion to their well-known fœdus æquum, concluded at this very time of the first Roman invasion of Etruria, and which existed to the end of the commonwealth, and nominally, at least, as the inscription above quoted shows, to the third century of the Christian era. It was in the territory of Camerinum also that L. Scipio was defeated by the Gauls and Samnites in the third Samnite war. The above inscription is given by Orelli, No. 920.

Fabius, having sent on his baggage and infantry during the night, followed himself with his cavalry about the middle of the day following; and on the next morning the whole army crossed the summit of the Ciminian ridge, and poured down into the plains beyond. Some of the Etruscan chiefs[101] assembled their peasantry, and attempted to stop the plunder of their lands; but they were defeated with great loss; and the invaders overran the country far and wide, and carried off cattle and prisoners in great numbers. How far they penetrated into Etruria is uncertain. According to Livy it was a mere plundering inroad, and could not have extended beyond the territory of Vulsinii; but, according to Diodorus,[102] the Roman army advanced into the very heart of Etruria, fought a great battle, and won a decided victory in the neighborhood of Perusia; insomuch that the siege of Sutrium was raised, and three of the greatest of the Etruscan cities, Perusia, Arretium, and Cortona, sued for peace, and concluded a truce for thirty years. Livy[103] represents the decisive victory as having been won near Sutrium after the return of the Romans from their expedition; an immense army of Etruscans, joined by the forces of some of the states of Umbria, hastened to pursue and take vengeance on the invaders, but did not overtake them within the Etruscan territory, and thus followed them to their old position in the neighborhood of Sutrium. Both accounts agree in describing the victory as signal, and in stating that it was followed by a peace with three of the principal cities of Etruria.

Samnium. The Romans are defeated, and L. Papirius Cursor is appointed dictator.

Meanwhile, the war was raging with no less fury in Samnium. C. Marcius, after having been recalled from Sutrium, had marched with his army into Apulia,[104] and there at first relieved the allies of Rome from the plundering incursions of the enemy. But the Samnites had no intention to act merely on the defensive; they were eager to crush the army of Marcius, while Fabius was engaged in Etruria; and they attacked him with such vigor[105] that the Roman annals themselves acknowledge that the issue of the battle was doubtful, and that it seemed to be unfavorable, owing to the loss of several superior officers, and especially as the consul himself was wounded. The truth is sufficiently evident that the Romans were, in fact, defeated. When the news of this battle reached Rome, the senate resolved immediately that L. Papirius Cursor should be again appointed dictator; but it was necessary that one of the consuls should name him, and as nothing certain was known of the fate of C. Marcius, a deputation was sent to Fabius in Etruria, to request that he would perform this office. Fabius and Papirius were personal enemies: the consul had not forgotten how nearly he had once fallen a sacrifice to Papirius' inexorable temper; and political difference had since, perhaps, contributed to keep alive the personal quarrel. The deputation sent to Fabius consisted, therefore, of senators[106] of consular rank, whose private influence with him might be supposed likely to aid the expressed wish of the senate, and to induce him to sacrifice his own personal feelings. He heard the senate's decree read, and listened to the arguments with which the deputies urged him to obey it; but he gave them no answer, either by look or word, and retired abruptly from the interview. In the dead of the night, however, according to the usual form, he pronounced the nomination of Papirius; but when the deputies ventured to thank him for his noble conquest over his feelings, he again heard them in silence, and finally dismissed them without any answer.

His great victory and splendid triumph.

The dictator found an army at once disposable in the troops which had been raised to cover Rome when Fabius began his march across the Ciminian hills. With this force he marched into Samnium; there

[101] The character of the Etruscan government is well given in Livy's short statement, "tumultuariæ agrestium Etruscorum cohortes repente a principibus regionis ejus concitatæ," IX. 36. These "principes" were the Lucomenes or nobles of Etruria, and the "agrestium cohortes" were their serfs, who, as in Russia and Poland, formed the bulk of the national armies.

[102] Livy, XX. 35.

[103] IX. 37.

[104] Diodorus, XX. 35.

[105] Livy, IX. 38.

[106] Livy, IX. 38.

he was joined by the wreck of the consul's army, and by the contingent of the Campanian allies of Rome; but he did not immediately venture upon a battle. Again all the previous movements of both armies are unknown, nor is even the scene of the battle mentioned, but we are told[107] that after a short time a general action took place, in which the dictator Papirius, his master of the horse, C. Junius Bubulcus, and his two lieutenants, M. Valerius and P. Decius, both men of consular rank, all alike distinguished themselves; and which ended in a complete victory on the side of the Romans. Papirius triumphed on the 15th of October;[108] and his triumph was distinguished by the splendor of the captured arms which were carried in the procession. There were a number of gilded and silvered shields[109] which had been borne by two different bands of Samnites in the late battle; the silvered shields had belonged to a band, each man of which had been pledged by solemn oaths, accompanied by a ceremonial of the most mysterious and appalling character, to return victorious or to die. As sacred soldiers, these men had worn in the field coats of white linen, and silvered arms; and had their station on the right wing, which was the post of honor. The band with gilded shields had worn coats of various colors, like a plaid; and both bands had plumes of an imposing height waving on their helmets. All these particulars of the Samnite arms are mentioned for the first time at the triumph of Papirius; which proves that on no former occasion had the Samnites sustained so great a defeat, or had attached such great importance to the issue of the contest, as to adopt the unwonted expedient of a sacred or devoted band. It is added that these gay shields were divided out amongst the several silversmiths in the Forum,[110] that they might hang them up to decorate their shops on those great festivals when the Forum was dressed up as a part of the pageant.

Confusions again in the chronology. Submission of Etruria.

The chronology is here again involved in confusion. According to the Fasti Capitolini, L. Papirius held his dictatorship for a whole year, during which there were no consuls; and Q. Fabius commanded in Etruria as proconsul, and triumphed in that office on the 13th of November. To this version of the story belongs, apparently, the account of a second Etruscan campaign of Q. Fabius, of a great victory gained by him over the Umbrians, and of a second gained over the Etruscans at the lake of Vadimon; then of the revolt and subsequent submission of Perusia, of the occupation of that strong city by a Roman garrison, and of embassies sent from the other cities of Etruria to sue for peace. It would be difficult indeed to find room for all these great achievements in the single year of Fabius' consulship; but, on the other hand, this second Etruscan campaign is unknown to Diodorus, and both he and Livy agree in making the second consulship of Q. Fabius follow immediately after his first, without any such interval as that mentioned in the Fasti. It is remarkable, also, that the little lake of Vadimon should have been the scene of two victories over the Etruscans, within a period of about thirty years; and we are tempted to ask whether the first of these battles has not been greatly exaggerated. Yet the Etruscans must have been signally humbled by Fabius; for, in the next year, when P. Decius invaded Etruria, he met with little opposition; the people of Tarquinii obtained a peace for forty years,[111] and the other Etruscan cities were glad to obtain a truce for a single year; and even this they

[107] Livy, IX. 40.

[108] Fasti Capitolini.

[109] Livy, IX. 40.

[110] These shops of the silversmiths lined the Via Sacra, which, on its course from the Velia to the foot of the Capitol, ran along the northern side of the Forum. They were like cells, open in front, built of peperino, and with a row of square massy supports, or piers, in front of them, supporting the first story of the houses above; exactly like the covered passages in which the shops are ranged in so many of the towns of Italy at this day. The shields were hung up on the outside front of the square piers, or pilæ, looking towards the Forum. The butchers' shops, which, in the time of the decemvirs, had occupied this side of the Forum, had lately disappeared with the growing magnificence of the city, and had been succeeded by the shops of goldsmiths and silversmiths. See Beschreibung der Stadt Rom, Vol. III. 2d part, p. 25.

[111] Livy, IX. 41. Diodorus, XX. 44.

purchased at the price of giving a year's pay to the consul's army, and two coats to each soldier.

Q. Fabius, who had been chosen consul for the third time as the colleague of P. Decius, had this year the conduct of the war in Samnium. But the Samnites were so weakened, that their speedy subjugation seemed inevitable; and this, we may suppose, filled the neighboring nations with a sense of their own danger if Samnium should fall, and induced not only the Marsians and Pelignians[112] to take part with the Samnites, but even shook the long-tried friendship of the Hernicans with Rome, and aroused the Sallentines, at the southern extremity of Italy, to look on the Samnite cause as their own. But all was of no avail, and the success of the Romans was uninterrupted. Nuceria Alfaterna, in Campania, which had revolted seven years before, was now recovered, the Marsians and Pelignians were defeated, and Fabius was enabled to leave his province without danger, and to hasten into Umbria;[113] the Umbrians, it is said, having raised so formidable an army as to threaten to march straight upon Rome, and P. Decius having thought it necessary to retreat from Etruria, in order to watch over the safety of the capital. Here, again, we cannot but suspect some exaggeration; for Fabius is said to have won an easy victory over the Umbrians, and the Umbrian towns immediately submitted. This may be doubtful; but it is certain that the people of Ocriculum concluded an alliance with Rome, and that Fabius obtained no triumph either for his victory over the Umbrians, or for those which he is said to have won in Samnium. Yet his command in Samnium was continued to him for another year, with the title of proconsul: the new consuls were Appius Claudius and L. Volumnius.

Continued successes of the Romans. Short war with the Umbrians.

As the Etruscan war was now over, and Q. Fabius continued to command the army in Samnium, only one of the consuls for this year was required to take the field. This was L. Volumnius, and he was sent against the Sallentines,[114] an Apulian or Iapygian people, who dwelt, as we have seen, at the extreme heel of Italy, and who were now attacked by the Romans, under pretence, we may suppose, of their having annoyed some of the Apulian allies of Rome. But Volumnius did nothing worthy of notice, although, according to Livy, he gained some victories, took several towns, and made himself very popular with his soldiers by his liberality in the disposal of the plunder. The Fasti Capitolini, however, show that he obtained no triumph; and one of the annalists, Piso,[115] omitted his consulship altogether, as if he doubted its reality.

War with the Sallentines.

Fabius,[116] on his part, defeated the Samnites near Allifæ, and obliged their army to surrender. The Samnites themselves he disarmed, and then dismissed them unhurt; but all the other prisoners, to whatever nation they belonged, were sold for slaves. Amongst this number, there were several who declared themselves to be Hernicans, and these were immediately sent off to Rome, and, by order of the senate, were committed to the custody of the several allied cities of the Latins. Q. Fabius then led his army home; but either his victory has been exaggerated, or it was balanced by some defeats which the Roman writers did not choose to mention, for he obtained no triumph.

The Hernicans become suspected by the Romans.

The new consuls were Q. Marcius Tremulus, and P. Cornelius Arvina. They brought the case of the Hernican prisoners before the senate, which, says Livy,[117] so exasperated the whole nation, that the people of Anagnia summoned a general council of deputies from every Hernican city, and all, with three exceptions, voted for war with Rome. It is manifest that something is omitted in this narrative, the decision of the senate upon the case which was brought before them. This it was, no doubt, which so exasperated the Hernicans; and no wonder, if, as there is every reason to believe, it ordered the pris-

The Hernicans revolt.

112 Livy, IX. 41.
113 Livy, IX. 41.
114 Livy, IX. 42.
115 Livy, IX. 44.
116 Livy, IX. 42.
117 Livy, IX. 42.

oners to be scourged and beheaded. Such a bloody execution would naturally excite a deep and general indignation, and the common feeling of the Hernican people would call aloud for vengeance.

Combined operations of the Hernican and Samnite armies.

Meanwhile the indomitable spirit of the Samnites kindled at the prospect of this accession to their league against Rome; and they thought that if they could clear the valley of the Liris, and thus open their communications with the country of the Hernicans, their combined forces might possibly again carry the war into the heart of Latium, through the great mountain-portal by Præneste. Accordingly, they attacked and carried the two posts of Calatia, on the Vulturnus, and Sora, on the upper Liris, and sold the prisoners as slaves.[118] Thus the communication with the Hernicans was opened, and a Samnite army must have taken up its position in the valley of the upper Liris, on the edge of the Hernican country. The Romans then hoped, by a combined operation of both the consular armies, to penetrate into the heart of the enemy's seat of war in two different directions; and Q. Marcius proceeded to invade the Hernican territory from the side of Latium, while P. Cornelius was to ascend the valley of the Liris from Campania, and to dislodge the Samnites from Sora. But the enemy held their ground so well,[119] and availed themselves so effectually of their central position, that the consuls could make no progress; and, being kept in total ignorance of each other's movements, it is likely that each successively sustained a severe check from a concentration of the enemy's force against his particular army. This state of affairs excited great alarm at Rome; all citizens within the military age were enlisted, and two regular armies of two legions each were raised, to be ready for any emergency.

The Hernicans solicit and obtain a truce. Samnium ravaged for five months by two consular armies.

Thus supported, Q. Marcius soon overbore the resistance of the Hernicans, and obliged them to purchase a truce for thirty days by furnishing the Roman army with two months' pay and rations of corn, and with clothing for each soldier. They then sued for peace, and were referred by the senate to the consul, who received accordingly their entire submission. He hastened to effect his junction with his colleague, and the Samnite army, oppressed by their united forces, was defeated with great slaughter.[120] Marcius returned to Rome and triumphed on the 30th of June,[121] and his services were accounted so eminent that an equestrian statue was set up in honor of him in the Forum,[122] in front of the temple of Castor, or rather of the twin heroes, Castor and Pollux. After his triumph, he rejoined his colleague in Samnium, and their two armies being completely masters of the field, ravaged, the whole country with the utmost perseverance for the space of nearly five months;[123] cutting down the fruit-trees, burning the houses that were not secured within the fortified towns, and doing all the mischief in their power, in the hope of forcing the enemy into submission. The consuls were thus detained so long in the field, that a dictator was named to hold the comitia; and L. Postumius and Ti. Minucius were elected consuls for the year following.

Final submission and settlement of the Hernicans.

Before the close of this year the senate had decided the fate of the Hernicans.[124] Three cities which had taken no part in the late war were left in the enjoyment of their municipal independence; but Anagnia and the other towns were obliged to receive the Roman franchise without the right of voting; or, in other words, to become the subjects of Rome, without any share either in the general government or in their own municipal administration. They were forbidden to hold any common meetings, or to intermarry with one another, and their magistrates were prohibited from exercising any other function than that of superintending the performance of the rites of religion.

118 Livy, IX. 43. Diodorus, XX. 80.

119 Livy, IX. 43.

120 Livy, IX. 43.

121 Fasti Capitolini.

122 Livy, IX. 43. Pliny, Hist. Nat. XXXIV. 6. The temple of Castor was on the southern side of the Forum, opposite to the line of the Via Sacra.

123 Diodorus, XX. 80.

124 Livy, IX. 43.

Decisive campaign in the heart of Samnium. Bovianum taken.

The long contest with the Samnites was now drawing to a conclusion. Before the new consuls took the field, and after Marcius and Cornelius had returned home, the Samnites revenged in some degree the devastation of their own country, by making several plundering inroads into the plain of Campania.[125] But when the legions opened the campaign, the power of the Romans was again irresistible. The seat of the war was now in the very heart of Samnium, on the north side of the Matese, in the country of the Pentrians; and the two consuls attacked the two cities of Tifernum and Bovianum. One last desperate effort was made by the Samnite imperator or captain-general, Statius Gellius, to relieve Bovianum: but it was vain, although the battle was so stoutly contested, that the Roman consul Ti. Minucius was mortally wounded, and did not live to reap the fruits of his victory. But Gellius was himself taken prisoner, and the greater part of his army destroyed. Bovianum then surrendered, and the consuls, on their return home, recovered the towns which had been lately lost in the valley of the Liris, Sora, Arpinum, and an unknown place, Cerennia,[126] or Censennia.

The Samnites and their allies submit to the Romans.

This campaign was decisive. The new consuls were P. Sulpicius and P. Sempronius, and Sulpicius immediately took the field in Samnium.[127] He gained some advantages, small perhaps in themselves, but important, as the last drop poured into the brimming vessel and causing the water to overflow. The Samnites at last sued for peace, and the Marrucinians, Marsians, Pelignians, and Frentanians followed the example. They were all obliged to become the allies of Rome, but the alliance was no longer on equal terms;[128] they became, in fact, politically subject, and consented to acknowledge and respect the majesty, or, in other words, the supremacy of Rome.

Accessions gained to the Roman dominion in the course of the war.

In comparison with such a full confession of the superior strength of the Romans, any partial acquisitions of territory were of slight importance. But the Romans had obtained in the course of the war the important position of Luceria in Apulia, which secured their ascendency in that part of Italy; and they had also won the whole line of the Liris, all those Volscian towns which had been the Samnite share of the spoil at the conclusion of the great Latin war. Campania had been retained, and its connection with Rome was rendered closer than ever; and above all, the timely extension of the full Roman franchise to so many of the Latin and Volscian cities in the neighborhood of Rome, had made the Roman power sound at the heart, and had consolidated that mass of citizens, and of allies scarcely less true than citizens, within the confines of Latium, of which neither the arms nor the arts of Hannibal could tempt a single individual to join his standard.

The conquest of the Hernicans gave the Romans, it is probable, a considerable accession of territory in the forfeited domain land of the several cities; and it put an end to the old equal alliance which entitled the Hernicans to a share of all plunder taken by the armies of the allied nations. The victories over the

[125] Livy, IX. 44. Diodorus, XX. 90.

[126] Diodorus calls it Serennia. Is not this place the "Cisauna" in Samnium, mentioned in the inscription on the tomb of L. Scipio Barbatus?

[127] This appears from the Fasti Capitolini, which state that Sulpicius obtained a triumph for his victories over the Samnites in this year.

[128] Dionysius, Excerpt. de Legation. p. 2331. Reiske. His words are, speaking of the Samnites, τοὺς ὑπηκόους ὁμολογήσαντας ἔσεσθαι. Livy says, "Fœdus antiquum Samnitibus redditum." This is because he never seems to have conceived that any nation could ever have been the equal ally of Rome, but that from the very beginning it must have acknowledged the Roman supremacy. Thus, when he speaks of the first treaty between Rome and Samnium in the year 401, he says that the Samnites solicited the friendship of Rome; that "Legatis eorum comiter ab senatu responsum; fœdere in societatem accepti." VII. 19. In the same manner he misrepresents the early relations between Rome and Latium. But the negotiations had broken off in the year 432 on this very point, because the Samnites would not become the dependent allies of Rome; and as the Romans never receded from the conditions on which they had once insisted, we may be sure that they would have granted no peace to the Samnites which did not include their complete submission; nor can we suppose that the Samnites would have persevered so long in carrying on the war amidst such repeated disasters, if they could have ended it on any terms less intolerable.

Etruscans and Umbrians had revealed the secret of the comparative weakness of those once dreaded nations, and had taught the Romans that their frontier might be extended as soon as they chose beyond the Ciminian hills.

Rome was now the first power in Italy.

Thus in the twenty years of the second Samnite war Rome had risen to the first place, beyond dispute, amongst the nations of Italy. And amidst the divisions and corruption of the several kingdoms which had grown up out of the fragments of Alexander's empire, there was scarcely a power in the civilized world, except Carthage, which could have contended successfully with Rome single-handed.

Half a century was yet to elapse before Carthage entered upon the contest. Meanwhile the Roman power was yet to be sharply tried; what Etruria and Samnium could neither singly nor by their joint efforts effect, they were to try again with the help of the Gauls; what they had failed to accomplish through barbarian aid, they were to attempt in their last struggle with the assistance of the arms and discipline of the Macedonian phalanx, and guided by the genius of Alexander's genuine successor, the hero-king of the race of Achilles.

CHAPTER XXXII.

INTERNAL HISTORY FROM 428 to 454—ABOLITION OF PERSONAL SLAVERY FOR DEBT—DICTATORSHIP OF C. MÆNIUS—CENSORSHIP OF APPIUS CLAUDIUS—CENSORSHIP OF Q. FABIUS AND P. DECIUS—THE OGULNIAN LAW.

"Nothing has contributed more than this lenity to raise the character of public men. Ambition is of itself a game sufficiently hazardous and sufficiently deep to inflame the passions, without adding property, life, and liberty to the stake."—EDINBURGH REVIEW, No. XCV. p. 161.

Altered position of parties at Rome. The new or lower popular party.

WE have seen that in the year immediately preceding the first campaign of the Samnite war, several symptoms had been manifested by a strong party amongst the patricians of the old jealousy towards the commons; M. Marcellus, a plebeian, had been forced to resign his dictatorship by the augurs, on the alleged reason that his appointment was invalid from some religious objection; and the most obstinate attempts were made to set aside the Licinian law, and to procure the election of two patrician consuls. In the course of the Samnite war occasional traces of the same feeling are discernible. But its shape was no longer what it had been in the earlier days of the commonwealth. It was no longer a struggle between an aristocracy in the exclusive possession of the government, and a people impatient of their own exclusion from it. It was no longer a struggle between the whole patrician order on one side, and the whole body of the commons on the other. A considerable portion of the patricians and a majority of the senate were well reconciled to the altered state of things, and cordially received the distinguished commoners who had made their way to the highest offices in the commonwealth, and composed a new nobility fully worthy to stand on equal terms by the side of the old. Thus the moderate patricians, the new nobility of the commons, and the mass of the old plebeians were now closely linked together; and their union gave that energy to the Roman councils and arms, which marks in so eminent a manner the middle of the fifth century. But as these elements had tended more and more towards each other, so they parted off on either side from other elements with which, at an earlier period, they had been respectively connected. The moderate patricians stood aloof from the high or more violent party, who still dreamt of recovering the old ascendency of their order: whilst a new popular party, though as yet very inconsiderable in power or influence, was growing up distinct from the old plebeians, regarding them with envy,[1] and regarded by them in turn with feelings of dislike and suspicion. This new party consisted of freedmen, and of citizens engaged in the various trades and occupations of a city life, who were despised by the old agricultural plebeians as a low and unwarlike populace, and who, by a strong public opinion, were excluded from all prospect of political distinctions. Many of these persons, indeed, had not even the right of voting, as they were not included in any tribe; and they bore this exclusion as impatiently as the old plebeians had borne their exclusion from the highest curule offices. This was a class which was daily becoming more numerous, in proportion as Rome grew in wealth and population, and it formed the origin of the popular party of the later period of the commonwealth; a party very different, both in its character and feelings, from the commons of its earlier history.

Coalition of the two extreme parties against the moderate party.

These extremes of civil society, the highest aristocrats and the lowest populace, have often made common cause with each other against that middle class which both hate equally. And when the malcontent aristocratical families are few in number, but of the highest nobility, any ambitious individual among them is tempted to court the populace for objects more directly personal; he tries to make them the instrument, not of the greatness of his order, but of his own. Thus it was commonly remarked of the tyrants of the ancient world, that they began by playing the demagogue. In such a union between the highest and the lowest classes of society, the gain is mostly for the former; the latter derived little advantage from the alliance, except the pleasure of the horse in the fable, when he saw his old enemy, the stag, effectually humbled. But the coalition is not solely one of political expediency; it arises partly out of certain moral affinities existing between those whose social and political conditions are the extremest opposites. The moral bond between them is their common impatience of law and good government; that anarchical and selfish restlessness, which sees in the existing order of society an equal restraint upon the pride and passion of the highest, and on the needy cupidity of the lowest.[2] This is the feeling which has so often brought together the proudest despot or the most insolent aristocrat and the lowest and most profligate populace; and it was this, though in a far milder degree, which associated in one common party

[1] This is the progress of all popular parties, from the necessity of the case. As the ruling body in the earliest state of society is extremely exclusive, the popular party then comprises what Sieyes would call the nation minus a privileged individual or a very small privileged class. Each success of this party satisfies the wishes of a portion of its members, and thus makes them for the future its enemies. And a repetition of this process would at last place the anti-popular party in that same position which was at first occupied by their adversaries; they would, in their turn, become the nation, minus a very small excluded class, a class, in fact, excluded by nothing but their own ignorance or profligacy. This would be the natural perfection of a state, but, unhappily, this as yet has never been attained to; the process has gone on healthfully in its first stages, satisfying successively all those whose exclusion was wholly unnatural, that is, who were excluded by distinctions purely arbitrary, or overbalanced by many more points of resemblance and fitness for political power. But when it reaches those who differ really from the governing body, as in the case of the rich and the poor, then convulsion and decline have mostly followed. The work of smoothing down these real differences is so difficult, that it has rarely or never been attempted; the excluding party, strengthened by all those who were once excluded, is now extremely powerful, and its power is moral as well as physical; the excluded or popular party, no longer a nation contending against a caste, but yet much more than a worthless faction contending against a nation, are conscious of a wrong done to them, and are embittered by this feeling; but being unable to carry their point, and, from their very inability to obtain a share of the benefits of society, becoming more and more morally unfit to enjoy them, their triumph and their continued exclusion are alike deplorable. Their triumph is but the triumph of slaves broken loose, full of brute ignorance and wickedness; their continued exclusion is a perpetual cancer, wasting away the nation's life; and it is a moral evil, moreover, because it involves injustice. The great and hardest problem of political wisdom is to prevent any part of society from becoming so socially degraded by poverty, that their political enfranchisement becomes dangerous, or even mischievous.

[2] *ἡ μὲν πενία ἀνάγκῃ τὴν τόλμαν παρέχουσα, ἡ δ' ἐξουσία ὕβρει τὴν πλεονεξίαν καὶ φρονήματι, . . . ἐξάγουσιν ἐς τοὺς κινδύνους.* Thucydides, II.

at Rome, in the period now before us, the humblest of the city populace and the representative of the proudest family in the commonwealth, Appius Claudius.

Character of such coalitions.

But in these coalitions, which are forever occurring in history, the two coalescing parties are far from deserving the same judgment. Historians have justly pronounced their full condemnation on the selfish hypocrisy of the tyrant, who talks of liberty in order to establish his own despotism. And for those who, despising all the honors and benefits of society which are fully open to them, aspire to a rank and greatness of a higher and more exclusive sort than the nature of society allows, no condemnation can be too severe, for no wickedness can be greater. But the lowest class, when they are misled into such alliances, deserve even in their worst excesses a milder sentence. Not only are they entitled to all the excuse which may be claimed by ignorance, and an ignorance arising rather from their condition than from their choice; but in their quarrel against the existing order of things, there is, and ever will be, amidst much of envy, and cupidity, and revenge, a certain mixture also of justice. Nothing is more horrible than the rebellions of slaves; yet it is impossible to regard even these with unmixed abhorrence. Nor can we ever place on the same level those who, being excluded from the benefits of society, do but seek a share of them, and those who, enjoying all these benefits in ample measure, cannot rest without something more. Neither are the middle classes apt to be wholly guiltless in their treatment of those below them; when they have established their own rights against the aristocracy, they become a new aristocracy themselves, and having themselves passed through the door, they shut it against those who would fain follow. But here, as in their own earlier contest with the old aristocracy, the fault does not consist in denying political rights to those who are not yet fit for them, for this may be often necessary and just; but in preventing them from ever becoming fit, by retaining institutions which have an inevitable tendency to keep the lowest classes morally degraded, or, at the best, by taking no pains to introduce such as may improve them.

Eminent men of this period. 1. Of the high aristocratical party, L. Papirius Cursor and Appius Claudius

In the high aristocratical party at Rome during the period now before us, two individuals are eminent: L. Papirius Cursor, and Appius Claudius. But their objects seem to have been different. Papirius appears to have been sincerely attached to the old aristocratical constitution, and to have honestly wished to restore what in his eyes was the uncorrupted discipline of the Roman commonwealth. Appius, like his ancestor the decemvir, or Dionysius of Syracuse, wished to overthrow the existing order of things, not in favor of the old patrician ascendency, but of his own personal dominion.

2. Of the middle or moderate party.

The moderate or middle party, composed as it was of the majority of the senate and of the whole body of the old commons, numbered amongst its members most of the distinguished men of the time. To this party belonged Q. Fabius Maximus, eminent alike in peace and in war, and who enjoyed the love[3] of his countrymen no less than he commanded their admiration and esteem. With him stood his friend P. Decius Mus, thrice his colleague in the consulship when Rome needed the services of her bravest and ablest generals against her foreign enemies; and his colleague also in that memorable censorship, which required and found in them all the statesman's wisdom. P. Decius might have disputed the palm of happiness in Solon's judgment with Tellus the Athenian. Born to the truest nobility, the son of that P. Decius, who, when consul, had devoted himself

Q. Fabius Maximus.

P. Decius Mus.

[3] When he died the people contributed by subscription a large sum for the expenses of his funeral, which seems to have been a method of expressing the public feeling towards the dead, even when his family was too wealthy to require it as an actual assistance. On this occasion, Q. Fabius Gurges, the son of the old Q. Fabius, employed the money in giving a public entertainment to one part of the people, epulum, and in sending portions of meat to the rest, visceratio. See the writer "de Viris Illustribus," in his life of Q. Fabius.

to death for his country in the great battle with the Latins, he, like his father, obtained the highest honors with the purest fame; and after having performed the greatest services in peace and in war, and having been rewarded in the fullest measure with the respect and affection of his fellow-citizens, he too, like his father, devoted himself to death to save Rome from defeat, and so consigned the glory of his life,[4] safe from all stain, and crowned with the yet higher glory of his death, to his countrymen's grateful memory forever. Of the same band, yet rather to be ranked first than third, was M. Valerius Corvus, to whom, no less than to Decius, Solon might have allowed the name of happy. His youth had caught the last rays of the romantic glory of earlier times; and his single combat with the giant Gaul, and the wonderful aid which the gods had then vouchsafed him, was sung in the same strains as the valiant acts of the heroes of old, of Camillus, or Cincinnatus, or Cornelius Cossus. His manhood was no less rich in glory of another sort, which, if less brilliant, was more real. Elected consul for the first time at three-and-twenty, five years afterwards, in his third consulship, he won this famous battle of Mount Gaurus against the Samnites, and gave in the victorious issue of the first encounter a happy omen of the final result of the long contest between the two nations. He was elected consul three times afterwards, and twice dictator; and in his political course, true to the character of his family, he finally relieved the long distress of the poorer commons, and appeased the most dangerous commotion which had ever yet threatened Rome; and he re-enacted the famous Valerian law in his fifth consulship, that great law of appeal from the sentence of the magistrate which the Romans regarded as the main bulwark of their freedom. In his sixth consulship he was nearly seventy years old, but he lived thirty years longer, and died at the full age of a hundred years,[5] after having witnessed the triumphant end of the long contest with the Samnites, which three generations earlier had been under his own auspices so successfully begun. Next to these three great men we may rank Q. Publilius Philo, the author of the Publilian laws, prætor,[6] dictator, censor, and four times consul, who was chosen consul with L. Papirius Cursor after the disaster of Caudium, as being with him the man most able to retrieve the honor of Rome. Nor should we omit C. Mænius,[7] twice dictator, a man odious to the high patrician party for the firmness with which he opposed their projects, but repelling their attacks by the spotless innocence of his public life. To the same party belonged also, in all probability, Q. Aulius Cerretanus,[8] twice consul, chosen master of the horse by Q. Fabius in his first dictatorship, who sacrificed his life in covering the retreat of the Romans in the route of Lautulæ, and M. Foslius, master of the horse to C. Mænius in his second dictatorship, like him obnoxious to the high patrician party,[9] and like him protected by his integrity.

M. Valerius Corvus.

Q. Publilius Philo.

C. Mænius.

Q. Aulius Cerretanus.

M. Foslius.

[4] *Δοκεῖ δέ μοι δηλοῦν ἀνδρὸς ἀρετὴν πρώτη τε μηνύουσα καὶ τελευταία βεβαιοῦσα ἡ νῦν τῶνδε καταστροφή.* Thucydid. II. 42. In Decius' case his death was not the "first indication" of his worth, but the "last confirmation" of it; it was the worthy close of a noble life.

[5] Pliny, Histor. Natur. VII. 48. Pliny says that forty six-years intervened between his first consulship and his sixth. His sixth consulship was in the year 453, according to Pliny's own chronology [446 Niebuhr], if we place it four years after the consulship of P. Sempronius and P. Sulpicius, which with Pliny is the year 449. (Hist. Natur. XXXIII. § 20.) His first consulship accordingly would fall in 406, but according to the Fasti Capitolini, which place his second consulship two years afterwards, in 407, it would fall in 405. His third according to the same chronology was in 410; and his fourth in 418. The Fasti are wanting at the period of his two last consulships, and they cannot be fixed positively. In his first consulship he was only three-and-twenty (Livy, VII. 26); which, following the chronology of the Fasti, would give 382 for the year of his birth. He lived, therefore, to the year 482 [475, Niebuhr]; that is, to the year after the capture of Tarentum, and the end of the fourth Samnite war.

[6] Livy, VIII. 15. VIII. 12. VIII. 17. For his four consulships see Livy, VIII. 12-22, IX. 7, and Diodorus, XIX. 66, and the Fasti Capitolini.

[7] For his second dictatorship, see Livy, IX. 26; for his first, see the fragments of the Fasti Capitolini, and note 61 of Chap. XXXI. of this volume.

[8] Livy, VIII. 37, IX. 15, and for his death see the Fasti Capitolini, and Diodorus, XIX. 72, Livy, IX. 23.

[9] Livy, IX. 26.

8. Of the new popular party. Cn. Flavius.

The third or new popular party could not be expected, from its very nature, to produce, as yet, any men of high distinction. Yet one individual belonging to it made himself remarkable, and will claim a place in this history, Cn. Flavius, the scribe or clerk, who divulged the secrets of the pontifical calendar, and of the technicalities of actions at law, and was rewarded with the curule ædileship in spite of his humble origin and occupation.

That we are able to notice so many individual characters at this period, shows that we are arrived at the dawn of what may be called real history. And this previous sketch of the parties of the commonwealth, and of their most eminent members, may, perhaps, make the account of the transactions in which they were engaged, not only clearer, but more interesting.

Abolition of personal slavery for debt.

During the first half of the Samnite war, but in what year[10] is uncertain, there was passed that famous law which prohibited personal slavery for debt; no creditor might for the future attach the person of his debtor, but he might only seize his property; and all those whose personal freedom was pledged for their debts (nexi), were released from their liability, if they could swear that they had property enough to meet their creditor's demands. It does not appear that this great alteration in the law was the work of any tribune, or that it arose out of any general or deliberate desire to soften the severity of the ancient practice. It was occasioned, we are told, by one scandalous instance of abuse of power on the part of a creditor towards his debtor, who, according to the old law, had been given over to him as a slave (addictus), because he had pledged his person for his debts, and had been unable to redeem his pledge. The outrage excited so general a feeling, that the senate immediately passed a bill for the effectual prevention of such atrocities for the future; and the consuls, or rather, as it would seem, the dictator, C. Pœtelius, was desired to propose it to the people, that it might become a law. But although personal slavery for debt was thus done away, yet the consequences of insolvency were much more serious at Rome than they are in modern Europe. He whose property had been once made over to his creditors by the prætor's sentence, became, ipso facto, infamous;[11] he lost his tribe, and with it all his political rights; and the forfeiture was irrevocable, even though he might afterwards pay his debts to the full; nor was it even in the power of the censors to replace him on the roll of citizens. So sacred a thing did credit appear in the eyes of the Romans; and so just did they consider it, that a failure in the discharge of one of the most important social obligations should be visited with a forfeiture of social and political rights.

State of parties with respect to the rising of the Tusculans and Privernatians.

As the internal history of Rome during this period can only be collected from a few detached notices, we are compelled to pass over in silence those memorable years which were marked by the rising of the Tusculans and Privernatians, and by the defeat at the pass of Caudium. This last disaster, indeed, was such as to still for a time all domestic disputes, and to make every Roman feel alike for the national calamity; and the election of L. Papirius Cursor and Q. Publilius as consuls for the following year, seems to show a common desire to appoint the two ablest generals of

[10] Livy places the story in the consulship of C. Pœtelius, in the very first year of the war; VIII. 28. But as Dionysius (Fragm. Vol. IV. p. 2338, Reiske) and Valerius Maximus (VI. 1, § 9) relate it as having happened after the affair of the pass of Caudium, Niebuhr refers it to the dictatorship of C. Pœtelius, in the 12th year of the war. (Livy, IX. 28.) A passage in Varro, de Ling. Lat. (VII. 105, ed. Müller), relates to this subject, but is so corrupt in the MSS. that its testimony cannot be appealed to with certainty. It runs "Hoc C. Popilio vocare Sillo dictatore sublatum ne fieret, ut omnes, qui bonam copiam jurarunt, ne essent nexi, sed soluti." Müller has corrected this into, "Hoc C. Popilio auctore Visolo dictatore sublatum." "Visolo" having been a conjecture of Anton. Augustino, and approved by Scaliger, because the cognomen of C. Pœtelius was Visolus, as we learn from the Fasti Capitolini. But I would rather read "C. Popilio provocante," in the former part of the sentence, than "C. Popilio auctore."

[11] "In pudoris notam capitis pœna conversa, bonorum adhibitâ proscriptione, suffundere maluit hominis sanguinem quam effundere."—Tertullian, Apologet. 4.

See also the strong language of Cicero pro Quintio, 15, 16.

the commonwealth, without any reference to party distinctions. But the war with Tusculum, Privernum, and Velitræ was of another character; and the claims of these cities, and the treatment which should be shown to them, must have been judged of very variously. Are we mistaken in supposing that the moderate or middle party supported the liberal policy which was actually pursued, while the new popular party, the party of the populace, called aloud for severity and vengeance? We know that L. Fulvius Curvus, who had so lately led the Tusculans to assail the city of Rome, was elected consul,[12] together with Q. Fabius; and that, six or seven years afterwards, he was appointed master of the horse[13] by L. Æmilius Mamercinus; and both Fabius and Æmilius were eminent amongst the leaders of the moderate party. We know also that M. Flavius, the tribune, who brought forward the bill for the punishment of the Tusculans, was a man of doubtful private character,[14] and that he was said to have owed his first tribuneship to a largess which he had given to the poorer citizens, in gratitude for having been acquitted by them when indicted by the ædiles on a criminal charge. It appears also that he must have been elected tribune twice, at least, within four years;[15] which, in a man of such character, seems to argue that he continued to practise the arts of a demagogue. If this be so, his bill for the punishment of the Tusculans exactly resembled, both in himself and in the personal and political character of its author, the famous bill of Cleon for the execution of the Mytileneans: and we have here another instance that a low popular party has as little claim as that of the high aristocracy to the title of high-principled and liberal.

Intrigues of the aristocratical party of the time of the revolt of Capua. C. Mænius dictator.

The six years which followed the affair of Caudium are to us, as far as regards domestic affairs, a blank; but in the year 439 (Niebuhr, 434), the defeat of Lautulæ and its consequences led to the second dictatorship of C. Mænius, an event of which the notices preserved to us are unusually full. Capua had revolted,[16] and as the consuls, M. Pœtelius and C. Sulpicius, were fully engaged with the Samnites, a dictator with a third army was appointed to reduce the Campanians. The battle of Cinna, as we have seen, terrified the Campanians into submission; and the principal leaders of the revolt perished by their own hands. But the dictator, C. Mænius,[17] during his inquiry into the origin of the revolt at Capua, gained some startling information, which showed that it had received encouragement from a powerful party in Rome itself; the spirit[18] of his commission, he argued, called upon him to follow up this investigation; and when he returned to Rome he pursued it with vigor. No proof, it seems, could be obtained of any direct act of treason; but there existed what were in Greece the well-known preparations for a revolution, a number of organized societies[19] for the purpose of influencing the elections, and procuring the appointment of particular candidates. These societies, it is implied, consisted partly of the highest members of the aristocracy, and partly of the lowest classes of citizens, both at present being combined in one common cause. The dictator, therefore, encountered a formidable opposition; the high patrician party recriminated upon him and upon his master of the horse, M. Foslius Flaccinator: "Men of the commons,[20] such as they were, needed undue means to secure their way to public offices, rather than the patricians, who derived from

[12] Livy, VIII. 38.

[13] Livy, IX. 21.

[14] Livy, VIII. 22.

[15] Compare Livy, VIII. 22, and 37. Huschké, in his work on the Constitution of Ser. Tullius, p. 730, refers to this M. Flavius the anecdote related by Valerius Maximus, VIII. 1, § 7. He ingeniously observes, that the anecdote must refer to a period when the number of the tribes was twenty-nine, which exactly tallies with the date of the story as given by Livy. According to Valerius Maximus, the curule ædile by whom Flavius was impeached was C. Valerius.

[16] Diodorus, XIX. 76.

[17] Livy, IX. 26.

[18] "Versa Romam interpretando res, non nominatim qui Capuæ, sed in universum qui usquam coissent conjurassentve adversus rempublicam, quæri senatum jussisse."—Livy, IX. 26.

[19] "Coitiones honorum adipiscendorum causâ factas."—Livy, IX. 26. These words are almost a translation of the description given by Thucydides of the aristocratical clubs of Athens, τὰς ξυνωμοσίας, αἵπερ ἐτύγχανον πρότερον ἐν τῇ πόλει οὖσαι ἐπὶ δίκαις καὶ ἀρχαῖς. VIII. 54.

[20] "Negare nobilium id crimen esse, quibus si nullâ obstetur fraude, pateat via ad honorem, sed hominum novorum."—Livy, IX. 26.

their noble birth a sufficient and an honorable title to the votes of their countrymen." Immediately the dictator and his master of the horse courted and called for the fullest inquiry into their conduct; they resigned their offices, were put upon their trial before the consuls, and, in spite of the efforts of the aristocratical party to prove them guilty, they were most honorably acquitted.[21] Q. Publilius Philo, the most distinguished commoner of his time, was accused by the same party on the same charge, and was acquitted no less completely. But by thus dexterously assailing their assailants, the high nobility gained a considerable advantage; it seemed as if both parties were open to accusation, and that an inquiry into an offence so universal must needs be fruitless. Besides, the most serious danger had been removed by the favorable turn of the events of the war; and when men's minds were no longer under the influence of alarm, the inquiry would cease to be supported by that strong public feeling which alone could enable it to proceed with effect. Accordingly, the societies triumphed; and the coalition between the high aristocracy and the populace, thus ineffectually attacked, began to manifest itself more freely and more decidedly.

Censorship of Appius Claudius.

Accordingly, two years afterwards, Appius Claudius was elected censor, together with C. Plautius. The censorship, it should be remembered, was, in point of rank, the highest office in the commonwealth: its power was almost unbounded; its command over the public money, and the opportunities of distinction and of influence which it afforded as originating and conducting all public works, made it an especial object of ambition to a man like Appius, who was less fitted to signalize himself as a general. Besides, he probably had from the first formed the design of prolonging his term of office for the full period of five years, in defiance of the Æmilian law; and so vast a power, enjoyed during so long a period, might be made to serve the wildest purposes of ambition.

His revision of the list of senators.

One of his earliest acts as censor was to revise the list of the senators. It was usual on these occasions to add to the list the names of such citizens as seemed best to deserve that honor; and the selection would commonly be made from those who, within the last five years, had been elected for the first time to any curule magistracy, and who, therefore, had not been in the senate at the last census. But, in addition to the deaths caused by the Samnite war (and the master of the horse could not have been the only senator who fell in the rout of Lautulæ), the year immediately preceding Appius' censorship had been marked by a visitation of pestilence, so that the names which he would have to add to the roll of the senate would be more than usually numerous. To the utter scandal of the old plebeians, no less than of the patricians, Appius passed over many names which other censors would have inserted, and filled up the vacancies with numbers of the low popular party, many of whom were the sons of freedmen,[22] and therefore, according to Roman law, the grandsons of nobody. The persons thus chosen were, probably, wealthy men, and many of them may have already filled the offices of tribune or plebeian ædile; but the time when the senate had been a purely patrician assembly was too recent to allow of its being thrown open not merely to commoners, but to men whose grandfathers had been slaves; and the attempt of Appius to fill the senate with those who would have been no better than his creatures, like some of his ancestor's colleagues in the decemvirate, was too violent a measure to be endured. Accordingly, the consuls of the next year, C. Junius Bubulcus and Q. Æmilius Barbula, set his list aside without hesitation, and summoned those only as senators whose names had been on the roll of the last previous censors, L. Papirius Crassus and C. Mænius.

Not discouraged, however, by this ill success, Appius acted on the same sys-

[21] "Publilius etiam Philo, multiplicatis summis honoribus post res tot domi belloque gestas, ceterum invisus nobilitati, causam dixit."—Livy, IX. 26.

[22] Diodorus, XX. 35, 36. Livy, IX. 29, 30.

tem when he proceeded to revise the rolls of the several tribes. His colleague, C. Plautius, unable to bear the shame of seeing his list of the senate utterly disregarded, had resigned his office at the end of the year.[23] If a censor died or resigned before the completion of the eighteen months fixed by the Æmilian law as the term of his authority, it was accounted unlucky to elect another in his place; and his colleague, on such occasions, usually resigned immediately, rather than incur the odium of wielding such vast powers alone. Appius, however, had no such scruples, and continued to act as sole censor. In his revision of the tribes he admitted a great number[24] of freedmen and citizens of low condition to the enjoyment of a full franchise; and he entered them purposely in all the tribes, that the influence of his party might extend to all. It will readily be understood that a large proportion of the members of the more remote tribes especially, would attend but seldom at the comitia; whilst the city populace and the tradesmen and artisans were always on the spot, and would be frequently the majority of voters in their respective tribes. Thus, the old agricultural commons saw themselves overwhelmed by their new tribesmen, and that share in the government which they had so hardly won was on the point of being wrested from them by men whom, according to the general feeling of the ancient world, they despised as little better than slaves.

He admits many freedmen into the tribes.

Thus far the conduct of Appius was not inconsistent with a mere desire to restore the old ascendency of the patricians; for the lowest classes, being as yet quite incapable of exercising dominion, might safely be used as auxiliaries for humbling the classes next above them; just as the feudal kings occasionally courted the commons, and were enabled through their aid to weaken the power of the nobles, without any danger of seeing their own authority subjected to the control of a representative assembly. But if it be true that Appius encouraged Cn. Flavius[25] in the acts which gave such offence to the aristocracy, we cannot conceive his objects to have been other than personal; for it was against the old patrician influence, much more than against the new plebeian nobility, that the proceedings of Flavius were directed. This man was the son of a freedman, a clerk or writer by his occupation, and at this time employed in the business of the censor's office under Appius. It was by Appius' instigation that he published his famous calendar or almanac; that is, he stuck up whited boards round the Forum, on which were marked down the days and parts of days in every month on which law business might lawfully be done; a knowledge which the people had hitherto been obliged to gain from the pontifices, or a few of the patricians who understood the pontifical law; and as the days did not recur regularly, and the principle which determined them was carefully kept a secret, the people were wholly at their instructors' mercy.[26] At the same time Flavius also published an account[27] of the forms to be observed in the several ways of proceeding at law; a work which, in after times, must have been exceedingly curious; but which must have utterly failed in practice, if its object was to enable a common man to conduct his own suit, without consulting some one learned in the law. Accordingly, it was to the publication of his calendar that Flavius owed his great popularity; he was elected soon after tribune;[28] he was appointed to one or two other important public offices, and six years later, as we shall see presently, he obtained the rank of curule ædile.

He encourages Cn. Flavius to publish his calendar and his account of the forms to be observed in actions at law.

Thus making it his pleasure to lessen all dignity and to diminish all influence but his own, offending in his pride the old aristocracy no less than the new, and the middle classes, Appius now, as sole censor, feel-

His public works.

[23] Livy, IX. 29.
[24] Diodorus, XX. 35, 36. Livy, IX. 46.
[25] "Appii Cœci scriba, cujus hortatu exceperat eos dies consultando assidue sagaci ingenio promulgaveratque."—Pliny, Hist. Natur. XXXIII. 6. Ed. Sillig.
[26] "Publicatis diebus fastis, quos populus a paucis principum *quotidie* petebat."—Pliny, XXXIII. 6.
[27] "Actiones composuit." See Cicero, de Orat. I. 41. Epp. ad Attic. VI. 1.
[28] Livy, IX. 46.

ing himself in possession of almost kingly power, resolved to distinguish his name by public works on a most magnificent scale, such as the greatest king might emulate. Without any authority from the senate,[29] he applied the large sums of public money which were paid into his hands by that multitude of persons who farmed the state property in all its manifold kinds, to the execution of two great works: one, the construction of a military road from Rome to Capua; the other, the bringing a constant supply of good water into the city from a distance of about eight miles from the Esquiline gate, partly by pipes under ground, and partly by an aqueduct.

The Appian Road to Capua.

The great road from Rome to Capua, which was afterwards continued to Brundisium, has, indeed, immortalized the name of its author; nor will the mightiest works of modern engineers ever rival the fame of the Appian Way. This has been owing to accidental causes; yet the road was a magnificent undertaking, and even without noticing the excellence of its pavement, which was added at a later period, we may justly admire the labor bestowed in order to keep its line generally on a level, the deep cuttings through hills, and the vast substructions of massy stones on which it was carried across valleys. The whole line from Rome to Capua was about 120 English miles; the road left the city at the Porta Capena, the gate of Capua; it passed in a straight line over the Campagna till it reached the foot of the Alban hills at Bovillæ; there it ascended to the higher grounds, and, passing through Aricia, and leaving Velitræ and the modern road to Naples on the left, it descended again into the plain nearly in the same straight line, and ran on to the Pontine marshes. At this point, as Niebuhr thinks, the road stopped; and the communication through the Pontine marshes was carried on by a canal almost as far as Tarracina. But the very excavation of the canal would, of itself, supply materials, in part, for an embankment by the side of it; and it is more likely that both it and the road were carried through the marshes together. Afterwards the road ascended the mountains behind Tarracina, thus avoiding the ill-omened pass of Lautulæ, and soon after descended again into the plain of Fundi, crossed the Liris at Minturnæ, and the Vulturnus at Casilinum, and three miles further it arrived at the termination of its course, the city of Capua.[30]

The Appian aqueduct.

The other work of Appius was less remarkable in itself, than as being the earliest of those famous aqueducts which still, amid their ruins, are such striking and characteristic monuments of Roman greatness. In fact, it can scarcely be called an aqueduct, for the water[31] was carried under ground throughout the whole of its course, with the exception of sixty Roman paces, or about a hundred yards, in the low ground by the Porta Capena, where it was conveyed partly on arches, and partly on a solid substruction of massy stones. Its termination was at the salt works by the river-side, close by the Porta Trigemina, and immediately under the northwest corner of the Aventine; and it seems to have been especially intended to supply water to the inhabitants of the low district about the Circus, who had hitherto been obliged to use the water of the river, or the rain-water collected in tanks or cisterns. When we remember that this part of Rome was particularly inhabited by the poorest citizens, we may suspect that Appius wished to repay the support which he had already received from them, or to purchase its continuance for the time to come; but we shall feel unmixed pleasure in observing that the first Roman aqueduct was constructed for the benefit of the poor, and of those who most needed it.

"These two works exhausted," says Diodorus, "the whole revenue of Rome."

[29] Diodorus, XX. 35, 36.

[30] It is well known that the ancient Capua did not stand on the Vulturnus, but about three miles to the south of it, on the site of the present S. Maria di Capua. The modern Capua corresponds with the ancient Casilinum.

[31] The whole account of this aqueduct is taken from the work of Frontinus. He was superintendent of the aqueducts in the reign of Nerva, and his account of them is exceedingly full and accurate.

How money and laborers were found for these works.

But, considering the unavoidable expenses of the war, to which the tributum was wholly appropriated, the disposable revenue from the vectigalia, or rents received by the commonwealth, must have been insufficient; and Niebuhr reasonably conjectures that Appius must have sold large portions of the state's domain, in order to raise the money which he required. The workmen employed consisted, doubtless in great measure, of the prisoners taken from the Samnites, either in battle or in the repeated invasions of their territory; the rest were the public or government slaves, or those furnished by the several contractors for the work: for such labors were held to be degrading to free citizens, and Appius would have acquired no popularity amongst the poorest classes, by offering to provide them with employment in making his road, or digging his water-course.

Appius retains his censorship beyond the legal term.

The regular term of the censor's office, eighteen months, was far too short for the completion of these works; and had they been finished by another censor, the glory of them would have been lost to Appius. Setting, therefore, all law and all opposition at defiance, Appius persisted in retaining his censorship when the eighteen months were expired; and although the tribune P. Sempronius Sophus,[32] one of the most eminent commoners of this period, threatened to send him to prison if he persisted in disobeying the law, and although six of the other tribunes supported their colleague, yet the remaining three promised Appius their protection; and as their negative was all-powerful, Appius was secured from any molestation so long as they continued in office. He found some tribunes equally devoted to him in the next year, for he retained his censorship four years, and in the fifth he endeavored to add to it the power and dignity of consul, and whilst he still continued to be censor, he declared himself a candidate for the consulship. Here, however, that negative power of the tribunes which had hitherto been his support was employed against him: L. Furius[33] forbade the business of the comitia to proceed, until Appius had resigned his censorship. Then, however, he was elected consul, and perhaps in this capacity finished and dedicated the two works of which he so greatly coveted the glory.

Wise moderation of the party opposed to him.

The extreme moderation of the party opposed to Appius deserves in all these transactions the highest praise. They composed probably the majority in the senate, and if they had exerted their whole strength they must have been also the majority in the comitia. Yet they suffered Appius to defy the laws for a period of two years and a half, and afterwards they allowed him to be elected consul without opposition, nor when he became a private citizen did they ever impeach him for the violence of his conduct. We cannot, in our ignorance of the details of these times, appreciate fully the wisdom of this conduct; but as violence begets violence, so unquestionably does moderation in political contests lead to moderation in return. The personal ambition of Appius had been gratified even beyond the law; and this his political opponents had endured at the time, nor did they seek to punish it afterwards. Nothing was attempted against him which could either irritate his own passions, or invest him in the eyes of the multitude with the character of a martyr in their cause. If he had ever carried his views still higher than to a five years' censorship, if the hope of regal dominion had ever floated before his eyes, the forbearance shown towards him deprived him not only of every pretext for further violence, but, appealing to the nobler part of his nature, restrained him for very shame from endeavoring to wrest more, where so much had been already yielded to him; it would not suffer him to assail that constitution which had shown itself towards him at once so confident and so placable. Ten years after his first consulship he was elected consul again in the midst of the third Samnite war, and he obtained the prætorship in the year following. He bore his part not

[32] Livy, IX. 33.

[33] Livy, IX. 42.

without honor, amongst the greatest generals of his day, in that most arduous contest when the Gauls again fought against Rome with the Etruscans and the Samnites to aid them; and in his old age he had the glory of determining the senate, by the last effort of his eloquence, not to treat with the ambassador of Pyrrhus.

Other public works. The Valerian Way.

The example which Appius had set in his public works was followed by the succeeding censors, M. Valerius Maximus and C. Junius Bubulcus. They also made some roads[34] through the country in the neighborhood of Rome; that is, they either improved the line of the existing local roads, or widened them, and constructed them of better materials. One of the roads, thus in a manner made anew, led from Rome to Tibur; and this being afterwards continued through the country of the Æquians by Carseoli and Alba, as far as Sulmo and Corfinium, and thus having become one of the greatest lines of communication in Italy, was known throughout its whole length by the name of the Valerian Way, because the first twenty miles of it from Rome to Tibur were made by the censor M. Valerius.

Trial of A. Atilius Calatinus.

In the same year, 447–8 (Nieb. 441), we may place the trial of A. Atilius Calatinus, on a charge of having betrayed the garrison of Sora to the Samnites. He had married a daughter of Q. Fabius, and had been left by his father-in-law in the command of the place, when he himself left his province of Samnium to return to Rome. Sora and Calatia were at this period[35] both surprised by the Samnites, and the troops who garrisoned them were sold for slaves. Atilius either made his escape, or was taken prisoner and allowed to be ransomed; but on his return to Rome he was accused of treason, a charge often made against unsuccessful officers, and listened to the more readily, because, while the soldiers had been led away into slavery, their commander had met with a fate so different. Perhaps in this accusation we may trace the influence possessed at this time in the comitia by the city populace, who were not commonly enlisted in the legions, and who were apt to judge the conduct of military men unfairly and severely, in proportion to their own total ignorance of war. It might have fared hardly with Atilius, had his father-in-law been any less distinguished man than Q. Fabius. But Fabius[36] came forward and declared to the people that the charge was groundless: "Had it been otherwise," said he, "I should not have allowed my daughter to remain the wife of a traitor."[37] The people, suspicious because they were ignorant, but meaning honestly, listened at once to the testimony of so great a general and so upright a man, and Atilius was acquitted. His son, the grandson of Q. Fabius, became one of the most distinguished citizens in the first Punic war; he was twice consul, dictator, and censor.[38]

Ædileship of Cn. Flavius, the clerk of Appius Claudius.

Two years afterwards the influence of the new popular party in the comitia reached its highest point, when Cn. Flavius, the clerk of Appius, and the man who had published the calendar and the forms of actions at law, was elected curule ædile. When the first votes were given in his favor, the ædile who presided at the comitia refused to receive them, saying that a clerk was not fit to hold a curule magistracy. It so happened[39] that Flavius himself was attending on the curule ædile at that very time in the way of his occupation; he had his tablets and his style in his hands, to record the votes. As soon as he heard the objection he stepped forwards; he laid

[34] Livy, IX. 43. Cassiodorus.

[35] Diodorus, XX. 80. Livy, IX. 43.

[36] Valerius Maximus, VIII. I. § 9.

[37] By which it appears, as Niebuhr well observes, that the practice of marrying without conventio in manum was common even amongst distinguished families. Thus the daughter still remained in her father's power, if, to bar her husband's right to her by prescription, she absented herself from him for three nights in the year. See p. 100.

[38] His epitaph said of him, in language resembling the epitaphs of the Scipios,

"Plurimæ consentiunt gentes
Populi primarium fuisse virum."

See Cicero, de Senect. 17.

[39] L. Piso, Annal. III. quoted by Gellius, VI. 9.

down his tablets, and declared upon oath that from that day forwards he would follow the business of a clerk no more. The ædile then received the votes that were given for him, and Cn. Flavius was duly elected. His colleague was Q. Anicius[40] of Præneste, who had only within the last few years become a Roman citizen; while two commoners of consular families, C. Pœtelius and Cn. Domitius, were unsuccessful candidates. The indignation of the patricians and of the old commons on this occasion was so great, that the senators laid aside their gold rings, and the young patricians, and wealthy commoners who formed the equestrian order, put off their chains of honor (phaleræ), as if so great a dishonor to the commonwealth required a general mourning. It should be remembered that the curule ædileship was at this time an office of high distinction, and that every curule magistracy was supposed to convey something of kingly and therefore of sacred dignity; so that it was a profanation if it were bestowed on a freedman's son, although he might have held the tribuneship of the commons without offence. Flavius, however, was a man of spirit, and was not abashed by these signs of displeasure; nay, he even enjoyed the mortification of the nobility; and a story[41] was told how on a time, when his colleague Q. Anicius was sick, Flavius went to visit him; and when he entered his room he found several noble youths who were sitting there with him. They, scorning the freedman's son, remained in their places, and would not rise as they were bound to do to the curule ædile. Upon which Flavius sent for his curule chair, and placed it in the doorway so that no one could pass, and then taking his seat in it, obliged them to see him in the enjoyment of his dignity. Yet, although he would not allow himself to be overborne by insolence, he could not bear to be the occasion of divisions between his countrymen; and he vowed to build a temple to Concord,[42] if he could succeed in effecting a reconciliation between the higher and lower classes of the commonwealth.

We must suppose, therefore, that he witnessed without opposition the decree of the senate that two censors should be immediately appointed, although not a year had elapsed since the last censors had resigned their office. Still less could he find fault with the choice of the comitia, which fell upon two of the most popular men in Rome, Q. Fabius and P. Decius.

Q. Fabius and P. Decius censors.

This censorship, according to Niebuhr, effected little less than a remodelling of the whole constitution; in particular, he supposes that the perplexing combination of tribes and centuries, which is known to have existed in the later periods of the commonwealth, was the work of Fabius and Decius; and that they adjusted, in a manner satisfactory to all parties, the ever-contending claims of nobility and wealth on the one hand and of numbers on the other. I cannot assert this, even on Niebuhr's authority, not only from the total want of all direct evidence, but because I am inclined to think that the mixture of tribes and centuries in the later form of the comitia centuriata was the work of the fourth century of Rome rather than of the fifth. Nor do I quite believe the story[43] that it was to his eminent services in this censorship that Q. Fabius owed his surname of Maximus.

Measures supposed to have been taken in their censorship.

What is actually recorded of the censors of this year is sufficiently probable;

[40] Pliny, Hist. Nat. XXXIII. 6.

[41] Piso, apud Gell. VI. 9. Livy IX. 46.

[42] "Flavius vovit ædem Concordiæ, si populo reconciliasset ordines." Niebuhr understands by populus the old patricians, and by ordines the plebs and the freedmen. But surely the old sense of populus is inapplicable here; and we must either understand "ordines" of the senate and the equestrian order, which is undoubtedly the meaning, if the words are Pliny's own; or if he copied them from an older writer, "ordines" may signify the clerks, scribæ, and the other trades or inferior callings, and populus means what Livy calls "integer populus," that is, the patricians and the old commons, as opposed to the "forensis factio."

[43] The story is told by Livy, IX. 46, and by several other writers. But Polybius asserts that the surname of Maximus was given to the dictator Q. Fabius in the second Punic war, on account of his great services at that period. III. 87. This is undoubtedly a mistake, but I believe the other story is no less so; and that the surname Maximus in the Fabian family, no less than in the Valerian and Carvilian, had reference originally to personal size rather than to greatness of mind or exploits; that it answered to the surname of Philip le Long, or of Edward

What was certainly effected was wise and beneficial.

and that it should have been accomplished not only without a contest, but as far as appears without exciting any thing but satisfaction, is one of the most extraordinary proofs of the political wisdom and moderation of the Roman people. The lower classes of the city, and those whose blood was not yet clear from the taint of slavery, had gained a political power much more than in proportion to their social importance; and there is in this something so unnatural, that it shocks even those who may be supposed to benefit by it, unless they have been previously corrupted by intolerable distress, no less fatal to wisdom and goodness than excessive enjoyment, or have been exasperated by previous insolence and oppression. Had there now been such a state of misery amongst the poorer classes as that which followed the Gaulish invasion, or had the old law of debtor and creditor existed still and been rigorously exercised, the lower people would have eagerly retained the power which fortune had thrown into their hands; they would have valued it as ensuring them at once protection and vengeance. But when all was prospering, when the state was victorious abroad and daily growing in wealth and magnificence at home; when the citizens of highest rank were also the worthiest; and the commonwealth seemed to enjoy a real aristocracy, which is as natural and excellent as its counterfeits are hateful; above all, when there was prevailing a general spirit of moderation, which dispelled all fears of tyranny,—why should men endure such an unfitness as that the lower should take the place of the higher, and that those who were of least account in society should exercise politically the greatest power? So Flavius, resigning all prospect of rising to higher honors, allowed that he had already risen too high for one of his class, and that more than one generation should elapse between the slave and the curule magistrate. Fabius and Decius removed all freedmen,[44] all artisans, and all other citizens of the lowest class, into four tribes only out of the one-and-thirty which then existed; so that they could influence at most but a little more than an eighth part of the whole comitia; and these four tribes were the old tribes of the city, as distinguished from those of the country, the Palatine, the Colline, the Esquiline, and the Suburran. Then Flavius, seeing the conditions of his vow fulfilled, built his temple to Concord,[45] a small chapel, of which the walls were plated with bronze, and which stood within the precinct of the temple of Vulcan, on the north side of the comitium. It was built with the money arising from the penalties paid by some wealthy men for having lent money at a rate of interest higher than was allowed by law; and Flavius, by virtue of his office of ædile, had prosecuted them before the comitia. When it was completed, the pontifex maximus, L. Cornelius Scipio,[46] refused to dictate the solemn form of dedication, which Flavius, according to custom, was to repeat after him; but the comitia, indignant at the spirit which dictated this refusal, passed a resolution which obliged the pontifex to retract it. Yet, afterwards, to complete the picture of moderation displayed by the people on this occasion, the comitia passed a bill proposed to them by the senate, enacting that for the time to come no man should be allowed to dedicate a temple without the sanction of the senate or of the majority of the tribunes of the commons. The aristocratical pride of the pontifex required to be restrained; yet it was not fit that he should be called to perform the solemnities of the national religion at the pleasure of an individual, or that a temple should be consecrated without the sanction of some public authority. Happy is that people which delivers itself from the evils of an aristo-

the First, rather than to that of Alexander or Charlemagne.

[44] Livy, IX. 46.

[45] Pliny, Hist. XXXIII. 6. In this notice of the founding of the temple by Cn. Flavius, Pliny adds, "inciditque in tabellâ æreâ eam ædem ccıv. annis post Capitolinam dedicatam." This is a very important passage for the chronology of Rome; for it declares that the consulship of P. Sempronius and P. Sulpicius, the last year of the second Samnite war, was believed by those who were then living, and by one who had an access to all existing monuments, to have been the 204th year from the beginning of the commonwealth.

[46] Livy, IX. 46.

cratical or priestly dominion, not by running wild into individual licentiousness, but by submitting to the wholesome sovereignty of law!

"The Carthaginians," says Aristotle,[47] "provide for the stability of their constitution, by continually sending out a portion of their commons to their settlements in the surrounding country." This policy was no less familiar to the Romans, and as some of the poorer citizens must have been discontented with the recent proceedings of the censors, so we find that three colonies were founded in the next two years, and that no fewer than fourteen thousand citizens were sent out as colonists.[48] The three places thus colonized were Sora, Alba, and Carseoli. Sora had been taken and retaken repeatedly in the late Samnite war, and its important position, just at the point where the Liris issues out from the mountains which confine its earlier course upon the high plain of Arpinum and Fibrenus, made it desirable to secure its permanent possession; Carseoli and Alba had been conquered in the late war with the Æquians. Carseoli was in the upper valley of the Anio, about thirty-eight miles from Rome. Alba stood on an isolated hill at a little distance from the lake Fucinus; and the strength of its fortifications was even at this time remarkable, for the walls which still exist are built of enormous polygonal blocks of the limestone of the Apennines, and belong to a period much more ancient than the fifth century of Rome.

Colonies founded at this time.

Places so recently conquered, and so exposed to fresh attacks whenever a war should break out again, must have been colonized by men who understood war, and might be able to maintain their own ground, as a sort of frontier garrison. The settlers sent thither could not, therefore, have consisted wholly of the unwarlike populace of the city, but of the poorer citizens of the old commons, who had been accustomed to serve in the legions, and who had the skill and courage of veteran soldiers. It is very probable, however, that a certain portion of the freedmen and of the city populace may have been mixed up with them.

Who were sent as settlers.

In appointing and supporting the censorship of Fabius and Decius, the patricians and the nobility of the commons must have acted in concert with each other. But three years afterwards, there was a feeble return of the old quarrel between the two orders, when two of the tribunes,[49] Q. and Cn. Ogulnius, proposed a bill for increasing the number of the pontifices and augurs by the addition of new members to be chosen from the commons. In Rome, as elsewhere, the civil equality of the two great orders of the state had been established, whilst the old religious distinctions between them still subsisted; a commoner might be consul, dictator, or censor, but he could not as yet be pontifex or augur. But this exclusion, although it related to religious offices, was maintained for political purposes, and could not, indeed, be justified on religious grounds. For, according to the old principle, that the priests of the gods must be of a certain race or caste, carefully preserved from any profane mixture, the Roman patricians had long since forfeited the purity of their blood by their frequent intermarriages with the commons. But politically, their exclusive possession of the offices of pontifex and augur might secure them some advantages. Twice within twenty-five years we have seen the appointment of a plebeian dictator annulled by the augurs, on the ground of certain religious objections of which they were the sole judges. All questions of augury depended on their decision; and this, in a state where nothing either political or military was done without consulting the auspices, conferred, necessarily, an immense power. The pontifices, in like manner, had the absolute control over every part of the ritual of religion, and as connected with it, over the calendar. What festivals were to be observed, and at what times; what public sacrifices

The Ogulnian bill for throwing open all sacred offices to the commons.

[47] Politic. II. 11.

[48] Six thousand were sent to Alba, four thousand to Sora, and as many to Carseoli. Livy, X. 1. 3.

[49] Livy 6, et seqq.

should be performed, and with what ceremonies; and what was an interference on the part of any individual with sacred places, persons, or things, were all points of their jurisdiction, against which it is doubtful whether even the tribunes would have ventured to interpose. It seems but reasonable, therefore, that as the patricians and commons were now become one people, and as both alike were admitted to those high and sacred dignities of consul and dictator, which involved the practice of augury, and the offering sacrifice to the peculiar gods of Rome, in the name of the Roman people, so the knowledge as well as the practice of the national religious system should be committed to both equally; that where no religious objection really existed, political ambition might no longer be able to shelter itself beneath its semblance.

P. Decius supports it, and it becomes a law.

Still, however, a party amongst the patricians, headed, as we are told, by Appius Claudius,[50] vehemently opposed the Ogulnian bill. It was supported by P. Decius; and no man could have pleaded for it with greater effect, when he appealed to his father's memorable death, and recalled him to the memory of some of his hearers, as they had seen him in the great battle with the Latins, with his toga wrapped around his head, and his feet on a javelin, devoting himself to the powers of death in behalf of the Roman people. "If my father," said he, "was no less fit than his patrician colleague to offer himself to the gods, as an accepted expiation for the whole people, how could he be unfit to direct their worship?" The question, in fact, could not be carried; some of the tribunes were at first engaged to interpose their negative, but the general feeling obliged them to forbear, and the Ogulnian bill became a law. The pontifices, who were then four in number, elected accordingly four commoners to complete their college to eight, or, including their head, the pontifex maximus, to nine. And the augurs, who were also four, elected five commoners to raise their college to the same number of nine, on the notion that each of the original tribes of Rome, the Ramnenses, the Titienses, and Luceres, was to be represented by an equal number of the public ministers of religion. It seems that the new appointments were fairly and wisely made; P. Decius himself,[51] and P. Sempronius Sophus, who had been both consuls and censors, were two of the new pontifices; and amongst the augurs, besides T. Publilius, C. Genucius, and C. Marcius, all of them members of the most eminent families of the commons, we find the name of P. Ælius Pætus, a man of no great political or military distinction, but who probably showed a remarkable fondness for the study of the pontifical and augural discipline, inasmuch as we find an unusual number of his descendants[52] filling the offices of pontifex and augur, as if those sacred duties were almost the hereditary calling of their race and name.

The Valerian law re-enacted.

In the same year,[53] M. Valerius, one of the consuls, re-enacted, for the third time, the famous law which bore the name of his family, and which was, in fact, the Roman law of trial by jury, as it permitted every citizen to appeal from the sentence of a magistrate in capital cases to the judgment of his country. It is not certain whether the consul who brought forward this law was M. Valerius Maximus, or M. Valerius Corvus: it must have been the latter, however, if the common statement be true that he was six times elected consul; and we should be glad to ascribe the measure to a man so worthy of it. The law denounced the violation of its provisions as a crime, but named no fixed penalty; leaving it open to the accuser to demand, and to the judges to award, a milder or a heavier sentence, according to the nature of the particular case, as was so generally the practice at Athens. But why this law should have been

[50] Livy, X. 7.

[51] Livy, X. 9.

[52] Q. Ælius Pætus, who fell at Cannæ, was pontifex, Livy, XXIII. 21. P. Ælius Pætus was appointed augur in the place of Marcellus, Livy. XXVII. 36: and on his death he was succeeded by Q. Ælius Pætus. Livy, XLI. 21. Nor must we forget that Ælius whom Ennius honored with the title of "egregiè cordatus homo."

[53] Livy, X. 9.

re-enacted at this particular time we know not. No recent instances of arbitrary power are mentioned, nor do we hear of any consul of this period who is charged with a disposition to cruelty. Perhaps the object of Valerius was simply to satisfy the humbler citizens that the government was not unmindful of their personal security, although it had diminished their political power; and that whilst the more distinguished commoners were completing their own equality with the patricians, they did not mean to allow the poorer members of their order to be oppressed with impunity. Thus, the re-enactment of the Valerian law, taken in conjunction with the passing of the Ogulnian, seems to form an æra in the constitutional history of Rome; when the commons obtained a confirmation of their great charter of personal freedom for the mass of their order, and for those of their members who might rise to eminence, a perfectly equal share in all the honors of the commonwealth, religious no less than civil.

This period is followed by one very obscurely known.

In some of the transactions recorded in this chapter, we seem almost to have emerged into the light of day, and to be able to trace events and their actors with much of the clearness of real history. But even in those which are in themselves most vivid, we find a darkness on either side, concealing from our view their causes and their consequences; as in dreams, single scenes and feelings present themselves with wonderful distinctness: but what brought us to them, or what is to follow after them, is left altogether a mystery. Some of the many difficult questions which belong to this period, I propose to lay before the reader in the appendix to this volume, as I feel that I can offer no explanation of them so satisfactory as to claim the name of history. In this number I would place especially the famous question as to the later constitution of the comitia of centuries, a problem which not even Niebuhr could fully solve, and which has equally baffled other writers who have more recently attempted it. But in the following period of about fourteen years, which elapsed between the passing of the Ogulnian law and the dictatorship of Q. Hortensius, there is scarcely a single fact in the domestic history of Rome which can be discerned clearly, and we are left to ask what circumstances could have produced so great a change; and how, after a state of things so peaceable and so prosperous, and a settlement of the constitution apparently so final, we are brought back again so suddenly to the circumstances of a long past period, to a heavy burden of debt, to quarrels between the different orders in the state from this cause, and to a new secession of the commons to the Janiculum.

In the mean time we must carry on for a while the foreign history of Rome, and describe that short but decisive war, in which the Romans triumphed over the triple coalition of the Etruscans, the Samnites, and the Gauls.

CHAPTER XXXIII.

FOREIGN HISTORY FROM 450 TO 464 (443 TO 456, NIEBUHR)—CONQUEST OF THE ÆQUIANS—THIRD SAMNITE WAR—COALITION OF THE ETRUSCANS, SAMNITES, AND GAULS—GREAT BATTLE OF SENTINUM, AND DEATH OF P. DECIUS—FINAL VICTORY OF Q. FABIUS OVER THE SAMNITES—C. PONTIUS IS LED IN TRIUMPH AND PUT TO DEATH IN COLD BLOOD.

"Ter totum fervidus irâ
Lustrat Aventini montem; ter saxea tentat
Limina nequidquam; ter fessus valle resedit."
VIRG. Æn. VIII. 230.

"Thrice did the indignant nations league their might,
Thrice the red darkness of the battle's night
Shrouded the recreant terror of their flight."
MILMAN, Judicium Regale.

War with the Æquians.

THE peace with Samnium was immediately followed by a war with the Æquians. Since the Gaulish invasion, the very name of this people has vanished out of our sight, except on one single occasion in the year immediately following the recovery of the city, when Camillus is said to have taken from them the town of Bola.[1] As they took no part in the subsequent attacks made by the Volscians upon Rome, and did not even join their neighbors of Præneste, when they, from the allies of the Romans, became their enemies, so we may conclude with Niebuhr, that the Gaulish invasion had been even more fatal to them than to the Romans; that they must have been so weakened by some great disaster sustained at that period, as to have fallen back altogether from their advanced position on the edge of the Campagna to their older country in the upper valleys of the Turano[2] and the Salto, and near the western shore of the lake Fucinus. From their towns on the edge of the Campagna they were, probably, expelled by the Latins; and acquisitions of territory from the Æquians may have been among the causes which raised Tibur and Præneste after the Gaulish invasion to greatness far above the rest of their countrymen. Meanwhile, the Æquians were left unmolested in their remaining territory, and for nearly eighty years from the burning of Rome by the Gauls they seem to have remained perfectly neutral. But towards the end of the second Samnite war, when the Hernicans, in their jealousy of the growing power of Rome, took up arms against her, the Æquians also, probably from similar motives, were induced to join in the quarrel. Æquian soldiers[3] were found, it was said, together with Hernicans, in that Samnite army which Q. Fabius, when proconsul in the year 447, had defeated at Allifæ; and after the Hernican war in the year following, the whole Æquian people joined the Samnites. Thus, when the Samnites, in the year 450, were obliged to sue for peace, the Æquians were left in a position of no small danger. Rome, it appears, was willing to forgive them on no other terms than those just imposed on the Hernicans; namely, that they should become citizens of Rome without the right of voting in the comitia; in other words,

[1] Livy, VI. 2.

[2] The Turano is the stream which, rising at the back of the hills which form the northern boundary of the valley of the Anio, flows thence in a northerly direction, and joins the Velino just below Rieti. The Salto rises very near to the lake Fucino, and, in its earlier course, is called the Imele; but it sinks into a fissure in the limestone, a little below the famous battle-field of Scurgola, the scene of Conradin's defeat by Charles of Anjou, and when it reappears it receives the name of Salto. It flows through the pastoral country of the Cicolano, and falls into the Velino above Rieti. See Bunsen's article, "Esame del sito dei più antichi stabilimenti Italici," &c. in the Annals of the Archæological Society of Rome, Vol. VI. p. 110.

[3] Livy, IX. 45.

that they should submit to become Roman subjects. Hopeless as their condition was, their old spirit would not yet allow them to yield, and they resolved to abide a contest with the whole undivided power of the Roman commonwealth.

Both consuls, P. Sempronius and P. Sulpicius,[4] with two consular armies, marched at once into the Æquian territory. Such a force, amounting to about 40,000 men, confounded all plans of resistance. Few Æquians of that generation had ever seen war; their country had not been exposed to the ravages of an enemy within the memory of any man then living. Abandoning all hope of maintaining the field against the invaders, they took refuge in their several towns, hoping there to baffle the first assault of the enemy, and trusting that time might bring some of the neighboring people to their aid. But their towns were small, and were thus each weak in the number of their defenders: the Romans well knew the effect of a first impression, and in the places which they first stormed, they probably, according to their usual practice, made a bloody execution, in order to strike terror into the rest. We have seen, under the influence of a general panic, some of the strongest fortresses and one of the most warlike nations of modern Europe taken and conquered in the space of two months; so that we cannot wonder that fifty days were sufficient to complete the Æquian war, and that forty-one towns were taken within that period,[5] the greater part of which were destroyed and burnt. The polygonal walls of many of them are still in existence, and are to be found scattered along the pastoral upland valley of the Himella or Salto, from Alba almost to the neighborhood of Reate. The Romans, however, did their work of destruction well; for although the style of the walls in these ruins denotes their high antiquity, yet no traces are to be found of the name, or race, or condition of their inhabitants: the actual remains will tell as little of the history of the Æquian people as we can glean from the scanty reports of their conquerors.

Their country is overrun, and their towns taken.

The fate which the Æquians had vainly striven to avert now fell upon the remnant of their nation, after the greatest portion of the people had perished or been led away into slavery. The survivors, after seeing the greatest portion of their territory converted into Roman domain land, were obliged to become Roman citizens without suffrage. But five years afterwards, when war with Etruria and with the Samnites was again threatening, the Romans admitted them to the full franchise,[6] and they formed a considerable part of the citizens enrolled in the year 455 in the two tribes then created, the Aniensian and Terentine.

They submit, and receive the Roman franchise.

When the Samnites had made peace with Rome, they were required to restore Lucania to its independence; that is, they were obliged to give back the hostages whom they had kept as a pledge of the nation's fidelity, and to withdraw their garrisons from the Lucanian towns. The Roman party in Lucania, upon this, regained its ascendency, and the foreign relations of the country were so changed, that, from having been in alliance with the Samnites and Tarentines against Rome, the

The Roman party predominant in Lucania. Rome and Lucania at war with Tarentum. The Tarentines call Cleonymus, the Spartan, to their aid.

[4] Livy, IX. 45.

[5] Livy, IX. 45. Diodorus, XX. 101.

[6] "Majores nostri," says Cicero, "Æquos in civitatem acceperunt." De Officiis, I. 11. That they were admitted into the tribes Aniensis and Terentina is not expressly stated by any ancient writer; but the date of the creation of these tribes connects them with the Æquians, and the tribe Aniensis must have included the upper valley of the Anio, which was Æquian. The tribe Terentina contained at a later period, as we know, the people of the Volscian city of Atina (Cicero pro Plancio, 8, 16, 22); and Niebuhr thinks that they were included in it, because it was in their neighborhood. But the Arpinatians, who lived nearer to the Æquian country than the people of Atina, were included in the Cornelian tribe (Livy, XXXVIII. 36): and we cannot always conclude that a tribe contained only the people of one particular district. The origin of the name Terentina is quite unknown. We know of no town Terentum which could have given it its name, nor of any river Terens. What was the ancient name of the Turano, which, as it runs near to the site of Carseoli, must have flowed through the Æquian territory? Bunsen has shown that it is a mere mistake to suppose that the Tolenus or Telonius was the Turano. (Annali dell' Instituto, &c. tom. VI. p. 104.) Could the Turano have been anciently called Terens, or Terentus, and could the tribe Terentina have been named from this river, as the Aniensis was from the Anio?

Lucanians now took part with Rome against Tarentum. During the Samnite war, the Tarentines, covered as they were by the territory of their allies, had nothing to fear from the Roman armies; and by sea, as the Roman navy was very inconsiderable, they carried on the contest with advantage. But now a consular army,[7] supported by their old enemies, the Lucanians, might, at any moment, appear under their very walls; and they looked out, therefore, for some foreign aid. They sent to Greece, and to their own mother-city, Sparta, imploring that an army might be sent to help them, and that Cleonymus might be its general. Cleonymus was the younger son of Cleomenes,[8] king of Sparta, and the grandson of Cleombrotus, who fell at Leuctra. His nephew Areus, Cleomenes' grandson by his elder son Acrotatus, had been now for about six years on the throne; and Cleonymus, like Dorieus of old, not liking to remain in Sparta as a private citizen, was eager for any opportunity of distinguishing himself abroad. Areus was no less ready to let him go; and accordingly he complied at once with the invitation of the Tarentines, and having levied at their expense about 5000 Greek mercenaries, he crossed over into Italy. There he raised 5000 mercenaries more, and the native forces of Tarentum are reckoned at 20,000 foot and 2000 horse.[9] Most of the Italian Greeks, together with the Sallentines, who had already been engaged in hostilities with Rome, joined his standard; and had Cleonymus possessed the ability of Pyrrhus, he might have rallied around him the Samnites and Etruscans, and, after the exhaustion of a twenty years' war, the Romans would have found it no easy matter to withstand him.

Peace between Rome and Tarentum.

As it was, the display of his force terrified the Lucanians, and they made their peace with Tarentum.[10] It is remarkable that Diodorus, who states this in express terms, and who had just before named the Romans as being also at war with the Tarentines, yet makes no mention of any peace between Tarentum and Rome. A treaty, however, must have been concluded, for the attack made by the Tarentines on a Roman fleet, eleven years afterwards, is said[11] to have been occasioned by a violation of the conditions of the peace between the two nations; and had it not been made at this time, we cannot conceive that Cleonymus could so immediately have engaged in other enterprises. It seems probable that no other terms were required on either side than the renewal of a preceding treaty; and this treaty was originally concluded at a period when the only conceivable intercourse between Rome and Tarentum could have been by sea. It stipulated[12] in the usual language that no Roman ships, meaning, probably, ships of war, were to advance along the south coast of Italy nearer to Tarentum than the headland of Lacinium, which forms the southern extremity of the Tarentine gulf. There was, no doubt, a similar stipulation, restraining the Tarentines from advancing with their ships of war nearer to Rome than the headland of Circeii.

Cleonymus, being thus no longer needed by the Tarentines, employed his arms with various success in plundering operations along the eastern coast of Italy, till at last he was beaten off by the inhabitants and obliged to return to Greece. He is not heard of again till he invited Pyrrhus to assist him in his attempt to seize the throne of Sparta.

Short war with the Marsians.

Two years after the end of the Samnite war, the Marsians, who had then, as we have seen, made peace with Rome like the other allies of the Samnites, were again engaged in hostilities. The Roman account[13]

[7] Diodorus says expressly, *Ταραντῖνοι πόλεμον ἔχοντες πρὸς Λευκανοὺς καὶ Ῥωμαίους.* XX. 104.

[8] Pausanias, III. 6. Plutarch, Agis, 3, and Pyrrhus, 26. Compare the article on the kings of Sparta in the Appendix to the second volume of Mr. Fynes Clinton's Fasti Hellenici.

[9] Diodorus, XX. 104.

[10] Diodorus, XX. 104.

[11] Appian, Samnitic. VII.

[12] *Δημαγωγὸς . . παλαιῶν τοὺς Ταραντίνους ἀνεμίμνησκε συνθηκῶν, μὴ πλεῖν Ῥωμαίους πρόσω Λακινίας ἄκρας.*—Appian, Samnitic. VII.

[13] Livy, X. 3. At this point we lose the connected history of Diodorus. The last consulship noticed in his twentieth book is that of M. Livius and M. Æmilius, which was the second year after the end of the Samnite war, and, according to Diodorus, the third year of the hun-

states that they resisted the settlement of a Roman colony at Carseoli, one of the Æquian towns lately conquered, and themselves maintained the place by force. This is scarcely credible, for they had made no opposition to the colonizing of Alba, a more important position, and one much nearer to their own country. However, the war, whatever was the cause, was short, and ended in the speedy submission of the Marsians, who were obliged to cede a portion of their domain. The same penalty had been paid in the preceding year by the Hernicans of Frusino, for an alleged attempt to excite their countrymen to revolt; and these acquisitions of land by the Romans are memorable, not so much as increasing their power against foreign enemies, but for their effect on their own state of society at home. We must remember that the land thus gained was mostly held in occupation by the Roman nobility, and often to a much larger extent than the Licinian law allowed; and that this great increase of their wealth, and accumulation of extensive domains, "Latifundia," led gradually to a system of slave cultivation, and contributed, more than any other cause, to the great diminution of the free population throughout Italy.

The Vestinians and Picentians in alliance with Rome.

In the same year the Vestinians,[14] of whom we have heard nothing since their unfortunate war with Rome in 429, are said to have sought the friendship of the Romans, and to have concluded with them a treaty of alliance. Since the conquest of the Æquians the Roman frontier had become contiguous to theirs; so that relations with Rome, either friendly or hostile, were become inevitable. Through this treaty, Rome completely separated the Samnites from the Etruscans; as her own territory or that of her allies reached now across the whole width of Italy from the mouth of the Tiber to that of the Aternus, on the Adriatic. Two or three years[15] afterwards the Picentians, whose country stretched along the coast of the Adriatic northward of the Vestinians, lapping, as it were, round Umbria on the east, and reaching as far as the settlements of the Senonian Gauls on the Metaurus and the Æsis, became also the allies of Rome. Their friendship was of importance; for not only were the Etruscans and Umbrians already at war with Rome, but it was known that the Gauls had been solicited to take part in the contest; and the situation of Picenum was most favorable for carrying the war into the Gauls' own country, if they should attempt to stir, or for threatening the flank and rear of the Etruscans and Umbrians, if they should move either on Rome or towards Samnium.

A new Etruscan war. Siege of Nequinum, in Umbria.

Meanwhile the Etruscan war, which was so soon to kindle a new war with the Samnites, broke out partially in the year 453. Its origin is ascribed to the internal factions of the Etruscan city of Arretium;[16] the powerful house of the Cilnians, of which Mecænas was a descendant, was at variance with the people or commons of Arretium, and was suspected also, by some of the neighboring cities, as likely to endanger their independence.

dred and nineteenth Olympiad. Although we have numerous fragments of his later books, yet these can ill supply the place of a regular narrative, which, with all its faults, has certainly preserved to us some very valuable and probable accounts of many events in the Roman history. We miss also his notices of the several writers from whom his work was compiled, and his occasional mention of obscure nations and cities, of which we have scarcely any other knowledge. Thus, for the third Samnite war Livy is almost our sole authority.

[14] Livy, X. 3.

[15] Livy, X. 10. Another year is inserted by the chronologers between the consulship of M. Livius and M. Æmilius, and that of M. Valerius and Q. Appuleius. Like two or three other years in the fifth century of Rome, it is said to have been a year without consuls, and marked only by a dictatorship. Thus the chronology becomes more and more confused, for these dictatorships, if real, could not have lasted more than six months, and the next consuls would therefore come into office half a year after their predecessors' term was expired. In this manner the beginning of the consular year was continually varying, and these portions of years being reckoned as whole years, the reckoning fell more and more in disorder. How constantly do the perplexities of the Roman Fasti remind one of the truth of Thucydides' remark, that the natural chronology of the seasons of the year was the only sure guide; the civil chronology, he says, was a perpetual source of mistakes: *οὐ γὰρ ἀκριβές ἐστιν οἷς καὶ ἀρχομένοις καὶ μεσοῦσι, καὶ ὅπως ἔτυχέν τῳ, ἐπεγένετό τι.*—V. 20.

[16] Livy, X. 3.

The Cilnians applied f. r aid to Rome, already known as the natural supporter of the high aristocratical party throughout Italy, and thus, we are told, a Roman army was sent into Etruria. The details, as is so often the case, are utterly conflicting; but it is said that the Cilnians were reconciled to the popular party, and hostilities ended for the present. In the next year, 454, we find one of the consuls besieging the Umbrian town of Nequinum,[17] on the Nar, on what provocation we know not. The siege, however, was protracted till the year following; for the inhabitants well availed themselves of the strong site of their town, built on a narrow ledge in the mountain side, with an almost abrupt ascent above, and a descent no less steep down into the narrow gorge of the Nar below. At last the town was betrayed to the Romans; and they immediately sent a colony to occupy the spot,[18] which from henceforth took the name of Narnia. It commands the defile which leads from the valley of the Tiber into the plain of Interamna or Terni, one of the richest tracts of central Italy.

The Samnites exert themselves vigorously to form a new coalition against Rome.

Some accounts[19] related that the Samnites had supported the people of Nequinum in their obstinate resistance, and had sent troops to their succor. It is manifest that the Samnite government was at this period making the greatest exertions, in the hope, probably, that the Etruscans would create a diversion in their favor, by drawing off a part of the forces of Rome to her northern frontier. The Samnite plans were, moreover, unexpectedly furthered by a new inroad of the Gauls; new hordes had lately arrived from beyond the Alps,[20] and their countrymen in the plains of the Po, having no room for them, were anxious to speed them on their way southwards; they encouraged them to cross the Apennines, and even joined themselves in the enterprise. The Etruscans had already, perhaps, engaged their services against the Romans; so that the Gauls marched through Etruria still onwards, and with an Etruscan force co-operating with them, they poured into the Roman dominions.[21] It is probable that they followed their old line by the valley of the Clanis into Umbria, and that their ravages were carried on rather in the territory of the allies of Rome than in that of Rome itself. But the invaders won a great spoil without any opposition, and the Gauls recrossed the Apennines to carry it home in safety. They would have been tempted, probably, by their success, to renew their inroad in the next year; but, fortunately for the Romans, they quarrelled with one another about the division of their plunder,[22] and the greatest part of their multitude were destroyed by each other's swords. Whilst the Gauls, however, were on the left bank of the Tiber, the whole force of Rome was watching their movements; and the Samnites seized the opportunity to march into Lucania.[23] The appearance of a Samnite army revived the Samnite party in Lucania; the Roman party was everywhere overpowered; town after town was recovered to the Samnite alliance; and the partisans of Rome sent an embassy in all haste to the senate, praying for instant succor. But the Samnite government did not stop here; their ambassadors endeavored to rouse all the nations of Italy to arms,

[17] Livy, X. 9.

[18] Livy, X. 10.

[19] "M. Fulvius Cn: F. Cn. N. Pætinus Cos. De Samnitibus Nequinatibusque. Ann: CD . . . VII. K. Oct."—Fasti Capitol.

[20] Polybius, II. 19. This account is again different from that of Livy, who represents the Gauls as quarrelling with the Etruscans about the terms of their service, and thus as not invading the Roman dominion at all. There can be no doubt that Polybius has preserved the truer version of these events. He fixes also this Gaulish invasion at about eighty-seven years after the first invasion, when Rome was taken, that is, according to his reckoning, Olym. 120–1, or B. C. 300. The common reckoning places it in 299, a difference not worth dwelling upon.

[21] ἐκ μὲν τῆς Ῥωμαίων ἐπαρχίας ἀσφαλῶς ἐπανῆλθον.—Polyb. II. 19.

[22] Polybius, II. 19.

[23] Livy, X. 11. Dionysius, XVI. 11. For these sudden revolutions in the condition of Lucania, we may compare the conquest of Bœotia by Myronides, and its loss a few years afterwards through the event of the battle of Coronea; and also the accession of Achaia to the Athenian alliance, a little before the thirty years' peace, and its loss again, through the stipulations of that treaty. It is manifest that the Roman and Samnite parties in Lucania, or, in other words, the aristocratical and popular parties, each as they gained the ascendency, took to themselves the name of the Lucanian nation, and spoke of the foreign supporters of the opposite party as the national enemies.

and to form one great coalition against Rome. They solicited the Picentians to join them;[24] but there the influence of the Roman party was predominant; and the Picentian government made a merit of communicating instantly to the Romans the attempt of the Samnites to shake their faith. Old jealousies probably influenced the Marsians, Marrucinians, and Pelignians; they had often found the Samnites restless neighbors, and dreaded the restoration of their former power. But the Sabines[25] seem to have listened to the Samnite overtures; there the ties of blood drew the two people towards one another; and the new Roman tribes, lately created in the Æquian territory, brought the Romans into too close neighborhood to Reate and the valley of the Velinus. Etruria was already engaged in a quarrel of her own with Rome; so far as the endless party revolutions in the Etruscan cities might allow any dependence on the stability of her counsels. The weakness of Umbria might yield to fear, if Etruria on one side and the Sabines on the other, and the Gauls hanging on her northern frontier, should together call upon her to join the confederacy. Nor were the Samnites neglectful of the nations of the south: they had already, as we have seen, recovered the greatest part of Lucania, and their arms, giving timely aid to their party within the country, must at this period have won also the majority of the Apulian nation to desert the Roman alliance, and to acknowledge once again the supremacy of Samnium.[26] The indefatigable Samnite government, after all these efforts, might have well remonstrated, like the Homeric goddess, with that hard destiny which was to render them all fruitless—

> *πῶς ἐθέλεις ἅλιον θεῖναι πόνον ἠδ' ἀτέλεστον,*
> *ἱδρῶ θ' ὃν ἵδρωσα μόγῳ; καμέτην δέ μοι ἵπποι*
> *λαὸν ἀγειρούσῃ, Πριάμῳ κακὰ τοῖό τε παισίν.*

The Romans, as might have been expected, readily listened to the prayer of their friends in Lucania. An alliance[27] was concluded with the Lucanian people, and hostages, taken probably from some of the families of the Samnite party, were given to the Romans as a pledge of their allies' fidelity. Ambassadors were sent into Samnium to require the Samnites to withdraw their troops from Lucania, and with a threat of instant war if the demand were not complied with. The Samnites ordered the ambassadors to leave Samnium without an audience; and the general council of the Samnite nation resolved that each separate state of their union should make its preparations for the support of the common cause. On the other side, the Romans made a formal declaration of war; and thus the desperate struggle began again with increased animosity.

Beginning of the third Samnite war.

When we read of the Samnites, Etruscans, and Gauls, with the Lucanians and Apulians, some of the Sabines, and most of the Umbrian states, engaged in one great confederacy against Rome, we are first inclined to wonder how the Romans could have escaped destruction. But when we consider that under the name of Rome were included all those nations which were in her alliance, and of whose forces she had the supreme disposal, we find that it was but a weaker and far worse organized confederacy opposed to one stronger in itself, and much more firmly united. From the Ciminian Hills to the bay of Naples, the territory of the Romans, Latins, and Campanians presented a compact mass of states and people, far superior in population, in resources, and in union, to the long and ill-organized line of its enemies; whilst, in the cen-

Superior strength of the Roman confederacy.

[24] Livy, X. 11.

[25] Amiternum, a Sabine town in the upper valley of the Aternus, was taken from the Samnites by the Romans in 461. Livy, X. 39. This implies a previous occupation of it by the Samnites, and an alliance therefore between the two countries. And an inscription relating to Appius Claudius the blind states, that he "defeated an army of Sabines and Etruscans" in his consulship, namely, in the year 458. See Orelli, Inscript. Latin. Collectio, No. 539.

[26] Because in the year 457 we find an Apulian army in the field in aid of the Samnites; and P. Decius is said to have defeated it at Maleventum, when on its march to join the Samnite army. Livy, X. 15.

[27] Livy, X. 11, 12. Dionysius, XVI. 11, 12.

tre of Italy, and reaching to the coast of the Adriatic, the Marsians, Pelignians, Marrucinians, Frentanians, Vestinians, and Picentians, formed a separate mass of Roman allies, who, by their position, might either obstruct the enemies' communication, or threaten their rear. In fact, it was only the desperate resolution of the Samnite people, and the great energy and ability of their leaders, which could afford any chance of success, where the resources of the contending parties were so unequal. The Gauls were, like all barbarians, uncertain and unmanageable; and the repeated vacillations of the Etruscan counsels made the alliance of Etruria as unsafe a support as that of Egypt to the kings of Juda: to lean on the Etruscans was indeed to lean on a broken reed.

First campaign of the war.

No combined plan of operations on the part of the enemies of Rome can be traced in the first campaign of the war. The Gauls could not be prevailed on as yet to take the field; and the Roman party in Lucania was not entirely put down, so that the Samnites were still employed in that quarter, and could not send an army into Etruria.

Uncertain and varying accounts of the campaign.

The Roman consuls of the year 456, the first year of the renewed Samnite war, were L. Cornelius Scipio and Cn. Fulvius Centumalus.[28] L. Scipio was the great-grandfather of the conqueror of Hannibal; he is the first Roman of whom a contemporary record has reached our times; the famous epitaph[29] on his tomb, which declares him to have been "a brave man and a wise, whose form well matched his nobleness." Yet such are the perplexities of the uncertain history of these times, that no one action recorded in Scipio's epitaph is noticed by Livy, while no action which Livy ascribes to him is mentioned in his epitaph. The accounts of his colleague's exploits are no less varied; some making him win a great battle in northern Samnium,[30] and saying that he afterwards besieged and took Bovianum and Aufidena; while others placed the seat of his campaign on the Lucanian frontier, and extolled[31] the ability with which he had conducted his operations against a superior enemy. A third account is followed by the Fasti Capitolini, that Fulvius triumphed over the Samnites and Etruscans; which seems to contradict the story followed by Livy, that Scipio invaded Etruria, advanced as far as Volaterræ, and gained a hardly won victory under the walls of that city. It is only certain that this year was really marked by no great successes on the part of the Romans; on the contrary, they looked forward to the next campaign with great anxiety, and therefore[32] they pressed Q. Fabius to accept the consulship, notwithstanding his advanced age, and although he was not legally eligible, as ten years had not elapsed since he was consul before. It was in vain that he remonstrated; a dispensation,[33] according to a practice afterwards so frequent, was passed in his favor; and the people proceeded to elect him. He then entreated of them that he

[28] Livy, X. 11.

[29] The sarcophagus which contained the bones of L. Cornelius Scipio was discovered in 1780, and is now in the Vatican Museum. The epitaph is as follows, written in the old Saturnian verse:

"Cornelius Lucius Scipio Barbatus Gnaivod
Patre prognatus fortis vir sapiensque
Quoius forma virtutei parisuma fuit,
Consol censor aidilis quei fuit apud vos,
Taurasia Cisauna Samnio cepit
Subigit omne Loucana opsidesque abdoucit."

"Gnaivod" in the first line would, in modern Latin, be "Cnæo," and "quoius" in the third line is "cujus." I have copied the inscription from Bunsen and Platner's "Beschreibung Roms," Vol. III. p. 616. It may be found also in Orelli's Collection of Inscriptions, No. 550, and an engraving of the sarcophagus, exhibiting also the epitaph, is given in the Gentleman's Magazine for April, 1787.

[30] Livy, X. 12.

[31] See the stories in Frontinus, Strategem, I. 6, § 1, 2, and I. 11, § 2, already referred to by Niebuhr. But the authority of the particular anecdotes contained in such collections as that of Frontinus is but small, and it is not in itself to be set in comparison with that of any moderately careful historian. In the present instance the anecdotes are curious, as showing how many different versions of the same events were in circulation, as long as no real historian existed to sift them all, and to choose the truest or the most probable; but they do not appear to me to be entitled to any peculiar credit.

[32] Livy, X. 13.

[33] "Tribuni plebis . . . aiebant, se ad populum laturos ut legibus solveretur."—Livy, X. 13. Legibus solvi is the regular expression used when any one has a dispensation granted him, to release him from complying with the enactments of some particular law.

might recommend to them P. Decius as his colleague: Decius and himself, he said, had been censors together, and there was no man with whom he could act so well as consul. Accordingly, Q. Fabius and P. Decius were elected together: L. Scipio, the consul of the preceding year, served[34] under Fabius as his lieutenant, and a Fulvius[35] and a Valerius are named amongst his military tribunes.

Second campaign. Destructive invasion of Samnium by Q. Fabius and P. Decius.

At this moment, when the Romans expected to be assailed by the whole force of the enemies' confederacy, they found it suddenly paralyzed. Etruria for some reason or other was not ready to act,[36] and the Roman frontier on that side might be safely left without an army. Accordingly, both consuls marched into Samnium,[37] Fabius by Sora and the upper Liris, Decius by the country of the Sidicinians and the line of the Vulturnus. Fabius was met by the main Samnite army, which he defeated after a most obstinate battle; while Decius had encountered the Apulians near Beneventum on their march to join their allies, and defeated them also. The Samnites then acted on the defensive, and were obliged to suffer their country to be laid waste without opposition. Both of the Roman armies remained in Samnium, it is said, for five months,[38] moving about from one part of it to another, and carrying on their ravages so systematically, that Decius was recorded to have encamped his legions in forty-five several places, and Fabius in as many as eighty-six. But the Samnites must have driven their cattle to their mountain pastures, and many of these were so surrounded by forests, and so fenced round with precipitous cliffs, that a small force could have defended them with success against an army. The low country,[39] however, was no doubt grievously wasted, and the Romans must have found plunder enough to encourage them to continue their invasion. Towards the end of the year Fabius returned to Rome to hold the comitia; after which he resumed his command, and both he and his colleague were ordered to remain in Samnium[40] for six months longer, with the title and power of proconsul.

Lucania and Apulia recovered to the Roman alliance.

It was probably in this winter that the Samnite influence in Lucania and Apulia was completely overthrown, and both those countries returned to the Roman alliance. In both the aristocratical party was of itself eager to re-establish this connection; and the presence of two Roman armies, and the inability of the Samnites to keep the field against them, destroyed the ascendency of the popular party,[41] and changed accordingly the foreign relations of the whole people. It was now too, it seems, that L. Scipio, as lieutenant of the proconsul, Q. Fabius, had so great a share in effecting the revolution in Lucania, as to be able to boast, in the words of his

[34] Livy, X. 14. "Fabius . . . Scipionem legatum hastatos primæ legionis subtrahere . . . jubet."

[35] Livy, X. 14. The reading in the modern editions of Livy is "M. Fulvium et M. Valerium," but most of the MSS. read "Maximum Fulvium," and Niebuhr observes that Maximus was a surname of the Fulvian family, as appears from the Fasti Capitolini. It is probable that the military tribunes here spoken of were the sons respectively of Cn. Fulvius and of M. Valerius, who had been consuls in 454 and 456.

[36] "Ab Sutrio et Nepete et Faleriis legati, auctores concilia Etruriæ populorum de petendâ pace haberi."—Livy, X. 14. This perpetual vacillation in the Etruscan counsels arose no doubt from the balanced state of their domestic parties. If any difficulty arose in obtaining the expected aid from the Gauls, the Cilnii of Arretium, and other friends of the Roman connection, would urge the danger of opposing Rome single-handed, and would advise delay; and fear and weakness, counterfeiting prudence, would easily be tempted to listen to them.

[37] Livy, X. 14.

[38] Livy, X. 15. The circumstantial statement of the number of encampments in this campaign deserves credit; and the account of Fabius' victory is moderate and probable.

[39] In the former war the consuls of the year 448 had ravaged Samnium during five months, burning all the scattered houses, and destroying the fruit-trees. Diodorus, XX. 80. But no enemy could have penetrated within the rocky walls of the Matese, and many other spots must have been equally secure.

[40] Livy, X. 16.

[41] "Lucanorum seditiones a plebeiis et agentibus ducibus ortas summâ optimatium voluntate per Q. Fabium proconsulem, missum eo cum vetere exercitu, compresserat."—Livy, X. 18. Nothing is mentioned of the Apulians after their defeat at Beneventum; but as they do not appear again as the allies of the Samnites, it is probable that they followed the example of the Lucanians, and returned in this winter to their old connection with Rome.

epitaph, that he had "subdued all Lucania and carried off hostages." The hostages would be demanded from the principal families of the popular or Samnite party, as a security that they should not again excite their countrymen to revolt from Rome.

Revival of the war in Etruria.

Thus having recovered Lucania and Apulia, having overrun Samnium without resistance during several months, and having succeeded apparently, through the influence of their party in the Etruscan cities, in separating Etruria from the coalition, the Romans thought that their work was done; the two proconsular armies marched home and were disbanded, and the consuls of the year, L. Volumnius and App. Claudius, after having hitherto remained quiet at Rome, were ordered to march with their newly raised legions[42] into Samnium, as if to receive the final submission of their exhausted enemy. But scarcely had the consuls left the city, when tidings came that the cities of Etruria were in arms,[43] that several of the Umbrian states had joined them, that they were engaging the services of a large force of Gaulish auxiliaries; and that a Samnite general, with a Samnite army, was in the midst of this mass of enemies, to cement their union, and to breathe into their counsels a new spirit of decision and energy.

March of Gellius Egnatius from Samnium into Etruria, to organize the war against Rome.

There is no finer scene in history than the embassy of Demosthenes to Thebes, when Philip had occupied Elatea. Triumphing alike over all old prejudices and all present fears, the great orator, almost in the very presence of the Macedonian army, and in spite of the influence of a strong Macedonian party in Thebes itself, prevailed upon the Thebans to throw themselves into the arms of Athens, and to share her fortune for life or for death in her contest against the common enemy of independent Greece. Most unlike to this action of Demosthenes in glory, yet not inferior to it in vigorous resolution, was the march of the Samnite general, Gellius Egnatius, into Etruria, in order by his presence to determine the wavering counsels of the Etruscans to a zealous co-operation against Rome. Seizing the moment when the proconsuls had left Samnium, and the new consuls had not yet taken the field, he fearlessly abandoned his own country to the attacks of the enemy, and with a select army, marched through the land of the Sabines into Umbria, and fron thence crossing the Tiber, arrived in the heart of Etruria. His sudden appearance raised the spirits of the friends of the Samnite alliance, and struck terror into the Cilnii and the party attached to Rome. The Etruscans resolved to renew the war, and, as we have seen, many of the Umbrian states and an army of Gauls were expected to join them.

Third campaign. Both consuls in Etruria. The Samnites invade Campania.

On the first tidings of this march of the Samnite general, the senate sent orders to Appius Claudius to follow him without delay. Appius, with the first and fourth Roman legions and 12,000 allies, was probably on his march towards the northern parts of Samnium, by the Latin road and the upper valley of the Liris, and thus could be sent into Etruria more readily than his colleague, who, we may suppose, had marched by the Appian Road to attack the southern frontier of Samnium from Campania. Appius hastened into Etruria,[44] and the appearance of a Roman army at first revived the hopes of the partisans of Rome: but one consul was unequal to the combined forces of the enemy, and L. Volumnius was obliged to evacuate Samnium also, and hasten to join his colleague. No sooner was the whole force of

[42] The accounts which Livy followed represent the proconsuls as being still in Samnium when the new consuls took the field, X. 18. But Niebuhr observes that his narrative contradicts itself, for the legions raised by the consuls are expressly said to have been the 1st, 2d, 3d, and 4th, as usual; whereas, had two consular armies been under arms at that time, the new legions must have been the 5th, 6th, 7th, and 8th. Besides, some of the annals reported that Appius Claudius and Volumnius both carried on war in Samnium (Livy, X. 17, ad finem); and it is not likely, as Niebuhr remarks, that four armies should have been employed before the war broke out in Etruria, and that two of them should then have been disbanded, just when their services were most needful.

[43] Livy, X. 18.

[44] Livy, X. 18.

Rome thus employed in Etruria, than the Samnites took the field with the forces which had been left to defend their own county, and burst into Campania.[45] There they laid waste not only the lands of the allies of Rome, but of all those Roman citizens who had obtained settlements in the Falernian district, and composed the Falerian tribe.

The march of Gellius Egnatius had thus completely attained its object; Samnium was wholly relieved, and the war was carried into the actual territory of Rome. Even the mere suddenness of this change was enough to increase its terrors; the Roman government ordered all legal business to be suspended,[46] and troops to be raised for the defence of the city; nor were the levies confined to the military age, or to free-born commons of the country tribes, but citizens above five-and-forty, and even freedmen of the four city tribes, were enrolled in the legions raised to meet the emergency. All these measures were directed in the absence of the consuls by P. Sempronius Sophus, the prætor. Meanwhile L. Volumnius had received intelligence of the invasion of Campania, and was hastening back from Etruria to his own province. It is apparent from the stories which have been preserved of the meeting of the two consuls in Etruria, that there was no harmony between them; and thus the public service was likely to suffer the less from the division of their forces. We may believe also, that their junction for a time had revived the Roman interest in the Etruscan cities; and we may admit, not indeed the account given by Livy of a complete victory won over the Etruscan and Samnite armies, but that some advantages were gained[47] which saved Appius from his perilous situation, and enabled his colleague to leave him when a still more pressing danger called him into Campania. Volumnius marched with the utmost rapidity, and on his reaching the scene of action, he obliged the Samnites instantly to retreat into their own country, and overtaking a party of them on their way, he defeated them with considerable loss,[48] and recovered a great portion of the spoil which they were carrying with them. This gleam of success was most welcome to the Romans; the usual course of business was resumed, after having been suspended for eighteen days, and a thanksgiving was ordered in the name of the consul for the favor which the gods had shown to the commonwealth under his auspices.

Alarm at Rome. The consul Volumnius marches back from Etruria to deliver Campania.

Still, however, the aspect of affairs was most critical. In order to protect the Falernian district from the ravages of the Samnites, it was resolved that two Roman colonies should be planted there; one at Minturnæ[49] at the mouth of the Liris, and the other at Sinuessa, on the hills which divide the waters running to the Liris from those that feed the Savone. But settlements in this quarter were considered so insecure, and so exposed to perpetual ravages from the Samnites, that few were willing to accept a grant of land on such terms. As the consular elections drew near, L. Volumnius was recalled from Campania to hold the comitia; and the unanimous voice of the people again called upon Q. Fabius to accept the office of consul. He again yielded to the general wish, but begged, as before, that P. Decius might be his colleague; and Decius was accordingly elected consul with him.[50] Appius Claudius, who was still with his army in Etruria, was appointed prætor, and L. Volumnius had his command prolonged for another year as proconsul. L. Cornelius Scipio, who had served under Fabius in his last consulship, Cn. Fulvius, who had been consul in the year 456, and had conducted the first campaign of this war in Samnium, together with L. Postumius Megel-

Great preparations for the ensuing campaign. Q. Fabius and P. Decius again chosen consuls.

[45] Livy, X. 20.

[46] Livy, X. 21.

[47] In the midst of the battle, Appius vowed to build a temple to Bellona, if the goddess would grant him victory; and this temple was afterwards built. See Orelli, Inscript. Latinar. Collect. No. 539. This may be taken as evidence that Appius repulsed the enemy and saved his own army, but it by no means proves that he won a decided victory. We have only to remember Coruña and Albuhera.

[48] Livy, X. 20, 21.

[49] Livy, X. 21.

[50] Livy, X. 22-26.

lus, were appointed also to commands in this great campaign, with the title of proprætors.

A. U. C. 459. B. C. 295. Reported omens of the fate of the war.

The anxiety occasioned by the impending contest may be measured by the particular accounts of prodigies and their expiations which were to be found in the annals of this year. From the altar[51] of the temple of the Capitoline Jupiter there flowed for three successive days, so said the annals, first blood, then honey, and on the third day milk. The blood was interpreted as a sign that the blood of thank-offerings for victory should soon stream on the altar of Jupiter, but the favors of the gods would not be unmixed; for honey was the medicine of the sick, and foreshowed a heavy visitation of sickness: milk was the food of those whose corn had failed them, and was the sign of a coming famine. To avert the threatened anger of the gods, and to confirm them in their promised favor, solemn prayers[52] were ordered to be offered during two whole days; and frankincense and wine were furnished to every one at the public expense, that the prayers might be universal and unceasing.

App. Claudius in Etruria. Winter march of Fabius to relieve him.

The consuls at this time came into office about the beginning of the year; and as the snow was still thick on the Apennines, the Gauls could not yet take the field to march into Etruria, and the campaign would not be opened till the spring. But the position of Appius Claudius in the enemy's country was exceedingly perilous; and he himself, in the opinion of Fabius, was scarcely equal to the difficulties of his situation. Accordingly, Fabius himself, having raised[53] a small force of 4000 foot and 600 horse, out of a great multitude who were eager to serve under so renowned a general, set out at once for Etruria. He found Appius Claudius busily employed in strengthening the fortifications of his camp, and the soldiers from thus acting solely on the defensive were dispirited, and mistrusted both themselves and their general. Fabius ordered them to level their fortifications; and having sent Appius home, he took the command of the army in person, and kept it continually in movement, marching rapidly from place to place, and restoring to the men their accustomed feeling of confidence. He then stationed one division[54] in the country of the Camertian Umbrians, the allies of the Romans, to observe the pass by which the Gauls were likely to cross the Apennines, apparently that of La Scheggia on the Flaminian road, descending on Nocera and Foligno. This was placed under the command of L. Scipio; while Fabius himself returned to Rome to concert measures with his colleague for the operations of the approaching spring.

Forces of the Romans and their allies employed in active operations.

Two consular armies[55] were destined to take the field, consisting each of two Roman legions, and an unusually large force of Roman cavalry; together with 500 Campanian cavalry, and a force of allies still larger than that of the Romans themselves. Amongst the allies were undoubtedly the Lucanians[56] and Campanians, and in all probability the Marsians, Pelignians, Marrucinians, and Vestinians, as well as the contingents of the colonies founded in the late war, and those of the still independent cities of the Latins. All the forces of the Picentians which could be spared from the defence of their own country, as well as those of the Camertians, were employed, we may suppose, with the army of L. Scipio, watching the movements of the enemy in Umbria.

Their armies of reserve.

Whilst this large force, consisting at least of between fifty and sixty thousand men, was to take the field in the north, two more Roman legions, with a proportionate number of allies, were to invade Samnium[57]

[51] Zonaras, VIII. 1.
[52] Livy, X. 23.
[53] Livy, X. 25.
[54] Livy, X. 25.
[55] Livy, X. 26.

[56] The Lucanians are mentioned as among the regular allies of the Romans, and quartered within the consuls' camp, in the year immediately following.—See Livy, X. 33.
[57] Livy, X. 27.

under L. Volumnius as proconsul. A third army, under Cn. Fulvius as proprætor,[58] was to be stationed as a reserve in the Faliscan territory, at once to defend the passage of the Tiber, and preserve the communications of the main army with Rome; and also to create a diversion, if opportunity should offer, by acting on the offensive against Etruria. And lastly, a fourth army, commanded by L. Postumius Megellus,[59] also proprætor, was to be encamped in the Vatican district, on the right bank of the Tiber, to cover Rome itself.

L. Scipio's division is defeated by the Gauls and Samnites.

This account of the dispositions of the Romans is clear and perfectly credible; but, unfortunately, we are left in total ignorance as to the numbers, movements, and position of the enemy. Why the Etruscans and Samnites did not crush Scipio's army, even before the arrival of the Gauls, we can scarcely understand, unless we suppose that party struggles again paralyzed the force of the Etruscans, and kept it in inactivity under a show of caution, till the whole army of the alliance should be assembled. At last the Gauls commenced their movement before the consuls had left Rome; they hastened to force the passage of the Apennines, and no sooner had they arrived on the scene of war than they began to act in earnest. L. Scipio's army[60] was attacked by the Gauls and Samnites, and completely defeated; one legion, it is said, was cut to pieces; the rest of his division took shelter, probably, within some of the neighboring towns, and the Gaulish horsemen overrunning the country, fell in suddenly with the two consular armies, which had now taken the field, and first acquainted them with the defeat of their countrymen, by exhibiting the heads of the slain Romans affixed to their long lances, or hanging round the necks of their horses.

The Etruscans and Umbrians leave their allies. The Gauls and Samnites retreat behind the Apennines.

Exactly at this critical point of the campaign, Livy's narrative fails us, and all that passed between the destruction of the legion and the final battle at Sentinum is a total blank; it is as much loss to us as a country travelled over during the night; we were in one sort of scenery yesterday, and we find ourselves in another this morning; each is distinct in itself, but we know not the connection between them. Earnestly must Gellius Egnatius have labored to bring on a decisive battle in the plains of Umbria; the allies had begun the campaign with happy omens, their whole force was united, the ground was favorable; nothing could be gained, and every thing would be hazarded by delay. But whether the fault rested once again with the Etruscans, or whether the Picentians caused a timely diversion, by threatening to invade the country of the Gauls, or whether the consuls fell back upon Spoletum, and were able to avoid an action for the moment, we know not. But they sent orders to the proprætors, Cn. Fulvius and L. Postumius, to advance into the heart of Etruria, and no sooner did the tidings of this movement reach the enemy's army, than the Etruscans and Umbrians insisted on marching to the defence of the Etruscan territory, and the Gauls and Samnites, indignant at their desertion, and refusing to follow them, had no choice themselves but to fall back behind the Apennines, and to resign their hopes of a victorious march upon Rome.

The Romans follow them. The two armies meet at Sentinum.

The Romans pursued them instantly, with two consular armies certainly, and with the wreck of L. Scipio's division; perhaps also with the two legions of L. Volumnius, which may have been recalled from Samnium. They found the enemy in the country of Sentinum, an Umbrian town on the north side of the Apennines,[61] just under the central chain, in a

[58] Livy. X. 27.

[59] Livy, X. 27.

[60] Livy, X. 26. Polybius, II. 19. We learn from Polybius, that the Samnites were engaged in this action as well as the Gauls, and that it was not a surprise, but a regular battle, *παρετάξαντε Ῥωμαίοις*. It was fought in the country of the Camertians, or people of Camerinum, perhaps near the point where the modern road from Ancona to Rome crosses the Apennines to descend upon Foligno.

[61] The ancient Sentinum stood on or near the site of the modern town of Sassoferrato, as is known by inscriptions which have been discovered there. See Orelli, Nos. 3861 and 4949. But I have no good information as to the details of the topography.

small valley which runs down into the larger valley of the Æsis or Esino, and not far on the right hand of the Flaminian road, at the point where it crosses the watershed of the mountains. It was of the utmost importance to the Roman generals to bring the contest to an issue whilst they had only the Gauls and Samnites to encounter, and in this they easily succeeded, for the Gauls had never yet fought the Romans without conquering them, and Gellius Egnatius knew enough of the inconstant humor of barbarians to be aware that they would soon be tired of a protracted war, and that if the Gauls too deserted him, his heroic march from Samnium would have been made in vain. So the two armies met by common consent in fair field; Q. Fabius was on the Roman right, opposed to Gellius Egnatius and his Samnites;[62] P. Decius was on the left over against the Gauls. If L. Volumnius was present with the legions from Samnium, he probably, like Cn. Servilius at Cannæ, who had also been consul in the year before the battle, had his place in the centre. The Samnites could not alone have contended with Q. Fabius, whose right wing was equal to a regular consular army; and the Gauls must have been more than enough to overpower P. Decius. It is probable, therefore, that the Gauls composed the greater part of the enemy's line of battle, and that only the extreme left was held by Gellius Egnatius and his Samnites.

A favorable omen encourages the Romans.

While the two armies fronted each other, and were on the very eve of battle, a hind,[63] said the Roman story, came running down from the mountains between the two opposing lines, with a wolf in chase of her. She ran in amongst the Gaulish ranks, and the Gauls transfixed her with their long javelins. The wolf ran towards the Romans, and they instantly gave free passage to the beast which had given suck to the founder of their city; and whose image they had only in the preceding year[64] set up beneath that very sacred fig-tree in the comitium, which tradition pointed out as the scene of the miracle. "See," cried out one of the soldiers, "Diana's sacred hind has been slain by the barbarians, and will bring down her wrath upon them; while the Roman wolf, unhurt by sword or spear, gives us a fair omen of victory, and bids us think on Mars and on Quirinus, our divine founder." So the Roman soldiers, as encouraged by a sign from the gods, rushed cheerfully to the onset.

Battle of Sentinum.

This story, with some other circumstances related of the battle itself, are blended strangely with the perfectly historical substance of the general narrative. When the armies closed,[65] the Roman left wing struggled vigorously against the numbers, and strength, and courage of the Gauls. Twice, it is said, did the Roman and Campanian cavalry charge with effect the Gaulish horsemen; but in their second charge they were encountered by a force wholly strange to them, the war chariots of the enemy, which broke in upon them at full speed, and with the rattling of their wheels, and their unwonted appearance, so startled the horses of the Romans, that they could not be brought to face them, and horses and men fled in confusion. Uncouth and almost ridiculous as these chariots may seem to our notions, yet a force which terrified Cæsar's veterans, and which that great master of war speaks of as formidable, could not have been ridiculous in reality; and the undoubted effect of the British chariots against the legions of Cæsar, may well convince us that the Gaulish chariots at Sentinum must have struck terror into the soldiers of Decius.

P. Decius devotes himself to death.

The Roman cavalry were driven back upon their infantry; the first line of the legions was broken, and the Gauls, following their advantage, pressed on with the masses of their infantry. Decius strove in vain to stop the flight of his soldiers; one way alone was left by which he might yet serve his country; he bethought him of his father at the battle by Vesuvius, and calling to M. Livius, one of the pontifices who attended him in the field, he desired him to dictate to him the fit words for self-devotion. Then, in the same

[62] Livy, X. 27.
[63] Livy, X. 27.
[64] Livy, X. 23.
[65] Livy, X. 27, 28.

dress, and with all the same ceremonies, he pronounced also the same form of words which had been uttered by his father, and devoting himself and the host of the enemy with him to the grave and to the powers of the dead, he rode into the midst of the Gaulish ranks and was slain.

The Gauls resist obstinately.

His last act as consul had been to invest the pontifex M. Livius[66] with the command of his legions as proprætor, and to order his lictors to follow the new general. Fabius also, learning the danger of his colleague, had sent two of his own lieutenants, L. Scipio and C. Marcius, to his aid, with reinforcements drawn from his own reserve; and thus the flight of the Romans was stayed, while the manner of Decius' death encouraged rather than dismayed his soldiers, as they believed that it was the price paid for their victory. But the Gauls, though checked, were yet neither beaten nor disheartened; they gathered into thick masses, with their huge shields covering almost their whole bodies, and wielding their heavy broadswords, they stood unbroken and unassailed; till the Romans picked up from the field of battle the javelins which had been discharged earlier in the action, and with these missiles endeavored to wear down the mass of their enemies. The pila pierced through the wooden shields of the Gauls, encumbering them, even when they inflicted no wound; but the Gauls stood as firm as the "Scottish circle deep" under the hail of the English arrows at Flodden; and no efforts of the left wing of the Romans could secure the victory.

Fabius defeats the Samnites, and at last forces the Gauls to give way. Complete victory of the Romans.

Meanwhile, Fabius,[67] on the right, after a long and arduous contest with the Samnites, and finding that his infantry could not break them, at last succeeded in charging their flank with his cavalry, and at the same moment bringing all his reserves of infantry into action, he assailed their line in front, and decided the victory. The Samnites fled to their camp, and thus left exposed the flank of the Gauls, who were still maintaining their ground. Fabius saw his opportunity, and detached the Campanian cavalry, with the principes of the third legion, to attack the Gauls in the rear; while he himself closely pursued the Samnites, and vowed aloud that if he won the day, he would build a temple and offer all the spoils of the enemy to Jupiter the victorious. The Samnites rallied under the ramparts of their camp, and still disputed the victory; but the Gauls, assailed on all sides, were now hopelessly broken, and the last hope of the Samnites vanished, when their commander, Gellius Egnatius, fell. Still, when the day was utterly lost, these brave men would neither surrender nor disperse; they left the field in a body, and immediately began their retreat to their own country.

Loss on both sides.

The Roman accounts of this bloody battle[68] state the loss of their enemies at 25,000 killed, and 8000 prisoners: their own they make to have amounted to 8200 killed; but they give no report of the number of wounded. Of the total loss, only 1200 are said to have fallen in the right wing, while in the army of Decius there were killed 7000. The great slaughter in ancient warfare always took place when the line of battle was broken; and the disparity of loss on the two wings of the Roman army is therefore such as might have been expected.

Operations in Etruria.

Meanwhile, Cn. Fulvius[69] had, according to his instructions, penetrated into Etruria; and had not only laid waste a large tract of country, but had defeated in the field an army sent out by the two cities of Perusia and Clusium to check his ravages.

[66] Livy, X. 29.

[67] Livy, X. 29.

[68] Livy, X. 29. Duris of Samos, a contemporary writer, but whose information of these events could come only from common report, and who delighted to exaggerate the disasters of the Gauls, related that in the Gaulish and Samnite army 100,000 men had fallen.—See Diodorus, XXI. Frag. Hoeschel. p. 490. Duris supposed that the Etruscans were engaged in the battle; and some of the Roman writers gave the same account, and made the allied army to consist of a million of men.—See Niebuhr, Vol. III., note 647.

[69] Livy, X. 30.

It is quite plain that the Etruscans were at this time suffering the full evil of distracted counsels, and that they were neither unanimous for peace nor for war. What was become of the forces of Arretium, of Volaterræ, of Russellæ, of Cortona, and of Vulsinii, when Clusium and Perusia were left to resist the Roman invasion alone?

The body of Decius[70] was found under a heap of slaughtered Gauls, and honorably buried. Fabius celebrated his funeral, and pronounced his funeral oration; a fit tribute from one who had been twice his colleague in the consulship and once in the censorship; nor had any man enjoyed better opportunities of knowing his excellence. He had proved his skill and courage in war, and his wisdom and moderation in peace; and he had experienced also the noble frankness of his nature, which never allowed any selfish jealousy to stand in the way of his private friendship, and much less of his devotion to his country's service.

Funeral of Decius.

Such was the great battle of Sentinum, the Austerlitz of the third Samnite war. But as more than eighteen months elapsed between the battle of Austerlitz and the peace of Tilsit, so neither was the coalition against Rome dissolved at once by the victory of Sentinum. The Gauls, indeed, remained quiet after their defeat, for their interest in the war was only that of mercenary soldiers, and they were not tempted to a service which seemed likely to bring with it more loss than profit. But even Etruria would not yet submit to Rome, and the Samnites, hoping still to keep the war at a distance from their own country, were eager to renew the contest.

The Gauls cannot be induced to serve again against Rome.

Yet the Romans could not but feel great relief from their victory. The armies of the proprætors, Cn. Fulvius and L. Postumius, were recalled to Rome[71] and disbanded; and Fabius marched into Etruria with his consular army, and was strong enough to obtain fresh advantages over the Perusians, who alone of all the Etruscan people ventured, it seems, to meet the Romans in the field. He then returned to Rome, and triumphed on the 4th of September over the three principal powers of the late coalition, the Etruscans, the Gauls, and the Samnites; and the soldiers who followed his chariot, in the rude verses which they were accustomed to utter on such occasions, commemorated the death of Decius as fully equal in glory to their own general's safe and victorious return. It is mentioned[72] that each soldier received out of the spoil taken in the late battle, eighty-two *ases*, and a coat, and military cloak; "rewards," says Livy, sadly feeling how whole districts of Italy had in his days been portioned out amongst the legions of Augustus, "which the soldiers of those times did not think despicable."

Triumph of Fabius.

The wreck of the Samnite army,[73] still, it is said, amounting to 5000 men, made its way unhurt or unopposed through the countries of the Picentians and Vestinians, and from thence proceeded towards Samnium through the country of the Pelignians, by Sulmo and the Five-mile plain to the valley of the Sagrus or Sangro. The Pelignians, more zealous in the quarrel, because they were nearer neighbors to the Samnites, and their lands, no doubt, had often suffered from Samnite incursions, endeavored to cut off the retreating army. But the Samnites, with some loss, beat off this new enemy, and entered their own country in safety.

The Samnite army forces its way back to Samnium.

[70] Livy, X. 29.

[71] This appears from the circumstance that Fabius marched into Etruria and engaged the Perusians; which shows that Cn. Fulvius must have already been recalled, and also because App. Claudius, the prætor, was ordered to support L. Volumnius in Samnium with the remains of the army of Decius: had the proprætor's armies been still embodied, one of them would probably have been employed on that service. I have followed Niebuhr in placing Fabius' victories over the Perusians before his triumph, whereas Livy makes him march back to Etruria after his triumph. But, as Niebuhr says, his army would be disbanded as a matter of course after his triumph, and the Fasti Capitolini say that he triumphed over the Etruscans, as well as the Samnites and Gauls; which he could not have done had he only triumphed for his victory at Sentinum, as no Etruscans were engaged there.

[72] Livy, X. 30.

[73] Livy, X. 30.

It is manifest that during this year Samnium enjoyed a complete respite from invasion; and that L. Volumnius, even if we suppose that he was not called away to the great seat of war in Umbria, was not a match for the Samnite forces opposed to him.

Operations in Samnium and Campania during this campaign.

His defeat of a Samnite army which had taken refuge in the Matese is entitled to no credit whatever; on the contrary, we find that the Samnites again invaded the Roman territory in two different directions;[74] that one army descended into the districts of Formiæ and Vescia, and another laid waste the banks of the Vulturnus apparently where it first issues out on the plain of Campania. After the battle of Sentinum, the legions of Decius were recalled from Etruria, and put under the command of Appius Claudius, the prætor, and he and L. Volumnius, acting together with their two armies, obliged the Samnites to retreat within their frontier. But as the Etruscans had not yet made peace with Rome, the Samnites were not discouraged, and trusted that another year might enable them to retrieve their defeat at Sentinum.

The events of the next year, however, are involved in such confusion that it is impossible to disentangle them. L. Postumius Megellus, one of the proprætors of the year before, was now consul, and M. Atilius Regulus was his colleague. The seat of war was again transferred to Apulia,[75] where the Samnites, well understanding the importance of acting on the offensive, laid siege to Luceria. Here there was fought a bloody and indecisive battle, in which the Romans were in such danger that the consul vowed to build a temple to Jove, the stayer of flight, if his army were saved from total rout. At the end of the campaign the Roman army wintered at Interamna,[76] in the valley of the Liris, to save that country from the ravages of the enemy; and the consul returned to Rome to hold the comitia. His colleague had been recalled from Samnium earlier in the season to carry on the war in Etruria; and this he did, according to the Roman accounts, with such success,[77] that Vulsinii, Perusia, and Arretium sued for peace, and obtained a truce for forty years. But which consul it was who fought at Luceria, and which had marched into Etruria, the annalists did not know, and therefore guessed variously.[78] Some accounts went so far as to say that both consuls triumphed;[79] but most said that only one obtained that honor, and again they did not agree in determining which consul it was. It is probable that neither of the consuls triumphed; nor does it seem likely that the Romans obtained any advantages in this year, except, perhaps, over the ever-restless but ever-vacillating and divided Etruscans. The Samnites, therefore, resolved to try their fortune once again.

A. U. C. 460. A. C. 294. Fifth campaign The Romans obtain no advantages in it.

The next year was undoubtedly marked by great successes on the side of the Romans; but its history is still uncertain in the details, and much of the geography of the campaign is wholly inexplicable. The consuls were L. Papirius Cursor, son of that Papirius who had

A. U. C. 461. A. C. 293. Sixth campaign. Consulship of L. Papirius and Sp. Carvilius.

[74] Livy, X. 31. He describes the scene of the Samnite inroad in these words, "in Æserninum quæque Vulturno adjacent flumini." The word which, in the modern editions of Livy, is printed as "Æserninum" varies, however, in the MSS. greatly. Æsernia, in Samnium, seems out of the question, for it was only in the beginning of the first Punic war that the Romans planted a colony there; unless we suppose that portions of its domain had already been ceded to the Romans in the second Samnite war, which, however, considering how deep the city lies in the heart of Samnium, seems improbable.

[75] Livy, X. 35.

[76] Livy, X. 36.

[77] Livy, X. 37.

[78] Livy says that Atilius fought at Luceria, and Postumius marched into Etruria. Claudius Quadrigarius, as quoted by Livy, maintained exactly the contrary; and Fabius, whose narrative of this war seems to have depended chiefly on the memoirs of the Fabian family, and to have become uncertain where they failed him, did not venture to say which it was.—See Livy, X. 37.

[79] Fasti Capitolini.—Livy says that Atilius did not triumph, but that Postumius did, by his own authority, without the sanction of the senate. But this story is referred by Dionysius to Postumius' third consulship three years afterwards; and Claudius said that Postumius never triumphed at all. It does not appear that the narrative of Fabius gave a triumph to either of them.—Livy, X. 37.

Orosius' description of the events of this year is far nearer the truth, I think, than the account of Livy. "Sequitur annus quo Romani instaurato a Samnitibus bello victi sunt, atque in castra fugerunt." III. 22.

been so famous in the second Samnite war, and Sp. Carvilius Maximus. Carvilius took the command[80] of the army which had wintered near Interamna, on the Liris; Papirius commanded two new legions, and both consuls were ordered to invade Samnium.

Desperate resolution of the Samnites.

The Samnites, on their part, are said to have raised an army with unusual care, and to have bound their soldiers by the most solemn oaths, taken amidst the most mysterious and horrid ceremonies, that they would either conquer or die. The men thus pledged were arrayed in a peculiar manner, with waving plumes on their helmets, and with coats of white linen, exactly as had been done fifteen years before, when the old Papirius, the father of the present consul, was appointed dictator to encounter them; and the repetition of these same ceremonies by the Samnites now made the Romans, for the omen's sake, appoint another Papirius Cursor to be consul; as if the Papirian family[81] was chosen by the gods to meet and to overcome the most desperate efforts of their Samnite enemies.

They retain their hold on the country of the Sabines.

It was no doubt the failure of all co-operation in Etruria, and the knowledge, therefore, that they would have to withstand the whole force of Rome, which led the Samnites to apply these extraordinary excitements to the courage of their soldiers. Yet it seems as if they had not abandoned all hopes of Etruscan aid, and that they had learned from their enemies the wisdom of acting on the offensive; for the first operations of the Roman armies were the capture of Amiternum,[82] and the ravaging of the country of Atina. This seat of war implies that the Samnites still obstinately retained their line of communication with Etruria amidst all the invasions of their own country, and with this view still held fast to their alliance those Sabine and Volscian cities which, at the beginning of the coalition, had been forced or persuaded to espouse their cause.

And ravage Campania.

A Samnite army was also sent into Campania to ravage the territory[83] of the Romans and their allies on the Liris and Vulturnus, whilst another was kept in Samnium for home defence; and it was, perhaps, to the soldiers of this last army, consisting of the oldest and youngest men capable of bearing arms, that the excitements of enthusiasm were applied, to make up for their inferiority in strength and in experience.

Both the Roman consuls invade Samnium. Operations on the north of the Matese.

The Roman consuls[84] having jointly laid waste the territory of Atina, proceeded to enter Samnium. The seat of war lay apparently in the country of the Pentrian Samnites on the north of the Matese: Carvilius laid siege to Cominium: Papirius, after having taken Duronia, marched against Aquilonia, where the Samnite army was stationed; all these three places are quite unknown to us, and we can only conclude that they lay on the north side of the Matese, because two of them are described as being near to Bovianum, the site of which is known. The Samnites, attacked at once by two consular armies, were compelled to divide their forces; and eight thousand men were detached from the army before Aquilonia to relieve Cominium. A deserter acquainted Papirius with this movement, and he instantly sent off a messenger to warn his colleague, while he himself attacked the enemy at the moment when he knew their force to be thus untimely weakened. The auspices had been reported to be most favorable; "the fowls ate so eagerly," so said their keeper to the consul, "that some of the corn dropped from their mouths on the ground."[85] This was the best possible omen; but just as the consul was on the point of giving the signal for action, his nephew, Sp. Papirius, came to tell him that the

[80] Livy, X. 39.
[81] Livy, X. 38, 39.
[82] Livy, X. 39.
[83] Zonaras, VIII. 1.
[84] Livy, X. 39.
[85] "Pullarius auspicium mentiri ausus tripudium solistimum."—Livy, X. 40. "Quia quum pascuntur (aves) necesse est aliquid ex ore cadere et terram pavire, terripavium primo, post terripudium dictum est: hoc quidem jam tripudium dicitur. Quum igitur offa cecidit ex ore pulli, tum auspicanti tripudium solistimum nuntiant."—Cicero, de Divinat. II. 34.

keeper had made a false report. "Some of his comrades have declared the truth," said the young man: "and far from eating eagerly, the fowls would not touch their food at all." "Thou hast done thy duty, nephew, in telling me this," replied his uncle, "but let the keeper see to it if he has belied the gods. His report to me is, that the omens are most favorable, and therefore I forthwith give the signal for battle. But do you see," he added to some centurions who stood by, "that this keeper and his comrades be set in the front ranks of the legions." Ere the battle-cry was raised on either side, a chance javelin struck the guilty keeper, and he fell dead. His fate was instantly reported to the consul. "The gods," he exclaimed, "are amongst us; their vengeance has fallen on the guilty." While he spoke, a crow was heard just in front of him to utter a full and loud cry. "Never did the gods more manifestly declare their presence and favor," exclaimed the consul, and forthwith the signal was given, and the Roman battle-cry arose loud and joyful.

The Samnites met their enemies bravely;[86] but the awful rites under which they had been pledged gave them a gloomy rather than a cheerful courage; they were more in the mood to die than to conquer. On the Roman side, the consul's blunt humor, which he had inherited from his father, spread confidence all around him. In the heat of the battle, when other generals would have earnestly vowed to build a temple to the god whose aid they sought, if he would grant them victory, Papirius called aloud to Jupiter the victorious, "Ah, Jupiter,[87] if the enemy are beaten, I vow to offer to thee a cup of honeyed wine before I taste myself a drop of wine plain." Such irreverent jests do not necessarily imply a scoffing spirit; they mark superstition or fanaticism quite as much as unbelief; nor would the consul's language shock those who heard it, but rather assure them that he spoke in the full confidence of being heard with favor by the gods, as a man in hours of festivity would smile at the familiarity of an indulged servant. Besides, Papirius performed well the part of a general; he is said to have practised the trick which was so successful at Bannockburn;[88] the camp servants were mounted on the baggage mules, and appeared in the midst of the action on the flank and rear of the Samnites; the news ran through both armies, that Sp. Carvilius was come up to aid his colleague, and a general charge of the Roman cavalry and infantry at this moment broke the Samnite lines, and turned them to flight. The mass of the routed army fled either to their camp, or within the walls of Aquilonia; but the cavalry, containing all the chiefs and the nobility of the nation, got clear from the press of the fugitives, and escaped to Bovianum.

Victory gained by L. Papirius.

The Romans[89] followed up their victory, and stormed the Samnite camp, and scaled the walls of Aquilonia, which was abandoned by the enemy during the night. Carvilius meanwhile had taken Cominium, while the detachment sent to relieve it had been recalled to the main army when Papirius began his attack, and thus had wasted the day in marching backwards and forwards, without being present at either scene of action. These soldiers, however, having halted during the night in the neighborhood of Aquilonia, pursued their march the next day, and with a very trifling loss effected their retreat to Bovianum, which was now the common rallying point.

Successes of Sp. Carvilius.

Both Aquilonia[90] and Cominium were given up to be plundered by the conquerors, and were then set on fire. It was late in the season, (a circumstance which shows how imperfect are our accounts of these wars,) but the consuls having now no enemy in the field, wished

The consuls attack the Samnite towns on the east of the Matese.

[86] Livy, X. 41.

[87] "Voverat Jovi Victori, si legiones hostium fudisset, pocillum mulsi priusquam temetum biberet sese facturum." Livy, X. 42. Mulsum was "honeyed wine," a favorite beverage of the Romans in the early times; temetum, in the older Latin, was merely "wine." See Pliny, Hist. Natur. XIV. 13, § 90, Ed. Sillig.

[88] Livy, X. 40, 41.

[89] Livy, X. 41–43.

[90] Livy, X. 44, 45.

to follow up their blow, and to attack the several Samnite cities; a service most welcome to the soldiers, as it offered to them the prospect of plunder. Bovianum, however, was too strong to be attacked as yet; so the consuls moved on further into the heart of the country, and fixed the seat of war on the eastern side of the Matese. Here Papirius laid siege to Sæpinum, a place not far from the sources of the Tamarus, near the modern road from Benevento to Campobasso, the capital of Molise. Carvilius attacked a town, called variously in the MSS. of Livy, Vella, Velia, or Volana, but the position of which is altogether unknown.

Sp. Carvilius is recalled and sent into Etruria.

The tidings of these successes[91] were received at Rome with the greatest joy; and thanksgivings were offered for four days; the longest period of public rejoicings for victory which has been hitherto mentioned in the Roman annals. Just at this time, as we are told, there came complaints from the Roman allies on the Etruscan frontier, that is, we must suppose from the people of Sutrium, that the Etruscans were again in arms, and that the Faliscans, hitherto the allies of Rome, had now taken part with the enemy. It is vain to attempt to explain all these movements in Etruria; or to decide whether the Etruscans were tempted to renew the contest by the employment of both consuls in Samnium, or whether the Romans were encouraged by their victories there to take vengeance for past offences on the Etruscans. At any rate, the consuls were ordered to determine by lot which of them should march into Etruria; and the lot fell upon Carvilius. His soldiers were glad to go, it is said, because the cold of Samnium was becoming intolerable; but they had other reasons besides the cold, for wishing to change their seat of war; for whatever might be the plunder of the Samnite towns, it was not always to be easily won; and though Carvilius had taken three of them, yet it had been at the cost of two actions in the field, in which his own loss had exceeded that of the enemy. Papirius, on his side, was detained for a long time before Sæpinum; the Samnites made repeated sallies, and would not allow him even to form the siege of the place; and their resistance was so protracted, that when at last they were overpowered, and the town was taken, the winter was so far advanced, that any further operations were impracticable, and Papirius having, as we may suppose, burnt Sæpinum, evacuated Samnium.

Triumphs of both consuls.

The operations of Sp. Carvilius in Etruria[92] were short and successful; Troilium and some small mountain fortresses were taken, and the Faliscans purchased a truce for a year by the payment of 100,000 ases, and a year's pay to the soldiers of the Roman army. Both consuls enjoyed a splendid triumph;[93] and a very large treasure of copper and of silver was brought home by Papirius, and paid by him into the treasury, his victorious soldiers receiving nothing. Carvilius brought home also a large treasure; but he divided a part of it amongst his troops, and their pay had already been provided to them out of the contribution paid by the Faliscans; so that the ungracious conduct of Papirius was doubly odious,—for his soldiers received nothing from the plunder, and the war tax, or tributum, was made to furnish them with their pay; and thus his victories brought to the poorer citizens no relief from the burdens of war. The captured arms[94] were so numerous, that the allies and colonies of Rome received a large share to ornament their own cities; and Sp. Carvilius[95] made out of those which fell to his portion a colossal statue of Jupiter, of such magnitude, that when it was set up on the Capitoline Hill at Rome, it could be seen from the temple of the Latin Jupiter on the summit of the mountain of Alba; a distance in a straight line of not less than twelve English miles.

[91] Livy, X. 45.
[92] Livy, X. 46.
[93] Carvilius triumphed on the 13th of January, and Papirius on the 13th of February. Fasti Capitolini. The weight of silver taken from the temples and houses of the several cities of Samnium which had been captured amounted to 1330 lbs.; the copper money which had been obtained by the ransom or sale of the prisoners, amounted to 2,033,000 ases of full weight, that is, to so many pounds' weight of copper.
[94] Livy, X. 46.
[95] Pliny, Hist. Nat. XXXIV. § 43, Ed. Sillig.

After such an issue of this campaign, we read with astonishment that Papirius led back his army to winter in the neighborhood of Vescia,[96] because that country was still infested by the incursions of the Samnites. And in the next year we find, after a long interval, C. Pontius of Telesia once more at the head of the Samnite armies; we find him carrying on war in Campania, and again victorious. Austria lost five armies in the campaign of 1796, before she would consent to treat for peace; and when the French were besieging Cadiz, and had won almost all the fortresses of the kingdom, Spain still continued to resist, and the Guerillas often inflicted defeat upon their triumphant enemy. But the Samnite victory obtained over Fabius Gurges in Campania in the year immediately following the triumphs of Papirius and Carvilius, is more extraordinary than the fortitude either of Austria or Spain; and so far as the circumstances are known to us, it can only be paralleled by the triumphant career of the Vendeans in Bretagne, when, after repeated defeats in their own country, they effected their desperate expedition beyond the Loire.

C. Pontius again commands the Samnite armies.

We may ask why the Roman government, little apt to hold its hands till the work was fully done, and having nothing to fear on the side of Etruria, contented itself with sending a single consular army into the field in the year following the great victories of Papirius and Carvilius, instead of employing its whole force, and thus again overrunning the enemy's country. The reason, probably, is to be found in the severe visitation of pestilence which at this time fell upon Rome;[97] and this may further explain why the legions of Papirius wintered in Campania; for as such disorders are generally more or less local, an army might be in perfect health on the hills by Vescia, while, had it remained in or near Rome, it would have been losing men daily. However, the new consul, Q. Fabius Gurges,[98] son of the great Fabius, took the command of the army in Campania, and proceeded towards the frontiers of Samnium. C. Pontius Herennius, of whom nothing is known since the affair of the pass of Caudium, again commanded the Samnite army; whether it was that he was now called upon in the extreme danger of his country, as the only man capable of saving it, or whether the southern Samnites, or Caudinians, had in fact taken no part in the war for many years, and only now, when the Pentrians were nearly exhausted, came forward to uphold their cause.

A. U. C. 462. A. C. 292. Q. Fabius Gurges, the new consul, is sent alone to invade Samnium.

The ravages which the pestilence was at this time making in Rome encouraged the enemy;[99] and C. Pontius boldly invaded Campania. Q. Fabius, forgetting how formidable is the last struggle of the hunted lion, thought that to meet the Samnites was to conquer them; and when he fell in with some of their look-out parties, and they retired before him, he believed the whole Samnite army to be retreating, and leaving his bag-

Seventh campaign. The Romans are defeated by C. Pontius.

96 Livy, X. 46.

97 Livy, X. 47. Zonaras, VIII. 1.

98 Livy, X. 47. In the last chapter of his tenth book, Livy names the consuls who were elected for the year 462, Q. Fabius Gurges, and D. Junius Brutus. And here the first decade of Livy's history ends, and as the second decade is lost, we shall now be without his assistance for the remainder of this volume. We should be glad to possess the eleventh book, which contained the account of the secession to the Janiculum and of the Hortensian laws: yet, on the whole, a careful study of the ninth and tenth books will dispose us to be more patient of the loss of those which followed them. How little does the tenth book tell us of the internal state of Rome, how uncertain are its accounts of the several wars! Its most valuable information consists in the miscellaneous notices with which Livy generally concludes his account of every year; such as his notice of the paving of part of the Appian road, and of the building of several temples. But we might cheerfully resign, not the second decade only, but the first, third, and fourth, in short, every line of Livy's history which we at present possess, if we could so purchase the recovery of the eighth and ninth decades, which contained the history of the Italian war, and of the civil war of Marius and Sylla which followed it. For this period, of which we know, as it is, so little, Livy's history would have been invaluable. He would have been writing of times and events sufficiently near to his own to have been perfectly understood by him; his sources of information would have been more numerous and less doubtful, and then his fair and upright mind, and the beauty of his narrative, would have given us a picture at once faithful, lively, and noble.

99 Zonaras, VIII. 2.

gage behind him, he pushed on as to a certain victory. His men were already tired and disordered by the haste of their march, when they found the Samnite army in perfect order ready to receive them. They were presently defeated; 3000 men were killed on the place,[100] many were wounded, and night alone saved the army from destruction. But they could not retreat to their baggage,[101] and passed a miserable night in the open country, without any means of relieving their wounded, whose sufferings filled the whole army with horror and dismay. Day dawned, and the Romans expected to be attacked by the conquerors: but Pontius, it is said, heard that the old Fabius was close at hand, coming up with a second army to support his son, and therefore he allowed the beaten Romans to retreat unmolested. This is improbable,[102] but the truth is lost beyond recovery, and it is vain to attempt to restore the details of this most important campaign.

The old Q. Fabius serves under his son as his lieutenant.

The defeat of Fabius excited great indignation at Rome; and the political adversaries of his father, such as Appius Claudius and L. Papirius, the latter of whom was now prætor, would not fail to exaggerate his misconduct. It was moved in the senate that he should be recalled from the army, in other words, that his imperium or consular power should be taken from him; a measure without example in Roman history, except in the case of L. Cinna. The simple course would have been to order the consul to name a dictator; and he would in that case have named his father, who, by universal consent, was the man best fitted to meet the need. But the more violent course was preferred by the party opposed to Fabius, and would have been carried, had not the old Fabius[103] moved the senate by offering to go himself to the army, not in the majesty of the dictator's office, as most befitted his age and glory, but merely as lieutenant to his son. This could not be refused, and the old man followed his son to the field, leading with him, we may be sure, sufficient reinforcements; for every Roman loved the old Q. Fabius, and felt confident that in marching under his command he was marching to victory.

C. Pontius is defeated and taken prisoner.

A second battle followed; where fought, or how brought about, we know not. The old Fabius was the Talbot of the fifth century of Rome; and his personal prowess, even in age, was no less celebrated than his skill as a general. When the consul was surrounded by the enemy in the heat of the battle,[104] his aged father led the charge to his rescue; and the Romans, animated by such an example, could not be resisted, and won a complete victory. C. Pontius was taken prisoner, and 4000 Samnites shared his fate, while 20,000 were slain on the field.

[100] Eutropius, II. Suidas, in Φάβιος Μάξιμος. We should like to know from whom Suidas borrowed this article; but who, except Niebuhr, has a sufficient power of divination to discover it?

I owe my knowledge of the passage in Suidas to Freinsheim's supplement of the eleventh book of Livy; and as he has consulted almost every passage in the ancient writers which relates to these times, I have in other instances been indebted to him in like manner. But it is right to state, that I have always consulted the passages to which he refers, and have myself verified them: and of this the reader may be assured, that no quotation has been made in these notes which I have not myself verified; if it has ever happened that I have not had the book within my reach, the circumstance has been and will be especially noticed.

[101] Zonaras, VIII. 2.

[102] Zonaras, who copies Dion Cassius, represents the old Fabius as having been appointed lieutenant to his son at the beginning of the campaign; and he says that the consul left Rome before his father, and was anxious to fight the Samnites, before he joined him, that the glory of the action might be his own. Livy, (Epitom. XI.) Eutropius, and the writer from whom Suidas copied his article, "Fabius Maximus," say that the old man was only made his son's lieutenant after his defeat, and upon his own request, in order to save him from being deprived of his command. But if this be true, and it seems the more probable account, how could Pontius expect the arrival of the old Fabius on the instant after his son's defeat? Perhaps the consul fought with only a part of his army, and his lieutenant brought up the other part to his rescue from the camp which he had left so rashly; and something of this sort is probable, for if Q. Fabius had been defeated by the enemy in a fair battle without any fault of his own, the senate, according to its usual practice, would not have treated his defeat so severely.

[103] Livy, Epit. XI. Dion Cass. Fragm. Peiresc. XXXVI.

[104] Orosius, III. 22.

What resources of hope or of despair could still be left to the Samnites after a disaster so irreparable? Yet they resisted for another year, during which the war was carried on by two consular armies[105] in the heart of their country: many of their towns were taken; and amongst the rest, Venusia, a place on the frontiers of Lucania and Apulia, and important both from its strength and its position. So completely, indeed, was the power of Samnium broken, that now, for the first time, the Romans resolved to establish a colony in its territory. Venusia was the spot chosen for this purpose; but it marks the sense still entertained of the Samnite spirit of resistance, that no fewer than 20,000 colonists were sent out to occupy and maintain the new settlement.

A. U. C. 463. A. C. 291. Eighth campaign. Samnium again ravaged by two consular armies.

After his victory, Q. Fabius, the consul, was continued in his command for some time as proconsul. It was not, therefore, till the summer of the year 463 that he returned to Rome, and triumphed. While he was borne along in his chariot, according to custom, his old father rode on horseback behind him as one of his lieutenants,[106] delighting himself with the honors of his son. But at the moment when the consul and his father having arrived at the end of the Sacred Way turned to the left to ascend the hill of the Capitol, C. Pontius, the Samnite general, who, with the other prisoners of rank, had thus far followed the procession, was led aside to the right hand to the prison[107] beneath the Capitoline Hill, and there was thrust down into the underground dungeon of the prison, and beheaded. One year had passed since his last battle; nearly thirty since he had spared the lives and liberty of two Roman armies, and, unprovoked by the treachery of his enemies, had afterwards set at liberty the generals who were given up into his power as a pretended expiation of their country's perfidy. Such a murder, committed or sanctioned by such a man as Q. Fabius, is peculiarly a national crime, and proves but too clearly that in their dealings with foreigners the Romans had neither magnanimity, nor humanity, nor justice.

Triumph of Q. Fabius Gurges. C. Pontius is led prisoner in the procession and put to death.

In the year 464, P. Cornelius Rufinus and M'. Curius Dentatus were chosen consuls. Both entered Samnium with their armies,[108] but it was rather to entitle themselves to the honor of a triumph, than to overbear any real opposition. Every resource of the Samnites was exhausted, and they again submitted. They were again received as dependent allies of Rome; what territory was taken from them besides that of Venusia, we are not told, or what other sacrifices were required of them. Such was the end of the third Samnite war.

A. U. C. 464. A. C. 290. Ninth campaign. The Samnites lay down their arms and submit to Rome.

[105] By L. Postumius, the consul, with his own army, and by Q. Fabius, the consul of the former year, as proconsul. Dionysius, XVI. 16.

[106] Plutarch in Fab. Maxim. c. 24.

[107] So the well-known passage in Cicero, Verres, Act. II. v. 30, where he describes and even approves of this atrocious practice. "Supplicia quæ *debentur* hostibus victis."

[108] Eutropius, II.

CHAPTER XXXIV.

INTERNAL HISTORY, FROM THE PASSING OF THE OGULNIAN LAW TO THE LANDING OF PYRRHUS IN ITALY—SECESSION TO THE JANICULUM—DICTATORSHIP OF Q. HORTENSIUS—HORTENSIAN AND MÆNIAN LAWS.—FROM A. U. C. 454 TO 474.

"Clearly a difficult point for government, that of dealing with these masses;—if indeed it be not rather the sole point and problem of government, and all other points mere accidental crotchets, superficialities, and beatings of the wind."—CARLYLE, Hist. of French Revolution, Vol. I. p. 48.

Changes for the worse in the internal state of Rome.

THERE is often in well-contrived works of fiction a point in the middle of the story, at which all its circumstances seem tending towards a happy catastrophe; and it is only because the reader knows that there is much of the story yet to come, and that something therefore must occur to spoil the fair prospect, that he doubts the stability of the hero's or heroine's good fortune. So promising was the domestic state of Rome in the year 454, when the censorship of Fabius and Decius on the one hand, followed by the Ogulnian and Valerian laws on the other, seemed to announce that society had arrived at its perfect settlement; in which every member of it had found his proper place, and the artificial institutions of man seemed to correspond faithfully to the model, existing in truth, though not in fact, which our reason declares to be the will of God.

These changes were social rather than political.

But it should ever be borne in mind, that history looks generally at the political state of a nation; its social state, which is infinitely more important, and in which lie the seeds of all the greatest revolutions, is too commonly neglected or unknown. What is called the constitution of Rome, as far as regards the relations of patricians and plebeians to each other, was, in fact, perfected by the Ogulnian law, and remained for centuries without undergoing any material change. By that law the commons were placed in all respects on a level with the patricians; and the contests between these two orders were brought to an end forever. The comitia, too, had assumed that form, whatever it was, which they retained to the end of the commonwealth; the powers of the magistrate as affecting the liberty of the citizen underwent but little subsequent alteration. But however stationary political institutions may remain, the social state of a nation is forever changing; peace affects this no less than war, and many times even more: nay, seasons of profound political quiet may be working far more extensive alteration than periods of faction, or even of civil war. And so it was with the years which followed the passing of the Ogulnian law. Politically they are almost a blank; they present no new law, nothing that deserves the name of a contest between orders in commonwealth, scarcely between indivdiuals; the public attention seems to have been fixed exclusively on the events of the war with Etruria and Samnium. Yet we know that they must have wrought great social changes; for so violent a measure as a secession could never have been so much as contemplated, had it not been preceded by long and general distress, producing social irritation first, and then political.

Occasioned partly by seasons of scarcity and pestilence.

In the seven years which followed immediately after the passing of the Ogulnian law, we find mention made of a season of great scarcity[1] (A. U. C. 454), and of two years[2] of pestilence (459 and 461). We also read of prosecutions by the ædiles in three several years for

[1] Livy, X. 11. 11.

[2] Livy, X. 31, 47.

violations of the Licinian law[3] (456, 458, 461); and also of prosecutions by the same magistrates for a breach of the law which forbade the taking of interest upon a debt[4] (358). Now, although there may be some caprice in Livy's notice or omission of such particulars, yet it is at least remarkable that he has recorded so many of them at this period; while in the twenty-three years previous to the Ogulnian law, a term which includes the whole of the second Samnite war, we have no mention of any one of them, with the exception of an uncertain report of a pestilence in the year 441.[5] And the argument is the stronger, because we do find notices before the second Samnite war of prosecutions both for the breach of the Licinian law, and for taking illegal interest[6] (398 and 411); so that we may fairly conclude that the second Samnite war itself was a period comparatively exempt, at any rate, from offences of this nature, as also from the visitations of pestilence and famine. The causes of these last evils belong, indeed, to a law of God's providence which is to us unknown; but the occurrence of particular crimes at particular periods may in general be explained, if we are fully acquainted with the history of the time; and even in the fifth century of Rome, meagre as our knowledge of it is, we may in some measure account for the facts presented to us.

Partly by the encroachments of the rich on the common pasture lands.

The close of the second Samnite war in 450, the conquest of the Æquians in the same year, that of the Hernican state of Frusino in the year following, and of the Marsians in 452, must have added greatly to the domain land of the Romans. It was but a small proportion of this which was assigned to the 14,000 colonists of Alba, Carseoli, and Sora; the remainder would be either let to the old inhabitants on payment of a rent or vectigal to Rome, or would be occupied or beneficially enjoyed by individual citizens of Rome or of her allies. Now, as slaves were not yet numerous, there would be a difficulty in procuring laborers to cultivate tracts of lands lying mostly at a distance from Rome, and, in many instances, liable to the incursions of an enemy in time of war. It would be more convenient, therefore, to the occupiers to throw their land into pasture wherever it was practicable; and large tracts of domain would be fit for nothing but pasture, such as the higher valleys, and the sides and summits of the mountains; and these would not be occupied by any one particular person, but would be common land, on which any one would have a right to turn out a certain number of sheep and oxen, limited by the Licinian law. Now, the acts of violence which were practised, even under the emperors, by powerful men against the property of their weaker neighbors, and the allusion to forcible ejectment, as to a thing of no unusual occurrence, in the language of the prætor's interdict, may warrant our believing that the cattle of a small proprietor, when turned out on the mountain pastures at a distance from Rome, would be liable to continual injuries, and that the common land would be exclusively enjoyed by wealthy men, who would little scruple to exceed the legal number of sheep and oxen which they were permitted to feed. These were the pecuarii whom Livy twice notices as impeached by the ædiles and heavily fined; but the temptation to violate the law was perpetually recurring; and the chances of a prosecution must have been very uncertain; nor was it always impossible for a powerful man[7] of fair military reputation to escape from his prosecutors, by getting the consul to name him as one of his lieutenants.

Partly by the continued wars.

Thus, on the one hand, the years which immediately followed the second Samnite war, furnished the rich with many opportunities of becoming richer. On the other hand, there were many causes at work which made the poor yet poorer. A season of extreme scarcity, such as that of the year 455, must have obliged many of the small tradesmen and artificers of the

[3] Livy, X. 13, 23, 47.
[4] Livy, X. 23.
[5] Livy, IX. 28.
[6] Livy, VII. 16, 28.
[7] As in the case of L. Postumius, which will be noticed hereafter.—See Livy, X. 46.

city to incur debts. Two or three years of pestilence following closely upon one another, as in 459, 461, and 462, must have created great distress not only amongst the town population, but also amongst the agricultural commons: where the father was carried off by the disorder, his wife and family, who were solely dependent on his labor, would be at once reduced to poverty, or again would be forced to relieve their immediate necessity by borrowing. If the pestilence was local, and raged most in Rome and its immediate neighborhood, yet the more distant tribes suffered from evils of another sort. The tribes on the Etruscan frontier suffered perhaps something in 455 from an inroad of the Gauls, which no doubt aggravated the scarcity of that year; the Falerian tribe in Campania was repeatedly, as we have seen, exposed to the invasions of the Samnites. The extraordinary military exertions of the Romans in the third Samnite war must have rendered necessary a heavy amount of taxation. In the great campaign of 459, six legions were raised, besides two armies of reserve; and in the preceding year there had been a levy[8] of the whole population of the city, which had been kept under arms for nearly three weeks, whilst the two consular armies were at the same time employed in the field. Nor were the services of the soldier required only for a few weeks in the summer or autumn; the legions were more than once[9] kept abroad during the whole winter; which in itself must have been a great hardship to the small landed proprietor, whose land could ill spare his presence and his labor. Besides, even in the unfair accounts which remain to us of the events of the war, it is confessed that the Roman loss in battle was often very severe; and although their writers do not acknowledge it, the Romans must have lost also many prisoners, whose ransom, if they were not left in hopeless captivity, was an additional burden upon their families. And when, after all this, the most valuable part of the spoil won in a successful campaign was wholly put into the treasury, as was done by L. Papirius in 461,[10] and the soldier received nothing but what he might have gained for himself in sacking one or more of the Samnite cities, the mass of the population would feel, that while the burdens of war were mostly borne by them, they had scarcely any share of its occasional advantage.

Obscurity of the history of this period. Friends and opponents of the popular cause.

Thus it is conceivable that, within three or four years after the end of the third Samnite war, a large portion of the Roman people should have been again involved in debt, and thus should have been irritated against their richer countrymen, and ready to catch fire on the smallest provocation. But the deepest obscurity involves this part of the Roman history: for Livy's tenth book ends with the consulship of L. Papirius and Sp. Carvilius, and from that time to the war with Pyrrhus, we have no other record of events than the meagre epitomes of Zonaras, Orosius, and Eutropius, and a few fragments and incidental notices from other writers. Even the Fasti Capitolini are wanting for this period; so that the very lists of consuls can only be made out from recent authorities.[11] Thus, we neither know the immediate causes, nor the leaders, nor the principal opponents, nor even the exact date of the great popular movement which was finally appeased by Q. Hortensius as dictator. We may conjecture that Appius Claudius, so far as his infirmities might

[8] Livy, X. 21. "Senatus—delectum omnis generis hominum haberi jussit, nec ingenui modo aut juniores sacramento adacti, sed seniorum etiam cohortes factæ, libertinique centuriati."

[9] App. Claudius' army was kept in Etruria during the winter of 458.—Livy, X. 25. The army of M. Atilius wintered near Interamna, on the Liris, in 460, and that of L. Papirius was kept out in the country of Vescia through the winter of 461.—Livy, X. 39, 46.

[10] Livy, X. 46.

[11] From Cassiodorus, from what are called the Fasti Siculi, published by Scaliger in his edition of Eusebius; from the anonymous Fasti, first published by Cardinal Noris from a manuscript in the imperial library at Vienna, and reprinted by Grævius in his great collection of Roman antiquities, Vol. XI. p. 355, and, lastly, from the Fasti, which go by the name of the Fasti of Idatius, published also by Grævius in the same volume, p. 247. The two last Fasti give only the cognomina of the consuls, and this is too often the case with the Sicilian Fasti also; they are also often corrupt, but such as they are, they are almost our sole authority for the consuls of this dark period.

permit him, was most zealous in his opposition to the demands of the people; and that L. Papirius Cursor took the same side. On the other hand, the claims of the popular party were supported, as is most probable, by one of the most eminent Romans of this period, M'. Curius Dentatus.

M'. Curius Dentatus opposes Appius Claudius.

This is a name familiar to every ear, and associated with our highest ideas of ancient Roman virtue. Yet there is not a single great man within the histórical period of Rome of whose life less is known to us. Like the Fulvii, and like Ti. Coruncanius, and C. Fabricius, he was not of Roman extraction; he came from one of the Latin towns which had received the full Roman franchise,[12] and he was a man of no inherited fortune. His merit as a soldier must have first brought him into notice; and the plain resoluteness of his character, not unlike that of Marius, and perhaps combined, as in his case, with a marked abhorrence of the wealthy aristocracy, caused him to be elected tribune of the commons. In his tribuneship[13] he resisted the most eloquent and overbearing of the patricians, Appius Claudius, who, when holding the comitia as interrex, refused to allow the election of a plebeian consul. Curius compelled the curiæ to ratify the choice of the centuries beforehand, on whomsoever it might fall; and thus the candidate, when elected by the comitia, needed no further confirmation of his title; he was at once consul. Such is the anecdote as related by Cicero; but we cannot with certainty fix the date of it.[14] It must, however, have occurred before the year 464, when Curius was consul, and, as we have seen, put an end to the Samnite war.

His conquest of the Sabines.

His consulship was rendered further memorable by the beginning and end of another war,[15] that with the Sabines. Some aid given by them to their kinsmen, the Samnites, afforded the Romans a pretext for attacking them, after the peace between the two nations had lasted since the year after the expulsion of the decemvirs; that is, during a period of a century and a half. The Sabines dwelt in the heart of Italy, in the valley of the Velinus, on the south of the central Apennines, and along the upper part of the course of the Aternus, which runs into the Adriatic. It was an extensive and populous country, for it came down to the left bank of the Tiber at Cures, only nineteen miles from Rome, and it stretched beyond the Apennines as far as the confines of the Vestinians and Picentians. It was rich in oil[16] and wine, and the acorns of its forests fattened innumerable herds of swine. But the long peace which had increased its wealth, had also made its people unwarlike; they fell almost without a struggle; and their conquest, according to the old historian, Fabius Pictor,[17] first made the Romans acquainted with riches. For his double victory over the Samnites and Sabines, Curius triumphed twice in the same year; and he declared of himself in the assembly of the people, on his return to Rome: "I

[12] This appears from the speech of Cicero, pro Sulla, 7, § 23; but we have no information, I believe, as to the particular town from which he came.

[13] Cicero, Brutus, 14, § 55.

[14] We find from Livy, X. 11, that Appius Claudius was interrex in the year 455, at the breaking out of the third Samnite war. But, as Niebuhr observes, Appius Claudius was interrex three several times, as appears from the inscription recording the principal dignities and actions of his life, Orelli, No. 529, so that we cannot tell in which of his three interregna the circumstance noticed by Cicero took place. When he was a candidate for his second consulship in 457, he earnestly endeavored to get Q. Fabius elected with himself, in order to exclude a plebeian, Livy, X. 15; but this must not be confounded with Cicero's story; it only shows the habitual temper of the man, and that he never lost sight of his object, of restoring the old ascendency of the patricians.

[15] Livy, Epitom. XI. Auctor, de Viris Illustr. in M'. Cur. Dentat.

[16] Strabo, V. 3, § 1, p. 228.

[17] Strabo, V. 3, § 1, p. 228. This contrasts strangely with our notions of Sabine simplicity and frugality: "hanc vitam veteres olim tenuêre Sabini," &c. But, possibly, Strabo did not give Fabius' meaning correctly; and the old historian may have spoken not of the Sabines only, but of them and the Samnites together, calling them both, perhaps, by the common name of "Sabellians," a term by which the Samnites are called in Livy, X. 19. Fabius meant, probably, to speak of the period of Curius' consulship, when he conquered both the Samnites and Sabines, and made the speech reported in the text. But that speech is especially referred by the author of the work "de Viris Illustribus" to the Samnite conquests of Curius, and not to his successes against the Sabines.

have conquered such an extent of country that it must have been left a wilderness, had the men whom I have made our subjects been fewer: I have subjected such a multitude of men, that they must have starved if the territory conquered with them had been smaller." The Sabines were obliged[18] to become subjects of Rome; that is, to receive the citizenship without the right of voting.

For his double victory over the Samnites and Sabines, Curius, it is recorded,[19] triumphed twice in the course of the year of his consulship. But a far harder contest, and one in which no triumphs could be gained, awaited him at Rome. He saw on the one hand the extreme distress of the poorer citizens, whom war and pestilence together had overwhelmed with misery; on the other hand, he had conquered large tracts of lands, which, if granted out under an agrarian law, might go far towards the relief of their sufferings; and, further, the grasping and insolent spirit of some of the nobility disgusted him with the system of the occupation of the domain lands by individuals. It was only in the preceding year that L. Postumius had employed a Roman army as his slaves,[20] and had made his soldiers clear a wide extent of public land won from the enemy, which he had been allowed to occupy for himself. The actual colleague of Curius in the consulship was P. Cornelius Rufinus,[21] a man already notorious for his rapacity and corruption, and who, doubtless, was turning his Samnite conquests to his own account, and appropriating to himself, at this very moment, the spoil won by the valor of his soldiers. So Curius thought that justice and the public good required that the conquests of the nation should be made available for the relief of the national distress; and he proposed an agrarian law which should allot to every citizen a portion of seven jugera.[22]

He brings forward an agrarian law.

He arrayed at once against him, not the patricians only, but many families, no doubt, of the new nobility, who, having attained to wealth and honors, felt entirely as the older members of the aristocracy. The ancestors of Lucullus, and of the Metelli, and of the orator Hortensius, already, we may believe, had joined that party which their descendants so constantly upheld. They made common cause with Appius Claudius, the uncompromising enemy of their whole order, who despised the richest of the Licinii as heartily as the poorest citizen of one of the city tribes. L. Scipio was likely to entertain the same spirit of resistance to the agrarian law of Curius, which Scipio Masica, nearly two hundred years afterwards, displayed so fiercely against the measures of Ti. Gracchus; and L. Papirius Cursor, with all his father's inflexible temper and unyielding courage, would be slow to comply with the demands of a plebeian multitude. The old Q. Fabius was respected and loved by all orders of his countrymen, and he had been opposed to the party of the high aristocracy; but perhaps his civil courage was not equal to his courage in the field; he had

Who were his principal opponents.

[18] Paterculus, I. 14. "Sabinis sine suffragio data civitas."

[19] Livy, Epitom. XI.

[20] A more detailed account of the mad conduct of Postumius in his consulship is given in a subsequent part of this chapter. His trial and fine took place, probably, in the very year when Curius and P. Cornelius Rufinus were consuls.

[21] Dion Cassius seems to have placed the well-known story of Fabricius voting for Rufinus at the consular comitia, because "he would rather be robbed than sold as a slave," in the first consulship of Rufinus, that is, in the year 464. See the mutilated fragment in Mai's Scriptor. Veter. Collect. Dion. XLI., which, when compared with the entire story as given by Cicero, de Oratore, II. 66, clearly relates to the same circumstance. Yet it is difficult to understand how, in either of Rufinus' consulships, the republic was in such perilous circumstances that great military skill was needed to save her from destruction, which is the meaning of Fabricius' words; and therefore Niebuhr thinks that the story may refer to the time of Rufinus' dictatorship just after the defeat of Lævinus by Pyrrhus.

[22] "Quaterna dena igri jugera viritim populo divisit." Auctor de Viris Illustribus.—M'. Curius. But these fourteen jugera must be understood of two separate agrarian laws, the one passed or proposed in the first consulship of Curius, the other in his second consulship, after the final defeat of Pyrrhus. It is not expressly stated that this first allotment was vehemently opposed; but the fragment from Appian, preserved by Suidas, and quoted below, proves that Curius was in a state of violent opposition to the senate, and this is likely to have been on account of his agrarian law. It may be, however, that he also brought forward some of those measures which were afterwards conceded by the aristocracy, and which were contained in the Hortensian laws.

shown on a former occasion[23] that he might be moved by the reproaches of his order, and if he took no part against Curius, yet we cannot believe that he supported him.

Tumults and violent state of parties. The agrarian law is passed.

I have tried to recall the individual actors in these troubles, in order to give to them something more of reality than can belong to a mere account of actions apart from the men who performed them. And the contest, no doubt, was violent; as it is said that Curius was followed by a band of eight hundred picked young men,[24] the soldiers, we may suppose, who had so lately conquered under his auspices, and who were ready to decide the quarrel, if needful, by the sword. They saved Curius from the fate of Ti. Gracchus, but it does not appear that they committed any acts of outrage themselves. But an impenetrable veil conceals from our view the particulars of all these disturbances; the law of Curius was finally passed, but we know not at what time, nor whether it was obtained by any other than peaceful and legal means.

Laws proposed for other popular objects. Secession of the people to the Janiculum.

Between the consulship of Curius and Cornelius Rufinus, and that of P. Dolabella and Cn. Domitius, when the Gaulish war broke out, there intervened a period of seven years, all the records of which have so utterly perished that not a single event can be fixed with certainty in any one particular year. But with all the chronology of these years we have lost also the history; we cannot ascertain the real character of the events which followed, nor the relations of parties to each other, nor the conduct of particular persons.[25] Some of the tribunes[26] proposed a law for the abolition of all debts; whether before or after the passing of Curius' agrarian law we know not. Nor can we tell whether Curius held on with the popular party till the end of the contest; or whether, as often happens with the leaders of the beginnings of civil dissensions, he thought that the popular cause was advancing too far, and either left it, or even joined the party of its opponents. We only know that the demands of the people[27] rose with the continuance of the struggle; that political questions were added to those of debtor and creditor; that points which, if yielded in time, would have satisfied all the wishes of the popular party, were contested inch by inch, till, when gained, they were only regarded as a step to something further; and that at last the mass of the people left Rome, and established themselves on the Janiculum.[28] Even then, if Zonaras may be trusted, the

[23] When he only refused to violate the Licinian law, and to return two patrician consuls, because he himself would have been one of them. Otherwise he is represented as saying that he would have complied with the wishes of the patricians, and have broken the law.—Livy, X. 15.

[24] *Δευτάτῳ κατὰ ζῆλον ἀρετῆς εἵπετο νέων λογάδων πλῆθος ὀκτακοσίων, ἐπὶ πάντα τὰ ἔργα ἕτοιμοι. καὶ βαρὺς ἦν τῇ βουλῇ παρὰ τὰς ἐκκλησίας.*

This is a quotation made from Appian by Suidas, and is to be found in Suidas' lexicon, in ζῆλος, or in Schweighauser's Appian, Samnitic. Extract. V.

[25] For example, a speech of Curius has been recorded, in which he said, "that the man must be a mischievous citizen who was not contented with seven jugera of land."—Pliny, Hist. Natur. XVIII. § 18. Ed. Sillig. But the application of this speech is most uncertain. According to Plutarch, it was spoken to reprove some violent supporters of the popular party, who thought that Curius' agrarian law did not go far enough, and that the whole of the state's domains ought to be allotted to separate proprietors, without allowing any portion to be occupied in great masses as at present.—Apothegm. p. 194. E. But Valerius Maximus transfers the speech to Curius' second consulship, and makes it accompany his refusal of an unusually large portion of land which the senate proposed to allot to himself—IV. 3, § 5. Frontinus also makes it accompany his refusal of an offer made to himself; but he places it in his first consulship, after the Sabine war. Strategemat. IV. 3, § 12. It might also have been spoken against the occupiers of large tracts of domain land, who would not be contented with an allotment of seven jugera as property, but wished to occupy whole districts. So impossible is it to see our way in the history of a period where the accounts are not only so meagre, but also at variance with one another.

[26] *δημάρχων τινῶν χρεῶν ἀποκοπὴν εἰσηγησαμένων.*—Zonaras, VIII. 2. The words *εἰσηγουμένων τῶν δημάρχων* are legible in a mutilated fragment of Dion Cassius relating to these times, which Mai has printed in such a state as to be in many parts absolutely unintelligible.—Fragm. XLII.

[27] This appears from the legible part of the fragment of Dion Cassius just noticed: *τελευτῶντες οὖν οὐδ' ἐθελόντων τῶν δυνατῶν πολλῷ πλείω τῶν κατ' ἀρχὰς ἐλπισθέντων σφίσιν ἀφεῖναι, συνηλλάγησαν.*

[28] Livy, Epitom. XI.

aristocracy would not yield, and it was only the alarm of a foreign enemy,[29] perhaps some gathering of the forces of Etruria, which at this time was meditating on a real and decisive trial of strength with Rome, which induced the senate to put an end at any price to the existing dissensions.

They are brought back by Q. Hortensius, who passes the Hortensian laws.

Accordingly, Q. Hortensius[30] was appointed dictator. He was a man of an old plebeian family, for we find an Hortensius amongst the tribunes of the year 332;[31] but, individually, he is unknown to us, and we cannot tell what recommended him to the choice of the consuls on this occasion. He assembled the people, including under that name the whole nation, those who had stayed in Rome no less than those who had withdrawn to the Janiculum, in a place called "the Oak Grove,"[32] probably without the walls of the city; and in that sacred grove were passed, and ratified probably by solemn oaths, the famous Hortensian laws.

Their provisions.

These contained, in the first place, an abolition,[33] or, at least, a great reduction of debts; 2d, an agrarian law on an extensive scale, allotting seven jugera of the domain land to every citizen; and 3d, one or more laws affecting the constitution; of which the most important was that which deprived the senate of its veto, and declared the people assembled[34] in their tribes to be a supreme legislative power. Accidental mention has been preserved to us of another law, or possibly of a particular clause in the former law, by which the nundinæ[35] or weekly market days which had hitherto been days of business for the commons only, and sacred or holy days for the patricians, were now made days of business for the whole nation alike. Was the object of this merely to abolish a marked distinction between the two orders; or was it to enable the patricians to take part in the meeting of the tribes in the Forum, which were held on the nundinæ, and had they hitherto belonged only to the tribes in that other, but to us undiscoverable form, in which they voted at the comitia of centuries on the field of Mars?

The legislative power of the tribes established.

Thus the sovereign legislative power of the assembly of the tribes in the Forum was fully established; and consequently, when C. Flaminius brought forward another agrarian bill, about fifty years afterwards, for a division of the recently conquered country of the Senones, the senate, how-

[29] Zonaras, VIII. 2.

[30] Livy, Epitom. XI. Pliny, Histor. Natur. XVI. § 37. Ed. Sillig.

[31] Livy, IV. 42.

[32] "Q. Hortensius, dictator, cum plebs secessisset in Janiculum, legem in esculeto tulit, ut quod ea jussisset omnes Quirites teneret."—Pliny, Hist. Nat. XVI. § 37. Ed. Sillig.

[33] This is not stated in direct terms in the scanty notices of these events, which alone have been preserved to us. But as the abolition of debts was the main thing required by the people, and as the fragment of Dion Cassius, above referred to, speaks of the people having their first demands granted, and then going on to insist upon others, and as we have seen an abolition of debts carried once before in the disturbances of 413, it does not seem too much to conclude that a similar measure was carried on on the present occasion also. With regard to the agrarian law, it may have been passed two or three years earlier; but from the statement already quoted (Auctor de Viris Illustribus, in M'. Curio), "that Curius granted fourteen jugera to each citizen," it is clear that an agrarian law proposed by him must have been carried at some time or other in the period between his consulship and the dictatorship of Hortensius. It may thus be numbered amongst the Hortensian laws, as belonging to the measures which the people at this period forced the aristocracy to concede to them.

[34] The statement in the text follows Niebuhr, who, as is well known, supposed that the Hortensian laws differed from the Publilian, inasmuch as the Publilian abolished the veto of the curiæ, and the Hortensian did away the veto of the senate. The tribes in the Forum and the senate were thus placed on a footing of equality; neither had a veto on the enactments of the other; and the tribunes had a veto upon both alike. Both also were considered as equal to laws; for "senatus consultum legis vicem obtinet" (Gaius, Institut. I. § 4); and by the Hortensian law, "plebiscita legibus exæquata sunt." (Gaius, Instit. I. § 3.) It may be doubted whether the limits of these two powers were ever very definitely settled; although one point is mentioned as lying exclusively in the power of the tribes, namely, the right of admitting any strangers to the franchise of Roman citizens.—Livy, XXXVIII. 36.

[35] Macrobius, Saturnal. I. 16. The reason assigned by Macrobius for this enactment of the Hortensian law may also be admitted; that it was made to suit the convenience of the citizens from the country, who, coming up to Rome on the market days, wished to be able to settle their legal business at the same time; but this could not be done, at least in the prætor's court, as there, according to the patrician usage, the market days were holydays, and consequently the court did not sit.

ever strongly averse to it, could not prevent it from becoming a law. The only check, therefore, which now remained on the absolute legislative power of the tribes, consisted in the veto of their own tribunes; and to secure the negative of a tribune became accordingly the ordinary resource of the aristocracy in the contests of the seventh century.

The Mænian law.

Another important law is supposed to have been passed at the same period with the law of Hortensius, though our knowledge of all particulars respecting it is still more scanty. A law bearing the name of Mænian,[36] and proposed, therefore, either by the good dictator C. Mænius himself, or, as is more probable, by one of his family, took away the veto which the curiæ had hitherto enjoyed in the election of curule magistrates. They were now to sanction beforehand the choice of the centuries, on whomsoever it might happen to fall. And thus their share in the elections being reduced to an empty form, they soon ceased to be assembled at all; and in later times of the commonwealth they were represented merely by thirty lictors, who were accustomed for form's sake to confirm the suffrages of the centuries, and to confer the imperium on the magistrates whom the centuries had elected.

These laws did not make the constitution of Rome a democracy.

But although supreme legislative power was now bestowed on the assembly of the tribes, and although the elections were freed from all direct legal control on the part of the aristocracy, yet we know full well that the Roman constitution was very far from becoming henceforward a democracy. To us, indeed, who are accustomed to enact more than five hundred new laws every year, and who see the minutest concerns of common life regulated by act of parliament, the possession of an independent legislative power by a popular assembly must seem equivalent to absolute sovereignty. But our own early history may teach us not to apply our present notions to other times and other countries. The legislative power, even in the days of the Tudors and Stuarts, was of small importance when compared with the executive and judicial. Now, the Hortensian law enabled the Roman people to carry any point on which they considered their welfare to depend; it removed all impediments, which after all do but irritate rather than hinder, out of the way of the strongly declared expression of the public will. But the public will was in the ordinary state of things quiescent, and allowed itself to be represented by the senate and the magistrates. It resigned to these even the power of taxation, and except in some rare or comparatively trifling cases, the whole judical power also: those judges who were appointed by the prætor to try questions of fact, in all the most important civil and criminal cases, were taken exclusively from the order of senators. All the ordinary administration was conducted by the senate; and its decrees on all particular points, like the ψηφίσματα of the Athenian popular assembly, had undoubtedly the force of laws.

According to Theophilus,[37] this was a concession made by the people to the

[36] What we know of the Mænian law comes chiefly from a passage of Cicero (Brutus, c. 14, § 55), in which he says of M'. Curius, that he "patres ante auctores fieri coegerit, quod fuit permagnum, nondum lege Mæniâ latâ." Livy must allude also to this law, when he says, "hodie—priusquam populus suffragium ineat, in incertum comitiorum eventum patres auctores fiunt." I. 17. It must be observed that the power taken away by the Mænian law from the "patres" was taken away from the senate no less than from the curiæ; for the senate in its original form was only a select assembly of the patres, whose great assembly was the comitia curiata. And gradually the senate drew to itself both the name and the power of the greater patrician assembly, so that what is said of the patres or patricians is commonly to be understood of the senate, and not of the curiæ, even although the senate had long ceased to be exclusively a patrician assembly. This view would coincide with Niebuhr's distinction between the Publilian and Hortensian laws. When the former were passed, the curiæ were still an efficient body, and the term "patres" therefore applied to them much more than to the senate. But in the fifty years that followed, the curiæ had dwindled away so much that the senate was become the principal assembly of the patres; and therefore the Hortensian law extended to the senate what had before been enacted by the Publilian law with respect to the curiæ.

[37] See Hugo, Geschichte des Rom. Rechts, p. 339. (9th Edit.) The passage in Theophilus is one which I have not verified, as I have not had an opportunity of consulting the book. But Hugo professes to quote it fully, and I have no doubt of his correctness.

Their effects were lasting and beneficial.

aristocracy, and embodied in the laws of Hortensius, that the decrees of the senate should be binding on the people, as the decrees or resolutions of the tribes were to be binding on the senate. At any rate, it is certain that the senate retained high and independent powers of its own, which were no less sovereign than those possessed by the assembly of the tribes; and in practice each of these two bodies kept up for a hundred and fifty years a healthy and vigorous life in itself, without interfering with the functions of the other. Mutual good sense and good feeling, and the continual moderating influence of the college of tribunes, whose peculiar position as having a veto on the proceedings both of the senate and people disposed them to regulate the action of each, prevented any serious collision, and gave to the Roman constitution that mixed character, partly aristocratic and partly popular, which Polybius recognized and so greatly admired. And thus the event seems to have given the highest sanction to the wisdom of the Hortensian laws: nor can we regard them as mischievous or revolutionary, when we find that from the time of their enactment the internal dissensions of the Romans were at an end for a hundred and fifty years, and that during this period the several parts of the constitution were all active; it was a calm not produced by the extinction of either of the contending forces, but by their perfect union.

Prospect of a new coalition against Rome.

It may be conjectured that the sickness which had visited Rome during three or four successive years at the close of the Samnite war returned, partially at least, in the concluding year of these domestic troubles, for Q. Hortensius died before the expiration of his dictatorship: an event hitherto unexampled in the Roman annals, and regarded as of evil omen; so that Augustine[38] makes it a reproach to the impotence of the god Æsculapius, that although he had been so lately brought from Greece with the utmost solemnity, and had been received at Rome with due honors, that his presence might stay the pestilence, he yet suffered the very dictator of the Roman people to fall its victim. Nearly about the same time also, if we can judge from the place and apparent drift of one of the fragments of Dionysius,[39] Rome suffered from an earthquake. And scarcely were the Hortensian laws passed, when the prospect of foreign war on a most extensive scale presented itself. Tarentum, it is said, was busily organizing a new coalition, in which the Lucanians, Samnites, and Bruttians in the south were to unite with the Etruscans, Umbrians, and Gauls in the north, and were again to try their combined strength against Rome.

Miscellaneous notices of domestic events.

In the mean time, before we trace the events of this great contest, we may bring together some few scattered notices of domestic affairs relating to the state of Rome in the middle of the fifth century.

Institution of the triumviri capitales.

A new magistracy had its origin[40] somewhere between the years 461 and 466; that of the triumviri capitales, or commissioners of police. These officers were elected by the people, the comitia being held by the prætor. Their business was to enforce the payment of fines due to the state;[41]

[38] De Civitate Dei, III. 17. Augustine's notice of the secession to the Janiculum is probably taken from Livy, and may be given here, as it contains one or two particulars not mentioned in any other existing record. "Post graves et longas Romæ seditiones ad ultimum plebs in Janiculum *hostile diremptione* secesserat: cujus mali tam dira calamitas erat, ut ejus rei causâ quod in extremis periculis fieri solebat, dictator crearetur Hortensius: qui plebe revocatâ in eodem magistratu expiravit, quod nulli dictatori ante contigerat."

[39] Ch. 39. Fragm. Dionys. apud Maium. Scriptor. Veter. Vatcian. Collect. Vol. II. p. 501.

[40] Livy Epitome, XI.

[41] Festus, in "Sacramentum." The appointment of the "triumviri capitales" was proposed, according to Festus, by L. Papirius, whom he calls "tribune of the commons." One cannot but suspect with Niebuhr, that the person meant was L. Papirius Cursor, who was *prætor* in the year 462 (Livy, X. 47); and then the appointment would coincide with the year when the plague was at its height, and when the deputation was sent to Epidaurus to invite Æsculapius to Rome. Varro, de L. L. V. 81. Ed. Müller. Pomponius, de Origine Juris, Digest I. Tit. II. § 39. Livy, XXV. 1. XXXII. 26. Valerius Maximus, V. 4. § 7.

Etymologicon Magn. in ἕνδεκα. See Herman, Pol. Antiq. of Greece, § 137.

to try by summary process all offenders against the public peace who might be taken in the fact; to have the care of the state prison, and to carry into effect the sentence of the law upon criminals. They resembled exactly in all these points the well-known magistracy of the eleven at Athens.

The creation of this office seems to mark an increase of ordinary crimes against person and property; and such an increase was the natural consequence of the distress which prevailed about this time, and particularly of the severe visitations of pestilence which occurred at this period. It is well known that such seasons are marked by the greatest outbreaks of all sorts of crime; and that never is a strong police more needed than when the prospect of impending death makes men reckless, and eager only to indulge their passions while they may.

The probable occasion of its institution.

The census of the year 461 gave a return of 262,322 Roman citizens;[42] that of the year 466, notwithstanding the havoc caused in the interval by the double scourge of pestilence and war, exhibited an increase of 10,000[43] upon the preceding return. This was owing to the conquest of the Sabines, and their consequent admission to the Roman franchise in the year 464: for the census included, as is well known, not only those citizens who were enrolled in the tribes, but those also who enjoyed the private rights of citizenship without as yet partaking in the right of suffrage.

Returns of the census at this period.

Amongst other traits of resemblance between the Spartan and the Roman aristocracies, we may notice the extreme moderation shown by each of them towards the faults of their distinguished citizens. It was not till after repeated proofs of his treasonable designs that the Spartan government would take any serious steps against Pausanias; and the forbearance of the Romans towards Appius Claudius was no less remarkable. Another memorable example of the same spirit occurred in the case of L. Postumius Megellus. He belonged to a family whose pride and hatred of the commons had been notorious in the political contests of the beginning of the fourth century;[44] and as Niebuhr has truly observed, the peculiar character of a Roman family was preserved from generation to generation, and it was rarely found that any of its members departed from it. He had been consul in 449, and again in 460, and had acquired in each of his commands the reputation of a brave and skilful soldier. But his conduct as a citizen was far less meritorious; and it was probably for some overbearing or oppressive behavior in his second consulship that he was threatened with impeachment by one of the tribunes as soon as he went out of office. In the crisis of the Samnite war, however, military merit atoned for all other defects; the consul Sp. Carvilius named him one of his lieutenants,[45] and the trial was delayed till the campaign should be over; but when it had ended triumphantly, the popularity and brilliant victories of Sp. Carvilius pleaded strongly in favor of his lieutenant, and the trial never was brought forward. Two years afterwards, in 463, Postumius was again chosen consul, when the great victory obtained in the preceding year by Q. Fabius made it probable that the war might soon be brought to a triumphant issue.

Story of L. Postumius Megellus.

His proud and bad nature was more irritated by having been threatened at first with impeachment, than softened by the favor shown to him afterwards; so that his conduct in his third consulship was that of a mischievous madman. His first act[46] was to insist on having Samnium assigned to him as his province, without referring the decision as usual to lot; and though his colleague, C. Junius Bubulcus, remonstrated against this arrogance, yet the nobility and powerful interest of Postumius prevailed, and C. Junius forbore to dispute what he perceived he could not resist with success.

His quarrels with his colleague in his third consulship.

Then followed, as usual, the levying of the legions for the service of the year;

42 Livy, X. 47.
43 Livy, Epitom. XI.
44 See Chap. XIII. of his history, note 48.
45 Livy, X. 46.
46 Dionysius, XVI. 15.

He employs his soldiers in clearing his own land.

but the Samnites were so humbled that nothing more was to be feared from them, and Q. Fabius Gurges still commanded an army in Samnium as proconsul. It was not necessary, therefore, for the consul to begin active operations immediately; but he, notwithstanding, took the field with his army, and advanced towards the enemy's frontier. In the course of the late campaigns, he had become the occupier of a large tract of the territory conquered from the Samnites; but much of it was uncleared land, and as slaves at Rome were yet but few, laborers were not easily to be procured in these remote possessions in sufficient numbers. Postumius did not scruple to employ his soldiers as though they had been his slaves: he set two thousand[47] men to work in felling his woods, and in this manner he engaged for a considerable time a large portion of a Roman army.

His behavior towards Q. Fabius Gurges.

When, at last, he was ready to commence active operations against the enemy, his pride displayed itself in a new form. Q. Fabius Gurges was still, as we have seen, commanding an army in Samnium as proconsul; and he was now laying siege to Cominium, which, though taken and burnt by the Romans two years before, appears to have been again occupied by the Samnites as a fortress; for the massy walls of their towns could not easily be destroyed, and these exist in many instances to this day, encircling nothing but desolation within them. The consul wrote to Fabius,[48] ordering him to withdraw from Samnium: Fabius pleaded the authority of the senate, by which he had been continued in his command; and the senate itself sent a deputation to Postumius, requiring him not to oppose their decree. But he replied to the deputies, that so long as he was consul it was for him to command the senate, not for the senate to dictate to him; and he marched directly towards Cominium, to compel Fabius to obedience by actual force. Fabius did not attempt to resist him; and the consul, having taken the command of both armies, immediately sent Fabius home.

He triumphs in spite of the prohibition of the senate.

In actual war Postumius again proved himself an able soldier: he took Cominium,[49] and several other places, and he conquered the important post of Venusia, and, well appreciating the advantages of its situation, he recommended that it should be made a Roman colony. The senate followed his advice, but would not appoint him one of the commissioners[50] for assigning the lands to the colonists, and superintending the foundation of the new settlement. He in his turn distributed all the plunder of the campaign amongst his soldiers, that he might not enrich the treasury; and he marched home and gave his soldiers leave of absence from their standards, without waiting for the arrival of his successor. Finally, when the senate refused to allow him to triumph,[51] he, having secured the protection of three of the tribunes, celebrated his triumph in defiance of the prohibition of the other seven, and in contempt of the senate's refusal.

He is tried and heavily fined.

For such a course of outrageous conduct, he was prosecuted as soon as he went out of office, by two of the tribunes, and was condemned by all the three-and-thirty tribes unanimously. But his accusers did not prosecute him capitally, they only sued him for a fine; and although the fine was the heaviest to which any Roman had been hitherto sentenced, for it amounted to 500,000 ases,[52] yet it was but small in comparison of the penalties imposed with far less provocation by the governments of Greece. It amounted, in Greek money, to no more than fifty thousand drachmæ, whereas Agis, the king of Sparta, had been condemned, even by the Spartans, to pay a fine of one hundred thousand[53] for a mere want of judgment in his military operations. Postu-

[47] Dionysius, XVI. 15. Livy, Epitome.

[48] Dionysius, XVI. 16.

[49] Dionysius, XVI. 17.

[50] Dionysius, XVI. 17.

[51] Dionys. XVI. 18. Livy relates this story of Postumius' second consulship, X. 37. But it agrees on every account better with his third consulship, of which it is related by Dionysius.

[52] Dionysius, XVI. 18.

[53] Thucydides, V. 63.

mius, in addition to his own large possessions, would probably have many wealthy clients, who were bound to pay their patron's fine. His family, at any rate, was not ruined or disgraced by his sentence, for his son was elected consul a few years afterwards, in the third year of the first Punic war.

Embassy sent to Epidaurus to invite the god Æsculapius to Rome.

Of the miscellaneous particulars recorded of this period one of the most remarkable is the embassy sent to Greece in the year 462, to invite the god Æsculapius to Rome, in order that he might put a stop to the plague which had then been raging for three years. The head of the embassy was Q. Ogulnius,[54] the proposer of the law by which the commons had been admitted to the sacred offices of pontifex and augur, and who more recently, as curule ædile, had caused the famous group of the she-wolf suckling Romulus and Remus to be placed by the sacred fig-tree in the comitium. The deputation arrived at Epidaurus, the peculiar seat of Æsculapius, and entreated permission to invite the god to Rome, and that they might be instructed how to offer him acceptable worship. This was no unusual request; for many cities had, in like manner, received his worship from Epidaurus; Sicyon,[55] Athens, Pergamus, and Cyrene. Accordingly, one of the snakes which were sacred to the god crawled from his temple to the city of Epidaurus, and from thence made its way to the sea-shore, and climbed up into the trireme of the Roman ambassadors, which was as usual drawn up on the beach. It was under the form of a snake that Æsculapius was said to have gone to Sicyon,[56] when his worship was introduced there; and the Romans, instructed by the Epidaurians, considered that he was now going to visit Rome in the same form, and they immediately sailed away with the sacred snake to Italy. But when they stopped at Antium, on their way home, the snake, so said the story,[57] left the ship, and crawled out into the precinct of the temple of Æsculapius, for the god it seems was worshipped at Antium also, and coiled himself round a tall palm-tree, where he remained for three days. The Romans anxiously waited for his return to the ship; and at last he went back, and did not move again till the ship entered the Tiber. Then when she came to Rome, he again crawled forth, but instead of landing with the ambassadors, he swam to the island in the middle of the Tiber, and there went on shore and remained quiet. A temple was built, therefore, to the god in the spot which he had himself chosen; and the island to this day preserves the memory of the story, for the travertino, which was brought there to form the foundation of the temple of the god, has been cut into a rude resemblance of a trireme, because it was on ship-board that Æsculapius had first visited the Romans, and received their worship.

The story not impossible.

There is no reason to doubt that the Romans did bring back with them a snake from Epidaurus, for there was a breed of snakes there, said to be peculiar to that country,[58] and perfectly harmless, which were accounted sacred to Æsculapius. And so complete is the ascendency which man's art has obtained over the brute creation, that it is very possible that they may have been trained to perform various feats at the bidding of their keepers; and if one of these, as is likely, went with the sacred snake to Rome, wonders may have really been exhibited to the Roman people, which they would have certainly supposed to be supernatural.

Mutual knowledge of each other possessed at this time by the Greeks and Romans.

This, if we except the doubtful story of the embassy to Athens immediately before the decemvirate, and one or two deputations to consult the oracle of Delphi, is the earliest instance recorded by the Roman annalists of any direct communication between their country and Greece since the beginning of the commonwealth. Greek writers, as we have seen, mentioned an embassy sent to Alexander at Babylon, and a remonstrance

[54] Valerius Maximus, I. 8. Auctor "de Viris Illustribus," in "Æsculap. Rom. advect."

[55] Pausanias, II. 10, 26.

[56] Pausanias, II. 10.

[57] As given by Valerius Maximus, I. 8, by the author "de Viris Illustribus," and above all by Ovid, Metamorphos. XV. 622, &c.

[58] Pausanias, II. 28.

made by Demetrius Poliorcetes against the piracies of the Antiatians, at a time when they were subject to the Romans. We may be sure, at any rate, that in the middle of the fifth century the two people were no strangers to each other; and whether it be true or not that Demetrius acknowledged the Romans to be the kinsmen of the Greeks, yet when the Epidaurians gave them their god Æsculapius, they would feel that they were not giving him to a people utterly barbarian, but to one which had for centuries paid divine honors to Greek heroes, which worshipped Hercules, and the twin gods Castor and Pollux; and which, within the memory of the existing generation, had erected statues in the comitium to the wisest and bravest of the men of Greece,[59] Pythagoras and Alcibiades. Nor can we doubt that Q. Ogulnius was sufficiently acquainted with the Greek language to address the Epidaurians, as L. Postumius a few years later addressed the Tarentines, without the help of an interpreter.

It becomes here necessary to describe the state of the east and the internal condition of Rome.

We are now arrived, however, at the period when the histories of Greece and Rome unavoidably intermix with one another; when the greatest prince and general of the Greek nation crossed over into Italy, and became the head of the last coalition of the Italian states against Rome. We must here then pause, and before we enter upon the new Samnite and Tarentine war, in which Pyrrhus so soon interfered, and before we notice those renewed hostilities with the Gauls, which owed their origin, in part at least, to the intrigues of the Tarentines, we must once more cross the sea, after an interval of more than a hundred years, and observe what was now the state of Greece and of the eastern world; what new powers had succeeded to Athens, Sparta, Thebes, and the great king who had inherited the fragments of the empire of Alexander, and what was the condition of the various states of the Grecian name in Greece itself and in Sicily. We must endeavor, too, to obtain some more lively notion of Rome and the Roman people at this same period, than could be gained from the imperfect record of political and military events; to conceive what that city was which Cineas likened to a temple; what was the real character of that people whose senate he described as an assembly of kings.

CHAPTER XXXV.

STATE OF THE EAST—KINGDOMS OF ALEXANDER'S SUCCESSORS—SICILY—GREECE—KINGDOM OF EPIRUS, AND EARLY FORTUNES OF PYRRHUS.

"When he was strong the great horn was broken; and for it came up four notable ones towards the four winds of heaven."—DANIEL VIII. 8.

The 124th Olympiad is a remarkable period in Grecian history.

THE hundred and twenty-fourth Olympiad witnessed, says Polybius,[1] the first revival of the Achæan league, and the deaths of Ptolemy, the son of Lagus, of Lysimachus, of Seleucus Nicator, and of Ptolemy Ceraunus. The same period was also marked by the Italian expedition of Pyrrhus, and immediately afterwards followed the great inroad of

[59] Pliny, Histor. Natural. XXXIV. § 26. Ed. Sillig. These statues were set up "bello Samniti," probably in the second war; and were erected in consequence of the command of the Delphian oracle, which the Romans had probably consulted after their disaster at the pass of Caudium, as they did afterwards after the defeat at Cannæ. Livy, XXII. 57.

[1] Polybius, II. 41. Some explanation may perhaps be required of the length of this chap-

the Gauls into Greece and Asia, their celebrated attack upon Delphi, and their establishment in the heart of Asia Minor, in the country which afterwards was called from them Galatia. This coincidence of remarkable events is enough of itself to attract attention; and the names which I have just mentioned contain, in a manner, the germ of the whole history of the eastern world; all its interests and all its most striking points may be fully comprehended, when these names have been rendered significant, and we have formed a distinct notion of the persons and people which they designate.

Seleucus is assassinated by Ptolemy Ceraunus, who seizes the throne of Macedonia.

Forty years[2] had elapsed since the death of Alexander, when Seleucus Nicator, the last survivor of his generals, was assassinated at Lysimachia[3] by Ptolemy Ceraunus. The old man, for Seleucus was more than seventy-five years old, had just before destroyed the kingdom of Lysimachus, the last survivor except himself of the immediate successors and former generals of Alexander; and after fifty years' absence, was returning as the sovereign of Asia to that country which he had left as an unknown officer in Alexander's army. But an oracle, it is said, had bidden him beware of Europe;[4] for that the appointed seat of his fortunes was Asia. And scarcely had he landed on the Thracian Chersonesus, when he was assassinated by one of his own followers, by Ptolemy Ceraunus,[5] the half brother of Ptolemy Philadelphus, the reigning king of Egypt, who had first been a refugee at the court of Lysimachus, and, after his death, had been taken into the service of Seleucus, and had been treated by him with the greatest kindness and confidence. Seleucus' vast kingdom, which reached from the Hellespont to the Indus, was inherited by his son Antiochus;[6] but his murderer seized upon the throne of Macedonia, which having been in rapid succession filled by various competitors, and having lastly been occupied by Lysimachus, now, in consequence of his overthrow and death, and of the murder of his conqueror, seemed to lie open to the first pretender.

Ptolemy the son of Lagus reigns in Egypt, Cyrene, and Cyprus.

Seleucus outlived by about two years[7] his old ally and his protector in his utmost need, Ptolemy the son of Lagus, king of Egypt. With more unbroken good fortune than any other of his contemporaries, Ptolemy had remained master of Egypt, first as satrap and afterwards as king, from the first division of Alexander's empire down to the period of his own death. The distinct and almost unassailable position of Egypt saved it from the sudden conquests which often changed the fortune of other countries; the deserts of the Nile formed a barrier not easily to be overcome. To Egypt, Ptolemy had added the old commonwealth of Cyrene,[8] where the domestic factions, according to the frequent fate of the Greek cities, had at last sacrificed their common independence to a foreign enemy. He was also master of the rich island of Cyprus,[9] and, after the defeat of Antigonus at Ipsus, he had extended his

ter, devoted as it is to matters not directly connected with the Roman history of the fifth century of Rome. But it is impossible to forget that all the countries here spoken of will successively become parts of the Roman empire; the wars in which they were engaged with Rome will hereafter claim our attention, and therefore their condition immediately before those wars cannot be considered foreign to my subject. Besides, the distinctness of the eastern empire from the western was productive of the most important consequences; and this distinctness arose from the spread of the Greek language and manners over Asia Minor, Syria, and Egypt, by Alexander's conquests, and the establishment of his successive kingdoms. As for the notices of Greece itself, of Sparta, of Thebes, and of Athens, they cannot plead quite the same justification; but I trust that they may be forgiven, as an almost involuntary tribute of respect and affection to old associations and immortal names, on which we can scarcely dwell too long or too often.

[2] Alexander died Olymp. 114-1-2, B. C. 323. Seleucus was murdered Olymp. 124-4, B. C. 280. See Fynes Clinton, Fasti Hellenici.

[3] Appian, Syriac. 62. Porphyry, apud Eusebium, Chronic. p. 63. Ed. Scaliger.

[4] Appian, Syriac. 63.

[5] Ptolemy Ceraunus was the son of Ptolemy Soter, by Eurydice, the daughter of Antipater; Ptolemy Philadelphus was his son by Berenice. Porphyry, apud Euseb. p. 63. Pausanias, I. 6.

[6] Memnon apud Photium, p. 226, Ed. Bekker.

[7] Ptolemy Soter, the son of Lagus, died just forty years after the death of Alexander, of whose actions he and Aristobulus were the earliest and most authentic historians. His death took place Olymp. 124-2, B. C. 283.

[8] Diodorus, XVIII. 21.

[9] Ptolemy reduced the several petty kings of

dominion in Syria, as far as the valley of the Orontes, the country known by the name of Cœle-Syria,[10] or the vale of Syria. His dominion, next to that of Seleucus, was by far the most extensive, as it was, without any exception, the most compact and secure of all the kingdoms formed out of Alexander's empire.

The Greek dominion was not shaken by Alexander's death.

When Alexander died at Babylon, only seven years had elapsed since his conquest of Persia, and not more than four since his victory over Porus and his campaign in India. That his conquests could not have been completely consolidated within so short a period is evident; but it affords a wonderful proof of the ascendency of the Greek race over the Asiatics, that the sudden death of the great conqueror did not destroy his unfinished work; that not a single native chief ventured to assert the independence of his country, but every province continued in the unity of the Macedonian empire, and obeyed without dispute a Macedonian satrap.[11] Nor did the subsequent wars between the Macedonian generals destroy the spell of their superiority. Eumenes and Antigonus carried on their contest in Susiana and Media, and disposed at their will of all the resources of those countries; and, after the murder of the last of Alexander's children, fourteen years after his own death, when obedience was no longer claimed even nominally for the blood and name of the great conqueror, still the Greek dominion was unshaken; and Seleucus, by birth a simple Macedonian subject, sat undisturbed in Babylon, on the throne of Nebuchadnezzar, and held the country of Cyrus as one amongst his numerous provinces.

This was owing partly to his conciliatory policy towards the Asiatics.

This continuance of the Macedonian power was owing, no doubt, in no small measure, to Alexander's comprehensive wisdom. He made a Macedonian soldier of his guard, Peucestes,[12] satrap of Persia; but the simple soldier, unfettered by any literary or philosophical pride, did not scruple to adopt the Persian dress, and to learn the Persian language; confirming his own and his nation's dominion by those very compliances which many of his more cultivated but less wise countrymen regarded as an unworthy condescension to the barbarians.[13] The youth of the Asiatic provinces[14] were enlisted in the Macedonian army, were taught the discipline of the phalanx, and the use of the Greek shield and pike; the bravest of them were admitted into the more distinguished bodies of cavalry and infantry known by the name of the king's companions; and the highest of the Persian nobility were made, together with the noblest of the Macedonians, officers of the king's body-guard. Thus, where the insulting display of superiority was avoided, its reality was felt and acknowledged without murmuring; and when the king's officers became independent satraps, the Asiatics saw their Macedonian comrades preferred, almost without a single exception, to these dignities, and they themselves remained the subjects of men whom they had so lately seen nominally their equals.

Spread of the Greek language and manners. Foundation of Greek cities in Asia.

Thus there was spread over Asia, from the shores of the Ægean to the Indus, and over the whole of Egypt also, an outer covering at the least of Greek civilization, however thinly it might have been laid on here and there, on the solid and heterogeneous mass below. The native languages were not extirpated, they were not even driven, as afterwards in the western provinces of the Roman empire, to a few mountainous or remote districts; they remained probably in general use for all the common purposes of life: but Greek was everywhere the medium of communication between the

the island, and made himself master of it, Olymp. 117-1, B. C. 312. [Diodorus, XIX. 79.] He afterwards lost it, in consequence of his great naval defeat by Demetrius near Salamis, Olymp. 118-2 [Diodorus, XX. 53], and finally recovered it after the victory of Ipsus. [Plutarch, Demetr. 35.]

[10] Diodorus, Fragm. Vatican. XXI. 1.

[11] See the account of the division of the provinces, and of the Macedonian generals appointed to be satraps over each, in Justin, XIII. 4, and Diodorus, XVIII. 3, 39. There is scarcely a single Asiatic name on the list; only Oxyartes, the father of Roxana, Alexander's queen, had the country of Paropamisadæ; and Porus and Taxilas retained for a time their governments on the Hydaspes and the Indus.

[12] Arrian, de Expedit. Alexand. VI. 30.

[13] Arrian, VII. 6.

[14] Arrian, VII. 6, 11.

natives of different countries; it was the language of the court, of the government, and of literature. Many new cities were also founded, where the predominant element of the population was Greek from the beginning: such as Antioch, Laodicea, Apamea, Seleucia in Syria,[15] Seleucia on the Tigris, and many other places built also by the same founder, Seleucus, in the several provinces of his empire. From these an influence was communicated to other cities in their neighborhood, which were older than the Greek conquest; and the Greek character was revived in places which, like Tarsus, claimed to be originally Grecian settlements,[16] but in the lapse of years had become barbarized.

Upper Asia was soon lost to the Greek dominion, and was again governed by native princes, the Arsacidæ.

In this manner Asia Minor and Syria were pervaded in every part by the language and institutions of Greece, and retained the impression through many centuries down to the period of the Saracen and Turkish conquerors. Upper Asia, from the Euphrates to the Indus, was effected much more slightly; and the connection of these countries with Greece was finally broken about thirty years after the period at which we are now arrived, by the restoration of a native monarchy, in the line of the Arsacidæ.[17] Seleucia on the Tigris then became the capital of a barbarian sovereign; and although it, with some of the other Greek cities founded by Seleucus[18] in Media and Parthia, had not lost their national character even in the time of Strabo, yet it was enough if they could retain it themselves; there was no possibility of communicating it in any degree to the nations around them.

Kingdoms half Greek half barbarian existing in Asia Minor.

We may be excused, however, from extending our view beyond the Euphrates, and may return to a more minute examination of those countries of western Asia and Africa which were all destined to become successively provinces of Rome. And here, although we at first sight see nothing but the two great monarchies of Syria and Egypt, yet a nearer view shows us some smaller kingdoms which had been overlooked by the strength of the first Macedonian kings, and established themselves boldly against the weakness of their successors: kingdoms ruled by a race of princes, partly or chiefly of barbarian descent, but where the Greek character notwithstanding gave the predominant color to their people, and even to themselves. Such were the kingdoms of Bithynia and Pontus on the northern side of Asia Minor. Another distinct state, if so it may be called, was formed in the 125th Olympiad by the settlement of the Gauls to the south of Bithynia, and to the northwest of Cappadocia: and the kingdom of Pergamus grew up not long afterwards on the coasts of the Ægean and the Propontis; but as yet it had not come into existence.

In the 124th Olympiad Zipætes[19] or Zibætes was still, at the age of more than

[15] Appian, Syriac. 57.

[16] Κτίσμα τῶν μετὰ Τριπτολέμου πλανηθήντων 'Αργείων κατὰ ζήτησιν 'Ιοῦς. Strabo, XIV. p. 673. One should not pay much regard to such a story, were there not other grounds for believing that the Greeks at a very early period had settled on the coasts of Cilicia. See the remarkable statement preserved in the Armenian translation of Eusebius, and copied by Eusebius from Alexander Polyhistor or Abydenus, that Sennacherib was called down from Nineveh by the news of a Greek descent on Cilicia, which he repelled after a very hard-fought battle. Compare Niebuhr's Kleine Schriften, p. 203. Might not the sons of Javan, to whom the Phœnicians sold Israelitish captives at a much earlier period (Joel iii. 6), be the Greek settlers on the Cilician coast as well as the more remote inhabitants of Greece itself?

[17] In Olymp. 132-3, B. C. 250. This was in the reign of Antiochus Theos. See Justin. XLI. 4, who makes a mistake, however, as to the reign, and Arrian, Parthic. apud Photium. p. 17. Ed. Bekker. See also Fynes Clinton, Fasti Hellenici, Vol. III. under the year B. C. 250, A. U. C. 404.

[18] Περιοικεῖται (ἡ Μηδία) πόλεσιν 'Ελληνίσι κατὰ τὴν ὑφήγησιν τὴν 'Αλεξάνδρου, φυλακῆς ἕνεκεν τῶν συγκυρούντων αὐτῇ βαρβάρων. Polybius, X. 27.

[19] He reigned from 336 B. C. to 278, and was born in 354. His father Bas was born in 397 B. C. Memnon apud Photium, p. 227, 228. Ed. Bekker.

This reference may perhaps require explanation for some readers. Photius, who was patriarch of Constantinople in the latter half of the ninth century, has left a sort of catalogue raisonné, or rather an abstract of the various books which he was in the habit of reading. In this work, which he called his library, there are preserved abridgments of many books which would otherwise have been altogether lost to us; and amongst the rest there is an abstract of a history of Heraclea on the Exuine sea, written by one Memnon, who flourished at a period not certainly known, but which cannot be placed earlier than the times of the early Roman emperors. In speaking of Heraclea, Mem-

Kingdom of Bithynia.

seventy, reigning over the Bithynians. His father had seen the torrent of Alexander's invasion pass by him without touching his dominions; and whilst the conqueror was engaged in Upper Asia, the Bithynian prince had repelled with success the attack of one of his generals, who was left behind to complete the conquest of the countries which Alexander had merely overrun. After Alexander's death, European Thrace and the southern coast of the Euxine were assigned in the general partition of the empire to Lysimachus; but the Bithynian princes held their ground against him, and still continued to reign over a territory more or less extensive, till Lysimachus and his dominions were conquered by Seleucus in the battle on the plain of Corus in Phrygia. Zipætes then was as jealous of Seleucus as he had been before of Lysimachus; and after Seleucus' death, he cherished the same feelings towards his son Antiochus, and continued to resist him with success till the end of his life.

Cappadocia and its divisions. Northern Cappadocia or Pontius.

In the geography of Herodotus[20] the name of Cappadocia is applied to the whole breadth of Asia Minor eastward of the Halys, from the chain of Taurus to the shores of the Euxine. The government of all this country had been bestowed by Darius,[21] the son of Hystaspes, on one of the Persian chiefs who had taken part with him in the conspiracy against Smerdis, and it had remained from that time forward with his posterity. But in the time of Xenophon,[22] the tribes along the Euxine were practically independent of any Persian satrap, and the name of Cappadocia was then, as afterwards, restricted to the southern and more inland part of the country. The same state of things prevailed in the early part of the reign of Philip of Macedon; Scylax, in his Periplus, notices a number of barbarian tribes between Colchis and Paphlagonia: yet immediately to the eastward of Paphlagonia he placed what he calls Assyria; and Syria, as we know, was the name anciently given by the Greeks to that country which they afterwards learnt to call by its Persian name Cappadocia.[23] But while the southern part of their old satrapy passed into other hands, the descendants of Darius' fellow-conspirator strengthened their hold on the northern part of their original dominion; and in the reign of Alexander, Mithridates, son of Ariobarzanes, is called[24] by Diodorus, "king," and his kingdom extended along the coast of the Euxine from the confines of Bithynia to those of Colchis. Though a king, however, he was regarded as a vassal by Alexander's general, Antigonus, when he, after the death of Eumenes, became master of all Asia from the Euphrates to the Ægean; and Antigonus suspecting his fidelity when he was on the eve of his decisive struggle against Cassander, Ptolemy, Seleucus, and Lysimachus, caused him to be put to death.[25] His son, Mithridates, notwithstanding, succeeded to his father's dominions, retained them during the lifetime of Seleucus, and for a period of nearly eighteen years afterwards, and having lived to witness the irruption[26] of the Gauls and their settlements on the very borders of his kingdom, died, after a reign of thirty-six years, immediately before the beginning of the first Punic war, and was succeeded in his turn by his son Ariobarzanes.

non was often led to notice the neighboring kings of Bithynia, and thus we are enabled to give the succession and the dates of the reigns of those obscure princes. So capricious is the chance which has preserved some portions of ancient history from oblivion, while it has utterly destroyed all record of others. But Photius' library, compiled in the ninth century, shows what treasures of Greek literature were then existing at Constantinople, which in the course of the six following centuries perished irrecoverably. In this respect the French and Venetian conquest in the thirteenth century was far more destructive than the Turkish conquest in the fifteenth.

[20] Herodot. I. 72, 76, compared with V. 49.

[21] Polybius, V. 43. Diodorus, XIX. 40. Appian, Mithridat. 9, 112, makes Mithridates to have been descended from Darius himself. We find no Mithridates or Ariobarzanes in either of the lists of the conspirators against Smerdis given by Herodotus and Ctesias.

[22] Anabas. VII. 8. In his time Mithridates was satrap of Cappadocia and Lycaonia.

[23] Herodot. I. 72. And in the Periplus of the Euxine ascribed to Marcianus of Heraclea (Hudson, Geogr. Min. p. 73), it is said that the Cappadocians were called by some White Syrians, and that the old geographers made Cappadocia extend as far as the coast of the Euxine.

[24] Diodorus, XVI. 90.

[25] Diodorus, XX. 111.

[26] Memnon, apud Photium, p. 220. Ed. Bekker. Diodorus, XX. 111.

Southern Cappadocia meanwhile had passed before the conquest of Alexander into the hands of a satrap named Ariarathes,[27] to whom Diodorus gives the title of king. Like every other prince and state in Asia, he had been unable to resist the power of the Macedonian invasion, but Alexander's death broke, as he supposed, the spell of the Greek dominion, and Ariarathes ventured to dispute the decision of the council of generals which had assigned Cappadocia to Eumenes, and to retain the possession of it himself. Such an example of resistance, if successful, might have at once dissolved the Macedonian empire, and Perdiccas hastened to put it down. He encountered Ariarathes,[28] defeated him, made him prisoner, and crucified him; and then, according to the arrangement of the council, bestowed the government of Cappadocia on Eumenes. The nephew and heir of Ariarathes, who also bore his name, took refuge[29] in Armenia, and there waited for better times. He saw the Macedonian power divided against itself; Perdiccas, his uncle's conqueror, had been killed by his own soldiers; Eumenes, who had been made satrap of Cappadocia, had been put to death by Antigonus; and Antigonus, who had become sovereign of all Asia Minor, was engaged in war with Seleucus the ruler of Mesopotamia and the eastern provinces. Amidst their quarrels Ariarathes, with the help of the prince of Armenia, made his way back to his country, drove out the Macedonian garrisons by which it was occupied, and made himself king of Cappadocia.

Southern Cappadocia.

The sovereignty of a native prince gratified the national feelings of the people, while from a Greek ruler they may have derived some improvements in art and civilization. But from neither were they like to receive the blessings of just and good government; and in this respect, probably, the Greek and barbarian rulers were perfectly on a level with each other. From time immemorial, indeed, in Asia, government had seemed to have no other object than to exact from the people the largest possible amount of revenue, and the system of finance consisted merely in the unscrupulous practice of oppression and fraud. Never was there a more disgraceful monument of an unprincipled spirit in such matters, than that strange collection of cases of open robbery or fraudulent dealing, which was so long ascribed to Aristotle, and which still is to be found amongst his works, under the title of the second book of the Economics. Its real date and author are unknown;[30] but it must have been written for the instruction of some prince or state in Asia, and it gives a curious picture of the ordinary ways and means of a satrap or dynast, as well as of the expedients by which they might supply their ordinary occasions. "A satrap's revenue," says the writer,[31] "arises from six sources: from his tithes of the produce of all the land in his satrapy; from his domains; from his customs; from his duties levied on goods within the country, and his market duties; from his pastures; and, sixthly, from his sundries," amongst which last are reckoned a poll tax,[32] and a tax on manufacturing labor. And amongst a king's ways and means is expressly mentioned, a tampering with the currency, and a raising or lowering the value of the coin[33] as it might suit his purposes.

All the Asiatic governments, whether Greek or barbarian, were alike oppressive and corrupt.

But far above the kingdoms of Asia, whether Greek or semi-barbarian, were those free Greek cities which lined the whole coast of Asia Minor, from Trapezus, at the south-eastern corner of the Euxine, to Soli and Tarsus, with their Greek or half Greek population, at the mouth of the Gulf of Issus, and almost on the frontier of Syria. Of these Greek cities, Sinope and Heraclea were the most famous on the north coast; the shore

Free Greek cities on the coasts of Asia Minor.

[27] Diodorus, XXXI. Excerpt. Photii.

[28] Diodorus, XXXI. apud Photium, and XVIII. 16.

[29] Diodorus, XXXI. apud Phot.

[30] See the article on this subject in Niebuhr's Kleine Schriften, p. 412, and another by Mr. Lewis, in the first volume of the Philological Museum.

[31] ἔστι δὲ εἴδη ἓξ τῶν προσόδων· ἀπὸ γῆς, ἀπὸ τῶν ἐν τῇ χώρᾳ ἰδίων γενομένων, ἀπὸ ἐμπορίων, ἀπὸ τελῶν, ἀπὸ βοσκημάτων, ἀπὸ τῶν ἄλλων. Œconomic. II. 1

[32] ἕκτη δὲ, ἡ ἀπὸ τῶν ἄλλων, ἐπικεφάλαιόν τε καὶ χειρωνάξιον προσαγορευομένη.

[33] περὶ τὸ νόμισμα λέγω, ποῖον καὶ πότε τίμιον ἢ εὔωνον ποιητέον.

of the Ægean was covered with towns whose names had been famous from remote ages; but the noblest state, not of Asia Minor only, but almost of the whole world, was the great and free and high-minded commonwealth of Rhodes.

Rhodes. Its wise and good government, and the just and heroic spirit of its citizens.

The island of Rhodes, till nearly the end of the Peloponnesian war, was divided between the three Dorian cities, Lindus,[34] Ialysus, and Camirus. But in the 93d Olympiad, about three years before the battle of Ægospotami, the three states agreed to found a common capital,[35] to which they gave the name of the island, and from that time forwards the city of Rhodes became eminent amongst the cities of the Greek name. It was built on the northern side of the island, after a plan given by Hippodamus of Miletus,[36] the most famous architect of his age, and it stood partly on the low ground nearly at the level of the sea, and partly, like Genoa, on the side of the hill, which formed a semicircle round the lower part of the town. Rhodes was famous alike in war and peace; the great painter, Protogenes, enriched it with pictures of the highest excellence, and which were universally admired; the famous colossal figure of the sun, more than a hundred feet in height, which bestrode the harbor's mouth, was reputed one of the wonders of the world; and the heroic resistance of the Rhodians against Demetrius Poliorcetes was no less glorious than the defence of the same city against the Turks in later times by the knights of St. John. But Rhodes could yet boast of a better and far rarer glory, in the justice and mutual kindness which distinguished her political institutions, and the social relations of her citizens;[37] and, above all, in that virtue so rare in every age, and almost unknown to the nations of antiquity, a spirit of general benevolence, and of forbearance even towards enemies. The naval power of Rhodes was great, but it was employed, not for purposes of ambition, but to put down piracy.[38] And in the heat of the great siege of their city, when Demetrius did not scruple to employ against them the pirates[39] whose crimes they had repressed, and when a thousand ships, belonging to merchants of various nations, had come to the siege, like eagles to the carcass, to make their profit out of the expected plunder of the town, and out of the sale of its citizens as slaves, this noble people rejected with indignation the proposal of some ill-judging orators, to pull down the statues of Antigonus and Demetrius,[40] and resolved that their present hostility to those princes should not tempt them to destroy the memorials of their former friendship. The Rhodians, in the midst of a struggle for life and death, allowed the statues of their enemies to stand uninjured in the heart of their city. The Romans, after all danger to themselves was over, could murder in cold blood the Samnite general, C. Pontius, to whom they owed not only the respect due to a brave enemy, but gratitude for the generosity with which he had treated them in his day of victory.

The literature of this period has almost wholly perished.

I have thus attempted to give a sketch of the state of Asia in the 125th Olympiad; but it should be remembered, that although the Greek literature of this period was very voluminous, yet it has so entirely perished, that hardly a single writer has escaped the wreck. Thus we know scarcely more of Greece and Asia in the middle of the fifth century of Rome, than we know of Rome itself; that is, we have in both cases the skeleton of political and military events, but we have no contemporary pictures of the real state of either nation. Almost the sole remains of the Greek literature of this period are, perhaps, that treatise on public economy or finance, which has been falsely ascribed to Aristotle,[41] and the corrupt fragments of Dicæar-

[34] Thucydides, VIII. 44.

[35] Diodorus, XIII. 75.

[36] Compare Strabo, XIV. p. 643, and Aristot. Politic. II. 6, and Diodorus, XIX. 45.

[37] Strabo, XIV. p. 652, 653, *πολιτευομένη κάλλιστα τῶν 'Ελλήνων*, is the character given of Rhodes by Diodorus, XX. 81.

[38] Diodorus, XXI. 81. Strabo, XIV. p. 652.

[39] Diodorus, XX. 82, 83.

[40] Diodorus, XX. 93.

[41] That it is not Aristotle's work seems to me certain; but I do not think that it can be much later than Aristotle's age, for the writer appears to regard the dominion of Alexander as still being one governed by the king, with his satraps in the several provinces, a notion which

chus, a scholar of Aristotle, and a friend of Theophrastus, on the topography of Greece. And not only the contemporary, but the later literature, which might have illustrated these times, has also for the most part perished; the entire and connected history of Diodorus ends for us with the 119th Olympiad, and the history of the subsequent years can be gleaned only from scattered and meagre sources; from one or two of the lives of Plutarch, from Justin's abridgment, from the mere sketches contained in Appian, and from the fragments of the chronologers, which are exclusively chronological, preserved to us by Eusebius.

Sicily. The Romans must have regarded with anxiety the great power of Agathocles.

The names of Sicily, of Syracuse, and of Agathocles, are never once mentioned in the ninth and tenth books of Livy, while he is giving the history of the second and third Samnite wars; nor would any one suspect, from his narrative, that there had existed during a period of twenty-eight years, from 436 to about 464 or 465,[42] separated from Italy only by a narrow strait, one of the greatest powers and one of the most remarkable men to be found at that time in the world. But this is merely one of the consequences of the absence of all Roman historians contemporary with the fifth century. Livy did and could only copy the annalists of the seventh, or of the middle of the sixth century, and the very oldest of these, separated by an interval of a hundred years from the Samnite wars, and having no original historian older than themselves, did but put together such memorials of the past as happened to be still floating on the stream of time, stories which had chanced to be preserved in particular families, or which had lived in the remembrance of men generally. Thus, as I have before observed, the military history of the Samnite wars is often utterly inexplicable: the detail of marches, the objects aimed at in each campaign, the combinations of the generals, and the exact amount of their success, are lost in oblivion; but particular events are sometimes given in great detail, and anecdotes of remarkable men have been preserved, while their connection with each other has perished. Agathocles never made war with the Romans, and his name therefore did not occur in the triumphal Fasti of any great Roman family. What uneasiness his power gave to the senate; how gladly they must have seen his arms employed in Africa;[43] how anxiously they must have watched his movements when his fleet invaded and conquered the Liparæan islands,[44] or when he crossed the Ionian gulf, and defended Corcyra with success against the power of Cassander;[45] above all, when he actually landed in Italy, with Etruscan and Ligurian soldiers in his service, and formed an alliance with the Apulians and Peucetians or Pediculans,[46] to assist him in his conquest of Bruttium: this no Roman tradition recorded, and therefore no later annalist has mentioned; but they who can represent to themselves the necessary relations of events, can have no difficulty in conceiving its reality.

It is mentioned also that Agathocles,[47] in his African wars, had many Samnite soldiers in his army as well as Etruscans, and in the year 446 or 447, an Etrus-

certainly may have outlasted the life of Alexander himself, for his generals for several years professed to be the subjects of his infant son, but which must have passed away, at any rate within a few years, when the generals assumed severally the kingly diadem.

[42] The beginning of Agathocles' dominion is placed by Diodorus in Olymp. 115-4, which, according to his synchronism, is the year of the consulship of M. Foslius and L. Plautius, and the ninth year of the second Samnite war. His death cannot be determined exactly, because of the confusions and different systems of the Roman chronology. It would fall in Olymp. 122-4, or B. C. 289; but whether that year would coincide with the consulship of M. Valerius and Q. Cædicius, one year after the end of the third Samnite war, or with one of the two succeeding consulships, it is impossible to fix certainly. Agathocles reigned in all twenty-eight years. See Diodorus, XXI. 12. Fragm. Hoeschel.

[43] During four years, from Olymp. 117-3 to 118-2 inclusive; that is, during the Etruscan campaigns of Q. Fabius in the second Samnite war.

[44] In Olymp. 119-1, the last year of the second Samnite war. Diodorus, XX. 101.

[45] In the 120th Olympiad, but the exact year is not known, and therefore, somewhere about the beginning of the third Samnite war. Diodorus, XXI. 2. Fragm. Hoeschel. Compare also Fragm. Vatican, XXI. 2.

[46] About the same period, just after his expedition to Corcyra. Diodorus, Fragm. Hoeschel, XXI. 3, 4.

[47] Diodorus, XX. 11 64.

His connection with some of the nations of Italy.

can fleet of eighteen ships[48] came to his relief at Syracuse, when he was blockaded by the Carthaginians, and enabled him to defeat the enemy and effect his passage once more to Africa. This was three or four years before the end of the second Samnite war, and just after the submission of the principal Etruscan states to Rome, in consequence of the great successes of Q. Fabius. We are told, also, that at one time the Tarentines[49] applied to him to command their forces against the Messapians and Lucanians, and that he went over to Italy accordingly, which, though the date is not mentioned, must have taken place in the latter part of his reign, when he was making war upon the Bruttians; that is, as nearly as we can fix it, in the 120th or 121st Olympiad, whilst the third Samnite war was raging. It is strange that neither the Samnites nor the Etruscans ever asked him to aid them against Rome, or, if they did, that he should not have been tempted to engage in so great a contest. But the nearer interest of humbling the Carthaginians, and of establishing his power on the south coast of Italy, prevented him from penetrating through the straits of Messana, and sending a fleet to the mouth of the Tiber. And no doubt, if he had attacked the Romans, they would have formed a close alliance with Carthage against him, as they did shortly afterwards against Pyrrhus; nay, it is probable that the renewal of the old league between the two countries, which took place in 448,[50] may have been caused in some degree by their common fear of Agathocles, who had at that period finally evacuated Africa, but had not yet made peace with Carthage.

Distracted state of Sicily during his government. Misery of his later years.

Agathocles died in the last year of the 122d Olympiad, about three years after the end of the third Samnite war. Had he lived fifty years earlier, he, like Dionysius, would have been known by no other title than that of tyrant; but now the successors of Alexander had accustomed men to tolerate the name of king, in persons who had no hereditary right to their thrones; and Agathocles certainly as well deserved the title as Lysimachus, or the ruffian Cassander. Polybius accused Timæus of calumniating him; but surely his own character of him must be no less exaggerated on the other side, when he says[51] that although in the beginning of his career he was most bloody, yet when he had once firmly established his power, he became the gentlest and mildest of men. Like Augustus, he was too wise to indulge in needless cruelty; but his later life was not so peaceful as that of Augustus, and whenever either cruelty or treachery seemed likely to be useful, he indulged in both without scruple. The devastation and misery of Sicily during his reign must have been extreme. Dinocrates, a Syracusan exile,[52] was at the head of an army of 20,000 foot and 3000 horse, and had made himself master of several cities, and so well was he satisfied with his buccaneer condition, that he rejected Agathocles' offer of allowing him to return to Syracuse, and of abdicating his own dominion that the exiles might return freely. Then Agathocles called the Carthaginians over to put Dinocrates down; and gave up to them as the price of their aid all the cities which they had formerly possessed in Sicily. The exiles were afterwards defeated, and Dinocrates was now glad to make his submission;[53] and from this time, A. U. C. 449, we hear of no further civil wars or massacres in Sicily, till the period immediately preceding Agathocles' death, which took place sixteen or seventeen years later. But his last days were full of misery. His son, Agathocles,[54] was murdered by his grandson Archagathus, and the old tyrant, who was now reduced almost to the brink of the grave by a painful and hopeless disorder, dreaded lest Archagathus should murder the rest of his family as soon as he should himself be no more. Accordingly, he resolved to send his wife, Texena,[55] with his two young sons, and all his treasure, to Egypt, her na-

[48] Diodorus, XX. 61. In Olymp. 118-2.
[49] Strabo, VI. p. 280.
[50] Livy, IX. 43.
[51] Polybius, IX. 23.
[52] Diodorus, XX. 77, 78.
[53] Diodorus, XX. 89, 90.
[54] Diodorus, XXI. 12. Fragm. Hoeschel.
[55] Justin, XXIII. 2. The account of the part-

tive country, whilst he himself should be left alone to die. On his death, the old democracy[56] was restored without a struggle, his property was confiscated, and his statues thrown down. But it was a democracy in name only, for we find that the same man, Hicetas, was continued in the office of captain-general for the next nine years[57] successively; and so long a term of military command in times of civil and foreign war was equivalent to a despotism or tyranny.

Excesses committed by the mercenary soldiers. They occupy Messana.

At the moment of Agathocles' death, there was a Syracusan army[58] in the field, consisting, as usual, chiefly of mercenaries, and commanded by the tyrant's grandson, Archagathus. But Mænon, who is said in Diodorus' account to have poisoned Agathocles, and who was now with the army of Archagathus, contrived to murder Archagathus, and to get the army into his own hands. He then attempted to get possession of Syracuse, and to make himself tyrant, and finding himself resisted by the new government and the captain-general, Hicetas, he too called in the Carthaginians. Syracuse was quite unable to resist, and submitted to the terms which they imposed. They gave 400 hostages, and consented to receive back all the exiles, under which term all Mænon's army were included. What was become of Mænon himself we know not; but the mercenaries, being mostly Samnite or Lucanian foreigners, were still looked upon as an inferior caste to the old Syracusan citizens; and as these last formed the majority of the people, none of the new citizens could ever get access to any public office. This led to fresh disturbances, but at last the strangers agreed to sell their properties within a certain time, and to leave Sicily. They accordingly came to Messana,[59] in order to cross the strait and return to Italy; but being admitted into the city, they rose by night and massacred the principal inhabitants, and kept the women and the city for themselves. From this time forwards the inhabitants of Messana were known by the name of Mamertini, sons of Mamers or Mars, that being the name by which these Italian soldiers of fortune had been used to call themselves.

Tyrants in the several cities of Sicily.

While Messana had thus fallen into the hands of a barbarian soldiery, the condition of the rest of Sicily was scarcely happier. Hicetas had the power of a tyrant in Syracuse, Phintias[60] was tyrant in Agrigentum, Tyndarion in Tauromenium, Heraclides in Leontini, and other men whose names have not reached posterity exercised the same dominion in the smaller cities. Hicetas and Phintias made war upon each other, made plundering inroads into each other's territories, and mutually reduced the frontier districts to a state of utter desolation. Gela was destroyed by Phintias, and its inhabitants removed to a new town which he founded on the coast near the mouth of the Himera, and called after his own name. And the Mamertines availed themselves of all this misery to extend their own power, even to the opposite side of the island; they sacked Camarina and Gela,[61] which had been again partially inhabited after its destruction by Phintias, and obliged several of the Greek cities to pay them tribute. Thus the Greek power in Sicily, which had been so formidable under Agathocles, was now quite prostrated, and the whole island seemed likely to become the spoil of the Carthaginians and Mamertines. This course of events on one side of the strait, and the extension of the Roman dominion a few years later to the extreme coast of Bruttium on the other side, tended inevitably to bring about a collision between Rome and Carthage, such as Pyrrhus foretold when he found it impossible to revive and consolidate the Greek interest, and restore in a manner the dominion of Agathocles.

ing between Agathocles and his family is given by Justin with much simplicity and good feeling, and it is much to his credit that he preferred this story to the horrible and incredible tales about the last days of Agathocles which Diodorus has copied apparently from Timæus.

56 Diodorus, Fragm. Hoeschel. XXI. 12.

57 Diodorus, Fragm. Hoeschel. XXII. 6. His expressions are, Ἱκέτας ἐννέα ἔτη δυναστεύσας—ἐκβάλλεται τῆς τυραννίδος.

58 Diodorus, Fragm. Hoeschel. XXI. 12, 13.

59 Diodorus, Fragm. Hoeschel. XXI. 13. Polybius, I. 7.

60 Diodorus, Fragm. Hoeschel. XXII. 2, 11.

61 Diodorus, Fragm. Hoeschel. XXIII. 2. Polybius, I. 8.

Greece. Its degraded condition. Attempt of the Greeks to throw off the Macedonian yoke after the death of Seleucus.

And now, before I speak of Pyrrhus himself and the fortunes of his early years, we must turn our eyes to Greece, the worn-out and cast-off skin from which the living serpent had gone forth to carry his youth and vigor to other lands. Greek power, Greek energy, Greek genius, might now be found indeed anywhere rather than in Greece. Drained of all its noblest spirits, for so hopeless was the prospect at home, that any foreign service[62] offered a temptation to the Greek youth to enter it; yet exposed to the miseries of war, and eagerly contended for by rival sovereigns, because its possession was still thought the most glorious part of every dominion; mocked by every despot in turn with offers of liberty, yet as soon as it was delivered from the yoke of one, condemned under some pretence to receive the garrison of another into its citadels; Greece, in the middle of the fifth century of Rome, seemed utterly exhausted, and lay almost as dead. Demetrius Poliorcetes had retained his hold upon it after his Asiatic dominion had been lost by the event of the battle of Ipsus; and even when he himself engaged in his last desperate attempt upon Asia, and whilst he was passing the last years of his life as a prisoner in the hands of Seleucus, Greece was still, for the most part, under the power of his son, Antigonus Gonatas. But upon the death of Seleucus Nicator, when Antigonus was disputing the sovereignty of Macedonia with Ptolemy Ceraunus, Seleucus' murderer, the Greeks made[63] a feeble attempt to assert their liberty. Sparta once more appeared at the head of the national confederacy, and Areus, the Spartan king, was intrusted with the conduct of the war. The Greeks attacked Ætolia, which appears at this time to have been in alliance with Antigonus, but they were repulsed with loss; and then, as usual, jealousy broke out, and the confederacy was soon dissolved. Yet, almost immediately afterwards, there was formed the first germ of a new confederacy, which existed from this time forwards till the total extinction of Grecian independence, and in which there was revived a faint image of the ancient glory of Greece, the pale martinmas summer of her closing year. This confederacy was the famous Achaian or Achæan league.

Formation of the Achæan league.

The Achaian name is conspicuous in the heroic ages of Greece, and in her last decline, but during the period of her greatness is scarcely ever brought before our notice. The towns of Achaia were small and unimportant, and the people lived for many generations in happy obscurity; but after the death of Ptolemy Ceraunus, when dread of a Gaulish invasion kindled a general spirit of exertion, and when Antigonus was likely to have sufficient employment on the side of Macedonia, four Achæan cities,[64] Dyme, Patræ, Tritæa, and Pharæ, formed a federal union for their mutual defence. According to the constitution of the league, each member was to appoint in succession, year by year, two captains-general,[65] and one secretary, or civil minister, to conduct the affairs of the union. These four states, like the forest cantons of Switzerland, were the original members, and in a manner the founders of the confederacy; and at the period of Pyrrhus' invasion of Italy, it consisted of these alone.

The cities of Peloponnesus mostly held in subjection by tyrants.

It is not possible to discover the condition of the several states of Greece, however much their ancient fame must excite an interest even for their last decay. But generally they were subjected to the Macedonian king, Antigonus,[66] either directly, by having a Macedonian garrison in their citadels, or indirectly, as being ruled by a tyrant from among their own people, who for his own sake upheld the Macedonian supremacy. Sicyon[67] had been governed by various tyrants ever since it had been taken by Demetrius Poliorcetes, when he destroyed the lower town, and removed

[62] Diodorus, XX. 40.
[63] Justin, XXIV. 1.
[64] Polybius, II. 41.
[65] Polybius, II. 43.
[66] Polybius, II. 41. IX. 29.
[67] Diodorus, XX. 102. Plutarch, Aratus, 9. He says that when Aratus delivered Sicyon in 251 B. C. some of the exiles whom he then restored had been in banishment fifty years. And Cicero, copying from the same source however, namely, Aratus' own memoirs, says the same thing. De Officiis, II. 23.

the whole population within the precincts of the old citadel. Megalopolis[68] about this time must have been under the dominion of its tyrant, Aristodemus, of Phigalea, who owed his elevation to factions in the oligarchy by which the city had been before governed. In Argos[69] Aristippus had the ascendency, through the support of king Antigonus. The Acropolis of Corinth[70] was held by one Alexander (we know not when or by what means he won it), and the strength of the place enabled him to enjoy a certain degree of independence; so that, after his death, Antigonus was obliged to employ stratagem in order to get it for himself out of the hands of Alexander's widow, Nicæa. Society was generally in a state of disorder, robbery and plundering forays were almost universal, and Greece could no longer boast that she had banished the practice of carrying arms in peace;[71] for men now went armed so commonly, that conspirators could meet and arm themselves in open day without exciting any suspicion.

Northern Greece. State of Bœotia. Disorders at Thebes.

Something more of life was to be seen in the states to the north of the isthmus of Corinth. When the Gauls invaded Greece in the second year of the 125th Olympiad, Athens, Megara, Bœotia, Phocis, Locris, and Ætolia sent a confederate army to Thermopylæ to oppose them; and the Bœotian force[72] amounted to 10,000 heavy-armed infantry, and 500 horse, a number equal to that which won the battle of Delium against the whole power of Athens in the Peloponnesian war. Thebes had twice revolted from Demetrius Poliorcetes, and had been twice reduced by him,[73] and after his second conquest of it he had pulled down its walls[74] and left it defenceless. Antigonus Gonatas retained possession of it till he succeeded in establishing himself in Macedonia; then his hold upon southern Greece was relaxed, except on those cities where he still kept a garrison of his soldiers, or where a tyrant who looked to him for protection governed almost as his officer. But Bœotia seems to have been left to itself, with nearly its old constitution; according to which Thebes enjoyed a certain supremacy over the other cities, but nothing like that dominion which she had claimed in the days of her greatness. The country was safe and flourishing when compared with Peloponnesus, and Tanagra is mentioned[75] as a place at once prosperous and deserving its prosperity; its citizens were wealthy yet simple in their manners, just, and hospitable. Thebes, on the contrary, is described as a scene of utter anarchy; acts of violence were constantly committed with impunity, and justice was so evaded or overborne by violence, that twenty-five or even thirty years[76] sometimes elapsed before the injured party could obtain a hearing for his cause before the magistrates. This was owing principally to the numerous societies or clubs which existed, avowedly for mere objects of convivial entertainments; but which becoming extremely wealthy, for men without children, and even some who had children, often left all their property to their club, were enabled no doubt to corrupt justice, in order to screen

[68] Pausanias, VIII. 27. He puts Aristodemus, however, too early, when he says that he became tyrant soon after the Lamian war, and confounds Acrotatus, son of Areus, with Acrotatus, son of Cleomenes. In 318 B. C. Megalopolis was governed by a strict oligarchy. See Diodorus, XVIII. 68. Compare Polybius, X. 25.

[69] Plutarch, Pyrrhus, 30.

[70] Plutarch, Aratus, 16, 17.

[71] Plutarch, Aratus, 6.

[72] Pausanias, X. 20.

[73] Plutarch, Demetrius, 39, 40.

[74] Diodorus, Fragm. Hoeschel. XXI. 10.

[75] Dicæarchus, Stat. Græc. p. 13. Ed. Hudson. The inscriptions of this period show that there was still a government for all Bœotia, *κοινὸν Παμβοιωτῶν συνέδριον*, and Bœotarchs, as in ancient times; there was also a magistrate called *ἄρχων ἐν κοινῷ Βοιωτῶν*, or *ἄρχων Βοιωτοῖς*, who seems to have been the head of the Bœotarchs, and of whom there is no mention, I believe, in the older constitution. Böckh thinks that it was one of the prerogatives of Thebes, that this magistrate should be always a Theban. Corpus Inscript. Vol. I. p. 729.

[76] Polybius, XX. 6. Dicæarchus, Stat. Græc. p. 15, et seqq. Hudson. The text in these fragments of Dicæarchus is often hopelessly corrupt; but they seem also, independently of such faults, to have been interpolated by some more modern writer, or rather their substance to have been given by him in his own language, not without many additions. We know the manner in which old topographical accounts are copied by one writer after another, each of whom adds something to them of his own; and thus the work of Dicæarchus seems to have formed the groundwork of the existing fragments, which have been wrought up by a later writer, and altered both in their language and matter.

the outrages of their members. A strong but not improbable picture of the worst abuses of such clubs, which even in their best state, and in the healthiest condition of society, are always fraught with evil either politically or morally.

Athens. The democracy overthrown by Antipater.

Forty years had now passed since Athens had lost Demosthenes. His death, as was most fitting, coincided exactly with the period of his country's complete subjection; within a month[77] after Antipater had established a Macedonian garrison in Munychia, Demosthenes escaped his vengeance by a sudden and painless death[78] in the island of Calauria. The shade of Xerxes might have rejoiced to see that his own people had a share in the humiliation of his old enemy; for in the army with which Antipater crushed the Greek confederates in the Lamian war there were Persian archers, slingers, and cavalry,[79] who had been brought to his aid from Asia by Craterus, and who thus strangely found, in their actual subjection to a Greek power, an opportunity of revenging the fatal days of Salamis and Platæa. That great democracy, with all its faults, by far the noblest example of free and just government which the world had then witnessed, was again destroyed by Antipater, after a duration of seventy-one years since its restoration by Thrasybulus. All citizens whose property fell short of 2000 drachmæ were deprived of their political rights; and more than half of the Athenian people were thus disfranchised. Lands in Thrace were offered to them, and they migrated thither in great numbers;[80] whilst the remnant, who were now exclusively the Athenian people, were left in mockery to the enjoyment of Solon's laws, while a Macedonian garrison occupied Munychia, and commanded the entrance into the harbor of Piræus.

And nominally restored by Demetrius Poliorcetes.

Then followed a period of fifteen years, during which Athens remained subject, first to Antipater and then to Cassander his son; and although the qualification of a citizen was reduced by Cassander[8] to 1000 drachmæ, only half of the sum fixed by his father, and thus the internal government became somewhat more popular, yet still, whilst Munychia and Piræus were in the power of a foreign prince, Athens could have no independent national existence. In the year of Rome 447, three years before the end of the second Samnite war, Cassander's garrisons were driven out by Demetrius Poliorcetes,[82] the old democracy was restored, and the Athenians were declared to be free. But it was only a shadow of the "fierce democratie," and of the real freedom of the days of Pericles and Demosthenes. The utmost baseness of flattery was lavished on Demetrius, such flattery as was incompatible with any self-respect, and which confessed that Athens was dependent[83] for the greatest national blessings not on itself, but on foreign aid.

Demetrius himself occupies Athens, and the Athenians drive out his garrisons.

A few years afterwards, when his fortune was ruined by the event of the battle of Ipsus, the Athenians refused to receive him into their city; and this so stung him that when his affairs began to mend, he laid siege to Athens, and having obliged it to surrender, he not only occupied Piræus and Munychia, but put a garrison into the city itself, converting the hill[84] of the Museum into a Macedonian citadel. It was recovered

[77] Plutarch, in Demosth. 28.

[78] Ibid. 30. The common story was that Demosthenes killed himself by a poison which he carried about him; but his nephew, Demochares, expressed his belief that his death was natural; or rather, in his own language, "that the gods, in their care for him, had rescued him from the cruelty of the Macedonians by a speedy and gentle death."

[79] Diodorus, XVIII. 16.

[80] Diodorus, XVIII. 18.

[81] Diodorus, XVIII. 74.

[82] Diodorus, XX. 45, 46.

[83] Who can help remembering Mr. Wordsworth's beautiful lines?

"So ye prop,
Sons of the brave who fought at Marathon!
Your feeble spirits. Greece her head hath bowed
As if the wreath of Liberty thereon
Would fix itself as smoothly as a cloud,
Which, at Jove's will, descends on Pelion's top.
* * * * * * *
Ah! that a conqueror's word should be so dear!
Ah! that a boon could shed such rapturous joys!
A gift of that which is not to be given
By all the blended powers of earth and heaven."

[84] Plutarch, Demetr. 30, 34. Pausanias, I. 25.

again, when he had been driven out of Macedonia by Lysimachus and Pyrrhus, by one of the last successful efforts of Athenian valor. Olympiodorus,[85] who had already acquired the reputation of a soldier and a general, led the whole population of Athens into the field; he defeated the Macedonians, stormed the Museum, and delivered Piræus and Munychia. This was in the second year of the 123d Olympiad: so that when Pyrrhus sailed for Italy seven years afterwards, Athens was really independent, for she had gained her freedom, not by the gift of another, but by her own sword.

Intellectual state of Athens. Zeno and Epicurus.

This, however, was almost a solitary gleam of light amidst the prevailing darkness. In general there were neither soldiers, statesmen, nor orators now to be found in Athens. The great tragedians had long since become extinct; and Thucydides has neither in his own country, whether free or in subjection, nor in any other country or age of the world, found a successor to rival him. Plato's divine voice was silent, and the "Master of the Wise"[86] had left none to inherit his acuteness, his boundless knowledge, and his manly judgment, at once so practical and so profound. The theatre, indeed, could boast of excellence, but it was only in the new comedy, the sickliest refinement of the drama, and a sure mark of a declining age. Still there was intellectual life of no common kind existing at this time in Athens. There were now living and teaching within her walls, two men whose doctrines in philosophy were destined to influence most widely and lastingly the characters and conduct of their fellow-creatures, the founders of the two great rival sects of the later age of the Roman republic,—Epicurus and Zeno.

Ætolia. Its bands of adventurers or "Pirates."

But Bœotia and Athens were no longer the principal powers of northern Greece; the half-barbarous Ætolians had risen to such an eminence, that we find them able, at a somewhat later period, to contend single-handed with the kingdom of Macedon. Their country was still, as in the days of Thucydides, separated from Acarnania[87] by the Achelous, and was stretched in length from the shores of the Gulf of Corinth to those of the Malian Bay, at the back of Locris, Doris, and Phocis. But a sort of federal government succeeded, in later times, to the multitude of scattered and independent villages which formerly composed the Ætolian nation; a general assembly of deputies from all the Ætolian towns met every year at Thermum to elect a captain-general,[88] a master of the horse, and a secretary for the general government of the confederacy; great fairs[89] and festivals, to which the people came up from all parts of the country, were held at the same place; and Thermum thus grew in wealth and magnificence, and its houses became noted for the magnificence of their furniture, as the inhabitants, on these great occasions, opened their doors to receive all comers, with a hospitality not common in Greece since the heroic ages. But there were other points in which the Ætolians equally retained the habits of an early state of society; in the best days of Grecian civ-

[85] Plutarch, Demetr. 46. Pausanias, I. 26.

[86] "Vidi 'l maestro di color che sanno
Seder tra filosofica famiglia."
DANTE, Inferno, IV.

[87] It had, however, acquired several towns situated in its neighborhood which had formerly been independent. The date of these several acquisitions is diffiult to fix precisely. The Ætolians had occupied the famous Cirrhæan plain just after the death of Seleucus; a repetition of the old Phocian sacrilege, which was the cause or pretence of a general attack upon them by the Peloponnesian Greeks under the supremacy of Sparta. But in this new sacred war, the authors of the sacrilege were more fortunate than the Phocians of old, and the Ætolians repelled their assailants with great loss. Justin, XXIV. 1. About the same time, in the year before the Gaulish invasion, the Ætolians obtained possession of Heraclea in Trachinia. (Pausanias, X. 20, § 9.) At a later period, Naupactus was become an Ætolian town, but we do not know when it was conquered.

[88] Polybius, V. 8, XXII. 15, § 10. The captain-general and secretary were officers also of the Achæan league. Whether the Ætolian league was formed on the Achæan model, or whether it existed earlier, we cannot tell.

[89] ἀγοραὶ καὶ πανηγύρεις. Polyb. V. 8. These fairs and religious festivals, held along with the assemblies for political purposes, remind us of the great Etruscan assemblies at the temple of Voltumna. The fairs seemed to imply that the towns in Ætolia were still little better than villages, so as to have but few shops for the regular supply of commodities.

ilization, when life and property were scarcely less secure at Athens than they are at this day in the best governed countries of Europe, the Ætolians went always armed;[90] and the character of a robber was still deemed honorable amongst them, as it had been in all parts of Greece in the Homeric age. As the nation became more powerful, this spirit was displayed on a larger scale, and Ætolian adventurers, countenanced, but not paid or organized, by the national government, made plundering expeditions on their own account both by land and sea, and were not very scrupulous in their choice of the objects of their attack. These adventurers were called "pirates," πειρατaί, a name[91] which occurs in the written language of Greece for the first time about this period, when the long wars between Alexander's successors and the general decline of good government had multiplied the number of such marauders.

Political relations of Ætolia.

The Ætolians will play an important part hereafter in this history, when their quarrels with Macedon and the Achæan league led them to conclude an alliance with Rome, and to array themselves with the Roman armies, on their first crossing the sea to carry on war in Greece. At present their place in the Greek political system seems not to have been definitely fixed; they were in alliance with Antigonus Gonatas[92] before he obtained possession of Macedon, at the time when their occupation of the Cirrhæan plain involved them in a sacred war with Peloponnesus, and they were also the allies of Pyrrhus and the Epirots; but their peculiar hostility to Macedon and to the Achæans had not as yet been called into existence. Polybius, from whom we derive most of our knowledge of them, was too much their enemy to do them full justice; and on the great occasion of the Gaulish invasion of Greece, they performed their duty nobly, and no state served the common cause more bravely or more effectually. Yet a people who made plunder their glory can have had little true greatness; and it must have been an evil time for Greece, when the Ætolians became one of the most powerful and most famous of the Grecian states.

Epirus. Its various tribes, their manner of living, and early history and traditions.

Northward of the Ambracian gulf, and lying without the limits of ancient as of modern Greece, the various Epirot tribes occupied the coast of the Ionian sea as far as the Acroceraunian promontory, reaching inland as far as the central mountains which turn the streams eastward and westward, and from the western boundary of Thessaly and Macedonia. Within these limits the Molossians, Thesprotians, Chaonians, and many other obscurer people, had from the earliest times led the same life, and kept the same institutions. They lived mostly in villages[93] or in small village-like towns, scattered over the mountains, in green glades opening amidst the forests, or along the rich valleys by which the mountains are in many places intersected, going always armed, and, with the outward habits, retaining also much of the cruelty and faithlessness of barbarians, attended by their dogs, a breed of surpassing excellence,[94] and maintaining themselves chiefly by pasturage, their ox-

[90] Thucydides, I. 5.

[91] Polybius, IV. 3. 6. Valckenaer says that the word πειρατὴς occurs, for the first time in the surviving Greek literature, in the Septuagint translation of the Bible. There it is to be found in Job XXV. 3, and Hosea VI. 10; in both instances, I think, signifying a robber by and rather than by sea. And so πειρατήριον is used in Genesis XLIX. 19. Thus the Scholiast on Pindar, Pyth. 62, says that πειραταὶ properly means οἱ ἐν ὁδῷ κακουργοῦντες. See Valckenaer on Ammonius, p. 194. The Greek translators of the Bible could not have got the word from old Greece, but the robber population of Isauria and Cilicia, who made the name of pirate so famous about two centuries afterwards, had probably already begun to be troublesome, and to molest the Egyptian merchant vessels.

[92] Justin, XXIV. 1. Dion Cassius, Fragm. Peiresc. XXXIX.

[93] οἰκοῦσι κατὰ κώμας, is the character given by Scylax of the Chaonians, Thesprotians, and Molossians equally. Periplus, p. 11. 12, Ed. Hudson. But we hear of some towns among them, although of none of any considerable size or importance.

[94] The ancient character of the Molcssian dogs is well known. Mr. Hughes found them as numerous and as fierce as they were in ancient days; the breed, he thinks, has in no respect degenerated. He describes them as "varying in color through different shades from a dark brown to a bright dun, their long fur being very soft, and thick and glossy; in size they are about equal to an English mastiff: they have a long nose, delicate ears finely point

en[95] being amongst the best of which the Greeks had any knowledge. In the heart of their country stood the ancient temple of Dodona, a name famous for generations before Delphi was yet in existence; the earliest seat of the Grecian oracles, whose ministers, the Selli, a priesthood of austerest life, received the answers of the god through no human prophet, but from the rustling voice of the sacred oaks which sheltered the temple. These traditions ascend to the most remote antiquity: but Epirus had its share also in the glories of the heroic age, and Pyrrhus the son of Achilles was said to have settled in the country of the Molossians after his return from Troy,[96] and to have been the founder of the line of Molossian kings. The government, indeed, long bore the character of the heroic period; the kings, on their accession, were wont, it is said, to meet their assembled people[97] at Passaron, and swore to govern according to the laws, while the people swore that they would maintain the monarchy according to the laws. In later times Epirus had become connected with Macedonia by the marriage of Olympias, an Epirot princess, with Philip the father of Alexander. Her brother, Alexander of Epirus, was killed, as we have seen, in Italy, where he had carried on war in defence of the Greek Italian cities against the Lucanians; and on his death his first cousin[98] Æacides succeeded to the throne. Æacides married Pthia, the daughter of Menon of Pharsalus, a distinguished leader in the last struggle between Greece and Macedon after the death of Alexander, and the children of this marriage were two daughters, Troias and Deidamia, and one son, Pyrrhus.

Early fortunes of Pyrrhus. He is brought up in exile in Illyria.

Æacides had taken part with his cousin Olympias,[99] when Cassander wanted to destroy all the family of Alexander in order to seat himself on the throne of Macedon. But Cassander had tampered with some of the Epirot chiefs; the cause of Olympias was not popular, and the Epirots did not wish to be involved in a quarrel with the party which was likely to be the ruling power in Macedon. They accordingly met in a general assembly, and deposed and banished their king. Æacides himself was out of their power, as he was still in the field on the frontiers of Macedonia with the few soldiers who remained true to him, and his daughter Deidamia was with Olympias. But Pyrrhus, then an infant, had been left at home, and the rebel chiefs[100] having murdered many of his father's friends, sought for him also to destroy him. He was hurried off in his nurse's arms by a few devoted followers, and carried safely into Illyria, where Glaucias, one of the Illyrian kings, protected him, and as his father was killed in battle soon afterwards,[101] Pyrrhus remained under Glaucius' care, and was brought up by him along with his own children.

He recovers his father's throne, loses it, and recovers it again.

Ten or eleven years afterwards, when the power of Cassander in Greece seemed to be tottering, and Demetrius Poliorcetes had re-established the democracy at Athens, Glaucias[102] entered Epirus with an armed force, and restored Pyrrhus to the throne. But again the face of affairs changed; the great league between Cassander, Ptolemy, Seleucus, and Lysimachus was formed, and Demetrius was obliged to loosen his hold on Greece, that he might help his father in Asia; thus Cassander's party recovered their influence in Epirus, and Pyrrhus, who was still only seventeen years old, was driven a second time into exile. He now joined Demetrius, who, besides their common enmity to Cassander, had married Deidamia his sister;

ed, magnificent tail, legs of a moderate length, with a body nicely rounded and compact." Travels in Albania, &c., Vol. I. p. 483.

[95] See Kruse's Hellas, Vol. I. p. 368, and the authorities there quoted.

[96] Pausanias, I. 11.

[97] Plutarch, Pyrrhus, 56.

[98] For the family of Pyrrhus, see Plutarch, Pyrrh. I. Pausanias, I. 11. Diodorus, XVI. 72, and XIX. 51. See also Justin, XVII. 3; but in his account there are some things which might mislead; as, for instance, he confounds Tharyntas or Tharypus, the great grandfather of Æacides, with Arybas his father, and makes Æacides and Alexander brothers instead of cousins, unless by the term "frater" he means frater patruelis" and not "frater germanus."

[99] Diodorus, XIX. 36.

[100] Plutarch, Pyrrh. 2.

[101] Diodorus, XIX. 74.

[102] Plutarch, Pyrrh. 3.

and with him he crossed over into Asia, and was present at the battle of Ipsus. After that great defeat he still remained faithful to Demetrius, and went as a hostage for him[103] into Egypt, when Demetrius had concluded a separate peace with Ptolemy Soter. Here fortune first began to smile upon him; he obtained the good opinion and regard of Ptolemy's queen, Berenice, and received in marriage Antigone, her daughter by a former husband. By Berenice's assistance he was supplied with men and money, and returned once more to Epirus. His kinsman, Neoptolemus, the son apparently of Alexander, who had died in Italy, had been placed on the throne, when he himself had been driven from it; but Neoptolemus was become unpopular, and Pyrrhus found many partisans. Dreading, however, lest Neoptolemus should apply to some foreign prince for aid, he entered into a compromise with him,[104] and the two rivals agreed to share the regal power between them. The end of such an arrangement could not be doubtful; suspicions arose, and Pyrrhus accusing Neoptolemus of forming designs against his life, did himself what he charged his rival with meditating, and having treacherously murdered him, after having invited him to his table as a guest, he remained the sole sovereign of Epirus.

He interferes in the quarrels between the sons of Cassander.

His old enemy Cassander died in the first year of the 121st Olympiad, five years after the battle of Ipsus. Not one of Alexander's successors had gained his power by more or worse crimes than Cassander; and as his house had been founded in blood, by the murder of Alexander's family, so now in its own blood was it to perish. His sons Antipater and Alexander[105] quarrelled for his inheritance. Antipater murdered his own mother, Thessalonica, the daughter of the great Philip of Macedon, and half-sister of Alexander; and now the last survivor of the old royal family of the race of Hercules. Alexander his brother applied to Pyrrhus for aid, and purchased it by ceding to him all that the Macedonian kings had possessed on the western side of Greece; Tymphæa and Parauæa,[106] just under the central ridge which turns the streams to the two opposite seas, and Ambracia, Acarnania, and Amphilochia, on the northern and southern shores of the Ambracian gulf. These were added permanently to the kingdom of Pyrrhus, and he fixed his capital at Ambracia.

Extinction of Cassander's family.

The price was thus paid, and Alexander drove out his brother, by Pyrrhus' help, and became king of Macedonia. Antipater fled to Lysimachus for protection, and was afterwards put to death by him.[107] Alexander was in his turn murdered by Demetrius Poliorcetes, who, after all his reverses, thus established his family on the throne of Macedon; and the bloody house of Cassander utterly perished.

Pyrrhus wins Macedonia and loses it. He reigns over Epirus and parts of the neighboring countries in peace for about six years.

Six or seven years afterwards the restless ambition of Demetrius leagued his old enemies, Seleucus, Ptolemy, and Lysimachus, once more against him, and they encouraged Pyrrhus to invade Macedonia. Pyrrhus dethroned Demetrius,[108] and obtained possession of a part of his dominions, the other part being claimed by Lysimachus.

[103] Plutarch, Pyrrh. 4. [104] Ibid. 5.

[105] Porphyry and Dexippus; apud Euseb. Chronic. Ed. Scaliger. p. 58, 63. Plutarch, Pyrrh. 6.

[106] Plutarch, Pyrrh. 6. The present text reads τήν τε Νυμφαίαν καὶ τὴν παραλίαν τῆς Μακεδονίας. Palmer had corrected Στυμφαίαν or Τυμφαίαν instead of Νυμφαίαν, and Niebuhr with no less certainty has restored Παραυαίαν for παραλίαν. Rom. Geschichte, Vol. III. p. 536. He observes that παραλίαν could only mean the coast between Dium and the Strymon, which it is absurd to suppose ceded to Pyrrhus. Tymphæa and Parauæa, Niebuhr adds, are mentioned together by Arrian, Exped. Alexand. I. 7, as countries which Alexander passed by on his march from Illyria into Thessaly. The Parauæans are reckoned along with the Epirot tribes by Thucydides, II. 80, and it appears that Alexander was but restoring to Pyrrhus countries which geographically belonged more to Epirus than to Macedon, and some of which had in earlier times been connected with it politically.

In Stephanus Byzant. in Χαονία, there is a quotation from Proxenus (an historian who wrote about Pyrrhus; see Dionys. Halic. XIX. 11, Fragm. Mai. and Fynes Clinton, Fasti Hellen. Vol. III. 563) enumerating the people of Chaonia. It runs, Τυμφαῖοι, Ταραύλιοι, Ἀμύμονες, where K. O. Muller corrects Τυμφαῖοι, Παραυαῖοι. "Uber die Makedoner. N. 33." His correction and Niebuhr's mutually confirm one another.

[107] Porphyry and Dexippus, apud Euseb. pp. 58–63. Plutarch, Pyrrh. 7. Demetrius, 36.

[108] Plutarch, Demetrius, 44. Pyrrh. 11.

But at the end of seven months[109] Lysimachus made himself master of the whole of Macedonia, and drove Pyrrhus across the mountains into his native kingdom of Epirus. There he reigned in peace for about six years, his dominions including not Epirus only, but those other countries which had been the price of his first interference in the quarrels of Cassander's sons, Tymphæa and Parauæa on the frontiers of Macedonia, and the coasts on both sides of the Ambracian gulf. He united himself in an alliance with his neighbors the Ætolians, which was renewed in the reign of his son. And thus he had leisure to ornament his new capital, Ambracia, which he enlarged by adding to it a new quarter[110] called after his own name, and decorated it with an unusual number of statues and pictures.

Revolutions during that period in other countries.

But although Pyrrhus himself was reigning peaceably in Epirus, yet the period which elapsed between his expulsion from Macedonia and his Italian expedition was marked by great revolutions elsewhere. Ptolemy, the founder of the Macedonian dynasty in Egypt, died after a reign or dominion of forty years from the death of Alexander. Demetrius Poliorcetes ended his days about the same time after a two years' captivity in Syria. Lysimachus was killed soon afterwards, as has been already mentioned, in a battle with Seleucus, and Seleucus himself, the last survivor of Alexander's immediate successors, was murdered seven months after his victory by Ptolemy Ceraunus. The murderer, who was half brother to Ptolemy Philadelphus, the second of the Macedonian kings of Egypt, took possession of the vacant throne of Macedonia, and became immediately involved in war with Antiochus, son of Seleucus, and with Antigonus, the son of Demetrius;[111] the first of whom wished to revenge his father's death, while the other was trying to recover Macedonia, which, as having been held by his father during six or seven years, he regarded as his lawful inheritance. In the mean time, he was actually the sovereign of Thessaly, and exercised a great power over all the states of Greece; and was in alliance with Pyrrhus and the Ætolians. The Greeks, as we have seen, made a fruitless attempt to assert their independence, by attacking his allies, the Ætolians; but they were easily beaten, and Antigonus seems to have reigned without further molestation in Thessaly and Bœotia, whilst Ptolemy Ceraunus still held his ill-gotten power in Macedonia.

Pyrrhus is invited by the Tarentines into Italy.

Things were in this state when ambassadors[112] from Tarentum entreated Pyrrhus to cross over into Italy, to protect both themselves and the other Greek cities of Italy from a barbarian enemy far more formidable than the Lucanians, the old enemies of his kinsman Alexander. Times were now so changed that the Lucanians and Samnites were leagued in one common cause with the Greeks, with whom they had been so long at enmity; the Etruscans had taken part also in the confederacy; yet the united efforts of so many states were too weak to resist the new power which had grown up in the centre of Italy, and was fast arriving at the dominion of the whole peninsula. To conquer these fierce barbarians, and to save so many Greek cities from slavery was a work that well became the kinsman of the great Alexander, the descendant of Achilles and Æacus.

The prayer of the Tarentines suited well with the temper and the circumstances of Pyrrhus. He promised them his aid, and began forthwith to prepare for his passage to Italy, and for his war with the Romans.

[109] Porphyry and Dexippus, apud Euseb. pp. 68-63.

[110] See Polybius, XXII. 10, 13.

[111] Justin, XXIV. 1. Memnon, apud Photium, p. 226. Ed. Bekker.

[112] Plutarch, Pyrrh. 13.

CHAPTER XXXVI.

ROME AND THE ROMAN PEOPLE AT THE BEGINNING OF THE WAR WITH THE TARENTINES AND WITH PYRRHUS.

"Privatus illis census erat brevis
Commune magnum; nulla decempedis
Metata privatis opacam
Porticus excipiebat Arcton,
Nec fortuitum spernere cespitem
Leges sinebant, oppida publico
Sumtu jubentes et deorum
Templa novo decorare saxo."
HORAT. Carmin. II. 15.

Sketch of the internal state of Rome.

THE preceding chapter has been compiled from materials which in their actual state are often fragmentary, and even when they are perfect, are not original. But yet they were derived from original sources; for although the contemporary histories of Alexander's successors have long since perished, yet they did once exist, and were accessible to the writers whom we read and copy now. We cross the Adriatic to inquire into the state of Italy, and not only are our existing materials the merest wreck of a lost history, not only would they tell their story to us at second hand, if they had been preserved entire; but even these very accounts could have been taken from no contemporary historians, for none such ever existed. In this absolute dearth of direct information, it is impossible that the following sketch should be other than meagre, and it must also rest partly on conjecture. Unsatisfactory as this is, yet the nature of the case will allow of nothing better; and I can but encourage myself, while painfully feeling my way amid such thick darkness, with the hope of arriving at length at the light, and enjoying all the freshness and fulness of a detailed contemporary history.

The divisions of the Roman people.

In the middle of the fifth century, the Roman people was divided into three-and-thirty tribes;[1] and the total number of citizens, which included, besides those enrolled in the tribes, the ærarians, and the people of those foreign states, which had been obliged to receive the civitas sine suffragio, amounted to 272,000.[2] What proportion of these were enrolled in the tribes, or, in other words, enjoyed the full rights of citizenship, we cannot tell, nor have we any means of estimating the number of the ærarians; nor again, can we draw any inference as to the population of the city of Rome, as distinguished from the country tribes; nor can we at all compute the proportion of slaves at this time to freemen. The class of ærarians, however, must have been greatly diminished, since freedmen and persons engaged in retail trade or manufactures had been enrolled in the tribes; and it could have only contained those

[1] That is to say, twenty tribes are known to have existed in the earliest period of the commonwealth, and another was added soon afterwards. The number of twenty-one continued till after the Gaulish invasion, when four more were added on the right bank of the Tiber, in 368; namely, the Stellatine, the Tromentine, the Sabatine, and the Arniensian. Two more were added in 397 for the inhabitants of the old Volscian lowlands near the Pomptine marshes, the Pomptine and the Publilian. Two more were added after the Latin war in 422, the Mæcian and the Scaptian, for the Lanuvians and some other people of Latium. In the second Samnite war, in 436–7, the Ufentine and Falerian tribes were created, which included the Privernatians, and the settlers in the Falernian plain. And, lastly, after the Æquian war, two more were added in 455, the Aniensian and the Terentine, in which were enrolled the Æquians.

All these are clearly local tribes, and their situation is well known. The same may be said of the four city tribes, the Colline, the Esquiline, the Palatine, and the tribe of Subura. But to the remaining seventeen, which are mostly named after some noble Roman family, as the Æmilian, the Cornelian, the Fabian, &c., it is extremely difficult to assign their proper locality.

[2] Livy, Epit. XI.

who had forfeited their franchise, either in consequence of their having incurred legal infamy, or by the authority of the censors.

Manner of life of the citizens of the country tribes.

The members of the country tribes, of those at least which had been created within the last century, lived on their lands, and probably only went up to Rome to vote at the elections, or when any law of great national importance was proposed, and there was a powerful party opposed to its enactment. They were also obliged to appear on the Capitol on the day fixed by the consuls for the enlistment of soldiers for the legions.[3] Law business might also call them up to Rome occasionally, and the Roman games, or any other great festival, would no doubt draw them thither in great numbers. With these exceptions, and when they were not serving in the legions, they lived on their small properties in the country; their business was agriculture, their recreations were country sports, and their social pleasures were found in the meetings of their neighbors at seasons of festival; at these times there would be dancing, music, and often some pantomimic acting, or some rude attempts at dramatic dialogue, one of the simplest and most universal amusements of the human mind. This was enough to satisfy all their intellectual cravings; of the beauty of painting, sculpture, or architecture, of the charms of eloquence and of the highest poetry, of the deep interest which can be excited by inquiry into the causes of all the wonders around us and within us, of some of the highest and most indispensable enjoyments of an Athenian's nature, the agricultural Romans of the fifth century had no notion whatsoever.

And of those of the city Study of the law. Appius Claudius, Ti. Coruncanius, and the Ogulnii.

But it was not possible that an equal simplicity should have existed at Rome. Their close and constant intercourse with other men sharpens and awakens the faculties of the inhabitants of cities; and country sports being by the necessity of the case denied to them, they learn earlier to value such pleasures as can be supplied by the art or genius of man. Besides, the conduct of political affairs on a large scale, much more when these affairs are publicly discussed either in a council or in a popular assembly, cannot but create an appreciation of intellectual power and of eloquence; and the multiplied transactions of civil life, leading perpetually to disputes, and these disputes requiring a legal decision, a knowledge of law became a valuable accomplishment, and the study of law, which is as wholesome to the human mind as the practice of it is often injurious, was naturally a favorite pursuit with those who had leisure, and who wished either to gain influence or to render services. Thus the family of the Claudii seem always to have aspired after civil rather than military distinction. Appius Claudius, the censor, was a respectable soldier, but he is much better known by his great public works and by his speech against making peace with Pyrrhus, than by his achievements in war; nay, it is said, that his plebeian colleague in the consulship, L. Volumnius, taunted him with his legal knowledge and his eloquence, as if he could only talk[4] and not fight. The Claudii, however, were distinguished by their high nobility, independently of any personal accomplishments; but the family of the Coruncanii owed its celebrity entirely, so far as it appears, to their acquaintance with the law. Ti. Coruncanius[5] was consul with P. Lævinus in the year when Pyrrhus came into Italy, and was named dictator more than thirty years afterwards for the purpose of holding the comitia. He left no writings behind him, but was accustomed to the very latest period of his life to give answers on points of law to all that chose to consult him; and his reputation was so high that he was the first plebeian[6] who was ever appointed to the dignity of pontifex maximus. The Ogulnii also appear to have been a family distinguished for knowledge and accomplishments. Two brothers of this name were, as we have seen, the authors of the law which threw open the offices of

[3] Polybius, VI. 19.
[4] Livy, X. 19.
[5] Pomponius, de Origine Juris, § 35, 38. Cicero, Brutus, 14. Cato Major, 9.
[6] Livy, Epit. XVIII.

augur and pontifex to the commons, and afterwards in their ædileship they ornamented the city with several works of art; and one of them, besides his embassy to Epidaurus, already noticed, was sent as one of three ambassadors[7] to Ptolemy Philadelphus, king of Egypt, soon after the retreat of Pyrrhus from Italy.

Total absence of all literature.

There was as yet no regular drama, for Livius Andronicus did not begin to exhibit his plays till after the first Punic war;[8] but there were pantomimic dances performed by Etruscan actors;[9] there were the saturæ[10] or medleys, sung and acted by native performers; and there were the comic or satirical dialogues on some ludicrous story (fabellæ atellanæ), in which the actors were of a higher rank, as this entertainment was rather considered an old national custom, than a spectacle exhibited for the public amusement. There were no famous poets, nor any Homer, to embody in an imperishable form the poetical traditions of his country; but there were the natural elements of poetry, and the natural love of it; and it was long the custom at all entertainments[11] that each guest in his turn should sing some heroic song, recording the worthy deeds of some noble Roman. So also there was no history, but there was the innate desire of living in the memory of after-ages; and in all the great families, panegyrical orations were delivered at the funeral of each of their members, containing a most exaggerated account of his life and actions.[12] These orations existed in the total absence of all other statements, and from these chiefly the annalists of the succeeding century compiled their narratives; and thus every war is made to exhibit a series of victories, and all the most remarkable characters in the Roman story are represented as men without reproach, or of heroic excellence.

Public amusements. The great games of the circus.

But whilst literature was unknown, and poetry, and even the drama itself, were in their earliest infancy, the Romans enjoyed with the keenest delight the sports of the circus, which resembled the great national games of Greece. Every year in the month of September[13] four days were devoted to the celebration of what were called indifferently, the Great or the Roman Games. Like all the spectacles of the ancient world, they were properly a religious solemnity, a great festival in honor of the three national divinities of the Capitoline temple, Jupiter, Juno, and Minerva. On the first day of the festival, the whole people went in procession[14] from the Capitol through the Forum to the circus; there the sacrifice was performed, and afterwards the exhibition of the various games began, which was so entirely a

[7] Dionysius, XX. 4. Fragm. Vatic. Valer. Maxim. IV. 3. § 9.

[8] Clinton, Fasti Hellenici, Vol. III. p. 25, B. C. 240.

[9] Livy, VII. 2.

[10] I am not venturing to determine the etymology of this word, but giving merely a description of the thing. "Olim carmen quod ex variis poematibus constabat, satyra vocabatur, quale scripserunt Pacuvius et Ennius." Diomedes, III. 9. Livy speaks of the saturæ or satyræ, as an intermediate state in the dramatic art between the acting of regular stories with a plot, and the mere rude *sparring* with coarse jests, "versum incompositum temere ac rudem alternis jaciebant," which used to go on between two performers. The saturæ appear, then, to have been comic songs in regular verse, in which a great variety of subjects were successively noticed, without any more connection than as being each of them points on which the hearers could be readily excited to laughter.

[11] Cicero, Brutus, 19.

[12] Cicero, Brutus, 16. Livy, VIII. 40.

[13] The fullest work on the games of the circus is, I suppose, that of Onuphrius Panvinius (Onofrio Panvini, a Veronese, who flourished in the latter part of the 16th century), published in the ninth volume of Grævius' Collection of Roman Antiquities. The view of the circus and the Palatine, given in Panvinius' work, is curious, as showing how greatly Rome has changed in the last 250 years. A shorter account may be found in Rosini and Dempster's work on Roman antiquities; and the topography of the circus is given in Bunsen and Platner's description of Rome, Vol. III. p. 91. Gibbon has given one of his lively and comprehensive sketches of the games of the circus, in his account of the reign of Justinian, which notices every important point in the subject. A representation of the circus is given on several coins which may be seen in Panvinius' work, and which enables us to form a sufficient notion of its appearance. The bands or factions of the drivers are noticed in numerous inscriptions.

[14] Tertullian, De Spectaculis, VII. His enumeration of the several parts of the great procession is full and lively. "De, simulacrorum serie, de imaginum agmine, de curribus, de thensis, de armamaxis, de sedibus, de coronis, de exuviis, quanta præterea sacra, quanta sacrificia præcedant, intercedant, succedant, quot collegia, quot sacerdotia, quot officia moveantur, sciunt homines illius urbis in quâ dæmoniorum conventus consedit."

national ceremony, that the magistrate of highest rank who happened to be in Rome gave the signal for the starting of the horses in the chariot race. The circus itself was especially consecrated to the sun, and the colors by which the drivers of the chariots were distinguished, were supposed to have a mystical allusion to the different seasons.[15] Originally there were only two colors, white and red, the one a symbol of the snows of winter, the other of the fiery heat of summer; but two others were afterwards added, the spring-like green, and the autumnal gray or blue. The charioteers, who wore the same colors, were called the red or white, or green or blue band (factio), and these bands became in later times the subject of the strongest party feeling; for men attached themselves either to the one or the other, and would have as little been induced to change their color in the circus as their political party in the commonwealth. It does not appear that these colors were connected with any real differences, social or political; there were no ideas of which they were severally the symbols; and thus, while the commonwealth lasted, the bands of the circus seem to have excited no deeper or more lasting interest than the wishes of their respective partisans for their success in the chariot race. But afterwards, when the emperor was known to favor any one color more than another, that color would naturally become the badge of his friends, and the opposite color the rallying point of his enemies; and when a real political feeling was connected with these symbols, it was not wonderful that the bands of the circus became truly factions, and that their quarrels in the lower empire should have sometimes deluged Constantinople with blood.

Public works. Numerous temples built and ornamented.

The Romans in the fifth century enjoyed the games as keenly as their descendants under the emperors; but the lavish magnificence of the imperial circus was as yet altogether unknown. Wooden boxes[16] supported on poles, like the simplest form of a stand on an English race-course, were the best accommodation as yet provided for the spectators; and it was only in the fifth century that the carceres[17] were first erected, a line of buildings of the common volcanic tufo of Rome itself, extending along one end of the circus, each with a door opening upon the course, from which the horses were brought out to take their places, before they started on the race. But although the works of this period were simple, yet they now began to be very numerous, and some of them were on a scale of very imposing grandeur. Livy has recorded the building of seven new temples[18] within ten years, between 452 and 462; for the period immediately following we have no detailed history, but the foundation of the temple of Æsculapius, about two years later, is noticed in the epitome of Livy's eleventh book; and many others may have been founded, of which we have no memorial. It is mentioned also that C. Fabius[19] ornamented one of these temples, that of Deliverance from Danger, with frescoes of his own execution, in consequence of which he obtained the surname of Pictor. The date of the Greek artists, Damophilus and Gorgasus,[20] who painted the frescoes of the temple of Ceres, close by the circus, we have no means of determining, but several notices show that a taste for the arts was beginning at this time to be felt at Rome. The colossal bronze statue of Jupiter, set up by Sp. Carvilius in the Capitol, in the year 461, has been already noticed, as well as the famous group of the she-wolf suckling Romulus and Remus, which was placed in the comitium three years before. And at the same time a statue of Jupiter in

[15] Tertullian, ibid. VIII. IX.

[16] Livy, I. 35.

[17] Livy, VIII. 20. Suetonius in Claud. 21. There are representations of the carceres in one or two of the engravings of Panvinius' work, copied from antiques.

[18] Namely, a temple of Bellona, vowed by Appius Claudius in 458 (Livy, X. 19); another of Jupiter the Victorious, vowed by Q. Fabius in the great battle of Sentinum (X. 29); a third near the circus, dedicated to Venus (X. 31); a fourth dedicated to Victory (X. 33); a fifth to Jupiter the Stayer of Flight (X. 37); a sixth to Fortis Fortuna (X. 46); and a seventh to Salus, or Deliverance from Danger, which was the temple painted by Fabius Pictor (Livy. X. 1).

[19] Pliny, Hist. Natur. XXXV. § 19.

[20] Pliny, Hist. Natur. XXXV. § 45.

a chariot drawn by four horses,[21] the work of an Etruscan artist, and wrought in clay, was erected on the summit of the Capitol.

The temple of Bellona, built by Appius Claudius[22] in fulfilment of a vow made on the field of battle, was decorated with a row of shields or escutcheons, on which were represented his several ancestors with scrolls recording the offices which they had filled, and the triumphs which they had won. Whoever of these had been the father of a family was represented with all his children by his side, as in some of our old monuments. In these and in all similar works, an exact likeness[23] was considered of much greater importance than any excellence of art; for the object desired was to transmit to posterity a lively image of those who had in their generation done honor to their name and family. For this purpose waxen busts, the scorn of the mere artist, were kept in cases ranged along the sides of the court in the houses of all great families; these were painted to the life, and being hollow, were worn like a mask[24] at funerals by some of the dependents of the family, who also put on the dress of the office of rank of him whose semblance they bore; so that it seemed as if the dead were attended to his grave by all the members of his race of past generations, no less than by those who still survived. None were so represented who had not in their lifetime filled some honorable public station, and thus the number of images worn at any funeral was the exact measure of the family's nobility.

Family images worn like masks at funerals.

No other aqueduct had yet been added to that constructed by Appius Claudius in his famous censorship; nor had any later road rivalled the magnificence of the Appian. This was paved with lava in the year 461, from the temple of Mars,[25] a little on the outside of the city walls, to Bovillæ, at the foot of the Alban hills.

The Appian road paved as far as Bovillæ.

The city itself was still confined within the walls of Servius Tullius. The Capitol and the Quirinal hills formed its northern limit, and looked down immediately on the open space of the Campus Martius, now covered with the greatest part of the buildings of modern Rome. Art or caprice had not yet effaced the natural features of the ground, by cutting down hills and filling up valleys, nor had the mere lapse of time as yet raised the soil by continued accumulations to a height far above its original level. The hills, with their bare, rocky sides, and covered in many parts with sacred groves, the remains of their primeval woods, rose distinctly and boldly from the valleys between them; on their summits were the principal temples and the houses of the noblest families; beneath were the narrow streets and lofty houses,[26] roofed only with wood, of the more populous quarters of the city, and in the midst, reaching from the Capitoline hill to the Palatine, lay the comitium and the Roman Forum.

Extent and aspect of the city.

A spot so famous well deserves to be described, that we may conceive its principal features, and image to ourselves the scene as well as the actors in so many of the great events of the Roman history. From the foot of the Capitoline hill[27] to that of the Palatine, there ran an open space of

Description of the Forum.

[21] Pliny, Hist. Natur. XXXV. § 158.

[22] Pliny (Hist. Nat. XXXV. § 2, 3) ascribes these shields to the first Appius Claudius, who was consul with P. Servilius in 259. But unless the words "qui consul cum Servilio fuit anno urbis CCLIX." are an unlucky gloss of some ignorant reader, as is most probable, they seem to show an extraordinary carelessness in Pliny himself; for to say nothing of the direct testimony, which ascribes the foundation of the temple of Bellona to Appius the Blind in 458, Pliny's own statement says, that Appius caused the figures of his ancestors, and scrolls recording the offices which they had filled, to be affixed to this temple: but who could have been the ancestors of the first Appius, and what offices could they have filled at Rome, when he himself was the first of his family who became a Roman?

[23] Pliny, Hist. Nat. XXXV. § 4. 6.

[24] Pliny, Hist. Nat. XXXV. § 6. Polybius, VI. 53.

[25] Livy, X. 47.

[26] Pliny, XVI. § 36, quoting from Cornelius Nepos.

[27] The whole of the following description of the Forum is taken from Bunsen's article in the third volume of the "Beschreibung der Stadt Rom." The substance of this article has been given by its author in another form, in a letter

unequal breadth, narrowing as it approached the Palatine, and enclosed on both sides between two branches of the Sacred Way. Its narrower end was occupied by the comitium, the place of meeting of the populus or great council of the burghers in the earliest times of the republic, whilst its wider extremity was the Forum, in the stricter sense, the market-place of the Romans, and therefore the natural place of meeting for the commons, who formed the majority of the Roman nation. The comitium was raised a little above the level of the Forum, like the dais or upper part of our old castle and college halls, and at its extremity nearest the Forum stood the rostra, such as I have already described it, facing at this period towards the comitium, so that the speakers addressed, not indeed the patrician multitude as of old, but the senators, who had, in a manner, succeeded to their place, and who were accustomed to stand in this part of the assembly, immediately in front of the senate-house, which looked upon the comitium from the northern side of the Via Sacra. The magnificent basilicæ, which at a later period formed the two sides of the Forum, were not yet in existence, but in their place there were two rows of solid square pillars of peperino, forming a front to the shops of various kinds, which lay behind them. These shops were like so many cells, open to the street, and closed behind, and had no communication with the houses which were built over them. Those on the north side of the Forum had been rebuilt or improved during the early part of the fifth century, and were called in consequence the new shops, a name which, as usual in such cases, they retained for centuries. On the south side, the line of shops was interrupted by the temple of Castor and Pollux, which had been built, according to the common tradition, by the dictator, A. Postumius, in gratitude for the aid afforded him by the twin heroes in the battle of the lake Regillus. On the same side also, but further to the eastward, and nearly opposite to the senate-house, was the temple of Vesta, and close to the temple was that ancient monument of the times of the kings which went by the name of the court of Numa.

Statues, &c., in the Forum.

In the open space of the Forum might be seen an altar which marked the spot once occupied by the Curtian pool, the subject of such various traditions. Hard by grew the three sacred trees[28] of the oldest known civilization, the fig, the vine, and the olive, which were so carefully preserved or renewed that they existed even in the time of the elder Pliny. Further towards the Capitol, at the western extremity of the Forum, were the equestrian statues of C. Mænius and L. Camillus, the conquerors of the Latins.

Statues and other objects of interest in the comitium.

Nor was the interior of the comitium destitute of objects entitled to equal veneration. There was the black stone which marked, according to one tradition, the grave of Faustulus, the foster-father of Romulus, according to another that of Romulus himself. There was the statue of Attius Navius, the famous augur; and there too was the sacred fig-tree, under whose shade the wolf had given suck to the two twins, Romulus and Remus. A group of figures representing the wolf and twins had been recently set up in this very place by the ædiles, Q. and Cn. Ogulnius, and the fig-tree

the Chevalier Canina, written in French (Rome, 1837). He has also prefixed to some impressions of his German article, which have been printed separately, all the passages in the ancient writers which throw any light on the topography of the Forum.

Since this chapter was written, I have seen Nibby's latest work on the topography of Rome, which was published in 1839. His plan of the Forum differs topographically from Bunsen's; he places it further to the west, and arranges the buildings differently. But historically his views are so imperfect, and he follows so contentedly the old popular accounts, without the slightest knowledge, so far as appears, of the light which Niebuhr has thrown on the Roman history, that his topography is necessarily rendered of less value. Bunsen has had every advantage of local knowledge no less than Nibby, but with his local knowledge he combines other qualities which Nibby is far from possessing equally.

However, the general correctness of the description of the Forum in the fifth century of Rome, as given in the text, is independent of the question whether the position of the Forum is to be fixed a certain number of yards more to the eastward or to the westward. And most of those buildings, the site of which has been so much disputed, were not in existence at the period to which this sketch relates.

[28] Pliny, Hist. Natur. XV. § 78.

itself had been removed by the power of Attius Navius, so said the story,[29] from its original place under the Palatine, that it might stand in the midst of the meetings of the Roman people. Nor were statues wanting to the comitium any more than to the Forum. Here were the three sibyls, one of the oldest works of Roman art; here also were the small figures of the Roman ambassadors who had been slain at Fidenæ by the Veientian king Tolumnius; and here too, at the edge of the comitium where it joined the Forum, were the statues which the Romans, at the command of the Delphian oracle, had erected in honor of the wisest and bravest of the Greeks, the statues of Pythagoras and Alcibiades.

Character of the population; the shops, &c.

The outward appearance of the Forum in the fifth century was very different from its aspect in the times of the Cæsars, and scarcely less different was the population by which it was frequented at either period. Rome was not yet the general resort of strangers from all parts of the world; the Tiber was as yet not only unpolluted by the Syrian Orontes, but its waters had received no accession from the purer streams of Greece; and the crowd which thronged the Forum, however numerous and busy, consisted mainly of the citizens, or at least of the inhabitants of Rome. The shops of the silversmiths had lately superseded those of a less showy character on the north side of the Forum; but, on the other side, the butchers' and cooks' shops still remained, as in the days of Virginius, and it marks the manners of the times, that the wealthier citizens used to hire cooks[30] from these places to bake their bread for them, having as yet no slaves who understood even the simplest parts of the art of cookery.

Great families of this period.

The names of the principal families, as well as of the most distinguished men of this period, have naturally been mentioned already in the course of the narrative. It is enough to remark that Appius Claudius was still alive, though now old and blind, that M. Valerius Corvus was also living, but his public career had been for some time ended; and that Q. Fabius, the hero of the third Samnite war, had died not long after its conclusion. Q. Publilius Philo was also dead, and with him expired the nobility of his family. But there were ready to meet Pyrrhus, the two victorious generals of the great campaign of 461, L. Papirius Cursor and Sp. Carvilius Maximus; M'. Curius Dentatus was still in the vigor of life, and Q. Fabius and P. Decius had both left sons to uphold the honor of their name. The great Cornelian house contributed eminent citizens for their country's service from three of its numerous branches; among the consuls of the fourth Samnite war we find a Cornelius Lentulus, a Cornelius Rufinus, and a Cornelius Dolabella. Two other names will demand our notice for the first time, those of C. Fabricius and L. Cæcilius Metellus, the first pre-eminent in the purest personal glory, but a glory destined to pass away from his family after one generation, "no son of his succeeding;" while L. Cæcilius, if he did not attain himself to the highest distinction, was yet "the father of a line of more than kings," of those illustrious Metelli who, from the first Punic war to the end of the commonwealth, were amongst the noblest and the best citizens of Rome.

Against a whole nation of able and active men the greatest individual genius of a single enemy must ever strive in vain. The victory of Pyrrhus at Heraclea was endangered by a rumor that he was slain, for in his person lay the whole strength of his army and of his cause. But had the noblest of the Fabii or Cornelii fallen at the head of a Roman army, the safety of the commonwealth would not have been for a single moment in jeopardy. This contrast alone was sufficient to ensure the decision of the great war on which we are now about to enter.

[29] The passage in Pliny which mentions this story, XV. § 77, is clearly corrupt, and various corrections of it have been attempted. Bunsen has given one in a note to his article on the Forum, Beschreib. der Stadt. Rom. III. p. 62.

[30] Pliny, Histor. Natur. XVIII. § 108. So in the Aulularia of Plautus, the cooks are hired in the Forum to go to Euclio's house, and dress his daughter's wedding dinner.

CHAPTER XXXVII.

FOREIGN HISTORY FROM 464 TO 479—WARS WITH THE ETRUSCANS, GAULS, AND TARENTINES—FOURTH SAMNITE WAR—PYRRHUS KING OF EPIRUS IN ITALY—BATTLES OF HERACLEA, ASCULUM, AND BENEVENTUM.

Non Simois tibi nec Xanthus nec Dorica castra
Defuerint; alius Latio jam partus Achilles.
VIRGIL, Æn. VI. 87.

Fourth Samnite war and coalition against Rome.

THE third Samnite war ended in the year 464, and Pyrrhus invaded Italy exactly ten years later, in the year 474. The events of the intervening period, both foreign and domestic, are, as we have seen, involved in the deepest obscurity; but as I have attempted to present an outline of the internal state of Rome, so I must now endeavor to trace the perplexed story of her foreign relations, from the first seeds of war, which the jealousy of the Tarentines either sowed or earnestly fostered, to the organization of that great coalition, in which the Gauls at first, and Pyrrhus afterwards, were principal actors.

State and dispositions of the Etruscans.

On the side of Etruria there had been for a long time past neither certain peace nor vigorous war. Jealousies between city and city, and party revolution in the several cities themselves, were, as we have seen, forever compromising the tranquillity and paralyzing the exertions of the Etruscan nation. In 461 the cities of southern Etruria had taken up arms, and had persuaded the Faliscans to join them; and in 462 we hear of victories obtained over the Faliscans by the consul, D. Junius Brutus.[1] No further particulars are known of the progress of the contest, but it appears from the epitome of Livy's eleventh book, that at some time or other within the next eight years, the people of Vulsinii took a principal part in it, and in 471 the whole, or nearly the whole, of the Etruscan nation were engaged in it once again.

Of the Gauls.

Further to the north "the Senonian Gauls remained quiet," says Polybius,[2] "for a period of ten years after the battle of Sentinum." If we take this statement to the letter, we must fix the renewal of the Gaulish war in 469; yet we cannot trace any act of hostility till the year 471. The Gauls appear first to have engaged as mercenaries in the Etruscan service, and afterwards to have joined the new coalition in their own name.

Of the Lucanians and Tarentines.

To the south of Rome, Lucania, during the third Samnite war, had remained faithful to the Romans, and in the year 460 we expressly read of Lucanian cohorts serving with the Roman legions.[3] Of Tarentum nothing is recorded after its short war with the Lucanians and Romans in 451, which appears to have been ended, as I have already observed,[4] by an equal treaty.

The Lucanians attack Thurii, and the Thurians apply to the Romans for aid.

Italy was in this state when the Lucanians attacked the Greek city of Thurii. We know not the cause or pretext of the quarrel, but those unfortunate Greek cities of Italy were at this time the prey of every spoiler; Agathocles had made repeated expeditions to that coast in the latter years of his reign, and had taken Croton and Hipponium,[5] while the Italian nations of the interior had from time immemorial regarded them as enemies. Thurii itself had been taken by Cleonymus in 452[6] when he was playing

[1] Zonaras, VIII. 1.
[2] Polybius, II. 19.
[3] Livy, X. 33.
[4] See chap. XXXIII.
[5] Diodorus, XXI. 4, 8, Fragm. Hoeschel.
[6] Livy, X. 2.

the buccaneer along all the coasts of Italy; and a Roman army had then come to its aid, but too late to prevent its capture. This was perhaps remembered now, when the city was threatened by the Lucanians, and the Romans were implored once again to bring help to the people of Thurii. The request was not at first granted; as far as we can make out the obscure story of these times, the first attacks must have been made about the period of the domestic troubles at Rome, when the commons occupied the Janiculum, and obliged the senate to consent to the Hortensian laws. During two successive summers, the Lucanians ravaged the territory of Thurii,[7] and so far as appears, there was no power of resistance in the inhabitants themselves, and no foreign sword was drawn to defend them.

The people in their tribes vote for war with the Lucanians.

Meanwhile the Hortensian laws were passed, and with them, or shortly before, an agrarian law had been passed also. The power of the assembly of the tribes had been acknowledged to be sovereign, and the popular party for some years from this time, feeling itself to have the disposal of all that the state might conquer, appears to have been as fond of war as ever was the Athenian democracy under Pericles, while the aristocratical party, for once only in the history of Rome, seems to have adopted the peaceful policy of Cimon and Nicias. C. Ælius, one of the tribunes, proposed and carried in the assembly of the tribes what Pliny[8] calls a law against Stenius Statilius,[9] the captain-general of the Lucanians; in other words, he moved that war should be declared against Stenius Statilius and all his followers and abettors; and the tribes gave their votes for it accordingly. The people of Thurii voted to Ælius, as a mark of their gratitude, a statue and a crown of gold, and probably a Roman army was sent to their aid, and relieved them from the present danger; but the Lucanians were not subdued, and it was evident that they would not be left to contend against Rome single-handed.

[7] The data for the arrangement of all these events in order of time are as follows: 1. The interposition of the Romans in behalf of the Thurians is mentioned in the epitome of the eleventh book of Livy, and the twelfth book began apparently with the consulship of Dolabella and Domitius in the year 471. 2. M'. Curius obtained an ovation or smaller triumph for his victories over the Lucanians. (Auctor de Viris Illustribus, in M'. Curio.) This must either have been in the year after his consulship, when he was perhaps prætor, or else in 471, when we know that he was appointed prætor after the defeat and death of L. Cæcilius. 3. But when C. Ælius carried his resolution for a war with the Lucanians, the Lucanian general Statilius had *twice* assailed the Thurians ("bis infestaverat, Pliny, Hist. Natur. XXXIV. § 32), which, I think, implies that he had ravaged their lands for two successive years; but the peace with the Samnites was only concluded in the year when Curius was consul; and throughout the war the Lucanians were in alliance with Rome, nor were they likely then to meddle with the Thurians. 4. C. Ælius passed his resolution as tribune; but before the Hortensian laws were carried, such a resolution was not likely to have been brought forward by a tribune, nor would it have been carried had the senate been opposed to it; and had they not been opposed to it, it would have been moved probably by one of the consuls with their authority. 5. There is a C. Ælius recorded in the consular Fasti, as having been consul in 468; we do not know whether this is the same person with the tribune; but if he were, his tribuneship, as preceding his consulship, must have taken place before the year 468. 6. The date of the Hortensian laws is unknown, but several modern writers place it in the very year 468, when C. Ælius was consul. On the whole, I would arrange these events in the following order:

A. U. C. 464. End of the third Samnite war.

A. U. C. 466, 467. Lucanians attack the Thurians.

A. U. C. 467. The Hortensian laws. C. Ælius, tribune, carries his motion in the assembly of the tribes for a war with the Lucanians.

A. U. C. 468. C. Ælius, consul, chosen perhaps as a reward for his popular conduct in his tribuneship.

A. U. C. 471. M'. Curius prætor. His ovation over the Lucanians.

A. U. C. 472. C. Fabricius consul. He defeats the Lucanians, and raises the siege of Thurii.

If it be thought that this scheme leaves too great an interval between the declaration of war against the Lucanians, and any recorded events of the war (although, in the total absence of all details of this period, this objection is not of much weight), then we must suppose that C. Ælius, the tribune, and C. Ælius, the consul, were different persons; and we might then place the resolution against the Lucanians a year or two later. But it seems more probable that the consul and the tribune were one and the same man, and then I think the above scheme offers fewer difficulties than any other.

[8] Histor. Natur. XXIV. § 32.

[9] It was probably a rogatio to the following effect: "Vellent juberentne cum Stenio Statilio Lucanorum prætore, quique ejus sectam secuti essent, bellum iniri." If there was a Roman party still predominant in any part of Lucania, it would explain why the rogatio should have rather specified Statilius personally than declared war against the whole Lucanian people.

These events appear to have taken place about six years after the conclusion of the third Samnite war, in the year 470, when C. Servilius Tucca and L. Cæcilius Metellus were consuls. Whatever was the cause, the Tarentines[10] at this period were most active in forming a new coalition against Rome. They endeavored to excite the Samnites to renew the war, and the Samnites, with the Lucanians, Apulians, and Bruttians, were to form a confederacy in the south of Italy, of which Tarentum was to be the head. The Romans sent C. Fabricius to the several Samnite and Apulian cities, to persuade them, if possible, to remain true to their alliance with Rome. But the states to whom he was sent laid hands on him and arrested him, and then dispatched an embassy with all speed into Etruria, to secure, if possible, the aid of the Etruscans, Umbrians, and Gauls. Fabricius, we may suppose, was made a hostage for the safety of those Samnite hostages who had been demanded by the Romans after the late peace, and his release was probably the stipulated price of theirs.

The Tarentines are busy in forming a coalition against Rome.

In the following year, 471, the Roman consuls were P. Cornelius Dolabella and Cn. Domitius Calvinus. The storm broke out against Rome in every direction. In the south the Samnites, Lucanians, Bruttians, and probably the Apulians, were now in a state of declared hostility; while in the north the mass of the Etruscans were in arms, and had engaged,[11] it seems, large bodies of the Senonian Gauls in their service, although the Senonians, as a nation, still professed to be at peace with Rome. In Arretium, however, the Roman party was still predominant; the Arretines would not join their countrymen against Rome; and accordingly Arretium[12] was besieged by an Etruscan army, of which a large part consisted, as we have seen, of Gaulish mercenaries.

General war. The Etruscans and Gauls besiege Arretium, which remains faithful to Rome.

A. U. C. 471. A. C. 283.

The new consuls came into office at this period, about the middle of April; so that the season for military operations had begun before they could be ready to take the field. Thus L. Cæcilius Metellus, the consul of the preceding year, had been left apparently with his consular army in Etruria during the winter; and when the Etruscans began the siege of Arretium, he marched at once to its relief. According to the usual practice of this period, he was elected prætor for the year following his consulship, and he seems to have just entered upon his new office when he led his army against the enemy. We know nothing of the particulars of the battle, but the result was most disastrous to the Romans.[13] L. Metellus himself, seven military tribunes, and 13,000 men were killed on the field; and the remainder of the army were made prisoners.

L. Cæcilius Metellus is defeated and slain in a battle near Arretium.

The consternation caused by such a disaster at such a moment must have been excessive. M'. Curius Dentatus was appointed prætor in the room of Metellus, and sent off with all haste with a fresh army to maintain his ground if possible. At the same time an embassy was sent to the Gauls to complain that their people were serving in the armies[14] of the enemies of Rome, while there was peace between the Gauls and Romans, and to demand that the prisoners taken in the late battle might be released. But the Gauls were at once elated and rendered savage by their late victory. The Romans assuredly had not sold their lives cheaply; many brave Gauls had fallen, and amongst the rest one of their noblest chiefs, Britomaris. His son, the young Britomaris, called for

The Gauls massacre the Roman ambassadors.

[10] Zonaras, VIII. 2, and Dion Cassius, Fragm. Ursin. CXLIV.

[11] Appian, de Rebus Gallic. XI. Samnitic. VI.

[12] Polybius, II. 19.

[13] Orosius, III. 22, and Augustine, de Civitate Dei, III. 17. Orosius dedicated his history to Augustine, and the exact similarity of the notices about the defeat of L. Metellus in both writers shows that both are taken from a common source, which doubtless was Livy. They vary from the account given by Polybius, in representing the murder of the Roman ambassadors as preceding the defeat of Metellus. Appian, copying from Dionysius, agrees with Polybius.

[14] Appian, Samnitic. Fragm. VI. Gallic. XI.

vengeance for his father's blood; and the Roman ambassadors, the sacred feciales themselves, were murdered by the barbarians, and their bodies hewed in pieces, and the mangled fragments cast out without burial.

Great victories obtained over the Senonian Gauls.

The consul, P. Dolabella, had already left Rome with the usual consular army, and was on his march into northern Etruria,[15] when he received the tidings of this outrage. Immediately he resolved on vengeance, and instead of advancing into Etruria, he turned to the right, marched through the country of the Sabines into Picenum, and from thence led his army into the territory of the Gauls. The flower of their warriors were absent in Etruria; those who were left, and endeavored to resist the invaders, were defeated with great slaughter: no quarter was given to any male able to bear arms: the women and children were carried off as slaves, the villages and houses were burnt, and the whole country was made a desert. Meanwhile the Gauls in Etruria, maddened at these horrors, and hoping to enjoy a bloody revenge, urged the Etruscans to seize the opportunity, and to march straight upon Rome. But Cn. Domitius, with the other consular army,[16] was covering the Roman territory; perhaps M'. Curius had joined him, or was hanging on the rear of the enemy during their march through Etruria, and was so at hand to co-operate in the battle. At any rate, the victory of the Romans was complete; and the Gauls who survived the battle slew themselves in despair. It was resolved by the senate to occupy their country without delay, and to plant in it a Roman colony.

And also over the Boian Gauls and Etruscans. Battle of the lake Vadimon.

These events had passed so rapidly that the season for military operations was not yet nearly at an end. The Boian Gauls,[17] the neighbors of the Senonians, enraged and alarmed at the total extermination of their countrymen, took up arms with the whole force of their nation, poured into Etruria, and encouraged the party adverse to Rome to try the fortune of war once again. What the Samnites and Lucanians were doing at this moment we know not; but probably a prætorian or proconsular army with the whole force of the Campanians, and perhaps of the Marsians and Pelignians, was in the field against them; and after the loss of C. Pontius we hear of no Samnite leader whose ability was equal to the urgency of the contest. Thus Dolabella and Domitius were enabled to turn their whole attention to the Etruscans and Gauls. Again, however, all details were lost, and we only know that the scene of the decisive action[18] was the valley of the Tiber, just below its junction with the Nar, and the neighborhood of the small lake of Vadimon, which lay in the plain at no great distance from the right bank of the river.

The victory of the Romans was complete;[19] the flower of the Etruscan army perished, while the Gauls suffered so severely that a very few of their number were all that escaped from the field.

A. U. C. 479. A. C. 282. The Gauls make peace with Rome.

The consuls of the ensuing year were C. Fabricius and Q. Æmilius Papus. Again the Etruscans and Gauls renewed their efforts, but one consular army was now thought enough to oppose to them, and Æmilius alone defeated them utterly, and obliged the Gauls to conclude a separate peace.[20] The Etruscans, who seemed to "like nor peace nor

[15] Appian, Samnitic. VI. Gallic. XI.

[16] Appian, Samnitic. VI. Gallic. XI.

[17] Polybius, II. 20.

[18] Polybius, II. 20. Dion Cassius, Mai Scriptor. Vatican. t. II. p. 536. Florus, II. 13. The lake Vadimon was esteemed sacred. See Pliny, Epist. VIII. 20, where he gives a description of it.

[19] Polybius, II. 20. One of the fragments of Dion Cassius, published by Mai in his Scriptor. Veter. Vatican. Collect. Vol. II. p. 536, states that Dolabella attacked the Etruscans as they were crossing the Tiber, and that the bodies of the enemy carried down by the stream brought the news of the battle to Rome before the arrival of the consul's messenger. The same story is told of one of the battles fought between Tarquinius Priscus and the Sabines; but there, at any rate, the scene of the action was within a very few miles of Rome. Livy, I. 37.

[20] Polybius, II. 20. It must have been Æmilius who defeated the Gauls, because we know that Fabricius was employed in the south: but the fragments of the Fasti Capitolini for this year contain only thus much:

"... eisque ..... III. Non. Mart."

Dionysius, however, says expressly that Æmilius, the colleague of Fabricius, commanded against the Etruscans in this year. XVIII. 5.

war," would not yet submit; or perhaps some states yielded while others continued the contest; but there remained only the expiring embers of a great fire; and the Roman party in the several cities was gradually gaining the ascendency, and preparing the way for that lasting treaty which was concluded two years afterwards.

Victories of Fabricius in the south over the Lucanians.

In the south, C. Fabricius was no less successful. He defeated the Samnites, Lucanians, and Bruttians in several great battles,[21] and penetrated through the enemy's country to the very shores of the Ionian sea, where Thurii was at that very time besieged by Statilius at the head of a Lucanian and Bruttian army. Fabricius defeated the enemy, stormed their camp, and raised the siege of Thurii;[22] for which service the Thurians expressed their gratitude as they had done two years before to the tribune, C. Ælius, by voting that a statue should be made and given to him, to be set up by him in Rome. Thus the coalition which the Tarentines had formed seemed to be broken to pieces, while its authors had not yet drawn the sword, and were still nominally at peace with the Romans.

A Roman fleet is sent to cruise on the coast of the Tarentines.

Fabricius left a garrison in Thurii, and led his army back to Rome with so rich a treasure of spoil,[23] that after having made a liberal distribution of money amongst his soldiers, and returned to all the citizens the amount of the war-taxes which they had paid in that year, he was still able to put four hundred talents into the treasury. In the mean time, as the army was withdrawn from Lucania, a fleet was sent to protect the Thurians, and to watch probably the movements of the Tarentines, whose dispositions must, ere this, have become sufficiently notorious. Accordingly, L. Valerius,[24] one of the two officers annually chosen to conduct the naval affairs of the commonwealth, with a fleet of ten ships of war, sailed on to the eastward of Thurii, and unexpectedly made his appearance before the walls of Tarentum,[25] and seemed to be preparing to force his way into the harbor.

The Tarentines attack and defeat it.

It was the afternoon[26] of the day, and as it was the season of the Dionysia, when the great dramatic contests took place and the prizes were awarded to the most approved poet, the whole Tarentine people were assembled in the theatre, the seats of which looked directly towards the sea. All saw a Roman fleet of ships of war, in undoubted breach of the treaty existing between the two states, which forbade the Romans to sail to the eastward of the Lacinian headland, attempting to make its way into their harbor. Full of wine, and in the careless spirits of a season of festival, they readily listened to a worthless demagogue, named Philocharis, who called upon them to

[21] Dionysius, XVIII. 5.

[22] Dionysius, XVIII. 5. Valerius Maximus, I. 8, § 6. Pliny, Hist. Natur. XXXIV. § 32. Mr. Fynes Clinton, by mistake, refers the account in Valerius Maximus to Fabricius' second consulship in 476. But the mention of the relief of Thurii shows clearly that it belongs to his first consulship.

The story in Valerius Maximus relates a wonderful appearance of a warrior of extraordinary stature, who led the Romans to the assault of the enemy's camp, and who was not to be found the next day when the consul was going to reward him with a mural crown. This, it was said, was no other than Mars himself, who fought on this day for his people. Compare the story in Herodotus of the gigantic warrior whose mere appearance struck the Athenian Epizelus blind at Marathon, VI. 117.

[23] Dionysius, XVIII. 16.

[24] Appian calls him "Cornelius," Samnitic. Fragm. VII. Dion Cassius, Fragm. Bekker. e libro IX. calls him "Valerius," and so does Zonaras, who copies Dion, VIII. 2.

[25] The harbor of Tarentum was a deep gulf, or land-locked basin, running far into the land, and communicating with the open sea by a single narrow passage. It is now called the Mare Piccolo. The ancient city formed a triangle, one side of which was washed by the open sea, and another by the waters of the harbor: the base was a wall drawn across from the sea to the harbor, and the point of the triangle came down to the narrow passage which was the harbor's mouth. Here at the extreme point of the city was the citadel, the site of which is occupied by the modern town. An enemy entering the harbor of Tarentum would therefore be as completely in the heart of the city, as in the great harbor of Syracuse; and Cicero's description will apply even more strongly to Tarentum than to Syracuse; "quo simul atque adisset non modo a latere sed etiam a tergo magnam partem urbis relinqueret."—Verres, Act. II. V. 38. See Keppel Craven, Tour through the southern provinces of Naples, p. 174, and Gagliardo, Descrizione di Taranto.

[26] Dion Cassius, Fragm. Ursin. CXLV. Zonaras, VIII. 2.

punish instantly the treachery of the Romans, and to save their ships and their city. Wiser citizens might remember, that by the Greek national law, ships of war belonging to a foreign power appearing under the walls of an independent city, in violation of an existing treaty,[27] were liable to be treated as enemies. But explanations and questionings were not thought of now: the Tarentines manned their ships, sailed out to meet the Romans, put them instantly to flight, sunk four of their ships without resistance, and took one, with all its crew. L. Valerius, the duumvir, was killed, and of the prisoners, the officers and soldiers serving on board were put to death, and the rowers were sold for slaves.

They expel the Romans from Thurii.

Thus fully committed, the Tarentines determined to follow up their blow. They taxed the Thurians[28] with preferring barbarian aid to that of Tarentum, a neighboring and a Greek city, and with bringing a Roman fleet into the Ionian sea. They attacked the town, allowed the Roman garrison to retire unhurt, on condition of their opening the gates without resistance, and having thus become masters of Thurii, they drove the principal citizens into exile, and gave up the property of the city to be plundered.

And insult the ambassadors, who are sent to demand satisfaction for these aggressions.

The Romans immediately sent an embassy to demand satisfaction for all these outrages. L. Postumius was the principal ambassador,[29] and the instant that he and his colleagues landed, they were beset by a disorderly crowd, who ridiculed their foreign dress, the white toga wrapped round the body like a plaid, with its broad scarlet border. At last they were admitted into the theatre, where the people were assembled, but it was again a time of festival, and the Tarentines were more disposed to coarse buffoonery and riot than to serious counsel. When Postumius spoke to them in Greek, the assembly broke out into laughter at his pronunciation, and at any mistakes in his language; but the Roman delivered his commission unmoved, gravely and simply, as though he had not so much as observed the insults offered to him. At last a worthless drunkard of known profligacy came up to the Roman ambassador, and purposely threw dirt in the most offensive manner upon his white toga. Postumius said, "We accept the omen; ye shall give us even more than we ask of you," and held up the sullied toga before the multitude, to show them the outrage which he had received. But bursts of laughter pealed from every part of the theatre, and scurril songs, and gestures, and clapping of hands, were the only answer returned to him. "Laugh on," said the Roman, "laugh on while ye may; ye shall weep long enough hereafter, and the stain on this toga shall be washed out in your blood." The ambassadors left Tarentum, and Postumius carefully kept his toga unwashed, that the senate might witness with their own eyes the insult offered to the Roman name.

A. U. C. 473. A. C. 281. The Romans declare war against the Tarentines.

He returned to Rome with his colleagues late in the spring of the year 473, after the new consuls, L. Æmilius Barbula and Q. Marcius Philippus, had already entered upon their office. Even now the Romans were reluctant to enter on a war with Tarentum, whilst they had so many enemies still in arms against them, and the debates in the senate lasted for several day. It was resolved[30] at last to declare war; but still, when

[27] The Corcyræans agreed to receive a single Athenian or Lacedæmonian ship into their harbor, but if a greater number appeared, they were to be treated as enemies. Thucyd. III. 71. And when the Athenian expedition coasted along Iapygia on its way to Syracuse, Tarentum would neither allow them to enter the city, nor even to bring their vessels to shore under the walls. Thucyd. VI. 44. So again the Camarinæans, although they had been in alliance with Athens a few years before, refused to admit more than a single ship of the Athenian armament within their harbor. VI. 52.

[28] Appian, Samnitic. Fragm. VII.

[29] Zonaras, VIII. 2. Dion Cassius, Fragm. Ursin. CXLV. Who this L. Postumius was is not known. He may have been one of the Postumii Albini, although the L. Postumius Albinus, who was consul in 520, was the son and grandson of two Auli Postumii. But it may have been the consul who had been fined for his mad conduct in 464, for with all his faults he was an able and resolute man, and the ambassadors sent to so great a city as Tarentum were likely to have been men of consular dignity.

[30] Dionysius, XVII. 10. Reiske has made Dionysius say just the contrary to this, by altering οὗτοι into αἱ. He gives no reason for the alteration, but merely says, "αἱ de meo dedi.

the consuls took the field as usual with their two consular armies, Q. Marcius was sent against the Etruscans, and L. Æmilius was ordered, not immediately to attack Tarentum, but to invade Samnium and subdue the revolted Samnites.

L. Æmilius invades and lays waste the Tarentine territory. Struggles of parties in Tarentum.

But whether the exhausted state of Samnium assured Æmilius that no great danger was to be apprehended there, or whether a prætorian army was sent to keep the Samnites in check, and to leave the consul at liberty for a march into southern Italy, it appears that instructions were sent to L. Æmilius soon after his arrival in Samnium,[31] to advance at once into the territory of Tarentum, and after offering once again the same terms which Postumius had proposed before, to commence hostilities immediately if satisfaction should still be refused. The terms were again rejected by the Tarentines, and Æmilius began to ravage their territory with fire and sword. But knowing that the aristocratical party in Tarentum, as elsewhere, were inclined to look up to Rome for protection, he showed much tenderness to some noble prisoners who fell into his hands,[32] and dismissed them unhurt. Nor did the result disappoint him, for the presence of the Roman army struck terror into the democratical party, while the mildness shown to those who had taken no part in the shameful outrages offered to the Romans, induced moderate men to hope that peace with Rome was a safer prospect for their country than an alliance with Pyrrhus. Agis, one of the aristocratical party, was chosen captain-general, and it was likely that the Tarentines would now in their turn offer that satisfaction which hitherto they had scornfully refused.

Pyrrhus is invited into Italy.

But before any thing could be concluded, the popular party regained their ascendency. An embassy to Pyrrhus, king of Epirus, had been sent off early in the summer,[33] inviting him over to Italy in the name of all the Italian Greeks, to be their leader against the Romans. All the nations of southern Italy, he was assured, were ready to join his standard; and he would find amongst them a force of 350,000 infantry, and 20,000 cavalry able to bear arms in the common cause.

He sends over Milo to occupy the citadel of Tarentum. The popular party recovers the ascendency.

Every Greek looked to foreign conquest only as a means of establishing his supremacy over Greece itself, the proudest object of his ambition. Victorious over the Romans,[34] thence easily passing over into Sicily, and from thence again assailing more effectually than Agathocles the insecure dominion of the Carthaginians in Africa, Pyrrhus hoped to return home with an irresistible force of subject allies, to expel Antigonus from Thessaly and Bœotia, and the ruffian Ptolemy Ceraunus from Macedonia, and to reign over Greece and the world, as became the kinsman of Alexander and the descendant of Achilles. He promised to help the Tarentines; but the force needed for such an expedition could not be raised in an instant; and when the invasion of the Roman army, and the probable ascendency of their political adversaries, made the call of the popular party for his aid more

pro vulg. οὗτοι." The old reading, however, is quite correct in grammar, and perfectly intelligible, and seems to be recommended by the general structure of the passage. It may be thought that it is inconsistent with Appian's account, who says that the consul Æmilius was already in Samnium when he received orders to march against the Tarentines (Samnitic. Fragm. VII. 3), whereas Dionysius makes him to have been present in the senate when the question of war or peace was debated; and had immediate war been then resolved upon, would he not, it may be said, have been ordered to attack Tarentum at once, instead of being sent into Samnium, and receiving a subsequent order to march against Tarentum? This, however, would not necessarily follow; for the senate may have thought it unsafe to hazard an army at the extremity of Italy till measures had been taken to secure it against an attack of the Samnites on its rear. When this was provided for, the consul might safely be ordered to advance upon Tarentum.

[31] The consuls came into office in April, and Æmilius was in the Tarentine territory before the corn was cut, for the Fragment of Dionysius, XVII. 12, clearly relates to this invasion: ἀρούρας τε ἀκμαῖον ἤδη τὸ σιτικὸν θέρος ἐχούσας πυρὶ διδούς. In 1818, Mr. Keppel Craven found the harvest going on briskly a little to the southwest of Tarentum on the 1st of June.—Tour through the southern provinces of Naples, p. 197.

[32] Zonaras, VIII. 2.

[33] Zonaras, VIII. 2. Plutarch, Pyrrh. 13.

[34] Plutarch, Pyrrh. 14.

urgent, he sent over Cineas,[35] his favorite minister, to assist his friends by his eloquence and address, and shortly afterwards Milo, one of his generals, followed with a detachment of 3000 men, and was put in possession of the citadel. A political revolution immediately followed;[36] Agis was deprived of his command, and succeeded by one of the popular leaders who had been sent on the embassy to Pyrrhus; all prospect of peace was at an end, and the democratical party held in their hands the whole government of the commonwealth.

The Roman army retreats from the Tarentine territory.

The Tarentines were masters of the sea, and the arrival of an experienced general and a body of veteran soldiers gave a strength to their land-forces, which in numbers were in themselves considerable. Winter was approaching, and Æmilius proposed to retreat into Apulia, to put his army into winter quarters in those mild and sunny plains. He was followed by the enemy,[37] and as his road lay near the sea, the Tarentine fleet prepared to overwhelm him with its artillery, as his army wound along the narrow road between the mountain sides and the water. Æmilius, it is said, put some of his Tarentine prisoners in the parts of his line of march most exposed to the enemy's shot, and as the Tarentines would not butcher their helpless countrymen, they allowed the Romans to pass by unmolested. The Roman army wintered in Apulia, and both parties had leisure to prepare their best efforts for the struggle of the coming spring.

Pyrrhus arrives at Tarentum. His strict discipline is irksome to the Tarentines.

It was still the depth of winter[38] when Pyrrhus himself arrived at Tarentum. His fleet had been dispersed by a storm on the passage, and he himself had been obliged to disembark on the Messapian coast with only a small part of his army, and to proceed to Tarentum by land. After a time, however, his scattered ships reached their destination safely, and he found himself powerful enough to act as the master rather than the ally of the Tarentines. He shut up the theatre, the public walks, and the gymnasia, obliged the citizens to be under arms all day, either on the walls or in the market-place, and stopped the feasts of their several clubs or brotherhoods, and all revelry, and all riotous entertainments throughout the city. Many of the citizens, as impatient of this discipline as the Ionians of old when Dionysius of Phocæa tried in vain to train them to a soldier's duties, left the city in disgust; but Pyrrhus, to prevent this for the future, placed a guard at the gates, and allowed no one to go out without his permission. It is further said that his soldiers were guilty of great excesses towards the inhabitants, and that he himself put to death some of the popular leaders, and sent others over to Epirus; and this last statement is probable enough, for the idle and noisy demagogues of a corrupt democracy would soon repent of their invitation to him, when they experienced the rigor of his discipline; and if they indulged in any inflammatory speeches to the multitude, Pyrrhus would consider such conduct as treasonable, and would no doubt repress it with the most effectual severity.

Amount of the forces of Pyrrhus.

So passed the winter at Tarentum. But the Italian allies, overawed perhaps by the Roman army in Apulia, were slow in raising their promised contingents,[39] and Pyrrhus did not wish to commence offensive preparations till his whole force was assembled. What number of men he had brought with him or received since his landing from Greece itself, it is not easy to estimate: 3000 men crossed at first under Milo; the king himself embarked with 20,000 foot, 3000 horse,[40] 2000 archers, 500 slingers, and 20 elephants, and Ptolemy Ceraunus is said to have lent him for two years the services of 5000 Macedonian foot, 4000 horse, and 50 elephants.[41] The Macedonian foot

[35] [36] Zonaras, VIII. 2.

[37] Zonaras, VIII. 2. Frontinus, Strategem. I. 4, § 1.

[38] Zonaras, VIII. 2. Plutarch, Pyrrh. 15, 16. Appian, Samnitic. Fragm. VIII.

[39] Plutarch, Pyrrh. 16.

[40] Plutarch, Pyrrh. 15. Zonaras agrees as to the number of elephants; of the numbers of the infantry and cavalry he gives no account.

[41] Justin, XVII. 2.

may have been included in the 20,000 men whom he himself brought into Italy; the cavalry and elephants of course cannot have been so, if the numbers are correctly given; but we find his cavalry afterwards spoken of as amounting only to 3000, and we can hardly think that he had at any time so many as 70 elephants. Some deductions must also be made, in all probability, for losses sustained by shipwreck, when the armament was dispersed by a storm in its passage. Yet still the Greek army with which Pyrrhus was ready to take the field from Tarentum in the spring of the year 474, must have been more numerous, both in foot, horse, and elephants, than that with which Hannibal, about sixty years later, issued from the Alps upon the plain of Cisalpine Gaul.

The Romans, on their part, finding that not Tarentum only, but so great a king and good a soldier as Pyrrhus was added to their numerous enemies, made extraordinary exertions to meet the danger. Even the proletarians,[42] or the poorest class of citizens, who were usually exempt from the military service, were now called out and embodied, and these probably formed a great part of the reserve army kept near Rome for the defence of the city. The new consuls were P. Valerius Lævinus and Ti. Coruncanius, of whom the latter was to command one consular army against the Etruscans, while the former was to oppose Pyrrhus in the south. No mention is made of the army of L. Æmilius, which had wintered in Apulia, so that we do not know whether it joined that of Lævinus, or was employed to watch the doubtful fidelity of the Apulians, and to prevent the Samnites from joining the enemy's army. We learn accidentally,[43] that a Campanian legion was placed in garrison at Rhegium, and other important towns were no doubt secured also with a sufficient force; but the whole disposition of the Roman armies in this great campaign cannot be known, from the scantiness of our remaining information respecting it.

And of the Romans. A. U. C. 474. A. C. 280.

It is briefly stated in the narrative of Zonaras[44] that the Romans chastised some of their allies who were meditating a revolt, and that some citizens of Præneste were suddenly arrested and sent to Rome, where they were imprisoned in the vaults of the ærarium on the Capitol, and afterwards put to death. If even the Latin city of Præneste could waver in its fidelity, what was to be expected from the more remote and more recent allies of Rome, from the Vestinians, Marsians, Pelignians, Sabines, and even from the Campanians, whose faith in the second Samnite war, little more than thirty years before, had been found so unstable? Yet one of the consuls for this year, Ti. Coruncanius, was a native of Tusculum, and those Latin, Volscian, and Æquian towns which had received the full rights of Roman citizenship were incorporated thereby so thoroughly into the Roman nation, that no circumstances could rend them asunder. Still the senate thought it best on every ground to keep the war, if possible, at a distance from their own territory, and Lævinus therefore marched into Lucania, to separate Pyrrhus from his allies, and to force him to a battle whilst he had only his own troops and the Tarentines to bring into the field.

State of the allies of Rome.

"Lævinus," says Zonaras,[45] "took a strong fortress in Lucania, and having left a part of his amy to overawe the Lucanians, he advanced with the remainder against Pyrrhus." Yet Pyrrhus, after all, fought, we are told, with an inferior army;[46] nor indeed can we conceive that so able a general would have exposed himself to the unavoidable disadvantage of seeming to dread an encounter with the enemy, had the number of his troops been equal to theirs. But a Roman consular army never contained more than 20,000 foot soldiers, and 2400 horse; and the army which Pyrrhus brought with him from Epirus was more numerous than this, without reckoning the Tarentines, and allowing that Milo and his detachment of 3000 men still garrisoned the

Lævinus, the Roman consul, marches against Pyrrhus.

[42] Orosius, IV. 1.
[43] Orosius, IV. 3. Polybius, I. 7.
[44] Zonaras, VIII. 3.
[45] VIII. 3.
[46] Justin, XVIII. 1.

citadel of Tarentum. It is clear, then, either that Lævinus had taken with him the whole or the greater part of the consular army which had wintered in Apulia, or that a prætorian army had marched under his command from the neighborhood of Rome, so that his force cannot be estimated at less than 30,000 foot and 3600 horse.

Pyrrhus endeavors to gain time till his allies should have joined him.

Pyrrhus not thinking himself strong enough to meet the enemy with the army actually at his disposal, endeavored to gain time by negotiation. He wrote to Lævinus,[47] offering his mediation between the Romans and his Italian allies, and saying that he would wait ten days for the consul's answer. But his offer was scornfully rejected; and in the same spirit, when one of his spies was detected in the Roman camp, Lævinus is said to have allowed the spy to observe his whole army on their usual parade,[48] and then to have sent him back unharmed, with a taunting message, that if Pyrrhus wished to know the nature of the Roman army, he had better not send others to spy it out secretly, but he should come himself in open day, and see it and prove it.

The Romans attack him. Battle of Heraclea.

Thus provoked, or more probably fearing to lose the confidence of his allies if he should seem to have crossed the sea only to lie inactive in Tarentum, Pyrrhus with his own army and with the Tarentines took the field and advanced towards the enemy. The Romans lay encamped on the right or southern bank of the Siris not far from the sea, and Pyrrhus having crossed the Aciris between the towns of Pandosia and Heraclea, encamped in the plain[49] which lies between the two rivers, and which was favorable at once for the operations of his heavy infantry, and for his cavalry and elephants. A nearer view of the strength of the Roman army determined him still to delay the battle, and he stationed a detachment of troops on the bank of the Siris, to obstruct, if possible, the passage of the stream. But the river, though wide, is shallow,[50] and while the legions prepared to cross directly in front of the enemy, the cavalry[51] passed above and below, so that the Greeks, afraid of being surrounded, were obliged to fall back towards their main body. Pyrrhus then gave orders to his infantry to form in order of battle in the middle of the plain, while he himself rode forward with his cavalry, in hopes of attacking the Romans before they should have had time to form after their passage of the river. But he found the long shields of the legionary soldiers advancing in an even line from the stream, and their cavalry in front ready to receive his attack. He charged instantly, but the Romans and their allies, although their arms were very unequal to those of the Greek horsemen, maintained the fight most valiantly, and a Frentanian captain[52] was seen to mark Pyrrhus himself so eagerly, that one of his officers noticed it, and advised the king to beware of that barbarian on the black horse with white feet. Pyrrhus, whose personal prowess was not unworthy of his hero-ancestry, replied, "What is fated, Leonatus, no man can avoid; but neither this man nor the stoutest soldier in Italy shall encounter with me for nothing." At that instant, the Frentanian rode at Pyrrhus with his levelled lance, and killed his horse; but his own was killed at the same instant, and while Pyrrhus was remounted instantly by his attendants, the brave Italian was surrounded and slain.

Finding that his cavalry could not decide the battle, Pyrrhus at length

[47] Dionysius, XVII. 15, 16.

[48] Dionysius, XVIII. 1. Zonaras, VIII. 3.

[49] Plutarch, Pyrrh. 16. At present a thick forest covers the western part of this plain, extending along the left bank of the Siris for several miles upwards from its mouth, as far as the point where the hills begin. See Keppel Craven, p. 203, and Zannoni's map. But in ancient times it is probable that the whole plain between the two rivers was open, and mostly corn land. The plain rises in a gradual slope from Policoro, supposed to be the site of the ancient Heraclea, for about three miles, and is for the most part highly cultivated.

[50] Keppel Craven, p. 204. Mr. Keppel Craven forded it below the point where the Roman army effected its passage.

[51] Plutarch, Pyrrh. 16.

[52] Plutarch, Pyrrh. 16. Dionysius, XVIII. 2–4. Part of this story of the Frentanian captain has been copied by Plutarch from Dionysius, but he has some other particulars which are not to be found in Dionysius, and which he got probably from Hieronymus.

ordered his infantry to advance and attack the line of the Roman legions.[53] He himself, knowing the importance of his own life to an army in which his personal ascendency was all in all, gave his own arms, and helmet, and scarlet cloak to Megacles, one of the officers of his guard, and himself put on those of the officer in exchange. But Megacles bought his borrowed splendor dearly: every Roman marked him, and at last he was struck down and slain, and his helmet and mantle carried to Lævinus, and borne along the Roman ranks in triumph. Pyrrhus feeling that this mistake was most dangerous, rode bareheaded along his line to show his soldiers that he was still alive; and the battle went on so furiously that either army seven times,[54] it is said, drove the enemy from the ground, and seven times was driven from its own.

Panic occasioned by the supposed death of Pyrrhus.

Lævinus, true to the tactic of his country, proposed to win the battle by keeping back his last reserve[55] till all the enemy's forces were in action. His triarii, it seems, were already engaged, and their long spears might enable them to encounter, on something like equal terms, the pikes of the phalanx; but Lævinus held back a chosen body of his cavalry, hoping that their charge might at last decide the day. They did charge, but Pyrrhus met them with a reserve still more formidable, his elephants. The Roman horses could not be brought to face monsters strange and terrible alike to them and to their riders; they fell back in confusion—the infantry were disordered by their flight; and Pyrrhus then charged with his Thessalian cavalry, and totally routed the whole Roman army. The vanquished fled over the Siris,[56] but did not attempt to defend their camp, which Pyrrhus entered without opposition. They retreated to a city in Apulia,[57] which Niebuhr supposes must have been Venusia, with a loss variously estimated as usual by different writers,[58] but sufficient at any rate to cripple their army, and to leave Pyrrhus undisputed master of the field.

The Romans are defeated, and their camp taken.

His Italian allies now joined him;[59] and though he complained of the tardiness of their aid, he distributed to them a share of the spoils of his victory. The allies of Rome began to waver; and the Roman garrisons in distant cities, cut off from relief, were placed in extreme jeopardy. The

Effects of the victory.

[53] Plutarch, Pyrrh. 17.

[54] Τροπὰς ἑπτὰ λέγεται φευγόντων ἀνάπαλιν καὶ διωκόντων γενέσθαι. Plutarch, Pyrrh. 17. From this and other circumstances related of this battle, it appears certain that only a very small part of Pyrrhus' infantry could have had the arms and array of the regular phalanx. For as the ground was open and level, and the two armies met front and front, if Pyrrhus' heavy-armed infantry had been numerous, they must have had the same advantage which the phalanx had at Cynocephalæ and at Pydna as long as it kept its line unbroken; and the Roman infantry could not have maintained the contest. While, on the other hand, if the phalanx did not keep its order, so that the Romans were able to penetrate it in several places, then they would have obtained an easy victory, as the phalanx when once broken became wholly helpless. But it would seem that the Greek infantry in this battle consisted mostly of peltastæ, or troops not formed in the close array of the phalanx; such were the Epirots generally, and such would be also the Ætolians and Illyrians, some of whom, it is said [Dion Cassius, Fragm. Peiresc. XXXIX.], were serving at this time in Pyrrhus' army. Thus the infantry in both armies were armed and formed in a manner not very different from each other; and this would account for the length and obstinacy of the action, and the number of slain on both sides.

[55] Zonaras, VIII. 3. Plutarch, Pyrrh. 17.

[56] The destruction of the Roman army was prevented, according to Orosius, by an accident. One Minucius, a soldier of the fourth legion, cut off with his sword the trunk of one of the elephants; which made the animal turn, and run back upon his own army. The confusion and delay thus occasioned enabled the Romans to escape over the Siris with the bulk of their army. Orosius, IV. 1.

[57] Zonaras, VIII. 3.

[58] Hieronymus, a contemporary, who in his account of the loss sustained in the battle of Asculum, is known to have copied Pyrrhus' own commentaries, makes the Roman loss in the first battle to have amounted to 7000 men, and that of Pyrrhus to less than 4000. Dionysius stated the Roman loss at 15,000 and that of Pyrrhus at 13,000, copying probably from the exaggerated accounts of some of the Roman annalists, perhaps from Valerius Antias himself. See Plutarch, Pyrrhus, 17. Orosius, copying from Livy, who in his turn probably followed Fabius, reckons the Roman loss at 11,880 killed, and 310 prisoners; while of their cavalry 243 were killed and 802 taken. He says also that twenty-two standards were taken. But what is curious, and which shows that neither he himself nor Livy could have at all consulted the Greek writers on this war, he asserts that of the loss on Pyrrhus' side no record had been preserved.

[59] Zonaras, VIII. 3. Plutarch, Pyrrh. 17.

The Roman garrison seizes Rhegium, and massacres the inhabitants.

Locrians rose upon the garrison of their city, and opened their gates to Pyrrhus.[60] At Rhegium[61] the garrison, which consisted of the eighth legion, composed of Campanian soldiers, acted like the garrison of Enna, in similar circumstances in the second Punic war: they anticipated the inhabitants by a general massacre of all the male citizens, and made slaves of the women and children. For this alone they might have received reward rather than punishment from the Roman government; and the Roman annalists would have pleaded necessity as a sanction for the act. But the Campanians, looking to the example of their Mamertine countrymen on the other side of the strait, and thinking that Rome was in no condition to enforce their allegiance any more, held the city in their own name, and refused to obey the consul's orders. Thus Rhegium, no less than Locri, was for the present lost to the Romans.

Pyrrhus resolves to send an embassy to Rome.

Pyrrhus, however, had not won his victory cheaply. Nearly four thousand of his men had fallen, and amongst these a large proportion of his best officers and personal friends; for the Greek loss must have fallen heavily on the cavalry, and when the king exposed his own life so freely, those immediately about his person must have suffered in an unusual proportion. The weather also, if we may trust some stories in Orosius,[62] was very unfavorable, and the state of the roads may have retarded the advance of the victorious army, and particularly of the elephants. Besides, so complete a victory, won by Pyrrhus with his own army alone, before the mass of his allies had joined him, might dispose the Romans to peace without the risk of a second battle. Accordingly, whilst the army advanced slowly from the shores of the Ionian sea towards central Italy, Cineas was sent to Rome with the king's terms of peace and alliance.[63]

He proposes terms of peace.

The conditions offered were these: peace, friendship, and alliance between Pyrrhus and the Romans;[64] but the Tarentines were to be included in it, and all the Greek states in Italy were to be free and independent. Further, the king's Italian allies, the Lucanians, Samnites, Apulians, and Bruttians, were to recover all towns and territories which they had lost in war to the Romans. If these terms were agreed to, the king would restore to the Romans all the prisoners whom he had taken without ransom.

Cineas sent as his ambassador.

Cineas, the ambassador of Pyrrhus on this memorable occasion, was, in the versatility and range of his talents, worthy of the best ages of Greece. He was a Thessalian,[65] and in his early youth he had heard Demosthenes speak; and the impression made on his mind by the great orator was supposed to have enkindled in him a kindred spirit of eloquence: the tongue of Cineas, it was said, had won more cities than the sword of Pyrrhus. Like Themistocles, he was gifted with an extraordinary memory; the very day after his arrival at Rome, he was able to address all the senators[66] and the citizens of the equestrian order by their several proper names. He had studied philosophy, like all his educated countrymen, and appears to have admired particularly the new doctrine of Epicurus;[67] which taught that war and state affairs were but toil and trouble, and that the wise man should imitate the blissful rest of the gods, who, dwelling in their own divinity, regarded not the vain turmoil

[60] Justin, XVIII. 1.

[61] Appian, Samnitic. Fragm. IX. Dion Cassius, Fragm. Peiresc. XL.

[62] Orosius, IV. 1. One of the Roman foraging parties, soon after the battle, was overtaken by so dreadful a storm, that thirty-four men were knocked down, and twenty-two left nearly dead; and many oxen and horses were killed or maimed.

[63] Appian, Samnitic. Fragm. X. Plutarch, Pyrrh. 18.

[64] Appian, Samnitic. Fragm. X. These terms showed sufficient respect on the part of Pyrrhus for the power and resolution of the Romans, but they would not satisfy the Roman vanity; and accordingly, Plutarch says that "the king merely asked for peace for himself and indemnity for the Tarentines, and offered to aid the Romans in conquering Italy." Pyrrh. 18.

[65] Plutarch, Pyrrh. 14.

[66] Pliny, Histor. Natur. VII. § 88.

[67] Cicero, de Senectut. 13. Plutarch, Pyrrh. 20.

of this lower world. Yet his life was better than his philosophy; he served his king actively and faithfully in peace and in war, and he wrote a military work,[68] for which he neither wanted ability nor practical knowledge. He excited no small attention as he went to Rome, and his sayings at the places through which he passed were remembered and recorded.[69] Some stories said that he was the bearer of presents to the influential senators, and of splendid dresses[70] to win the favor of their wives; all which, as the Roman traditions related, were steadily refused. But his proposals required grave consideration, and there were many in the senate who thought that the state of affairs made it necessary to accept them.

Appius Claudius is led to the senate, and speaks against the peace.

Appius Claudius, the famous censor, the greatest of his countrymen in the works of peace, and no mean soldier in time of need, was now, in the thirtieth year after his censorship, in extreme old age, and had been for many years blind. But his active mind triumphed over age and infirmity; and although he no longer took part in public business, yet he was ready[71] in his own house to give answers to those who consulted him on points of law, and his name was fresh in all men's minds, though his person was not seen in the Forum. The old man heard that the senate was listening to the proposals of Cineas, and was likely to accept the king's terms of peace. He immediately desired to be carried to the senate-house, and was borne in a litter by his slaves through the Forum. When it was known that Appius Claudius was coming, his sons and sons-in-law[72] went out to the steps of the senate-house to receive him, and he was by them led into his place. The whole senate kept the deepest silence as the old man arose to speak.

Similar scene in English history.

No Englishman can have read thus far without remembering the scene, in all points so similar, which took place within our fathers' memory in our own house of parliament. We recollect how the greatest of English statesmen, bowed down by years and infirmity like Appius, but roused, like him, by the dread of approaching dishonor to the English name, was led by his son and son-in-law into the house of lords, and all the peers, with one impulse, arose to receive him. We know the expiring words of that mighty voice, when he protested against the dismemberment of this ancient monarchy, and prayed that if England must fall, she might fall with honor. The real speech of Lord Chatham against yielding to the coalition of France and America, will give a far more lively image of what was said by the blind Appius in the Roman senate, than any fictitious oration which I could either copy from other writers, or endeavor myself to invent; and those who would wish to know how Appius spoke should read the dying words of the great orator of England.

The senate rejects the terms proposed.

When he had finished his speech, the senate voted that the proposals of Pyrrhus should be rejected, that no peace[73] should be concluded with him so long as he remained in Italy, and that Cineas should be ordered to leave Rome on that very day.

And prepare vigorously for war.

Even whilst the senate had been considering the king's proposals, there had been no abatement of the vigor of their preparations for war. Two new legions,[74] which must have been at least the ninth and tenth

[68] At least Cicero, in writing to Pætus, says, "Plane nesciebam te tam peritum esse rei militaris. Pyrrhi te libros et Cineæ video lectitasse." Ad Familiar. IX. 25. Now the commentaries of Pyrrhus are referred to by Plutarch, and it would seem therefore that the allusion to the writings of Cineas is also to be taken literally.

[69] At Aricia, on the Appian Way, Cineas had remarked the luxuriance of the vines, as they festooned on the very summits of the elms, and at the same time complained of the harshness of the wine. "The mother which bore this wine well deserves," he said, "to be hung on so high a gibbet." Pliny, Hist. Natur. XIV. § 12.

[70] Plutarch, Pyrrh. 18.

[71] Cicero, de Senectut. 6, 11. Tusculan. Disp. V. 38.

[72] Plutarch, Pyrrh. 18. He had four sons and five daughters, but how many of his daughters were married, we know not. See Cicero de Senect. 11. A speech was extant in Cicero's time purporting to be that which Appius spoke on this occasion. De Senectut. 6. Brutus, 16. But Cicero does not seem to have regarded it as genuine.

[73] Plutarch, Pyrrh. 19. Appian, Samnitic. X. 2. Zonaras, VIII. 4.

[74] Appian, Samnitic. X. 3. The Campanian

in number, were raised while Cineas was at Rome by voluntary enlistment, proclamation being made, that whoever wished to offer his services to supply the place of the soldiers who had fallen in battle, should enrol himself immediately. Niebuhr supposes that this was the period of P. Cornelius Rufinus' dictatorship, and that he superintended the recruiting of the armies. The new legions were sent to reinforce Lævinus, who, as Pyrrhus began to advance northwards, followed him hanging upon his rear, but not venturing to engage in a second battle.

Pyrrhus advances into Campania.

Cineas returned to the king, to tell him that he must hope for nothing from negotiation. He expressed, according to the writers[75] whom we are obliged to follow, the highest admiration of all that he had seen. "To fight with the Roman people was like fighting with the hydra, so inexhaustible were their numbers and their spirit." "Rome was a city of generals, nay, rather of kings," or, according to another and more famous version of the story, "The city was like a temple, the senate was an assembly of kings." Did we find these expressions recorded by Hieronymus of Cardia, who wrote before Rome was the object of universal flattery, we might believe them; but from the later Greek writers they deserve no more credit than if reported merely by the Romans themselves; and nothing is more suspicious than such statements of the language of admiration proceeding from the mouth of an enemy. But be this as it may, Pyrrhus now resolved to prosecute the war with vigor. At the head of a large army,[76] for the Italian allies had now joined him, he advanced through Lucania and Samnium into Campania. The territory of the allies of Rome had now for some years been free from the ravages of war,[77] and its scattered houses, its flourishing cultivation, and luxuriant fruit-trees, were a striking contrast to the wasted appearance of Samnium and Lucania. All was ravaged and plundered without mercy, by the Italians in revenge, by the Greeks to enrich themselves and force their enemy to submission, but in some instances it only provoked a firmer resistance, and Neapolis and Capua[88] were attacked, but refused to surrender, nor could Pyrrhus make himself master of either of them.

And through the Hernican country. He takes Præneste, and advances within eighteen miles of Rome.

From Campania he ascended the valley of the Liris, and followed the Latin road towards Rome. Fregellæ,[79] wrested formerly from the Volscians by the Samnites, and the occupation of which by the Romans had led to the second Samnite war, now yielded to the Greek conqueror. The Hernicans, who, under the name of Roman citizens, without the right of suffrage, were in fact no better than Roman subjects, received Pyrrhus readily, and Anagnia,[80] their principal city, opened its gates to him. Still advancing, he at last looked out upon the plain of Rome from the opening in the mountains under Præneste; and Præneste itself,[81] with its almost impregnable citadel, fell into his hands, for the Prænestines remembered the execution of their principal citizens a few months before, and longed for vengeance. Præneste is barely twenty-four miles distant from Rome, but Pyrrhus advanced yet six miles further,[82] and from the spot where the road

legion which garrisoned Rhegium had been the eighth. Orosius, IV. 3. But perhaps the proletarians raised to form the army of reserve had already formed a ninth and tenth legion, in which case those now raised would be the eleventh and twelfth. We cannot account for four legions in the two consular armies, two more under the proconsul, L. Æmilius; one or two, we know not which, forming the reserve army under the walls of Rome, and one in garrison at Rhegium. The legions of Lævinus had suffered so greatly in the battle that their numbers were no doubt very incomplete; but the reinforcements formed two fresh legions, and did not merely serve to recruit the old ones, as appears both by Appian's express language, and also by what is afterwards said of the punishment of the legions which had fought on the Siris, for it would have been very hard to have involved in their sentence the newly raised soldiers who had no share in the defeat.

[75] Plutarch, in Pyrrh. 19. Appian, Samnit. X. 3. Florus, I. 18. Dion Cassius apud Maium, Script. Veter. Collect. tom. II. p. 538.

[76] Zonaras, VIII. 4. Eutropius, II. Florus, I. 18.

[77] Dion Cassius, Fragm. 50. Script. Veter. Collect.

[78] Zonaras, VIII. 4.

[79] Florus, I. 18.

[80] Appian, Samnitic. X. 3.

[81] Florus, I. 18. Eutropius, II.

[82] "Milliario ab urbe octavodecimo." Eutropius. If this statement is correct, Pyrrhus must have passed beyond Zagarolo, and reached the spot where the road descends to the level

descends from the last roots of the mountains to the wide level of the Campagna he cast his eyes upon the very towers of the city.

One march more would have brought him under the walls of Rome, where, as he hoped, there was nothing to oppose him but the two legions, which, at the beginning of the campaign, had been reserved for the defence of the capital. But at this moment he was informed that the whole Etruscan nation had concluded a peace[83] with Rome, and Ti. Coruncanius, with his consular army, was returned from Etruria, and had joined the army of reserve. At the same time Lævinus was hanging on his rear, and before he could enter Rome, both consuls would be able to combine their forces, and he would have to deal with an army of eight or nine Roman legions, and an equal number of their Latin and other allies. Besides, his own army was feeling the usual evils of a force composed of the soldiers of different nations; the Italians complained of the Greeks,[84] and charged them with plundering the territory of friends and foes alike; the Greeks treated the Italians with arrogance, as if in themselves alone lay the whole strength of the confederacy. Pyrrhus retreated, loaded with plunder, and returned to Campania; Lævinus fell back before him, but it is said that when Pyrrhus[85] was going to attack him, and ordered his soldiers to raise their battle-cry, and the Greeks to strike their spears against their brazen shields, and when the elephants, excited by their drivers, uttered at the same time their fearful roarings, the Roman army answered with a shout so loud and cheerful, that he did not venture to bring on an action. Neither party made any further attempts at active operations; the Samnites and Lucanians wintered in their own countries, Pyrrhus himself returned to Tarentum, and the Romans remained within their own frontiers,[86] excepting only the legions which had been beaten in the first battle, and which were ordered to remain in the field during the winter in the enemy's country, with no other supplies than such as they could win by their own swords.

The Etruscans suddenly make peace with Rome, and the second consular army is employed against Pyrrhus. He retreats to Campania.

As soon as the campaign was over, the senate dispatched an embassy to Pyrrhus to request that he would either allow them to ransom his Roman prisoners, or that he would exchange them for an equal number of Tarentines and others of his allies who were prisoners at Rome.[87] The ambassadors sent to Pyrrhus were C. Fabricius, Q. Æmilius, and P. Dolabella, all of them men of the highest distinction; but Fabricius was the favorite hero of Roman tradition, and the stories of this embassy spoke of him alone. That Pyrrhus was struck with the circumstance of his being at once so eminent among his countrymen, and yet so simple in his habits, and even, according to a king's standard of wealth, so poor, is perfectly probable: he may have asked him to enter into his service, for the Greeks of that age thought it no shame to serve a foreign king; and if the Thessalian Cineas was his minister, he could not suppose that a similar office would be refused by the barbarian Fabricius. It was the misfortune of Pyrrhus to live in a state of society where

A Roman embassy sent to Pyrrhus. His interview with Fabricius.

of the Campagna, close by what is called the lake of Regillus, and just at the junction of the modern road from La Colonna. (Labici.)

[83] Zonaras, VIII. 4. See also Appian, X. 3, although his statement is not quite accurate as to time.

[84] Dion Cassius, Fragm. 50. Script. Veter. Collect.

[85] Zonaras, VIII. 4. Dion Cassius, Fragm. LI.

[86] Frontinus, Strategem. IV. 1. § 24. The name of the place to which Lævinus' army was sent is corrupt. Oudendorp and the Bipont edition read "Firmum," which, of course, must be wrong, as Firmum was far away from the seat of war. Niebuhr conjectures Samnium or Ferentinum, supposing that Ferentinum, the Hernican town, had revolted, and that these legions were employed in reducing it. But nothing can be decided with certainty.

[87] Appian, Samnitic. Fragm. X. 4, 5. The names of the Roman ambassadors, and long speeches put into the mouths of Pyrrhus and of Fabricius, are to be found in the fragments of Dionysius, XVIII. 5–26. The famous anecdotes, how Fabricius was neither to be bribed by the king's money, nor frightened by the sudden sight of one of his elephants, which at a signal given stretched out its trunk immediately over his head, are given by Plutarch, Pyrrh. 20. Speeches of Pyrrhus and of Fabricius in answer, declining the king's offers, are also preserved in the Vatican Fragments of Dion Cassius, LIII. LIV.

patriotism was become impossible; the Greek commonwealths were so fallen, and their inner life so exhausted, that they could inspire their citizens neither with respect nor with attachment, and the military monarchies founded by Alexander's successors could know no deeper feeling than personal regard for the reigning monarch; loyalty to his line could not yet have existed, and love for the nation under a foreign despotism is almost a contradiction. In Rome, on the other hand, the state and its institutions were in their first freshness and vigor, and so surpassed any individual distinction, that no private citizen could have thought of setting his own greatness on a level with that of his country, and the world could offer to him nothing so happy and so glorious as to live and die a Roman. But the particular anecdotes recorded of the king and Fabricius are so ill attested and so suspicious, and the speeches ascribed to them both are so manifestly the mere invention of the writers of a later age, that I have thought it best to exclude them from this history, and merely to give a slight mention of them in a note, on account of their great celebrity.

His generous treatment of the Roman prisoners.

Pyrrhus would neither ransom nor exchange his prisoners, unless the Romans would accept the terms of peace proposed to them by Cineas.[88] But to show how little he wished to treat them with harshness, he allowed Fabricius to take them all back with him to Rome to pass the Saturnalia, their winter holydays, at their several homes, on a solemn promise that they would return to him when the holydays were over, if the senate still persisted in refusing peace. The senate did persist in its refusal, and the prisoners returned to Pyrrhus; the punishment of death having been denounced by the Roman government against any prisoner who should linger in Rome beyond the day fixed for their return. And thus both parties prepared to try the fortune of war once again.

A. U. C. 475. A. C. 279. Second campaign. Both consuls are opposed to Pyrrhus in Apulia.

The new consuls were P. Sulpicius Saverrio, whose father had been consul in the last year of the second Samnite war, and P. Decius Mus, the son of the Decius who had devoted himself at Sentinum, and the grandson of him who had devoted himself in the great battle with the Latins. The legions required for the campaign were easily raised,[89] every citizen being eager to serve in such a season of danger, and C. Fabricius acted as lieutenant to one of the consuls; but beyond this we know nothing of the number or disposition of the Roman armies, nor of their plan of operations, nor of the several generals employed in different quarters. Nor do we know whether any of the places which had revolted to Pyrrhus during his advance upon Rome continued still to adhere to him after his retreat; nor, if they did, how much time and what forces were required to subdue them. We are only told that Pyrrhus took the field in Apulia, and reduced several places in that quarter;[90] and that he was employed in besieging Asculum when both consuls, with their two consular armies, advanced to relieve it and to offer him battle.

Preparations for battle on both sides.

The ancient Asculum, if its site was exactly the same with that of the modern Ascoli, stood on a hill of inconsiderable size[91] on the edge of the plains of Apulia; but, geologically speaking, it belongs to the plains, for the hill is composed only of beds of sand and clay, and the range of the limestone mountains sweeps round it at some distance on the west and south. The country is, for the most part, open, and must have been favorable for the operations of the king's phalanx and elephants, as the soil, which after the winter rains is stiff and heavy, must, later in the year, have recovered its hardness.

[88] Appian, Samnitic. Fragm. X. 4, 5. Zonaras, following Dion Cassius, and Dionysius also, place at this period the free release of all the Roman prisoners by Pyrrhus without ransom. And so also does the epitome of Livy, XIII. Plutarch agrees with Appian, and their account is so much the more probable of the two that I have not hesitated to follow it.

[89] Dion Cassius, Fragm. Vatic. LV. Orosius, IV. 1.

[90] Zonaras, VIII. 4.

[91] See Dr. Daubeny's Excursion to Amsanctus, p. 30. Ascoli is a poor town, though it contained in 1797, according to Giustiniani, 5270 souls. It has suffered repeatedly from earthquakes.

When the armies were opposed to each other, a rumor spread among Pyrrhus' soldiers[92] that the consul Decius intended to follow the example of his father and grandfather, and to devote himself, together with the enemy's army, to the powers of death, whenever they should join battle. The men were uneasy at this report, so that Pyrrhus thought it expedient to warn them against yielding to superstitious fears, and to describe minutely the dress worn by any person so devoting himself. "If they saw any one so arrayed," he said, "they should not kill him, but by all means take him alive;" and he sent a message to the consuls, warning them that if he should take any Roman practising such a trick, he would put him to an ignominious death as a common impostor. The consuls replied, that they needed no such resources, and trusted to the courage of Roman soldiers for victory.

Battle of Asculum.

The first encounter took place on rough ground,[93] and near the swampy banks of a river; and Pyrrhus having assailed the Romans in such a position, was repulsed with loss. But he manœuvred so as to bring them fairly into the plain, and there the two armies engaged. He kept his cavalry and elephants to act as a reserve; the Tarentines formed the centre of his line; the Lucanians, Bruttians, and Sallentines[94] were on the left, and the Greeks and Samnites on the right. The Romans, as usual, had their cavalry on the wings, and their own legions formed the first line, and also the reserve; the troops of their allies forming a second line between them. If this be true, the Romans must have suspected the fidelity of their allies; for their courage had been proved in a hundred battles; and the Marsians and Pelignians now, as at Pydna, would have thrown themselves on the pikes of the phalanx as fearlessly as the bravest Roman. On the other hand, Pyrrhus intermingled the Samnites with his Greek infantry, on purpose to combine the advantages of the Italian tactic[95] with those of the Macedonian; that if his line should be attacked in flank, or if the enemy should penetrate it in any quarter, the Samnites might meet the Romans with their own weapons, and allow the Greeks time to recover the position and close order which, to their mode of fighting, were indispensable.

The Romans are defeated.

But he had no occasion to try the effect of this disposition; for his phalanx kept its advantage, and as the nature of the ground obliged the Romans to attack it in front, they hewed in vain with their swords[96] at the invincible mass of the Macedonian pikes, or tried to grapple them with their hands and break them. The Greeks kept an even line, and the Romans, finding it impossible to get within the hedge of spears, were slaughtered without returning a wound. At last they gave way, and then the elephants charged, and completed the rout. The other parts of the line opposed to the Tarentines and Lucanians were obliged to follow the example, and the Roman army fled to its camp. This was so close at hand that the loss did not exceed six thousand men, while in the army of Pyrrhus there had fallen 3505 according to the statement copied by Hieronymus from the commentaries of the king himself. This loss must again have fallen on the cavalry, light troops, and peltastæ of Pyrrhus' army, unless it was sustained chiefly by his allies on the centre and left wing; for the circumstances of the battle make it certain that the victory of his heavy-armed Greek infantry must have been almost bloodless.

Exaggerated and false account of this battle.

In this account of the actual battle of Asculum, Plutarch luckily chose to copy Hieronymus; but immediately after it he follows Dionysius, and we have nothing but the usual exaggerations of Roman vanity, which leave the real facts of the campaign in utter darkness. The victory of Asculum was not improved, and at the end of the season the Romans wintered in Apulia, and Pyrrhus again returned to Tarentum. A victory followed by no

92 Zonaras, VIII. 5. Dion Cassius, Fragm. Vatican. LV.

93 Plutarch, Pyrrh. 21.

94 Frontinus, Stratagem. II. 3, § 21.

95 Polybius, XVIII. 11.

96 Plutarch, Pyrrh. 21, copying apparently from Hieronymus.

results is easily believed to be a defeat; and where there is no other memorial of events than unchecked popular report and unsifted stories, facts which have no witness in their permanent consequences are soon hopelessly perverted. Niebuhr declares from his own personal observation, that within a few days after the battle of Bautzen every Prussian who had not been actually engaged in the action, maintained that the allies had been victorious; and we can remember the extraordinary misrepresentation which for a moment persuaded the English public that Napoleon had been defeated at Borodino. The successive steps of Roman invention with respect to the battle of Asculum are so curious, that I have given a view of them in a note:[97] but it is not so easy to determine what were the real causes which neutralized to Pyrrhus the result of his victory, and made the issue of the campaign, as a whole, decidedly unfavorable to him.

It is attended with no results. League between the Romans and Carthaginians.

Both Zonaras and Dionysius relate that the baggage of Pyrrhus was plundered during the battle by his Italian allies; by the Apulians according to Zonaras, or according to Dionysius by the Samnites. If this were so, not only did it imply such bad discipline and bad feeling on the part of his allies as to make it impossible for Pyrrhus to depend on their co-operation for the future; but the loss of their plunder and baggage would greatly discourage his own soldiers, and indispose them to the continuance of the war. Besides, it was manifest that the brunt of every battle must fall on the Greeks; already Pyrrhus had lost many of his best officers, and as he never lost sight of his schemes of conquest in Greece, he would not be willing to sacrifice his bravest soldiers in a series of hard-won battles in Italy, for the sake of allies on whom he could place no reliance. It is likely also that the Apulian cities which he had taken, overawed by the Roman power, and disgusted with the arrogance and indiscriminate plundering of the Greeks, were ready to return to their alliance with Rome; and as the Roman army was certain to be speedily reinforced, whilst Pyrrhus could look for no additional soldiers from Epirus, it might be absolutely impossible for him to keep the field. Finally, the Romans had concluded a defensive alliance[98] with the Carthaginians, for their mutual support against Pyrrhus; and towards the autumn of the year Ptolemy Ceraunus, king of Macedon, was defeated and killed by the Gauls,[99] and the presence of these barbarians in Macedonia made it certain that no more soldiers could be spared from Epirus for foreign warfare, when their own frontier was in hourly danger of invasion.

Thus left with no prospect of further conquests in Italy, Pyrrhus eagerly listened during the winter to offers from other quarters, inviting him to a new field

The account in the text is Plutarch's, copied, as I have said, from Hieronymus of Cardia, a contemporary historian. And Justin agrees with it: "The issue of the second battle," he says, "was similar to that of the first," XVIII. 1. Livy, if we may trust the epitome of his 13th book, describes the action as a drawn battle: "dubio eventu pugnatum est." But Florus calls it a victory on the part of the Romans; and Eutropius and Orosius, copying apparently from the same source, says that Pyrrhus was wounded, many of his elephants destroyed, and 20,000 of his men killed, the Roman loss not exceeding 5000. Zonaras, copying from Dion Cassius, says that Pyrrhus was wounded, and that his army was defeated; owing chiefly to an attack made on his camp during the battle by a party of Apulians, which spread a panic among his soldiers. According to Dionysius, as quoted by Plutarch, Pyrrhus was wounded, the Samnites, and not the Apulians, assaulted his camp during the action, and the loss on both sides was equal, amounting to 15,000 men in each army. It is no less remarkable that, according to Cicero, the consul P. Decius did actually devote himself in this battle as his father and grandfather had done before him. De Finib. II. 19. Tusculan. Disp. I. 37. No other existing account notices this circumstance; and according to the author "de Viris Illustribus," Decius was alive some years afterwards, and was engaged in the last war with Volsinii. Probably it was either a forgetfulness in Cicero himself, or he followed some exaggerated account, which, as he was not writing a history of the period, he did not criticise, but adopted it without inquiry. But such enormous discrepancies in the several accounts show what is the character of the Roman history of this period, that, except in particular cases, it is merely made up of traditional stories and panegyrical orations, and can scarcely be called history at all. How different is the account given of the battle by the contemporary historian Hieronymus, who was writing from really good materials, not from guess or fancy, but from knowledge!

[98] Livy, Epitome, XIII. Polybius, III. 25 Justin, XVIII. 2.

[99] Plutarch, Pyrrh. 22.

of action. The death of Ptolemy Ceraunus and the anarchy which followed tempted him to win back his old dominion in Macedonia, while envoys from some of the principal cities of Sicily called upon him to aid them against Carthage, and promised to make him master of the whole island. He was thus eager to seize the first pretext for abandoning Italy, and early in the following spring such an occasion was afforded him. The new consuls, C. Fabricius and Q. Æmilius, were sent against him:[100] and he soon received a message from them to say that one of his servants had offered to poison him, and had applied to the Romans to reward his crime, but that the consuls, abhorring a victory gained by treason, wished to give the king timely notice of his danger. Pyrrhus upon this expressed his gratitude in the warmest terms, furnished all his prisoners with new clothing, and sent them back to their own country, without ransom and without conditions.[101] Immediately afterwards, without paying any regard to the remonstrances of his allies, he left Milo still in possession of the citadel of Tarentum,[102] and his second son Alexander at Locri, and set sail with the rest of his army for Sicily.

Pyrrhus crosses over into Sicily.

A. U. C. 476. A. C. 278.

It was apparently soon after the battle of Asculum, that a Carthaginian fleet of 120 ships[103] was sent to Ostia to offer aid to the Romans, and the senate declining this succor, the Carthaginian commander sailed away to the south of Italy, and there it is said proposed to Pyrrhus that Carthage should mediate between him and the Romans, his real object being to discover what were the king's views with respect to Sicily. Was then the Tarentine fleet wasting the coasts of Latium, so that Rome stood in need of naval aid? Or did so large a fleet contain a Carthaginian army, and was Rome wisely unwilling to see an African general making war in Italy, and carrying off the plunder of Italian cities? The insinuation against the good faith of the Carthaginian commander seems quite unfounded; this very armament helped the Romans[104] in attempting to recover Rhegium, and though the seige did not succeed, yet a large supply of timber, which the Campanians had collected for building ships, was destroyed, and the Carthaginians having made a league with the Mamertines of Messana, watched the strait with their fleet to intercept Pyrrhus on his passage. But it seems that their fleet was called off in the next year to be employed in the siege of Syracuse, so that Pyrrhus, avoiding Messana, crossed from Locri to Tauromenia[105] without opposition, and being welcomed there by the tyrant Tyndarion, landed his army, and marched to the deliverance of Syracuse. His operations in Sicily lasted more than two years;[106] his fortune, which at first favored him in every enterprise, was wrecked in a fruitless siege of Lilybæum;[107] disgusts arose, as in Italy, between him and his allies; they were unmanageable and he was tyrannical, so that when at length his Italian allies implored him to come once again to their aid, he was as ready to leave Sicily as he had before been anxious to invade it.

A Carthaginian fleet is sent to the aid of the Romans.

During his absence the Samnites, Lucanians, Bruttians, and Tarentines still

[100] Claudius Quadrigarius, quoted by A. Gellius, III. 8. Appian, Samnitic. Fragm. XI. Plutarch, Pyrrh. 21.

[101] Plutarch and Appian say that the senate released an equal number of Tarentine and Samnite prisoners, and that Cineas was again sent to Rome to negotiate a peace, but that the Romans refused to treat, while Pyrrhus remained in Italy. Yet Appian, in another fragment, says that Pyrrhus, "after his treaty with the Romans," μετὰ τὰς πρὸς Ῥωμαίους συνθήκας, went over to Sicily. Probably a truce for a certain period was agreed to, and with it a general exchange of prisoners. Whether Pyrrhus stipulated any thing for the Tarentines we cannot tell; but the consuls of the two succeeding years, although they triumphed over the Samnites and Lucanians, yet appeared to have obtained no triumph over Tarentum, and the success for which Fabricius triumphed "de Tarentinis" (Fasti Capitol.) may have been obtained in the early part of his consulship, before the truce with Pyrrhus was concluded.

[102] Justin, XVIII. 2. Zonaras, VIII. 5.

[103] Justin, XVIII. 2.

[104] Diodorus, Fragm. Hoeschel. XXII. 9.

[105] Diod., Fragm. Hoeschel. XXII. 11.

[106] From the middle of 476 to the latter end of 478. ἔτει τρίτῳ is Appian's expression, Samnitic. Fragm. XII., which Mr. Fynes Clinton wrongly understands of the year 479, for that, according to the Greek mode of reckoning, would not have been ἔτει τρίτῳ, but τετάρτῳ.

[107] Diodorus, Fragm. Hoeschel. XXII. 14. Plutarch, Pyrrh. 22, 23.

A. U. C. 476, 477. A. C. 278, 277. Progress of the war in Italy during the absence of Pyrrhus.

continued the war. They ventured no battles in the field, but resolutely defended their towns and fastnesses,[108] and sometimes, as always happens in such warfare, inflicted some partial loss on the enemy, without being able to change in any degree the general fortune of the contest. The consuls employed against them enjoyed a triumph at the end of each campaign; Fabricius at the end of the year 476,[109] C. Junius Brutus at the end of 477, and Q. Fabius Gurges at the end of 478. In the mean time P. Cornelius Rufinus, the colleague of C. Junius in 477, had recovered Croton and Locri; but as he was considered the principal cause of a severe repulse sustained by himself[110] and his colleague from the Samnites at the beginning of the year, he was not thought deserving of a triumph.

A. U. C. 478. A. C. 276. Pyrrhus returns to Italy.

It seems to have been in the autumn of 478 that Pyrrhus returned to Italy.[111] But his return was beset with enemies, for a Carthaginian fleet attacked him on his passage, and sunk seventy of his ships of war,[112] and when he landed on the Italian coast he found that the Mamertines had crossed over from Messana to beset his road by land, and he had to cut his way through them with much loss. Yet he reached Tarentum with a force nearly as large as that which he had first brought over from Epirus; as large in numbers, but of a very different quality, consisting principally of mercenaries raised in his Sicilian wars, men of all countries, Greek and Barbarian, and whose fidelity would last no longer than their general was victorious.

He plunders the temple of Proserpine at Locri.

No sooner had he arrived at Tarentum than he commenced active operations. The Roman consuls were employed in Lucania and in Samnium,[113] but he received no interruption from them, and recovered Locri. He next made an attempt upon Rhegium, a place so important from its position to the success of any new expedition to Sicily, but the Campanian garrison resisted Pyrrhus[114] as stoutly as they had resisted the Romans, and the king was obliged to retire with loss. His old allies, the Samnites and Lucanians,[115] received him coldly, and, however anxious to obtain his aid, they had not, exhausted as they were, the means of supplying him with money, even if they had been disposed to rely on his constancy in their cause. Thus embarrassed, as he passed by Locri on his return from Rhegium to Tarentum, he listened to the advice of some of his followers,[116] and plundered the temple of Proserpine. In the vaults underneath this temple was a large treasure, which had been buried for unknown generations, and no mortal eye had been allowed to look on it. This he carried off, and embarked his spoil on board of his ships, to transport it by sea to Tarentum. A storm, however, arose and wrecked the ships, and cast ashore the plundered treasure on the coast of Locri. Pyrrhus was moved, and ordered it to be replaced in the temple of the goddess, and offered sacrifices to propitiate her anger. But when there were no signs given that she accepted his offering, he put to death the three men who had advised him to commit the sacrilege, and even yet his mind was haunted by a dread of divine vengeance, and his own commentaries[117] recorded his belief that Proserpine's wrath was still

[108] Zonaras, VIII. 6.

[109] Fabricius triumphed in December, Brutus in January, thirteen months afterwards, and Fabius in the February of the year following, when Pyrrhus in all probability was already returned to Italy.

[110] Zonaras, VIII. 6.

[111] Zonaras expressly says that Pyrrhus returned in the year after the consulship of P. Rufinus, that is, in 478. VIII. 6.

[112] Appian, Samnitic. Fragm. XII. Plutarch, Pyrrh. 24. Pyrrhus had obtained this fleet chiefly from the Syracusans, who, on his first arrival in Sicily, gave up to him their whole navy, amounting to 140 ships of war. Diodorus, Fragm. Hoeschel. XXII. 11. The Carthaginians employed in their engagement with Duilius in the first Punic war a large ship, which they took from Pyrrhus probably on his retreat from Sicily. (Polybius, I. 23.) We must suppose that the ships of war were convoying the transports on which Pyrrhus had embarked his army; and that their resistance enabled the transports to escape.

[113] Zonaras, VIII. 6.

[114] Zonaras, VIII. 6.

[115] Plutarch, Pyrrh. 25. Dion. Cassius, Fragm. Peiresc. XLII.

[116] Dionysius, XIX. 9. Appian, Samnitic Fragm. XII.

[117] Dionysius, XIX., ὡς καὶ αὐτὸς ὁ Πύῤῥος ἐν τοῖς ἰδίοις ὑπομνήμασι γράφει.

pursuing him, and bringing on his arms defeat and ruin. If Pyrrhus nimself, after his long intercourse with the Epicurean Cineas, entertained such fears, they weighed far more heavily doubtless on the minds of many of his soldiers and his allies; and the sense of being pursued by the wrath of heaven may have well chilled the hearts of the bravest, and affected in no small degree the issue of the war.

This was fast approaching. The consuls chosen for the year 479 were M'. Curius Dentatus and L. Cornelius Lentulus. The Romans on their side also were visited by religious terrors; during the year 478 a fatal pestilence had raged amongst them,[118] and now the clay statue of Jupiter on the summit of the Capitoline temple was struck by lightning, and shattered to pieces. The head of the image was nowhere to be found, and the augurs declared that the storm had blown it into the Tiber, and commanded that it should be searched for in the bed of the river. It was found in the very place in which the augurs had commanded the search to be made.

Religious terrors at Rome. A. U. C. 479. A. C. 275.

Fears of the anger of the gods, together with the dread of the arms of Pyrrhus, made the Romans backward to enlist in the legions. Those who were summoned did not answer to their names, upon which the consul, M'. Curius,[119] commanded that the goods of the first defaulter should be publicly sold. A public sale of a man's property by the sentence of a magistrate rendered him incapable of exercising afterwards any political rights; but the necessity of a severe example was so felt that no tribune interposed in behalf of the offender, and the consul's order was carried into execution. The usual number of legions was then raised; Lentulus[120] marched into Lucania, Curius into Samnium.

Severity of the consul in the enlistment of soldiers.

Pyrrhus took the field against Curius with his own army, and the flower of the force of Tarentum, and a division of Samnites; the rest of the Samnite army was sent into Lucania to prevent Lentulus from coming to join his colleague. Curius, finding that Pyrrhus was marching against him, sent to call his colleague to his aid; and in the mean while the omens would not allow him to attack the enemy,[121] and he lay encamped in a strong position near Beneventum. There is much rugged and difficult country behind the town on the road towards Apulia, and there is a considerable extent of level ground in the valley of the Calore below it, which was the scene of the decisive battle between Manfred and Charles of Anjou. But whether they fought on the same ground which had witnessed the last encounter between Pyrrhus and the Romans, it is not possible to determine.

Pyrrhus and M'. Curius opposed to each other near Beneventum.

Pyrrhus resolved to attack Curius before his colleague joined him, and he planned an attack upon his camp by night.[122] He set out by torchlight, with the flower of his soldiers and the best of his elephants; but the way was long, and the country overgrown with wood, and intersected with steep ravines; so that his progress was slow, and at last the lights were burnt out, and the men were continually missing their way. Day broke before they reached their destination; but still the enemy were not aware of their approach till they had surmounted the heights above the Roman camp, and were descending to attack it from the vantage-ground. Then Curius led out his troops to oppose them; and the nature of the ground gave the Romans a great advantage over the heavy-armed Greek infantry, as soon as the attempt to surprise them had failed. But the action seems to have been decided

Unsuccessful night-march of Pyrrhus to surprise the Roman camp.

[118] Orosius, IV. 2. Livy, Epitom. XIV. Cicero, de Divinat. I. 10.

[119] Livy, Epitom. XIV. Valerius Maximus, VI. 3, § 4, adds to this story that Curius sold not only the property of the defaulter, but the man himself, saying "that the commonwealth wanted no citizen who did not know how to obey." If the tribunes did not interfere, the consul's power might indeed extend to any thing; and we know that the Romans were most tolerant even of the greatest severity when the public service seemed to require it. But the authority of a collector of anecdotes is so small, that Valerius' addition to the story must be considered very doubtful.

[120] Plutarch, Pyrrh. 25.

[121] Plutarch, Pyrrh. 25.

[122] Plutarch, Pyrrh. 25. Dionysius, XIX. 12-14.

by an accident; for one of Pyrrhus' elephants was wounded, and running wild among its own men, threw them into disorder; nor could they offer a long resistance, being almost exhausted with the fatigue of their night-march. They were repulsed with great loss;[123] two elephants were killed, and eight being forced into impracticable ground from which there was no outlet, were surrendered to the Romans by their drivers.

Battle of Beneventum. Pyrrhus is defeated.

Thus encouraged, Curius no longer declined a decisive action on equal ground; he descended into the plain,[124] and met Pyrrhus in the open field. On the one wing the Romans were victorious; on the other, oppressed by the weight of the elephants' charge, they were driven back to their camp.[125] But their retreat was covered by a shower of missiles from the guards on the rampart, and these so annoyed the elephants that they turned about, and fled through their own ranks, bearing down all before them. When the phalanx was thus disordered the Romans attacked it vigorously, and made their way into the mass; and then their swords had an immense advantage over the long spears of the enemy, and their victory was speedy and complete.

He finally leaves Italy and returns to Epirus.

What number of men were killed or taken is variously reported; but the overthrow was decisive; and Pyrrhus, retreating to Tarentum, resolved immediately to evacuate Italy. Yet, as if he still clung to the hope of returning hereafter, he left Milo with his garrison in the citadel of Tarentum, and then embarked for Epirus.[126] He landed in his native kingdom with no more than eight thousand foot and five hundred horse,[127] and without money to maintain even these. Thus he was forced to engage in new enterprises; and often victorious in battle, but never successful in war, he perished two or three years afterwards, as is well known, by a woman's hand, in his attack upon Argos.

CHAPTER XXXVIII.

GENERAL HISTORY FROM THE DEPARTURE OF PYRRHUS FROM ITALY TO THE BEGINNING OF THE FIRST PUNIC WAR—FINAL SUBMISSION OF SAMNIUM—CONQUEST OF TARENTUM—PICENTIAN AND VOLSINIAN WARS—ROME ACQUIRES THE SOVEREIGNTY OF ALL ITALY—DETACHED EVENTS AND ANECDOTES RELATING TO THIS PERIOD.—479 TO 489 A. U. C., 275 TO 265 A. C.

"France was now consolidated into a great kingdom. . . . And thus having conquered herself, if I may use the phrase, and no longer apprehensive of any foreign enemy, she was prepared to carry her arms into other countries."—HALLAM, Middle Ages, Chap. I. Part 11.

Relations between Rome and Carthage.

WE have seen that a Carthaginian fleet appeared on the coasts of Latium in the heat of the war with Pyrrhus, to offer its assistance to the Romans. The offer was then refused, but very soon afterwards a

[123] Dionysius, XIX. 14.

[124] Plutarch, Pyrrh. 25. The scene of the battle is placed by Orosius and Florus "in campis Arusinis," or "sub campis Arusinis," but this name is unknown to us, and does not enable us to determine the place exactly.

[125] Plutarch, Pyrrh. 25. The story which Dionysius and Plutarch relate of the first action is by Zonaras and Florus referred to the last and decisive battle; namely, that a young elephant having been wounded, and running about screaming, its cries were heard by its mother, and so excited her, that she, too, became ungovernable, and threw the Greek army into disorder, and that this accident first turned the fortune of the day.

[126] It is said that a report was purposely circulated by Pyrrhus, of the speedy arrival of reinforcements from the kings of Macedonia and Syria, and that the Romans therefore did not venture to advance upon Tarentum. Pausanias, I. 13; compare Niebuhr, Vol. III. p. 610, and note 927.

[127] Plutarch, Pyrrh. 26.

treaty was concluded between Rome and Carthage,[1] in which both nations engaged to reserve to themselves the right of assisting one another, even if either should conclude an alliance with Pyrrhus; that is to say, their alliance with him was to be subordinate to their alliance with each other, and instead of aiding him in his attacks against the other, they were in such a case to aid one another, even against him. Such were the relations subsisting between Rome and Carthage in the year 479; eleven years afterwards these friendly ties were broken to pieces, and the two nations were engaged in the first Punic war.

Preparation of events for the first Punic war.

In fact, from the moment that Pyrrhus embarked at Tarentum to return to Epirus, the whole stream of our history begins to set towards that great period when Rome and Carthage first became enemies. The relics of wars in Italy, which still remain to be noticed, are only like a clearing of the ground for that mightier contest; and the union of all Italy under one dominion is rather to be regarded for the present as the forging of that iron power by which Carthage was to be crushed, and the whole civilized world bowed into subjection, than as the completion of the magnificent and complicated fabric in which law and polity were to abide as in their appointed temple. The very barrenness of the political history of Rome during the half century which followed the war with Pyrrhus, is in itself a presumption that the energies of the Roman people at this time were employed abroad rather than at home. I shall therefore defer all notice of the internal state of Italy under the Roman sovereignty, till we come to the period of the second Punic war. Then, when Hannibal's sword was probing so deeply every unsound part in the Roman dominion, and when he was laboring to array Campania and Samnium and Lucania and Bruttium in a fifth coalition against Rome, the internal relations of the Italian states towards the Romans and towards each other will necessarily demand our attention. But for the present I shall merely regard them as blended into one great mass, which was presently to be engaged in deadly conflict with the dominion of Carthage.

A. U. C. 482. A. C. 272. Siege of Tarentum. Milo retires to Epirus. Surrender of the town.

After Pyrrhus left Italy, his general, Milo, retained the citadel of Tarentum for nearly four years. The aristocratical party, which had been from the beginning opposed to the Epirot alliance, now endeavored to rid themselves of it by force of arms. They failed, however, in their attempt to recover the citadel, and then leaving Tarentum, they occupied a fort in the neighborhood,[2] from whence they carried on a plundering warfare against the city, and were able to make their own peace with the Romans. Even the popular party were tired of the foreign garrison and its governor, but, feeling that they never could be forgiven by the Romans, they looked elsewhere for aid, and sent to the Carthaginian commanders[3] in Sicily to deliver them from Milo's dominion. A Carthaginian fleet appeared accordingly before the harbor, while L. Papirius Cursor, the Roman consul, was besieging the town by land. But Papirius, dreading the interference of Carthage, treated secretly with Milo,[4] and persuaded him to deliver up the citadel to the Romans, on condition of being allowed to retire in safety to Epirus with his garrison and all their baggage. Thus Tarentum was given up into the hands of the Romans, and the Carthaginian fleet returned to Sicily. The Roman government complained of its appearance on the coast of Italy,[5] when its assistance had not been requested by

[1] Polybius, III. 25.

[2] Zonaras, VIII. 6. This was like the aristocratical party in Corcyra, who, after their expulsion from the city, built a fort in the mountains, from whence they plundered the lands of their opponents. Thucyd. III. 85.

[3] Zonaras, VIII. 6. Orosius, IV. 3. But the account in Orosius is greatly distorted and exaggerated, for he makes the Tarentines call in the aid of Carthage not against Milo, but against Rome, and says that a regular action took place between the Roman and Carthaginian forces, in which the Romans were victorious.

[4] Zonaras, VIII. 6. Frontinus, Strategem. III. 3, § 1.

[5] Orosius, IV. 5. That the interference of the Carthaginians on this occasion was complained of by the Romans appears also from Livy, Epitom. XIV. and from Dion Cassius, Fragm. Vatican. LVII. Yet as Pyrrhus was the enemy of Carthage, the Carthaginians might lawfully aid the Tarentines against his officer; the of-

Rome; and the Carthaginians, now that Tarentum was actually in the Roman power, disavowed the expedition as an unauthorized act of their officers in Sicily.

Subjugation of Tarentum.

The death or banishment of the leaders of the democratical party at Tarentum atoned, no doubt, for the insult offered to the Roman ambassadors, and for the zealous enmity which had organized against Rome the fourth Samnite war. When vengeance was satisfied, policy demanded the complete humiliation of a city which had shown both the will and the power to injure.[6] Tarentum was dismantled, its fleet and all its stores of arms were surrendered, it was made to pay a yearly tribute, and a Roman garrison,[7] it seems, was quartered in the citadel. When thus effectually disarmed and fettered, the Tarentines were allowed to retain their municipal freedom, as the allies, and not the subjects of Rome.

Submission of the Samnites, Lucanians, and Bruttians.

In the same year, immediately before the fall of Tarentum, Samnium, Lucania, and Bruttium had made their final and absolute submission. L. Papirius Cursor and Sp. Carvilius Maximus, who had been consuls together one-and-twenty years earlier in the great campaign which decided the third Samnite war, were elected consuls together for the second time, to put the last stroke to the present contest. Carvilius invaded Samnium,[8] and received the submission of the Samnites; Papirius received that of the Lucanians and Bruttians. The three nations all retained their municipal freedom, or rather their several towns or districts were left free individually, but their national union was dissolved; and they were, probably, not even allowed to intermarry with or to inherit property from each other. Besides this, they made, undoubtedly, large cessions of territory, and were obliged to give hostages[9] for their future good behavior. It is mentioned in particular that the Bruttians ceded the half of their mountain and forest district, called Sila,[10] or the Weald; a tract rich to this day in all varieties of timber trees, and in wide ranges of well-watered pastures, and famous for yielding the best vegetable pitch known to the ancients. The right of preparing this pitch was let as usual by the censors, and brought into the republic a large revenue.

A. U. C. 484. A. C. 270. Punishment of the revolted garrison of Rhegium.

Thus the Romans had put down all their enemies in the south of Italy, except the rebellious soldiers of the eighth legion, who had taken possession of Rhegium. Those, however, were reduced two years later by the consul, C. Genucius.[11] A separate treaty concluded with the Mamertines of Messana[12] had cut them off from their most natural succor, and Hiero, who since Pyrrhus had left Sicily had been raised by his merit and services[13] to the throne of Syracuse, took an active part against them, and supplied the Roman besieging army not with corn only, but with an auxiliary force of soldiers. Thus the town of Rhegium was at last stormed, and most of the garrison put to the sword in the assault. Of the survivors, all except the soldiers of the original legion were executed[14] by the consul on the spot; but these, as Campanian citizens,[15] and, therefore, having all the private rights of citizens of Rome, were reserved for the judgment of the senate and people. When they were brought to Rome, one of the tribunes pleaded in their behalf that they

fence complained of, however, was, in all probability, the appearance of a foreign fleet, uninvited by the Romans, on the coasts of what they would consider the Roman dominion. But the Carthaginians might answer that the coast of Iapygia was not yet to be regarded as belonging to Rome.

[6] Zonaras, VIII. 6.

[7] In the interval between the first and second Punic wars, a legion was regularly stationed at Tarentum. Polybius, II. 24. Niebuhr thinks that this had been the case ever since the surrender of the city.

[8] Zonaras, VIII. 6.

[9] This appears from Zonaras, VIII. 7, where Lollius, a Samnite hostage, is said to have escaped from Rome.

[10] Dionysius, XX. 5. Sila is, doubtless, the same word as Silva and as ὕλη. For the actual state of this forest country, see Mr. Keppel Craven, Tour in the Southern Provinces of Naples, p. 242.

[11] Dionysius, XX. 7.

[12] Zonaras, VIII. 6.

[13] Polybius, I. 8, 9. Justin, XXIII. 4. Zonaras, VIII. 6.

[14] Orosius, IV. 3.

[15] See Niebuhr, Rom. Hist. Vol. II. p. 57. Eng. Transl.

were Roman citizens,[16] and ought not to be put to death, except by the judgment of the people; but the people were as little disposed to mercy as the senate, and the thirty-three tribes[17] condemned them unanimously. They were thus all scourged and beheaded, to the number of more than three hundred, and their bodies were cast out unburied. Rhegium and its territory were restored to the survivors of the old inhabitants.

In the next year one of the Samnite[18] hostages escaped from Rome, and revived a guerilla warfare in the country of the Caracenians in northern Samnium. Both consuls were employed to crush at once an enemy who might soon have become formidable, and the bands which had taken up arms were soon dispersed, and their strongholds taken, although not without some loss and danger on the part of the conquerors.

A. U. C. 485. A. C. 269. Short guerilla war in Samnium.

A war followed with a people whose name has only once before been heard of in Roman history, the Picentians, on the coast of the Adriatic. The Picentians had become the allies of Rome[19] thirty-one years before this period, at the beginning of the third Samnite war, and they had ever since observed the alliance faithfully. But in the year 486 we find two consular armies[20] employed against them, and after a short struggle they submitted at discretion. A portion of them was removed to the coast of the Tuscan sea, and settled in the country which had formerly belonged to the Samnites, on the shores of the gulf of Salernum.[21] It may have been that this migration had been commanded by the Roman government as a measure of state policy, in order to people the old Samnite coast with less suspected inhabitants, and to acquire as Roman domain the lands which the Picentians had left in their old country; and the Picentians, perhaps, like the Carthaginians in the third Punic war, unwilling to be torn from their native land, rose against Rome in mere despair. But whatever was the cause of the war, it ended in the speedy and complete conquest[22] of the Picentian people.

A. U. C. 486. A. C. 268. War with and conquest of the Picentians.

The last gleanings of Italian independence were gathered in during the two years which next followed. The Sallentines and Messapians had at one time taken part in the confederacy[23] of southern Italy against Rome, but they had withdrawn from the cause before its overthrow. Their repentance, however, availed them nothing, for the port of Brundisium, in the Sallentine territory, was a position which the Romans were very anxious to secure;[24] the more so as Alexander, the son of Pyrrhus, was reigning in Epirus, and had inherited much of the warlike temper of his

A. U. C. 487 and 488. A. C. 267 and 266. Conquest of the Messapians. Occupation of Brundisium.

[16] Valerius Maximus, II. 7, § 15. The same thing happened after the reduction of Capua in the second Punic war. The Campanians being Roman citizens, the senate could not determine their fate without being empowered by the people to do so; and accordingly the tribes voted that whatever sentence the senate might pass should have their authority for its full execution. Livy, XXVI. 33. It is remarkable that the power of taking up the Roman franchise at pleasure should be considered as so completely equivalent to the possession of the franchise actually, which is Niebuhr's explanation of the condition of the Campanians. Vol. II. note 136. Eng. Transl. It rather appears from the definition of the term municeps, given by Festus from Ser. Sulpicius the younger, that the Campanians, and others in the same relation to Rome, enjoyed actually all the private rights of Roman citizens, without forfeiting their own Campanian franchise; and this too seems implied by the fact of their forming a regular legion in war, instead of being reckoned merely as auxiliaries.

[17] Dionysius, XX. 7. Polybius, I. 7.

[18] Zonaras, VIII. 7. Dionysius, XX. 9.

[19] See page 331.

[20] The Fasti Capitolini record that both the consuls of the year, P. Sempronius and Appius Claudius, triumphed over the Picentians.

[21] Strabo, V. p. 251.

[22] The Picentian war is briefly noticed by Florus, I. 19, by Eutropius, and by Orosius, IV. 4. A great earthquake happened just as the Roman and Picentian armies were going to engage, upon which P. Sempronius, the consul, vowed to build a temple to the earth. The population of the Picentians, when they submitted to the Romans, amounted, according to Pliny (Hist. Natur. III. § 110), to 360,000 souls.

[23] They had fought under Pyrrhus at Asculum; see Frontinus Strategem. II. 3, § 21; and they are not mentioned as conquered by Papirius and Carvilius, when the Samnites, Lucanians, and Bruttians submitted, so that they had probably left the confederacy at an earlier period.

[24] Zonaras, copying from Dion Cassius, accuses the Romans of making war on the Sallentines because they wished to get possession of Brundisium. VIII. 7.

father; and whether for attack or defence, the possession of Brundisium, the favorite point of communication in later times with Greece and the East, appeared therefore to the Romans very desirable. Accordingly, the Sallentines and Messapians were reduced to submission, and Brundisium was ceded to the Romans. They did not send a colony thither till some years[25] afterwards, but the land must, in the mean while, have formed a part of their domain, and the port in all probability was occupied by a Roman garrison.

Conquest of the Sarsinatians.

In the midst of the Sallentine war, the consuls of the year 488 triumphed over the Sarsinatians,[26] a people of Umbria, and the countrymen of the comic poet Plautus. Livy's epitome[27] speaks of the Umbrians generally, and says that they, as well as the Sallentines, submitted to the Romans at discretion.

War with the Volsinians. A. U. C. 489. A. C. 265.

One more conquest still remained to be achieved, a conquest called for by political jealousy no less than by national ambition. The aristocracy of Volsinii[28] applied to Rome for aid against the intolerable tyranny of their former serfs or vassals, who were now in possession of the government. As the necessity of keeping up a large navy in the Persian invasions first led to the ascendency of the poorer classes at Athens, and as wars with foreign states had favored the liberties of the Roman commons, so the long wars in which Volsinii had been engaged with Rome had obliged the aristocracy to arm and train their vassals, till they, feeling their importance and power, had risen against their old lords, and had established their own complete ascendency. But in proportion as they had been more degraded and oppressed than the Roman commons, so was their triumph far less happy. Slaves let loose knew not how to become citizens; two only social relations had they ever known, those of oppressor and oppressed; and having ceased to be the one, they became immediately the other. They retaliated on their former masters the worst atrocities which they had themselves been made to suffer;[29] and when they found that some of the oppressed party had applied to Rome for aid, they put many of them to death,[30] as for an act of treason. This was more than sufficient to excite the Romans to interfere, and, as the present ruling party in Volsinii were regarded as little better than revolted slaves, the majority of the Roman commons would be ready to put them down no less than the senate. National ambition, no doubt, made the enterprise doubly welcome; perhaps too the accusation of Metrodorus[31] was not without foundation, when he ascribed the war to a baser passion, and said that the two thousand statues with which Volsinii was ornamented, tempted the Romans to attack it. Q. Fabius Gurges, one of the consuls of the year 489,

[25] In the latter part of the first Punic war. See Livy, Epitom. XIX. But Florus says [I. 20] that Brundisium, with its famous port, was reduced by M. Atilius, who was one of the consuls of the year 487. And so also does Eutropius.

[26] Fasti Capitolini.

[27] Epitom. XV. "Umbri et Sallentini victi in deditionem accepti sunt."

[28] Zonaras, VIII. 7. Auct. de Viris Illustrib. "Decius Mus." Florus, I. 21. Valerius Maximus, IX. 1, Extern. § 2. Orosius, IV. 5. All these writers call the revolution at Volsinii a rising of slaves against their masters; just as Herodotus represents a similar revolution at Argos, after the old citizens had been greatly weakened by their wars with Sparta. VI. 83. The story told in the work "de Mirabil. Auscultationibus," 94, Ed. Bekker, wrongly ascribed to Aristotle, relates undoubtedly to Volsinii, and shows the vague and exaggerated form in which even contemporary events in distant countries are related, when there is no real historian to sift them. According to this story, "the city is very strong; for in the midst of it there is a hill that runs up thirty stadia in height; and beneath there is a forest of all sorts of trees, and much water. So the people of the city, fearing lest any of them should become a tyrant, set up their freedmen to be their magistrates; and these freedmen rule over them, and others of the same sort are appointed in their place at the end of the year."

[29] Valerius Maximus, IX. 1. The worst of all the outrages there described was practised in some instances by the feudal aristocracy in modern Europe; and it is far more likely that the Volsinian serfs retaliated it upon their masters than that they should have been the first inventors of it.

[30] Zonaras, VIII. 7.

[31] Pliny, Hist. Natur. XXXIV. § 34. Metrodorus of Scepsis lived in the seventh century of Rome, and was intimate with Mithridates, whose hatred against the Romans he shared to such a degree, that he was called ὁ μισορώμαιος. His charge, whether true or false, is at least consistent with those other representations which speak of the growing wealth and increased love of wealth among the Romans at this period.

laid siege to Volsinii with a consular army;[32] but having been mortally wounded in one of the sallies of the besieged, he left the completion of his work to his successors.[33] In the following year Volsinii was taken; bloody executions took place, and the remnant of the new Volsinian citizens, who were not put to death, were given up as serfs once again to their former masters. But the old Volsinian aristocracy were not allowed to return to the city of their fathers. Volsinii was destroyed, its statues, no doubt, were carried to Rome, and its old citizens were settled in a new spot[34] on the lower ground near the shores of the lake, apparently on or near the site of the modern town of Bolsena.

Thus the whole extent of Italy from the Macra and the Rubicon to Rhegium and Brundisium was become more or less subject to Rome. But it was not merely that the several Italian nations were to follow in war where Rome might choose to lead them; nor yet that they paid a certain tribute to the sovereign state, such as Athens received from her subject allies. The Roman dominion in Italy had wrested large tracts of land from the conquered nations in every part of the peninsula; forests, mines, and harbors had become the property of the Roman people, from which a large revenue was derived; so that all classes of Roman citizens were enriched by their victories; the rich acquired a great extent of land to hold in occupation; the poor obtained grants of land in freehold by an agrarian law; while the great increase of revenue required a greater number of persons to collect it, and thus from the quæstors to the lowest collectors or clerks employed under them, all the officers of government became suddenly multiplied.

The Romans sovereigns of all Italy.

The changes, indeed, which were wrought in the course of ten years, from the retreat of Pyrrhus to the conquest of Volsinii, must have affected the whole life and character of the Roman people. Even the mere fragmentary notices, which are all that we possess of this period, record, first, the increase of the number of quæstors from four to eight:[35] secondly, a distribution of land, in portions of seven jugera[36] to each citizen, to the Roman commons generally: thirdly, a distribution of money amongst the citizens,[37] probably amongst those of the city tribes who did not wish to become possessors of land; the money so distributed having arisen from the sale of conquered territory: fourthly, the first adoption of a silver coinage, copper having been hitherto the only currency of the state:[38] fifthly, the appointment of several new magistrates or commissioners, such as the decemviri litibus judicandis,[39] or

Great changes which took place at this period in the condition of the Romans.

[32] Zonaras, VIII. 7.

[33] The author "de Viris Illustrib." ascribes the conquest of Volsinii to Decius Mus, who was consul in 475, and fought with Pyrrhus at Asculum. But whether Decius was employed as prætor, or as dictator, we know not. The same writer also says that Appius Claudius, the consul of the year 490, obtained the surname of Caudex, after his conquests of the Volsinians; but the Fasti Capitolini give the honor of the conquest to his colleague, M. Fulvius Flaccus, who triumphed "de Vulsiniensibus, An. CDXXCIX. K. Nov."

[34] Zonaras, VIII. 7.

[35] Livy, Epitom. XV.

[36] Columella, Præfat.

[37] Dionysius, XX. ad finem.

[38] Pliny, Hist. Natur. XXXIII. § 44. The silver coinage was first introduced in the year 485; and the coins struck were denarii, quinarii, and sestertii. It is still a great question in whose hands the right of coining money was placed. The devices on the consular denarii are so various, and refer so peculiarly to the house of the individual who coined them, that Niebuhr supposes them to have been really a private coinage, like the tokens occasionally issued in England, a coinage issued by private persons for their own profit, but sanctioned by the state, and controlled by the triumviri monetales. Quæstors are known to have coined money when employed under a proconsul as his paymaster, but these coins are equally without any peculiar national device, and relate to something in the quæstor's own family or in the circumstances of his general. Thus on the gold coins struck by P. Lentulus Spinther, when he was quæstor to Cassius in Asia, we see the device of a cap of liberty and a dagger, in manifest allusion to the assassination of Cæsar. Yet the two-horsed and four-horsed chariots which appear so often on the denarii are noticed by Pliny as a general device, from which the oldest silver coins received their name. It seems probable that there was no fixed rule with respect to the right of coining; that sometimes the state issued a coinage, that sometimes money was struck by particular magistrates for the immediate use of their own department of the public service; and that sometimes also it was struck by individuals for their own profit, just as a large part of our own circulation at this day consists in the notes issued by private bankers.

[39] "Pomponius de origine juris," 29. See Niebuhr. Rom. Gesch. III. p. 649.

the board of ten, who presided over the court of the centumviri or hundred judges; the board of four,[40] who had the care of the streets and roads; the board of five, who acted for the magistrates during the night,[41] the consuls' ordinary responsibility ceasing with the going down of the sun; and the board of three, who had the care of the coinage. All these things are recorded as having been introduced for the first time about the period between the war with Pyrrhus and the first war with Carthage, and they clearly show what manifold changes the Roman people were then undergoing.

Effects of these on the national manners. Anecdotes of Curius and Fabricius.

The conquest of Italy was, indeed, to Rome what the overthrow of the Athenian empire was to Sparta: the larger scale of all public transactions, the vast influx of wealth into the state, and the means of acquiring wealth unjustly which were put within the reach of many private individuals, were a severe shock to the national character. Many other Romans, no doubt, besides P. Cornelius Rufinus, were as corrupt and tyrannical as Gylippus and Lysander; and it was this very corruption which made men dwell so fondly on those who were untainted by it:[42] the virtue of Fabricius and Curius, like that of Callicratidas, shone the brighter, because the temptations which they resisted were so often yielded to by others. In the present state of Italy any eminent Roman might seriously affect the condition of any of the subject people either for good or for evil: hence the principal citizens of Rome were earnestly courted with compliments, and often, no doubt, propitiated with presents, and it was for refusing such presents when offered to them by the Samnites, that Fabricius and Curius became so famous. All know how deputies from Samnium came to Curius[43] at his Sabine farm to offer him a present of gold. They found him seated by the fireside, with a wooden platter before him, and roasting turnips in the ashes. "I count it my glory," he said, "not to possess gold myself, but to have power over those who do." So, again, other Samnite deputies came to bring a present[44] of ten pounds of copper, five of silver, and five slaves, to Fabricius as the patron of their nation. Fabricius drew his hands over his ears, eyes, nose, and mouth, and then along his neck and down his body; and said that whilst he was the master of his five senses and sound in body and limb, he needed nothing more than he had already. Thus, whether refusing to have clients, or to accept from them their customary dues, Curius and Fabricius lived in such poverty as to be unable to give a dowry to their daughters;[45] and in both cases the senate paid it for them. Men of this sort, so indifferent to money, and at the same time not without a roughness of nature which would delight in vexing the luxury and rapacity of others, were likely to struggle hard against the prevailing spirit of covetousness and expense. When Fabricius was censor in 479, he expelled P. Rufinus[46] from the senate because he had returned amongst his taxable possessions ten pounds weight of silver plate; for there is often a jealousy against any new mode of displaying wealth, when the greatest expenditure in old and accustomed ways excites no displeasure. Silver plate was a new luxury in the fifth century of Rome, and therefore attracted the censor's notice; three hundred years later, the possession of silver plate to any

[40] [41] Pomponius, § 30, 31.

[42] Pope has said, that

"Lucullus, when frugality could charm,
Had roasted turnips in the Sabine farm;"

as if the virtue of Curius had belonged to his age and not to himself. But this is the mistake of a satirist and fatalist, whose tendency it always is to depreciate human virtue. Had Lucullus lived in Curius' day, he would have shown in the possession of ten pounds of silver plate, the same spirit which, in his own days, was shown in the splendor of his feasts in the Apollo: had Curius lived in the days of Cicero, he would have displayed, like Cicero in the government of his province, the same spotless integrity which he proved actually in sitting by his cottage fire, and refusing the humble presents of the Samnites.

[43] Cicero, de Senectut. 16. Valerius Maxim. IV. 3, § 5.

[44] Julius Hyginus, apud Gellium, I. 14. Valerius Maximus, IV. 3, § 6.

[45] I borrow this from Niebuhr, who refers for the story to Apuleius.

[46] Livy, Epitom. XIV. Niebuhr supposes that Fabricius may have suspected this plate to have been a part of the spoils won by Rufinus at Croton, and have thought that he ought to have accounted for it to the treasury.

amount was fully allowed,[47] but gold plate was still unusual, and the senate, even in the reign of Tiberius, denounced it as an unbecoming extravagance. But Fabricius, no doubt, disliked the large domain lands held in occupation by Rufinus as much as his ten pounds of silver plate, thinking that great wealth in the hands of private persons, however employed, was injurious to the commonwealth.

First exhibition of gladiators. A. U. C. 490. A. C. 264.

It must not be forgotten, amongst the other changes of this period, that the consulship of Appius Claudius and M. Fulvius,[48] the year which witnessed the final reduction of Volsinii, was marked by the first exhibition of gladiators ever known at Rome. Two sons of D. Junius Brutus exhibited them, it is recorded, at the funeral of their father. The principle of this, as a part of the funeral solemnity, was very ancient and very universal;[49] that the dead should not go on his dark journey alone, but that a train of other departed souls, whether of enemies slain to avenge him, or of followers to do him honor, should accompany him to the unseen world. But the Romans, it is said,[50] borrowed the practice of substituting a combat for a sacrifice, that the victims might die by each other's swords, immediately from the Etruscans; and when we recollect that the capture of Volsinii took place in this very year, we may conjecture that the gladiators of M. and D. Brutus were Volsinian prisoners, perhaps slaves, who had been accustomed to fight before under the service of their former masters. The spectacle, from the very beginning, excited the liveliest interest at Rome; but for many years it was exhibited only at funerals, as an offering in honor of the dead; the still deeper wickedness of making it a mere sport, and introducing the sufferings and death of human beings as a luxury for the spectators in their seasons of the greatest enjoyment, was reserved for a later period.

Great prosperity of the Roman people at this period.

The ten years preceding the first Punic war were probably a time of the greatest physical prosperity which the mass of the Roman people ever knew. Within twenty years two agrarian laws had been passed on a most extensive scale; and the poorer citizens had received besides what may be called a large dividend in money out of the lands which the state had conquered. In addition to this, the farming of the state domains,[51] or of their produce, furnished those who had money with abundant opportunities of profitable adventure, while the accumulation of public business increased the demand for clerks and collectors in every branch of the service of the revenue. And the power of obtaining like advantages in all future wars seemed secured to the people by the Hortensian laws, which enabled them to pass an agrarian law whenever they pleased, in spite of the opposition in the senate. No wonder then that war was at this time popular, and that the tribes, more than once, resolved on taking up arms, when the senate would have preferred peace from considerations of prudence, and, we may hope, of national faith and justice. But our "pleasant vices" are ever made "instruments to scourge us:" and the first Punic war, into which the Roman people forced the senate to enter, not only in its own long course bore most heavily upon the poorer citizens, but from the feelings of enmity which it excited in the breast of Hamilcar, led most surely to

[47] Tacitus, Annal. II. 33.

[48] Valerius Maximus, II. 4, § 7.

[49] Every one remembers the slaughter of twelve Trojan prisoners over the funeral pile of Patroclus. When the Scythian kings died, some of all their servants were slain and were buried with them. (Herodotus, IV. 71.) In Thrace single combats took place at the funerals of the chiefs; and there also, as in India, the best beloved of the wives of the deceased was killed and buried with her husband. (Herodotus, V. 5, 8.) In Spain, too, when Viriathus was burnt on his funeral pile, there were single combats fought around in honor of him. Appian, de Rebus Hispan. 75. Cassander paid the same honor to Philip Arrhidæus and Eurydice at their funeral at Ægæ. Diyllus, apud Athenæum, IV. p. 155. Diodorus, XIX. 52.

[50] Nicolaus Damascenus, apud Athenæum, IV. p. 153.

[51] See the well-known passage in Polybius, where he notices the extent of patronage possessed by the senate. Πολλῶν γὰρ ἔργων ὄντων τῶν ἐκδιδομένων ὑπὸ τῶν τιμητῶν διὰ πάσης Ἰταλίας εἰς τὰς ἐπισκευὰς καὶ κατασκευὰς τῶν δημοσίων, ἅ τις οὐκ ἂν ἐξαριθμήσαιτο ῥᾳδίως, πολλῶν δὲ ποταμῶν, λιμένων, κηπίων, μετάλλων, χώρας, συλλήβδην ὅσα πέπτωκεν ὑπὸ τὴν Ῥωμαίων δυναστείαν, πάντα χειρίζεσθαι συμβαίνει τὰ προειρημένα διὰ τοῦ πλήθους, καὶ σχεδὸν, ὡς ἔπος εἰπεῖν, πάντας ἐνδεδέσθαι ταῖς ὠναῖς καὶ ταῖς ἐργασίαις ταῖς ἐκ τούτων.—IV. 17.

that fearful visitation of Hannibal's sixteen years' invasion of Italy, which destroyed forever, not indeed the pride of the Roman dominions, but the well-being of the Roman people.

Aqueduct of Curius. Tiles used for roofing the houses at Rome.

But that calamitous period was only to come upon the children of the existing generation, and in the mean time all was going on prosperously. Another aqueduct was constructed by M'. Curius,[52] when he was censor soon after the retreat of Pyrrhus, by which a supply of water was conveyed to the northern parts of the city from the Anio above Tibur: and tiles[53] at this time began to supersede wood as the roofing material for the common houses of Rome.

Embassy to Ptolemy Philadelphus, king of Egypt.

Their victories over Pyrrhus spread the fame of the Romans far and wide; and immediately after his return to Greece, when he was again becoming formidable by his victories over Antigonus in Macedonia, Ptolemy Philadelphus,[54] king of Egypt, sent an embassy to Rome to conclude an alliance with the Romans. The senate, delighted at such a compliment from so great a king, sent in return an embassy to Alexandria, consisting of three of the most eminent citizens in the commonwealth, Q. Fabius Gurges, who was then first senator (princeps senatus), Q. Ogulnius, who had gone to Epidaurus to invite Æsculapius to Rome, and Num. Fabius Pictor, the son of that Fabius who had painted the frescoes in the temple of Deliverance from Danger. The ambassadors found Alexandria at the height of its splendor, for these were the most brilliant days of the Greek-Egyptian kingdom; and Ptolemy Philadelphus,[55] with a fleet of 1500 ships of war, and a revenue of nearly 15,000 talents, reigned over the whole coast of the Mediterranean, from Cyrene to the Nile, and from the Nile to the Triopian headland at the southwestern extremity of Asia Minor, opposite to Rhodes; while to the south his power extended to the heart of Ethiopia or Abyssinia, and along both shores of the Red Sea. In his capital there met together the wisdom of Greece and of the east and of Egypt itself: Theocritus, Callimachus, and the seven tragedians of the Pleias;[56] the Jews who at this time began at Alexandria the translation of the Bible; and Manetho, the famous historian of the ancient dynasties of Egypt. The Roman ambassadors were honorably entertained and received valuable presents; which on their return home they laid before the senate, but which the senate immediately gave back to them, with permission to do with them as they thought proper.

Outrage to the ambassadors of Apollonia. The offenders given up to the Apollonians.

In the year 488,[57] the people of Apollonia, a Greek city on the coast of Epirus, sent an embassy to Rome, with what object we know not, but possibly to complain of some of the officers of the Roman government. Two Romans of rank, one of them a senator of the house of Fabius, insulted and beat the ambassadors, and were, in consequence of the outrage, given up to the Apollonians; one of the quæstors also was sent to escort

[52] Frontinus, de Aquæductibus, 6. The aqueduct of Curius was known by the name of "Anio vetus;" its whole length was forty-three miles; but, like the older aqueduct of Appius Claudius, it consisted mostly of pipes under ground, and was only conducted on an embankment above ground for a distance of something less than a quarter of a mile.

[53] See Cornelius Nepos quoted by Pliny, as already noticed, Hist. Natur. XVI. § 36.

[54] Livy, Epitom. XIV. Zonaras, VIII. 6. Dionysius, XX. 4. Valerius Maximus, IV. 3, § 9.

[55] The extent of Ptolemy Philadelphus' dominion, and the flourishing condition of Egypt during his reign, are described by Theocritus, an eye-witness, in his 17th Idyll, and in that remarkable inscription found at Adulis, on the western shore of the Red Sea, by Cosmas Indicopleustes, in the reign of Justin, the father of Justinian. Cosmas copied the inscription into his work, which is to be found in Montfaucon's Collectio Nova, &c. Vol. II. p. 142. Some remarkable particulars as to the amount of Ptolemy's revenue are preserved by Jerome in his Commentary on Daniel, XI. 5.

[56] They were called the Pleias from their number, in allusion to the constellation. Different lists of them are given (see Fynes Clinton, Fasti Hellen. Vol. III. year B. C. 259), but none of them are known to us by any existing works, if, as Mr. Fox and Niebuhr seem most justly to think, the Lycophron who wrote the Alexandra is a very different person from the Lycophron of the Pleias, and belongs to a later age. See Niebuhr's Kleine Schrift. p. 438–450.

[57] Zonaras, VIII. 7. Livy, Epitom. XV. Valer. Max. VI. 6, § 5.

the ambassadors and their prisoners to Brundisium, lest any attempt should be made to rescue them. But the Apollonians, measuring rightly their own utter inability to cope with so great a nation as the Romans, and judging that it would be unwise[58] to interpret too closely the sentence of the senate, restored both offenders unhurt.

Physical history. Severe winter of 484.

Our notices of the physical history of these times are very scanty. The winter of 484 was one of unusual severity;[59] the Tiber was frozen over to a great depth, the snow lay in the Forum for nearly six weeks, the olives and fig-trees were generally killed, and many of the cattle perished for want of pasture, as they were dependent, even in winter, on such food as they could find in the fields. This great frost happened about one hundred and thirty years after the frost of 355, and seems to have equalled it in severity. Volcanic phenomena[60] are recorded during the two following years, and in 488 we hear of a very destructive pestilence, which lasted for more than two years more, and is described as exceedingly fatal;[61] but the language of Augustine is indefinite, and that of Orosius clearly exaggerated, so that we can neither discover the nature and causes of the disease, nor estimate the amount of the mortality.

A new generation coming forward. Deaths of Curius and Fabricius.

Ten years, as they bring forward into active life a new generation, so they always sweep away some of the last survivors of former times, and bring down to a later period the range of living memory. Appius Claudius and Valerius Corvus, who were both alive when Pyrrhus was in Italy, died soon after his return to Epirus. L. Papirius Cursor, if he were still living, had yet appeared for the last time in a public station; neither he nor his colleague, Sp. Carvilius, are heard of again after their second censorship in the year 482. M'. Curius had obtained the censorship in that same year, three years after his victory at Beneventum; he employed the money arising from the spoils of his triumph in constructing, as we have seen, the second oldest of the Roman aqueducts; and after his censorship he was named by the senate one[62] of two commissioners for completing the work, but he died within a few days after his appointment. Thus one of the most honest and energetic men known to us in the Roman history, a man whose name is associated so closely with the uncorrupted period of the Roman character, was carried off apparently before he had arrived at old age. When Fabricius died we know not; but he was not heard of again after his censorship in 479, nor do we know any further particulars of him than that he was buried, by a special dispensation, within the city walls;[63] a rare honor, which strongly marks the general sense entertained of the purity of his virtue; "as if," says Niebuhr, "his bones could be no defilement to the temples of the heavenly gods, nor his spirit disturb the peace of the living."

Conclusion.

So passes away what may be called the spring-time of the Roman people. Wealth, and power, and dominion have brought on the ripened summer, with more of vigor indeed, but less of freshness. Beginning her career of conquest beyond the limits of Italy, Rome was now entering upon her appointed work, and that work was undoubtedly fraught with good. The conqueror and the martyr are alike God's instruments; but it is the priv-

[58] They may have remembered the wisdom of the Æginetans in like circumstances, when the Spartan king, Leutychidas, was given up to them by his countrymen, as an atonement for some wrong which he had done to them. A Spartan had warned them not to take the Spartan government at its word, nor to believe that they might really carry the king of Sparta away as their prisoner, and punish him at their discretion. See Herodotus, VI. 85.

[59] Zonaras, VIII. 6. Augustine, de Civit. Dei, III. 17.

[60] Orosius, IV. 4. The earthquake which happened in the Picentian war, just as the Romans and Picentians were going to engage, belongs to the volcanic phenomena of this period.

[61] Augustine, III. 17. Orosius, IV. 5.

[62] Frontinus, de Aquæduct, 6.

[63] Cicero, de Legibus, II. 23. Thus Brasidas was buried within the walls of Amphipolis, as having been the deliverer of the city. Thucyd. V. 11.

ilege of his conscious and willing instruments to be doubly and merely blessed; the benefits of their work to others are unalloyed by evil, while to themselves it is the perfecting and not the corrupting of their moral being; when it is done, they are not cast away as instruments spoiled and worthless, but partake of the good which they have given, and enjoy forever the love of men, and the blessing of God.

CHAPTER XXXIX.

CONSTITUTION AND POWER OF CARTHAGE.

Πολιτεύεσθαι δὲ δοκοῦσι καὶ Καρχηδόνιοι καλῶς.—ARISTOTLE, Politic. II.

THE name of Carthage has already occurred more than once in the course of this history; and I have already noticed the extent of her dominion, and the inherent causes of its unsoundness, inasmuch as the Carthaginians and their African subjects were separated from one another by broad differences of race, language, and institutions; so that they could not blend together into one nation. The isolation of Carthage from all the surrounding people offers a striking contrast to the position of Rome in Italy, where the allies and the Latin name were bound to the Romans and to each other by manifold ties, and the communication of the Roman franchise, or at least the prospect of obtaining it hereafter, was every year effacing the painful memory of the first conquest, and effecting that consolidation of various elements into one great and united people, in which alone conquest can find its justification. But as the Carthaginians will now occupy no small share of our attention, from the importance and long duration of their contest with the Romans, so it becomes desirable to look at them more closely, and see what was their internal state, and with what excellences and defects in their national character and institutions they encountered the iron strength of Rome.

Internal condition of Carthage.

The constitution of Carthage was compared to that of Sparta, as containing in it the elements of monarchy and of aristocracy, and of democracy. But in such mixed governments, one element is always predominant: first, in the natural course of things, the monarchical, next the aristocratical, and, lastly, the democratical or popular. The predominance of one element by no means implies, however, the total inactivity of the others; and in their common, although not equal action, consists the excellence of such constitutions; not simply that the working of the principal power is checked by the direct legal rights of the other two, but much more because the nation retains by their means those ideas and those points of character which they peculiarly suggest and encourage, and is thus saved from that narrow-minded uniformity of views and of tastes which the exclusive influence of any single element must necessarily occasion. In Carthage there is reason to believe that the monarchical part of the constitution had once the ascendency,[1] but during those times in which she is best known to us, the aristocratical element was predominant; the

Its government was mixed, but predominantly aristocratical.

[1] Aristotle says that Carthage had never suffered in any serious degree either from faction or from a tyrant. Politic. II. 11. Yet in another place he gives Carthage as an instance of a country where a tyranny had been succeeded by an aristocracy. V. 12. It seems, then, that this tyranny must be understood of the earlier times of the Carthaginian history, before that constitution existed on which Aristotle comments.

full development of the democratical was prevented by the premature destruction of the whole nation.

The suffetes or judges.

The Carthaginian aristocracy was partly one of birth, but chiefly, as it should seem, of wealth. Indeed, the older form of a pure aristocracy of birth must necessarily be rare in a colony, where the original settlers must almost always be a mixed body, and yet in their new settlement find themselves on an equality with each other. It appears, however, that nobility of birth was acknowledged in Carthage, and that their two chief magistrates, or judges,[2] suffetes, whom the Greeks called kings, were elected only from a certain number of families. How many these were, and what was the origin of their nobility, we are not informed. But wealth, contrary to the practice of the Roman government, was an indispensable qualification for all the highest offices. Nay, we are told that the very suffetes and captains-general of the commonwealth bought their high dignities:[3] whether this is to be understood of paying money to obtain votes, or, as is much more probable, that the fees or expenses of entering on an office were purposely made very heavy, to render it inaccessible to any but the rich.

The great council, and the council of elders.

The great council, σύγκλητος, was probably an assembly as numerous as the Roman senate, and, like the senate, was a mixed body, containing members of different ages, who, in whatever manner appointed, were a sort of representation of the general feelings of the aristocracy. But from this great council there were chosen one hundred members,[4] who formed what was called the council of elders, and who in fact were the supreme authority in the state. They were originally appointed as a check upon the power of the captains-general, and were a court before which every general, on his return from a foreign command, had to render an account of his conduct. But by degrees they became not only supreme criminal judges in all cases, but also a supreme executive council, of which the two suffetes or kings were the presidents. In this capacity they were legally, we may presume, no more than a managing committee for the great council, so they became in ordinary cases its substitute, and in all cases exercised such a control over it, that they are called a power for governing the general council itself.[5]

The commissions or boards of five.

The hundred, or the elders, were chosen for life from members of the great council, but not by the votes of the great council at large. On the contrary, they were chosen by certain bodies which Aristotle calls πενταρχίαι, or commissions of five, and which formed so many close corporations, filling up their own vacancies. This is nearly all the information which we possess on the subject; for Aristotle only adds, that these commissions had great and various powers, and that their members remained longer in office than the ordinary magistrates, inasmuch as they exercised an authority both before and after their regular term of magistracy. The most probable conjecture is, that the more important branches of the public administration were, as we should say, put in commission, and vested in boards of five members; that thus the treasury

[2] Aristotle, Politic. II. 11. Βέλτιον δὲ τοὺς βασιλεῖς μήτε κατὰ τὸ αὐτὸ εἶναι γένος μηδὲ τοῦτο τὸ τυχόν. It is obvious that "suffes," or "sufes," is the same word with the Hebrew שׁוֹפֵט, which was the title of those magistrates whom we call the judges. Now as the judges in the Scripture history are distinguished from the kings, and it was a great change when the Israelites, tired of their judges, or suffetes, desired to have a king; so it is probable that the suffetes at Carthage also were so named to show that they were not kings, and that the Greek writers, in calling them βασιλεῖς, have used a term likely to mislead.

[3] Polybius, VI. 56. Aristotle's account implies the same thing.

[4] "Centum ex numero senatorum judices deliguntur," says Justin, giving an account of the origin of this council of elders, XIX. 2. The council of elders, or γερουσία, is distinguished expressly from the larger council, or senate, σύγκλητος. See Polybius, X. 18, and XXXVI. 2. For the whole subject of the Carthaginian constitution I have been largely indebted to Heeren's Historical Researches on the African Nations, Vol. I. I have also derived some assistance from Kluge's Commentary on Aristotle's account of the Carthaginian constitution, published in 1824.

[5] Livy, XXX. 16. "Sanctius consilium, maximaque ad ipsum senatum regendum vis."

would be intrusted to one commission of five, the care of public manners and morals, the censor's office at Rome, would be given to another commission; the police, perhaps, to another; the navy to another; and so on. Nothing would hinder these commissioners from being members of the great council, and nothing would hinder them, therefore, from electing themselves to fill up vacancies in the council of elders; in fact, we are expressly told[6] that the treasurer's or quæstor's office led regularly to a seat amongst the hundred; and thus the same men being often members at one and the same time of one or perhaps more of these administrative commissions, and of the great council, and also of the council of elders, we can understand what Aristotle means when he says that it was a favorite practice with the Carthaginians to invest the same person with several offices together.

The aristocratical clubs.

All this was sufficiently aristocratical, or rather in the spirit of that worst form of aristocracy which the Greeks called oligarchy. And what was thus ordered by law, was to be maintained by feeling; the members of the aristocracy had their clubs,[7] where they habitually met at a common mess or public table, with the very object of binding them more closely to each other, and imbuing them entirely with the spirit of their order.

Diminution of the power of the suffetes.

Under such a constitution the power of the suffetes had been reduced from its originally almost kingly prerogatives to the state of the doge under the late constitution of Venice. In earlier times they had been invested with the two great characters of ancient royalty, those of general and of priest;[8] but now the first of these was commonly taken from him, and the office of general-in-chief is spoken of by Aristotle as distinct; nor was it even left in the suffetes' appointment. Still the two kings, as the Greek writers call them, were recognized as an essential branch of the government, and if they differed upon any proposed measure from the council of elders, then the question was referred to the assembly of the people.[9] It was thus, no doubt, that an opening was afforded for weakening the power of the aristocracy; for either of the suffetes was thus enabled to introduce the decision of the popular branch on points of government; and it is of the essence of a popular assembly, if called into activity, to become predominant: it may exist and yet be powerless, but only so long as few points are in practice submitted to its decision.

Judicial power. Court of the hundred and four.

But so long as the suffetes and council were agreed, the power of the Carthaginian people was exceedingly small. Nothing, it seems, could originate with the popular assembly; so that the exercise of its functions did not depend on its own will, but on the accidental disagreement of the other branches of the legislature. And as the mass of the people had so small a share practically in the legislation or in the administration of affairs, so they were destitute of judicial power: there were no juries as in England, nor any large popular courts where hundreds or even thousands of the poorest citizens sat in judgment as at Athens. All causes, civil and criminal, were tried by certain magistrates;[10] the highest matters, as we have seen, by the council of

[6] Livy, XXXIII. 46.—What is here said of the multiplication of offices in the hands of the same persons at Carthage, was also the case at Venice. Every member of the supreme criminal tribunal of forty had a seat ex-officio in the senate; and the three presidents of the Forty sat also in the council of the doge. "L'autorité du législateur," says Daru, "celle du juge, l'influence de l'administration et le pouvoir discrétionnaire de la police, se trouvaient réunis dans les mêmes mains."—Histoire de Venise, Livre XXXIX. Vol. VI. p. 68, and 146.

[7] Τὰ συσσίτια τῶν ἑταιριῶν. Aristotle, Politic. II. 11. It may be mentioned, as a mark of the aristocratical spirit of the Carthaginian government, that the senate and people had different baths.—Valer. Max. IX. 5. Ext. § 4.

[8] At least Hamilcar, who commanded the Carthaginians at the battle of Himera, and who was one of the suffetes, is described by Herodotus as sacrificing during the battle, and pouring libations with his own hand on the victims. VII. 167. And although the expression in Herodotus is ἐθύετο, and not ἔθυεν, yet the same expression is applied to the prophet Tisamenus, who was with the Greek army at Platæa; and, unless Hamilcar had been personally engaged in the sacrifice, we can scarcely suppose that he would have remained in the camp while it was going forward, instead of being present with his soldiers in the action.

[9] Aristotle, Politic. II. 11.

[10] Ἀριστοκρατικὸν, τὸ τὰς δίκας ὑπὸ τῶν ἀρχείων δικάζεσθαι πάσας, καὶ μὴ ἄλλας ὑπ' ἄλλων, καθάπερ ἐν

elders; but every magistracy seems to have had a judicial power attached to it, and only one court had a popular constitution. This was the court of the hundred and four,[11] the members of which were elected by the people at large; but public opinion required that they should be men of irreproachable characters; and therefore the election was conducted with care, and no one without merit was likely to be appointed. This court probably exercised jurisdiction especially in civil and mercantile causes; such as would be exceedingly numerous in so great a commercial country as Carthage.

Regular system of colonization.

Thus excluded in the ordinary course of things from the government, the legislature, and the courts of justice, the Carthaginian commons were kept for centuries in a state of contented acquiescence with their country's constitution, because provision was happily and wisely made for their physical wants. Colonization, as a provision for the poorer citizens, was an habitual resource of the Carthaginian government. And not only did their numerous settlements along the coast of Africa enable them to make grants of land to whole bodies of their people, but individuals[12] were employed in various offices under the government, as clerks, or as custom-house officers, where opportunities of acquiring money would not be wanting. With such means of relief, largely offered by fortune and wisely used, the Carthaginian people were saved from that worst cause of revolutions, general distress; and the mass of mankind are so constituted, that so long as their physical wants are satisfied, the cravings of their intellectual and moral nature are rarely vehement.

Meagreness of our accounts of Carthage from the total want of all Carthaginian literature.

Every one who is accustomed to make history a reality must feel how unsatisfactory are these accounts of mere institutions, which, at the best, can offer us only a plan, and not a living picture. Was the Carthaginian aristocracy, with its merchant-nobles, its jealous tribunals, its power abroad and its weakness at home, an older sister of that Venetian republic, whose fall, less shameful than the long stagnation of its half existence, Nemesis has in our own days rejoiced in? Or did the common voice in France speak truly, when it called England the modern Carthage? Or is Holland the truer parallel; and do the contests of the house of Nassau with the Dutch aristocracy represent the ambition of the house of Barca, and the triumph of the popular party over the old aristocratical constitution? We cannot answer these questions certainly, because Carthage on the stage of history is to us a dumb actor; no poet, orator, historian, or philosopher, has escaped the wreck of time, to show us how men thought and felt at Carthage. There were Carthaginian

Λακεδαίμονι. Aristot. Politic. II. 11. Πάσας ἀρχαί τινες κρίνουσι τὰς δίκας, III. 1. For the statement in the text these passages are a sufficient warrant; but the first offers, as is well known, much difficulty in itself; and Kluge's explanation is not satisfactory. In the latter passage Carthage and Lacedæmon are said to resemble each other in the aristocratical principle of vesting the judicial power in magistrates, and not in juries taken from the people at large. This is perfectly clear; but one does not see why it should be more aristocratical to give all these magistrates a universal jurisdiction, rather than, as at Sparta, to assign civil causes to one court, and criminal to another. It is strange, too, that in one of these passages Sparta and Carthage should be said to manage their courts of justice on the same principle; that is, on one of an antipopular character, τὸν αὐτὸν δὲ τρόπον καὶ περὶ Καρχηδόνα, if in the other passage they are meant to be contrasted with one another. Is it not possible therefore to refer the words καθάπερ ἐν Λακεδαίμονι to the whole of the clause preceding it, rather than to the words καὶ μὴ ἄλλας ὑπ' ἄλλων, and to understand these last words not of the Lacedæmonian practice of submitting different causes to different magistrates, but of a more democratical system by which not all causes were tried by magistrates, as at Carthage, but some by magistrates, and others by juries; "some by one authority, and others by another?"

[11] The number of this court is supposed by Niebuhr (Vol. I. note 851) to have reference to the number of weeks in the solar year, as if there were two judges for each week. The numbers were elected, says Aristotle, οὐκ ἐκ τῶν τυχόντων ἀλλ' ἀριστίνδην. This can only mean that public opinion required for the office so high a qualification in point of character, that the appointment was in the truest sense of the word aristocratical; whereas at Sparta, a lower standard being fixed for the characters of the Ephori, persons of very ordinary qualifications were often chosen, if party feelings recommended them.

[12] Aristot. Politic. VI. 5. 'Αεί τινας ἐκπέμποντες τοῦ δήμου πρὸς τὰς περιοικίδας ποιοῦσιν εὐπόρους. Kluge understands this passage as I have done; Heeren objects to this interpretation, and explains it of colonies sent out in the mass.

writers, we know. Sallust had heard translations of passages in their historical records;[13] and the Roman senate, when Carthage was destroyed, ordered Mago's work on agriculture to be translated into Latin.[14] Nor were geographical accounts of their voyages of discovery wanting; imperfect translations of, or rather extracts from, two of which into Greek[15] and Latin, have descended to our times. But of poets, orators, and philosophers we hear nothing; nor probably were the writers who were translated to Sallust deserving of the name of historians; at least all that he quotes from them relates to times beyond real historical memory, as if they had but recorded floating popular traditions, without attempting critical or contemporary history. It was a Greek who gave what may be looked upon as a Carthaginian account[16] of the first Punic war; and it was to two Greeks[17] that Hannibal committed the task of recording his own immortal expedition to Italy. Their language, indeed, shut the Carthaginians out from the prevailing civilization of the ancient world: it was easy for a Roman to learn Greek, which was but a sister language to his own; but neither Greek nor Latin have any near resemblance to Phœnician; nor were there any Carthaginian names or stories which poets and artists had made famous amongst all civilized nations like those of Thebes and Troy. Thus, as I said before, Carthage, not having spoken of what was in her heart, it has passed along with herself into destruction; and we can now only know something of what she did, without understanding what she was.

Growth of the popular party, headed by Hamilcar Barca and his family.

Polybius[18] has said that during the wars with the Romans, the Carthaginian constitution became more democratical, and he ascribes the victory of the Romans in some measure to the superior wisdom of their aristocratical government, and the instability of popular counsels in Carthage. It is, indeed, evident, that the family of Barca rested on popular support, and were opposed by the party of the aristocracy; and that they could maintain their power so long in spite of such an opposition, shows, undoubtedly, that the popular part of the constitution must have gained far more strength than it possessed in the days of Aristotle. Hamilcar and his family seem to have stood in the position of Pericles at Athens; both have often been taxed with having injured irreparably the constitution of their two countries; and both, perhaps, had the natural weakness of great men, that feeling themselves to be better than any institutions, they removed too boldly things which to them were hindrances, but to the mediocrity of ordinary men are supports or useful guides; so that when they died, and no single men arose able to fill their place, what they had undone found nothing to succeed to it, and then the overthrow of the older system appeared an irreparable mischief. But the question is amongst the most difficult in political science; Venice shows that no democracy, no tyranny, can be so vile as the dregs of an aristocracy suffered to run out its full course; and with respect to the conduct of a war, the Roman senate is no fair specimen of aristocracies in general; the affairs of Athens and Carthage were

[13] Sallust, Bell. Jugurth. 20.

[14] Pliny, Histor. Natur. XVIII. § 22. It appears from this passage that on the destruction of Carthage the Carthaginian libraries were given by the senate to "the princes of Africa," "regulis Africæ;" that is chiefly, no doubt, to Masinissa. And thus the Carthaginian books from which Sallust quotes were said, he tells us, to have belonged to king Hiempsal, Masinissa's grandson. And further, Mago's work was committed for translation to persons who understood Carthaginian, of whom the man who knew it best was a member of the Junian family, D. Silanus. Still a knowledge of Carthaginian must have been a rare accomplishment; which makes us wonder at the introduction of speeches in that language upon the Roman stage, as in the Pœnulus of Plautus. It seems to me by no means certain that all of what is there given is genuine Carthaginian. Was Plautus likely to have learnt the language, and for what object would pure Carthaginian have been introduced, when apparently the only purpose answered by Hanno's speaking in a foreign language is to cause a laugh at Milphio's burlesque interpretation of it?

[15] Such as a Greek translation of a voyage of Hanno, published by Hudson in his Geographi Minores; and Festus Avienus' Latin version of certain parts of the voyage of Himilcon, which Heeren has given in the Appendix to his work on Carthage.

[16] Philinus of Agrigentum.

[17] Sosilus of Lacedæmon, and Silanus or Silenus. Vid. Cornel. Nepot. in Hannibal, 13.

[18] VI. 51.

never conducted so ably as when the popular party was most predominant; nor have any governments ever shown in war greater feebleness and vacillation and ignorance than those of Sparta, and, but too often, of England.

Enterprising spirit of the Carthaginian government.

A great commercial state, where wealth was largely gained and highly valued, was always in danger, according to the opinion of the ancient philosophers, of losing its spirit of enterprise. But in this Carthage resembled the government of British India; necessity at first made her merchants soldiers; and when she became powerful, then the mere impulse of a great dominion kept up her energy; she had much to maintain, and what she already possessed gave her the power, and with it the temptation, of acquiring more. Besides, it is a very important point in the state of society in the ancient world, that the business of a soldier was no isolated profession, but mixed up essentially with the ordinary life of every citizen. Hence those who guided the counsels of a state were ready also to conduct its armies; and military glory was a natural object of ambition to many enterprising minds which, in modern Europe, could only hope for distinction in the cabinet or in parliament. The great families of Carthage, holding amongst them a monopoly of all the highest offices, might safely calculate on obtaining for all their members some opportunity of distinguishing themselves: if the father fell in the service of his country, his son not unfrequently became his successor, and the glory of finishing what he had begun was not left to a stranger. Thus the house of Mago for three generations conducted the Carthaginian invasions of Sicily: and thus Hamilcar Barca, according to his own expression,[19] reared his three sons, Hannibal, Hasdrubal, and Mago, as lion's whelps to prey upon the Romans.

Inferiority of the Carthaginian people as soldiers. Want of fortresses in the Carthaginian territory.

History can produce no greater statesmen and generals than some of the members of the Carthaginian aristocracy. But the Carthaginian people were wholly unfit to contend with the people of Rome. No military excellence in arms or tactic is ever ascribed to them; nor does it appear that they were regularly trained to war, like the citizens of Rome and Italy. The Carthaginian armies were composed of Africans and Numidians, of Gauls and Spaniards, but we scarcely hear of any Carthaginian citizens except as generals or officers. With this deficiency in native soldiers, there was also a remarkable want of fortresses; a point of no small importance at all periods, but especially so in ancient warfare. The walls exist in Italy to this day of many towns whose very names have perished; but we know that, small as they were, they could have delayed the progress of an invader; and how inestimable were the services rendered to the Romans in their greatest danger by the fortifications of Nola and Casilinum! But in the Carthaginian territory an invader found nothing but a rich and defenceless spoil. Agathocles conquered 200 towns[20] with scarcely any opposition; and Hannibal himself, after one defeat in the field, had no resource but submission to the conqueror. Had a French army ever effected a landing in England during the last war, the same want of fortresses would have enabled the enemy to overrun the whole country, and have taught us by fatal experience to appreciate in this respect the improvidence of Carthage.

Carthage was unequal to Rome.

Thus, with abler leaders and a richer treasury, but with a weaker people, an unguarded country, and with subjects far less united and attached to her government, Carthage was really unequal to the contest with Rome. And while observing this inequality in the course of our story, we shall have more reason to admire that extraordinary energy and genius of Hamilcar Barca and his family, which so long struggled against it, and even in spite of nature, almost made the weaker party victorious.

[19] Valerius Maximus, IX. 3.

[20] Diodorus, XX. 17.

CHAPTER XL.

FIRST PUNIC WAR—THE ROMANS INVADE SICILY—SUBMISSION OF HIERO—THE ROMANS CREATE A NAVY—NAVAL VICTORIES OF MYLÆ AND ECNOMUS—EXPEDITION OF M. REGULUS TO AFRICA; HIS SUCCESSES, HIS ARROGANCE IN VICTORY, HIS DEFEAT AND CAPTIVITY—WAR IN SICILY—SIEGE OF LILYBÆUM AND NAVAL ACTIONS CONNECTED WITH IT—HAMILCAR BARCA AT EIRCTE AND ERYX—NAVAL BATTLE OF THE ÆGATES—PEACE CONCLUDED—A. U. C. 490 TO 513—A. C. 264 TO 241.

Μελετήσομεν καὶ ἡμεῖς ἐν πλέονι χρόνῳ τὰ ναυτικά, καὶ ὅταν τὴν ἐπιστήμην ἐς τὸ ἴσον καταστήσωμεν, τῇ γε εὐψυχίᾳ δή που περιεσόμεθα· ὃ γὰρ ἡμεῖς ἔχομεν φύσει ἀγαθόν, ἐκείνοις οὐκ ἂν γένοιτο διδαχῇ· ὃ δ' ἐκεῖνοι ἐπιστήμῃ προύχουσι, καθαιρετέον ἡμῖν ἐστὶ μελέτῃ.—THUCYD. I. 121.

A. U. C. 490. A. C. 264. Introduction to the history of the first Punic war.

THE first Punic war lasted, without intermission, for more than two-and-twenty years,[1] a longer space of time than the whole period occupied by the wars of the French revolution, if we omit to reckon the nineteen months of the peace or rather truce of Amiens. And we have now, for the first time, the guidance of a careful and well-informed historian, who, having been born little more thirty years after the end of the war,[2] had studied the written accounts given of its events by each of the contending parties, had learned something, no doubt, concerning it, from the mouths both of Romans and Carthaginians, and who judged what he had heard and read with understanding, and for the most part impartially. The actions, then, of this war may be known, and some of them deserve to be described particularly; nor does it indeed seem possible to communicate any interest to history, if it must only record results and not paint actions. But in military matters, especially, much that may and ought to be told at length by a contemporary historian, ought not to be repeated by one who writes after an interval of many centuries: and therefore I must, of necessity, pass over slightly many battles and sieges, in order to relate others in full detail, and yet avoid the fault of too great prolixity.

The Mamertines of Messana apply to Rome for aid against the Carthaginians and Hiero.

It was the eleventh year after the defeat of Pyrrhus at Beneventum, and Appius Claudius Caudex and M. Fulvius Flaccus were consuls, when a deputation[3] arrived at Rome from the Mamertines of Messana, praying that the Romans, the sovereigns of Italy, would not suffer an Italian people to be destroyed by Greeks and Carthaginians. Hiero, king of Syracuse, was their open enemy; the Carthaginians, under pretence of saving them from his vengeance, were trying to get possession of their citadel; but the Mamertines, true to their Italian blood, sought to put themselves under the protection of their own countrymen, and it greatly concerned the Romans not to allow the Carthaginians to become masters of Messana, and to gain a station for their fleets within thirty stadia of the coast of Italy.

Six years had not elapsed since the Romans had extirpated the brethren and

[1] From the middle, perhaps, of the year 490 to the middle of the year 513; nearly twenty-three years, if we reckon from the arrival of the first Mamertine embassy at Rome, to the conclusion of the definitive treaty. The whole period of the revolution wars, from April, 1792, to July, 1815, is but a very little longer, and it becomes very much shorter if the interval of peace be deducted, which extends from October, 1801, to May, 1803.

[2] The exact year of Polybius' birth is uncertain. He was under 30 in 573, but as he was appointed ambassador to Egypt in that year, he could not have been many years younger. See Fynes Clinton, Fasti Hellen. Vol. III. p. 75.

[3] Polybius, I. 10. Zonaras, VIII. 8.

imitators of the Mamertines, who had done to Rhegium what the Mamertines had done to Messana; and Hiero, king of Syracuse, had zealously aided them in the work, and, as it appears,[4] was actually at this time their ally. The Mamertines were a horde of adventurers and plunderers, who were the common enemies of mankind, and whose case the Romans had prejudged already by their exemplary punishment of the very same conduct in the Campanians of Rhegium, while Hiero and the Carthaginians were the friends and allies of Rome. The senate, therefore, we are assured,[5] after long debates, could not resolve to interfere in such a quarrel.

The senate hesitates to grant it.

But the consuls, who, if true to the hereditary character of their families, were both of them ambitious men and unscrupulous, brought the petition of the Mamertines before the assembly of the people. The ready topics of aiding the Italian people against foreigners, and of restraining the power of Carthage, whose establishments in Corsica, Sardinia, and the Liparæan islands, were already drawn, like a chain, round the Roman dominion, were, no doubt, urged plausibly; it might have been said too that the Carthaginians had already undertaken to protect the Mamertines, so that they could not reproach the Romans for upholding the very same cause. Besides, the Roman people had a fresh remembrance of the assignations of land, the rich spoil, and lucrative employments which had followed from their late conquests in Italy; the fertility of Sicily was proverbial; and the well-known riches of Carthage made a war with her as tempting a prospect to the Romans as a war with Spain has been ere now to Englishmen. So the Roman people resolved to protect the Mamertine buccaneers, and to receive them as their friends and allies.

But the people in their tribes resolve to assist them.

The vote of the comitia was, by the actual constitution of Rome, paramount to every other authority except the negative of the tribunes; and as the tribunes did not interpose, the hesitation of the senate availed nothing. Accordingly the senate now resolved to assist the Mamertines; and Appius Claudius was ordered to carry the resolution into effect. But before he could be ready to act with a consular army, C. Claudius, with a small force, was sent to the spot with orders to communicate as quickly as possible with the Mamertines. In a small boat[6] he crossed the strait to Messana, and was introduced before the Mamertine assembly. With the language so invariably repeated afterwards whenever a Roman army appeared in a foreign country, C. Claudius assured the Mamertines that he was come to give them their freedom, and he called on the Carthaginians either to evacuate the city, for since the Mamertine embassy to Rome they had been put in possession of the citadel by their partisans in Messana, or to explain the grounds on which they occupied it. His address received no answer; upon which he said, "This silence proves that the Mamertine people are not their own masters, and that the Carthaginians have no just defence of their conduct to offer. For the sake of our common Italian blood, and because our aid has been implored, we will do the Mamertines justice."

C. Claudius crosses over to Messana, and promises to the Mamertines the aid of Rome.

But the strait of Messana, guarded by a Carthaginian fleet, was a barrier not easy to surmount. The Romans, since their conquest of Tarentum and their possession of all the coasts of Italy, seem to have given up their navy altogether, and we hear at this time of no duumviri or naval commanders as regular officers of the commonwealth. From the Greek cities in their alliance, Neapolis,[7] Velia, and Tarentum, they obtained a few triremes and penteconters; but they had not a single quinquereme, the class of ships which may be called the line-of-battle-ships of that period. Their attempt to cross to Sicily was therefore easily baffled, and some of their triremes,[8] with

The Roman fleet, in attempting to cross the strait, is repulsed by the Carthaginians.

[4] Zonaras, VIII. 8. Dion Cassius, Fragm. Vatican. LVIII.

[5] Polybius, I. 11.

[6] Zonaras, VIII. 8. Dion Cassius, Fragm. Vatican. LVIII.

[7] Polybius, I. 20.

[8] Dion Cassius, Fragm. Vatic. LIX. Zonaras, VIII. 8.

the soldiers whom they were transporting, fell into the hands of the Carthaginians.

Hanno, the Carthaginian governor of Messana, sent back the ships and the prisoners to the Romans, calling upon them not to break the peace with Carthage, nor to venture again on the hopeless attempt of crossing the strait in defiance of his naval superiority.[9] C. Claudius rejected his overtures, and repeated his determination to deliver Messana. Hanno exclaimed, that since they were so arrogant, he would not suffer the Romans to meddle with the sea so much as to wash their hands in it. Yet his vigilance did not justify this language, for Claudius with a few men effected his passage, apparently in a single ship, and finding the Mamertines assembled at the harbor to receive him, he again proceeded to address them, professed his wish to leave their choice of protectors to their own free decision, and urged that Hanno should be invited to come down from the citadel, that the Roman and Carthaginian commanders might each plead the claim of his own country to be received as the ally and defender of Messana.

Claudius again crosses to Messana, and invites the Carthaginian governor to a conference.

With this proposal Hanno[10] was induced to comply, as overscrupulous, it seems, to remove every ground of suspicion against the good faith of Carthage as Claudius was unscrupulous in serving the ambition of Rome. When the Carthaginian governor appeared, the discussion began; neither party would yield, and at last Claudius ordered his soldiers to seize Hanno and detain him as a prisoner. The Mamertines applauded the act, and Hanno, to procure his liberty, engaged to withdraw his garrison from the citadel, and to leave Messana in the hands of the Romans.

The governor is treacherously seized, and surrenders the citadel to purchase his freedom.

The Carthaginian council of elders,[11] always severe in its judgments upon military commanders, ordered Hanno forth to be crucified; and dispatched another officer of the same name with a fleet and army to Sicily. Hiero, provoked by the treachery of the Romans, concluded an alliance with Carthage against them, and the two allied powers jointly blockaded Messana. Hiero lay encamped on the south side of the town, Hanno stationed himself on the north, and his fleet lay close by, at the headland of Pelorus, where the strait is narrowest, to prevent the Romans from reinforcing their garrison.

Messana is besieged by the joint force of Carthage and of Syracuse.

Things were in this state[12] when Appius Claudius, with his consular army arrived at Rhegium. After some fruitless attempts at negotiation, he prepared to force his passage. We want here a consistent account of the details; but negligence there must have been on the part of the Carthaginians,[13] to allow an army of twenty thousand men to be embarked, conveyed over the strait, and landed on the coast of Sicily, without loss or serious interruption. The landing was effected at night, and on the south of Messana, near the camp of the Syracusans. Appius immediately led his soldiers to attack Hiero, who, confounded at the appearance of the Romans, and believing that the Carthaginians must have betrayed the passage, still marched out to meet the enemy. The Syracusan cavalry supported its old renown, and obtained some advantage, but the infantry were never much esteemed, and on this occasion they were, probably, inferior in numbers. Hiero was defeated and driven to his camp, and the very next night, suspecting his allies, and perceiving

Appius Claudius crosses the strait with a consular army, and defeats the Syracusans.

[9] Zonaras, VIII. 9. Dion Cassius, Fragm. Vatic. LIX.

[10] Zonaras, VIII. 9. Dion Cassius, Fragm. Vatic. LX.

[11] Zonaras, VIII. 9. Polybius, I. 11. Diodorus, Fragm. Hoeschel. XXIII. 2.

[12] Polybius, I. 11. Diodorus, Fragm. Hoeschel. XXIII. 2. 4. Zonaras, VIII. 9.

[13] Zonaras says of Appius, ὡς εὗρε συχνοὺς αὐτῶν πολλαχῇ κατὰ πρόφασιν ἐμπορίας ἐλλιμενίζοντας, ἐξηπάτησε σφᾶς ὅπως διέλθῃ τὸν πορθμὸν ἀσφαλέστατα. It is not easy to ascertain the exact meaning of Zonaras' Greek, but I believe that κατὰ πρόφασιν ἐμπορίας does not mean "under pretence of trafficking," but when "they had an occasion of trafficking." Compare in Thucydides, VII. 13, ἐπ' αὐτομολίας προφάσει. It would seem then that the Carthaginian sailors were trafficking in the port of Messana when they ought to have been at sea, watching the movements of the Romans.

that he had ventured on an ill-advised contest, he raised the siege and retreated to Syracuse.

Thus delivered from one enemy, Appius next attacked the Carthaginians.[14] Their position was strong, and he was repulsed; but this success tempted them to meet him on equal ground, and they were then defeated with loss. Messana was now completely relieved; the Carthaginian army retreated, and was divided into detachments to garrison the towns of the Carthaginian part of the island. Appius overran the open country in every direction, and the soldiers, no doubt, congratulated themselves on their decision in the comitia at Rome, which, in so short a time, had enriched them with the plunder of Sicily. But an attempt to take Egesta was repulsed with considerable slaughter, and when Appius advanced even to the very walls of Syracuse, and pretended to besiege the city, he found that he could not always be successful; his men suffered from the summer and autumn fevers of the marsh plain of the Anapus, and he retreated to Messana, with the Syracusan army pressing upon his rear. The Syracusans, however, long accustomed to regard the Carthaginians as their worst enemies, were unwilling to support the evils of war in their cause; the Syracusan advanced posts held frequent communications with the Romans, and although Hiero could not yet consent to make peace with the protectors of the Mamertines, yet the manifest disposition of his subjects was not to be resisted, and the Romans reached Messana in safety. Appius left a garrison there, and returned with the rest of his army to Rome; the strait was now clear of the enemy's ships, for in ancient warfare a fleet was dependent upon land co-operation,[15] and could not act without great difficulty upon a coast which was wholly in the possession of an enemy.

He defeats the Carthaginians, raises the siege of Messana, and pursues Hiero under the walls of Syracuse.

When Appius returned to Rome, he found that the war with Volsinii was at an end, for his colleague, M. Fulvius Flaccus, triumphed for his victories over the Volsinians on the first of November.[16] The whole force of Rome was therefore now at liberty, and as the Carthaginians seem to have despaired of defending the straits of Messana, two consular armies,[17] amounting to about 35,000 men, crossed over into Sicily in the spring of 491. All opposition was overborne, and Hiero, after having lost sixty-seven towns,[18] was glad to obtain peace on condition of restoring all the Roman prisoners without ransom, of paying a large sum of money, and of becoming the ally of the Roman people. He had the wisdom to maintain this alliance unbroken to the hour of his death, having found that the friendship of Rome would secure him from all other enemies, whereas the allies of Carthage were exposed to suffer from her tyranny, but could not depend on her protection. Hiero retained nearly the same extent of territory which had belonged to Syracuse in old times, before the tyranny of the first Dionysius; but all the rest of his dominion was ceded to the Romans.

Second campaign in Sicily. Hiero makes peace with Rome. A. U. C. 491. A. C. 263.

Having now only one enemy to deal with,[19] and having the whole power of Syracuse transferred from the Carthaginian scale to their own, the Roman generals went on prosperously. Many towns were taken from the Carthaginians, and

Zonaras, VIII. 9. Polybius, I. 12. Diodorus, Fragm. Hoeschel. XXIII. 4.

[15] The failure of Pompey's fleet in either preventing Cæsar from crossing the Ionian sea from Brundusium, or in effectually cutting off his communications with Italy afterwards, is one of the most striking instances of the defects of the ancient naval service. But with respect to the invasion of Sicily from Italy, we must remember that not even the British naval force, while every point in Sicily was in our possession, could prevent the French from throwing across a division of about 3000 men, in September, 1810, whose defeat was effected by our land forces solely, after they had effected their landing in safety.

[16] Fasti Capitolini.

[17] Polybius, I. 16.

[18] Diodorus, Fragm. Hoeschel. XXIII. 5. The terms of the peace with Hiero are variously reported. Diodorus says that he obtained a peace for fifteen years on giving up his Roman prisoners without ransom, and on paying 150,000 drachmæ; Polybius makes the sum 100 talents, and says nothing of any term when the peace was to expire; Zonaras names no specific sum, and Orosius and Eutropius set it at 200 talents.

[19] Polybius, I. 17-20.

Third and fourth campaigns. Siege of Agrigentum. The Romans resolve to build a fleet. A. U. C. 492-3. A. C. 262, 261.

in the following year, 492, Agrigentum[20] was reduced after a long and obstinate siege, and all the inhabitants sold for slaves. The consuls of the year 493 were no less successful, but the Carthaginians had at last begun to exert their naval power effectually; many towns on the Sicilian coasts[21] which had yielded to the Roman armies were recovered by the Carthaginian fleets; the coasts of Italy were often ravaged, so that the Romans found it necessary to encounter their enemy on his own element: they resolved to dispute with the Carthaginians their dominion of the sea.

They find a model for their ships, and train their seamen.

Immediately at the close of the year 493, they began to fell their timber. But no Italian shipwright knew how to build the line-of-battle ships of that period, called quinqueremes, and their build was so different from that of the triremes, that the one would not serve as a model for the other. Shipwrights might have been procured from the king of Egypt, but to send thither would have caused too great a delay. It happened that a Carthaginian quinquereme[22] had run ashore on the Bruttian coast when Appius Claudius was first crossing over to Sicily, and it was noted as a curious circumstance that the Roman soldiers had taken a ship of war. This quinquereme, which had probably been sent to Rome as a trophy, was now made the shipwright's model, and a hundred ships were built after her pattern, and launched in two months after the first felling of the timber.[23] The seamen, partly Roman proletarians, or citizens of the poorest class, partly Etruscans, or Greeks from the maritime states of Italy, were all unaccustomed to row in quinqueremes, and the Romans had, perhaps, never handled an oar of any sort. While the ships were building, therefore, to lose no time, the future crew of each quinquereme[24] were arranged upon benches ashore, in the same order, that to us undiscoverable problem, in which they were hereafter to sit on board; the keleustes, whose voice or call regulated the stroke in the ancient galleys, stood in the midst of them, and at his signal they went through their movements, and learned to keep time together, as if they had been actually afloat. With such ships and such crews the Romans put to sea early in the spring, to seek an engagement with the fleet of the first naval power in the world.

Defects in the ancient naval service.

An English reader is tempted here either to suspect extreme exaggeration in the accounts of the Roman inexperience in naval matters, or to entertain great contempt for the fleets and sailors of the ancient world altogether. There are no braver men than the Austrians, but there would be something ludicrous in the idea of an Austrian fleet, manned chiefly by peasants from the inland provinces of the empire, and commanded by officers of the land service, venturing a general action with an English or American squadron. But the accounts of these events are trustworthy; and had the Romans encountered the Athenian navy in the days of its greatness instead of the Carthaginian, the result, in the first years of the war at least, would probably have been different. However, there is no doubt that the naval service of the ancient nations was out of all proportion inferior to their land service; the seamen were altogether an inferior class, and the many improvements which had been made in the military art on shore seemed never to have reached naval warfare. Ships worked with oars were still exclusively used as ships of war; and although the use of engines, well deserving the name of artillery, was familiar in sieges, yet it had never been adopted in sea-fights,[25] and the old method of attempting to sink

[20] Polybius, I. 18, 19. Orosius, IV. 7. Zonaras, VIII. 10.

[21] Polybius, I. 20.

[22] Polybius, I. 20. Auctor de Viris Illustrib. in Appio Claud. Caudic. "quinqueremem hostium copiis pedestribus cepit." So in the invasion of Holland in 1795, the French triumphed greatly in the capture of some Dutch ships of war by a party of their cavalry: the ships were locked up in the ice, and the French cavalry took them without any resistance.

[23] Pliny, Histor. Natur. XVI. § 192. Florus, II. 2.

[24] Polybius, I. 21.

[25] Vegetius, writing in the fourth century after the Christian era, speaks of the use of artillery in sea-fights as a thing of common practice; but I do not recollect any mention of it as early as the Punic wars.

or disable an enemy's vessel by piercing her just below the water with the brazen beak affixed to every ship's bows, was still universally practised. The system of fighting, therefore, necessarily brought the ships close to one another; and if the fighting men on one side were clearly superior to those on the other, boarding, if it could be effected, would insure victory. The fighting men in the ancient ships, as is well known, were quite distinct from their rowers or seamen, and their proportion to these varied, as boarding was more or less preferred to manœuvring. In the Ionian revolt, about 500 B. C., we find forty soldiers[26] employed on each of the China ships out of a crew of 200; the Corinthians and Corcyræans, about seventy years afterwards, had nearly as many,[27] but the Athenians, in the most flourishing state of their navy, had commonly no more than ten. In the quinqueremes now used, we find the Romans employing on one occasion 300 seamen and 120 soldiers; this, however, was perhaps something above their usual proportion; but there can be no doubt that the soldiers on board of each ship were numerous, and if they could board the enemy their victory over what Niebuhr justly calls the mere rabble of an African crew was perfectly certain.

Machine invented by the Romans to enable them to board the enemy.

The object of the Romans was therefore to enable their men, in every case, to decide the battle by boarding. For this purpose they contrived in each ship what may be called a long drawbridge, thirty-six feet long, by four wide, with a low parapet on each side of it. This bridge was attached by a hole at one end of it to a mast twenty-four feet high, erected on the ship's prow, and the hole was large and oblong, so that the bridge not only played freely all around the mast, but could be drawn up so as to lie close and almost parallel to it, the end of it being hoisted by a rope passing through a block at the mast-head, just as our cutters' booms are hoisted by what is called the topping lift. The bridge was attached to the mast at the height of about twelve feet from the deck, and it had a continuation of itself reaching down to the deck, moving, I suppose, on hinges,[28] and serving as a ladder by which it might be ascended. Playing freely round the mast, and steered by the rope above-mentioned, the bridge was let fall upon an enemy's ship, on whatever quarter she approached; and as a ship's beak was commonly her only weapon, an enemy ventured without fear close to her broadside or her stem, as if she were there defenceless. When the bridge fell, a strong iron spike, fixed at the bottom of it, was driven home by the mere weight of the fall into the deck of the enemy's ship, and held it fast; and then the soldiers, in two files, rushed along it by an inclined plane down upon the deck of the enemy, their large shields and

[26] Herodotus, VI. 15.

[27] Thucydides, I. 49. He says that the ships had many heavy-armed soldiers on board, and many archers and dartmen, after the ancient fashion. That the number of fighting men on board the Athenian ships in the most flourishing state of their navy was no more than ten, appears from a comparison of several passages in Thucydides, II. 92, 102. III. 95, and IV. 76, 101.

[28] This is the difficult part of Polybius' description, I. 22, which he by no means makes very intelligible. "The ladder, or bridge, was put round the mast after the first twelve feet of its own length:" the object being apparently to attach it to the mast at such a height above the deck, as to make it form an inclined plane down to the deck of the enemy. But unless the lower end of the ladder had been fixed to the deck, the men could not have ascended by it; and had it been all one piece with the upper part, the moment the bridge was lowered to fall on the enemy's deck, the lower part must immediately have gone up into the air. And, of course, it is absurd to suppose that the men could have gone upon the bridge before it was fixed on the enemy's ship. I can only suppose, then, that what Polybius calls "the first twelve feet of the ladder" served as a permanent ascent from the deck to the end of the bridge, where it went round the mast, and that it was so far distinct from the bridge, that it remained in its own place when the bridge was lowered, although, when the bridge was hoisted up to lie close to the mast, both it and the bridge seemed to be a continuation of each other.

Folard's engraving and description of this machine are altogether erroneous: but he mentions a story which well illustrates the object of attaching the bridge to the mast at a height of twelve feet above the deck. "The Maltese seamen," he says, "have been known to mount on the main-yard preparatory to boarding, and when the ship runs on board of the enemy, one yard-arm is lowered, and the men are thus dropped one after another on the enemy's deck." I will not answer for the truth of the story, but it evidently contains the same notion of boarding by an inclined plane, which appears to have suggested to the Romans the arrangement of their bridge.

the parapet of the bridge together completely sheltering their flanks from the enemy's missiles, while the two file leaders held their shields in front of them, and so covered the bridge lengthways. So with these bridges drawn up to their masts, and exhibiting a strange appearance, as the regular masts were always lowered previously to going into action, the Roman fleet put to sea in quest of their enemy.

C. Duilius commands the Roman fleet. Sea-fight of Mylæ.

It was commanded by one of the consuls, Cn. Cornelius Scipio,[29] but as he allowed himself to be taken with seventeen ships, in an ill-advised attempt on the Liparæan islands, his colleague, C. Duilius, the descendant probably of that upright and moderate tribune who took so great a part in the overthrow of the decemvirs' tyranny, was sent for from his army to conduct the fleet. He found the Carthaginian fleet under the command of Hannibal, the same officer who had defended Agrigentum in the late siege, ravaging the coast of Mylæ, the modern Melazzo, on the north coast of Sicily, not far from the strait of Messana. The Carthaginians advanced in the full confidence of victory, and though surprised at the masts and tackle on the prows of the Roman ships, they yet commenced the action boldly. But the thirty ships which formed their advanced squadron, including that of Hannibal himself, were immediately grappled by the Roman bridges, boarded and taken. Hannibal escaped in his boat to his main battle, which was rapidly advancing; but the disaster of their first division startled them, and when they found, that even if they approached the Roman ships on their broadside or on their stern, still these formidable bridges were wheeled round and lowered upon them, they were seized with a panic and fled. Their whole loss, including that of the advanced squadron,[30] amounted to about fifty ships sunk or taken, and in men to three thousand killed and seven thousand prisoners.

Results of the battle, and honors allowed to Duilius The Duilian column.

The direct consequence of this victory was the raising of the siege of Egesta,[31] which the Carthaginians had well-nigh reduced to extremity, and the taking of Macella by assault. But its moral results were far greater, inasmuch as the Romans were now confident of success by sea as well as on shore, and formed designs of wresting from the Carthaginians all their island possessions, Sardinia and Corsica no less than Sicily. Duilius, as was to be expected, obtained a triumph, and he was allowed[32] for the rest of his life to be escorted home with torches borne before him, and music playing whenever he went out to supper, an honor which he enjoyed for many years afterwards. A pillar also was set up in the Forum to commemorate his victory, with an inscription recording the amount of the spoil which he had taken; and an ancient copy of this inscription,[33] retaining the old forms of the words, is still preserved, though in part illegible.

Indecisive war in Sicily. Roman expedition to Corsica and Sardinia. Conspiracy at Rome.

The events of the three next years may be passed over briefly. Towns were taken and retaken in Sicily, much plunder was gained, enormous havoc made, and many brave actions[34] performed, but with no decisive result. Hamilcar, one of the Carthaginian generals, de-

[29] Polybius, I. 21. [30] Polybius, I. 23.
[31] Polybius, I. 24.
[32] Cicero, de Senectute, 13. It appears that this continuation of his triumph during his whole life was his own act, and that it was thought right and proper, as he had done such good service; "quæ sibi nullo exemplo privatus sumpserat: tantum licentiæ dabat gloria." This no doubt is more correct than those other statements which represent it as an honor specially conferred upon him by the senate or people.
[33] A temple of Janus, built by C. Duilius at this time, was restored in the early part of the reign of the Emperor Tiberius. (Tacitus, Annal. II. 49.) It is possible that the column and its inscription may have been restored in the reign of Augustus; for the restoration of the temple had been begun by him, and was only completed by his successor.
[34] Such as that noble act of a military tribune in the army of the consul A. Atilius Calatinus, in the year 496, who sacrificed himself and a cohort of 400 men to cover the retreat of the army out of a dangerous defile in which they had been surprised by the enemy. Cato complained of the injustice of fortune which had given so scanty a share of fame to this tribune, while Leonidas for an act of no greater heroism had acquired such undying glory. In fact, the tribune's very name is uncertain, for we find the action ascribed to three different persons. See A. Gellius, III. 7, who quotes at length the passage of the Origines in which Cato describes the action.

stroyed the town of Eryx and removed its inhabitants to Drepanum, a place on the sea-side close beneath the mountain where they had lived before, and provided with an excellent harbor.[35] It was not far from Lilybæum, and these two posts both being strongly fortified were intended to be the strongholds of the Carthaginian power in Sicily. On the other hand, the Romans invaded Sardinia and Corsica[36] and carried off great numbers of prisoners. But as they extended their naval operations they unavoidably became acquainted with the violence of the Mediterranean storms; and the terrors of the sea were very dreadful to the inland people of Italy, who were forced to furnish seamen to man the Roman fleets, a service utterly foreign to the habits of their lives. Thus in the year 495[37] some Samnites, who were waiting in Rome till the fleet should be ready for sea, entered into a conspiracy with some slaves who had been lately carried off as captives from Sardinia and Corsica, to make themselves masters of the city. The seamen, however, of the ancient world were always chosen from the poorest classes of freemen, and their making common cause with the slaves showed at once that their attempt had nothing of the character of a national revolt. In fact, their own Samnite commander informed the Roman government of their conspiracy, which was thus prevented and punished. The higher classes in the allied states, who served as soldiers, liked the war probably as much as the Romans did; and with one doubtful exception,[38] we read of no symptoms of disaffection to Rome during the whole course of the war.

Naval action off the Liparæan islands.

Besides their expeditions to Sardinia and Corsica, and their naval co-operation with the consular armies engaged in Sicily, the Romans gained an advantage over the Carthaginian fleet in the year 497, off the Liparæan islands,[39] for which the Consul C. Atilius obtained, like Duilius, a naval triumph.

Great armament of the Romans.

A. U. C. 498. A. C. 256. They prepare to invade Africa.

This success, although in itself very indecisive, yet encouraged the Romans to attempt operations on a far grander scale, and to carry the war into Africa. Great efforts were made during the winter, and a fleet of 330 ships was prepared,[40] manned by nearly 300,000 seamen, exclusive of soldiers or fighting men. This vast number could scarcely have been furnished either by Rome itself or its Italian allies; but the thousands of captives carried off from Corsica and Sardinia, or from the cities of Sicily, no doubt were largely employed as galley-slaves; and if they worked in chains, as is most probable, the free rowers who were in the ships with them would be a sufficient guard to deter them from mutiny. The two consuls for the ensuing year were L. Manlius Vulso and Q. Cædicius; but Q. Cædicius died soon after he came into office, and was succeeded M. Atilius Regulus. The two consular armies had apparently wintered in Sicily; for the fleet sailed through the strait of Messana, doubled Cape Pachynus,[41] and took the legions on board at Ecnomus, a small place on the southern coast, between

[35] Diodorus, Fragm. Hoeschel. XXIII. Zonaras, VII. 11.

[36] Zonaras, VIII. 11. Polybius, I. 24. The Fasti Capitolini record L. Scipio's triumph over the Sardinians and Corsicans in the year 494, that is, according to the common reckoning, 495; and they record also a triumph of C. Sulpicius over the Sardinians in the year following. The Lucius Scipio who triumphed over the Corsicans was the son of L. Scipio who was defeated by the Gauls in the third Samnite war. His epitaph has been preserved, as well as his father's, and it tells of him, how "he won Corsica and the city of Aleria." Aleria is the Alalia of Herodotus, an old Greek colony founded by the Phocæans when they fled from the generals of Cyrus.

[37] Zonaras, VIII. 11. Scipio on his return from Corsica in 495 had encountered a violent storm, and built a temple to the powers of the weather in gratitude for his escape from destruction. This is noticed in his epitaph, "Dedit tempestatibus æde merito," and also by Ovid in his Fasti.

[38] Polybius says that in 495 or 496, the allies quarrelled with the Romans in Sicily, complaining that their services in the field were not sufficiently acknowledged, and that they consequently encamped apart from the Romans, and were attacked in their separate position by the Carthaginian general, and cut to pieces, I. 24. But it does not appear that these were the Italian allies of Rome, and it is possible that they may have been the Mamertines.

[39] Polybius, I. 25. Fasti Capitolini. Zonaras, VIII. 12.

[40] Polybius, I. 25. Each Roman ship had on board 300 rowers and 120 fighting men.

[41] Polybius, I. 25.

Gela and Agrigentum. Forty thousand men were here embarked, and the Carthaginians, who had assembled a still larger fleet of three hundred and fifty ships, had already crossed over to Lilybæum, and from thence, advancing eastward along the Sicilian coast, were arrived at Heraclea Minoa, and were ready to give the Romans battle. Both consuls were on board the Roman fleet; the Carthaginians were commanded by Hanno, who had been defeated at Agrigentum during the siege of that town, and by Hamilcar, who had so lately founded Drepanum.

Battle of Ecnomus. Defeat of the Carthaginian fleet off the south coast of Sicily.

The Roman fleet at Ecnomus contained 140,000 men, while less than 20,000 British seamen were engaged at Trafalgar. Yet it is not only in our generation, when Trafalgar and its consequences are fresh in our memory, that its fame will surpass a hundred-fold the fame of the battle of Ecnomus. For the twenty-seven ships which Nelson commanded at Trafalgar, by crushing the naval force of France, changed the destiny of all Europe; whilst the three hundred and thirty ships which fought at Ecnomus produced only a brief result, which within five years was no more perceivable. A fleet that could be built in a few months was no irreparable loss if destroyed; and the poor slaves who worked at the oar might be replaced by the plunder of the next campaign. The battle of Ecnomus was obstinately contested, but at last the Romans were completely victorious. They lost twenty-four ships,[42] in which not more than 2880 soldiers could have perished, if we suppose, what rarely happened, that not a man was picked up by the other ships; but they destroyed thirty of the enemy's fleet, and took sixty-four with all their crews. The Carthaginians with the rest of their ships made all speed to reach Carthage, that they might be still in time to defend their country against the expected invasion.

The consuls cross over to Africa, occupy Clypea, and begin to lay waste the country.

The way to Africa was now open, and the consuls,[43] after having victualled their ships with more than their usual supplies, as they knew not what port would next receive them, prepared to leave the coast of Sicily and to cross the open sea to an unknown world. The soldiers and even one of the military tribunes murmured;[44] they had been kept from home during one whole winter, and now they were to be carried to a strange country, into the very stronghold of their enemy's power, to a land of scorching heat, and infested with noisome beasts and monstrous serpents,[45] such as all stories of Africa had told them of. Regulus, it is said, threatened the tribune with death, and forced the men on board. The fleet did not keep together, and thirty ships reached the African shore unsupported,[46] and might have been destroyed before the arrival of the rest, had not the Carthaginians in their confusion neglected their opportunity. When the whole fleet was reassembled under the headland of Hermes, Cape Bon, they stood to the southward along the coast, and disembarked the legions near the place called Aspis or Clypea,[47] in English, shield—a fortress built by Agathocles about fifty years before, and deriving its name from its walls forming a circle upon the top of a conical hill. They immediately drew their ships up on the beach, after the ancient manner, and secured them with a ditch and rampart; and having taken Clypea, and dispatched mes-

[42] Polybius, I. 27, 28.

[43] Polybius, I. 29.

[44] Florus, II. 2.

[45] "Libya to the west of the lake Tritonis," that is, the present pashalik of Tunis, the ancient territory of Carthage, "is very hilly," says Herodotus, "and overgrown with woods, and full of wild beasts. For here are *the monstrous serpents*, and the lions, and the elephants, and the bears, and the asps, and the asses with horns, and the dog-heads, and the creatures with no heads, whose eyes are in their breasts, at least as the Libyans say, and the wild men and the wild women, and a great many other creatures besides." IV. 191. This description is very remarkable, following, as it does, a detailed and most exact account not only of all the African tribes on the coast from Egypt to the lesser Syrtis, but also of those in the interior. But the Carthaginian territory was rendered so inaccessible to foreigners, that all sorts of exaggerations and fables were circulated respecting it. Herodotus seems to have known nothing of its fertility, but only of its woods and its wild beasts, the terrors of which the Carthaginians no doubt purposely magnified.

[46] Diodorus, Fragm. Vatican. XXIII. 3.

[47] Polybius, I. 29. Strabo, XVII. p. 834.

sengers to Rome with the news of their success, and to ask for further instructions, they began to march into the country; and the ravages of forty thousand men were spread far and wide over that district which, for its richness and flourishing condition, was unmatched probably in the world.

Description of the country south of Carthage. One consul returns home. Regulus is left in Africa.

From Cape Bon, the Hermean headland, the African coast runs nearly north and south for as much as three degrees of latitude as far as the bottom of the lesser Syrtis. This was the most highly prized country of the Carthaginian dominion, filled with their towns, and covered with the villas of their wealthier citizens. In their old commercial treaties[48] with Rome no Roman vessel was allowed to approach this coast; they wished to keep it hidden from every foreigner, that its surpassing richness might not tempt the spoiler. Here grew those figs which Cato the censor showed in the Roman senate, to prove how the fruits of Italy were outdone by those of Africa; and here grew those enormous harvests of corn which in later times[49] constantly fed the people of Rome. But now the aspect of the country resembled the approach to Genoa, or the neighborhood of Geneva, or even the most ornamented parts of the valley of the Thames above London. Everywhere were to be seen single houses[50] standing in the midst of vineyards, and olive-grounds, and pastures; for as in Judea in its golden days, every drop of rain was carefully preserved in tanks or cisterns on the high grounds, and a plentiful irrigation spread life and freshness on every side, even under the burning sun of Africa. On such a land the hungry soldiers of the Roman army were now let loose without restraint. Villas were ransacked and burnt, cattle and horses were driven off in vast numbers, and twenty thousand persons, many of them doubtless of the highest condition, and bred up in all the enjoyments of domestic peace and affluence, were carried away as slaves. This havoc continued for several weeks, till the messengers sent from Rome returned with the senate's orders. One of the consuls,[51] with one consular army and forty ships, was to remain in Africa; the other was to return home with the second consular army, the fleet, and the plunder. L. Manlius accordingly embarked, and arrived safely at Rome with his division of the army, and with the spoil. M. Regulus, with 15,000 foot and 500 horse, was left in Africa.

He defeats the Carthaginians, and fixes his head-quarters at Tunes.

The defenceless state of the country, and the apparent helplessness of the Carthaginian government, seem to have encouraged the Roman senate to hope that a single consular army might at any rate be able to maintain its ground and harass the enemy, even if it could not force them to submission. And the example of Agathocles, who, during four years, had set the power of Carthage at defiance, no doubt increased their confidence. The incapacity of the Carthaginian government and generals was enough indeed to embolden the Romans. Their army, strong in cavalry and elephants, kept on the hills[52] where neither could act, and were attacked and defeated, and their camp taken by the Romans. Regulus then overran the whole country without opposition; the Romans[53] boasted that he took and plundered more than three hundred walled villages or towns, but none of these deserved the name of a fortified place; and even Tunes[54] itself, within twenty miles of Carthage, fell into their hands with little resistance. Here Regulus established his head-quarters, and here he seems to have remained through the winter.[55]

[48] See Polybius, III. 22, 23.

[49] Horace's expressions are well known, "Frumenti quantum metit Africa," "quicquid de Libycis verritur areis," &c. See also Tacitus, Annal. XII. 43.

[50] See the description of this country as it appeared to the soldiers of Agathocles. Diodorus, XX. 8. The irrigation is especially noticed, πολλῶν ὑδάτων διωχετευμένων καὶ πάντα τόπον ἀρδευόντων. It is the neglect of this which has so reduced the productiveness of Africa in modern times, but still the soil is described as extremely fertile. Sir G. Temple counted ninety-seven shoots or stalks on a single plant of barley, which was by no means one of the largest in the field; he was assured that plants were often seen with three hundred. Excursions in the Mediterranean, Vol. II. p. 108.

[51] Polybius, I. 29.

[52] Polybius, I. 30.

[53] Florus, II. 2.

[54] Polybius, I. 30.

[55] Zonaras, VIII. 13.

Meanwhile, to increase the distress of the Carthaginians, the Numidians,[56] or the roving tribes of the interior, then as now always ready to attack and plunder the civilized settlers of the sea-coast, joined the Romans, and, like the Cossacks, being most expert in such desultory and plundering warfare, they outdid the Romans in their devastations. From all quarters fugitives from the country crowded into Carthage, and it was feared that the city was unable to feed so great a multitude as were now confined within its walls. Alarm and distress prevailed, and the council of elders sent three of its own members to the Roman consul to sue for peace.

A. U. C. 498, 499. A. C. 256, 257. The Numidian tribes joined him. Distress of Carthage.

Regulus, like Fabricius and Curius, was in his own country a poor man; it is a well-known story[57] that he complained of the loss which his small portion of land must sustain from his absence, and that the senate promised to maintain his wife and children till his return. Such a man's head could not but be turned by his present position, when the plunder of Africa had given him the power of acquiring riches beyond all his conceptions, and when the noblest citizens of the wealthiest state in the world came as suppliants to his head-quarters. He treated them with the insolence shown by some of the French generals during the revolution to the ambassadors of the old sovereigns of Europe. Carthage[58] must evacuate Sicily and Sardinia, ransom all her own prisoners, and give up without ransom all those whom she had taken from the Romans; must make good all the expenses of the war, and pay a yearly contribution besides; above all, she must follow wherever the Romans should lead, and make neither alliance nor war without their consent; she must not send to sea more than a single ship of war on her own account, but if the Romans required her aid she must send them a fleet of fifty ships. The Carthaginian ambassadors protested against terms so extravagant. "Men who are good for any thing," replied Regulus, "should either conquer or submit to their betters."[59] And with threatening and insolent expressions to the ambassadors personally, he ordered them to begone with all speed from the Roman camp.

Regulus imposes intolerable terms on the Carthaginians who come to sue for peace.

The council of the elders called together the great council on this emergency;[60] and the whole body of the aristocracy of Carthage with one voice rejected conditions so intolerable. But great was the danger, and great the general alarm. The gods were to be propitiated by no common sacrifices, and those horrid offerings to Moloch, which had been made when Agathocles was threatening Carthage with ruin, were now again repeated. The figure of the god stood with outstretched arms to receive his victims; young children of the noblest families were placed in the hands of the image, and from thence rolled off into a furnace which burnt before him. Nor were there wanting those who with something of a better spirit threw themselves into the fire, willing to pay with their own lives the atonement for their country.

His terms are rejected.

In the midst of this distress, an officer returned[61] who had been sent to Greece to engage Greek soldiers of fortune in the Carthaginian service. Among others he brought with him a Spartan named Xanthippus, a man who had been trained in his country's discipline, and had added to it much of actual military experience. He might have

Xanthippus, a Spartan soldier, arrives at Carthage, and directs the operations of the Carthaginians.

[56] Polybius, I. 31. Diodorus, Fragm. Vatican. XXIII. 4.

[57] Auctor de Viris Illustrib. in Regul. Valer. Maxim. IV. 4, § 6.

[58] Dion Cassius, Fragm. Ursin. CXLVIII. Regulus was so elated by his successes, that he wrote home to the senate to say that "he had sealed up the gates of Carthage by the terror of his arms." Zonaras, VIII. 13.

[59] Diodorus. Fragm. Vatican. XXIII. 4.

[60] Polybius, I. 31. Diodorus, Fragm. Vatican, XXIII. 4. And for a particular description of the human sacrifices offered in such emergencies, see Diodorus, XX. 14.

[61] Polybius, I. 32. Some years afterwards, when Ptolemy Euergetes overran the whole kingdom of Seleucus Callinicus, he committed his conquests beyond the Euphrates to the care of "*Xantippus*, one of his two generals-in-chief." Jerome, in Daniel, XI. 9. Could this Xantippus or Xanthippus be the conqueror of Regulus, whose glory in Africa recommended him to the notice of the king of Egypt after his return from Carthage, so that he became a general in the Egyptian armies?

fought with Acrotatus against Pyrrhus in that gallant defence of Sparta; and in all likelihood he had followed king Areus[62] to Athens to save the city from the dominion of Antigonus, when Sparta and Athens fought for the last time side by side in defence of the independence of Greece. Xanthippus[63] condemned the conduct of the Carthaginian generals in the strongest terms; his reputation gave weight to his words; the government sent for him, and he so justified his opinion and explained so clearly the causes of their defeats, that they intrusted him with the direction of their forces. Hope was already rekindled; but when he reviewed the soldiers without the walls, and made them go through the movements which were best fitted to meet the peculiar tactic of the Romans, loud shouts burst from the ranks, and there was a universal cry to be led out to battle. The generals of the commonwealth did not hesitate to comply, and although they had no more than 12,000 foot, yet relying on their cavalry, four thousand in number, and on their elephants, amounting to no fewer than a hundred, they boldly marched out, and no longer keeping the high grounds, encamped in the open plain, and thus checked at once the devastation of the country.

He prepares to give battle to the Romans.

Regulus was obliged to risk a battle,[64] for as soon as he ceased to be master of the field, his men would be destitute of provisions. He encamped within little more than a mile of the enemy, and the sight of the Roman legions, so long victorious, made the resolution of the Carthaginian generals waver. But the soldiers were clamorous for battle, and Xanthippus urged the generals not to lose the precious opportunity. They yielded, and requested him to form the army on his own plan. Accordingly, he placed his cavalry on the flanks, together with some of the light-armed mercenaries, slingers perhaps from the Balearian islands, and archers from Crete. The heavy-armed mercenaries, we know not of what nation, whether Gauls, or Spaniards, or Greeks, or a mixed band of all, were on the right in the line of battle; the Africans, with some Carthaginian citizens, were on the left and centre; the whole line being covered by the elephants, which formed a single rank at some distance in advance. The Romans were in their usual order, their cavalry on the wings, and their velites or light-armed troops in advance of the heavy-armed soldiers; but their line was formed of a greater depth than usual, to resist the elephants' charge.

And totally defeats them. Regulus is taken prisoner.

When the signal was given, the Carthaginian cavalry and elephants immediately advanced, and the Romans, clashing their pila against the iron rims of their shields and cheering loudly, rushed on to meet them. The left wing, passing by the right of the line of elephants, attacked the Carthaginian mercenaries and routed them; Xanthippus rode up to rally them,[65] threw himself from his horse, and fought amongst them as a common soldier. Meantime his cavalry had swept the Roman and Italian horse from the field, and then charged the legions on the rear; while the elephants, driving the velites before them into the intervals of the maniples, broke into the Roman main battle, and with irresistible weight and strength and fury trampled under foot and beat down and dispersed the bravest. If any forced their way forwards through the elephants' line, they were received by the Carthaginian infantry, who, being fresh and in unbroken order, presently cut them to pieces. Two thousand men of the left of the Roman army escaped after they had driven the mercenaries to their camp, and found that all was lost behind them. Regulus himself, with 500 more, fled also from the rout, but was pursued, overtaken, and made prisoner. The rest of the Roman army was destroyed to a man on the field of battle.

Rejoicings at Carthage

The few fugitives from the left wing made their escape to Clypea; Tunes, it seems, was lost immediately, and, except Clypea, the Romans did not retain a foot of ground in Africa. We have no Carthaginian histo-

[62] See Justin, XXVI. 2. Pausanias, III. 6, § 8.

[63] Polybius, I. 32.

[64] Polybius, I. 33.

[65] Diodorus, Fragm. Vatic. XXIII. 5.

rian to describe the triumphant return of the victorious army to Carthage; how the Roman prisoners and Regulus, lately so insolent, were led through the streets bound and half naked; how the bands of noble citizens met at their public tables, sworn companions and brethren to each other in peace and war, and remembered with joyful tears their comrades who had fallen; how the whole city was full of festivity,[66] and every temple was crowded by wives and mothers offering their thanksgivings for this great deliverance. The feasting, after the Carthaginian manner, continued deep into the night; but other sounds and other fires than those of revelry and rejoicing were to be seen and heard amid the darkness; the fires of Moloch again were blazing, and some of the bravest of the prisoners were burnt alive as a thank-offering.

A. U. C. 499. A. C. 255. The Romans send a fleet to bring off the remains of their army from Africa.

Xanthippus, crowned with glory,[67] and no doubt richly rewarded, returned to Greece soon after his victory, before admiration and gratitude had time to be changed to envy. Clypea was besieged, but the Roman garrison held out desperately, and the senate no sooner learned the disaster of their army, than they sent a fleet to bring off the survivors. The Carthaginians, dreading a second invasion, raised a fleet to meet the enemy at sea, but the number of their ships was greatly inferior, and they were completely defeated. The Romans, however, had no intention of landing again in Africa; so total a destruction of their whole army impressed them with a dread of the enemy's elephants, which they could not for a long time shake off: they contented themselves with taking on board the garrison of Clypea, and sailed back to Sicily.

The fleet is wrecked on its return off the south coast of Italy.

The Romans had now for five years sent fleets to sea, and had as yet had little experience of its terrors. This increased their natural confidence, and they thought that Romans[68] might sail at any season, and that it was only cowardice which was restrained by pretended signs of bad weather. So, in the month of July, in spite of the warnings of their pilots, they persisted in coasting homewards along the southern coasts of Sicily, at the very time when violent gales from the south and southwest make that coast especially perilous. The fleet was off Camarina when the storm came on, and taught the Romans that fair-weather seamen may mistake ignorant presumption for courage. Above 260 ships were wrecked, which must have had on board 78,000 seamen, without counting the soldiers, who were probably at least as many as 25,000, and the whole coast from Camarina to Pachynus was covered with wrecks and bodies. The men[69] who escaped to shore were most kindly relieved by Hiero, who fed and clothed them, and conveyed them to Messana.

War in Sicily. Agrigentum recovered by the Carthaginians. The Romans take Panormus.

This great disaster encouraged the Carthaginians to redouble their efforts in Sicily. Carthalo, an able and active officer,[70] immediately recovered Agrigentum, and Hasdrubal was sent over with 140 elephants, to take the chief command of all the Carthaginian forces in the island. But the Romans, with indomitable spirit, fitted out a new fleet of 220 ships in the space of three months; and the consuls of the following

[66] Polybius, I. 36. For the description of the Carthaginian human sacrifices after a victory, see Diodorus, XX. 65.

[67] Polybius, I. 36. Niebuhr supposes that Regulus was defeated towards the end of the consular year 499, so that the sea-fight off Clypea took place early in the consulship of Cn. Cornelius and A. Atilius, that is, in the consular year 500. He thinks that Ser. Fulvius and M. Æmilius were already proconsuls when they obtained their victory, because it appears from the Fasti Capitolini that they were proconsuls when they obtained their triumph. But it is more probable that they were both employed as proconsuls in Sicily for a whole year after their consulship, and thus that their triumph was delayed. Zonaras says expressly that they were consuls when they were sent out to bring off the garrison of Clypea, and we can hardly extend the operations of Regulus in Africa to a period of a year and a half.

[68] Polybius, I. 37.

[69] Diodorus, Fragm. Hoeschel. XXIII. 14. The language of these fragments must surely be very modern, for in this passage the writer says that along the whole coast, τὰ σώματα καὶ τὰ ἄλογα καὶ τὰ ναυάγια ἔκειντο· τὰ ἄλογα must here mean "the horses," which is the common meaning of the word in modern Greek, but no writer of the Augustan age would have so used it.

[70] Diodorus, Fragm. Hoeschel. XXIII. 14. Polybius, I. 38.

year, A. Atilius and Cn. Cornelius, crossing over to Messana, and there being joined by the remnant of the other fleet which had escaped the storm, sailed along the northern coast of Sicily, took Cephalœdium, and although obliged by Carthalo to raise the siege of Drepanum, yet they besieged and took the important town of Panormus, obtained a sum of nearly 470 talents from those of the inhabitants who could afford to pay the stipulated ransom, and sold 13,000 of the poorer class as slaves. A garrison was left in Panormus, and several other smaller places revolted also to the Romans.

A. U. C. 493. A. C. 261.

For this service Cn. Cornelius justly obtained a triumph.[71] But we are surprised to find the same honor bestowed on one of his successors, C. Sempronius Blæsus. For Sempronius and his colleague, Cn. Servilius Cæpio,[72] having carried their fleet over to the coast of Africa, made some descents and plundered the country near the sea, but were able to effect nothing of importance; and after having been obliged to throw all their plunder overboard to enable their ships to float over the shallows of the Lesser Syrtis, they were finally, when sailing across from Panormus to the Lucanian coast, overtaken by another storm, which wrecked more than 150 of their ships. Upon this the Romans resolved to attempt the sea no more, and to keep only a fleet of sixty ships, to supply their armies with provisions, and to protect the coasts of Italy.

A. U. C. 501. A. C. 254. Another Roman fleet is wrecked between Panormus and the coast of Italy.

The two following years were full of discouragement to the Romans. Their armies remained in Sicily, but did little to advance the conquest of the island; because the terror of the elephants was so great that their generals were afraid to risk a general action. Such a state of things is very injurious to the discipline of an army, and we find that the service was so unpopular that 400 of the Roman horsemen,[73] all of them men of birth and fortune, refused to obey the consul, C. Aurelius Cotta, when he ordered them to work at some fortifications, and were by him reported to the censors, who degraded them all from their rank, and deprived them of their franchise of voting. And on other occasions Cotta ordered two of his officers to be scourged publicly by his lictors for misconduct;[74] one of them a kinsman of his own, and the other a military tribune, and a patrician of the noble name and house of the Valerii. Yet with the aid of some ships which he procured from Hiero, he attacked and reduced the island of Lipara, the largest of the Liparæans;[75] and for this and the capture of Therma, which had risen up on the site of the ancient Himera, he obtained after all a triumph.

A. U. C. 502. A. C. 252. A. U. C. 503. A. C. 251. The Roman armies in Sicily are in a bad state of discipline.

In the spring of the third year, when C. Atilius Regulus and L. Manlius Vulso were chosen each for the second time consuls, the Romans resolved somewhat to extend their naval operations, and to build fifty new ships.[76] But before the consuls left Rome, the tidings came of a most complete victory in Sicily, and of the total destruction of the dreaded Carthaginian elephants. Resuming then all their former confidence, the Romans increased their fleet to two hundred ships,[77] and sent out both consuls with two consular armies to form at once the siege of Lilybæum, the strongest and almost the only place still held by the Carthaginians in Sicily.

A. U. C. 504. A. C. 250.

This most brilliant and seasonable victory had been won by L. Cæcilius Metellus, who had been consul in the preceding year; and when his colleague, C. Furius, had gone home at the end of the campaign, Metellus[78] was left in Sicily with his own army as proconsul. It appears that Hasdrubal, the Carthaginian general, was taunted for

Battle of Panormus. Great victory obtained by L. Metellus over Hasdrubal. The Carthaginian elephants are taken.

[71] Fasti Capitolini.

[72] Polybius, I. 39. Zonaras, VIII. 14. Orosius, IV. 9.

[73] Valerius Maximus, II. 9, § 7. Frontinus, Strategem. IV. 1, § 22.

[74] Frontinus, Strategem. IV. 1, § 30, 31. Val. Max. II. 7, § 4.

[75] Diodorus, Fragm. Hoeschel. XXIII. 15. Zonaras, VIII. 14. Polybius, I. 39.

[76] Polybius, I. 39.

[77] Polybius, I. 41.

[78] Zonaras, VIII. 14. Polyb. I. 40.

his inactivity;[79] and relying, besides, too much on the terror of his elephants, he crossed the mountains from Selinus, and descended into the plain of Panormus. Metellus kept close within the walls of the town, till Hasdrubal, not content with having laid waste the open country, advanced towards Panormus, and drew out his army in order of battle, as if in defiance. Then the proconsul[80] keeping his regular infantry within one of the gates on the left of the enemy, so that by a timely sally he could attack them in flank, scattered his light troops in great numbers over the ground immediately in front of them, with orders, if hard pressed, to leap down into the ditch for refuge. Meantime all the idle hands in the town were employed in throwing down fresh supplies of missile weapons at the foot of the wall within the ditch, that the light troops might not exhaust their weapons. The elephants charged, drove the enemy before them, and advanced to the edge of the counterscarp, or outer side of the ditch. Here they were overwhelmed with missiles of all sizes; some fell into the ditch, and were there dispatched by thrusts of pikes; the rest turned about, and, becoming ungovernable, broke into the ranks of their own army, which was advancing behind them, and threw it into great confusion. Philinus,[81] who favored the Carthaginians, said that the Gauls in their army had indulged so freely in the wines which foreign traders sent to Sicily to tempt the soldiers to traffic with their plunder, as to be incapable of doing their duty. But there was no need of drunkenness to increase the disorder, when more than a hundred elephants, driven to fury by their wounds, were running wild amidst the Carthaginian ranks. Then Metellus sallied, attacked the enemy in flank, and completely defeated them. Ten elephants were taken with their drivers still mounted on them;[82] the rest had thrown off their drivers, and the Romans knew not how to take them alive, till Metellus made proclamation that any prisoner who should secure an elephant should be set at liberty. This induced the drivers to exert themselves, and in the end all the elephants were secured, and conveyed safely to Rome,[83] to be exhibited in the conqueror's triumph. And the device of an elephant, which is frequent on the coins of the Cæcilian family, shows the lasting sense entertained by the Metelli in after-times of the glory of their ancestor's victory.

Triumph and subsequent honors of Metellus.

The battle of Panormus was fought about midsummer, and Metellus returned to Rome with his army and his trophies, and triumphed on the seventh of September.[84] The captured elephants were exhibited in the circus maximus,[85] and hunted up and down it by men armed only with pointless spears, to teach the people not to be afraid of them; after which they were shot at with real weapons and destroyed. Metellus must have lived for nearly fifty years after his triumph,[86] full of honors and glory. He was a second time chosen consul, he was appointed once master of the horse, and once dictator, and he was also created pontifex maximus, in which last office he acquired a new glory, by rescuing the sacred palladium from the temple of Vesta when it was on fire, at the risk of his life, and to the actual loss of his sight. For this act of piety he was allowed ever after to be drawn to the senate in a chariot, an extraordinary honor, as the chariot was accounted one of the marks of kingly state, and therefore not to be used by the citizen of a commonwealth.

Thirteen noble Carthaginians[87] had been taken at Panormus, and had been led

[79] Diodorus, Fragm. Hoeschel. XXIII. 15.
[80] Polybius, I. 40.
[81] Diodorus, Fragm. Hoeschel. XXIII. 15.
[82] Polybius, I. 40. Zonaras, VIII. 14.
[83] They were carried across the straits on rafts composed of a number of casks lashed together, with a sort of flooring fastened together upon them. The flooring or deck was fenced in with high bulwarks, and covered over with earth, so that the elephants were not aware of their situation, and were conveyed over the sea quietly. Zonaras, VIII. 14. Frontinus, Strategem. I. 7, § 1. Pliny, Hist. Natur. VIII. § 16.
[84] Fasti Capitolini.
[85] Pliny, Histor. Natur. VIII. § 17.
[86] He lived to the age of a hundred years (Pliny, Histor. Natur. VII. § 157), and we can scarcely suppose him to have been much more than fifty when he obtained his first consulship. For his other honors see Pliny, Hist. Nat. VII. § 139. He was appointed dictator just after the Gaulish invasion of 529. See Fasti Capitolini.
[87] Livy, Epitom. XIX. Zonaras, VIII. 15. Orosius, IV. 10.

Embassy from Carthage to propose an exchange of prisoners. Regulus accompanies it. His magnanimous counsel. Return to Carthage and death.

in the triumphal procession of the conqueror. The Carthaginians, wishing to recover these and others of their citizens, sent an embassy to Rome to propose an exchange of prisoners, and M. Regulus was allowed to accompany the ambassadors, upon his promise given to return with them to Carthage if the negotiation failed. Pyrrhus had given a similar permission to his Roman prisoners, with the hope, no doubt, that in order to avoid returning to captivity, they would use their influence to procure the acceptance of his terms. But Regulus, thinking that the proposed exchange would be to the advantage of the Carthaginians, nobly dissuaded the senate from consenting to it; he himself would be ill-exchanged, he said, for a Carthaginian general in full health and strength, for the Carthaginians, he believed, had given him a secret poison,[88] and he felt that he could not live long. The exchange was refused; Regulus returned to Carthage, and soon after died. His springs of life had been poisoned, not by the deliberate crime of the Carthaginians, but by mortification, shame, a pining after his country, and the common miseries of a prisoner's condition, at a period when the courtesies of war were unknown. Afterwards the story prevailed, that the Carthaginians, in their disappointment, had put him to a death of lingering torment; whilst the Carthaginians told a similar story of the cruel treatment of two noble Carthaginian prisoners[89] by the wife and sons of Regulus, into whose hands they had been given as hostages, and Regulus' natural death was made, according to the story, the pretext for wreaking their cruelty upon the unfortunate Carthaginians in their power. We may hope that these stories are both untrue; but even if the Carthaginians had exercised towards Regulus the full severity of the ancient laws of war, it ill became the Romans to complain of it, when their habitual treatment, even of generous and magnanimous enemies, was such as we have seen it exemplified in the execution of the Samnite, C. Pontius.

The Romans form the siege of Lilybæum.

Never had the prospects of the Romans been fairer than when, in the autumn of the fifteenth year of the war, the consuls, C. Atilius and L. Manlius, began the siege of Lilybæum. This place and Drepanum were the only two points in Sicily still retained by the Carthaginians; and here they concentrated all their efforts, destroying even Selinus,[90] their earliest conquest from the Greeks, and removing to Lilybæum its inhabitants and its garrison. But from this time forward to the very end of the war the victories of the Romans ceased, and during a period of eight successive years the Fasti record not a single triumph, a blank not to be paralleled in any other part of the Roman annals. Lilybæum and Drepanum remained unconquered to the last, after the former had sustained a siege which for its length and the efforts made both by besiegers and besieged is not to be surpassed in history.

Situation of Lilybæum and its ports. Forces employed on both sides in the siege.

The general difficulty of ascertaining precisely the position of the ancient towns and harbors is felt particularly when we attempt to fix the topography of Lilybæum. It seems that the ancient city, covering more ground than the modern town of Marsala, must have occupied the extreme point of Sicily, now called Cape Boeo; and to have had two sea fronts, one looking N. W. and the other S. W., while on the land side the wall ran across the point from sea to sea, facing eastwards, and forming the base of a triangle, of which the two sea fronts meeting at the point of Cape Boeo formed the sides. Polybius speaks of the harbors of Lilybæum, as if there were more than one; and as the ancient harbors were almost always basins closed by artificial moles, it is probable that there would be one at each sea front of the town. But the principal harbor looked towards Africa, on the S. W. side of Lilybæum, and its entrance was very narrow, because at a little distance[91] from the shore

[88] A. Gellius, VI. 4. Zonaras, VIII. 15.

[89] Diodorus, Fragm. de Virtut. et Vitiis, XXIV. A. Gellius, II. 4.

[90] Diodorus, Fragm. Hoeschel. XXIV. 1.

[91] See Captain Smyth's Hydrographical Remarks on the coast of Sicily, p. xxvi., and his plan of the anchorages and shoals in the neighborhood of Trapani, in his Sicilian Atlas.

there extends a line of shoals nearly rising in some places to the water's edge, and running parallel to the coast, and the passages through these shoals, or round their extremity, were exceedingly narrow and intricate. The land side was fortified by a wall with towers at intervals,[92] and covered by a ditch ninety feet wide and sixty deep. The garrison consisted at first of ten thousand regular soldiers besides the inhabitants, and the governor Himilcon was an able and active officer, equal to the need. The Romans employed in the siege two consular armies, and the seamen of a fleet of two hundred ships of war, and a great multitude of small craft; so that as the seamen worked regularly at the trenches, the besieging force may well have amounted to 110,000 men.[93]

Attempts of the Romans to stop up the entrances into the harbor.

The Romans attacked the land front of the town in form:[94] they carried mounds across the ditch, and battered the towers in succession; whilst a formidable artillery covered their operations, and played upon the defenders of the walls. On the sea side they endeavored to block up the harbor by sinking stone ships in the channels through the shoals, but a violent storm[95] raised such a sea that every thing was swept away, and the harbor still remained open.

Able and successful attempts of the Carthaginian naval officers to throw succors into the place.

But material fortifications, however strong, must yield at last to a persevering enemy. The real strength of Lilybæum lay in the courage and ability which the long war had at last enkindled among the Carthaginian officers; so that now all was energy and wisdom, in complete contrast to the weakness and timidity of former generals. Himilcon was defending Lilybæum with the utmost ability and vigor; Adherbal, a man no less brave and able, had the command at Drepanum, and had with him a worthy associate in Carthalo; while Hannibal, one of his intimate friends, was sent from Carthage to carry succors to Himilcon. And here, for the first time, the Carthaginians displayed the combined skill and coolness of true seamen. Hannibal sailed from Carthage[96] with fifty ships, and lay waiting his time at the small Ægusan islands which lie to the north of Lilybæum. At length the wind blew fresh from the north, setting full into the harbor's mouth; Hannibal placed his soldiers on the decks ready for battle, hoisted every sail, and knowing the channels well, he ran down before the wind to the entrance between the shoals, dashed through the narrow passage, whilst the Romans in astonishment and awkwardness did not put out a single ship to stop him, and amidst the cheers and shouts of the whole garrison and people of Lilybæum, who had crowded to the walls to watch the event, he landed ten thousand men in safety within the harbor. Other officers of single ships passed several times backwards and forwards with equal success,[97] acquainting the Carthaginian government with

Diodorus, Fragm. Hoesch. XXIV. 1. Polybius, I. 42.

[93] The amount given by Diodorus, XXIV. 1.

[94] Diodorus, Fragm. Hoeschel. XXIV. 1. Polybius, I. 42.

[95] Diodorus, Fragm. Hoeschel. XXIV. 1, copying, probably, from Philinus. Polybius ascribes the failure of the work to the depth of the sea and the force of the current in the narrow channels. But for more than a mile off the land the water is shallow, nowhere exceeding four fathoms, and it is inconceivable that in fair weather such a depth of water could have been a serious impediment to a people like the Romans, when they had at their command the labor of a hundred thousand men. According to Captain Smyth, some of the stones thrown in by the Romans in this siege have been weighed by an English wine merchant residing near Marsala, and have been used by him to build a very respectable mole opposite to his own establishment, nearly at what must have been the southeast corner of the ancient town. One would be glad to know the exact spot at which these stones were weighed up; but Captain Smyth does not mention it. See his Survey of Sicily, p. 234.

[96] Polybius, I. 44. It is not easy to ascertain whether Hannibal ran into the harbor on the N. W. front of Lilybæum, or into that on the S. W. front. Probably it was the latter, so that he passed between Cape Boeo and the shoals which lie a little off the land, and so ran on in a direction parallel to the line of the coast till he came to the actual entrance between the moles in the harbor.

[97] Polybius, I. 46, 47. There is a passage in this description which, if we could discover the line of the ancient walls of Lilybæum, might determine the position of the harbor. The way to enter the harbor, says Polybius, was "to approach it from the side towards Italy, and to bring the tower on the sea-shore in a line with all the towers of the wall looking towards Africa, so as to cover them all." I. 47. The "tower on the sea-shore" must mean the tower

every particular of the siege, and confounding the Romans by their absolute command, as it seemed, of the winds and waves.

But the courage of the Roman soldiers was as firm as ever. Immediately after Hannibal's arrival, Himilcon made a general sally[98] to destroy the works of the besiegers, but the Romans maintained their ground and he was repulsed with loss. The land wall of the town was carried,[99] but Himilcon, meanwhile, had raised a second wall within, parallel to the first; so that when the first was taken the Romans had to begin all their approaches over again; and a second attempt[100] to burn the works, being favored by a strong wind, was completely successful. All the Roman engines, their covered galleries, and towers, were burnt to ashes, and the consuls, in despair, turned the siege into a blockade.

Sally of the garrison. They burn the Roman works.

During the winter the sufferings of the Romans were very great. Thousands of men had perished in the course of the siege,[101] and the loss of seamen had been so great, as they, it seems, were chiefly employed in the works, that the fleet was useless for want of hands to work it. Besides, the troops were ill-supplied with corn, and were obliged to subsist chiefly on meat;[102] a change of diet most unwelcome and hurtful to the Romans, who were accustomed then as now to live almost wholly on their polenta and on vegetables. Fevers broke out amongst them, and were very fatal; but Hiero again came to their assistance, and supplied them with corn. But no progress was made with the siege, when the following summer brought the new consul, P. Claudius, to Sicily to take the command.

Sufferings of the Romans during the winter.

P. Claudius was the son of Appius Claudius, the famous censor, and he inherited, even in over measure, the pride and overbearing temper of his family. He loudly reproached the former consuls for their inactivity;[103] and complaining that the discipline of the army was gone to ruin, he exercised the greatest severities on all under his command, whether Romans or Italians. He renewed with equal ill-success the attempt to block up the entrance to the harbor, and being impatient to distinguish himself, he no sooner received a reinforcement of 10,000 seamen from Rome than he resolved to put to sea and attack Adherbal, who was lying with the Carthaginian fleet in the harbor of Drepanum. It seems that his own officers[104] foreboded the failure of his attempt, but none could hope to move a Claudius from his purpose. The consul's pride disdained alike the warnings of gods and men; as he was going to sail it was reported to him that the omens were unfavorable, for the sacred chickens refused to eat. "Then they shall drink," was Claudius' answer, and he ordered them immediately to be thrown into the sea.

A. U. C. 505. A. C. 249. P. Claudius takes the command at Lilybæum. He sails to attack Adherbal at Drepanum. His obstinacy and profaneness.

Adherbal did not expect the attack;[105] but so great was his promptitude, that on the first sight of the enemy he manned all his ships with his seamen and soldiers, and keeping close under the land, stood out of the harbor while the enemy were actually entering it. Claudius, confounded at this, ordered his ships to put about and stand out to sea again. Some ran foul of each other in doing this, but at last he got clear of the harbor

Battle of Drepanum. Great victory of Adherbal over the Roman fleet under P. Claudius.

nearest to the extreme point of Cape Boeo, but whether the line of towers looking towards Africa followed the line of the coast, so that to bring them into a line with the "tower on the sea side," a vessel must advance in a course nearly S. E., or whether they ran due eastward from Cape Boeo, in the direction of the modern Marsala, and therefore did not follow the line of the coast, can hardly be ascertained without a further and more careful examination of the ground.

[98] Polybius, I. 45.

[99] Diodorus, Fragm. Hoeschel. XXIV. 1.

[100] Polybius, I. 48.

[101] Diodorus, Fragm. Hoeschel. XXIV. 1. Polybius, I. 49.

[102] κρεωβοροῦντες μόνον εἰς τὴν νόσον ἔπιπτον. Diodorus, Fragm. Hoeschel. XXIV. 1. We may compare the distress of Cæsar's soldiers on the coast of Epirus, when, although they had meat in plenty, yet they wanted corn, and nothing could make up to them for the loss of their bread. Cæsar, Bell. Civil. III. 40.

[103] Diodorus, Fragm. de Virtut. et Vitiis, XXIV. Fragm. Hoeschel. XXIV. 1. Polybius, I. 49.

[104] Cicero de Nat. Deor. II. 3. Valer. Maxim. I. 4, § 3.

[105] Polybius, I. 49–51. Orosius, IV. 10. Diodorus, Fragm. Hoeschel. XXIV. 1.

and formed his fleet under the land, with the ships' heads turned to the sea. Adherbal, who had brought his own fleet safely into the open sea, now formed his line of battle and attacked the Romans. We hear no more of Duilius' bridges for boarding; whether the Carthaginians had discovered some means of baffling them, or whether the practised soldiers now on board the Carthaginian ships rendered such a contrivance no longer formidable. Adherbal's victory was complete; Claudius escaped with only thirty ships, and the rest, amounting to ninety-three, were taken; with a loss in men, although some escaped to land, of not fewer than 8000 killed and 20,000 prisoners. The conquerors did not lose a single ship, and the number of their killed and wounded was very inconsiderable.

The Carthaginians follow up their success with vigor.

They followed up their victory with vigor.[106] Thirty ships sailed to Panormus, and carried off from thence the Roman magazines of corn, which were sent to supply the garrison of Lilybæum. Carthalo arrived with seventy ships from Carthage, and being reinforced by Adherbal, attacked the remains of the Roman fleet which had been drawn up on shore at Lilybæum under the protection of the army, carried off five ships and destroyed others. Meanwhile the other consul, L. Junius Pullus, had sailed from Rome with a large fleet of ships laden with corn and other supplies for the army at Lilybæum, which he convoyed with a hundred and twenty ships of war. Being himself detained at Syracuse to wait for some of the ships of his convoy, and to collect corn from some of the districts in the interior of the island, he intrusted about four hundred of the corn-ships with some of his ships of war to his quæstors, and sent them on to Lilybæum, where the want of corn was severely felt. Carthalo was lying at Heraclea, near Agrigentum, looking out for the Roman fleet; and when he heard of their approach he put out to sea to intercept them. The quæstors being in no condition to fight, fled to the small bay of Phintias, not far from Ecnomus, the scene of the great naval battle seven years before, and there mooring their ships at the bottom of the bay, and mounting the artillery of the town on the cliffs on each side of them, they waited for the enemy's attack. Carthalo was disappointed to find them so well prepared, and as their resistance was obstinate, he only carried off a few of the corn-ships, and returned to Heraclea, watching for the time when they should venture to continue their voyage.

Two Roman fleets are totally wrecked.

He had not waited long when his look-out ships[107] announced that the rear-division of the Roman fleet under the consul in person had doubled Cape Pachynus, and was advancing along the southern coast of Sicily. Wishing to meet these ships before they could join their other division in the bay of Phintias, he sailed in pursuit of them with all speed. The consul made for the shore near Camarina, dreading an open and rocky coast, and the danger of the southwest gales, less than an engagement with an enemy so superior. Carthalo, not choosing to attack him in this situation, stationed his fleet off a headland between Phintias and Camarina, and there lay, watching the movements of both the Roman divisions. Meanwhile it began to blow hard from the south, and there were signs of a coming storm which were not lost on the experienced Carthaginian pilots, who urged Carthalo to run in time for shelter. With great exertions he got around Cape Pachynus, and there lay safely in smooth water. But the storm burst with all its fury on the Romans, and overwhelmed both their fleets with such utter destruction, that all the corn-ships, amounting to nearly 800, and 105 ships of war, were dashed to pieces. With two ships of war only did the unfortunate consul arrive at Lilybæum.

P. Claudius is recalled, and a dictator appointed.

These accumulated disasters broke the resolution of the Romans. P. Claudius was recalled to Rome,[108] and required to name a dictator, that he might himself be brought to trial for misconduct. He named one of his own clerks, M. Claudius Glicia, as if he delighted to express

[106] Diodorus, Fragm. Hoeschel. XXIV. 1. Polybius, I. 52, 53.

[107] Diodorus, Fragm. Hoeschel. XXIV. 1 Polybius, I. 53, 54.

[108] Livy, Epitom. XIX. Zonaras, VIII. 15.

his scorn of his country when it no longer held him in honor. The senate obliged Glicia to resign his office immediately, and appointed by their own authority, as in ancient times, A. Atilius Calatinus. Atilius named L. Metellus his master of horse, and they both set out without delay to take the command in Sicily.

A. U. C. 505, 506. A. C. 249, 248. Trial of P. Claudius.

P. Claudius was tried before the people for his profane contempt of the auspices; but, according to the most probable account,[109] the trial was broken off by a sudden storm, which if noticed by any one present obliged the comitia to separate. It was done, in all likelihood, on an understanding that the accused would by his own act satisfy the justice of the people; and the Romans at this period shrank from shedding noble blood by the hands of the executioner. We only know that three years afterwards P. Claudius was no longer alive; for his sister, being pressed by the crowd of spectators as she was going home from the circus, said aloud that she wished her brother could come to life, and command another fleet, that he might make the streets less crowded. For this speech she was impeached[110] by the ædiles, and heavily fined: and this trial is recorded to have taken place three years after the defeat at Drepanum.

and of his colleague, L. Junius.

L. Junius[111] was not more fortunate than his colleague, although he had on shore endeavored to make up for his disasters at sea, and had stormed and occupied the mountain and town of Eryx, immediately above Drepanum. He too was tried for having put to sea in defiance of the auspices, and finding his condemnation certain he killed himself.

A. U. C. 507. A. C. 247. Hamilcar Barca is appointed to the command in Sicily. His system of warfare.

It was about this period of the contest that Hamilcar Barca,[112] the father of the great Hannibal, was appointed to command the Carthaginian forces in Sicily. The Romans had resigned the sea to their enemy, but their superiority by land was at present irresistible; the terror of the elephants had vanished, and Sicily, in general, is not a country peculiarly suited to the action of cavalry. It was Hamilcar's object, which he pursued steadily to the end of his life, to form an infantry which should be a match for the Roman legions; and this could only be done by avoiding for the present all pitched battles, and at the same time carrying on an incessant warfare of posts, in which his soldiers would be constantly trained, and learn to feel confidence in their general and in each other. This was the method by which alone Pompey could have resisted Cæsar's veterans; but Pompey, although he saw what was right, had not the firmness to persevere in it, and Pharsalia was the reward of his weakness. Hamilcar possessed patience equal to his ability, and his influence with the government enabled him to turn both to the best advantage.

A. U. C. 507—511. A. C. 247—243. His long occupation of the table-mountain near Panormus, and of Eryx.

During six years, therefore, Hamilcar made Sicily a training school for the Carthaginian soldiers, as he afterwards made Spain. He first occupied the summit of a table-mountain near Panormus,[113] now called Monte Pellegrino, rising immediately above the sea, with precipitous cliffs on every side, and with a level surface of considerable extent on the summit, and abundant springs of water. A steep descent led to a little cove where ships could be drawn upon the beach with safety;[114] and here he kept a light fleet always at hand, with which he made repeated plundering descents on the coasts of Italy, while by land he was continually breaking out and making inroads into the territory of the Roman allies, even as far as the eastern coast of the island.[115] Year after year the consuls were em-

[109] Valer. Maximus, VIII. 1, § 4.

[110] A. Gellius, X. 6.

[111] Polybius, I. 55. Cicero, de Natur. Deor. II. 3.

[112] Polybius, I. 56. Hamilcar seems to have succeeded Carthalo. Zonaras, VIII. 16.

[113] Polybius, I. 56. Monte Pellegrino is famous in modern times for the cave in which Sta. Rosolia's bones were said to have been found in 1624, and where a church has since been built in her honor.

[114] Apparently the small bay of Mondello, between Capo di Gallo and Monte Pellegrino.

[115] A fragment of Diodorous speaks of Hamilcar as making war in the neighborhood of Catana. Fragm. Hoeschel. XXIV. 2.

ployed against him, but they never could gain any pretence for claiming a triumph. During the latter part of this remarkable warfare Hamilcar recovered, and fixed his head-quarters at the town of Eryx,[116] although the summit of the mountain above him was occupied by the Romans, and a Roman army lay also below him, nominally engaged in blockading Drepanum. It appears that the Romans still continued also to blockade or rather to be encamped before Lilybæum; but as the sea was perfectly open, their presence produced no effect on the garrison.

Internal state of Rome. Depreciation of the copper coinage.

We wish in vain to catch any glimpses of the internal state of Rome after twenty years of such destructive warfare. If the varying numbers of the MSS. of Livy's epitomes can be trusted, the Roman citizens at the end of the war were fewer by one-sixth part than they had been ten years before: the census sank from 297,797 to 251,222,[117] and the decrease amongst the Latins and Italian allies must have been at least equal. We find also that the As towards the end of the war was reduced five-eighths of its original weight; from having weighed twelve ounces it was brought down to two;[118] and although it is certain that this reduction was gradual, inasmuch as Ases of several intermediate weights are still in existence, yet Pliny may be so far correct that the As, having weighed a full pound, or nearly so, down to the beginning of the first Punic war, was reduced to two ounces before the end of it. No rise in the value of copper could possibly have justified such a reduction, which could only have been one of the ordinary tricks of distressed governments; it is clear also that the silver denarii coined a few years before must have vanished out of circulation, as otherwise, if the general payments of the government were made in silver, they would have gained nothing by the depreciation of the copper coinage. Besides, the constant employment of such immense armaments in Sicily must have drained Italy of its silver, as even the Sicilian states, and much more the foreign merchants, who always gathered in numbers where war was going on on a large scale, would have been unwilling to take the Roman copper money. And this great scarcity of money would perhaps explain the very low reported prices of provisions at Rome[119] on one or two occasions during the war, if those prices were indeed to be depended on; for if the government did not want to make purchases of corn for its armies, a plentiful harvest would create a great glut of it in the market: the actual war, and the general jealousy of the ancient world on that point, making it alike impossible to dispose of it by exportation.

Heavy taxation. Foundation of one or two colonies, and great assignation of lands.

Twenty years before, the Roman people, we are told, had voted for engaging in the war with Carthage, while the senate sat hesitating; and the plunder of Sicily, in the first campaigns, made them doubtless rejoice in their decision. At a later period, something was occasionally gained by the soldiers in the same way, but from the beginning of the siege of Lilybæum it ceased altogether, and the warfare with Hamilcar was as unprofitable to the Roman armies as it was laborious and dangerous. Meanwhile the taxation must have been very heavy; for the building of such large fleets, though not to be measured by the cost of our ships of war, was still expensive, and armaments of a hundred thousand men, including soldiers and seamen together, such as were often sent out in the course of the war, must have greatly

[116] Polybius, I. 58. Diodorus, Fragm. Hoeschel. XXIV. 2.

[117] Livy, Epitom. XVIII. XIX.

[118] Pliny, Hist. Nat. XXXIII. § 44.

[119] Pliny, Hist. Natur. XVIII. § 17, quoting from Varro, says that at the time of L. Metellus' triumph, the modius or peck of corn sold for a single As, and that the congius of wine, and twelve pounds of meat, were sold also at the same price. Some accident must have occasioned these prices, unless indeed we are to understand the As before its depreciation, or rather that the reckoning was made according to the old standard and not the later and reduced one. It is very strange, however, that in the very winter after this season of plenty, the Romans should have been in such great distress for corn at Lilybæum. See p. 441. The low prices at the time of Metellus' triumph were not probably market prices, but merely the rate at which he made distributions of corn and wine to the people in honor of his success.

drained the treasury. To all this was to be added, since the disasters of the Roman fleets, the ravage of the coast of Italy by the enemy; for Hamilcar, from his stronghold near Panormus, more than once put to sea with his ships of war, and wasted not only the Bruttian and Lucanian coasts, but the shores of the gulf of Salernum, and even of the bay of Naples as far as Cumæ.[120] On the other hand, private citizens were allowed to fit out the government ships of war on their own account,[121] and some plunder was thus taken, but very insufficient to make up for the losses of the war. Two or three colonies were planted, such as Alsium and Fregenæ on the Etruscan coast near the mouth of the Tiber, and Brundisium; but these were more for public objects, the two in Etruria being founded probably as outposts to check the descents of the Carthaginian fleet, than for the relief of the poorer citizens. An accidental notice in Pliny[122] informs us that L. Metellus was in the course of his life appointed one of fifteen commissioners for granting out lands; a larger number of commissioners than we find on any other occasion named for that purpose. It would be important to fix the date of this appointment, but this can only be done by conjecture; it could scarcely, however, have been as early as the great assignation of lands made after the fourth Samnite war, for that was twenty years before Metellus obtained his first consulship; nor could it have been much later than the period of Hamilcar's warfare in Sicily, for in the beginning of the last year[123] of the war he was already pontifex maximus, and in the year following he lost his sight in saving the palladium. The probability is, therefore, that an assignment of lands on the largest scale took place about the close of the war, either to the poorer citizens generally, or, as after the second Punic war, to the old soldiers who had undergone such hard and unprofitable service in Sicily.

Effects of the war on Carthage.

On the other side, Carthage maintained no large fleets since the Romans had laid aside theirs, purposely to avoid so great an expense. Hamilcar's army could not have been very large, and the agriculture and internal trade of Africa suffered little or nothing from the war. But the contest was tedious and wearing, and in Sicily it was almost wholly defensive, which in itself is apt to sicken a nation of continuing it; nor were ordinary minds likely to enter into the views of Hamilcar, and await patiently the result of his system of creating an effective army. Besides, the unsoundness of the Carthaginian power in Africa was always felt in seasons of pressure; and at this very time hostilities[124] were going on against some of the African people, which, however successful, were necessarily an expense and a distraction to the government. It seemed, therefore, that in spite of Hamilcar's ability, the possession of Lilybæum and Drepanum was held but by a thread, which a single unfortunate event might sever.

A. U. C. 512. A. C. 240. The Romans resolve to send another fleet to sea.

The Roman government at last, in the twenty-fourth year of the war, roused itself for one more decisive effort. But so exhausted was the treasury, that a fleet could only be raised by a patriotic loan; that is to say, one, two, or three wealthy persons, according to their means, advanced money to build a quinquereme, which was to be repaid to them in better times.[125] In this way two hundred ships were constructed; and the Romans had an excellent model in one of the best sailing of the Carthaginian ships, which had been taken some years before off Lilybæum. The consuls of the year were C. Lutatius Catulus and A. Postumius Albinus. Lutatius was the founder of the nobility of his house, and a man worthy to have been the ancestor of that Q. Catulus whose pure virtue bore the hardest of trials, the triumph of his own party. Postumius belonged to a family scarcely second to the Claudii in overbearing pride; and it was perhaps not without some suspicion of his

120 Polybius, I. 56.
121 Zonaras, VIII. 16.
122 VII. § 139.
123 Valerius Maximus, I. 1, § 2.
124 Diodorus, Fragm. de Virtut. et Vitiis, XXIV. Polybius, I. 73.
125 Polybius, I. 59.

following the example of P. Claudius at Drepanum, that the pontifex maximus,[126] Metellus, forbade him to take any foreign command, because, as he was flamen of Mars, his religious duties required his constant presence at Rome. The fleet therefore was intrusted to C. Lutatius.

Anxiety for its success.

The anxiety for the success of this enterprise was naturally great. On such occasions omens and prophecies were never wanting; and the consul himself longed to discover his future fate, and wished to consult the famous lots kept in the temple of Fortune at Præneste.[127] But the senate forbade him, resolving that the consul of the Roman people should go forth with no auspices but those vouchsafed to him by the gods of Rome.

C. Lutatius Catulus arrives with the fleet at Drepanum.

The fleet sailed at an unusual season; for if Eutropius' date of the battle be correct, the ships must have left the Tiber as early as the month of February. Lutatius, accordingly, found that the Carthaginian ships had all gone back to Carthage[128] for the winter, so that he occupied the harbor of Drepanum without opposition, and began vigorously to besiege the town. As Q. Valerius, the prætor, accompanied him to Sicily, it is probable that two consular armies were employed, and so large a force obliged Hamilcar to remain quiet in Eryx, and made it certain that Drepanum must fall, unless relieved by a fleet from Carthage.

A Carthaginian fleet is sent over from Africa to oppose him.

Lutatius, expecting to be attacked by sea,[129] was indefatigable in exercising his seamen both in rowing and in manœuvring, and he attended carefully to their food and manner of living, that they might be in the best possible condition. The Carthaginians, on their part, equipped a fleet with all haste, and appointed Hanno to command it, an officer who had acquired distinction by his services against the Africans. But they had lately so neglected their navy that their seamen and soldiers on board were alike, for the most part, without experience; and the ships, besides, were heavily laden with provisions and other stores for the relief of Drepanum.

Catulus is anxious to intercept them.

Hanno first put in at the small island of Hiera,[130] which lies some miles out to sea off the western point of Sicily. His hope was to dash over unperceived to the coast of Drepanum, to land his stores, and to take Hamilcar and his veterans on board from Eryx; which being effected, he would not fear to encounter the Romans. This Catulus was above all things anxious to hinder, and he resolved to bring on the action, if possible, before the enemy could communicate with Hamilcar. He had himself been badly wounded a little before in some skirmish with the garrison of Drepanum, and was unable to leave his bed; but Q. Valerius, the prætor, was ready to take the command, and kept earnestly watching for the enemy.

Battle of Ægusa or of the Ægates. Great victory of the Romans.

It was the morning of the 10th of March;[131] the Roman fleet having taken on board picked soldiers from the legions, had sailed on the preceding evening to the island of Ægusa, which lies between Hiera and the Sicilian coast, and had there spent the night. When day broke, the wind was blowing fresh from the west, and rolling a heavy sea in upon the land; the Carthaginians took advantage of it, hoisted their sails, and ran down before the wind towards Drepanum. The Roman fleet, notwithstanding the heavy sea and the adverse wind, worked out to intercept them, and formed in line of battle with their heads to windward, cutting off the enemy's passage. Then the Carthaginians lowered their masts and sails, and prepared of necessity to fight. But their heavy ships and raw seamen and soldiers were too unequal to the contest, and the fortune of the day was soon decided. Fifty ships were sunk, and seventy taken; the rest fled, and the wind, happily for them, shifting just in time, they again hoisted their sails, and escaped to Hiera.

[126] Valerius Maxim. I. 1, § 4.
[127] Cicero, de Divinat. II. 41.
[128] Polybius, I. 59.
[129] Polybius, I. 59, 60.
[130] Polybius, I. 60. Zonaras, VIII. 17. Valer. Maxim. II. 8, § 2.
[131] Eutropius, II. Polybius, I. 60.

To continue the war was now impossible, and orders were sent to Hamilcar to negotiate for peace.[132] Lutatius, whose consulship was on the point of expiring, readily received his overtures; but he required that Hamilcar's army should give up their arms, and all the Roman deserters who had fled to them, as the price for being allowed to return to Carthage. This demand was rejected by Hamilcar with indignation: "Never," he replied, "would he surrender to the Romans the arms which his country had given him to use against them;" and he declared that sooner than submit to such terms, he would defend Eryx to the last extremity. Lutatius thought of Regulus, and of the vengeance which had punished his abuse of victory, and he withdrew his demand. It was then agreed, "that the Carthaginians should evacuate Sicily, and make no war upon Hiero or his allies; that they should release all Roman prisoners without ransom; and pay to the Romans in twenty years 2200 Euboic talents." These were the preliminaries, which were subject to the approval of the Roman government; the senate and people would not, however, ratify them, but sent over ten commissioners with full powers to conclude a treaty.[133] These plenipotentiaries required that the money to be paid should be increased to 3200 talents, and the term of years reduced to ten; and they insisted that the Carthaginians should also give up all the islands between Sicily and Italy. This clause was intended apparently to prevent their forming any establishments on the Liparæan Islands, which, although not at present in their power, they might after the peace have attempted to reoccupy, as some of them were uninhabited, and none possibly had been as yet formally occupied by the Romans.

The Carthaginians sue for peace. Terms of the treaty

Hamilcar would not break off the negotiation on such points as these. His views were now turned to Spain, a wide field of enterprise which might amply compensate for the loss of Sicily. And he wished to see his country relieved from the burden of the war with Rome, and enabled to repair and consolidate its resources. The peace, therefore, was concluded: Hamilcar evacuated Eryx,[134] and his troops were embarked at Lilybæum for Carthage. But their unseasonable and bloody rebellion which immediately followed, and which for more than three years involved the Carthaginians in a war far more destructive than that with the Romans, deranged all his plans, and delayed probably for many years the renewal of the contest between the two rival nations.

Hamilcar evacuates Sicily.

Such was the end of the first Punic war, in which, although the contest was long and wearisome, yet both parties fought as it were at arm's length, and if we except the short expedition of Regulus, neither struck a blow at any vital part of his enemy. But the next struggle was sure to be of a more deadly character, to be fought, not so much for dominion as for life and death. In this new contest, the genius of Hamilcar and of his son determined that in the mortal assault Carthage should anticipate her rival; and Italy for fifteen years was laid waste by a foreign invader. The state of the Roman supremacy in Italy, when it was exposed to this searching trial, the fate of the several Italian nations under the Roman dominion, and their dispositions, whether of attachment or of hatred, will form, therefore, the fit beginning of the succeeding portion of this history, which will embrace the third period of the Roman commonwealth; the period of its foreign conquests, before Rome,

Conclusion.

"——whom mighty kingdoms curtsied to,
Like a forlorn and desperate castaway,
Did shameful execution on herself."

[132] Polybius, I. 62. Diodorus, Fragm. Vatican. XXIV. 4. Cornel. Nepos in Hamilcar, 1.

[133] Polybius, I. 63.

[134] Polybius, I. 66.

CHAPTER XLI.

STATE OF ITALY AFTER THE ROMAN CONQUEST—POLITICAL RELATIONS OF THE INHABITANTS, AND DIFFERENT TENURES OF LAND—LATIN COLONIES.

Πόλεσι γὰρ—ἐπελθόντες,—καὶ ναῦς καὶ ἵππους καὶ μεγέθη ἐχούσαις οὐ δυνάμενοι ἐπενεγκεῖν οὔτε ἐκ πολιτείας τι μεταβολῆς τὸ διάφορον αὐτοῖς, ᾧ προσήγοντο ἄν, οὔτ' ἐκ παρασκευῆς πολλῷ κρείσσους ὄντες, σφαλλόμενοι δὲ τὰ πλείω,—ἠπόρουν.—Thucyd. VII. 55.

Establishment of the Roman dominion over Italy.

The first and second Punic wars were separated by an interval of two-and-twenty years; and the first Punic war, as we have seen, had lasted for a period of exactly the same duration. The end of the fourth Samnite war, and the final submission of the Samnites, Lucanians, and Bruttians, took place[1] eight years before the beginning of the contest with Carthage; and the treaty which permanently settled the relations of Rome with the Etrurians was concluded eight years earlier still.[2] Thus, when Hannibal, in the spring of the year 537, invaded Etruria, few living Etrurians had seen their country independent, except in their childhood or earliest youth; and all who were still in the vigor of manhood had been born since it had become the dependent ally of Rome. And when, after his victory at the lake Thrasymenus, he marched into Samnium, and encouraged the Samnites to take up arms once more in their old national quarrel, fifty-five years had passed since the Samnites, abandoned by Pyrrhus, and having tried fortune and hope to the uttermost, had submitted to the consul Sp. Carvilius Maximus. So in Samnium, as well as in Etruria, the existing generation had grown up in peace and alliance with the Romans; and many a Samnite may have been enriched by the plunder of Sicily, and must have shared with the Romans in the memorable vicissitudes of the first Punic war; in the defeat of Drepanum, and the disastrous shipwrecks which followed it; in the five years of incessant fighting with Hannibal's father at Eryx and by Panormus; in the long and painful siege of Lilybæum; in the brilliant victory of S. Metellus, and in the final triumph of C. Lutatius at the Ægates. It is true, that fifty-five years of constrained alliance had not extinguished the old feelings of hatred and rivalry; and the Samnites joined Hannibal, as a hundred and fifty years afterwards they joined the younger Marius, against the same enemy, the dominion of the Roman aristocracy. But that their rising was not universal,[3] nor persisted in with more desperate resolution; that Etruria, with some doubtful exceptions,[4] offered no encouragement to the Carthaginian general; that the fidelity of Picenum, of Umbria, of the Vestinians, Marsians, Pelignians, Marrucinians, and Sabines never wavered; that the "Latin name" remained true to a man; and that even in Campania the fidelity of Nola and of Cuma was as marked as the desertion of Capua;—all this is to be attributed mainly to the system of government which the Romans had established after their conquest of Italy, and which, so far as it can be traced, we must now proceed to examine in its complicated details. Not that we should by any means regard this system of government as a constitution founded upon justice,

[1] In 482 A. U. C. See chap. XXXVIII. p. 410.

[2] In 474 A. U. C. See chap. XXXVIII. p. 401.

[3] The Pentrian Samnites, that is to say, the Samnites on the north of the Matese, in whose territory Æsernia had formerly been, and who still held Bovianum, did not revolt from Rome at all. See Livy, XXII. 61. A wealthy Samnite of Bovianum, Numerius Decimius, distinguished himself on the Roman side, in an action fought by M. Minucius against Hannibal, in the year preceding the battle of Cannæ. Livy, XXII. 24.

[4] Such as the alleged disaffection of the people of Arretium in the eleventh year of the second Punic war, which however displayed itself in no overt acts. Livy, XXVII. 21, 24.

and granting to all whom it embraced within its range the benefits of equal law. Its praise is rather, that it secured the Roman dominion, without adopting the extreme measures of tyranny; that its policy was admirable, its iniquity and oppression not intolerable. And so small a portion of justice has usually been dealt to the mass of mankind, that their highest hopes have commonly aspired to nothing more than an escape from extravagant tyranny. If life, and property, and female honor, and domestic, national, and religious feelings, have not been constantly and capriciously invaded and outraged, lesser evils have been contentedly endured. Political servitude, a severe conscription, and a heavy taxation, habitual arrogance on the part of the governors, and occasional outbreaks of insolence and cruelty, have been considered no less incident to the condition of humanity, than the visitations of poverty, disease, and death. The dominion of the Romans over the people of Italy, therefore, as it allowed the ordinary enjoyment of many rights, and conferred some positive advantages, was viewed by its subjects, notwithstanding its constant absoluteness and occasional tyranny, as a condition quite as likely, if overthrown, to be changed for the worse as for the better.

Aristocratical character of the Roman sovereignty.

"The Lacedæmonians," says Thucydides,[5] "maintained their supremacy over their allies, by taking care that an oligarchy such as suited their own interests should be everywhere their allies' form of government." This also was one of the means by which the Romans secured their dominion in Italy. They universally supported[6] the aristocratical party, and thus made the principal inhabitants of every city willing instruments to uphold their sovereignty; a fact which alone would prove, if the point were otherwise doubtful, that the constitution of Rome itself, even since the passing of the Hortensian laws, was much more an aristocracy than a democracy.

Its advantages.

I have said that the Roman dominion in Italy allowed its subjects the ordinary enjoyment of many rights, and conferred on them some positive advantages. Moreover, it held out to them hopes more or less definite of rising to a higher political condition hereafter. These three points will give us the fair side of the Roman sovereignty, and they shall now be considered in order.

Ancient rights retained under it.

I. According to the general practice of the ancient world, the relation between Rome and her Italian subjects was nominally that of alliance; and the very term alliance implies something of distinctness; for the members of the same commonwealth cannot be each other's allies. Thus it is understood at once, that most of the Italian states retained their municipal independence: they had their own magistrates; they could pass laws for their internal government; and their ancient[7] laws of inheritance, and marriage, as well as their criminal law, were still preserved in full force. But this applies only to single states, or to the separate parts of a nation; for every thing like a national council or diet was carefully prohibited. Arretium, Perusia, and Volaterræ, might each legislate for themselves; but we hear no more of any general congress of the Lucumones, or chiefs of the whole Etruscan nation, at the temple of Voltumna. Nay, in some recorded instances,[8] and probably in many others not

[5] I. 19, 76, 144.

[6] In the second Punic war, Livy says, "unus velut morbus invaserat omnes Italiæ civitates, ut plebes ab optimatibus disentirent; senatis Romanis faveret, plebs ad Pœnos rem traheret." XXIV. 2. So it was at Nola; Livy, XXIII. 15. But we have the same thing already existing in the Samnite wars: where some of the Ausonian aristocracy betray their cities to the Romans, and the Lucanian aristocracy is attached to the Roman alliance, while the popular party favor the Samnites. See page 269 of this history.

[7] The Latins retained some peculiar laws relating to marriage, till they obtained the full Roman franchise after the great Italian war in the middle of the seventh century. A. Gellius, IV. 4. And their law of interest, being different from that of Rome, enabled Roman creditors to evade their own law, by nominally transferring their debts to a Latin, who, according to his law, might exact a greater rate of interest than was permitted at Rome. Livy, XXXV. 7

[8] As in the case of the Latins after the great Latin war, Livy, VIII. 14; of the Hernicans, after their revolt, in the second Samnite war, Livy, IX. 43; and of the Macedonians, after the battle of Pydna, Livy, XLV. 29.

recorded, the several states or districts of the same nation were so isolated from each other, that the citizens of one could neither intermarry with, nor inherit, nor purchase land, from those of another. Thus the allies were left in possession of their municipal independence; but all free national action amongst them was totally destroyed.

Benefits conferred by it.

II. Besides the benefits which the Roman dominion did not take away from its subjects, there were some others which it conferred upon them, and which they could not have enjoyed without it. The first and greatest of these was the extinction of internal war. From the Rubicon to the straits of Messana, there were no more of the intolerable miseries of a plundering border warfare, no more wasting of lands, driving away of cattle, burning of houses, and carrying off the inhabitants into slavery. Those cities which had survived the Roman conquest, were thenceforward secure from destruction; their gods would be still worshipped in their old temples; their houses were no longer liable to be laid in ruins by a victorius enemy; their people would not be massacred, made slaves, or scattered over the face of the earth, and their very name and memory extinguished. The Americans feel truly that, whatever may be the inconveniences of their federal union, it has still the inestimable advantage of banishing war from the whole of their vast continent; and this blessing was conferred on ancient Italy by the Roman dominion, and was so far even more valuable, as wars between independent states in the ancient world were far more frequent than now, and produced a far greater amount of human misery.

Again, the allies of Rome, while they escaped the worst miseries of war, were enabled by the great power of their confederacy to reap largely its advantages. In the plunder of Sicily the Italian allies and the Roman legions shared equally; and after the fourth Samnite war the Campanians received as their share of the spoil a large portion of the coast[9] of the Gulf of Salerno, which had formerly belonged to the Samnites. Individuals also amongst the allied states might enjoy the benefits of an occupation of the Roman domain land; a privilege which would naturally bind many of the wealthiest families throughout Italy to the Roman interest, some already possessing it, and others hoping to obtain it.

Hopes held out by it.

III. With these actual benefits the Roman dominion also held out hopes to its subjects of rising sooner or later to a higher political condition. The regular steps appear to have been, that an allied state should first receive the Roman franchise without the right of voting; and after the lapse of years these imperfect citizens gradually gained the full franchise, and were either formed into one or more new tribes, or were admitted into one of the tribes already existing. It is true that the first step in this process was generally an unwelcome one; because it involved, under ordinary circumstances, the forfeiture of all municipal independence, and the entire adoption of a foreign system of law. But there were cases in which it was stripped of these degradations, and became, as far as appears, a mere benefit: such seems to have been the condition of a large portion of the Campanians at the beginning of the second Punic war. Capua at that time was, beyond all doubt, municipally independent: it had its own laws and magistrates, and its own domain lands:[10] yet it is no less certain that the Campanian aristocracy, at any rate, were Roman citizens in all respects, except in the right of suffrage.[11] Other allied states might expect the same reward of their continued fidelity; and from this condition the advance to the full franchise was always to be looked for in the course of time; and would, in all probability, have been the reward of Capua itself, had the Campanians devoted

[9] This appears from the statement, that the Roman colonies of Salernum and Buxentum, founded after the second Punic war, were settled on land which had belonged to Capua. Livy, XXXIV. 45. As the coast of the Gulf of Salernum had originally belonged to the Samnites, we may conclude that the Campanians obtained it as their share of the spoil after the third or fourth Samnite war.

[10] Livy, XXIII. 3, foll. XXVIII. 46.

[11] Livy, VIII. 14. See Niebuhr, Vol. II. note 136.

their whole strength to the support of Rome after the battle of Cannæ, instead of opening their gates to Hannibal.

Its oppressiveness.

Living in such a state, with so much not taken from them, with so much given to them, and with the hope of one day obtaining so much more; and being further bound to their sovereigns by geographical position in all cases, and in most by something of an acknowledged affinity in race and language, the Roman allies had many inducements to acquiesce in their actual condition, and to regard themselves as united indissolubly with Rome, whether for better or for worse. But they had also much to bear; nor can we wonder if the descendants of C. Pontius, or Gellius Egnatius, or Stimius Statilius, or of the Calavii of Capua, should have thought life intolerable under the absolute dominion of that people, against whom their fathers had fought in equal rivalry. England, for many generations, upheld a system of domestic slavery in her colonies, while her own law so abhorred it, that any slave landed upon English ground became immediately a freeman. What the four seas were to England, that the line running round the city at the distance of a mile from the walls, was to Rome: it was the boundary between law and despotism. Within this precinct the sentences of the magistrates were the sentence of the law (*legitima judicia*); and their power was controlled by the sacred interposition of the tribunes. But without this limit all was absolute dominion, *imperium:* there the magistrate wielded the sword with full sovereignty; and judicial sentences were held to proceed not from the law, but from his personal power, so that their validity lasted in strictness no longer than the duration of his authority. Even Roman citizens had no present protection from this tyranny; they had only the resource of seeking for redress afterwards from the courts of Rome. But the allies had not even this relief, except in cases of extraordinary atrocity: for the imperium of the Roman magistrates conferred a plenitude of dominion over the persons and property of the subjects of Rome: any thing might be done on the plea of the service of the Roman people, or of maintaining the dignity of its officers; and the least opposition was held to be rebellion. Therefore, although barefaced robberies of private property were as yet mostly restrained by public opinion, which would not allow a magistrate to use his power for purposes of personal plunder; yet acts of insolence and cruelty, far more galling than any mere spoliations of property, were no doubt frequent from the very beginning of the Roman dominion over Italy, and arose partly out of the very position of the Roman officers with respect to the allies, and partly out of the inherent coarseness and arrogance of the Roman national character.

Differences in the condition of the allies.

Thus far we have considered the subjects or allies of Rome, in their relations to Rome generally, without noticing any differences in their condition which distinguished them more or less from each other; indeed, in that distant view of the sixth century of Rome, which is all that we are permitted to enjoy, these differences are scarcely perceptible; greatly as they must have affected the internal state of the Italian people, yet in their recorded outward movements we see scarcely any thing but the equal working of the Roman power, which all were alike obliged to obey. The treaties which fixed the relations of the several allied states with Rome, varied considerably in their conditions. Camerinum, in Umbria, and Heraclea, on the Ionian Sea, are noticed as having treated with the Romans on almost equal terms;[12] and Etruria, making peace at the very moment when Pyrrhus was advancing victoriously upon Rome, must surely have secured more favorable conditions than could be obtained by the exhausted Samnites and Lucanians, when in utter helplessness they submitted to their triumphant enemy. But we neither know what these differences were, nor, if we did, would the knowledge be of much importance, without much fuller

[12] Livy, XXVIII. 46. Camertes, quum æquo fœdere cum Romanis essent. On Heraclea, see Cicero pro Arch. c. 4.

information on the other points than we can now ever recover. One great distinction, however, claims the attention of the most general history,—that which separated all the other Italian allies from those of the Latin name.

When Mago brought to Carthage the tidings of the victory of Cannæ, and told the council how, not only the Bruttians and Apulians, but even some of the Lucanians and Samnites, and above all, the great city of Capua itself, had in consequence of it joined the Carthaginians, the leader of the party opposed to Hannibal is represented as asking, whether a single people of the Latin name had revolted, or a single citizen of the thirty-five tribes deserted to the enemy?[13] Unfaithfulness to Rome was thought to be not more impossible in her very citizens than in her Latin allies: Samnium and Capua might revolt; but the fidelity of the Latin name was never to be shaken. What, then, were the ties which bound the two nations together so indissolubly?

The Latin name.

In order to answer this question, we must first explain what was meant in the sixth century of Rome by the "Latin name." Now, if we remember that almost all the cities of ancient Latium were long since become Roman, so that scarcely any except Tibur and Præneste could any longer be included under the name of allies, we may wonder how the Latin name could still be spoken of as so powerful, or where could be found those eighty-five thousand Latins, who were returned as able to bear arms in the census of the great Gaulish war.[14]

Its extent.

The answer is, that the Latin name was now extended far beyond its old geographical limits, and was represented by a multitude of flourishing cities scattered over the whole of Italy, from the frontier of Cisalpine Gaul to the southern extremity of Apulia. The people of the Latin name in the sixth century of Rome were not the Tiburtines merely and the Prænestines,[15] but the inhabitants of Circeii and Ardea on the old coast of Latium, of Cora and Norba on the edge of the Volscian highlands, of Fregellæ and Interamna in the valley of the Liris, of Sutrium and Nepete under the Ciminian hills, of Cales, Suessa Aurunca, and Saticula on the edge of the Campanian plain, of Alba in the country of the Marsians, of Æsernia and Beneventum in the heart of Samnium, of Narnia and Spoletum in Umbria, of Luceria and Venusia in or close to the frontiers of Apulia, of Hadria and Firmum in Picenum, and finally of Brundisium, far to the south, where the Adriatic opens into the Ionian Sea, and of Ariminum on the frontiers of the Cisalpine Gauls, where the Apennines first leave the shores of the Adriatic, and make room for the vast plain of northern Italy.[16] All these states, with others which I have not noticed, formed the Latin name in the sixth century; not that they were Latins in their origin, or connected with the cities of the old Latium: on the contrary, they were by extraction Romans; they were colonies founded by the Roman people, and consisting of Roman citizens: but the Roman government had resolved, that in their political relations they should be considered, not as Romans, but as Latins; and the Roman settlers, in consideration of the advantages which they enjoyed as colonists, were content to descend politically to a lower condition than that which they had received as their birthright.

Privileges belonging to it.

The states of the Latin name, whether cities of old Latium or Roman colonies, all enjoyed their own laws and municipal government, like the other allies; and all were, like the other allies, subject to the sovereign dominion of the Romans. They were also so much regarded as foreigners, that they could not buy or inherit land from Roman citizens; nor had they generally the right of intermarriage with Romans. But they had two peculiar privileges: one, that any Latin who left behind him a son in his own city, to perpetuate his family there, might remove to Rome, and acquire the Roman franchise; the other, that every person who had held any magistracy or distinguished

[13] Livy, XXIII. 12.
[14] Polybius, II. 24.
[16] Livy, XXVII. 9, 10. Savigny, on the Jus Latii, in the Philological Museum, I. 56.

office in a Latin state, might become at once a Roman citizen. So that in this manner all the principal families in the Latin cities had a definite prospect assured to them of arriving in time at the rights of citizens of Rome.

Yet it is remarkable that when twelve of the Latin colonies, in the middle of the second Punic war, renounced the sovereignty of Rome, the consuls, in their remonstrance with them, are represented as appealing, not to their peculiar political privileges, but to their sense of duty and gratitude towards their mother-country. "They were originally Romans, settled on lands conquered by the Roman arms for the very purpose of rearing sons to do their country service; and whatever duties children owed to their parents, were owed by them to the commonwealth of Rome."[17] And as no age made a son, according to the Roman law, independent of his father, but entire obedience was ever due to him, without any respect of the greater or less benefits which the son might have received from his kindness, so the Romans thought that the allegiance of their colonies was not to depend on a sense of the advantages which their connection with Rome gave to them, but was a plain matter of duty. When they called on the Campanians not to desert them after the battle of Cannæ, they appealed to their gratitude for the boon of political or social privileges: "We gave you," they said, "the enjoyment of your own laws, and to a great proportion of your people we communicated the rights of our own franchise."[18] How different is this language from the simple admonition of the Latin colonies, "that they were the children of Rome, and should render to their parent a child's obedience!"

Its relation to Rome.

Yet the sense of filial duty might have been quickened in the Latin colonies by a recollection of what they owed to Rome, and how much of their political existence depended on her protection. The colonists of Beneventum and Æsernia, of Luceria and Spoletum, were not the only inhabitants of those cities: they had not been sent as settlers into a wilderness, where every work of man around them was to be their own creation. According to the Roman notions of a colony, they had been sent to occupy cities already built and inhabited, to enter into the possession of lands which man's labor had long since made productive. They were to be the masters and citizens of their new city and its territory, while the old inhabitants were to be their subjects, and strangers, as it were, in their own land. And as long as they remained true to their duties as Roman colonies, the power of Rome would maintain their dominion: but if Rome no longer upheld them, there was no slight danger of their being expelled by the old population of the colony, aided, as the latter would soon be, by their countrymen in the neighboring cities; and Beneventum and Æsernia would then no longer be Latin colonies, but return to their old condition of independent states of Samnium.

Condition of the Latin colonies.

It may be asked, however, why the Romans refused to their own colonies the private rights, at any rate, of Roman citizens; and as in some instances colonies of Roman citizens were founded, why was not this made the general rule, and why were the great majority of the colonies obliged to content themselves with the name and franchise of Latins? I do not believe that any existing ancient writer has answered this question directly; and the uncertain history of the early times of Rome embarrasses our conjectures. But it is probable that colonies founded during the equal alliance between Rome and Latium, such as Norba and Ardea, were properly Latin cities, to which the Latins sent colonists equally with the Romans; so that they did not belong exclusively to Rome. It is more difficult to understand why Sutrium and Nepete, colonies planted on the Etrurian frontier, and at a period when the old Latin alliance was virtually at an end, still received the Latin franchise, and not the Roman; and why Cales, and the other colonies founded after the great Latin war, were colonies, not of the Roman, but

[17] Livy, XXVII. 9. [18] Livy, XXIII. 5.

of the Latin name. We may suppose, perhaps, that in all these settlements the population of the colony was mixed from the beginning—colonists from Latin cities, some of which were always friendly to Rome, being amongst the original settlers; and after the Latin war, we may conceive that there were many Latins, whom, either as a reward or a precaution, the Romans may have been glad to establish in a colony out of their own country. We may understand also, that as the Roman colonists were often taken, not only from the class of poorer citizens, but also from the freedmen, the government would be glad to get them off from the roll of Roman citizens, which could only be done by their consenting to join a Latin colony, in consideration of its providing them with a grant of land. And generally, as the country of a Greek or a Roman was essentially a single city, it was natural that men leaving that city, and settling in another at a distance, should, in the common course of things, cease to be citizens of their old country. In the Greek colonies the connection was broken off altogether: but, as this would have defeated the very purpose for which Rome founded hers, it was not entirely severed, but exchanged for the relation of subject and sovereign, or, in the Roman language, of child and parent.

Subjects of Rome enjoying the lower franchise of the city, under the jurisdiction of præfects.

Besides the allies and the Latin name, there was yet a third class of Roman subjects, those who were Romans in their private rights, but not in their political, who possessed the rights of intermarriage, and of inheritance, or purchase of land by mancipation, *connubium* and *commercium*, but had no vote in the comitia, and were ineligible to all public offices of authority. This condition, although it was often a preparatory step to receiving the full Roman franchise, was yet in itself considered far inferior to that of the allies or of the Latin name, inasmuch as it implied the complete forfeiture of all a nation's laws and institutions, and a complete adoption of the laws and customs of Rome. It was a natural consequence of this state, that it did away all municipal government. A people thus become subject to Rome had properly no magistrates of its own; such public officers as it still retained had merely an honorary office: they were to superintend the sacrifices, preside at festivals, and direct other matters of pageantry and ceremonial. The administration of justice was vested in the hands of a præfect sent from Rome; and districts so governed were properly called præfectures. These præfectures were probably very numerous all over Italy; for the magistrates of the cities had no jurisdiction beyond the city walls; and even in the territories of the colonies themselves the country district was called a præfecture, although in these cases the præfect was not sent from Rome, but appointed by the colony. It is possible that this may explain what otherwise seems so puzzling, the application of the terms præfectura and municipium to the same places, and that too in cases where municipium undoubtedly expresses the existence of a municipal government, as at Cumæ, Fundi, and Formiæ.[19] In these instances the towns were municipia, and had their own magistrates; but the country around them may have been a præfecture; and the præfect was not appointed, as in the colonies, by the government of what may be called its local capital, but was sent immediately from Rome.

Various tenures of land.

This intermixture of different kinds of government, within the same geographical limits, may lead us to consider another point of some importance: the variety of the tenures of land which the Roman conquest had introduced into every part of Italy; so that in each separate country, for instance in Etruria, Umbria, Samnium, or Lucania, as there were great differences of political condition, so also was there the greatest diversity in the tenures of property. There might be found everywhere three sorts of land,—1st, Land held by the old inhabitants, whether it had never been forfeited, or, if forfeited at the period of their conquest, formally restored to them by the Roman

[19] Festus, v. Præfecturæ.

government; 2dly, Land held by a Roman or Latin colony, by grant from the Roman people; and 3dly, Land still held by the Roman people as domain, whether it was let or farmed by the government, or was in the occupation of individuals, whether Romans, Latins, or Italians of other nations. We have no Domesday-book of Italy remaining, which would enable us to determine the relative proportion of these three kinds of land; but the amount of the third kind, or domain land, was absolutely enormous; for the Roman people retained their full right of property, as we have seen before, in all land occupied (possessus) by individuals; whereas a large proportion of the manors which Domesday-book records as belonging to the crown, when granted, as they soon were, to private persons, ceased to be domain, and became to all intents and purposes private property. Thus in England, and in other countries of modern Europe, the domain lands have become gradually less and less extensive; but as at Rome nothing could alienate them except a regular assignation, and as various circumstances from time to time added to their amount, on the whole their extent went on increasing rather than diminishing; and we are astonished at the vast proportion of domain land belonging to the commonwealth, even at the end of the seventh century, all of which would have come within the disposal of a general agrarian law.

Effects of the domain land on the state of Italy.

The later effects of these enormous tracts of domain land are well known, and will require our notice hereafter. But from the beginning they must have greatly injured the spirit and life of Italy. The whole spring of social and civil activity in the ancient world lay in its cities; and domain land and cities could not exist together. Towns, therefore, which had been taken at the first conquest of the country, and their inhabitants massacred or sold for slaves, becoming in many instances the domain of the conqueror, were condemned to perpetual desolation. Their old population was dispersed or destroyed; and the wealthy Roman, who became the occupant of their territory, allowed a large part of it perhaps to lie waste, and settled the slaves whom he employed in cultivating the remainder, rather in farm buildings or workhouses in the country, than in the houses of the old town. Thus a scanty and scattered slave population succeeded in the place of those numerous free cities, which, small as they were, yet well answered the great object of civil society, in bringing out at once the faculties and affections of mankind; while by the frequent interposition of these large and blank districts, the free towns which were left became more isolated, and their resources diminished, because they too had lost a part of their territory to the conqueror. The larger cities had in many instances become Latin colonies, and were lost to their old nation: and thus, when the Samnites joined Hannibal, it was like the insurrection of a peasantry, where all the fortresses are in possession of the enemy. Beneventum and Æserina, the principal cities remaining in Samnium, were Latin colonies, or in other words Roman garrisons; the Samnite towns were all inconsiderable; and as soon as Hannibal's protection was withdrawn, the first Roman army which invaded the country recovered them almost without resistance.

Many questions might be asked concerning the state of Italy, to which the above sketch contains no answer. Many, indeed, I could not answer satisfactorily; and the discussion of doubtful points of law or antiquities, where the greatest men have been unable to arrive at any certain conclusions, seems to me to encumber history, rather than illustrate it. Some points I have forborne to notice at present, because their bearing on the general course of the story is not yet manifest. I have wished, not to write an essay on the condition of ancient Italy in the abstract, but to connect my notices of it with the history of the period, that this chapter may catch some portion of the interest attached to Hannibal's great invasion; whilst it may render the narrative of that invasion more intelligible, and may enable me to pursue it with fewer interruptions.

Meantime we must follow the course of events abroad and at home, through the two-and-twenty years which still separate us from the beginning of the expedition of Hannibal.

CHAPTER XLII.

GENERAL HISTORY FROM THE FIRST TO THE SECOND PUNIC WAR—ILLYRIAN WAR—GREAT GAULISH INVASION—MUSTER OF THE FORCES OF ALL ITALY—DEFEAT OF THE GAULS—ROMAN INVASIONS OF CISALPINE GAUL—M. MARCELLUS AND C. FLAMINIUS. A. U. C. 513 TO 535. A. C. 241 TO 219.

Eminent Romans of this period.

ALREADY at the end of the first Punic war some eminent Romans were in their full manhood, whose names are enduringly associated with the events of the second. Q. Fabius Maximus, the great dictator, "who by his caution saved the Roman state," was consul eight years after the conclusion of the treaty with Carthage; Q. Fulvius Flaccus, the conqueror and butcher of Capua, obtained his first consulship four years earlier, in the year 517; and M. Claudius Marcellus, the conqueror of Syracuse, must have been thirty years old at the end of the first Punic war, had already won honors by his personal prowess as a soldier in Sicily, and had held the office of curule ædile. The earliest Roman historians, C. Fabius Pictor, and L. Cincius Alimentus, must have been at this time old enough to retain some impression of things around them; Nævius, the earliest known Roman poet, had served in the last war in Sicily; Livius Andronicus, the oldest dramatist, brought his first piece upon the stage in the very year after the conclusion of the war. Hannibal himself, whose genius was to be the mover and controller of the future invasion of Italy, was already born; but he was as yet an innocent child, only six years old, playing in his father's house at Carthage.

A. U. C. 513. A. C. 241.

State of Rome after the war.

The transition from war to peace, which we remember five or six and twenty years ago, after a contest of very nearly the same length as the first Punic war, brought rather an increase than an abatement of embarrassment. A great stimulant was withdrawn; but a great burden remained to be borne; and the end is not yet manifest. But no sooner do the marks of battles pass away from the fields where they were fought, than the effects even of an exhausting war were shaken off in ancient times by nations not yet fallen into decline; because wars in those days were not maintained at the expense of posterity. The sole debt which Rome had contracted had been incurred for the building of her last fleet; and this could be paid off immediately by the Carthaginian contributions. Population repairs its losses with wonderful rapidity; and to the dominions which the Romans had possessed before the war, was now added the greatest portion of Sicily. Q. Lutatius, the brother and successor of the consul who had won the decisive victory of the Ægates, passed the whole summer of his consulship in Sicily after the conclusion of the peace, and settled the future condition of the Roman part of the island.[1] Sicily was the earliest Roman province; and in it was first exhibited that remarkable system of provincial government, which was gradually extended over so large a part of the ancient world. The peculiar character of this system did not consist in the absolute dominion of the Roman magistrates; for their power was no less uncontrolled in Italy itself, everywhere beyond the immediate precinct of Rome, than it could be in the provinces. But the nations of Italy, like the allies of Lacedæmon, aided the sovereign state with their arms, and paid no tribute; while the provinces were disarmed, like the allies of Athens, and served their sovereign with their money, and not with their men. Hence the perpetual difference in Roman law between land in Italy and land in the provinces; that the former

[1] Zonaras, VIII. 17.

might be held by individuals as their freehold, and was liable to no payments of tithe or land tax; while the property of the latter was vested solely in the Roman people. When we hear that a Sicilian state had its forfeited lands restored to it,[2] this means only that they were restored subjected to the sovereign rights of the conqueror; and therefore they were still burdened with the payment of tithes, as an acknowledgment that they were not held by their possessors in full property.

Sources of wealth opened to the farmers of the revenues.

No sooner was the provincial system established in Sicily, than the moneyed men of Rome, the famous Publicani, began to flock over to the island to farm the tithes and the various other revenues which came in from a province to the Roman people. Then were opened all those sources of acquiring wealth at the expense of the provincials, which rich or influential Roman citizens drained so unsparingly. Many Sicilian states were hindered from buying land in each other's territories;[3] but the Roman could purchase everywhere; and competition being thus restricted, he was enabled to purchase at greater advantage. If any state, or any individual in it, had sustained losses which disabled them from paying what they owed to the government at the appointed time, a wealthy Roman was always ready to lend them money; and as the Roman law of interest did not extend to the provinces, he lent it on his own terms, and availed himself of the necessities of the borrower to the utmost. Even in common commercial transactions the Roman merchant in the provinces came into the market with great advantages. If he wished to buy, a provincial would often be afraid to bid against him: if he sold at a high price, the provincial dealers in the same commodity would be afraid to undersell him. The money thus gained by Roman citizens in the provinces gave them influence at Rome; and this again made their friendship or enmity of importance to the Roman provincial governors. Thus they were armed not only with the general authority of the Roman name, but with the direct countenance and support of the Roman magistrates; and those magistrates held the lives and properties of the provincials at their absolute disposal.

Two new tribes, raising the number to thirty-five.

While the wealthy had these means afforded them of becoming more wealthy, the end of a long war seemed a fit season for rewarding the faithful services of some of the poorer citizens, and of the subjects of the commonwealth I have already noticed the large assignation of lands which took place somewhere about this period, and for the direction of which no fewer than fifteen commissioners were appointed. And the censors of the year 513 created two new tribes of Roman citizens, the Quirinian and the Velinian,[4] containing, as the names show, the Sabines of the neighborhood of Cures and of the valley of the Velinus, and the people possibly of some other towns and districts also. These new tribes raised the whole number of tribes to thirty-five: and none were ever added afterwards. Nearly sixty years had elapsed since the last creation of two tribes, the Aniensian and Terentine, between the second and third Samnite wars. But before another period of sixty years could elapse, Hannibal's invasion had so changed the state of Italy and of the Roman people, that the old practice was never again repeated: and thus the Roman tribes remained fixed at the number of thirty-five, rather from accident, as I believe, than from deliberate design.

Destruction of agricultural laborers supplied by slaves.

But the remedy in human affairs is seldom commensurate with the evil. Neither the assignation of lands by the fifteen commissioners, nor the grant of the full Roman franchise to a portion of the Sabine people, could compensate to Italy for the wide destruction of the poorest classes of free citizens occasioned by the naval losses of the first Punic war. "The Romans," says Polybius,[5] "lost in battle and by shipwreck, in the course of the war, no fewer than 700 quinqueremes." They lost besides, at one

[2] Cicero in Verrem, III. 6.
[3] Cicero in Verrem, II. 50, III. 40.
[4] Livy, Epitom. XIX.
[5] I. 63.

time, nearly 800 corn ships in the great storm which wrecked the two fleets ot L. Junius, on the south coast of Sicily, in the year 505. Now the seamen, as is well known, were taken exclusively from the poorest class of freemen; from those who, in many instances no doubt, like the corresponding class in Greece, lived only by their labor; who in Etruria, especially, and elsewhere, resembled the Coloni, so well known from the law books of the latter empire, a class of men humble and dependent, but not slaves. As the war drained this class more and more, it had at the same time supplied the slave market beyond all former example. Nor did the supply cease with the war against Carthage; for several years afterwards we read of expeditions against the Ligurians, Sardinians, oı Corsicans:[6] and every expedition brought off slaves as a part of its plunder. "Sardinians for sale"[7] became a proverb to express any thing of the least possible value; and the Corsicans were a race so brutish, according to the judgment of the slave dealers of the Augustan age, that they would fetch only the smallest price in the market.[8] These poor wretches therefore would not pay the expense of carrying them to the distant markets of Greece or Asia: they must be sold at home; and their purchasers would commonly be the holders of large estates of domain land, who employed them there in the place of free laborers. Thus began that general use of slave labor in Italy, which in the course of a hundred years had in some places almost extirpated the free population.

War with the Faliscans.

At the end of the summer of 513, the consul Q. Lutatius returned home from the settlement of Sicily: but before he went out of office in the following spring, both he and his colleague, A. Manlius, were obliged to employ the whole force of the commonwealth against an enemy scarcely thirty miles distant from the walls of Rome. These enemies were the Faliscans, or people of Falerii:[9] a name which has not been heard of in Roman history for more than a hundred and fifty years; when it is said that the four new tribes created after the recovery of Rome from the Gauls, in the year 368, were composed partly out of the inhabitants of the territory of Falerii. What could tempt a single city to brave the power of Rome at a period when there was no foreign war to make a diversion in its favor, we know not, and can scarcely conjecture. But the Romans thought the example so dangerous, that they exerted their whole force to put an immediate stop to it; and in six days the Faliscans, after a desperate resistance, were obliged to submit at discretion. They were forced to surrender all their arms, horses, and movable property, and half of their domain land: their city was destroyed; and they were removed to another spot less strongly situated; a condition similar to that which had been imposed on the people of Volsinii, four-and-twenty years earlier. For this conquest both consuls obtained a triumph.

Employments during three years of peace.

With the exception of this six days' war, the three years which followed the treaty with Carthage were to Rome a period of perfect peace. While the Carthaginians in Africa were struggling for their existence against their revolted subjects and their rebellious mercenary soldiers, the Roman annals record nothing but friendly embassies, works of internal improvement, new festivals, and new kinds of amusement. Ambassadors were sent to Ptolemy Euergetes, king of Egypt, to offer him the aid of Rome against the king of Syria;[10] but it was declined with thanks, as the war was already at an end. A carriage road was made to the top of the Aventine by the ædiles, L. and M. Publicius, with the fines which they had recovered from persons convicted of pasturing their cattle illegally on the domains of the commonwealth: with another portion of these same fines was defrayed the expense of the games of

[6] Zonaras, VIII. 18.

[7] Sardi venales. Aurelius Victor, de Vir. Ill. c. LVII. attributes the origin of this saying to the time of the conquest of Sardinia by Tiberius Gracchus.

[8] Strabo, V. p. 224.

[9] Livy, Epitom. XIX. Zonaras, VIII. 18. Polybius, I. 65. Eutropius, II. 28. Orosius, IV. 11.

[10] Eutropius, III. 1.

Flora,[11] now for the first time instituted, and celebrated from henceforward every year, beginning on the 28th of April: and in 514, as I have already mentioned, the first regular drama was exhibited at Rome by L. Livius Andronicus.[12] It may be noticed as a curious coincidence, that the next year, 515, witnessed the birth of Q. Ennius, who may be called the father of the existing poetry of the Latin language.

This season of peace appears to have infused a spirit of unwonted moderation and honesty into the Roman councils. Some Italian vessels carrying corn to the African rebels were interrupted by the Carthaginians, and the crews thrown into prison.[13] The Romans sent an embassy to require their liberation, which the Carthaginians granted; and this ready compliance so gratified the Roman government, that they released without ransom all the Carthaginian prisoners still left in their hands, permitted supplies of all kinds to be carried to Africa for the use of the Carthaginians, while they strictly forbade all traffic with the rebels; and even, it is said, allowed the Carthaginians to levy soldiers in their dominions; that is, to enlist, as they had been wont in times long past, Lucanian, or Samnite, or Bruttian mercenaries. Nor was this all; for when the mercenaries in Sardinia revolted from Carthage, and called in the Romans to their aid, their request was not listened to; and when the people of Utica, dreading the vengeance of the Carthaginians, offered to give themselves up to Rome, the Romans rejected this offer also.

Friendly relations with Carthage.

But when Hamilcar's genius had delivered his country from its extreme peril, when the rebel mercenaries were destroyed, and when Utica and the other revolted towns and people of Africa had been obliged to submit at discretion, when perhaps also rumors were already abroad of Hamilcar's intended expedition to Spain, then the jealousy of the Romans seems to have revived, and their whole conduct towards Carthage underwent a total change. The mercenaries of Sardinia, after having revolted from Carthage, and applied at that time vainly for the aid of the Romans, were overpowered by the natives and obliged to fly from the island.[14] They took refuge in Italy, and had probably never ceased soliciting the Roman government to espouse their quarrel, and take possession of Sardinia for themselves. But now the Romans began to listen to them; and it was resolved to send over a fleet to Sardinia to restore them. The Carthaginians meanwhile, having recovered their dominion in Africa, were proceeding to reduce the revolted islands; and an armament was prepared to attack Sardinia. Then the Romans complained that the Carthaginians, while employing their fleet to prevent the African rebels from receiving supplies by sea, had committed many outrages upon Roman subjects sailing to and from Africa; that this had manifested their hostile feeling towards Rome; and that the armament, prepared ostensibly for the recovery of Sardinia, was intended to attack Italy. Accordingly, the senate and people passed a resolution for war with Carthage. The Carthaginians, utterly unable to engage in a new contest, offered any terms for the sake of peace; and the Romans not only obliged them to make a formal cession of Sardinia, but required them to pay 1200 talents, in addition to the sum stipulated by the last treaty, as a compensation for the injuries sustained by the Roman merchants, and a penalty for their meditated aggression.[15] Hamilcar advised compliance with these demands; but he hastened, no doubt, with tenfold eagerness, the preparations for his expedition to Spain.

Beginning of new disputes.

A. U. C. 516. A. C. 238.

When all was ready, the general performed a solemn sacrifice, to propitiate the gods for the success of his enterprise.[16] The omens were declared favorable; Hamilcar had poured the libation on the victim, which

Hannibal's vow.

[11] Ovid, Fast. V. 279-294. Festus, v. Publicius.
[12] Cicero, Tusc. Quæst. I. 1. Brut. 18.
[13] Polybius, I. 83.
[14] Polybius, I. 29.
[15] Polybius, I. 88. Appian de Reb. Punic. c. 5.
[16] Polybius, III. 11.

was duly offered on the altar, when on a sudden he desired all his officers, and the ministers of the sacrifice, to step aside to a little distance, and then called his son Hannibal. Hannibal, a boy of nine years old, went up to his father, and Hamilcar asked him kindly, if he would like to go with him to the war. The boy eagerly caught at the offer, and with a child's earnestness implored his father to take him. Then Hamilcar took him by the hand, and led him up to the altar, and bade him, if he wished to follow his father, lay his hand upon the sacrifice, and swear "that he would never be the friend of the Romans." Hannibal swore, and never to his latest hour forgot his vow. He went forth devoted to his country's gods as the appointed enemy and destroyer of their enemies; and the thought of his high calling dwelt ever on his mind, directing and concentrating the spirit and enthusiasm of his youth, and mingling with it the forecast, the great purposes, and the deep and unwavering resolution of the maturest manhood.

Renewed disputes with Carthage.

This story of his solemn vow was told by Hannibal himself many years afterwards to Antiochus, king of Syria; but, at the time, it was heard by no other ears than his father's; and when he sailed with Hamilcar to Spain, none knew that he went with any feelings beyond the common light-hearted curiosity of a child. But the Romans viewed Hamilcar's expedition with alarm, and were probably well aware that he would brook his country's humiliation only so long as he was unable to avenge it. More than once they renewed their complaints that the Carthaginians annoyed their merchants at sea, and that they were intriguing with the Sardinians, to excite them to revolt from Rome. A fresh sum of money was paid by Carthage; but the complaints still continued; and the Romans, for the second time it is said, passed a resolution for war. Embassy after embassy was sent to Rome by the Carthaginian government, to deprecate a renewal of the contest;[17] and at last ten of the principal members of the council of elders were appointed ambassadors, if perhaps their rank and dignity might at once move the Romans to pity, and inspire confidence in the peaceful intentions of Carthage. Still the Romans were for a long time inexorable; till Hanno, the youngest of the ambassadors, and, if he was, as is probable, the famous opponent of Hannibal, himself sincerely inclined to maintain the peace, remonstrated with the senate plainly and boldly. "If you will not have peace with us," he said, "then give us back Sardinia and Sicily; for we yielded them to you, not to purchase a brief truce, but your lasting friendship."[18] Then the Romans were persuaded; and the treaty of peace was again renewed and ratified. This was in the year of Rome 519, in the consulship of T. Manlius Torquatus and C. Atilius Bulbus. It was, apparently, to assure the Carthaginians that the peace thus ratified was to be sincere and lasting, that the old ceremony of shutting the gates of Janus was now performed;[19] for the first time, it was said, since the reign of King Numa; for the last time also until they were closed by Augustus after his conquest of Egypt.

A. U. C. 519. A. C. 235.

A. U. C. 521. A. C. 233. Divers wars.

But in this very year, as well as for several years before and after it, the Roman arms found employment against barbarian enemies in Sardinia, in Corsica, in Liguria, and in Cisalpine Gaul.[20] These wars served to exercise the citizens in arms, to furnish the consuls with an occasion of triumphs, and to bring fresh multitudes of slaves into Italy. Q. Fabius Maximus, afterwards so famous, was consul for the first time in 521, and obtained a triumph for his victories over the Ligurians.[21]

Twelve years after the end of the first Punic war, and six after the solemn confirmation of the treaty, a Roman army was sent, for the first time, across the Ionian

[17] Zonaras, VIII. 18. Orosius, IV. 12.
[18] Dion Cassius, Fragm. Ursin. CL.
[19] Eutropius, III. 3. Orosius, IV. 12.
[20] For the wars in Corsica and Sardinia, see Zonaras, VIII. 28; Livy, Epit. XX.; Valerius Maximus, VI. 3, § 3; Eutropius, III. 3. For the war in Liguria, Dion Cassius, Fragm. Peiresc. XLV.; and for that in Cisalpine Gaul, Polybius, II. 21.
[21] Plutarch, Fabius, 2.

The Romans cross the Adriatic.

gulf. More than forty years had now passed since the death of Pyrrhus; his family in the second generation had become extinct; and the Epirots were governing themselves without a king. But their power had sunk almost to nothing; and the only name now dreaded in those parts was that of the Illyrians.

The Illyrians.

The various tribes of the Illyrian nation occupied the whole eastern coast of the Adriatic, from its most northern extremity to its mouth. Their extent inland can scarcely be determined: in the later Roman geography, the name of Illyricum was applied to the whole country between Macedonia and the Danube,[22] while the early Greek writers distinguished the Illyrians from the Pæonians or Pannonians, and appear to have confined the Illyrian name to the tract of country more or less narrow where the streams flow into the Adriatic; and placed other nations, the Triballians, Pæonians, and Thracians, in the country beyond the watershed, where the streams run northward to the Danube. In truth, all these nations were probably connected with each other; and their language, if it belonged, as seems likely, to the Sclavonic branch of the great Indo-Germanic family, was not wholly foreign either to the Hellenic, spoken on their southern borders, or to the various dialects of Italy, from which they are so little distant on their western frontier. The Illyrians on the Adriatic coast, and on the western border of Upper Macedonia, were held by the Greeks in great respect for their courage; but, like most barbarians, they loved to maintain themselves by plunder instead of labor; and the innumerable harbors along their coast tempted them to plunder by sea rather than by land. Seventy years before this, they were already formidable to all who navigated the Adriatic: but now, since the fall of the Epirot power, the coast to the southward lay unprotected; and their vessels made frequent plundering descents, not only on Epirus, but even on the western shores of Peloponnesus, on Elis, and on Messenia. This brought them more in the way of the merchant ships of Italy, which were engaged in traffic with Greece and the East; and complaints of the Illyrian piracies had been frequently brought before the Roman government.

A. U. C. 525. A. C. 229.

These were for a time neglected, but at last they became more numerous and pressing; and they were further supported by the people of the island of Issa, a Greek colony, who, being attacked by the Illyrians, sent to implore the protection of the Romans.

Ambassadors sent to Illyria put to death.

The senate accordingly sent, as was its custom, three ambassadors to Illyria, to learn the state of the Illyrian power,[23] and to find out what friends the Romans would be likely to have within the country itself, if they should have occasion to declare war. The ambassadors found the king of the Illyrians dead; and his widow, Teuta, as the Illyrian law permitted, was governing in the name of her step-son, Pinnes, who was still a child. At the moment when the ambassadors arrived, the Illyrian queen was besieging Issa, and was highly elated with the recent success of her fleet, which had returned loaded with spoil from a plundering expedition against Epirus. She was in no mood therefore to brook the peremptory language always used by Roman ambassadors; and one of the three so offended her, that she sent one of her ships after them on their return home, to seize them. Two of them were killed, and the third was brought to the queen, and thrown into prison.[24]

War with the Illyrians.

The Romans, without delay, declared war against the Illyrians, and both consuls, Cn. Fulvius Centumalus and L. Postumius Albinus, were sent across the Adriatic with a fleet and army such as had rarely been seen in those parts. As usual, they found allies within the country; Deme-

[22] Zonaras, VIII. 19. Appian, Illyr. I.

[23] Polybius, II. 8. Dion, Fragm. Ursin. CLI. Zonaras, VIII. 19.

[24] Polybius, II. 8, gives Caius and Lucius Coruncancius as the names of the ambassadors. Pliny, XXXIV. 11, says that statues (*tripedaneæ*) were raised by the republic to P. Junius and Titus Coruncancius, who were killed by Teuta, queen of the Illyrians. "Hoc a republica tribui solebat injuria cæsis."

trius, a Greek of the island of Pharos, who was holding Corcyra for the Illyrian queen, surrendered it at once to the Roman fleet,[25] and guided the consuls in all their subsequent operations. A Roman fleet of two hundred quinqueremes, and a regular consular army of 22,000 men, were, as opposed to the piratical barks and robber soldiery of Queen Teuta, like a giant amongst pigmies. Town after town, and tribe after tribe, yielded to them, and Teuta, having taken refuge in Rhizon, which was almost her last remaining stronghold, was glad to obtain peace on the conqueror's terms. The greater part of her former dominion was bestowed on Demetrius; she was to pay a fixed tribute to the Romans, and was never to allow more than two of her ships together, and these not armed vessels, to sail to the south of the port of Lissus, the last place in the Illyrian dominions.[26] In the course of this short war, not only Corcyra, but Apollonia also, and Epidamnus, submitted to the Romans at discretion, and received their liberty, as was afterwards the fate of all Greece, as a gift from the Roman people.

Roman embassies into Greece.

The Illyrian war having been settled rather by the Roman fleet than by the army, Cn. Fabius, who had commanded the fleet, returned home alone to obtain a triumph; while his colleague, L. Postumius, was left with a small force at Corcyra. He sent ambassadors to the Ætolians and the Archæan league, to explain the grounds on which the Romans had crossed the sea, and to read the treaty which had been concluded with the Illyrians. As all the Greeks had suffered from or dreaded the Illyrian piracies, the Roman ambassadors had met with a most friendly reception, and were welcomed as the benefactors of Greece. Soon afterwards the Romans sent other embassies to Corinth and to Athens, with no other object, so far as appears, than of introducing themselves to some of the most illustrious states of the Greek name, which many of the Romans had already learnt to admire. At Corinth they received the solemn thanks of the Corinthians for the services they had rendered to the Greek nation; and the Romans were allowed to take part in the Isthmian games, as if they were acknowledged to have some connection with the Hellenian race.[27] The Athenians, it is said, went further, granted to the Roman people the honorary franchise of Athenian citizens, and admitted them to the Eleusinian mysteries. That this honor was not despised by the highest Roman nobility may be concluded from the fact, that A. Manlius Torquatus, who was censor in 506, and consul in 509 and 512, has the surname of Atticus, in the Capitoline Fasti, a name borne, so far as we know, by no other member of his family, either before or afterwards.

Death of Hamilcar.

Nearly about the time when the consuls, Cn. Fulvius and L. Postumius, left Rome on their expedition to Illyria, the Romans must have heard the tidings of the death of Hamilcar. From his first landing in Spain he had advanced with uninterrupted success, training his army in this constant warfare with the bravest of barbarians, and gaining fresh popularity and influence both at home and with his soldiers, by his free distribution of his spoils; spoils not to be estimated by the common poverty of barbarians, but rich in silver and gold, the produce of the still abundant mines of Spain. In the ninth year of his command he had reached the Tagus, when he was killed in a battle with the Vettonians, a tribe who dwelt between the Tagus and the Douro, and was succeeded by his son-in-law, Hasdrubal.[28]

Hasdrubal's progress in Spain. Measures taken by the Romans to check him.

The work which Hamilcar had begun by the sword, was continued and consolidated by the policy of his successor. Hasdrubal was one of those men who are especially fitted to exercise an ascendency over the minds of barbarians;[29] his personal appearance was engaging; he understood the habits and feelings of the Spaniards, and spared no pains to

[25] Polybius, II. 11.
[26] Polybius, II. 12.
[27] Polybius, II. 12. Zonaras, VIII. 19.
[28] Polybius, II. 1. Zonaras, VIII. 19. Nepos, Diodor. Ecl. lib. XXV.
[29] Polybius, II. 13, 36. Appian, VI. 4, 6.

accommodate himself to them. Thus the native princes, far and near, sought his friendship, and were eager to become the allies of Carthage; while by the foundation of New Carthage, or Carthagena, a place possessing one of the best harbors in the Mediterranean, and naturally strong on the land side, he was enabled to command the heart of Spain, from a position close at hand, instead of beginning his operations from a distant corner of the country, like Gades. The Romans observed his progress with no small alarm; but their dread of an approaching Gaulish invasion made them unwilling to provoke a war at this moment with Carthage. They endeavored therefore to secure themselves by treaty, and concluded a convention with Hasdrubal, by which he bound himself not to extend his conquests to the north of the Iberus or Ebro[30] By this stipulation the Romans hoped to keep him at a sufficient distance, not from Italy only, but from their old allies, the people of Massalia, some of whose colonies had been founded south of the Pyrenees, along the coast of what is now Catalonia. Nor were they abandoning to him the whole country southward of the Iberus; for they had lately formed an alliance with the Saguntines, a people partly of Greek, or at any rate not of Spanish extraction, who lived near the coast between the Iberus and the Sucro, and who, in their fear of the Carthaginian power, had put themselves under the protection of Rome.[31] The treaty concluded with Hamilcar, at the end of the first Punic war, had contained a clause forbidding either of the contracting parties to molest the allies of the other;[32] Saguntum, therefore, was safe from attack; and the Romans hoped, no doubt, to secure their footing in Spain through its means, and from thence, so soon as the Gaulish war was over, to sap the newly formed dominion of Carthage, by offering their aid to all the native tribes who might wish to escape from it.

A. U. C. 526. A. C. 228.

But these hopes and fears for their dominion in Spain were overpowered at present by a nearer anxiety, the dread of a Gaulish invasion. The Cisalpine Gauls had for the last ten years resumed their old hostile dispositions, which before that time had slumbered for nearly forty-five years, since their great defeat by the consul Q. Æmilius Papus, two years before the invasion of Pyrrhus.[33] In that interval they had seen two Roman colonies founded on the land which had formerly been theirs; Sena, immediately after the war,[34] and Ariminum, about fourteen years afterwards, or four years before the beginning of the war with Carthage. But neither of these occupations of what they must have considered their own land, provoked them, as it seems, to attack the Romans; and they remained quiet through the whole of the first Punic war, when the Romans, engaged year after year in Sicily, would have resisted them at the greatest disadvantage. But three years after the peace with Carthage, we find the Roman consuls invading the territory of the Gauls. It is difficult to believe that these renewed hostilities were wholly owing, as Polybius says,[35] to the innate restlessness of the Gaulish character, and to the rising up of a new generation who had forgotten the defeats of their fathers. But this new generation must have been ready for war at least ten years earlier; and their impatience would scarcely have waited so long only to break forth at last when the favorable opportunity was over.

Threatenings of an invasion by the Gauls.

The Cisalpine Gauls called in their brethren from beyond the Alps to aid them; but these new-comers excited jealousies; and on one occasion there was a regular battle fought between them and the Cisalpine Gauls, with such slaughter on both sides as relieved the Romans from all present danger.[36] But afterwards, in the year 521, when Fabius Maximus was for the first time consul, an agrarian law was proposed and carried by C. Fla-

Preparations of the Gauls for war.

[30] Polybius, II. 13. III. 27, 9.
[31] Polybius, III. 15, 21, 30.
[32] Polybius, III. 21.
[33] A. U. C. 472. Chap. XXXVII. p. 390 of this history.
[34] Polybius, II. 19. [35] II. 21.
[36] Polybius, II. 21.

minius, one of the tribunes, for a general assignation of the land between Ariminum and Sena,[37] a measure which not only ejected, perhaps, many of the old Gaulish inhabitants, who had still been suffered to enjoy their former possessions, but seemed an earnest of the intention of the Romans to extirpate the Gauls altogether from every portion of Gaulish territory which the fortune of war might hereafter give them. Accordingly, there was now a unanimous cry amongst the Gauls for war, and for obtaining the aid of their Transalpine countrymen. Their preparations were made with unusual patience; there was no premature movement; but they endeavored to provide themselves with money, of which they had none of their own, by selling various commodities, wool and hides, and, above all, captive slaves, to merchants who would pay for them in gold and silver.[38] Thus they were enabled to engage the services of a large body of Transalpine Gauls, whom they tempted besides with the prospect of a permanent settlement in Italy; whilst the Romans, knowing full well that the storm was gathering, yet unwilling to provoke it by commencing hostilities, were kept year after year in a state of anxious preparation, till the invasion at last, as it seems, actually burst upon them unexpectedly.

A. U. C. 528. A. C. 226.

Superstitious terrors.

In this state of suspense, superstitious terrors possessed men's minds readily. The Capitol was struck with lightning, an unwonted prodigy; and the Sibylline books were consulted in consequence. The books said, "When the lightning shall strike the Capitol and the temple of Apollo, then must thou, O Roman, beware of the Gauls."[39] And another prophecy said that a time should come "when the race of the Greeks and the race of the Gauls should occupy the Forum of Rome." It is characteristic of superstition to transfer to its idols that mockery of truth which itself so delights in, and to believe that they care not for wickedness, if it be done to promote their service. A man and woman of the Gaulish race, with a Greek man and woman, were buried alive in the Forum Boarium, that the prophecy might be fulfilled in word, and might, so the Romans hoped, be proved to be in spirit a lie.[39]

Revolt of Sardinia.

It was the spring of the year 529, and the consuls chosen were L. Æmilius Papus and C. Atilius Regulus, son of that Regulus who had been so famous in the first Punic war. The Transalpine Gauls had not yet crossed the Alps; and, on the other hand, tidings arrived that the Sardinians, impatient of the dominion of a Roman prætor, to which they had now, for the first time, been made regularly subject, had broken out into a general revolt. Accordingly, C. Regulus, with one consular army, was sent over to Sardinia to put down the revolt.[40]

Preparations for the great Gaulish war.

He was already arrived in his province, when the Transalpine Gauls, on the first melting of the snows, crossed the Alps; and the Cisalpine Gauls, joining them with all their own disposable forces, the invasion of Italy was no longer delayed. The alarm was given at Rome; and then was seen with what vast power and energy the Roman government could meet an emergency of real danger. The whole free population of Italy, of an age to bear arms, was reported to Rome in the returns of the census of the several states; and in a contest with barbarians such as the Gauls, every state and every man could be depended on; for no evil could equal the victory of such an enemy. Thus knowing the whole extent of its resources, the government prepared accordingly its active armies, and its armies of reserve, while every important city was duly provisioned, and provided with

A. U. C. 527. A. C. 227.

[37] Cicero, De Senectute, c. 4, places this law in 526, when Q. Fabius, *consul iterum*, C. Flaminio, quoad potuit, restitit, agrum Picentem et Gallicum viritim contra senatus auctoritatem dividenti. But from Polybius, II. 21, it appears that the law was carried into effect by M. Lepidus, who was consul in 523; so that it must have been passed in the previous year, when Fabius was consul along with M'. Pomponius Matho.

[38] Zonaras, VIII. 19.

[39] See the fragments of Dion, published by Mai, p. 185.

[39] Orosius, IV. 13. Plutarch, Marcell. 3. Zonaras, VIII. 19.

[40] Polybius, II. 23. Zonaras, VIII. 19.

large magazines of arms, and the system being never forgotten of securing allies to act on the enemy's flank or rear, the friendship of the Cenomanians and Venetians was timely obtained, whose country, lying along the lower part of the course of the Po, and on the shores of the Adriatic, was in direct communication with the Romans at Ariminum, and commanded the whole eastern frontier of the hostile Gauls, so as to threaten their territory with invasion, as soon as their army should begin to march southwards. In fact, this desertion of the Gaulish cause by the Cenomanians and Venetians crippled the invasion at the very outset; for a large force was kept at home to cover the frontier, and the invading army, according to Polybius, did not finally amount to more than 50,000 foot, and 20,000 cavalry and war-chariots.[41]

Position of the Roman armies.

Two roads led from Cisalpine Gaul into the heart of Italy; the one by Ariminum and Umbria, the other by Etruria. Of these the former was covered by a consular army of 27,000 men, by the disposable force of the Umbrians, amounting to 20,000 men, and by the Cenomanian and Venetian auxiliaries, who are computed at 20,000 men more. The Umbrians and the barbarian auxiliaries were stationed on the edge of the Gaulish frontier, westward, probably, of Sarsina, to be ready to pour down upon the Boian country, near the modern towns of Forli and Faenza; while the consul, L. Æmilius, was posted at some point in the direction of Ariminum: but whether he was actually at Ariminum to defend the frontier, or in some position nearer to Rome, from whence he might more easily co-operate with the army covering Etruria, the narrative of Polybius does not state clearly.[42] On the other line, which led through Etruria, there lay an army of 54,000 Sabines and Etruscans, commanded by a Roman prætor; whilst Rome itself was covered by a reserve army of more than 50,000, under the command, we may suppose, of the prætor of the city. These forces were actually called out and organized; but the returns of the population capable of bearing arms, and which, in case of need, might recruit and support the troops already in the field, presented, it is said, a sum total, inclusive of the soldiers really enlisted, of no fewer than 750,000.[43]

A. U. C. 529. A. C. 225. The Gauls invade Etruria, and are defeated.

The invaders seem to have conducted their march skilfully; for passing between the Roman armies, they descended from the Apennines into the valley of the upper Arno, followed it down nearly to Arretium, and from thence advanced towards Clusium, in the very heart of Etruria, after having ravaged the whole country near the line of their march without any opposition. When the Roman prætor became aware that the enemy were between him and Rome, he put his army in motion to pursue them. The Gauls met him and defeated him, but were prevented from completing the destruction of his army by the sudden appearance of the consul L. Æmilius, who had also hastened to the scene of action, when he heard that the enemy were in Etruria.[44] Then the Gauls, enriched, but at the same time encumbered, with their plunder, and having been entirely successful hitherto, determined to carry off their prisoners and spoil in safety to their own country, and afterwards, when their army was again fit for action, to repeat their invasion. As the Roman armies were between them and the Apennines, they resolved to retreat by the coast road into Liguria, and descended into the valley of the Ombrone with that object. But when they had reached the coast, and were marching northwards towards the mouth of the Arno, they suddenly encountered a new enemy. The consul, C. Regulus, having been recalled from Sardinia, had just landed at Pisa, and was now on his march by the very same coast road towards Rome.[45] The Gauls were thus placed between two enemies; for L. Æmilius was hanging on

[41] II. 23.

[42] Δεύκιον Αἰμίλιον . . . ἐξαπέστειλαν ὡς ἐπ' Ἀριμίνου.

[43] Polybius, II. 24. Eutropius, III. 5. Polybius, after giving this enormous muster, adds, ἐφ' οὓς Ἀννίβας, ἐλάττους ἔχων δισμυρίων, ἐπέβαλεν εἰς τὴν Ἰταλίαν.

[44] Polybius, II. 25, 26.

[45] Polybius, II. 27.

their rear; and they were obliged to engage both the consular armies at once. The battle was long and bloody, and the Romans lost one of their consuls, C. Regulus; but in the end they won a complete victory, and the Gaulish army was almost destroyed.[46] Immediately after the victory, L. Æmilius hastened to invade the Gaulish territory by the same road which the Gauls had intended to make their line of retreat; and as the Gauls were mostly on their other frontier, to oppose the Umbrians and their barbarian allies, the consul overran the country without resistance. He returned to Rome and triumphed; and the golden chains worn by the Gauls round their necks and arms were hung up as a splendid monument of the victory in the temple of the Capitoline Jupiter.[47]

Conquest of the Boians and Insubrians.

This great success encouraged the Romans to press the war against the Gauls with the utmost vigor, in the hope of completing their destruction, and effecting the conquest of their country. Trusting to their treaty with Hasdrubal, they thought they should have time to deal with their nearer enemies, before they turned their attention seriously to the affairs of Spain. Accordingly for the next three years both consuls were each year employed in Cisalpine Gaul, and with such success, that the Boian and Insubrian nations, whose country stretched from the Apennines to the Alps across the whole plain of Northern Italy, and extended from the neighborhood of Ariminum westward as far as the Ticinus, were obliged one after the other to submit at discretion.[48]

Campaign of 530.

The details of battles fought with barbarians are rarely worth recording; but among the consuls of these three years were men whose personal fame attracts our notice; and some of the circumstances connected with their military proceedings will lead us naturally to a subject of far deeper interest, the political state of Rome on the eve of the second Punic war.

The consuls of the year 530, who succeeded L. Æmilius and C. Regulus, had both of them been consuls before, and censors; and in their censorship they had been colleagues, as now in their second consulship. These were T. Manlius Torquatus and Q. Fulvius Flaccus, men of kindred character; Manlius possessing all the traditional sternness of his race, and Q. Fulvius, in his unyielding and unrelenting nature, rivalling the proudest patricians in Rome. They were made consuls together, in the hope that the Gaulish war, under their conduct, would be brought to a speedy conclusion; but in this they disappointed their countrymen; for although they reduced the Boians to submission, yet they could do nothing against the Insubrians, owing to an unusually rainy season, which, filling all the streams, made the country about the Po impracticable, and occasioned epidemic diseases among the soldiers.[49] The consuls were apparently required to abdicate before the end of the year; for the old and blind L. Metellus, the pontifex maximus, was named dictator, to hold the comitia; and by him were elected the consuls of the following year, C. Flaminius Nepos and P. Furius Philus.

A. U. C. 530. A. C. 224.

Flaminius defeats the Gauls and triumphs in spite of the senate.

Flaminius, as we have seen, had been tribune ten years before, and had then carried an agrarian law for a general assignation of the land formerly conquered from the Gauls near Ariminum. It was perhaps from some expectation that, if he made fresh conquests, he would propose a similar assignation of them, that the people elected him consul: the senate, on the other hand, used their utmost endeavors to make his consulship wholly inactive. He was already in the field with his colleagues, and had entered the enemy's country, when the senate sent orders to both the consuls to return instantly to Rome. Dreadful prodigies had been manifested; three moons had been seen at once in the sky; a vulture had haunted the Forum; and a stream in Picenum had run blood.[51] The augurs declared that the omens had

[46] Polybius, II. 28-31.
[47] Polybius, II. 31.
[48] Polybius, II. 32-35. Zonaras, VIII. 19. Orosius, IV. 13.
[49] Polybius, II. 31.
[51] Zonaras, VIII. 20. Orosius, IV. 13.

not been duly observed at the election of the consuls; they must therefore be forthwith recalled. Flaminius, guessing the purport of the senate's dispatches, and receiving them when he was on the very eve of a battle, would not read them till the action was over; and having gained a complete victory, he declared, when he did read them, that the gods themselves had solved the senate's scruples as to the lawfulness of his appointment, and that it was needless for him now to return. He continued his operations therefore till the end of the season with much success; he took a great many prisoners, and a large amount of plunder, all of which he distributed to his soldiers; and on his return to Rome he demanded a triumph. The senate, resenting his disobedience, refused it; but he obtained it, as the popular consuls Horatius and Valerius had done 220 years before, by a decree of the comitia.[52]

A. U. C. 531. A. C. 223.

Flaminius was through life the enemy of the aristocratical party; and our accounts of these times come from writers whose feeling was strongly aristocratical. Besides, his defeat and death at Thrasymenus made the Romans in general unfriendly to his memory; as national pride is always ready to ascribe disasters in war to the incapacity either of the general or the government. But Flaminius was a brave and honest man, over-confident, it is true, and over-vehement, but neither a demagogue, nor a mere blind partisan. Like many others of the noblest of the plebeians, he was impatient of that craft of augury, which he well knew was no genuine and simple-hearted superstition, but an engine of aristocratical policy used by the nobility against those whom they hated or feared. Yet the time was not come when the people at large saw this equally; and therefore Flaminius shared the fate, and incurred the blame, of those premature reformers, who, putting the sickle to the corn before it is ripe, reap only mischief to themselves, and obtain no fruit for the world.

Character of Flaminius.

Flaminius and Furius were succeeded in the consulship by M. Claudius Marcellus and Cn. Cornelius Scipio. Marcellus, afterwards so famous, was at this time nearly fifty years old, and in his natural character seems greatly to have resembled Flaminius. Like him he was a brave and hardy soldier, open in his temper, active and enterprising in the highest degree; but so adventurous and imprudent, that even in old age he retained the thoughtlessness of a boy, and perished at sixty by plunging into a snare which a stripling might have expected and shunned. But he attached himself to the aristocracy, which Flaminius opposed; and all his military successes met with their full share of honor and reward. In this his first consulship he encountered Britomarus, or Viridomarus, one of the Gaulish chiefs, in single combat, and slew him in the sight of his army. For this exploit he was ranked with Romulus and Cornelius Cossus, who, like him, when commanding the Roman armies, had slain the enemy's general with their own hand; and he offered the Spolia Opima, or choice spoils, of the slain chief to Jupiter Feretrius, as the most striking part of the spectacle of his splendid triumph.[53]

A. U. C. 532. A. C. 222. Character of Marcellus.

The two following years, 533 and 534, were only marked by wars with new barbarian enemies; the Istrians, whose country ran out like a peninsula into the Adriatic, at the very head of the gulf, to the east of the country of the Venetians, and the Gaulish or mixed Gaulish tribes, which lived to the north of the Insubrians, on the very roots of the Alps. The Istrians, a people of kindred race and habits to the Illyrians of the more southern parts of the Adriatic, were accused like them of having committed acts of piracy on the Roman merchant vessels. They were defeated, but not without a severe loss on the side of the Romans. One of the consuls employed against them was M. Minucius Rufus, so famous four years afterwards as master of the horse to the dictator Q. Fabius.[54]

A. U. C. 533. A. C. 221. War with the Istrians.

[52] Zonaras, VIII. 20.

[53] Plutarch, Marcell. 7, 8. Livy, Epit. XX. Eutropius, III. 6.

[54] Zonaras, VIII. 20. Orosius, IV. 13. Eutropius, III. 7.

The year of Rome 534 was marked by the censorship of L. Æmilius Papus and C. Flaminius; a censorship distinguished by several memorable regulations and public works, and which throws great light on the character of Flaminius, and through him on the general state of parties in the commonwealth. In the first place, we may be quite certain that no mere demagogue, nor any one who was considered a bad or unwise man, would have been elected a censor at this period. The high dignity of the office repelled from it all but citizens of the very first reputation; nor were the bravery and activity of a good soldier the qualities which most fitted a man to discharge its many important duties. Flaminius had carried an agrarian law, and had continued to command his army as consul, in direct opposition to the majority of the senate; but he knew how to distinguish between the selfishness and jealousy of an aristocracy, and those aristocratical elements which are essential to all good government; and the great measure of his censorship was a repetition of the regulation made by the famous censors Q. Fabius Rullus and P. Decius, about eighty years before: he removed all freedmen from the country tribes, and enrolled them in the four city tribes, the Palatine, the Esquiline, the Colline, and the Suburran.

Censorship of Flaminius.

A single line in the epitome of Livy's twentieth book contains all our information respecting this measure, and it relates the fact merely, without a word of explanation. We must suppose that the regulation of Fabius and Decius had been regarded as a remedy for a crying evil at a particular time, and not as a general rule to be observed forever. In common times the freedman, being still closely connected with his old master, who was now become his patron, patronus, would be enrolled in his patron's tribe; and this would seem the most natural course, when the particular case was considered, without reference to the political consequences of the system, so soon as it was generally adopted. These consequences would be to give political influence to a class of men in all respects unlike the old agricultural commons. The class of freedmen contained many rich citizens, and many poor ones; but rich and poor alike lived by trade rather than by agriculture,—in Rome, rather than in the country. It is said that the freed negro in America is confined by public feeling to the exercise of two or three trades or callings only, and these humble ones; but the freedman of the ancient world labored under no such restriction. He might keep a little stall in the Forum, or he might be a merchant trafficking with Egypt and with Carthage: or again, he might be a moneyed man, and live on the interest of his loans; or he might go out as a farmer of the taxes to Sicily, and acquire an immense fortune at the expense of the province. But in no case were his habits like those of the agricultural citizen; and Flaminius, like M. Curius, and P. Decius, and like C. Marius in later times, was an enemy to every thing which might elevate the mercantile and moneyed classes, and still more the small shopkeepers and low populace of the city, above the proprietors and cultivators of the land.

Transfer of the freedmen to the city tribes.

It was probably in the same spirit that Flaminius shortly afterwards supported the bill of an unknown tribune, Q. Claudius, which forbade all senators and sons of senators from being the owners of a ship of the burden of more than 300 amphoræ. The express object of this bill was to hinder the Roman aristocracy from becoming, like the Venetian nobles, a company of wealthy merchants. The corn ships which the Istrians were accused of intercepting, belonged, no doubt, to some of the nobility, and were engaged in carrying the corn grown on their extensive occupation lands in Picenum and the coast of Umbria, to the markets of Greece and Macedonia. Flaminius thought that traffic was unworthy of the Roman nobility: perhaps he fancied that they who derived their wealth from foreign trade would be too much afraid of offending their customers, and would compromise their country's honor for the sake of their own profit. But on this occasion he stood alone in the senate: neither Q. Fabius, nor T. Manlius, nor M. Marcellus, nor any of the Atilii,

Bill to check the growth of a mercantile spirit among the senators.

or Sempronii, or Sarvilii, supported him; but as the comitia by the Hortensian law enjoyed the supreme legislative power, the opposition of the senate was vain, and the bill was passed.[55]

Yet, while Flaminius imitated Fabius and Decius in their political regulations, he rivalled Appius Claudius in the greatness of his public works. He perfected the direct communication between Rome and Ariminum,[56] the great road, which, turning to the right after crossing the Milvian bridge, ascended the valley of the Tiber, leaving Soracte on its left, till it again joined the line of the modern road where it recrosses the Tiber and ascends to Ocriculum; which then ascended the valley of the Nar to Narnia and Interamnia, passed over the lofty ridge of the Monte Somma, descended on the newly founded colony of Spoletum, and passed through the magnificent plain beyond, till it reached Fulginia; which there again penetrating into the green valley of the Calcignolo, wound its way along the stream to Nuceria; which then, by an imperceptible ascent, rose through the wide upland plain of Helvillum (Sigillo) to the central ridge of the Apennines; which, the moment it had crossed the ridge, plunged precipitately down into the deep and narrow gorge of the Cantiano, and, hemmed in between gigantic walls of cliff, struggled on for many miles through the defile, till it came out upon the open country, where the Cantiano joins the Metaurus; which then, through a rich and slightly varied plain, followed the left bank of that fateful stream till it reached the shores of the Adriatic; and which finally kept the line of the low coast to Ariminum, the last city of Italy, on the very edge of Cisalpine Gaul. This great road, which is still one of the chief lines of communication in Italy, and which still exhibits in its bridges, substructions, and above all in the magnificent tunnel of Furlo, splendid monuments of Roman greatness, has immortalized the name of C. Flaminius, and was known throughout the times of the Commonwealth and the Empire as the Flaminian Way.

Public works. The Flaminian Way.

His other great work was the building of a circus in the Campus Martius, which was also called by his name, and which, like the Greek theatres, was used not only for the exhibition of games, but also occasionally for meetings of the senate and assemblies of the people, when they were held without the walls of the city.

The Flaminian Circus.

Flaminius, although opposed to the overbearing rule of the aristocracy, stood aloof, as we have seen, from the party of the populace, and wished to do no more than to tread in the steps of the best citizens of former times, of Fabius Rullus and Decius, of M. Curius and Fabricius. But we find symptoms of the growth of another party, which, in the later times of the Commonwealth, was almost the sole representative of the popular cause, the party of the poorer classes within Rome itself, the Forum populace, as they were called, in whom the ancient political writers saw the worst form of democracy. By the influence of this party, it seems C. Tarentius Varro, a butcher's son, had already been raised to the quæstorship, and had been made plebeian and curule ædile, and was now looking forward to still higher distinctions. But the war with Carthage crushed it for the present, and delayed its revival for nearly a hundred years, and established the power of the aristocracy on the firmest base, that of the public respect and love, feelings which their conduct in the great national struggle had justly earned for them.

Growth of a lower democratical party.

Hasdrubal had died in the year before Flaminius' censorship, having been assassinated in his tent by a Gaulish slave, in revenge for the death of his master.[57] The voice of the army had immediately called Hannibal to the command, and the government of Carthage had ratified their choice. He had made two campaigns, and had so put down all opposition to the Carthaginian dominion, that the Saguntines, ex-

Death of Hasdrubal: Hannibal takes the command; ambassadors sent to Hannibal and to Carthage.

[55] Livy, XXI. 63.
[56] Livy, Epit. XX.
[57] Polybius, II. 36. Appian, Hispan. 5.

pecting to be attacked next, as the only people still left independent, sent earnest embassies to Rome, to request the interference of the Romans in their behalf.[58] Towards the close of the year 534, Roman ambassadors visited Hannibal in his winter-quarters at New Carthage, warning him not to attack Saguntum, which was an ally of Rome, nor to carry his arms beyond the Iberus. Receiving unsatisfactory answers, they proceeded to Carthage, and declared to the government that the Romans would consider any attack upon Saguntum, or any advance of the Carthaginians beyond the Iberus, as acts of direct hostility against Rome. They could not imagine that Carthage would dare to incur such a penalty; she had paid money and ceded parts of her territory to escape the resentment of the Romans; would she now voluntarily brave it by acts of aggression? Hannibal's party could not have obtained so complete an ascendency; and his opponents would surely recover their influence, when his policy threatened to involve his country in the dreaded evils of another war with Rome. So L. Æmilius Paullus and M. Livius were chosen consuls for the year 535, as if the peace would not be broken; and they were both sent over to Illyria with two consular armies to chastise the revolt of Demetrius of Pharus, who, relying on his intimate connection with the court of Macedon, had committed various breaches of treaty, and was setting the Romans at defiance.[59]

L. Æmilius was a brave and able officer; and he and his colleague did their work effectually; they reduced all the enemy's strongholds, took Pharus itself, and obliged Demetrius to escape for his life to Macedonia, and finally received the submission of all Illyria, and settled its affairs at their discretion. They returned to Rome at the end of the season, and obtained a triumph, the last that was for some years enjoyed by any Roman officer; for already the falsehood of the Roman calculations was manifest; Saguntum, unaided by Rome, had been taken and destroyed: war with Carthage was no longer doubtful; and the seat of that war was likely to be no longer Spain, but Italy.

A. U. C. 535. A. C. 219. War in Illyria.

CHAPTER XLIII.

SECOND PUNIC WAR.

HANNIBAL—MARCH OF HANNIBAL FROM SPAIN TO ITALY—PASSAGE OF THE ALPS—BATTLES OF THE TREBIA, AND OF THRASYMENUS—Q. FABIUS MAXIMUS DICTATOR—BATTLE OF CANNÆ—A. U. C. 535 TO 538.

TWICE in history has there been witnessed the struggle of the highest individual genius against the resources and institutions of a great nation; and, in both cases, the nation has been victorious. For seventeen years Hannibal strove against Rome; for sixteen years Napoleon Bonaparte strove against England: the efforts of the first ended in Zama, those of the second in Waterloo.

A. U. C. 535. A. C. 219. Second Punic war.

True it is, as Polybius has said, that Hannibal was supported by the zealous exertions of Carthage;[1] and the strength of the opposition to his policy has been very possibly exaggerated by the Roman writers.

Greatness of Hannibal.

[58] Polybius, III. 15. Appian, Hispan. 11. Livy, XXI. 10.

[59] Polybius, III. 16, 18. Zonaras, VIII. 20.

[1] Polybius, III. 10.

But the zeal of his country in the contest, as Polybius himself remarks in another place,[2] was itself the work of his family. Never did great men more show themselves the living spirit of a nation than Hamilcar, and Hasdrubal, and Hannibal, during a period of nearly fifty years, approved themselves to be to Carthage. It is not, then, merely through our ignorance of the internal state of Carthage that Hannibal stands so prominent in all our conceptions of the second Punic war: he was really its moving and directing power; and the energy of his country was but a light reflected from his own. History therefore gathers itself into his single person: in that vast tempest which, from north and south, from the west and the east, broke upon Italy, we see nothing but Hannibal.

Greatness of Rome. The success of Rome has been for the good of mankind.

But if Hannibal's genius may be likened to the Homeric god, who in his hatred of the Trojans rises from the deep to rally the fainting Greeks, and to lead them against the enemy; so the calm courage with which Hector met his more than human adversary in his country's cause, is no unworthy image of the unyielding magnanimity displayed by the aristocracy of Rome. As Hannibal utterly eclipses Carthage, so on the contrary Fabius, Marcellus, Claudius Nero, even Scipio himself, are as nothing when compared to the spirit, and wisdom, and power of Rome. The senate which voted its thanks to its political enemy, Varro, after his disastrous defeat, "because he had not despaired of the Commonwealth," and which disdained either to solicit, or to reprove, or to threaten, or in any way to notice the twelve colonies which had refused their accustomed supplies of men for the army, is far more to be honored than the conqueror of Zama. This we should the more carefully bear in mind, because our tendency is to admire individual greatness far more than national; and as no single Roman will bear comparison with Hannibal, we are apt to murmur at the event of the contest, and to think that the victory was awarded to the least worthy of the combatants. On the contrary, never was the wisdom of God's providence more manifest than in the issue of the struggle between Rome and Carthage. It was clearly for the good of mankind that Hannibal should be conquered: his triumph would have stopped the progress of the world. For great men can only act permanently by forming great nations; and no one man, even though it were Hannibal himself, can in one generation effect such a work. But where the nation has been merely enkindled for a while by a great man's spirit, the light passes away with him who communicated it; and the nation, when he is gone, is like a dead body, to which magic power had for a moment given an unnatural life: when the charm has ceased, the body is cold and stiff as before. He who grieves over the battle of Zama, should carry on his thoughts to a period thirty years later, when Hannibal must, in the course of nature, have been dead, and consider how the isolated Phœnician city of Carthage was fitted to receive and to consolidate the civilization of Greece, or by its laws and institutions to bind together barbarians of every race and language into an organized empire, and prepare them for becoming, when that empire was dissolved, the free members of the commonwealth of Christian Europe.

Hannibal takes Saguntum.

Hannibal was twenty-six years of age when he was appointed commander-in-chief of the Carthaginian armies in Spain, upon the sudden death of Hasdrubal. Two years, we have seen, had been employed in expeditions against the native Spaniards; the third year was devoted to the siege of Saguntum. Hannibal's pretext for attacking it was, that the Saguntines had oppressed one of the Spanish tribes in alliance with Carthage;[3] but no caution in the Saguntine government could have avoided a quarrel, which their enemy was determined to provoke. Saguntum, although not a city of native Spaniards, resisted as obstinately as if the very air of Spain had breathed into foreign settlers on its soil the spirit so often, in many different ages, displayed by the Spanish people. Saguntum was defended like Numantia and Gerona: the siege lasted

[2] Polybius, IX. 22.

[3] Polybius, III. 15. Appian, Hispan. XI.

eight months; and when all hope was gone, several of the chiefs kindled a fire in the market-place, and after having thrown in their most precious effects, leapt into it themselves, and perished. Still the spoil found in the place was very considerable: there was a large treasure of money, which Hannibal kept for his war expenses; there were numerous captives, whom he distributed amongst his soldiers as their share of the plunder; and there was much costly furniture from the public and private buildings, which he sent home to decorate the temples and palaces of Carthage.[4]

Ambassadors sent to Carthage, who declare war.

It must have been towards the close of the year, but apparently before the consuls were returned from Illyria, that the news of the fall of Saguntum reached Rome. Immediately ambassadors were sent to Carthage; M. Fabius Buteo, who had been consul seven-and-twenty years before, C. Licinius Varus, and Q. Bæbius Tamphilus. Their orders were simply to demand that Hannibal and his principal officers should be given up for their attack upon the allies of Rome, in breach of the treaty, and, if this were refused, to declare war. The Carthaginians tried to discuss the previous question, whether the attack on Saguntum was a breach of the treaty; but to this the Romans would not listen. At length M. Fabius gathered up his toga, as if he was wrapping up something in it, and holding it out thus folded together, he said, "Behold, here are peace and war; take which you choose!" The Carthaginian suffete, or judge, answered, "Give whichever thou wilt." Hereupon Fabius shook out the folds of his toga, saying, "Then here we give you war;" to which several members of the council shouted in answer, "With all our hearts we welcome it." Thus the Roman ambassadors left Carthage, and returned straight to Rome.

Hannibal's preparations for war.

But before the result of this embassy could be known in Spain, Hannibal had been making preparations for his intended expedition, in a manner which showed, not only that he was sure of the support of his government, but that he was able to dispose at his pleasure of all the military resources of Carthage. At his suggestion fresh troops from Africa were sent over to Spain to secure it during his absence, and to be commanded by his own brother, Hasdrubal; and their place was to be supplied by other troops raised in Spain;[6] so that Africa was to be defended by Spaniards, and Spain by Africans, the soldiers of each nation, when quartered amongst foreigners, being cut off from all temptation or opportunity to revolt. So completely was he allowed to direct every military measure, that he is said to have sent Spanish and Numidian troops to garrison Carthage itself; in other words, this was a part of his general plan, and was adopted accordingly by the government. Meanwhile he had sent ambassadors into Gaul, and even across the Alps, to the Gauls who had so lately been at war with the Romans, both to obtain information as to the country through which his march lay, and to secure the assistance and guidance of the Gauls in his passage of the Alps, and their co-operation in arms when he should arrive in Italy. His Spanish troops he had dismissed to their several homes at the end of the last campaign, that they might carry their spoils with them, and tell of their exploits to their countrymen, and enjoy, during the winter, that almost listless ease which is the barbarian's relief from war and plunder. At length he received the news of the Roman embassy to Carthage, and the actual declaration of war; his officers also had returned from Cisalpine Gaul. "The natural difficulties of the passage of the Alps were great," they said, "but by no means insuperable; while the disposition of the Gauls was most friendly, and they were eagerly expecting his arrival."[7] Then Hannibal called his soldiers together, and told them openly that he was going to lead them into Italy. "The Romans," he said, "have demanded that I and my

A. U. C. 536. A. C. 218.

[4] Livy, XXI. 14. Polybius, III. 18.

[5] Livy, XXI. 18 Polybius, III. 20. Zonaras, VIII. 32.

[6] Polybius, III. 33. Livy, XXI. 21.

[7] Polybius, III. 34.

principal officers should be delivered up to them as malefactors. Soldiers, will you suffer such an indignity? The Gauls are holding out their arms to us, inviting us to come to them, and to assist them in revenging their manifold injuries. And the country which we shall invade, so rich in corn, and wine, and oil, so full of flocks and herds, so covered with flourishing cities, will be the richest prize that could be offered by the gods to reward your valor." One common shout from the soldiers assured him of their readiness to follow him. He thanked them, fixed the day on which they were to be ready to march, and then dismissed them.

Hannibal's sacrifice.

In this interval, and now on the very eve of commencing his appointed work, to which for eighteen years he had been solemnly devoted, and to which he had so long been looking forward with almost sickening hope, he left the head-quarters of his army to visit Gades, and there, in the temple of the supreme god of Tyre, and all the colonies of Tyre, to offer his prayers and vows for the success of his enterprise.[8] He was attended only by those immediately attached to his person; and amongst these was a Sicilian Greek, Silenus, who followed him throughout his Italian expedition, and lived at his table. When the sacrifice was over, Hannibal returned to his army at New Carthage; and every thing being ready, and the season sufficiently advanced, for it was now late in May, he set out on his march for the Iberus.

His vision.

And here the fulness of his mind, and his strong sense of being the devoted instrument of his country's gods to destroy their enemies, haunted him by night as they possessed him by day. In his sleep, so he told Silenus, he fancied that the supreme god of his fathers had called him into the presence of all the gods of Carthage, who were sitting on their thrones in council. There he received a solemn charge to invade Italy; and one of the heavenly council went with him and with his army, to guide him on his way. He went on, and his divine guide commanded him, "See that thou look not behind thee." But after a while, impatient of the restraint, he turned to look back; and there he beheld a huge and monstrous form, thick-set all over with serpents; wherever it moved, orchards, and woods, and houses fell crashing before it. He asked his guide in wonder, what that monster form was? The god answered, "Thou seest the desolation of Italy; go on thy way, straight forward, and cast no look behind."[9] Thus, with no divided heart, and with an entire resignation of all personal and domestic enjoyments forever, Hannibal went forth, at the age of twenty-seven,[10] to do the work of his country's gods, and to redeem his early vow.

Miscalculations of the Romans.

The consuls at Rome came into office at this period on the fifteenth of March: it was possible therefore for a consular army to arrive on the scene of action in time to dispute with Hannibal not only the passage of the Rhone, but that of the Pyrenees. But the Romans exaggerated the difficulties of his march, and seem to have expected that the resistance of the Spanish tribes between the Iberus and the Pyrenees, and of the Gauls between the Pyrenees and the Rhone, would so delay him that he would not reach the Rhone till the end of the season. They therefore made their preparations leisurely.

Their preparations for war.

Of the consuls for this year, the year of Rome 536, and 218 before the Christian era, one was P. Cornelius Scipio, the son of L. Scipio, who had been consul in the sixth year of the first Punic war, and the grandson of L. Scipio Barbatus, whose services in the third Samnite war are recorded in his famous epitaph. The other was Ti. Sempronius Longus, probably, but not certainly, the son of that C. Sempronius Blæsus who had been consul in the year 501. The consuls' provinces were to be Spain and Sicily; Scipio, with two Roman legions, and 15,600 of the Italian allies, and with a fleet of sixty quinqueremes, was to command in Spain; Sempronius, with a somewhat larger

[8] Livy, XXI. 21. Compare Polybius, XXXIV. 9. Valerius Maximus, I. 7, 1, Externa. Zonaras, VIII. 22.

[9] Cicero de Div. I. 24. Livy, XXIV. 22. [10] Nepos, Hannibal, c. 3.

army, and a fleet of 160 quinqueremes, was to cross over to Lilybæum, and from thence, if circumstances favored, to make a descent on Africa. A third army, consisting also of two Roman legions, and 11,000 of the allies, was stationed in Cisalpine Gaul, under the prætor, L. Manlius Vulso.[11] The Romans suspected that the Gauls would rise in arms ere long; and they hastened to send out the colonists of two colonies, which had been resolved on before, but not actually founded, to occupy the important stations of Placentia and Cremona on the opposite banks of the Po. The colonists sent to each of these places were no fewer than six thousand; and they received notice to be at their colonies in thirty days. Three commissioners, one of them, C. Lutatius Catulus, being of consular rank, were sent out, as usual, to superintend the allotment of lands to the settlers; and these 12,000 men, together with the prætor's army, were supposed to be capable of keeping the Gauls quiet.[12]

It is a curious fact, that the danger on the side of Spain was considered to be so much the less urgent, that Scipio's army was raised the last, after those of his colleague and of the prætor, L. Manlius.[13] Indeed, Scipio was still at Rome, when tidings came that the Boians and Insubrians had revolted, had dispersed the new settlers at Placentia and Cremona, and driven them to take refuge at Mutina, had treacherously seized the three commissioners at a conference, and had defeated the prætor, L. Manlius, and obliged him also to take shelter in one of the towns of Cisalpine Gaul, where they were blockading him.[14] One of Scipio's legions, with five thousand of the allies, was immediately sent off into Gaul under another prætor, C. Atilius Serranus; and Scipio waited till his own army should again be completed by new levies. Thus, he cannot have left Rome till late in the summer; and when he arrived with his fleet and army at the mouth of the eastern branch of the Rhone, he found that Hannibal had crossed the Pyrenees; but he still hoped to impede his passage of the river.

Revolt of the Gauls.

Hannibal meanwhile, having set out from New Carthage with an army of 90,000 foot and 12,000 horse, crossed the Iberus;[15] and from thenceforward the hostile operations of his march began. He might, probably, have marched through the country between the Iberus and the Pyrenees, had that been his sole object, as easily as he made his way from the Pyrenees to the Rhone; a few presents and civilities would easily have induced the Spanish chiefs to allow him a free passage. But some of the tribes northward of the Iberus were friendly to Rome: on the coast were the Greek cities of Rhoda and Emporiæ, Massaliot colonies, and thus attached to the Romans as the old allies of their mother city: if this part of Spain were left unconquered, the Romans would immediately make use of it as the base of their operations, and proceed from thence to attack the whole Carthaginian dominion. Accordingly, Hannibal employed his army in subduing the whole country, which he effected with no great loss of time, but at a heavy expense of men, as he was obliged to carry the enemy's strongholds by assault, rather than incur the delay of besieging them. He left Hanno with eleven thousand men to retain possession of the newly conquered country; and he further diminished his army by sending home as many more of his Spanish soldiers, probably those who had most distinguished themselves, as an earnest to the rest, that they too, if they did their duty well, might expect a similar release, and might look forward to return ere long to their homes full of spoil and of glory. These detachments, together with the heavy loss sustained in the field, reduced the force with which Hannibal entered Gaul to no more than 50,000 foot and 9000 horse.[16]

Hannibal conquers the north of Spain.

From the Pyrenees to the Rhone his progress was easy. Here he had no wish to make regular conquests; and presents to the chiefs mostly succeeded in con-

[11] Polybius, III. 40, 41.
[12] Polybius, III. 40.
[13] Livy, XXI. 26.
[14] Polybius, III. 40.
[15] Polybius, III. 35. Livy, XXI. 23.
[16] Polybius, III. 35.

ciliating their friendship, so that he was allowed to pass freely. But on the left bank of the Rhone the influence of the Massaliots with the Gaulish tribes had disposed them to resist the invader; and the passage of the Rhone was not to be effected without a contest.

He marches to the Rhone.

Scipio, by this time, had landed his army near the eastern mouth of the Rhone; and his information of Hannibal's movements was vague and imperfect. His men had suffered from sea-sickness on their voyage from Pisa to the Rhone; and he wished to give them a short time to recover their strength and spirits, before he led them against the enemy. He still felt confident that Hannibal's advance from the Pyrenees must be slow, supposing that he would be obliged to fight his way; so that he never doubted that he should have ample time to oppose his passage of the Rhone. Meanwhile he sent out 300 horse, with some Gauls, who were in the service of the Massaliots, ordering them to ascend the left bank of the Rhone, and discover, if possible, the situation of the enemy. He seems to have been unwilling to place the river on his rear, and therefore never to have thought of conducting his operations on the right bank, or even of sending out reconnoitring parties in this direction.[17]

Scipio's movements.

The resolution which Scipio formed a few days afterwards, of sending his army to Spain, when he himself returned to Italy, was deserving of such high praise, that we must hesitate to accuse him of over caution or needless delay at this critical moment. Yet he was sitting idle at the mouth of the Rhone, while the Gauls were vainly endeavoring to oppose Hannibal's passage of the river. We must understand that Hannibal kept his army as far away from the sea as possible, in order to conceal his movements from the Romans; therefore he came upon the Rhone, not on the line of the later Roman road from Spain to Italy, which crossed the river at Tarasco, between Avignon and Arles, but at a point much higher up, above its confluence with the Durance, and nearly half way, if we can trust Polybius' reckoning, from the sea to its confluence with the Isere.[18] Here he obtained from the natives on the right bank, by paying a fixed price, all their boats and vessels of every description with which they were accustomed to traffic down the river: they allowed him also to cut timber for the construction of others; and thus in two days he was provided with the means of transporting his army. But finding that the Gauls were assembled on the eastern bank to oppose his passage, he sent off a detachment of his army by night with native guides, to ascend the right bank, for about two-and-twenty miles, and there to cross as they could, where there was no enemy to stop them. The woods, which then lined the river, supplied this detachment with the means of constructing barks and rafts enough for the passage; they took advantage of one of the many islands in this part of the Rhone, to cross where the stream was divided; and thus they all reached the left bank in safety. There they took up a strong position, probably one of those strange masses of rock which rise here and there with steep cliffy sides like islands out of the vast plain, and rested for four-and-twenty hours after their exertions in the march and the passage of the river.

Hannibal's preparations for passing the Rhone.

Hannibal allowed eight-and-forty hours to pass from the time when the detachment left his camp; and then, on the morning of the fifth day after his arrival on the Rhone, he made his preparations for the passage of his main army. The mighty stream of the river, fed by the snows of the high Alps, is swelled rather than diminished by the heats of summer; so that, although the season was that when the southern rivers are generally at their lowest, it was rolling the vast mass of its waters along with a startling fulness and rapidity. The heaviest vessels were therefore placed on the left, highest up the stream, to form something of a breakwater for the smaller craft crossing below; the small boats held the flower of the light-armed foot, while the cavalry

The army crosses the river.

[17] Polybius, II. 41. Livy, XXI. 26.

[18] Polybius, III. 42.

were in the larger vessels; most of the horses being towed astern swimming, and a single soldier holding three or four together by their bridles. Every thing was ready, and the Gauls on the opposite side had poured out of their camp, and lined the bank in scattered groups at the most accessible points, thinking that their task of stopping the enemy's landing would be easily accomplished. At length Hannibal's eye observed a column of smoke rising on the farther shore, above or on the right of the barbarians. This was the concerted signal which assured him of the arrival of his detachment; and he instantly ordered his men to embark, and to push across with all possible speed. They pulled vigorously against the rapid stream, cheering each other to the work; while behind them were their friends, cheering them also from the bank; and before them were the Gauls singing their war-songs, and calling them to come on with tones and gestures of defiance. But on a sudden a mass of fire was seen on the rear of the barbarians; the Gauls on the bank looked behind, and began to turn away from the river; and presently the bright arms and white linen coats of the African and Spanish soldiers appeared above the bank, breaking in upon the disorderly line of the Gauls. Hannibal himself, who was with the party crossing the river, leapedon shore amongst the first, and forming his men as fast as they landed, led them instantly to the charge. But the Gauls, confused and bewildered, made little resistance; they fled in utter rout; whilst Hannibal, not losing a moment, sent back his vessels and boats for a fresh detachment of his army; and before night his whole force, with the exception of his elephants, was safely established on the eastern side of the Rhone.[19]

Arrival of emissaries from the Cisalpine Gauls.

As the river was no longer between him and the enemy, Hannibal early on the next morning sent out a party of Numidian cavalry to discover the position and number of Scipio's forces, and then called his army together, to see and hear the communications of some chiefs of the Cisalpine Gauls, who were just arrived from the other side of the Alps. Their words were explained to the Africans and Spaniards in the army by interpreters; but the very sight of the chiefs was itself an encouragement; for it told the soldiers that the communication with Cisalpine Gaul was not impracticable, and that the Gauls had undertaken so long a journey for the purpose of obtaining the aid of the Carthaginian army against their old enemies, the Romans. Besides, the interpreters explained to the soldiers that the chiefs undertook to guide them into Italy by a short and safe route, on which they would be able to find provisions; and spoke strongly of the great extent and richness of Italy, when they did arrive there, and how zealously the Gauls would aid them. Hannibal then came forward himself and addressed his army: their work, he said, was more than half accomplished by the passage of the Rhone; their own eyes and ears had witnessed the zeal of their Gaulish allies in their cause; for the rest, their business was to do their duty, and obey his orders implicitly, leaving every thing else to him. The cheers and shouts of the soldiers again satisfied him how fully he might depend upon them; and he then addressed his prayers and vows to the gods of Carthage, imploring them to watch over the army, and to prosper its work to the end, as they had prospered its beginning. The soldiers were now dismissed, with orders to prepare for their march on the morrow.[20]

Scipio sends his army to Spain, and returns to Italy.

Scarcely was the assembly broken up, when some of the Numidians who had been sent out in the morning, were seen riding for their lives to the camp, manifestly in flight from a victorious enemy. Not half of the original party returned; for they had fallen in with Scipio's detachment of Roman and Gaulish horse, and, after an obstinate conflict, had been completely beaten. Presently after, the Roman horsemen appeared in pursuit; but when they observed the Carthaginian camp, they wheeled about and rode off, to carry back word to their general. Then at last Scipio put his army in motion, and

[19] Polybius, III. 42, 43. [20] Polybius, III. 44.

ascended the left bank of the river to find and engage the enemy.[21] But when he arrived at the spot where his cavalry had seen the Carthaginian camp, he found it deserted, and was told that Hannibal had been gone three days, having marched northwards, ascending the left bank of the river. To follow him seemed desperate: it was plunging into a country wholly unknown to the Romans, where they had neither allies nor guides, nor resources of any kind; and where the natives, over and above the common jealousy felt by all barbarians towards a foreign army, were likely, as Gauls, to regard the Romans with peculiar hostility. But if Hannibal could not be followed now, he might easily be met on his first arrival in Italy; from the mouth of the Rhone to Pisa was the chord of a circle, while Hannibal was going to make a long circuit; and the Romans had an army already in Cisalpine Gaul; while the enemy would reach the scene of action exhausted with the fatigues and privations of his march across the Alps. Accordingly, Scipio descended the Rhone again, embarked his army and sent it on to Spain under the command of his brother, Cnæus Scipio, as his lieutenant; while he himself, in his own ship, sailed for Pisa, and immediately crossed the Apennines to take the command of the forces of the two prætors, Manlius and Atilius, who, as we have seen, had an army of about 25,000 men, over and above the colonists of Placentia and Cremona, still disposable in Cisalpine Gaul.[22]

Wisdom of this resolution.

This resolution of Scipio to send his own army on to Spain, and to meet Hannibal with the army of the two prætors, appears to show that he possessed the highest qualities of a general, which involve the wisdom of a statesman no less than of a soldier. As a mere military question, his calculation, though baffled by the event, was sound; but if we view it in a higher light, the importance to the Romans of retaining their hold on Spain would have justified a far greater hazard; for if the Carthaginians were suffered to consolidate their dominion in Spain, and to avail themselves of its immense resources, not in money only, but in men, the hardiest and steadiest of barbarians, and, under the training of such generals as Hannibal and his brother, equal to the best soldiers in the world, the Romans would hardly have been able to maintain the contest. Had not P. Scipio then dispatched his army to Spain at this critical moment, instead of carrying it home to Italy, his son in all probability would never have won the battle of Zama.

The elephants are carried over the Rhone.

Meanwhile Hannibal, on the day after the skirmish with Scipio's horse, had sent forward his infantry, keeping the cavalry to cover his operations, as he still expected the Romans to pursue him; while he himself waited to superintend the passage of the elephants. These were thirty-seven in number; and their dread of the water made their transport a very difficult operation. It was effected by fastening to the bank large rafts of 200 feet in length, covered carefully with earth: to the end of these smaller rafts were attached, covered with earth in the same manner, and with towing lines extended to a number of the largest barks, which were to tow them over the stream. The elephants, two females leading the way, were brought upon the rafts by their drivers without difficulty; and as soon as they came upon the smaller rafts, these were cut loose at once from the larger, and towed out into the middle of the river. Some of the elephants, in their terror, leaped overboard, and drowned their drivers; but they themselves, it is said, held their huge trunks above water, and struggled to the shore; so that the whole thirty-seven were landed in safety.[23] Then Hannibal called in his cavalry, and covering his march with them and with the elephants, set forward up the left bank of the Rhone to overtake the infantry.

Hannibal's march through Gaul.

In four days they reached the spot where the Isere,[24] coming down from the main Alps, brings to the Rhone a stream hardly less full or mighty than his own. In the plains above the confluence two Gaulish

[21] Polybius, III. 45.
[22] Polybius, III. 47.
[23] Polybius, III. 46. Livy, XXI. 28.
[24] Polybius, III. 49.

brothers were contending which should be chief of their tribe; and the elder called in the stranger general to support his cause. Hannibal readily complied, established him firmly on the throne, and received important aid from him in return. He supplied the Carthaginian army plentifully with provisions, furnished them with new arms, gave them new clothing, especially shoes, which were found very useful in the subsequent march, and accompanied them to the first entrance on the mountain country, to secure them from attacks on the part of his countrymen.

Difficulty of determining his line of march.

The attentive reader, who is acquainted with the geography of the Alps and their neighborhood, will perceive that this account of Hannibal's march is vague. It does not appear whether the Carthaginians ascended the left bank of the Isere, or the right bank; or whether they continued to ascend the Rhone for a time, and leaving it only so far as to avoid the great angle which it makes at Lyons, rejoined it again just before they entered the mountain country, a little to the left of the present road from Lyons to Chamberri. But these uncertainties cannot now be removed, because Polybius neither possessed a sufficient knowledge of the bearings of the country, nor sufficient liveliness as a painter, to describe the line of the march so as to be clearly recognized. I believe, however, that Hannibal crossed the Isere, and continued to ascend the Rhone; and that afterwards, striking off to the right across the plains of Dauphiné, he reached what Polybius calls the first ascent of the Alps, at the northern extremity of that ridge of limestone mountains, which, rising abruptly from the plain to the height of 4000 or 5000 feet, and filling up the whole space between the Rhone at Belley and the Isere below Grenoble, first introduces the traveller coming from Lyons to the remarkable features of Alpine scenery.

Hannibal finds the mountaineers ready to oppose him.

At the end of the lowland country, the Gaulish chief, who had accompanied Hannibal thus far, took leave of him: his influence probably did not extend to the Alpine valleys; and the mountaineers, far from respecting his safe-conduct, might be in the habit of making plundering inroads on his own territory. Here then Hannibal was left to himself; and he found that the natives were prepared to beset his passage. They occupied all such points as commanded the road; which, as usual, was a sort of terrace cut in the mountain side, overhanging the valley whereby it penetrated to the central ridge. But as the mountain line is of no great breadth here, the natives guarded the defile only by day, and withdrew when night came on to their own homes, in a town or village among the mountains, and lying in the valley behind them.[25] Hannibal, having learnt this from some of his Gaulish guides whom he sent among them, encamped in their sight just below the entrance of the defile; and as soon as it was dusk, he set out with a detachment of light troops, made his way through the pass, and occupied the positions which the barbarians, after their usual practice, had abandoned at the approach of night.

He baffles them.

Day dawned; the main army broke up from its camp, and began to enter the defile; while the natives, finding their positions occupied by the enemy, at first looked on quietly, and offered no disturbance to the march. But when they saw the long narrow line of the Carthaginian army winding along the steep mountain side, and the cavalry and baggage-cattle struggling at every step with the difficulties of the road, the temptation to plunder was too strong to be resisted; and from many points of the mountain above the road they rushed down upon the Carthaginians. The confusion was terrible; for the road or track was so narrow, that the least crowd or disorder pushed the heavily loaded baggage-cattle down the steep below; and the horses, wounded by the barbarians' missiles, and plunging about wildly in their pain and terror, increased the mischief. At last Hannibal was obliged to charge down from his position, which commanded the whole scene of confusion, and

Polybius, III. 50.

to drive the barbarians off. This he effected; yet the conflict of so many men on the narrow road made the disorder worse for a time; and he unavoidably occasioned the destruction of many of his own men.[26] At last, the barbarians being quite beaten off, the army wound its way out of the defile in safety, and rested in the wide and rich valley which extends from the lake of Bourget, with scarcely a perceptible change of level, to the Isere at Montmeillan. Hannibal meanwhile attacked and stormed the town, which was the barbarians' principal stronghold; and here he not only recovered a great many of his own men, horses, and baggage-cattle, but also found a large supply of corn and cattle belonging to the barbarians, which he immediately made use of for the consumption of his soldiers.

Difficulties of the march.

In the plain which he had now reached, he halted for a whole day, and then, resuming his march, proceeded for three days up the valley of the Isere on the right bank, without encountering any difficulty. Then the natives met him with branches of trees in their hands, and wreaths on their heads in token of peace: they spoke fairly, offered hostages, and wished, they said, neither to do the Carthaginians any injury, nor to receive any from them. Hannibal mistrusted them, yet did not wish to offend them; he accepted their terms, received their hostages, and obtained large supplies of cattle; and their whole behavior seemed so trustworthy, that at last he accepted their guidance, it is said, through a difficult part of the country, which he was now approaching.[27] For all the Alpine valleys become narrower, as they draw nearer to the central chain; and the mountains often come so close to the stream, that the roads in old times were often obliged to leave the valley and ascend the hills by any accessible point, to descend again when the gorge became wider, and follow the stream as before. If this is not done, and the track is carried nearer the river, it passes often through defiles of the most formidable character, being no more than a narrow ledge above a furious torrent, with cliffs rising above it absolutely precipitous, and coming down on the other side of the torrent abruptly to the water, leaving no passage by which man or even goat could make its way.

Attacks of the mountaineers.

It appears that the barbarians persuaded Hannibal to pass through one of these defiles, instead of going round it; and while his army was involved in it, they suddenly, and without provocation, as we are told, atacked him. Making their way along the mountain sides above the defile, they rolled down masses of rock on the Carthaginians below, or even threw stones upon them from their hands, stones and rocks being equally fatal against an enemy so entangled. It was well for Hannibal, that, still doubting the barbarians' faith, he had sent forward his cavalry and baggage, and covered the march with his infantry, who thus had to sustain the brunt of the attack. Foot soldiers on such ground were able to move, where horses would be quite helpless; and thus at last Hannibal, with his infantry, forced his way to the summit of one of the bare cliffs overhanging the defile, and remained there during the night, whilst the cavalry and baggage slowly struggled out of the defile.[28] Thus again baffled, the barbarians made no more general attacks on the army; some partial annoyance was occasioned at intervals, and some baggage was carried off; but it was observed, that wherever the elephants were, the line of march was secure; for the barbarians beheld those huge creatures with terror, having never had the slightest knowledge of them, and not daring to approach when they saw them.

Hannibal reaches the summit of the Alps.

Without any further recorded difficulty, the army on the ninth day after they had left the plains of Dauphiné arrived at the summit of the central ridge of the Alps. Here there is always a plain of some

[26] Polybius, III. 51.
[27] Polybius, III. 52.
[28] Polybius, III. 53.

extent, immediately overhung by the snowy summits of the high mountains, but itself in summer presenting in many parts a carpet of the freshest grass, with the chalets of the shepherds scattered over it, and gay with a thousand flowers. But far different is its aspect through the greatest part of the year: then it is one unvaried waste of snow; and the little lakes, which on many of the passes enliven the summer landscape, are now frozen over and covered with snow, so as to be no longer distinguishable. Hannibal was on the summit of the Alps about the end of October: the first winter snows had already fallen; but two hundred years before the Christian era, when all Germany was one vast forest, the climate of the Alps was far colder than at present, and the snow lay on the passes all through the year. Thus the soldiers were in dreary quarters; they remained two days on the summit, resting from their fatigues, and giving opportunity to many of the stragglers, and of the horses and cattle, to rejoin them by following their track; but they were cold, and worn, and disheartened; and mountains still rose before them, through which, as they knew too well, even their descent might be perilous and painful.

Looks down upon Italy.

But their great general, who felt that he now stood victorious on the ramparts of Italy, and that the torrent which rolled before him was carrying its waters to the rich plains of Cisalpine Gaul, endeavored to kindle his soldiers with his own spirit of hope. He called them together; he pointed out the valley beneath, to which the descent seemed the work of a moment: "That valley," he said, "is Italy; it leads us to the country of our friends the Gauls; and yonder is our way to Rome." His eyes were eagerly fixed on that point of the horizon; and as he gazed, the distance between seemed to vanish, till he could almost fancy that he was crossing the Tiber, and assailing the capitol.[29]

Descent.

After the two days' rest the descent began. Hannibal experienced no more open hostility from the barbarians, only some petty attempts here and there to plunder; a fact strange in itself, but doubly so, if he was really descending the valley of the Doria Baltea, through the country of the Salassians, the most untamable robbers of all the Alpine barbarians. It is possible that the influence of the Insubrians may partly have restrained the mountaineers; and partly also they may have been deterred by the ill success of all former attacks, and may by this time have regarded the strange army and its monstrous beasts with something of superstitious terror. But the natural difficulties of the ground on the descent were greater than ever. The snow covered the track so that the men often lost it, and fell down the steep below: at last they came to a place where an avalanche had carried it away altogether for about three hundred yards, leaving the mountain side a mere wreck of scattered rocks and snow. To go round was impossible; for the depth of the snow on the heights above rendered it hopeless to scale them; nothing therefore was left but to repair the road. A summit of some extent was found, and cleared of the snow; and here the army was obliged to encamp, whilst the work went on. There was no want of hands; and every man was laboring for his life; the road therefore was restored, and supported with solid substructions below; and in a single day it was made practicable for the cavalry and baggage-cattle, which were immediately sent forward, and reached the lower valley in safety, where they were turned out to pasture. A harder labor was required to make a passage for the elephants: the way for them must be wide and solid; and the work could not be accomplished in less than three days. The poor animals suffered severely in the interval from hunger; for no forage was to be found in that wilderness of snow, nor any trees whose leaves might supply the place of other herbage. At last they too were able to proceed with safety:[30] Hannibal overtook his cavalry and baggage; and in three days more the whole army had got clear of the Alpine val-

[29] Polybius, III. 54. Livy, XXI. 35.

[30] Polybius, III. 54, 55.

leys, and entered the country of their friends, the Insubrians, on the wide plain of northern Italy.

Arrival in Italy. Losses on the march.

Hannibal was arrived in Italy, but with a force so weakened by its losses in men and horses, and by the exhausted state of the survivors, that he might seem to have accomplished his great march in vain. According to his own statement, which there is no reason to doubt, he brought out of the Alpine valleys no more than 12,000 African and 8000 Spanish infantry, with 6000 cavalry;[31] so that his march from the Pyrenees to the plains of northern Italy must have cost him 33,000 men; an enormous loss, which proves how severely the army must have suffered from the privations of the march and the severity of the Alpine climate; for not half of these 33,000 men can have fallen in battle. With his army in this condition, some period of repose was absolutely necessary; accordingly, Hannibal remained in the country of the Insubrians, till rest, and a more temperate climate, and wholesome food, with which the Gauls plentifully supplied him, restored the bodies and spirits of his soldiers, and made them again ready for action.[32] His first movement was against the Taurinians, a Ligurian people, who were constant enemies of the Insubrians, and therefore would not listen to Hannibal, when he invited them to join his cause. He therefore attacked and stormed their principal town, put the garrison to the sword, and struck such terror into the neighboring tribes, that they submitted immediately, and became his allies. This was his first accession of strength in Italy, the first fruits, as he hoped, of a long succession of defections among the allies of Rome, so that the swords of the Italians might effect for him the conquest of Italy.

Scipio marches to meet him.

Meanwhile Scipio had landed at Pisa, had crossed the Apennines, and taken the command of the prætors' army, sending the prætors themselves back to Rome, had crossed the Po at Placentia, and was ascending its left bank, being anxious to advance with all possible haste, in order to hinder a general rising of the Gauls by his presence.[33] Hannibal, for the opposite reason, was equally anxious to meet him, being well aware that the Gauls were only restrained from revolting to the Carthaginians by fear, and that on his first success in the field they would join him.[34] He therefore descended the left bank of the Po, keeping the river on his right; and Scipio having thrown a bridge over the Ticinus, had entered what are now the Sardinian dominions, and was still advancing westward, with the Po on his left, although, as the river here makes a bend to the southward, he was no longer in its immediate neighborhood.[35]

Engagement on the Ticinus.

Each general was aware that his enemy was at hand, and both pushed forward with their cavalry and light troops in advance of their main armies, to reconnoiter each other's position and numbers. Thus was brought on accidentally the first action between Hannibal and the Romans in Italy, which, with some exaggeration, has been called the battle of the Ticinus.[36] The Numidians in Hannibal's army, being now properly supported by heavy cavalry, were able to follow their own manner of fighting, and, falling on the flanks and rear of the Romans, who were already engaged in front with Hannibal's heavy horsemen, took ample vengeance for their defeat on the Rhone. The Romans were routed; and the consul himself was severely wounded, and owed his life, it is said, to the courage and fidelity of a Ligurian slave.[37] With their cavalry thus crippled, it was impossible to act in such an open country; the Romans therefore hastily retreated, recrossed the Ticinus, and broke down the bridge, yet with so much hurry and confusion, that 600 men were left on the right bank, and fell into the enemy's hands; and then, crossing the Po also, established themselves under the walls of their colony, Placentia.

31 Polybius, III. 56.
32 Polybius, III. 60.
33 Polybius, III. 56.
34 Polybius, III. 60.
35 Polybius, III. 64.
36 Polybius, III. 65.
37 Polybius, III. 66. Livy, XXI. 46.

Hannibal's advance.

Hannibal, finding the bridge over the Ticinus destroyed, reascended the left bank of the Po till he found a convenient point to cross, and then, having constructed a bridge with the river boats, carried over his army in safety. Immediately, as he had expected, the Gauls on the right bank received him with open arms; and again descending the river, he arrived on the second day after his passage in sight of the Roman army, and on the following day offered them battle. But as the Romans did not move, he chose out a spot for his camp, and posted his army five or six miles from the enemy, and apparently on the east of Placentia, cutting off their direct communication with Ariminum and Rome.[38]

Campaign in Sicily. Sempronius joins Scipio.

On the first news of Hannibal's arrival in Italy, the senate had sent orders to the other consul, Ti. Sempronius, to return immediately to reinforce his colleague.[39] No event of importance had marked the first summer of the war in Sicily. Hannibal's spirit so animated the Carthaginian government, that they were everywhere preparing to act on the offensive; and before the arrival of Sempronius, M. Æmilius, the prætor, had already had to fight a naval action with the enemy, in order to defend Lilybæum.[40] He had defeated them, and prevented their landing, but the Carthaginian fleets still kept the sea; and whilst Sempronius was employing his whole force in the conquest of the island of Melita, the enemy were cruising on the northern side of Sicily, and making descents on the coast of Italy. On his return to Lilybæum he was going in pursuit of them, when he received orders to return home and join his colleague. He accordingly left part of his fleet with the prætor in Sicily, and part he committed to Sex. Pomponius, his lieutenant, for the protection of the coasts of Lucania and Campania; while, from a dread of the dangers and delays of the winter navigation of the Adriatic, his army was to march from Lilybæum to Messana, and, after crossing the strait, to go by land through the whole length of Italy, the soldiers being bound by oath to appear on a certain day at Ariminum. They completed their long march, it is said, in forty days; and from Ariminum they hastened to the scene of action, and effected their junction with the army of Scipio.[41]

Position of the Roman army.

Sempronius found his colleague no longer in his original position, close by Placentia and the Po, but withdrawn to the first hills which bound the great plain on the south, and leave an interval here of about six miles between themselves and the river.[42] But Hannibal's army lying, as it seems, to the eastward, the Roman consul retreated westward, and leaving Placentia to its own resources, crossed to the left bank of the Trebia, and there lay encamped, just where the stream issues from the last hills of the Apennines. It appears that the Romans had several magazines on the right bank of the Po above Placentia, on which the consul probably depended for his subsistence; and these posts, together with the presence of his army, kept the Gauls on the immediate bank of the river quiet, so that they gave Hannibal no assistance. When the Romans fell back behind the Trebia, Hannibal followed them, and encamped about five miles off from them, directly between them and Placentia.[43] But his powerful cavalry kept his communications open in every direction; and the Gauls who lived out of the immediate control of the Roman army and garrisons, supplied him with provisions abundantly.

Hannibal's policy.

It is not explained by any existing writer how Sempronius was able to effect his junction with his colleague without any opposition from Hannibal. The regular road from Ariminum to Placentia passes through a country unvaried by a single hill; and the approach of a large army should have been announced to Hannibal by his Numidian cavalry, soon enough to allow him to interrupt it. But so much in war depends upon trifling accidents,

[38] Polybius, III. 66.
[39] Polybius, III. 61.
[40] Livy, XXI. 49, 50.
[41] Polybius, III. 61, 68. Livy, XXI. 51.
[42] Polybius, III. 67.
[43] Polybius, III. 68.

that it is in vain to guess where we are without information. We only know that the two consular armies were united in Scipio's position on the left bank of the Trebia; that their united forces amounted to 40,000 men; and that Hannibal, with an army so reinforced by the Gauls since his arrival in Italy, that it was little inferior to his enemy's,[44] was so far from fearing to engage either consul singly, that he wished for nothing so much as to bring on a decisive battle with the combined armies of both. Depending on the support of the Gauls for his subsistence, he must not be too long a burden to them; they had hoped to be led to live on the plunder of the enemy's country, not to maintain him at the expense of their own. In order to force the Romans to a battle, he began to attack their magazines. Clastidium, now Castiggio, a small town on the right bank of the Po, nearly opposite to the mouth of the Ticinus, was betrayed into his hands by the governor; and he here found large supplies of corn.[45]

Sempronius commands the Roman army, and is anxious to engage.

On the other hand, Sempronius, having no fears for the event of a battle, was longing for the glory of a triumph over such an enemy as Hannibal;[46] and as Scipio was still disabled by his wound, he had the command of the whole Roman army. Besides, the Gauls who lived in the plain between the Trebia and Placentia, not knowing which side to espouse, had been plundered by Hannibal's cavalry, and besought the consuls to protect them. This was no time, Sempronius thought, to neglect any ally who still remained faithful to Rome: he sent out his cavalry and light troops over the Trebia to drive off the plunderers; and in such skirmishes he obtained some partial success, which made him the more disposed to risk a general battle.[47]

His rashness.

For this, as a Roman officer, and before Hannibal's military talents were fully known, he ought not to be harshly judged; but his manner of engaging was rash, and unworthy of an able general. He allowed the attacks of Hannibal's light cavalry to tempt him to follow them to their own field of battle. Early in the morning the Numidians crossed the river, and skirmished close up to the Roman camp: the consul first sent out his cavalry, and then his light infantry, to repel them;[48] and when they gave way and recrossed the river, he led his regular infantry out of his camp, and gave orders for the whole army to advance over the Trebia and attack the enemy.

Commencement of the battle on the Trebia.

It was mid-winter, and the wide pebbly bed of the Trebia, which the summer traveller may almost pass dry-shod, was now filled with a rapid stream running breast-high. In the night it had rained or snowed heavily; and the morning was raw and chilly, threatening sleet or snow.[49] Yet Sempronius led his soldiers through the river, before they had eaten any thing; and wet, cold, and hungry as they were, he formed them in order of battle on the plain. Meanwhile Hannibal's men had eaten their breakfast in their tents, and had oiled their bodies, and put on their armor around their fires. Then, when the enemy had crossed the Trebia, and were advancing in the open plain, the Carthaginians marched out to meet them; and about a mile in front of their camp, they formed in order of battle. Their disposition was simple: the heavy infantry, Gauls, Spaniards, and Africans, to the number of 20,000, were drawn up in a single line; the cavalry, 10,000 strong, was, with the elephants, on the two wings; the light infantry and Balerian slingers were in the front of the whole army. This was all Hannibal's visible force. But near the Trebia, and now left in their rear by the advancing Roman legions, were lying close hid in the deep and overgrown bed of a small water-course, two thousand picked soldiers, horse and foot, commanded by Hannibal's younger brother, Mago, whom he had posted there during the night, and whose ambush the Romans passed with no suspicion. Arrived on the field of battle, the legions were formed in their usual order, with the allied infantry on the wings; and their weak cavalry

44 Polybius, III. 72. Livy, XXI. 52.
45 Polybius, III. 69.
46 Polybius, III. 70.
47 Polybius, III. 69.
48 Polybius, III. 71.
49 Polybius, III. 72.

of 4000 men, ill able to contend with the numerous horsemen of Hannibal, were on the flanks of the whole line.

Defeat of the Roman light infantry and cavalry.

The Roman velites, or light infantry, who had been in action since daybreak, and had already shot away half their darts and arrows, were soon driven back upon the hastati and principes, and passed through the intervals of the maniples to the rear. With no less ease were the cavalry beaten on both wings, by Hannibal's horse and elephants. But when the heavy infantry, superior in numbers and better armed both for offence and defence, closed with the enemy, the confidence of Sempronius seemed to be justified: and the Romans, numbed and exhausted as they were, yet, by their excellence in all soldierly qualities, maintained the fight with equal advantage.[50]

Rout of the whole army.

On a sudden a loud alarm was heard; and Mago, with his chosen band, broke out from his ambush, and assaulted them furiously in the rear. Meantime both wings of the Roman infantry were broken down by the elephants, and overwhelmed by the missiles of the light infantry, till they were utterly routed, and fled towards the Trebia. The legions in the centre, finding themselves assailed on the rear, pushed desperately forwards, forced their way through the enemy's line, and marched off the field straight to Placentia. Many of the routed cavalry made off in the same direction, and so escaped. But those who fled towards the river were slaughtered unceasingly by the conquerors till they reached it; and the loss here was enormous. The Carthaginians, however, stopped their pursuit on the brink of the Trebia: the cold was piercing, and to the elephants so intolerable that they almost all perished; even of the men and horses many were lost, so that the wreck of the Roman army reached their camp in safety; and when night came on, Scipio again led them across the river, and, passing unnoticed by the camp of the enemy, took refuge with his colleague within the walls of Placentia.[51]

Hannibal winters in Gaul.

So ended Hannibal's first campaign in Italy. The Romans, after their defeat, despaired of maintaining their ground on the Po; and the two consular armies retreated in opposite directions, Scipio's upon Ariminum, and that of Sempronius across the Apennines into Etruria. Hannibal remained master of Cisalpine Gaul; but the season did not allow him to besiege Placentia and Cremona; and the temper of the Gauls rendered it evident that he must not make their country the seat of war in another campaign. Already they bore the burden of supporting his army so impatiently, that he made an attempt, in the dead of the winter, to cross the Apennines into Etruria, and was only driven back by the extreme severity of the weather, the wind sweeping with such fury over the ridges, and through the passes of the mountains, that neither man nor beast could stand against it.[52] He was forced therefore to winter in Gaul; but the innate fickleness and treachery of the people led him to suspect that attempts would be made against his life, and that a Gaulish assassin might hope to purchase forgiveness from the Romans for his country's revolt, by destroying the general who had seduced them. He therefore put on a variety of disguises to baffle such designs; he wore false hair, appearing sometimes as a man of mature years, and sometimes with the gray hairs of old age;[53] and if he had that taste for humor which great men are seldom without, and which some anecdotes of him imply, he must have been often amused by the mistakes thus occasioned, and have derived entertainment from that which policy or necessity had dictated.

Flaminius is chosen consul and takes the command.

We should be glad to catch a distinct view of the state of Rome, when the news first arrived of the battle of the Trebia. Since the disaster of Caudium, more than a hundred years before, there had been known no defeat of two consular armies united; and the surprise

[50] Polybius, III. 73.
[51] Polybius, III. 74.
[52] Livy, XXI. 58.
[53] Polybius, III. 78.

and vexation must have been great. Sempronius, it is said, returned to Rome to hold the comitia; and the people resolved to elect as consul a man who, however unwelcome to the aristocracy, had already distinguished himself by brilliant victories in the very country which was now the seat of war. They accordingly chose C. Flaminius for the second time consul; and with him was elected Cn. Servilius Geminus, a man of an old patrician family, and personally attached to the aristocratical party, but unknown to us before his present consulship. Flaminius' election was most unpalatable to the aristocracy; and as numerous prodigies were reported, and the Sibylline books consulted, and it was certain that various rites would be ordered to propitiate the favor of the gods,[54] he had some reason to suspect that his election would again be declared null and void, and he himself thus deprived of his command. He was anxious therefore to leave Rome as soon as possible: as his colleague was detained by the religious ceremonies, and by the care of superintending the new levies, Flaminius, it is said, left the city before the 15th of March, when his consulship was to begin, and actually entered upon his office at Ariminum, whither he had gone to superintend the formation of magazines, and to examine the state of the army.[55] But the aristocracy thought it was no time to press party animosities; they made no attempt to disturb Flaminius' election; and he appears to have had his province assigned him without opposition, and to have been appointed to command Sempronius' army in Etruria, while Servilius succeeded Scipio at Ariminum. The levies of soldiers went on vigorously; two legions were employed in Spain; one was sent to Sicily, another to Sardinia, and another to Tarentum; and four legions, more or less thinned by the defeat at the Trebia, still formed the nucleus of two armies in Ariminum and in Etruria. It appears that four new legions were levied, with an unusually large proportion of soldiers from the Italian allies and the Latin name; and these being divided between the two consuls, the armies opposed to Hannibal on either line, by which he might advance, must have been, in point of numbers, exceedingly formidable. Servilius, as we have seen, had his head-quarters at Ariminum; and Scipio, whom he superseded, sailed as proconsul into Spain, to take command of his original army there. Flaminius succeeded to Sempronius in Etruria, and lay encamped, it is said, in the neighborhood of Arretium.[56]

A. U. C. 537. A. C. 217.

Thus the main Roman armies lay nearly in the same positions which they had held eight years before, to oppose the expected invasion of the Gauls. But as the Gauls then broke into Etruria unperceived by either Roman army, so the Romans were again surprised by Hannibal on a line where they had not expected him. He crossed the Apennines, not by the ordinary road to Lucca, descending the valley of the Macra, but, as it appears, by a straighter line down the valley of the Anser or Serchio; and leaving Lucca on his right, he proceeded to struggle through the low and flooded country which lay between the right bank of the Arno and the Apennines below Florence, and of which the marsh or lake of Fucecchio still remains a specimen. Here again the sufferings of the army were extreme; but they were rewarded when they reached the firm ground below Fæsulæ, and were let loose upon the plunder of the rich valley of the upper Arno.[57]

Hannibal enters Etruria.

Flaminius lay quietly at Arretium, and did not attempt to give battle, but sent messengers to his colleague, to inform him of the enemy's appearance in Etruria. Hannibal was now on the south of the Apennines, and in the heart of Italy; but the experience of the Samnites and of Pyrrhus had shown that the Etruscans were scarcely more to be relied on than the Gauls; and it was in the south, in Samnium, and Lucania, and Apulia, that the only materials existed for organizing a new Italian war against Rome. Accord-

Advances towards Perugia.

54 Livy, XXI. 62.
55 Livy, XXI. 63.
56 Livy, XXII. 2.
57 Polybius, III. 78, 79.

ingly Hannibal advanced rapidly into Etruria, and finding that Flaminius still did not move, passed by Arretium, leaving the Roman army in his rear, and marching, as it seemed, to gain the great plain of central Italy, which reaches from Perusia to Spoletum, and was traversed by the great road from Ariminum to Rome.

Flaminius follows him.

The consul Flaminius now at last broke up from his position, and followed the enemy. Hannibal laid waste the country on every side with fire and sword, to provoke the Romans to a hasty battle; and leaving Cortona on his left untouched on its mountain seat, he approached the lake of Thrasymenus, and followed the road along its northeastern shore, till it ascended the hills which divide the lake from the basin of the Tiber.[58] Flaminius was fully convinced that Hannibal's object was not to fight a battle, but to lay waste the richest part of Italy: had he wished to engage, why had he not attacked him when he lay at Arretium, and while his colleague was far away at Ariminum? With this impression he pressed on his rear closely, never dreaming that the lion would turn from the pursuit of his defenceless prey, to spring on the shepherds who were dogging his steps behind.

Difficulty of marking out the field of battle.

The modern road along the lake, after passing the village of Passignano, runs for some way close to the water's edge on the right, hemmed in on the left by a line of cliffs, which make it an absolute defile. Then it turns from the lake and ascends the hills; yet, although they form something of a curve, there is nothing to deserve the name of valley; and the road, after leaving the lake, begins to ascend almost immediately, so that there is a very short distance during which the hills on the right and left command it. The ground therefore does not well correspond with the description of Polybius, who states that the valley in which the Romans were caught was not the narrow interval between the hills and the lake, but a valley beyond this defile, and running down to the lake, so that the Romans, when engaged in it, had the water, not on their right flank, but on their rear.[59] Livy's account is different, and represents the Romans as caught in the defile beyond Passignano, between the cliff and the lake. It is possible that if the exact line of the ancient road could be discovered, it might assist in solving the difficulty: in the mean time the battle of Thrasymenus must be one of the many events in ancient military history, where the accounts of historians, differing either with each other or with the actual appearances of the ground, are to us inexplicable.

Flaminius advances to attack Hannibal.

The consul had encamped in the evening on the side of the lake, just within the present Roman frontier, and on the Tuscan side of Passignano: he had made a forced march, and had arrived at his position so late that he could not examine the ground before him.[60] Early the next morning he set forward again; the morning mist hung thickly over the lake and the low grounds, leaving the heights, as is often the case, quite clear. Flaminius, anxious to overtake his enemy, rejoiced in the friendly veil which thus concealed his advance, and hoped to fall upon Hannibal's army while it was still in marching order, and its columns encumbered with the plunder of the valley of the Arno. He passed through the defile of Passignano, and found no enemy; this confirmed him in his belief that Hannibal did not mean to fight. Already the Numidian cavalry were on the edge of the basin of the Tiber: unless he could overtake them speedily, they would have reached the plain; and Africans, Spaniards, and Gauls, would be rioting in the devastation of the garden of Italy. So the consul rejoiced as the heads of his columns emerged from the defile, and, turning to the left, began to ascend the hills, where he hoped at least to find the rear-guard of the enemy.

At this moment the stillness of the mist was broken by barbarian war-cries on

[58] Polybius, III. 82. Livy, XXII. 3.
[59] III. 83.
[60] Polybius, III. 83, 84.

every side; and both flanks of the Roman column were assailed at once. Their right was overwhelmed by a storm of javelins and arrows, shot as if from the midst of darkness, and striking into the soldier's unguarded side, where he had no shield to cover him; while ponderous stones, against which no shield or helmet could avail, came crashing down upon their heads. On the left were heard the trampling of horse, and the well-known war-cries of the Gauls; and presently Hannibal's dreaded cavalry emerged from the mist, and were in an instant in the midst of their ranks; and the huge forms of the Gauls and their vast broadswords broke in upon them at the same moment. The head of the Roman column, which was already ascending to the higher ground, found its advance also barred; for here was the enemy whom they had so longed to overtake; here were some of the Spanish and African foot of Hannibal's army drawn up to wait their assault. The Romans instantly attacked these troops, and cut their way through: these must be the covering parties, they thought, of Hannibal's main battle; and, eager to bring the contest to a decisive issue, they pushed forward up the heights, not doubting that on the summit they should find the whole force of the enemy. And now they were on the top of the ridge, and to their astonishment no enemy was there; but the mist drew up, and, as they looked behind, they saw too plainly where Hannibal was: the whole valley was one scene of carnage, while on the sides of the hills above were the masses of the Spanish and African foot witnessing the destruction of the Roman army, which had scarcely cost them a single stroke.

Destruction of the main body of the Romans.

The advanced troops of the Roman column had thus escaped the slaughter; but being too few to retrieve the day, they continued their advance, which was now become a flight, and took refuge in one of the neighboring villages. Meantime, while the centre of the army was cut to pieces in the valley, the rear was still winding through the defile beyond, between the cliffs and the lake. But they too were attacked from the heights above by the Gauls, and forced in confusion into the water. Some of the soldiers, in desperation, struck out into the deep water swimming, and, weighed down by their armor, presently sank: others ran in as far as was within their depth, and there stood helplessly, till the enemy's cavalry dashed in after them. Then they lifted up their hands, and cried for quarter; but on this day of sacrifice, the gods of Carthage were not to be defrauded of a single victim; and the horsemen pitilessly fulfilled Hannibal's vow.

Of the rear-guard.

Thus, with the exception of the advanced troops of the Roman column, who were about 6000 men, the rest of the army was utterly destroyed. The consul himself had not seen the wreck consummated. On finding himself surrounded, he had vainly endeavored to form his men amidst the confusion, and to offer some regular resistance: when this was hopeless, he continued to do his duty as a brave soldier, till one of the Gaulish horsemen, who is said to have known him by sight from his former consulship, rode up and ran him through the body with his lance, crying out, "So perish the man who slaughtered our brethren, and robbed us of the lands of our fathers."[61] In these last words we probably rather read the unquenchable hatred of the Roman aristocracy to the author of an agrarian law, than the genuine language of the Gaul. Flaminius died bravely, sword in hand, having committed no greater military error than many an impetuous soldier, whose death in his country's cause has been felt to throw a veil over his rashness, and whose memory is pitied and honored. The party feelings which have so colored the language of the ancient writers respecting him, need not be shared by a modern historian: Flaminius was indeed an unequal antagonist to Hannibal; but in his previous life, as consul and as censor, he had served his country well; and if the defile of Thrasymenus witnessed his rashness, it also contains his honorable grave.

Death of Flaminius.

[61] Livy, XXII. 6.

The battle must have been ended before noon; and Hannibal's indefatigable cavalry, after having destroyed the centre and rear of the Roman army, hastened to pursue the troops who had broken off from the front, and had for the present escaped the general overthrow. They were supported by the light-armed foot and the Spaniards, and finding the Romans in the village to which they had retreated, proceeded to invest it on every side. The Romans, cut off from all relief, and with no provisions, surrendered to Maharbal, who commanded the party sent against them. They were brought to Hannibal: with the other prisoners taken in the battle, the whole number amounted to 15,000. The general addressed them by an interpreter; he told the soldiers who had surrendered to Maharbal, that their lives, if he pleased, were still forfeited, for Maharbal had no authority to grant terms without his consent: then he proceeded with the vehemence often displayed by Napoleon in similar circumstances, to inveigh against the Roman government and people, and concluded by giving all his Roman prisoners to the custody of the several divisions of his army. Then he turned to the Italian allies: they were not his enemies, he said; on the contrary, he had invaded Italy to aid them in casting off the yoke of Rome; he should still deal with them as he had treated his Italian prisoners taken at the Trebia; they were free from that moment, and without ransom.[62] This being done, he halted for a short time to rest his army, and buried with great solemnity thirty of the most distinguished of those who had fallen on his own side in the battle. His whole loss had amounted only to 1500 men, of whom the greater part were Gauls. It is said also that he caused careful search, but in vain, to be made for the body of the consul, Flaminius, being anxious to give him honorable burial.[63] So he acted afterwards to L. Æmilius and to Marcellus; and these humanities are worthy of notice, as if he had wished to show that, though his vow bound him to unrelenting enmity towards the Romans while living, it was a pleasure to him to feel that he might honor them when dead.

Capture of the advanced guard. Conduct of Hannibal to the prisoners.

The army of Hannibal now broke up from the scene of its victory, and, leaving Perusia unassailed, crossed the infant stream of the Tiber, and entered upon the plains of Umbria. Here Maharbal, with the cavalry and light troops, obtained another victory over a party of some thousand men, commanded by C. Centenius, and killed, took prisoners, or dispersed the whole body.[64] Then that rich plain, extending from the Tiber under Perusia to Spoletum, at the foot of the Monte Somma, was laid waste by the Carthaginians without mercy. The white oxen of the Clitumnus, so often offered in sacrifice to the gods of Rome by her triumphant generals, were now the spoil of the enemy, and were slaughtered on the altars of the gods of Carthage, amidst prayers for the destruction of Rome. The left bank of the Tiber again heard the Gaulish war-cry; and the terrified inhabitants fled to the mountains or into the fortified cities from this unwonted storm of barbarian invasion. The figures and arms of the Gauls, however formidable, might be familiar to many of the Umbrians; but they gazed in wonder on the slingers from the Balearian islands, on the hardy Spanish foot, conspicuous by their white linen coats bordered with scarlet;[65] on the regular African infantry, who had not yet exchanged their long lances and small shields for the long shield and stabbing sword of the Roman soldier; on the heavy cavalry, so numerous, and mounted on horses so superior to those of Italy; above all, on the bands of wild Numidians, who rode without saddle or bridle, as if the rider and his horse were one creature, and who scoured over the country with a speed and impetuosity defying escape or resistance. Amidst such a scene the colonists of Spoletum deserved well of their country, for shutting their gates boldly, and not yielding to the general panic; and when the Numid-

He ravages Umbria.

62 Polybius, III. 85.

63 Livy, XXII. 7. Compare Valerius Maximus, V. 1, Ext. 6.

64 Polybius, III. 86.

65 Polybius, III. 114. Livy, XXII. 46.

ian horsemen reined up their horses, and turned away from its well-manned walls, the colonists, with an excusable boasting, might claim the glory of having repulsed Hannibal.[66]

But Hannibal's way lay not over the Monte Somma, although its steep pass, rising immediately behind Spoletum, was the last natural obstacle between him and Rome. Beyond that pass the country was full, not of Roman colonies merely, but of Roman citizens: he would soon have entered on the territory of the thirty-five Roman tribes, where every man whom he would have met was his enemy. His eyes were fixed elsewhere: the south was entirely open to him; the way to Apulia and Samnium was cleared of every impediment. He crossed the Apennines in the direction of Ancona, and invaded Picenum: he then followed the coast of the Adriatic, through the country of the Marrucinians and Frentanians, till he arrived in the northern part of Apulia, in the country called by the Greeks Daunia.[67] He advanced slowly and leisurely, encamping after short marches, and spreading devastation far and wide: the plunder of slaves, cattle, corn, wine, oil, and valuable property of every description, was almost more than the army could carry or drive along. The soldiers, who, after their exhausting march from Spain over the Alps, had ever since been in active service, or in wretched quarters, and who from cold and the want of oil for anointing the skin had suffered severely from scorbutic disorders, were now revelling in plenty in a land of corn and olives and vines, where all good things were in such abundance that the very horses of the army, so said report, were bathed in old wines to improve their condition.[68] Meanwhile, wherever the army passed, all Romans or Latins, of an age to bear arms, were, by Hannibal's express orders, put to the sword.[69] Many an occupier of domain land, many a farmer of the taxes, or of those multiplied branches of revenue which the Roman government possessed all over Italy, collectors of customs and port duties, surveyors and farmers of the forests, farmers of the mountain pastures, farmers of the salt on the sea-coast, and of the mines in the mountains, were cut off by the vengeance of the Carthaginians; and Rome, having lost thousands of her poorer citizens in battle, and now losing hundreds of the richer classes in this exterminating march, lay bleeding at every pore.

He marches into Apulia.

But her spirit was invincible. When the tidings of the disaster of Thrasymenus reached the city, the people crowded to the Forum, and called upon the magistrates to tell them the whole truth.[70] The prætor peregrinus, M. Pomponius Matho, ascended the rostra, and said to the assembled multitude, "We have been beaten in a great battle; our army is destroyed; and C. Flaminius, the consul, is killed." Our colder temperaments scarcely enable us to conceive the effect of such tidings on the lively feelings of the people of the south, or to image to ourselves the cries, the tears, the hands uplifted in prayer, or clenched in rage, the confused sounds of ten thousand voices, giving utterance with breathless rapidity to their feelings of eager interest, of terror, of grief, or of fury. All the northern gates of the city were beset with crowds of wives and mothers, imploring every fresh fugitive from the fatal field for some tidings of those most dear to them. The prætors, M. Æmilius and M. Pomponius, kept the senate sitting for several days from sunrise to sunset, without adjournment, in earnest consultation on the alarming state of their country.

State of Rome on hearing the news of the battle.

Peace was not thought of for a moment: nor was it proposed to withdraw a single soldier from Spain, or Sicily, or Sardinia; but it was resolved that a dictator ought to be appointed, to secure unity of command. There had been no dictatorship for actual service since that of A. Atilius Colatinus, two-and-thirty years before, in the disastrous consulship of

Fabius Maximus is appointed dictator.

[66] Livy, XXII. 9.
[67] Polybius, III. 86. Livy, XXII. 9.
[68] Polybius, III. 87, 88.
[69] Polybius, III. 86.
[70] Polybius, III. 85. Livy, XXII. 7.

P. Claudius Pulcher and L. Junius Pullus. But it is probable that some jealousy was entertained of the senate's choice, if, in the absence of the consul, Cn Servilius, the appointment, according to ancient usage, had rested with them: nor was it thought safe to leave the dictator to nominate his master of the horse. Hence an unusual course was adopted: the centuries in their comitia elected both the one and the other, choosing one from each of the two parties in the state; the dictator, Q. Fabius Maximus, from one of the noblest, but at the same time the most moderate families of the aristocracy, and himself a man of a nature no less gentle than wise; the master of the horse, M. Minucius Rufus, as representing the popular party.[71]

Measures to propitiate the gods.

Religion in the mind of Q. Fabius was not a mere instrument for party purposes: although he may have had little belief in its truth, he was convinced of its excellence, and that a reverence for the gods was an essential element in the character of a nation, without which it must assuredly degenerate. Therefore, on the very day that he entered on his office, he summoned the senate, and dwelling on the importance of propitiating the gods, moved that the sibylline books should forthwith be consulted.[72] They directed, among other things, that the Roman people should vow to the gods what was called "a holy spring;" that is to say, that every animal fit for sacrifice born in the spring of that year, between the first day of March and the thirtieth of April, and reared on any mountain or plain or river-bank or upland pasture throughout Italy, should be offered to Jupiter.[73] Extraordinary games were also vowed to be celebrated in the Circus Maximus; prayers were put up at all the temples; new temples were vowed to be built; and for three days those solemn sacrifices were performed, in which the images of the gods were taken down from their temples, and laid on couches richly covered, with tables full of meat and wine set before them, in the sight of all the people, as if the gods could not but bless the city where they had deigned to receive hospitality.

Plan of Fabius for the campaign.

Then the dictator turned his attention to the state of the war. A long campaign was in prospect; for it was still so early in the season that the prætors had not yet gone out of their provinces; and Hannibal was already in the heart of Italy. All measures were taken for the defence of the country; even the walls and towers of Rome were ordered to be made good against an attack. Bridges were to be broken down; the inhabitants of open towns were to withdraw into places of security; and in the expected line of Hannibal's march, the country was to be laid waste before him, the corn destroyed, and the houses burnt.[74] This would probably be done effectually in the Roman territory; but the allies were not likely to make such extreme sacrifices; and this of itself was a reason why Hannibal did not advance directly upon Rome.

Roman levies.

More than thirty thousand men, in killed and prisoners, had been lost to the Romans in the late battle. The consul Cn. Servilius commanded above thirty thousand in Cisalpine Gaul; and he was now retreating in all haste, after having heard of the total defeat of his colleague. Two new legions were raised, besides a large force out of the city tribes, which was employed partly for the defence of Rome itself, and partly, as it consisted largely of the poorer citizens, for the service of the fleet. This last indeed was become a matter of urgent necessity; for the Carthaginian fleet was already on the Italian coast, and had taken a whole convoy of corn-ships, off Cosa, in Etruria, carrying supplies to the army in Spain; while the Roman ships, both in Sicily and at Ostia, had not yet been launched after the winter.[75] Now all the ships at Ostia and in the Tiber were sent to sea in haste, and the consul Cn. Servilius commanded them; whilst the dictator and master of the horse, having added the two newly raised legions to the consul's army, proceeded through Campania and

71 Polybius, III. 87. Livy, XXII. 8.
72 Livy, XXII. 9.
73 Livy, XXII. 10.
74 Livy, XXII. 11.
75 Livy, XXII. 11.

Samnium into Apulia, and, with an army greatly superior in numbers, encamped at the distance of about five or six miles from Hannibal.[76]

Hannibal ravages Samnium and enters Campania.

Besides the advantage of numbers, the Romans had that of being regularly and abundantly supplied with provisions. They had no occasion to scatter their forces in order to obtain subsistence; but keeping their army together, and exposing no weak point to fortune, they followed Hannibal at a certain distance, watched their opportunity to cut off his detached parties, and above all, by remaining in the field with so imposing an army, overawed the allies, and checked their disposition to revolt.[77] Thus Hannibal, finding that the Apulians did not join him, recrossed the Apennines, and moved through the country of the Hirpinians into that of the Caudinian Samnites. But Beneventum, once a great Samnite city, was now a Latin colony; and its gates were close shut against the invader. Hannibal laid waste its territory with fire and sword, then moved onwards under the south side of the Matese, and took possession of Telesia, the native city of C. Pontius, but now a decayed and defenceless town: thence descending the Calor to its junction with the Vulturnus, and ascending the Vulturnus till he found it easily fordable, he finally crossed it near Allifæ, and passing over the hills behind Calatia, descended by Cales into the midst of the Falernian plain, the glory of Campania.[78]

Fabius follows him.

Fabius steadily followed him, not descending into the plain, but keeping his army on the hills above it, and watching all his movements. Again the Numidian cavalry were seen scouring the country on every side; and the smoke of burning houses marked their track. The soldiers in the Roman army beheld the sight with the greatest impatience: they were burning for battle, and the master of the horse himself shared and encouraged the general feeling. But Fabius was firm in his resolution; he sent parties to secure even the pass of Tarracina, lest Hannibal should attempt to advance by the Appian road upon Rome; he garrisoned Casilinum on the enemy's rear; the Vulturnus from Casilinum to the sea barred all retreat southwards; the colony of Cales stopped the outlet from the plain by the Latin road; while from Cales to Casilinum the hills formed an unbroken barrier, steep and wooded, the few paths over which were already secured by the Roman soldiers.[79] Thus Fabius thought that Hannibal was caught as in a pitfall; that his escape was cut off, while his army, having soon wasted its plunder, could not possibly winter where it was, without magazines, and without a single town in its possession. For himself, he had all the resources of Campania and Samnium on his rear; while on his right the Latin road, secured by the colonies of Cales, Casinum, and Fregellæ, kept his communications with Rome open.

Hannibal's artifice to escape the Roman army.

Hannibal, on his part, had no thought of wintering where he was; but he had carefully husbanded his plunder, that it might supply his winter consumption, so that it was important to him to carry it off in safety. He had taken many thousand cattle; and his army besides was encumbered with its numerous prisoners, over and above the corn, wine, oil, and other articles, which had been furnished by the ravage of one of the richest districts in Italy. Finding that the passes in the hills between Cales and the Vulturnus were occupied by the enemy, he began to consider how he could surprise or force his passage without abandoning any of his plunder. He first thought of his numerous prisoners; and dreading lest in a night march they should either escape or overpower their guards and join their countrymen in attacking him, he commanded them all, to the number it is said of 5000 men, to be put to the sword. Then he ordered 2000 of the stoutest oxen to be selected from the plundered cattle, and pieces of split pine wood, or dry vine wood, to be fastened to their horns. About two hours before midnight the drovers began to

[76] Polybius, III. 88.
[77] Polybius, III. 90.
[78] Polybius, III. 90. Livy, XXII. 13.
[79] Livy, XXII. 15.

drive them straight to the hills, having first set on fire the bundles of wood about their heads; while the light infantry following them till they began to run wild, then made their own way to the hills, scouring the points just above the pass occupied by the enemy. Hannibal then commenced his march; his African infantry led the way, followed by the cavalry; then came all the baggage; and the rear was covered by the Spaniards and Gauls. In this order he followed the road in the defile, by which he was to get out into the upper valley of the Vulturnus, above Casilinum and the enemy's army.[80]

Its success

He found the way quite clear; for the Romans who had guarded it, seeing the hills above them illuminated on a sudden with a multitude of moving lights, and nothing doubting that Hannibal's army was attempting to break out over the hills in despair of forcing the road, quitted their position in haste, and ran towards the heights to interrupt or embarrass his retreat. Meanwhile Fabius, with his main army, confounded at the strangeness of the sight, and dreading lest Hannibal was tempting him to his ruin as he had tempted Flaminius, kept close within his camp till the morning. Day dawned only to show him his own troops who had been set to occupy the defile, engaged on the hills above with Hannibal's light infantry. But presently the Spanish foot were seen scaling the heights to reinforce the enemy; and the Romans were driven down to the plain with great loss and confusion; while the Spaniards and the light troops, having thoroughly done their work, disappeared behind the hills, and followed their main army.[81] Thus completely successful, and leaving his shamed and baffled enemy behind him, Hannibal no longer thought of returning to Apulia by the most direct road, but resolved to extend his devastations still further before the season ended. He mounted the valley of the Vulturnus towards Venafrum, marched from thence into Samnium, crossed the Apennines, and descended into the rich Pelignian plain by Sulmo, which yielded him an ample harvest of plunder, and thence retracing his steps into Samnium, he finally returned to the neighborhood of his old quarters in Apulia.

His plan for the winter.

The summer was far advanced; Hannibal had overrun the greater part of Italy: the meadows of the Clitumnus and the Vulturnus, and the forest glades of the high Apennines, had alike seen their cattle driven away by the invading army; the Falernian plain and the plain of Sulmo had alike yielded their tribute of wine and oil; but not a single city had as yet opened its gates to the conqueror, not a single state of Samnium had welcomed him as its champion, under whom it might revenge its old wrongs against Rome. Everywhere the aristocratical party had maintained its ascendency, and had repressed all mention of revolt from Rome. Hannibal's great experiment therefore had hitherto failed. He knew that his single army could not conquer Italy; as easily might king William's Dutch guards have conquered England: and six months had brought Hannibal no fairer prospect of aid within the country itself, than the first week after his landing in Torbay brought to king William. But among Hannibal's greatest qualities was the patience with which he knew how to abide his time; if one campaign had failed of its main object, another must be tried; if the fidelity of the Roman allies had been unshaken by the disaster of Thrasymenus, it must be tried by a defeat yet more fatal. Meantime he would take undisputed possession of the best winter-quarters in Italy; his men would be plentifully fed; his invaluable cavalry would have forage in abundance; and this at no cost to Carthage, but wholly at the expense of the enemy. The point which he fixed upon to winter at was the very edge of the Apulian plain, where it joins the mountains: on one side was a boundless expanse of corn, intermixed with open grass land, burnt up in summer, but in winter fresh and green; whilst on the other side were the wide pastures of the mountain forests, where his numerous cattle might be turned out till the first snows of autumn fell. These were

[80] Polybius, III. 93. Livy, XXII. 16, 17.

[81] Polybius, III. 94. Livy, XXII. 18.

as yet far distant; for the corn in the plain, although ripe, was still standing; and the rich harvests of Apulia were to be gathered this year by unwonted reapers.

Descending from Samnium, Hannibal accordingly appeared before the little town of Geronium, which was situated somewhat more than twenty miles northwest of the Latin colony of Luceria, in the immediate neighborhood of Larinum.[82] The town, refusing to surrender, was taken, and the inhabitants put to the sword; but the houses and walls were left standing, to serve as a great magazine for the army; and the soldiers were quartered in a regularly fortified camp without the town. Here Hannibal posted himself; and, keeping a third part of his men under arms to guard the camp and to cover his foragers, he sent out the other two-thirds to gather in all the corn of the surrounding country, or to pasture his cattle on the adjoining mountains. In this manner the storehouses of Geronium were in a short time filled with corn.

He takes Geronium.

Meanwhile the public mind at Rome was strongly excited against the dictator. He seemed like a man who, having played a cautious game, at last makes a false move, and is beaten; his slow defensive system, unwelcome in itself, seemed rendered contemptible by Hannibal's triumphant escape from the Falernian plain. But here too Fabius showed a patience worthy of all honor. Vexed as he must have been at his failure in Campania, he still felt sure that his system was wise; and again he followed Hannibal into Apulia, and encamped, as before, on the high grounds in his neighborhood. Certain religious offices called him at this time to Rome; but he charged Minucius to observe his system strictly, and on no account to risk a battle.[83]

Unpopularity of Fabius.

The master of the horse conducted his operations wisely: he advanced his camp to a projecting ridge of hills, immediately above the plain, and sending out his cavalry and light troops to cut off Hannibal's foragers, obliged the enemy to increase his covering force, and to restrict the range of his harvesting. On one occasion he cut off a great number of the foragers, and even advanced to attack Hannibal's camp, which, owing to the necessity of detaching so many men all over the country, was left with a very inferior force to defend it. The return of some of the foraging parties obliged the Romans to retreat; but Minucius was greatly elated, and sent home very encouraging reports of his success.[84]

Minucius adopts a bolder system.

The feeling against Fabius could no longer be restrained. Minucius had known how to manage his system more ably than he had done himself; such merit at such a crisis deserved to be rewarded; nor was it fit that the popular party should continue to be deprived of its share in the conduct of the war. Even among his own party Fabius was not universally popular: he had magnified himself and his system somewhat offensively, and had spoken too harshly of the blunders of former generals. Thus it does not appear that the aristocracy offered any strong resistance to a bill brought forward by the tribune M. Metilius, for giving the master of the horse power equal to the dictator's. The bill was strongly supported by C. Terentius Varro, who had been prætor in the preceding year, and was easily carried.[85]

His authority is made equal to the dictator's.

The dictator and master of the horse now divided the army between them, and encamped apart, at more than a mile's distance from each other. Their want of co-operation was thus notorious; and Hannibal was not slow to profit by it. He succeeded in tempting Minucius to an engagement on his own ground; and having concealed about 5000 men in some ravines and hollows close by, he called them forth in the midst of the action to fall on the enemy's rear. The rout of the Trebia was well-nigh repeated; but Fabius was near enough to come up in time to the rescue; and his fresh legions checked the

He is routed, and Fabius saves him.

82 Polybius, III. 100. Livy, XXII. 23.

83 Polybius, III. 94. Livy, XXII. 18.

84 Polybius, III. 101, 102. Livy, XXII. 24.

85 Polybius, III. 103. Livy, XXII. 25, 26.

pursuit of the conquerors, and enabled the broken Romans to rally. Still the loss already sustained was severe; and it was manifest that Fabius had saved his colleague from total destruction. Minucius acknowledged this generously: he instantly gave up his equal and separate command, and placed himself and his army under the dictator's orders.[86] The rest of the season passed quietly; and the dictator and master of the horse resigning their offices as usual at the end of six months, the army during the winter was put under the command of the consuls; Cn. Servilius having brought home and laid up the fleet, which he had commanded during the summer, and M. Atilius Regulus having been elected to fill the place of Flaminius.

State of feeling at Rome.

Meanwhile the elections for the following year were approaching; and it was evident that they would be marked by severe party struggles. The mass of the Roman people were impatient of the continuance of the war in Italy; not only the poorer citizens, whom it obliged to constant military service through the winter, and with no prospect of plunder, but still more perhaps the moneyed classes, whose occupation as farmers of the revenue was so greatly curtailed by Hannibal's army. Again, the occupiers of domain lands in remote parts of Italy could get no returns from their property; the wealthy graziers, who fed their cattle on the domain pastures, saw their stock carried off to furnish winter provisions for the enemy. Besides, if Hannibal were allowed to be unassailable in the field, the allies, sooner or later, must be expected to join him; they would not sacrifice every thing for Rome, if Rome could neither protect them nor herself. The excellence of the Roman infantry was undisputed: if with equal numbers they could not conquer Hannibal's veterans, let their numbers be increased, and they must overwhelm him. These were, no doubt, the feelings of many of the nobility themselves, as well as of the majority of the people; but they were imbittered by party animosity: the aristocracy, it was said, seemed bent on throwing reproach on all generals of the popular party, as if none but themselves were fit to conduct the war; Minucius himself had yielded to this spirit by submitting to be commanded by Fabius, when the law had made him his equal: one consul, at least, must be chosen, who would act firmly for himself and for the people; and such a man, to whose merits the bitter hatred of the aristocratical party bore the best testimony, was to be found in C. Terentius Varro.[87]

A. U. C. 538. A. C. 216. Election of the new consuls: Varro and Æmilius Paullus.

Varro, his enemies said, was a butcher's son; nay, it was added, that he had himself been a butcher's boy,[88] and had only been enabled by the fortune which his father had left him to throw aside his ignoble calling, and to aspire to public offices. So Cromwell was called a brewer; but Varro had been successively elected quæstor, plebeian and curule ædile, and prætor, while we are not told that he was ever tribune; and it is without example in Roman history, that a mere demagogue, of no family, with no other merits, civil or military, should be raised to such nobility. Varro was eloquent, it is true; but eloquence alone would scarcely have so recommended him; and if in his prætorship, as is probable, he had been one of the two home prætors, he must have possessed a competent knowledge of law. Besides, even after his defeat at Cannæ, he was employed for several years in various important offices, civil and military; which would never have been the case had he been the mere factious braggart that historians have painted him. The aristocracy tried in vain to prevent his election: he was not only returned consul, but he was returned alone, no other candidate obtaining a sufficient number of votes to entitle him to the suffrage of a tribe.[89] Thus he held the comitia for the election of his colleague; and considering the great influence exercised by the magistrate so presiding, it is creditable to him, and to the temper of the people generally,

[86] Polybius, III. 104, 105. Livy, XXI. 28, 29. Plutarch, Fabius, 13.

[87] Livy, XXII. 34.

[88] Valerius Maximus, III. 4, 4.

[89] Livy, XXII. 35.

that the other consul chosen was L. Æmilius Paullus, who was not only a known partisan of the aristocracy, but having been consul three years before, had been brought to trial for an alleged misappropriation of the plunder taken in the Illyrian war, and, although acquitted, was one of the most unpopular men in Rome. Yet he was known to be a good soldier; and the people, having obtained the election of Varro, did not object to gratify the aristocracy by accepting the candidate of their choice.

No less moderate and impartial was the temper shown in the elections of prætors. Two of the four were decidedly of the aristocratical party, M. Marcellus and L. Postumius Albinus; the other two were also men of consular rank, and no way known as opponents of the nobility, P. Furius Philus and M. Pomponius Matho. The two latter were to have the home prætorships; Marcellus was to command the fleet, and take charge of the southern coast of Italy; L. Postumius was to watch the frontier of Cisalpine Gaul.

New prætors.

The winter and spring passed without any military events of importance. Servilius and Regulus retained their command as proconsuls for some time after their successors had come into office; but nothing beyond occasional skirmishes took place between them and the enemy. Hannibal was at Geronium, maintaining his army on the supplies which he had so carefully collected in the preceding campaign: the consuls apparently were posted a little to the southward, receiving their supplies from the country about Canusium, and immediately from a large magazine, which they had established at the small town of Cannæ, near the Aufidus.[90]

Position of the armies.

Never was Hannibal's genius more displayed than during this long period of inactivity. More than half of his army consisted of Gauls, of all barbarians the most impatient and uncertain in their humor, whose fidelity, it was said, could only be secured by an ever open hand; no man was their friend any longer than he could gorge them with pay or plunder. Those of his soldiers who were not Gauls were either Spaniards or Africans; the Spaniards were the newly conquered subjects of Carthage, strangers to her race and language, and accustomed to divide their lives between actual battle and the most listless bodily indolence; so that, when one of their tribes first saw the habits of a Roman camp, and observed the centurions walking up and down before the prætorium for exercise, the Spaniards thought them mad, and ran up to guide them to their tents, thinking that he who was not fighting could do nothing but lie at his ease and enjoy himself.[91] Even the Africans were foreigners to Carthage: they were subjects harshly governed, and had been engaged within the last twenty years in a war of extermination with their masters. Yet the long inactivity of winter-quarters, trying to the discipline of the best national armies, was borne patiently by Hannibal's soldiers: there was neither desertion nor mutiny amongst them; even the fickleness of the Gauls seemed spell-bound; they remained steadily in their camp in Apulia, neither going home to their own country, nor over to the enemy. On the contrary, it seems that fresh bands of Gauls must have joined the Carthaginian army after the battle of Thrasymenus, and the retreat of the Roman army from Ariminum. For the Gauls and the Spaniards and the Africans were overpowered by the ascendency of Hannibal's character: under his guidance they felt themselves invincible: with such a general the yoke of Carthage might seem to the Africans and Spaniards the natural dominion of superior beings; in such a champion the Gauls beheld the appointed instrument of their country's gods to lead them once more to assault the capitol.

Wisdom shown by Hannibal during the winter.

Silanus, the Greek historian, was living with Hannibal daily;[92] and though not intrusted with his military and political secrets, he must have seen and known him as a man; he must have been familiar with his

Silanus.

[90] Polybius, III. 107.
[91] Strabo, p. 164.
[92] Nepos, Hannib. c. XIII.

habits of life, and must have heard his conversation in those unrestrained moments when the lightest words of great men display the character of their minds so strikingly. His work is lost to us; but had it been worthy of his opportunities, anecdotes from it must have been quoted by other writers, and we should know what Hannibal was. Then, too, the generals who were his daily companions would be something more to us than names: we should know Maharbal, the best cavalry officer of the finest cavalry service in the world: and Hasdrubal, who managed the commissariat of the army for so many years in an enemy's country; and Hannibal's young brother, Mago, so full of youthful spirit and enterprise, who commanded the ambush at the battle of the Trebia. We might learn something, too, of that Hannibal, surnamed the Fighter, who was the general's counsellor, ever prompting him, it was said, to deeds of savage cruelty,[93] but whose counsels Hannibal would not have listened to, had they been merely cruel, had they not breathed a spirit of deep devotion to the cause of Carthage, and of deadly hatred to Rome, such as possessed the heart of Hannibal himself. But Silanus saw and heard without heeding or recording; and on the tent and camp of Hannibal there hangs a veil, which the fancy of the poet may penetrate; but the historian turns away in deep disappointment; for to him it yields neither sight nor sound.

Opening of the campaign; Hannibal takes Cannæ.

Spring was come, and well-nigh departing; and in the warm plains of Apulia the corn was ripening fast, while Hannibal's winter supplies were now nearly exhausted. He broke up from his camp before Geronium, descended into the Apulian plains, and whilst the Roman army was still in its winter position, he threw himself on its rear, and surprised its great magazine at Cannæ.[94] The citadel of Cannæ was a fortress of some strength; this, accordingly, he occupied, and placed himself, on the very eve of harvest, between the Roman army and its expected resources, while he secured to himself all the corn of southern Apulia. It was only in such low and warm situations that the corn was nearly ready; the higher country, in the immediate neighborhood of Apulia, is cold and backward; and the Romans were under the necessity of receiving their supplies from a great distance, or else of retreating, or of offering battle. Under these circumstances the proconsuls sent to Rome, to ask what they were to do.

The Roman army.

The turning point of this question lay in the disposition of the allies. We cannot doubt that Hannibal had been busy during the winter in sounding their feelings; and now it appeared that, if Italy was to be ravaged by the enemy for a second summer without resistance, their patience would endure no longer. The Roman government therefore resolved to risk a battle; but they sent orders to the proconsuls to wait till the consuls should join them with their newly raised army; for a battle being resolved upon, the senate hoped to secure success by an overwhelming superiority of numbers. We do not exactly know the proportion of the new levies to the old soldiers; but when the two consuls arrived on the scene of action, and took the supreme command of the whole army, there were no fewer than eight Roman legions under their orders, with an equal force of allies; so that the army opposed to Hannibal must have amounted to 90,000 men.[95] It was evident that so great a multitude could not long be fed at a distance from its resources; and thus a speedy engagement was inevitable.

Varro resolves to bring on a battle.

But the details of the movements by which the two armies were brought in presence of each other on the banks of the Aufidus, are not easy to discover. It appears that the Romans, till the arrival of the new consuls, had not ventured to follow Hannibal closely; for when they did follow him, it took them two days' march to arrive in his neighborhood, where they encamped at about six miles distance from him.[96] They found him on the

[93] Polybius, IX. 24, 5.
[94] Polybius, III. 107.
[95] Polybius, III. 107.
[96] Polybius, III. 110.

left bank of the Aufidus, about eight or nine miles from the sea, and busied, probably, in collecting the corn from the early district on the coast, the season being about the middle of June. The country here was so level and open, that the consul, L. Æmilius, was unwilling to approach the enemy more closely, but wished to take a position on the hilly ground further from the sea, and to bring on the action there.[97] But Varro, impatient for battle, and having the supreme command of the whole army alternately with Æmilius every other day, decided the question irrevocably on the very next day, by interposing himself between the enemy and the sea, with his left resting on the Aufidus, and his right communicating with the town of Salapia.

Æmilius crosses the Aufidus.

From this position Æmilius, when he again took the command in chief, found it impossible to withdraw. But availing himself of his great superiority in numbers, he threw a part of his army across the river, and posted them in a separate camp on the right bank, to have the supplies of the country south of the Aufidus at command, and to restrain the enemy's parties who might attempt to forage in that direction. When Hannibal saw the Romans in this situation, he also advanced nearer to them, descending the left bank of the Aufidus, and encamped over against the main army of the enemy, with his right resting on the river.

Preparatory manœuvres and skirmishes.

The next day, which, according to the Roman calendar, was the last of the month Quinctilis, or July, the Roman reckoning being six or seven weeks in advance of the true season, Hannibal was making his preparations for battle, and did not stir from his camp; so that Varro, whose command it was, could not bring on an action. But on the first of Sextilis, or August, Hannibal being now quite ready, drew out his army in front of his camp and offered battle. Æmilius, however, remained quiet, resolved not to fight on such ground, and hoping that Hannibal would soon be obliged to fall back nearer the hills, when he found that he could no longer forage freely in the country near the sea.[98] Hannibal, seeing that the enemy did not move, marched back his infantry into his camp, but sent his Numidian cavalry across the river to attack the Romans on that side, as they were coming down in straggling parties to the bank to get water. For the Aufidus, though its bed is deep and wide, to hold its winter floods, is a shallow or a narrow stream in summer, with many points easily fordable, not by horse only, but by infantry. The watering parties were driven in with some loss, and the Numidians followed them to the very gates of the camp, and obliged the Romans, on the right bank, to pass the summer night in the burning Apulian plain without water.

Hannibal draws out his army.

At daybreak on the next morning, the red ensign, which was the well-known signal for battle, was seen flying over Varro's head-quarters;[99] and he issued orders, it being his day of command, for the main army to cross the river, and form in order of battle on the right bank. Whether he had any further object in crossing to the right bank, than to enable the soldiers on that side to get water in security, we do not know; but Hannibal, it seems, thought that the ground on either bank suited him equally; and he too forded the stream at two separate points, and drew out his army opposite to the enemy. The strong town of Canusium was scarcely three miles off in his rear; he had left his camp on the other side of the river; if he were defeated, escape seemed hopeless. But when he saw the wide, open plain around him, and looked at his numerous and irresistible cavalry, and knew that his infantry, however inferior in numbers, were far better and older soldiers than the great mass of their opponents, he felt that defeat was impossible. In this confidence his spirits were not cheerful merely, but even mirthful; he rallied one of his officers jestingly, who noticed the overwhelming numbers of the Romans; those near him

[97] Polybius, III. 110.
[98] Polybius, III. 111. Livy, XXII. 45.
[99] Plutarch, Fabius, 15.

laughed; and as any feeling at such a moment is contagious, the laugh was echoed by others; and the soldiers, seeing their great general in such a mood, were satisfied that he was sure of victory.[100]

Its position.

The Carthaginian army faced the north, so that the early sun shone on their right flank, while the wind, which blew strong from the south, but without a drop of rain, swept its clouds of dust over their backs, and carried them full into the faces of the enemy.[101] On their left, resting on the river, were the Spanish and Gaulish horse; next in the line, but thrown back a little, were half of the African infantry armed like the Romans; on their right, somewhat in advance, were the Gauls and Spaniards, with their companies intermixed; then came the rest of the African foot, again thrown back like their comrades; and on the right of the whole line were the Numidian light horsemen.[102] The right of the army rested, so far as appears, on nothing; the ground was open and level; but at some distance were hills overgrown with copsewood, and furrowed with deep ravines, in which, according to one account of the battle, a body of horsemen and of light infantry lay in ambush. The rest of the light troops, and the Balearian slingers, skirmished as usual in front of the whole line.

That of the Roman army,

Meanwhile the masses of the Roman infantry were forming their line opposite. The sun on their left flashed obliquely on their brazen helmets, now uncovered for battle, and lit up the waving forest of their red and black plumes, which rose upright from their helmets a foot and a half high.

They stood brandishing their formidable pila, covered with their long shields, and bearing on their right thigh their peculiar and fatal weapon, the heavy sword, fitted alike to cut and to stab.[103] On the right of the line were the Roman legions; on the left the infantry of the allies; while between the Roman right and the river were the Roman horsemen, all of them of wealthy or noble families; and on the left, opposed to the Numidians, were the horsemen of the Italians and of the Latin name. The velites or light infantry covered the front, and were ready to skirmish with the light troops and slingers of the enemy.

drawn up in columns.

For some reason or other, which is not explained in any account of the battle, the Roman infantry were formed in columns rather than in line, the files of the maniples containing many more than their ranks.[104] This seems an extraordinary tactic to be adopted in a plain by an army inferior in cavalry, but very superior in infantry. Whether the Romans relied on the river as a protection to their right flank, and their left was covered in some manner which is not mentioned,—one account would lead us to suppose that it reached nearly to the sea,[105]—or whether the great proportion of new levies obliged the Romans to adopt the system of the phalanx, and to place their raw soldiers in the rear, as incapable of fighting in the front ranks with Hannibal's

[100] Plutarch, Fabius, 15. *Εἰπόντος δέ τινος τῶν περὶ αὐτὸν ἀνδρὸς ἰσοτίμου, τοὔνομα Γίσκωνος, ὡς θαυμαστὸν αὐτῷ φαίνεται τὸ πλῆθος τῶν πολεμίων συναγαγὼν τὸ πρόσωπον ὁ Αννίβας, "ἕτερον," εἶπεν, "ὦ Γίσκων, λέληθέ σε τούτου θαυμασιώτερον." Ἐρομένου δὲ τοῦ Γίσκωνος "Τὸ ποῖον·" "Ὅτι" ἔφη "τούτων ὄντων τοσούτων, οὐδεὶς ἐν αὐτοῖς Γίσκων καλεῖται." Γενομένου δὲ παρὰ δόξαν αὐτοῖς τοῦ σκώμματος ἐμπίπτει γέλως πᾶσι· καὶ κατέβαινον ἀπὸ τοῦ λόφου τοῖς ἀπαντῶσιν ἀεὶ τὸ πεπαιγμένον ἀπαγγέλλοντες, ὥστε διὰ πολλῶν πολὺν εἶναι τὸν γέλωτα καὶ μηδ' ἀναλαβεῖν ἑαυτοὺς δύνασθαι τοὺς περὶ Ἀννίβαν. Τοῦτο τοῖς Καρχηδονίοις ἰδοῦσι θάῤῥος παρέστη λογιζομένοις ἀπὸ πολλοῦ καὶ ἰσχυροῦ τοῦ καταφρονοῦντος ἐπιέναι γελᾶν οὕτω καὶ παίζειν τῷ στρατηγῷ παρὰ τὸν κίνδυνον.*

[101] Livy, XXII. 46. Plutarch, Fabius, 16.

[102] Polybius, III. 113. Livy, XXII. 46.

[103] Polybius, III. 114. Livy, XXII. 45.

[104] Polybius, III. 113. *ποιῶν πολλαπλάσιον τὸ βάθος ἐν ταῖς σπείραις τοῦ πετώπου.* Raleigh suggests that "this had been found convenient against the Carthaginians in the former war. It was indeed no bad way of resistance against elephants, to make the ranks thick and short, but the files long, as also to strengthen well the rear, that it might stand fast compacted as a wall, under shelter whereof the disordered troops might rally themselves. Thus much, it seems, that Terentius had learned of some old soldiers; and therefore he now ordered his battles accordingly, as meaning to show more skill than was in his understanding. But the Carthaginians had here no elephants with them in the field: their advantage was in horse, against which this manner of imbattailing was very unprofitable, forasmuch as their charge is better sustained in front, than upon a long flank."

[105] Appian, VII. 21. *οἱ τὸ λαιὸν ἔχοντες ἐκ τῇ θαλάσσῃ.*

veterans,—it appears at any rate that the Roman infantry, though nearly double the number of the enemy, yet formed a line of only equal length with Hannibal's.

The skirmishing of the light-armed troops preluded as usual to the battle: the Balearian slingers slung their stones like hail into the ranks of the Roman line, and severely wounded the consul Æmilius himself. Then the Spanish and Gaulish horse charged the Romans front to front, and maintained a standing fight with them, many leaping off their horses and fighting on foot, till the Romans, outnumbered and badly armed, without cuirasses, with light and brittle spears, and with shields made only of ox-hide, were totally routed, and driven off the field.[106] Hasdrubal, who commanded the Gauls and Spaniards, followed up his work effectually; he chased the Romans along the river till he had almost destroyed them; and then, riding off to the right, he came up to aid the Numidians, who, after their manner, had been skirmishing indecisively with the cavalry of the Italian allies. These, on seeing the Gauls and Spaniards advancing, broke away and fled; the Numidians, most effective in pursuing a flying enemy, chased them with unweariable speed, and slaughtered them unsparingly; while Hasdrubal, to complete his signal services on this day, charged fiercely upon the rear of the Roman infantry.

Defeat of the Roman cavalry.

He found its huge masses already weltering in helpless confusion, crowded upon one another, totally disorganized, and fighting each man as he best could, but struggling on against all hope by mere indomitable courage. For the Roman columns on the right and left, finding the Gaulish and Spanish foot advancing in a convex line or wedge, pressed forwards to assail what seemed the flanks of the enemy's column; so that, being already drawn up with too narrow a front by their original formation, they now became compressed still more by their own movements, the right and left converging towards the centre, till the whole army became one dense column, which forced its way onwards by the weight of its charge, and drove back the Gauls and Spaniards into the rear of their own line. Meanwhile its victorious advance had carried it, like the English column at Fontenoy, into the midst of Hannibal's army; it had passed between the African infantry on its right and left; and now, whilst its head was struggling against the Gauls and Spaniards, its long flanks were fiercely assailed by the Africans, who, facing about to the right and left, charged it home, and threw it into utter disorder. In this state, when they were forced together into one unwieldy crowd, and already falling by thousands, whilst the Gauls and Spaniards, now advancing in their turn, were barring further progress in front, and whilst the Africans were tearing their mass to pieces on both flanks, Hasdrubal with his victorious Gaulish and Spanish horsemen broke with thundering fury upon their rear. Then followed a butchery such as has no recorded equal, except the slaughter of the Persians in their camp, when the Greeks forced it after the battle of Platæa. Unable to fight or fly, with no quarter asked or given, the Romans and Italians fell before the swords of their enemies, till, when the sun set upon the field, there were left out of that vast multitude no more than three thousand men alive and unwounded; and these fled in straggling parties, under cover of the darkness, and found a refuge in the neighboring towns.[107] The consul Æmilius, the proconsul Cn. Servilius, the late master of the horse M. Minucius, two quæstors, twenty-one military tribunes, and eighty senators, lay dead amidst the carnage; Varro with seventy horsemen had escaped from the rout of the allied cavalry on the right of the army, and made his way safely to Venusia.

Of the whole army.

But the Roman loss was not yet completed. A large force had been left in the camp on the left bank of the Aufidus, to attack Hannibal's camp during the action, which it was supposed that, with his inferior numbers, he could not leave adequately guarded. But it was defended

Capture of the camps.

[106] Polyb. III. 115. Livy, XXII. 47. [107] Polybius, III. 116. Livy, XXII. 49.

so obstinately, that the Romans were still besieging it in vain, when Hannibal, now completely victorious in the battle, crossed the river to its relief. Then the besiegers fled in their turn to their own camp, and there, cut off from all succor, they presently surrendered. A few resolute men had forced their way out of the smaller camp on the right bank, and had escaped to Canusium; the rest who were in it followed the example of their comrades on the left bank, and surrendered to the conqueror.

Results of the battle.

Less than six thousand men of Hannibal's army had fallen: no greater price had he paid for the total destruction of more than eighty thousand of the enemy, for the capture of their two camps, for the utter annihilation, as it seemed, of all their means for offensive warfare. It is no wonder that the spirits of the Carthaginian officers were elated by this unequalled victory. Maharbal, seeing what his cavalry had done, said to Hannibal, "Let me advance instantly with the horse, and do thou follow to support me; in four days from this time thou shalt sup in the capitol."[108] There are moments when rashness is wisdom; and it may be that this was one of them. The statue of the goddess Victory in the capitol may well have trembled in every limb on that day, and have dropped her wings, as if forever, but Hannibal came not; and if panic had for one moment unnerved the iron courage of the Roman aristocracy, on the next their inborn spirit revived; and their resolute will, striving beyond its present power, created, as is the law of our nature, the power which it required.

CHAPTER XLIV.

PROGRESS OF THE WAR IN ITALY AFTER THE BATTLE OF CANNÆ—REVOLT OF CAPUA, AND OF THE PEOPLE OF SOUTHERN ITALY, TO HANNIBAL—GREAT EXERTIONS OF THE ROMANS—SURPRISE OF TARENTUM—SIEGE OF CAPUA—HANNIBAL MARCHES ON ROME—REDUCTION AND PUNISHMENT OF CAPUA.—A. U. C. 538 TO 543.

Change in the character of the war.

FROM New Carthage to the plains of Cannæ, Hannibal's march resembled a mighty torrent, which, rushing along irresistible and undivided, fixes our attention to the one line of its course: all other sights and sounds in the landscape are forgotten, while we look on the rush of the vast volume of waters, and listen to their deep and ceaseless roar. Therefore I have not wished to draw away the reader's attention to other objects, but to keep it fixed upon the advance of Hannibal. But from Cannæ onwards the character of the scene changes. The single torrent, joined by a hundred lesser streams, has now swelled into a wide flood, overwhelming the whole valley; and the principal object of our interest is the one rock, now islanded amid the waters, and on which they dashed furiously on every side, as though they must needs sweep it away. But the rock stands unshaken: the waters become feebler; and their streams are again divided: and the flood shrinks; and the rock rises higher and higher; and the danger is passed away. In the next part of the second Punic war, our attention will be mainly fixed on Rome, as it has hitherto been on Hannibal. But in order to value aright the mightiness of her energy, we must consider the multitude of her enemies; how all southern Italy, led by Hannibal, struggled with her face to face; how Sicily and Macedon struck at her from be-

[108] Livy, XXII. 51.

hind; how Spain supplied arms to her most dangerous enemy. Yet her policy and her courage were everywhere: Sicily was struck to the earth by one blow; Macedon obliged to defend himself against his nearer enemies; the arms which Spain was offering to Hannibal were torn out of his grasp; revolted Italy was crushed to pieces; and the great enemy, after all his forces were dispersed and destroyed, was obliged, like Hector, to fight singly under his country's walls, and to fall like Hector, with the consolation of "having done mighty deeds, to be famed in after ages."

The news of the defeat reaches Rome.

The Romans, knowing that their army was in presence of the enemy, and that the consuls had been ordered no longer to decline a battle, were for some days in the most intense anxiety. Every tongue was repeating some line of old prophecy, or relating some new wonder or portent; every temple was crowded with supplicants; and incense and sacrifices were offered on every altar. At last the tidings arrived of the utter destruction of both the consular armies, and of a slaughter such as Rome had never before known. Even Livy felt himself unable adequately to paint the grief and consternation of that day;[1] and the experience of the bloodiest and most imbittered warfare of modern times would not help us to conceive it worthily. But one simple fact speaks eloquently: the whole number of Roman citizens able to bear arms had amounted at the last census to 270,000;[2] and supposing, as we fairly may, that the loss of the Romans in the late battle had been equal to that of their allies, there must have been killed or taken, within the last eighteen months, no fewer than 60,000, or more than a fifth part of the whole population of citizens above seventeen years of age. It must have been true, without exaggeration, that every house in Rome was in mourning.

Measures taken by the senate.

The two home prætors summoned the senate to consult for the defence of the city. Fabius was no longer dictator; yet the supreme government at this moment was effectually in his hands; for the resolutions which he moved were instantly and unanimously adopted. Light-horsemen were to be sent out to gather tidings of the enemy's movements; the members of the senate, acting as magistrates, were to keep order in the city, to stop all loud or public lamentations, and to take care that all intelligence was conveyed in the first instance to the prætors: above all, the city gates were to be strictly guarded, that no one might attempt to fly from Rome, but all abide the common danger together.[3] Then the Forum was cleared, and the assemblies of the people suspended; for at such a moment had any one tribune uttered the word "peace," the tribes would have caught it up with eagerness, and obliged the senate to negotiate.

Arrival of dispatches from Varro.

Thus the first moments of panic passed; and Varro's dispatches arrived, informing the senate that he had rallied the wrecks of the army at Canusium, and that Hannibal was not advancing upon Rome.[4] Hope then began to revive; the meetings of the senate were resumed, and measures taken for maintaining the war.

Marcellus is sent into Apulia.

M. Marcellus, one of the prætors for the year, was at this moment at Ostia, preparing to sail to Sicily. It was resolved to transfer him at once to the great scene of action in Apulia; and he was ordered to give up the fleet to his colleague, P. Furius Philus, and to march with the single legion which he had under his command into Apulia, there to collect the remains of Varro's army, and to fall back as he best could into Campania, while the consul returned immediately to Rome.[5]

Varro's manly conduct.

In the mean time the scene at Canusium was like the disorder of a ship going to pieces, when fear makes men desperate, and the instinct of self-preservation swallows up every other feeling. Some young men

[1] Livy, XXII. 54.
[2] Livy, Epit. XX.
[3] Livy, XXII. 55.
[4] Livy, XXII. 56.
[5] Livy, XXII. 57. Plutarch, Marcellus, 9.

of the noblest families, a Metellus being at the head of them, looking upon Rome as lost, were planning to escape from the ruin, and to fly beyond sea, in the hope of entering into some foreign service. Such an example at such a moment would have led the way to a general panic: if the noblest citizens of Rome despaired of their country, what allied state, or what colony, could be expected to sacrifice themselves in defence of a hopeless cause? The consul exerted himself to the utmost to check this spirit, and aided by some firmer spirits amongst the officers themselves, he succeeded in repressing it.[6] He kept his men together, gave them over to the prætor Marcellus, on his arrival at Canusium, and prepared instantly to obey the orders of the senate by returning to Rome. The fate of P. Claudius and L. Junius in the last war might have warned him of the dangers which threatened a defeated general; he himself was personally hateful to the prevailing party at Rome; and if the memory of Flaminius was persecuted, notwithstanding his glorious death, what could he look for, a fugitive general from that field where his colleague and all his soldiers had perished? Demosthenes dared not trust himself to the Athenian people after his defeat in Ætolia; but Varro, with a manlier spirit, returned to bear the obloquy and the punishment which the popular feeling, excited by party animosity, was so likely to heap on him. He stopped, as usual, without the city walls, and summoned the senate to meet him in the Campus Martius.

The senate thank him.

The senate felt his confidence in them, and answered it nobly. All party feeling was suspended; all popular irritation was subdued; the butcher's son, the turbulent demagogue, the defeated general, were all forgotten; only Varro's latest conduct was remembered, that he had resisted the panic of his officers, and, instead of seeking shelter at the court of a foreign king, had submitted himself to the judgment of his countrymen. The senate voted him their thanks, "because he had not despaired of the commonwealth."[7]

A dictator appointed.

It was resolved to name a dictator; and some writers related that the general voice of the senate and people offered the dictatorship to Varro himself, but that he positively refused to accept it.[8] This story is extremely doubtful; but the dictator actually named was M. Junius Pisa, a member of a popular family, and who had himself been consul and censor. His master of the horse was T. Sempronius Gracchus, the first of that noble but ill-fated name who appears in the Roman annals.[9]

The senate refuses to ransom the prisoners.

Already, before the appointment of the dictator, the Roman government had shown that its resolution was fixed to carry on the war to the death. Hannibal had allowed his Roman prisoners to send ten of their number to Rome to petition that the senate would permit the whole body to be

[6] The author would, doubtless, have explained his reasons for ascribing the suppression of this conspiracy to leave Italy to Varro. By Livy, XXII. 53, by Valerius Maximus, V. 6, 7, by Dion, Fragm. Peiresc. XLIX., it is attributed to Scipio. See also Silius Italicus, X. 426, fol. It is somewhat remarkable that Polybius makes no mention of the fact, either in the account of the battle of Cannæ, or in the character of Scipio, X. 1–6, where he speaks of Scipio's early exploits. According to Livy, with whose accounts Dion's concurs, the fugitives at Canusium were headed by four tribunes, who voluntarily submitted to the command of Scipio and Appius Claudius, two of their number; and Scipio, by a characteristic act of youthful heroism, stifled the plot. Meanwhile Varro is represented to have been at Venusia. Appian's account, too, VII. 26, though differing as to the order of the events, and plainly inaccurate—since it makes Varro resign the command to Scipio, instead of Marcellus, when he went to Rome—implies that Scipio distinguished himself at Canusium. Dion's statement is the more trustworthy, as he did not join in the cry against Varro, but speaks with high praise of his conduct after the defeat. Ἐς τὸ Κανύσιον ἐλθὼν τά τε ἐνταῦθα κατεστήσατο, καὶ τοῖς πλησιοχώροις φρουρὰς ὡς ἐκ τῶν παρόντων ἔπεμψεν, προσβάλλοντάς τε τῇ πόλει ἱππέας, ἀπεκρούσατο· τό τε σύνολον οὔτ' ἀθυμήσας, οὔτε καταπτήξας, ἀλλ' ἀπ' ὀρθῆς διανοίας ὥσπερ μηδενὸς σφίσι δεινοῦ συμβεβηκότος, πάντα τὰ πρόσφορα τοῖς παροῦσι καὶ ἐβούλευσε καὶ ἔπραξεν. Zonaras was so careless in abridging his author, that he transfers what Dion here says of Varro to Scipio.

[7] Livy, XXII. 61. Plutarch, Fabius, 18. See also Florus, II. 6.

[8] Valerius Maximus, III. 4, § IV. 5, § 2. Frontinus, IV. 5, 6. "Honoribus, quum, ei deferrentur a populo, renuntiavit, dicens, felicioribus, magistratibus reipublicæ opus esse."

[9] Livy, XXII. 57.

ransomed by their friends at the sum of three minæ, or 3000 ases for each prisoner. But the senate absolutely forbade the money to be paid, neither choosing to furnish Hannibal with so large a sum, nor to show any compassion to men who had allowed themselves to fall alive into the enemy's hands.[10] The prisoners therefore were left in hopeless captivity; and the armies which the state required were to be formed out of other materials. The expedients adopted showed the urgency of the danger.

When the consuls took the field at the beginning of the campaign, two legions had been left, as usual, to cover the capital. These were now to be employed in active service; and with them was a small detachment of troops, which had been drawn from Picenum and the neighborhood of Ariminum, where their services were become of less importance. The contingents from the allies were not ready; and there was no time to wait for them. In order, therefore, to enable the dictator to take the field immediately, eight thousand slaves were enlisted, having expressed their willingness to serve; and arms were provided by taking down from the temple the spoils won in former wars.[11] The dictator went still further: he offered pardon to criminals and release to debtors, if they were willing to take up arms; and amongst the former class were some bands of robbers, who then, as in later times, infested the mountains, and who consented to serve the state on receiving an indemnity for their past offences.[12] With this strange force, amounting, it is said, to about twenty-five thousand men, M. Junius marched into Campania; whilst a new levy of the oldest and youngest citizens supplied two new legions for the defence of the capital, in the place of those which followed the dictator into the field. M. Junius fixed his head-quarters at Teanum,[13] on high ground upon the edge of the Falernian plain, with the Latin colony of Cales in his front, and communicating by the Latin road with Rome.

Measures to raise troops.

The dictator was at Teanum, and M. Marcellus with the army of Cannæ, whom we left in Apulia, is described as now lying encamped above Suessula,[14] that is, on the right bank of the Vulturnus, on the hills which bound the Campanian plain, ten or twelve miles to the east of Capua, on the right of the Appian road as it ascends the pass of Caudium towards Beneventum. Thus we find the seat of war removed from Apulia to Campania; but the detail of the intermediate movements is lost; and we must restore the broken story as well as we can, by tracing Hannibal's operations after the battle of Cannæ, which are undoubtedly the key to those of his enemies.

Position of the Roman army.

The fidelity of the allies of Rome, which had not been shaken by the defeat of Thrasymenus, could not resist the fiery trial of Cannæ. The Apulians joined the conqueror immediately, and Arpi and Salapia opened their gates to him. Bruttium, Lucania, and Samnium were ready to follow the example;[15] and Hannibal was obliged to divide his army, and send officers into different parts of the country, to receive and protect those who wished to join him, and to organize their forces for effective co-operation in the field. Meanwhile he himself remained in Apulia, not perhaps without hope that this last blow had broken the spirit as well as the power of the enemy, and that they would listen readily to proposals of peace. With this view he sent a Carthaginian officer to accompany the deputation of the Roman prisoners to Rome, and ordered him to encourage any disposition on the part of the Romans to open a negotiation.[16] When he found, therefore, on the return of the deputies, that his officers had not been allowed to enter the city, and that the Romans had refused to ransom their prisoners, his disappointment betrayed him into acts of the most

Revolt of the allies; conduct of Hannibal.

[10] Polybius, VI. 58. Livy, XII. 58–61. Appian, VII. 28. Cicero de Off. I. 13, 32. III. 32. Aulus Gellius, VII. 18.
[11] Livy, XXII. 57.
[12] Livy, XXIII. 14.
[13] Livy, XXIII. 24.
[14] Livy, XXII. 14.
[15] Livy, XXII. 61. Polybius, III. 118. Appian, VII. 31.
[16] Livy, XXII. 58.

inhuman cruelty. The mass of the prisoners left in his hands he sold for slaves; and so far he did not overstep the recognized laws of warfare; but many of the more distinguished of them he put to death; and those who were senators he obliged to fight as gladiators with each other in the presence of his whole army. It is added, that brothers were in some instances brought out to fight with their brothers, and sons with their fathers; but that the prisoners refused so to sin against nature, and chose rather to suffer the worst torments than to draw their swords in such horrible combats.[17] Hannibal's vow may have justified all these cruelties in his eyes; but his passions deceived him, and he was provoked to fury by the resolute spirit which ought to have excited his admiration. To admire the virtue which thwarts our dearest purposes, however natural it may seem to indifferent spectators, is one of the hardest trials of humanity.

Hannibal enters Campania: revolt of Capua.

Finding the Romans immovable, Hannibal broke up from his position in Apulia, and moved into Samnium. The popular party in Compsa opened their gates to him; and he made the place serve as a dépôt for his plunder, and for the heavy baggage of his army.[18] His brother Mago was then ordered to march into Bruttium with a division of the army, and after having received the submission of the Hirpinians on his way, to embark at one of the Bruttian ports, and carry the tidings of his success to Carthage.[19] Hanno, with another division, was sent into Lucania, to protect the revolt of the Lucanians;[20] while Hannibal himself, in pursuit of a still greater prize, descended once more into the plains of Campania. The Pentrian Samnites, partly restrained by the Latin colony of Œsernia, and partly by the influence of their own countryman, Num. Decimius of Bovianum, a zealous supporter of the Roman alliance, remained firm in their adherence to Rome: but the Hirpinians and the Caudinian Samnites all joined the Carthaginians; and their soldiers no doubt formed part of the army with which Hannibal invaded Campania.[21] There all was ready for his reception. The popular party in Capua were headed by Pacuvius Calavius, a man of the highest nobility, and married to a daughter of Appius Claudius, but whose ambition led him to aspire to the sovereignty, not of his own country only, but, through Hannibal's aid, of the whole of Italy, Capua succeeding, as he hoped, to the supremacy now enjoyed by Rome. The aristocratical party were weak and unpopular, and could offer no opposition to him; while the people, wholly subject to his influence, concluded a treaty with Hannibal, and admitted the Carthaginian general and his army into the city.[22] Thus the second city in Italy, capable, it is said, of raising an army of 30,000 foot and 4000 horse,[23] connected with Rome by the closest ties, and which for nearly a century had remained true to its alliance under all dangers, threw itself into the arms of Hannibal, and took its place at the head of the new coalition of southern Italy, to try the old quarrel of the Samnite wars once again.

Marcellus encamps at Suessula.

This revolt of Capua, the greatest result, short of the submission of Rome itself, which could have followed from the battle of Cannæ, drew the Roman armies towards Campania. Marcellus had probably fallen

[17] Diodorus, XXVI. Exc. de. Virtut. et Vitiis. Appian, VII. 28. Zonaras, IX. 2. Valerius Maximus, IX. 2, Ext. 2. But as even Livy does not mention these stories, though they would have afforded such a topic for his rhetoric,—nor does Polybius, either in IX. 24, when speaking of Hannibal's alleged cruelty, or in VI. 58, where he gives the account of the mission of the captives, and adds that Hannibal, when he heard that the Romans had refused to ransom them, *κατεπλάγη τὸ στάσιμον καὶ τὸ μεγαλόψυχον τῶν ἀνδρῶν ἐν τοῖς διαβουλίοις*,—there must doubtless be a great deal of exaggeration in them, even if they had any foundation at all. The story in Pliny, VIII. 7, that the last survivor of these gladiatorial combats had to fight against an elephant, and killed him, and was then treacherously waylaid and murdered by Hannibal's orders, was probably invented with reference to this very occasion. The remarks of Polybius should make us slow to believe the stories of Hannibal's cruelties, which so soon became a theme for the invention of poets and rhetoricians.

[18] Livy, XXIII. 1.

[19] Livy, XXIII. 11.

[20] Livy, XXIII. 37.

[21] Livy, XXII. 61, 24.

[22] Livy, XXIII. 2–4.

[23] Livy, XXIII. 5. See Niebuhr, Vol. II. note 145.

back from Canusium by the Appian road through Beneventum, moving by an interior and shorter line; whilst Hannibal advanced by Compsa upon Abellinum, descending into the plain of Campania by what is now the pass of Monteforte. Hannibal's cavalry gave him the whole command of the country; and Marcellus could do no more than watch his movements from his camp above Suessula, and wait for some opportunity of impeding his operations in detail.

How came it that Rome was not destroyed?

At this point in the story of the war, the question arises, how was it possible for Rome to escape destruction? Nor is this question merely prompted by the thought of Hannibal's great victories in the field, and the enormous slaughter of Roman citizens at Thrasymenus and Cannæ; it appears even more perplexing to those who have attentively studied the preceding history of Rome. A single battle, evenly contested and hardly won, had enabled Pyrrhus to advance into the heart of Latium; the Hernican cities and the impregnable Præneste had opened their gates to him; yet Capua was then faithful to Rome; and Samnium and Lucania, exhausted by long years of unsuccessful warfare, could have yielded him no such succor, as now, after fifty years of peace, they were able to afford to Hannibal. But now, when Hannibal was received into Capua, the state of Italy seemed to have gone backwards a hundred years, and to have returned to what it had been after the battle of Lautulæ in the second Samnite war,[24] with the immense addition of the genius of Hannibal and the power of Carthage thrown into the scale of the enemies of Rome. Then, as now, Capua had revolted, and Campania, Samnium, and Lucania, were banded together against Rome; but this same confederacy was now supported by all the resources of Carthage: and at its head in the field of battle was an army of thirty thousand veterans and victorious soldiers, led by one of the greatest generals whom the world has ever seen. How could it happen that a confederacy so formidable was only formed to be defeated?—that the revolt of Capua was the term of Hannibal's progress?—that from this day forwards his great powers were shown rather in repelling defeat than in commanding victory?—that, instead of besieging Rome, he was soon employed in protecting and relieving Capua?—and that his protection and succors were alike unavailing?

Causes which saved her.

No single cause will explain a result so extraordinary. Rome owed her deliverance principally to the strength of the aristocratical interest throughout Italy,—to her numerous colonies of the Latin name,—to the scanty numbers of Hannibal's Africans and Spaniards, and to his want of an efficient artillery. The material of a good artillery must surely have existed in Capua; but there seem to have been no officers capable of directing it; and no great general's operations exhibit so striking a contrast of strength and weakness, as may be seen in Hannibal's battles and sieges. And when Cannæ had taught the Romans to avoid pitched battles in the open field, the war became necessarily a series of sieges, where Hannibal's strongest arm, his cavalry, could render little service, while his infantry was in quality not more than equal to the enemy, and his artillery was decidedly inferior.

Military measures in Campania.

With two divisions of his army absent in Lucania and Bruttium, and while anxiously waiting for the reinforcements which Mago was to procure from Carthage, Hannibal could not undertake any great offensive operation after his arrival in Campania. He attempted only to reduce the remaining cities of the Campanian plain and sea-coast, and especially to dislodge the Romans from Casilinum, which, lying within three miles of Capua, and commanding the passage of the Vulturnus, not only restrained all his movements, but was a serious annoyance to Capua, and threatened its territory with continual incursions. Atilla and Calatia had revolted to him already with Capua: and he took Nuceria, Alfaterna, and Acerræ. The Greek cities on the coast, Neapolis and Cumæ, were firmly attached to Rome, and were too strong to be besieged

[24] See Chap. XXXI.

with success; but Nola lay in the midst of the plain nearly midway between Capua and Nuceria; and the popular party there, as elsewhere, were ready to open their gates to Hannibal. He was preparing to appear before the town; but the aristocracy had time to apprise the Romans of their danger; and Marcellus, who was then at Casilinum, marched round behind the mountains to escape the enemy's notice, and descended suddenly upon Nola from the hills which rise directly above it. He secured the place, repressed the popular party by some bloody executions, and when Hannibal advanced to the walls, made a sudden sally, and repulsed him with some loss.[25] Having done this service, and left the aristocratical party in absolute possession of the government, he returned again to the hills, and lay encamped on the edge of the mountain boundary of the Campanian plain, just above the entrance of the famous pass of Caudium. His place at Casilinum was to be supplied by the dictator's army from Teanum; but Hannibal watched his opportunity, and anticipating his enemies this time, laid regular siege to Casilinum, which was defended by a garrison of about 1000 men.

Conduct of the garrison of Casilinum.

This garrison had acted the very same part towards the citizens of Casilinum, which the Campanians had acted at Rhegium in the war with Pyrrhus.[26] About 500 Latins of Præneste, and 450 Etruscans of Perusia, having been levied too late to join the consular armies when they took the field, were marching after them into Apulia by the Appian road, when they heard the tidings of the defeat of Cannæ. They immediately turned about, and fell back upon Casilinum, where they established themselves, and for their better security massacred the Campanian inhabitants, and, abandoning the quarter of the town which was on the left bank of the Vulturnus, occupied the quarter on the right bank.[27] Marcellus, when he retreated from Apulia with the wreck of Varro's army, had fixed his head-quarters for a time at Casilinum; the position being one of great importance, and there being some danger lest the garrison, while they kept off Hannibal, should resolve to hold the town for themselves rather than for the Romans. They were now left to themselves; and dreading Hannibal's vengeance for the massacre of the old inhabitants, they resisted his assaults desperately, and obliged him to turn the siege into a blockade. This was the last active operation of the campaign: all the armies now went into winter-quarters. The dictator remained at Teanum; Marcellus lay in his mountain camp above Nola; and Hannibal's army was at Capua.[28] Being quartered in the houses of the city, instead of being encamped by themselves, their discipline, it is likely, was somewhat impaired by the various temptations thrown in their way: and as the wealth and enjoyments of Capua at that time were notorious, the writers who adopted the vulgar declamations against luxury, pretended that Hannibal's army was ruined by the indulgences of this winter, and that Capua was the Cannæ of Carthage.[29]

Progress of the war in other quarters.

This intermission of active warfare will afford us an opportunity of noticing the progress of events elsewhere, which we have hitherto unavoidably neglected. From the banks of the Iberus Hannibal had made his way without interruption to Capua; and the countries which he left behind him sink in like manner from the notice of the historian. We must now see what had happened in each of them since Hannibal's passage.

A. U. C. 537. A. C. 217. Success of the Romans in Spain.

It has been mentioned above, that P. Scipio, when he returned from the Rhone to Italy, to be ready to meet Hannibal in Cisalpine Gaul, sent his army into Spain under the command of his brother.[30] After his consulship was over, his province of Spain was still continued to him as proconsul; and he went thither accordingly to take the command. He found that his brother had already effected much: he had defeated and made

25 Livy, XXIII. 14–17. Plutarch, Marcellus, 11.

26 See Vol. II. p. 398.

27 Livy, XXIII. 17.

28 Livy, XXIII. 18.

29 Livy, XXIII. 45. Florus, II. 6. Valerius Maximus, IX. Ext. 1.

30 Above, p. 477.

prisoner the Carthaginian general, Hanno, whom Hannibal left to maintain his latest conquests in Spain, and had driven the Carthaginians beyond the Iberus.[31] His own arrival in Spain took place in the summer of the year 537, three or four months after the battle of Thrasymenus; and although little was done in the field before the end of the season, the Carthaginian governor of Saguntum was persuaded to set at liberty all the Spanish hostages left in his custody; and the Spaniard who had advised this step under the mask of good will to Carthage, as a means of securing the affections of the Spanish people, had no sooner received the hostages with orders to take them back to their several homes, than he delivered them up to the Romans. Thus Scipio enjoyed the whole credit of restoring them to their friends, and made the Roman name generally popular.[32] In the following year, Hasdrubal, the son of Hamilcar, having received orders to march into Italy to co-operate with his brother, was encountered by the Romans near the Iberus, and defeated;[33] so that his invasion of Italy was for the present effectually prevented.

A. U. C. 538. A. C. 216. Its great importance.

The importance of this Spanish war cannot be estimated too highly; for, by disputing the possession of Spain, the Romans, deprived their enemy of his best nursery of soldiers, from which otherwise he would have been able to raise army after army for the invasion of Italy. But its importance consisted not so much in the particular events, as in its being kept up at all; nor is there any thing requiring explanation in the success of the Romans. Their army had originally consisted of 20,000 men; and P. Scipio had brought some reinforcements; while Hasdrubal and Hanno in their two armies had a force not much superior: hence, after the total defeat of Hanno, Hasdrubal could not meet the Romans with any chance of success. For Spanish levies were now no longer to be depended on, while the Romans were inviting the nations of Spain to leave the Carthaginians, and come over to them. In this contest between the two nations, which should most influence the minds of the Spaniards, the ascendency of the Roman character was clearly shown; and the natives were drawn, as by an invincible attraction, to the worthier.

Tranquillity of Cisalpine Gaul.

While Spain was thus the scene of active warfare, Cisalpine Gaul, after Hannibal's advance into Italy, seems to have sunk back into a state of tranquillity, such as it had enjoyed in the first Punic war. It is very remarkable, that the colonies of Placentia and Cremona, so far in advance of the Roman frontier, and surrounded by hostile tribes, were left unassailed from the time when Hannibal crossed the Apennines into Etruria. We are only told that L. Postumius Albinus, one of the prætors of the year 538, was sent with an army into Gaul, when Varro and Æmilius marched into Apulia, with the express object of compelling the Gauls in Hannibal's service to return to the defence of their own country.[34] What he did in the course of that summer we know not: at the end of the consular year he was still in his province, and was elected consul for the year following, with Ti. Sempronius Gracchus. But before his consulship began, early in March apparently, according to the Roman calendar, he fell into an ambuscade, while advancing into the enemy's country, and was cut to pieces[35] with his whole army. We are told that the Romans found it utterly impossible to replace the army thus lost, and that it was resolved for the present to leave the Gauls to themselves.[36] But it was not so certain that the Gauls, if unopposed, would leave the Romans to themselves; and we find that M. Pomponius Matho, who had been city prætor in 538, was sent, on the expiration of his office, with proconsular power to Ariminum, and that he remained on that frontier for two years with an army of two legions,[37] while C. Varro with another legion was quartered in Picenum, to support him in

[31] Polybius, III. 76.
[32] Polybius, III. 98, 99.
[33] Livy, XXIII. 27, 28, 29.
[34] Polybius, III. 106.
[35] Livy, XXIII. 24. Polybius, III. 118.
[36] Livy, XXIII. 25.
[37] Livy, XXIV. 10, 44. See Duker's note on the former passage.

time of need.[38] Still the inaction of the Gauls is extraordinary, the more so as we find them in arms immediately after the end of the war with Carthage, and attacking Placentia and Cremona, which they had so long left in peace.[39] We can only suppose that the absence of a large portion of their soldiers, who were serving in Hannibal's army, crippled the power of the Gauls who were left at home; and that long experience had taught them that, unless when conducted by a general of a more civilized nation, they could not carry on war successfully with the Romans. The older Gaulish chiefs also were often averse to war, when the younger chiefs were in favor of it;[40] and the Romans were likely to be lavish of presents at a time so critical, to confirm their friends in their peaceful sentiments, and to win over their adversaries. It seems probable that some truce was concluded, which restrained either the Gauls or Romans from invading each other's territory; and the Romans were contented not to require the recall of the Gauls serving with Hannibal; some of whom, we know, continued to be with him till a much later period. The multitude of the Gauls rejoiced, perhaps, that they had won thus much from their proud enemy, and were well content that the war should be carried on far from their own frontiers, and yet that they should share in its advantages. But wiser men might regret that better use was not made of the favorable moment; that no Carthaginian officer had been left with them to organize their armies and conduct them into the field; that the Roman encroachments on their soil were still maintained; and that there was no Gellius Gnatius in northern Italy to rouse the Etruscans and Umbrians to unite their forces with those of the Gauls on the south of the Apennines, and, while Hannibal lay triumphant in Capua, to revenge the defeat of Sentinum by a second victory on the Alia or the Tiber.

Resources of the Romans.

Whatever was the cause, the inactivity of the Gauls, after their great victory over L. Postumius, might strengthen the arguments of those Greeks who ascribed the conquests of the Romans to their good fortune. It was no less timely than the peace with Etruria, concluded at the very moment when Pyrrhus was advancing upon Rome, or than the quiet of these same Gauls during the first Punic war. The consequence was, that the Romans had the whole force of Etruria and Umbria disposable for the contest in the south; and that any disposition to revolt, which might have existed in those countries, was unable to show itself in action. Their soldiers served as allies in the Roman armies, and with the Sabines, Picentians, Vestinians, Frentanians, Marrucinians, Marsians, and Pelignians, together with the cities of the Latin name, composed the Roman confederacy after the revolt of southern Italy. That revolt made the drain, both of men and money, press more heavily on the states which still remained faithful; and the friends of Rome must everywhere have had the greatest difficulty in persuading their countrymen not to desert a cause which seemed so ruinous. Under such a pressure, the Roman government plainly told its officers in Sardinia and Sicily, that they must provide for their armies as they best could, for that they must expect no supplies of any kind from home.[41] The proprætor of Sicily applied to the never-failing friendship of Hiero, and obtained from him, almost as the last act of his long life, money enough to pay his soldiers, and corn for six months' consumption. But the proprætor of Sardinia had no such friend to help him; and he was obliged to get both corn and money from the people of the province.[42] The money, it seems, like the benevolences of our own government in old times, was nominally a free-will offering of the loyal cities of Sardinia to the Roman people: but the Sardinians knew that it was a gift which they could not help giving; and impatient of this addition to their former burdens, they applied to Carthage for aid, and broke out the following year into open revolt.[43]

[38] Livy, XXIII. 32.
[39] Livy, XXXI. 10.
[40] See, for instance, Cæsar, B. G. II. 17.
[41] Livy, XXIII. 21.
[42] Livy, XXIII. 21.
[43] Livy, XXIII. 32.

It is not without reason that the Roman government had abandoned its officers in the provinces to their own resources. Their financial difficulties were enormous. Large tracts of land, arable, pasture, and forest, from which the state ordinarily derived a revenue, were in the hands of the enemy; the number of tax-payers had been greatly diminished by the slaughter of so many citizens in battle; and in many cases their widows and children would be unable to cultivate their little property, and would be altogether insolvent. If the poorer citizens were again obliged, as after the Gaulish invasion, to borrow money of the rich, discontent and misery would have been the sure consequence; and the debtor would regard his creditor as a worse enemy than Hannibal. Accordingly three commissioners were appointed, on the proposition of the tribune Minucius, like the five commissioners of the year 403, with the express object of facilitating the circulation, and assisting the distressed tax-payer.[44] Their measures are not recorded; but we may suppose that they acted like the former commissioners, and allowed the poor citizens to pay their taxes in kind, when they could not procure money, and did not force them to sell their property, when it must have been sold at a certain loss.[45] The war must no doubt have raised the value of money, and diminished that of land; and the agricultural population, who had to pay a fixed amount of taxation in money, were thus doubly sufferers. As a mere financial operation, the commissioners' measures may not have been very profitable; but the government had the wisdom to see that every thing depended on the unanimity and devotion of all classes to the cause of their country; and it was worth a great pecuniary sacrifice, even in the actual financial difficulties, to attach the people heartily to the government, and to prevent that intolerable evil of a general state of debt, which must speedily have led to a revolution, and laid Rome prostrate at the feet of Hannibal.

Their financial difficulties.

Neither Rome nor Carthage could be said to have the undisputed mastery of the sea. Roman fleets sometimes visited the coasts of Africa; and Carthaginian fleets in the same way appeared off the coasts of Italy. Hannibal received supplies from Carthage, which were landed in the ports of Bruttium; and when the Carthaginians wished to assist the revolt of the Sardinians, the expedition which they sent, although it suffered much from bad weather, was neither delayed nor prevented by the enemy.[46] On the other hand, the Romans had gained a naval victory of some importance in Spain;[47] and their cruising squadrons in the Ionian Gulf, having the ports of Brundisium and Tarentum to run to in case of need, were of signal service, as we shall see hereafter, in intercepting the communications which the king of Macedon was trying to open with Hannibal.[48]

Events of the naval war.

Meantime the news of the battle of Cannæ had been carried to Carthage, as we have seen, by Hannibal's brother Mago, accompanied with a request for reinforcements. Nearly two years before, when he first descended from the Alps into Cisalpine Gaul, his Africans and Spaniards were reduced to no more than 20,000 foot and 6000 horse. The Gauls, who had joined him since, had indeed more than doubled this number at first; but three great battles, and many partial actions, besides the unavoidable losses from sickness during two years of active service, must again have greatly diminished it; and this force was now to be divided: a part of it was employed in Bruttium, a part in Lucania, leaving an inconsiderable body under Hannibal's own command. On the other hand, the accession of the Campanians, Samnites, Lucanians, and Bruttians supplied him with auxiliary troops in abundance, and of excellent quality; so that large reinforcements from home were not required,

Reinforcements from Carthage.

[44] Livy, XXIII. 21. Compare VII. 21.

[45] Salmasius (de Usuris. p. 510) conceives that the reduction of the as to an ounce, which, Pliny (XXXIII. 13) says, took place in the dictatorship of Fabius Maximus, was a measure of these commissioners.

[46] Livy, XXIII. 43, 34.

[47] Polybius, III. 96.

[48] Livy, XXIII. 32, 34.

but only enough for the Africans to form a substantial part of every army employed in the field; and above all, to maintain his superiority in cavalry. It is said that some of the reinforcements which were voted on Mago's demand, were afterwards diverted to other services;[49] and we do not know what was the amount of force actually sent over to Italy, nor when it arrived.[50] It consisted chiefly, if not entirely, of cavalry and elephants; for all the elephants which Hannibal had brought with him into Italy had long since perished; and his anxiety to obtain others, troublesome and hazardous as it must have been to transport them from Africa by sea, speaks strongly in favor of their use in war, which modern writers are perhaps too much inclined to depreciate.[51]

Feelings of the Campanians.

We have no information as to the feelings entertained by Hannibal and the Campanians towards each other, while the Carthaginians were wintering in Capua. The treaty of alliance had provided carefully for the independence of the Campanians, that they might not be treated as Pyrrhus had treated the Tarentines. Capua was to have its own laws and magistrates; no Campanian was to be compelled to any duty, civil or military, nor to be in any way subject to the authority of the Carthaginian officers.[52] There must have been something of a Roman party opposed to the alliance with Carthage altogether; though the Roman writers mention one man only, Decius Magius, who was said to have resisted Hannibal to his face with such vehemence, that Hannibal sent him prisoner to Carthage.[53] But three hundred Campanian horsemen of the richer classes, who were serving in the Roman army in Sicily when Capua revolted, went to Rome as soon as their service was over, and were there received as Roman citizens;[54] and others, though unable to resist the general voice of their countrymen, must have longed in their hearts to return to the Roman alliance. Of the leaders of the Campanian people we know little: Pacuvius Calavius, the principal author of the revolt, is never mentioned afterwards; nor do we know the fate of his son Perolla, who, in his zeal for Rome, wished to assassinate Hannibal at his own father's table, when he made his public entrance into Capua.[55] Vibius Virrius is also named as a leading partisan of the Carthaginians;[56] and amid the pictures of the luxury and feebleness of the Campanians, their cavalry, which was formed entirely out of the wealthiest classes, is allowed to have been excellent;[57] and one brave and practised soldier, Jubellius Taurea, had acquired a high reputation amongst the Romans when he served with them, and had attracted the notice and respect of Hannibal.[58]

Measures to fill up the senate. Two dictators at the same time.

During the interval from active warfare afforded by the winter, the Romans took measures for filling up the numerous vacancies which the lapse of five years, and so many disastrous battles, had made in the numbers of the senate.[59] The natural course would have been to elect censors, to whom the duty of making out the roll of the senate properly belonged; but the vacancies were so many, and the censor's power in admitting new citizens, and degrading old ones, was so enormous, that the senate feared, it seems, to trust to the result of an ordinary election; and resolved that the censor's business should be performed by the oldest man in point of standing, of all those who had already been censors, and that he should be appointed dictator for this especial duty, although there was one dictator already for the conduct of the war. The person thus selected was M. Fabius Buteo, who had been censor six-and-twenty years before, at the end of the first Punic war, and who

[49] Livy, XXIII. 13, 32.

[50] He is represented as having elephants at the siege of Casilinum. Livy, XXIII. 18. If this be correct, the reinforcements must already have joined him.

[51] See the interesting dissertation on elephants by A. W. Schlegel, in his *Indische Bibliothek*, Vol. I. 173, foll.

[52] Livy, XXIII. 7.

[53] Livy, XXIII. 7, 10.

[54] Livy, XXIII. 4, 7, 31.

[55] Livy, XXIII. 8, 9.

[56] Livy, XXIII. 6.

[57] Frontinus, Strateg. IV. 7, 29.

[58] Livy, XXIII. 8, 46, 47. XXVI. 15. Valerius Maximus, V. 3. Ex. 1.

[59] Livy, XXIII. 22.

had more recently been the chief of the embassy sent to declare war on Carthage after the destruction of Saguntum. That his appointment might want no legal formality, C. Varro, the only surviving consul, was sent for home from Apulia to nominate him, the senate intending to detain Varro in Rome till he should have presided at the comitia for the election of the next year's magistrates. The nomination as usual took place at midnight; and on the following morning M. Fabius appeared in the Forum with his four-and-twenty lictors, and ascended the rostra to address the people. Invested with absolute power for six months, and especially charged with no less a task than the formation, at his discretion, of that great council which possessed the supreme government of the commonwealth, the noble old man neither shrunk weakly from so heavy a burden, nor ambitiously abused so vast an authority. He told the people that he would not strike off the name of a single senator from the list of the senate, and that, in filling up the vacancies, he would proceed by a defined rule; that he would first add all those who had held curule offices within the last five years, without having been admitted as yet into the senate; that in the second place he would take all who within the same period had been tribunes, ædiles, or quæstors; and thirdly, all those who could show in their houses spoils won in battle from an enemy, or who had received the wreath of oak for saving the life of a citizen in battle. In this manner 177 new senators were placed on the roll; the new members thus forming a large majority of the whole number of the senate, which amounted only to three hundred. This being done forthwith, the dictator, as he stood in the rostra, resigned his office, dismissed his lictors, and went down into the Forum a private man. There he purposely lingered amidst the crowd, lest the people should leave their business to follow him home; but their admiration was not cooled by this delay; and when he withdrew at the usual hour, the whole people attended him to his house.[60] Such was Fabius Buteo's dictatorship, so wisely fulfilled, so simply and nobly resigned, that the dictatorship of Fabius Maximus himself has earned no purer glory.

Varro, it is said, not wishing to be detained in Rome, returned to his army the next night, without giving the senate notice of his departure. The dictator, M. Junius, was therefore requested to repair to Rome to hold the comitia; and Ti. Gracchus and M. Marcellus were to come with him to report on the state of their several armies, and concert measures for the ensuing campaign.[61] There is no doubt that the senate determined on the persons to be proposed at the ensuing elections, and that, if any one else had come forward as a candidate, the dictator who presided would have refused to receive votes for him. Accordingly the consuls and prætors chosen were all men of the highest reputation for ability and experience: the consuls were L. Postumius, whose defeat and death in Cisalpine Gaul were not yet known in Rome, and Ti. Gracchus, now master of the horse. The prætors were M. Valerius Lævinus, Ap. Claudius Pulcher, a grandson of the famous censor, Appius the blind, Q. Fulvius Flaccus, old in years, but vigorous in mind and body, who had already been censor, and twice consul, and Q. Mucius Scævola.[62] When the death of L. Postumius was known, his place was finally filled by no less a person than Q. Fabius Maximus: whilst Marcellus was still to retain his command with proconsular power, as his activity and energy could ill be spared at a time so critical.[63]

Election of officers for year 539.

A. U. C. 539. A. C. 215.

The officers for the year being thus appointed, it remained to determine their several provinces, and to provide them with sufficient forces.[64] Fabius was to succeed to the army of the dictator, M. Junius; and his head-quarters were advanced from Teanum to Cales, at the northern extremity of the Falernian plain, about seven English miles from Casilinum and the

Distribution of provinces and troops.

[60] Livy, XXIII. 23.
[61] Livy, XXIII. 24.
[62] Livy, XXIII. 30.
[63] Livy, XXIII. 31.
[64] Livy, XXIII. 31, 32.

Vulturnus, and less than ten from Capua. The other consul, Ti. Sempronius, was to have no other Roman army than two legions of volunteer slaves, who were to be raised for the occasion; but both he and his colleague had the usual contingent of Latin and Italian allies. Gracchus named Sinuessa on the Appian road, at the point where the Massic hills run out with a bold headland into the sea, as the place of meeting for his soldiers; and his business was to protect the towns on the coast, which were still faithful to Rome, such as Cuma and Neapolis. Marcellus was to command two new Roman legions, and to lie as before in his camp above Nola; while his old army was sent into Sicily to relieve the legions there, and enable them to return to Italy, where they formed a fourth army under the command of M. Valerius Lævinus, the prætor peregrinus, in Apulia. The small force which Varro had commanded in Apulia was ordered to Tarentum, to add to the strength of that important place; while Varro himself was sent with proconsular power into Picenum, to raise soldiers, and to watch the road along the Adriatic by which the Gauls might have sent reinforcements to Hannibal. Q. Fulvius Flaccus, the prætor urbanus, remained at Rome to conduct the government, and had no other military command than that of a small fleet for the defence of the coast on both sides of the Tiber. Of the other two prætors, Ap. Claudius was to command in Sicily, and Q. Mucius in Sardinia; and P. Scipio as proconsul still commanded his old army of two legions in Spain. On the whole, including the volunteer slaves, there appeared to have been fourteen Roman legions in active service at the beginning of the year 539, without reckoning the soldiers who served in the fleets; and of these fourteen legions, nine were employed in Italy. If we suppose that the Latin and Italian allies bore their usual proportion to the number of Roman soldiers in each army, we shall have a total of 140,000 men, thus divided: 20,000 in Spain, and the same number in Sicily; 10,000 in Sardinia; 20,000 under each of the consuls; 20,000 with Marcellus; 20,000 under Lævinus in Apulia; and 10,000 in Tarentum.

Extraordinary exertions of the Romans, military and financial.

Seventy thousand men were thus in arms, besides the seamen, out of a population of citizens which at the last census before the war had amounted only to 270,213,[65] and which had since been thinned by so many disastrous battles. Nor was the drain on the finances of Rome less extraordinary. The legions in the provinces had indeed been left to their own resources as to money; but the nine legions serving in Italy must have been paid regularly; for war could not there be made to support war; and if the Romans had been left to live at free quarters upon their Italian allies, they would have driven them to join Hannibal in mere self-defence. Yet the legions in Italy cost the government in pay, food, and clothing, at the rate of 541,800 denarii a month; and as they were kept on service throughout the year, the annual expense was 6,501,600 denarii; or in Greek money, reckoning the denarius as equal to the drachma, 1083 Euboic talents. To meet these enormous demands on the treasury, the government resorted to the simple expedient of doubling the year's taxes, and calling at once for the payment of one-half of this amount, leaving the other to be paid at the end of the year.[66] It was a struggle for life and death; and the people were in a mood to refuse no sacrifices, however costly: but the war must have cut off so many sources of wealth, and agriculture itself must have so suffered from the calling away of so many hands from the cultivation of the land, that we wonder how the money could be found, and how many of the poorer citizens' families could be provided with daily bread.

Other military means of the Romans.

In addition to the five regular armies which the Romans brought into the field in Italy, an irregular warfare was also going on, we know not to what extent; and bands of peasants and slaves were armed in many parts of the country to act against the revolted Italians, and to ravage their territory. For instance, a great tract of forest in Bruttium, as we have

[65] Livy, Epit. XX.

[66] Livy, XXIII. 31.

seen, was the domain of the Roman people; this would be farmed like all the other revenues; and the publicani who farmed it, or the wealthy citizens who turned out cattle to pasture in it, would have large bodies of slaves employed as shepherds, herdsmen, and woodsmen, who, when the Bruttian towns on the coast revolted, would at once form a guerilla force capable of doing them great mischief. And lastly, besides all these forces, regular and irregular, the Romans still held most of the principal towns in the south of Italy; because they had long since converted them into Latin colonies. Brundisium on the Ionian sea, Pæstum on the coast of Lucania, Luceria, Venusia, and Beneventum in the interior, were all so many strong fortresses, garrisoned by soldiers of the Latin name, in the very heart of the revolted districts;[67] whilst the Greek cities of Cumæ and Neapolis in Campania, and Rhegium on the straits of Messina, were held for Rome by their own citizens with a devotion no way inferior to that of the Latin colonies themselves.[68]

Hannibal's resources.

Against this mass of enemies, the moment that they had learnt to use their strength, Hannibal, even within six months after the battle of Cannæ, was already contending at a disadvantage. We have seen that he had detached two officers with two divisions of his army, one into Lucania, the other into Bruttium, to encourage the revolt of those countries, and then to organize their resources in men and money for the advancement of the common cause. Most of the Bruttians took up arms immediately as Hannibal's allies, and put themselves under the command of his officer, Himilcon; but Petelia, one of their cities, was for some reason or other inflexible in its devotion to Rome, and endured a siege of eleven months, suffering all extremities of famine before it surrendered.[69] Thus Himilcon must have been still engaged in besieging it long after the campaign was opened in the neighborhood of Capua. The Samnites also had taken up arms, and apparently were attached to Hannibal's own army: the return of their whole population of the military age, made ten years before during the Gaulish invasion, had stated it at 70,000 foot and 7000 horse;[70] but the Pentrians, the most powerful tribe of their nation, were still faithful to Rome; and the Samnites, like the Romans themselves, had been thinned by the slaughter of Thrasymenus and Cannæ, which they had shared as their allies. It is vexatious that we have no statement of the amount of Hannibal's old army, any more than of the allies who joined him, at any period of the war later than the battle of Cannæ. His reinforcements from home, as we have seen, were very trifling; while his two divisions in Lucania and Bruttium, and the garrisons which he had been obliged to leave in some of the revolted towns, as, for example, at Arpi in Apulia,[71] must have considerably lessened the force under his own personal command. Yet, with the accession of the Samnites and Campanians, it was probably much stronger than any one of the Roman armies opposed to him; quite as strong, indeed, in all likelihood, as was consistent with the possibility of feeding it.

Fall of Casilinum.

Before the winter was over, Casilinum fell. The garrison had made a valiant defence, and yielded at last to famine: they were allowed to ransom themselves by paying each man seven ounces of gold for his life and liberty. The plunder which they had won from the old inhabitants enabled them to discharge this large sum; and they were then allowed to march out unhurt, and retire to Cumæ. Casilinum again became a Campanian town; but its important position, at once covering Capua, and securing a passage over the Vulturnus, induced Hannibal to garrison it with seven hundred soldiers of his own army.[72]

67 Livy, XXVII. 10.
68 Livy, XXIII. 1, 36, 37. XXIV. 1.
69 Polybius, VII. 1. Livy, XXII. 61. XXIII. 20, 30. Appian, VII. 28. Valerius Maximus, VI. 6. Ext. 2.
70 Polybius, II. 24, 10.
71 Livy, XXIV. 46, 47. Appian, VII. 31.
72 Livy, XXIII. 19, 20.

The season for active operations was now arrived. The three Roman armies of Fabius, Gracchus, and Marcellus, had taken up their positions round Campania; and Hannibal marched out of Capua, and encamped his army on the mountain above it, on that same Tifata where the Samnites had so often taken post in old times, when they were preparing to invade the Campanian plain.[73] Tifata did not then exhibit that bare and parched appearance which it has now; the soil, which has accumulated in the plain below, so as to have risen several feet above its ancient level, has been washed down in the course of centuries, and after the destruction of its protecting woods, from the neighboring mountains; and Tifata, in Hannibal's time, furnished grass in abundance for his cattle in its numerous glades, and offered cool and healthy summer quarters for his men. There he lay waiting for some opportunity of striking a blow against his enemies around him, and eagerly watching the progress of his intrigues with the Tarentines, and his negotiations with the king of Macedon. A party at Tarentum began to open a correspondence with him immediately after the battle of Cannæ;[74] and since he had been in Campania he had received an embassy from Philip, king of Macedon, and had concluded an alliance, offensive and defensive, with the ambassadors, who acted with full powers in their master's name.[75] Such were his prospects on one side, while, if he looked westward and southwest, he saw Sardinia in open revolt against Rome:[76] and in Sicily the death of Hiero at the age of ninety, and the succession of his grandson Hieronymus, an ambitious and inexperienced youth, were detaching Syracuse also from the Roman alliance. Hannibal had already received an embassy from Hieronymus, to which he had replied by sending a Carthaginian officer of his own name to Sicily, and two Syracusan brothers, Hippocrates and Epicydes, who had long served with him in Italy and in Spain, being, in fact, Carthaginians by their mother's side, and having become naturalized at Carthage, since Agathocles had banished their grandfather, and their father had married and settled in his place of exile.[77] Thus the effect of the battle of Cannæ seemed to be shaking the whole fabric of the Roman dominion; their provinces were revolting; their firmest allies were deserting them; while the king of Macedon himself, the successor of Alexander, was throwing the weight of his power, and of all his acquired and inherited glory, into the scale of their enemies. Seeing the fruit of his work thus fast ripening, Hannibal sat quietly on the summit of Tifata, to break forth like the lightning flash when the storm should be fully gathered.

Hannibal encamps on Mount Tifata. Rome deserted by her allies.

Thus the summer of 539 was like a breathing-time, in which both parties were looking at each other, and considering each other's resources, while they were recovering strength after their past efforts, and preparing for a renewal of the struggle. Fabius, with the authority of the senate, issued an order, calling on the inhabitants of all the country which either actually was, or was likely to become, the seat of war, to clear their corn off the ground, and carry it into the fortified cities, before the first of June, threatening to lay waste the land, to sell the slaves, and burn the farm buildings, of any one who should disobey the order.[78] In the utter confusion of the Roman calendar at this period, it is difficult to know whether in any given year it was in advance of the true time, or behind it; so that we can scarcely tell whether the corn was only to be got in when ripe without needless delay, or whether it was to be cut when green, lest Hannibal should use it as forage for his cavalry. But at any rate, Fabius was now repeating the system which he had laid down in his dictatorship, and hoped, by wasting the country, to oblige Hannibal to retreat; for his means of transport were not sufficient for him to feed his army from a distance: hence, when the resources in his immediate neighborhood were exhausted, he was obliged to move elsewhere.

Measures of Fabius to cut off Hannibal's supplies.

[73] Livy, XXIII. 36. VII. 29.
[74] Livy, XXII. 61. Appian, VII. 32.
[75] Livy, XXIII. 33. Zonaras, IX. 4.
[76] Livy, XXIII. 32, 34.
[77] Livy, XXIII. 4, 6. Polybius, VII. 2.
[78] Livy, XXIII. 32.

Meanwhile Gracchus had crossed the Vulturnus near its mouth, and was now at Liternum, busily employed in exercising and training his heterogeneous army. The several Campanian cities were accustomed to hold a joint festival every year at a place called Hamæ, only three miles from Cumæ.[79] These festivals were seasons of general truce, so that the citizens even of hostile nations met at them safely: the government of Capua announced to the Cumæans, that their chief magistrate and all their senators would appear at Hamæ, as usual, on the day of the solemnity; and they invited the senate of Cumæ to meet them. At the same time they said that an armed force would be present to repel any interruption from the Romans. The Cumæans informed Gracchus of this; and he attacked the Capuans in the night, when they were in such perfect security, that they had not even fortified a camp, but were sleeping in the open country, and massacred about 2000 of them, among whom was Marius Alfius, the supreme magistrate of Capua. The Romans charge the Capuans with having meditated treachery against the Cumæans, and say that they were caught in their own snare; but this could only be a suspicion, while the overt acts of violence were their own. Hannibal no sooner heard of this disaster, than he descended from Tifata, and hastened to Hamæ, in the hope of provoking the enemy to battle in the confidence of their late success. But Gracchus was too wary to be so tempted, and had retreated in good time to Cumæ, where he lay safe within the walls of the town.[80] It is said that Hannibal, having supplied himself with all things necessary for a siege, attacked the place in form, and was repulsed with loss, so that he returned defeated to his camp at Tifata. A consular army defending the walls of a fortified town was not indeed likely to be beaten in an assault; and neither could a maritime town, with the sea open, be easily starved; nor could Hannibal linger before it safely, as Fabius, with a second consular army, was preparing to cross the Vulturnus.

Massacre of 2000 Capuans at a festival by Gracchus.

Casilinum being held by the enemy, Fabius was obliged to cross at a higher point behind the mountains, nearly opposite to Allifæ; and he then descended the left bank to the confluence of the Calor with the Vulturnus, crossed the Calor, and passing between Taburnus and the mountains above Caserta and Maddaloni, stormed the town of Saticula, and joined Marcellus in his camp above Suessula.[81] He was again anxious for Nola, where the popular party were said to be still plotting the surrender of the town to Hannibal: to stop this mischief, he sent Marcellus with his whole army to garrison Nola, while he himself took his place in the camp above Suessula. Gracchus, on his side, advanced from Cumæ towards Capua; so that three Roman armies, amounting in all to about sixty thousand men, were on the left bank of the Vulturnus together; and all, so far as appears, in free communication with each other. They availed themselves of their numbers and of their position to send plundering parties out on their rear to overrun the lands of the revolted Samnites and Hirpinians; and as the best troops of both these nations were with Hannibal on Tifata, no force was left at home sufficient to check the enemy's incursions. Accordingly, the complaints of the sufferers were loud, and a deputation was sent to Hannibal imploring him to protect his allies.[82]

Strength of the Roman armies.

Already Hannibal felt that the Roman generals understood their business, and had learnt to use their numbers wisely. On ground where his cavalry could act, he would not have feared to engage their three armies together; but when they were amongst mountains, or behind walls, his cavalry were useless, and he could not venture to attack them: besides, he did not wish to expose the territory of Capua to their ravages; and therefore he did not choose lightly to move from Tifata. But the prayers of the Samnites were urgent: his partisans in Nola might require his aid, or might be able to admit

Hannibal receives his reinforcements.

[79] Livy, XXIII. 35.
[80] Livy, XXIII. 36.
[81] Livy, XXIII. 39.
[82] Livy, XXIII. 41, 42.

him into the town; and his expected reinforcement of cavalry and elephants from Carthage had landed safely in Bruttium, and was on its way to join him, which the position of Fabius and Marcellus might render difficult, if he made no movement to favor it. He therefore left Tifata, advanced upon Nola, and timed his operation so well that his reinforcements arrived at the moment when he was before Nola; and neither Fabius nor Marcellus attempted to prevent their junction.[83]

Advantages gained by Marcellus. Hannibal marches into Apulia.

Thus encouraged, and perhaps not aware of the strength of the garrison, Hannibal not only overran the territory of Nola, but surrounded the town with his soldiers, in the hope of taking it by escalade. Marcellus was alike watchful and bold; he threw open the gates and made a sudden sally, by which he drove back the enemy within their camp; and this success, together with his frank and popular bearing, won him, it is said, the affections of all parties at Nola, and put a stop to all intrigues within the walls.[84] A more important consequence of this action was the desertion of above 1200 men, Spanish foot, and Numidian horse, from Hannibal's army to the Romans;[85] as we do not find that their example was followed by others, it is probable that they were not Hannibal's old soldiers, but some of the troops which had just joined him, and which could not, as yet, have felt the spell of his personal ascendency. Still their treason naturally made him uneasy, and would for the moment excite a general suspicion in the army: the summer too was drawing to a close; and wishing to relieve Capua from the burden of feeding his troops, he marched away into Apulia, and fixed his quarters for the winter near Arpi. Gracchus, with one consular army, followed him; while Fabius, after having ravaged the country round Capua, and carried off the green corn, as soon as it was high enough out of the ground, to his camp above Suessula, to furnish winter food for his cavalry, quartered his own army there for the winter, and ordered Marcellus to retain a sufficient force to secure Nola, and to send the rest of his men home to be disbanded.[86]

Complete success of the Romans in Sardinia.

Thus the campaign was ended, and Hannibal had not marked it with a victory. The Romans had employed their forces so wisely, that they had forced him to remain mostly on the defensive: and his two offensive operations, against Cumæ and against Nola, had both been baffled. In Sardinia their success had been brilliant and decisive. Mucius, the prætor, fell ill soon after he arrived in the island; upon which the senate ordered Q. Fabius, the city prætor, to raise a new legion, and to send it over into Sardinia, under any officer whom he might think proper to appoint. He chose a man, in age, rank, and character, most resembling himself, T. Manlius Torquatus, who in his first consulship, twenty years before, had fought against the Sardinians, and obtained a triumph over them. Manlius' second command in the island was no less brilliant than his first: he totally defeated the united forces of the Sardinians and Carthaginians, took their principal generals prisoners, reduced the revolted towns to obedience, levied heavy contributions of corn and money as a punishment of their rebellion, and then embarked with the troops which he had brought out with him, only leaving the usual force of a single legion in the island, and returned to Rome to report the complete submission of Sardinia. The money of his contributions was paid over to the quæstors, for the payment of the armies; the corn was given to the ædiles to supply the markets of Rome.[87]

Capture of the Macedonian ambassadors. Expedition to Greece.

Fortune in another quarter served the Romans no less effectually. The Macedonian ambassadors, after having concluded their treaty with Hannibal at Tifata, made their way back into Bruttium in safety, and embarked to return to Greece. But their ship was taken off the Calabrian coast by the Roman squadron on that station; and the ambassa-

[83] Livy, XXIII. 43.
[84] Livy, XXIII. 44, 45, 46.
[85] Livy, XXIII. 46.
[86] Livy, XXIII. 46, 48.
[87] Livy, XXIII. 34, 41.

dors, with all their papers, were sent prisoners to Rome.[88] A vessel which had been of their company escaped the Romans, and informed the king what had happened. He was obliged, therefore, to send a second embassy to Hannibal, as the former treaty had never reached him; and although this second mission went and returned safely, yet the loss of time was irreparable, and nothing could be done till another year.[89] Meanwhile the Romans, thus timely made aware of the king's intentions, resolved to find such employment for him at home as should prevent his invading Italy. M. Valerius Lævinus was to take the command of the fleet at Tarentum and Brundisium, and to cross the Ionian Gulf, in order to rouse the Ætolians, and the barbarian chiefs whose tribes bordered on Philip's western frontier, and, with such other allies as could be engaged in the cause, to form a Greek coalition against Macedon.[90]

Measures of the Romans to raise money: a loan.

These events, and the continued successes of their army in Spain, revived the spirits of the Romans, and encouraged them to make still greater sacrifices, in the hope that they would not be made in vain. The distress of the treasury was at its height: P. Scipio, in announcing his victories, reported that his soldiers and seamen were in a state of utter destitution; that they had no pay, corn, or clothing; and that the two latter articles must at any rate be supplied from Rome.[91] His demands were acknowledged to be reasonable; but the republic had lost so large a portion of her foreign revenue, that her chief resource now lay in the taxation of her own people: this had been doubled in the present year, yet was found inadequate; and to increase it, or even to continue it at its present amount, was altogether impossible. Accordingly the city prætor, Q. Fulvius, addressed the people from the rostra, explained the distress of the government to them, and appealed to the patriotism of the moneyed class to assist their country with a loan. Fabius did not mean to hold out an opportunity to the public creditor of investing his money to advantage, subject only to the risk of a national bankruptcy: on this Roman loan no interest was to be paid; the creditors were simply assured that, as soon as the treasury was solvent, their demands should be discharged before all others; in the mean time their money was totally lost to them. But, on the other hand, opportunities of investing money profitably must have been greatly diminished by the war; to lend it to the government was not, therefore, so great a sacrifice. Still a public spirit was shown in the ready answer to the prætor's appeal, such as merchants have often honorably displayed in seasons of public danger; mixed up, however —for when are human motives altogether pure?—with a considerable regard to personal advantage. Three companies were formed, each, as it seems, composed of eighteen members and a president, or chairman; and these were to supply the corn and clothing which the armies might require. But in return they demanded an exemption from military service, whilst they were thus serving the state with their money; and they also required the government to undertake the whole sea risk, whether from storms, or from the enemy: whatever articles were thus lost were to be the loss of the nation, and not of the companies.[92] It will be seen hereafter how some of the contractors abused this equitable condition, and wilfully destroyed cargoes of small value, in order to recover the insurance upon them from the government. That a citizen should enrich himself by frauds practised on his country in such a season of distress and danger is sufficiently monstrous; but the spirit of what is so emphatically called jobbing is inveterate in human nature; and we cannot wonder at its existence among Roman citizens, while Rome was struggling for life or death, when it has been known to find its way into the prison of Christian martyrs.[93]

Yet neither the ordinary taxation, nor the loan in addition to it, were sufficient

[88] Livy, XXIII. 38.
[89] Livy, XXIII. 39.
[90] Livy, XXIII. 38, 48. XXIV. 10. Zonaras, IX. 4.
[91] Livy, XXIII. 48.
[92] Livy, XXIII. 49.
[93] See Cyprian, Epp. X. XXII. Ed. Rigalt.

Property tax.

for the vast expenditure of the war. The hostility of Macedon had made it necessary to raise an additional fleet; for the coasts of Italy must be protected; and Hannibal's free communications with Africa must be restrained; and now another fleet was required, by the threatening aspect of affairs in Sicily. Accordingly a graduated property tax for the occasion was imposed on all citizens whose property amounted to or exceeded 100,000 ases; that is, they were required to furnish a certain number of their slaves as seamen, to arm and equip them, and to provide them with dressed provisions for thirty days, and with pay, in some cases for six months, in others for a whole year.[94] The senators, who were rated higher than all other citizens, were obliged in this manner each to provide eight seamen, with pay for the longer term of the whole year.

A. U. C. 540. A. C. 214. Fabius holds the comitia.

Whilst the commonwealth was making these extraordinary efforts, it was of the last importance that they should not be wasted by incompetent leaders, either at home or abroad. Gracchus was watching Hannibal in Apulia; so that Fabius went to Rome to hold the comitia. It was not by accident, doubtless, that he had previously sent home to fix the day of the meeting, or that his own arrival was so nicely timed, that he reached Rome when the tribes were actually met in the Campus Martius; thus, without entering the city, he passed along under the walls, and took his place as presiding magistrate at the comitia,[95] while his lictors still bore the naked axe in the midst of their fasces, the well-known sign of that absolute power which the consul enjoyed everywhere out of Rome. Fabius, in concert no doubt with Q. Fulvius and T. Manlius, and other leading senators, had already determined who were to be consuls: when the first century, in the free exercise of its choice, gave its vote in favor of T. Otacilius and M. Æmilius Regillus, he at once stopped the election, and told the people that this was no time to choose ordinary consuls; that they were electing generals to oppose Hannibal, and should fix upon those men under whom they would most gladly risk their sons' lives and their own, if they stood at that moment on the eve of battle. "Wherefore, crier," he concluded, "call back the century to give its votes over again."[96]

Fabius and Marcellus are elected consuls.

Otacilius, who was present, although he had married Fabius' niece, protested loudly against this interference with the votes of the people, and charged Fabius with trying to procure his own re-election. The old man had always been so famous for the gentleness of his nature, that he was commonly known by the name of "the Lamb;"[97] but now he acted with the decision of Q. Fulvius or T. Manlius; he peremptorily ordered Otacilius to be silent, and bade him remember that his lictors carried the naked axe: the century was called back, and now gave its voice for Q. Fabius and M. Marcellus. All the centuries of all the tribes unanimously confirmed this choice.[98] Q. Fulvius was also re-elected prætor; and the senate, by a special vote, continued him in the prætorship of the city, an office which put him at the head of the home government. The election of the other three prætors, it seems, was left free: so the people, as they could not have Otacilius for their consul, gave him one of the remaining prætorships, and bestowed the other two on Q. Fabius, the consul's son, who was then curule ædile, and on P. Cornelius Lentulus.

Great exertions of the Romans; armies abroad.

Great as the exertions of the commonwealth had been in the preceding year, they were still greater this year. Ten legions were to be employed in different parts of Italy, besides the reserve army of the two city legions, which was to protect the capital. Two legions were to

[94] Livy, XXIV. 11. Comp. XXVI. 36. XXXIV. 6.

[95] Livy, XXIV. 7.

[96] Livy, XXIV. 8.

[97] Ovicula, see Aurelius Victor de Vir. Illustr. c. 43. Plutarch, Fabius, c. 1. Ὁ δὲ Ὀουικούλας σημαίνει τὸ προβάτιον· ἐτέθη δὲ πρὸς τὴν πρᾳότητα καὶ βαρύτητα τοῦ ἤθους ἔτι παιδὸς ὄντος. Τὸ γὰρ ἡσύχιον αὐτοῦ καὶ σιωπηλὸν καὶ μετὰ πολλῆς εὐλαβείας τῶν παιδικῶν ἀπτόμενον ἡδονῶν, βραδέως δὲ καὶ διαπόνως δεχόμενον τὰς μαθήσεις, εὔκολον δὲ πρὸς τοὺς συνήθεις καὶ κατήκοον ἀβελτερίας τινὸς καὶ νωθρότητος ὑπόνοιαν εἶχε παρὰ τοῖς ἐκτός· ὀλίγοι δ' ἦσαν οἱ τὸ δυσκίνητον ὑπὸ βάθους καὶ τὸ μεγαλόψυχον καὶ λεοντῶδες ἐν τῇ φύσει καθορῶντες αὐτοῦ.

[98] Livy, XXIV. 9.

hold Sardinia, where the sparks of revolt were probably not altogether extinguished: two were sent to Sicily, with a prospect of no inactive service; and two were stationed in Cisalpine Gaul, there being some likelihood, we must suppose, that the Gauls would soon require a force in their neighborhood; or possibly the colonies of Placentia and Cremona were thought insecure, if they were left to their own resources, insulated as they were in the midst of the enemy's country. Finally, the Scipios still commanded their two legions in Spain; and the naval service in Sicily, and on the coast of Calabria, required no fewer than a hundred and fifty ships of war.[99]

Distribution of those in Italy.

The Italian armies were disposed as follows: Cales, and the camp above Suessula and Nola, were again to be the head-quarters of the two consuls, each of whom was to command a regular consular army of two legions. Gracchus, with proconsular power, was to keep his own two legions, and was at present wintering near Hannibal in the north of Apulia. Q. Fabius, one of the new prætors, was to be ready to enter Apulia with an army of equal strength, so soon as Gracchus should be called into Lucania and Samnium, to take part in the active operations of the campaign. C. Varro, with his single legion, was still to hold Picenum; and M. Lævinus, also with proconsular power, was to remain at Brundisium with another single legion.[100] The two city legions served as a sort of dépôt, to recruit the armies in the field in case of need; and there was a large armed population, serving as garrisons in the Latin colonies, and in other important posts in various parts of the country, the amount of which it is not possible to estimate. Nor can we calculate the numbers of the guerilla bands, which were on foot in Lucania, Bruttium, and possibly in Samnium, and which hindered Hannibal from having the whole resources of those countries at his disposal. The Roman party was nowhere probably altogether extinct: wealthy Lucanians, who were attached to Rome, would muster their slaves and peasantry, and either by themselves, or getting some Roman officer to head them, would ravage the lands of the Carthaginian party, and carry on a continued harassing warfare against the towns or districts which had joined Hannibal. Thus the whole south of Italy was one wide flood of war, the waters were everywhere dashing and eddying, and running in cross-currents innumerable; whilst the regular armies, like the channels of the rivers, held on their way, distinguishable amidst the chaos by their greater rapidity and power.

Hannibal marches into Campania.

Hannibal watched this mass of war with the closest attention. To make head against it directly being impossible, his business was to mark his opportunities, to strike wherever there was an opening; and being sure that the enemy would not dare to attack him on his own ground, he might maintain his army in Italy for an indefinite time, whilst Carthage, availing herself of the distraction of her enemy's power, renewed her efforts to conquer Spain and recover Sicily. He hoped ere long to win Tarentum; and, if left to his own choice, he would probably have moved hither at once, when he broke up from his winter-quarters: but the weakness or fears of the Campanians hung with encumbering weight upon him; and an earnest request was sent to him from Capua, calling on him to hasten to its defence, lest the two consular armies should besiege it.[101] Accordingly he broke up from his winter-quarters at Arpi, and marched once more into Campania, where he established his army as before on the summit of Tifata.

Fabius collects the Roman armies around Hannibal.

The perpetual carelessness and omissions in Livy's narrative, drawn as it is from various sources, with no pains to make one part correspond with another, render it a work of extreme difficulty to present an account of these operations, which shall be at once minute and intelligible. We also miss that notice of chronological details, which is essential to the history of a complicated campaign. Even the year in which important

[99] Livy, XXIV. 11. [100] Livy, XXIV. 12, 10. [101] Livy, XXIV. 12.

events happened is sometimes doubtful; yet we want, not to fix the year only, but the month, that we may arrange each action in its proper order. When Hannibal set out on his march into Campania, Fabius was still at Rome; but the two new legions, which were to form his army, were already assembled at Cales; and Fabius, on hearing of Hannibal's approach, set out instantly to take the command. His old army, which had wintered in the camp above Suessula, had apparently been transferred to his colleague, Marcellus; and a considerable force had been left at the close of the last campaign to garrison Nola. Fabius, however, wished to have three Roman armies co-operating with each other, as had been the case the year before; and he sent orders to Gracchus to move forwards from Apulia, and to occupy Beneventum; while his son Q. Fabius, the prætor, with a fourth army, was to supply the place of Gracchus at Luceria.[102] It seemed as if Hannibal, having once entered Campania, was to be hemmed in on every side, and not permitted to escape: but these movements of the Roman armies induced him to call Hanno to his aid, the officer who commanded in Lucania and Bruttium, and who, with a small force of Numidian cavalry, had an auxiliary army under his orders consisting chiefly of Italian allies. Hanno advanced accordingly in the direction of Beneventum, to watch the army of Gracchus, and if an opportunity offered, to bring it to action.[103]

Hannibal offers sacrifice at the lake Avernus.

Meanwhile Hannibal, having left some of his best troops to maintain his camp at Tifata, and probably to protect the immediate neighborhood of Capua, descended into the plain towards the coast, partly in the hope of surprising a fortified post which the Romans had lately established at Puteoli, and partly to ravage the territory of Cumæ and Neapolis. But the avowed object of his expedition was to offer sacrifice to the powers of the unseen world, on the banks of the dreaded lake of Avernus.[104] That crater of an old volcano, where the very soil still seemed to breathe out fire, while the unbroken rim of its basin was covered with the uncleared masses of the native woods, was the subject of a thousand mysterious stories, and was regarded as one of those spots where the lower world approached most nearly to the light of day, and where offerings paid to the gods of the dead were most surely acceptable. Such worship was a main part of the national religion of the Carthaginians; and Hannibal, whose latest act before he set out on his great expedition, had been a journey to Gades to sacrifice to the god of his fathers, the Hercules of Tyre, visited the lake of Avernus, it is probable, quite as much in sincere devotion, as in order to mask his design of attacking Puteoli. Whilst he was engaged in his sacrifice, five noble citizens of Tarentum came to him, entreating him to lead his army into their country, and engaging that the city should be surrendered as soon as his standard should be visible from the walls. He listened to their invitation gladly; they offered him one of the richest cities in Italy, with an excellent harbor, equally convenient for his own communication with Carthage, and for the reception of the fleet of his Macedonian allies, whom he was constantly expecting to welcome in Italy. He promised that he would soon be at Tarentum; and the Tarentines returned home to prepare their plans against his arrival.[105]

He marches against Tarentum,

With this prospect before him, it is not likely that he would engage in any serious enterprise in Campania. Finding that he could not surprise Puteoli, he ravaged the lands of the Cumæans and Neapolitans. According to the ever suspicious stories of the exploits of Marcellus, he made a third attempt upon Nola, and was a third time repulsed; Marcellus having called down the army from the camp above Suessula to assist him in defending the town. Then, says the writer whom Livy copied, despairing of taking a place which he had so often attacked in vain, he marched off at once towards Tarentum.[106] The truth probably is, that, finding a complete consular army in Nola, and

[102] Livy, XXIV. 12.
[103] Livy, XXIV. 14.
[104] Livy, XXIV. 12, 13.
[105] Livy, XXIV. 13.
[106] Livy, XXIV. 17.

having left his light cavalry, and some of the flower of his infantry, in the camp on Tifata, he had no thought of attacking the town, but returned to Tifata to take the troops from thence; and having done this, and stayed long enough in Campania for the Capuans to get in their harvest safely, he set off on his march for Tarentum. None of the Roman armies attempted to stop him, or so much as ventured to follow him. Fabius and Marcellus took advantage of his absence to besiege Casilinum with their united forces;[107] Gracchus kept wisely out of his reach, whilst he swept on like a fiery flood, laying waste all before him, from Tifata to the shores of the Ionian sea.[108] He certainly did not burn or plunder the lands of his own allies, either in Samnium or Lucania; but his march lay near the Latin colony of Venusia; and the Lucanians and Samnites in his army would carefully point out those districts which belonged to their countrymen of the Roman party; above all, those ample tracts which the Romans had wrested from their fathers, and which were now farmed by the Roman publicani, or occupied by Roman citizens. Over all these, no doubt, the African and Numidian horse poured far and wide; and the fire and sword did their work.

but fails.

Yet, after all, Hannibal missed his prey. Three days before he reached Tarentum, a Roman officer arrived in the city, whom M. Valerius Lævinus had sent in haste from Brundisium to provide for its defence.[109] There was probably a small Roman garrison in the citadel, to support him in case of need; but the aristocratical party in Tarentum itself, as elsewhere, was attached to Rome; and with their aid Livius, the officer whom Lævinus had sent, effectually repressed the opposite party, embodied the population of the town, and made them keep guard on the walls, and selecting a certain number of persons whose fidelity he most suspected, sent them off as hostages to Rome. When the Carthaginian army therefore appeared before the walls, no movement was made in their favor; and after waiting a few days in vain, Hannibal was obliged to retreat. His disappointment, however, did not make him lose his temper; he spared the Tarentine territory, no less when leaving it, than when he first entered it, in the hope of winning the city; a moderation which doubtless produced its effect, and confirmed the Tarentines in the belief that his professions of friendship had been made in honesty. But he carried off all the corn which he could find in the neighborhood of Metapontum and Heraclea, and then returned to Apulia, and fixed his quarters for the winter at Salapia. His cavalry overran all the forest country above Brundisium, and drove off such numbers of horses which were kept there to pasture, that he was enabled to have four thousand broken in for the service of his army.[110]

The Romans take Casilinum.

Meanwhile the Roman consuls in Campania were availing themselves of his absence, to press the siege of Casilinum. The place was so close to Capua, that it was feared the Capuans would attempt to relieve it; Marcellus, therefore, with a second consular army, advanced from Nola to cover the siege. The defence was very obstinate; for there were seven hundred of Hannibal's soldiers in the place, and two thousand Capuans; and Fabius, it is said, was disposed to raise the siege; but his colleague reminded him of the loss of reputation, if so small a town were allowed to baffle two consular armies; and the siege was continued. At last the Capuans offered to Fabius to surrender the town, on condition of being allowed to retire to Capua; and it appears that he accepted the terms, and that the garrison had begun to march out, when Marcellus broke in upon them, seized the open gate from which they were issuing, cut them down right and left, and forced his way into the city. Fabius, it is said, was able to keep his faith to no more than fifty of the garrison, who had reached his quarters before Marcellus arrived, and whom he sent unharmed to Capua. The rest of the Capuans and of Hannibal's soldiers were sent prisoners

107 Livy, XXIV. 19.
108 Livy, XXIV. 20.
109 Livy, XXIV. 20.
110 Livy, XXIV. 20.

to Rome; and the inhabitants were divided amongst the neighboring cities, to be kept in custody till the senate should determine their fate.[111]

After this scandalous act of treachery, Marcellus returned to Nola, and there remained inactive, being confined, it was said, by illness,[112] till the senate, before the end of the summer, sent him over to Sicily to meet the danger that was gathering there. Fabius advanced into Samnium, combining his operations, it seems, with his son, who commanded a prætorian army in Apulia, and with Gracchus, who was in Lucania, and whose army formed the link between the prætor in Apulia and his father in Samnium. These three armies were so formidable, that Hanno, the Carthaginian commander in Lucania, could not maintain his ground, but fell back towards Bruttium, leaving his allies to their own inadequate means of defence. Accordingly the Romans ravaged the country far and wide, and took so many towns that they boasted of having killed or captured 25,000 of the enemy.[113] After these expeditions, Fabius, it seems, led back his army to winter-quarters in the camp above Suessula Gracchus remained in Lucania; and Fabius the prætor wintered at Luceria.

Fabius ravages Samnium.

I have endeavored to follow the operations of the main armies on both sides throughout the campaign, without noticing those of Gracchus and Hanno in Lucania. But the most important action of the year, if we believe the Roman accounts, was the victory obtained by Gracchus near Beneventum, when he moved thither out of Apulia to co-operate with the consuls in Campania, and Hanno was ordered by Hannibal to march to the same point out of Lucania. Hanno, it is said, had about 17,000 foot, mostly Bruttians and Lucanians, and 1200 Numidian and Moorish horse; and Gracchus, encountering him near Beneventum, defeated him with the loss of almost all his infantry; he himself and his cavalry being the only part of the army that escaped.[114] The numbers, as usual, are probably exaggerated immensely; but there is no reason to doubt that Gracchus gained an important victory; and it was rendered famous by his giving liberty to the volunteer slaves, by whose valor it had mainly been won. Some of these had behaved ill in the action, and were afraid that they should be punished, rather than rewarded; but Gracchus first set them all free without distinction, and then, sending for those who had misbehaved, made them severally swear that they would eat and drink standing, so long as their military service should last, by way of penance for their fault. Such a sentence, so different from the usual merciless severity of the Roman discipline, added to the general joy of the army; the soldiers marched back to Beneventum in triumph; and the people poured out to meet them, and entreated Gracchus that they might invite them all to a public entertainment. Tables were set out in the streets; and the freed slaves attracted every one's notice by their white caps, the well-known sign of their enfranchisement, and by the strange sight of those who, in fulfilment of their penance, ate standing, and waited upon their worthier comrades. The whole scene delighted the generous and kind nature of Gracchus: to set free the slave and to relieve the poor appear to have been hereditary virtues in his family: to him, no less than to his unfortunate descendants, beneficence seemed the highest glory. He caused a picture to be painted, not of his victory over Hanno, but of the feasting of the enfranchised slaves in the streets of Beneventum, and placed it in the temple of Liberty on the Aventine, which his father had built and dedicated.[115]

Gracchus defeats Hanno, and enfranchises the slaves in his army.

The battle of Beneventum obliged Hanno to fall back into Lucania, and perhaps as far as the confines of Bruttium. But he soon recruited his army, the Lucanians and Bruttians, as well as the Picentines, who lived on the shores of the gulf of Salerno, being very zealous in the cause; and

Hanno retrieves his loss.

[111] Livy, XXIV. 19.
[112] Livy, XXIV. 20.
[113] Livy, XXIV. 20.
[114] Livy, XXIV. 14, 15, 16.
[115] Livy, XXIV. 16.

ere long he revenged his defeat by a signal victory over an army of Lucanians of the Roman party, whom Gracchus had enlisted to act as an irregular force against their countrymen of the opposite faction. Still Hanno was not tempted to risk another battle with a Roman consular army; and when Gracchus advanced from Beneventum into Lucania, he retired again into Bruttium.[116]

There seems to have been no further dispute with regard to the appointment of consuls. Fabius and the leading members of the senate appear to have nominated such men as they thought most equal to the emergency; and no other candidates came forward. Fabius again held the comitia; and his son, Q. Fabius, who was prætor at the time, was elected consul together with Gracchus. The prætors were entirely changed. Q. Fulvius was succeeded in the city prætorship by M. Atilius Regulus, who had just resigned the censorship, and who had already been twice consul; the other three prætors were M. Æmilius Lepidus, Cn. Fulvius Centumalus, and P. Sempronius Tuditanus. The two former were men of noble families: Sempronius appears to have owed his appointment to his resolute conduct at Cannæ, when he cut his way from the camp through the surrounding enemies, and escaped in safety to Canusium.[117]

Comitia for new officers.

Thus another year passed over; and although the state of affairs was still dark, the tide seemed to be on the turn. Hannibal had gained no new victory; Tarentum had been saved from his hands; and Casilinum had been wrested from him. Public spirit was rising daily; and fresh instances of the patriotic devotion which possessed all classes of the commonwealth were continually occurring. The owners of the slaves whom Gracchus had enfranchised refused to receive any price for them: the wealthy citizens who served in the cavalry determined not to take their pay; and their example was followed by the centurions of the legions. Trust moneys belonging to minors, or to widows and unmarried women, were deposited in the treasury; and whatever sums the trustees had occasion to draw for, were paid by the quæstor in bills on the banking commissioners, or triumviri mensarii: it is probable that these bills were actually a paper currency, and that they circulated as money, on the security of the public faith. In the same way we must suppose that the government contracts were also paid in paper; for the censors, we are told, found the treasury unable to supply the usual sums for public works and entertainments; there was no money to repair or keep up the temples, or to provide horses for the games of the circus. Upon this the persons who were in the habit of contracting for these purposes, came forward in a body to the censors, and begged them to make their contracts as usual, promising not to demand payment before the end of the war. This must mean, I conceive, that they were to be paid in orders upon the treasury, which orders were to be converted into cash, when the present difficulties of the government should be at an end.[118]

A.U.C. 541. A.C. 213. Public spirit shown by the Romans.

While such was the spirit of the people, any severity exercised by the government towards the timid or the unpatriotic was sure to be generally acceptable. The censors, M. Atilius Regulus and P. Furius Philus, summoned all those persons, most of them members of noble, and all of wealthy families, who had proposed to fly from Italy after the battle of Cannæ. L. Metellus, who was said to have been the first author of that proposal, was at this time quæstor; but he and all who were concerned in it were degraded from the equestrian order, and removed from their respective tribes. Two thousand citizens of lower rank were also removed from their tribes, and deprived of their political franchise, for having evaded military service during the last four years; and the senate inflicted an additional punishment by ordering that they should serve as foot soldiers in Sicily, along with the remains of the army of Cannæ, and

Severe measures of the censors.

[116] Livy, XXIV. 20.
[117] Livy, XXIV. 43.
[118] Livy, XXIV. 18.

should continue to serve so long as the enemy was in Italy.[119] The case of Metellus seems to have been considered a hard one: in spite of the censor's sentence, he was elected one of the tribunes in the following year. He then impeached the censors before the people; but the other nine tribunes interposed, and would not allow the trial to proceed.[120] If Metellus had been wronged, the people had made up for it by electing him tribune; but it was thought a dangerous precedent to subject the censors to a trial for the exercise of their undoubted prerogative, when there was no reason to suspect the honesty of their motives.

Distribution of the Roman armies

The forces to be employed in Italy in the approaching campaign were to consist of nine legions, three fewer than in the year before. The consuls were each to have their two legions, Gracchus in Lucania, and Fabius in Apulia. M. Æmilius was to command two legions also in Apulia, having his head-quarters at Luceria; Cn. Fulvius with two more was to occupy the camp above Suessula; and Varro was to remain with his one legion in Picenum. Two consular armies of two legions each were required in Sicily; one commanded by Marcellus as proconsul, the other by P. Lentulus as proprætor: two legions were employed in Cisalpine Gaul under P. Sempronius, and two in Sardinia under their old commander, Q. Mucius. M. Valerius Lævinus retained his single legion and his fleet, to act against Philip on the eastern side of the Ionian sea; and P. Scipio and his brother were still continued in their command in Spain.[121]

Opening of the campaign.

Hannibal passed the winter at Salapia, where, the Romans said, was a lady whom he loved, and who became famous from her influence over him.[122] Whether his passion for her made him careless of every thing else, or whether he was really taken by surprise, we know not; but the neighboring town of Arpi was attacked by the consul Fabius, and given up to him by the inhabitants; and some Spaniards, who formed part of the garrison, entered into the Roman service.[123] Gracchus obtained some slight successes in Lucania; and some of the Bruttian towns returned to their old alliance with Rome; but a Roman contractor, T. Pomponius Veientanus, who had been empowered by the government to raise soldiers in Bruttium, and to employ them in plundering the enemies' lands, was rash enough to venture a regular action with Hanno, in which he was defeated and made prisoner.[124] This disaster checked the reaction in Bruttium for the present.

Hannibal lingers near Tarentum.

Meanwhile Hannibal's eyes were still fixed upon Tarentum; and thither he marched again as soon as he took the field, leaving Fabius behind him in Apulia. He passed the whole summer in the neighborhood of Tarentum, and reduced several small towns in the surrounding country: but his friends in Tarentum made no movement; for they dared not compromise the safety of their countrymen and relations, who had been carried off as hostages to Rome. Accordingly the season wore away unmarked by any memorable action. Hannibal still lingered in the country of the Sallentines, unwilling to give up all hope of winning the prize he had so long sought; and to lull the suspicions of the Romans, he gave out that he was confined to his camp by illness, and that this had prevented his army from returning to its usual winter-quarters in Apulia.[125]

Conspiracy to betray it to Hannibal.

Matters were in this state, when tidings arrived at Tarentum, that the hostages, for whose safety their friends had been so anxious, had been all cruelly put to death at Rome for having attempted to escape from their captivity.[126] Released in so shocking a manner from their former hesitation, and burning to revenge the blood of their friends, Hannibal's partisans no longer

[119] Livy, XXIV. 18.
[120] Livy, XXIV. 43.
[121] Livy, XXIV. 44.
[122] Appian, VII. 43. Pliny, III. 16. See Lucian, Dial. Mortuor. XII. and Hemsterhuis' note.
[123] Livy, XXIV. 46, 47.
[124] Livy, XXV. 1.
[125] Polybius, VIII. 28. Livy, XXV. 8.
[126] Livy, XXV. 7.

delayed. They communicated secretly with him, arranged the details of their attempt, and signed a treaty of alliance, by which he bound himself to respect the independence and liberty of the Tarentines, and only stipulated for the plunder of such houses as were occupied by Roman citizens.[127] Two young men, Philemenus and Nicon, were the leaders of the enterprise. Philemenus, under pretence of hunting, had persuaded the officer at one of the gates to allow him to pass in and out of the town by night without interruption. He was known to be devoted to his sport; he scarcely ever returned without having caught or killed some game or other; and by liberally giving away what he had caught, he won the favor and confidence, not only of the officer of the gate, but also of the Roman governor himself, M. Livius Macatus, a relation of M. Livius Salinator, who afterwards defeated Hasdrubal, but a man too indolent and fond of good cheer to be the governor of a town threatened by Hannibal. So little did Livius suspect any danger, that on the very day which the conspirators had fixed for their attempt, and when Hannibal with ten thousand men was advancing upon the town, he had invited a large party to meet him at the Temple of the Muses near the market-place, and was engaged from an early hour in festivity.[128]

Situation of Tarentum favorable to the conspirators.

The city of Tarentum formed a triangle, two sides of which were washed by the water; the outer or western side by the Mediterranean; the inner or north-eastern side by that remarkable land-locked basin, now called the Little Sea, which has a mouth narrower than the entrance into the Norwegian Fiords, but runs deep into the land, and spreads out into a wide surface of the calmest water, scarcely ruffled by the hardest gales. Exactly at the mouth of this basin was a little rocky knoll, forming the apex of the triangle of the city, and occupied by the citadel: the city itself stood on low and mostly level ground; and its south-eastern wall, the base of the triangle, stretched across from the Little Sea to the Mediterranean.[129] Thus the citadel commanded the entrance into the basin, which was the port of the Tarentines; and it was garrisoned by the Romans, although many of the officers and soldiers were allowed to lodge in the city. All attempts upon the town by land must be made then against the south-eastern side, which was separated from the citadel by the whole length of the city: and there was another circumstance which was likely to favor a surprise; for the Tarentines, following the direction of an oracle, as they said, buried their dead within the city walls; and the street of the tombs was interposed between the gates and the inhabited parts of the town.[130] This the conspirators turned to their own purposes: in this lonely quarter two of their number, Nicon and Tragiscus, were waiting for Hannibal's arrival without the gates. As soon as they perceived the signal which was to announce his presence, they, with a party of their friends, were to surprise the gates from within, and put the guards to the sword; while others had been left in the city to keep watch near the museum, and provent any communication from being conveyed to the Roman governor.[131]

Carelessness of the governor.

The evening wore away; the governor's party broke up; and his friends attended him to his house. On their way home they met some of the conspirators, who, to lull all suspicion, began to jest with them, as though themselves going home from a revel, and joining the party amidst riotous shouts and loud laughter, accompanied the governor to his own door. He went to rest in joyous and careless mood; his friends were all gone to their quarters; the noise of revellers returning from their festivities died away through the city; and when midnight was come, the conspirators alone were abroad. They now divided into three parties: one was posted near the governor's house, a second secured the approaches to the market-place, and the third hastened to the quarter of the tombs, to watch for Hannibal's signal.[132]

127 Polybius, VIII. 26, 27. Livy, XXV. 8.
128 Polybius, VIII. 28, 29. Livy, XXV. 8, 9.
129 Strabo, VI. p. 278.
130 Polybius, VIII. 30.
131 Polybius, VIII. 29, 30. Livy, XXV. 9.
132 Polybius, VIII. 29.

They did not watch long in vain; a fire in a particular spot without the walls assured them that Hannibal was at hand. They lit a fire in answer; and presently, as had been agreed upon, the fire without the walls disappeared. Then the conspirators rushed to the gate of the city, surprised it with ease, put the guards to the sword, and began to hew asunder the bar by which the gates were fastened. No sooner was it forced, and the gates opened, than Hannibal's soldiers were seen ready to enter; so exactly had the time of the operations been calculated. The cavalry were left without the walls as a reserve; but the infantry, marching in regular column, advanced through the quarter of the tombs to the inhabited part of the city.[133]

Hannibal enters one of the gates.

Meantime Philemenus with a thousand Africans had been sent to secure another gate by stratagem. The guards were accustomed to let him in at all hours, whenever he returned from his hunting expeditions; and now, when they heard his usual whistle, one of them went to the gate to admit him. Philemenus called to the guard from without to open the wicket quickly; for that he and his friends had killed a huge wild boar, and could scarcely bear the weight any longer. The guard, accustomed to have a share in the spoil, opened the wicket; and Philemenus and three other conspirators, disguised as countrymen, stepped in, carrying the boar between them. They instantly killed the poor guard, as he was admiring and feeling their prize; and then let in about thirty Africans, who were following close behind. With this force they mastered the gate-house and towers, killed all the guards, and hewed asunder the bars of the main gates to admit the whole column of Africans, who marched in on this side also in regular order, and advanced towards the market-place.[134]

Another is opened to him by Philemenus.

No sooner had both Hannibal's columns reached their destination, and as it seems without exciting any general alarm, than he detached three bodies of Gaulish soldiers to occupy the principal streets which led to the market-place. The officers in command of these troops had orders to kill every Roman who fell in their way; but some of the Tarentine conspirators were sent with each party to warn their countrymen to go home and remain quiet, assuring them that no mischief was intended to them. The toils being thus spread, the prey was now to be enticed into them. Philemenus and his friends had provided some Roman trumpets; and these were loudly blown, sounding the well-known call to arms to the Roman soldier. Roused at this summons, the Romans quartered about the town armed themselves in haste, and poured into the streets to make their way to the citadel. But they fell in scattered parties into the midst of Hannibal's Gauls, and were cut down one after another. The governor alone had been more fortunate; the alarm had reached him in time; and being in no condition to offer any resistance,—for he felt, says Polybius, that the fumes of wine were still overpowering him,—he hastened to the harbor, and getting on board a boat, was carried safely to the citadel.[135]

Slaughter of the Roman troops.

Day at last dawned, but did not quite clear up the mystery of the night's alarm to the mass of the inhabitants of Tarentum. They were safe in their houses, unmassacred, unplundered; the only blast of war had been blown by a Roman trumpet; yet Roman soldiers were lying dead in the streets; and Gauls were spoiling their bodies. Suspense at length was ended by the voice of the public crier summoning the citizens of Tarentum, in Hannibal's name, to appear without their arms in the market-place; and by repeated shouts of "Liberty! Liberty!" uttered by some of their own countrymen, who ran round the town calling the Carthaginians their deliverers. The firm partisans of Rome made haste to escape into the citadel, while the multitude crowded to the market-place. They found it regularly occupied by Car-

Hannibal addresses the Tarentines, and promises to protect them.

[133] Polybius, VIII. 30, 31.
[134] Polybius, VIII, 31.
[135] Polybius, VIII. 32. Livy, XXV. 10.

thaginian troops; and the great general, of whom they had heard so much, was preparing to address them. He spoke to them, in Greek apparently, declaring, as usual, that he was come to free the inhabitants of Italy from the dominion of Rome. "The Tarentines therefore had nothing to fear; they should go home, and write each over his door, *a Tarentine's house;* those words would be a sufficient security; no door so marked should be violated. But the mark must not be set falsely upon any Roman's quarters; a Tarentine guilty of such treason would be put to death as an enemy; for all Roman property was the lawful prize of the soldiers." Accordingly all houses where Romans had been quartered were given up to be plundered; and the Carthaginian soldiers gained a harvest, says Polybius, which fully answered their hopes. This can only be explained by supposing that the Romans were quartered generally in the houses of the wealthier Tarentines, who were attached to the Roman alliance; and that the plunder was not the scanty baggage of the legionary soldiers, but the costly furniture of the richest citizens in the greatest city of southern Italy.[136]

He drags the Tarentine fleet through the town, and returns into Apulia.

Thus Tarentum was won; but the citadel on its rocky knoll was still held by the Romans; and its position at once threatened the town, and shut up the Tarentine fleet useless in the harbor. Hannibal proceeded to sink a ditch, and throw up a wall along the side of the town towards the citadel, in order to repress the sallies of the garrison. While engaged in these works he purposely tempted the Romans to a sally, and having lured them on to some distance from their cover, turned fiercely upon them, and drove them back with such slaughter, that their effective strength was greatly reduced. He then hoped to take the citadel: but the garrison was reinforced by sea from Metapontum, the Romans withdrawing their troops from thence for this more important service; and a successful night-sally destroyed the besiegers' works, and obliged them to trust to a blockade. But as this was hopeless, while the Romans were masters of the sea, Hannibal instructed the Tarentines to drag their ships overland, through the streets of the city, from the harbor to the outer sea; and this being effected without difficulty, as the ground was quite level, the Tarentine fleet became at once effective, and the sea communications of the enemy were cut off. Having thus, as he hoped, enabled the Tarentines to deal by themselves with the Roman garrison, he left a small force in the town, and returned with the mass of his troops to his winter-quarters in the country of the Sallentines, or on the edge of Apulia.[137]

What were the Romans doing?

It will be observed that the only events recorded of this year, 541, are the reduction of Arpi by Fabius, the unimportant operations of Gracchus in Lucania, and Hannibal's surprise of Tarentum; which last action, however, did not happen till the end of the campaign, about the middle of the winter. According to Livy, Hannibal had passed the whole summer near Tarentum; he must therefore have been some months in that noigborhood; and what was going on elsewhere the while? Gracchus, we are told, was engaged in Lucania; but where was the consul Fabius, with his father? and what was done by the four Roman legions, Fabius' consular army, and the prætorian army of M. Æmilius, which were both stationed in Apulia? Allowing that Cn. Fulvius, with his two legions in the camp above Suessula, was busied in watching the Campanians, yet Fabius and Æmilius had nearly forty thousand men at their disposal; and yet Capua was not besieged; nor was Hannibal impeded in his attempts upon Tarentum. Is it to be conceived that so large a portion of the power of Rome, directed by old Fabius himself, can have been totally wasted during a whole summer, useless alike for attack or defence?

Chronological difficulties.

The answer to this question depends upon another point, which is itself not easy to fix; the true date, namely, of the surprise of Tarentum. Livy tells us that it was placed by different writers in different

136 Polybius, VIII. 33. Livy, XXV. 10.

137 Polybius, VIII. 34-36. Livy, XXV. 11.

years; and he himself prefers the later date,[138] yet does not give it correctly. For, as Tarentum was surprised in the winter, the doubt must have been, whether to fix it towards the end of the consulship of Fabius and Gracchus, or of Fulvius and Appius Claudius: it could never have been placed so early as the consulship of Fabius and Marcellus. Livy describes it after he has mentioned the coming into office of Fulvius and Claudius, as if it belonged to their year; yet he places it before the opening of the campaign, which implies that it must have occurred in the preceding winter, whilst Fabius and Gracchus were still in office. Polybius evidently gave the later date, that is, the year of Fulvius and Appius, but the end of it: according to him, it followed the death of Gracchus, and the various events of the summer of 542. And there are some strong reasons for believing this to be the more probable position. If this were so, we must suppose that the summer of 541 was passed without any important action, because Hannibal, after the loss of Arpi, continued to watch the two Roman armies in Apulia; and that either the fear of losing Tarentum, or the hope of recovering Salapia and other Apulian towns, detained Fabius in the southeast, and delayed the siege of Capua.

Disorders at Rome.

In the mean time men's minds at Rome were restless and uneasy; and the government had enough to do to prevent their running wild in one direction or another. The city had suffered from a fire, which lasted a whole day and two nights, and destroyed all the buildings along the river, with many of those on the slope of the Capitoline hill, and between it and the Palatine.[139] The distress thus caused would be great; and the suspicions of treason and incendiarism, the constant attendants of great fires in large cities, would be sure to imbitter the actual suffering. At such a time every one would crave to know what the future had in store for him; and whoever professed to be acquainted with the secrets of fate found many to believe him. Faith in the gods of Rome was beginning to be shaken: if they could not, or would not save, other powers might be more propitious; and sacrifices and prayers to strange gods were offered in the Forum and Capitol; while prophets, deceiving or deceived, were gathering crowds in every street, making a profit of their neighbors' curiosity and credulity.[140] Nor were these vagabond prophets the only men who preyed upon the public distress: the wealthy merchants, who had come forward with patriotic zeal to supply the armies when the treasury was unable to bear the burden, were now found to be seeking their own base gain out of their pretended liberality. M. Postumius, of Pyrgi, was charged by public rumor with the grossest frauds: he had demanded to be reimbursed for the loss of stores furnished by him at sea, when no such loss had occurred; he had loaded old rotten vessels with cargoes of trifling value; the sailors had purposely sunk the ships, and had escaped in their boats; and then Postumius magnified the value of their cargo, and prayed to be indemnified for the loss.[141] Even the virtue of Roman matrons could not stand the contagion of this evil time: more than one case of shame was brought by the ædiles before the judgment of the people.[142] Man's spirit failed with woman's modesty: the citizens of the military age were slow to enlist; and many from the country tribes would not come to Rome when the consuls summoned them.[143] All this unsoundness at home may have had its effect on the operations of the war, and tended to make Fabius more than usually cautious, as another defeat at such a moment might have extinguished the Roman name.

A. U. C. 542. A. C. 212. Vigorous measures of the senate.

Against this weight of evils the senate bore up vigorously. The superstitions of the people, their worship of strange gods, and their shrinking from military service, required to be noticed without delay. The city prætor, M. Atilius, issued an edict forbidding all public sacrifices

138 Livy, XXV. 11.
139 Livy, XXIV. 47.
140 Livy, XXV. 1, 12.
141 Livy, XXV. 3, 4.
142 Livy, XXV. 2.
143 Livy, XXV. 5.

to strange gods, or with any strange rites. All books of prophecies, all formularies of prayer or of sacrifice, were to be brought to him before the first of April; that is, before he went out of office.[144] The great ceremonies of the national religion were celebrated with more than usual magnificence; the great games of the circus were kept up for an additional day; two days were added to the celebration of the games of the commons; and they were further marked by a public entertainment given in the precincts of the temple of Jupiter on the capitol to all the poorer citizens.[145] A great military effort was to be made the ensuing campaign; old Q. Fulvius Flaccus, one of the ablest as well as severest men in Rome, was chosen consul for the third time; and Appius Claudius was elected as his colleague.[146] The armies, notwithstanding the difficulty of enlisting soldiers, were to be augmented; two extraordinary commissions, of three members each, were appointed, one to visit all the country tribes within fifty miles of Rome, and the other such as were more remote. Every free-born citizen was to be passed in review; and boys under seventeen were to be enlisted, if they seemed strong enough to bear arms; but their years of service were to count from their enlistment; and if they were called out before the military age began, they might claim their discharge before it ended.[147]

Punishment of Postumius.

While dealing thus strictly with the disorders and want of zeal of the multitude, the senate, it might have been supposed, would not spare the fraud of the contractor Postumius. But with that neglect of equal justice, which is the habitual sin of an aristocracy, they punished the poor, but were afraid to attack the wealthy; and although the city prætor had made an official representation of the tricks practised by Postumius, no steps were taken against him. Amongst the new tribunes, however, were two of the noble house of the Carvilii, who, indignant at the impunity of so great an offender, resolved to bring him to trial. They at first demanded no other penalty than that a fine of 200,000 ases should be imposed on him; but when the trial came on, a large party of the moneyed men broke up the assembly by creating a riot, and no sentence was passed. This presumption, however, overshot its mark; the consuls took up the matter and laid it before the senate: the senate resolved that the peace of the commonwealth had been violently outraged; and the tribunes now proceeded against Postumius and the principal authors of the disturbance capitally. Bail was demanded of them; but they deserted their bail, and went into exile; upon which the people, on the motion of the tribunes, ordered that their property should be sold, and themselves outlawed.[148] Thus the balance of justice was struck; and this, doubtless, contributed to conciliate the poorer citizens, and to make them more ready to bear their part in the war.

Resolution to besiege Capua.

It was resolved that Capua should be besieged without delay. In the preceding year, 112 noble Capuans had left the city, and come over to the Romans, stipulating for nothing but their lives and properties.[149] This shows that the aristocratical party in Capua could not be depended on: if the city were hard pressed, they would not be ready to make any extraordinary sacrifices in its behalf. Hannibal was far away in the farthest corner of Italy; and as long as the citadel of Tarentum held out, he would be unwilling to move towards Campania. Even if he should move, four armies were ready to oppose him; those of the two consuls, of the consul's brother, Cn. Fulvius, who was prætor in Apulia, and of another prætor, C. Claudius Nero, who commanded two legions in the camp above Suessula. Besides this mass of forces, Ti. Gracchus, the consul of the preceding year, still retained his army as proconsul in Lucania, and might be supposed capable of keeping Hanno and the army of Bruttium in check.

144 Livy, XXV. 1.
145 Livy, XXV. 2.
146 Livy, XXV. 3.
147 Livy, XXV. 5.
148 Livy, XXV. 4.
149 Livy, XXIV. 47.

It was late in the spring before the consuls took the field. One of them succeeded to the army of the late consul, Fabius; the other took the two legions with which Cn. Fulvius Centumulas had held the camp above Suessula.[150] These armies marching, the one from Apulia, the other from Campania, met at Bovianum: there, at the back of the Matese, in the country of the Pentrian Samnites, the faithful allies of Rome, the consuls were making preparations for the siege of Capua, and, perhaps, were at the same time watching the state of affairs in the south, and the movements of Hannibal. The Campanians suspected that mischief was coming upon them, and sent a deputation to Hannibal praying him to aid them. If they were to stand a siege, it was important that the city should be well supplied with provisions; and their own harvest had been so insufficient, owing to the devastation caused by the war, that they had scarcely enough for their present consumption. Hannibal would therefore be pleased to order that supplies should be sent to them from the country of his Samnite and Lucanian allies, before their communications were cut off by the presence of the Roman armies.[151]

The Campanians apply to Hannibal for aid.

Hannibal was still near Tarentum, whether hoping to win the town or the citadel, the doubtful chronology of this period will not allow us to decide. He ordered Hanno, with the army of Bruttium, to move forward into Samnium; a most delicate operation, if the two consuls were with their armies at Bovianum, and Gracchus in Lucania itself, in the very line of Hanno's march, and if C. Nero, with two legions more, was lying in the camp above Suessula. But the army from Suessula had been given to one of the consuls, and the legions which were to take its place were to be marched from the coast of Picenum, and perhaps had hardly reached their destination. The Lucanians themselves seem to have found sufficient employment for Gracchus; and Hanno moved with a rapidity which friends and enemies were alike unprepared for. He arrived safely in the neighborhood of Beneventum, encamped his army in a strong position about three miles from the town, and dispatched word to the Capuans that they should instantly send off every carriage and beast of burden in their city, to carry home the corn which he was going to provide for them. The towns of the Caudine Samnites emptied their magazines for the purpose, and forwarded all their corn to Hanno's camp. Thus far all prospered; but the negligence of the Capuans ruined every thing: they had not carriages enough ready; and Hanno was obliged to wait in his perilous situation, where every hour's delay was exposing him to destruction.[152] Beneventum was a Latin colony, in other words, a strong Roman garrison, watching all his proceedings; from thence, information was sent to the consuls at Bovianum; and Fulvius with his army instantly set out, and entered Beneventum by night. There he found that the Capuans with their means of transport were at length arrived; and all disposable hands had been pressed into the service; that Hanno's camp was crowded with cattle and carriages, and a mixed multitude of unarmed men, and even of women and children; and that a vigorous blow might win it with all its spoil: the indefatigable general was absent, scouring the country for additional supplies of corn. Fulvius sallied from Beneventum a little before daybreak, and led his soldiers to assault Hanno's position. Under all disadvantages of surprise and disorder, the Carthaginians resisted so vigorously, that Fulvius was on the point of calling off his men, when a brave Pelignian officer threw the standard of his cohort over the enemy's wall, and desperately climbed the rampart and scaled the wall to recover it. His cohort rushed after him; and a Roman centurion then set the same example, which was followed with equal alacrity. Then the Romans broke into the camp on every side, even the wounded men struggling on with the mass, that they might die within the enemy's ramparts. The slaughter was great, and the prisoners many; but above all, the

He sends Hanno to relieve them, who fails through their negligence.

150 Livy, XXV. 3.

151 Livy, XXV. 13.

152 Livy, XXV. 13.

whole of the corn which Hanno had collected for the relief of Capua was lost, and the object of his expedition totally frustrated. He himself, hearing of the wreck of his army, retreated with speed into Bruttium.[153]

Again the Capuans sent to Hannibal requesting him to aid them ere it was too late. Their negligence had just cost him an army, and had frustrated all his plans for their relief; but, with unmoved temper, he assured them that he would not forget them, and sent back 2000 of his invincible cavalry with the deputation, to protect their lands from the enemy's ravages. It was important to him not to leave the south of Italy till the very last moment; for since he had taken Tarentum, the neighboring Greek cities of Metapontum, Heraclea, and Thurii, had joined him; and as he had before won Croton and Locri, he was now master of the whole coast from the straits of Messana to the mouth of the Adriatic, with the exception of Rhegium and the citadel of Tarentum. Into the latter the Romans had lately thrown supplies of provisions; and the garrison was so strong, that Hannibal was unwilling to march into Campania, while such a powerful force of the enemy was left behind in so favorable a position.[154]

The Capuans again apply for aid.

The consuls meanwhile, not content with their own two armies, and with the two legions expected, if not yet arrived, in the camp above Suessula, sent to Gracchus in Lucania, desiring him to bring up his cavalry and light troops to Beneventum, to strengthen them in that kind of force, in which they fully felt their inferiority. But before he could leave his own province, he was drawn into an ambuscade by the treachery of a Lucanian in the Roman interest, and perished.[155] His quæstor, Cn. Cornelius, marched with his cavalry towards Beneventum, according to the consul's orders; but the infantry, consisting of the slaves whom he had enfranchised, thought that their services were ended by the death of their deliverer, and immediately dispersed to their homes.[156] Thus Lucania was left without either a Roman army or general; but M. Centenius, an old centurion, distinguished for his strength and courage, undertook the command there, if the senate would intrust him with a force equal to a single legion. Perhaps, like T. Pomponius Veientanus, he was connected with some of the contractors and moneyed men, and owed his appointment as much to their interest as to his own reputation. But he was a brave and popular soldier; and so many volunteers joined him on his march, hoping to be enriched by the plunder of Lucania, that he arrived there with a force, it is said, amounting to near sixteen thousand men. His confidence and that of his followers was doomed to be wofully disappointed.[157]

Death of Gracchus: Centenius raises an army in Lucania.

The consuls knew that Hannibal was far away; and they did not know that any of his cavalry were in Capua. They issued boldly, therefore, from the Caudine Forks on the great Campanian plain, and scattered their forces far and wide to destroy the still green corn. To their astonishment the gates of Capua were thrown open; and with the Campanian infantry they recognized the dreaded cavalry of Hannibal. In a moment their foragers were driven in; and as they hastily formed their legions in order of battle to cover them, the horsemen broke upon them like a whirlwind, and drove them with great loss and confusion to their camp.[158] This sharp lesson taught them caution; but their numbers were overwhelming; and their two armies, encamped before Capua, cut off the communications of the city, and had the harvest of the whole country in their power.

The Romans are repulsed by a sally from Capua.

But ere many days had elapsed, an unwelcome sight was seen on the summit of Tifata; Hannibal was there once more with his army. He descended into Capua; two days afterwards he marched out to

Hannibal returns to Tifata.

153 Livy, XXV. 14. Valerius Maximus, III. 2, 20.

154 Livy, XXV. 15, Appian, VII. 35.

155 Livy, XXV. 16.

156 Livy, XXV. 20.

157 Livy, XXV. 19.

158 Livy, XXV. 18.

battle; again his invincible Numidians struck terror into the Roman line, when the sudden arrival of Cn. Cornelius with the cavalry of Gracchus' army broke off the action; and neither side, it is said, knowing what this new force might be, both, as if by common consent, retreated.[159] How Hannibal so outstripped Cornelius as to arrive from Tarentum on the scene of action two or three days before him, who was coming from Lucania, we are not told, and can only conjecture. But the arrival of this reinforcement, though it had saved the consuls from defeat, did not embolden them to hold their ground: they left their camps as soon as night came on; Fulvius fell down upon the coast, near Cumæ; Appius Claudius retreated in the direction of Lucania.

He enters Capua.

Few passages in history can offer a parallel to Hannibal's campaigns; but this confident gathering of the enemies' overflowing numbers round the city of his nearest allies, his sudden march, the unlooked-for appearance of his dreaded veterans, and the instant scattering of the besieging armies before him, remind us of the deliverance of Dresden in 1813, when Napoleon broke in upon the allies' confident expectations of victory, and drove them away in signal defeat. And like the allies in that great campaign, the Roman generals knew their own strength; and though yielding to the shock of their adversary's surpassing energy and genius, they did not allow themselves to be scared from their purpose, but began again steadily to draw the toils which he had once broke through. Great was the joy in Capua, when the people rose in the morning and saw the Roman camps abandoned: there needs no witness to tell us with what sincere and deep admiration they followed and gazed on their deliverer; how confident they felt that, with him for a shield, no harm could reach them. But almost within sight and hearing of their joy, the stern old Fulvius was crouching, as it were, in his thicket, watching the moment for a second spring upon his prey; and when Hannibal left that rejoicing and admiring multitude to follow the traces of Appius, he passed through the gates of Capua, to enter them again no more.

On his return into Lucania he destroys the army of Centenius;

Appius retreated in the direction of Lucania: this is all that is reported of his march; and then, after a while, having led his enemy in the direction which suited his purposes, he turned off by another road, and made his way back to Campania.[160] With such a total absence of details, it is impossible to fix the line of his march exactly. It was easy for Appius to take the round of the Matese; retiring first by the great road to Beneventum, then turning to his left and regaining his old quarters at Bovianum, from whence, the instant that Hannibal ceased to follow him, he would move along under the north side of the Matese to Æsernia, and descend again upon Campania by the valley of the Vulturnus. Hannibal's pursuit was necessarily stopped as soon as Appius moved northwards from Beneventum: he could not support his army in the country of the Pentrian Samnites, where every thing was hostile to him; nor did he like to abandon his line of direct communication with southern Italy. He had gained a respite for Capua, and had left an auxiliary force to aid in its defence: meanwhile other objects must not be neglected; and the fall of the citadel of Tarentum might of itself prevent or raise the siege of Capua. So he turned off from following Appius, and was marching back to the south, when he was told that a Roman army was attempting to bar his passage in Lucania. This was the motley multitude commanded by Centenius, which had succeeded, as we have seen, to the army of Gracchus. With what mad hope, or under what false impression, Centenius could have been tempted to rush upon certain destruction, we know not: but in the number, no less than in the quality of his troops, he must have been far inferior to his adversary. His men fought bravely; and he did a centurion's duty well, however he may have failed

[159] Livy, XXV. 19.

[160] Livy, XXV. 19.

as a general; but he was killed, and nearly fifteen thousand men are said to have perished with him.[161]

Thus Lucania was cleared of the Romans; and as the firmest partisan of the Roman interest among the Lucanians had been the very man who had betrayed Gracchus to his fate, it is likely that the Carthaginian party was triumphant through the whole country. Only one Roman army was left in the south of Italy, the two legions commanded by Cn. Fulvius Flaccus, the consul's brother, in Apulia. But Cn. Fulvius had nothing of his brother's ability; he was a man grown old in profligacy; and the discipline of his army was said to be in the worst condition. Hannibal, hoping to complete his work, moved at once into Apulia, and found Fulvius in the neighborhood of Herdonea. The Roman general met him in the open field without hesitation, and was presently defeated; he himself escaped from the action, but Hannibal had occupied the principal roads in the rear of the enemy with his cavalry; and the greatest part of the Roman army was cut to pieces.[162]

And that of Cn. Fulvius in Apulia.

We naturally ask what result followed from these two great victories; and to this question we find no recorded answer. Hannibal, we are told, returned to Tarentum; but finding that the citadel still held out, and could neither be forced nor surprised, and that provisions were still introduced by sea, a naval blockade in ancient warfare being always inefficient, he marched off towards Brundisium, on some prospect that the town would be betrayed into his hands. This hope also failed him; and he remained inactive in Apulia, or in the country of the Sallentines, during the rest of the year. Meantime the consuls received orders from the senate to collect the wrecks of the two beaten armies, and to search for the soldiers of Gracchus' army, who had dispersed, as we have seen, after his death. The city prætor, P. Cornelius, carried on the same search nearer Rome; and these duties, says Livy, were all performed most carefully and vigorously.[163] This is all the information which exists for us in the remains of the ancient writers; but assuredly this is no military history of a campaign.

What were the results of these victories.

It is always to be understood that Hannibal could not remain long in an enemy's country, from the difficulty of feeding his men, especially his cavalry. But the country round Capua was not all hostile; Atella and Calatia, in the plain of Campania itself, were still his allies; so were many of the Caudine Samnites, from whose cities Hanno had collected the corn early in this year for the relief of Capua. Again, we can conceive how the number of the Roman armies sometimes oppressed him; how he dared not stay long in one quarter, lest a greater evil should befall him in another. But at this moment three great disasters, the dispersion of the army of Gracchus, and the destruction of those of Centenius and Fulvius, had cleared the south of Italy of the Romans; and his friends in Apulia, in Lucania, at Tarentum, and in Bruttium, could have nothing to fear, had he left them for the time to their own resources. Why, after defeating Fulvius, did he not retrace his steps towards Campania, hold the field with the aid of his Campanian and Samnite allies till the end of the military season, and then winter close at hand, on the shores of the gulf of Salerno, in the country of his allies, so as to make it impossible for the Romans either to undertake or to maintain the siege of Capua?

Difficulties of Hannibal's situation.

That his not doing this was not his own fault, his extraordinary ability and energy may sufficiently assure us. But where the hindrance was, we cannot for certain discover. His army must have been worn by its long and rapid march to and from Campania, and by two battles fought with so short an interval. His wounded must have been numerous; nor can we tell how such hard service in the heat of summer may have tried the health of

His probable reasons for wintering in Apulia.

[161] Livy, XXV. 19.
[162] Livy, XXV. 20, 21.
[163] Livy, XXV. 22.

his soldiers. His horses, too, must have needed rest; and to overstrain the main arm of his strength would have been fatal. Perhaps, too, great as was Hannibal's ascendency over his army, there was a point beyond which it could not be tried with safety. Long marches and hard-fought battles gave the soldier, especially the Gaul and the Spaniard, what in his eyes was a rightful claim to a season of rest and enjoyment: the men might have murmured had they not been permitted to taste some reward of their victories. Besides all these reasons, the necessity of a second march into Campania may not have seemed urgent: the extent of Capua was great; if the Roman consuls did encamp before it, still the city was in no immediate danger; after the winter another advance would again enable him to throw supplies into the town, and to drive off the Roman armies. So Capua was left for the present to its own resources, and Hannibal passed the autumn and winter in Apulia.

The Romans surround Capua with a double wall.

Immediately the Roman armies closed again upon their prey. Three grand magazines of corn were established, to feed the besieging army during the winter, one at Casilinum within three miles of Capua; another at a fort built for the purpose at the mouth of the Vulturnus; and a third at Puteoli. Into these two last magazines the corn was conveyed by sea from Ostia, whither it had already been collected from Sardinia and Etruria.[164] Then the consuls summoned C. Nero from his camp above Suessula; and the three armies began the great work of surrounding Capua with double continuous lines, strong enough to repel the besieged on one side, and Hannibal on the other, when he should again appear in Campania. The inner line was carried round the city, at a distance of about a quarter of a mile from the walls; the outer line was concentric with it; and the space between the two served for the cantonments and magazines of the besiegers. The lines, says Appian,[165] looked like a great city, inclosing a smaller city in the middle; like the famous lines of the Peloponnesians before Platæa. What time was employed in completing them we know not; they were interrupted by continual sallies of the besieged; and Jubellius Taurea and the Capuan cavalry were generally too strong for the Roman horsemen.[166] But their infantry could do nothing against the legions; the besieging army must have amounted nearly to sixty thousand men; and slowly but surely the imprisoning walls were raised, and their circle completed, shutting out the last gleams of light from the eyes of the devoted city.

Their offer to allow any of the citizens to come out safely is rejected. A.U.C. 543. A.C. 211.

Before the works were closed all round, the consuls, according to the senate's directions signified to them by the city prætor, announced to the Capuans, that whoever chose to come out of the city with his family and property before the ides of March, might do so with safety, and should be untouched in body or goods.[167] It would seem then that the works were not completed till late in the winter; for we cannot suppose that the term of grace would have been prolonged to a remote day, especially as the ides of March were the beginning of the new consular year; and it could not be known long beforehand whether the present consuls would be continued in their command or no. The offer was received by the besieged, it is said, with open scorn; their provisions were as yet abundant, their cavalry excellent; their hope of aid from Hannibal, as soon as the campaign should open, was confident. But Fulvius waited his time; nor was his thirst for Capuan blood to be disappointed by his removal from the siege at the end of the year: it would seem as if the new consuls were men of no great consideration, appointed probably for that very reason, that their claims might not interfere with those of their predecessors. One of them, P. Sulpicius Galba, had filled no curule office previously: the other, Cn. Fulvius Centumalus, had been prætor two years before, but was not distinguished by any remarkable action. The siege of Capua was still to be con-

[164] Livy, XXV. 22.
[165] VII. 37.
[166] Appian, VII. 37. Livy, XXVI. 4.
[167] Livy, XXV. 22.

ducted by Appius Claudius and Fulvius; and they were ordered not to retire from their positions till they should have taken the city.[168]

What was the state of affairs in Capua meantime, we know not. The Roman stories are little to be credited, which represent all the richer and nobler citizens as abandoning the government, and leaving the office of chief magistrate, Meddix Tuticus, to be filled by one Seppius Lesius, a man of obscure condition, who offered himself as a candidate.[169] Neither Vibius Virrius nor Jubellius Taurea wanted resolution to abide by their country to the last; and it was expressly said that, down to the latest period of the siege, there was no Roman party in Capua; no voice was heard to speak of peace or surrender; no citizen had embraced the consul's offers of mercy.[170] Even when they had failed to prevent the completion of the Roman lines, they continued to make frequent sallies; and the proconsuls could only withstand their cavalry by mixing light-armed foot soldiers amongst the Roman horsemen, and thus strengthening that weakest arm in the Roman service. Still, as the blockade was now fully established, famine must be felt sooner or later: accordingly a Numidian was sent to implore Hannibal's aid, and succeeded in getting through the Roman lines, and carrying his message safely to Bruttium.[171]

State of Capua.

Hannibal listened to the prayer, and leaving his heavy baggage and the mass of his army behind, set out with his cavalry and light infantry, and with thirty-three elephants.[172] Whether his Samnite and Lucanian allies joined him on the march is not stated; if they did not, and if secrecy and expedition were deemed of more importance than an addition of force, the troops which he led with him must have been more like a single corps than a complete army. Avoiding Beneventum, he descended the valley of the Calor towards the Vulturnus, stormed a Roman post, which had been built apparently to cut off the communications of the besieged with the upper valley of the Vulturnus, and encamped immediately behind the ridge of Tifata. From thence he descended once more into the plain of Capua, displayed his cavalry before the Roman lines in the hope of tempting them out to battle, and finding that this did not succeed, commenced a general assault upon their works.

Hannibal comes to its relief.

Unprovided with any artillery, his best hope was, that the Romans might be allured to make some rash sally: his cavalry advanced by squadrons up to the edge of the trench, and discharged showers of missiles into the lines; while his infantry assailed the rampart, and tried to force their way through the palisade which surmounted it. From within, the lines were attacked by the Campanians and Hannibal's auxiliary garrison; but the Romans were numerous enough to defend both fronts of their works; they held their ground steadily, neither yielding nor rashly pursuing; and Hannibal, finding his utmost efforts vain, drew off his army.[173] Some resolution must be taken promptly; his cavalry could not be fed where he was, for the Romans had previously destroyed or carried away every thing that might serve for forage; nor could he venture to wait till the new consuls should have raised their legions, and be ready to march from Rome and threaten his rear. One only hope remained; one attempt might yet be made, which should either raise the siege of Capua or accomplish a still greater object: Hannibal resolved to march upon Rome.

Hannibal attacks the Roman lines ineffectually, and resolves to march against Rome.

A Numidian was again found, who undertook to pass over to the Roman lines as a deserter, and from thence to make his escape into Capua, bearing a letter from Hannibal, which explained his purpose, and conjured the Capuans patiently to abide the issue of his attempt for a little while.[174] When this letter reached Capua, Hannibal was already gone; his camp-fires had

He sets out suddenly by night.

168 Livy, XXVI. 1. Frontinus, III. 18, 3.
169 Livy, XXVI. 6.
170 Livy, XXVI. 12.
171 Livy, XXVI. 4. Frontinus, IV. 7, 29.
172 Livy, XXVI. 5.
173 Polybius, IX. 3. Livy, XXVI. 5.
174 Polybius, IX. 5. Livy, XXVI. 7.

been seen burning, as usual, all night in his accustomed position on Tifata; but he had begun his march the preceding evening, immediately after dark, while the Romans still thought that his army was hanging over their heads, and were looking for a second assault.[175]

Difficulty of making out his line of march.

His army disappeared from the eyes of the Romans behind Tifata; and they knew not whither he was gone. Even so it is with us at this day; we lose him from Tifata; we find him before Rome; but we know nothing of his course between. Conflicting and contradictory accounts have made the truth undiscoverable: what regions of Italy looked with fear or hope on the march of the great general and his famous soldiers, it is impossible from our existing records to determine. Whether he followed the track of Pyrrhus, and spread havoc through the lands of the numerous colonies on the Latin road, Cales, Casinum, Interamna, and Fregellæ;[176] or whether, to baffle the enemy's pursuit, and avoid the delay of crossing the Vulturnus, he plunged northwards into the heart of Samnium,[177] astonished the Latin colonists of Œsernia with his unlooked-for passage, crossed the central Apennines into the country of the Pelignians, and then, turning suddenly to his left, broke down into the land of the Marsians, passing along the glassy waters of Fucinus, and under the ancient walls of Alba, and scaring the upland glades and quiet streams of the aboriginal Sabines, with the wild array of his Numidian horsemen; we cannot with any confidence decide. Yet the agreement of all the stories as to the latter part of his march seems to point out the line of its beginning. All accounts say that, descending nearly by the old route of the Gauls, he kept the Tiber on his right, and the Anio on his left; and that, finally, he crossed the Anio, and encamped at a distance of less than four miles from the walls of Rome.[178]

Terror in Rome; fortitude of the senate.

Before the sweeping pursuit of his Numidians, crowds of fugitives were seen flying towards the city, while the smoke of burning houses arose far and wide into the sky. Within the walls the confusion and terror were at their height: he was come at last, this Hannibal, whom they had so long dreaded; he had at length dared what even the slaughter of Cannæ had not emboldened him to venture; some victory greater even than Cannæ must have given him this confidence; the three armies before Capua must be utterly destroyed; last year he had destroyed or dispersed three other armies, and had gained possession of the entire south of Italy; and now he had stormed the lines before Capua, had cut to pieces the whole remaining force of the Roman people, and was come to Rome to finish his work. So the wives and mothers of Rome lamented, as they hurried to the temples; and there, prostrate before the gods, and sweeping the sacred pavement with their unbound hair in the agony of their fear, they remained pouring forth their prayers for deliverance. Their sons and husbands hastened to man the walls and the citadel, and to secure the most important points without the city; whilst the senate, as calm as their fathers of old, whom the Gauls massacred when sitting at their own doors, but with the energy of manly resolution, rather than the resignation of despair, met in the Forum, and there remained assembled, to direct every magistrate on the instant how he might best fulfil his duty.[179]

Rome is preserved from an assault.

But God's care watched over the safety of a people whom he had chosen to work out the purposes of his providence: Rome was not to perish. Two city legions were to be raised, as usual, at the beginning of the year; and it so happened that the citizens from the country tribes were to meet at Rome on this very day for the enlistment for one of these legions; while the soldiers of the other, which had been enrolled a short time before, were to appear at Rome on this same day in arms, having been allowed, as the custom was, to return home for a few days after their enlistment, to prepare for active service.

175 Polybius, IX. 5.

176 Livy, XXVI. 9.

177 Polybius, IX. 5.

178 Polybius, IX. 6. Livy, XXVI. 9. Appian, VII. 38.

179 Polybius, IX. 6. Livy, XXVI. 9.

Thus it happened that ten thousand men were brought together at the very moment when they were most needed, and were ready to repel any assault upon the walls.[180] The allies, it seems, were not ordinarily called out to serve with the two city legions; but on this occasion it is mentioned that the Latin colony of Alba, having seen Hannibal pass by their walls, and guessing the object of his march, sent his whole force to assist in the defence of Rome; a zeal which the Greek writers compared to that of Platæa, whose citizens fought alone by the side of the Athenians on the day of Marathon.[181]

Hannibal ravages the country round.

To assault the walls of Rome was now hopeless; but the open country was at Hannibal's mercy, a country which had seen no enemy for near a hundred and fifty years, cultivated and inhabited in the full security of peace. Far and wide it was overrun by Hannibal's soldiers; and the army appears to have moved about, encamping in one place after another, and sweeping cattle and prisoners and plunder of every sort, beyond numbering, within the inclosure of its camp.[182]

He rides up to the walls of Rome.

It was, probably, in the course of these excursions, that Hannibal, at the head of a large body of cavalry, came close up to the Colline gate, rode along leisurely under the walls to see all he could of the city, and is said to have cast his javelin into it as in defiance.[183] From farthest Spain he had come into Italy; he had wasted the whole country of the Romans and their allies with fire and sword for more than six years, had slain more of their citizens than were now alive to bear arms against him; and at last he was shutting them up within their city, and riding freely under their walls, while none dared meet him in the field. If any thing of disappointment depressed his mind at that instant; if he felt that Rome's strength was not broken, nor the spirit of her people quelled, that his own fortune was wavering, and that his last effort had been made, and made in vain; yet thinking where he was, and of the shame and loss which his presence was causing to his enemies, he must have wished that his father could have lived to see that day, and must have thanked the gods of his country that they had enabled him so fully to perform his vow.

Fulvius returns to Rome, and the Romans march out to check Hannibal.

For some time, we know not how long, this devastation of the Roman territory lasted without opposition. Meanwhile the siege of Capua was not raised; and Fabius, in earnestly dissuading such a confession of fear, showed that he could be firm no less than cautious, when boldness was the highest prudence. But Fulvius, with a small portion of the besieging army, was recalled to Rome: Fabius had ever acted with him, and was glad to have the aid of his courage and ability; and when he arrived, and by a vote of the senate was united with the consuls in the command, the Roman forces were led out of the city, and encamped, according to Fabius' old policy, within ten stadia of the enemy, to check his free license of plunder.[184] At the same time, parties acting on the rear of Hannibal's army had broken down the bridges over the Anio, his line of retreat, like his advance, being on the right bank of that river, and not by the Latin road.

Hannibal retires.

Hannibal had purposely waited to allow time for his movement to produce its intended effect in the raising of the siege of Capua. That time, according to his calculations, was now come: the news of his arrival before Rome must have reached the Roman lines before Capua; and the armies from that quarter, hastening by the Latin road to the defence of their city, must have left the communication with Capua free. The presence of Fulvius with his army in Latium, which Hannibal would instantly discover, by the thrice-repeated sounding of the watch, as Hasdrubal found out Nero's arrival in the camp of Livius near Sena, would confirm him in his expectation that the other proconsul was on his march with the mass of the army; and he accord-

180 Polybius, IX. 6.
181 Appian, VII. 39.
182 Polybius, IX. 6.
183 Livy, XXVI. 10. Pliny, XXXIV. 15.
184 Livy, XXVI. 8, 9, 10. Polybius, IX. 7. Appian, VII. 40.

ingly commenced his retreat by the Tiburtine road, that he might not encounter Appius in front, while the consuls and Fabius were pressing on his rear.

Accordingly, as the bridges were destroyed, he proceeded to effect his passage through the river, and carried over his army under the protection of his cavalry, although the Romans attacked him during the passage, and cut off a large part of the plunder which he had collected from the neighborhood of Rome.[185] He then continued his retreat; and the Romans followed him, but at a careful distance, and keeping steadily on the higher grounds, to be safe from the assaults of his dreaded cavalry.[186]

The Romans follow him at a distance.

In this manner Hannibal marched with the greatest rapidity for five days, which, if he was moving by the Valerian road, must have brought him at least as far as the country of the Marsians, and the shores of the lake Fucinus.[187] From thence he would again have crossed by the Forca Carrosa to the plain of the Pelignians, and so retraced his steps through Samnium towards Capua. But at this point he received intelligence that the Roman armies were still in their lines, that his march upon Rome had therefore failed, and that his communications with Capua were as hopeless as ever. Instantly he changed all his plans; and feeling obliged to abandon Capua, the importance of his operations in the south rose upon him in proportion. Hitherto he had not thought fit to delay his march for the sake of attacking the army which was pursuing him; but now he resolved to rid himself of this enemy; so he turned fiercely upon them, and assaulted their camp in the night. The Romans, surprised and confounded, were driven from it with considerable loss, and took refuge in a strong position in the mountains. Hannibal then resumed his march, but, instead of turning short to his right towards Campania, descended towards the Adriatic and the plains of Apulia, and from thence returned to what was now the stronghold of his power in Italy, the country of the Bruttians.[188]

He marches down into Bruttium.

The citadel of Tarentum still held out against him; but Rhegium, confident in its remoteness, had never yet seen his cavalry in its territory, and was now less likely than ever to dread his presence, as he had so lately been heard of in the heart of Italy, and under the walls of Rome. With a rapid march therefore he hastened to surprise Rhegium. Tidings of his coming reached the city just in time for the Rhegians to shut their gates against him; but half their people were in the country, in the full security of peace; and these all fell into his power.[189] We know not whether he treated them kindly, as hoping through their means to win Rhegium, as he had won Tarentum; or whether disappointment was now stronger than hope, and, despairing of drawing the allies of Rome to his side, he was now as inveterate against them as against the Romans. He retired from his fruitless attempt to win Rhegium only to receive the tidings of the loss of Capua.

He misses taking Rhegium.

The Romans had patiently waited their time, and were now to reap their reward. The consuls were both to command in Apulia with two consular armies; one of them therefore must have returned to Rome, to raise the two additional legions which were required. Fulvius hastened back to the lines before Capua. His prey was now in his power; the straitness of the blockade could no longer be endured, and aid from Hannibal was not to be hoped. It is said that mercy was still promised to any Capuan who should come over to the Romans before a certain day, but that none availed themselves of the offer, feeling, says Livy, that their offence was beyond forgiveness.[190] This can only mean that they believed the Romans to be as faithless as they were cruel, and felt sure that every promise of mercy would be evaded or openly broken. One last attempt was made to summon Hannibal again to their aid; but the Numidians employed on the service were detected this time in the

The Romans press the siege of Capua.

[185] Polybius, IX. 7.
[186] Appian, VII. 40.
[187] Polybius, IX. 7.
[188] Polybius, IX. 7. Appian, VII. 41–43.
[189] Polybius, IX. 7.
[190] Livy, XXVI. 12.

Roman lines, and were sent back torn with stripes, and with their hands cut off, into the city.[191]

No Capuan writer has survived to record the last struggle of his country; and never were any people less to be believed than the Romans, when speaking of their enemies. Yet the greatest man could not have supported the expiring weakness of an unheroic people; and we hear of no great man in Capua. Some of the principal men in the senate met, it is said, at the house of one of their number, Vibius Virrius, where a magnificent banquet had been prepared for them; they ate and drank, and when the feast was over, they all swallowed poison. Then, having done with pleasure and with life, they took a last leave of each other; they embraced each other, lamenting with many tears their own and their country's calamity; and some remained to be burned together on the same funeral pile, while others went away to die at their own homes. All were dead before the Romans entered the city.[192]

The chief senators of Capua poison themselves.

In the mean while the Capuan government, unable to restrain their starving people, had been obliged to surrender to the enemy. In modern warfare the surrender of a besieged town involves no extreme suffering; even in civil wars, justice or vengeance only demands a certain number of victims, and the mass of the population scarcely feels its condition affected. But surrender, *deditio*, according to the Roman laws of war, placed the property, liberties, and lives of the whole surrendered people at the absolute disposal of the conquerors; and that not formally, as a right, the enforcement of which were monstrous, but as one to abate which in any instance was an act of free mercy. In this sense Capua was surrendered; in the morning after Vibius Virrius' funeral banquet, the gate of Jupiter, which looked towards the Roman head-quarters, was thrown open; and a Roman legion, with its usual force of cavalry doubled, marched in to take possession. It was commanded by C. Fulvius, the brother of the proconsul, who immediately placed guards at all the gates, caused all the arms in the city to be brought to him, made prisoners of the Carthaginian garrison, and sent all the Capuan senators into the Roman camp, to abide his brother's sentence.

Surrender of the city.

No Roman family has preserved a more uniform character of pride and cruelty through successive generations than the Claudii; but in the treatment of the Capuans, Q. Fulvius was so much the principal actor, that, according to some of the annals, Appius Claudius was no longer alive, having been mortally wounded some time before the end of the siege.[193] His daughter had been married to a Campanian; and the senators of Capua might perhaps seem to him worthier of regard than the commons of Rome. But whether Appius was living or dead, he was unable to arrest the course of his colleague's vengeance. The Capuan senators were immediately chained as bond-slaves, were commanded to give up all their gold and silver to the quæstors, and were then sent in custody, five-and-twenty to Cales, and twenty-eight to Teanum. Ere the next night was over, Fulvius, with 2000 chosen horsemen, left the camp, and arrived at Teanum by daybreak. He took his seat in the Forum, ordered the magistrates of Teanum to bring forth their prisoners, and saw them all scourged and beheaded in his presence. Then he rode off to Cales, and repeated the same tragedy there.[194]

Fulvius puts all the senators to death.

Atilla and Calatia followed the example of Capua, and surrendered at discretion to the Romans. There, also, about twenty senators were executed, and about three hundred persons of noble birth, in one or other of the three cities, were sent to Rome, and thrown into the Mamertine prison, there to die of starvation and misery, while others met a similar fate

Severe treatment of all the Campanians.

[191] Livy, XXVI. 12.
[192] Livy, XXVI. 14.
[193] Livy, XXVI. 15. Zonaras, IX. 6.
[194] Livy, XXVI. 15. Valerius Maximus, III. 8, 1.

in the various allied cities whither they were sent prisoners.[195] The besieging army was then relieved from its long services; part of it was probably sent home, or transferred to one of the consuls to form his army in Apulia. C. Nero, the proprætor, was sent with about 13,000 men into Spain, where the Roman affairs were in a most critical state;[196] while Q. Fulvius remained still as proconsul in Capua, exercising the utmost severity of conquest over the remnant of the unfortunate people.

Decrees about them.

A few months afterwards, on the night of the 18th of March in the following year, a fire broke out at Rome in several places at once, in the neighborhood of the Forum. The temple of Vesta, and its eternal fire, the type of the life of the commonwealth, were saved with great difficulty. This fire was said to be the work of some noble Capuans whose fathers had been beheaded by Q. Fulvius; they were accused by one of their slaves; and a confession of the charge having been forced from their other slaves by torture, the young men were put to death.[197] Fulvius made this a pretence for fresh severities against the Capuans; and no doubt it had an influence upon the senate when the fate of the three revolted cities of Campania was finally decided. As the Capuans had enjoyed the franchise of Roman citizens, the senate was obliged to obtain an act of the comitia, empowering them to determine their future condition. A number of decrees were passed accordingly, as after the great Latin war, distinguishing the punishment of different classes, and even of different individuals. All who had been senators, or held any office, were reduced to utter beggary, their lands being forfeited to Rome, together with the whole Campanian territory, and their personal property of every kind being ordered to be sold. Some were sold, besides, for slaves, with their wives and children; and it was especially ordered that they should be sold at Rome, lest some of their countrymen or neighbors should purchase them for the purpose of restoring their liberty. All who had been in Capua during the siege were transported beyond the Tiber, and forbidden to possess lands or houses above a certain measure, or out of certain specified districts; those who had not been in Capua, or in any other revolted city, during the war, were only transported beyond the Liris; while those who had gone over to the Romans before Hannibal entered Capua, were removed no further than across the Vulturnus. In their exiled state, however, they were still to be personally free, but were incapable of enjoying either the Roman franchise or the Latin.[198] The city of Capua, bereaved of all its citizens, was left to be inhabited by that mixed multitude of resident foreigners, freedmen, and half-citizens, who, as shopkeepers and mechanics, had always formed a large part of the population; and all political organization was strictly denied to them; and they were placed under the government of a præfect sent thither every year from Rome.[199] The Campanian plain, the glory of Italy, and all the domain lands which Capua had won in former wars, when she was the ally of Rome, as her share of the spoils of Samnium, were forfeited to the Roman people. In the domain lands some colonies were planted soon after the war;[200] but the Campanian plain was held in occupation by a number of Roman citizens; and the vectigal, or rent, which they paid to the state, was for a hundred and fifty years an important part of the Roman revenue.[201] Only two individuals were found deserving of favor, it is said, among the whole Capuan people: these were two women, one of whom had daily sacrificed in secret during the siege for the success of the Romans; and the other had secretly fed some Roman prisoners. These had their property restored to them by a special decree of the senate; and they were desired to go to Rome and to petition the senate, if they thought proper, for some additional reward.[202]

195 Livy, XXVI. 16.
196 Livy, XXVI. 17.
197 Livy, XXVI. 27.
198 Livy, XXVI. 33, 34.
199 Livy, XXVI. 16.
200 Livy, XXVI. 45.
201 Cicero, De Leg. Agrar. II. 39.
202 Livy, XXVI, 33, 34.

I have given the settlement of Campania and the fate of the Capuans in detail, because it seems taken from authentic sources, and is characteristic of the stern determination with which the Roman government went through its work. It is no less characteristic that when Q. Fulvius applied for a triumph, after his most important and splendid success, the senate refused to grant it, because he had only recovered what had belonged to Rome before; and the mere retrieving of losses, and restoring the dominion of the commonwealth to its former extent, was no subject of extraordinary exultation.[203]

Fulvius is refused a triumph.

But although not rewarded by a triumph, the conquest of Capua was one of the most important services ever rendered by a Roman general to his country. It did not merely deprive Hannibal of the greatest fruit of his greatest victory, and thus seem to undo the work of Cannæ; but its effect was felt far and wide, encouraging the allies of Rome, and striking terror into her enemies; tempting the cities which had revolted to return without delay to their allegiance, and filling Hannibal with suspicions of those who were still true to him, as if they only waited to purchase their pardon by some act of treachery towards his garrisons. By the recovery of Capua his great experiment seemed decided against him. It appeared impossible, under any circumstances, to rally such a coalition of the Italian states against the Roman power in Italy, as might be able to overthrow it. We almost ask, with what reasonable hopes could Hannibal from this time forward continue the war? or why did he not change the seat of it from Southern Italy to Etruria and Cisalpine Gaul?

Importance of the taking of Capua.

But with whatever feelings of disappointment and grief he may have heard of the fall of Capua, of the ruin of his allies, and the bloody death of so many of the Capuan senators, and of the brave Jubellius Taurea, whom he had personally known and honored, yet the last campaign was not without many solid grounds of encouragement. Never had the invincible force of his army been more fully proved. He had overrun half Italy, had crossed and recrossed the passes of the Apennines, had plunged into the midst of the Roman allies, and had laid waste the territory of Rome with fire and sword. Yet no superiority of numbers, no advantage of ground, no knowledge of the country, had ever emboldened the Romans to meet him in the field, or even to beset his road, or to obstruct and harass his march. Once only, when he was thought to be retreating, had they ventured to follow him at a cautious distance; but he had turned upon them in his strength; and the two consuls, and Q. Fulvius with them, were driven before him as fugitives to the mountains, their camp stormed, and their legions scattered. It was plain, then, that he might hold his ground in Italy as long as he pleased, supporting his army at its cost, and draining the resources of Rome and her allies, year after year, till in mere exhaustion the Roman commons would probably join the Latin colonies and the allies in forcing the senate to make peace.

Hannibal' favorable prospects.

At this very moment Etruria was restless, and required an army of two legions to keep it quiet:[204] the Roman commons, in addition to their heavy taxation and military service, had seen their lands laid waste, and yet were called upon to bear fresh burdens: and there was a spirit of discontent working in the Latin colonies, which a little more provocation might excite to open revolt. Spain, besides, seemed at last to be freed from the enemy; and the recent defeats and deaths of the two Scipios there held out the hope to Hannibal, that now at length his brother Hasdrubal, having nothing to detain him in Spain, might lead a second Carthaginian army into Italy, and establish himself in Etruria, depriving Rome of the resources of the Etruscan and Umbrian states, as she had already lost those of half Samnium, of Lucania, Bruttium, and Apulia.

Unfavorable circumstances of the Romans in Italy and in Spain.

[203] Valerius Maximus, II. 8, 4.

[204] Livy, XXVI. 1, 28; XXVII. 7. Comp. XXVII. 21, 22, 24.

Then, assailed at once by two sons of Hamilcar, on the north and the south, the Roman power, which one of them singly had so staggered, must, by the joint efforts of both, be beaten to the ground and destroyed. With such hopes, and with no unreasonable confidence, Hannibal consoled himself for the loss of Capua, and allowed his army, after its severe marching, to rest for the remainder of the year in Apulia.[205] And now, as we have brought the war in Italy to this point, it is time to look abroad, and to observe the course of this mighty contest in Spain, in Greece, and in Sicily.

CHAPTER XLV.

PROGRESS OF THE WAR IN SPAIN, SICILY, AND GREECE—OPERATIONS OF THE SCIPIOS IN SPAIN—THEIR DEFEAT AND DEATH—MACEDON AND GREECE—REVOLUTIONS OF SYRACUSE—MARCELLUS IN SICILY—SIEGE OF SYRACUSE—ARCHIMEDES—SACK OF SYRACUSE, AND REDUCTION OF SICILY—MUTINES, THE NUMIDIAN, IN SICILY.—A. U. C. 538 TO 543.

When wars ought to be related circumstantially.

WARS must of necessity form a large part of all history; but in most wars the narrative of military operations is without interest for posterity, and should only be given by contemporary writers. It was right for Thucydides to relate every little expedition of the Peloponnesian war at length; but modern writers do wrong in following his example; for the details of petty warfare are unworthy to survive their own generation. And there are also wars conducted on a great scale, and very important in their consequences, the particulars of which may safely be forgotten. For military events should only be related circumstantially to after ages, when they either contain a great lesson in the art of war, or are so striking in their incidents, as to acquire the interest of a romance, and thus retain their hold on the imaginations and moral feelings of all ages and countries. Hannibal's campaigns in Italy have this double claim on our notice: they are a most valuable study for the soldier, whilst for readers in general they are a varied and eventful story, rich in characters, scenes, and actions. But the war in Spain, although most important in its results, and still more the feeble bickerings rather than wars of the decayed states of Greece, may and ought to be related summarily. A closer attention must be given to the war in Sicily: there again the military and the general interest of the story are great; we have the ancient art of defence exhibited it its highest perfection; we have the immortal names of Syracuse and Archimedes.

Campaign of 541 in Spain.

There is another reason, however, why we should not give a minute account of the Spanish war: because we really know nothing about it. The Roman annalists, whom Livy has copied here, seem to have outdone their usual exaggerations in describing the exploits of the two Scipios; and what is the truth concealed beneath this mass of fiction, we are wholly unable to discover. Spain, we know, has in later wars been overrun victoriously and lost again in a single summer; and no one can say how far the Scipios may at times have penetrated into the heart of the country: but it is certain that in the first years of their command they made no lasting impression south of the Iberus. Still their maintaining their ground at all in Spain was of signal service to Rome.

205 Compare Livy, XXVI. 37.

The Carthaginians, on the other hand, knew the importance of expelling them; but it appears that in the year 541, they became engaged in a war with Syphax, one of the kings or chiefs of the Numidians; and a war in Africa was always so alarming to them, that they recalled Hasdrubal, Hannibal's brother, from Spain, with a part of their forces employed in that country, and thus took off the pressure from the Romans at a most critical moment.[1] The Scipios availed themselves of this relief ably; and now they seemed to have advanced into the heart of Spain with effect, to have drawn over many of the Spanish tribes to the Roman alliance, and thus to have obtained large recruits for their own army, which received but slight reinforcements from Rome. It is said that 20,000 Celtiberians were raised to serve under the Scipios, and that at the same time 300 noble Spaniards were sent into Italy to detach their countrymen there from Hannibal's service.[2] Cn. Scipio, we are told, was greatly loved and reverenced by the Spaniards;[3] and his influence probably attracted the Celtiberians to the Roman armies; but we know not where he found money to pay them, as the Roman treasury was in no condition to supply him, and he was obliged to make war support war. However, careful economy of the plunder which he may have won from some of the allies of Carthage, assisted perhaps by loans from some of the Spanish chiefs attached to himself and to Rome, had enabled him to raise a large army; so that, when Hasdrubal returned from Africa, apparently late in 542, although there were two other Carthaginian generals in Spain,[4] each commanding a separate army, yet the Roman generals thought themselves strong enough to act on the offensive; and they concerted a grand plan for the campaign of 543, by which they hoped to destroy all the armies opposed to them, and to drive the Carthaginians out of Spain. With this confidence they divided their forces, and having crossed the Iberus, marched each in pursuit of a separate enemy. Cn. Scipio was to attack Hasdrubal, while his brother was to fall on the other two Carthaginian generals, Hasdrubal the son of Giscon, and Mago.[5]

A. U. C. 541. A. C. 213.

They had wintered, it seems, in the country of their new auxiliaries, or, according to one account, even further to the south, in the valley of the Bætis or Guadalquiver.[6] But it is as impossible to disentangle the geography of this war as its history. The Carthaginian generals owed their triumph—and more than this we cannot ascertain—to the ascendency of Hasdrubal's name and personal character; for the Celtiberians, when brought into his neighborhood, were unable to resist his influence, and abruptly left the Roman camp, and returned home.[7] Thus abandoned, and at a great distance from all their resources, the two Roman generals were successively attacked by the Carthaginians, defeated and killed.[8] Of the wreck of their armies, some fled to the towns of their Spanish allies for refuge, and were in some instances slain by them, or betrayed to the Carthaginians: a remnant, which had either been left behind the Iberus before the opening of the campaign, or had effected its retreat thither, was still held together by Scipio's lieutenant, T. Fonteius, and by L. Marcius.[9] Marcius was only a simple Roman knight, that is, a man of good fortune, who therefore served, not in the infantry of the legions, but in the cavalry: he had a natural genius for war, and was called irregularly, it seems, by the common voice of the soldiers to take the command; and we need not doubt that by some timely advantages gained over some of the enemies' parties, he raised the spirits of the men, and preserved the Roman cause in Spain from utter extinction. But the extravagant fables of his victories over the victorious Carthaginians, and of his storming their camps,

Campaign of 543: defeat and death of the Scipios.

A. U. C. 543. A. C. 211.

[1] Appian, VI. 15. Livy, XXIV. 48.
[2] Livy, XXV. 32. XXIV. 49.
[3] Livy, XXV. 36. Appian, VI. 15.
[4] Livy, XXV. 32. Appian, VI. 16.
[5] Livy, XXV. 32.
[6] Appian, VI. 16.
[7] Livy, XXV. 33.
[8] Livy, XXV. 34-36. Appian, VI. 16.
[9] Livy, XXV. 36-39.

show too clearly out of what wretched materials the Roman history has to be written.[10]

If the defeat of the Scipios took place, as seems probable, early in the year 543, that is, a few weeks before the fall of Capua, we may again admire the wonderful disposal of events by which the ruin of the Roman cause in Spain was delayed till their affairs in Italy had passed over their crisis, and were beginning to mend. The Scipios' army was replaced by that of C. Nero, which the fall of Capua set at liberty:[11] a year earlier this resource would not have been available. Still the Carthaginians immediately recovered all the states south of the Ebro, which had before revolted, and the Romans were confined to a narrow strip of coast between the Iberus and the Pyrenees,[12] from which the overwhelming force of their enemies was likely ere long to drive them. And so it would, had not the external weakness of the Roman cause been now upheld for the first time by individual genius; so that a defeated and dispirited army became, in the hands of the young P. Scipio, the instrument by which all Spain was conquered.

The Romans are driven to the foot of the Pyrenees.

Seventy years before this period, a Greek army under Pyrrhus had shaken the whole power of Rome: yet the kingdom of Pyrrhus was little more than a dependency of Macedon, and Pyrrhus had struggled against the arms of the Macedonain kings vigorously, but without success. Now a young, warlike, and popular king was seated on the throne of Macedon:[13] he had just concluded a war victoriously with the only state in Greece which seemed capable of resisting his power. What Pyrrhus had almost done alone, would surely be easy for Philip to accomplish, with Hannibal and his invincible army to aid him; and what could Rome have done, if to the irresistible African cavalry there had been joined a body of heavy-armed Macedonians, and a force of artillery and engineers such as Greek science alone could furnish? The strangest and most unaccountable blank in history is the early period of the Macedonian war, before the Ætolians became the allies of Rome and a coalition was formed against Philip in Greece itself. Philip's treaty with Hannibal was concluded in the year 539, or early enough, at any rate, to allow of his commencing operations in the year 540.[14] The Ætolians concluded their treaty with Rome in 543, after the fall of Capua.[15] More than three precious years seem to have been utterly wasted; and during all this time M. Valerius Lævinus, commanding at Brundisium with a single legion and a small fleet, was allowed to paralyze the whole power of Macedon.[16]

Strange inefficiency of Macedon,

The cause of this is to be found in that selfish attention to separate objects which has so often been the ruin of coalitions. Philip's object, or rather that of Demetrius of Pharos, whose influence appears plainly in all this war with Rome, was to undo the work of the late Roman victories in Illyria, and to wrest the western coast of Epirus from their dominion. In his treaty with Hannibal, Philip had especially stipulated that the Romans should not be allowed to retain their control over Corcyra, Apollonia, Epidamnus, Pharus, Dimalla or Dimalus, the country of the Parthinians, and Atintania;[17] places which in the Illyrian wars had either submitted to, or been conquered by the Romans. Philip does not appear to have understood that all these were to be reconquered most surely in Italy; that it was easier to crush Lævinus at Brundisium, than to repel him from Epirus; more prudent to march against him

arising from Philip's selfishness.

[10] Livy, XXV. 39. According to one account, 37,000 men were slain on the Carthaginian side. Valerius Antias returned 17,000 killed, and 4330 prisoners. Appian (XI. 17) substitutes Marcellus by mistake for Marcius, but says he did nothing brilliant, so that the Carthaginian power increased, and spread almost over the whole of Spain.

[11] Livy, XXVI. 17.

[12] Appian, VI. 17.

[13] Philip was not more than seventeen years old in the archonship of Ariston, A. U. C. 534. Polybius, IV. 5. For his popular and warlike character see Polybius, IV. 77, 82, 1.

[14] Livy, XXIII. 33, 39. Above, p. 514.

[15] Livy, XXVI. 24.

[16] Livy, XXIV. 10, 44. XXV. 3. XXVI. 24.

[17] Polybius, VII. 9.

at the head of the Greeks of Italy, than to let him come to the aid of the Greeks on the coast of Illyria. Thus he trifled away his strength in petty enterprises, and those not always successful, till the Romans found the time come to carry on the war against him in earnest; and they were not apt either to neglect their opportunities or to misuse them.

Philip was personally brave, and could on occasion show no common activity and energy. But he had not that steadiness of purpose, without which energy in political affairs is worthless. Thus he was lightly deterred from an enterprise by dangers which he was not afraid of, but rather did not care to encounter. The naval power of Greece had long since sunk to nothing; Philip had no regular navy, and the small vessels which he could collect were no match for the Roman quinqueremes; so that a descent upon Italy appeared hazardous, while various schemes opened upon him nearer home, which his own temper, or the interests of his advisers, led him to prefer. Hence, he effected but little during three years. He neither took Epidamnus, nor Apollonia, nor Corcyra; but he won Lissus, and the strong fortress which served as its citadel;[18] and he seems also to have conquered Dimalus or Dimallus, and to have enlarged his dominion more or less nominally with the countries of the Parthinians and Atintanians, of which the sovereignty had belonged to the Romans.[19] From all this Hannibal derived no benefit, and Rome sustained no serious injury.

He wastes his time on petty objects.

In the year of Rome 491, in the second year of the first Punic war, Hiero, king of Syracuse, had made peace with the Romans, and had become their ally.[20] Forty-seven years had passed away since, when the tidings of the battle of Cannæ arrived at Syracuse, and seemed to announce that a great part of Sicily was again to change its masters, and to be subjected once more to the Carthaginian dominion. But Hiero, although about ninety years of age, did not waver. Far from courting the friendship of Carthage, he increased his exertions in behalf of Rome: he supplied the Roman army in Sicily with money and corn at a time when all supplies from home had failed;[21] and about a year afterwards, when a fleet was prepared to meet the hostile designs of Philip of Macedon, Hiero again sent 50,000 medimni of wheat and barley to provision it.[22] This must nearly have been his last public act. Towards the close of the year 539, after a life of ninety years, and a reign of fifty-four, but still retaining all his faculties, sound in mind and vigorous in body, Hiero died.[23]

Hiero's faithful friendship to the Romans: his death;

A. U. C. 539. A. C. 215.

He had enjoyed and deserved the constant affection of his people, and had seen his kingdom flourishing more and more under his government. One only thing had marred the completeness of his fortune: his son Gelon had died before him, with whom he had lived in the most perfect harmony, and who had ever rendered him the most devoted and loving obedience.[24] He had still two daughters, Damarata and Heraclea, who were married to two eminent Syracusans, Andranodorus and Zoippus; and he had one grandson, a boy of about fifteen, the son of Gelon, Hieronymus.[25]

preceded by that of his son Gelon.

It is the most difficult problem in an hereditary monarchy, how to educate the heir to the throne, when the circumstances of his condition, so much more powerful than any instruction, are apt to train him for evil far more surely than the lessons of the wisest teachers can train him for good. In the ancient world, moreover, there was no fear of God to sober the mind, which was raised above all fear or respect for man; and if the philosophers spoke of the superiority of virtue and wisdom over all the gifts of

He is succeeded by his grandson Hieronymus; his character.

[18] Polybius, VIII. 15, 16.
[19] In Livy, XXIX. 12, we find these attacked by the Romans, as being subject to Macedon.
[20] See p. 427.
[21] Livy, XXIII. 22. See above, p. 508.
[22] Livy, XXIII. 38.
[23] Polybius, VII. 8.
[24] Polybius, VII. 8.
[25] Livy, XXIV. 4.

fortune, their own example, when they were seen to sue for the king's favor, and to dread his anger, no less than ordinary men, made their doctrines regarded either as folly or hypocrisy. Hieronymus at fifteen became king of Syracuse; a child in understanding, but with passions precociously vigorous, because he had such large means of indulging them; insolent, licentious, and cruel, yet withal so thoughtless and so mere a slave of every impulse, that he was sure to be the instrument of his own ruin.

He joins the Carthaginians,

We have already noticed his early communication with Hannibal, and the arrival of Hippocrates and Epicydes at Syracuse, Syracusans by extraction, but born at Carthage, and by education and franchise Carthaginians, whom Hannibal had sent to Hieronymus to confirm him in his alienation from Rome.[26] They won the youth's ear by telling him of Hannibal's marches and victories; for in those days events that were two or three years old were still news to foreigners; common fame had reported the general facts, but the details could only be gathered accidentally; and Hieronymus listened eagerly to Hippocrates and Epicydes, when they told him stories of their crossing the Rhone, of their passage of the Alps and Apennines, of the slaughter of the Romans at Thrasymenus, and of their late unequalled victory at Cannæ, of all which they had themselves been eye-witnesses.[27] And when they saw Hieronymus possessed with a vague longing that he too might achieve such great deeds, they asked him who had such claims as he to be king of all Sicily. His mother was the daughter of Pyrrhus; his father was Hiero's son; with this double title to the love and homage of all Sicilians, he should not be contented to divide the island either with Rome or Carthage: by his timely aid to Hannibal he might secure it wholly to himself. The youth accordingly insisted that the sovereignty of all Sicily should be ceded to him as the price of his alliance with Carthage; and the Carthaginians were well content to humor him, knowing that if they could drive the Romans out of the islands, they had little to fear from the claims of Hieronymus.[28]

and deserts the Romans.

Appius Claudius, the Roman prætor in Sicily, aware of what was going on, sent some of his officers to Syracuse, to warn the king not to break off his grandfather's long friendship with Rome, but to renew the old alliance in his own name.[29] Hieronymus called his council together, and Hippocrates and Epicydes were present. His native subjects, afraid to oppose his known feelings, said nothing; but three of his council, who came from old Greece, conjured him not to abandon his alliance with Rome. Andranodorus alone, his uncle and guardian, urged him to seize the moment, and become sovereign of all Sicily. He listened, and then, turning to Hippocrates and Epycides, asked them, "And what think you?" "We think," they answered, "with Andranodorus." "Then," said he, "the question is decided; we will no longer be dependent on Rome." He then called in the Roman ambassadors, and told them that "he was willing to renew his grandfather's league with Rome, if they would repay him all the money and corn with which Hiero had at various times supplied them; if they would restore the costly presents which he had given them, especially the golden statue of Victory, which he had sent to them only three years since, after their defeat at Thrasymenus; and, finally, if they would share the island with him equally, ceding all to the east of the river Himeras."[30] The Romans considered this answer as a mockery, and went away without thinking it worthy of a serious reply. Accordingly, from this moment Hieronymus conceived himself to be at war with Rome: he began to raise and arm soldiers, and to form magazines; and the Carthaginians, according to their treaty with him, prepared to send over a fleet and army to Sicily.

Meanwhile his desertion of the Roman alliance was most unwelcome to a strong

[26] Polybius, VII. 34. Livy, XXIV. 6. See above, p. 514.

[27] Polybius, VII. 4.

[28] Polybius, VII. 4. Livy, XXIV. 6.

[29] Polybius, VII. 5. Livy, XXIV. 6.

[30] Polybius, VII. 5. See Livy, XXII. 37.

party in Syracuse. A conspiracy had already been formed against his life, which was ascribed, whether truly or not, to the intrigues of this party;[31] and now that he had actually joined the Carthaginians, they became more bitter against him; and a second conspiracy was formed with better success. He had taken the field to attack the cities in the Roman part of the island. Hippocrates and Epicydes were already in the enemy's country; and the king, with the main body of his army, was on his march to support them, and had just entered the town of Leontini.[32] The road, which was also the principal street of the city, lay through a narrow gorge, with abrupt cliffs on each side; and the houses ran along in a row, nestling under the western cliff, and facing towards the small river Lissus, which flowed through the gorge between the town and the eastern cliff.[33] An empty house in this street had been occupied by the conspirators: when the king came opposite to it, one of their number, who was one of the king's guards, and close to his person, stopped just behind him, as if something had caught his foot; and whilst he seemed trying to get free, he checked the advance of the following multitude, and left the king to go on a few steps unattended. At that moment the conspirators rushed out of the house and murdered him. So sudden was the act, that his guards could not save him: seeing him dead, they were seized with a panic and dispersed. The murderers hastened, some into the market-place of Leontini, to raise the cry of liberty there, and others to Syracuse, to anticipate the king's friends, and secure the city for themselves and the Romans.[34]

He is murdered by a conspiracy.

Their tidings, however, had flown before them; and Andranodorus, the king's uncle, had already secured the island of Ortygia, the oldest part of Syracuse, in which was the citadel, and where Hiero and Hieronymus had resided.[35] The assassins arrived just at nightfall, displaying the bloody robe of Hieronymus, and the diadem which they had torn from his head, and calling the people to rise in the name of liberty. This call was obeyed: all the city, except the island, was presently in their power; and in the island itself a strong building, which was used as a great corn magazine for the supply of the whole city, was no sooner seized by those whom Andranodorus had sent to occupy it, than they offered to deliver it up to the opposite party.[36]

Insurrection at Syracuse.

The general feeling being thus manifested, Andranodorus yielded to it. He surrendered the keys of the citadel and of the treasury; and in return he and Themistus, who had married a sister of Hieronymus, were elected among the captains-general of the commonwealth, to whom, according to the old Syracusan constitution, the executive government was to be committed. But their colleagues were mostly chosen from the assassins of Hieronymus; and between such opposites there could be no real union. Suspicions and informations of plots were not long wanting. An actor told the majority of the captains-general, that Andranodorus and Themistus were conspiring to massacre them and the other leaders of their party, and to re-establish the tyranny: the charge was made out to the satisfaction of those who were so well disposed to believe it: they stationed soldiers at the doors of the council-chamber; and as soon as Andranodorus and Themistus entered, the soldiers rushed in and murdered them.[37] The members of the council decided that they were rightfully slain; but the multitude were inclined to believe them less guilty than their murderers, and beset the council, calling for vengeance. They were persuaded, however, to hear what the perpetrators of the deed could say in its defence; and Sopater, one of the captains-general, who was concerned both in the recent murder and in that of Hieronymus, arose to justify himself and his party. The tyrannies in the ancient world were so hateful, that they were put by common

Murder of Andranodorus and Themistus.

[31] Polybius, VII. 2. Livy, XXIV. 5.
[32] Livy, XXIV. 7.
[33] Polybius, VII. 6.
[34] Livy, XXIV. 7.
[35] Livy, XXIV. 21.
[36] Livy, XXIV. 21, 22.
[37] Livy, XXIV. 23, 24.

feeling out of the pale of ordinary law: when Sopater accused Andranodorus and Themistus of having been the real authors of all the outrages committed by the boy Hieronymus; when he inveighed against their treacherous submission to their country's laws, and against their ingratitude in plotting the deaths of those who had so nobly forgiven all their past offences; and when he said, finally, that they had been instigated to all these crimes by their wives, that Hiero's daughter and grand-daughter could not condescend to live in a private station; there arose a cry from some, probably of their own tutored partisans, which the whole multitude, in fear or in passion, immediately echoed, "Death to the whole race of the tyrants; not one of them shall be suffered to live."[38]

And of all the descendants of Hiero.

They who had purposely roused the multitude to fury, were instantly ready to secure it for their own bloody ends. The captains-general proposed a decree for the execution of every person of the race of the tyrants; and the instant it was passed, they sent parties of soldiers to carry it into effect. Thus the wives of Andranodorus and Themistus were butchered: but there was another daughter of Hiero, the wife of Zoippus, who was so far from sharing in the tyranny of Hieronymus, that when sent by him as his ambassador to Egypt, he had chosen to live there in exile. His innocent wife, with her two young maiden daughters, were included in the general proscription. They took refuge at the altar of their household gods, but in vain: the mother was dragged from her sanctuary and murdered; the daughters fled wildly into the outer court of the palace, in the hope of escaping into the street, and appealing to the humanity of the passers-by; but they were pursued and cut down by repeated wounds. Ere the deed was done, a messenger came to say that the people had revoked their sentence; which seems to show that the captains-general had taken advantage of some expressions of violence, and had done in the people's name what the people had never in earnest agreed to. At any rate, their rage was now loud against their bloody government; and they insisted on having a free election of captains-general to supply the places of Andranodorus and Themistus; a demand which implies that some preceding resolutions or votes of the popular assembly had been passed under undue influence.[39]

The Carthaginian party rallies.

The party which favored the Roman alliance had done all that wickedness could to make themselves odious. The reaction against them was natural; yet the same foreign policy which these butchers supported, had been steadily pursued by the wise and moderate Hiero. Every party in that corrupt city of Syracuse wore an aspect of evil: the partisans of Carthage were in nothing better than those of Rome. When Hieronymus had been murdered, Hippocrates and Epicydes were at the moment deserted by their soldiers, and returned to Syracuse as private individuals. There they applied to the government for an escort to convey them back to Hannibal in safety: but the escort was not provided immediately; and in the interval they perceived that they could serve Hannibal better by remaining in Sicily. They found many amongst the mercenary soldiers of the late king, and amongst the poorer citizens, who readily listened to them, when they accused the captains-general of selling the independence of Syracuse to Rome; and their party was so strengthened by the atrocities of the government, that, when the election was held to choose two new captains-general in the place of Andranodorus and Themistus, Hippocrates and Epicydes were nominated and triumphantly elected.[40] Again, therefore, the government was divided within itself; and Hippocrates and Epicydes had been taught by the former conduct of their colleagues that one party or the other must perish.

The Roman party had immediately suspended hostilities with Rome, obtained a truce from Appius Claudius renewable every ten days, and sent ambassadors to

[38] Livy, XXIV. 25.
[39] Livy, XXIV. 26.
[40] Livy, XXIV. 23, 27.

him to solicit the revival of Hiero's treaty. A Roman fleet of a hundred ships was lying off the coast a little to the north of Syracuse, which the Romans, on the first suspicion of the defection of Hieronymus, had manned by the most extraordinary exertions, and sent to Sicily. On the other hand, Himilco, with a small Carthaginian fleet, was at Pachynus, Rome and Carthage each anxiously watching the course of events in Syracuse, and each being ready to support its party there. Matters were nicely balanced; and the Roman fleet, in the hope of turning the scale, sailed to Syracuse, and stationed itself at the mouth of the great harbor.[41]

The Roman fleet sails to the mouth of the harbor.

Strengthened by this powerful aid, the Roman party triumphed; even moderate men not wishing to provoke an enemy who was already at their gates. The old league with Rome was renewed, with the stipulation, that whatever cities in Sicily had been subject to king Hiero should now in like manner be under the dominion of the Syracusan people. It appears that, since the murder of Hieronymus, his kingdom had gone to pieces, many of the towns, and Leontini in particular, asserting their independence. These were, like Syracuse, in a state of hostility against Rome, owing to Hieronymus' revolt; but they had no intention of submitting again to the Syracusan dominion. Still, when the Romans threatened them, they sent to Syracuse for aid; and as the Syracusan treaty with Rome was not yet ratified or made public, the government could not decline their request. Hippocrates accordingly was sent to Leontini, with a small army, consisting chiefly of deserters from the Roman fleet: for, in the exigency of the time, the fleet had been manned by slaves furnished by private families in a certain proportion, according to their census; and the men thus provided, being mostly unused to the sea, and forced into the service, deserted in unusually large numbers, insomuch that there were two thousand of them in the party which Hippocrates led to the defence of Leontini.[42]

The Roman party becomes the more powerful.

This auxiliary force did good service; and Appius Claudius, who commanded the Roman army, was obliged to stand on the defensive. Meanwhile M. Marcellus had arrived in Sicily, having been sent over thither, as we have seen, after the close of the campaign in Italy, to take the supreme command. As the negotiations with Syracuse were now concluded, Marcellus required that Hippocrates should be recalled from Leontini, and that both he and Epicydes should be banished from Sicily. Epicydes upon this, feeling that his personal safety was risked by remaining longer at Syracuse, went also to Leontini; and both he and his brother inveighed loudly against the Roman party who were in possession of the government; they had betrayed their country to Rome, and were endeavoring, with the help of the Romans, to enslave the other cities of Sicily, and to subject them to their own dominion. Accordingly, when some officers arrived from Syracuse, requiring the Leontines to submit, and announcing to Hippocrates and Epicydes their sentence of expulsion from Sicily, they were answered, that the Leontines would not acknowledge the Syracusan government, nor were they bound by its treaties. This answer being reported to Syracuse, the leaders of the Roman party called upon Marcellus to fulfil his agreement with them, and to reduce Leontini to submission.[43] That city was now the refuge and centre of the popular party in Sicily, as Samos had been in Greece, when the four hundred usurped the government of Athens; and Hippocrates and Epicydes looked upon their army as the true representative of the Syracusan people, just as Thrasybulus and Thrasyllus, and the Athenian fleet at Samos, regarded themselves, during the tyranny of the aristocratical party at home, as the true people of Athens.

Marcellus arrives in Sicily; Leontini, the head of the Carthaginian party.

But, as we have noticed more than once before, nothing could less resemble

[41] Livy, XXIV. 27.
[42] Livy, XXIV. 28, 29.
[43] Livy, XXIV. 29.

Marcellus takes Leontini; his cruelties there

the slowness and feebleness of Sparta than the tremendous energy of Rome. The prætor's army in Sicily at the beginning of the year consisted of two legions; and it is probable that Marcellus had brought one at least of the two legions which had formed his consular army. With this powerful force Marcellus instantly attacked Leontini, and stormed it; and in addition to the usual carnage on the sack of a town, he scourged and in cold blood beheaded two thousand of the Roman deserters, whom he found bearing arms in the army of Hippocrates; Hippocrates and his brother escaping only with a handful of men, and taking refuge in the neighboring town of Herbessus.[44]

excite general indignation.

For nearly thirty years war had been altogether unknown in Sicily; fifty years had passed since a hostile army had made war in the territory of Syracuse. All men therefore were struck with horror at the fate of Leontini: if Ætna had rolled down his lava flood upon the town, its destruction would scarcely have been more sudden and terrible. But with horror indignation was largely mingled: the bloodiness of the Romans in the sack of towns went far beyond the ordinary practice of the Greeks; the Syracusan government had betrayed their countrymen of Leontini to barbarians more cruel than the Mamertines.

The Syracusan army refuses to march,

The tidings spread far and wide, and met a Syracusan army, which two of the captains-general, Sosis and Dinomenes, both of them assassins of Hieronymus, and devoted to the cause of Rome, were leading out to co-operate with Marcellus. The soldiers, full of grief and fury, refused to advance a step further: their blood, they said, would be sold to the Romans, like that of their brethren at Leontini. The generals were obliged to lead them back to Megara, within a few miles of Syracuse: then hearing that Hippocrates and Epicydes were at Herbessus, and dreading their influence at a moment like this, they led their troops to attack the town where they had taken refuge.[45]

and to act against Hippocrates and Epicydes.

Hippocrates and his brother threw open the gates of Herbessus, and came out to meet them. At the head of the Syracusan army marched six hundred Cretans, old soldiers in Hiero's service, whom he had sent over into Italy to act as light troops in the Roman army against Hannibal's barbarians, but who had been taken prisoners at Thrasymenus, and with the other allies or auxiliaries of Rome had been sent home by Hannibal unhurt. They now saw Hippocrates and Epicydes coming towards them with no hostile array, but holding out branches of olive tufted here and there with wool, the well-known signs of a suppliant. They heard them praying to be saved from the treachery of the Syracusan generals, who were pledged to deliver up all foreign soldiers serving in Sicily to the vengeance of the Romans. The Cretans felt that the cause of Hippocrates and Epicydes was their own, and swore to protect them. In vain did Sosis and Dinomenes ride forward to the head of the column, and trying what could be done by authority, order the instant arrest of the two suppliants. They were driven off with threats; the feeling began to spread through the army; and the Syracusan generals had no resource but to march back to Megara, leaving the Cretan auxiliaries, it seems, with Hippocrates and Epicydes in a state of open revolt.[46]

Triumph of the popular party in Syracuse.

Meantime the Cretans sent out parties to beset the roads leading to Leontini; and a letter was intercepted, addressed by the Syracusan generals to Marcellus, congratulating him on his exploit at Leontini, and urging him to complete his work by the extermination of every foreign soldier in the service of Syracuse. Hippocrates took care that the purport of this letter should be quickly made known to the army at Megara; and he followed closely with the Cretans to watch the result. The army broke out into mutiny: Sosis and Dinomenes, protesting in vain that the letter was a mere forgery of the

[44] Livy, XXIV. 30.
[45] Livy, XXIV. 30.
[46] Livy, XXIV. 30, 31.

enemy, were obliged to escape for their lives to Syracuse: even the Syracusan soldiers were accused of sharing in their generals' treason, and were for a time in great danger from the fury of the foreigners, their comrades. But Hippocrates and Epicydes prevented this mischief, and being received as leaders by the whole army, set out forthwith for Syracuse. They sent a soldier before them, most probably a native Syracusan, who had escaped from the sack of Leontini, and could tell his countrymen as an eye-witness what acts of bloodshed, outrage, and rapine the Romans had committed there. Even in moderate men, who for Hiero's sake were well inclined to Rome, the horrors of Leontini overpowered all other thoughts and feelings: within Syracuse and without, all followed one common impulse. When Hippocrates and Epicydes arrived at the gates, the citizens threw them open: the captains-general in vain endeavored to close them; they fled to Achradina, the lower part of the city, with such of the Syracusan soldiers as still adhered to them, whilst the stream of the hostile army burst down the slope of Epipolæ, and, swelled by all the popular party, the foreign soldiers, and the old guards of Hiero and Hieronymus, came sweeping after them with irresistible might. Achradina was carried in an instant; some of the captains-general were massacred; Sosis escaped to add the betrayal of his country hereafter to his multiplied crimes. The confusion raged wild and wide; slaves were set free; prisoners were let loose; and amidst the horrors of a violent revolution, under whatever name effected, the popular party, the party friendly to Carthage, and adverse to aristocracy and to Rome, obtained the sovereignty of Syracuse.[47]

A. U. C. 541. A. C. 213. Marcellus besieges Syracuse,

Sosis, now in his turn a fugitive, escaped to Leontini, and told Marcellus of the violence done to the friends of Rome. The fiery old man, as vehement at sixty against his country's enemies, as when he slew the Gaulish king in single combat in his first consulship, immediately moved his army upon Syracuse. He encamped by the temple of Olympian Jupiter, on the right bank of the Anapus, where two solitary pillars still remain, and serve as a sea-mark to guide ships into the great harbor. Appius Claudius with the fleet beset the city by sea; and Marcellus did not doubt that in the wide extent of the Syracusan walls some unguarded spot would be found, and that the punishment of Leontini would soon be effaced by a more memorable example of vengeance.[48]

by land and by sea;

Thus was commenced the last siege of Syracuse; a siege not inferior in interest to the two others which it had already undergone, from the Athenians, and from the Carthaginians. It should be remembered that the city walls now embraced the whole surface of Epipolæ, terminating, like the lines of Genoa, in an angle formed by the converging sides of the hill or inclined table-land, at the point where it becomes no more than a narrow ridge, stretching inland, and connecting itself with the hills of the interior. The Romans made their land attack on the south front of the walls, while their fleet, unable, as it seems, to enter the great harbor, carried on its assaults against the sea-wall of Achradina.

is baffled by Archimedes.

The land attack was committed to Appius Claudius, while Marcellus in person conducted the operations of the fleet. The Roman army is spoken of as large, but no details of its force are given: it cannot have been less than twenty thousand men, and was probably more numerous. No force in Sicily, whether of Syracusans or Carthaginians, could have resisted it in the field; and it had lately stormed the walls of Leontini as easily, to use the Homeric comparison, as a child tramples out the towers and castles which he has scratched upon the sand of the sea-shore. But at Syracuse it was checked by an artillery such as the Romans had never encountered before, and which, had Hannibal possessed it, would long since have enabled him to bring the war to a

[47] Livy, XXIV. 31, 32.

[48] Livy, XXIV. 33.

triumphant issue. An old man of seventy-four, a relation and friend of king Hiero, long known as one of the ablest astronomers and mathematicians of his age, now proved that his science was no less practical than deep; and amid all the crimes and violence of contending factions, he alone won the pure glory of defending his country successfully against a foreign enemy. This old man was Archimedes.[49]

His extraordinary engines to defend the city.

Many years before, at Hiero's request, he had contrived the engines which were now used so effectively.[50] Marcellus brought up his ships against the sea-wall of Achradina, and endeavored by a constant discharge of stones and arrows to clear the walls of their defenders, so that his men might apply their ladders, and mount to the assault. These ladders rested on two ships lashed together broadside to broadside, and worked as one by their outside oars; and when the two ships were brought close up under the wall, one end of the ladder was raised by ropes passing through blocks affixed to the two mast-heads of the two vessels, and was then let go, till it rested on the top of the wall. But Archimedes had supplied the ramparts with an artillery so powerful, that it overwhelmed the Romans before they could get within the range which their missiles could reach; and when they came closer, they found that all the lower part of the wall was loopholed; and their men were struck down with fatal aim by an enemy whom they could not see, and who shot his arrows in perfect security. If they still persevered, and attempted to fix their ladders, on a sudden they saw long poles thrust out from the top of the wall, like the arms of a giant; and enormous stones, or huge masses of lead, were dropped from these upon them, by which their ladders were crushed to pieces, and their ships were almost sunk. At other times machines like cranes, or such as are used at the turnpikes in Germany, and in the market-gardens round London, to draw water, were thrust out over the wall; and the end of the lever, with an iron grapple affixed to it, was lowered upon the Roman ships. As soon as the grapple had taken hold, the other end of the lever was lowered by heavy weights, and the ship raised out of the water, till it was made almost to stand upon its stern; then the grapple was suddenly let go, and the ship dropped into the sea with a violence which either upset it, or filled it with water. With equal power was the assault on the land side repelled; and the Roman soldiers, bold as they were, were so daunted by these strange and irresistible devices, that if they saw so much as a rope or a stick hanging or projecting from the wall, they would turn about and run away, crying, "that Archimedes was going to set one of his engines at work against them." Their attempts, indeed, were a mere amusement to the enemy, till Marcellus, in despair, put a stop to his attacks; and it was resolved merely to blockade the town, and to wait for the effect of famine upon the crowded population within.[51]

Difficulties in the history of the Sicilian war.

Thus far, keeping our eyes fixed upon Syracuse only, we can give a clear and probable account of the course of events. But when we would extend our view further, and connect the war in Sicily with that in Italy, and give the relative dates of the actions performed in the several countries involved in this great contest, we see the wretched character of our materials, and must acknowledge that, in order to give a comprehensive picture of the whole war, we have to supply, by inference or conjecture, what no actual testimony has recorded. We do not know for certain when Marcellus came into Sicily, when he began the siege of Syracuse, or how long the blockade was continued. We read of Roman and Carthaginian fleets appearing and disappearing at different times in the Sicilian seas; but of the naval operations on either side we can give no connected report. Other difficulties present themselves, of no great importance, but perplexing because they shake our confidence in the narra-

[49] Livy, XXIV. 34. Polybius, VIII. 7.
[50] Plutarch, Marcellus, 14.
[51] Polybius, VIII. 6–9. Livy, XXIV. 34. Plutarch, Marcellus, 15–17.

tive which contains them. So easy is it to transcribe the ancient writers; so hard to restore the reality of those events of which they themselves had no clear conception.

The first attacks upon Syracuse are certainly misplaced by Livy, when he classes them among the events of the year 540.[52] The Sicilian war belongs to the year following, to the consulship of Q. Fabius, the dictator's son, and of Ti. Gracchus. Even when this is set right, it is difficult to reconcile Polybius' statement,[53] "that the blockade of Syracuse lasted eight months," with the account which places the capture of the city in the autumn of 542. Instead of eight months, the blockade would seem to have lasted for more than twelve: nor is there any other solution of this difficulty, than to suppose that the blockade was not persevered in to the end, and was in fact given up as useless, as the assaults had been before. I notice these points, because the narrative which follows is uncertain and unsatisfactory, and no care can make it otherwise.

Chronology of the war.

The year 541 saw the whole stress of the war directed upon Sicily. Little or nothing, if we can trust our accounts, was done in Italy; there was a pause also in the operations in Spain; but throughout Sicily the contest was raging furiously. Four Roman officers were employed there: P. Cornelius Lentulus held the old Roman province, that is, the western part of the island; and his head-quarters were at Lilybæum: T. Otacilius had the command of the fleet:[54] Appius Claudius and Marcellus carried on the war in the kingdom of Syracuse; the latter certainly as proconsul; the former as proprætor, or possibly only as the lieutenant, legatus, of the proconsul. Marcellus, however, as proconsul, must have had the supreme command over the island; and all its resources must have been at his disposal; so that the fleet which he conducted in person at the siege of Syracuse, was probably a part of that committed to T. Otacilius, Otacilius himself either serving under the proconsul, or possibly remaining still at Lilybæum. It is remarkable that, although he is said to have had the command of the fleet continued to him for five successive years,[55] yet his name never occurs as taking an active part in the siege of Syracuse; and how he employed himself we know not. Nor is it less singular that he should have retained his naval command year after year, though he was so meanly esteemed by the most influential men in Rome, that his election to the consulship was twice stopped in the most decided manner, first by Q. Fabius in 540, and again by T. Manlius Torquatus in 544.[56] But the clue to this, as to other things which belong to the living knowledge of these times, is altogether lost.

Sicily becomes the main seat of war.

While the whole of Sicily was become the scene of war, an army of nine or ten thousand old soldiers was purposely kept inactive by the Roman government, and was not even allowed to take part in any active operations. These were the remains of the army of Cannæ, and a number of citizens who had evaded their military service: as we have seen they had been all sent to Sicily in disgrace, not to be recalled till the end of the war.[57] Now, however, that there was active service required in Sicily itself, these condemned soldiers petitioned Marcellus that they might be employed in the field, and have some opportunity of retrieving their character. This petition was presented to him at the end of the first year's campaign in Sicily, and was referred by him to the senate. The answer was remarkable: "The senate could see no reason for intrusting the service of the commonwealth to men who had abandoned their comrades at Cannæ, while they were fighting to the death: but if M. Claudius thought differently, he might use his discretion; provided always that none of these soldiers should receive any honorary exemption or reward,

Wise conduct of the senate towards the fugitives from Cannæ.

[52] Livy, XXIV. 34.
[53] Polybius, VIII. 9.
[54] Livy, XXIV. 10.
[55] Livy, XXII. 32. XXIV. 10, 44. XXV & XXVI. 1.
[56] Livy, XXIV. 9. XXVI. 22.
[57] Livy, XXIII. 25. See above, p. 523.

however they might distinguish themselves, nor be allowed to return to Italy till the enemy had quitted it."[58] Here was shown the consummate policy of the Roman government, in holding out so high a standard of military duty, while, without appearing to yield to circumstances, they took care not to push their severity so far as to hurt themselves. Occasions might arise, when the services of these disgraced soldiers could not be dispensed with; in such a case Marcellus might employ them. Yet even then their penalty was not wholly remitted; it was grace enough to let them serve their country at all; nothing that they could do was more than their bounden duty of gratitude for the mercy shown them; they could not deserve exemption or reward. It was the glory and happiness of Rome that her soldiers could bear such severity. Sicily was full of mercenary troops, whose swords were hired by foreigners to fight their battles; and if these disgraced Romans had chosen to offer their services to Carthage, they might have enjoyed wealth and honors, with full vengeance on their unforgiving country. Greek soldiers at this time would have done so: the proudest of the nobility of France in the sixteenth century did not scruple to revenge his private wrongs by treason. But these ten thousand Romans, although their case was not only hard, but grievously unjust, inasmuch as their rich and noble countrymen, who had escaped like them from Cannæ, had received no punishment, still bowed with entire submission to their country's severity, and felt that nothing could tempt them to forfeit the privilege of being Romans.

Use of these troops.

We must not suppose, however, that these men were useless, even while they were kept at a distance from the actual field of war. As soon as Syracuse became the enemy of Rome, it was certain that the Carthaginians would renew the struggle of the first Punic war for the dominion of Sicily; and the Roman province, from its neighborhood to Carthage, was especially exposed to invasion. Lilybæum, therefore, and Drepanum, Eryx, and Panormus, required strong garrisons for their security; and the soldiers of Cannæ, by forming these garrisons, set other troops at liberty who must otherwise have been withdrawn from active warfare. As it was, these towns were never attacked; and the keys of Sicily, Lilybæum at one end of the island, and Messana at the other, remained throughout in the hands of the Romans.

Efforts of the Carthaginians in Sicily.

Yet the example of Syracuse produced a very general effect. The cities which had belonged to Hiero's kingdom mostly followed it, unless where the Romans secured them in time with sufficient garrisons. Himilconi, the Carthaginian commander, who had been sent over to Pachynus with a small fleet to watch the course of events, sailed back to Carthage, as soon as the Carthaginian party had gained possession of Syracuse, and urged the government to increase its armaments in Sicily.[59] Hannibal wrote from Italy to the same effect; for Sicily had been his father's battle-field for five years; he had clung to it till the last moment; and his son was no less sensible of its importance. Accordingly, Himilcon was supplied with an army, notwithstanding the pressure of the Numidian war in Africa, and landing on the south coast of Sicily, he presently reduced Heraclea, Minoa, and Agrigentum, and encouraged many of the smaller towns in the interior of the island to declare for Carthage. Hippocrates broke out of Syracuse and joined him. Marcellus, who had left his camp to quell the growing spirit of revolt among the Sicilian cities, was obliged to fall back again; and the enemy, pursuing him closely, encamped on the banks of the Anapus. Meanwhile a Carthaginian fleet ran over to Syracuse, and entered the great harbor; its object being apparently to provision the place, and thus render the Roman blockade nugatory.[60]

Difficulties of the Romans.

It was clear that Marcellus could not make head against a Carthaginian army supported by Syracuse and half the other cities of Sicily. The fleet also was unequal to the service required of it; many

[58] Livy, XXV. 5-7. [59] Livy, XXIV. 35. [60] Livy, XXIV. 35, 36.

ships had probably been destroyed by Archimedes; Lilybæum could not be left unguarded, and some ships were necessarily kept there; and in the general revolt of the Sicilian cities, the Roman army could not always depend on being supplied by land, and would require corn to be brought sometimes from a distance by sea. Besides, the reinforcements which Marcellus so needed must be sent in ships and embarked at Ostia; for Hannibal's army cut off all communication by the usual line, through Lucania to Rhegium, and over the strait to Messana. Thirty ships therefore had to sail back to Rome, to take on board a legion and transport it to Panormus; from whence, by a circuitous route along the south coast of the island, the fleet accompanying it all the way, it reached Marcellus' head-quarters safely. And now the Romans again had the superiority by sea; but by land Himilcon was still master of the field; and the Roman garrison at Murgantia, a little to the north of Syracuse, was betrayed by the inhabitants into his hands.[61]

Massacre of the inhabitants of Enna.

This example was no doubt likely to be followed, and should have increased the vigilance of the Roman garrisons. But it was laid hold of by L. Pinarius, the governor of Enna, as a pretence for repeating the crime of the Campanians at Rhegium, and of the Prænestines more recently at Casilinum. Standing in the centre of Sicily on the top of a high mountain platform, and fenced by precipitous cliffs on almost every side, Enna was a stronghold nearly impregnable, except by treachery from within; and whatever became of the Roman cause in Sicily, the holders of Enna might hope to retain it, as the Mamertines had kept Messana. Accordingly Pinarius, having previously prepared his soldiers for what was to be done, on a signal given ordered them to fall upon the people of Enna, when assembled in the theatre, and massacred them without distinction. The plunder of the town Pinarius and his soldiers kept to themselves, with the consent of Marcellus, who allowed the necessity of the times to be an apology for the deed.[62]

Revolt of the Sicilians: Marcellus winters before Syracuse.

The Romans alleged that the people of Enna were only caught in their own snare; that they had invited Hippocrates and Himilcon to attack the city, and had vainly tried to persuade Pinarius to give them the keys of the gates, that they might admit the enemy to destroy the garrison. But the Sicilians saw that, if the people of Enna had meditated treachery, the Romans had practised it: a whole people had been butchered, their city plundered, and their wives and children made slaves, when they were peaceably met in the theatre in their regular assembly; and this new outrage, added to the sack of Leontini, led to an almost general revolt. Marcellus having collected some corn from the rich plains of Leontini, carried it to the camp before Syracuse, and made his dispositions for his winter-quarters. Appius Claudius went home to stand for the consulship, and was succeeded in his command by T. Quinctius Crispinus, a brave soldier, who was afterwards Marcellus' colleague as consul, and received his death-wound by his side, when Marcellus was killed by Hannibal's ambush. Crispinus lay encamped near the sea, not far from the temple of Olympian Jupiter, and also commanded the naval force employed in the siege; while Marcellus, with the other part of the army, chose a position on the northern side of Syracuse, between the city and the peninsula of Thapsus, apparently for the purpose of keeping up his communications with Leontini.[63] As to the blockade of Syracuse, it was in fact virtually raised; all the southern roads were left open; and as a large part of the Roman fleet was again called away either to Lilybæum or elsewhere, supplies of all sorts were freely introduced into the town by sea from Carthage.

A. U. C. 542. A. C. 232. Intrigues of the Roman party in Syracuse.

The events of the winter were not encouraging to the Romans. Hannibal had taken Tarentum; and the Tarentine fleet was employed in besieging the Roman garrison, which still held the citadel. Thus the Roman naval force was still further divided, as it was necessary

[61] Livy, XXIV. 36. [62] Livy, XXIV. 37–39. [63] Livy, XXIV. 39.

to convey supplies by sea to the garrison; so that, when spring returned, Marcellus was at a loss what to attempt, and had almost resolved to break up from Syracuse altogether, and to carry the war to the other end of Sicily. But Sosis, and other Syracusans of the Roman party, were intriguing actively with their countrymen within the city; and although one conspiracy, in which eighty persons were concerned, was detected by Epicydes, and the conspirators all put to death, yet the hopes they had held out of obtaining easy terms from the Romans were not forgotten; and the lawlessness of the Roman deserters, and of the other foreign soldiers, made many of the Syracusans long for a return of the happy times under Hiero, when Rome and Syracuse were friends.[64]

The Syracusans send to solicit aid from Macedon.

Thus the spring wore away; and the summer had come, and had reached its prime, and yet the war in Sicily seemed to slumber: for the greater part of the cities which had revolted to Carthage were undisturbed by the Romans; yet the Carthaginians were not strong enough to assail the heart of the Roman province, and to besiege Drepanum or Lilybæum. In this state of things, the Syracusans turned their eyes to Greece, and thought that the king of Macedon, who was the open enemy of Rome, and the covenanted ally of Carthage, might serve his own cause no less than theirs by leaving his ignoble warfare on the coast of Epirus, and crossing the Ionian sea to deliver Syracuse. Damippus, a Lacedæmonian, and one of the counsellors of Hieronymus and of Hiero, was accordingly chosen as ambassador, and put to sea on his mission to solicit the aid of king Philip.[65]

The Romans prepare to scale the walls at the festival of Diana.

Again the fortune of Rome interposed to delay the interference of Macedon in the contest. The ship which was conveying Damippus was taken by the Romans on the voyage. The Syracusans valued him highly, and opened a negotiation with Marcellus to ransom him. The conferences were held between Syracuse and the Roman camp; and a Roman soldier, it is said, was struck with the lowness of the wall in one particular place, and having counted the rows of stones, and so computed the whole height, reported to Marcellus that it might be scaled with ladders of ordinary length. Marcellus listened to the suggestion; but the low point was for that very reason more carefully guarded, because it seemed to invite attack; he therefore thought the attempt too hazardous, unless occasion should favor it.[66] But the great festival of Diana was at hand, a three days' solemnity, celebrated with all honors to the guardian goddess of Syracuse. It was a season of universal feasting; and wine was distributed largely among the multitude, that the neighborhood of the Roman army might not seem to have banished all mirth and enjoyment. One vast revel prevailed through the city; Marcellus, informed of all this by deserters, got his ladders ready; and soon after dark two cohorts were marched in silence and in a long thin column to the foot of the wall, preceded by the soldiers of one maniple, who carried the ladders, and were to lead the way to the assault.

They gain possession of Tyche and Neapolis;

The spot selected for this attempt was in the wall which ran along the northern edge of Epipolæ, where the ground was steep, and where apparently there was no gate, or regular approach to the city. But the vast lines of Syracuse inclosed a wide space of uninhabited ground; the new quarters of Tyche and Neapolis, which had been added to the original town since the great Athenian siege, were still far from reaching the top of the hill; and what was called the quarter of Epipolæ only occupied a small part of the sloping ground known in earlier times by that name. Thus, when the Romans scaled the northern line, they found that all was quiet and lonely; nor was there any one to spread the alarm, except the soldiers who garrisoned the several towers of the wall itself. These however, heavy with wine, and dreaming of no

64 Livy, XXV. 23.

65 Livy, XXV. 23.

66 Livy, XXV. 23. Plutarch, Marcellus, 18. Polybius, Vol. V. p. 32, 33.

danger, were presently surprised and killed; and the assailants, thus clearing their way as they went, swept the whole line of the wall on their right, following it up the slope of the hill towards the angle formed at the summit by the meeting of the northern line with the southern. Here was the regular entrance into Syracuse from the land side; and this point, being the key of the whole fortified inclosure, was secured by the strong work called Hexapylon, or the Six Gates; probably from the number of barriers which must be passed before the lines could be fully entered. To this point the storming party made their way in the darkness, not blindly, however, nor uncertainly, for a Syracusan was guiding them,—that very Sosis,[67] who had been one of the assassins of Hieronymus, and one of the murderers of Hiero's daughters, and who, when he was one of the captains-general of Syracuse, must have become acquainted with all the secrets of the fortifications. Sosis led the two Roman cohorts towards Hexapylon: from that commanding height a fire-signal was thrown up, to announce the success of their attempt; and the loud and sudden blast of the Roman trumpets from the top of the walls called the Romans to come to the support of their friends, and told the bewildered Syracusans that the key of their lines was in the hands of the enemy.[68]

and take the Hexapylon.

Ladders were now set, and the wall was scaled in all directions; for the main gates of Hexapylon could not be forced till the next morning; and the only passage immediately opened was a small side-gate at no great distance from them. But when daylight came, Hexapylon was entirely taken, and the main entrance to the city was cleared; so that Marcellus marched in with his whole army, and took possession of the summit of the slope of Epipolæ.

Marcellus looking down on Syracuse, sheds tears.

From that high ground he saw Syracuse at his feet, and, he doubted not, in his power. Two quarters of the city, the new town as it was called, and Tyche, were open to his first advance; their only fortification being the general inclosure of the lines, which he had already carried. Below, just overhanging the sea, or floating on its waters, lay Achradina and the island of Ortygia, fenced by their own separate walls, which till the time of the first Dionysius had been the limit of Syracuse, the walls which the great Athenian armament had besieged in vain. Nearer on the right, and running so deeply into the land, that it seemed almost to reach the foot of the heights on which he stood, lay the still basin of the great harbor, its broad surface half hidden by the hulls of a hundred Carthaginian ships; while further on the right was the camp of his lieutenant, T. Crispinus, crowning the rising ground beyond the Anapus, close by the temple of Olympian Jupiter. So striking was the view on every side, and so surpassing was the glory of his conquest, that Marcellus, old as he was, was quite overcome by it: unable to contain the feelings of that moment, he burst into tears.[69]

His troops plunder the captured parts of the city.

A deputation from the inhabitants of Tyche and Neapolis approached him, bearing the ensigns of suppliants, and imploring him to save them from fire and massacre. He granted their prayer, but at the price of every article of their property, which was to be given up to the Roman soldiers as plunder. At a regular signal the army was let loose upon the houses of Tyche and Neapolis, with no other restriction than that of offering no personal violence. How far such a command would be heeded in such a season of license, we can only conjecture. The Roman writers extol the humanity of Marcellus; but the Syracusans regarded him as a merciless spoiler, who had wished to take the town by assault, rather than by a voluntary surrender, that he might have a pretence for seizing its plunder.[70] Such a prize, indeed, had never before been won by a Roman army; even the wealth of Taren-

[67] Livy, XXVI. 21.
[68] Livy, XXV. 24. Plutarch, Marcellus, 18.
[69] Livy, XXV. 24.
[70] Livy, XXVI. 30.

tum was not to be compared with that of Syracuse. But as yet the appetites of the Roman soldiers were fleshed rather than satisfied; less than half of Syracuse was in their power; and a fresh siege was necessary to win the spoils of Achradina and Ortygia. Still what they had already gained gave Marcellus large means of corruption; the fort of Euryalus, on the summit of Epipolæ, near Hexapylon, which might have caused him serious annoyance on his rear while engaged in attacking Achradina, was surrendered to him by its governor, Philodemus, an Argive; and the Romans set eagerly to work to complete their conquest. Having formed three camps before Achradina, they hoped soon to starve the remaining quarters of the city into a surrender.[71]

The Carthaginian army attempting to relieve Syracuse, is destroyed by a fever.

Epicydes meanwhile showed a courage and activity worthy of one who had learned war under Hannibal. A squadron of the Carthaginian fleet put to sea one stormy night, when the Roman blockading ships were driven off from the mouth of the harbor, and ran across to Carthage to request fresh succors. These were prepared with the greatest expedition: while Hippocrates and Himilcon, with their combined Carthaginian and Sicilian armies, came from the western end of the island to attack the Roman army on the land side. They encamped on the shore of the harbor, between the mouth of the Anapus and the city, and assaulted the camp of Crispinus, while Epicydes sailed from Achradina to attack Marcellus. But Roman soldiers fighting behind fortifications were invincible; their lines at Capua in the following year repelled Hannibal himself; and now their positions before Syracuse were maintained with equal success against Hippocrates and Epicydes. Still the Carthaginian army remained in its camp on the shore of the harbor, partly in the hope of striking some blow against the enemy, but more to overawe the remains of the Roman party in Syracuse, which the distress of the siege, and the calamities of Neapolis and Tyche, must have rendered numerous and active. Meanwhile the summer advanced; the weather became hotter and hotter; and the usual malaria fevers began to prevail in both armies, and also in Syracuse. But the air here, as at Rome, is much more unhealthy without the city than within; above all, the marshy ground by the Anapus, where the Carthaginian army lay, was almost pestilential; and the ordinary summer fevers in this situation soon assumed a character of extreme malignity. The Sicilians immediately moved their quarters, and withdrew into the neighboring cities; but the Carthaginians remained on the ground, till their whole army was effectually destroyed. Hippocrates and Himilcon both perished with their soldiers.[72]

Their fleet fails in a like attempt.

The Romans suffered less; for Marcellus had quartered his men in the houses of Neapolis and Tyche; and the high buildings and narrow streets of the ancient towns kept off the sun, and allowed both the sick and the healthy to breathe and move in a cooler atmosphere. Still the deaths were numerous; and as the terror of Archimedes and his artillery restrained the Romans from any attempts to batter or scale the walls, they had nothing to trust to save famine or treason. But Bomilcar was on his way from Carthage with 130 ships of war, and a convoy of seven hundred storeships, laden with supplies of every description: he had reached the Sicilian coast near Agrigentum, when prevailing easterly winds checked his further advance, and he could not reach Pachynus. Alarmed at this most unseasonable delay, and fearing lest the fleet should return to Africa in despair, Epicydes himself left Syracuse, and went to meet it, and to hasten its advance. The storeships, which were worked by sails, were obliged to remain at Heraclea; but Epicydes prevailed on Bomilcar to bring on his ships of war to Pachynus, where the Roman fleet, though inferior in numbers, was waiting to intercept his progress. The east winds at length abated, and Bomilcar stood out to sea to double Pachynus. But when the Roman fleet advanced against him, he suddenly changed his plans, it is said; and

[71] Livy, XXV. 25.

[72] Livy, XXV. 26.

having dispatched orders to the storeships at Heraclea to return immediately to Africa, he himself, instead of engaging the Romans, or making for Syracuse, passed along the eastern coast of Sicily, without stopping, and continued his course till he reached Tarentum.[73]

Here again the story in its present state greatly needs explanation. It is true that Hannibal was very anxious at this time to reduce the citadel of Tarentum; and he probably required a fleet to co-operate with him, in order to cut off the garrison's supplies by sea. But Bomilcar had been sent out especially to throw succors into Syracuse; and we cannot conceive his abandoning this object on a sudden, without any intelligible reason. The probability is, that the easterly winds still kept the storeships at Heraclea; and if they could not reach Syracuse, nothing was to be gained by a naval battle. And then, as the service at Tarentum was urgent, he thought it best to go thither, and to send back the convoy to Africa, rather than wait inactive on the Sicilian coast, till the wind became favorable. After all, Syracuse did not fall for want of provisions: the havoc caused by sickness, both in the city and in the Carthaginian camp on the Anapus, must have greatly reduced the number of consumers, and made the actual supply available for a longer period. It seems to have been a worse mischief than the conduct of Bomilcar, that Epicydes himself, as if despairing of fortune, withdrew to Agrigentum, instead of returning to Syracuse; for from the moment of his departure the city seems to have been abandoned to anarchy. At first the remains of the Sicilian army, which now occupied two towns in the interior, not far from Syracuse, began to negotiate with Marcellus, and persuaded the Syracusans to rise on the generals left in command by Epicydes, and to put them to death. New captains-generals were then appointed, probably for the Roman party; and they began to treat with Marcellus for the surrender of Syracuse, and for the general settlement of the war in Sicily.[74]

Epicydes quits the city, which becomes a prey to anarchy.

Marcellus listened to them readily: but his army was longing for the plunder of Achradina and Ortygia; and he knew not how to disappoint them: for we may be sure that no pay was issued at this period to any Roman army serving out of Italy; in the provinces, war was by fair means or foul to support war. Meanwhile the miserable state of affairs in Syracuse was furthering the wish of the Roman soldiers. A besieged city, with no efficient government, and full of foreign mercenaries, whom there was no native force to restrain, was like a wreck in mutiny: utter weakness and furious convulsions were met in the same body. The Roman deserters first excited the tumult, and persuaded all the foreign soldiers to join them; a new outbreak of violence followed; the Syracusan captains-general were massacred in their turn; and the foreign soldiers were again triumphant. Three officers, each with a district of his own, were appointed to command in Achradina, and three more in Ortygia.[75]

Insurrection of the mercenaries in the city;

The foreign soldiers now held the fate of Syracuse in their hands; and they began to consider that they might make their terms with the Romans, although the Roman deserters could not. Their blood was not called for by the inflexible law of military discipline; by a timely treachery they might earn not impunity merely, but reward. So thought Mericus, a Spaniard, who had the charge of a part of the sea-wall of Achradina. Accordingly he made his bargain with Marcellus, and admitted a party of Roman soldiers by night at one of the gates which opened towards the harbor. As soon as morning dawned, Marcellus made a general assault on the land front of Achradina; the garrison of Ortygia hastened to join in the defence; and the Romans then sent boats full of men round into the great harbor, and, effecting a landing under the

who betray it to the Romans.

[73] Livy, XXV. 27.
[74] Livy, XXV. 28.
[75] Livy, XXV. 29.

walls, carried the island with little difficulty. Meanwhile Mericus had openly joined the Roman party, whom he had admitted into Achradina; and Marcellus, having his prey in his power, called off his soldiers from the assault, lest the royal treasures, which were kept in Ortygia, should be plundered in the general sack of the town.[76]

Syracuse is taken and plundered. Archimedes is slain.

In the respite thus gained, the Roman deserters found an opportunity to escape out of Syracuse. Whether they forced their way out, or whether the soldiers, hungry for plunder, and not wishing to encounter the resistance of desperate men, obliged Marcellus to connive at their escape, we know not: but with them all wish or power to hold out longer vanished from Syracuse; and a deputation from Achradina came once more to Marcellus, praying for nothing beyond the lives and personal freedom of the citizens and their families. This, it seems, was granted; but as soon as Marcellus had sent his quæstor to secure the royal treasures in Ortygia, the soldiers were let loose upon the city to plunder it at their discretion. They did not merely plunder, however: blood was shed unsparingly, partly by the mere violence of the soldiers, partly by the axes of the lictors, as the punishment of rebellion against the majesty of Rome. Amidst the horrors of the sack of the city, Archimedes was slain.[77] The stories of his death vary; and which, if any of them, is the true one, we cannot determine. But Marcellus, who made it his glory to carry all the finest works of art from the temples of Syracuse to Rome,[78] would no doubt have been glad to have seen Archimedes walking amongst the prisoners at his triumph. He is said to have shown kindness to the relations of Archimedes for his sake;[79] and if this be true, he earned a glory which few Romans ever deserved, that of honoring merit in an enemy.

Miserable condition of the Syracusans.

Old as Archimedes was, the Roman soldier's sword dealt kindly with him, in cutting short his scanty term of remaining life, and saving him from beholding the misery of his country. It was a wretched sight to see the condition of Syracuse when the sack was over, and what was called a state of peace and safety had returned. Every house was laid bare, every temple stript; and the empty pedestals showed how sweeping the spoiler's work had been. The Syracusans beheld their captive gods carried to the Roman quarters, or put on shipboard to be conveyed to Rome; the care with which they were handled, lest the conqueror's triumph should lose its most precious ornaments, only adding to the grief and indignation of the conquered. Those fathers and mothers, who were so happy as to gather all their children safe around them when the plunder was over, had escaped the sword, indeed, and they and their sons and daughters were not yet sold as slaves; but their only choice was still between slavery or death. They had lost every thing. What food was still remaining in the besieged city, the sack had either carried off or destroyed; and if food had been at hand, they had no money to buy it. And this came upon them after a heavy visitation of sickness; when the body, reduced by that weakening malaria fever, needed all tender care and comfort to restore it, instead of being harassed by alarm and anxiety, and exposed to destitution and starvation. Many therefore sold themselves to the Roman soldiers, to escape dying by hunger; and the family circle, which the sack of the city had spared, was again broken up forever. Those who, being unmarried and childless, had given no hostages to fortune, and who might yet hope to live in personal freedom, were only the more able to feel the ruin and degradation of their country.[80] Syracuse, who had led captive the hosts of Athens, and seen the invading armies of Carthage melt away by disease under her walls, till scarce any remained to fly—Syracuse, where Dionysius had reigned, which Timoleon had freed, which Hiero

[76] Livy, XXV. 30.

[77] Livy, XXV. 31. Plutarch, Marcellus, 19. Valerius Maximus, VIII. 7, 7.

[78] Livy, XXV. 40. Polybius, IX. 10. Cicero, in Verrem, IV. 54.

[79] Livy, XXV. 31. Plutarch, Marcellus, 19.

[80] Diodorus, XXVI. Fragm. Mai.

had cherished and sheltered under his long paternal rule—was now become subject to barbarians, whom she had helped in their utmost need, and who were repaying the unshaken friendship of Hiero with the plunder of his city and the subjugation of his people. If there was yet a keener pang to be felt by every noble Syracusan, it was to behold their countrymen, who had fought in the Roman army, returning in triumph, establishing themselves in the empty houses ot the slaughtered defenders of their country, and insulting the general misery by displaying the rewards of their treason. Among these was Sosis, assassin, murderer, and traitor, who was looking forward to the triumph of Marcellus, as one to whom the shame of his country was his glory, and her ruin the making of his fortune.[81]

Syracuse had fallen; and the cities in the eastern part of Sicily had no other hope now, than to obtain pardon, if it might be, from Rome, by immediate submission. But it was too late: they were treated as conquered enemies;[82] that is to say, Marcellus put to death those of their citizens who were most obnoxious, and imposed such forfeitures of land on the cities, and such terms of submission for the time to come, as he judged expedient. It became the fashion afterwards to extol his humanity, and even his refinement,[83] because he showed his taste for the works of Greek art by carrying the statues of the Syracusan temples to Rome. But his admiration of Greek art did not make him treat the Greeks themselves with less severity; and the Sicilians taxed him with perfidy as well as cruelty, and regarded him as the merciless oppressor of their country.[84]

Cruelty of Marcellus.

Meantime Hannibal's comprehensive view had not lost sight of Sicily. When he heard of the havoc caused by the epidemic sickness, and of the death of Hippocrates, he sent over another of his officers to share with Epicydes, and with the general who came from Carthage, in the command of the war. This was Mutines, or Myttonus, a half-caste Carthaginian, excluded on that account from civil honors;[85] but Hannibal's camp recognized no such distinctions; and brave and able men, whatever was their race or condition, were sure to be employed and rewarded there. Mutines proved the unerring judgment of Hannibal in his choice of officers. His arrival in Sicily was equivalent to an army: being put at the head of the Numidian cavalry then serving under Epicydes and Hanno, he overran the whole island, encouraging the allies of Carthage, harassing those of Rome, and defying pursuit or resistance by the rapidity and skill of his movements. He renewed the system of warfare which Hamilcar had maintained so long in the last war; and having the strong place of Agrigentum to retire to in case of need, he perplexed the Roman generals not a little. Marcellus was obliged to take the field, and march from Syracuse westward as far as the Himera, where the enemy's army lay encamped. But he met with a rough reception; the Numidian cavalry crossed the river, and came swarming round his camp, insulting and annoying his soldiers on guard, and confining his whole army to their intrenchments; and when on the next day, impatient of this annoyance, he offered battle in the field, Mutines and his Numidians broke in upon his lines with such fury, that he was fain to retreat with all speed, and seek the shelter of his camp again. It appears that other arms were then tried with better success: the Numidians were tampered with; their irregular habits and impatient tempers made them at all times difficult to manage; and a party of them having left the Carthaginian camp in disgust, Mutines went after them to pacify and win them back to their duty, earnestly conjuring Hanno and Epicydes not to venture a battle till he should return. But Hanno was jealous of Hannibal's officers; and holding his own commission directly from the government of Carthage, he could not

Hannibal sends Mutines to Sicily; his successes.

A. U. C. 543. A. C. 211.

[81] Livy, XXVI. 21.
[82] Livy, XXV. 40.
[83] Cicero, in Verrem, IV. 52–59.
[84] Livy, XXVI. 29–32. Plutarch, Marcellus, 23.
[85] Livy, XXV. 40. Polybius, IX. 22.

bear to be restrained by a half-caste soldier, sent to Sicily from Hannibal's camp, by the mere authority of the general. His rank probably gave him a casting vote, when only one other commander was present, so that Epicydes in vain protested against his imprudence.[86] A battle was ventured; and not only was the genius of Mutines wanting, but the Numidians whom he had left with Hanno, thinking their commander insulted, would take no active part in the action, and Hanno was defeated with loss.

Marcellus returns to Rome.

Marcellus, rejoiced at having thus retrieved his honor, had no mind to risk another encounter with Mutines: he forthwith retreated to Syracuse;[87] and as the term of his command was now expired, his thoughts were all turned to Rome, and to his expected triumph. He left Sicily after the fall of Capua, towards the end of the summer of 543, and about a year after the conquest of Syracuse; but he was not allowed to carry his army home with him; and M. Cornelius Cethegus, one of the prætors, who succeeded him in his command, found that his province was far from being in a state of peace. The Carthaginians had reinforced their army: Mutines, with his Numidians, was scouring the whole country; the soldiers were discontented because they had not been permitted to return home; and the Sicilians were driven desperate by the oppressions which Marcellus had commanded or winked at, and were ready to break out in revolt again.[88]

A. U. C. 544. A. C. 210.

Lævinus is sent to Sicily.

In fact, it appears that in the year 544, nearly two years after the fall of Syracuse, there were as many as sixty-six towns in Sicily in a state of revolt from Rome, and in alliance with Carthage.[89] So greatly had Mutines restored the Carthaginian cause, that it was thought necessary to send one of the consuls over with a consular army, to bring the war to an end. Accordingly, M. Valerius Lævinus, who had been employed for the last three or four years on the coast of Epirus, conducting the war against Philip, and who was chosen consul with Marcellus in the year 544, carried over a regular consular army into Sicily; while L. Cincius, one of the new prætors, and probably the same man who is known as one of the earliest Roman historians, took the command of the old province, and of the soldiers of Cannæ who were still quartered there.[90] The army with which Marcellus had won Syracuse was now at last disbanded, and the men were allowed to return home with as much of their plunder as they had not spent or wasted: but four legions were even now employed in Sicily, besides a fleet of one hundred ships; and yet Mutines and his Numidians were overrunning all parts of the island, and the end of the war seemed as distant as ever.

Mutines is insulted by Hanno, and betrays Agrigentum to the Romans.

Lævinus advanced towards Agrigentum, with small hope, however, of taking the place; for Mutines sallied whenever he would, and carried back his plunder in safety whenever he would: whilst the neighborhood of Carthage made relief by sea always within calculation, whatever naval force the Romans might employ in the blockade. In this state of things, Lævinus to his astonishment received a secret communication from Mutines, offering to put Agrigentum into his power. The half-caste African, the officer of Hannibal, the sole stay of the Carthaginian cause in Sicily, was on all these accounts odious to Hanno; and it is likely that Mutines did not bear his glory meekly, and that he expressed the scorn which Hannibal's soldier was likely to feel for the pride and incapacity of the general sent out by the government at home, and probably by the party opposed to Hannibal, and afraid of his glory. But whatever was the secret of the quarrel, its effects were public enough: Hanno ventured to deprive Mutines of his command. The Numidians, however, would obey no other leader, while him they would obey in every thing; and at his bidding they rose in open mutiny, took possession of one of the gates

86 Livy, XXV. 40.
87 Livy, XXV. 41.
88 Livy, XXVI. 21.
89 Livy, XXVI. 40.
90 Livy, XXVI. 28.

of the town, and let in the Romans. Hanno and Epicydes had just time to fly to the harbor, to hasten on board a ship, and escape to Carthage; but their soldiers, surprised and panic-struck, were cut to pieces with little resistance; and Lævinus won Agrigentum. He treated it more severely than Marcellus had dealt with Syracuse; after executing the principal citizens, he sold all the rest for slaves, and sent the money which he received for them to Rome.[91]

Lævinus accomplishes the conquest of Sicily,

This blow was decisive. Twenty other towns, which still held with the Carthaginians, were presently betrayed to the Romans, either by their garrisons, or by some of their own citizens; six were stormed by the Roman army; and the remainder, to the number of forty, then submitted at discretion. The consul dealt out his rewards to the traitors who had betrayed their country; and his lictors scourged and beheaded the brave men who had persevered the longest in their resistance: thus at last he was able to report to the senate that the war in Sicily was at an end.

and reduces it to entire submission.

Four thousand adventurers of all descriptions, who in the troubled state of Sicily had taken possession of the town of Agathyrna on the north coast of the island, and were maintaining themselves there by robbery, Lævinus carried over into Italy at the close of the year, and landed them at Rhegium, to be employed in a plundering warfare in Bruttium. Having thus cleared the island of all open disturbers of its peace, he obliged the Sicilians, says Livy, to turn their attention to agriculture, that its fruitful soil might grow corn to supply the wants of Italy and of Rome.[92] And he assured the senate, at the end of the year, that the work was thoroughly done; that not a single Carthaginian was left in Sicily; that the towns were repeopled by the return of their peaceable inhabitants, and the land was again cultivated; that he had laid the foundation of a state of things equally happy for the Sicilians and for Rome.[93]

Deplorable condition of Sicily.

So Lævinus said; and so he probably believed. But with the return of peace to the island, there came a host of Italian and Roman speculators; who, in the general distress of the Sicilians, bought up large tracts of land at a low price, or became the occupiers of estates which had belonged to Sicilians of the Carthaginian party, and had been forfeited to Rome after the execution or flight of their owners. The Sicilians of the Roman party followed the example, and became rich out of the distress of their countrymen. Slaves were to be had cheap; and corn was likely to find a sure market, whilst Italy was suffering from the ravages of war. Accordingly, Sicily was crowded with slaves, employed to grow corn for the great landed proprietors, whether Sicilian or Italian, and so ill-fed by their masters, that they soon began to provide for themselves by robbery. The poorer Sicilians were the sufferers from this evil; and as the masters were well content that their slaves should be maintained at the expense of others, they were at no pains to restrain their outrages. Thus, although nominally at peace, though full of wealthy proprietors, and though exporting corn largely every year, yet Sicily was teeming with evils, which, seventy or eighty years after, broke out in the horrible atrocities of the Servile War.[94]

[91] Livy, XXVI. 40.
[92] Livy, XXVI. 40.
[93] Livy, XXVII. 5.
[94] Diodorus, XXXIV. Excerpt. Photii, p. 525, &c. and Excerpt. Valesii, p. 599. Florus, III. 19.

CHAPTER XLVI.

STATE OF ITALY—DISTRESS OF THE PEOPLE—TWELVE COLONIES REFUSE TO SUPPORT THE WAR—EIGHTEEN COLONIES OFFER ALL THEIR RESOURCES TO THE ROMANS—EVENTS OF THE WAR—DEATH OF MARCELLUS—FABIUS RECOVERS TARENTUM—MARCH OF HASDRUBAL INTO ITALY—HE REACHES THE COAST OF THE ADRIATIC—GREAT MARCH OF C. NERO FROM APULIA TO OPPOSE HIM—BATTLE OF THE METAURUS, AND DEATH OF HASDRUBAL.—A. U. C. 543 TO A. U. C. 547.

A. U. C. 543. A. C. 211. Intermission of hostilities after the taking of Capua.

IN following the war in Sicily to its conclusion we have a little anticipated the course of our narrative; for we have been speaking of the consulship of M. Lævinus, whilst our account of the war in Italy has not advanced beyond the middle of the preceding year. The latter part of the year 543 was marked, however, by no military actions of consequence; so great an event as the fall of Capua having, as was natural, produced a pause, during which both parties had to shape their future plans according to the altered state of their affairs and of their prospects.

Hannibal abandons the west of Italy.

Hannibal on his side had retired, as we have seen, into Apulia, after his unsuccessful attempt upon Rhegium, and there allowed his soldiers to enjoy an interval of rest. The terrible example of Capua shook the resolution of his Italian allies, and made them consider whether a timely submission to Rome might not be their wisest policy; nay, it became a question whether their pardon might not be secured by betraying Hannibal's garrisons, and returning to their duty not empty-handed. Hannibal therefore neither dared to risk his soldiers by dispersing them about in small and distant towns; nor could he undertake, even if he kept his army together, to cover the wide extent of country which had revolted to him at different periods of the war. His men would be worn out by a succession of flying marches; and after all, the Roman armies were so numerous, that he would always be in danger of arriving too late at the point attacked. Accordingly he found it necessary to abandon many places altogether; and from some he obliged the inhabitants to migrate, and made them remove within the limits which he still hoped to protect. In this manner, it is probable, the western side of Italy, from the edge of Campania to Bruttium, was at once left to its fate; including what had been the territory of the Capuans on the shores of the Gulf of Salernum, the country of the Picentians, and Lucania; while Apulia and Bruttium were carefully defended. But in evacuating the towns which they could not keep, and still more in the compelled migrations of the inhabitants, Hannibal's soldiers committed many excesses; property was plundered, and blood was shed; and thus the minds of the Italians were still more generally alienated.[1]

Movements of the Roman armies.

We have seen that, immediately after the fall of Capua, C. Nero, with a part of the troops which had been employed on the blockade, had been sent off to Spain.[2] Q. Fulvius remained at Capua, with another part, amounting to a complete consular army;[3] and some were probably sent home. The two consuls marched into Apulia, which was to be their province;[4] but no active operations took place during the remainder of the season; and at the end of the year P. Sulpicius was ordered to pass over into Epirus, and succeed M. Lævinus in the command of the war against Philip. The home administration was left in the hands of C. Calpurnius Piso, the city prætor.

About the time that the two consuls took the command in Apulia, M. Corne-

[1] Livy, XXVI. 38.
[2] Livy, XXVI. 17.
[3] Livy, XXVI. 28.
[4] Livy, XXVI. 22.

lius Cethegus, who had obtained that province as prætor at the beginning of the year, was sent over to Sicily to command the army there, Marcellus having just left the island to return to Rome. Marcellus was anxious to obtain a triumph for his conquest of Syracuse: but the war in Sicily was still raging; and Mutines was in full activity. The senate therefore would not grant a triumph for an imperfect victory, but allowed Marcellus the honor of the smaller triumph or ovation. He was highly dissatisfied at this, and consoled himself by going up in triumphal procession to the temple of Jupiter on the highest summit of the Alban hills, and offering sacrifice there, a ceremony which by virtue of his imperium he could lawfully perform: he might go in procession where he pleased, and sacrifice where he pleased, except within the limits of Rome itself. On the day after his triumph on the hill of Alba, he entered Rome with the ceremony of an ovation, walking on foot according to the rule, instead of being drawn in a chariot in kingly state, as in the proper triumph. But the show was unusually splendid: for a great picture of Syracuse with all its fortifications was displayed, and with it some of the very artillery which Archimedes had made so famous in his defence of them; besides an unwonted display of the works of art of a more peaceful kind, the spoils of Hiero's palace, and of the temples in his city, silver and bronze figures, embroidered carpets and coverings of couches, and, above all, some of the finest pictures and statues. Men also observed the traitor Sosis walking in the procession, with a coronet of gold on his head, as a benefactor of the Roman people: he was further to be rewarded with the Roman franchise, with a house at his own choice out of those belonging to the Syracusans who had remained true to their country, and with five hundred jugera of land, which had either been theirs, or part of the royal domain.[5]

Marcellus is unable to obtain a triumph; his splendid ovation.

At the end of the year Cn. Fulvius was summoned to Rome from Apulia to preside at the consular comitia. On the day of the election, the first century of the Veturian tribe, which had obtained the first voice by lot, gave its votes in favor of T. Manlius Torquatus and T. Otacilius Crassus. As the voice of the tribe first called was generally followed by the rest, Manlius, who was present, was immediately greeted by the congratulations of his friends: but, instead of accepting them, he made his way to the consul's seat, and requested him to call back the century which had just voted, and allow him to say a few words. The century was summoned again, all men wondering what was about to happen. Manlius had been consul five-and-twenty years before, in the memorable year when the temple of Janus was shut in token of the ratification of peace with Carthage; twenty years had passed since he was censor; and though his vigor of body and mind was still great, he was an old man, and age had made him nearly blind. "I am unfit to command," he said; "for I can only see through the eyes of others. This is no time for incompetent generals; let the century make a better choice." But the century answered unanimously, "that they could not make a better; that they again named Manlius and Otacilius consuls." "Your tempers and my rule," said the old man, "will never suit. Give your votes over again; and remember that the Carthaginians are in Italy, and that their general is Hannibal." A murmur of admiration burst from all around, and the voters of the century were moved. They were the younger men of their tribe; and they besought the consul to summon the century of their elders, that they might be guided by their counsel. Fulvius accordingly summoned the century of elders of the Veturian tribe; and the two centuries retired to confer on the question. The elders recommended that Fabius and Marcellus should be chosen; or, if a new consul were desirable, that they should take one of these, and with him elect M. Lævinus, who for some years past had done good service in conducting the war against Philip. Their advice was adopted, and the century gave its votes now in favor of Marcellus

A. U. C. 544. A. C. 210. Comitia: noble conduct of Manlius; Marcellus and Lævinus are elected consuls.

[5] Livy, XXVI. 21.

and Lævinus. All the other centuries confirmed their choice; and thus T. Otacilius was for the second time, by an extraordinary interference with the votes of the centuries, deprived of the consulship, to which some uncommonly amiable qualities, or some peculiar influence, had twice recommended him, in spite of his deficient ability.[6]

He probably never knew of this second disappointment; for scarcely was the election over, when news arrived from Sicily of his death.[7] Cn. Fulvius returned to his army in Apulia; and as M. Lævinus was still absent in Epirus, Marcellus on the usual day, the ides of March, entered upon the consulship alone. Q. Fulvius was still at Capua; but Q. Fabius and T. Manlius were at Rome; and their counsels, together with those of Marcellus, were of the greatest influence in the senate, and probably directed the government.

Alarming posture of Roman affairs. Patriotic proposition of Lævinus: self-devotion of the senators: their example followed by the whole people.

There was need for all their ability and all their firmness, for never had the posture of affairs been more alarming. Hannibal's unconquered and unconquerable army, although it had not saved Capua, had wasted Italy more widely than ever in the last campaign; and it had struck particularly at countries which had hitherto escaped its ravages, the valleys of the Sabines, and the country of the thirty-five tribes themselves, up to the very gates of Rome. Many of the citizens had not only lost their standing crops, but their cattle had been carried off, and their houses burned to the ground.[8] Actual scarcity was added to other causes of distress; insomuch that the modius of wheat rose to nearly three denarii, which, in a plentiful season eight years afterwards, was sold at four ases, or the fourth part of one denarius.[9] The people were becoming unable to bear further burdens; and some of the Latin colonies, which had hitherto been the firmest support of the commonwealth, were suspected to be not only unable, but unwilling. It was probably to meet the urgent necessity of the case that the armies were somewhat reduced this year, four legions, it seems, being disbanded.[10] But this fruit of the fall of Capua was in part neutralized by the necessity of raising fresh seamen; for unless the commonwealth maintained its naval superiority, Sicily would be lost, and Philip might be expected on the coasts of Italy; and the supply of corn which was looked for from Egypt in the failure of all nearer resources, would become very precarious.[11] Accordingly a tax was imposed, requiring all persons to provide a certain number of seamen, in proportion to the returns of their property at the last census, with pay and provisions for thirty days. But our own tax of ship-money did not excite more opposition, though on different grounds. The people complained aloud: crowds gathered in the Forum, and declared that no power could force from them what they had not got; that the consuls might sell their goods, and lay hold on their persons, if they chose; but they had no means of payment.[12] The consuls—for Lævinus was by this time returned home from Macedonia—with that dignity which the Roman government never forgot for an instant, issued an order, giving the defaulters three days to consider their determination; thus seeming to grant as an indulgence, what necessity obliged them to yield. Meanwhile they summoned the senate; and when every one was equally convinced of the necessity of procuring seamen, and the impossibility of carrying through the tax, Lævinus, in his colleague's name and his own, proceeded to address the senators. He told them that, before they could call on the people to make sacrifices, they must set the example. "Let each senator," he said, "keep his gold ring, and the rings of his wife and children: let him keep the golden bulla worn by his sons under age, and one ounce of gold for ornaments for his wife, and an ounce for each of his daughters. All the rest of the gold which we possess, let us offer

6 Livy, XXVI. 22.
7 Livy, XXVI. 23.
8 Livy, XXVI. 26.
9 Polybius, IX. 44. Livy, XXXI. 5.
10 Livy, XXVI. 28.
11 Polybius, IX. 10.
12 Livy, XXVI. 36.

for the public service. Next, let all of us who have borne curule offices, reserve the silver used in the harness of our war-horses; and let all others, including those just mentioned, keep one pound of silver, enough for the plate needful in sacrifices, the small vessel to hold the salt, and the small plate or basin for the libation; and let us each keep five thousand ases of copper money. With these exceptions, let us devote all our silver and copper to our country's use, as we have devoted all our gold. And let us do this without any vote of the senate, of our own free gift, as individual senators, and carry our contributions at once to the three commissioners for the currency. Be sure that first the equestrian order, and then the mass of the people, will follow our example." He spoke to hearers who so thoroughly shared his spirit, that they voted their thanks to the consuls for this suggestion. The senate instantly broke up; the senators hastened home, and thence came crowding to the Forum, their slaves bearing all their stores of copper, and silver, and gold, each man being anxious to have his contribution recorded first; so that, Livy says, neither were there commissioners enough to receive all the gifts that were brought, nor clerks enough to record them. The example, as the consuls knew, was irresistible; the equestrian order and the commons poured in their contributions with equal zeal; and no tax could have supplied the treasury so plentifully as this free-will offering of the whole people.[13]

Value of these sacrifices.

There is no doubt that the money thus contributed was to be repaid to the contributors, when the republic should see better days; but the sacrifice consisted in this, that, while the prospect of payment was distant and uncertain, the whole profit of the money in the mean time was lost: for the Roman state creditors received no interest on their loans. Therefore it was at their own cost mainly, and not at the cost of posterity, that the Romans maintained their great struggle; and from our admiration of their firmness and heroic devotion to their country's cause, nothing is in this case to be abated.

Complaints of the severity of Fulvius and Marcellus.

Nor is it less striking, that the senate at this very moment listened to accusations brought by vanquished enemies against their conquerors, and these conquerors men of the highest name and greatest influence in the commonwealth, Marcellus and Q. Fulvius. When Lævinus passed through Capua on his way to Rome, he was beset by a multitude of the Capuans, who complained of the intolerable misery of their condition under the dominion of Q. Fulvius, and besought him to take them with him to Rome, that they might implore the mercy of the senate. Fulvius made them swear that they would return to Capua within five days after they received their answer, telling Lævinus that he dared not let them go at liberty; for if any Capuan escaped from the city, he instantly became a brigand, and scoured the country, burning, robbing, and murdering all that fell in his way; even at Rome, Lævinus would find the traces of Capuan treason, for the late destructive fire in the city was their work. So a deputation of Campanians, thus hardly allowed to go, followed Lævinus towards Rome; and when he approached the city, a similar deputation of Sicilians came out to meet him, with like complaints against Marcellus.[14]

The Sicilians entreat that Marcellus may not be sent into Sicily.

The provinces assigned to the consuls were this year to be the conduct of the war with Hannibal, and Sicily; and Sicily fell by lot to Marcellus. The Sicilians present were thrown into despair when this was announced to them: they put on mourning and beset the senate-house, weeping and bewailing their hard fate, and saying that it would be better for their island to be sunk in the sea, or overwhelmed with the lava floods of Ætna, than given up to the vengeance of Marcellus. Their feeling met with much sympathy in the senate; and this was made so intelligible, that Marcellus, without waiting for any resolution on the subject, came to an agreement with his colleague, and they exchanged their provinces.[15]

This having been settled, the Sicilians were admitted into the senate, and

[13] Livy, XXVI. 36. [14] Livy, XXVI. 27. [15] Livy, XXVI. 29.

Their complaint is heard by the senate; counter-statement of Marcellus.

brought forward their complaint. It turned principally on the cruelty of making them responsible for the acts, first of Hieronymus, and then of a mercenary soldiery which they had no means of resisting; while the long and tried friendship of Hiero, proved by the Romans in the utmost extremity of their fortune, had been forgotten. Marcellus insisted that the deputation should remain in the senate, and hear his statement,—answer he would not call it, and far less defence, as if a Roman consul could plead to the accusations of a set of vanquished Greeks,—but his statement of their offences, which had justly brought on all that they had suffered. He said that they had acted as enemies, had rejected his frequent offers of peace, and had resisted his attacks with all possible obstinacy, instead of doing as Sosis, whom they called a traitor, had done, and surrendering their city into his hands. He then left the senate-house together with the Sicilians, and went to the Capitol to carry on the enlistment of the newly raised legions.[16]

Decree of the senate. Marcellus becomes the patronus of Syracuse.

There was a strong feeling in the senate that Syracuse had been cruelly used; and old T. Manlius expressed this as became him, especially urging the unworthy return which had been made to the country of Hiero for all his fidelity to Rome. But a sense of Marcellus' signal services, and of the urgency of the times, prevailed; and a resolution was passed confirming all that he had done, but declaring that for the time to come the senate would consult the welfare of the Syracusans, and would commend them especially to the care of Lævinus. A deputation of two senators was then sent to the consul to invite him to return to the senate; the Syracusans were called in, and the decree was read. Then the Syracusan deputies threw themselves at the feet of Marcellus, imploring him to forgive all that they had said against him, to receive them under his protection, and to become the patronus of their city.[17] He gave them a gracious answer, and accepted the office; and from that time forward the Syracusans found it their best policy to extol the clemency of Marcellus; and later writers echoed their language, not knowing, or not remembering, that these expressions of forced praise were their own strongest refutation.

Severe treatment of the Campanians.

The Campanian deputation was heard with less favor; but still it was heard; and the senate took their complaint into consideration. But in this case no mercy was shown; and it was now that those severe decrees were passed, fixing the future fate of the Campanian people, which I have already mentioned by anticipation, at the end of the story of the siege of Capua.[18]

Opening of the campaign; the army of Fulvius is destroyed by Hannibal.

The military history of this year is again difficult to comprehend, owing to the omissions and incoherence in Livy's narrative. Two armies, as we have seen, were employed against Hannibal: that of Cn. Fulvius, the consul of the preceding year, in Apulia; and that of Marcellus in Samnium. Where Hannibal had passed the winter, or the end of the preceding summer, we know not; not a word being said of his movements after his ineffectual attempt upon Rhegium, till we hear of his march against Fulvius. We may suppose, however, that he had wintered in Apulia; and we are told that, Salapia having been betrayed to the Romans, and a detachment of Numidians having been cut off in it, Hannibal again retreated into Bruttium.[19] With two armies opposed to him, it was of importance not to let either of them advance to attack Tarentum and the towns on the coast, while he was engaged with the other. He was obliged therefore to abandon his garrisons in Samnium and Apulia to their own resources, and kept his army well in hand, ready to strike a blow whenever opportunity should offer. As usual, he received perfect information of the enemy's proceedings through his secret emissaries; and having earned that Fulvius was in the neighborhood of Herdonea, trying to win the

[16] Livy, XXVI. 30, 31.
[17] Livy, XXVI. 32.
[18] Above, p. 540, foll. Livy, XXVI. 33.
[19] Livy, XXVII. 1.

place, and that, relying on his distance from the Carthaginian army, he was not sufficiently on his guard, Hannibal conceived the hope of destroying this army by an unexpected attack. Again the details are given variously; but the result was, that Hannibal's attempt was completely successful. The army of Fulvius was destroyed, and the proconsul killed; and Hannibal, having set fire to Herdonea, and executed those citizens who had been in correspondence with the enemy, sent away the rest of the population into Bruttium, and himself crossed the mountains into Lucania, to look after the army of Marcellus.[20]

Marcellus adopts the policy of Fabius.

Marcellus, on the news of his colleague's defeat, left Samnium, and advanced into Lucania: his object now was to watch Hannibal closely, lest he should again resume the offensive; all attempts to recover more towns in Samnium or elsewhere must for the time be abandoned. And this service he performed with great ability and resolution, never leaving Hannibal at rest, and taking care not to fall into any ambush, but unable, notwithstanding the idle stories of his victories, to do any thing more than keep his enemy in sight, as Fabius had done in his first dictatorship. Thus the rest of the season passed away unmarked by any thing of importance: Marcellus wintered apparently at Venusia; Hannibal in his old quarters, in the warm plains near the sea.[21]

Advantages gained by the Romans out of Italy.

In spite, therefore, of the reduction of Capua, the Roman affairs in Italy had made no progress. On the contrary, another army had been totally destroyed; and the war, with all its burdens, seemed interminable. But in other quarters this year had been more successful: Lævinus had ended the war in Sicily, and the resources of that island were now at the disposal of the Romans; while the Carthaginian fleets had no point nearer than Carthage itself to carry on their operations, whether to the annoyance of the enemy's coasts, or the relief of their own garrisons at Tarentum, and along the southern coast of Italy. In addition to this, the alliance which Lævinus had concluded with the Ætolians before he quitted Epirus, had left a far easier task to his successor, P. Sulpicius, and removed all danger of Philip's co-operating with Hannibal. Meanwhile Lævinus was summoned home to hold the comitia, Marcellus being too busily employed with Hannibal to leave his army; and accordingly he crossed over directly from Lilybæum or Panormus to Ostia, accompanied by the African, Mutines, who was now to receive the reward of his desertion, in being made a citizen of Rome by a decree of the people.[22]

Alarming news from Africa.

Before his departure from Sicily, Lævinus had sent the greater part of his fleet over to Africa, partly to make plundering descents on the coast, but chiefly to collect information as to the condition and plans of the enemy. Messalla, who had succeeded to T. Otacilius in the command of the fleet, accomplished this expedition in less than a fortnight; and the information which he collected was so important, that, finding Lævinus was gone to Rome, he forwarded it to him without delay. Its substance bore, that the Carthaginians were collecting troops with great diligence, to be sent over into Spain; and that the general report was, that these soldiers were to form the army of Hasdrubal, Hannibal's brother, and were to be led by him immediately into Italy. This intelligence so alarmed the senate, that they would not detain the consul to hold the comitia, but ordered him to name a dictator for that purpose, and then to return immediately to his province.[23]

A. U. C. 545. A. C. 209. A dictator appointed to hold the comitia: Fabius and Fulvius chosen consuls.

With all the patriotism of the Romans, it was not possible that personal ambition and jealousy should be wholly extinct among them; and the influence exercised at the present crisis by Q. Fabius, and his preference of Q. Fulvius and Marcellus to all other commanders, was no doubt regarded by some as excessive and overbearing. The

[20] Livy, XXVII. 1.
[21] Livy, XXVII. 2, 4, 12-14, 20.
[22] Livy, XXVII. 5.
[23] Livy, XXVII. 5.

magistrate who presided at the comitia enjoyed so great a power over the elections, that the choice of the dictator on this occasion was of some consequence; and Lævinus intended to name the commander of his fleet, M. Messala, not without some view, possibly, to his own re-election, if the comitia were held under the auspices of a man not entirely devoted to Fabius and Fulvius. But when he declared his intention to the senate, it was objected that a person out of Italy could not be named dictator; and the consul was ordered to take the choice of the people, and to name whomsoever the people should fix upon. Indignant at this interference with his rights as consul, Lævinus refused to submit the question to the people, and forbade the prætor, L. Manlius Acidinus, to do so. This, however, availed him nothing; for the tribunes called the assembly, and the people resolved that the dictator to be named should be Q. Fulvius. Lævinus probably expected this, and, as his last resource, had left Rome secretly on the night before the decision, that he might not be compelled to go through the form of naming his rival dictator. Here was a new difficulty, for the dictator could only be named by one of the consuls: so it was necessary to apply to Marcellus; and he nominated Q. Fulvius immediately.[24] The old man left Capua forthwith, and proceeded to Rome to hold the comitia, at which the century first called gave its votes in favor of Fulvius himself and Fabius. This, no doubt, had been preconcerted: but two of the tribunes shared the feelings of Lævinus, and objected to such a monopoly of office in the hands of two or three men; they also complained of the precedent of allowing the magistrate presiding at the election to be himself elected. Fulvius, with no false modesty, or what in our notions would be real delicacy, maintained that the choice of the century was good, and justified by precedents; and at last the question was submitted by common consent to the senate. The senate determined that, under actual circumstances, it was important that the ablest men and most tried generals should be at the head of affairs; and they therefore approved of the election. Accordingly Fabius and Fulvius were once more appointed consuls; the former for the fifth time, the latter for the fourth.[25]

Plan for the campaign.

Thus was the great object gained of employing the three most tried generals of the republic, Fabius, Fulvius, and Marcellus, against Hannibal in the approaching campaign. Each was to command a full consular army, Marcellus retaining that which he now had, with the title of proconsul; and the plan of operations was, that, while Marcellus occupied Hannibal on the side of Apulia, a grand movement should be made against Tarentum and the other towns held by the enemy on the southern coast. Fabius was to attack Tarentum, while Fulvius was to reduce the garrisons still retained by Hannibal in Lucania,[26] and then to advance into Bruttium; and that band of adventurers from Sicily, which Lævinus had sent over to Rhegium to do some service in that quarter, was to attempt the siege of Caulon, or Caulonia. Every exertion was to be made to destroy Hannibal's power in the south, before his brother could arrive in Italy to effect a diversion in the north.[27] Lævinus, it seems, paid the penalty of his opposition to Fulvius' election, in being deprived of his consular army, which he was ordered to send over to Italy to be commanded by Fulvius himself; and he and the proprætor, L. Cincius, were left to defend Sicily with the old soldiers of Cannæ, and the remains of the defeated armies of the two Fulvii, the prætor and the proconsul, which had been condemned to the same banishment, together with the forces which they had themselves raised within the island, partly native Sicilians, and partly Numidians, who had come over to the Romans with Mutines.[28] With these resources, and with a fleet of seventy ships, Sicily was firmly held; and Lævinus, it is said, was able in the course of the year to send supplies of corn to Rome, and also to the army of Fabius before Tarentum.[29]

[24] Livy, XXVII. 5.
[25] Livy, XXVII. 6.
[26] Livy, XXVII. 7.
[27] Livy, XXVII. 12.
[28] Livy, XXVII. 7.
[29] Livy, XXVII. 8.

But before the consuls could take the field, a storm burst forth more threatening than any which the republic had yet experienced. The soldiers of the army defeated at Herdonea, who were now to be sent over to Sicily, were in a large proportion Latins of the colonies; and as they were to be banished for the whole length of the war, fresh soldiers were to be levied to supply their places in Italy. This new demand was the drop which made the full cup overflow. The deputies of twelve of the colonies, who were at Rome as usual to receive the consul's orders, when they were required to furnish fresh soldiers, and to raise money for their payment, replied resolutely that they had neither men nor money remaining.[30]

Twelve of the Latin colonies refuse fresh supplies.

"The Roman people," says Livy, "had at this period thirty colonies; of which number twelve thus refused to support the war any longer. The number mentioned by the historian has occasioned great perplexity; but its coincidence with the old number of the states of the Latin confederacy leaves no doubt of its genuineness; and when the maritime colonies are excepted, which stood on a different footing, as not being ordinarily bound to raise men for the regular land-service, it agrees very nearly with the list which we should draw up of all the Latin colonies mentioned to have been founded before this period. But what particular causes determined the twelve recusant colonies more than the rest to resist the commands of Rome, we cannot tell. Amongst them we find the name of Alba, which two years before had shown, such zeal in hastening to the assistance of Rome unsummoned, when Hannibal threatened its very walls; we also find some of the oldest colonies, Circeii, Ardea, Cora, Nepete, and Sutrium; Cales, which had so long been an important position during the revolt of Capua, Carseoli, Suessa, Setia, Narnia, and Interamna, on the Liris. The consuls, thunderstruck at their refusal, attempted to shame them from their purpose by rebuke. "This is not merely declining to furnish troops and money," they said; "it is open rebellion. Go home to your colonies; forget that so detestable a thought ever entered your heads; remind your fellow-citizens that they are not Campanians nor Tarentines, but Romans, Roman born, and sent from Rome to occupy lands conquered by Romans, to multiply the race of Rome's defenders. All duty owed by children to their parents, you owe to the senate and people of Rome." But in vain did Fabius and Fulvius, with all the authority of their years and their great name, speak such language to the deputies. They were coldly answered, "that it was useless to consult their countrymen at home; the colonies could not alter their resolution: for they had no men nor money left." Finding the case hopeless, the consuls summoned the senate, and reported the fatal intelligence. The courage which had not yielded to the slaughter of Cannæ, was shaken now. "At last," it was said, "the blow is struck, and Rome is lost: this example will be followed by all our colonies and allies: there is doubtless a general conspiracy amongst them to give us up bound hand and foot to Hannibal."[31]

The consuls remonstrate with them in vain.

The consuls bade the senate to take courage; the other colonies were yet true; "even these false ones will return to their duty, if we do not condescend to entreat them, but rather rebuke them for their treason." Every thing was left to the consuls' discretion: they exerted all their influence with the deputies of the other colonies privately; and having ascertained their sentiments, they then ventured to summon them officially, and to ask, "Whether their appointed contingents of men and money were forthcoming?" Then M. Sextilius of Fregellæ stood up and made answer in the name of the eighteen remaining colonies: "They are forthcoming; and if more are needed, more are at your disposal. Every order, every wish of the Roman people, we will with our best efforts fulfil: to do this we have means enough, and will more than enough." The consuls replied, "Our thanks are all too little for your desert: the whole senate must thank you themselves." They

Patriotic spirit of the other eighteen colonies; the senate resolves to take no notice of the twelve.

[30] Livy, XXVII. 9.

[31] Livy, XXVII. 9.

led the deputies into the senate-house; and thanks were voted to them in the warmest terms. Then the consuls were desired to lead them before the people, to remind the people of all the services which the colonies had rendered to them and to their fathers, services all surpassed by this last act of devotion. The thanks of the people were voted no less heartily than those of the senate. "Nor shall these eighteen colonies even now," says Livy, "lose their just glory. They were the people of Signia, of Norba, of Saticula, of Brundisium, of Fregellæ, of Luceria, of Venusia, of Hadria, of Firmum, and of Ariminum; and from the lower sea, the people of Pontia, and of Pæstum, and of Cosa; and from the midland country, the people of Beneventum, and of Æsernia, and of Spoletum, and of Placentia, and of Cremona." The aid of these eighteen colonies on that day saved the Roman empire. Satisfied now, and feeling their strength invincible, the senate forbade the consuls to take the slightest notice of the disobedient colonies; they were neither to send for them, nor to detain them, nor to dismiss them; they were to leave them wholly alone.[32]

Magnanimity of their conduct. Singular coincidence in the subsequent destinies of the house of Fulvius and of Fregellæ.

It is enough for the glory of any nation, that its history in two successive years should record two such events as the magnanimous liberality of the senate in sacrificing their wealth to their country, and the no less magnanimous firmness and wisdom of their behavior towards their colonies. An aristocracy endowed with such virtue deserved its ascendency; for its inherent faults were now shown only towards the enemies of Rome; its nobler character alone was displayed towards her citizens. But when M. Sextilius of Fregellæ was standing before Q. Fulvius, promising to serve Rome to the death, and the old consul's stern countenance was softened to admiration and joy, and his lips, which had so remorselessly doomed the Capuan senators to a bloody death, were now uttering thanks and praises to Rome's true colonists, how would each have started, could he have looked for a moment into futurity, and seen what events were to happen, before a hundred years were over! By a strange coincidence, each would have seen the selfsame hand red with the blood of his descendants, and extinguishing the country of the one and the family of the other. Within ninety years, the Roman aristocracy were to become utterly corrupted; and its leader, L. Opimius, as base personally as he was politically cruel, was to destroy Fregellæ, and treacherously in cold blood to slay an innocent youth, the last direct representative of the great Q. Fulvius, after he had slain M. Fulvius, the youth's father, in civil conflict within the walls of Rome.[33] Fregellæ, to whose citizens Rome at this time owed her safety, was within ninety years to be so utterly destroyed by the Roman arms, that at this day its very site is not certainly known: the most faithful of colonies has perished more entirely than the rebellious Capua.[34]

The sacred treasure is brought out.

Rome could rely on the fidelity of the majority of her colonies; but their very readiness made it desirable to spare them to the utmost. Therefore a treasure, which was reserved in the most sacred treasury for the extremest need, was now brought out; amounting, it is said, to four thousand pounds weight of gold; and which had been accumulating during a period of about 150 years, being the produce of the tax at five per cent. on the value of every emancipated slave, paid by the person who gave him his liberty. With this money the military chests of the principal armies were well replenished; and supplies of clothing were sent to the army in Spain, which P. Scipio was now commanding, and was on the point of leading to the conquest of New Carthage.[35]

Samnium and Lucania submit to the Romans: the Bruttians treat about submission.

At length the consuls took the field. Marcellus, according to the plan agreed upon, broke up from his quarters at Venusia, and proceeded to watch and harass Hannibal; while Fabius advanced upon Tarentum, and Fulvius marched into Lucania. Caulonia at the

[32] Livy, XXVII. 10.

[33] Velleius, II. 6, 4. II. 7, 2. Plutarch, C. Gracchus, c. xvi. Appian, B. C. I. 26.

[34] Velleius, II. 6, 4. Strabo, V. p. 363. Auctor ad Herennium, IV. 15.

[35] Livy, XXVII. 10.

same time was besieged by the band of adventurers from Sicily. The mass of forces thus employed was overwhelming; and Hannibal, while he clung to Apulia and Bruttium, was unable to retain his hold on Samnium and Lucania. Those great countries, or rather the powerful party in both, which had hitherto been in revolt from Rome, now made their submission to Q. Fulvius, and delivered up such of Hannibal's soldiers as were in garrison in any of their towns. They had apparently chosen their time well; and by submitting at the beginning of the campaign they obtained easy terms. Even Fulvius, though not inclined to show mercy to revolted allies, granted them full indemnity: the axes of his lictors were suffered this time to sleep unstained with blood. This politic mercy had its effect on the Bruttians also: some of their leading men came to the Roman camp to treat concerning the submission of their countrymen on the terms which had been granted to the Samnites and Lucanians; and the base of all Hannibal's operations, the southern coast of Italy, was in danger of being torn away from him, if he lingered any longer in Apulia.[36]

Hannibal's brilliant exploits. Tarentum is betrayed to the Romans.

Then his indomitable genius and energy appeared once more in all its brilliancy. He turned fiercely upon Marcellus, engaged him twice, and so disabled him, that Marcellus, with all his enterprise, was obliged to take refuge within the walls of Venusia, and there lay helpless during the remainder of the campaign.[37] Freed from this enemy, Hannibal flew into Bruttium: the strength of Tarentum gave him no anxiety for its immediate danger; so he hastened to deliver Caulonia. The motley band who were besieging it fled at the mere terror of his approach, and retreated to a neighboring hill; thither he pursued them, and obliged them to surrender at discretion.[38] He then marched back with speed to Tarentum, hoping to crush Fabius, as he had crushed Marcellus. He was within five miles of the city when he received intelligence that it was lost. The Bruttian commander of the garrison had betrayed it to Fabius: the Romans had entered it in arms: Carthalo, the Carthaginian commander, and Nico and Philemenus, who had opened its gates to Hannibal, had all fallen in defending it: the most important city and the best harbor in the south of Italy were in the hands of the Romans.[39]

Hannibal tries to draw Fabius into a snare, but fails.

The news of the fall of Paris, when Napoleon was hastening from Fontainebleau to deliver it, can scarcely have been a heavier disappointment to him, than the news of the loss of Tarentum was to Hannibal. Yet, always master of himself, he was neither misled by passion nor by alarm: he halted and encamped on the ground, and there remained quiet for some days, to show that his confidence in himself was unshaken by the treason of his allies. Then he retreated slowly towards Metapontum, and contrived that two of the Metapontines should go to Fabius at Tarentum, offering to surrender their town and the Carthaginian garrison, if their past revolt might be forgiven. Fabius, believing the proposal to be genuine, sent back a favorable answer, and fixed the day on which he would appear before Metapontum with his army. On that day Hannibal lay in ambush close to the road leading from Tarentum, ready to spring upon his prey. But Fabius came not: his habitual caution made him suspicious of mischief; and it was announced that the omens were threatening: the haruspex, on inspecting the sacrifice, which was offered to learn the pleasure of the gods, warned the consul to beware of hidden snares, and of the arts of the enemy. The Metapontine deputies were sent back to learn the cause of the delay; they were arrested, and, being threatened with the torture, disclosed the truth.[40]

He remains master of the field.

The remaining operations of the campaign are again unknown: the Romans, however, seem to have attempted nothing further; and Hannibal kept his army in the field, marching whither he would without op-

[36] Livy, XXVII. 15.
[37] Livy, XXVII. 12–14.
[38] Livy, XXVII. 15, 16.
[39] Livy, XXVII. 15, 16.
[40] Livy, XXVII. 16.

position, and again laying waste various parts of Italy with fire and sword.[41] So far as we can discover, he returned at the end of the season to his old winter-quarters in Apulia.

Dissatisfaction at Rome; complaints against Marcellus, who nevertheless is elected consul.

It is not wonderful that this result of a campaign, from which so much had been expected, should have caused great disappointment at Rome. However much men rejoiced in the recovery of Tarentum, they could not but feel that even this success was owing to treason; and that Hannibal's superiority to all who were opposed to him was more manifest than ever. This touched them in a most tender point; because it enabled him to continue his destructive ravages of Italy, and thus to keep up that distress which had long been felt so heavily. Above all, indignation was loud against Marcellus;[42] and if in his lifetime he indulged in that braggart language, which his son used so largely after his death, the anger of the people against him was very reasonable. If he called his defeats victories, as his son no doubt called them afterwards, and as the falsehood through him has struck deep into Roman history, well might the people be indignant at hearing that a victorious general had shut himself up all the summer within the walls of Venusia, and had allowed the enemy to ravage the country at pleasure. The feeling was so strong, that C. Publicius, one of the tribunes, a man of an old and respected tribunician family, brought in a bill to the people to deprive Marcellus of his command. Marcellus returned home to plead his cause, when Fulvius went home also to hold the comitia; and the people met to consider the bill in the Flaminian circus, without the walls, to enable Marcellus to be present; for his military command hindered his entering the city. It is likely that the influence of Fulvius was exerted strongly in his behalf; and his own statement, if he told the simple truth, left no just cause of complaint against him. He had executed his part of the compaign to the best of his ability: twice had he fought with Hannibal to hinder him from marching into Bruttium; and it was not his fault, if the fate of all other Roman generals had been his also; he had but failed to do what none had done, or could do. The people felt for the mortification of a brave man, who had served them well from youth to age, and in the worst of times had never lost courage: they not only threw out the bill, but elected Marcellus once more consul, giving him, as his colleague, his old lieutenant in Sicily, T. Quintius Crispinus, who was now prætor, and during the last year had succeeded to Fulvius in the command at Capua.[43]

A.U.C. 546. A.C. 208. Jul. Cæsar prætor.

It marks our advance in Roman history, that among the prætors of this year we find the name of Sex. Julius Cæsar; the first Cæsar who appears in the Roman Fasti.

Doubts about the fidelity of Etruria.

For some time past the Romans seem to have mistrusted the fidelity of the Etruscans; and an army of two legions had been regularly stationed in Etruria, to check any disposition to revolt. But now C. Calpurnius Piso, who commanded in Etruria, reported that the danger was becoming imminent, and he particularly named the city of Arretium as the principal seat of disaffection.[44] Why this feeling should have manifested itself at this moment, we can only conjecture. It is possible that the fame of Hasdrubal's coming may have excited the Etruscans. It is possible that Hannibal may have had some correspondence with them, and persuaded them to co-operate with his brother. But other causes may be imagined; the continued pressure of the war upon all Italy, and the probability that the defection of the twelve colonies must have compelled the Romans to increase the burdens of their other allies. If, as Niebuhr thinks,[45] the Etruscans were not in the habit of serving with the legions in the regular infantry, their contributions in money, and in seamen for the fleets,

[41] Livy, XXVII. 20. "Vagante per Italiam Hannibale."

[42] Livy, XXVII. 20.

[43] Livy, XXVII. 20, 21.

[44] Livy, XXVII. 21.

[45] See page 505.

would have been proportionably greater; and both these would fall heavily on the great Etruscan chiefs, or Lucumones, from whose vassals the seamen would be taken, as their properties would have to furnish the money. Again, in the year 544, when corn was at so enormous a price, we read of a large quantity purchased in Etruria by the Roman government for the use of their garrison in the citadel of Tarentum.[46] This corn the allied states were bound to sell at a fixed price; so that the Etruscan landowners would consider themselves greatly injured, in being forced to sell at a low price, what in the present condition of the markets was worth four or five times as much. But whatever was the cause, Marcellus was sent into Etruria, even before he came into office as consul, to observe the state of affairs, that, if necessary, he might remove the seat of war from Apulia to Etruria. The report of his mission seemed satisfactory; and it did not appear necessary to bring his army from Apulia.[47]

Yet some time afterwards, before Marcellus left Rome to take the field, the reports of the disaffection of Arretium became more serious; and C. Hostilius, who had succeeded Calpurnius in the command of the army stationed in Etruria, was ordered to lose no time in demanding hostages from the principal inhabitants. C. Terentius Varro was sent to receive them, to the number of 120, and to take them to Rome. Even this precaution was not thought sufficient; and Varro was sent back to Arretium to occupy the city with one of the home legions, while Hostilius, with his regular army, was to move up and down the country, that any attempt at insurrection might be crushed in a moment.[48] It appears also that, besides the hostages, several sons of the wealthy Etruscans were taken away to serve in the cavalry of Marcellus' army, to prevent them at any rate from being dangerous at home.[49]

Disaffection of Arretium.

The two consuls were to conduct the war against Hannibal, whilst Q. Claudius, one of the prætors, with a third army, was to hold Tarentum, and the country of the Sallentines. Fulvius with a single legion resumed his old command at Capua. Fabius returned to Rome, and from this time forward no more commanded the armies of his country, although he still in all probability directed the measures of the government.[50]

Disposition of the Roman armies. Fabius retires from military service.

Crispinus had left Rome before his colleague, and, with some reinforcements newly raised, proceeded to Lucania, to take the command of the army which had belonged to Fulvius. His ambition was to rival the glory of Fabius, by attacking another of the Greek cities on the southern coast. He fixed upon Locri, and having sent for a powerful artillery from Sicily, with a naval force to operate against the sea front of the town, commenced the siege. Hannibal's approach, however, forced him to raise it; and as Marcellus had now arrived at Venusia, he retreated thither to co-operate with his colleague. The two armies were encamped apart, about three miles from each other: two consuls, it was thought, must at any rate be able to occupy Hannibal in Apulia, while the siege of Locri was to be carried on by the fleet and artillery from Sicily, with the aid of one of the two legions commanded by the prætor Q. Claudius at Tarentum. Such was the Roman plan of campaign for the year 546, the eleventh of this memorable war.[51]

Plan of the campaign.

The two armies opposed to Hannibal must have amounted at least to 40,000 men; he could not venture to risk a battle against so large a force: but his eye was everywhere; and he was neither ignorant nor unobservant of what was going on in his rear, and of the intended march of the legion from Tarentum to carry on the siege of Locri by land. So confident was he in his superiority, that he did not hesitate to detach a force of 3000 horse and 2000 foot from his already inferior numbers, to intercept these

Hannibal destroys a legion sent to besiege Locri.

[46] Livy, XXV. 15.
[47] Livy, XXVII. 21.
[48] Livy, XXVII. 24.
[49] Livy, XXVII. 26.
[50] Livy, XXVII. 22.
[51] Livy, XXVII. 25.

troops on their way: and while the Romans marched on in confidence, supposing that Hannibal was far away in Apulia, they suddenly found their road beset; and Hannibal's dreaded cavalry broke in upon the flanks of their column. The rout was complete in an instant; the whole Roman division was destroyed or dispersed; and the fugitives, escaping over the country in all directions, fled back to Tarentum.[52] The fleet from Sicily were obliged therefore to carry on the siege of Locri as well as they could, with no other help.

Position of the two armies. Marcellus is killed in an ambush.

This signal service rendered, Hannibal's detachment returned to his camp, bringing back their numerous prisoners. Frequent skirmishes took place between the opposed armies; and Hannibal was continually hoping for some opportunity of striking a blow. A hill covered with copsewood rose between the two armies, and had been occupied hitherto by neither party; only Hannibal's light cavalry were used to lurk amongst the trees at its foot, to cut off any stragglers from the enemy's camp. The consuls, it seems, wished to remove their camp—for the two consular armies were now encamped together—to this hill; or, at any rate, to occupy it as an intrenched post, from which they might command the enemy's movement. But they resolved to reconnoitre the ground for themselves; and, accordingly, they rode forward with two hundred cavalry, and a few light-armed soldiers, leaving their troops behind in the camp, with orders to be in readiness on a signal given to advance and take possession of the hill.[53] The party ascended the hill without opposition, and rode on to the side towards the enemy, to take a view of the country in that direction. Meantime the Numidians, who had always one of their number on the lookout, to give timely notice of any thing that approached, as they were lurking under the hill, were warned by their scout, that a party of Romans were on the heights above them. No doubt he had marked the scarlet war-cloaks of the generals, and the lictors who went before them, and told his companions of the golden prize that fortune had thrown into their hands. The Numidians stole along under the hill, screened by the trees, till they got round it, between the party on the summit and the Roman camp; and then they charged up the ascent, and fell suddenly upon the astonished enemy. The whole affair was over in an instant: Marcellus was run through the body with a spear, and killed on the spot; his son and Crispinus were desperately wounded; the Etruscan horsemen, who formed the greater part of the detachment, had no inclination to fight in a service which they had been forced to enter; the Fregellans, who formed the remainder of it, were too few to do any thing; all were obliged to ride for their lives, and to leap their horses down the broken ground on the hill-sides to escape to their camp. The legions in the camp saw the skirmish, but could not come to the rescue in time. Crispinus and the young Marcellus rode in covered with blood, and followed by the scattered survivors of the party; but Marcellus, six times consul, the bravest and stoutest of soldiers, who had dedicated the spoils of the Gaulish king, slain by his own hand, to Jupiter Feretrius in the capitol, was lying dead on a nameless hill; and his arms and body were Hannibal's.[54]

The Roman army retreats. Hannibal raises the siege of Locri.

The Numidians, hardly believing what they had done, rode back to their camp to report their extraordinary achievement. Hannibal instantly put his army in motion, and occupied the fatal hill. There he found the body of Marcellus, which he is said to have looked at for some time with deep interest, but with no word or look of exultation: then he took the ring from the finger of the body, and ordered, as he had done before in the case of Flaminius and Gracchus, that it should be honorably burned, and that the ashes should be sent to Marcellus' son.[55] The Romans left their camp under cover of the night, and retreated to a position of greater security: they no longer

[52] Livy, XXVII. 26.
[53] Livy, XXVII. 26.
[54] Livy, XXVII. 27.
[55] Plutarch, Marcellus, c. 20.

thought of detaining Hannibal from Bruttium; their only hope was to escape out of his reach. Then Hannibal flew once more to the relief of Locri: the terror of the approach of his Numidian cavalry drove the Romans to their ships; all their costly artillery and engines were abandoned; and the siege of Locri, no less disastrous to the Roman naval force than to their land army, was effectually raised.[56]

During the rest of the season the field was again left free to Hannibal; and his destructive ravages were carried on, we may be sure, more widely than even in the preceding year. The army of Marcellus lay within the walls of Venusia; that of Crispinus retreated to Capua;[57] officers having been sent by the senate to take the command of each provisionally. Crispinus was desired to name a dictator for holding the comitia; and he accordingly nominated the old T. Manlius Torquatus; soon after which he died of the effect of his wounds; and the republic, for the first time on record, was deprived of both its consuls before the expiration of their office, by a violent death.[58]

He continues master of the field. The consul Crispinus dies of his wounds.

The public anxiety about the choice of new consuls was quickened in the highest degree by the arrival of an embassy from Massilia. The Massilians, true to their old friendship with Rome, made haste to acquaint their allies with the danger that was threatening them. Hasdrubal, Hannibal's brother, had suddenly appeared in the interior of Gaul; he had brought a large treasure of money with him, and was raising soldiers busily. Two Romans were sent back to Gaul with the Massilian ambassadors to ascertain the exact state of affairs; and these officers, on their return to Rome, informed the senate, that, through the connections of Massilia with some of the chiefs in the interior, they had made out that Hasdrubal had completed his levies, and was only waiting for the first melting of the snows to cross the Alps. The senate therefore must expect in the next campaign to see two sons of Hamilcar in Italy.[59]

The Massilians send tidings of Hasdrubal's being in Gaul.

Reserving the detail of the war in Spain for another place, I need only relate here as much as is necessary for understanding Hasdrubal's expedition. Early in the season of 546, while the other Carthaginian generals were in distant parts of the peninsula, Hasdrubal had been obliged with his single army to give battle to Scipio at Baccula, a place in the south of Spain, in the upper part of the valley of the Bætis; and having been defeated there, had succeeded, nevertheless, in carrying off his elephants and money, and had retreated first towards the Tagus, and then towards the western Pyrenees, whither Scipio durst not follow him, for fear of abandoning the sea-coast to the other Carthaginian generals.[60] By this movement Hasdrubal masked his projects from the view of the Romans; they did not know whether he had merely retired to recruit his army, in order to take the field against Scipio, or whether he was preparing for a march into Italy.[61] But even if Italy were his object, it was supposed that he would follow the usual route, by the eastern Pyrenees along the coast of the Mediterranean; and Scipio accordingly took the precaution of securing the passes of the mountains in this direction, on the present road between Barcelona and Perpignan;[62] perhaps also he secured those other passes more inland, leading from the three valleys which meet above Lerida into Languedoc, and to the streams which feed the Garonne. But Hasdrubal's real line of march was wholly unsuspected: for passing over the ground now so famous in our own military annals, near the highest part of the course of the Ebro, he turned the Pyrenees at their western extremity, and entered Gaul by the shores of the ocean, by the Bidassoa and the Adour.[63] Thence striking eastward, and avoiding the neighborhood of

His route out of Spain through Gaul.

56 Livy, XXVII. 28.
57 Livy, XXVII. 29.
58 Livy, XXVII. 33.
59 Livy, XXVII. 36.
60 Livy, XXVII. 18, 19. Polybius, X. 38, 39.
61 Polybius, X. 39, 7. Livy, XXVII. 20.
62 Polybius, X. 40, 11.
63 Livy, XXVII. 20.

the Mediterranean, he penetrated into the country of the Arverni; and so would cross the Rhone near Lyons, and join Hannibal's route for the first time in the plains of Dauphiné, at the very foot of the Alps. This new and remote line of march concealed him so long, even from the knowledge of the Massilians, and obliged them to seek intelligence of his movements from the chiefs of the interior.[64]

Doubts at Rome about the choice of consuls.

Now then the decisive year was come, the year of the great struggle so long delayed, but which the Carthaginians had never lost sight of, when Italy was to be assailed at once from the north and from the south by two Carthaginian armies, led by two sons of Hamilcar. And at this moment Marcellus, so long the hope of Rome, was gone; Fabius and Fulvius were enfeebled by age; Lævinus, whose services in Macedonia and Sicily had been so important, had offended the ruling party in the senate by his opposition to the appointment of Fulvius as dictator two years before; and no important command would as yet be intrusted to him. In this state of things the general voice pronounced that the best consul who could be chosen was C. Claudius Nero.[65]

A. U. C. 547. A. C. 207. C. Nero.

C. Nero came of a noble lineage, being a patrician of the Claudian house, and a great-grandson of the famous censor, Appius the blind. He had served throughout the war, as lieutenant to Marcellus in 540; as prætor and proprætor at the siege of Capua, in 542 and 543; as proprætor in Spain in 544; and lastly as lieutenant of Marcellus in 545.[66] Yet it is strange that the only mention of him personally before his consulship which has reached us, is unfavorable: he is said to have shown a want of vigor when serving under Marcellus in 540, and a want of ability in his command in Spain.[67] But these stories are, perhaps, of little authority; and if they are true, Nero must have redeemed his faults by many proofs of courage and wisdom; for his countrymen were not likely to choose the general rashly, who was to command them in the most perilous moment of the whole war; and we know that their choice was amply justified by the event.

M. Livius.

But if Nero were one consul, who was to be his colleague? It must be some one who was not a patrician, to comply with the Licinian law, and the now settled practice of the constitution. But there was no Decius living, no Curius, no Fabricius; and the glory of the great house of the Metelli had hitherto, during the second Punic war, been somewhat in eclipse, bearing the shame of that ill-advised Metellus, who dared after the rout of Cannæ to speak of abandoning Italy in despair. The brave and kindly Gracchus, the bold Flaminius, the unwearied and undaunted Marcellus, had all fallen in their country's cause. Varro was living, and had learnt wisdom by experience, and was serving the state well and faithfully; but it would be of evil omen to send him again with the last army of the commonwealth to encounter a son of Hamilcar. At last men remembered a stern and sullen old man, M. Livius, who had been consul twelve years before, and had then done good service against the Illyrians, and obtained a triumph, the last which Rome had seen;[68] but whose hard nature had made him generally odious, and who, having been accused before the people of dividing the Illyrian spoil amongst his soldiers unfairly, had been found guilty and fined.[69] The shame and the sense of wrong had so struck him—for though ungracious and unjust from temper, he was above corruption—that for some years he lived wholly in the country; and though he had since returned to Rome, and the last censors had obliged him to resume his place in the senate, yet he had never spoken there, till this very year, when the attacks made on his kinsman, the governor of Tarentum, had induced him to open his lips in

[64] Livy, XXVII. 39.

[65] Livy, XXVII. 34.

[66] Livy, XXIV. 17. XXV. 2, 3, 22. XXVI. 17. XXVII. 14.

[67] Livy, XXIV. 17. XXVII. 14.

[68] See above, p. 470.

[69] Frontinus, IV. I. 45.

his defence. He was misanthropical to all men, and especially at enmity with C. Nero: yet there were qualities in him well suited to the present need; and the senators suggested to their friends, and tribesmen, and dependents, that no better consuls could be appointed than C. Nero and M. Livius.[70]

The people might agree to choose Livius, but would he consent to be chosen? At first he refused altogether: "If he were fit to be consul, why had they condemned him? if he had been justly condemned, how could he deserve to be consul?" But the senators reproved him for this bitterness, telling him "that his country's harshness was to be borne like a parent's, and must be softened by patient submission." Overpowered, but not melted, he consented to be elected consul.

He consents reluctantly to be chosen consul;

Then the senators, and especially Q. Fabius, besought him to be reconciled to his colleague. "To what purpose?" he replied: "we shall both serve the commonwealth the better, if we feel that an enemy's eye is watching for our faults and negligences." But here again the senate's authority prevailed; and the consuls were publicly reconciled.[71] Yet the vindictive temper of Livius still burnt within him so fiercely, that, before he took the field, when Q. Fabius was urging him not to be rash in hazarding a battle, until he had well learnt the strength of his enemy, he replied, "that he would fight as soon as ever he came in sight of him;" and when Fabius asked him why he was so impatient, he answered, "Because I thirst either for the glory of a victory, or for the pleasure of seeing the defeat of my unjust countrymen."[72]

and is reconciled to Nero.

It is worth while to remark what gigantic efforts the Romans made for this great campaign. One consul was to have Cisalpine Gaul for his province, the other Lucania and Bruttium; each with the usual consular army of two legions, and an equal force of Italian allies. The army of the north was supported by two others of equal force; one, commanded by L. Porcius, one of the prætors, was to co-operate with it in the field; the other, commanded by C. Varro, was to overawe Etruria, and form a reserve. In like manner the consul of the army of the south had two similar armies at his disposal, besides his own; one in Bruttium, of which old Q. Fulvius once more took the command, and another in the neighborhood of Tarentum. Besides these twelve legions, one legion occupied Capua, and two new home legions were raised for the immediate defence of Rome. Thus fifteen legions, containing 75,000 Roman citizens, besides an equal number of Italian allies, were in arms this year for the protection of Italy. In this same year the return of the whole population of Roman citizens of an age to bear arms according to the census, amounted only to 137,108; and in addition to the forces employed in Italy, eight legions were serving abroad; two in Sicily, two in Sardinia, and four in Spain.[73]

Enormous armament of the Romans.

Soldiers were raised with a strictness never known before; insomuch that even the maritime colonies were called upon to furnish men for the legions, although ordinarily exempted from this service, on the ground that their citizens were responsible for the defence of the sea-coast in their neighborhood. Only Antium and Ostia were allowed to retain their customary exemption; and the men within the military age in both these colonies were obliged to swear that they would not sleep out of their cities more than thirty nights, so long as the enemy should be in Italy. The slaves also were again invited to enlist; and two legions were composed out of them; and after all, so perilous was the aspect of affairs in the north from the known disaffection of Etruria, and even of Umbria, that P. Scipio is said to have draughted 10,000 foot and 1000 horse from the forces of his province, and sent them by sea to reinforce the army of the north; while the prætor commanding in Sicily sent 4000 archers and slingers for

Means taken to raise troops.

[70] Livy, XXVII. 34.

[71] Livy, XXVII. 35. Valerius Maximus, IV. 3, 1. 2, 2. VII. 2, 6.

[72] Livy, XXVII. 40. Valerius Maximus, IX.

[73] Livy, XXVII. 36.

the army of the south. The lot decided that M. Livius was to be opposed to Hasdrubal, C. Nero to Hannibal.[74]

Hasdrubal crosses the Alps, and advances upon Ariminum.

Meantime Hasdrubal had begun his march from the plains between the Rhone and the Isere, and proceeded to cross the Alps by the route formerly followed by his brother. It is said that he found the obstacles of all kinds, both those presented by nature, and those offered by the hostility of the inhabitants, far less than had been experienced by Hannibal. The inhabitants were now aware that the stranger army meant them no ill; that it was merely passing through their valleys on its way to a distant land, to encounter its enemies there. Nay, it is added that traces of Hannibal's engineering were still in existence, that the roads which he had built up along the steep mountain-sides, and the bridges which he had thrown over the torrents, and the cuttings which he had made through the rocks, after having been exposed for eleven years to the fury of the avalanches, and the chafing of the swollen streams, were even now serviceable to Hasdrubal. At any rate, Hasdrubal appeared in Italy sooner than either friend or foe had expected him;[75] and having issued from the Alpine valleys, and crossed the Po, he descended along its right bank, and sat down before the Latin colony of Placentia. But the colony was one of the faithful eighteen, and did not forget its duty. It closed its gates; and Hasdrubal had no artillery to batter down its walls; he only lay before it therefore long enough for the Cisalpine Gauls and Ligurians to join him, and then pressed forward on his march by the line of the later Æmilian road, towards Ariminum and the shores of the Adriatic. The prætor L. Porcius retreated before him; and Hasdrubal sent off four Gaulish horsemen and two Numidians to his brother, to announce his approach, and to propose that they should unite their two armies in Umbria, and from thence advance by the Flaminian road straight upon Rome.[76] Livius had by this time arrived on the scene of action, and had effected his junction with L. Porcius; yet their combined forces were unable to maintain their ground on the frontier of Italy; Ariminum was abandoned to its fate; they fell back behind the Metaurus; and still keeping the coast road,—for the later branch of the Flaminian road, which ascends the valley of the Metaurus, was not yet constructed,—they encamped about fourteen miles further to the south, under the walls of the maritime colony of Sena.[77]

Nero encamps at Venusia.

On the other side of Italy, C. Nero, availing himself of the full powers with which the consuls were invested for this campaign, had incorporated the two legions, which Q. Fulvius was to have commanded in Bruttium, with his own army, leaving Fulvius at the head of a small army of reserve at Capua. With an army thus amounting to 40,000 foot and 2500 horse, Nero fixed his head-quarters at Venusia; his object being by all means to occupy Hannibal, and to hinder him from moving northwards to join his brother.[78]

Difficulties in the history of this campaign.

At no part of the history of this war do we more feel the want of a good military historian, than at the opening of this memorable campaign. What we have in Livy is absolutely worthless; it is so vague, as well as so falsified, that the truth from which it has been corrupted can scarcely be discovered. We are told that Hannibal moved later from his winter-quarters than he might have done, because he thought that his brother could not arrive in Cisalpine Gaul so early as he actually did; and we are told that he received information of his having reached Placentia.[79] Yet, after having heard this, he wastes much time in moving about in the south, first into Lucania, then to Apulia, thence falling back into Bruttium, and finally advancing again into Apulia, and there remaining idle, till the fatal blow had been struck in the north. It is added, that in the course of these movements he was several times engaged with the

[74] Livy, XXVII. 38.
[75] Livy, XXVII. 39. Appian, VII. 52.
[76] Livy, XXVII. 43.
[77] Appian, VII. 52.
[78] Livy, XXVII. 40.
[79] Livy, XXVII. 39.

Romans, and lost nearly 15,000 men, killed or taken.[80] Putting aside these absurdities, in which we cannot but recognize the perversions of Valerius Antias, or some annalist equally untrustworthy, we must endeavor as far as possible to conjecture the outline of the real story.

Hannibal's movements.

With 40,000 men under an active general opposed to him in the field, and with 20,000 more in his rear in the neighborhood of Tarentum, Hannibal could only act on the offensive by gathering all his remaining garrisons into one mass, and by raising additional soldiers, if it were possible, amongst the allies who yet adhered to him. This was to be accomplished in the face of a superior enemy, and, as Hasdrubal was already arrived on the Po, without loss of time. It was for this object apparently that he entered Lucania, to raise soldiers amongst his old partisans there; with this view he crossed back into Apulia, and then moved into Bruttium to join the new Bruttian levies, which had been collected by Hanno, the governor of Metapontum. All this he effected, baffling the pursuit of Nero, or beating off his attacks; and having amassed a force sufficient for his purpose, he again turned northwards, re-entered Apulia, advanced, followed closely by Nero, to his old quarters near Canusium, and there halted.[81] Whether he was busy in collecting corn for his further advance, or whether he was waiting for more precise intelligence from his brother, we know not; but we do not find that he moved his army beyond Canusium.

He waits for tidings from his brother.

Admitting, however, that Hannibal was aware of Hasdrubal's arrival before Placentia, we can understand why his own movements could not but be suspended, after he had collected all his disposable force together, till he should receive a fresh communication from his brother. For from Placentia Hasdrubal had a choice of roads before him; and it was impossible for Hannibal to know beforehand which he might take. But on this knowledge his own plans were to depend; if Hasdrubal crossed the Apennines into Etruria, in order to rally the disaffected Etruscans around him, Hannibal might then advance into Samnium and Campania: if, on the other hand, Hasdrubal were to move eastward towards the Adriatic, thinking it desirable that the two armies should act together, then Hannibal also would keep near the coast, and retracing the line of his own advance after the battle of Thrasymenus, would be ready to meet his brother in Picenum, or in Umbria. And it was in order to determine Hannibal's movements, that Hasdrubal, when he left Placentia, sent off the six horsemen, as has been already mentioned, to say that he was marching upon Ariminum, instead of upon Etruria, and that the two brothers were to effect their junction in Umbria.

Hasdrubal's messengers are taken prisoners, and brought to Nero.

With marvellous skill and good fortune Hasdrubal's horsemen made their way through the whole length of Italy. But Hannibal's rapid movement into Bruttium disconcerted them; they attempted to follow him thither; but mistaking their way, and getting too near to Tarentum, they fell in with some foragers of the army of Q. Claudius, and were made prisoners. The prætor instantly sent them under a strong escort to Nero. They were the bearers of a letter from Hasdrubal to his brother, containing the whole plan of their future operations; it was written, not in cipher, but in the common Carthaginian language and character; and the interpreter read its contents in Latin to the consul.[82]

Nero leaves his camp.

Nero took his resolution on the instant. He dispatched the letter to the senate, urging the immediate recall of Fulvius with his army from Capua to Rome, the calling out every Roman who could bear arms, and the marching forward the two home legions to Narnia, to defend that narrow gorge of the Flaminian road against the invader. At the same time he told the senate what he was going to do himself. He picked out 7000 men, of whom 1000 were horse, the flower of his whole army; he ordered them to hold them-

[80] Livy, XXVII. 41, 42. [81] Livy, XXVII. 42. [82] Livy, XXVII. 43.

selves in readiness for a secret expedition into Lucania, to surprise one of Hannibal's garrisons; and as soon as it was dark, he put himself at their head, leaving his lieutenant, Q. Catius, in the command of the main army, and began his march.[83]

His march was not towards Lucania. Already before he left his camp had he sent forward horsemen on the road leading to Picenum and Umbria, with the consul's orders, that all the provisions of the country should be brought down to the road-side, that all horses and draught cattle should be led thither also, and carriages for the transport of the weak and wearied soldiers. Life and death were upon his speed, the life and death of his country. His march was towards the camp of his colleague, before Sena; his hope was to crush Hasdrubal with their combined and overwhelming forces, whilst Hannibal, waiting for that letter which he would never receive, should remain still in Apulia.

and marches to join Livius.

When Nero had reached a sufficient distance from Hannibal, he disclosed the secret of his expedition to his soldiers. They felt the glory of their mission, and shared the spirit of their leader. Nor was it a little thing to witness the universal enthusiasm which everywhere welcomed their march. Men and women, the whole population of the country, crowded to the road-side; meat, drink, clothing, horses, carriages, were pressed upon the soldiers; and happy was the man from whom they would accept them. Every tongue blessed them as deliverers; incense rose on hastily built altars, where the people, kneeling as the army passed, poured forth prayers and vows to the gods for their safe and victorious return. The soldiers would scarcely receive what was offered to them: they would not halt; they ate standing in their ranks; night and day they hastened onwards, scarcely allowing themselves a brief interval of rest.[84] In six or seven days the march was accomplished: Livius had been forewarned of his colleague's approach; and, according to his wish, Nero entered the camp by night, concealing his arrival from Hasdrubal no less successfully than he had hidden his departure from Hannibal.[85]

Nero joins Livius.

The new-comers were to be received into the tents of Livius' soldiers; for any enlargement of the camp would have betrayed the secret; and they were more than seven thousand men: for their numbers had been swelled on their march; veterans who had retired from war, and youths too young to be enlisted, having pressed Nero to let them share in his enterprise. A council was held the next morning; and though Livius and L. Porcius, the prætor, urged Nero to allow his men some rest before he led them to battle, he pleaded so strongly the importance of not losing a single day, lest Hannibal should be upon their rear, that it was agreed to fight immediately. The red ensign was hoisted as soon as the council broke up; and the soldiers marched out and formed in order of battle.[86]

They determine to fight without delay.

The enemy, whose camp, according to the system of ancient warfare, was only half a mile distant from that of the Romans, marched out and formed in line to meet them. But as Hasdrubal rode forward to reconnoitre the Roman army, their increased numbers struck him; and other circumstances, it is said, having increased his suspicions, he led back his men into their camp, and sent out some horsemen to collect information. The Romans then returned to their own camp; and Hasdrubal's horsemen rode round it at a distance to see if it were larger than usual, or in the hope of picking up some stragglers. One thing alone, it is said, revealed the secret: the trumpet which gave the signal for the several duties of the day, was heard to sound as usual once in the camp of the prætor, but twice in that of Livius. This, we are told, satisfied Hasdrubal that both the consuls were before him; unable to understand

Hasdrubal retreats.

[83] Livy, XXVII. 43.
[84] Livy, XXVII. 45.
[85] Livy, XXVII. 46.
[86] Livy, XXVII. 46.

how Nero had escaped from Hannibal, and, dreading the worst, he resolved to retire to a greater distance from the enemy; and having put out all his fires, he set his army in motion as soon as night fell, and retreated towards the Metaurus.[87]

Whose narrative Livy has followed here, we cannot tell; it is not that of Polybius, except in part; and some points speak ill for the credibility of its author. According to this account, Hasdrubal marched back fourteen miles to the Metaurus: but his guides deserted him and escaped unobserved in the darkness, so that, when the army reached the Metaurus, they could not find the fords, and began to ascend the right bank of the river, in the hope of passing it easily when daylight came, and they should be arrived at a higher part of its course. But the windings of the river, it is said, delayed him: as he ascended further from the sea, he found the banks steeper and higher; and no ford was to be gained.[88]

along the banks of the Metaurus.

The Metaurus, in the last twenty miles of its course, flows through a wide valley or plain, the ground rising into heights rather than hills, while the mountains from which it has issued ascend far off in the distance, and bound the low country near the sea with a gigantic wall. But, as is frequently the case in northern Italy, the bed of the river is like a valley within a valley, being sunk down between steep cliffs, at a level much below the ordinary surface of the country; which yet would be supposed to be the bottom of the plain by those who looked only at the general landscape, and did not observe the kind of trough in which the river was winding beneath them. Yet this lower valley is of considerable width; and the river winds about in it from one side to the other, at times running just under its high banks, at other times leaving a large interval of plain between it and the boundary. The whole country, both in the lower valley and in the plain above, is now varied with all sorts of cultivation, with scattered houses and villages, and trees; an open, joyous, and habitable region, as can be found in Italy. But when Hasdrubal was retreating through it, the dark masses of uncleared wood still, no doubt, in many parts covered the face of the higher plain, overhanging the very cliffs of the lower valley; and the river below, not to be judged of by its present scanty and loitering stream, ran like the rivers of a half-cleared country, with a deep and strong body of waters.

Description of the course of the Metaurus.

These steep cliffs would, no doubt, present a serious obstacle to an army wishing to descend to the edge of the river; and if their summits were covered with wood, they would at once intercept the view, and make the march more difficult. Thus Hasdrubal was overtaken by the Romans, and obliged to fight. It is clear from Polybius that he had encamped for the night after his wearisome march; and retreat being fatal to the discipline of barbarians, the Gauls became unmanageable, and indulged so freely in drinking, that, when morning dawned, many of them were lying drunk in their quarters, utterly unable to move.[89] And now the Roman army was seen advancing in order of battle; and Hasdrubal, finding it impossible to continue his retreat, marched out of his camp to meet them.[90]

The Romans overtake Hasdrubal,

No credible authority tells us what was the amount of his army: that the Roman writers extravagantly magnified it, is certain; and that he was enormously outnumbered by his enemy is no less so. Polybius[91] says, that he deepened his lines, diminishing their width, and drawing up his whole force in a narrow space, with his ten elephants in front. We hear nothing of his cavalry, the force with which his brother had mainly won his victories; and he had probably brought scarcely any African horse from Spain: what Gaulish horsemen had joined him since he had crossed the Alps, we know

who draws up his army for battle.

87 Livy, XXVII. 47.
88 Livy, XXVII. 47.
89 Polybius, XI. 3.
90 Livy, XXVII. 48.
91 Polybius, XI. 1.

not. His Gaulish infantry, as many as were fit for action, were stationed on his left, in a position naturally so strong as to be unassailable in front; and its flank would probably be covered by the river. He himself took part with his Spanish infantry, and attacked the left wing of the Roman army, which was commanded by Livius. Nero was on the Roman right, the prætor in the centre.[92]

He is defeated and slain.

Between Hasdrubal and Livius the battle was long and obstinately disputed, the elephants being, according to Polybius, an equal aid, or rather an equal hindrance, to both parties;[93] for, galled by the missiles of the Romans, they broke sometimes into their own ranks, as well as into those of the enemy. Meanwhile Nero, seeing that he could make no progress on his front, drew off his troops out of the line, and passing round on the rear of the prætor and of Livius, fell upon the right flank and the rear of the enemy. Then the fate of the day was decided; and the Spaniards, outnumbered and surrounded, were cut to pieces in their ranks, resisting to the last. Then too, when all was lost, Hasdrubal spurred his horse into the midst of a Roman cohort, and there fell sword in hand, fighting, says Livy with honorable sympathy, as became the son of Hamilcar and brother of Hannibal.[94]

Effects of the victory.

The conquerors immediately stormed the Carthaginian camp, and there slaughtered many of the Gauls, whom they found still lying asleep in the helplessness of brute intoxication.[95] The spoil of the camp was rich, amounting in value to 300 talents: of the elephants, six were killed in the action; the other four were taken alive. All the Carthaginian citizens who had followed Hasdrubal were either killed or taken; and 3000 Roman prisoners were found in the camp, and restored to liberty. The loss of men on both sides was swelled prodigiously by the Roman writers, ambitious, it seems, of making the victory an exact compensation for the defeat of Cannæ; but Polybius[96] states it at 10,000 men on the side of the vanquished, and 2000 on that of the Romans; a decisive proof that Hasdrubal's army actually engaged cannot have been numerous, for of those in the field few can have escaped. But the amount of the slain mattered little; Hasdrubal's army was destroyed, and he himself had perished; and Hannibal was left to fight out the war with his single army, which, however unconquerable, could not conquer Italy.

Value of Hasdrubal's life.

Polybius[97] praises the heroic spirit of Hasdrubal, saying that he knew when it was time for him to die; that, having been careful of his life, so long as there was any hope of accomplishing his grand enterprise, when all was lost, he gave his country, what Pericles calls the greatest and noblest gift of a true citizen, the sacrifice of his own life. And doubtless none can blame the spirit of self-devotion to the highest known duty: Hasdrubal was true to his country in his death as in his life. Yet the life of a son of Hamilcar was to Carthage of a value beyond all estimate: Hasdrubal's death outweighed the loss of many armies; and had he deigned to survive his defeat, he might again have served his country, not only in peace as Hannibal did after his defeat at Zama, but as the leader of a fresh army of Gauls and Ligurians, of Etruscans and Umbrians, co-operating with his brother in marching upon Rome.

Hannibal receives intelligence of his brother's death.

With no less haste than he had marched from Apulia, Nero hastened back thither to rejoin his army. All was quiet there: Hannibal still lay in his camp, waiting for intelligence from Hasdrubal. He received it too soon; not from Hasdrubal, but from Nero: the Carthaginian prisoners were exhibited exultingly before his camp; two of them were set at liberty, and sent to tell him the story of their defeat; and a head was thrown down in scorn before his outposts, if his soldiers might know whose it was. They took it up, and brought to Hannibal the head of his brother.[98] He had not

92 Livy, XXVII. 48.
93 XI. 1.
94 Livy, XXVII. 49. Polybius, XI. 2.
95 Polybius, XI. 3.
96 XI. 3.
97 XI. 2.
98 Livy, XXVII. 51.

dealt so with the remains of the Roman generals: but of this Nero recked nothing; as indifferent to justice and humanity in his dealings with an enemy, as his imperial descendants showed themselves towards Rome, and all mankind.

Anxiety and joy at Rome.

Meanwhile, from the moment that Nero's march from the south had been heard of at Rome, intense anxiety possessed the whole city. Every day the senate sat from sunrise to sunset; and not a senator was absent: every day the Forum was crowded from morning till evening, as each hour might bring some great tidings; and every man wished to be among the first to hear them. A doubtful rumor arose, that a great battle had been fought, and a great victory won only two days before: two horsemen of Narnia had ridden off from the field to carry the news to their home; it had been heard and published in the camp of the reserve army, which was lying at Narnia to cover the approach to Rome. But men dared not lightly believe what they so much wished to be true; and how, they said, could a battle fought in the extremity of Umbria be heard of only two days after at Rome? Soon, however, it was known that a letter had arrived from L. Manlius Acidinus himself, who commanded the army at Narnia: the horsemen had certainly arrived there from the field of battle, and brought tidings of a glorious victory. The letter was read first in the senate, and then in the Forum from the rostra: but some still refused to believe: fugitives from a battle-field might carry idle tales of victory to hide their own shame: till the account came directly from the consuls it was rash to credit it.[99] At last word was brought that officers of high rank in the consuls' army were on their way to Rome; that they bore a dispatch from Livius and Nero. Then the whole city poured out of the walls to meet them, eager to anticipate the moment which was to confirm all their hopes. For two miles, as far as the Milvian bridge over the Tiber, the crowd formed an uninterrupted mass; and when the officers appeared, they could scarcely make their way to the city, the multitude thronging around them, and overwhelming them and their attendants with eager questions. As each man learnt the joyful answers, he made haste to tell them to others: "The enemy's army is destroyed; their general slain; our own legions and both the consuls are safe." So the crowd re-entered the city; and the three officers, all men of noble names, L. Veturius Philo, P. Licinius Varus, and Q. Metellus, still followed by the thronging multitude, at last reached the senate-house. The people pressed after them into the senate-house itself: but even at such a moment the senate forgot not its accustomed order; the crowd was forced back; and the consuls' dispatch was first read to the senators alone. Immediately afterwards the officers came out into the Forum; there L. Veturius again read the dispatch; and as its contents were short, and it told only the general result of the battle, he himself related the particulars of what he had seen and done. The interest of his hearers grew more intense with every word, till at last the whole multitude broke out into a universal cheer, and then rushed from the Forum in all directions to carry the news to their wives and children at home, or ran to the temples to pour out their gratitude to the gods. The senate ordered a thanksgiving of three days; the prætor announced it in the Forum; and for three days every temple was crowded; and the Roman wives and mothers, in their gayest dresses, took their children with them, and poured forth their thanks to all the gods for this great deliverance. It was like the burst of all nature, when a long frost suddenly breaks up, and the snow melts, and the ground resumes its natural coloring, and the streams flow freely. The Roman people seemed at last to breathe and move at liberty; confidence revived; and with it the ordinary business of life regained its activity: he who wanted money found that men were not afraid to lend it; what had been hoarded came out into circulation; land might be bought without the dread that the purchase would be rendered worthless by Hannibal's ravages; and in the joy and confidence of the

[99] Livy, XXVII. 50.

moment, men almost forgot that their great enemy with his unbroken army was still in Italy.[100]

The consuls triumph.

At the end of the year both consuls returned to Rome, and triumphed. Many years had passed since this spectacle had been exhibited in its full solemnity; for Marcellus had only obtained the smaller triumph, or ovation, in which the general passed through the streets on foot. But now the kingly chariot once more carried a Roman consul in the pomp of kingly state up to the temple of the Capitoline Jupiter; and the streets once more resounded with the shouts and rude jests of the victorious soldiers, as they moved in long array after their general. The spoil of Hasdrubal's camp was large; each soldier received a donation of three denarii and a half; and three millions of sesterces in silver, besides 80,000 pounds of the old Italian copper money, were carried into the treasury. Nero rode on horseback by the side of his colleague's chariot; a distinction made between them, partly because Livius had happened to have the command on the day of the battle, and partly because Nero had come without his army; his province still requiring its usual force, as Hannibal was there. But the favor of the multitude, if we can trust the writers under Augustus, when they speak of his adopted son's ancestor, amply compensated to Nero for this formal inferiority: they said that he was the real conqueror of Hasdrubal, while his name, even in absence, had overawed Hannibal.[101] One thing, however, is remarkable, that Nero was never employed again in a military command: we only hear of him after his consulship as censor. Fabius and Fulvius and Marcellus had been sent out year after year against Hannibal; whilst the man whose military genius eclipsed all the Roman generals hitherto engaged in Italy, was never opposed to him again. Men's eyes were turned in another direction; and the conqueror of the Metaurus was less regarded than a young man whose career of success had been as brilliant as it was uninterrupted, and who was now almost entitled to the name of conqueror of all Spain. It is time that we should trace the events of the war in the west, and describe the dawn of the glory of Scipio.

CHAPTER XLVII.

P. CORNELIUS SCIPIO—HIS OPERATIONS IN SPAIN—SIEGE AND CAPTURE OF NEW CARTHAGE—BATTLE OF BÆCULA—THE CARTHAGINIANS EVACUATE THE SPANISH PENINSULA—SCIPIO RETURNS TO ROME, AND IS ELECTED CONSUL.—A. U. C. 543 TO A. U. C. 548.

Family of the Scipios.

THREE generations of Scipios have already been distinguished in Roman history: L. Scipio Barbatus, who was actively engaged in the third Samnite war; L. Scipio, his son, who was consul early in the first Punic war, and obtained a triumph; and Publius and Cnæus Scipio, the sons of L. Scipio, who served their country ably in Spain in the second Punic war, and, as we have seen, were at last cut off there by the enemy towards the end of the siege of Capua. Publius Scipio, who was killed in Spain, left two sons behind him, Lucius and Publius: of these, Lucius, the elder, became afterwards the conqueror of king Antiochus; Publius, the younger, was the famous Scipio Africanus.

Athens abounded in writers at the time of the Peloponnesian war; but, had

[100] Livy, XXVII. 51.

[101] Livy, XXIX. 37.

Contradictory accounts of Scipio's character.

not Thucydides been one of them, how hard would it be rightly to estimate the characters of the eminent men of that period! And even Thucydides seems in one instance to have partaken of the common weaknesses of humanity: his personal gratitude and respect for Antiphon has colored, not indeed his statement of his actions, but his general estimate of his worth: he attributes an over-measure of virtue to the conspirator, who scrupled not to use assassination as a means of overthrowing the liberty and independence of his country. But Polybius, whose knowledge of Rome was that of a foreigner, and for a long time of a prisoner, could not be to Roman history what Thucydides is to that of Greece, even if in natural powers he had approached more nearly to him; and all his accounts of the Scipios are affected by his intimacy with the younger Africanus, and are derived from partial sources, the anecdotes told by the elder Lælius, or the funeral orations and traditions of the family. On the other hand, there was a large party in Rome to whom Scipio was personally and politically obnoxious, and their writers would naturally circulate stories unfavorable to him. Hence, the accounts of his early life and character are varying, and sometimes contradictory; and points, apparently the most notorious, are stated very differently, so that we know not what to believe. His friend and companion, Lælius, told Polybius,[1] that in his first battle, when only seventeen, he saved his father's life; but Cœlius Antipater said that this was a false pretension; that the consul, P. Scipio, was saved, not by his son, but by the fidelity of a Ligurian slave.[2] By his friends again Scipio is represented as one who, amid all temptations of youth and power, maintained the complete mastery over his passions:[3] while his enemies said that his youth was utterly dissolute; and that the famous story of his noble treatment of the Spanish captive maiden was invented to veil conduct which had really been of the very opposite nature.[4] His common admirers extolled his singular devotion to the gods: he delighted, it was said, to learn their pleasure, and to be guided by their counsel; nor would he ever engage in any important matter, public or private, till he had first gone up to the capitol, and entered the temple of Jupiter, and there sat for a time alone, as it seemed, in the presence of the god, and doubtless enjoying unwonted communications from his divine wisdom.[5] But Polybius, by temper and by circumstances a rationalist, is at great pains to assure his readers, that Scipio owed no part of his greatness to the gods, and that his true oracle was the clear judgment of his own mind.[6] According to him Scipio did but impose upon and laugh at the credulity of the vulgar; speaking of the favor shown him by the gods, while he knew the gods to be nothing. Livy, with a truer feeling, which taught him that a hero cannot be a hypocrite, suggests a doubt, though timidly, as if in fear of the skepticism of his age, whether the great Scipio was not really touched by some feelings of superstition,[7] whether he did not in some degree speak what he himself believed.

His religious spirit.

A mind like Scipio's, working its way under the peculiar influences of his time and country, cannot but move irregularly; it cannot but be full of contradictions. Two hundred years later, the mind of the dictator Cæsar acquiesced contentedly in Epicureanism: he retained no more of enthusiasm than was inseparable from the intensity of his intellectual power, and the fervor of his courage, even amidst his utter moral degradation. But Scipio could not be like Cæsar. His mind rose above the state of things around him; his spirit was solitary and kingly; he was cramped by living among those as his equals, whom he felt fitted to guide as from some higher sphere; and he retired at last to Liternum to breathe freely,[8] to enjoy the simplicity of childhood, since

[1] X. 3.
[2] Livy, XXI. 46.
[3] Polybius, X. 18, 19. Livy, XXVI. 49, 50.
[4] Cn. Nævius and Valerius Antias, quoted by A. Gellius, VI. 8.
[5] Polybius, X. 2, 5, 11. Livy, XXVI. 19.
[6] Polybius, X. 2, 5, 7.
[7] XXVI. 19. Sive et ipse capti quadam superstitione animi.
[8] Livy, XXXVIII. 52, 53. Valerius Maximus, V. 3, 2.

he could not fulfil his natural calling to be a hero king. So far he stood apart from his countrymen, admired, reverenced, but not loved. But he could not shake off all the influences of his time; the virtue, public and private, which still existed at Rome, the reverence paid by the wisest and best men to the religion of their fathers, were elements too congenial to his nature not to retain their hold on it; they cherished that nobleness of soul in him, and that faith in the invisible and divine, which two centuries of growing unbelief rendered almost impossible in the days of Cæsar. Yet how strange must the conflict be, when faith is combined with the highest intellectual power, and its appointed object is no better than paganism! Longing to believe, yet repelled by palpable falsehood, crossed inevitably with snatches of unbelief, in which hypocrisy is ever close at the door, it breaks out desperately, as it may seem, into the region of dreams and visions, and mysterious communings with the invisible, as if longing to find that food in its own creations, which no outward objective truth offers to it. The proportions of belief and unbelief in the human mind in such cases, no human judgment can determine: they are the wonders of history; characters inevitably misrepresented by the vulgar, and viewed even by those who in some sense have the key to them as a mystery, not fully to be comprehended, and still less explained to others. The genius which conceived the incomprehensible character of Hamlet, would alone be able to describe with intuitive truth the character of Scipio or of Cromwell.

Its effect on his life.

In both these great men, the enthusiastic element which clearly existed in them, did but inspire a resistless energy into their actions, while it in no way interfered with the calmest and keenest judgment in the choice of their means: nor in the case of Scipio did it suggest any other end of life, than such as was appreciated by ordinary human views of good. Where religion contained no revelation of new truth, it naturally left men's estimate of the end of their being exactly what it had been before, and only furnished encouragement to the pursuit of it. It so far bore the character of magic, that it applied superhuman power to the furtherance of human purposes: the gods aided man's work; they did not teach and enable him to do theirs.

Charge against him.

The charge of early dissoluteness brought against Scipio by his enemies is likely to have been exaggerated, like the stories of our Henry V. Yet the sternest and firmest manhood has sometimes followed a youth marked with many excesses of passion; and what was considered an unbecoming interruption to the cares of public business, was held to be in itself nothing blamable. That sanction of inherited custom, which at Rome at this period was the best safeguard of youthful purity, Scipio was not inclined implicitly to regard.

Comparison between his character and Hannibal's.

With all his greatness there was a waywardness in him, which seems often to accompany genius; a self-idolatry, natural enough where there is so keen a consciousness of power and of lofty designs; a self-dependence, which feels even the most sacred external relations to be unessential to its own perfection. Such is the Achilles of Homer, the highest conception of the individual hero, relying on himself, and sufficient to himself. But the same poet who conceived the character of Achilles, has also drawn that of Hector; of the truly noble, because unselfish hero, who subdues his genius to make it minister to the good of others, who lives for his relations, his friends, and his country. And as Scipio lived in himself and for himself, like Achilles, so the virtue of Hector was worthily represented in the life of his great rival Hannibal, who, from his childhood to his latest hour, in war and in peace, through glory and through obloquy, amid victories and amid disappointments, ever remembered to what purpose his father had devoted him, and withdrew no thought or desire or deed from their pledged service to his country.

Scipio had fought at Cannæ, and, after the battle, had been forward, it was said, in putting down that dangerous spirit, which showed itself among some of high birth and name, when they were purposing to abandon Italy in despair, and seek their fortune in Greece, or Egypt, or Asia.[9] His early manhood had attracted the favor of the people; and although the details are variously given, it is certain that he was made curule ædile at an early age, and with strong marks of the general good-will.[10] But he had filled no higher office than the ædileship, when his father and uncle were killed in Spain, and when C. Nero, after the fall of Capua, was sent out as proprætor to command the wreck of their army, and joining it to the force which he brought from Italy, to maintain the almost desperate cause of the Roman arms in the west.

His first office.

A. U. C. 543.

He held his ground, and even ventured, if we may believe a story overrun with improbabilities, to act on the offensive, and to penetrate into the south of Spain, as far as the Bætis.[11] The faults of the Carthaginian generals were ruining their cause, and vexing the spirit of Hasdrubal, the son of Hamilcar, who alone knew the value of the present opportunity, and was eager to make use of it. But the other Hasdrubal and Mago thought their work was done, and were only anxious to enrich themselves out of the plunder of Spain. They disgusted the Spanish chiefs by their insolence and rapacity, while they were jealous of each other, and both, as was natural, hated and dreaded the son of Hamilcar.[12] Accordingly, all concert between the Carthaginian generals was at an end; they engaged in separate enterprises in different parts of the country: Hasdrubal, the son of Gisco, and Mago, moved off to the extreme west of the peninsula, to subdue and plunder the remoter Spanish tribes; and only Hasdrubal, the son of Hamilcar, remained to oppose the Romans. Nero, therefore, whether he acted on the offensive or no, was certainly unassailed behind the Iberus; and at the end of the year 544, eighteen months at least after the defeat of the Scipios, the Roman arms had met with no fresh disaster; and the coast of the Mediterranean between the Pyrenees and the Iberus still acknowledged the Roman dominion.

A. U. C. 544. A. C. 210. War in Spain after the death of the Scipios.

It was at this period that the government resolved to increase its efforts in Spain, to employ a larger army there, and to place it under the command of an officer of higher rank than Nero, who was only proprætor. It was probable that Hasdrubal's expedition to Italy was now seriously meditated, and that the Romans, being aware of this, were anxious to detain him in Spain; but, even without this special object, the importance of the Spanish war was evident; and it was not wise to leave the Roman cause in Spain it its present precarious state, in which it was preserved only by the divisions and want of ability of the enemy's generals. Accordingly, the tribes were to meet to appoint a proconsul, who should carry out reinforcements to Spain, and, with a proprætor acting under him, take the supreme command of the Roman forces in that country.

A.U.C. 545. A. C. 209. The Romans resolve to prosecute it with more vigor.

To the surprise of the whole people, P. Scipio, then only in his twenty-seventh year, and who had filled no higher office than that of curule ædile, came forward as a candidate.[13] It is said that he had no competitors, all men being deterred from undertaking a service which seemed so unpromising; whereas Scipio himself had formed a truer judgment of the state of affairs in Spain, and felt that they might be restored, and that he himself was capable of restoring them. He expressed his confidence strongly in all his addresses to the people; and there was that in him which distinguished his boldness from a young man's idle boastings, and communicated his hope to his hearers.[14] At the same age, and nearly under the same circumstances, in which Napoleon was appointed in 1796 to take the command of the French army

Scipio is elected proconsul for the Spanish war,

[9] Livy, XXII. 53. See above, p. 502.
[10] Polybius, X. 4. Livy, XXV. 2.
[11] Livy, XXVI. 17.
[12] Polybius, IX. 11. X. 36.
[13] Livy, XXVI. 18. Polybius, X. 6.
[14] Livy, XXVI. 19. Polybius, X. 6.

of Italy, was P. Scipio chosen by the unanimous voice of the Roman people, to take the command of their army in Spain. And great as were the consequences of the appointment of Napoleon, those which followed the appointment of Scipio were greater and far more lasting.

And goes with large reinforcements to Spain.

At the same time a new propraetor was to be sent out in the room of C. Nero, whose year of command was come to an end. His successor was M. Junius Silanus,[15] who had been prætor two years before, and since that time had been employed in overawing the party disaffected to Rome in Etruria. The two new generals were to take with them large reinforcements, amounting to 10,000 foot, 1000 horse, and a fleet of thirty quinqueremes. The troops were embarked at the mouth of the Tiber; and the fleet proceeded along the coasts of Etruria, Liguria, and Gaul, till it arrived safely at Emporiæ, a Massaliot colony, lying immediately on the Spanish side of the Pyrenees. Here the soldiers were disembarked, and proceeded by land to Tarraco; the fleet followed; and the head-quarters of the proconsul were established at Tarraco for the winter, as it was too late in the season to admit of any active operations immediately.[16]

View of Spain.

And now that Spain has received that general and that army, by whom her fate was fixed through all after time,—for the expulsion of the Carthaginians from the peninsula decided its subjection to the Romans, and though the work of conquest was slow, and often interrupted, it was not the less sure,—let us for a moment survey the earliest known state of this great country; what Spain was, and who were the earliest Spaniards, before Romans, Goths, and Moors, had filled the land with stranger races, and almost extirpated the race and language of its original people.

Description of the Spanish peninsula.

The Spanish peninsula, joined to the main body of Europe by the isthmus of the Pyrenees, may be likened to one of the round bastion towers which stand out from the walls of an old fortified town, lofty at once and massy. Spain rises from the Atlantic on one side, and the Mediterranean on the other, not into one or two thin lines of mountains divided by vast tracts of valleys or low plains, but into a huge tower, as I have called it, of table-land, from which the mountains themselves rise again like the battlements on the summit. The plains of Castile are mountain plains, raised nearly 2000 feet above the level of the sea; and the elevation of the city of Madrid is nearly double that of the top of Arthur's Seat, the hill or mountain which overhangs Edinburgh. Accordingly the centre of Spain, notwithstanding its genial latitude, only partially enjoys the temperature of a southern climate; while some of the valleys of Andalusia, which lie near the sea, present the vegetation of the tropics, the palm-tree, the banana, and the sugar-cane. Thus the southern coast seemed to invite an earlier civilization; while the interior, with its bleak and arid plains, was fitted to remain for centuries the stronghold of barbarism.

Early Phœnician settlements in Spain. The Basques, a remnant of the aboriginal inhabitants.

Accordingly the first visits of the Phœnicians to Spain are placed at a very remote period. Some stories ascribed the foundation of Gades to Archelaus, the son of Phœnix—Phœnix and Cadmus being the supposed founders of Tyre and Sidon, and belonging to the earliest period of Greek tradition; while other accounts of a more historical character made the origin of Gades contemporary with the reign of the Athenian Codrus, that is, about a thousand years before the Christian era.[17] Three hundred years later, the Prophet Isaiah[18] describes the downfall of Tyre as likely to give deliverance to the land of Tarshish; that is, to the south of Spain, where the Phœnicians had established their dominion. In the time of Ezekiel, the Tyrian trade with Spain was most flourishing; and the produce of the Spanish mines, silver, iron, tin, and lead, are especially mentioned as the ar-

[15] Livy, XXVI. 19.
[16] Livy, XXVI. 19, 20.
[17] Velleius, I. II. 5.
[18] XXIII. 10.

ticles which came from Tarshish to the Phœnician ports.[19] Nor did the Phœnicians confine themselves to a few points on the sea-coast; they were spread over the whole south of Spain; and the greatest number of the towns of Turditania were still inhabited in Strabo's time by people of Phœnician origin.[20] They communicated many of the arts of life to the natives, and among the rest the early use of letters; for the characters which the Iberians used in their writing before the time of the Romans,[21] can scarcely have been any other than Phœnician. The Phœnicians visited Spain at a very remote period; but they found it already peopled. Who the aboriginal inhabitants were, and from whence they came, it is impossible to determine. The Greeks called them Iberians, and said that, although they were divided into many tribes, and spoke many various dialects, they yet all belonged to the same race.[22] It cannot be doubted that their race and language still exist; that the Basques, who inhabit the Spanish provinces of Guipuscoa, Biscay, Alava, and Navarre, and who in France occupy the country between the Adour and the Bidassoa, are the genuine descendants of the ancient Iberians. Their language bears marks of extreme antiquity; and its unlikeness to the other languages of Europe is very striking, even when compared with Welsh, or with Sclavonic. The affinities of the Welsh numerals with those of the Teutonic languages, and the Greek and Latin, are obvious at the first glance; and the same may be said of most of the Sclavonic numerals: but the Basque are so peculiar, that it is difficult to identify any one of them, except "sei," "six," with those of other languages.[23] And an evidence of its great antiquity seems furnished by the fact, that the inflexions of the nouns and verbs are manifestly so many distinct words, inasmuch as they exist in a separate form as such. We suspect this reasonably of the terminations of the nouns and verbs of Greek and Latin; but in the Basque language it can be proved beyond question.[24]

We have seen that the Phœnicians were settled amongst the Iberians in the south; and Keltic tribes were said to be mixed up with them in parts of the north and centre, forming a people, whom the Greeks called Keltiberians. How far strangers of other races were to be found in Iberia, it is difficult to decide. One or two Greek colonies from Massalia, such as Rhoda and Emporiæ, were undoubtedly planted on the shore of the Mediterranean, just within the limits of Iberia, immediately to the south of the Pyrenees.[25] These belong to the times of certain history; but stories are told of invasions of Spain, and of colonies founded on its territory, on which in their present form we can place no reliance. Carthaginian writers spoke of a great expedition of the Tyrian

Various traditions of early settlements.

[19] XXVII. 12.

[20] III. p. 149.

[21] Strabo, III. p. 139.

[22] Herodotus, in a fragment of Stephanus Byzantius, v. Ἰβηρίαι, preserved by Constantine Porphyrogenitus, and given by Berkelius: Τὸ Ἰβηρικὸν γένος—διώρισται ὀνόμασιν, ἓν γένος ἐὸν, κατὰ φῦλα.

[23] I give the Welsh from Pughe's Welsh Grammar, Denbigh, 1832; the Sclavonic (Bohemian), from Dobrowsky, Lehrgebäude der Böhmischen Sprache, Prag. 1819; the Basque from Larramendi, Arte de la Lingua Bascongada, Salamanca, 1729.

Numerals from 1 *to* 10.

	WELSH.	SCLAVONIC.	BASQUE.
One	Un	Geden	Bat
Two	Dau	Dwa	Bi
Three	Tri	Tri	Hirú
Four	Pedwar	Etyn	Lau
Five	Pump	Pět	Bost
Six	Chwech	Ssest	Sei
Seven	Saith	Sedm	Zazpi
Eight	Wyth	Osm	Zortzi
Nine	Naw	Dewět	Bederatzi
Ten	Deg	Deset	Amár.

[24] See W. Humboldt's Dissertation on the Basque Language in Adelung's Mithridates, vol. iv. p. 314–332.

[25] Strabo, III. pp. 159, 160.

Hercules into Spain, at the head of an army of Medes, Persians, Armenians, and other nations of the east.[26] Megasthenes,[27] the Greek traveller and historian of India, said that Tearco, king of Æthiopia, and Nabuchodonosor, king of the Chaldæans, had both carried their arms as far as Spain. Amongst the innumerable countries which were made the scene of the adventures of the Greek chiefs on their return from Troy, after they had been scattered by the famous storm, the coasts of Iberia, and even its coasts upon the ocean, are not forgotten.[28] Other stories, as we have seen, claimed a Greek origin for Saguntum; while others again called it a Rutulian colony, from the Tyrrheno-Pelasgian city of Ardea.[29] The settlements of the Greek chiefs on their way home from Troy are mere romances, as unreal as the famous siege of Paris by the Saracens in the days of Charlemagne, or as the various adventures and settlements of Trojan exiles, which were invented in the middle ages. Whether any real events are disguised in the stories of the expeditions of Hercules, of Tearco, and of Nabuchodonosor, is a question more difficult to answer: for the early migrations from the east to the west are buried in impenetrable obscurity. But the Persians and Æthiopians may have made their way into Spain before historical memory, as the Vandals and Arabs invaded it in later times; the fact itself is not incredible, if it rested on any credible authority.

State of agriculture in Spain.

Not knowing, then, what strange nations may at one time or other have invaded or settled in Spain, we cannot judge how much the Iberian character and manners were affected by foreign influence. Agriculture was practised from a period beyond memory: but the vine and olive, and perhaps the flax, were first introduced into the south of Spain by the Phœnicians, and only spread northwards gradually, the vine and fig advancing first, and the olive, as becomes its greater tenderness, following them more slowly and cautiously. Even in Strabo's time the vine had scarcely reached the northern coast of Spain; and the olive, when Polybius wrote, appears not to have been cultivated north of the Sierra Morena.[30] Butter supplied the place of oil to the inhabitants of the northern coast, and beer that of wine.[31]

Character of the Iberians.

In the character of the people some traits may be recognized, which even to this day mark the Spaniard. The grave dress,[32] the temperance and sobriety, the unyielding spirit, the extreme indolence, the perseverance in guerilla warfare, and the remarkable absence of the highest military qualities, ascribed by the Greek and Roman writers to the ancient Iberians, are all more or less characteristics of the Spaniards of modern times. The courtesy and gallantry of the Spaniard to women has also come down to him from his Iberian ancestors: in the eyes of the Greeks it was an argument of an imperfect civilization, that among the Iberians the bridegroom gave, instead of receiving, a dowry; that daughters sometimes inherited to the exclusion of sons, and, thus becoming the heads of the family, gave portions to their brothers, that they might be provided with suitable wives.[33] In another point, the great difference between the people of the south of Europe, and those of the Teutonic stock, was remarked also in Iberia: the Iberians were ignorant, but not simple-hearted; on the contrary, they were cunning and mischievous, with habits of robbery almost indomitable, fond of brigandage, though incapable of the great combinations of war.[34] These, in some degree, are qualities common to almost all barbarians; but they offer a strong contrast to the character of the Germans, whose words spoke what was in their hearts, and of whose most powerful tribe it is recorded, that their ascendency was maintained by no other arms than those of justice.[35]

[26] Sallust, Jugurth. c. XVIII.

[27] Quoted by Strabo, XV. 1, § 6, p. 687, and by Josephus, Antiq. X. 11, § 1, and contr. Apion. I. 20. Strabo's character of Megasthenes is not favorable: *διαφερόντως ἀπιστεῖν ἄξιον Δηϊμάχῳ τε καὶ Μεγασθένει.* II. 1, p. 70.

[28] Strabo, III. pp. 149, 150.

[29] Livy, XXI. 7. See Niebuhr, vol. i. note 127.

[30] III. p. 164.

[31] Strabo, III. p. 155. Polybius in Athenæus, I. 28.

[32] Strabo, III. p. 145, *μελανείμονες ἅπαντες.*

[33] Strabo, III. p. 165. [34] Strabo, III. p. 154.

[35] Tacitus, German. 22, 35.

Spanish soldiers had for more than two centuries formed one of the most efficient parts of the Carthaginian armies;[36] and on this account the Carthaginian government set a high value on its dominion in Spain. But this dominion furnished Carthage with money, no less than with men. The Spanish mines had been worked for some centuries; first by the Phœnicians of Asia, and latterly by their Carthaginian descendants; yet they still yielded abundantly. And some of them have been worked for two thousand years since the Carthaginians were driven out of the country; and to this hour their treasures are unexhausted.[37]

Importance of Spain to the Carthaginians.

These mines existed for the most part in the mountains which divide the streams running to the Guadiana from those which feed the Guadalquiver.[38] This is the chain so well known by the name of the Sierra Morena; but the several arms which it pushes out towards the sea eastward and southward, were also rich in precious metals; and some mines were worked in the valley of the Guadalquiver itself, as low down as Seville. The streams, moreover, which flowed from these mountains, brought down gold mingled with their sand and gravel;[39] and this was probably collected long before the working of the regular mines began. But in the time of the second Punic war the mines were worked actively; and a hundred years earlier the cinnabar, or sulphuret of quicksilver, of the famous mines of Almaden, was well known in the markets of Greece.[40] The Carthaginians honored as a hero or demi-god, the man who first discovered the most productive silver mines; and one of these was in the immediate neighborhood of New Carthage itself.[41] Others were nearer the Guadalquiver, at Castulo and Ilipa; or on the feeders of the Guadiana, as at Sisapo,[42] the ancient name of the place near to which the great quicksilver mines were worked, now known as the mines of Almaden. One large and most productive silver mine, yielding three hundred pounds daily, is said to have been opened by Hannibal himself,[43] who, while he was in Spain, had married the daughter of one of the chiefs of Castulo,[44] and perhaps had acquired some possessions through her in the mining district, as Thucydides had through his wife in Thrace.

Spanish mines.

The immense resources which the Carthaginians derived from their Spanish dominion, seemed now more than ever secured to them, by the destruction of the Roman army under the two Scipios, and the consequent retreat of the Romans behind the Iberus. But the divisions between their generals, and the arrogance with which their officers now treated the Spaniards, as if it was no longer worth while to conciliate them, had made a fatal opening, exposing their power to the most deadly blow which it had yet sustained. Scipio, with intuitive sagacity, observed this opening, and with decision no less admirable struck his blow to the heart of his enemy. He formed his plans at Tarraco during the winter; as soon as the season allowed his fleet to co-operate with him, he put it and his army in motion; and while the three Carthaginian generals were in places equally remote from one another, and from the point threatened by the enemy, Scipio crossed the Iberus, and led his land and sea forces to besiege New Carthage.[45]

Scipio's first measures in Spain.

His early and most intimate friend, C. Lælius, commanded the fleet; the proprætor, M. Silanus, was left behind the Iberus with 3000 foot and 500 horse, to protect the country of the allies of Rome, while Scipio himself led 25,000 foot and 2500 horse on his expedition. Polybius declares that the march from the Iberus to New Carthage was performed in seven days; but as, according to his own reckoning, the distance was

A. U. C. 545. A. C. 209. He marches against New Carthage.

[36] Herodotus, VII. 165.
[37] Strabo, III. 146–148.
[38] Strabo, III. p. 142.
[39] Strabo, III. p. 146.
[40] Strabo, III. p. 147.
[41] Polybius, X. 10, 11. Strabo, III. p. 148.
[42] Polybius, X. 38, 7. Strabo, III. p. 142.
[43] Pliny, XXXIII. 31.
[44] Livy, XXIV. 41.
[45] Polybius, X. 6–9. Livy, XXVI. 42.

not less than 325 Roman miles, the accuracy of one or both of his statements may well be questioned.[46] Three degrees of latitude divide Carthagena from the Ebro; and the ordinary windings and difficulties of a road in such a distance must make it all but an impossibility that an army with its baggage should have marched over it in a single week. However, the march was undoubtedly rapid; and the Roman army established itself under the walls of New Carthage, while all succor was far distant, and when the actual garrison of a place so important did not exceed a thousand men. To the protection of a force so small was committed the capital of the Carthaginian dominion in Spain, the base of their military operations, their point of communication with Africa, their treasures and magazines, and the hostages taken from the different Spanish tribes to secure their doubted fidelity.[47]

Position of New Carthage.

The present town of Carthagena stands at the head of its famous harbor, built partly on some hills of tolerable height, and partly on the low ground beneath them, with a large extent of marshy ground behind it, which is flooded after rains, and its inner port surrounded by the buildings of the arsenal, running deeply into the land on its western side. But in the times of the second Punic war, the marshy ground behind was all a lagoon, and its waters communicated artificially with those of the port of the arsenal; so that the town was on a peninsula, and was joined to the main land only by a narrow isthmus, which had itself been cut through in one place, to allow the lagoon-water to find an outlet.[48] Scipio then encamped at the head of this isthmus; and having fortified himself on the rear, with the lagoon covering his flank, he left his front open, that nothing might obstruct the free advance of his soldiers to storm the city.[49]

Scipio attacks it,

Accordingly, without delay, he was preparing to lead on his men to the assault, when he was himself assailed by Mago, who, with his scanty garrison, made a desperate sally along the isthmus against the Roman camp. After an obstinate struggle, the besieged were beaten back into the town with loss; and the Romans, following them, fixed their ladders to the walls, and began to mount. But the height of the walls was so great, that the long ladders necessary to reach their summit broke in some instances under the weight of the soldiers who crowded on them; and the enemy made their defence so good, that towards afternoon Scipio found it expedient to recall his men from the assault.[50]

and carries the walls.

He had told his men before the assault began, that the god Neptune had appeared to him in his sleep, and had promised to give him aid in the hour of need, so manifest, that all the army should acknowledge his interposition.[51] For the lagoon, it seems, was so shallow, that even the slight fall of the tide in the Mediterranean was sufficient to leave much of it uncovered, as is the case at this day in parts of the harbor of Venice. This would take place in the afternoon, and Scipio ordered five hundred men to be ready with ladders, to march across the lagoon as soon as the ebb began. Then he renewed his assault by the isthmus; and whilst this in itself discouraged the enemy, who had hoped that their work for the day was over, and whilst the soldiers again swarmed up the ladders, and the missiles of the besieged were beginning to fail, the five hundred men who were in readiness, boldly rushed across the lagoon, and, having guides to show them the hardest parts of it, reached the foot of the walls in safety, applied their ladders where there were no defenders, and mounted without opposition.[52]

No sooner had they won the walls, than they hastened to the main gate of the

[46] Polybius, X. 9, 7. III. 39, 5. XXVI. 42.
[47] Polybius, X. 8.
[48] Polybius, X. 10. Livy, XXVI. 42.
[49] Polybius, X. 11.
[50] Polybius, X. 12, 13. Livy, XXVI. 45.
[51] Polybius, X. 11. Livy, XXVI. 45.
[52] Polybius, X. 14. Livy, XXVI. 46.

city, towards the isthmus; and when they had burst it open, their comrades from without rushed in like a torrent. At the same moment the scaling parties on each side of the main gate overbore the defenders, and were now overflowing the ramparts. Mago reached the citadel in safety; but Scipio in person pushed thither with a thousand picked men; and the governor, seeing the city lost, surrendered. The other heights in the town were stormed with little difficulty; and the soldiers, according to the Roman practice, commenced a deliberate massacre of every living creature they could find, whether man or beast, till, after the citadel had surrendered, a signal from their general called them off from slaughter, and turned them loose upon the houses of the town to plunder. Yet it marks the Roman discipline, that even before night fell, order was restored. Some of the soldiers marched back to the camp, from whence the light troops were sent for to occupy one of the principal heights of the town; Scipio himself, with a thousand men, went to the citadel; and the tribunes got the soldiers out of the houses, and made them bring all their plunder into one heap in the market-place, and pass the night there quietly, waiting for the regular division of the spoil, which was to take place on the following morning.[53]

The town is taken and plundered.

When the morning came, whilst the usual distribution of the money arising from the sale of the plunder was made by the tribunes, Scipio proceeded to inspect his prisoners. All were brought before him together, to the number of nearly 10,000. He first caused them to be divided into three classes. One consisted of all the citizens of New Carthage, with their wives and families: all these Scipio set at liberty, and dismissed them to their homes unhurt. The second class contained the workmen of handicraft trades, who were either slaves, or, if free, only sojourners in the city, enjoying no political rights. These men were told, that they were now the slaves of the Roman people, but that, if they worked well and zealously in their several callings, they should have their liberty at the end of the war. Meantime they were all to enter their names with the quæstor; and a Roman citizen was set over every thirty of them as an overseer. These workmen were in all about two thousand. The third class contained all the rest of the prisoners, domestic slaves, seamen, fishermen, and the mixed populace of the city; and from these Scipio picked out the most ablebodied, and employed them in manning his fleet: for he found eighteen ships of the enemy at New Carthage; and these he was able to add to his own naval force immediately, by putting some of his own seamen into them, and filling up their places with some of the captives, taking care, however, that the number of these should never exceed a third of the whole crew. The seamen thus employed were promised their liberty at the end of the war, like the workmen, if they did their duty faithfully.[54]

Scipio's conduct to the prisoners.

The Carthaginian prisoners and the Spanish hostages were still to be attended to. The former were committed to the care of Lælius, to be taken forthwith to Rome; and there were amongst them fifteen members of the great or ordinary council of Carthage, and two members of the council of elders. The Spanish hostages were more than three hundred; and amongst them were many young boys. To show kindness to these was an obvious policy; accordingly Scipio made presents to them all, and desired them to write home to their friends, and assure them that they were well and honorably treated, and that they would all be sent back safely to their several countries, if their countrymen were willing to embrace the Roman alliance. Particular attention was shown to the wife of a Spanish chief of high rank, who had been recently seized as a hostage by Hasdrubal Gisco, because her husband had refused to comply with his demands for money. Her treatment had been rude and insolent, if not worse; but Scipio assured her that he would take as delicate care of her and of the other

His kind treatment of the Spanish hostages.

[53] Polybius, X. 15. Livy, XXVI. 46.

[54] Polybius, X. 16, 17. Livy, XXVI. 47.

Spanish women, as he would of his own sisters or daughters. This honorable bearing of the young conqueror, for Scipio was not more than twenty-seven years of age, produced a deep impression all over Spain.[55]

After this important conquest, Scipio remained for a time at New Carthage, and busied himself in exercising his soldiers and seamen, and in setting his workmen to labor in manufacturing arms.[56] He had taken a considerable artillery in the place, a large sum of money, abundant magazines of corn, and about sixty-three merchant-ships in the harbor, with their cargoes; so that, according to Livy, the least valuable part of the conquest of New Carthage was New Carthage itself.[57]

Magazines taken in the city.

Lælius with his prisoners arrived at Rome after a voyage of thirty-four days, and brought the welcome news of this great restoration of the Roman affairs in Spain.[58] Amidst the confusions of the chronology of the Spanish war, it is not easy to ascertain the exact time at which Lælius reached Rome. But it is probable that he arrived there early in the year 545, perhaps at that critical moment when the disobedience of the twelve colonies excited such great alarm, and when the destruction of the army of Cn. Fulvius at Herdonea was still fresh in men's memories. Scipio's victory was therefore doubly welcome; and his requests for supplies were favorably listened to; for his army, although victorious, was still in want of many things, the old soldiers especially, who had been ill clothed and worse paid during several years. Accordingly we find that a sum of fourteen hundred pounds' weight of gold was brought out from the treasure reserved for the most extraordinary occasions, and expended in purchasing clothing for the army in Spain.[59]

Lælius carries the news of this conquest to Rome.

Scipio himself returned from New Carthage to Tarraco, taking his Spanish hostages with him.[60] It was early in the season; but we hear of no other military action during the remainder of the year. This on Scipio's part is easily intelligible: his army was too weak to hold the field against the combined forces of the enemy; and it was his object to strengthen himself by alliances with the natives, and to draw them off from the service of Carthage, if he could not induce them to enter that of Rome. He had struck one great blow with vigor, surprising the enemy by his rapidity: but what had been won by vigor might be lost by rashness; and after so great an action as the conquest of New Carthage, he could well afford to lie quiet for the rest of the year, waiting for his supplies of clothing from Rome, and strengthening his interest amongst the chiefs of Spain. The inactivity of the Carthaginian generals would be more surprising, if we did not make allowance for the paralyzing effect of their mutual jealousies. No efficient co-operation could be contrived between them; and Hasdrubal, Hannibal's brother, was too weak to act alone, and, disgusted with the conduct of his colleagues, was probably anxious to husband his own army carefully, looking forward now more than ever to the execution of his long projected march upon Italy. Thus there was a pause from all active operations in Spain for several months; whilst in Italy Fabius had recovered Tarentum, and he and Fabius were on the point of being succeeded in the consulship by Marcellus and Crispinus.

The rest of the year passes in inaction.

The loss of Tarentum made it more important than ever that Hasdrubal should join his brother in Italy; while the growing disposition of the Spaniards to revolt to Rome rendered the prospect of success in Spain less encouraging. But with no Carthaginian accounts remaining, and amidst the confusions, omissions, and contradictions of the Roman historians, it is almost impossible to give a satisfactory explanation of the events of the ensuing year, 546, in Spain. Masinissa, then a very young man, the son

A.U.C. 546. A.C. 208. Decline of the Carthaginian influence in Spain.

55 Polybius, X. 18. Livy, XXVI. 47, 49.
56 Polybius, X. 20.
57 XXVI. 47. Polybius, X. 19.
58 Livy, XXVII. 7.
59 Livy, XXVII. 10.
60 Livy, XXVII. 17. Polybius, X. 34.

of a Numidian king, named Gala, was sent over from Africa with a large body of Numidian cavalry to reinforce Hasdrubal, the son of Hamilcar, principally, it is said, in order to his march into Italy.[61] Still Hasdrubal made no forward movement, but remained in a very strong position near a place called variously Bæcula or Bebula, situated in the upper valley of the Guadalquiver, near the mining district; and there he seemed rather disposed to await Scipio's attack, than to assume the offensive.[62] He saw that the fidelity of the Spaniards to Carthage was deeply shaken, not only by the loss of their hostages, but by the encouraging treatment which the hostages themselves had received from the Romans. This feeling had been working ever since the fall of New Carthage; and now its fruits were daily becoming more manifest; insomuch that, when the time at which Scipio was expected to take the field drew near, Mandonius and Indibilis, two of the most influential of the Spanish chiefs, retired with all their followers from Hasdrubal's camp, and established themselves in a strong position, from which they might join the Romans, as soon as their army should appear in the south.[63] On the other hand, Scipio's Roman force was strengthened, by his having laid up his fleet, and draughted the best of his seamen into the legions, to increase the number of his soldiers. And although a combined effort of the three Carthaginian generals might yet have recovered New Carthage, or at any rate kept Scipio behind the Iberus, nothing of this sort was attempted; and Hasdrubal Gisco, jealous, it seems, both personally and politically of Hannibal's brother, left him unaided to sustain the first assault of the enemy.

Hasdrubal leaves Spain.

Hasdrubal, the son of Hamilcar, therefore, under these circumstances, was doubtless anxious to carry into effect his expedition into Italy. Yet, not wishing it to be said that he had abandoned his colleagues, he resolved first to try his strength with Scipio, to see what Spanish tribes would actually join him, and whether, by offering battle in a favorable position, he could repulse the enemy, and thus break that spell of Scipio's fortune which was working so powerfully. But in this hope he was disappointed. Scipio advanced from the Iberus to the valley of the Bætis, or Guadalquiver, before Hasdrubal saw any thing of the armies of his colleagues hastening to his aid: many Spanish tribes joined the Roman army at the Iberus; Mandonius and Indibilis hastened to it as soon as it approached the place where they were posted; and Hasdrubal, unable to maintain his strong position, and, if we believe Scipio's statement, seeing it in the act of being carried by the enemy at the close of a successful assault, retreated accordingly, not towards the southern sea, nor towards the western ocean, but northwards towards the Tagus,[64] and from thence, as we have seen, towards the western Pyrenees; there recruiting his army from those tribes which had not yet come under the influence of Rome, and preparing for that great expedition to Italy, of which we have already related the progress and the event.

Increase of Scipio's influence.

Before Hasdrubal finally retreated, he had lost many prisoners. All those who were Spaniards, were sent home free without ransom by the politic conqueror; and he liberally rewarded those Spanish chiefs who had already come over to his side. They, on their part, saluted him with the title of king. The first Hasdrubal, the founder of New Carthage, had lived in kingly state amongst the Spaniards; and they probably thought that Scipio meant to do the same, and would pass the rest of his life in their country. But the name of king, although perhaps not ungrateful to Scipio's ears, was intolerable to those of his countrymen; nor would he have been contented to reign in Spain over barbarians: his mind was already turned towards Africa, and anticipated the glory of conquering Carthage. So he repressed the homage of the Spanish chiefs, and desired them to call him, not king, but general. He then

[61] Livy, XXIV. 49. XXV. 34.

[62] Polybius, X. 38. Livy, XXVII. 18. Appian, VI. 24.

[63] Polybius, X. 35. Livy, XXVII. 17.

[64] Polybius, X. 38, 39. Livy, XXVII. 17, 18. Appian, VI. 25–28.

took possession of the strong position which Hasdrubal had evacuated; and there he remained during the rest of the season, watching, so it is said, the movements of Hasdrubal Gisco, and Mago, who were now come upon the scene of action. On the approach of winter he again returned to Tarraco.[65]

Such is the account given by Polybius of the events of the war in Spain during the summer of the year 545; and such, no doubt, was the statement given by Scipio himself, and obtained by Polybius from Scipio's old friend and companion, C. Lælius. What Silenus said of these events we know not; and it is possible that Hasdrubal's account of them was never known, owing to his subsequent fate, so that Silenus may have had no peculiar information about them, and may have passed them over slightly. It is evident that Scipio's pretended victory at Bæcula was of little importance. Hasdrubal carried off all his elephants, all his treasure, and a large proportion of his infantry: he was not pursued; he retreated in the direction which best suited his future movements; and these movements he effected without the slightest interruption from the enemy. Scipio did not follow him, says Polybius,[66] because he dreaded the arrival of the other Hasdrubal and Mago: he remained in the south, therefore, to keep them in check, and to prevent them from attacking New Carthage; and not doubting that Hasdrubal would follow his brother's route, and attempt to enter Gaul by the eastern Pyrenees, he detached some troops from his army to secure the passes of the mountains, and other defensible positions between the Iberus and the frontiers of Gaul.[67] It is probable that his notions of the geography of the western parts of Spain and Gaul were so vague, that he had no conception of the possibility of Hasdrubal's marching towards the Alps without coming near the Mediterranean. The line which he actually took from the western Pyrenees to the upper part of the course of the Rhone, through the interior of Gaul, was one of which Scipio, in all probability, did not even suspect the existence.

Difficulties in the account of the campaign.

It may be asked why Hasdrubal, whose great object was to reach Italy, did not commence his march at the beginning of the year, without waiting so long at Bæcula; especially after the desertion of Mandonius and Indibilis had taught him that the Spaniards were no longer to be relied on. But he had himself on a former occasion won over the Celtiberians from the army of Scipio's father; and any reverse sustained by the Romans might tempt the Spanish chiefs to return to their old alliance. It is possible also that he waited so long at Bæcula for another reason, because he wished to carry with him as large a sum of money as possible; and he was daily drawing a supply from the abundant silver mines in the neighborhood. The success of his expedition depended on his being able to raise soldiers amongst the Cisalpine Gauls, as well as amongst the tribes of northwestern Spain; and for both these purposes ready money was most desirable.

Reasons for Hasdrubal's delay.

A more inexplicable point in the story of these transactions is the alleged discord between Hasdrubal and the other Carthaginian generals; when one of them, Mago, was his own brother, and was not only a soldier of tried ability, but is expressly said to have conducted the war in Spain in accordance with Hannibal's directions, after Hasdrubal had marched into Italy.[68] Whether Mago was placed under Hasdrubal Gisco's orders, and could not act independently, or whether jealousy, or any other cause, really made him careless of his brother's success and safety, we cannot pretend to determine: the interior of a Carthaginian camp, and still more the real characters and feelings of the Carthaginian generals, are entirely unknown to us.

Jealousies of the Carthaginian generals.

The one great advantage possessed by Scipio, far more important than his pretended victory at Bæcula, was the remarkable ascendency which he had obtained over the minds of the Spaniards. Every thing in him was at once attractive and imposing; his youth, and the

Ascendency of Scipio over the minds of the Spaniards.

[65] Polybius, XXXVIII. 40. Livy, XXVII. 19.
[66] X. 39.
[67] Polybius, X. 40.
[68] Polybius, IX. 22.

mingled beauty and majesty of his aspect; his humanity and courtesy to the Spanish hostages and to their friends; his energy and ability at the head of his army. Above all, there was manifest in him that consciousness of greatness, and that spirit, at once ardent, lofty, and profound, which naturally bows the hearts and minds of ordinary men, not to obedience only and respect, but to admiration, and almost to worship. The Carthaginian generals felt, it is said, that no Spanish troops could be trusted, if brought within the sphere of his influence; Mago must go over to the Balerian islands, and raise soldiers there, who might be strangers to the name of Scipio; while Masinissa should follow the course pursued by Mutines in Sicily, and scour the whole country with his Numidian cavalry, relieving the allies of Carthage, and harassing the states which had revolted.[69] But Masinissa himself was not secure from Scipio's ascendency: his nephew had been made prisoner at Bæcula, and had been sent back to him without ransom:[70] some conciliatory messages were probably addressed to him at the same time, and Scipio never lost sight of him, till two years afterwards he gratified the Numidian's earnest wish for a personal interview, and then attached him forever to the interests of Rome.[71]

A. U. C. 547. Hasdrubal evades Scipio, and marches into Italy.

Meanwhile that memorable year was come, when the fortune of Rome was exposed to its severest trial, and rose in the issue signally triumphant. Vainly did Scipio's guards keep vigilant watch in the passes of the eastern Pyrenees, looking out for the first signs of Hasdrubal's approach, and hoping to win the glory of driving him back defeated, and of marring his long-planned expedition to Italy. They sat on their mountain posts, looking earnestly southwards, while he for whom they waited was passing far on their rear northwards, winning his way through the deep valleys of the chain of Cebenna, or the high and bleak plains of the Arverni, till he should descend upon the Rhone, where it was as yet unknown to the Massaliot traders, flowing far inland in the heart of Gaul. Hasdrubal had accomplished his purpose: his Spanish soldiers were removed out of the reach of Scipio's ascendency; the accumulated treasures of his Spanish mines had purchased the aid of a numerous band of Gauls; and the Alps had seemed to smooth their rugged fastnesses to give him an easy passage. All the strength which Rome could gather was needed for the coming struggle; and Scipio, as we have seen, sent a large detachment from his own army, both of Roman soldiers and of Spaniards, to be conveyed by sea from Tarraco to Etruria, and to assist in conquering the enemy in Italy, whose march he had been unable to stop in Spain.

A. U. C. 547. A. C. 207. The campaign of 547 not marked by any decisive events.

Thus, with Hasdrubal's army taken away from the Carthaginian force in Spain, and with the Roman army weakened by its contributions to the defence of Italy, the Spanish war was carried on but feebly during the summer of the year 547. A new general of the name of Hanno had been sent over to take Hasdrubal's place; and he and Mago proceeded to raise soldiers amongst the Celtiberians in the interior,[72] while Hasdrubal Gisco was holding Bætica, and while Scipio was still in his winter-quarters at Tarraco. But some Celtiberian deserters informed Scipio of the danger; and he sent M. Silenus with a division of his army to put it down. A march of extreme rapidity enabled him to surprise the enemy; the best of Hanno's new levies were cut to pieces, the rest dispersed. Hanno himself was made prisoner; but Mago carried off his cavalry and his old infantry without loss, and joined Hasdrubal Gisco safely in Bætica.[73] The formation of a Carthaginian army in the centre of Spain was thus effectually prevented; and Scipio, encouraged by this success, ventured to resume the offensive, and to advance in pursuit of Hasdrubal Gisco into the south. Hasdrubal, instead of risking a general action, broke up his army into small detachments, with which he garrisoned the more important towns. Scipio

[69] Livy, XXVII. 20.
[70] Livy, XXVII. 19.
[71] Livy, XXVIII. 35.
[72] Livy, XXVIII. 1.
[73] Livy, XXVIII. Appian, VI. 31.

shrank from the tedious and difficult service of a series of sieges, in a country at a distance from his resources, and where Mago and Masinissa with their cavalry would be sure to obstruct, if not destroy, all his communications. But to avoid the discredit of retreating without having done any thing, he singled out one of the wealthiest and strongest of the towns thus garrisoned against him, by name Oringis, and sent his brother, L. Scipio, with a large division of his army to attack it. It was stormed after an obstinate resistance; and the conqueror, true to his brother's policy, after carrying off his Carthaginian prisoners in the garrison, restored the town unplundered to its Spanish inhabitants.[74] Thus much having been achieved for the honor of the Roman arms, Scipio carried back his whole army behind the Iberus, sent off L. Scipio to Rome, with Hanno and his other prisoners of distinction, and himself went into winter-quarters as usual at Tarraco.[75]

A. U. C. 548. A. C. 206. Scipio becomes anxious for a decisive action.

But before the end of the season he must have received intelligence of the battle of the Metaurus. The troops which he had sent to Italy were probably, in part at least, sent back to him; and every motive combined to make him desirous of marking the next campaign by some decisive action. Nero, whom he had succeeded in Spain, had won the greatest glory by his victory over Hasdrubal: it became Scipio to show that he too could serve his country no less effectively.

Strength and position of the two armies.

The Carthaginian general, whether he had been reinforced from Africa, or whether he had used extraordinary vigor in his levies of soldiers in western Spain, took the field early in the spring of the year 548, with an army greatly superior to that of his enemy. If Polybius, or rather Scipio may be trusted, he had 70,000 foot, 4000 horse, and thirty-two elephants; while the Roman army, with all the aids which Scipio could gather from the Spanish chiefs in the Roman alliance, did not exceed 45,000 foot, and 3000 horse.[76] Hasdrubal took up a position in the midst of the mining district, near a town which is variously called Elinga and Silpia;[77] but neither its real name nor its exact situation can be determined. His camp lay on the last hills of the mountain country, with a wide extent of open plain in front of it. He wished to fight, and if possible on this ground, favorable at once to his superior numbers, and to his elephants.

Preparations for battle.

Scipio, no less anxious to bring on a general battle, marched straight towards the enemy. But when he saw their numbers, he was uneasy lest the faith of his Spanish allies should fail, as it had towards his father; he dared not lay much stress on them; yet without them his numbers were too weak for him to risk a battle. His object therefore was to use his Spaniards for show, to impose upon the enemy, while he won the battle with his Romans. And thus, when the day came on which he proposed to fight, he suddenly changed his dispositions. For some days previously, both armies had been drawn up in order of battle before their camps; and their cavalry and light troops had skirmished in the interval between. All this time the Roman troops had formed the centre of Scipio's line, opposite to Hasdrubal's Africans, while the Spanish auxiliaries in both armies were on the wings. But on the day of the decisive battle, the Spaniards formed the centre of Scipio's army, while his Roman and Italian soldiers were on the right and left. The men had eaten their breakfast before day; and the cavalry and light troops pushed forward close under the camp of the enemy, as if challenging him to come out and meet them. Behind this cloud of skirmishes, the infantry were fast forming, and advancing to the middle of the plain; and when the sun rose, it shone upon the Roman line with its order completed; the Spaniards in the centre, the Romans and Italians on the right and left; the left commanded by M. Silanus and L. Marcius, Scipio in person leading his right.[78]

[74] Livy, XXVIII. 3.

[75] Livy, XXVIII. 4.

[76] Polybius, XL. 20. Livy, XXVIII. 12.

[77] Elinga in the MS. and old text of Polybius, has been altered into Ilipa, on the authority of Strabo; in the text of Livy the name stands Silpia.

[78] Polybius, XL. 22. Livy, XXVIII. 14.

The assault of the Roman cavalry and light troops called out Hasdrubal's army; the Carthaginians poured forth from their camp without waiting to eat, just as the Romans had done at the Trebia; their cavalry and light troops engaged the enemy; while their infantry formed in its usual order, with the Spanish auxiliaries on the wings, and the Africans in the centre. In this state the infantry on both sides remained for a time motionless; but when the day was advanced, Scipio called off his skirmishers, sent them to the rear, through the intervals of his maniples, and formed them behind his infantry on both wings; the light infantry immediately behind the regular infantry, and the cavalry covering all.

The armies engage.

For a few moments the Roman line seemed advancing evenly to meet the line of the enemy. But suddenly the troops on the right wing began to wheel round to the left, and those on the left wing wheeled to the right, changing their lines into columns; while the cavalry moved round from the rear, and took up its position on the outside of the columns; and both infantry and cavalry now advanced with the utmost fury against the enemy. Thus the centre of the Roman army was held back by the rapid advance of its wings; and the Africans in Hasdrubal's centre were standing idle, doing nothing, whilst the battle was raging on their right and left, and yet not venturing to move from their position to support their wings, because of the enemy in their front, who threatened every moment to attack, yet still advanced as slowly as possible to give time for the attacks on the two wings to complete their work. And this work was not long; Roman and Italian veterans were opposed to newly raised Spaniards; men well fed to men exhausted by their long fast; men perfect in all their movements, and handled by their general with masterly skill, to barbarians confused by evolutions which neither they nor their officers could deal with. As usual, the elephants did as much mischief to friends as to foes; and the Carthaginian wings, broken and slaughtered, began to fly. Then the Africans in the centre commenced their retreat also; slowly at first, as men who had not themselves been beaten; but the flight of their allies infected them; and the Romans pressed them so hardly, that they too rushed towards their camp with more haste than order.[79] The battle was won; and Scipio said that the camp would have been won also, had not a violent storm suddenly burst on the field of battle, and the rain fallen in such a deluge, that the Romans could not stand against it, but were obliged to seek the shelter of their own camp. Their work, however, was done; not least probably by the effect which the battle would have on the minds of the Spaniards. In the Carthaginian army, their countrymen had been exposed to defeat and slaughter, while the Africans looked on tamely, and moved neither hand nor foot to aid them; on the other hand, the Spaniards in Scipio's army had obtained a victory, with no loss to themselves; it had been purchased altogether by the blood of the Romans.

Scipio gains a complete victory.

Accordingly, the Carthaginian generals found that the contest in Spain was virtually ended. The Spanish soldiers in their army went over in large bodies to the enemy; the Spanish towns opened their gates to the Romans, and put the Carthaginian garrisons into their hands. Hasdrubal and Mago, closely followed by the enemy, retreated by the right bank of the Bætis to the shores of the ocean, and effected their escape by sea to Gades. Masinissa left them, and went home to Africa, not, it is said, without having a secret interview with M. Silanus, and settling the conditions and manner of its defection. Scipio himself returned by slow marches to Tarraco, inquiring by the way into the merits or demerits of the various native chiefs, who came crowding around him to plead their services, and to propitiate the favor of the new conqueror of Spain. Silanus, whom he had left behind in the south, to witness the final dispersion of the army of Hasdrubal, soon after rejoined him at

Destruction of the Carthaginian dominion in Spain.

79 Polybius, XI. 23, 24. Livy, XXVIII. 15, 16.

Tarraco, and reported to him that the war was over, that no enemy was to be found in the field, from the Pyrenees to the Pillars of Hercules.[80] Scipio therefore sent off his brother to Rome, to announce the completion of his work.

Scipio crosses to Africa, and negotiates with Syphax.

His own mind was already turned to another field of action: the expulsion of the Carthaginians from Spain seemed to him only to be valued as it might enable him the easier to carry the war into Africa. He had already won the support of Masinissa: but he desired to secure a more powerful ally; and accordingly he sent Lælius over to Africa, to sound the dispositions of the Masæsylian king, Syphax, the most powerful of all the African princes, and who, although at present in alliance with the Carthaginians, had been, not many years since, their enemy. Syphax told Lælius that he would negotiate only with the Roman general in person; and Scipio, relying on his own personal ascendency, and affecting in all things what was extraordinary, did not hesitate to leave his province, and to cross over from New Carthage to Africa, with only two quinqueremes, in order to visit the Masæsylian king. No less fortunate than Napoleon, when returning from Egypt to France in his solitary frigate, Scipio crossed the sea without accident, and entered the king's port in safety, with the wind so brisk and fair as to carry him into the harbor in a straight course, in a very short time after his ships had first been seen from the shore.[81] In the harbor, by the strangest of chances, were seven ships of the Carthaginians, which had just brought Hasdrubal from Spain with the very same object as Scipio, to secure the alliance of king Syphax; it having been known, probably, that a Roman officer had lately visited his court, with purposes which could not be doubtful. Hasdrubal and Scipio met under the roof of Syphax; and by his special request, they were present at the same entertainment.[82] Lælius, who had accompanied his friend to Africa, magnified the charms of his address and conversation, according to his usual practice, and told Polybius, many years afterwards, that Hasdrubal had expressed to Syphax his great admiration of Scipio's genius, which, he said, appeared to him more dangerous in peace than in war.[83] Lælius further declared that Syphax was so overcome by Scipio's influence, as to conclude a treaty of alliance with him,[84] which treaty, however, we may be very sure, was not one of those which Polybius found preserved in the capitol. It is very possible that Syphax amused Scipio with fair promises; but in reality Hasdrubal negotiated more successfully than his Roman rival; and the beauty of his daughter, Sophonisba, was more powerful over the mind of Syphax, than all the fascinations of Scipio's eloquence and manners.[85] Scipio, however, was satisfied with the success of his mission, and returned again to New Carthage.

Insurrection of the Spaniards.

It is manifest that, when Scipio and Silanus returned from the south of Spain to Tarraco, after the dispersion of the Carthaginian army, they imagined that their work was done; and they cannot have expected to be called out again to active operations in the same year. But, after Scipio's return from his voyage to Africa, we find him again taking the field in the south: we find a general revolt of the Spanish chiefs, who had so lately joined him; and what is most startling, we find his own Roman army breaking out into an alarming mutiny. Livy's explanation is, simply, that the present appeared a favorable opportunity to punish those Spanish towns which had made themselves most obnoxious to Rome in the course of the war, and on which it would not have been expedient to take vengeance earlier.[86] But surely, if any such intention had been entertained a few weeks sooner, the Roman army would never have been marched back behind the Iberus, but would have proceeded at once to attack the obnoxious towns, as soon as Hasdrubal and Mago had retired to Gades, and the

[80] Livy, XXVIII. 16.
[81] Livy, XXVIII. 17.
[82] Livy, XXVIII. 18.
[83] XI. Fragm. Mai. Livy, XXVIII. 18.
[84] Livy, XXVIII. 18.
[85] Livy, XXIX. 23.
[86] Livy, XXVIII. 19.

Carthaginian army was broken up. Either the Spaniards must have given some new provocation, which called Scipio again into the field; or some new motive must have influenced him, which hitherto he had not felt, and, outweighing all other considerations, forced him to retrace his steps to the south.

Either of these causes is sufficiently probable. Mago had by this time received instructions from Hannibal; and acting under such direction, he was not likely to abandon Spain to the Romans without another struggle. We read of a Carthaginian garrison in Castulo, which is said to have fled thither after the dispersion of Hasdrubal's army;[87] but it may also have been sent thither by Mago from Gades, to assist in organizing a new rising against the Romans. The mines were still in his hands; and he probably employed their treasures liberally. Nor were causes wanting to rouse the Spaniards, without any foreign instigation. If they had admired Scipio, they had since found that his virtues did not restrain the license of his army; the Roman soldiers had fleshed themselves with the plunder of Spain, and were likely to return after a moment's respite, and fall again upon their prey. On the other hand, the Roman army, like the Spaniards afterwards in America, may have been so eager to prosecute their conquest, and to win more of the wealth of Spain, that their general found it impossible not to gratify them; or they may have shown symptoms of license and turbulence, which made it desirable to keep them actively employed, that they might not have leisure to contrive mischief: whatever was the cause, the Roman army again marched into the south of Spain. L. Marcius was ordered to attack Castulo; Scipio himself laid siege to Illiturgi.

Probable causes of it.

Illiturgi stood on the north, or right bank of the Bætis, near to the site of the present town of Andujar, and not far therefore from Baylen, and from the scene of the almost solitary triumph of the Spanish arms in the war with Napoleon. Its people had been allies of the Carthaginians, and had revolted to Rome, when the two Scipios first advanced into the south of Spain;[88] but after their defeat and death, Illiturgi had gone back to the alliance of Carthage; and the Roman fugitives from the rout of the two Scipios, who escaped to Illiturgi, were either cut off by the inhabitants, or given up by them to the Carthaginians. Such was the Roman account of the matter; and Castulo was charged with a similar defection after the defeat of the Scipios, a defection however not aggravated, as at Illiturgi, by any particular acts of hostility.[89]

Situation and state of Illiturgi.

Vengeance was now to be taken for this alleged treason. Without any terms of peace offered or solicited on either side, the Romans prepared to attack Illiturgi, and the Spaniards with all their national obstinacy to defend it. They fought so stoutly, that the Romans were more than once repulsed; and Scipio was at last obliged to offer to lead the assault in person, and was preparing to mount the first ladder, when a general shout of his soldiers called upon him to forbear: with an overwhelming rush of numbers they crowded up the ladders in many places at once, and drove the defenders by main force from the ramparts. At the same moment, Lælius scaled the walls on the opposite side of the city; and some African deserters, who were now in the Roman service, men trained to all feats of daring activity, climbed up the almost precipitous cliff on which the citadel was built, and surprised it without resistance.[90] Then followed a horrible massacre, in which neither age nor sex was spared; and when the sword had done its work upon the people, fire was let loose upon the buildings of the city, and Illiturgi was totally destroyed.

Its capture and destruction.

Scipio then marched to Castulo to support L. Marcius, who had been able, it seems, to make no impression with the force under his separate command. But Scipio's arrival, fresh from the storming of Illiturgi, struck terror into the besieged; and the Spaniards hoped to make their

Capture of Castulo:

87 Livy, XXVIII. 20.
88 Livy, XXIII. 49.
89 Livy, XXVIII. 19.
90 Livy, XXVIII. 19, 20.

peace by surrendering, not their town only, but a Carthaginian garrison, which was engaged jointly with them in its defence. The Romans treated Castulo, says Livy, more mildly than they had treated Illiturgi; which seems to imply that even at Castulo blood was shed after the town was taken, though it did not amount to an indiscriminate massacre.[91]

Of Astapa: self-devotion of its inhabitants.

After the second conquest, Scipio left it to L. Marcius to complete the work, whether of vengeance or of ambition, by the subjugation of the other towns of Bætica, while he himself returned to New Carthage.[92] Marcius crossed the Bætis, and received the submission of some of the towns on the left bank; but the inhabitants of one place, Astapa, which had rendered itself obnoxious, by carrying on an active guerilla warfare against the Roman detached parties and communications, exhibited one of those shocking instances of desperation which testify so painfully to the miserable lot of the vanquished in ancient warfare. They erected a great pile in the middle of their city, on which they threw all their ornaments and most valuable property, and then bade their wives and children ascend it, and sit down quietly on the top. Fifty chosen men were left to keep watch beside the pile, while the rest of the citizens sallied out against the Romans, determined to fight till they were cut to pieces. They fell to a man, selling their lives dearly: in the mean while the fifty men left by the pile performed their dreadful task; they set it on fire; they butchered the women and children who were placed on it, and then threw themselves into the flames. The Roman soldiers lost their plunder, and exclaimed against the desperate ferocity of the people of Astapa.[93]

Offer to surrender Gades

After this tragedy, the neighboring towns submitted; and Marcius returned to his general at New Carthage. But he was not allowed to rest: for a secret deputation came to Scipio from Gades, offering to surrender the city to him, along with the Carthaginian fleet and garrison employed in maintaining it, and Mago their general, Hannibal's brother. Again therefore Marcius took the field with a light division of the army; and Lælius accompanied him by sea with a small squadron, to ascertain whether the offer could really be executed.[94]

Scipio's illness: mutiny in the Roman army.

It was now late in the summer; and the season, combined with the fatigue and excitement which he had undergone, brought on a serious illness upon Scipio, which rumor magnified, spreading the tidings over Spain that the great Roman general could not live. At once, it is said, the fidelity of the Spanish chiefs was shaken: Mandonius and Indibilus, who had regarded Scipio with such extreme veneration, cared nothing for the Roman people, and prepared to assert their country's independence, by driving out the Roman army.[95] But a worse mischief was threatening; a division of eight thousand Roman or Italian soldiers, who were quartered in a stationary camp on the Sucro, at once as a reserve for the army engaged in the field, and as a covering force to keep the more northern parts of Spain quiet, broke out into open mutiny; and having driven their tribunes from the camp, they conferred the command on two private soldiers, the one C. Atrius, of the allied people of the Umbrians, and the other C. Albius, of the Latin colony of Cales. It is probable that this division of Scipio's army consisted almost entirely of Latins and Italian allies; and the generals chosen accordingly represented both of these, and assumed the full state of Roman generals, causing the lictors to go before them, and to bear the rods and axes, which were the symbol of the consul's imperium, his absolute power of life and death.[96]

Its causes; Scipio's recovery.

The alleged grievance of the mutinous soldiers was, that their pay was greatly in arrears. This indeed was likely to be the case, the treasury of Rome being ill able to meet the numerous demands for the public

[91] Livy, XXVIII. 20.
[92] Livy, XXVIII. 21.
[93] Livy, XXVIII. 22, 23. Appian, VI. 33.
[94] Livy, XXVIII. 23.
[95] Livy, XXVIII. 24.
[96] Livy, XXVIII. 25.

service; and as the Spanish army had avowedly been left to its own resources as to money, it is probable that the soldiers were allowed to plunder the more freely, in order to reconcile them to their not being paid in the regular manner. Scipio himself was charged with injuring the discipline of his army by his indulgence: here, as in other things, it was in his character to rely on his own personal ascendency; and he thought that he might dispense with the constant strictness necessary to ordinary men, as he was sure that his soldiers would never be disobedient to him. But however lax his discipline was, troops at a distance from the seat of war, and quartered amongst a friendly or submissive people, must be somewhat restrained in their license of plunder; and accordingly, even before Scipio's illness, the soldiers on the Sucro complained that they were neither paid regularly as in peace, nor allowed to provide for themselves as in war. And when they heard that Scipio was at the point of death, and that the Spaniards in the north were revolting from Rome, they hoped to draw their own profit out of these troubled waters, and, following the example of the Campanians at Rhegium, to secure a city for themselves, and to live in luxury upon the plunder and the tributes of the surrounding people.[97] It is said that Mago from Gades sent them money, to prevail on them to enter into the service of Carthage, and that they took the money, but did no more than appoint their own generals, take oath of fidelity to one another, and remain in a state of open revolt from Rome.[98] They probably thought that they might establish themselves in Spain without serving any government at all; and that their own swords were more to be relied on than Mago's promises. While this was the state of affairs on the Sucro, tidings came, not of Scipio's death, but of his convalescence; and presently seven military tribunes arrived in the camp, sent by Scipio to prevent the soldiers from breaking out into any worse outrage. The tribunes affected to rejoice that matters had not been carried to any greater extremity; they acknowledged the former services of the troops, and said that Scipio was not a man to forget or leave them unrewarded; meanwhile the general would endeavor to raise money from the subject tribes of Spain, to make good their arrears of pay. Accordingly soon afterwards a proclamation appeared, inviting the soldiers to come to New Carthage to receive it.[99]

The mutineers come to New Carthage.

Scipio's recovery was felt from one end of Spain to the other; the revolted Spaniards gave up their hostile purposes, and returned quietly to their homes; and the soldiers on the Sucro, moved at once by the fear of resisting one whom the gods seemed to favor in all things, and by the hope of receiving, not only pardon for their fault, but the very pay which they demanded, resolved to march in a body to New Carthage. As they drew near to that city, the seven tribunes, who had visited their camp on the Sucro, came to meet them, gave them fair words, and mentioned, as if incidentally, that M. Silanus, with the troops at New Carthage, was to march the next morning to put down the revolt of Mandonius and Indibilis. Delighted to find that Scipio would thus be left without any force at his disposal, they entered New Carthage in high spirits: there they saw the troops all busy in preparations for their departure; and they were told that the general was rejoiced at their seasonable arrival, to supply the place of the soldiers who were going to leave him. In perfect confidence they dispersed to their quarters for the night.[100]

They are surrounded.

Thus the prey had run blindly into the snare. The seven tribunes, who met the soldiers on their march, had each been furnished with the names of five of the principal ringleaders, whom they were to secure in the course of the evening without disturbance. Accordingly they invited them to supper in their quarters, seized them all, and kept them in close custody till the next morning. But all else was quiet: the baggage of the army which was

[97] Livy, XXVIII. 24.
[98] Appian, VI. 34.
[99] Livy, XXVIII. 25.
[100] Livy, XXVIII. 26.

to take the field against the Spaniards began to move before daybreak; about dawn the columns of the troops formed in the streets, and marched out of the town. But they halted at the gates; and parties were sent round to every other gate to secure them all, and to take care that no one should leave the city. In the mean time the troops from the Sucro were summoned to the forum to meet their general; and they crowded impatiently to the place, without their arms, as was the custom of the Greek soldiers on similar occasions. No sooner were they all assembled, than the columns from the gates marched into the town, and occupied all the streets leading to the market-place. Then Scipio presented himself on his tribunal, and sat a while in silence. But as soon as he heard that the prisoners, who had been secured on the preceding evening, were brought up, the crier, with his loud clear voice, commanded silence, and Scipio arose to speak.[101]

The mutiny is quelled by the punishment of the ringleaders.

The scene had been prepared with consummate art; and its effect was overwhelming. The mutinous soldiers saw themselves completely in their general's power; they listened in breathless anxiety to his address, and with joy beyond all hope heard his concluding sentence, that he freely pardoned the multitude, and that justice would be satisfied with the punishment of those who had misled them. The instant he ceased speaking, the troops posted in the adjoining streets clashed their swords on their shields, as if they were going to attack the mutineers; and the crier's voice was again heard calling the names of the thirty-five ringleaders, one after another, to receive the punishment to which they had been condemned. They were brought forth, already stripped and bound; each was fastened to his stake; and all underwent their sentence, being first scourged, and then beheaded. When all was finished the bodies were dragged away, to be thrown out of the city; the place of execution was cleansed from the blood; and the soldiers from the Sucro heard the general and the other officers swear to grant them a free pardon with an entire amnesty for the past. They were then summoned by the crier, one by one, to appear before the general to take the usual military oath of obedience, after which each man received his full arrears of pay.[102] Never was mutiny quelled with more consummate ability; and Scipio's ascendency over his soldiers after this memorable scene was doubtless more complete than ever.

The revolted Spaniards are subdued.

The punishment of the mutineers, however, we are told, rendered the revolted Spaniards desperate. Thinking that they had already done enough to draw down Scipio's vengeance, they resolved to try the chances of war, and again took the field, and began to attack the allies of the Romans on the north of the Iberus. Scipio lost not a moment in marching in pursuit of them: he was not sorry to employ his soldiers against the enemy, as the surest means of effacing the recollection of their recent disorders; and he spoke of the Spaniards with bitter contempt, as barbarians equally powerless and faithless, on whom he was resolved to take signal vengeance. In ten days he marched from New Carthage to the Iberus; and on the fourth day after crossing the river he came in sight of the enemy. He engaged and totally defeated them, not, however, without a loss of more than four thousand men killed and wounded; and immediately after the battle the chiefs threw themselves on his mercy. He required nothing more than the immediate payment of a sum of money, which was to make good the money lately advanced or borrowed to pay the soldiers after the mutiny; and then, leaving Silanus at Tarraco, he returned to New Carthage.[103]

Scipio's interview with Masinissa.

Even yet he would not allow himself to rest. Leaving the mass of his army at New Carthage, he joined L. Marcius, his lieutenant, in the neighborhood of Gades, for the sole purpose, it is said, of gratifying Masinissa's earnest desire of a personal interview. Masinissa had returned from Africa to Gades, and was professedly consulting with Mago how one more

[101] Livy, XXVIII. 26.

[102] Polybius, XI. 30. Livy, XXVIII. 29. Appian, VI. 36.

[103] Polybius, XI. 31-33. Livy, XXVIII. 31-34.

attempt might be made to restore the Carthaginian dominion in Spain. But his mind was already made up to join the Romans; and he took the opportunity of a pretended plundering excursion with his Numidian cavalry to arrange and effect a meeting with Scipio. He too, it is said, like all other men, was overawed at once, and delighted by Scipio's personal appearance, manner, and conversation; he promised the most zealous aid to the Romans, and urged Scipio to cross over as soon as possible into Africa, where he might be able to serve him most effectually.[104] Scipio's keen discernment of character taught him the value of Masinissa's friendship; and his journey from New Carthage to Gades, in order to secure it, was abundantly rewarded afterwards; for had Masinissa fought in Hannibal's army, Scipio, in all probability, would never have won the day at Zama.

Mago evacuates Spain, and makes preparations in Minorca for invading Italy.

Mago heard of the termination of the mutiny in the Roman army, and of the defeat of the revolted Spaniards in the north; and he found that the Roman army was again returned to New Carthage, and that all hopes of making head against Rome in Spain were, for the present, at an end. Hannibal summoned him to Italy; and the Carthaginian government, acting, as it seems, cordially upon Hannibal's views, ordered him to obey his brother's call. It was not the least bold enterprise of this great war, to plan the invasion of Italy from Gades, at a time when the whole of Spain, from the Pillars of Hercules to the Pyrenees, was possessed by the enemy. But Scipio, to strengthen his land forces, had laid up the greater part of his fleet; and the exertions of the Carthaginian government, or his own, had provided Mago with a naval force, small probably in point of numbers, but consisting of excellent ships manned by skilful seamen, and capable, if ably used, of rendering essential service. He was supplied with money from Carthage; and he levied large contributions, it is said, on the people of Gades, and even emptied their treasury, and stripped their temples.[105] He then put to sea, so late in the season, that Scipio was gone back to Tarraco, and was preparing to return to Rome; and the Roman army being gone into its winter-quarters behind the Iberus, New Carthage was left to the protection of its own garrison. This encouraged Mago to attempt to surprise the place; but in this he failed: he then crossed over to the Island of Pityusa (Iviza), which was held by the Carthaginians; and having there received supplies of provisions and of men, he proceeded to attack the two Balerian islands, now called Majorca and Minorca. He was repulsed from the larger island, but made himself master of the smaller: there he landed his men, and drew up his ships, and purposed to pass the winter, the season securing him from any attack by sea, perhaps even hiding his movements altogether from the knowledge of the Romans; while he lay in readiness to catch the first return of spring, and to run over to Italy, and establish himself on the coast of Liguria, in the midst of a warlike population, furnishing the materials of a future army.[106]

Treaty with Gades. Scipio returns to Rome.

Spain was thus abandoned by the Carthaginians; and Gades, left to itself, went over to the Roman alliance, and concluded a treaty with L. Marcius, which for two centuries formed the basis of its relations with Rome.[107] He had probably been left in command at New Carthage, when Scipio returned to Tarraco. Scipio himself was known to be desirous of leaving Spain, and offering himself as a candidate for the consulship; and accordingly L. Lentulus and L. Manlius Acidius were appointed proconsuls to succeed him and M. Silanus in the command of the Roman army and province. Scipio meanwhile, accompanied by C. Lælius, returned to Rome; he could not have a triumph, because he had been neither consul nor prætor; but he entered the city with some display, with an immense treasure of silver, in money and in ingots, which he deposited in the treasury; and his name was so popular, that he was

[104] Livy, XXVIII. 35.
[105] Livy, XXVIII. 36.
[106] Livy, XXVIII. 37.
[107] Livy, XXVIII. 37. Appian, VI. 37. See Cicero pro Cornelio, c. XVII.

elected consul immediately, with an almost unanimous feeling in his favor. His colleague was P. Licinius Crassus, who at that time held the dignity of Pontifex Maximus.[108]

Prospects of the war in Italy.

Thus the war, being altogether extinguished in Spain, was reduced as it were to Italy only; and there it smoldered rather than blazed; for Hannibal with his single army could do no more than maintain his ground in Bruttium. Was it possible that Mago might kindle a fierce flame in Liguria? might blow up the half-extinguished ashes in Etruria, and reviving the fire in the south, spread the conflagration around the walls of Rome? This was not beyond possibility: but Scipio, impatient of defensive warfare, and himself the conqueror of a vast country, was eager to stop the torrent at its source, rather than raise barriers against it, when it was sweeping down the valley: he was bent on combating Hannibal, not in Italy, but in Africa.

SUPPLEMENT.

[WITH the preceding chapter the work is unfortunately terminated. From a note in the margin, that chapter appears to have been finished on the 5th of May; on the 12th of June the author breathed his last. Two more chapters at least would have been requisite to bring the history down to the end of the Second Punic War; for the heading of the forty-eighth chapter shows what it was intended to contain:—Last years of the war in Italy—Consulship of P. Scipio—Scipio in Sicily—Siege of Locri—Scipio in Africa—His victories over Hasdrubal Gisco and Syphax—The Carthaginians recall Hannibal and Mago from Italy—A. U. C. 548 to A. U. C. 551.

Every reader of the foregoing narrative of one of the most interesting and eventful periods in ancient history, must regret that the author was not allowed to carry it on to the close of the war. As the best substitute for that which we should have had, the following account of the last years of the war, written by Dr. Arnold in the year 1823, for the life of Hannibal in the Encyclopædia Metropolitana, is here inserted.]

Adventures and death of Mago.

The defeat and destruction of Hasdrubal's army reduced Hannibal to the necessity of acting entirely on the defensive. It had been for some time evident, that his single army could not overthrow the supremacy of Rome in Italy. Still, while the fate of the war was balanced in Spain and Sicily, and while he was looking forward to the arrival of his brother to co-operate with him, he might be justified in making himself as troublesome as possible to the enemy, even though by so doing he might sometimes incur the danger of some loss. But now his policy was altered: to maintain his ground in Italy, till another effort could be made by his government to support him, was become his most important duty. He was obliged to abandon several towns which had revolted to him from the Romans; and he forced the inhabitants of others to desert their homes, and to retire with him into the remotest part of Bruttium. The superiority of his personal character was so great, that the Romans never dared to attack him; and thus he might repose for a while, watching the first favorable opportunity of issuing from his retreat, and attempting once more to accomplish the design with which he had originally invaded Italy. The death of Hasdrubal had not extinguished all his hopes. Mago, after the total wreck of the

108 Livy, XXVIII. 38.

Carthaginian interest in Spain, was ordered, as we have seen, to attempt a diversion in Italy, and transporting a small force with him by sea, landed in Liguria, and surprised the town of Genoa.[1] The name of his family urged the Gauls and Ligurians to flock to his standard; and his growing strength excited much alarm among the Romans, and obliged them to keep a large army in the north of Italy to watch his movements. The details of his adventures are unknown; nor are we informed what cause prevented him from attempting to penetrate into Tuscany. We only find that he became so formidable an enemy as to maintain an obstinate contest against an army of four Roman legions, a few weeks before the final evacuation of Italy by Hannibal; nor were the Romans certain of victory, till Mago was mortally wounded, and obliged to leave the field. From the scene of this battle, which is said to have been in the country of the Insubrian Gauls, he retreated with as much expedition as his wound would allow, to the coast of Liguria; and there he found orders from Carthage that he should immediately return to Africa, to oppose the alarming progress of P. Scipio. He accordingly embarked with his troops, and commenced his voyage homewards: but his exertions and anxiety of mind had proved too great for his strength; and he had scarcely passed the coast of Sardinia, when he expired. So unwearied was the zeal, and so great the ability, with which the sons of Hamilcar maintained the cause of their country, almost solely by their personal efforts, against the overbearing resources and energy of the Roman people.

When the Carthaginian government sent for Mago from Italy, they also recalled Hannibal. The account of his operations during the three or four years that preceded his return to Africa is peculiarly unsatisfactory. The Roman writers have transmitted some reports of victories obtained over him in Italy, too audacious in falsehood for even themselves to have believed. But, in truth, the terror with which he continued to inspire his enemies, after his career of success was closed, is even more wonderful than his first brilliant triumphs. For four years after the death of Hasdrubal, he remained in undisputed possession of Bruttium, when the Romans had reconquered all the rest of Italy. Here he maintained his army, without receiving any supplies from home, and with no other naval force at his disposal, than such vessels as he could build from the Bruttium forests, and man with the sailors of the country. Here too he seems to have looked forward to the renown which awaited him in aftertimes; and as if foreseeing the interest with which posterity would follow his progress in his unequalled enterprise, he recorded many minute particulars of his campaigns on monumental columns, erected at Lacinium,[2] a town situated in that corner of Italy, which was so long like a new country acquired by conquest, for himself and his soldiers. At length, when it was plain that no new diversion could be effected in his favor, and when the dangerous situation of his country called for his presence, as the last hope of Carthage, he embarked his troops without the slightest interruption from the Romans; and moved only by the disasters of others, while his own army was unbroken and unbeaten, he abandoned Italy fifteen years after he had first entered it, having ravaged it with fire and sword from one extremity to the other, and having never seen his numerous victories checkered by a single defeat.

Hannibal evacuates Italy.

Scipio, meanwhile, after his important services in Spain, had returned to Rome, and been elected consul, hoping to carry into execution the design which he had for some time conceived, of forcing Hannibal to leave Italy, by attacking the Carthaginians in Africa. But according to the invariable policy of Rome, he was desirous of securing the aid of some ally in the country which he was going to make the seat of war. For this end, as we have seen, he had already opened a communication with Syphax, the most considerable of the Numidian princes, and, according to Livy, had actually concluded a treaty with him. But Syphax was won over to the interests of Carthage by

A. U. C. 550. A. C. 204. Scipio carries the war into Africa.

[1] Livy, XXVIII. 46. XXX. 18.

[2] Polybius, III. 33, 56.

the charms of Sophonisba, the daughter of Hasdrubal Gisco; and a short time before Scipio crossed over into Africa, he sent to inform him of his new connection, and to dissuade him from his intended expedition, as he should now be obliged to join the Carthaginians in opposing him. Scipio, however, was not yet without the prospect of finding allies in Africa. Masinissa had deserted the Carthaginian cause after its disasters in Spain, and had privately pledged himself to support the Romans on the first opportunity. Since that time he had been deprived of his paternal dominions by the united efforts of Syphax and the Carthaginians; but though his power was thus reduced, his zeal in the cause of Rome was likely to be the more heightened; and as his personal character was high among his countrymen, many of them might be expected to join him, when they saw him supported by a Roman army. Accordingly, he united himself[3] to Scipio so soon as he had landed in Africa; and his activity, and perfect familiarity with the country and its inhabitants, made him a very valuable auxiliary. The landing had been effected within a few miles of Carthage itself; and after some plunder, amongst which eight thousand prisoners to be sold for slaves are particularly specified, had been collected from the adjoining country, the army formed the siege of Utica, whilst a considerable fleet co-operated with it on the side of the sea. But the approach of Hasdrubal Gisco and Syphax, at the head of two immense armies of Carthaginians and Numidians, induced Scipio to raise the siege, and to remove his troops to a strong position near the sea, where he proposed to remain, as winter was fast approaching, and secure of subsistence, through the co-operation of his fleet, to wait for some favorable opportunity of striking a vigorous blow.

He destroys the Carthaginian and Numidian army.

His first hope was[4] to win over Syphax again to the Roman cause; and with this view his emissaries were continually going and returning between the Roman and Numidian camps. Their temptations to Syphax were ineffectual: but their report of the manner in which the Carthaginian and Numidian armies were quartered, suggested to Scipio the possibility of insuring success by other means than negotiation. They related, that the Carthaginians were lodged in huts constructed of stakes or hurdles, and covered with leaves, and that the Numidian quarters were composed of similar materials, of reeds, thatch, and dried leaves. Upon this intelligence Scipio conceived the plan of setting fire to both the camps of the enemy. In order to gain a more perfect knowledge of their situation, and the approaches to them, he pretended to listen to the terms of peace which Syphax had before proposed to him in vain. Under pretence of negotiation, he was for some months in constant correspondence with the Numidian king; and disguising some of his most intelligent soldiers in the dress of slaves, he procured them an easy entrance into the enemy's camp, as forming part of the suite of the officers employed in the negotiation. At last, when the season for military operations was returning, and his seemingly sincere desire of peace had thrown the enemy into a state of perfect security, he suddenly broke off all communication with them, declaring that, however disposed he himself was to agree to the proposed terms, the other members of the military council were fixed on rejecting them. This sudden rupture disappointed Syphax; but neither he nor the Carthaginian general had any suspicion of Scipio's real designs; when suddenly the Roman army marched out by night in two divisions, the one commanded by Scipio, and the other by Lælius, his second in command, and advanced against the camps of the enemy, which were not more than six miles from their own. Lælius, assisted by Masinissa, first silently approached the encampment of the Numidians, and set fire to the first tents that he met with. The flames spread so rapidly, that the Numidians were soon precluded from approaching the quarter where they had first broken out, and thus, having no suspicion that they had been kindled by the enemy, crowded

[3] Livy, XXIX. 29.

[4] Polybius, XIV. 1, &c.

together in the utmost disorder to effect their escape out of the camp. Numbers were trampled to death in the confusion at the several outlets; numbers were overtaken by the flames and burnt to death; and the rest, on reaching the open country, found themselves intercepted by Masinissa, who had posted his troops in the quarter to which he knew that the fugitives were most likely to direct their flight. In this manner the whole Numidian army, amounting to sixty thousand men, was completely destroyed or dispersed, with the exception of Syphax himself and a few horsemen.

Meanwhile the Carthaginians, when they first saw the camp of their allies on fire, not doubting that it was occasioned by accident, began partly to run with assistance to the Numidians, and the rest rushed hastily out of their tents, without their arms, and stood on the outside of the camp, contemplating the progress of this fearful conflagration with dismay. In this helpless state they found themselves attacked by the enemy, under the command of Scipio in person: some were instantly cut down; and the rest, driven back into their camp, saw it set on fire by their pursuers. They then understood the whole extent of the calamity which had befallen their allies and themselves; but resistance and flight were alike impracticable; the fire spread with fury to every quarter; and every avenue was choked up by a struggling crowd of men and horses, all striving with the same distracted efforts to effect their escape. In this attempt, Hasdrubal and a few followers alone succeeded; thirty thousand men, who had composed the Carthaginian army, perished. The annals of war contain no bloodier tragedy.

He gains another victory.

Hasdrubal, hopeless of delaying the progress of the enemy, continued his flight to Carthage; while Syphax had retreated into the opposite direction towards his own dominions, and was endeavoring to rally the wrecks of his army. After much debate in the Carthaginian supreme council, it was resolved that the fortune of war should be tried once more. Syphax was prevailed upon to join his troops to theirs, instead of confining himself to the defence of Numidia; and the recent arrival of four thousand Spaniards, who had been enlisted by Carthaginian agents in Spain, encouraged the two confederates to hope for a successful issue. Scipio was so engrossed with the siege of Utica, which he had pushed with additional vigor after his late victory, that he allowed the enemy to unite their forces, and appear again in the field with no fewer than thirty thousand men. But when he heard of their junction, he lost no time in advancing to meet them; and engaging them a second time, in little more than a month after the destruction of their former armies, he again totally defeated them, and obliged their two generals to fly once more, Syphax to Numidia, and Hasdrubal to Carthage.

A. U. C. 552. A. C. 202. Defeat and capture of Syphax. The Carthaginians sue for peace.

The victors now divided their forces: Lælius and Masinissa were dispatched in pursuit of Syphax; and in a short time Masinissa recovered his father's kingdom; and Syphax, having risked a third battle, was not only defeated as before, but was himself made prisoner, and his capital fell into the hands of the enemy. Scipio meantime overran the country towards Carthage, receiving or forcing the submission of the surrounding towns, and enriching his soldiers with an immense accumulation of plunder. The chief part of this, in order to lighten his army, he sent back to his winter-quarters before Utica; and then he advanced as far as Tunis, and finding that important place abandoned by its garrison, posted himself there, hoping by his presence in the immediate neighborhood of the capital, to terrify the Carthaginians into complete submission. But they had not yet abandoned more resolute counsels; and instead of suing for peace, they determined to send messengers to Italy, to recall Hannibal and Mago, and, in the mean time, to make an attempt to raise the blockade of Utica, by destroying the Roman fleet. The attempt was made, and was partly successful; but this slight advantage was so far overbalanced by the defeat and capture of Syphax, intelligence of which reached Carthage about the same time, that the further prosecution of the war appeared desperate, and a deputation from the council of elders was sent to Scipio to solicit terms of peace. It is said that these deputies forgot their own and their country's dignity in the humbleness of their entreaties: they moved Scipio, however, to dictate such conditions as he might well deem a sufficient recompense of his victories; conditions which, by obliging the Carthaginians to evacuate Italy and Gaul,—to cede Spain and all the islands between Italy and Africa,—to give up all their ships of war, except twenty,—and to pay an immense contribution of corn and money,—sufficiently declared the complete triumph of the Roman arms. Hard as they were, the Carthaginians judged them sufficiently favorable to be accepted without difficulty. A truce was concluded with Scipio; and ambassadors were sent to Rome to procure the ratification of the senate and people.

Interruption of the negotiations.

With regard to the transactions that followed, we are more than ever obliged to regret the want of a Carthaginian historian. Wherever the family of Scipio is concerned the impartiality of Polybius becomes doubtful; and besides, we have only fragments of this part of his narrative, so that we cannot exactly fix the dates of the several events, a point which here becomes of considerable importance. According to our only existing authorities, the Carthaginians, emboldened by the arrival of Hannibal, or, according to Livy, by the mere expectation of his arrival, wantonly broke the truce subsisting between them and Scipio, by detaining some Roman transports which had been driven by a storm into the bay of Carthage; and then denied satisfaction to the officers whom Scipio sent to complain of this outrage; and lastly, in defiance of the law of nations, endeavored to seize the officers themselves on their way back to the Roman camp at Utica. By such conduct the resentment of Scipio is described to have been very naturally provoked; and the war was renewed with greater animosity than ever. This, no doubt, was Scipio's own report of these transactions, which Polybius, the intimate friend of his adopted grandson, and deriving his information, in part at least, from Lælius, in all probability sincerely believed. But it is probable that a Carthaginian narrative of the war in Africa would so represent the matter, that posterity would esteem the behavior of the Carthaginians, in breaking off the truce when it suited their purposes, as neither more nor less dishonorable than the conduct of Scipio himself, when he set fire to the camps of Syphax and Hasdrubal; and that, although the success was different, yet the treachery in both cases, whatever it may have been, was pretty nearly equal.

Battle of Zama.

Hannibal, we are told, landed at Leptis,[5] at what season of the year we know not; and after refreshing his troops for some time at Adrumetum, he took the field, and advanced to the neighborhood of Zama, a town situated, as Polybius describes it, about five days' journey from Carthage, towards the west. It seems that Scipio was busied in overrunning the country, and in subduing the several towns, when he was interrupted in these operations by the approach of the Carthaginian army. He is said to have detected some spies sent by Hannibal to observe his position; and by causing them to be led carefully round his camp, and then sent back in safety to Hannibal, he so excited the admiration of his antagonist, as to make him solicit a personal interview, with the hope of effecting a termination of hostilities. The report of this conference, and of the speeches of the two generals, savors greatly of the style of Roman family memoirs, the most unscrupulous in falsehood of any pretended records of facts that the world has yet seen. However, the meeting ended in nothing; and the next day the two armies were led out into the field for the last decisive struggle. The numbers on each side we have no knowledge of; but probably neither was in this respect much superior. Masinissa, however, with four thousand Numidian cavalry, besides six thousand infantry, had joined Scipio a few days before the battle; while Hannibal, who had so often been indebted to the

[5] Livy, XXX. 25, &c. Polybius, XV. 1, &c.

services of Numidians, had now, on this great occasion, only two thousand horse of that nation to oppose to the numbers, and fortune, and activity of Masinissa. The account of the disposition of both armies, and of the events of the action, was probably drawn up by Polybius from the information given to him by Lælius, and perhaps from the family records of the house of Scipio. And here we may admit its authority to be excellent. It states that the Roman legions were drawn up in their usual order, except that the maniples of every alternate line did not cover the intervals in the line before them, but were placed one behind another, thus leaving avenues in several places through the whole depth of the army from front to rear. These avenues were loosely filled by the light-armed troops, who had received orders to meet the charge of the elephants, and to draw them down the passages left between the maniples, till they should be enticed entirely beyond the rear of the whole army. The cavalry, as usual, was stationed on the wings; Masinissa, with his Numidians, on the right, and Lælius, with the Italians, on the left. On the other side, Hannibal stationed his elephants, to the number of eighty, in the front of his whole line. Next to these were placed the foreign troops in the service of Carthage, twelve thousand strong, consisting of Ligurians, Gauls, inhabitants of the Balearian islands, and Moors. The second line was composed of those Africans who were the immediate subjects of Carthage, and of the Carthaginians themselves; while Hannibal himself, with his veteran soldiers, who had returned with him from Italy, formed a third line, which was kept in reserve, at a little distance behind the other two. The Numidian cavalry were on the left, opposed to their own countrymen under Masinissa; and the Carthaginian horse on the right, opposed to Lælius and the Italians. After some skirmishing of the Numidians in the two armies, Hannibal's elephants advanced to the charge; but being startled by the sound of the Roman trumpets, and annoyed by the light-armed troops of the enemy, some broke off to the right and left, and fell in amongst the cavalry of their own army on both the wings; so that Lælius and Masinissa, availing themselves of this disorder, drove the Carthaginian horse speedily from the field. Others advanced against the enemy's line, and did much mischief; till at length, being frightened, and becoming ungovernable, they were enticed by the light-armed troops of the Romans to follow them down the avenues which Scipio had purposely left open, and were thus drawn out of the action altogether. Meantime the infantry on both sides met: and after a fierce contest, the foreign troops in Hannibal's army, not being properly supported by the soldiers of the second line, were forced to give ground; and in resentment for this desertion, they fell upon the Africans and Carthaginians, and cut them down as enemies; so that these troops, at once assaulted by their fellow-soldiers, and by the pursuing enemy, were also, after a brave resistance, defeated and dispersed. Hannibal, with his reserve, kept off the fugitives, by presenting spears to them, and obliging them to escape in a different direction; and he then prepared to meet the enemy, trusting that they would be ill able to resist the shock of a fresh body of veterans, after having already been engaged in a long and obstinate struggle. Scipio, after having extricated his troops from the heaps of dead which lay between him and Hannibal, commenced a second, and a far more serious contest. The soldiers on both sides were perfect in courage and in discipline; and as the battle went on, they fell in the ranks where they fought, and their places were supplied by their comrades with unabated zeal. At last Lælius and Masinissa returned from the pursuit of the enemy's beaten cavalry, and fell, in a critical moment, upon the rear of Hannibal's army.[6] Then his veterans, surrounded and overpowered, still maintained their

[6] The battle of Marengo forms, in many points, an exact parallel with that of Zama. The Austrians having routed the advanced divisions of the French army, commenced an entirely new action with the reserve, which Bonaparte, like Hannibal, had kept at a distance from the scene of the first engagement. The struggle, which was obstinately maintained, was decided, as at Zama, by a timely charge of cavalry on the flank of the enemy's infantry; but the victorious cavalry in the two battles did not belong to the armies whose situations cor-

high reputation; and most of them were cut down where they stood, resisting to the last. Flight, indeed, was not easy; for the country was a plain, and the Roman and Numidian horse were active in pursuit; yet Hannibal, when he saw the battle totally lost, with a nobler fortitude than his brother had shown at the Metaurus, escaped from the field to Adrumetum. He knew that his country would now need his assistance more than ever; and as he had been in so great a degree the promoter of the war, it ill became him to shrink from bearing his full share of the weight of its disastrous issue.

Results of the battle.

On the plains of Zama twenty thousand of the Carthaginian army were slain, and an equal number taken prisoners; but the consequences of the battle far exceeded the greatness of the immediate victory. It was not the mere destruction of an army, but the final conquest of the only power that seemed able to combat Rome on equal terms. In the state of the ancient world, with so few nations really great and powerful, and so little of a common feeling pervading them, there was neither the disposition nor the materials for forming a general confederacy against the power of Rome; and the single efforts of Macedonia, of Syria, and of Carthage herself, after the fatal event of the second Punic war, were of no other use than to provoke their own ruin. The defeat of Hannibal insured the empire of the ancient civilized world.

Terms of the peace granted to Carthage.

The only hope of the Carthaginians now rested on the forbearance of Scipio; and they again sent deputies to him, with a full confession of the injustice of their conduct in the first origin of the war, and still more in their recent violation of the truce, and with a renewal of their supplications for peace. The conqueror, telling them that he was moved solely by considerations of the dignity of Rome, and the uncertainty of all human greatness, and in no degree by any pity for misfortunes which were so well deserved, presented the terms on which alone they could hope for mercy. "They were to make amends for the injuries done to the Romans during the truce; to restore all prisoners and deserters; to give up all their ships of war, except ten, and all their elephants; to engage in no war at all out of Africa, nor in Africa without the consent of the Romans; to restore to Masinissa all that had belonged to him or any of his ancestors; to feed the Roman army for three months, and pay it till it should be recalled home; to pay a contribution of ten thousand Euboic talents, at the rate of two hundred talents a year, for fifty years; and to give a hundred hostages, between the ages of fourteen and thirty, to be selected at the pleasure of the Roman general." At this price the Carthaginians were allowed to hold their former dominion in Africa, and to enjoy their independence, till it should seem convenient to the Romans to complete their destruction. Yet Hannibal strongly urged that the terms should be accepted, and, it is said, rudely interrupted[7] a member of the supreme council at Carthage, who was speaking against them. He probably felt, as his father had done under circumstances nearly similar, that for the present resistance was vain; but that by purchasing peace at any price, and by a wise management of their internal resources, his countrymen might again find an opportunity to recover their losses. Peace was accordingly signed; the Roman army returned to Italy; and Hannibal, at the age of forty-five, having seen the schemes of his whole life utterly ruined, was now beginning, with equal patience and resolution, to lay the foundation for them again.

Wise domestic policy of Hannibal; he is forced to quit Carthage, and goes to Antiochus.

From our scanty notices of the succeeding years of his life, we learn that his conduct, as a citizen, displayed great wisdom and great integrity. He is said to have reduced the exorbitant[8] power of an order of perpetual judges, whose authority was very extensive, and had been greatly abused. He turned his attention also to the employment of the public

respond with one another; for at Zama the reserve was defeated by the charge of Lælius; while it was victorious at Marengo, owing to the attack made by Kellerman. See Gen. Matthieu Dumas, *Campagne de 1800*, and *Victoires et Conquêtes des Français*, tome xiii.

[7] Polybius, XV. 19.

[8] Livy, XXXIII. 45, 46, &c.

revenue, much of which he found to be embezzled by persons in office, while the people were heavily taxed to raise the yearly contributions due to the Romans by the last treaty. When a man of such high character raised his voice against so gross an abuse, there was yet vigor enough in the popular part of the Carthaginian constitution to give him effectual support; and it appears that the evil was removed, and the public revenue henceforward applied to public services. Hannibal, however, had thus created many powerful enemies; and ere long they found an opportunity of gratifying their hatred. The war between Rome and Macedonia had lately been concluded; and the success of the Romans, and their commanding interference in the affairs of Greece, awakened the fears and jealousy of Antiochus, king of Syria, whose kingdom was the greatest possessed by any of the successors of Alexander. He seemed disposed to take up the contest which Philip, king of Macedonia, had been compelled to resign; and the Romans were either informed, or fancied, that Hannibal was using all his influence at Carthage to persuade his countrymen to join him. Accordingly a commission was sent to the Carthaginian government, requiring them to punish Hannibal as a disturber of the peace between the two nations. Hannibal, knowing that he should be unable to resist the efforts of his domestic enemies, when thus supported by the influence of Rome, seems at last to have surrendered his long-cherished hopes of restoring his country to her ancient greatness. He found means to escape from Carthage, and procured a vessel to transport him to Tyre, where he was received with all the honors due to a man who had shed such glory on the Phœnician name, and from whence he easily reached the court of Antiochus, at Antioch. Finding that the king was already set out on his way towards Greece, he followed and overtook him at Ephesus; and being cordially received, he contributed powerfully to fix him in his determination to declare war on the Romans, and was retained near his person, as one of his most valuable counsellors.

War of Antiochus. Hannibal goes to the court of Prusias: his death.

The ability of Hannibal was displayed again on this new occasion, by the plans which he recommended for the prosecution of the war. He first and most strongly urged that he should be sent[9] with an army into Italy; there, he said, the Romans were most vulnerable; and an attack made upon their own country might distract their counsels, and at least lessen their means of carrying on hostilities in Greece or Asia. When this measure was abandoned, owing, as it is said, to the king's jealousy of the glory which Hannibal would gain by its success, his next proposal was[10] that the alliance of Philip, king of Macedon, should be purchased at any price. Macedon was a power strong enough to take a substantial part in the war, and would be too important to escape, as the little second or third-rate states might do, by forsaking its ally as soon as he should experience any reverses. This counsel was also neglected; and Philip united himself with the Romans against Antiochus; so that Hannibal, employed only in a subordinate naval command, a duty for which his experience had in no way fitted him, could render the king no essential service; and in a short time, when the Romans had brought the war to a triumphant end, he was obliged to seek another asylum, as Antiochus had agreed, by one of the articles[11] of the treaty, to surrender him up to the Roman government. His last refuge was the court of Prusias, king of Bithynia. With that prince he remained about five years; and it is mentioned by Cornelius Nepos, that he gained a victory, while commanding his fleet, over his old enemy Eumenes, king of Pergamus. All his own prospects had long since been utterly ruined; and the condition of such a man, reduced to the state of a dependent exile, under the protection of so humble a sovereign as Prusias, might have satisfied the most violent hatred of the Romans. But it seems they could not be free from uneasiness while Hannibal lived; and when a Roman embassy was sent to the court of Pru-

[9] Livy, XXXIV. 60. [10] Livy, XXXVI. 7. [11] Polybius, XXI. 14.

sias, that king, whether spontaneously, or at the solicitation of the ambassadors, promised to put their great enemy into their hands. His treachery, however, was suspected by Hannibal; and when he found the avenues to his house secured by the king's guards, he is said to have destroyed himself by a poison which he had long carried about him for such an emergency. Some particulars are added by Livy and Plutarch, which, not being credibly attested, nor likely to have become publicly known, it is needless to insert here. It is sufficient to say, that Hannibal died by his own hand, to avoid falling into the power of the Romans, at Nicomedia, in Bithynia; and, as nearly as we can ascertain, in the sixty-fourth year of his age.

His character.

If the characters of men be estimated according to the steadiness with which they have followed the true principle of action, we cannot assign a high place to Hannibal. But if patriotism were indeed the greatest of virtues, and a resolute devotion to the interests of his country were all the duty that a public man can be expected to fulfil, he would then deserve the most lavish praise. Nothing can be more unjust than the ridicule with which Juvenal has treated his motives, as if he had been actuated merely by a romantic desire of glory. On the contrary, his whole conduct displays the loftiest genius, and the boldest spirit of enterprise, happily subdued and directed by a cool judgment to the furtherance of the honor and interests of his country; and his sacrifice of selfish pride and passion, when after the battle of Zama he urged the acceptance of peace, and lived to support the disgrace of Carthage, with the patient hope of one day repairing it, affords a strong contrast to the cowardly despair with which some of the best of the Romans deprived their country of their service by suicide. Of the extent of his abilities, the history of his life is the best evidence: as a general, his conduct remains uncharged with a single error; for the idle censure which Livy presumes to pass on him for not marching to Rome after the battle of Cannæ, is founded on such mere ignorance, that it does not deserve any serious notice. His knowledge of human nature, and his ascendency over men's minds, are shown by the uninterrupted authority which he exercised alike in his prosperity and adversity over an army composed of so many various and discordant materials, and which had no other bond than the personal character of the leader. As a statesman, he was at once manly, disinterested, and sensible; a real reformer of abuses in his domestic policy, and in his measures, with respect to foreign enemies, keeping the just limit between weakness and blind obstinacy. He stands reproached, however, with covetousness by the Carthaginians, and with cruelty by the Romans. The first charge is sustained by no facts that have been transmitted to us; and it is a curious circumstance, that the very same vice was long imputed by party violence to the great duke of Marlborough, and that the imputation has been lately proved by his biographer to have been utterly calumnious. Of cruelty indeed, according to modern principles, he cannot be acquitted; and his putting to death all the Romans whom he found on his march through Italy, after the battle of the lake Thrasymenus, was a savage excess of hostility. Yet many instances of courtesy are recorded of him, even by his enemies, in his treatment of the bodies of the generals who fell in action against him; and certainly, if compared with the ordinary proceedings of Roman commanders, his actions deserve no peculiar brand of barbarity. Still it is little to his honor, that he was not more careless of human suffering than Marcellus or Scipio; nor can the urgency of his circumstances, or the evil influence of his friends, to both which Polybius attributes much of the cruelty ascribed to him, be justly admitted as a defence. It is the prevailing crime of men in high station to be forgetful of individual misery, so long as it forwards their grand objects; and it is most important, that our admiration of great public talents and brilliant successes should not lead us to tolerate an indifference to human suffering.

CONSULS AND MILITARY TRIBUNES.

FROM THE BEGINNING OF THE COMMONWEALTH TO THE TAKING OF ROME BY THE GAULS.

CONSULS AND MILITARY TRIBUNES.

Year of the Commonwealth.	Year of Rome, common reckoning.	Year before the Christian Era.	Olympiads.	Fasti Capitolini.	LIVY.	DIODORUS.	DIONYSIUS.
1	245	508	68-1			[The tenth book of Diodorus being lost, we have no lists of Consuls from him earlier than the 21st year of the Commonwealth, according to Livy's Fasti.]	L. Junius Brutus L. Tarquinius Collatinus
2	246	507	68-2				P. Valerius II. T. Lucretius Dionys. V. 20.
3	247	506	68-3		L. Junius Brutus L. Tarquinius Collatinus, afterwards, in the same year, P. Valerius Publicola M. Horatius Pulvillus		P. Valerius III. M. Horatius II.[1] V. 21.
4	248	505	68-4	M. Valer . . . . . Cos. . . . CCXLVIII P. Post . . . . . Cos. . . . CCXLVIII	P. Valerius II. T. Lucretius Livy, II. 8.		Sp. Lartius T. Herminius V. 36.
5	249	504	69-1	P. Valerius . . . Poplicol . . .	P. Lucretius P. Valerius Publicola III. II. 15.		M. Valerius P. Postumius V. 37.
6	250	503	69-2	P. Postumi . . . Cos. II. . . . Ann. CCL Agrippa M . . . Cos. . . . Ann. CCL	M. Valerius P. Postumius II. 16.		P. Valerius IV. T. Lucretius II. V. 40.
7	251	502	69-3	Sp. Cassius . . . Cos. . . . Ann. CCLI	P. Valerius IV. T. Lucretius II. II. 16.		Agrippa Menenius P. Postumius V. 44.
8	252	501	69-4		Agrippa Menenius P. Postumius II. 16.		Opiter Virginius Sp. Cassius V. 49.
9	253	500	70-1		Opiter Virginius Sp. Cassius II. 17.		Postumus Cominius T. Lartius V. 50.
10	254	499	70-2		Postumus Cominius T. Lartius II. 18.		Ser. Sulpicius M'. Tullius V. 52.
11	255	498	70-3		Ser. Sulpicius M'. Tullius II. 19.		P. Veturius P. Æbutius V. 58.
12	256	497	70-4		T. Æbutius C. Veturius II. 19.		T. Lartius Q. Clœlius Siculus V. 59.
13	257	496	71-1		Q. Clœlius T. Lartius II. 21.		A. Sempronius M. Minucius V. 77.
14	258	495	71-2		A. Sempronius M. Minucius II. 21.		A. Postumius T. Virginius VI. 2.
15	259	494	71-3		A. Postumius T. Virginius II. 21.		Ap. Claudius P. Servilius VI. 23.
16	260	493	71-4		Ap. Claudius P. Servilius II. 21.		A. Virginius T. Veturius VI. 34.
17	261	492	72-1		A. Virginius T. Veturius II. 28.		Postumus Cominius Sp. Cassius II. VI. 49.
18	262	491	72-2		Sp. Cassius Postumus Cominius II. 33.		T. Geganius P. Minucius VII. 1.
19	263	490	72-3		T. Geganius P. Minucius II. 34.		M. Minucius A. Sempronius VII. 20.
20	264	489	72-4		M. Minucius A. Sempronius II. 34.		Q. Sulpicius Ser. Lartius VII. 68.

[1] Dionysius agrees also with Livy in making P. Valerius and M. Horatius consuls in this year after the banishment of Collatinus and the death of Brutus.

Year of the Common-wealth.	Year of Rome.	Year before the Christian Era.	Olympiads.	Fasti Capitolini.	LIVY.	DIODORUS.	DIONYSIUS.
21	265	488	73-1		Sp. Nautius Sex. Furius II. 39.		C. Julius P. Pinarius VIII. 1.
22	266	487	73-2		T. Sicinius C. Aquillius II. 40.		Sp. Nautius Sex. Furius VIII. 16.
23	267	486	73-3		Sp. Cassius Proculus Virginius II. 41.		C. Aquillius T. Siccius VIII. 64.
24	268	485	73-4		Ser. Cornelius Q. Fabius II. 41.		Proculus Virginius Sp. Cassius III. VIII. 68.
25	269	484	74-1		L. Æmilius K. Fabius II. 42.		Q. Fabius Ser. Cornelius VIII. 77.
26	270	483	74-2		M. Fabius L. Valerius II. 42.		L. Æmilius K. Fabius VIII. 83.
27	271	482	74-3	. . . . . Vibulanus II.	Q. Fabius C. Julius II. 43.		A.U.C. 270 according to Dionysius M. Fabius L. Valerius VIII. 87.
28	272	481	74-4	. . . N . . . . Fusus	K. Fabius Sp. Furius II. 43.		C. Julius Q. Fabius VIII. 90.
29	273	480	75-1	. . . . ibulanus II.	M. Fabius Cn. Manlius II. 43.	Sp. Cassius Proclus Virginius XI. 1.	K. Fabius II. Sp. Furius IX. 1.
30	274	479	75-2	. . . T. N. . . . Tricost Rutil. . . .	K. Fabius T. Virginius II. 48.	Q. Fabius Silvanus Ser. Cornelius XI. 27.	Cn. Manlius M. Fabius II. IX. 5.
31	275	478	75-3	. . . . . ctus Ahala	L. Æmilius C. Servilius II. 49.	K. Fabius L. Æmilius XI. 38.	K. Fabius T. Virginius IX. 14.
32	276	477	75-4	. . . . . Lanatus	C. Horatius T. Menenius II. 51.	M. Fabius L. Valerius XI. 41.	L. Æmilius C. Servilius IX. 16.
33	277	476	76-1	. . . . uctus	A. Virginius Sp. Servilius II. 51.	Kæso Fabius Sp. Furius XI. 48.	C. Horatius T. Menenius IX. 18.
34	278	475	76-2	. . . . utilus . . . . eisque Ann. CCLXXIIX	C. Nautius P. Valerius II. 52.	M. Fabius Cn. Manlius XI. 50.	Ser. Servilius A. Virginius IX. 25.
35	279	474	76-3	. . . um F VIII . . . . Ann. CCLXXIX	L. Furius C. Manlius II. 54.	K. Fabius T. Virginius XI. 51.	P. Valerius C. Nautius IX. 28.
36	280	473	76-4	. . . . Iulus	L. Æmilius Opiter Virginius, or Vopiscus Julius II. 54.	L. Æmilius Mamercus C. Cornelius Lentulus XI. 52.	A. Manlius L. Furius IX. 36.
37	281	472	77-1	. . . . sus	L. Pinarius P. Furius II. 56.	T. Minucius C. Horatius XI. 53.	L. Æmilius Vopiscus Julius IX. 37.
38	282	471	77-2		Ap. Claudius T. Quintius II. 56.	A. Virginius Tricostus C. Servilius Structus XI. 54.	L. Pinarius P. Furius IX. 40.
39	283	470	77-3		L. Valerius Ti. Æmilius II. 61.	P. Valerius C. Nautius Rufus XI. 60.	T. Quintius Ap. Claudius IX. 43.
40	284	469	77-4		T. Numicius A. Virginius II. 63.	L. Furius† Mediolanus† M. Manlius Vaso XI. 63.	L. Valerius II. Ti. Æmilius IX. 51.
41	285	468	78-1	A.CCXX	T. Quintius Q. Servilius II. 64.	L. Æmilius Mamercus L. †Studius† I[illegible]us XI. 65.	A. Virginius T. Numicius IX. 56.
42	286	467	78-2		Ti. Æmilius Q. Fabius III. 1.	L. Pinarius Mamertinus P. Furius† Fifron† XI. 66.	T. Quintius Capitolinus II. Q. Servilius Priscus IX. 57.
43	287	466	78-3	Sp. Postumius A.F.P.N. Albus Regi	Q. Servilius Sp. Postumius III. 2.	Ap. Claudius T. Quintius Capitolinus XI. 67.	Ti. Æmilius II. Q. Fabius IX. 59.

Year of the Commonwealth.	Year of Rome.	Year before the Christian Era.	Olympiads.	Fasti Capitolini.	LIVY.	DIODORUS.	DIONYSIUS.
44	288	465	78-4	Q. Fabius M.F.K.N. Vibulan	Q. Fabius T. Quintius III. 2.	L. Valerius Publicola T. Æmilius Mamercus XI. 69.	Sp. Postumius Albinus Q. Servilius Priscus II. IX. 60.
45	289	464	79-1	A. Postumius A.F.P.N. Albus Regill	A. Postumius Sp. Furius III. 4.	A. Virginius T. Minucius XI. 70.	T. Quintius Capitolinus III. Q. Fabius Vibulanus II. IX. 61.
46	290	463	79-2	P. Servilius Sp : F.P.N. Prisc.	L. Æbutius { Kal. Sext. P. Servilius { ineunt magistrat. III. 6.	T. Quintius Q. Servilius Structus XI. 71.	A. Postumius Albus Ser. Furius IX. 62.
47	291	462	79-3	L. Lucretius T.F.T.N. Tricipitinu	L. Lucretius { A. d. III. T. Veturius { Id. Sext. III. 8.	Q. Fabius Vibulanus Ti. Æmilius Mamercus XI. 74.	L. Æbutius P. Servilius Priscus IX. 67.
48	292	461	79-4	P. Volumnius M.F.M.N. Amintin. Galus.	P. Volumnius Ser. Sulpicius III. 10.	Q. Servilius Sp. Postumius Albinus XI. 75.	L. Lucretius T. Veturius Geminus IX. 69.
49	293	460	80-1	P. Valerius P. F. Volusi N. Poplicola II. in Mag Mortuus est. In ejus L.F.E. L. Quinctius L.F.L.N. Cincinnatus	C. Claudius P. Valerius III. 15.	Q. Fabius T. Quintius Capitolinus XI. 77.	P. Volumnius Ser. Sulpicius Camerinus X. 1.
50	294	459	80-2	Q. Fabius M.F.K.N. Vibulanus III. . . . . . Maluginesis V.	Q. Fabius Vibulanus L. Cornelius Malugin III. 15.	A. Postumius Regulus XI. 78. Sp. Furius† Mediolanus†	P. Valerius C. Claudius Sabinus X. 9.
51	295	458	80-3	C. Nautius Sp : F. Sp : N. Rutilus II. . . . Carven . . . In M . . . . Mortuus est. In ejus L. F. est L. Minucius P.F.M.N. Esquilin. Augurin	L. Minucius C. Nautius III. 25.	P. Servilius Structus L. Æbutius Alvas XI. 79.	Q. Fabius Vibulanus III. L. Cornelius X. 20.
52	296	457	80-4	C. Horatius M.F.L.N. Pulvillus II. Q. Minucius P.F.M.N. Esquilinus	Q. Minucius C. Horatius III. 30.	L. Lucretius XI. 81. T. Veturius† Cichorinus†	C. Nautius II. L. Minucius X. 22.
53	297	456	81-1	M. Valerius M'.F. Volusi N. Maxumus Sp. Virginius A.F.A. . . . Tricost. Cæliomont.	M. Valerius Sp. Virginius III. 31.	Ser. Sulpicius XI. 84. P. Volumnius Amentinus	C. Horatius Q. Minucius X. 26.
54	298	455	81-2	T. Romilius T.F.T.N. Rocus Vaticanus C. Veturius P. . . . . Cicurinus	T. Romilius C. Veturius III. 31.	P. Valerius C. Clodius Regillus XI. 85.	M. Valerius Sp. Virginius X. 31.
55	299	454	81-3	Sp. Tarpeius M.F.M.N. Montan. Capitolin. A. Aternius . . . . Varus Fontinalis	Sp. Tarpeius A. Aterius III. 31.	Q. Fabius Vibulanus L. Cornelius Curitinus XI. 86.	T. Romilius C. Veturius X. 33.
56	300	453	81-4	Sex. Quintilius Sex. F.P.N. . . . . P. Curiati . . . . N. Fistus Trigemin	P. Curiatius Sex. Quintilius III. 32.	C. Nautius Rutilus L. Minucius† Carutianus† XI. 88.	Sp. Tarpeius A. †Termenius† X. 48.
57	301	452	82-1	P. Sestius Q.F. Vibi N. Capito . . . . . ticanus T. Menen . . . . F. Agripp. N. Lanatus	C. Menenius P. Sestius III. 32.	[This year is wanting.]	P. Horatius Sex. Quintilius X. 53.
58	302	451	82-2	Ap. Claudius Ap. F.M.N. Crassin . . . gill Sabinus II. T. Genu . . . . . . Augurinus Ap. Claudius, Ap. F.M.N. Crassin . T. Genucius L.F.L.N. Augurin : Sp. Veturius, Sp. F.P.N. Cr. . . . sus Cicurinus, C. Julius C.F.L.N. Iulus. A. Manlius, Cn. F.P.N. Vulso Decemviri Consular . . . . . rio Legibus S . . .	Ap. Claudius { Coss. design. T. Genucius { Ap. Claudius, T. Genucius, P. Sestius, L. Veturius, C. Iulius, A. Manlius, Ser. Sulpicius, P. Curatius, T. Romilius, Sp. Postumius. Decemviri, Legg. scribendis. III. 33.	L. Postumius M. Horatius XI. 91.	L. Menenius P. Sestius X. 54.
59	303	450	82-3	Ap. Claudius . . . . Crassin Regil. . . Sabin M. Cor . . . . . . r. N. Maluginesis . . . . Esquilin . . . . linus Augurin . . . . Mere . . .	Ap. Claudius, M. Cornelius, Maluginensis, M. Sergius, L. Minucius, Q. Fabius, Vibulanus, Q. Pœtelius, T. Antonius, Merenda, K. Duilius, Sp. Oppius Cornicen, M'. Rabuleius. Decemviri Legg. scribendis. III. 35.	L. Quintius Cincinnatus M. Fabius Vibulanus XII. 3.	Ap. Claudius { Coss. design. T. Genucius { X. 56. Ap. Claudius, T. Genucius, P. Sestius, P. Postumius, Ser. Sulpicius, A. Manlius, T. Romilius, C. Iulius, T. Veturius, P. Horatius. Decemviri legibus scribendis.

Year of the Common-wealth.	Year of Rome.	Year before the Christian Era.	Olympiads.	Fasti Capitolini.	LIVY.	DIODORUS.	DIONYSIUS.
60	304	449	82-4	. . . tius M.F . . . . Barbatus . . . Sabin . . . Ann: CCCIV VII K. Sept: . . . . ius F.F.P.N. Poplicola Potit . . . . De Æqueis Idibus Sextil. Ann: CCCIV.	The same Decemvirs III. 38.	M. Valerius Lactuca Sp. Virginius Tricostus XII. 4.	Ap. Claudius, Q. Fabius, M. Cornelius, M. Sergius, L. Minucius, T. Antonius, M'. Rabuleius, Q. Pœtilius, Kæso Duillius, Sp. Oppius. Decemviri Legg. scribendis. X. 58.
61	305	448	83-1		L. Valerius M. Horatius III. 55.	T. Romilius Vaticanus XII. 5. C. Veturius †Cichorius†	The Decemvirs as before. X. 61.
62	306	447	83-2		Lar Herminius T. Virginius III. 65.	Sp. Tarpeius XII. 6. A. †Asterius † Fontinius†	L. Valerius Potitus M. Horatius Barbatus XI. 45.
63	307	446	83-3		M. Geganius Macerinus C. Julius III. 65.	Sex. †Quintius† . . . . . Trigeminus XII. 7.	Lar Herminius T. Virginius XI. 51.
64	308	445	83-4		T. Quinctius Capitolinus IV. Agrippa Furius III. 66.	T. Menenius P. Sestius Capitolinus XII. 22.	M. Ge[ganius XI. 51. C. Julius] The names are almost lost in the MS.
65	309	444	84-1		M. Genucius C. Curtius IV. 1.	Decemvirs: names given corruptly. XII. 23.	[This year is wanting.]
66	310	443	84-2	nius M . . . . . inus . . . . De . . . . Ann. CCCX . . . . nis Sep . . .	A. Sempronius, L. Atilius, T. Clœlius } Tribb. Milit. IV. 7.	Decemvirs: names again corrupt. XII. 24.	M. Genucius C. Quintius XI. 52.
67	311	442	84-3		M. Geganius Macerinus II. T. Quinctius Capitolinus V. IV. 8.	†Cancus † Horatius L. Valerius † Turpinus† XII. 26.	A. Sempronius Atrat., L. Atilius Longus, T. Clœlius Siculus } Tribb. Milit. XI. 62.
68	312	441	84-4		M. Fabius Vibulanus Postumus Æbutius Cornicen IV. 11.	Larinus Herminius T. †Stertinius † Structus XII. 27.	M. Geganius Macerinus II. T. Quinctius Capitolinus V. XI. 63.
69	313	440	85-1		C. Furius Pacilus M. Papirius Crassus IV. 12.	L. Julius M. Geganius XII. 29.	Here the regular history of Dionysius breaks off; the rest being lost, with the exception of fragments.
70	314	439	85-2		Proculus Geganius Macerinus L. Menenius Lanatus IV. 12.	T. Quintius Agrippa Furius XII. 30.	
71	315	438	85-3		T. Quintius Capitolinus VI. Agrippa Menenius IV. 3.	M. Genucius Agrippa Ourtius Chilo. XII. 31.	
72	316	437	85-4	. . . . us . . . . Ann. CCCXVI Idib. Se	Mam. Æmilius, L. Quinctius Cincinnatus, L. Julius } Tribb. Milit. IV. 16.	A. Sempronius, L. Atilius, T. Quintius } Tribb. Milit. XII. 32.	
73	317	436	86-1		M. Geganius Macerin. III. L. Sergius Fidenas IV. 17.	T. Quinctius XII. 33. M. Geganius Macerinus	
74	318	435	86-2		M. Cornelius Maluginensis L. Papirius Crassus IV. 21.	M. Fabius XII. 34. Postum. Æbutius † Vulecus †	
75	319	434	86-3		C. Julius II. L. Virginius IV. 21.	Q. Furius Fusus M'. Papirius Crassus XII. 35.	
76	320	433	86-4		M. Manlius, Q. Sulpicius } or { C. Julius III., L. Virginius II. IV. 23.	T. Menenius Proclus Geganius Macerinus XII. 36.	
77	321	432	87-1		M. Fabius Vibulanus, M. Foslius, L. Sergius Fidenas } Tribb. Milit. IV. 25.	T. Quinctius † Nittus † Menenius XII. 37.	

Year of the Commonwealth.	Year of Rome.	Year before the Christian Era.	Olympiads.	Fasti Capitolini.	LIVY.	DIODORUS.	DIONYSIUS.
78	322	431	87-2		L. Pinarius Mamercinus L. Furius Medullinus Sp. Postumius Albus } Tribb. Milit. IV. 2.	M'. Æmilianus Mamercus C. Julius L. Quintius } Tribb. Milit. IV. 38.	
79	323	430	87-3		T. Quintius Cincinnatus C. Julius Mento IV. 26.	M. Geganius L. Sergius XII. 43.	
80	324	429	87-4		L. Papirius Crassus L. Julius IV. 30.	L. Papirius XII. 46. A. Cornelius† Macerinus†	
81	325	428	88-1		L. Sergius Fidenas II. Hostus Lucretius Tricipitinus IV. 30.	C. Julius Proclus Virginius Tricostus XII. 49.	
82	326	427	88-2		A. Cornelius Cossus T. Quintius Pennus II. IV. 30.	M. Manlius Q. Sulpicius Prætextatus Sor. Cornelius Cossus } Tribb. Milit.	
83	327	426	88-3		C. Servilius Ahala L. Papirius Mugillanus. IV. 30.	M. Fabius M. † Falinius † L. † Servilius † } Tribb. Milit. XII. 58.	A. Cornelius Cossus II. T. Quintius II. XII. 3. Frag. Vatican.
84	328	425	88-4		T. Quintius C. Furius M. Postumius A. Cornelius Cossus } Tribb. Milit. IV. 31.	L. Furius Sp. Pinarius C. † Metellus † } Tribb. Milit. XII. 60.	
85	329	424	89-1		A. Sempronius Atratinus L. Quintius Cincinnatus L. Furius Medullinus L. Horatius Barbatus } Tribb. Milit. IV. 35.	T. Quintius C. Julius XII. 65.	
86	330	423	89-2		Ap. Claudius Sp. Nautius Rutilus L. Sergius Fidenas Sex. Julius } Tribb. Milit. IV. 35.	C. Papirius L. Julius XII. 72.	
87	331	422	89-3	. . . . Mugillan.	C. Sempronius Atratinus Q. Fabius Vibulanus IV. 37.	Opiter Lucretius L. Sergius Fidenas XII. 73.	
88	332	421	89-4	. . . . tolin Barbat. N. Fabius . . .	L. Malinus Capitolinus Q. Antonius Merenda L. Papirius Mugillanus } Tribb. Milit. IV. 42.	T. Quintius A. Cornelius Cossus XII. 75.	
89	333	420	90-1	. . . . Cincinnatus II. M. Manl . . . . dullinus III. A. Sempro . . .	N. Fabius Vibulanus T. Quintius Capitolinus. IV. 43.	L. Quintius A. Sempronius XII. 77.	
90	334	419	90-2	. . . . ripp. N. Lanatus Sp. Nautius . . . . Tricipitinus C. Servilius	L. Quintius Cincinnatus III. L. Furius Medullinus II. M. Manlius A. Sempronius Atratinus } Tribb. Milit. IV. 44.	L. Papirius Mugillanus C. Servilius Structus XII. 78.	
91	335	418	90-3	. . . . Mugillanus. C. Servilius Q.F.C.N. Axilla II. L. Sergius C.F.C.N. Fidenas III. Q. Servilius P.F. Sp: N. Priscus Fidenas II. D . . . C . . . . . . Q.F.C.N. Axilla Mag . . . . . . Cens. L. Papirius M'. F.	Agrip. Menenius Lanatus P. Lucretius Tricipitinus Sp. Nautius Rutilus } Tribb. Milit. IV. 45.	C. Furius T. Quintius M. Postumius A. Cornelius } Tribb. Milit. XII. 80.	

Year of the Common-wealth.	Year of Rome.	Year before the Christian Era.	Olympiads.	Fasti Capitolini.	LIVY.	DIODORUS.	DIONYSIUS.
92	336	417	90-4	P. Lucretius Hosti F . . . . Agrippa Menenius T.F.	L. Sergius Fidenas M. Papirius Mugillanus C. Servilius Priscus } Tribb. Milit. IV. 45.	L. Furius L. Quintius A. Sempronius } Tribb. Milit. XII. 81.	
93	337	416	91-1	A. Sempronius L.F.A.N. . . . . Q. Fabius Q.F.M.N.	Agrip. Menenius Lanatus II. L. Servilius Structus II. P. Lucretius Tricipitinus II. Sp. Rutilius Crassus } Tribb. Milit. IV. 47.	T. Claudius Sp. Nautius L. †Sentius† Sex. Julius } Tribb. Milit. XII. 82.	
94	338	415	91-2	P. Cornelius P.N. . . . . C. Valerius L.F. Volusi N.	A. Sempronius Atratinus III. M. Papirius Mugillanus II. Sp. Nautius Rutilus II. } Tribb. Milit. IV. 47.	† Sergius Lucius † M. Papirius M. Servilius } Tribb. Milit. XIII. 2.	
95	339	414	91-3	Q. Fabius Q.F.M.N. . . . . P. Postumius A F.A.N.	P. Cornelius Cossus C. Valerius Potitus Q. Quintius Cincinnatus N. Fabius Vibulanus } Tribb. Milit. IV. 49.	P. Lucretius C. Servilius Agrippa Menenius Sp. Veturius } Tribb. Milit. XIII. 7.	
96	340	413	91-4		Cn. Cornelius Cossus L. Valerius Potitus Q. Fabius Vibulanus II. M. Postumius Regillensis } Tribb. Milit. IV. 49.	A. Sempronius M. Papirius Q. Fabius Sp. Nautius } Tribb. Milit. XIII. 9.	
97	341	412	92-1		A. Cornelius Cossus L. Furius Medullinus } Coss. IV. 51.	P. Cornelius C. Fabius . . . . . . } Tribb. Milit. XIII. 34.	
98	342	411	92-2		Q. Fabius Ambustus C. Furius Pacilus } Coss. IV. 52.	T. Postumius C. Cornelius C. Valerius K. Fabius } Tribb. Milit. XIII. 38.	
99	343	410	92-3		M. Papirius Atratinus C. Nautius Rutilus } Coss. IV. 52.	M. Cornelius L. Furius } Coss. XIII. 43.	
100	344	409	92-4	. . . . . A.F.M.N. . . . . Medullin : II.	M'. Æmilius C. Valerius Potitus } Coss. IV. 53.	Q. Fabius C. Furius } Coss. XIII. 54.	
101	345	408	93-1	TR. MIL. . . . . Vospisci N. Iulus . . . . A.F.M.N. Cossus . . . . F.Q.N. Ahala	Cn. Cornelius Cossus L. Furius Medullinus II. } Coss. IV. 54.	M. Papirius Sp. Nautius } Coss. XIII. 68.	
102	346	407	93-2	. . . . . . Potit : Volusus II. C. Servilius P.F.Q.N. Ahala II. TR. MIL. . . . . Medullinus N. Fabius Q.F.M.N. Vibulanus II.	C. Julius Iulus P. Cornelius Cossus C. Servilius Ahala } Tribb. Milit. IV. 56.	C. †Manius† Æmilius C. Valerius } Coss. XIII. 76.	
103	347	406	93-3	. . . . tilus Cossus L. Valerius L. F. P. N. Potitus II. . . . . Cossus N. Fabius M.F.Q.N. Ambustus.	L. Furius Medullinus III. C. Valerius Potitus II. N. Fabius Vibulanus II. C. Servilius Ahala II. } Tribb. Milit. IV. 57.	L. Furius Cn. † Pompeius † } Coss. XIII. 80.	

Year of the Common-wealth.	Year of Rome.	Year before the Christian Era.	Olympiads.	Fasti Capitolini.	LIVY.	DIODORUS.	DIONYSIUS.
104	348	405	93-4	. . . . Iulus II. M' Aimilius Mam. F.M.N. Mamercinus. . . . . lin. Barb : L. Furius L. F. Sp.: N. Medullinus II. . . . . nnatus. Tr. Mil. A. Manlius A.F. Cn : N. Vulso Capolin.	P. Cornelius Cossus Cn. Cornelius Cossus N. Fabius Ambustus L. Valerius Potitus } Tribb. Milit. IV. 58.	C. Julius P. Cornelius C. Servilius } Tribb. Milit. XIII. 104.	
105	349	404	94-1	. . . . uginensis Sp : Nautius Sp : F. Sp : N. . . . utilus III. . . . . sus II. C. Valerius L. F. Vol : N. Potit : Volus : III. . . . . F.Q.N. Ambustus M' Serg. . . . . . . Fidenas Tr. Mil.	T. Quintius Capitolinus Q. Quintius Cincinnatus C. Julius Iulus II. A. Manlius L. Furius Medullinus III. M'. Æmilius Mamercinus } Tribb. Milit. IV. 61.	C. Furius C. Servilius C. Valerius N. Fabius } Tribb. Milit. XIV. 3.	
106	350	403	94-2	. . . ius Mam. F.M.N. . . n. II. M. Fur . . . . Fusus . . . . dius P.F. Ap : N. . . . . . . s. Tr. Mil. L. Juli . . . Iulus . . . . nctilius L.F.L.N. . . . . s. L. Valer . . . P.N. Potitus III. . . . ens. M. Furius L.F. Sp : N.C. . . . . . Postumius A F A.N. Albinus Regillens. L.F. XVI.	C. Valerius Potitus III. M'. Sergius Fidenas P. Cornelius Maluginensis Cn. Cornelius Cossus K. Fabius Ambustus Sp. Nautius Rutilus II. } Tribb. Milit. IV. 61.	P. Cornelius N. Fabius L. Valerius † Terentius Maximus † } Tribb. Milit. XIV. 12.	
107	351	402	94-3	. . . rvilius P.F.Q.N. Ahal . . . Q. Sulpicius Ser : F. Ser : N. Camerin. Cornut. . . . . Q.F.P.N. Fiden. A. Manlius A.F. Cn : N. Vulso Capitol : II. . . irginius L. F. Opetr. N. Tricost : Esqui . . M' Sergius L.F.L.N. Fidenas II. Tr. Mil.	M'. Æmilius Mamercinus II. L. Valerius Potitus III. Ap. Claudius Crassus M. Quintillus Varus L. Julius Iulus M. Postumius M. Furius Camillus M. Postumius Albinus } Tribb. Milit. V. 1.	T. Quintius C. Julius A. Manlius . . . . } Tribb. Milit. XVI. 17.	
108	352	401	94-4	. . . urius L.F. Sp : N. Camillus L. Julius L.F. Vopisci N. Iulus . . . rnelius P.F.A.N. Cossus III. M' Aimilius Mam : F.M.N. Mamercinus III. . . . rius L.F.P.N. Potitus IV. K. Fabius M.F.Q.N. Ambustus II. Tr. Mil.	C. Servilius Ahala III. Q. Servilius L. Virginius Q. Sulpicius A. Manlius II. M. Sergius Fidenas II. } Tribb. Milit. V. 8.	P. Cornelius K. Fabius Sp. Nautius C. Valerius M'. Sergius † Junius Lucullus † } Tribb. Milit. XIV. 19.	
109	353	400	95-1	. . . lius M.F. Cn : N. Vulso P. Maelius Sp : F. C.N. Capitolinus . . . . . us P.F.P.N. Calvus Esquilinus Sp. F . . . ius L.F. Sp : N. Medullinus . . . . . us L.F.M'N. Pansa Saccus L. Poblilius L.F. Voler. N. Philo Vulcus Tr. Mil.	L. Valerius Potitus IV. M. Furius Camillus II. M'. Æmilius Mamercinus III. Cn. Cornelius Cossus II. K. Fabius Ambustus II. L. Julius Iulus } Tribb. Milit. V. 10.	M'. Claudius M. Quintius L. Julius M. Furius L. Valerius } Tribb. Milit. XIV. 35.	
110	354	399	95-2	. . . cius M.F.M.N. Augurinus C. Duilius K.F.K.N. Longus . . . . . s L.F.L.N. Priscus M. Veturius Ti. F. Sp . N. Crass. Cicurin. . . . onius L.F.L.N. Rufus Voler. Poblilius P.F. Voler. N. Philo. Tr. Mil.	P. Licinius Calvus P. Mænius L. Tatinius P. Mælius L. Furius Medullinus II. L. Publilius Volcus } Tribb. Milit. V. 12.	C. Servilius L. Virginius Q. Sulpicius A. Manlius † Capitus † Claudius M. † Ancus † } Tribb. Milit. XIV. 38.	

Year of the Common-wealth.	Year of Rome.	Year before the Christian Era.	Olympiads.	Fasti Capitolini.	LIVY.	DIODORUS.	DIONYSIUS.
111	355	398	95-3	. . . . . s L.F.PN. Potitus V. L. Furiu . F. Sp : N. Medullin. III. . . . . M.F.M.N. Lactucin. Maxum. Q. Servilius. . . . . us II. Q. Sulpicius Ser. . . . . . Tr. Mil.	M. Veturius M. Pomponius C. Duilius Volero Publilius Cn. Genucius L. Atilius } Tribb. Milit. V. 13.	L. Iulius M. Furius M. Æmilius Cn. Cornelius K. Fabius Sex. † Paulus † } Tribb. Milit. XIV. 44.	
112	356	397	95-4	. . . . . s II. L. Sergius M'F.L.N. . . . . nus IV. P. Cornelius P.F. . . . . nsis A. Manlius A.F.C.	L. Valerius Potitus V. M. Valerius Maximus M. Furius Camillus III. L. Furius Medullinus III. Q. Servilius Fidenas II. Q. Sulpicius Camerinus II. } Tribb. Milit. V. 14.	P. Manlius Sp. † Manius † L. Furius . . . . } Tribb. Milit. XIV. 47.	
113	357	396	96-1	. . . accus II. . . squilinus II. Q. Manlius A. F. . . . . . Cn. Genucit. . . . . Capitolinus II. L. Atilius L. . . . . N. . . . . Camillus Di . . . . . . F.M.N. Maluginensis Mag . . .	L. Julius Iulus L. Furius Medullinus IV. L. Sergius Fidenas A. Postumius Regillensis P. Cornelius Maluginensis A. Manlius } Tribb. Milit. V. 16.	Cn. Genucius L. Atilius M. Pomponius C. Duilius M. Veturius †Valerius †Publilius } Tribb. Milit. XIV. 54.	
114	358	395	96-2	. . . . . Cossus L. Fu . . . . Scipio . . . . stus III.	P. Licinius Calvus L. Titinius P. Mænius P. Mælius Cn. Genucius L. Atilius } Tribb. Milit. V. 18.	L. Valerius M. Furius Q. Servilius Q. Sulpicius Claudius † Ugo † † Marius Appius † } Tribb. Milit. XIV. 82.	
115	359	394	96-3	. . . . s III.	P. Cornelius Cossus P. Cornelius Scipio M. Valerius Maximus II. K. Fabius Ambustus III. L. Furius Medullinus V. Q. Servilius III. } Tribb. Milit. V. 24.	L. Sergius A. Postumius P. Cornelius Sex. † Censius † Q. Manlius † Anitius † Camillus } Tribb. Milit. XIV. 85.	
116	360	393	96-4		M. Furius Camillus IV. L. Furius Medullinus VI. C. Æmilius L. Valerius Publicola Sp. Postumius P. Cornelius II. } Tribb. Milit. V. 26.	L. Titinius P. Licinius P. Mælius Q. Manlius Cn. Genucius L. Atilius } Tribb. Milit. XIV. 90.	
117	361	392	97-1		L. Lucretius Flavus Ser. Sulpicius Camerinus } Coss. V. 29.	P. † Sextus † Cornelius Crassus † K. Fabius L. Furius Q. Servilius M. Valerius } Tribb. Milit. XIV. 94.	

Year of the Commonwealth.	Year of Rome.	Year before the Christian Era.	Olympiads.	Fasti Capitolini.	LIVY.	DIODORUS.	DIONYSIUS.
118	362	391	97-2		L. Valerius Potitus, M. Manlius Capitolinus } Coss. V. 31.	M. Furius, C. Æmilius, † Catulus Verus † } Tribb. Milit. XIV. 97.	
119	363	390	97-3		L. Lucretius, Ser. Sulpicius, M. Æmilius, L. Furius Medullinus VII., Agrippa Furius, C. Æmilius II. } Tribb. Milit. V. 32.	L. Lucretius, Ser. † Casson † } Coss. XIV. 99.	
120	364	389	97-4		Q. Fabius Ambustus, Fabius Ambustus, Fabius Ambustus, Q. Sulpicius Longus, Q. Servilius IV., Ser. Cornelius Maluginensis } Tribb. Milit. V. 36.	L. Valerius, A. Manlius } Coss. XIV. 103.	
121	365	388	98-1		L. Valerius Publicola II., L. Virginius, P. Cornelius, A. Manlius, L. Æmilius, L. Postumius } Tribb. Milit. VI. 1.	L. Lucretius, Ser. Sulpicius, C. Æmilius, C. † Rufus † } Tribb. Milit. XIV. 107.	
122	366	387	98-2			Q. † Kæso †, † Ænus † Sulpicius, K. Fabius, Q. Servilius, P. Cornelius, M. † Claudius † } Tribb. Milit. XIV. 110.	
123	367	386	98-3			M. Furius, † Caius †, † Æmilius † } Tribb. Milit. XV. 2.	
124	368	385	98-4			L. Lucretius, Ser. Sulpicius } Coss. XV. 8.	
125	369	384	99-1			L. Valerius, A. Manlius } Coss. XV. 14.	
126	370	383	99-2			L. Lucretius, † Sentius † Sulpicius, L. Æmilius, L. Furius } Tribb. Milit. XV. 15.	
127	371	382	99-3			Q. Sulpicius, C. Fabius, Servilius Cornelius, P. † Ugo †, Sex. † Anius †, Caius † Marcus † } Tribb. Milit. XV. 20.	
128	372	381	99-4			P. Cornelius, L. Virginius, L. Papirius, M. Furius, A. Valerius, L. Manlius, Q. Postumius } Tribb. Milit. XV. 22.	

EXPLANATION OF THE FIRST TABLES.

The preceding tables exhibit a view of the lists of consuls and military tribunes from the beginning of the commonwealth to the Gaulish invasion, according to four distinct authorities: the remains of the Fasti Capitolini, Livy, Diodorus Siculus, and Dionysius of Halicarnassus. And I have endeavored to arrange each list according to the chronology adopted by its own particular author; so that as this chronology varies, the same year will be found marked by the names of different sets of consuls, according as we prefer one of these four authorities to the other.

I. The principal fragments of the Fasti Capitolini were discovered in the year 1546, in the course of some excavations which were then being made on the ground of the ancient Forum. They have been preserved in the museum of the Capitol, and their contents have been long known to the world, as they have been often published. My extracts have been taken from the edition of Sigonius; and I have been careful to give them in their genuine state, without noticing the additions by which Sigonius attempted to supply from conjecture the lost or effaced words of the original marble.

It happened, however, that about two hundred and seventy years after the discovery of these fragments, two other fragments of the same marble were brought to light in the course of a new excavation in the Forum, on the very spot where the former remains had been found. This was in the years 1817 and 1818; and Signor Borghesi, an eminent Italian antiquary, published a fac-simile of these new portions of the Fasti, and illustrated them in two able memoirs published at Milan in the year 1818. The new pieces joined on exactly with those discovered before; so that in several instances a word, of which only one syllable had been preserved in the former fragments, was now completed by the discovery of the remaining syllable, after an interval of nearly three centuries. I have, therefore, copied their contents from Borghesi's edition, and incorporated them with the older fragments published long ago by Sigonius.

These Fasti do not notice the Greek Olympiads; but they preserve in several places notices of the years from the foundation of Rome. Thus the consulship of Sex. Quinctilius and P. Curiatus is placed in the year 300, and the triumph of the consuls who immediately succeeded the decemvirate, M. Horatius and L. Valerius, is assigned to the month of August, 304. It appears, then, that these Fasti only allow two years to the decemvirate, and not three; and, moreover, that they place its commencement in the year 302, agreeing in that respect with the chronology of Livy.

II. Livy also makes no mention of the Greek chronology; but he too, from time to time, notices the years from the building of Rome. Thus he places the first institution of the military tribuneship in 310 (IV. 7), and the beginning of the decemvirate in 302 (III. 33). Taking these two dates for my starting points, I have calculated from them the dates of the years before and after them, according to Livy's list of consuls. This brings the date of the expulsion of the Tarquins to the year 247; but then it seems probable that Livy has omitted the consuls of the fourth year of the commonwealth by accident; and it seems as if he had omitted those of one or two years more at the beginning of the great Volscian war of Coriolanus. With the addition of these three years, the first year of the commonwealth would become the year 244, which would agree with Livy's own calculation of the reigns of the several kings; but as my object in these tables was rather to give the actual chronology of the several authorities than to endeavor to correct it, I have reckoned no greater number of consulships in the table of the Fasti according to Livy, than Livy himself allows for.

III. Dionysius regularly gives the Olympiads along with the Roman consulships, so that the synchronistic part of his chronology can be ascertained with certainty. With him, the first year of the commonwealth is the first year of the sixty-eighth Olympiad (I. 74); and the Gaulish invasion falls in the first year of the ninety-eighth Olympiad; so that there were just one hundred and twenty years between them. Again, the first year of the commonwealth is the two hundred and forty-fifth from the foundation of Rome (I. 75); so that the Gaulish invasion falls, according to Dionysius, in the year of Rome 365, and the intermediate years can, therefore, be determined without difficulty But as the remaining part of Dionysius' history ends at the year of Rome 312, we can not compare his lists of the consuls and military tribunes, from 313 to 365, with those of the Fasti Capitolini, of Livy, and of Diodorus.

IV. Diodorus gives the Olympiads also, but his synchronistic system does not agree with that of Dionysius. We have not his list of the early consulships, because his tenth book which contained them is lost: but the seventy-fifth Olympiad falls, according to him, in the consulship of Sp. Cassius and Proclus Virginius, whereas that same consulship is by Dionysius placed five years earlier, in the last year of the seventy-third Olympiad. Accordingly, if the list of consuls in the two writers had continued to agree with one another, the invasion of the Gauls would have fallen, by Diodorus' reckoning, in the second year of the ninety-ninth Olympiad. And yet he does place it in the second year of the ninety-eighth Olympiad. This is the date assigned to it by Polybius (I. 6), and it was probably so generally agreed upon, that Diodorus thought himself obliged to conform his reckoning to it. He had already introduced into his list several variations from the Fasti followed by Dionysius. For instance, he had omitted the consulship of C. Julius and Q. Fabius, which Dionysius places in Olymp. 74-4; and he had then inserted two consulships unknown to Dionysius, to Livy, and to the Fasti Capitolini, in Olymp. 82-2, and 82-3. Thus the first year of the decemvirate, which according to Dionysius was Olymp. 82-3, is with Diodorus Olymp. 84-1. The difference is then reduced by one year, because Diodorus assigns only two years to the decemvirate instead of three; and thus the famous consulship of L. Valerius and M. Horatius is placed by him five years later than by Dionysius, in Olymp. 84-3 instead of Olymp. 83-2. But after this he inserts another consulship in Olymp. 90-1, so that the difference is again raised to six years, and the Gaulish invasion ought consequently to have been placed in Olymp. 99-3. To prevent this, and to bring it to Olymp. 98-2, he strikes out the consulships and military tribuneships of five years from Olymp. 91-2 to Olymp. 92-2 inclusive, so that the tribunes whom he places in Olymp. 91-2 are L. Sergius, M. Papirius, and M. Servilius, whom he ought, according to his own system, to have placed in Olymp. 92-3. The object desired is thus accomplished, and the Gaulish invasion is in this manner thrown back to Olymp. 98-2. But so resolved was Diodorus to follow his own system in his general chronology, although he had felt himself in a manner forced to depart from it in giving the date of the Gaulish invasion, that, in order to return to it, he fills up the five years following Olymp. 98-2 with the very same consulships and tribuneships which he had already given for it and the four years preceding it; so that the military tribunes of Olymp. 99-4 are, in fact, the tribunes of the year next after the Gaulish invasion, and those of Olymp. 99-3 are evidently, although the names are grievously corrupted, the very same with the tribunes whom he had before placed in Olymp. 98-2, and under whose tribuneship he had given his account of the Gaulish war.

Thus much will suffice in illustration of the table. It may be observed, however, as a proof of the confusion of the early chronology of Rome, that the only instance in which the Roman annals of this period attempted any synchronism with the events of foreign history, tends but to perplex the subject still more. The annals of the year of Rome 323, according to Livy's reckoning, that is, the year of the consulship of T. Quintius and C. Julius, had recorded that in that year the Carthaginians first crossed over with an army into Sicily, having been invited to take part in the domestic wars of the Sicilian states. Now this year, according to Dionysius, was Olymp. 87-4, and according to Diodorus it would be Olymp. 89-1. But the Carthaginians crossed over into Sicily, for the first time since the reign of Gelon, in Olymp. 92-3, according to Diodorus, XIII. 43, and this is confirmed by Xenophon, Hellenic. I. 1, ad finem, so that the true date of this event is nineteen years later than the date assigned to it in the Roman annals, if we follow the reckoning of Dionysius, and fourteen years later if we follow that of Diodorus. Niebuhr supposes that the Roman annalists confused the Carthaginian invasion with the first appearance of an Athenian fleet in Sicily, namely, with the expedition of Laches, in the fifth year of the Peloponnesian war (Thucydides, III. 86), that is, in Olymp. 88-2. But this is one of the very few conjectures of Niebuhr which appear to me quite improbable. The expedition of Laches consisted only of twenty ships, and its operations were so insignificant that it cannot be conceived to have attracted the attention of the Romans. But the Carthaginian expedition which Hannibal led against Selinus consisted, according to the lowest computation, of one hundred thousand men and sixty ships of war; and his great success in the destruction of so powerful a city as Selinus was likely to have spread terror through all the neighboring countries. Yet how is it possible to make the ninety-second Olympiad synchronize with the consulship of T. Quinctius and C. Iulius, that is, with the year 323 or 324 of Rome?

Note.—I have said that Livy places the beginning of the decemvirate in the year 302. His words are, "Anno trecentesimo altero quam condita Roma erat." III. 33. But Sigonius understands this to mean the year 301, although he finds it difficult to make out nine years in Livy's narrative between the first decemvirate and the institution of the military tribuneship, which Livy places beyond all dispute in the year 310. As to the grammatical question, although I am aware that the point has been contested, yet it seems to me certain that "Anno trecentesimo altero" must signify the year 302, and not 301. For "alter" must immediately precede "tertius," and there can be no doubt that "Anno trecentesimo tertio" would signify the year 303. The confusion seems to have arisen from such expressions as "alter ab undecimo," which, although Servius interprets even this to mean the "thirteenth," may yet, I suppose, be fairly understood to be the twelfth, because here the inclusive system of reckoning is followed, and the eleventh year itself is counted as the first, the twelfth as the second from the eleventh, the thirteenth as the third, and so on. Thus the thirteenth of March is, according to the Roman reckoning, the third day before the Ides, or fifteenth, because the fifteenth itself is reckoned as the first. But in abstract numeral expressions, such as "trecentesimo altero," it is different, for here the inclusive system is not followed, and "alter" is therefore the "second" in our sense of the word, and "trecentesimo primo" would be the date of the year preceding it. The usage of the Greek word δεύτερος is exactly analogous to this. Δευτέρῳ ἔτει μετὰ την μάχην would be the year next after the battle, which we should more naturally call the "first year" after it. But 'Ολυμπιὰς δευτέρα πρὸς ταῖς ἑκατὸν is not the one hundred and first, but the one hundred and second Olympiad. If Sigonius' interpretation could be shown to be right, it would only embarrass his system still more; for if "trecentesimo altero" means what we should call "the three hundred and first," then "trecentesimo decimo" in Livy, IV. 7, must be what we should call the "three hundred and ninth," it being certain that in all reckonings "alter" is immediately followed by "tertius."

CONSULS AND MILITARY TRIBUNES.

Year of the Common-wealth.	Year of Rome, common reckoning.	Year before the Christian Era.	Olympiad.	Fasti Capitolini.	DIODORUS.	LIVY.	Fasti Siculi.	Fasti Cuspiniani sive Norisiani.
123	367	387	98-2		*Tribb. Milit.*—XIV. 110. Q. † Kæso † † Ænus † Sulpicius K. Fabius Q. Servilius P. Cornelius M. † Claudius †	*Tribb. Milit.*—VI. 4. T. Quintius Cincinnatus Q. Servilius Fidenas V. L. Julius Julus L. Aquillius Corvus L. Lucretius Tricipitinus Ser. Sulpicius Rufus		Capitolino & Corbo.
124	368	386	98-3		*Tribb. Milit.*—XV. 2. M. Furius † Caius † † Æmilius †	*Tribb. Milit.*—VI. 5. L. Papirius C. Cornelius C. Sergius L. Æmilius II. L. Menenius L. Valerius Publicola III.		Cursore & Lanato.
125	369	385	98-4		*Coss.*—XV. 8. L. Lucretius Ser. Sulpicius	*Tribb. Milit.*—VI. 6. M. Furius Camillus Ser. Cornelius Maluginensis Q. Servilius Fidenas VI. L. Quintius Cincinnatus L. Horatius Pulvillus P. Valerius		Maluginense & Cincinnato.
126	370	384	99-1		*Coss.*—XV. 14. L. Valerius A. Manlius.	*Tribb. Milit.*—VI. 11. A. Manlius P. Cornelius T. Quintius } Capitolini L. Quintius } L. Papirius Cursor II. C. Sergius II.		Capitolino & Cincinnato.
127	371	383	99-2		*Tribb. Milit.*—XV. 15. L. Lucretius † Sentius † Sulpicius L. Æmilius L. Furius	*Tribb. Milit.*—VI. 18. Ser. Cornelius Maluginensis III. P. Valerius Potitus II. M. Furius Camillus Ser. Sulpicius Rufus II. C. Papirius Crassus T. Quintius Cincinnatus II.		Rufo & Camillo.
128	372	382	99-3		*Tribb. Milit.*—XV. 20. Q. Sulpicius C. Fabius Servilius Cornelius P. † Ugo † Sex. † Anius † Caius † Marcus †	*Tribb. Milit.*—VI. 21. L. Valerius IV. A. Manlius III. Ser. Sulpicius III. L. Lucretius L. Æmilius III. M. Trebonius	Genucius & Curtius Γαλάται καὶ Κελτοὶ Ῥώμης ἐκράτησαν πλὴν τοῦ Καπετωλίου.	Publicola III. & Flacco III.

Year of the Common-wealth.	Year of Rome.	Year before the Christian Era.	Olympiad.	Fasti Capitolini	DIODORUS.	LIVY.	Fasti Siculi.	Fasti Cuspiniani sive Norisiani.
129	373	381	99-4		*Tribb. Milit.*—XV. 22. F. Cornelius L. Virginius L. Papirius M. Furius A. Valerius L. Manlius Q. Postumius	*Tribb. Milit.*—VI. 22. Sp. Papirius L. Papirius Ser. Cornelius Maluginensis IV. Q. Servilius Ser. Sulpicius L. Æmilius IV.	Macrinus II. & Capitolinus IV.	Fidenas & Crasso.
130	374	380	100-1		*Tribb. Milit.*—XV. 23. T. Quintius L. Servilius L. Julius Aquillius Decius Lucretius Ancus Ser. Sulpicius	*Tribb. Milit.*—VI. 22. M. Furius Camillus VII. A. Postumius Regillensis L. Postumius Regillensis L. Furius L. Lucretius M. Fabius Ambustus	Vibulanus & Elva	Publicola IV. & Tricipitino.
131	375	379	100-2		*Tribb. Milit.*—XV. 24. L. Palpirius C. Cornelius L. Mallius C. Servilius A. Valerius Q. Fabius	*Tribb. Milit.*—VI. 27. L. Valerius V. P. Valerius III. C. Sergius III. L. Menenius II. Sp. Papirius Ser. Cornelius Maluginensis	† Pacelaus † & Crassus	Publicola V. & Mamertino VI.
132	376	378	100-3		*Tribb. Milit.*—XV. 25. M. Cornelius Q. Servilius M. Furius L. Quintius	*Tribb. Milit.*—VI. 30. P. Manlius C. Manlius L. Julius C. Sextilius M. Albinius L. Antistius	Macrinus III. & Lænas	Capitolino & Albino.
133	377	377	100-4		*Tribb. Milit.*—XV. 28. L. Papirius M. † Publius † T. Cornelius L. Quintius	*Tribb. Milit.*—VI. 31. Sp. Furius Q. Servilius II. C. Licinius P. Clœlius M. Horatius L. Geganius	† Manlius † & Capitolinus V.	Fidenas II. & Siculo.
134	378	376	101-1		*Tribb. Milit.*—XV. 36. Ser. Sulpicius L. Papirius T. Cornelius M. Quintius	*Tribb. Milit.*—VI. 32. L. Æmilius P. Valerius IV. C. Veturius Ser. Sulpicius L. Quintius } Cincinnati C. Quintius }	Macrinus IV. & Fidenas	Mamertino & Cincinnato.
135	379	375	101-2		*Tribb. Milit.*—XV. 38. L. Valerius Crispus † Mallius Fabius † Ser. Sulpicius Lucretius	[Omitted in Livy, through some confusion in his reckoning.]	Malogennesius & Crassus	Lanato III. & Prætextato.

Year of the Common-wealth.	Year of Rome.	Year before the Christian Era.	Olympiad.	Fasti Capitolini.	DIODORUS.	LIVY.	Fasti Siculi.	Fasti Cuspiniani sive Norisiani.
136	380	374	101-3		*Tribb. Milit.*—XV. 41. Q. Crassus † Servilius † Cornelius Sp. Papirius † Fabius † Albus†	VI. 35. No curule Magistrates	Julius & Virginius	Bacho † Solo †
137	381	373	101-4		*Tribb. Milit.*—XV. 48. M. Furius L. Furius A. Postumius L. Lucretius M. Fabius L. Postumius	VI. 35. No curule Magistrates	Capitolinus VI. & Camerinus	Papirio & † Ninio †
138	382	372	102-1	. . . actus est . . . t . . dedicavit	*Tribb. Milit.*—XV. 50. L. Valerius P. † Ancus † C. Terentius L. Menenius C. Sulpicius T. Papirius L. Æmilius M. Fabius	VI. 35. No curule Magistrates	Pœnus & † Melito †	† Scarabiense † & Celimontano.
139	383	371	102-2	. . . opilcola V. . . . ext. III. . . luginensis VI. Tr. Mil.	*Tribb. Milit.*—XV. 51. P. Manlius C. † Erenucius † C. † Sextus † Tib. Julius L. Albinius P. Trebonius C. Mallius L. Anthestius	VI. 35. No curule Magistrates	Crassus & Tullius	Prisco & Cominio.
140	384	370	102-3	. . . . . Cossus . . . . uginensis. M. Fabius K.F.M.N. Ambustus II. Tr. Mil.	*Tribb. Milit.*—XV. 57. Q. Servilius L. Furius C. Licinius P. Clœlius	VI. 35. No curule Magistrates	Tricipitinus & Fidenas II.	Mamertino & † Solo †
141	385	369	102-4	. . . . . . pitolin. . . . . . luginensis VII. . extat. IV. Tr. Mil. Sp. Servilius C.F.C.N. Structus L. Papirius Sp. F.C.N. Crassus. L. Veturius L.F. Sp. N. Crassus Cicurinus. . . . llus IV. Dict. Rei Gerundæ Causa. . . . . amercinus Mag. Eq. . . . . um in Milites ex. S.C. abdicarunt. In eorum locum facti sunt . . . pitolinus. Dict. Seditionis sedandæ et R.G.C. . . . . mus e Plebe Mag. eq.	*Tribb. Milit.*—XV. 61. L. Æmilius C. Virginius Ser. Sulpicius L. Quintius C. Cornelius C. Valerius	*Tribb. Milit.*—VI. 36. L. Furius A. Manlius Ser. Sulpicius Ser. Cornelius P. Valerius C. Valerius	Cossus & Pœnus II.	Medullino & Polito.

Year of the Commonwealth.	Year of Rome.	Year before the Christian Era.	Olympiad.	Fasti Capitolini.	DIODORUS.	LIVY.	Fasti Siculi.	Fasti Cuspiniani sive Norisiani.
142	386	368	103-1	. . . . ssus II. . . . . aluginensis II. . . . . acerinus L. Veturius L.F. Sp. N. Crassus Cicurinus II. P. Valerius L.F.L.N. Potitus Poplicola VI. P. Manlius A.F.A.N. Capitolinus II. . . . amillus V. Dict. Rei Gerund. Causa. . . . . Mag. eq.	*Tribb. Milit.*—XV. 71. L. Papirius L. Menenius Ser. Cornelius Ser. Sulpicius	*Tribb. Milit.*—VI. 36. Q. Servilius C. Veturius A. Cornelius M. Cornelius Q. Quintius M. Fabius	† Achillas † & Mugillanus	Fidenas III. & Maluginense.
143	387	367	103-2	. . . EBE PRIMUM CREARI CŒPTI. . . . mercinus L. Sextius Sex. F.N.N. Sextin. Lateran. Primus e plebe. . . . . . Regillensis Albinus C. Sulpicius M.F.Q.N. Peticus.	XV. 75. Anarchy	*Tribb. Milit.*—VI. 38. T. Quintius Ser. Cornelius Ser. Sulpicius Sp. Servilius L. Papirius L. Veturius	Atratinus & Vibulanus	Capitolino & Structo
144	388	366	103-3	. . . tinensis Q. Servilius Q.F.Q.N. Ahala . .	*Tribb. Milit.*—XV. 76. L. Furius Paulus Mallius Ser. Sulpicius Ser. Cornelius	*Tribb. Milit.*—VI. 42. A. Cornelius II. M. Cornelius II. M. Geganius P. Manlius L. Veturius P. Valerius VI.	Capitolinus VII. & Vibulanus II.	Cosso II. & Grasso.
145	389	365	103-4	. . . Peticus C. Licinius C.F.P.N. Calvus	*Tribb. Milit.*—XV. 77. Q. Servilius C. Veturius A. Cornelius M. Cornelius M. Fabius	*Coss.*—VII. 1. L. Sextius L. Æmilius Mamercinus	Mugillanus II. & Rutilius	Mamercino & Laterano.
146	390	364	104-1	. . . ercinus II. Cn. Genucius. M.F.M.N. Aventinensis. . . . mperiossus. Dict. . . . Natta. Mag. eq.	*Tribb. Milit.*—XV. 78. T. Quintius Ser. Cornelius Ser. Sulpicius	*Coss.*—VII. 1. L. Genucius Q. Servilius	Æmilius & Rusticus	Abentinense & Haala.
147	391	363	104-2	. . . Ahala II. L. Genucius. M.F.M.N. Aventinensis II. Regillensis. Dict. Rei Gerundæ Causa. . Sci . . . Mag. eq.	*Coss.*—XV. 82. L. Æmilius Mamercus L. Sextius Laterius	*Coss.*—VII. 2. C. Sulpicius Peticus C. Licinius Stolo	† Cossus † Medullinus	Petico & Calbo.
148	392	362	104-3	. . . . C. Sulpicius M.F.Q.N. Peticus II. . . . Capitolinus Crispinus. Dict. . . . . M.N. Maluginensis. Mag. eq. Rei Gerundæ Causa. . . alibus . . . o CCCXCII.	*Coss.*—XV. 90. L. Genucius Q. Servilius	*Coss.*—VII. 3. Cn. Genucius L. Sextius Mamercinus II.	Flavus & Camerinus	Mamertino & Abentinense.

Year of the Commonwealth.	Year of Rome.	Year before the Christian Era.	Olympiad.	Fasti Capitolini.	DIODORUS.	LIVY.	Fasti Siculi.	Fasti Cuspiniani sive Norisiani.
149	393	361	104-4	. . . . . mbustus C. Pœtelius C.F.Q.N. Libo. Visolus. . . . Ahala. Dict. Rei. Gerund. Causa . . . Capitolin. Crispinus. Mag. eq. . . . . Cos. De Galleis et Tiburtibus. . . . . rt. M. Fabius N.F.M.N. Ambustus. Cos. Ovans. De Herniceis. Ann. CCCXCIII. Non. Sept.	*Coss.*—XV. 95. C. Sulpicius C. Licinius	*Coss.*—VII. 4. Q. Servilius Ahala L. Genucius	Potitus & Capitolinus	Haala II. & Abentinense.
150	394	360	105-1	. . . . Lænas Cn. Manlius L.F.A.N. Capitolin. Imperioss.	*Coss.*—XVI. 2. Cn. Genucius L. Æmilius	*Coss.*—VII. 9. C. Sulpicius C. Licinius Calvus	Genucius & † Cubius †	Stolo & Petico.
151	395	359	105-2	. . . . . . mbustus. C. Plautius P.F.P.N. Proculus C. Sulpicius M.F.Q.N. Peticus II. Dict. Galleis. Ann. CCCXCV. Nonis Mai. C. Plautius P.F.P.N. Proculus. Cos. De Herniceis. Ann. CCCXCV. Idibus Mai.	*Coss.*—XVI. 4. Q. Servilius L. Genucius	*Coss.*—VII. 11. C. Pœtelius Balbus M. Fabius Ambustus	Mamertinus & Lateranus	Ambusto & Proculo.
152	396	358	105-3	. . . . . . C. Marcius L.F.C.N. Rutilus. Cos. De Privernatibus. Ann. CCCXCVI. Kal. Jun.	*Coss.*—XVI. 6. C. Licinius C. Sulpicius	*Coss.*—VII. 12. M. Popillius Lænas Cn. Manlius	Petitus & Galba	Rutilo & Capitolino.
153	397	357	105-4	. . . . C. Marcius L.F.C.N. Rutilus. Dict. De Tusceis. Ann. CCCXCVII. Pridie Non. Mai.	*Coss.*—XVI. 9. M. Fabius C. Pœtelius	*Coss.*—VII. 12. C. Fabius C. Plautius	Mamertinus II. & † Sulla †	Ambusto & Lænas II.
154	398	356	106-1		*Coss.*—XVI. 15. M. Popilius Lænas Cn. Manlius Imperiosus	*Coss.*—VII. 16. C. Marcius Cn. Manlius	† Allus † & Genucius	Rutilo & Capitolino.
155	399	355	106-2	. . . . M. Fabius N.F.M.N. Ambustus II. Cos. III. De Tiburtibus. Ann. CCCXCIX. III. Non. Jun.	*Coss.*—XVI. 23. M. Fabius C. Plotius	*Coss.*—VII. 17. M. Fabius Ambustus II. M. Popillius Lænas II.	Stolo & Petinus	Ambusto II. & Lænas II.
156	400	354	106-3		*Coss.*—XVI. 28. C. Marcius Cn. Manlius	*Coss.*—VII. 18. C. Sulpicius Peticus III. M. Valerius Publicola "Quadringentesimo anno quam urbs Roma condita erat, quinto tricesimo quam a Gallis reciperata."	Libo & Lænas	Petico & Publicola.

Year of the Common-wealth.	Year of Rome.	before the Christian Era.	Olympiad.	Fasti Capitolini.	DIODORUS.	LIVY.	Fasti Siculi.	Fasti Cuspiniani sive Norisiani.
157	401	353	106-4		*Coss.*—XVI. 32. M. Fabius M. Popillius	*Coss.*—VII. 18. M. Fabius Ambustus III. T. Quintius "in quibusdam annalibus pro T. Quintio M. Popilium consulem invenio."	Ambustus & Proculus	Ambusto III. & Capitolino.
158	402	352	107-1		*Coss.*—XVI. 37. C. Sulpicius M. Valerius	*Coss.*—VII. 19. C. Sulpicius Peticus IV. M. Valerius Publicola II.	Rusticius & Capitolinus	Petico IV. & Publicola II.
159	403	351	107-2	. . . lius M C.F.N. Lænas Cos. III. . . . alleis. Ann. CDIII. Quirinalibus.	*Coss.*—XVI. 40. M. Fabius T. Quintius	*Coss.*—VII. 21. P. Valerius Publicola C. Marcius Rutilus	Ambustus II. & Lænas	Publicola & Rutilo II.
160	404	350	107-3	. . . audius P.F. . . . Regil . . . . . biit . . . Dict. . . . Mag. eq. Comit. Habend. Causa.	*Coss.*—XVI. 64. M. Valerius C. Sulpicius	*Coss.*—VII. 22. C. Sulpicius Peticus T. Quintius Pennus	† Potitus & Publicola †	Petico V. & Penno II.
161	405	349	107-4	. . . . erius M.F.M.N. Corvus . . . Dict. Comit. Habend. Causa.	*Coss.*—XVI. 52. C. Marcius P. Valerius	*Coss.*—VII. 23. M. Popilius Lænas N. Cornelius Scipio	Rusticius II. & †Pœnus †	Lænas IV. & Scipione.
162	406	348	108-1	. . . . rioss. Torquat . .	*Coss.*—XVI. 53. C. Sulpicius C. Quintius	*Coss.*—VII. 24. L. Furius Camillus Ap. Claudius Crassus	Scipio & Lænas	Camilo & Crasso.
163	407	347	108-2	. . . . Visolus. . . . erius M.F.M.N. Corvus. Cos. II. . . . Antiatibus Volsceis Satricaneisque. Ann. CDVII. K. Febr.	*Coss.*—XVI. 56. C. Cornelius M. Popillius	*Coss.*—VII. 26. M. Valerius Corvus M. Popilius Lænas IV.	Camillus & Crassus	Lænas IV. & Corvino.
164	408	346	108-3		*Coss.*—XVI. 59. M. Æmilius T. Quintius	*Coss.*—VII. 27. T. Manlius Torquatus C. Plautius	Corvinus & Lænas II.	Venno & Torquato.
165	409	345	108-4		*Coss.*—XVI. 66. M. Fabius Ser. Sulpicius	*Coss.*—VII. 27. M. Valerius Corvus II. C. Pœtelius	Venox & Torquatus	Corvo & Visulo.
166	410	344	109-1	. . rius . M.F.M.N. Corvus. De Samnitibus Anno CDX. X. K. Oct. . . nelius P.F.A.N. Cossus Arvina . . os. De Samnitibus. Ann. CDX VIII. K. Oct.	*Coss.*—XVI. 69. M. Valerius M. Popillius	*Coss.*—VII. 28. M. Fabius Dorso Ser. Sulpicius Camerinus	Corvinus II. & Libo	Dorsus & Rufa.
167	411	343	109-2		*Coss.*—XVI. 70. C. Plautius T. Manlius	*Coss.*—VII. 28. C. Marcius Rutilus III. T. Manlius Torquatus II.	Vulso & Camerinus	Rutilo III. & Torquato.
168	412	342	109-3		*Coss.*—XVI. 72. M. Valerius C. Pœtelius	*Coss.*—VII. 28. M. Valerius Corvus III. A. Cornelius Cossus	Rutilus & Torquatus	Corvo III. & Cosso III.

Year of the Commonwealth.	Year of Rome.	Year before the Christian Era.	Olympiad.	Fasti Capitolini.	DIODORUS.	LIVY.	Fasti Siculi.	Fasti Cuspiniani sive Norisiani.
169	413	341	109-4	. . . anlius L.F.A.N. Imperiossus Torquat. . . os III. De Latineis Campaneis Si dicineis . . urunceis. A: CDXIII. XV. K. Junias.	*Coss.*—XVI. 74. C. Marcius T. Manlius Torquatus	*Coss.*—VII. 38. C. Marcius Rutilus Q. Servilius	Corvinus III. & Cossus	Haala III. & Rutilo IIII.
170	414	340	110-1	. . ubilius Q.F.Q.N. Philo Cos. De Latineis Ann. CDXIV. Idib. Janar.	*Coss.*—XVI. 77. M. Valerius A. Cornelius	*Coss.*—VIII. 1. C. Plautius II. L. Æmilius Mamercinus	† Allus † & Rutilius	Venno II. & Mamerco.
171	415	339	110-2	L. Furius Sp. F.M.N. Camilus Cos. De Pedaneis et Tiburtibus. An. CDXV. IV. K. Oct. C. Mænius. P.F.P.N. Cos. De Antiatibus Lavineis Veliterneis. Ann. CDXV. Pridie K. Oct.	*Coss.*—XVI. 82. Q. Servilius Marcius Rutilus	*Coss.*—VIII. 3. T. Manlius Torquatus III. P. Decius Mus	Venox II. & † Mamertinus †	Torquato III. & Mure.
172	416	338	110-3		*Coss.*—XVI. 84. L. Æmilius C. Plotius	*Coss.*—VIII. 12. Ti. Æmilius Mamercinus Q. Publilius Philo	Torquatus III. & Muso	Mamercino & Philo.
173	417	337	110-4		*Coss.*—XVI. 89. T. Manlius Torquatus P. Decius	*Coss.*—VIII. 13. L. Furius Camilus C. Mænius	† Mamertinus † & † Silo †	Camillo & † Nepote †.
174	418	336	111-1	M. Valerius M.F.M.N. Corvus III. Cos. IV. De Calensis. Ann. CDXIIX. Idib. Mart.	*Coss.*—XVI. 99. Q. Publilius Ti. Æmilius Mamercus	*Coss.*—VIII. 15. C. Sulpicius Longus P. Ælius Pætus	Camillus & † Minius †	Pæto & Longo
175	419	335	111-2		*Coss.*—XVII. 2. L. Furius C. Mænius	*Coss.*—VIII. 16. L. Papirius Crassus K. Duilius	† Phistus † & Longus	Crasso & † Hella †.
176	420	334	111-3		*Coss.*—XVII. 17. C. Sulpicius L Papirius	*Coss.*—VIII. 16. M. Valerius Corvus IV. M. Atilius Regulus	Crassus & † Dulius †	† Caleno † & Corvo IV.
177	421	333	111-4		*Coss.*—XVII. 29. K. Valerius L. Papirius	*Coss.*—VIII. 16. T. Veturius Sp. Postumius	Regulus & Corvinus	Caudino & Calvino.
178	422	332	112-1		*Coss.*—XVII. 40. M. Atilius M. Valerius	*Coss.*—VIII. 17. A. Cornelius II. Cn. Domitius	† Albinus † & Calvinus	† Hoc anno Dictatores non fuerunt †.
179	423	331	112-2		*Coss.*—XVII. 49. Sp. Postumius T. Veturius	*Coss.*—VIII. 18. M. Claudius Marcellus C. Valerius	Albinus II. & Cossus	Calvino & Arvinus II.
180	424	330	112-3	. . Aimilius L . . . N. Mamercin. Privernas. Cos. II. De Privernatibus. Ann. CDXXIV. K. Mart. C. Plautius P.F.P.N. Decianus Cos. de Privernatibus. Ann. CDXXIV. K. Mart.	*Coss.*—XVII. 62. C. Domitius A. Cornelius	*Coss.*—VIII. 19. L. Papirius Crassus II. L. Plautius Venno	Potitus & Marcellus	Petito & Marcello.
181	425	329	112-4		*Coss.*—XVII. 74. C. Valerius M. Clodius	*Coss.*—VIII. 20. L. Æmilius Mamercinus C. Plautius	† Brassus † & Venox	Crasso II & Vennc.

Year of the Common-wealth.	Year of Rome.	Year before the Christian Era.	Olympiad.	Fasti Capitolini.	DIODORUS.	LIVY.	Fasti Siculi.	Fasti Cuspiniani sive Norisiani.
182	426	328	113-1		*Coss.*—XVII. 82. L. Plotius L. Papirius	*Coss.*—VIII. 22. P. Plautius Proculus P. Cornelius Scapula	Mamertinus II. & Decianus	† Privernas † II. & Deciano.
183	427	327	113-2	Q. Publilius Q.F.Q.N. Philo II. Primus Pro Cos. De Samnitibus Palæpolitaneis. Ann. CDXXVII. K. Mai.	*Coss.*—XVII. 87. P. Cornelius A. Postumius	*Coss.*—VIII. 22. L. Cornelius Lentulus Q. Publilius Philo II.	Venox & Scipio	Deciano II. & Barbato.
184	428	326	113-3		*Coss.*—XVII. 110. L. Cornelius Q. Publilius	*Coss.*—VIII. 23. C. Pœtelius L. Papirius	Lentulus & † Silo †	Lentulo & Philo.
185	429	325	113-4	L. Papirius Sp. F.L.N. Cursor. Dict. De Samnitibus. An. CDXXIX. III. Non. Mart.	. . . . .	*Coss.*—VIII. 29. L. Furius Camillus II. Junius Brutus Scæva	Libo & Cursor	Libone III. & Cursore II.
186	430	324	114-1		*Coss.*—XVII. 113. C. Pœtelius Papirius	*Coss.*—VIII. 37. C. Sulpicius Q. Æmilius or Aulius	Camillus & Brutus	Camillo II. & Bruto.
187	431	323	114-2	L. Fulvius L.F.L.N. Curvus Cos. De Samnitibus. Ann. CDXXXI. Quirinalibus. Q. Fabius M.F.N.N. Maximus Rullianus Cos. De Samnitibus et Apuleis Ann. CDXXXI. XII. K. Mart.	*Coss.*—XVIII. 2. L. Furius Dec. Junius	*Coss.*—VIII. 38. Q. Fabius L. Fulvius	Longus & Ceratanus	† Hoc anno Dictatores non fuerunt †.
188	432	322	114-3		*Coss.*—XVIII. 26. C. Sulpicius C. Ælius	*Coss.*—IX. 1. T. Veturius Calvinus Sp. Postumius	Cursor II. & † Sullus †	Longo II. & Cerretano.
189	433	321	114-4	C. Ma . . . M. Fos . . . L. Corn . . L. Papiriu . . . T. Manli . . . L. Papiriu . .	. . . .	*Coss.*—IX. 7. Q. Publilius Philo L. Papirius Cursor	Calvinus & † Balbinus †	† Corvo † & Rulliano.
190	434	320	115-1	L. Papirius. . . . L. Papirius Sp. F.L.N. Cursor II. Cos. III. De Samnitibus. Ann. CDXXXIV. X. K. Septem. Cens. . . . . C. . . . cius . . .	. . .	*Coss.*—IX. 15. Q. Aulius Cerretanus II. L. Papirius	Cursor III. & † Silo †	Calvino II. & Albino.
191	435	319	115-2	M. Plautius L.F.L.N. Venno L. Foslius C.F. . . N. Flaccina . . . Cens. L. Papirius L.F.M.N. Crassus C. Mainius P.F.P.N. Lustrum Fecer. X. V.	*Coss.*—XVIII. 44. Q. Publilius Q. † Publius †	*Coss.*—IX. 20. M. Foslius Flaccinator L. Plautius Venno	† Papinius † & Ceratanus	Cursore II. & Philo III.
192	436	318	115-3	Q. Aimilius Q.F.L.N. Barbula. C. Junius C.F.C.N. Bubulcus. Brutus.	*Coss.*—XVIII. 58. Q. Ælius L. Papirius	*Coss.*—IX. 20. C. Junius Bubulcus Q. Æmilius Barbula	Venox & Flaccus	† Murillano † & Ceretano.
193	437	317	115-4	Sp. Nautius Sp. F. Sp. N. Rutilus M. Popilius M.F.M.N. Lænas. L. Aimilius L.F.L.N. Mamerc. Privernas. Dict. L. Fulvius L.F.L.N. Curvus. Mag. eq. Rei Gerund. Causa.	*Coss.*—XIX. 2. L. Plotius M'. Fulvius	*Coss.*—IX. 21. Sp. Nautius M. Popillius	Barbula & Bubulcus	Venno & Flaccinatore.

Year of the Commonwealth.	Year of Rome.	Year before the Christian Era.	Olympiad.	Fasti Capitolini.	DIODORUS.	LIVY.	Fasti Siculi.	Fasti Cuspiniani sive Norisiani.
194	438	316	116-1	L. Papirius Sp. F.L.N. Cursor IV. . . . oblilius . . F.Q.N. Philo IV. . . Fabius M.F.N.N. Maximus Rullianus. Dict. . . Aulius . . F. Ai. N. Cerretan. In Prælio occisus est. In ejus L.F. est. Mag. eq. R.G.C. . . Fabius M.F.N.N. Ambustus. Mag. eq.	*Coss.*—XIX. 17. C. Junius Q. Æmilius	[Names omitted.]	Rutilus & Lænas	Barbula & Bruto.
195	439	315	116-2	M. Pœtelius M.F.M.N. Libo. C. Sulpicius Ser. F.Q.N. Longus . . . C. Mainius P.F.P.N. Dict. Rei Gerund. Causa. M. Foslius C.F.M.N. Flaccinator. Mag. eq. C. Sulpicius Ser. F.Q.N. Longus Cos. III. De Samnitibus. Ann. CDXXXIX. K. Quint.	*Coss.*—XIX. 55. Sp. Nautius M. Popillius	*Coss.*—IX. 24. M. Pætelius C. Sulpicius	Cursor IV. & Lænas II.	Lucillo & Lænas.
196	440	314	116-3	L. Papirius Sp. F.L.N. Cursor. . . C. Junius C.F.C.N. Bubulcus. Brutus . . C. Pœtelius C.F.C.N. Libo. Visolus. Dict. M. . . . . . M.F.M.N. Libo. Mag. eq. Rei Gerund. Causa.	*Coss.*—XIX. 66. L. Papirius IV. Q. Publilius II.	*Coss.*—IX. 28. L. Papirius V. C. Junius Bubulcus	Cursor V. & Bubulcus II.	Cursore IV. & Philo IIII.
197	441	313	116-4	M. Valerius M.F.M.N. Maximus. P. Decius P.F.Q.N. Mus. C. Sulpicius Ser. F.Q.N. Longus Dict. R.G.C. C. Junius C.F.C.N. Bubulcus. Brutus Mag. eq. Cens. Ap. Claudius C.F. Ap. N. Cæcus. C. Plautius C.F.C.N. Qui in hoc honore. Venox appellatus est. L.F. XXVI. M. Valerius M.F.M.N. Maximus. Cos. De Samnitibus Soraneisq. Ann. CDXXXXI. Idib. Sext.	*Coss.*—XIX. 73. M. Pætelius C. Sulpicius	*Coss.*—IX. 28. M. Valerius P. Decius	. . . .	Libone & Longo III.
198	442	312	117-1	C. Junius C.F.C.N. Bubulcus. Brutus III. Q. Aimilius Q.F.L.N. Barbula II. C. Junius. C.F.C.N. Bubulcus. Brutus. Cos. III. De Samnitibus. An. CDXLII. Nonis Sext. Q. Aimilius Q.F.L.N. Barbula. Cos. II. De Etrusceis. An. CDXLII. Idib. Sext.	*Coss.*—XIX. 77. L. Papirius V. C. Junius	*Coss.*—IX. 30. C. Junius Bubulcus III. Q. Æmilius Barbula II.	Maximus & Muso	Cursore V. & Bruto II.
199	443	311	117-2	Q. Fabius M.F.N.N. Maxim. Rullian. C. Marcius C.F.L.N. Rutilus. Qui postea Censorinus appellatus est.	*Coss.*—XIX. 105. M. Valerius P. Decius	*Coss.*—IX. 33. Q. Fabius C. Marcius Rutilus	Bubulcus IV. & Barbula	Maximo & Mure.
200	444	310	117-3	L. Papirius Sp. F.L.N. Cursor. Dict. C. Junius C.F.C.N. Bubulcus Brutus. Mag. eq. Rei Gerund. Causa. Hoc anno Dictator et Magist: Eq. sine Cos. fuerunt L. Papirius Sp. F.L.N. Cursor III. Dict. II. De Samnitibus. An. CDXLIV. Idibus Oct. Q. Fabius M.F.N.N. Maximus Rullian. II. Pro Cos. De Etrusceis. An. CDXLIV. Idib: Nov.	*Coss.*—XX. 3. C. Junius Q. Æmilius	*Coss.*—IX. 41. Q. Fabius P. Decius	Rullus & Rutilius	Bruto III. & Barbula II.

Year of the Common-wealth.	Year of Rome	Year before the Christian Era.	Olympiad.	Fasti Capitolini.	DIODORUS.	LIVY.	Fasti Siculi.	Fasti Cuspiniani sive Norisiani.
201	445	309	117-4	P. Decius P.F.Q.N. Mus. Q. Fabius M.F.N.N. Maximus Rullian. III.	*Coss.*—XX. 27. Q. Fabius II. C. Marcius	*Coss.*—IX. 42. Ap. Claudius L. Volumnius	Muso II. & Rullus II.	Rulliano II. & Rutilo II.
202	446	308	118-1	Ap. Claudius C.F. Ap. N. Cæcus. L. Volumnius C.F.C.N. Flamma Violens. Cens. M. Va erius M.F.M.N. Maximus. C. Junius C.F.C.N. Bubulcus Brutus. L. F. XXVII.	† *Coss.* †—XX. 36. † Ap. Claudius † † L. Plautius †	*Coss.*—IX. 42. P. Cornelius Arvina Q. Marcius Tremulus	Appius & Violens	† Hoc anno Dictatores non fuerunt †
203	447	307	118-2	.... Tr .. ulus P. Corn .... Q. Marcius Q.F.Q.N. Tremulus Cos. De Anagnineis Herniceisq. Ann. CDXLVII. Prid. K. Quint. ... N. Scipio Barbatus. ..... Mus.	*Coss.*—XX. 45. Ap. Claudius L. Volumnius	*Coss.*—IX. 44. L. Postumius Ti. Minucius	† Remulus † & † Albinus †	† Mure II. & Rulliano III. †
204	448	306	118-3	..... Megellus. Ti. Mi..... M..... M. Fulvius L.F.L.N. Curvus. Pætinus Cos. De Samnitibus. Ann. CDXLIX. III. Non. Oct.	*Coss.*—XX. 73. Q. Marcius P. Cornelius	*Coss.*—IX. 45. P. Sulpicius Saverrio P. Sempronius Sophus	† Metellus † & Minucius	Cæco & Violense.
205	449	305	118-4	..... C. N. Sophus. P. S .... N. N. Maximus Rullianu . P. Sempronius P.F.C.N. Sophus Cos. de Æqueis Ann. CDXLIX. VII. K. Oct. P. Sulpicius Ser. F.P.N. Saverrio. Cos. De Samnitibus. Ann. CDXLIX. IIII. K. Nov.	*Coss.*—XX. 81. L. Postumius Ti. Minucius	*Coss.*—X. 1. L. Genucius Ser. Cornelius	Sempronius & † Faverius †	Tremulo & Arvina.
206	450	304	119-1	..... n. F. Cn. N. Lentulus.	*Coss.*—XX. 91. P. Sempronius P. Sulpicius	*Coss.*—X. 1. M. Livius Denter M. Æmilius	Lentulus & † Aventesius †	Megello & Augurino.
207	451	303	119-2	...... C. N. Den ... . N. Bubulcus B ..... C. Junius C.F.C.N. Bubulcus Brutus II. Dict. De Æqueis Ann. CDLI. III. K. Sext.	*Coss.*—XX. 102. Ser. Cornelius L. Genucius	*Coss.*—X. 6. M. Valerius V. Q. Appuleius	Dentonius & Æmilius	Sofo & Saberio.
208	452	302	119-3	.... M.F.N.N. Max .... ilius L.F.L.N. ... . no Dictat .... M.F.M.N. .... onius ... M. Valer .... IV. Dict. II. .... X. K. De ..	*Coss.*—XX. 106. M. Livius M. Æmilius	*Coss.*—X. 9. M. Fulvius Pætinus T. Manlius Torquatus. Huic suffectus M. Valerius.	Corvinus & Pansa	Rufo & Adventinense.

Year of the Commonwealth.	Year of Rome.	Year before the Christian Era.	Olympiad.	Fasti Capitolini.	DIODORUS.	LIVY.	Fasti Siculi.	Fasti Cuspiniani sive Norisiani.
209	453	301	119-4	. . . . . F.C.N	[The regular history of Diodorus ends with the 20th book, at the third year of the 119th Olympiad, and his lists of consuls here terminate.]	*Coss.*—X. 11. L. Cornelius Scipio Cn. Fulvius	Petitus & Torquatus	† Dextro † & Paulo.
210	454	300	120-1	. . . . M. Fulvius Cn. F. Cn. N. Pætinus Cos. De Samnitibus Nequinatibusque. Ann. CD . VII. K. Oct.		*Coss.*—X. 14. Q. Fabius Maximus IV. P. Decius III.	Scipio & Maximus	† Corvo II. & Rulliano II. †
211	455	299	120-2	. . . . Cn. Fulvius Cn. F. Cn. N. Max. Centumalus. Cos. De Samnitibus Etrusceisque. Ann. CDLV. Idibus Nov.		*Coss.*—X. 16. L. Volumnius Ap. Claudius	† Rullus III. & Muso III. †	Corvo V. & Pansa.
212	456	298	120-3	. . .		*Coss.*—X. 22. Q. Fabius Maximus V. P. Decius IV.	† Claudius & Violens †	Petino & Torquato.
213	457	297	120-4	. . . . ens		*Coss.*—X. 32. L. Postumius Megellus M. Atilius Regulus	Rullus IV. & Muso IV.	Scipione & Centumalo.
214	458	296	121-1	. . . . M. Rull. . . . . e devovit. Q. Fabius M.F.N.N. Maximus Rullianus III. Cos. V. De Samnitibus et Etrusceis Galleis. Ann. CDLIIX. Prid. Non. Sept.		*Coss.*—X. 38, 39. L. Papirius Cursor Sp. Carvilius	Claudius & Violens II.	Rulliano IV. & Mure III.
215	459	295	121-2	. . . . N. Megellu . . . . lus. . . . . . . Cornelius A.F.P.N. Arvin . . . . I. est . . . . XX. L. Postumius L.F. Sp. N. Megell. Coss. II. De Samnitib. et Etrusceis VI. K. April. CDLIX. M. Atilius M.F.M.N. Regulus Cos. De Volsonibus et Samnitib. A. CDLIX. V. K. Apr.		*Coss.*—X. 47. Q. Fabius Gurges D. Junius Brutus	Rullus V. & Muso V.	Cæco & Violense.
216	460	294	121-3	L. Papirius L.F. Sp. N. Cursor S . . . . mus. Sp. Carvilius C.F.C.N. Maximus Cos. De Samnitibus. Ann. CDLX. Idibus Jan. . . . . L.F. Sp. N. Cursor . . . . . itibus . . . Ann. CDLX. Idibus Febr.		[Here the 10th book of Livy ends; and the ten following books being lost, his lists of consuls are wanting till the period of the second Punic war.]	† Metellus † & Regulus	Rulliano V. & Mure IV.
217	461	293	121-4	. . . .			† Cursor & Maximus	Megello II. & Regulo.
218	462	292	122-1	. . . . ximus . . . Ann. D. CDLXII. K. Sext.			Maximus & Gracchus	Gurgis & Scævola.

Year of the Common-wealth.	Year of Rome.	Year before the Christian Era.	Olympiad.	Fasti Capitolini.	DIODORUS.	LIVY.	Fasti Siculi.	Fasti Cuspiniani sive Norisiani.
219	463	291	122-2				Metellus II. & Bulbus	Megello III. & Bruto.
220	464	290	122-3				Maximus II. & Muso VI.	Dentato & Rufino.
221	465	289	122-4				† Cremolus † & † Albinus †	Corvino II. & Noctua.
222	466	288	123-1				Marcellus & Rutilius	Tremulo II. & Arvina.
223	467	287	123-2				Potitus & † Petitus †	Marcellino & Rutilo.
224	468	286	123-3				Lepidus & † Cecinna †	Maximo & Pæto.
225	469	285	123-4				† Tacitus † & † Dento †	Canina & Lepido.
226	470	284	124-1				Dolabella & Maximus	Tucca & Metello.
227	471	283	124-2	. . . . . eisque . . . III. Non. Mart.			† Lucius † & Pappus	Calvo & Maximo.
228	472	282	124-3	. . cius Q.F.Q N. Philippus . . . Etrusceis. Ann. CDLXXII. K. Apr.			Barbula & Philippus	Luscinio & Labo.
229	473	281	124-4	. . . uncanius Ti. F. Ti. N. Cos. . e Vulsiniensibus et Vulcientib. Ann. CDLXXIII. K. Febr. . . milius Q.F.Q.N. Barbalu Pro Cos. De Tarentineis Samnitibus et Sallentineis. Ann. DCLXXIII. VI. Idus Quint.			Levinus & Coruncanius	Barbula & Filippo.
230	474	280	125-1				Severio & Muro	Levino & Coruncanio.
231	475	279	125-2	C. Fabricius C.F.C.N. Luscinus II. Cos. II. De Lucaneis Bruttieis Tarentin. Samnitibus. Ann. CDLXXV. Idibus Decembr.			Luscinus & Pappus	Saberio & † Prorico †.
232	476	278	125-3	C. Junius C.F.C.N. Brutus Bubulc. Cos. II. De Lucaneis et Bruttieis. Ann. CDLXXVI. Non. Jan.			Rufinus & Bubulcus	Luscino II. & Pæto.
233	477	277	125-4	Q. Fabius Q.F.M.N. Maximus. Gurges II. Cos. II. De Samnitibus Lucaneis Bruttieis. Ann. CDLXXVII. Quirinalib.			Gorges & Clepsinus	Rufino II. & Bruto II.
234	478	276	126-1	M' Curius M'F.M'N. Dentat. IV. . . . . . nitib. et Rege Pyrrho. A. CDLXXIIX . . . . ebr. . . . Ti. F. Ser. N. Lentul. . . os. De Samnitibus et . . Ann. CDLXXIIX. K. Mart.			† Benacus † & Lentulus	Gurgis II. & Clepsina.
235	479	275	126-2				† Benacus † & Merenda	Dentato II. & Lentulo.
236	480	274	126-3	. . . C. N. Canina . . . . neis Samnitibus . Ann. CDXXC. Quirinalibus.			Licinius & † Cambius †	Dentato III. & Merenda.

Year of the Commonwealth.	Year of Rome.	Year before the Christian Era.	Olympiad.	Fasti Capitolini.	DIODORUS.	LIVY.	Fasti Siculi.	Fasti Cuspiniani sive Norisiani.
237	481	273	126-4	. . . ximus II. . . . . . Tarenti . . . . An. CD . . . L. Papirius L. . . . Cos. II. De Ta . . . . . Bruttieis			Cursor & Maximus	† Lucino † & † Cinna †.
238	482	272	127-1				Claudius & Clepsinas	Cursore II. & Maximo.
239	483	271	127-2	. . . . Corne . . . . . . assi			Gallus & Pictor	† Claudo † & Clepsina.
240	484	270	127-3				Sempronius & Rufus	Clepsina II. & Læsio †.
241	485	269	127-4	. . . . . onius P.F. . . . . De Peicentibus . . Ap. Claudius Ap. F . . . Cos. De Peicen . . .			Regulus & Libo	Gallo & Pictore.
242	486	268	128-1	M. Atilius M.F.L.N. . . . . . Cos. De Sallentineis . . . . VIII. L. Julius L.F.L.N. Libo. Cos. De Sallentineis. An. C . . . . VII . . Febr.			Fabius Pictor & † Peta †	Sofo & † Ruffo †.
243	487	267	128-2	D. Junius D.F.D.N. Pera Cos. De Sassinatibus An. CDXXCVII. V. K. Octobr. N. Fabius C.F.M.N. Pictor II. Cos. De Sassinatibus. An. CDXXCVII. III. Non. Oct. N. Fabius C.F.M.N. Pictor II. Cos. De Salentineis Messapieisque. An. CDXXCVII. K. Febr. D. Junius D.F.D.N. Pera II. Cos. De Sallentineis Messapieisque. An. CDXXCVII. Non. Febr.			Maximus & Vitulus	Regulo & Libone.
244	488	266	128-3	Cens. Cn. Cornelius L. F. N. Blasio C. Marcius C.F.L.N. Rutilus Qui. L.F. XXXV. in hoc honore Censorin. appel. e.			† Thaugatus † & Flaccus	Pera & Pictore.
245	489	265	128-4	BELLUM PUNICUM PRIMUM. Ap. Claudius C.F. Ap. N. Caudex. M. Fulvius Q.F.M.N. Flaccus. M. Fulvius Q.F.M.N. Flaccus Cos. De Vulsiniensibus. An. CDXXCIX. K. Nov.			Maximus II. & Crassus	Maximo & Vitulo.
246	490	264	129-1	M' Valerius M.F.M.N. Maximus. Qui in hoc honore Messal. appel. e. M' Otacilius C.F.M'N. Crassus. Cn. Fulvius Cn.F.Cn. Maxim. Centumalus. Dict. } Clavi figend. causa. Q. Marcius Q.F.Q.N. Philippus Mag. eq. } M' Valerius M.F.M.N. Maxim. Messalla Cos. De Pœneis et Rege Siculor. Hierone. An. CDXC. XVI. K. April.			Albinus & Vitulus	Caudex & Flacco.
247	491	263	129-2	L. Postumius L.F.L.N. Megellus Q. Mamilius Q.F.M.N. Vitulus.			Flaccus II. & Crassus II.	Maximo & Grasso.

Year of the Common-wealth.	Year of Rome.	Year before the Christian Era.	Olympiad.	Fasti Capitolini.	DIODORUS.	LIVY.	Fasti Siculi.	Fasti Cuspiniani sive Norisiani.
248	492	262	129-3	L. Valerius M.F.L.N. Flaccus T. Otacilius C.F.M'N. Crassus.			Scipio & Duilius	Megello & Vitulo.
249	493	261	129-4	Cn. Cornelius L.F.Cn.N. Scipio Asina. C. Duilius M.F.M.N. C. Duilius M F.M.N. Cos. Primus Navalem De Sicul. et classe Pœnica egit An. CDXCIII. K. Interka ar.			Scipio II. & Florus	Flacco & Grasso.
250	494	260	130-1	L. Cornelius L.F.Cn.N. Scipio C. Aquilius M.F.C.N. Florus L. Cornelius L.F.Cn.N. Scipio Cos. De Pœneis et Sardin. Corsica An. CDXCIV. V. Id. Mart.			† Catacinus † & Paterculus	Asina & Duillio.
251	495	259	130-2	A. Atilius A.F.C.N. Calatinus C. Sulpicius Q.F.Q.N. Paterculus C. Aquilius M.F.C.N. Florus Pro Cos. De Pœneis An. CDXCV. IIII. Non. Octob. C. Sulpicius Q.F.Q.N. Paterculus Cos. De Pœneis et Sardeis An. CDXC . . . . III . . . Cens. C. Duilius M.F.M . . . . cipi			Regulus & Blesus	Scipione & Floro.
252	496	258	130-3	C. Atilius M.F.M.N. Regulus Cn. . . . . . Q. Ogulnius L.F.A.N. Gallus Dict. Latinar. Fer. Causa. M. Lætorius M.F.M.N. Plancianus Mag. eq. A. Atilius A F.C.N. Calatinus Pr. ex Sicilia De Pœnis. An. . . . . XIIII. K. F . . . C. Atilius M.F.M.N. Regulus Cos. De Pœnis Navalem egit VIII. . . .			Vulso & † Decius †	Calatino & Paterculo.
253	497	257	130-4	L. Manlius A.F.P.N. Vulso Longus. Q. Cædicius Q.F.Q.N. In Mag. mort. e. in ejus locum factus est M. Atilius M.F.L.N. Regulus. L. Manlius A.F.P.N. Vulso Long. Cos. De Pœnis Navalem egit VII . . . An. . .			Petinus & Paullus	Rugulo & Blesio.
254	498	256	131-1	Ser. Fulvius M.F.M.N. Pætin. Nobilior M. Aimilius M.F.L.N. Paullus.			Scipio & †Catacion†	Longo & Regulo.
255	499	255	131-2	Cn. Cornelius L.F. Cn. N. Scipio Asina A. Atilius A.F.C.N. Calatinus. Ser. Fulvius M.F.M.N. Pætinus Nobilior Pro Cos. De Cossurensibus et Pœneis Navalem egit XIII. K. Febr. A. CDXCIX. M. Aimilius M.F.L.N. Paullus Pro Cos. De Cossurensibus et Pœnis Navalem egit XII. K. Febr. An. CDXCIX.			Capito & Blesus II.	Nobiliore & Paulo.

Year of the Common-wealth.	Year of Rome.	Year before the Christian Era.	Olympiad.	Fasti Capitolini.	DIODORUS.	LIVY.	Fasti Siculi.	Fasti Cuspiniani sive Norisiani.
256	500	254	131-3	Cn. Servilius Cn. F. Cn. N. Cæpio C. Sempronius Ti. F. Ti. N. Blæsus Cens. D. Junius D.F.D.N. Pera. Abd. L. Postumius L.F.L.N. Megell. Idem qui Pr. erat. In mag. m. est. Cn. Cornelius L.F. Cn. N. Scipio Asina Pro Cos. De Pœnis X. K. April. An. D. C. Sempronius Ti. F. Ti. N. Blæsus Cos. De Pœnis K. April. An. D.			Cotta & Geminus	Asina II. & Calatino II.
257	501	253	131-4	C. Aurelius L.F.C.N. Cotta. P. Servilius Q.F.Cn.N. Geminus Cens. M' Valerius M.F.M.N. Maxim. Messal. P. Sempronius P.F.P.N. Sophus L.F. XXXVII. C. Aurelius L.F.C.N. Cotta Cos. De Pœneis et Siculeis. Idibus April. An. DI.			Metellus & † Pappus †	Cepio & Blesio.
258	502	252	132-1	L. Cæcilius L.F.C.N. Metellus C. Furius C.F.C.N. Pacilus			Regulus II. & Vulso	Cotta & Gemino.
259	503	251	132-2	C. Atilius M.F.M.N. Regulus II. L. Manlius A.F.P.N. Vulso II. L. Cæcilius L.F.C.N. Metellus Pro Cos. De Pœnis VII. Idus Septemb. A. DII .			Pulcher & † Pulcher †	Metello & Pacilo.
260	504	250	132-3	P. Claudius Ap. F.C.N. Pulcher . L. Junius C.F.L.N. Pullus. M. Claudius C.F. Glicia. qui scriba fuerat. Dictator. coact. abdic. Sine Mag. eq. In ejus locum factus est A. Atilius A.F.C.N. Calatinus Dict. L. Cæcilius L.F.C.N. Metellus Mag. eq. Rei Gerund. Causa.			Cotta II. & Geminus II.	Regulo II. & Vulso.
261	505	249	132-4	C. Aurelius L.F.C.N. Cotta II. P. Servilius Q.F.Cn.N. Geminus II.			Metellus II. & Buteo	Pulcro & Pullo.
262	506	248	133-1	L. Cæcilius L.F.C.N. Metellus II. N. Fabius M.F.M.N. Buteo. Cens. A. Atilius. A.F.C.N. Calatinus A. Manlius T.F.T.N. Torquat. Attic. L.F. XXXVIII.			Crassus & Licinius	Cotta II. & Gemino II.
263	507	247	133-2	M' Otacilius C.F.M.N. Crassus II. M. Fabius M.F.M.N. Licinus. Ti. Coruncanius Ti. F. Ti. Nepos. Dict. M. Fulvius Q.F.M.N. Flaccus Mag. eq. Comit. Habend. Causa.			Buteo II. & Bulbus	Metello & † Rutilo †.

Year of the Common-wealth.	Year of Rome.	Year before the Christian Era.	Olympiad.	Fasti Capitolini.	DIODORUS.	LIVY.	Fasti Siculi.	Fasti Cuspiniani sive Norisiani.
264	508	246	133-3	M. Fabius M.F M.N. Buteo. C. Atilius A.F.A.N. Bulbus .			Torquatus & Blesus	Grasso II. & Licino II.
265	509	245	133-4	A. Manlius T.F.T.N. Torquat. Attic. C. Sempronius Ti. F. Ti. N. Blæsus II.			Fundulus & Gallus	Buteo & Pullo.
266	510	244	134-1	C. Fundanius C.F.Q.N. Fundulus C. Sulpicius C.F. Ser. N. Gallus			Catulus & Albinus	Attico & Blæso.
267	511	243	134-2	C. Lutatius C.F.C.N. Catulus A. Postumius A.F.L.N. Albinus.			Torquatus & † Cato †	Fundulo & Gallo.
268	512	242	134-3	A. Manlius T.F.T.N. To . . . Attic. II. Q. Lutatius . . . C.N. Ce . . . Cens. C. Aurelius L . . . . . . C. Lutatius C.F.C.N. Catulus Pro Cos. De Pœnis ex Sicil . . . e . . . egit. IIII. Non. Oct. A. DXII. Q. Valerius Q.F.P.N. Falto Pro Pr. ex Sicilia Navalem egit Prid. Non. Octob. An. DXII. Q. Lutatius C.F.C.N. Cerco Cos. De Falisceis K. Mart. An. DXII. A. Manlius T.F.T.N. Torquatus Atticus. Cos. II. De Falisceis IV. Non. M . . . Ann. DXII.			Cento & † Tudinatus †	Catuto & Albino.
269	513	241	134-4	C. Claudius. Ap. F.C.N. Centho. M. Sempronius C.F.M.N. Tuditanus.			† Toncinus † & Falco	Attico II. & Cerco.

EXPLANATION OF THE SECOND TABLES.

I HAVE continued the tables of military tribunes and consuls from the point of time at which they ended in the preceding ones, to the end of the first Punic war. I have given, as before, the lists of consuls from Livy and Diodorus so far as their remaining works contain them; and I have now given the fragments of the Fasti Capitolini which relate to the period contained in the tables without any omission, and at the same time without adding to the words or even letters which exist on the fragments of the marble hitherto discovered.

The Fasti of Diodorus end with the year 452, and those of Livy with the year 459; and the Fasti Capitolini are wanting for several years here and there both before and after that period. I have, therefore, given two other sets of Fasti, one of which goes by the name of the Sicilian Fasti, because Onufrio Panvini found the MS. containing it in Sicily. Casaubon copied the MS. and gave his copy to Scaliger, who published it in his edition of Eusebius, pp. 227–299, under the title of ἐπιτομὴ χρόνων.

The other Fasti were first made known by John Cuspiniani, who published extracts from them in his commentary on Cassiodorus in the sixteenth century. They have been since published entirely by Noris towards the end of the seventeenth century, and they may be found, with his dissertation on them, in the eleventh volume of Grævius' Collection of Roman Antiquities. The MS. containing them is in the imperial library at Vienna, and, according to Noris, they were compiled about the year 354 of the Christian era.

These last Fasti are no doubt older and more correct than the Sicilian, which are full of errors; but both are useless for the period of the military tribuneships, because, representing all the years of the commonwealth as marked by consulships, they never give to any year the names of more than two magistrates. But the author of the Sicilian Fasti seems to have copied his lists from some writer who, like Cassiodorus, gave only the consulships, and purposely omitted the years of military tribuneships; and not being aware of this, and supposing that the lists of consuls were continuous in point of time, he has marked the years immediately preceding the first plebeian consulship with the names of the consuls who preceded the Gaulish invasion; insomuch that, placing that invasion in the third year of the 99th Olympiad, he notwithstanding makes it fall in the consulship of M. Genucius and C. Curtius, who were consuls only five years after the expulsion of the decemvirs. Both the Sicilian Fasti and those of Noris give merely the cognomen, or last name, of each consul: it seems as if they had looked hastily up some Fasti where all the names were given at length, and had, to save trouble, merely copied down the name which came last. Sometimes the recurrence of the same names near to each other has misled them; as, for instance, in the third Samnite war, the Sicilian Fasti give three consulships of Q. Fabius and P. Decius instead of two, and two of Ap. Claudius and Volumnius instead of one. The corruptions of the Roman names are as bad as those in the Fasti of Diodorus: Calatinus is corrupted into "Catacion," Dentatus into "Benacus," Cædicius into "Decius," Caudex into "Thaugatus," Canina, a rather uncommon cognomen of one branch of the Claudian house, becomes "Cambius" in the Sicilian Fasti, and "Cinna" in those of Noris; and many others recur which it is in general easy to correct from the corresponding years in the Fasti Capitolini, or from any correct list of the consuls. Some corruptions, however, cannot easily be restored, nor is it always easy to ascertain how much must be ascribed to mere errors of the copyist, and where the authors really meant to give different consuls from those named in the other Fasti.

With regard to Livy's Chronology, the fixed point from which we must set out is the year of Rome 400, which, according to his express statement, VII. 18, was the thirty-fifth year after the expulsion of the Gauls, and was marked by the consulship of C. Sulpicius Peticus and M. Valerius Publicola. Reckoning the years from this point, according to Livy's own statement of events, the consulship of Q. Fabius Gurges and D. Junius

Brutus, the last mentioned in his tenth book, would fall in the year 459. But Sigonius places it one year later, and makes the year 422 to have been wholly taken up by interregna, and so to have been marked by no consuls' names. This he does, in order to reconcile Livy with himself, because his reckonings elsewhere require, as he thinks, the insertion of a year more than he has actually accounted for. That is to say, Livy, in the beginning of the 31st book, says that the sixty-three years which passed between the beginning of the first Punic war and the end of the second, had furnished him with matter for as many books as the four hundred and seventy-eight years which had elapsed from the foundation of Rome to the consulship of Ap. Claudius, when the first Punic war began. Such are the numbers in almost all the MSS. But as the number four hundred and seventy-eight would agree with no system of chronology, it has been long since corrected in the printed editions to "four hundred and eighty-eight." Sigonius, however, argued that the true reading was four hundred and eighty-six, the Roman numerals CDLXXVIII. having, as he thinks, been corrupted from CDLXXXVI. the third X having been altered to V, and the V separated into II. He therefore places the beginning of the first Punic war in 486, having, as I have above mentioned, inserted a whole year of interregna, not noticed by Livy, which he makes out to be the year 422. Now, without this additional year, the first Punic war does actually, as I think, according to Livy, begin in 487; for Sigonius omits two consulships between the retreat of Pyrrhus and the consulship of Ap. Claudius and M. Fulvius, namely, those of Q. Ogulnius and C. Fabius in 485, and of Q. Fabius Gurges and L. Mamilius in 489. The first of these is mentioned expressly by Pliny, Hist. Natur. XXXIII. § 44, as well as by Zonaras, VIII. 7, and by the Sicilian Fasti and those of Noris, and is admitted by Sigonius himself in his commentary on the Fasti Capitolini. The consulship of Q. Fabius and L. Mamilius is mentioned by the Sicilian Fasti and by those of Noris, and is required by the dates of the Fasti Capitolini, which place the consulship of D. Junius Pera and N. Fabius in 487, and that of Ap. Claudius and M. Fulvius in 489, manifestly making an interval of a year between them, although the names of the intermediate consuls are lost. Zonaras speaks of Fabius as being sent against the Volsinians, and expressly says that he was consul in that year with "Æmilius," according to the present text of Zonaras in the edition of Du Cange, Venice, 1729. But in the second chapter of the same eighth book of Zonaras, L. Æmilius, the colleague of Q. Marcius Philippus in 473, is in one MS. called Μανίλιον, which shows how readily the names Αἰμίλιος and Μαμίλιος may be confounded with each other. And further, Sigonius acknowledges this consulship of Q. Fabius and L. Mamilius in his commentary on the Fasti Capitolini. Thus, according to Livy, there would be, in fact, the events of 486 years related in his fifteen first books, and the sixteenth book began with the year 487—that is, with the consulship of Ap. Claudius and M. Fulvius; and the fifteen next books did contain also the events of sixty three years—from the year 487 to the year 550, the consulship of Cn. Cornelius and P. Ælius Pætus, before the expiration of which the war with Carthage was concluded—as the first Punic war had begun about the middle of 487. And thus the correctness of Sigonius' alteration of Livy's date from CDLXXVIII. to CDLXXXVI. is indeed established, although, as I think, his way of justifying it is erroneous, and so also is his interpretation of it; for Livy does not say that App. Claudius was consul in 486, but that his own fifteen first books, which stopped at the beginning of App. Claudius' consulship, had contained the events of 486 years. And, therefore, according to Livy, the first year of the war with Pyrrhus would fall in 471, the first year of the first Punic war in 487, and the end of the second Punic war in 550.

Meantime I follow the common chronology of the years of Rome, because it is hopeless now to endeavor to supersede it by any other system, and it would be a mere perplexity to my readers if they were to find every action recorded in this history fixed to a different year from that with which they had been accustomed to connect it. Nor does there seem any adequate object to be gained by the attempt. The era of the foundation of Rome is itself a point impossible to fix accurately; nor can we determine the chronology of the fourth and fifth centuries of Rome either in itself or as compared with the chronology of Greece. Our existing authorities are too uncertain and too conflicting to allow of this; and, as I have said already in another place, the uncertainty of the history and chronology act mutually on each other, and a sure standing-place is not to be found. The five years of anarchy during the discussions on the Licinian laws are, indeed, utterly improbable, and we may safely assume that they could not have happened exactly as they are represented. But Cn. Flavius, in the middle of the fifth century, recorded on his Temple of Concord[1] that it was dedicated 204 years after the dedication

[1] Pliny, Hist. Natur. XXXIII. § 19. Ed. Sillig.

of the Capitol; and this agrees exactly with the Fasti Capitolini, which place the ædileship of Flavius and the censorship of Fabius and Decius in the year of Rome 449. It is, indeed, probable that the Gaulish invasion should be placed later than its common date; and the five years of the anarchy may well be inserted in the early part of the commonwealth, a period for which we have neither a history nor a chronology that will bear any inquiry. Yet Polybius followed the common date of the Gaulish invasion, and his chronology of the subsequent Gaulish wars is all based on the assumption that Rome was taken in the 98th Olympiad, and not later. Polybius doubtless may have been misled, and Cn. Fulvius may have had no sufficient authority for fixing the interval between the dedication of his temple of Concord and that of the Capitol; but if they were both mistaken, where are we to find surer guides? and if the records on which they relied were uncertain, as indeed they very possibly were, what evidence or what probability can we find now, so as to be enabled to arrive at a more certain conclusion?

I follow, then, the common chronology of Rome; not, indeed, as thinking with the authors of "L'Art de vérifier les Dates," that it is possible to fix the very year, and even the day of the month, on which the several consuls of the fifth century entered upon their office, but because it is a convenient standard of reference; and if not correct, which in all probability it is not, yet is quite as much so as any other system which could be set up in its room. And this has determined me not to adopt Niebuhr's dates even on his authority, because I cannot persuade myself that the certainty of his amended chronology is so clear as to compensate for the manifest inconvenience of departing from a system which is fixed in the memories of all the readers of Roman history throughout Europe.

CORRECTION OF NOTE 15.—PAGE 37.

I might have spared the first part of this note had I known, when I wrote it, that the reading, "Turrianum a Fregellis accitum," is undoubtedly corrupt. The Bamberg MS reads "vulcaniveis accitum;" one of those at Paris (called by Harduin and Brotier "Regius II." and numbered at present in the Catalogue of the Library, 6797) reads "at vul gamulis accitum:" both show that the common text, like so many others in Pliny, is merely a false restoration of a passage which in the oldest and best MSS. is unintelligible, but which clearly contained a meaning very different from that exhibited in the later MSS. Sillig, in his Dictionary of ancient Artists, has conjectured that the true reading was "et Volsiniis accitum;" but in his edition of Pliny he approves rather of Jahn's conjecture, "Vulcanium a Veiis accitum," as agreeing more nearly with the traces preserved in the Bamberg MS. At any rate, Pliny is relieved from an apparent contradiction, and Turrianus or Turianus should no longer be quoted as an artist on Pliny's authority. I find that Mr. Millingen had already anticipated me in correcting "Fregenis" instead of "Fregellis," he not knowing, I suppose, any more than I did, that we were but fighting with a shadow.

ADDENDA.

THE following notes are extracted from manuscripts of the Author's, some of them written while he was collecting materials for the latter portion of this history, but the chief part in 1833, when he was thinking of converting the series of Biographies in the Encyclopædia Metropolitana into a continuous history of Rome, which was to open with the first Punic war, the period where Niebuhr's great work had just been broken off by his death. As they contain information, and express opinions on several interesting questions connected with Roman history, it has been thought expedient to insert them.

NOTE A, to p. 455, l. 54.

If we endeavor to picture to ourselves what the Roman people were at the beginning of the sixth century of their history; to represent to ourselves the size and aspect of their city and its neighborhood; their language, their manners, their social and domestic habits, their wealth, private and public, their principles of religion and of law; their character and condition, in short, as men and as citizens; where are the eyes so piercing as to discern the almost vanishing forms of these objects amidst the dimness of antiquity? or how can we supply, and arrange into an intelligible whole, the disjointed and seemingly unmeaning images, which our fragments of information offer, as perplexing and incongruous as the chaos of a dream?

The city of Rome, properly so called, was still contained at the beginning of the sixth century, and for some centuries afterwards, within the walls ascribed to Servius Tullius. Its circumference was about seven miles; but this enclosure was far from being all built over. Sacred groves, the remains of the forest which in the earliest times had covered all the higher grounds, were still very numerous; gardens, orchards, perhaps copse-wood, such as still grows on the sides of the Monte Testaccio, also occupied a considerable space.[1] As in so many other towns in their original state, the walls did not come down close to the river,[2] but ran parallel to it at some distance, passing from the Capitol to the Aventine by what is called the Janus Quadrifons, and the western extremity of the Circus Maximus. But, as was natural, one of the earliest suburbs sprang up in this quarter; and the space between the walls and the Tiber, without the Porta Flumentana, was already covered with houses in the time of the second Punic war.[3] Buildings had probably grown up beyond the Tiber also, connecting the fortress on the Janiculus with the city: on the eastern side of Rome, from the Esquiline to the end of the Quirinal, the space before the walls seems to have been open.

The streets were narrow and winding,[4] and the houses lofty; the different floors[5] being occupied by different families, according to the practice still so common in Scotland and on the continent. There was as yet little of ornamental

[1] Bunsen's Beschreibung der Stadt Rom, Vol. I. p. 678.

[2] Bunsen, p. 628, &c. Niebuhr, Rom. Hist. Vol. III. p. 360, note 525.

[3] Niebuhr, Abriss der Geschichte de Stadt [in Bunsen's Rome, p. 112].

[4] Tacitus, Annal. XV. 43.

[5] This is said expressly by Dionysius, X. 32, of the houses on the Aventine.

architecture, such as was introduced at a later period from Greece; and of the style of the older temples we have no means of judging. Those great works which peculiarly characterize Rome, her aqueducts and her roads, were as yet in their infancy. Of the former, only two were in existence, the Appia and the Anio Vetus; but these were not carried upon a long line of magnificent arches, like the aqueducts of a later age; their course was almost wholly underground;[6] for it was not yet beyond possibility that the Romans might see an invading enemy in the neighborhood of their city, and it was of the utmost importance to conceal the line by which they obtained their supplies of water. Of the roads there existed the Appian, which in the year 459 had been paved with basalt,[7] as far as Bovillæ, that is, to the foot of the Alban hills, ten miles from Rome; and according to Niebuhr, there must also have existed the Latin, the Salarian, the Nomentan, and the oldest Tiburtine. Whether these were as yet paved, we have, I believe, no information.

If we look to the neighborhood of Rome, we shall find that many of the old towns with which Latium was so thickly set in early times, had already been utterly destroyed. Nothing more surprises those who fancy the Campagna of Rome to be like Champagne, or like the great chalk plains of Hampshire and Wiltshire, than the sight of its actual scenery. The swellings of the ground continually end in little precipitous cliffs; and the numerous streams flow between deep rocky banks, offering exactly such situations as the old Italians loved to choose for the citadels of their towns. Accordingly, Pliny reckons up the names of fifty-three[8] people of Latium, who had all perished without leaving a trace of their existence behind. Many of these indeed were destroyed at a period not only beyond historical memory, but even beyond the reach of those traditions which once passed for history; some, however, occur in the early annals of the commonwealth, and are afterwards lost to us altogether, as Crustimeria, Corioli, Longula, Polusca, &c., while others, as Gabii and Fidenæ, though not actually destroyed, fell into such a state of decay that they became a proverb to express the extremity of loneliness and desolateness.[9] No doubt the law of conquest had been applied to these states in its full extent; and their lands, having been taken in war, had mostly been occupied by the patricians, and thus became, in fact, though not in law, the property of individual Romans. Thus, at a very early period, we find that the fortunes of the nobility consisted chiefly in land[10] conquered from an enemy; the old Ager Romanus, or original territory of Rome, extending only about five miles[11] from the city towards Alba, and still less in other directions. Accordingly, Strabo says expressly that Antemnæ and Fidenæ, the latter five miles from Rome, the former less than three, were in his time the property of private persons. By *property*, *κτήσεις*, he meant *possessiones*, land which had been originally won from an enemy, and never divided out as a colony; which was the possession of individuals, sold, let, and bequeathed, like actual property, so long as the state did not choose to exercise its right of resuming it.

Polybius has remarked,[12] that the old Latin language differed so much from

[6] Frontinus, de Aquæductibus, 7, 18. The Aqua Appia had its source near the road to Præneste, between the seventh and eighth milestones from Rome; and the whole length of its course to the point at which the distribution of the water took place, near the Porta Trigemina (at the foot of the Aventine, looking towards the Palatine), was 11 miles and 190 paces. It was carried underground the whole of the distance, except for sixty paces close to the Porta Capena (in the low ground, just under the southern end of the Cælian). The Anio Vetus was contracted for in the year 482 (481 according to Frontinus), and completed a few years afterwards. Its source was twenty miles from Rome, above Tibur; and the whole length of its course was forty-three miles, all of which, except 221 paces, was underground. Frontinus, c. 6.

[7] Livy X. 47. Silice perstrata est. Silex is lava basaltina, of a blackish gray color, made up of a crystallized mass of augite, leucite, zeolite, &c. See Bunsen's Rome, p. 50, note.

[8] III. 5.

[9] Gabiis desertior atque Fidenis Vicus. See also Cicero, pro Plancio.

[10] Livy, IV. 48. Nec enim ferme quicquam agri, ut in urbe alieno solo positâ, non armis partum erat.

[11] Strabo, V. p. 159. Compare Livy, I. 28, and II. 39.

[12] III. 22.

that spoken in his time, that even those of the Romans who understood it best met with expressions in it which they found great difficulty in interpreting. This refers to the language spoken at the beginning of the commonwealth; and the famous hymn of the Fratres Arvales, which has been preserved to our own times, enables us to confirm the truth of the statement. But in the Punic wars the Latin language was substantially the same as in the age of Cicero and Virgil: the inscription on the Duillian column, and that on the tomb of L. Scipio, who was consul in 495, are both perfectly intelligible to us, and only differ in the forms of the words from the writings of the Augustan age.

The free male population of Italy of an age to bear arms, exclusive of Bruttium, of the Greek cities of Magna Græcia, and of the whole country north of the Rubicon and the Macra, is said by Polybius to have amounted to 770,000 men, in the year 529. It is not clear however whether there is not some confusion[13] in the reckoning, and whether the sum total ought not to be reduced by nearly 50,000. Even adopting the lower number, we get a free population of 1,440,000 persons in the vigor of life; and if we add half as many for those of both sexes who were under seventeen or above sixty, it makes the whole free population of Italy, with the important omissions already noticed, to amount to 2,120,000 souls. The slave population it is impossible to calculate. In Campania the slaves must have been numerous: in Etruria those who were not reckoned amongst the citizens, that subject population who, though not strictly slaves, are often carelessly called so, must have greatly outnumbered those properly called Etruscans. But in Latium, in Samnium, amongst the Sabines, and in Rome itself, the slaves were as yet perhaps a minority of the whole population. Still, if we reckon the whole population, free and slave together, at five millions, and consider the number and populousness of the Greek cities, of which no account is given, the sum for the whole peninsula south of the Macra and the Rubicon will appear sufficiently great. No doubt it had once been far greater; but the long and bloody wars which led to the Roman conquest of Italy, must have diminished it enormously, to say nothing of the wasting invasions of the Gauls.

Extensive tracts of land had been seized by the Romans, and were mostly held in occupation by a small number of proprietors; nor must we conceive of these large estates, as of the large farms of modern times, which are supposed to be so favorable to agriculture. On the contrary, they were cultivated carelessly and partially: and ground, which the necessities of the small proprietor had forced into productiveness, was allowed to return to its natural barrenness. Besides, the extent of the woodlands must have been much greater than at present; and if some spots were then well peopled, which the malaria has now rendered uninhabitable, yet, on the other hand, there were places, as particularly in the valley of the Arno, which have only been reclaimed in later times from the state of impracticable marshes; and the number of individuals supported by trade, or by any other means than agriculture, was beyond all comparison smaller than in modern Italy.

I know of only one fact which seems to indicate the existence of a commercial spirit among the Romans at the period with which we are now engaged. This is the law of Q. Claudius,[14] one of the tribunes, passed a short time before the second Punic war, which made it unlawful for any senator, or father of a senator, to possess a ship of the burden of more than three hundred amphoræ.

[13] Polybius reckons the four Roman legions employed in the field, and the reserve which covered the city, as *exclusive* of the census of the Romans and Campanians; that is, the complete census, including the legions stationed in Sicily and Tarentum, would have given a sum total of 324,900. But the census for the year 532, gives only 270,213 citizens. Now if, as Niebuhr supposes, the census included all those citizens of foreign states, who were municipes of Rome, it would on this occasion comprise the Campanians; and we thus get a number very closely agreeing with the sum of the Romans and Campanians as given by Polybius, 273,000, if we suppose that he ought to have included the soldiers actually employed in this amount, instead of reckoning them separately.

[14] Livy, XXI. 63.

The avowed object of this law was to exclude the nobility from engaging in maritime commerce; the professed reason for the exclusion was, that trade was degrading to the dignity of a senator: but the circumstance that it was resisted strenuously by the whole senate, and carried in despite of their opposition, proves that they felt the restriction much more as an injury than an honor, and makes it probable that the real object of the friends of the law was to monopolize the profits of trade to the middling classes, and to exclude the competition of the nobility, whose superior wealth would have given them great advantages in every market. But the commercial spirit of the Romans had no time to develop itself; the invasion of Hannibal was fatal to the security, and much more to the acquisition of capital; and after the struggle was over, society had undergone a change which fixed the attention of the people on other objects. Trade therefore contributed but little to the greatness of Rome: indeed it is ridiculous to speak of the trade of a country, where some of the simplest callings[15] were as yet unknown, and where silver money had been coined[16] for the first time only five years before the first Punic war.

Were the manners of Rome, then, as pure as those writers would imagine, who consider an agricultural people to be placed in so much healthier a moral condition than a commercial or manufacturing one? Undoubtedly the Roman character before the second Punic war was full of nobleness; but it is idle to connect its excellence with the preference given to agriculture, rather than to trade. The Roman people were as yet in the youth of their existence; and their minds enjoyed a youthful freshness. They had not lost the feelings of admiration and veneration; feelings which knowledge and experience, inasmuch as their field is an evil world, surely lessen; feelings whose destruction is the worst degradation of human nature. Respect for the gods, respect for the laws, respect for the aged, respect for the judgment of the good and the wise, powerfully influenced a Roman's mind; and, opposed to these, self-confidence and self-indulgence could as yet do nothing. What there was of crime was not the mere wickedness of individual gratification: of whatever offences a Roman was guilty, his idol was not that vilest of all, his own single pleasure or pride. He was cruel and treacherous to foreigners; for such conduct might save the majesty of Rome from humiliation: if a patrician, he might be oppressive and insolent to the commons, or *the mob of the forum, turba forensis;* but he was striving against the confusion of sacred things with vile, against dishonoring the images of his ancestors, whose spirits watched over the welfare of their race, and required of their descendants in every generation to transmit its honor and dignity to their children unimpaired. So in Rome, as in more corrupted states, there was violence and injustice, and towards foreigners cruelty and falsehood; but there was, withal, a surrender of self to some more general interest; and where the commands of that interest were in accordance with truth and justice, there was exhibited virtue in some of its most heroic forms, resolute control of appetite, obedience even to death, unshaken fortitude, and entire self-devotion in the cause of duty.

In such a state of things the domestic relations are purely and faithfully discharged; for on these points law and public opinion always speak the language of nature and of truth; it is only individual wickedness that leads to the violation of these plain duties. Accordingly we find that the marriage tie was seldom broken, either by adultery or by divorce;[17] and the obedience of children

[15] Barbers were unknown at Rome, according to Varro (Pliny, VII. 59), till the year 554; bakers, or rather bread-makers, till the year 580. (Pliny, XVIII. 11.) But the oldest food of the Romans was *puls*, a sort of paste made of spelt (far); like the polenta of maize, so commonly eaten in Italy now.

[16] Pliny, XXXIII. 3.

[17] It is a well-known story that Sp. Carvilius was the first Roman who divorced his wife; and that this took place after the end of the first Punic war (See Aul. Gellius, IV. 3. Valor. Maximus, II. 1, §4). Niebuhr (Rom. Hist. Vol. III. p. 414) and Hugo (Geschichte des Rom. Rechts, p. 114) consider this as a mistake; and possibly it is not to be taken to the letter. But

to their parents was secured at once by the general feeling and by law. The laws indeed relating to the *patria potestas* confer on the parent an exclusive authority, and even profane one of the most sacred of human relations by placing it on the footing of that of master and slave. Yet so strong is parental affection, that there is little danger of a father's tyrannizing over his children; and this natural love makes the great distinction between domestic government and political; neglect and disobedience on the part of the child being the evil most to be dreaded in the one, as oppression on the part of the rulers is in the other.

But although in the early times of Rome, the marriage tie was most rarely broken, yet we are not to imagine that the standard of morals approached nearly to the purity required by Christianity. As if compromising with passions which it could not wholly extirpate, public opinion almost tolerated some kinds of sensual indulgence, in order more effectually to put down others. The plays of Plautus, although the stories are of Greek origin, could not have been relished by a Roman audience, had not the state of morals which they describe resembled actual life at Rome, no less than that at Athens. So universal is the tendency of our nature to impurity, that we could readily believe, even without express testimony,[18] that the conversation of the Romans at their entertainments, even in the most ancient times, was unfit for a modest woman to hear. Nor can we wonder that the young Romans acted in the entertainments known by the name of Fabulæ Atellanæ,[19] without any degradation, although these[20] in the coarseness of their ribaldry went far beyond the regular drama. It seems as if the ancient commonwealths acted on the famous principle of Aristotle, and deemed it wise to give the passions their full range on particular occasions, that their violence might so be exhausted, and the general course of life preserved safe from their dominion. Thus, while the purity of the Athenian tragedy has been guarded with such scrupulous care, the comedy of the same people indulged in the grossest indecencies; and thus, as the slaves had their season of liberty at the Saturnalia, so the Floralia, the Liberalia, and other religious festivals, gave free license to the lowest and most slavish passions of our nature; and abominations were then practised and publicly sanctioned, which would be utterly inconsistent with the severity of the Roman discipline in other respects, did we not believe that they were looked upon as a sort of safety-valve, whereby it was possible to regulate the escape of feelings too powerful to be repressed altogether

Note B, to page 460, l. 39.

The expression in Varro is remarkable, "T. Manlio Consule bello Carthaginiensi primo confecto" (Ling. Lat. IV. p. 39, Ed. Varior. 1619), and again in Livy,

if, as the story seems to imply, Carvilius divorced his wife in order to marry another (and this is the notion of the word "Divortium," given in Scholium on Cicero de Oratore, I. 40, Divortium est, quoties dissoluto matrimonio alter eorum alteras nuptias sequitur), then it may have been one of the earliest instances of such a divorce, if not absolutely the very earliest. For the Romans in early times, no less than the Germans in the days of Tacitus, abhorred second marriages (Valor. Maxim. II. 1, § 3). Again, marriages celebrated with the religious ceremonies known by the name of *Confarreatio* were held to be indissoluble, except by the performance of certain other ceremonies, which were purposely made horrid and revolting, in order to deter any one from having recourse to them. This shows the old feeling with regard to divorce; for marriage by *Confarreatio* was doubtless considered originally as the only true and solemn marriage. And therefore, in later times, when divorces were frequent, it fell into disuse, as did, in fact, the *Conventio in Manum* altogether; and a less formal marriage came into general use, founded merely on the consent of the parties, which could be dissolved more readily.

[18] See Fragm. Varro, Satyr. Menipp. in Agathon.

[19] Livy, VII. 2. Festus in Personata Fabula.

[20] Augustine, Civit. Dei, II. 8. "Hæc sunt scenicorum tolerabilia ludorum, comœdiæ scilicet et tragœdiæ, hoc est, fabulæ, poetarum agendæ in spectaculis, multâ rerum turpitudine, sed nullâ saltem, sicut alia multa, verborum obscœnitate compositæ." That the "alia multa" include the Atellanæ Fabulæ is clear from the distinction between them and regular comedy, and from Livy's words, "Juventus, histrionibus fabellarum actu relicto, ipsa inter se more antiquo ridicula intexta versibus jactitare cœpit."

I. 19, "T. Manlio Consule, post Punicum primum perfectum bellum." This cannot allude to the first treaty concluded by Catulus six years before, but must relate to the apparently entire termination of all disputes by the solemn confirmation of it in 518–19. And thus, according to the expression of Paterculus, "Certæ pacis argumentum Janus geminus clausus dedit." The gate of Janus was the Porta Janualis, one of the gates of the original Rome on the Palatine. Afterwards, by the addition of the Sabine settlement on the Quirinal and Capitol, it became a passage gate, rather than an entrance gate, being now in the middle of the city, just like Temple Bar. It stood near the present arch of Septimius Severus, on the edge of the Forum, and close upon the Via Sacra. Livy places it in the Argiletum; that is, in the low ground between the Capitol and the Tiber, near the site of the existing arch of Janus Quadrifons; but this is probably a confusion, as we read of a temple of Janus in this quarter, but one which had been built by C. Duillius in the first Punic war. (Tacitus, Annal. II. 49.) The notion of opening the gates of Janus in war was, that this god, who under his name of Quirinus was worshipped by the old Italians, as the god of battles, might go out to war in defence of his people. And his statue was set up at the Porta Janualis, rather than at any other place, because tradition recorded, that in the battle between the Romans and Sabines, in the reign of Romulus, he had wrought a signal deliverance for Rome on that very spot. See Macrobius, Saturnal. I. 9. I am aware that Niebuhr (Vol. I. p. 202, 2d edit.) gives a different explanation of the origin of the custom, and supposes that the Porta Janualis, connecting the Roman and Sabine towns with each other, was closed in peace, to show that they were distinct and independent states, but opened in war to imply that then they were allies, and rendered one another mutual aid. This seems to me rather forced; whereas the statement given above from Macrobius is simple and probable. Besides, Virgil, a high authority in such matters, declares that the custom of opening the gates of Janus in time of war was not of Roman origin, but borrowed from the general practice of the Latins. (Æn. VII. 601.) It could not, therefore, have referred to any local peculiarities in the situation of Rome.

Note C, to p. 461, l. 19.

Nothing is known of the language or customs of the Illyrians, by which we can confidently ascertain their race. A legend recorded by Appian (Illyrica, c. I.), which makes Keltus, Illyrius, and Gala to have been three brothers, the sons of the Cyclops Polyphemus, is grounded probably on the known intermixture of Keltic tribes, the Boii, the Scordisci, and the Taurisci, amongst the Illyrians at a later period; and the Japodes, a tribe on the borders of Istria, are described by Strabo (IV. p. 143) as half Kelts, half Illyrians. In the practice of tattooing their bodies, the Illyrians resembled the Thracians (Strabo, VII. p. 218, Herodot. V. 6); the custom of one of their tribes, the Dalmatians, to have a new division of their lands every seven years (Strabo, VII. p. 218) resembles the well-known practice of the Germans, only advanced somewhat further towards civilized life; and the names of Teuta and Teutus might make us fancy a connection between them and the Teutonic race. The author of the Periplus ascribed to Scylax speaks of the great influence enjoyed by their women, whose lives in consequence he describes as highly licentious; but Scymnus Chius, writing about a hundred years before the Christian era, calls them "a religious people, just and kind to strangers, loving to be liberal, and desiring to live orderly and soberly," a character which often marks the first growth of the virtues of peace amongst a people newly reclaimed from barbarism; while they yet retain the simplicity of their earlier state, but have laid aside its lawlessness and cruelty. These happy fruits of Roman conquest and dominion were exhibited in Illyria in the time of Scymnus Chius, as at a later period they were displayed among the Cisalpine Gauls, who in the time of Pliny preserved a simplicity and purity of manners unknown in the rest of Italy. (Pliny, Epist. I. 14.) But at the time of the first Illyrian war, the Illyrians were as yet merely barbarous, dreaded for their ferocity, and with that low sense of justice or true nobleness which commonly characterizes the barbarian.

Note D, to p. 463, l. 3.

The Spaniards value the harbor of Carthagena so highly, that, according to their proverb, "there are four harbors in the Mediterranean :—Carthagena, June, July, and August."

Note E, to p. 464, l. 29.

From the mention of Greeks on this and other similar occasions (as in Livy, XXII. 57), Niebuhr concludes that the prophecies referred to cannot have been of Greek origin, and therefore not what were properly called "Sibylline books," but rather of Etruscan origin, or Latin, some of which were kept together with the Sibylline books, under the care of the same officers. But it does not appear that the prophecy and the method of evading it were contained in the same books; nor is it likely, for no prophecy would seek to render itself nugatory. If the books were Greek, they were likely to contain prophecies of Greek triumphs; and such must undoubtedly have been the meaning of the declaration, that the Greeks should take possession of Rome. Prophecies relating to the Gauls may have been of Etruscan origin, dictated by that fear of the Gaulish arms, which the Etruscans had learnt in earlier ages, when the Gauls had driven them from their settlements on the north of the Apennines. The evasion of these prophecies was merely the commentary of the Roman pontifices, such as was generally practised in order to avert a prediction, whose authority it was not thought proper to deny. Niebuhr refers to a similar trick practised by the Apulians against the Brundisians. An oracle had declared that the Ætolians, the followers of Diomedes, should possess Brundisium forever; so, when the Apulians had expelled them from Brundisium, and they on the assurance of this oracle sent an embassy to reclaim it, the Apulians put the ambassadors to death, and buried them within the city; thus fulfilling the prophecy, and preventing its fulfilment in any other sense. (Justin, XII. 2.)

Note F, to p. 465, l. 23.

Nothing shows more clearly the great rarity of geographical talent, than the praise which has been commonly bestowed on Polybius as a good geographer. He seems indeed to have been aware of the importance of geography to history, and to have taken considerable pains to gain information on the subject; but this very circumstance proves the more the difficulty of the task; for his descriptions are so vague and imperfect, and so totally devoid of painting, that it is scarcely possible to understand them. For instance, in his account of the march of the Gauls into Italy, and of the subsequent movements of their army and of the Romans, there is an obscurity, which never could have existed, had he conceived in his own mind a lively image of the seat of war as a whole, of the connection of the rivers and chains of mountains with each other, and of the consequent direction of the roads and most frequented passes. The Gauls, he tells us, crossed the Apennines into Tuscany, and advanced to Clusium; and thus placed themselves on the rear of the prætor's army, which had been destined to cover th

Etruscan frontier. We must suppose, then, that the prætor's army was posted between Fæsulæ and Pistoria, expecting the Gauls to cross the Apennines nearly by the line of the present road from Modena to Florence by Pistoria; and that the Gauls, instead of taking this line, came in the direction of the modern road from Bologna; except that after descending the main chain of the Apennines, near Moncarelli, they followed the Val Mugello, or Valley of the Sieve, to their left, and thus came out on the Valdarno, about half way between Florence and Incisa: from thence they may either have ascended the Valdarno, till they crossed over from it to the Val di Chiana by the line of the Valdambra; or else, as is more probable, they may have moved at once in the direction of Sienna, and then crossed from Sienna, by the upper part of the Val d'Ombrone, and Montepulciano, to Chiusi or Clusium.

NOTE G, to p. 466, l. 38.

The text of Polybius (II. 25) places this battle at *Fæsulæ;* this should clearly be corrected into *Rusalæ.* The Italian names of places in our manuscripts of Polybius are continually corrupt, as the Constantinople copyist knew nothing about them.

Note H, to p. 466, l. 1.

In Polybius, the Gauls are said to be intercepted, περὶ Τελαμῶνα τῆς Τυῤῥηνίας. This is evidently a mistake. Frontinus (I. 2, 7) places the scene of the battle at Poplonia, which is far more intelligible.

NOTE I, to p. 466, l. 20.

It was probably about eighty years after this period that the historian Polybius travelled through Cisalpine Gaul, and was struck with the unrivalled productiveness of the country. It yielded wine and all sorts of grain in the greatest abundance; its oak woods, scattered at intervals over the plain, fed the largest part of those immense droves of swine which were annually consumed in Italy, or required for the use of the Roman army; and travellers at the inns were provided plentifully with every thing that they wanted after their day's journey, at the rate of a quarter of an obulus for each person. Such are the fruits of the first application of the security and energy of civilization to a soil highly favored by nature. The earth is in its first freshness and vigor; the woods thinned, but not destroyed: the population flourishing and increasing, but far below the number of inhabitants capable of being maintained in comfort; and whilst the vices of barbarism have been put down, those of corrupted and ill-watched civilization have not yet had time to grow up. But this was the state of Cisalpine Gaul after it had been subjected for more than half a century to the dominion of Rome. It must have presented a very different aspect to the first Roman settlers of the year 534. The roads or tracts were cut through a wide extent of forest and marshes; and only a small space of the most inviting character had been hardly recovered from its natural wildness by the lazy and careless cultivation of the Gauls. Towns were nowhere to be seen; the population was scattered about in unwalled villages, if the name of village may be given to a collection of wretched huts, so devoid of the commonest articles of furniture, that "man's life" spent in them was literally "as cheap as beasts'." And along with this state of physical degradation, there was the total absence of civil society. There were men in the country; there were families, bands, and hordes; but there was no commonwealth. One relation alone, beyond those of blood, seems to have been acknowledged; the same which, introduced into Europe six hundred years afterwards by the victories of the German barbarians, has deeply tainted modern society down to this hour; the relation of chief and followers, or, as it was called in its subsequent form, lord and vassals. The head of a family distinguished for his strength and courage, gathered around him a numerous train of followers from other families; and they formed his clan, or band, or followers, bound to him for life and death, bestowing on him those feelings of devoted attachment, which can be safely entertained only towards the commonwealth and its laws, and rendering him that blind obedience, which is wickedness when paid to any less than God. This evil and degrading bond is well described by the Greek and Roman writers, by words expressive of unlawful and antisocial combinations ("Factio," Cæsar, de Bell. Gallic. VI. 11; ἑταιρεία, Polybius, II. 17): it is the same which in other times and countries has appeared in the shape of sworn brotherhoods, factions, parties, sects, clubs, secret societies, and unions, everywhere and in every form the worst enemy both of individual and of social excellence, as it substitutes other objects in place of those to which as men and citizens we ought only to be bound, namely, God and Law.

Note K, to p. 468, l. 42.

The remova of the freedmen into the four city tribes is recorded in the Epitome of the 20th book, nearly in the same words as in the Epitome of the 9th. There it is said, "forensis factio cum comitia et campum turbaret . . . a Q. Fabio censore in quatuor tribus redacta est, quas urbanas appellavit." In the 20th Epitome it is said, "libertini in quatuor tribus redacti sunt, cum antea dispersi per omnes fuissent, Esquilinam, Palatinam, Suburranam, Collinam." The "forensis factio" of the 9th book is said to have consisted of "humiles," "humillimi;" and they are called also "forensis turba," as if their occupation were described rather than their birth. In the 20th book, the persons removed are called simply "libertini." But libertini in general must have followed city employments from the necessity of the case; few can have had landed property. We must therefore suppose that Fabius' measure was considered as a remedy for a crying evil, rather than a general rule for the time to come; and that, when slaves were set free, they were generally entered in their late master's tribe, which, as he was still in a close relation with them, that of patronus, would be the most natural course to take, when no particular political excitement was stirring. But that such an excitement was stirring in the years immediately preceding the second Punic war, appears from what Livy says of C. Varro: "Proclamando pro sordidis hominibus causisque adversus rem et famam bonorum primum in notitiam populi, deinde ad honores pervenit." XXII. 26. Varro was prætor in 536, and before that time had been quæstor, ædile, and curule ædile; so that he must have come into notice before the censorship of Flaminius. Now it is easy to conceive that, under such circumstances, the aristocracy would wish to lessen the influence of the poorer citizens in the tribes; but the wonder is, how C. Flaminius should have become their instrument in doing this, after his violent contests with them about his Agrarian law, and afterwards about his recall from Cisalpine Gaul, both of which took place before his censorship. Nor could his colleague have done it against his will, according to the well-known law, "Melior est conditio prohibentis."

The solution can only be, that Flaminius was a very honest man, and, whilst he liked the agricultural commons, did not like the populace of the Forum. He was like M. Curius, who also vehemently upheld an Agrarian law, yet sold as a slave a citizen who refused to serve as a soldier. He was, like P. Decius, the colleague of Fabius in the former clearing of the tribes, yet forward as a supporter of the Ogulnian law. He was, like Marius, the stoutest opposer of the aristocracy, yet a resolute opposer also of a Lex Frumentaria. (Plutarch, Marius, 4.) Perhaps, too, his notions were wholly against giving political influence to any thing but agriculture ; and his support of the Claudian law, the object of which was to prevent the senators from becoming merchants, was perhaps conceived in the same spirit as his removing the freedmen into the four city tribes. In this, and perhaps in the vehemence of his temper, he seems to have resembled Cato the censor.

Note L, to p. 478, l. 25.

The question, in what direction this famous march was taken, has been agitated for more than eighteen hundred years ; and who can undertake to decide it ? The difficulty to modern inquirers has arisen chiefly from the total absence of geographical talent in Polybius. That this historian indeed should ever have gained the reputation of a good geographer, only proves how few there are who have any notion what a geographical instinct is. Polybius indeed labored with praiseworthy diligence to become a geographer ; but he labored against nature ; and the unpoetical character of his mind has in his writings actually lessened the accuracy, as it has totally destroyed the beauty of history. To any man who comprehended the whole character of a mountain country, and the nature of its passes, nothing could have been easier than to have conveyed at once a clear idea of Hannibal's route, by naming the valley by which he had ascended to the main chain, and afterwards that which he followed in descending from it. Or admitting that the names of barbarian rivers would have conveyed little information to Greek readers, still the several Alpine valleys have each their peculiar character, and an observer with the least power of description could have given such lively touches of the varying scenery of the march, that future travellers must at once have recognized his description. Whereas the account of Polybius is at once so unscientific and so deficient in truth and liveliness of painting, that persons who have gone over the several Alpine passes for the very purpose of identifying his descriptions, can still reasonably doubt whether they were meant to apply to Mont Genevre, or Mont Cenis, or to the Little St. Bernard.

On the whole, it appears to me most probable, that the pass by which Hannibal entered Italy was that which was known to the Romans by the name of the Graian Alps, and to us as the Little St. Bernard. Nor was this so circuitous a line as we may at first imagine. For Hannibal's object was not simply to get into Italy, but to arrive in the country of those Cisalpine Gauls with whom he had been corresponding, and who had long been engaged in wars with the Romans. Now these were the Boii and Insubrians ; and as the Insubrians, who were the more westerly of the two, lived between the Addi and the Ticinus, the pass of the Little St. Bernard led more directly into the country of his expected allies, than the shorter passage into Italy by the Cottian Alps, or Mont Genevre.

Note M, to p. 481, l. 2.

Such is the story of the earliest recorded passage of the Alps by civilized men, the earliest and the most memorable. Accustomed as we are, since the completion of the great Alpine roads in the present century, to regard the crossing of the Alps as an easy summer excursion, we can even less than our fathers conceive the difficulties of Hannibal's march, and the enormous sacrifices by which it was accomplished. He himself declared that he had lost above thirty thousand men since he had crossed the Pyrenees, and that the remnant of his army, when he reached the plains of Italy, amounted to no more than twenty thousand foot, and six thousand horsemen : nor does Polybius seem to suspect any exaggeration in the statement. Yet eleven years afterwards Hasdrubal crossed the Alps in his brother's track without sustaining any loss deserving of notice; and "a few accidents"[21] are all that occurred in the most memorable passage of modern times, that of Napoleon over the Great St. Bernard. It is evident that Hannibal could have found nothing deserving the name of a road, no bridges over the rivers, torrents, and gorges, nothing but mere mountain-paths, liable to be destroyed by the first avalanche or landslip, and which the barbarians neither could nor cared to repair, but on the destruction of which they looked out for another line, such as for their purposes of communication it was not difficult to find. It is clear also, either that Hannibal passed by some much higher point than the present roads over the Little St. Bernard, or Mount Cenis; or else, as is highly probable,[22] that the limit of perpetual snow reached to a much lower level in the Alps than it does at present. For the passage of the main chain is described as wholly within this limit; and the "old snow" which Polybius speaks of was no accidental patch, such as will linger through the summer at a very low level in crevices or sunless ravines; but it was the general covering of the pass, which forbade all vegetation, and remained alike in summer as in winter. How great a contrast to the blue lake, the green turf, the sheep and cattle freely feeding on every side tended by their shepherds, and the bright hues of the thousand flowers which now delight the summer traveller on the Col of the Little St. Bernard!

I have little doubt as to Hannibal's march up the Tarentaise; but the Val d'Aosta puzzles me. According to any ordinary rate of marching, an army could never get in three days from the Little St. Bernard to the plains of Ivrea; not to mention that the Salassians of that valley were such untameable robbers, that they once even plundered Cæsar's baggage, and Augustus at last extirpated them by wholesale. And yet Hannibal, on the Italian side of the main chain, sustains little or no annoyance. I have often wished to examine the pass which goes by the actual head of the Isere, by Mont Iseran, and descends by Usseglio, not exactly on Turin, but nearly at Chivasso, where the Po, from running N. and S., turns to run E. and W. In some respects also, I think, Mont Cenis suits the description of the march better than any other pass. I lay no stress on the Roche blanche; it did not strike me when I saw it as at all conspicuous; nor does the λευκόπετρον mean any remarkably white cliff, but simply one of those bare limestone cliffs, which are so common both in the Alps and Apennines.

Note N, to p. 484, l. 2.

There is a passage in the third volume of Niebuhr's life, in a letter to the Count de Serre, in which he says that Hannibal at the Trebia acted like Napoleon at Marengo, throwing himself between the Romans and the line of their retreat, by Placentia and Ariminum. I believe that this is right, and that Hannibal was on the right bank of the Trebia between the Romans and Placentia, so that the expression in Livy is correct. The Romans had several emporia on the right bank of the Po, above Placentia, Clastidium, Victumviæ, &c. From these, their army, I suppose, was fed; and the taking of Clastidium thus helped to force them to a battle. Polybius' words are equally clear with Livy's. The front

[21] "On n'eut que peu d'accidens." Napoleon's Memoirs, Vol. I. p. 261.

[22] Even as late as the year 1646, Evelyn's description of the passage of the Simplon in September can scarcely be recognized by those who know only its present state. He speaks of the house in which he lodged at Sempione, as "half covered with snow," and says that "there is not a tree or bush growing within many miles;" whereas now the pines are so luxuriant about the village, that the road seems to run through an ornamental park. And again above Sempione, Evelyn was told by the country people that "the way had been covered with snow since the creation; no man remembered it to be without." And he speaks of the descent towards Brieg by the old road as being made for some way "through an ocean of snow." Memoirs, Vol. I. p. 220, 221.

of the Roman centre, he says, despaired of retreating to their own camp κωλυόμενοι διὰ τὸν ποταμὸν καὶ τὴν ἐπιφορὰν καὶ συστροφὴν τοῦ κατὰ κεφαλὴν ὄμβρου (the rain having made the river deeper than it had been in the morning:) τηροῦντες δὲ τὰς τάξεις ἀθρόοι μετ'ἀσφαλείας ἀπεχώρησαν εἰς Πλακεντίαν. It is still a difficulty how Sempronius could have been allowed to effect his junction with Scipio, while Hannibal was actually lying between them; but I suppose that he must have turned off to the hills before he approached Placentia, and so have left Hannibal in the plain on his right.

Note O, p. 486, l. 35.

Niebuhr in the same letter speaks of the following view of Thrasymenus as absolutely certain. Flaminius, with Servilius, was originally at Ariminum, expecting Hannibal by that road. But when he heard that Hannibal had entered Etruria by the marshes of the Lower Arno, he hastened over the Apennines to Arezzo, eager to cover the road to Rome. He moved then by Cortona upon Perugia; but Hannibal turned to the right, and followed the western side of the lake towards Chiusi; then turning short round, occupied the defile of Passignano, and spreading out his right upon the hills, forced the long Roman column by a flank attack into the lake, while he engaged the head of it in the defile. Polybius and Livy differ decidedly as to the scene of the main battle: the latter represents it as taking place in the defile of Passignano, where the Romans had their right flank to the lake. But Polybius says, that only the rear was caught there; most of the army had cleared the defile, and turned to the left into a valley running down at right angles to the lake, so that the lake was exactly on their rear. And the modern road does so turn from the lake tc ascend the hills towards Perugia: the only difficulty is (I have been twice on the ground), that there is nothing that can be called a valley; for the road ascends almost from the edge of the lake: still it is true that the hills do form a small comb, so that an army ascending from the lake might have an enemy on both its flanks on the hill-sides above it.

Note P, to p. 505, l. 43.

It seems to me that the Latin colonies and Hannibal's want of artillery were the main causes of his failure. The Romans had in these colonies, not one of which he ever took, fortresses in the heart of the countries which revolted to him. Thus Apulia revolted; but the Romans still held Luceria, Venusia, and Brundisium: Samnium revolted; but the Romans held Æsernia and Beneventum; and so on. Casilinum cost him a siege of several weeks, but the Romans recovered it in a much shorter time. If he had engaged Archimedes as his engineer in chief, and got Philip to send him artillery, he would have done far better; for the Macedonian princes seemed to have carried their artillery to great perfection. As it was, his only very strong arm was his cavalry: for his infantry, veterans as they were, could never beat the Roman raw levies behind works. It appears to me that the sieges are the great defect of Hannibal's operations in Italy; and thus as soon as his army moved from any place, the inhabitants who had joined him were at the mercy of the Roman garrisons. And their colonies were very strong garrisons: Venusia was originally settled with 20,000 colonists.

Note Q, to p. 536, l. 25.

According to Livy, Hannibal collects all the boats which are to be found on the Vulturnus, orders his men to provide themselves with provisions for ten days, and *crosses in the night.* (XXVI. 7.)

He *remains on the right bank the next day and night*, then moves by Cales in Agrum Sidicinum, and there *remains one day plundering.*

He advances by the Latin road, per Suessanum, Allifanumque et Casinatem agrum. He then *remains for two days under Casinum*, plundering the country in all directions.

He goes on by Interamna and Aquinum to Fregellæ, where he finds the bridges over the Liris broken down; he ravages the ager Fregellanus with peculiar spite for that reason; and then advances by Frusino, Ferentinum, and Anagnia, in Agrum Lavicanum.

From thence he goes over Algidus to Tusculum, descends to Gabii, thence marches down in Pupiniam, and pitches his camp eight miles from Rome.

He moves his camp ad Anienem, three miles from Rome, and there establishes stativa; he himself advancing along under the walls from the Colline gate to the temple of Hercules, to look about him.

On the next day he crosses the Anio, and offers battle to the enemy; a storm breaks off the action.

Next day he offers battle again, and there comes a second storm. He falls back ad Tutiam fluvium, six miles from Rome.

He plunders the temple of Feronia, and marches to Eretum: from thence he goes to Reate, Cutiliæ, and Amiternum. From thence through the Marsian and Marrucinian territory by Sulmo, through the Pelignian territory into Samnium, and from Samnium into Campania. From Campania into Lucania, thence into Bruttium, and thence to Rhegium.

Here are traces of two accounts jumbled together. The march from the Vulturnus, as far as the camp in Pupinia, eight miles from Rome, is all highly consistent and probable, and comes, I suspect, either from Fabius or Cincius. But the advance to the Anio, the crossing it to offer battle, and then the retreat ad Tutiam, belong to a different story, that namely which made Hannibal advance upon Rome from Reate. For in advancing by the Latin road, or the Via Gabina, he had nothing to do with the Anio; and if he crossed the Anio to offer battle, he must have been between Rome and the Roman army, and the Roman army would have been between him and the Tutia. This then is all absurd and inconsistent.

Again, according to Livy, Fulvius had heard beforehand of Hannibal's design, and had warned the senate of it; he receives an answer from Rome, selects 15,000 foot, and 1000 horse, crosses the Vulturnus on rafts after a long delay, because Hannibal had burnt all the boats, advances to Rome by the Appian way, and arrives by the Porta Capena just as Hannibal had reached Pupinia. Now, according to Polybius, Hannibal set out for Rome only five days after his arrival before Capua: there was no time therefore for Fulvius to send to Rome and get an answer before Hannibal set out. Again, Casilinum being in the power of the Romans, the passage of the Vulturnus was in their own hands, and the story about the rafts is an absurdity.

Appian says, that Hannibal marched with urgent haste through many and hostile nations, some of whom could not and some did not try to stop him; and thus he arrived on the Anio, and encamped at 32 stadia from Rome. The Romans break down the bridge over the Anio; and two thousand men from Alba Marsorum come valiantly to the aid of Rome. This all agrees with Cælius, and supposes evidently that Hannibal advanced through Samnium and by Reate. The "many and hostile nations" are the Pelignians, Marsians, Marrucinians, and Sabines. Thus, too, he arrives naturally on the Anio; and the Albensians, seeing him pass through their country, set off at once by the Valerian road to Rome, to be ready to meet him. Had he advanced by the Latin road, they would have known nothing about his march, and he would have been between them and Rome.

Fulvius then, according to Appian, hastens to Rome, and meets Hannibal on the Anio, with the river between them. Hannibal ascends the right bank of the river to turn it by its source. Fulvius ascends the left bank watching him. Hannibal leaves some Numidians behind, who cross the river when Fulvius was gone, plunder all the country round the walls, and then rejoin Hannibal. Hannibal goes round by the sources of the river; and, as it was only a little way to Rome, he steals out by night with three squires to have a look at it, and then takes fright and returns to Capua. Fulvius follows him; and Hannibal, in attempting to surprise his camp on the road, is sadly foiled. He then marches off to *winter in Lucania*; and Fulvius rejoins Appius before Capua. This is beneath criticism; but I observe that the story of Fulvius being too cunning for Hannibal is given by Livy at the assault of the Roman lines before Capua, and is probably as true of one as of the other. Again, the line of retreat here indicated is by the Latin road; the ascending the Anio shows this, and is inconsistent with the retreat by Reate.

Cælius Antipater had expressly given Hannibal's advance upon Rome thus:—

From Campania into Samnium, and thence to the Pelignians, that is, by the present great road up the Vulturnus to Venafro; thence by Isernia and Castel di Sangro to the Five Mile plain; then passing by Sulmo to the Marrucinians; thence by Alba to the Marsians; thence to Amiternum and Foruli: from Amiternum, by Cutiliæ, Reate, and Eretum, upon the Anio.

What a confusion! which neither Nauta nor Prinsterer meddle with. The road from Sulmo to Amiternum is simple enough; descending along the Gizio to the Aterno or Pescara at Popoli, thence ascending to the high upland plain by Navelli and Città Retenga, and so by Aquila to Amiternum, S. Vittorino. But conceive a man,—to say nothing of an army in a hurry,—going down from Popoli to Chieti, then turning back to Sulmona, and going over by the Forchetta to Celano, and thence by Rocca di Mezzo into the valley of Aquila. All this folly arises from the untimely correction where the MS. gives corruptly in Marrucinos, Martinos, Martianos, Maceranos, &c. Cælius supposed that Hannibal, instead of descending from Sulmo towards Popoli, turned to his left, and crossed the mountains by the Forchetta[23] to Cilano, and thence either by Rocca di Mezzo over the mountains to Aquila, or else by the Cicolano, and down the valley of Tornimparte. Instead of Marrucinos, the better condition would be Marrubios, or Marruvios; the people of Marruvium, a Pelignian town on the E. or S. E. shore of the lake Fucinus.

According to Polybius, Hannibal, five days after his arrival before Capua, left his fires burning at night, and set off after supper. He marched by *vigorous and uninterrupted marches through Samnium*, always exploring and preoccupying the ground near the road with his advanced guard; and whilst all at Rome were thinking only of Capua, he suddenly crossed the Anio, and encamped at a distance of not more than four miles from Rome. He intended the next day to assault the city; but the consuls with their two newly raised legions encamped before the walls. He then gives up the assault, and sets about plundering the country and burning the houses in all directions. After this (how long after is not said, nor why, but we must suppose after Fulvius had arrived from Capua) the consuls advance boldly, and encamp within ten stadii of Hannibal. Then Hannibal, having filled his army with plunder, and thinking that his diversion must now have taken effect at Capua, commenced his retreat. But the bridges over the Anio had been broken down; and in fording the river he was attacked and sustained some loss: his cavalry, however, served him so well, that the Romans returned to their camp, ἄπρακτοι. He continued his march hastily, which the enemy thought was through fear; so they followed him close, but keeping to the higher grounds. He was moving in haste upon Capua; but *on the fifth day of his retreat*, learning that the Romans there were still in their

[23] At Raiano. This is still a carriageable road. Keppel Craven calls the pass, Furca Caruso.

lines, he halted to wait for his pursuers, and turning upon them attacked their camp by night, and stormed it. The Romans rallied by daybreak on a steep hill which he could not force; so he would not wait to besiege them, but marched through Apulia and Bruttium, and nearly succeeded in surprising Rhegium.

Again what a narrative! with no details of time or place, jumping at once from a five days' march from Rome into Apulia, and merely implying that Hannibal's retreat was on the right bank of the Anio. But this mention of the Anio, connected with the expression "marching through Samnium," seems to show that Polybius, like Cælius, made Hannibal advance by a circuitous route upon Rome, and not by the Latin road.

The season of the year must have been early, according to the Roman calendar, not later than April, whatever that was by true time; because the levy of the two city legions was only half finished. But, unless the Roman calendar was at least two months behind true time, how could Hannibal have passed such defiles as that of Rocca, Vall' Osuira; or such passes as those between Isernia and Castel di Sangro? Would not the snow have covered the ground at such a season?

APPENDIX.

I.—NOTE ON THE TRIAL AND DEATH OF MANLIUS.

ZONARAS, whose history is taken generally from Dion Cassius, relates that Manlius was holding the Capitol against the government, and that a slave, having offered to betray him, went up to the Capitol as a deserter, and begged to speak with Manlius. He professed to be come to him on the part of the slaves of Rome, who were ready to rise and join him; and while Manlius was speaking to him apart on the edge of the cliff, the slave suddenly pushed him down it, and he was then seized by some men who had been previously placed there in ambush, and was by them carried off as a prisoner. Then he was tried in the Campus Martius; and as the people could not condemn him in sight of the Capitol, the trial was adjourned, and the people met again in another place out of sight of the Capitol, and then condemned him. The scene of the second trial is said by Livy to have been the Peteline Grove. Now we find that on two other occasions after a secession assemblies were held in groves without the city walls, and not in the Campus Martius; once after the revolt of the soldiers and secession of the commons in 413, in this very Peteline Grove (Livy, VII. 41), and once after the last secession to the Janiculum, in the Oak Grove, "in Esculeto." (Pliny, Hist. Nat. XVI. § 37.) Now as there is little reason to doubt that there was a secession also in the disturbance caused by Manlius, it is likely that when peace was restored the terms would have been settled in an assembly held in some sacred grove, and that there a general amnesty would be passed, and any exceptions to the amnesty discussed and determined. And if Manlius had fallen into the power of his enemies in the manner described by Zonaras, his partisans, having thus lost their leader, would have been ready to submit, and could not have opposed his execution, if it were insisted upon by the government as a necessary sacrifice to public justice. The story of his trial before the centuries in the Campus Martius is every way suspicious, and may possibly have been invented to account for the fact of his death having been decreed in an assembly held in the Peteline Grove. It was obvious that trials before the centuries, the only tribunal which could legally try a Roman citizen capitally, were held in the Campus Martius; and as the fact of the secession was more and more glossed over, so the real nature of the assembly in the Peteline Grove would be less understood; and then it was attempted to be explained as a mere adjourned meeting of the centuries, held in an unusual place, because the deliverer of the Capitol could not be condemned in the Campus Martius, where his judges had the Capitol directly before their eyes.

I may observe that the law which forbade any patrician's residing from henceforth in the Capitol strongly confirms the fact of an actual secession. Manlius had occupied the citadel as a fortified position, and had held it with an armed force against the government; and this pointed out the danger of allowing any one to reside within its precincts.

II.—ON THE LATER CONSTITUTION OF THE CENTURIES.

THE constitution of the comitia of the centuries, as it originally existed, is perfectly familiar to every reader. But it is remarkable that this well-known form of it never existed during those times of which we have a real history; and the form which had succeeded to it is a complete mystery. It is strange, but true, that we know how the centuries were constituted in the times of the later kings, but that we do not know what was their constitution in the time of Cicero and Cæsar.

It is quite clear that the old constitution of the centuries gave a decided ascendency to wealth. The first class, together with the centuries of the knights, formed a majority of the whole comitia. Thus every election would have been in the hands of the rich, and such a state of things as existed in the last years of the commonwealth, when the aristocracy had no other decided influence than what they could gain by bribery, is altogether inconceivable.

Again, the division of the people into tribes had nothing to do with the earlier constitution of the centuries; the votes were taken by classes, and a man's class depended on the amount of his property. But in the later constitution the votes were taken by tribes, and a man's tribe, except in the case of the four city tribes, implied nothing as to his rank or fortune. The agents employed to purchase votes were called divisores tribuum; such and such tribes are mentioned as interested in behalf of particular candidates (Cicero pro Plancio); and some one tribe was determined by lot to exercise the privilege of voting before the rest. In short, the tribes are mentioned as commonly at the comitia in the Campus Martius, whether held for trials or for elections, as at the comitia held in the Forum.

On the other hand, the division by classes continued to exist in the later constitution. Cicero speaks of the comitia of centuries differing from the comitia of tribes, inasmuch as in the former, he says, "the people are arranged according to property, rank, and age, while in the latter no such distinctions are observed." De Legibus, III. 19. The centuries of the first class are spoken of both in trials (Livy, XLIII. 16) and in elections (Cicero, Philippic. II. 33); and in the second oration of the pseudo-Sallust to Cæsar, de Republicâ Ordinanda, the author notices, as a desirable change in the actual constitution, that a law formerly proposed by C. Gracchus should be again brought forward and enacted, that the centuries should be called by lot from all the five classes indiscriminately. This proves not only that the division into classes existed to the end of the commonwealth, but also that the first class continued to enjoy certain advantages above the others. The problem, therefore, is to determine how the system of classes was blended with that of tribes, and in what degree the centuries of the historical period of the commonwealth retained or had forfeited the strong aristocratical character impressed on them by their original constitution.

Various solutions of this problem have been offered at different times by scholars of great ability. Octavius Pantagathus in the 16th century supposed that each of the five classes had two centuries belonging to it in each of the tribes, and that the Equites had one century in each tribe, making the whole number of centuries to amount to 385, out of which those of the Equites and the first class together would amount to 105, while those of the other classes were 280; so that the two former, instead of being a majority of the whole comitia, stood to the other centuries only in the proportion of 3 to 8. This notion of seventy centuries in each class, or ten centuries in each tribe, has been maintained also by Savigny, according to Zumpt; and by Walther, in his History of the Roman Law, Vol. I. p. 136. This also is the opinion of another living authority of the highest order, who has expressed to me his full acquiescence in it.

Niebuhr, on the contrary, held that the whole division into five classes was done away with; that each tribe contained two centuries only, one of older men, the other of younger; that the thirty-one country tribes constituted the first class under this altered system, and the four city tribes the second class; and that besides these two classes there were no more. He held the aristocratical character of the comitia of centuries, as compared with the assembly of the tribes, to consist in the following points: that the plebeian knights voted distinctly from the rest of the commons, and that the patricians also had their separate votes in the sex suffragia, or six old centuries of knights; 2d, that the centuries of each tribe were divided according to their age, one of older men, and the other of younger; 3d, that the proletarians, or those who possessed property under four thousand ases, were altogether excluded; and 4th, that the auspices were necessarily taken at the comitia of centuries, and that they were thus subjected to the influence of the augurs. Niebuhr held also that the prerogative century could only be chosen out of the tribes of the first class, and never out of the four city tribes.

Zumpt, in a recent essay on the constitution of the comitia of centuries, read before the Prussian academy in 1836, maintains that the old centuries of Ser. Tullius subsisted to the end of the commonwealth without any material alteration, except that those of the first class were reduced from eighty to seventy. He then supposes that two of these centuries were allotted to each of the thirty-five tribes, together with three centuries from the four remaining classes; and of these three one, he thinks, was taken from the fifth class, and two-thirds of a century from the second, third, and fourth classes. Thus the richer citizens still retained an influence in the comitia more than in proportion to their numbers, although much less than it had been in the original constitution of Ser. Tullius.

Lastly, Professor Huschke, of Breslau, in his work on the constitution of Ser. Tullius, published in 1838, agrees with Niebuhr in supposing that the whole number of centuries was reduced to seventy, each tribe containing two, one of older men and the other of younger; but these seventy centuries were divided, he thinks, into five classes; so that about ten tribes, or twenty centuries, would contain the citizens of the first class, a certain number of tribes would, in like manner, contain all the citizens of the second class, and so on to the end: some tribes, according to this hypothesis, consisting only of richer citizens, and others only of poorer.

But I confess that all these solutions, including even that of Niebuhr himself, are to me unsatisfactory. If the first class had contained thirty-one out of the thirty-five tribes, while each tribe contained only two centuries, we should hear rather of the tribes of the first class, than of the centuries; whilst on the other hand the positive testimony of the pseudo-Sallust, who, according to Niebuhr himself, could not have lived later than the second century after the Christian era, to the existence of five classes down to the time of the civil war, seems to be on that point an irresistible authority.

It appears to me to be impossible to ascertain with certainty either the number of the centuries in the later constitution, or their connection with the five classes. To guess at points of mere detail seems hopeless, and positive information on the subject there is none. But we know that the comitia of centuries differed from those of the tribes expressly in this, that whereas all the members of a tribe voted in the comitia tributa without any further distinction between them, and, as far as appears, without any subdivisions within the tribe itself, so in the comitia of centuries the members of the same tribe were distinguished from each other; the older men certainly voted distinctly from the younger men, and probably the richer men also voted distinctly from the poorer: so that the centuries were a less democratical body than the tribes.

In the account given by Polybius of the composition of the Roman army, we find traces at once of the existence of something like the old system of classes, and of the changes which it must have undergone. All citizens whose property exceeded four thousand ases, were now enlisted into the legions, whereas in old times none had been required to provide themselves with arms whose property fell short of twelve thousand five hundred ases. But one hundred thousand ases still appear to have been the qualification for the first class; and it is remarkable that the peculiar distinction of this class, the coat of mail, was the same as it had been in the oldest known system of the classes. All distinctions of arms, offensive or defensive, between the second, third, and fourth classes, seem to have been abolished: but the fifth class still, as in old times, supplied the light-armed soldiers of the legions, or the velites.

But however much of the old system of the classes was preserved in the later constitution of the centuries, the difference in the political spirit of the tribes and centuries is scarcely, I think, perceivable. We do not find the votes of the centuries ever relied upon by the aristocracy to counterbalance the popular feeling of the tribes. It might have been conceived that a popular assembly, where wealth conferred any ascendency, would have been decidedly opposed to one of a character purely democratical; that the centuries, in short, like our own House of Commons, during more than one period of our history, should have sympathized more and more with the senate, and have counteracted to the utmost of their power on the Campus Martius the policy embraced by the tribes in the Forum. But this is not the case; the spirit of the Roman people, as distinguished from the senate and the equestrian order, appears to have been much the same whether they were assembled in one sort of comitia or another; the centuries elected Flaminius and Varro to the consulship in the second Punic war, although their opposition to the aristocracy seems to have been one of their chief recommendations; and in later times the centuries elected many consuls who advocated the popular cause not less violently than the most violent of the tribunes elected by the tribes.

The cause of this is to be found in the great wealth of the equestrian order and of the senate, which drew a broad line of separation between them and the richest of the plebeians, and thus drove the members of the first class to sympathize with those below them rather than with those above them. While the possession of the judicial power was disputed by the senate and the equestrian order, it was only after many years that any share of it was communicated to the richest of the plebeians. Thus it is probable that the middle classes at Rome, as elsewhere, repelled by the pride of the highest classes, were forced back, as it were, into the mass of the lower; and entered as bitterly into all measures galling to the aristocracy, as the poorest citizens of the tribes.

If this be so, the question as to the exact form of the comitia of centuries in later times, however curious in itself, is of no great importance to our right understanding of the subsequent history. For whether the influence of the first class as compared with that of the lower classes was greater or less, it does not appear that the character of the comitia was altered from what it would have been otherwise; the first class was as little attached to the aristocracy as the fourth or fifth. After the unsuccessful attempts of so many men of ability and learning, I have no confidence that I could approach more nearly to the true solution of the problem; and, in fact, there seem difficulties in the way of every theory, which our present knowledge can hardly enable us to remove. I must at present express my belief that the exact arrangement of the classes in the later comitia of centuries is a problem no less inexplicable than that of the disposition of the rowers in the ancient ships of war.

III.—OF THE ROMAN LEGION IN THE FIFTH CENTURY OF ROME.

THE accounts of the Roman legion in the fourth and fifth centuries of Rome are full of perplexity. Nor is this to be wondered at, for as there were no contemporary historians, and as the military system afterwards underwent considerable changes, the older state of things could be known only from accidental notices of it in the stories of the early wars, or from uncertain memory. How little help in these inquiries is to be expected from Livy, may be understood from this single fact: that although he himself in two several places (I. 43 and VIII. 8) has expressly stated that the ancient Roman tactic was that of the phalanx, yet in no one of his descriptions of battles are any traces to be found of such a system; but the sword and not the pike is spoken of as the most efficient weapon, just as it was in the tactic of the second Punic war, or of the age of Marius and of Cæsar.

Livy, however, has preserved in one place a detailed account of the earlier legion, as it existed in the great Latin war in the beginning of the fifth century. And Polybius, as is well known, has described at length the arms and organization of the legion of his time, that is, of the latter part of the sixth and the beginning of the seventh century of Rome. I shall notice the similar and dissimilar points in these two accounts, and then see how far we can explain the changes implied in them; and, finally, notice some statements in other writers which relate to the same subject.

Both accounts acknowledge the existence of four divisions of fighting men in the legion: the light-armed (γροσφόμαχοι, Polyb. rorarii, Livy), the hastati, the principes, and the triarii. But to these there was in the older legion a fifth added, the accensi, or supernumeraries; who, in ordinary cases, were not armed, but went to the field to be ready to take arms and supply the places of those who fell.

In both accounts the hastati, when the legion is drawn up in order of battle, are placed in front of the principes, and the principes in front of the triarii. But in the old legion the greater part of the light-armed soldiers are described as stationed with the triarii in the third line, and only about a fourth part of them are with the hastati in the front. Whereas, in the later legion, the light troops are divided equally among the three lines.

Again, in the older legion the triarii were equal in numbers to the hastati and principes, respectively, each division consisting of somewhat more than nine hundred men. Whereas, in the later legion, the triarii were never more than six hundred men; while the hastati and principes were regularly twelve hundred each, and sometimes exceeded this number.

In the older legion the light-armed troops carried each man a pike, "hasta," and two or more javelins, "gæsa.' These were the arms of the fourth class in the Servian constitution, "nihil præter hastam et verutum datum:" verutum and gæsa alike signifying missile weapons or javelins as opposed to the hasta or pike. But in the later legion, the light-armed soldier carried no pike, but had a round shield, πάρμη, and a dirk or cutlass, μάχαιρα, together with his javelins.

In the older legion again the hastati, principes, and triarii, all bore the arms of the second and third classes in the Servian constitution; that is to say, the large oblong shield, "scutum," the pike, and the sword, "gladius." But in the later legion, the hastati and principes had both dropped the pike, and were armed instead of it with two large javelins, of about six feet in length, which Polybius calls ὑσσοί, and which were no other than the formidable pila.

Further, we have a remarkable notice that there was a time when the triarii alone carried pila, and were called pilani, while the hastati and principes still carried pikes.[2]

Again, the older legion was divided into forty-five maniples or ordines; fifteen of hastati, fifteen of principes, and fifteen of triarii; but as the triarii were, in fact, a triple division, so their maniples contained one hundred and eighty-six, or possibly one hundred and eighty-nine men each, while those of the hastati and principes contained only sixty-three men each.

In the later legion, the hastati, principes, and triarii contained ten maniples each; and those of the two former divisions consisted of one hundred and twenty men each, while those of the triarii contained only sixty. The light troops were divided into thirty divisions, one of which was added to each maniple of the heavy-armed troops, in just proportion to its respective strength; that is, that twenty-four light-armed men were added to each maniple of the triarii, and forty-eight to each maniple of the hastati and principes. It may be, however, that the divisions of the light-armed troops were all equal: in which case they would have raised each maniple of the triarii to one hundred men, and each maniple of the hastati and principes to one hundred and sixty.

In the older legion, each maniple contained two centurions; that is, it consisted of two centuries. Therefore the century of the old legion consisted of thirty men.

In the later legion each maniple also had two centurions; but the maniples being of unequal numbers, the centuries were unequal also; the centuries of the triarii contained thirty men each, as in the older legion, but those of the hastati and principes had each sixty.

On comparing these two forms of the legion, it is manifest that in the older there is retained one of the characterestic points of the system of the phalanx, or of fighting in columns, the keeping of the light-armed or worst-armed men mostly in the rear. The old legion consisted of a first division of about nineteen hundred men, of whom only three hundred and fifteen had inferior arms; and of a second division of nearly twenty-eight hundred men, of whom only nine hundred and thirty were well armed; nine hundred and thirty were light armed, and the remaining nine hundred and thirty, the accensi, were not armed at all. Nay, it appears doubtful whether even the triarii, properly so called, were quite equal to the hastati and principes; for in the Latin war it seems to be a mistake of Livy's to suppose that they carried pikes; they appear at that time to have borne only pila and swords, and were therefore less fitted than the hastati and principes for the peculiar manner of fighting then in use in the Roman army.

But even in this earlier form of the legion there seems to have been some change introduced from a form still earlier. The mixture of light-armed soldiers in the front ranks of the phalanx, unless we are to suppose that they were always thrown forward as mere skirmishers, and had no place in the line, seems to show that a modification of the tactic of the phalanx had already been found necessary, and that the use of the javelin instead of the pike was already rising in estimation.

This alteration seems to derive its origin from the Gaulish wars. The Gauls used javelins themselves, and the weight of their charge was such that the full-armed soldiers of the Roman legions were not numerous enough to withstand them; it became of importance, therefore, to improve the efficiency of the light-armed soldiers, and at the same time to enable the Roman line to reply to the Gaulish missiles, if the enemy preferred a distant combat to fighting hand to hand.

That something of this sort was done is directly stated; but as usual the accounts are conflicting and inconsistent with themselves. Dionysius makes Camillus say to his soldiers, that whereas "the Gauls had only javelins, they had arrows, a weapon of deadly effect." 'Αντὶ λόγχης δϊστὸς, ἄφυκτον βέλος. Fragm. Vatic. XXX. Plutarch says that Camillus instructed his soldiers "to use their long javelins as weapons for close fight," τοῖς ὑσσοῖς μακροῖς διὰ χειρὸς χρῆσθαι, Camill. 40, and in the next chapter he describes the Gauls as grappling with the Romans, and trying to push aside their javelins, which evidently supposes them to have been used as pikes. And yet in the very sentence before he talks of the Gaulish shields as being weighed down by the Roman javelins, which had run through them, and hung upon them, τοὺς δὲ θυρεους συμπεπάρθαι καὶ βαρύνεσθαι τῶν ὑσσῶν ἐφελκομένων (Camill. 41), a description applicable only to weapons thrown at the enemy, and not used as pikes.

A passage in Livy seems to offer the solution of this difficulty. When the Gauls attacked the Roman camp in their invasion of the Roman territory in the year 405, only ten years before the Latin war, the triarii were engaged in throwing up works, and the

[2] Livy says that the hastati and principes were called antepilani—VIII. 8. Varro (Ling. Lat. V. § Ed. Müller) and Ovid (Fasti, III. 129) call the triarii expressly pilani.

hastati and principes covered them. Then, as the Gauls advanced up hill to attack the Roman position, "all the pila and spears," "pila omnia hastæque," "took effect," says Livy, "from their own weight; and the Gauls had either their bodies run through, or their shields weighed down by the darts that were sticking in them." VII. 23. It appears, then, that both the pilum and hasta could be used as missiles; but both also could be used as pikes, for the pilum was six feet in length, and therefore it is very possible that Camillus may have shortened the spear of the hastati, to render it available as a missile, and also strengthened and lengthened the pilum to make it serve on occasion the purposes of a pike.

Thus the hastati and principes were armed with swords, with large oblong shields, scuta, and with spears, hastæ; but the large shield already fitted them for a more independent and personal mode of fighting than that of the phalanx, and the spear might be used as a javelin, no less than as a pike. The Samnite wars, following so soon afterwards, decided the Romans to give up the tactic of the phalanx still more entirely: the spear which might be used as a javelin, but was more fitted for close fight, was now given only to the soldiers of the third line; while the pilum, which might be used as a pike, but was properly a missile, was taken from the third line, and given to the soldiers of the first and second lines. At the same time those citizens whose properties were rated between four thousand ases and twelve thousand five hundred, and who were not formerly required to provide themselves with arms, were now called upon to do so, and therefore the accensi are no more heard of; while the rorarii, who seem to have belonged to the fifth class of the old Servian division, and to have gone to battle with no other weapons than slings, were now called upon to provide themselves with light arms of a better description, and became the velites of the new legion. Why the triarii should have been also reduced in number does not certainly appear; except that as the whole Roman tactic was now become a very active system of personal combats along the whole line, it was necessary to have as many men as possible available for the two first divisions, and that the mere reserve, which was not to form any part of the fighting force, except on emergency, should be kept low, and confined to the older soldiers who had no longer sufficient activity to be employed in the constantly moving battle of the regular line.

Niebuhr has attempted to explain the number of centuries in the legion, and of men in each century, by a reference to the varying number of tribes, and to the centuries in the classes of the Servian constitution. But his explanation does not seem to me satisfactory; and the question is not essential to our understanding of the military character of the legion. It may be observed, however, that the germ of the division of the legion into ten cohorts, may be traced already in the legion of the time of Polybius, as a tenfold division existed in it in each of the three lines of the hastati, principes, and triarii. A cohort then would be merely one maniple of each of these three lines; a miniature legion, presenting the same variety of force on a small scale, which the legion itself did on a large scale. And thus the cohorts of the legion of four thousand two hundred men would consist of four hundred and twenty men each, as afterwards in the imperial legion they consisted properly of six hundred men each.

Sallust, it is well known, makes Cæsar say that the Romans had borrowed their arms, offensive and defensive, from the Samnites. (Bell. Catilinar. 51.) And although the Samnites are not named, yet the order of time seems to show that they must, partly at least, be intended, where Diodorus says, Fragm. Vatic. XXIII. 1, that the Romans, having first adopted the tactic of the phalanx in their wars with the Etruscans, afterwards exchanged it for the system of fighting in cohorts (*σπειραῖς* being a certain correction for *πειραῖς*, which has no meaning at all), and with the large oblong shield, *θυρεοῖς*, because the nations whom they subsequently encountered used this tactic. And it probably is true, that the peculiar form of the Roman legion was owing to the wars with the Gauls and Samnites, which led to the total disuse of the phalanx, and to the perfecting of those weapons, such as the sword and the javelin, which, in the system of the phalanx, are of the least importance.

THE END.

www.ingramcontent.com/pod-product-compliance
Lightning Source LLC
LaVergne TN
LVHW021048110826
845150LV00001B/17

* 9 7 8 1 4 2 5 5 6 8 4 6 7 *